Key to the road maps   Pages 64-248

SHETLAND
233
Lerwick

232
Kirkwall
ORKNEY

Thurso
Wick

228–9
Stornoway
Ullapool
231
OUTER HEBRIDES

Inverness
SCOTLAND
Portree 222–3
224–5
226–7

Aberdeen

Fort William
216–7
218–9
Pitlochry
Forfar
220–1
Tobermory

ATLANTIC
OCEAN

Dundee
210–1
212–3
214–5
Oban
Perth
St. Andrews
230

NORTH

204–5
Stirling
206–7
208–9
EDINBURGH
GLASGOW

SEA

198–9
200–1
Berwick-
upon-
Tweed
Ayr
Selkirk
202–3

192–3
194–5
Alnwick
196–7

Dumfries
246–7
Londonderry
248
Larne
Stranraer
184–5
Carlisle
186–7
188–9
Newcastle
upon Tyne
190–1
Donegal
NORTHERN
IRELAND
BELFAST

Sligo
Darlington
Middlesbrough
178–9
180–1
182–3
Kendal
Scarborough
154
Douglas
Newry
242–3
244–5
ISLE OF MAN
172–3
174–5
176–7
York
Westport
REPUBLIC OF
Blackpool
Bradford
LEEDS
Kingston upon
Hull
Preston
168–9
170–1
Galway
DUBLIN
IRELAND
240–1
MANCHESTER
Huddersfield
238–9
154–5
Holyhead
156–7
158–9
160
Doncaster
162–3
164–5
LIVERPOOL
SHEFFIELD
Lincoln
Limerick
Chester
146–7
Boston
142–3
144–5
148–9
150–1
152–3
Dolgellau
STOKE ON
TRENT
Nottingham
King's Lynn
234–5
Cork
236–7
Shrewsbury
Derby
130–1
132–3
Wolverhampton
Leicester
Norwich
Great
Yarmouth
Aberystwyth
134–5
136–7
138–9
140
Newtown
Coventry
Cambridge
Lowestoft
118–9
120–1
BIRMINGHAM
124–5
126–7
128–9
Killarney
Waterford
Worcester
Northampton
Fishguard
Hereford
122–3
ENGLAND
Ipswich
104–5
Carmarthen
Brecon
110–1
Oxford
Luton
Colchester
106–7
108–9
Gloucester
112–3
114–5
Harwich
WALES
Swansea
Newport
Reading
LONDON
Southend-on-Sea
92–3
CARDIFF
94–5
Bristol
96–7
98–9
100–1
102–3
Margate
Bath
Guildford
Maidstone
CELTIC
Barnstaple
Salisbury
Winchester
Royal
Tunbridge
Wells
Canterbury
SEA
80–1
82–3
84–5
86–7
88–9
90–1
Dover
Taunton
Southampton
Brighton
NETHERLANDS
Okehampton
Bournemouth
Portsmouth
Eastbourne
BELGIUM
70–1
72–3
74–5
76–7
78–9
Exeter
Weymouth
66–7
Torquay
ATLANTIC
Newquay
Plymouth
OCEAN
Penzance
Truro
68–9
ISLES OF SCILLY
64–5
64
ENGLISH CHANNEL

FRANCE

CHANNEL ISLANDS
74–5

The Complete Driver's Atlas of Britain & Ireland

The Complete Driver's Atlas of Britain & Ireland

Published by the Reader's Digest Association Ltd

London • New York • Sydney • Montreal

Contents

Planning your route

6–14

Route planning

Four maps, Southern Britain (including most of Wales), Central Britain, Northern Britain (including most of Scotland) and Ireland show in outline form all the major routes and destinations in Great Britain and Ireland. Use them to plan your trip and move on to the Road Maps for more detailed information.

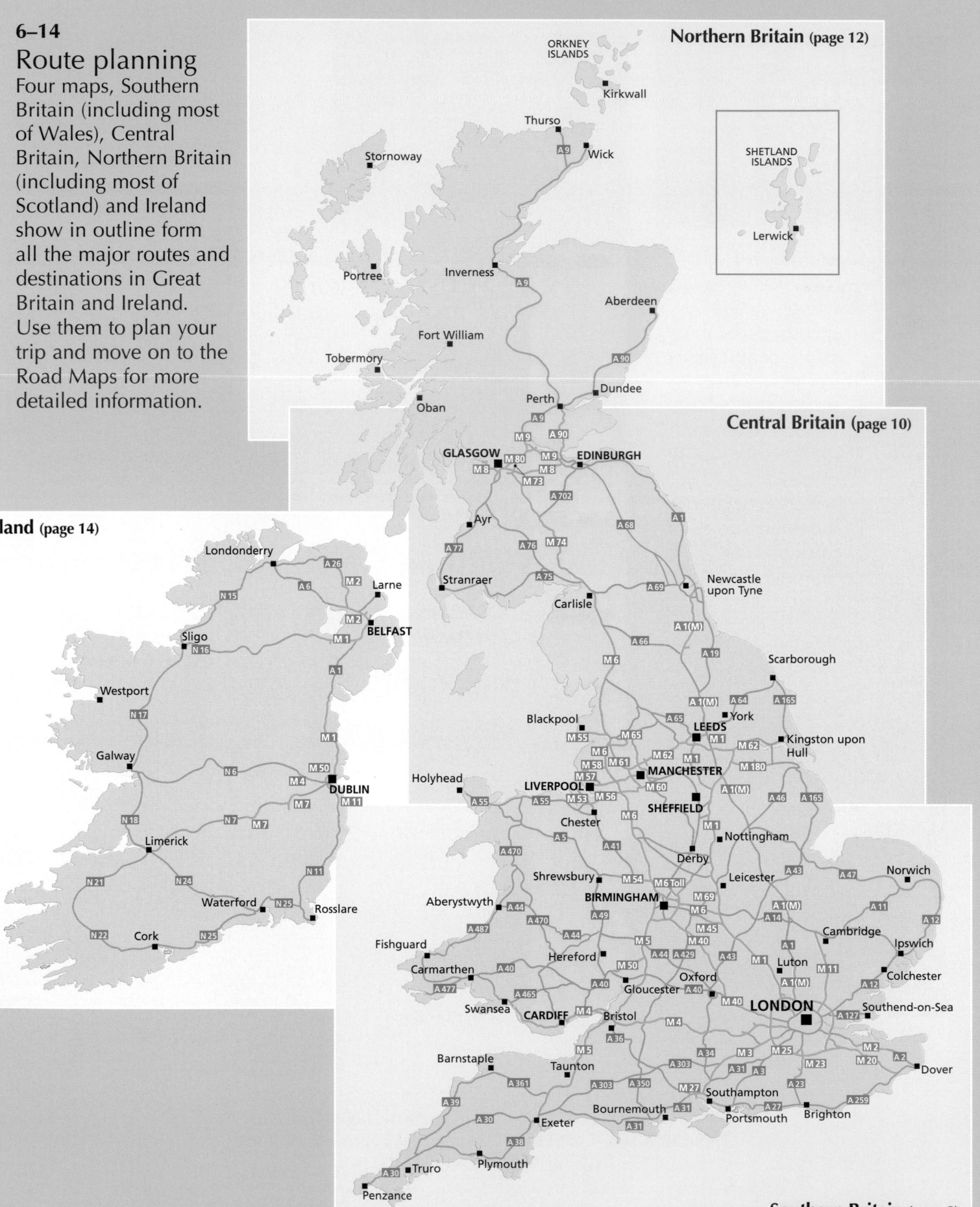

Northern Britain (page 12)

ORKNEY ISLANDS

Kirkwall

Thurso

Stornoway

Wick

A9

SHETLAND ISLANDS

Lerwick

Portree

Inverness

A9

Aberdeen

Fort William

A90

Tobermory

Dundee

Oban

Perth

A9

Central Britain (page 10)

M9 A90

GLASGOW M9 M80 M9 **EDINBURGH**

M8 M8

M73

A702

Ayr

A68 A1

A77 A76 M74

Stranraer A75

Newcastle upon Tyne

A69

Carlisle

A1(M)

A66 A19

M6

Scarborough

A1(M) A64 A165

Blackpool A65

Leeds York

M55 M65 M1 M62

Kingston upon Hull

M6 M61 M62 M1

M58 **MANCHESTER** M180

Holyhead

M57 A1(M)

LIVERPOOL M60 A46 A165

A55 M53 M56

Chester **SHEFFIELD**

A55 M6

M1

A5 Nottingham

A470 A41

Derby

Shrewsbury M6 Toll Leicester A43 A47 Norwich

BIRMINGHAM M69

Aberystwyth A44 M6 A1(M) A11

A470 A14

Fishguard A44 M5 M45 Cambridge A12

A487 M40 A1 Ipswich

Hereford A44 A429 A43 M1 Luton

Carmarthen A40 M50 Oxford M11 Colchester

A477 A40 Gloucester A40 A1(M) A12

Swansea A465 **CARDIFF** M4 M40 **LONDON** Southend-on-Sea

Bristol M4 A127

M5 A36 M2 A2

Barnstaple A34 M3 M25 A20 Dover

Taunton A303 M23

A39 A361 A303 A350 M27 Southampton A23 A259

Bournemouth A31 A27 Brighton

A30 Portsmouth

Exeter A31

A38

A30 Truro Plymouth

Penzance

Southern Britain (page 8)

Ireland (page 14)

Londonderry

A26

N15 A6 M2 Larne

M2

Sligo M1 **BELFAST**

N16

A1

Westport

N17

M1

Galway M50

N6 M4 **DUBLIN**

N18 M7 M11

N7 M7

Limerick

N11

N21 N24

Waterford N25 Rosslare

N22 Cork N25

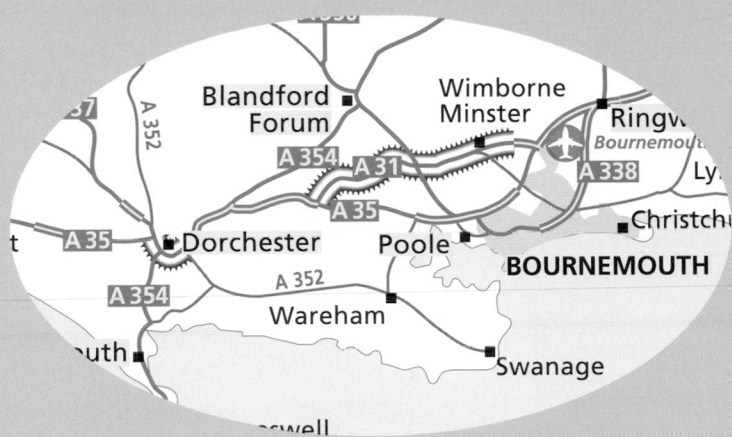

15–33
Congestion blackspots

Even the best-planned journeys can end in frustrating delays because of road black spots that could be avoided with a bit a forewarning. This section identifies the stretches of road that regularly cause the worst traffic problems, allowing you to devise an alternative route or time your trip to escape holdups.

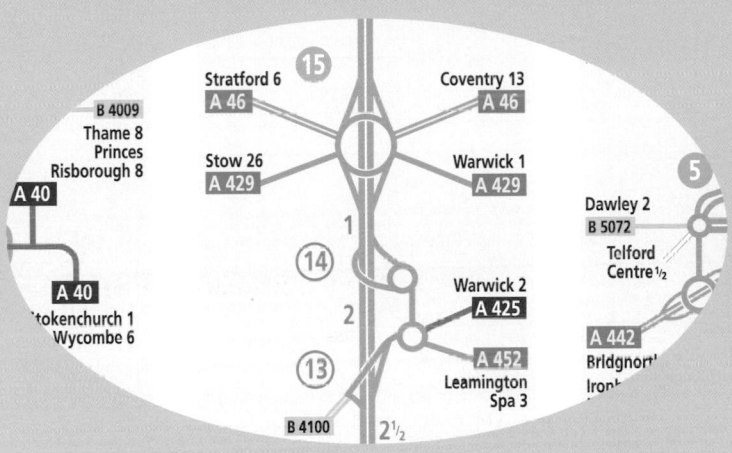

34–57
Motorway plans

Find your way around the major motorways using a series of clear, linear diagrams. Each plan includes all the junctions, where to turn off for major towns and cities, and all the service stations along the route. The orbital motorways around London, Manchester and Birmingham are shown as unique circular diagrams.

58–59
Rail routes and airports

All major rail routes in Great Britain and Ireland are shown in outline, along with the airports which carry the largest number of passengers. Telephone contact numbers for the rail operating companies and airports are also given.

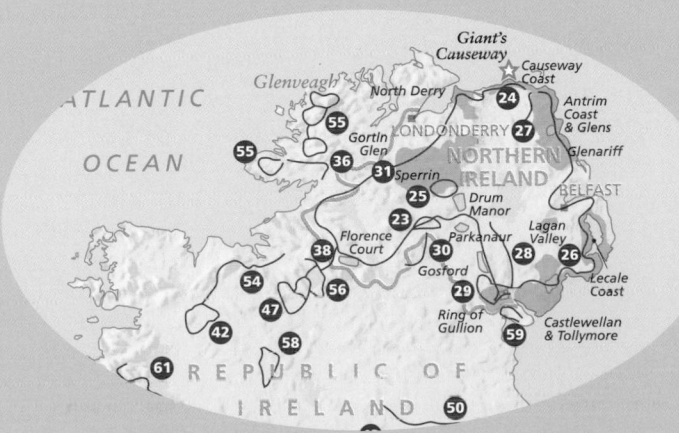

60–61
Scenic Britain & Ireland

The most unspoiled parts of Great Britain and Ireland are highlighted here, including National Parks, Areas of Outstanding Natural Beauty, Forest Parks, National Trails in England and Wales and Waymarked Ways in Ireland. Also included are phone numbers for all the National Parks, walks and trails.

Legend

M 1	Motorway with number
	Motorway under construction
	Full access junction
	Restricted access junction
	Service area
A 23	Primary route, single and dual carriageway
Swindon	Primary route destination
A 32	Other 'A' road
	Vehicle ferry
80	Index to maps in road map section

MILES
0   10   20   30   40

0   20   40   60
KILOMETRES

ANGLESEY

Holywell
Northwich
Buxton
Bangor
Bethesda
Denbigh
Queensferry
CHESTER
Sandbach
Kidsgrove
Leek
Caernarfon
Llanrwst
Ruthin
Mold/Yr Wyddgrug
Crewe
STOKE-ON-TRENT
Newcastle-under-Lyme
Betws-y-coed
Corwen
Ruabon
Wrexham
Nantwich
Llanberis
Beddgelert
Porthmadog
Ffestiniog
Llangollen
Whitchurch
Stone
Stafford
142 143 144 145 146
Pwllheli
Criccieth
Bala
Ellesmere
Market Drayton
Abersoch
Harlech
Oswestry
Newport
Dolgellau
Shrewsbury
Telford
WOLVERHAMPTON
Barmouth
Mallwyd
Welshpool
Church Stretton
Bridgnorth
Dudley
Tywyn
Machynlleth
Llanbrynmair
Stourbridge
130 131 132 133 BIRMINGHAM
Aberdyfi
Caersws
Newtown
Kidderminster
Aberystwyth
Llanidloes
Bromsgrove
Llangurig
Knighton
Ludlow
Redd
Cardigan Bay
Aberaeron
Rhayader/Rhaeadr Gwy
Llandrindod Wells
Leominster
Tenbury Wells
Droitwich
New Quay
Tregaron
Kington
Worcester
118 119 120 121 122 Pershore
Cardigan/Aberteifi
Lampeter
Builth Wells/Llanfair-ym-Muallt
Bromyard
Great Malvern
Broadw
Llanwrtyd Wells
Hay-on-Wye
Hereford
Ledbury
Eve
Fishguard/Abergwaun
Newcastle Emlyn
Llandovery/Llanymddyfri
Llyswen
Talgarth
Pontrilas
St David's
Carmarthen/Caerfyrddin
Llandeilo
Brecon/Aberhonddu
Ross-on-Wye
Gloucester
Chelter
Haverfordwest/Hwlffordd
St Clears/Sanclêr
Abergavenny/Y Fenni
North
104 105 106 107 108 109 110
Narberth
Ammanford
Merthyr Tydfil/Merthyr Tudful
Ebbw Vale
Monmouth/Trefynwy
Stroud
Milford Haven/Aberdaugleddau
Hirwaun
Lydney
Nailsworth
Cirence
Pembroke Dock/Doc Penfro
Pontarddulais
Aberdare
Pontypool
Usk
Tetbury
Pembroke
Tenby/Dinbych-y-Pysgod
Neath/Castell Nedd
Treorchy
Caerphilly
Cwmbran
Chepstow/Cas-Gwent
Llanelli
SWANSEA/ABERTAWE
Pontypridd
Newport/Casnewydd
Malmesbury
Rosslare Harbour
Port-Eynon
Port Talbot
94 95 96 Chippenham
Ringaskiddy (Cork)
92 93 Porthcawl
Bridgend/Pen-y-Bont ar Ogwr
CARDIFF/CAERDYDD
Clevedon
BRISTOL
Bath
Trowbridge
Bristol Channel
Weston-super-Mare
Churchill
Cheddar
Westbury
Lynton
Minehead
Burnham-on-Sea
Wells
Frome
Warminster
Ilfracombe
Watchet
Shepton Mallet
Braunton
Barnstaple
Bridgwater
Glastonbury
Street
80 81 82 83 84 Wincanton
Bideford
South Molton
Taunton
Langport
Ilchester
Great Torrington
Wellington
Illminster
Yeovil
Sherborne
Shaftesbury
Bude
Holsworthy
Tiverton
Chard
Crewkerne
Blandford Forum
Wimb
Mins
Okehampton
Crediton
Honiton
Axminster
Dorchester
BOURNEMO
70 71 72 73 74 75
Launceston
EXETER
Seaton
Lyme Regis
Bridport
Poole
Padstow
Tavistock
Chudleigh
Sidmouth
Weymouth
Wareham
Wadebridge
Bodmin
Newton Abbot
Dawlish
Teignmouth
Bill of Portland
Fortuneswell
Newquay
Liskeard
PLYMOUTH
Torquay
Paignton
Guernsey & Jersey
66 67 68 69 Brixham
Lostwithiel
Saltash
Plympton
St Austell
Looe
Dartmouth
Redruth
Truro
Kingsbridge
St Ives
Penryn
Salcombe
Penzance
St Mawes
Falmouth
St Just
Helston
64 65 Santander (seasonal)
Roscoff
Land's End
Lizard
ENGLISH
Isles of Scilly (seasonal)

Bristol Channel

Cardigan Bay

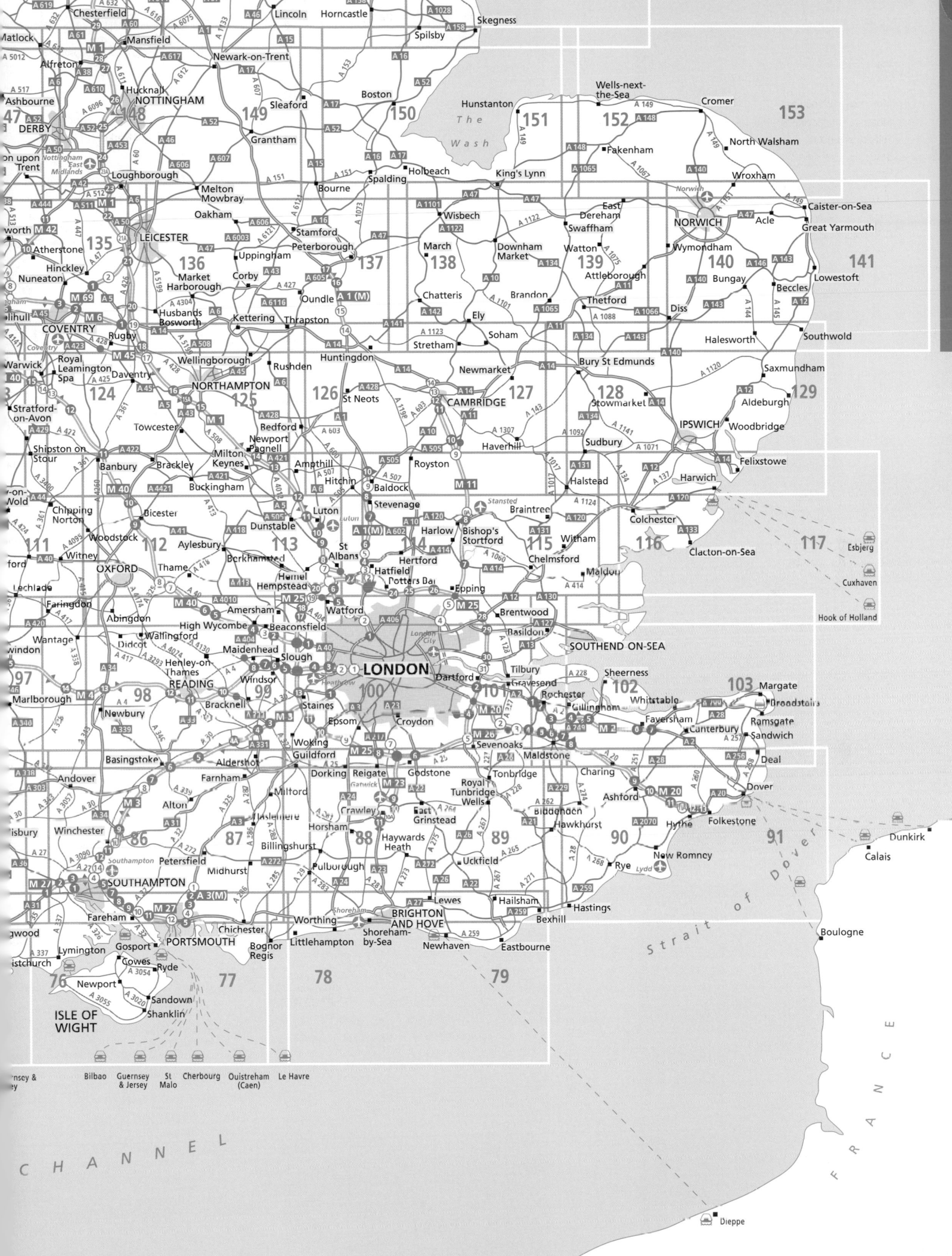

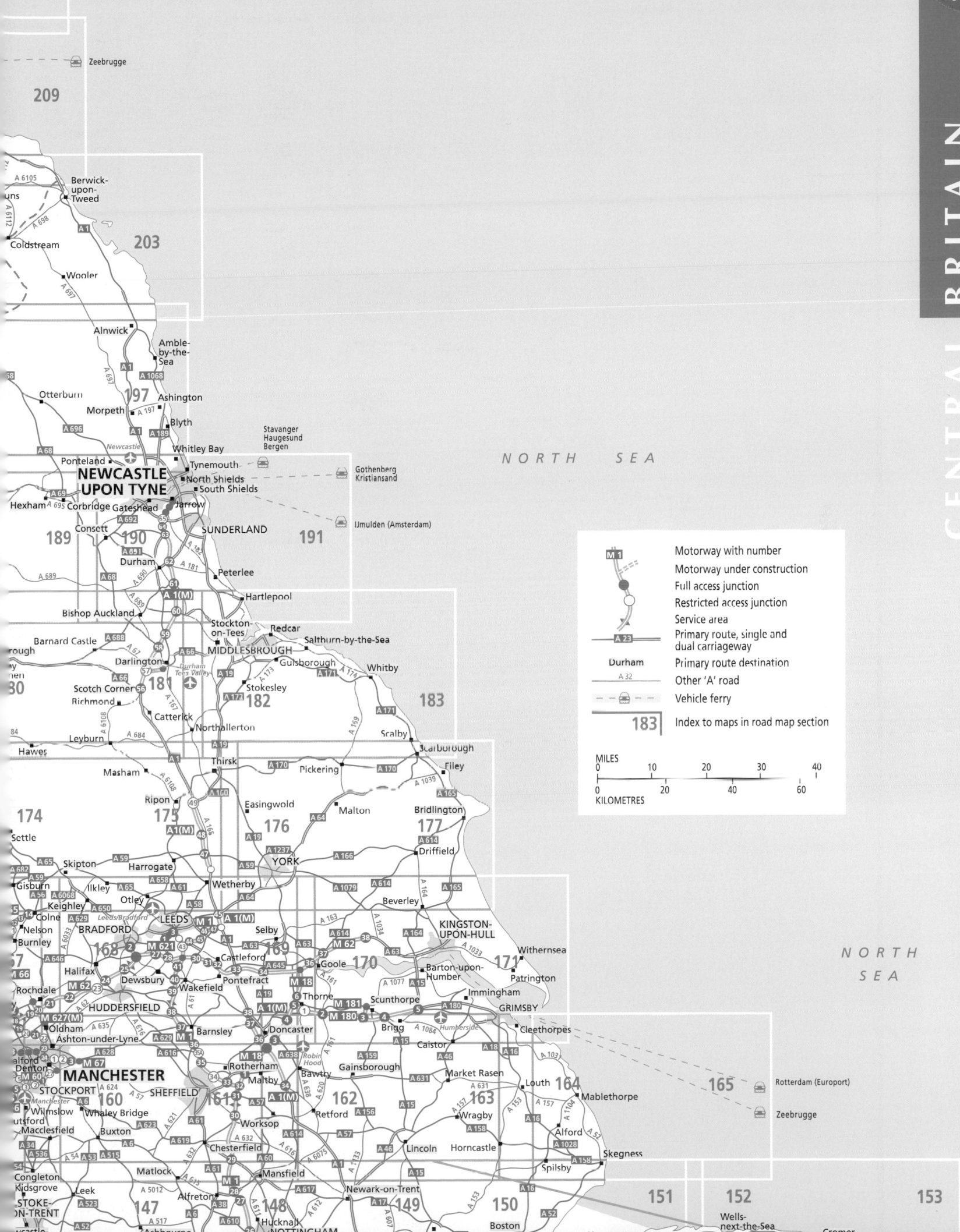

209

Zeebrugge

A 6105
Berwick-upon-Tweed
A 6112
A 698
Coldstream
203
A 697
Wooler
Otterburn
A 1068
Alnwick
Amble-by-the-Sea
197
Ashington
A 696
Morpeth
A 197
A 1
A 189
Blyth
Whitley Bay
Newcastle
Tynemouth
Ponteland
North Shields
A 68
NEWCASTLE UPON TYNE
South Shields
Hexham
A 69
Corbridge Gateshead
Jarrow
A 695
189
190
SUNDERLAND
191
Consett
A 692
A 691
65
63
A 693
Durham
62
A 182
A 181
Peterlee
A 689
A 68
A 690
61
Hartlepool
Bishop Auckland
A 1(M)
60
Stockton-on-Tees
Redcar
59
Barnard Castle
A 688
A 67
58
A 66
MIDDLESBROUGH
Salthurn-by-the-Sea
Darlington
Durham Tees Valley
A 19
Guisborough
Whitby
A 173
A 171
A 66
57
181
Scotch Corner 56
Stokesley
182
A 171
Richmond
A 6108
A 167
A 159
Catterick
Northallerton
Scalby
Leyburn
A 684
A 19
Scarborough
Hawes
A 1
Thirsk
Filey
Masham
A 6108
Pickering
A 170
A 170
Ripon
49
A 160
A 1039
A 165
174
175
Easingwold
Malton
Bridlington
A 64
176
A 19
177
A1(M)
48
A 614
A 166
Settle
47
A 59
A 1237
Driffield
Skipton
A 59
YORK
A 65
Harrogate
A 682
A 59
A 658
A 61
Wetherby
A 614
A 165
Gisburn
Ilkley
A 64
A 56
A 6068
Otley
A 1079
Keighley
A 650
A 58
Beverley
A 629
Leeds/Bradford
A 164
Colne
M 1
A 1(M)
KINGSTON-UPON-HULL
Nelson
BRADFORD
LEEDS
Selby
Withernsea
Burnley
168
A 1
A 163
A 614
A 6033
A 63
170
A 646
M 621
Castleford
A 63
Goole
171
M 66
Halifax
Dewsbury
Pontefract
A 645
A 1034
Patrington
M 62
Wakefield
A 19
Barton-upon-Humber
Rochdale
HUDDERSFIELD
Thorne
A 161
Immingham
M 62
A 61
M 18
A 1077
A 15
M 627(M)
Oldham
A 635
Barnsley
A 1(M)
Scunthorpe
GRIMSBY
Ashton-under-Lyne
A 629
Doncaster
M 181
A 180
Salford
A 628
M 18
Brigg
Cleethorpes
Denton
Rotherham
Robin Hood
Humberside
Caistor
MANCHESTER
A 616
Maltby
Bawtry
Gainsborough
Market Rasen
A 46
A 18
STOCKPORT
SHEFFIELD
A 159
Louth
164
Mablethorpe
Wilmslow
160
161
A 1(M)
162
A 631
165
Rotterdam (Europort)
Whaley Bridge
163
Retford
A 156
Wragby
A 16
Alford
Buxton
Worksop
A 57
A 158
Skegness
Congleton
Chesterfield
A 46
Lincoln
Horncastle
Spilsby
Kidsgrove
Matlock
A 61
A 15
STOKE-ON-TRENT
Leek
Mansfield
M 1
Newark-on-Trent
150
151
152
153
147
148
149
Boston
Ashbourne
NOTTINGHAM
Wells-next-the-Sea
Hunstanton
Cromer

Legend

M 1   Motorway with number

Motorway under construction

Full access junction

Restricted access junction

Service area

A 23   Primary route, single and dual carriageway

Durham   Primary route destination

A 32   Other 'A' road

Vehicle ferry

183   Index to maps in road map section

MILES
0   10   20   30   40
0   20   40   60
KILOMETRES

NORTH SEA

NORTH SEA

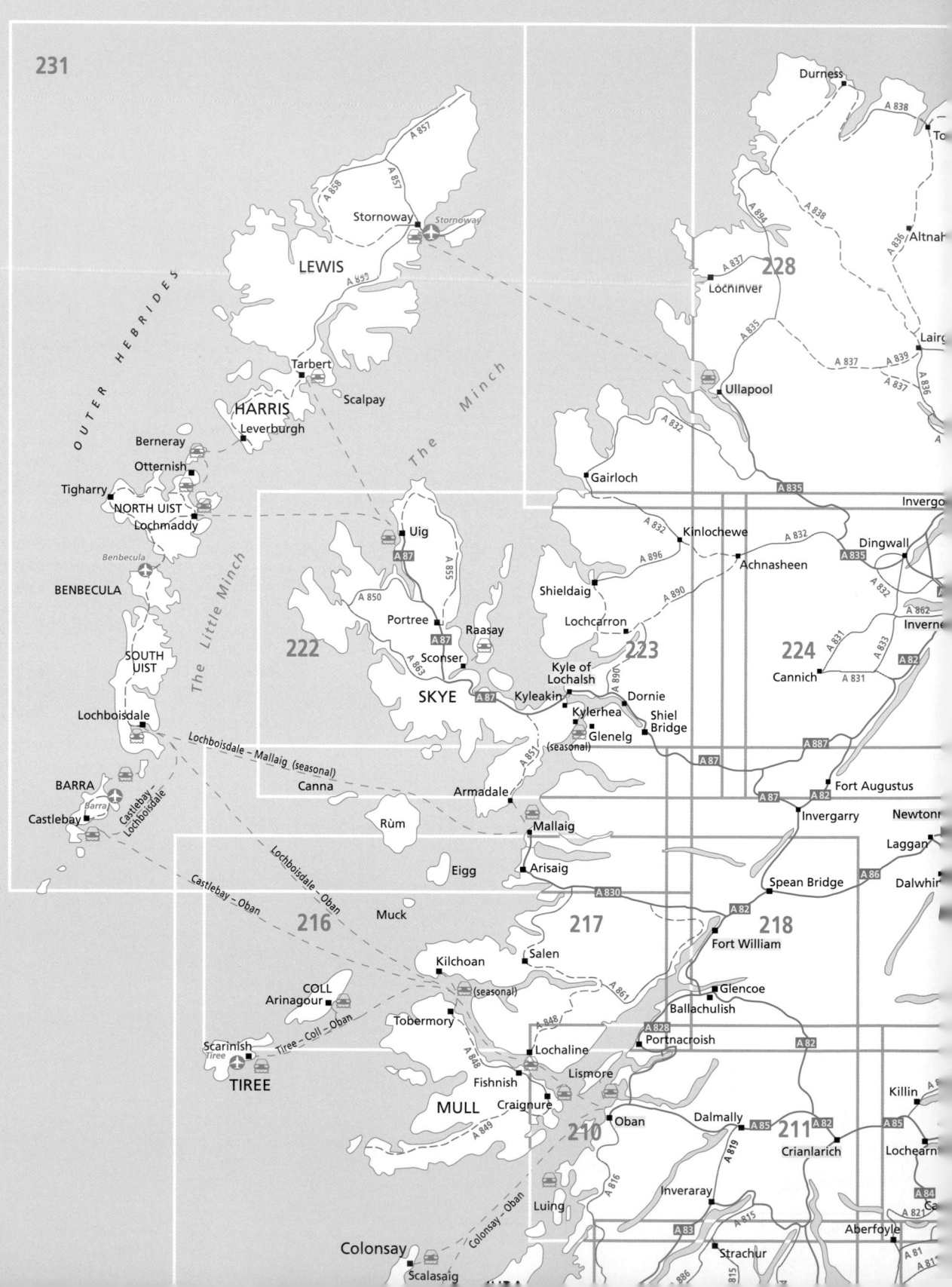

231

Durness

A 838

LEWIS

A 857

A 858

A 857

Stornoway

Stornoway

A 859

228

Lochinver

A 837

A 838

A 836

Altnah

A 834

To

Tarbert

HARRIS

Scalpay

The Minch

A 835

A 839

Laird

A 837

A 836

A 837

Ullapool

Leverburgh

Berneray

Otternish

Tigharry

NORTH UIST

Lochmaddy

OUTER HEBRIDES

The Minch

Gairloch

A 832

Kinlochewe

A 832

Achnasheen

A 835

Dingwall

Invergo

Benbecula

BENBECULA

Uig

A 87

A 855

A 896

Shieldaig

A 890

Lochcarron

A 862

Inverne

SOUTH
UIST

The Little Minch

A 850

Portree

A 87

Raasay

Sconser

A 863

SKYE

Kyle of
Lochalsh

Kyleakin

223

A 831

A 833

224

Cannich

A 831

A 82

Lochboisdale

Dornie

Kylerhea

Shiel
Bridge

A 887

222

Lochboisdale – Mallaig (seasonal)

Canna

BARRA

Castlebay –
Lochboisdale

Castlebay

Barra

Glenelg
(seasonal)

A 851

Armadale

A 87

A 82

Fort Augustus

Invergarry

Newtonr

Laggan

Rùm

Mallaig

Lochboisdale – Oban

Eigg

Castlebay – Oban

216

Muck

A 830

Spean Bridge

A 86

Dalwhir

217

A 82

218

Fort William

Kilchoan

Salen

A 861

Glencoe

COLL

Arinagour

(seasonal)

Tiree – Coll – Oban

Tobermory

Ballachulish

A 948

Portnacroish

A 828

A 82

Scarinish

Tiree

A 848

Lochaline

Lismore

TIREE

Fishnish

Craignure

MULL

A 849

Oban

210

Dalmally

A 85

211

A 82

Killin

A 8

A 85

Lochearn

A 819

Crianlarich

Colonsay

Colonsay – Oban

A 816

Luing

A 83

Inveraray

A 815

A 821

A 84

Ca

Aberfoyle

A 81

Strachur

Scalasaig

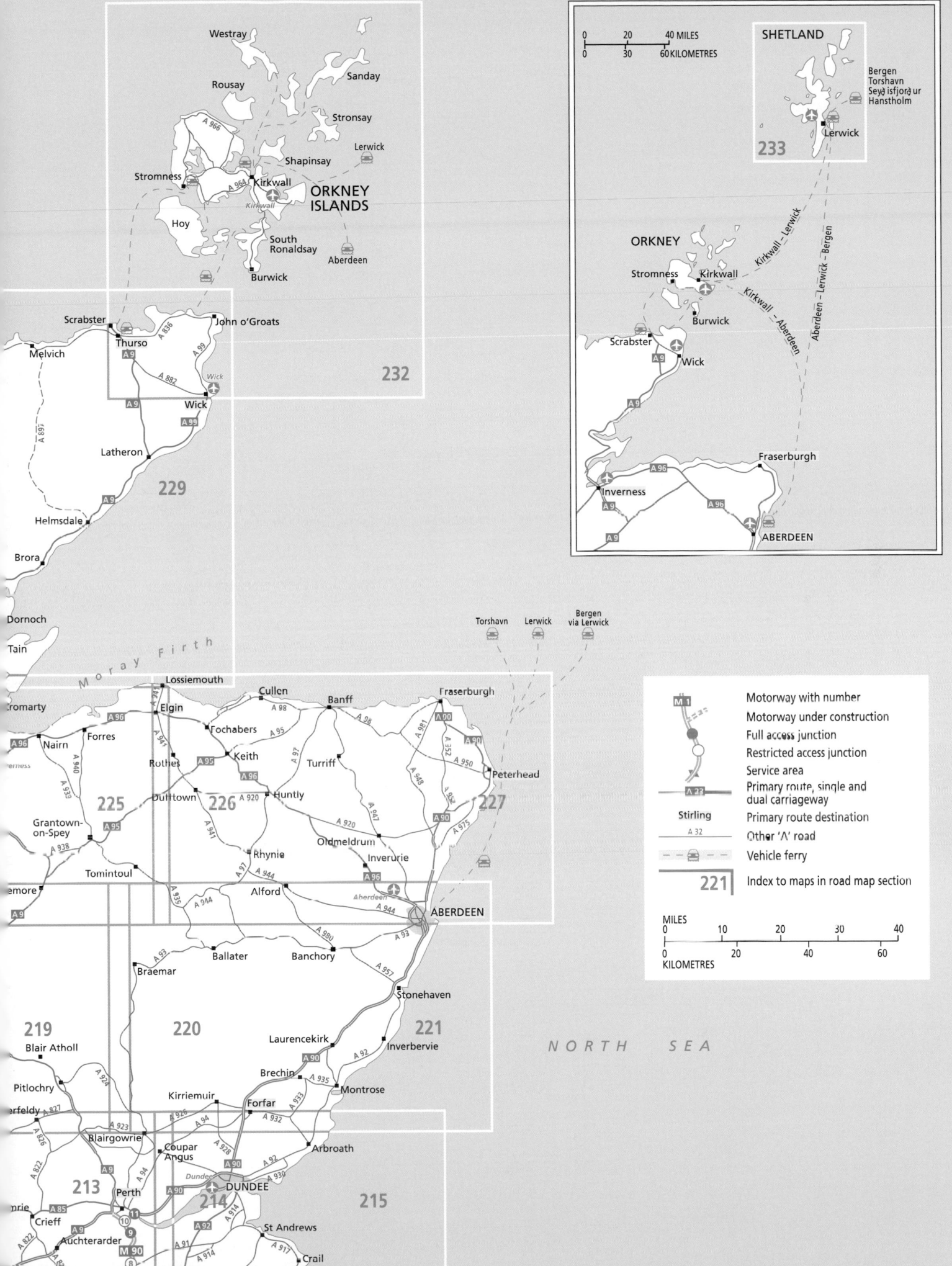

Westray
Rousay
Sanday
Stronsay
Shapinsay
Lerwick
Stromness
Kirkwall
ORKNEY
ISLANDS
Kirkwall
Hoy
South
Ronaldsay
Aberdeen
Burwick

SHETLAND
Bergen
Torshavn
Seyðisfjörður
Hanstholm
Lerwick
233

ORKNEY
Kirkwall – Lerwick
Aberdeen – Lerwick – Bergen
Kirkwall – Aberdeen
Stromness
Kirkwall
Burwick
Scrabster
A9
Wick

232

Fraserburgh
A 96
Inverness
A 96
A 9
ABERDEEN

Scrabster
Thurso
A 836
A 99
John o'Groats
A 9
Melvich
A 882
Wick
Wick
A 99
A 897
Latheron
229
A 9
Helmsdale
Brora

Dornoch
Tain
Moray Firth
Cromarty
Lossiemouth
Cullen
Banff
Fraserburgh
Elgin
A 96
A 98
A 98
A 90
Forres
Fochabers
A 95
A 981
A 90
Nairn
A 96
Keith
A 97
Turriff
A 352
A 950
A 940
Rothes
A 95
A 948
Peterhead
A 933
A 96
Huntly
Inverness
225
Dufftown
226
A 920
A 941
A 920
A 941
A 90
Grantown-
on-Spey
A 95
A 941
A 975
227
A 938
Rhynie
Oldmeldrum
Tomintoul
A 97
A 944
Inverurie
A 9
A 935
Alford
A 96
Aberdeen
A 944
A 944
ABERDEEN

Motorway with number
Motorway under construction
Full access junction
Restricted access junction
Service area
Primary route, single and
dual carriageway
Primary route destination
Other 'A' road
Vehicle ferry
Index to maps in road map section

Torshavn
Lerwick
Bergen
via Lerwick

Stirling
A 32
221

MILES
0   10   20   30   40
0   20   40   60
KILOMETRES

A 93
Ballater
Banchory
Braemar
A 957
Stonehaven
219
220
221
Blair Atholl
A 924
Laurencekirk
A 92
Inverbervie
Pitlochry
Brechin
A 935
Montrose
erfeldy
A 927
Kirriemuir
A 933
A 823
Forfar
A 932
Blairgowrie
A 926
A 94
Coupar
Angus
A 928
Arbroath
rie
A 85
Dundee
A 90
A 92
215
213
Perth
214
DUNDEE
A 914
St Andrews
Crieff
A 91
A 917
Auchterarder
A 92
A 914
Crail
M 90
A 917
Anstruther
unblane
A 92
Elie
Kinross
A 91
Glenrothes
Zeebrugge
Stirling
A 907
Firth of
Forth

NORTH SEA

NORTHERN BRITAIN

IRELAND

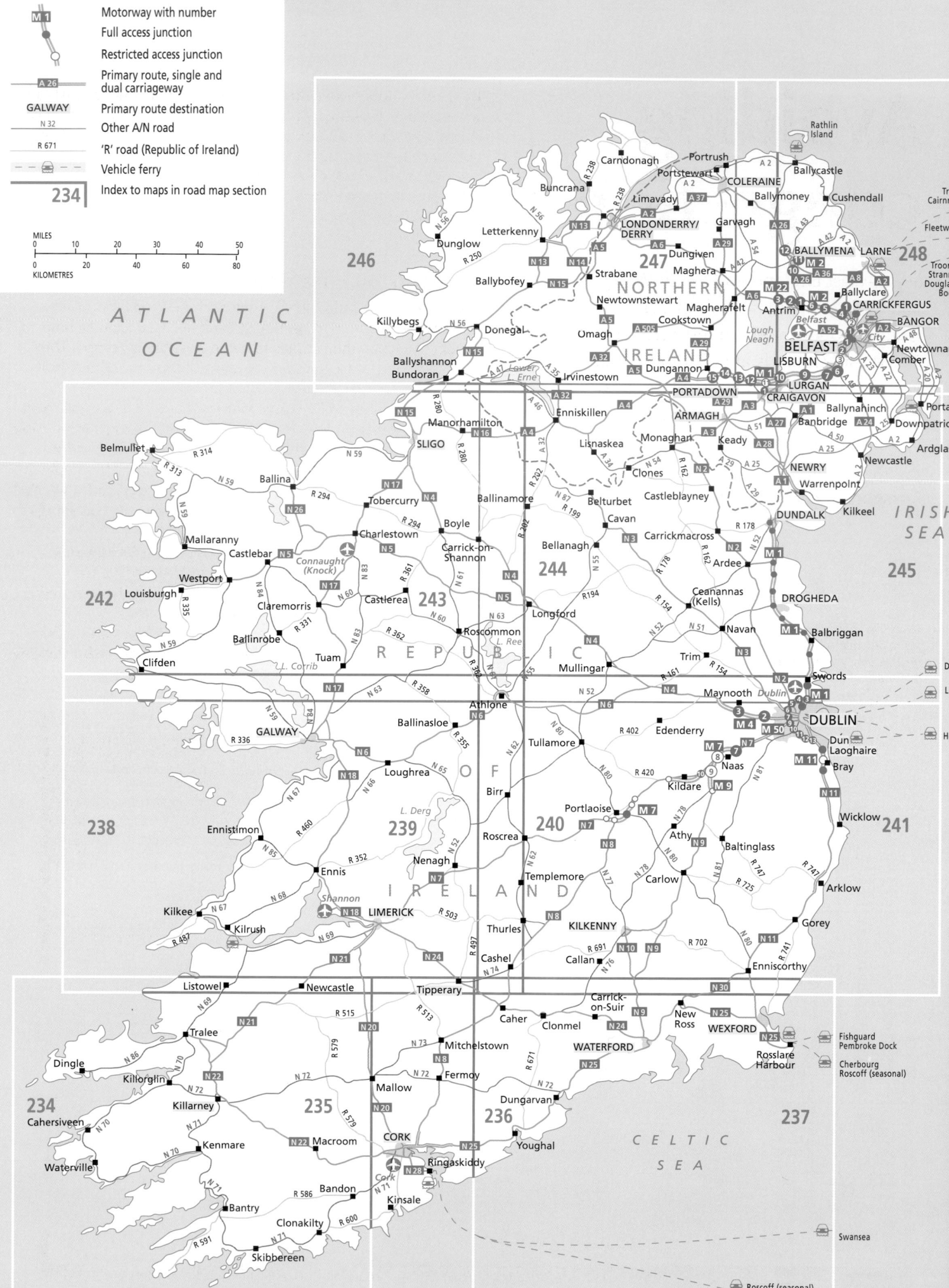

Legend

M 1 — Motorway with number
● — Full access junction
○ — Restricted access junction
A 26 — Primary route, single and dual carriageway
GALWAY — Primary route destination
N 32 — Other A/N road
R 671 — 'R' road (Republic of Ireland)
🚗 — Vehicle ferry
234 — Index to maps in road map section

MILES
0   10   20   30   40   50
KILOMETRES
0   20   40   60   80

Avoiding congestion

Using the maps Areas where congestion occurs are indicated using notched red lines. The green boxes are arrowed in to the heavy traffic zones and offer a clear explanation of why delays occur and the times to avoid using those roads.

In 1996, it was estimated that 1.6 billion hours were wasted by drivers and passengers as a result of congestion. It is not hard to see why. In the past 25 years, the numbers of vehicles using our roads has risen by 96 per cent, to around 28 million vehicles, most of which are cars. More than 70 per cent of the workforce now use their cars to travel to work. New roads such as the M25, built to help absorb traffic, have ironically now become some of Britain's most congested.

Bypassing the 'hot spots'

The maps which follow have been designed to pinpoint the roads where traffic jams are most likely to occur and to help travellers to plan their routes to avoid possible hold-ups. They include major motorways and A roads as well as more minor routes into popular towns.

Some stretches of road are congested only during peak rush hour travel times (8–9.30am and 4.30–6pm). Others are en route to holiday destinations where in the summer months and at weekends, the weight of traffic frequently outstrips the capacity of local roads. In certain cases, routes have heavy traffic all year round, a situation only likely to be alleviated by the building of additional roads.

If you can, check for problems on the roads before you start your journey. The AA and RAC regularly update the travel information on their web sites – **www.theaa.co.uk** and **www.rac.co.uk**. The Highways Agency web site, at **www.highways.gov.uk**, also has details of problem areas. For information while you are driving, tune in to local radio stations – their frequencies are listed on main map borders.

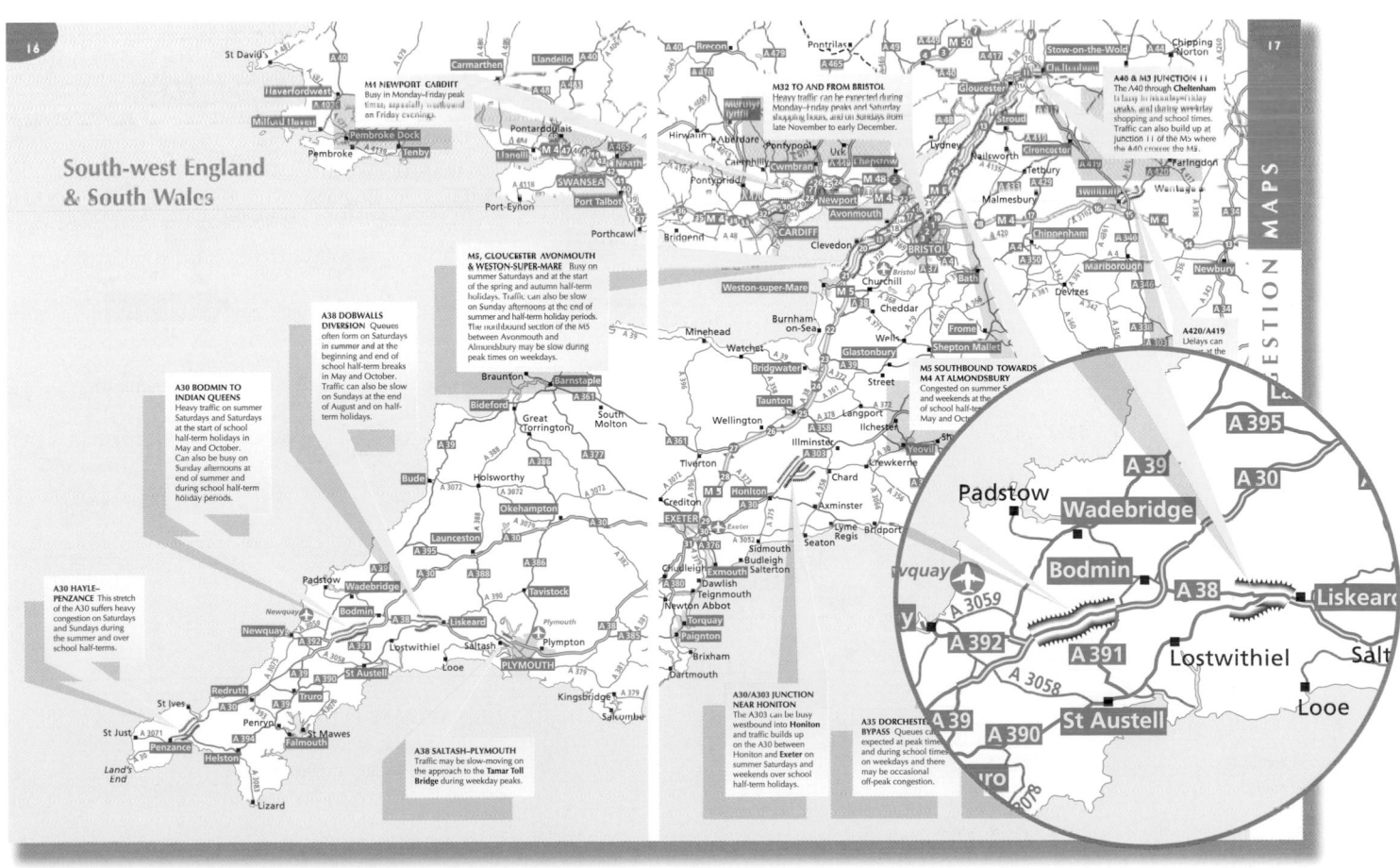

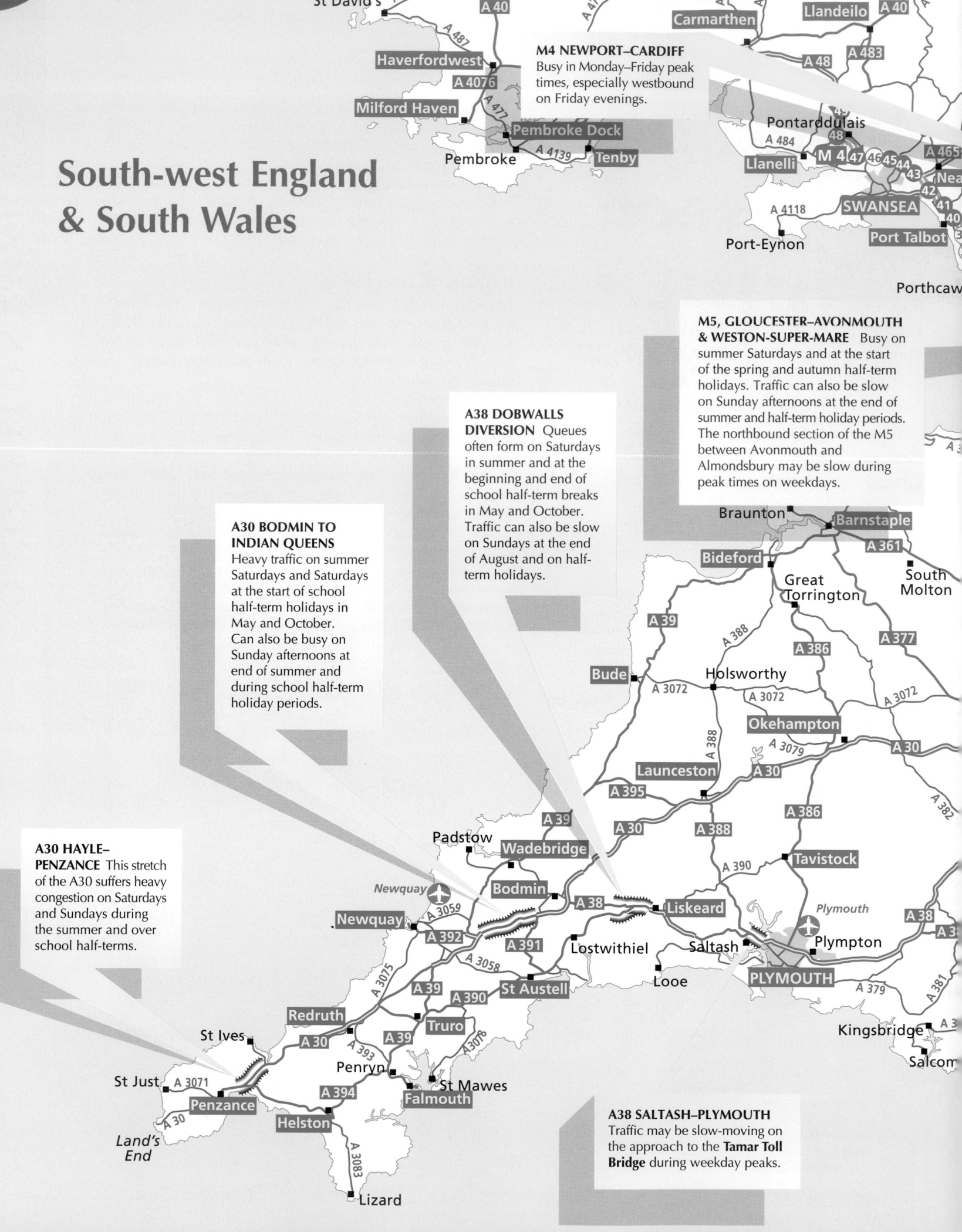

South-west England & South Wales

M4 NEWPORT–CARDIFF Busy in Monday–Friday peak times, especially westbound on Friday evenings.

M5, GLOUCESTER–AVONMOUTH & WESTON-SUPER-MARE Busy on summer Saturdays and at the start of the spring and autumn half-term holidays. Traffic can also be slow on Sunday afternoons at the end of summer and half-term holiday periods. The northbound section of the M5 between Avonmouth and Almondsbury may be slow during peak times on weekdays.

A38 DOBWALLS DIVERSION Queues often form on Saturdays in summer and at the beginning and end of school half-term breaks in May and October. Traffic can also be slow on Sundays at the end of August and on half-term holidays.

A30 BODMIN TO INDIAN QUEENS Heavy traffic on summer Saturdays and Saturdays at the start of school half-term holidays in May and October. Can also be busy on Sunday afternoons at end of summer and during school half-term holiday periods.

A30 HAYLE– PENZANCE This stretch of the A30 suffers heavy congestion on Saturdays and Sundays during the summer and over school half-terms.

A38 SALTASH–PLYMOUTH Traffic may be slow-moving on the approach to the **Tamar Toll Bridge** during weekday peaks.

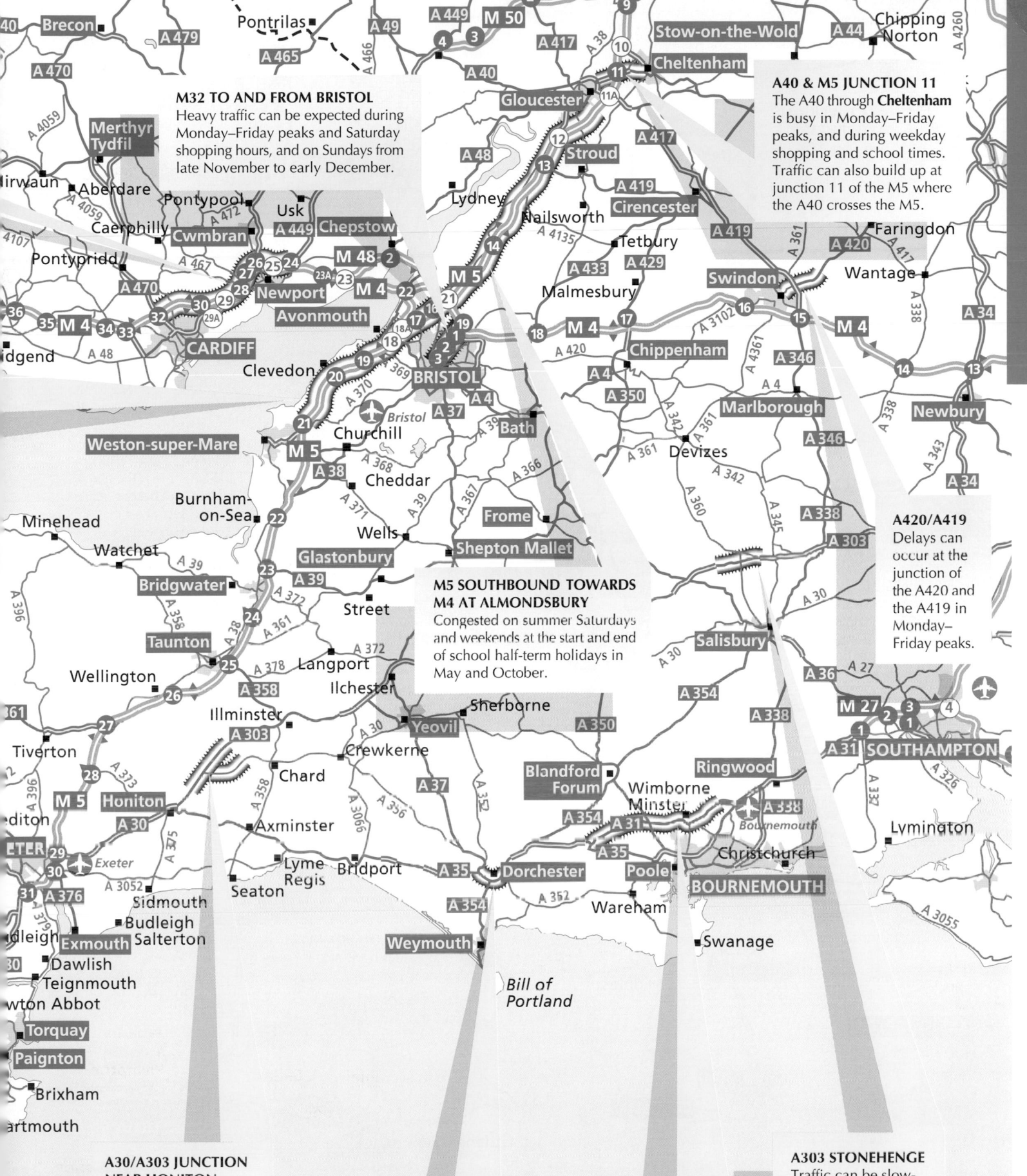

M32 TO AND FROM BRISTOL
Heavy traffic can be expected during Monday–Friday peaks and Saturday shopping hours, and on Sundays from late November to early December.

A40 & M5 JUNCTION 11
The A40 through **Cheltenham** is busy in Monday–Friday peaks, and during weekday shopping and school times. Traffic can also build up at junction 11 of the M5 where the A40 crosses the M5.

M5 SOUTHBOUND TOWARDS M4 AT ALMONDSBURY
Congested on summer Saturdays and weekends at the start and end of school half-term holidays in May and October.

A420/A419
Delays can occur at the junction of the A420 and the A419 in Monday–Friday peaks.

A30/A303 JUNCTION NEAR HONITON
The A303 can be busy westbound into **Honiton** and traffic builds up on the A30 between Honiton and **Exeter** on summer Saturdays and weekends over school half-term holidays.

A35 DORCHESTER BYPASS Queues can be expected at peak times and during school times on weekdays and there may be occasional off-peak congestion.

A31 AROUND POOLE & BOURNEMOUTH
Heavy holiday traffic on weekends in the summer months and over school half-terms often causes long delays.

A303 STONEHENGE
Traffic can be slow-moving westbound between **Thruxton** and **Stonehenge** on weekends through the summer and during school half-term holidays in May and October.

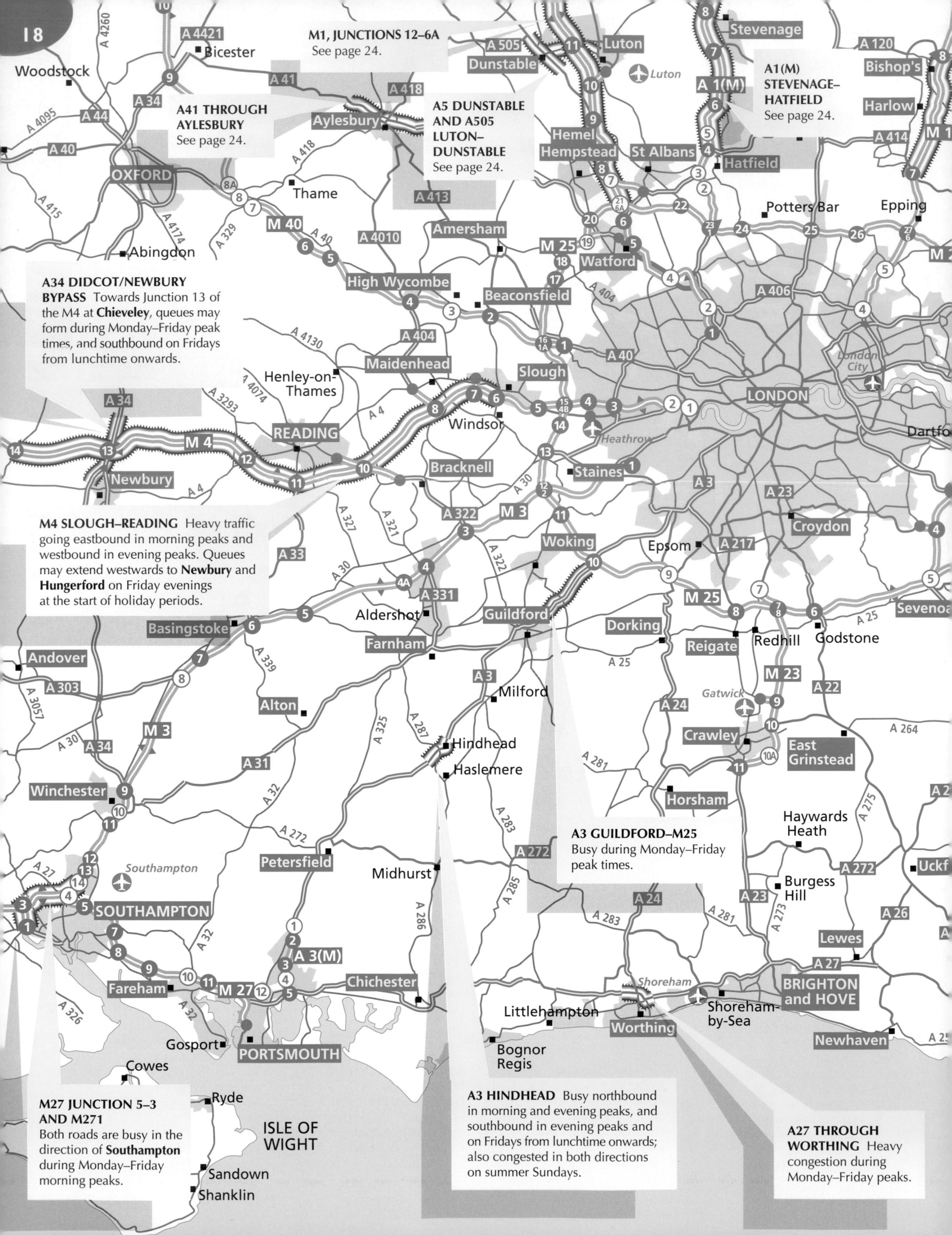

18

M1, JUNCTIONS 12–6A
See page 24.

A1(M) STEVENAGE–HATFIELD
See page 24.

A41 THROUGH AYLESBURY
See page 24.

A5 DUNSTABLE AND A505 LUTON–DUNSTABLE
See page 24.

A34 DIDCOT/NEWBURY BYPASS Towards Junction 13 of the M4 at **Chieveley**, queues may form during Monday–Friday peak times, and southbound on Fridays from lunchtime onwards.

M4 SLOUGH–READING Heavy traffic going eastbound in morning peaks and westbound in evening peaks. Queues may extend westwards to **Newbury** and **Hungerford** on Friday evenings at the start of holiday periods.

A3 GUILDFORD–M25 Busy during Monday–Friday peak times.

M27 JUNCTION 5–3 AND M271 Both roads are busy in the direction of **Southampton** during Monday–Friday morning peaks.

A3 HINDHEAD Busy northbound in morning and evening peaks, and southbound in evening peaks and on Fridays from lunchtime onwards; also congested in both directions on summer Sundays.

A27 THROUGH WORTHING Heavy congestion during Monday–Friday peaks.

Woodstock · Bicester · Aylesbury · Stevenage · Bishop's · Harlow
A 4260 · A 4421 · A 505 · Luton · Dunstable · A 120
A 34 · A 44 · OXFORD · A 41 · A 418 · Hemel Hempstead · St Albans · Hatfield · A 414 · M 1
A 4095 · A 40 · Thame · Aylesbury · Luton · A 413 · Potters Bar · Epping
Abingdon · M 40 · Amersham · Watford · M 25 · A 406
A 4174 · A 329 · A 4010 · High Wycombe · Beaconsfield · A 404 · A 40
Henley-on-Thames · Maidenhead · Slough · LONDON · London City · Dartfo
A 34 · A 3293 · A 4074 · A 4130 · Windsor
READING · Bracknell · Staines · A 3 · A 23 · Croydon
M 4 · Newbury · A 4 · A 30 · A 322 · M 3 · Woking · Epsom · A 217 · A 25 · Sevenoa
A 33 · Aldershot · A 331 · Guildford · Dorking · Reigate · Redhill · Godstone
Basingstoke · Farnham · Reigate · M 23 · A 22
Andover · A 339 · A 3 · Milford · Gatwick · Crawley · A 264
A 303 · A 3057 · Alton · A 287 · Hindhead · A 24 · East Grinstead
M 3 · A 30 · A 34 · A 325 · Haslemere · Horsham · Haywards Heath · A 275
Winchester · A 31 · A 32 · A 281 · A 272
A 27 · Petersfield · Midhurst · A 283 · Burgess Hill · A 23 · A 272 · Uckf
Southampton · A 272 · A 285 · A 286 · A 24 · A 283 · A 281 · A 273 · A 26
SOUTHAMPTON · A 32 · A 3(M) · Lewes · A 27
A 326 · Fareham · M 27 · Chichester · Shoreham · BRIGHTON and HOVE
Gosport · PORTSMOUTH · Littlehampton · Worthing · Shoreham-by-Sea · Newhaven
Cowes · Bognor Regis
Ryde · ISLE OF WIGHT
Sandown · Shanklin

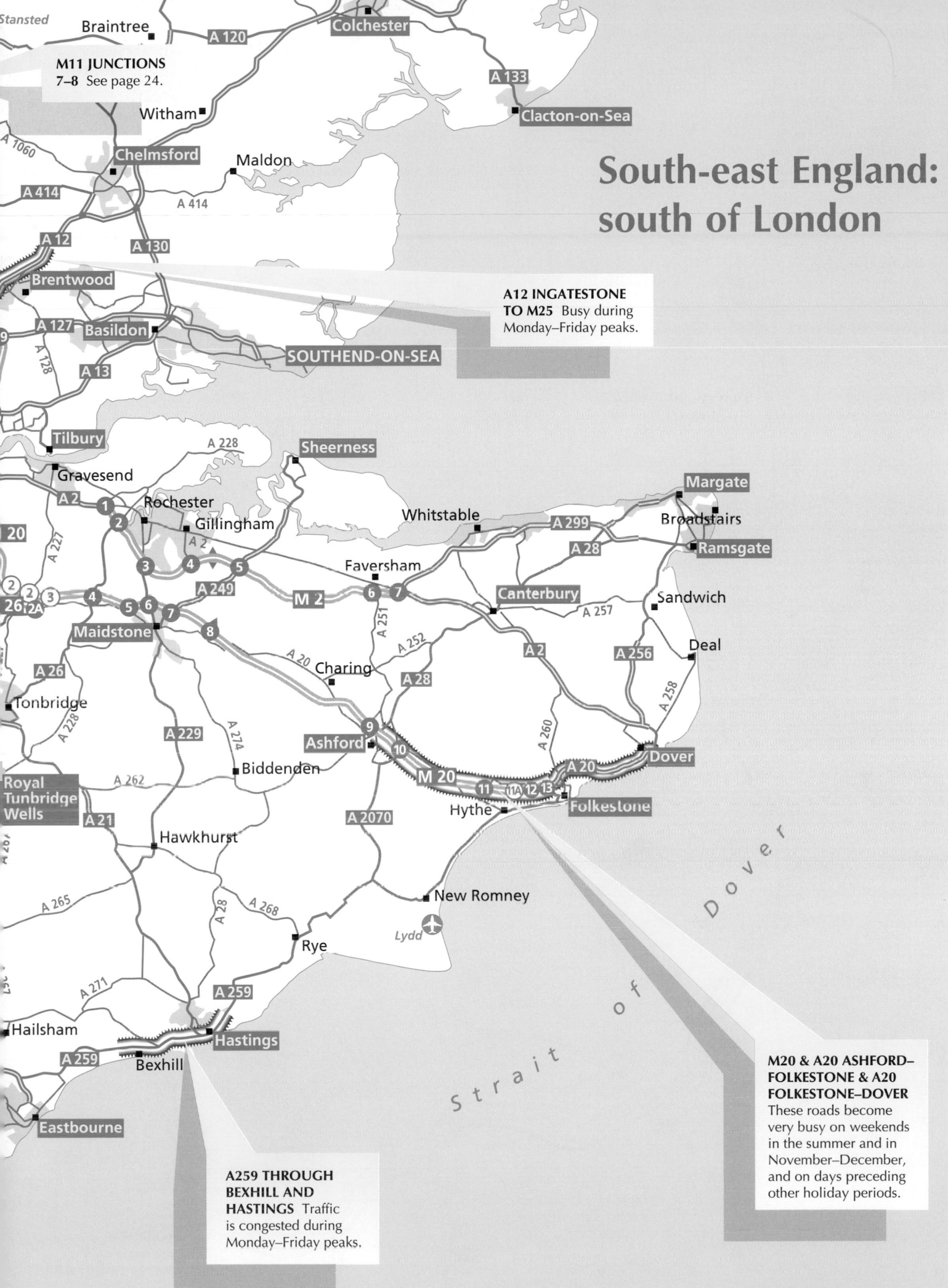

South-east England: south of London

Stansted

Braintree

Colchester

M11 JUNCTIONS 7–8 See page 24.

A 120

A 133

Witham

Clacton-on-Sea

Chelmsford

Maldon

A 1060

A 414

A 414

A 130

A 12

Brentwood

A12 INGATESTONE TO M25 Busy during Monday–Friday peaks.

A 127

Basildon

SOUTHEND-ON-SEA

A 128

A 13

Tilbury

Gravesend

A 228

Sheerness

Margate

A 2

Rochester

Whitstable

Broadstairs

1

A 299

20

2

Gillingham

A 28

Ramsgate

A 227

A 2

Faversham

2

3

4

5

6

7

Canterbury

Sandwich

2

2A

3

4

A 249

M 2

A 251

A 257

26 2A

5

6

7

A 252

A 2

Deal

Maidstone

8

A 20

Charing

A 256

A 26

A 28

A 258

Tonbridge

A 228

A 274

A 260

Royal Tunbridge Wells

A 229

9

Ashford

Dover

A 262

10

A 20

A 21

M 20

11

1A 12 13

Hawkhurst

A 2070

Hythe

Folkestone

A259 THROUGH BEXHILL AND HASTINGS Traffic is congested during Monday–Friday peaks.

A 265

A 28

A 268

New Romney

Lydd

Rye

A 271

A 259

Strait of Dover

Hailsham

Hastings

A 259

Bexhill

Eastbourne

Strait of Dover

M20 & A20 ASHFORD–FOLKESTONE & A20 FOLKESTONE–DOVER These roads become very busy on weekends in the summer and in November–December, and on days preceding other holiday periods.

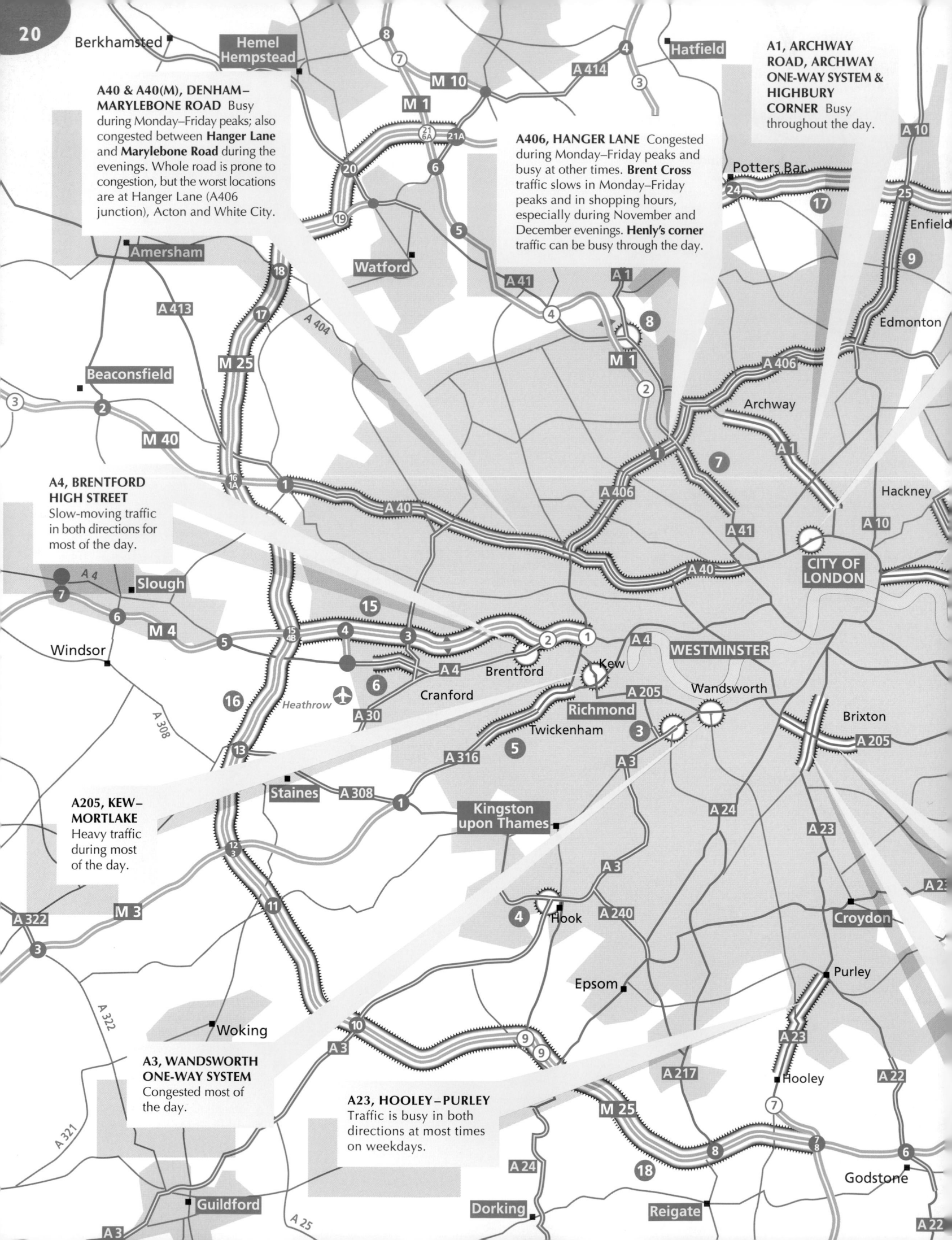

20

Berkhamsted

Hemel Hempstead

A40 & A40(M), DENHAM–MARYLEBONE ROAD Busy during Monday–Friday peaks; also congested between **Hanger Lane** and **Marylebone Road** during the evenings. Whole road is prone to congestion, but the worst locations are at Hanger Lane (A406 junction), Acton and White City.

A406, HANGER LANE Congested during Monday–Friday peaks and busy at other times. **Brent Cross** traffic slows in Monday–Friday peaks and in shopping hours, especially during November and December evenings. **Henly's corner** traffic can be busy through the day.

A1, ARCHWAY ROAD, ARCHWAY ONE-WAY SYSTEM & HIGHBURY CORNER Busy throughout the day.

Hatfield

A414

Potters Bar

Enfield

Edmonton

Amersham

A413

Watford

Archway

Hackney

Beaconsfield

A4, BRENTFORD HIGH STREET Slow-moving traffic in both directions for most of the day.

Windsor

Slough

M 4

Heathrow

Brentford

Cranford

Kew

WESTMINSTER

Wandsworth

Brixton

CITY OF LONDON

Richmond

Twickenham

A205, KEW–MORTLAKE Heavy traffic during most of the day.

Staines

Kingston upon Thames

Woking

A3, WANDSWORTH ONE-WAY SYSTEM Congested most of the day.

A23, HOOLEY–PURLEY Traffic is busy in both directions at most times on weekdays.

Hook

Epsom

Purley

Croydon

Hooley

Godstone

Guildford

Dorking

Reigate

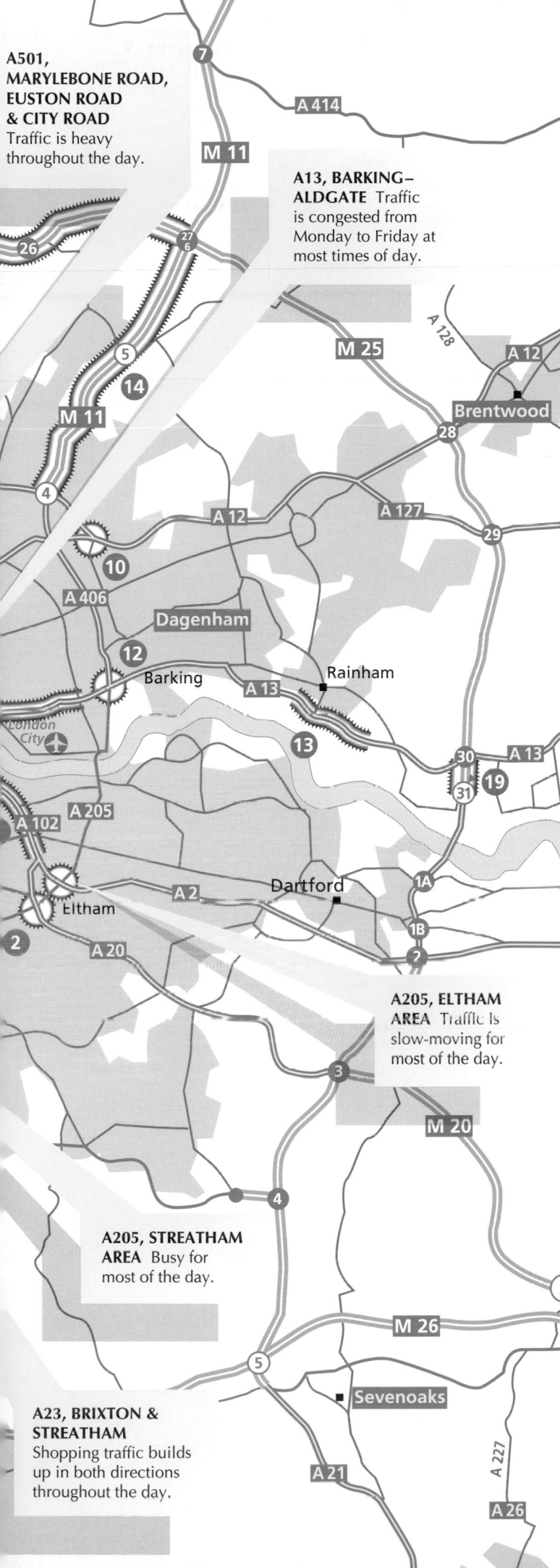

A501, MARYLEBONE ROAD, EUSTON ROAD & CITY ROAD Traffic is heavy throughout the day.

A13, BARKING–ALDGATE Traffic is congested from Monday to Friday at most times of day.

Brentwood

Dagenham

Barking

Rainham

London City

Dartford

Eltham

A205, ELTHAM AREA Traffic is slow-moving for most of the day.

A205, STREATHAM AREA Busy for most of the day.

Sevenoaks

A23, BRIXTON & STREATHAM Shopping traffic builds up in both directions throughout the day.

Greater London: within the M25

This map shows some of the worst congestion blackspots in London. However, most of the principal routes can be heavily congested at peak times, so it is advisable to allow extra time for journeys through or around London.

❶ A102, BLACKWALL TUNNEL SOUTHERN APPROACH
Congested from Monday to Friday at peak times in both directions.

❷ A20, ELTHAM AT WESTHORNE AVENUE ROUNDABOUT (JUNCTION WITH A205)
The junction is busy during Monday–Friday peaks, and sometimes throughout the day.

❸ A3, TIBBETT'S CORNER
Traffic is heavy during weekday peaks and often during off-peak times too.

❹ A3, HOOK
Congested in Monday–Friday peaks and also through the evening in November and early December as a result of heavy shopping traffic in the Kingston area.

❺ A316, TWICKENHAM–RICHMOND
Congested on weekdays at peak times and also when rugby matches are played.

❻ A4, CRANFORD
Very busy in both directions during peak times from Monday to Friday.

❼ A41, FINCHLEY ROAD & SWISS COTTAGE
Can be very congested during Monday–Friday peaks, and on Saturdays. Also often busy at off-peak times.

❽ A41 & A1, MILL HILL, NORTHWAY CIRCUS 'APEX CORNER'
Congested during peak times on weekdays and also on Sunday evenings.

❾ A10, ENFIELD–EDMONTON
Heavy traffic during Monday–Friday peaks and during school times.

❿ A12, GANTS HILL
Heavy congestion can be expected during peak times from Monday to Friday.

⓫ A12, HACKNEY–BLACKWALL TUNNEL
Busy in both directions in Monday–Friday peaks.

⓬ A406–A13, BARKING
Congested during weekday peaks and occasionally at off-peak times.

⓭ A13, RAINHAM BYPASS
Traffic builds up during Monday–Friday peaks.

⓮ M11, JUNCTION 6–4
Congestion occurs during Monday–Friday peaks.

⓯ M4, JUNCTION 1–4B
Traffic builds up during Monday–Friday peaks and occasionally at off-peak times too.

⓰ M25, WESTERN SECTOR (JUNCTIONS 10–21A)
Busy in both directions during Monday–Friday peak times, Saturday shopping times and on Sunday evenings. Also congested throughout the day on Saturdays and Sundays from late November to early December and during school holiday periods.

⓱ M25, JUNCTIONS 23–27
Heavy traffic during weekday peaks and on Sunday evenings.

⓲ M25, JUNCTIONS 10–7
Slow-moving during Monday–Friday peak times, especially during the summer months, as a result of heavy airport traffic.

⓳ M25, JUNCTIONS 30–31B
Shopping traffic can cause delays during evenings and weekends in November and early December.

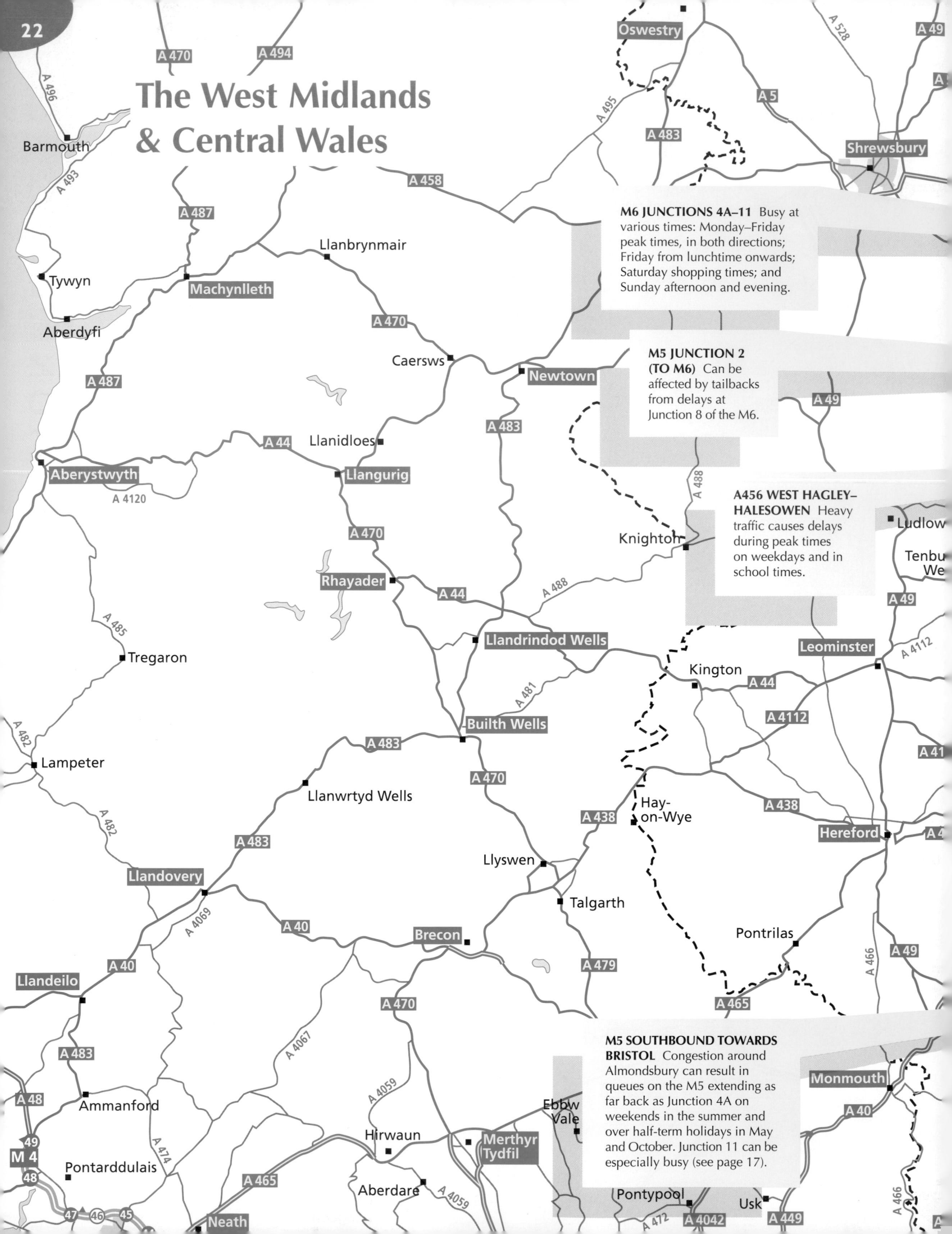

The West Midlands & Central Wales

M6 JUNCTIONS 4A–11 Busy at various times: Monday–Friday peak times, in both directions; Friday from lunchtime onwards; Saturday shopping times; and Sunday afternoon and evening.

M5 JUNCTION 2 (TO M6) Can be affected by tailbacks from delays at Junction 8 of the M6.

A456 WEST HAGLEY–HALESOWEN Heavy traffic causes delays during peak times on weekdays and in school times.

M5 SOUTHBOUND TOWARDS BRISTOL Congestion around Almondsbury can result in queues on the M5 extending as far back as Junction 4A on weekends in the summer and over half-term holidays in May and October. Junction 11 can be especially busy (see page 17).

Barmouth
Oswestry
Shrewsbury
Tywyn
Machynlleth
Llanbrynmair
Aberdyfi
Caersws
Newtown
Llanidloes
Ludlow
Aberystwyth
Llangurig
Knighton
Tenbu We
Rhayader
Llandrindod Wells
Leominster
Tregaron
Kington
Lampeter
Builth Wells
Llanwrtyd Wells
Hay-on-Wye
Hereford
Llyswen
Llandovery
Talgarth
Pontrilas
Brecon
Llandeilo
Ammanford
Hirwaun
Merthyr Tydfil
Ebbw Vale
Monmouth
Pontarddulais
Aberdare
Neath
Pontypool
Usk

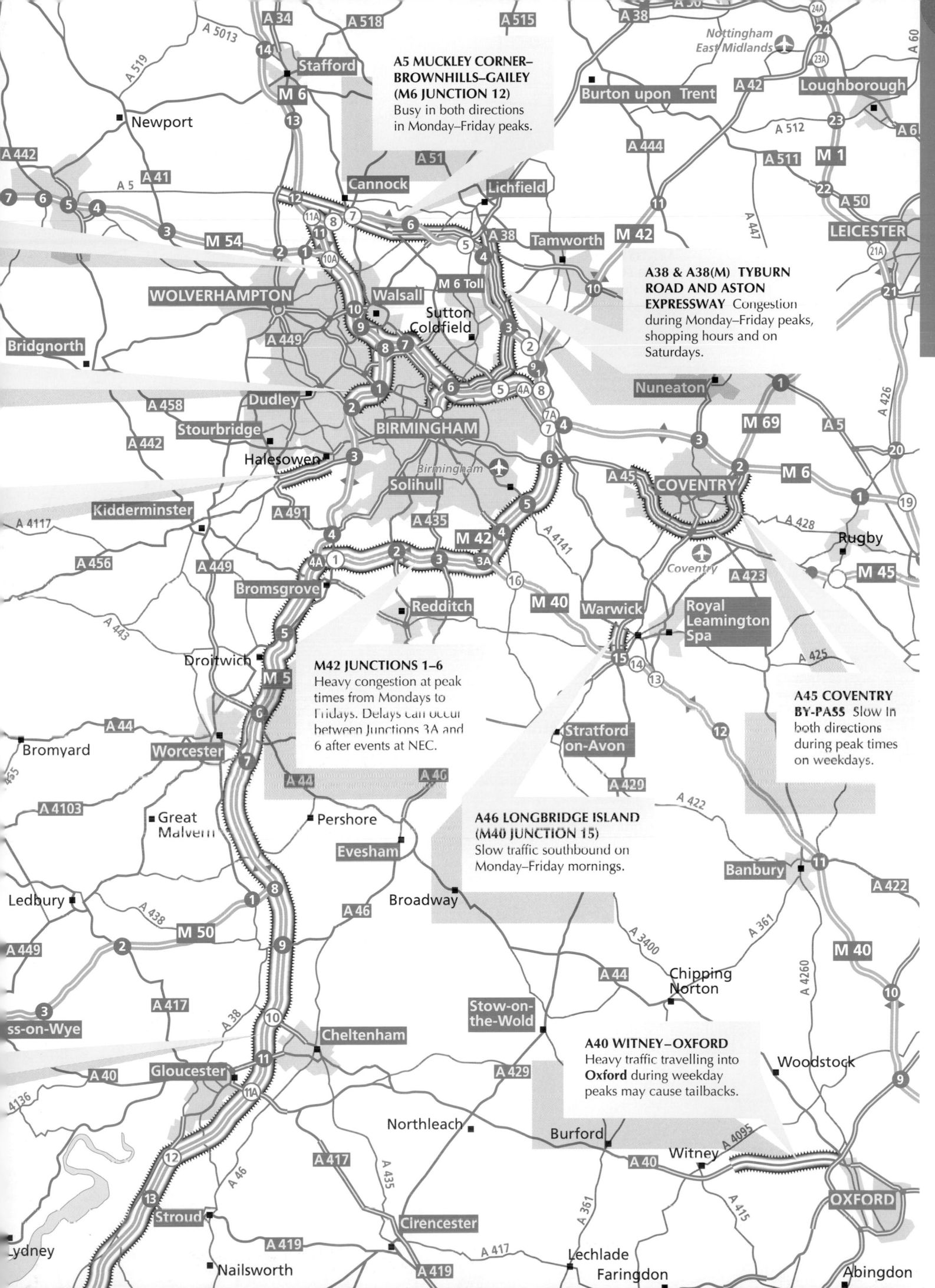

A5 MUCKLEY CORNER–BROWNHILLS–GAILEY (M6 JUNCTION 12) Busy in both directions in Monday–Friday peaks.

A38 & A38(M) TYBURN ROAD AND ASTON EXPRESSWAY Congestion during Monday–Friday peaks, shopping hours and on Saturdays.

M42 JUNCTIONS 1–6 Heavy congestion at peak times from Mondays to Fridays. Delays can occur between Junctions 3A and 6 after events at NEC.

A45 COVENTRY BY-PASS Slow in both directions during peak times on weekdays.

A46 LONGBRIDGE ISLAND (M40 JUNCTION 15) Slow traffic southbound on Monday–Friday mornings.

A40 WITNEY–OXFORD Heavy traffic travelling into **Oxford** during weekday peaks may cause tailbacks.

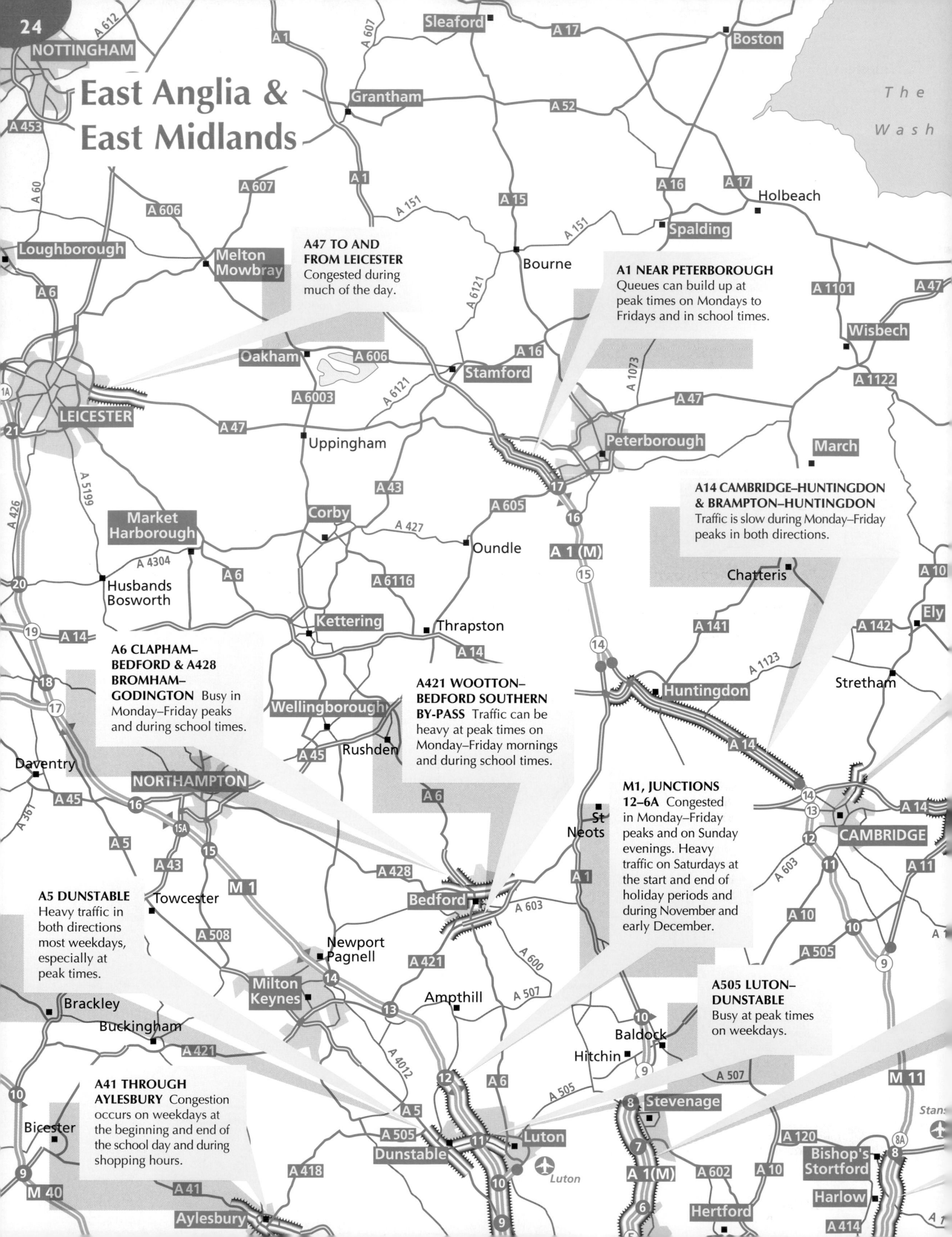

East Anglia & East Midlands

A47 TO AND FROM LEICESTER Congested during much of the day.

A1 NEAR PETERBOROUGH Queues can build up at peak times on Mondays to Fridays and in school times.

A14 CAMBRIDGE–HUNTINGDON & BRAMPTON–HUNTINGDON Traffic is slow during Monday–Friday peaks in both directions.

A6 CLAPHAM– BEDFORD & A428 BROMHAM– GODINGTON Busy in Monday–Friday peaks and during school times.

A421 WOOTTON– BEDFORD SOUTHERN BY-PASS Traffic can be heavy at peak times on Monday–Friday mornings and during school times.

M1, JUNCTIONS 12–6A Congested in Monday–Friday peaks and on Sunday evenings. Heavy traffic on Saturdays at the start and end of holiday periods and during November and early December.

A5 DUNSTABLE Heavy traffic in both directions most weekdays, especially at peak times.

A505 LUTON– DUNSTABLE Busy at peak times on weekdays.

A41 THROUGH AYLESBURY Congestion occurs on weekdays at the beginning and end of the school day and during shopping hours.

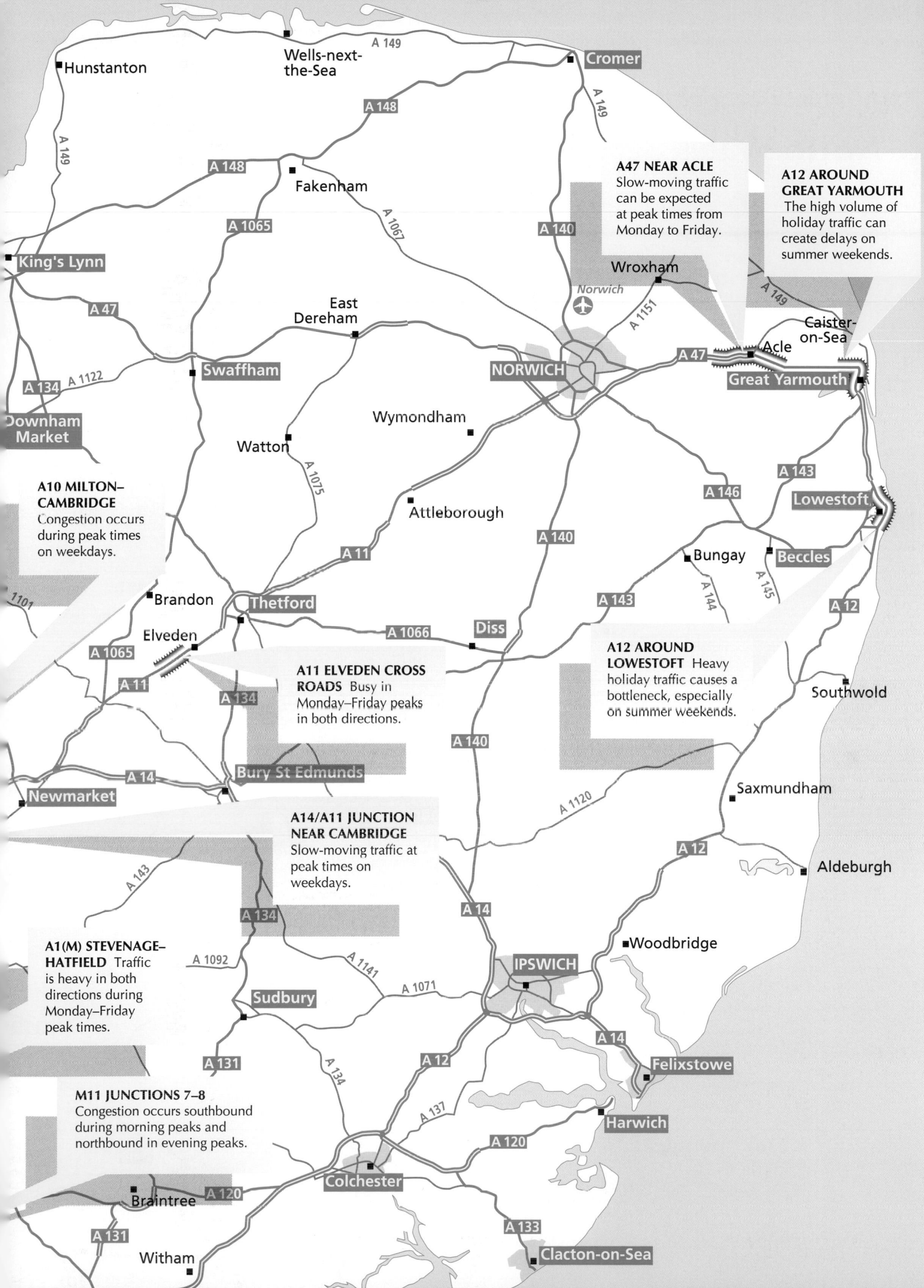

A47 NEAR ACLE Slow-moving traffic can be expected at peak times from Monday to Friday.

A12 AROUND GREAT YARMOUTH The high volume of holiday traffic can create delays on summer weekends.

A10 MILTON–CAMBRIDGE Congestion occurs during peak times on weekdays.

A11 ELVEDEN CROSS ROADS Busy in Monday–Friday peaks in both directions.

A12 AROUND LOWESTOFT Heavy holiday traffic causes a bottleneck, especially on summer weekends.

A14/A11 JUNCTION NEAR CAMBRIDGE Slow-moving traffic at peak times on weekdays.

A1(M) STEVENAGE–HATFIELD Traffic is heavy in both directions during Monday–Friday peak times.

M11 JUNCTIONS 7–8 Congestion occurs southbound during morning peaks and northbound in evening peaks.

North-west England & North Wales

IRISH   SEA

A565, FORMBY–LIVERPOOL
Can be very busy during Monday–Friday peaks and at shopping times.

A55, CHESTER–CONWY Carries holiday traffic to North Wales during July and August so is busy on summer weekends. There may be heavy traffic on Saturdays at the start of half term holidays and Sunday afternoons at the end of half term.

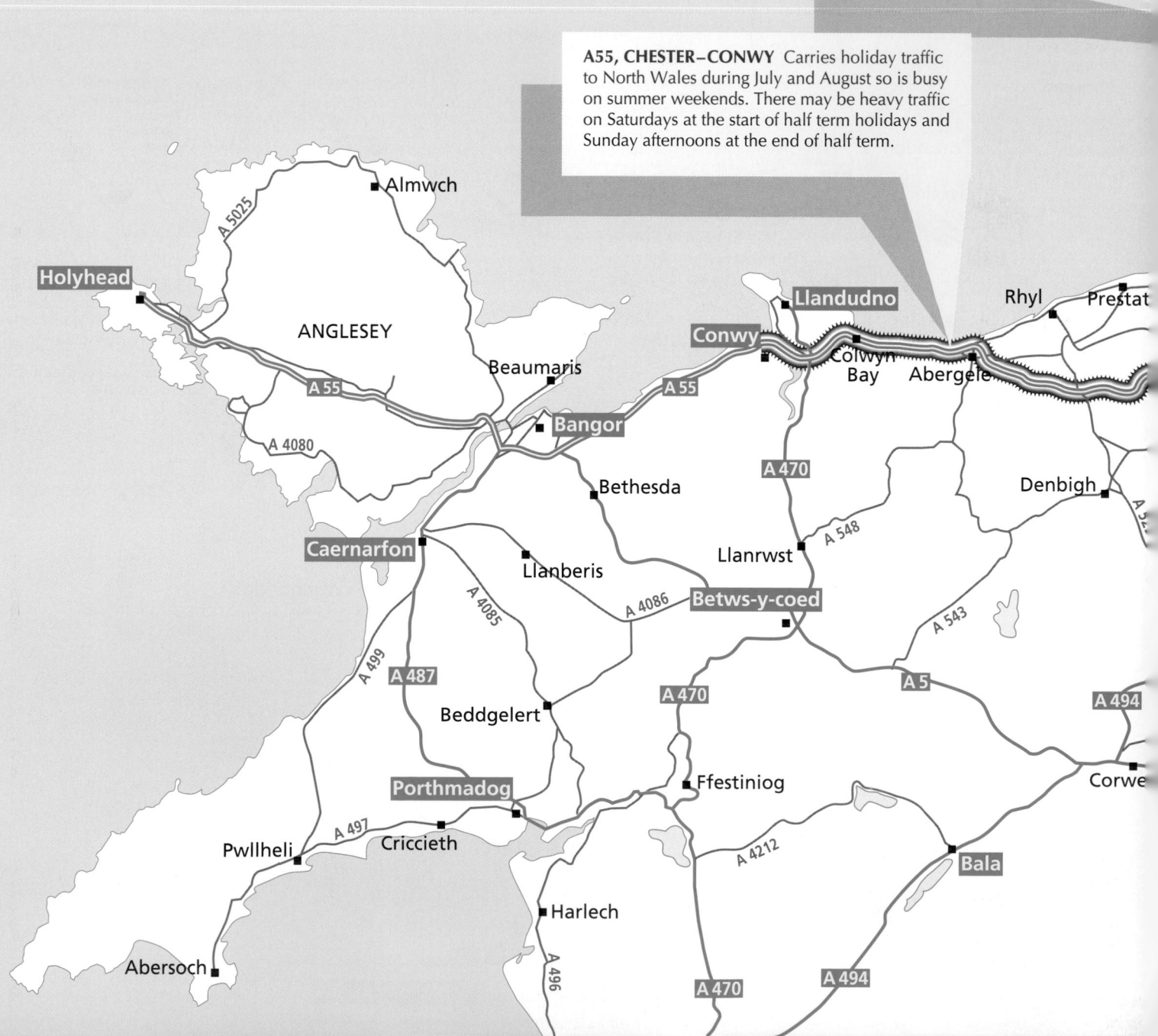

Holyhead

ANGLESEY

A 5025

Almwch

A 4080

A 55

Beaumaris

Bangor

A 55

Conwy

Llandudno

Colwyn Bay

Abergele

Rhyl

Prestat

Caernarfon

Bethesda

A 470

Denbigh

Llanberis

A 548

Llanrwst

A 4086

Betws-y-coed

A 543

A 4085

A 499

A 487

Beddgelert

A 470

A 5

A 494

Porthmadog

Ffestiniog

Corwe

Pwllheli

A 497

Criccieth

A 4212

A 496

Bala

Harlech

A 470

A 494

Abersoch

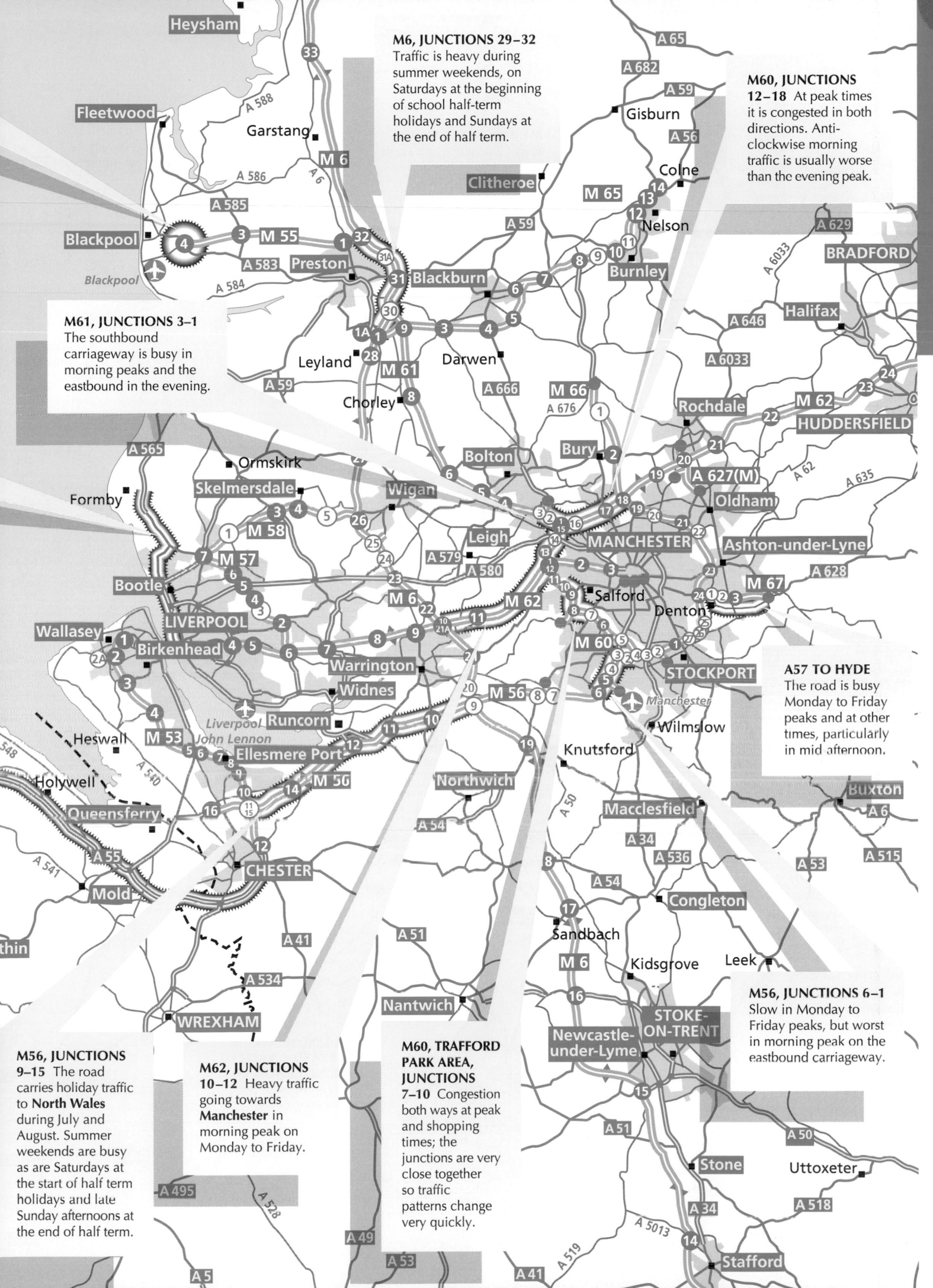

M6, JUNCTIONS 29–32 Traffic is heavy during summer weekends, on Saturdays at the beginning of school half-term holidays and Sundays at the end of half term.

M60, JUNCTIONS 12–18 At peak times it is congested in both directions. Anticlockwise morning traffic is usually worse than the evening peak.

M61, JUNCTIONS 3–1 The southbound carriageway is busy in morning peaks and the eastbound in the evening.

A57 TO HYDE The road is busy Monday to Friday peaks and at other times, particularly in mid afternoon.

M56, JUNCTIONS 6–1 Slow in Monday to Friday peaks, but worst in morning peak on the eastbound carriageway.

M56, JUNCTIONS 9–15 The road carries holiday traffic to **North Wales** during July and August. Summer weekends are busy as are Saturdays at the start of half term holidays and late Sunday afternoons at the end of half term.

M62, JUNCTIONS 10–12 Heavy traffic going towards **Manchester** in morning peak on Monday to Friday.

M60, TRAFFORD PARK AREA, JUNCTIONS 7–10 Congestion both ways at peak and shopping times; the junctions are very close together so traffic patterns change very quickly.

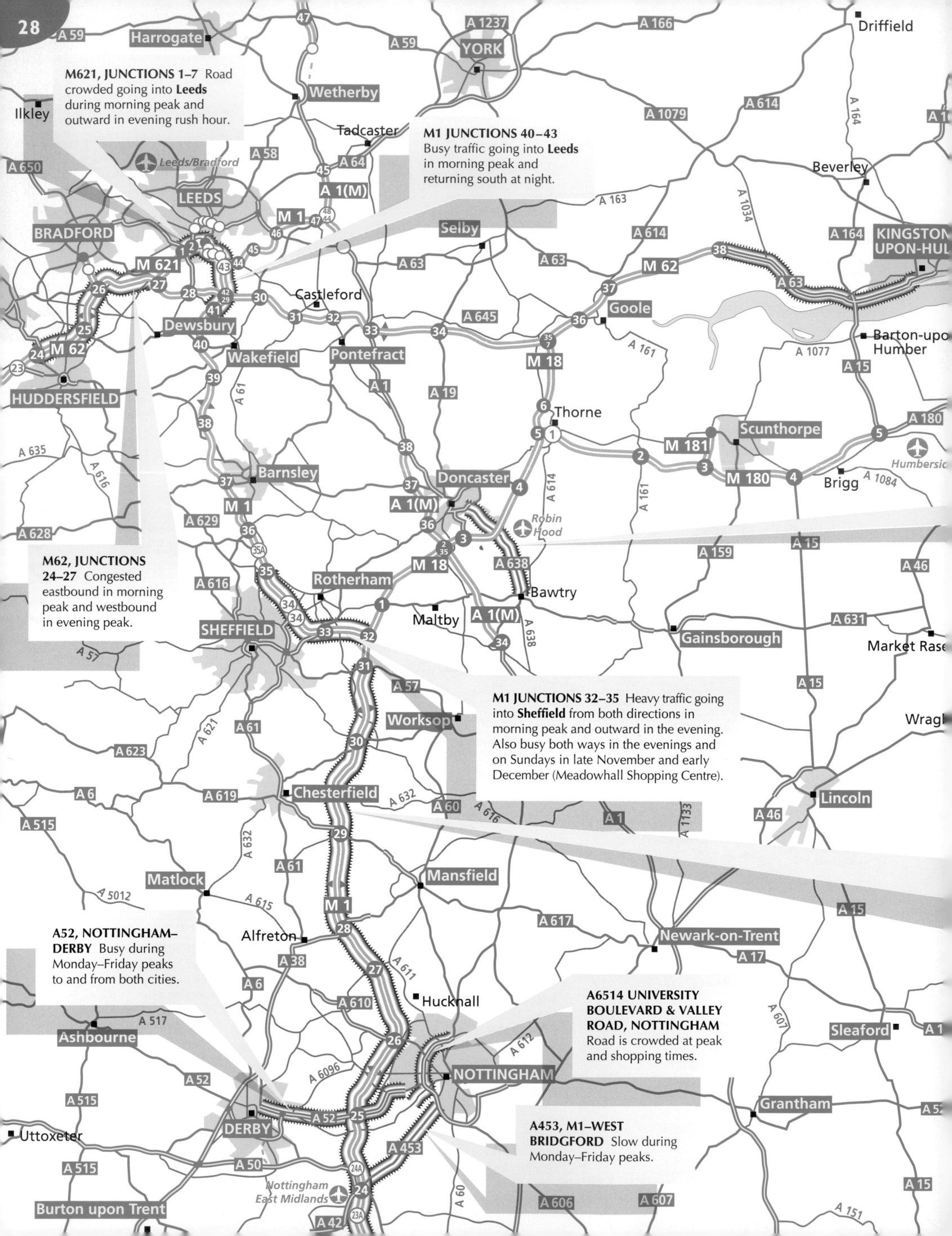

M621, JUNCTIONS 1–7 Road crowded going into **Leeds** during morning peak and outward in evening rush hour.

M1 JUNCTIONS 40–43 Busy traffic going into **Leeds** in morning peak and returning south at night.

M62, JUNCTIONS 24–27 Congested eastbound in morning peak and westbound in evening peak.

M1 JUNCTIONS 32–35 Heavy traffic going into **Sheffield** from both directions in morning peak and outward in the evening. Also busy both ways in the evenings and on Sundays in late November and early December (Meadowhall Shopping Centre).

A52, NOTTINGHAM–DERBY Busy during Monday–Friday peaks to and from both cities.

A6514 UNIVERSITY BOULEVARD & VALLEY ROAD, NOTTINGHAM Road is crowded at peak and shopping times.

A453, M1–WEST BRIDGFORD Slow during Monday–Friday peaks.

Driffield

Harrogate

Ilkley

Wetherby

Tadcaster

YORK

Leeds/Bradford

LEEDS

BRADFORD

Beverley

Selby

KINGSTON UPON-HULL

Castleford

Goole

Dewsbury

Barton-upon Humber

Wakefield

Pontefract

HUDDERSFIELD

Scunthorpe

Thorne

Brigg

Barnsley

Doncaster

Humberside

Rotherham

Robin Hood

Maltby

Bawtry

Gainsborough

SHEFFIELD

Market Rasen

Worksop

Lincoln

Chesterfield

Wragby

Matlock

Mansfield

Newark-on-Trent

Alfreton

Sleaford

Ashbourne

Hucknall

NOTTINGHAM

Grantham

DERBY

Uttoxeter

Nottingham East Midlands

Burton upon Trent

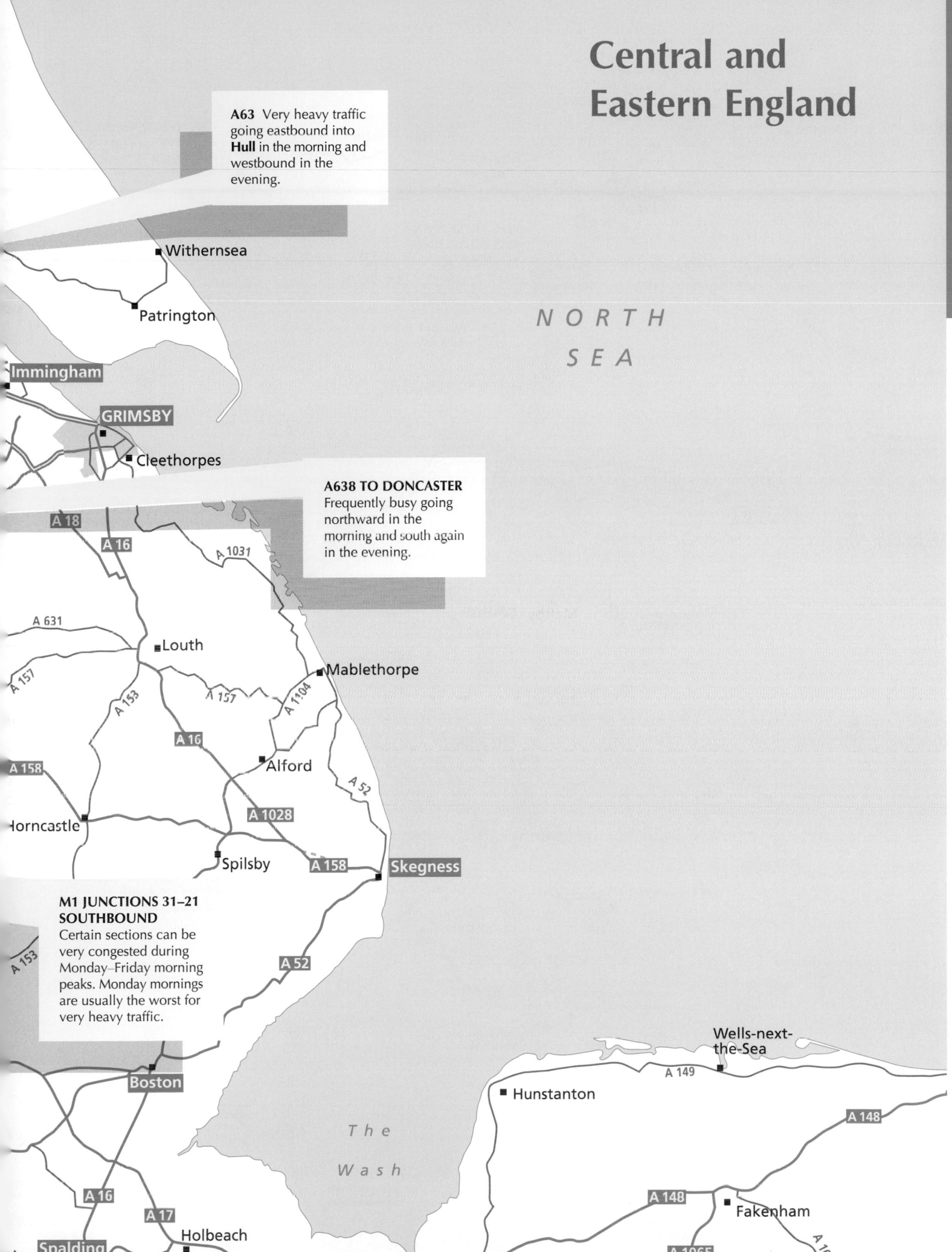

Central and Eastern England

A63 Very heavy traffic going eastbound into **Hull** in the morning and westbound in the evening.

A638 TO DONCASTER
Frequently busy going northward in the morning and south again in the evening.

M1 JUNCTIONS 31–21 SOUTHBOUND
Certain sections can be very congested during Monday–Friday morning peaks. Monday mornings are usually the worst for very heavy traffic.

NORTH SEA

The Wash

Withernsea

Patrington

Immingham

GRIMSBY

Cleethorpes

A 18

A 16

A 1031

A 631

A 157

Louth

Mablethorpe

A 157

A 153

A 157

A 1104

A 16

A 158

Alford

A 52

Horncastle

A 1028

Spilsby

A 158

Skegness

A 153

A 52

Wells-next-the-Sea

A 149

Boston

Hunstanton

A 148

A 16

A 148

A 17

Fakenham

Holbeach

A 1065

A 1067

Spalding

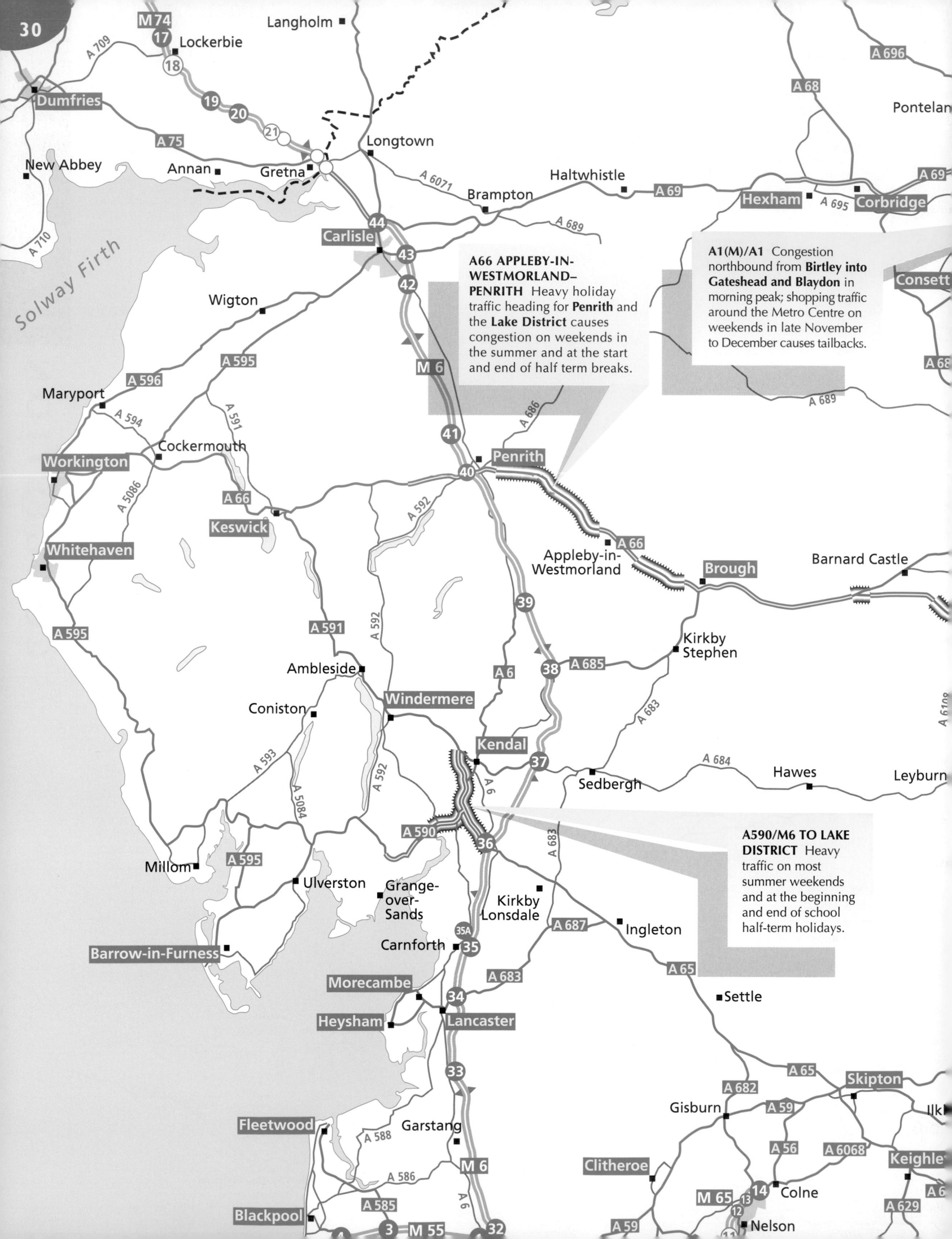

A66 APPLEBY-IN-WESTMORLAND–PENRITH Heavy holiday traffic heading for **Penrith** and the **Lake District** causes congestion on weekends in the summer and at the start and end of half term breaks.

A1(M)/A1 Congestion northbound from **Birtley into Gateshead and Blaydon** in morning peak; shopping traffic around the Metro Centre on weekends in late November to December causes tailbacks.

A590/M6 TO LAKE DISTRICT Heavy traffic on most summer weekends and at the beginning and end of school half-term holidays.

Solway Firth

Dumfries
New Abbey
Annan
Gretna
Longtown
Langholm
Lockerbie
Haltwhistle
Brampton
Hexham
Corbridge
Pontelan
Consett

Carlisle
Wigton
Maryport
Cockermouth
Workington
Whitehaven
Keswick
Penrith
Appleby-in-Westmorland
Brough
Barnard Castle
Kirkby Stephen
Ambleside
Coniston
Windermere
Kendal
Sedbergh
Hawes
Leyburn
Millom
Ulverston
Grange-over-Sands
Kirkby Lonsdale
Ingleton
Barrow-in-Furness
Carnforth
Morecambe
Heysham
Lancaster
Settle
Fleetwood
Garstang
Gisburn
Skipton
Ilk
Blackpool
Clitheroe
Keighle
Colne
Nelson

M74
M6
M55
M65

A709
A75
A710
A596
A594
A595
A591
A5086
A592
A593
A5084
A588
A586
A585
A6071
A689
A69
A695
A68
A696
A686
A66
A685
A683
A684
A6108
A687
A65
A682
A59
A56
A6068
A629
A6

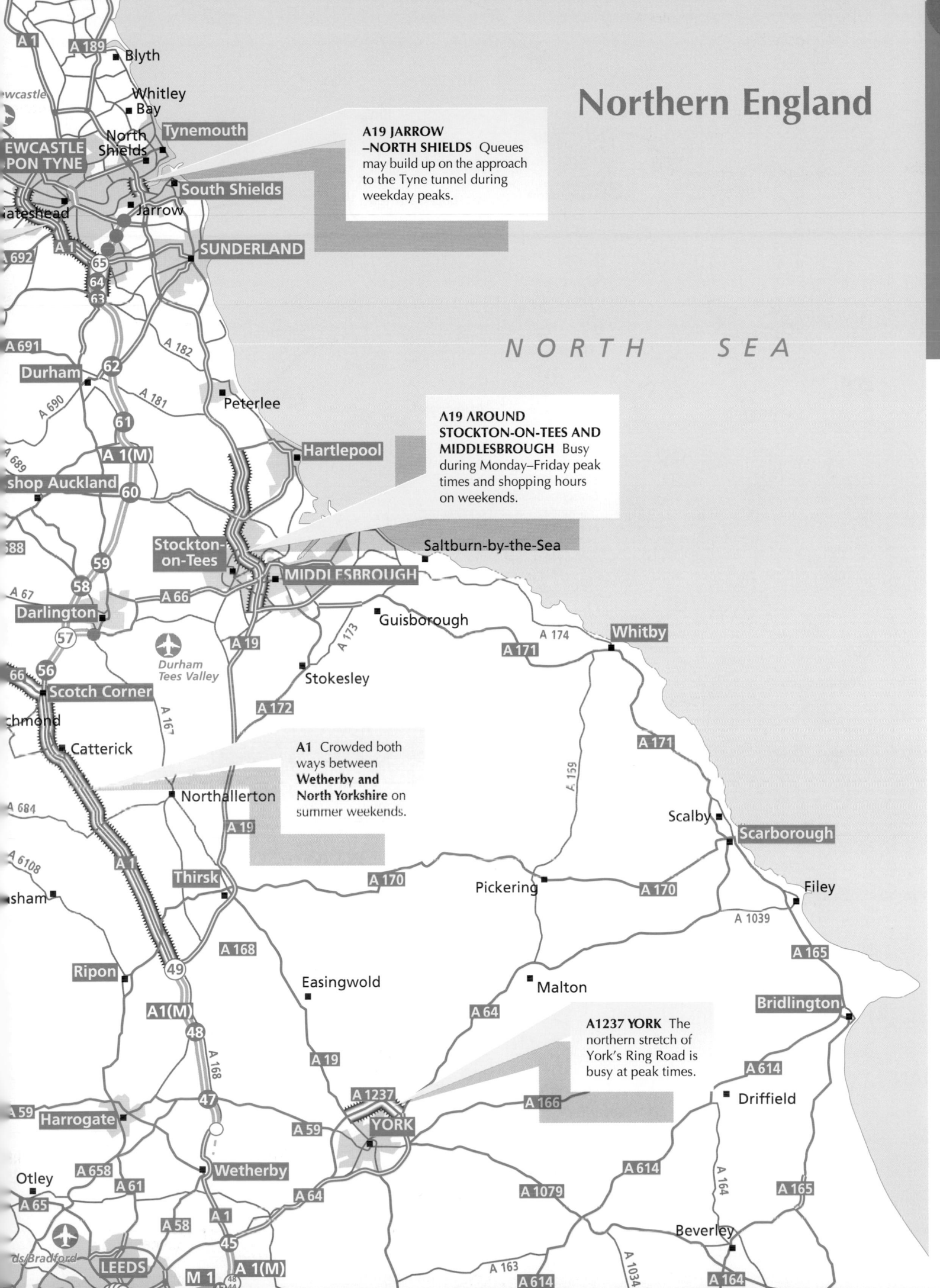

Northern England

A19 JARROW –NORTH SHIELDS Queues may build up on the approach to the Tyne tunnel during weekday peaks.

A19 AROUND STOCKTON-ON-TEES AND MIDDLESBROUGH Busy during Monday–Friday peak times and shopping hours on weekends.

A1 Crowded both ways between **Wetherby and North Yorkshire** on summer weekends.

A1237 YORK The northern stretch of York's Ring Road is busy at peak times.

NORTH SEA

Blyth
Whitley Bay
Tynemouth
wcastle
North Shields
EWCASTLE PON TYNE
South Shields
ateshead
Jarrow
SUNDERLAND
A 189
A 1
A 692
A 1
65
64
63
A 691
A 182
Durham
62
A 690
A 181
Peterlee
61
A 1(M)
Hartlepool
shop Auckland
60
A 689
688
59
Stockton-on-Tees
Saltburn-by-the-Sea
A 67
58
MIDDLESBROUGH
Darlington
A 66
Guisborough
Whitby
57
A 19
A 173
A 174
Durham Tees Valley
A 171
66
56
Scotch Corner
Stokesley
chmond
A 172
A 171
Catterick
A 167
A 684
Northallerton
Scalby
Scarborough
A 6108
A 19
Filey
A 1
A 170
Pickering
A 170
Thirsk
A 159
A 1039
sham
A 168
A 165
Ripon
Easingwold
Malton
A 1(M)
Bridlington
49
A 64
A 614
48
A 168
A 19
A 1237 YORK
Driffield
A 59
Harrogate
A 1237
A 166
47
Otley
A 658
A 59
YORK
A 658
A 61
Wetherby
A 614
A 59
A 164
A 165
A 65
A 64
A 1
A 1079
A 58
Beverley
LEEDS
45
ds Bradford
M 1
A 1(M)
A 163
A 614
A 1034
A 164

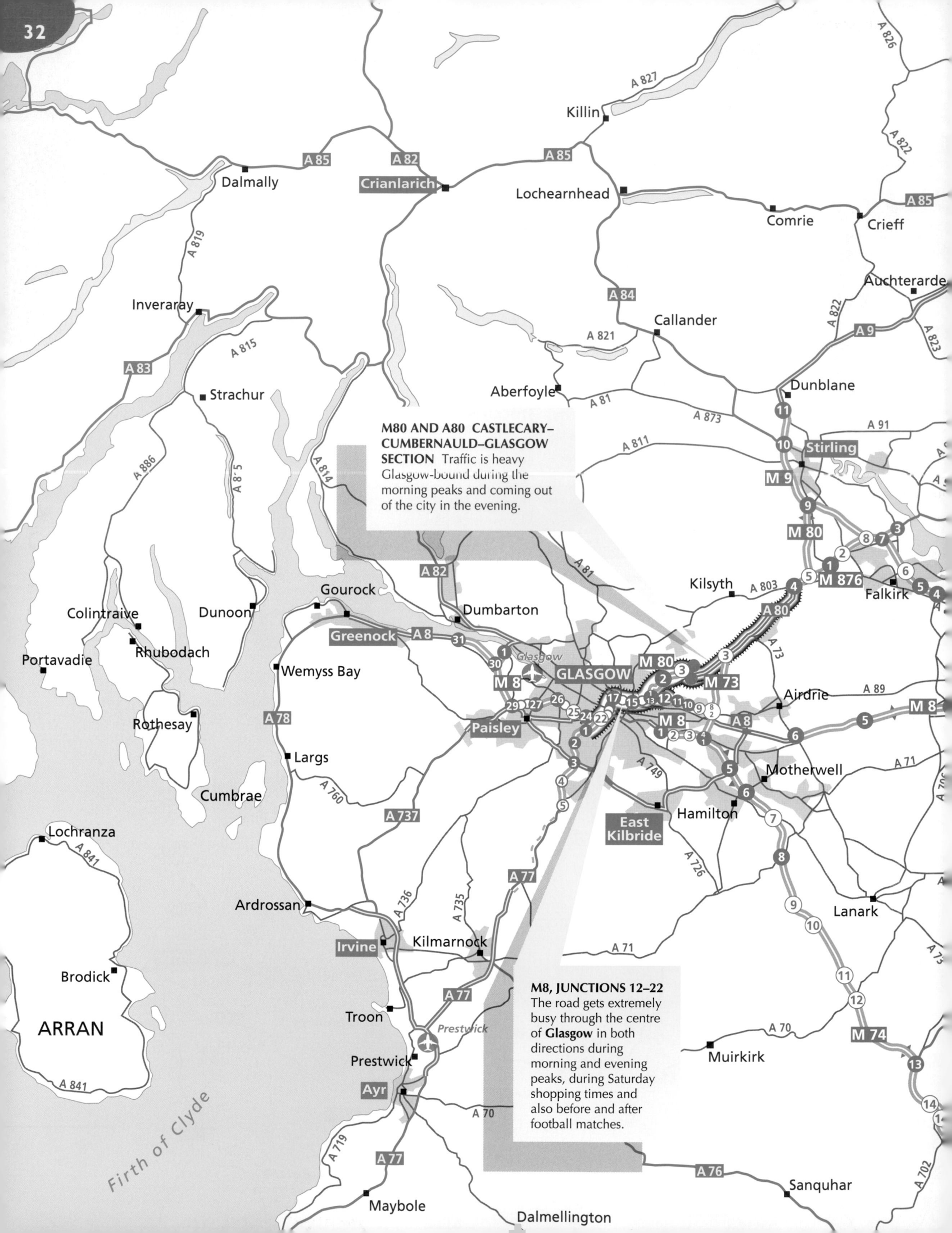

A 826

A 827

Killin

A 85

Dalmally

A 82

Crianlarich

A 85

Lochearnhead

Comrie

Crieff

A 85

A 822

A 819

A 84

Auchterarde

Inveraray

A 815

Callander

A 822

A 9

A 823

A 821

A 83

Strachur

Aberfoyle

A 81

Dunblane

A 91

M80 AND A80 CASTLECARY–CUMBERNAULD–GLASGOW SECTION Traffic is heavy Glasgow-bound during the morning peaks and coming out of the city in the evening.

A 873

11

A 811

10

Stirling

A 886

A 8'5

A 814

M 9

9

A 82

M 80

8 7 3

2

Gourock

A 82

Dumbarton

A 81

Kilsyth

A 803

1 M 876

Falkirk

Colintraive

Dunoon

A 80

4 5

A 80

Rhubodach

Glasgow

M 80

3

Portavadie

Wemyss Bay

31

1

M 73

A 73

Airdrie

A 89

M 8

30

2 3

A 78

M 8

29 1 27

26

17 15

13 12 11 10 9

8 2

A 8

M 8

Paisley

25 24 22

1

M 8

A 8

6

5

Rothesay

1

2

A 760

2

1 2 3 4

A 749

5

Largs

A 737

3

Motherwell

A 71

Cumbrae

4

5

6

Lochranza

A 841

East Kilbride

Hamilton

7

A 726

Ardrossan

A 736

A 735

8

A 77

Brodick

9

Lanark

A 73

10

Irvine

Kilmarnock

ARRAN

11

A 77

A 71

M8, JUNCTIONS 12–22 The road gets extremely busy through the centre of **Glasgow** in both directions during morning and evening peaks, during Saturday shopping times and also before and after football matches.

12

Troon

Prestwick

Muirkirk

A 70

M 74

Prestwick

13

Ayr

A 841

A 76

14

Firth of Clyde

A 719

A 70

A 702

A 77

Maybole

Dalmellington

Sanquhar

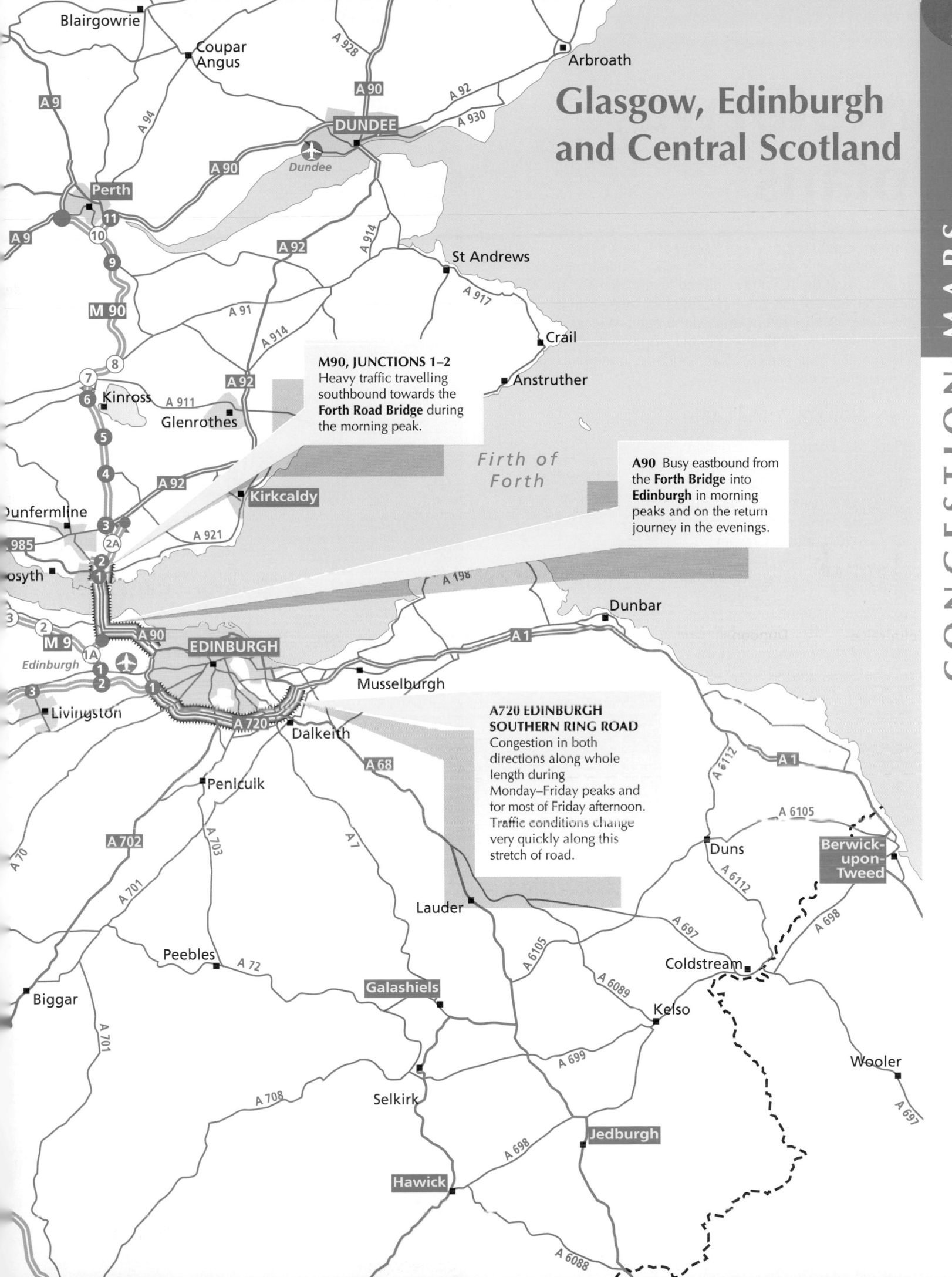

Glasgow, Edinburgh and Central Scotland

M90, JUNCTIONS 1–2
Heavy traffic travelling southbound towards the **Forth Road Bridge** during the morning peak.

A90 Busy eastbound from the **Forth Bridge** into **Edinburgh** in morning peaks and on the return journey in the evenings.

A720 EDINBURGH SOUTHERN RING ROAD
Congestion in both directions along whole length during Monday–Friday peaks and for most of Friday afternoon. Traffic conditions change very quickly along this stretch of road.

Blairgowrie
Coupar Angus
Arbroath
DUNDEE
Dundee
Perth
St Andrews
Crail
Kinross
Glenrothes
Anstruther
Firth of Forth
Kirkcaldy
Dunfermline
Dunbar
EDINBURGH
Edinburgh
Musselburgh
Livingston
Dalkeith
Penicuik
Duns
Berwick-upon-Tweed
Lauder
Peebles
Coldstream
Galashiels
Kelso
Biggar
Wooler
Selkirk
Jedburgh
Hawick

Motorway plans

The principal motorways of Britain and Ireland are shown as strip plans, with details of junctions and interchanges. Each plan starts at the junction with the lowest number and reads from the base of the column to the top, then continues from the base of the adjacent strip on the right. Mileages between the first and last destinations of the strips on each page are given at the foot; where a plan continues on the next page, a separate mileage is given.

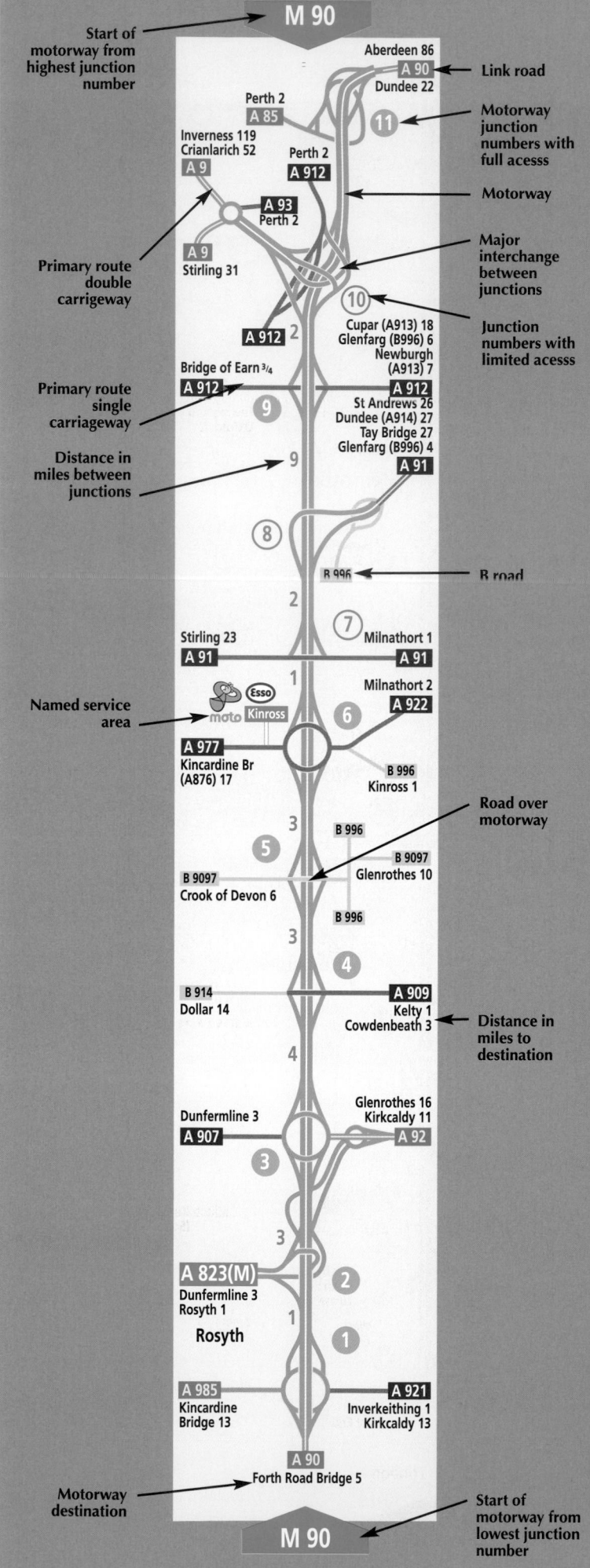

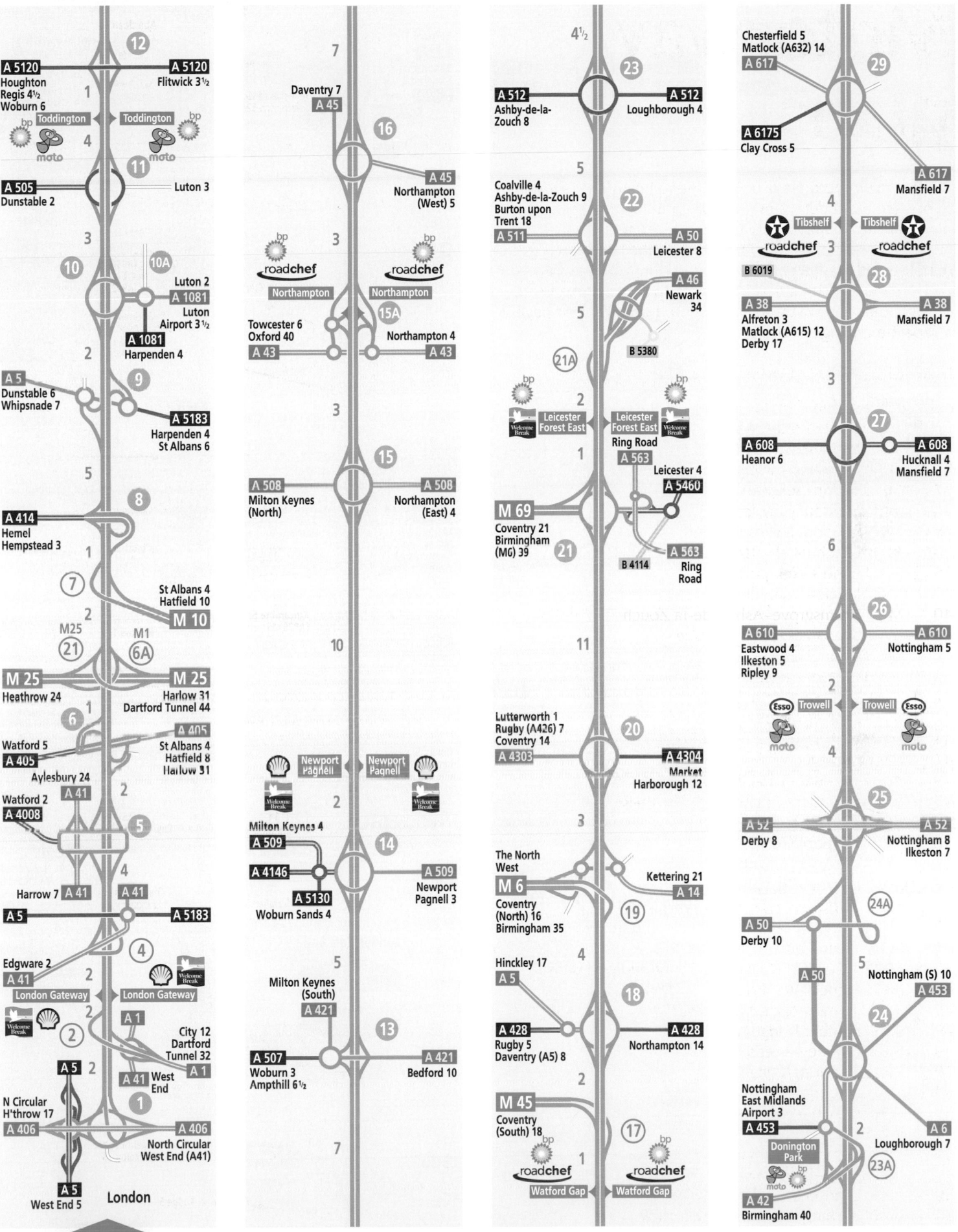

M1 London–Chesterfield 138 miles

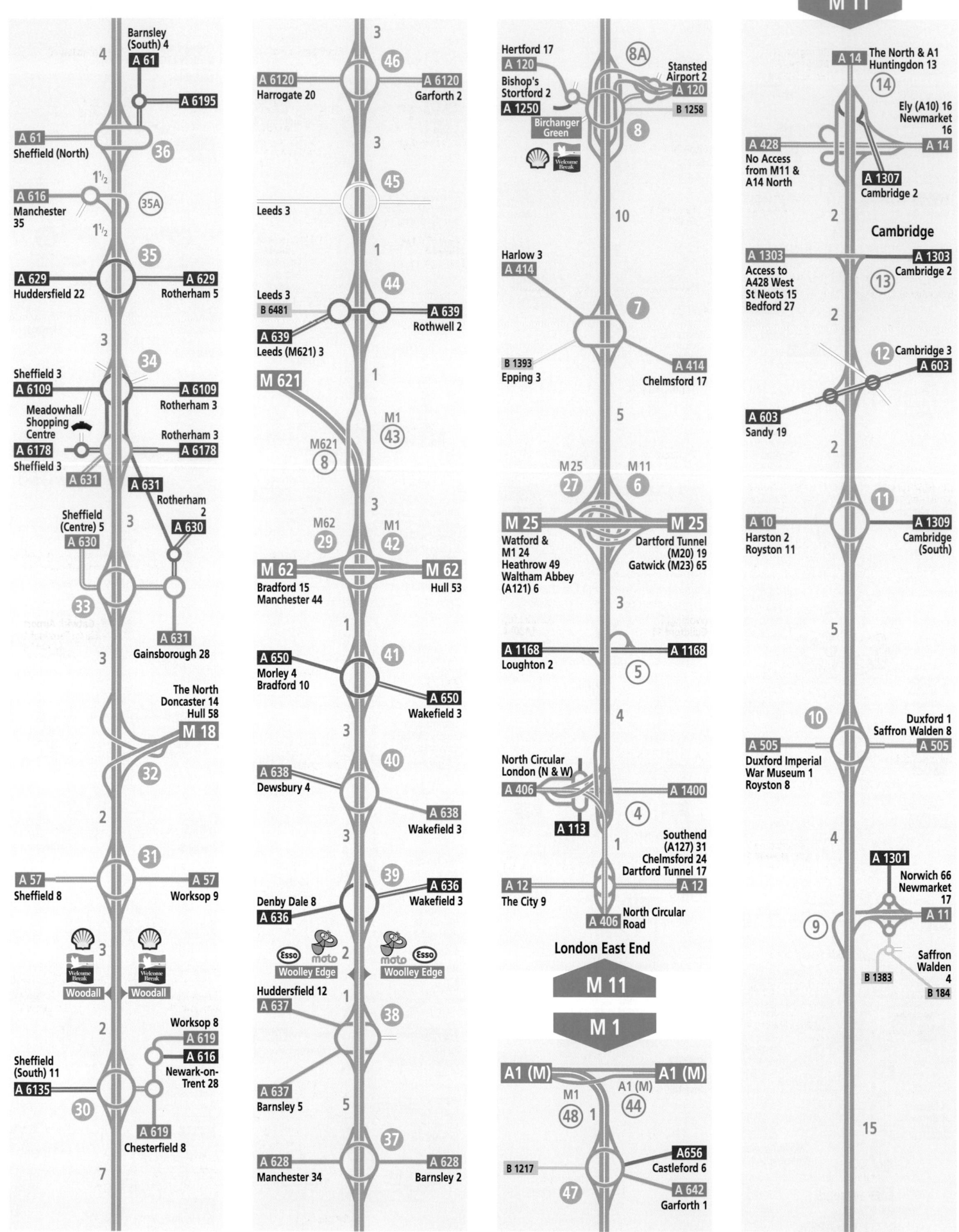

M1 Chesterfield–Garforth 57 miles • M11 London–Cambridge 61 miles

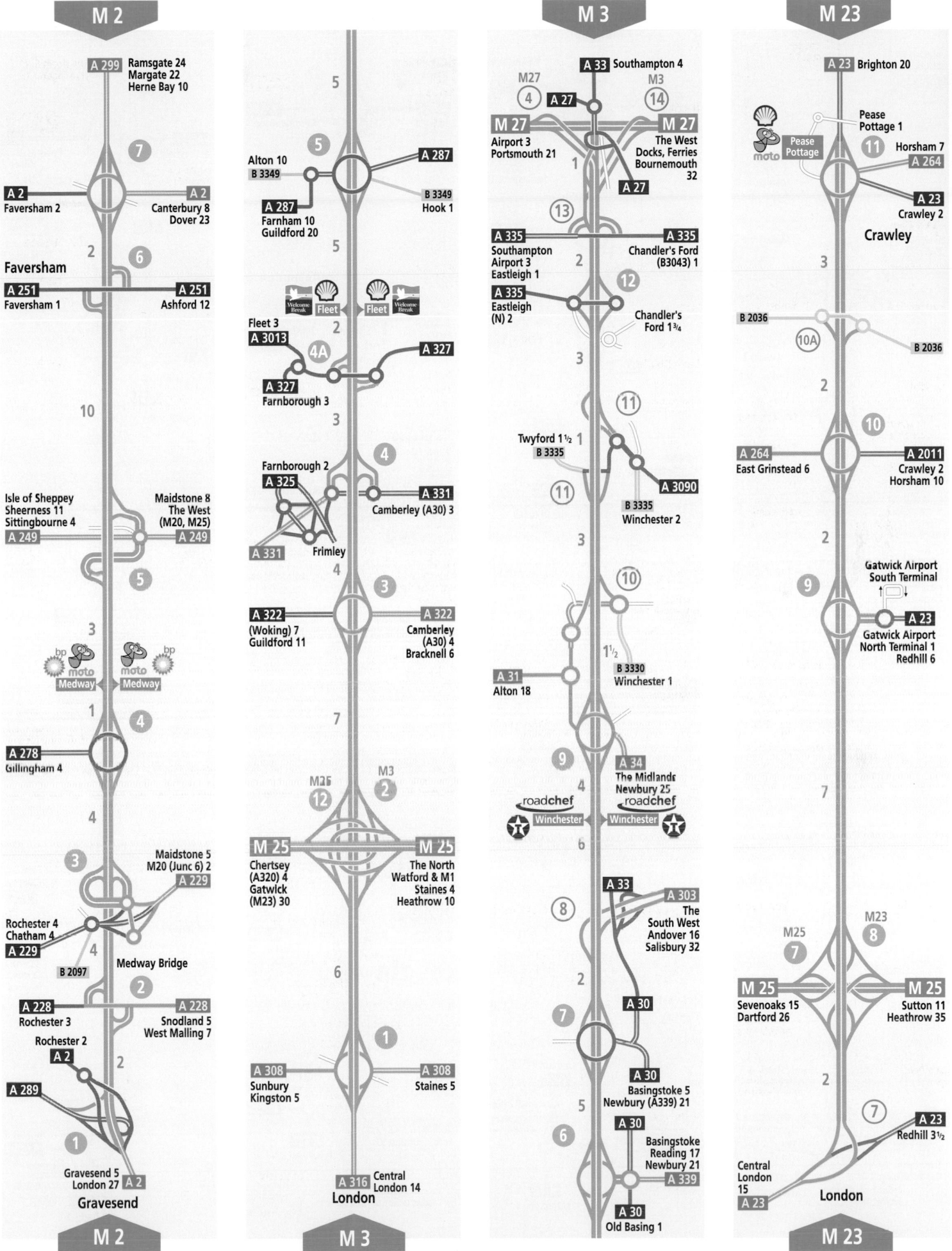

M2 Gravesend–Faversham 33 miles • M3 London–Southampton 80 miles • M23 London–Crawley 28 miles

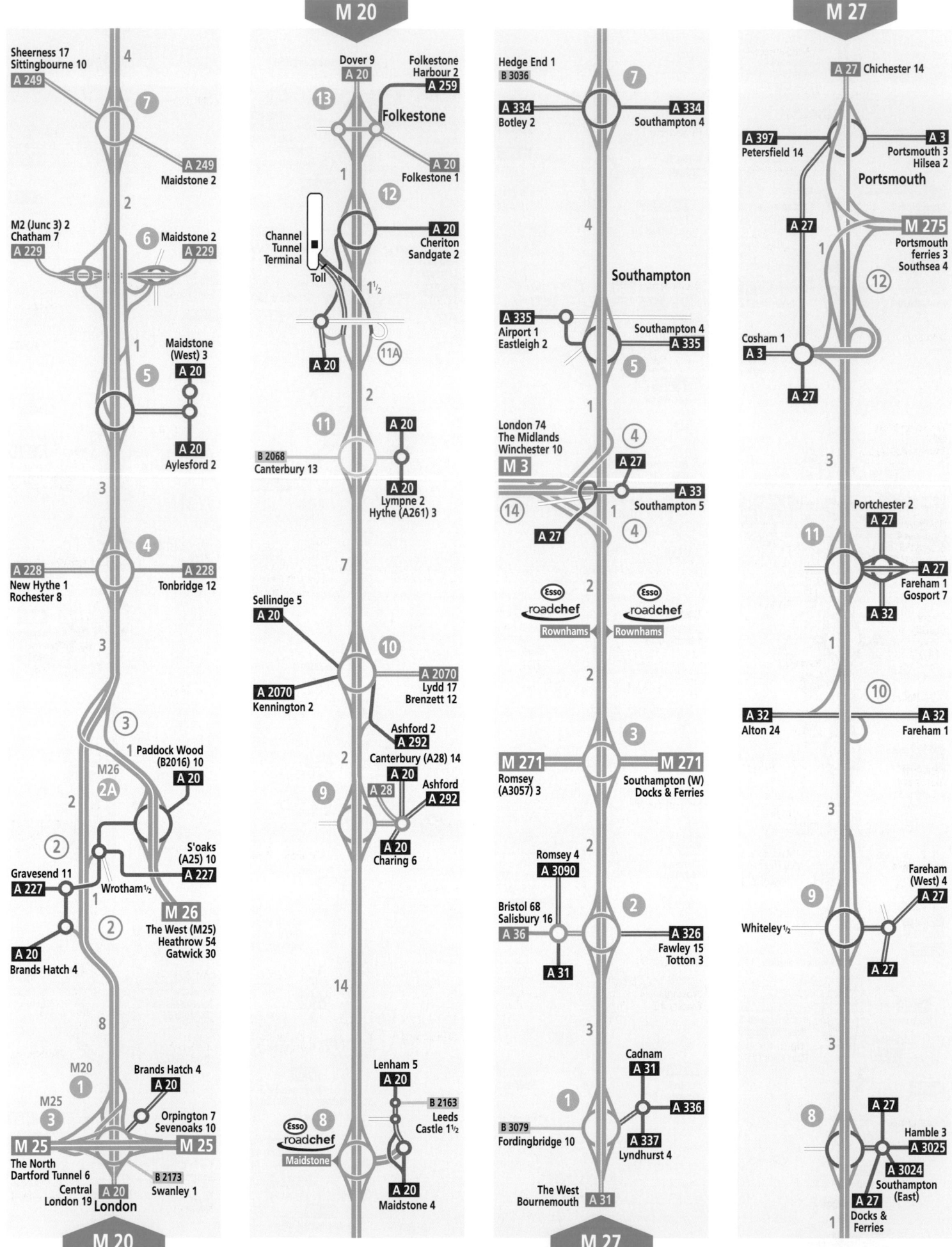

M20 London–Folkestone 73 miles • M27 Lyndhurst–Portsmouth 34 miles

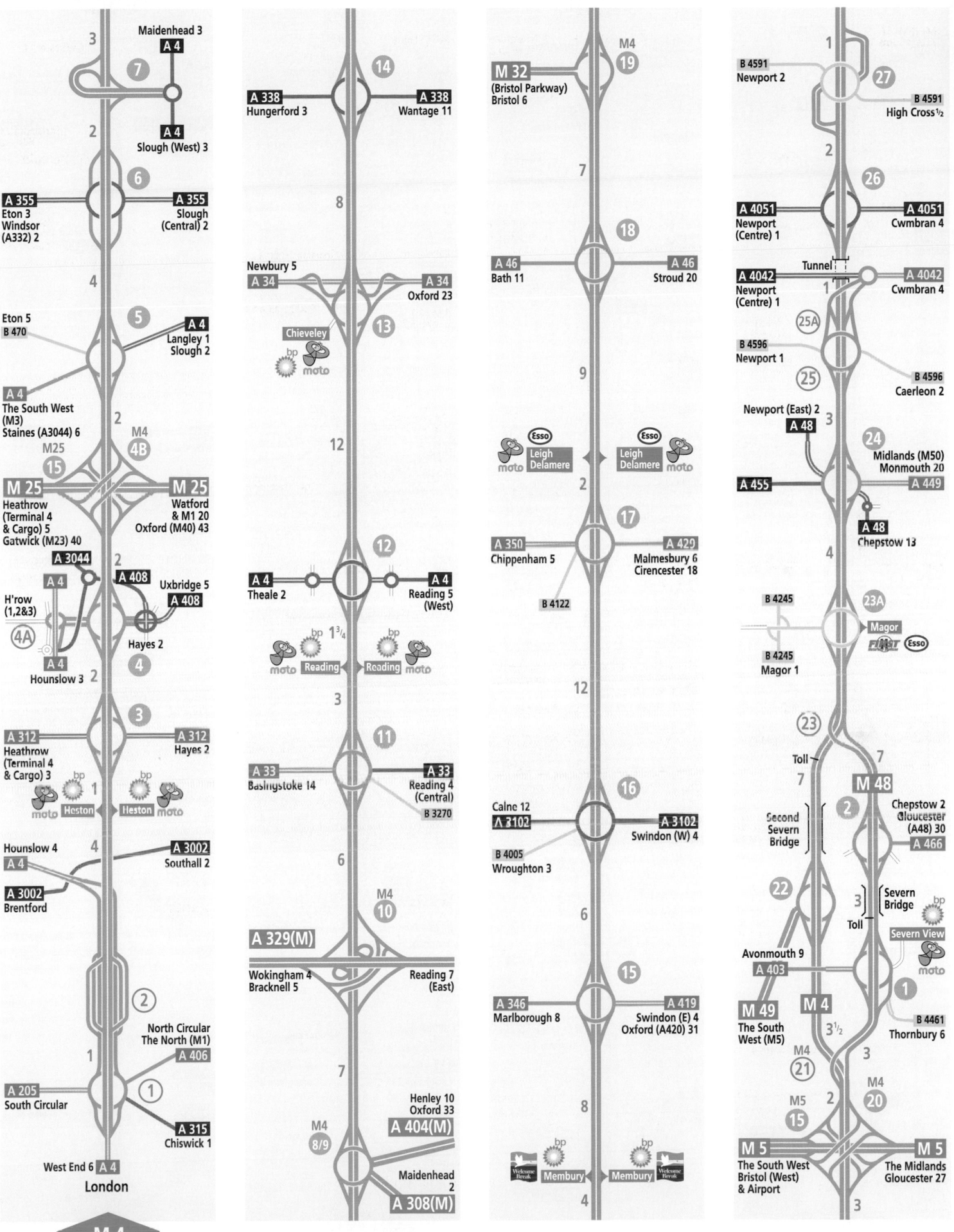

M4 London–Newport 138 miles

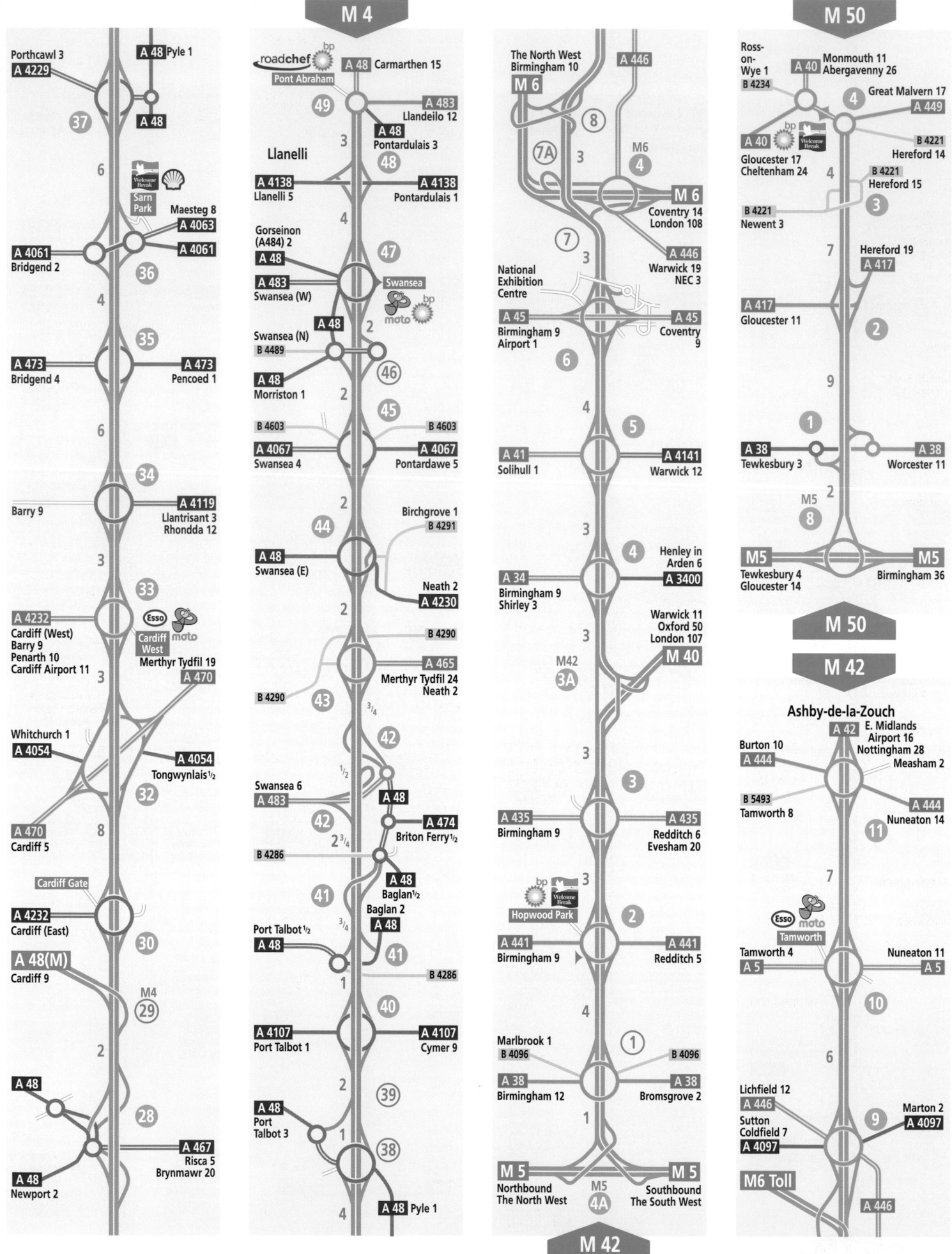

M4 Newport–Llanelli 64 miles • M42 Bromsgrove–Ashby-de-la-Zouch 49 miles
M50 Strensham–Ross-on-Wye 22 miles

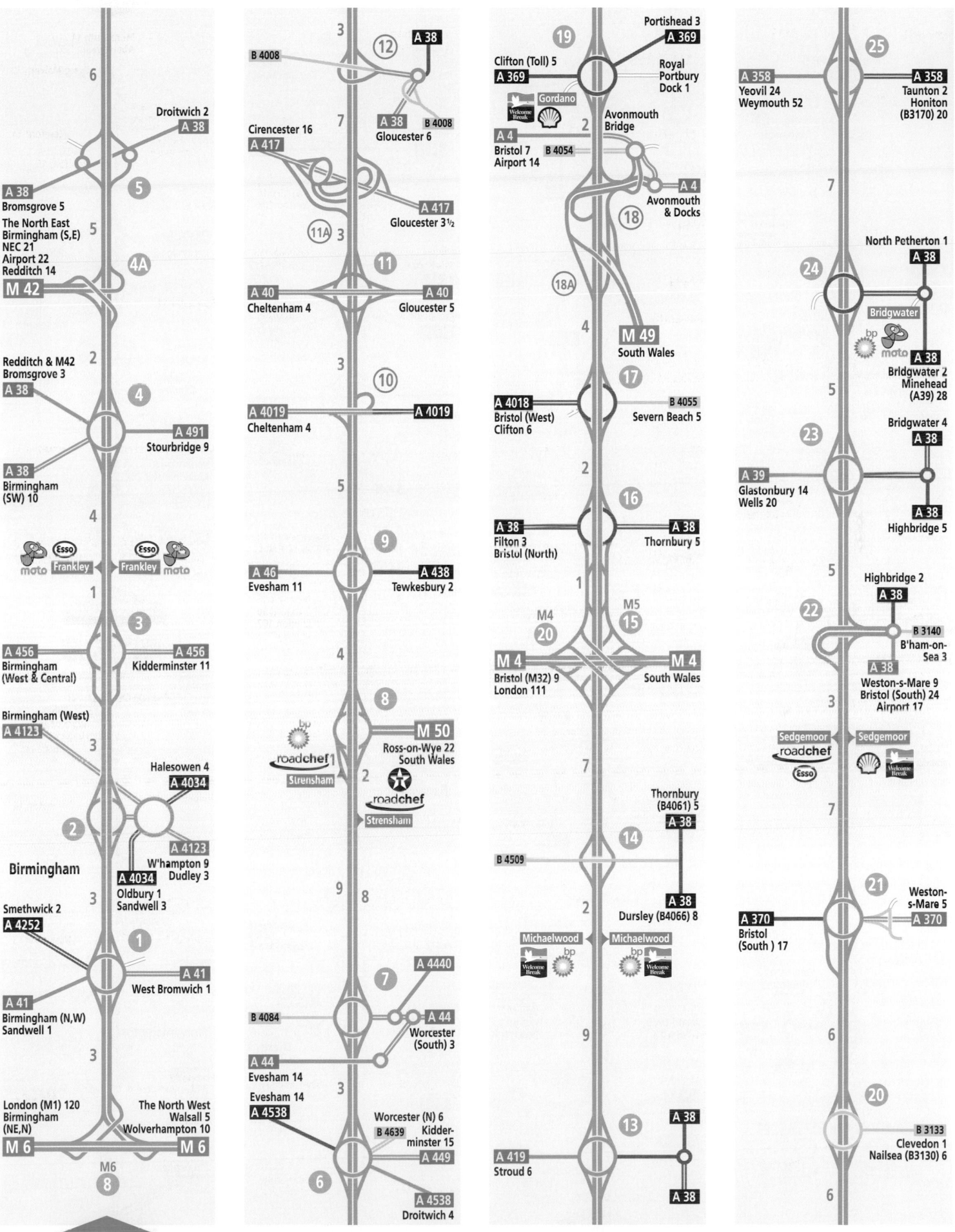

M5 Birmingham–Taunton 130 miles

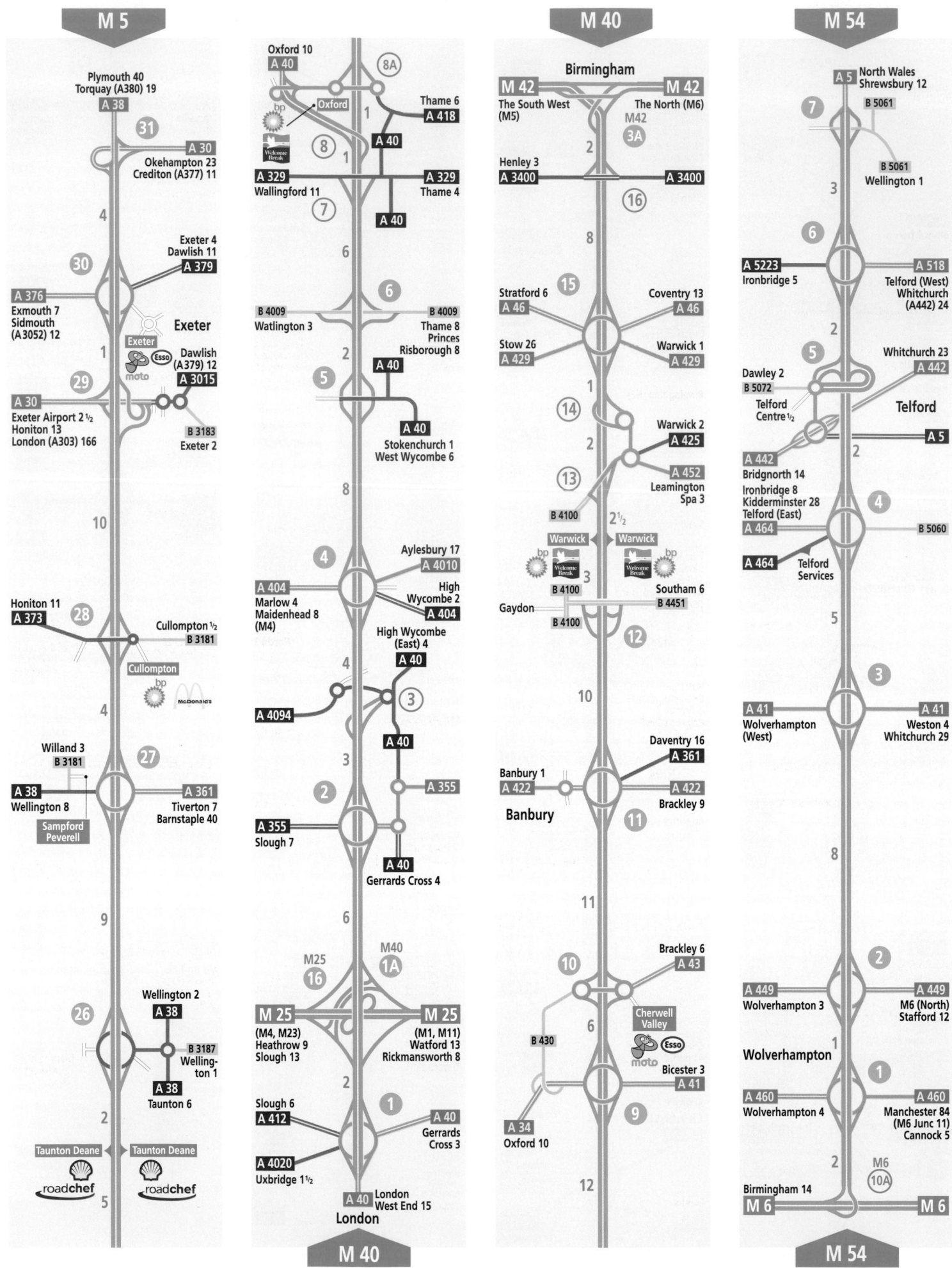

M5 Taunton–Exeter 35 miles • M40 London–Birmingham 120 miles • M54 Wolverhampton–Telford 23 miles

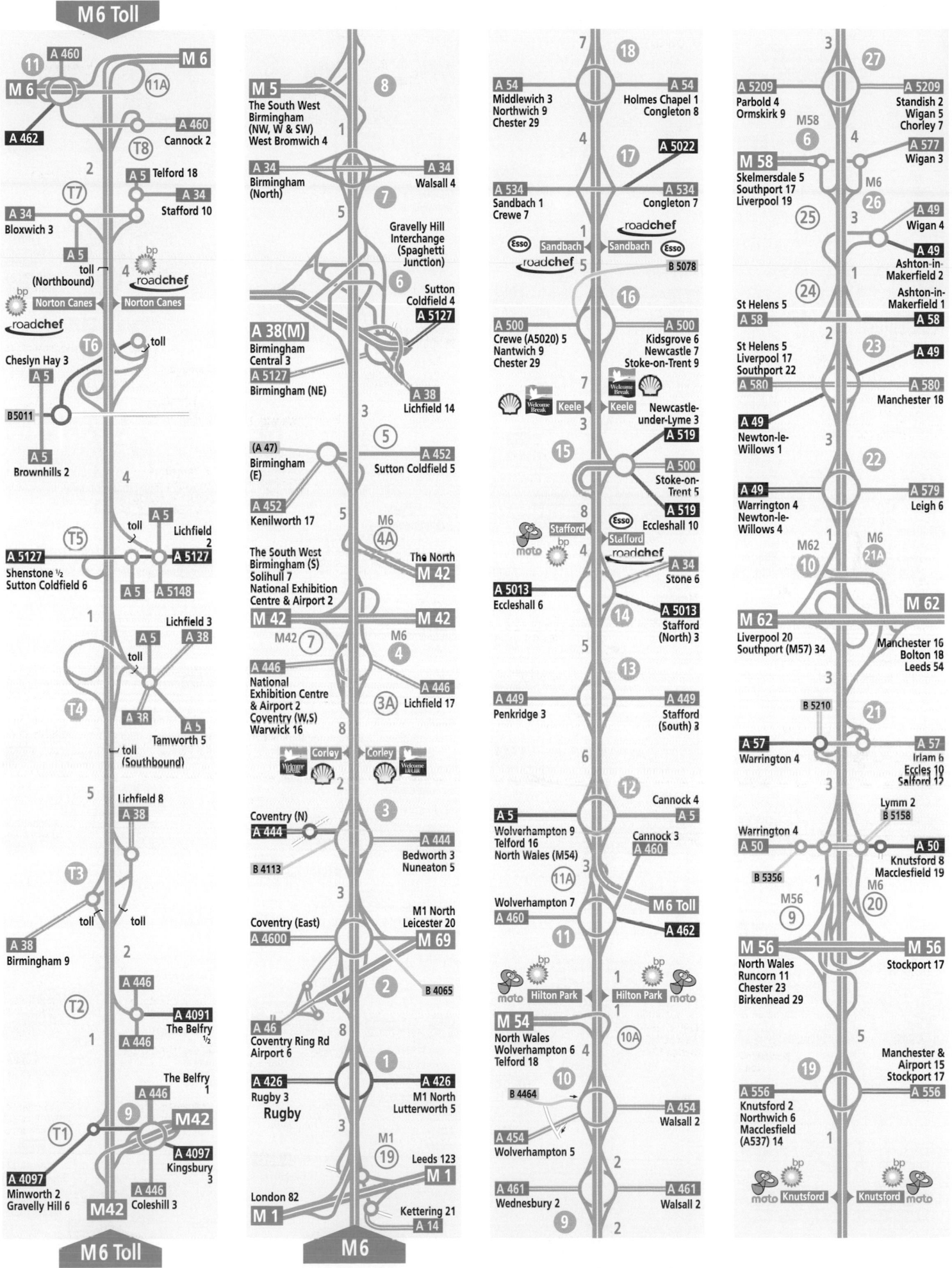

M6 Toll 27 miles • M6 Rugby–Standish 110 miles

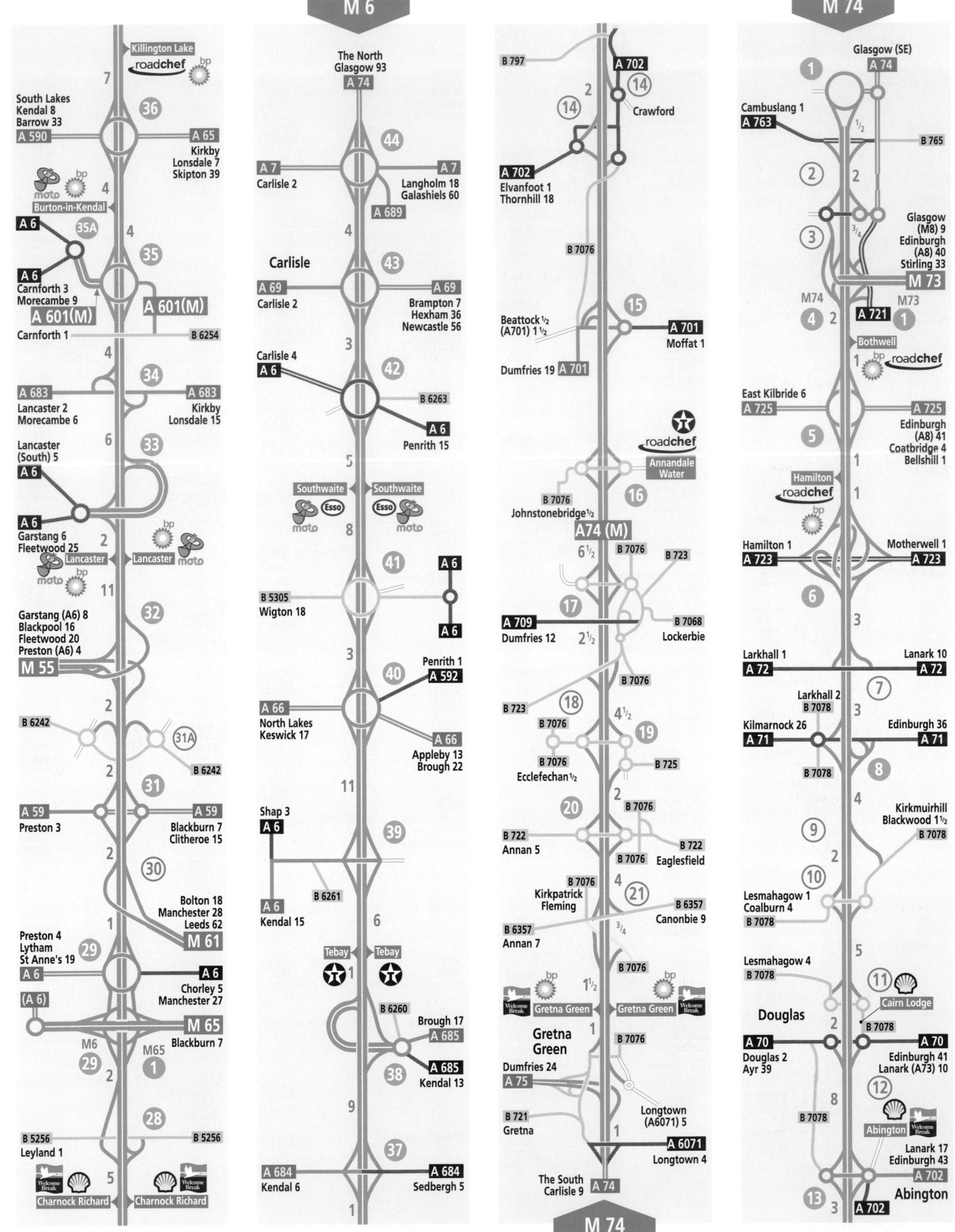

M6 M74 Standish–Glasgow 208 miles

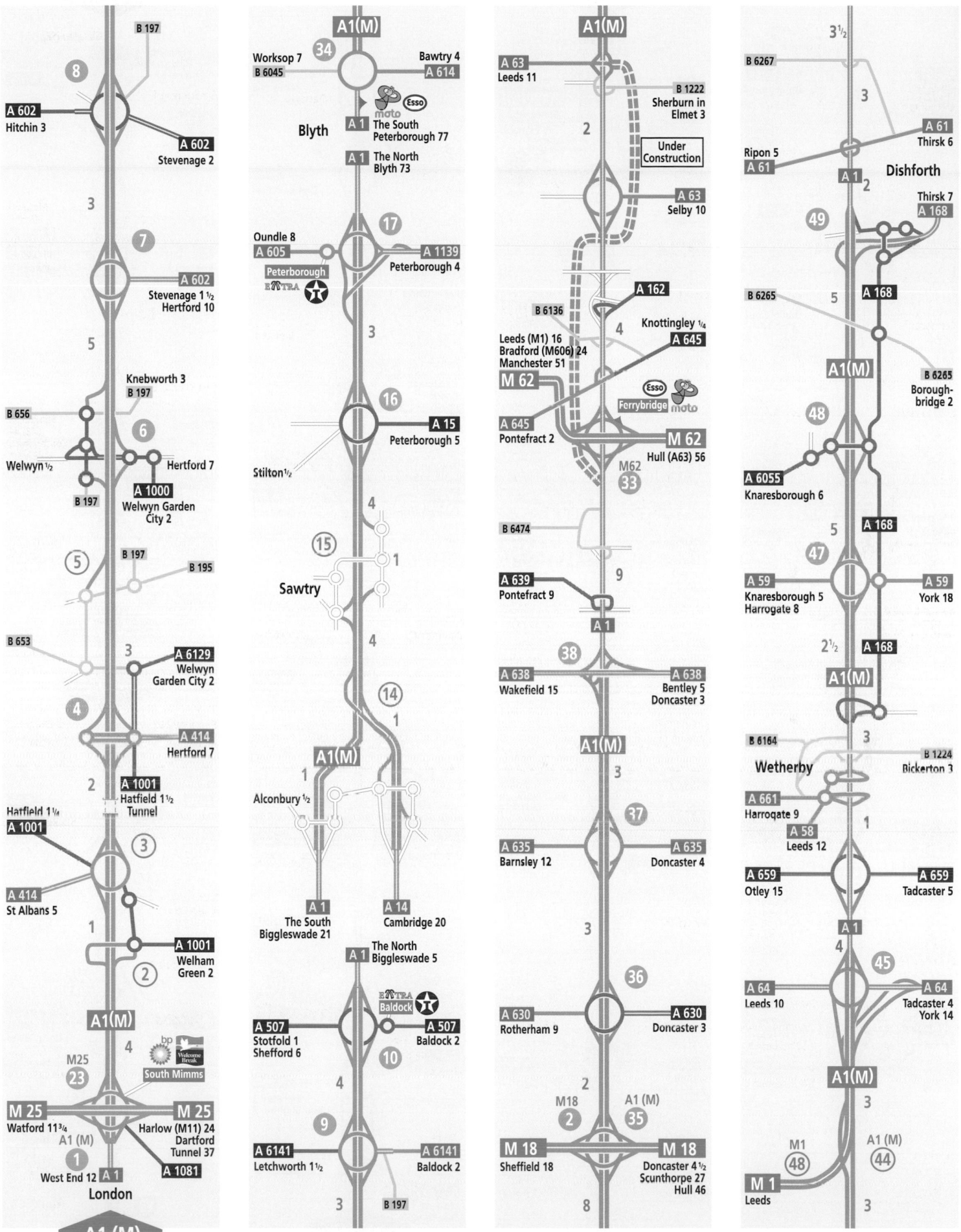

A1(M) London–Biggleswade 25 miles,   Alconbury–Peterborough 12 miles, Blyth–Ripon 65 miles, Wetherby–Dishforth 16 miles

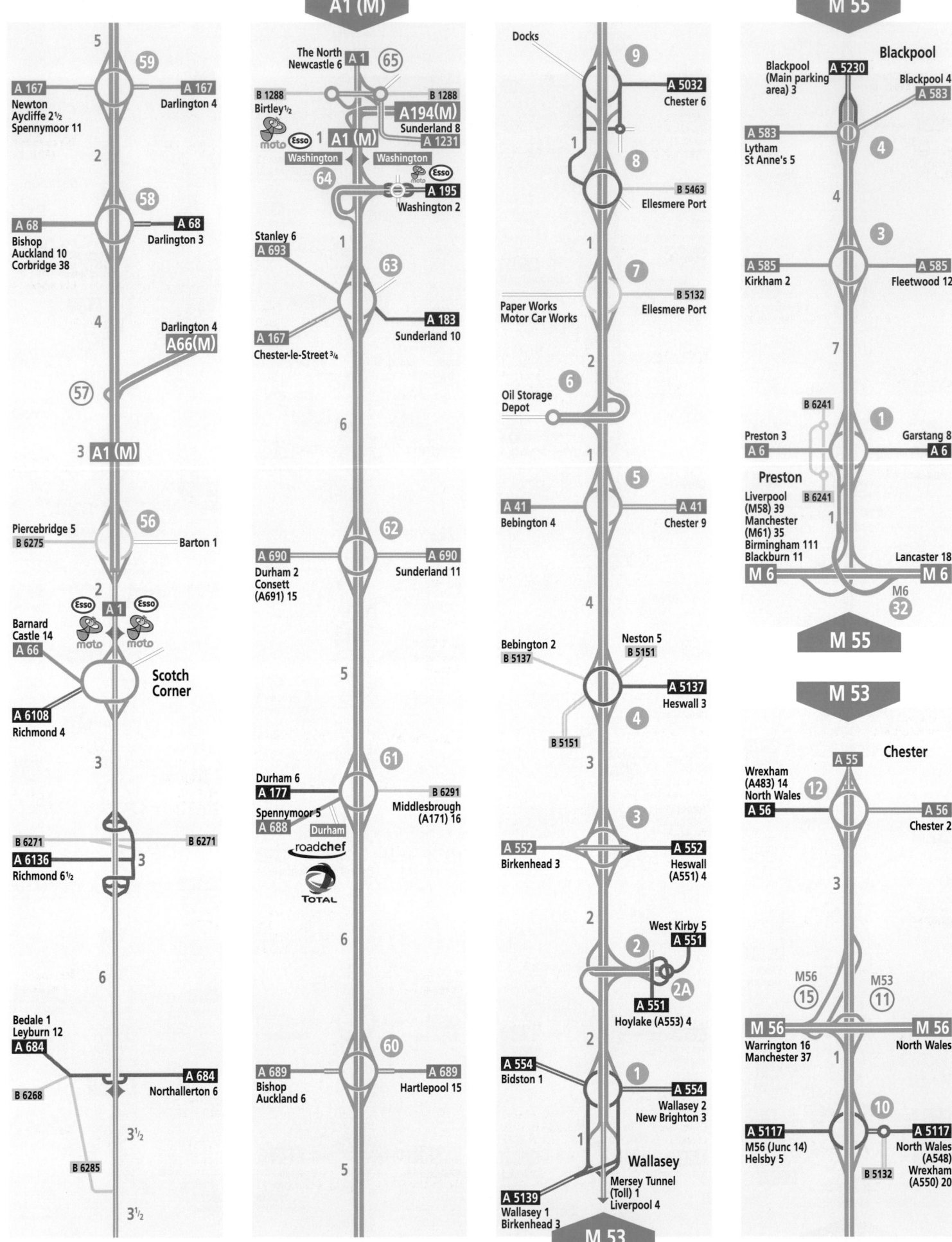

A1(M) Ripon–Newcastle 53 miles • M53 Wallasey–Chester 24 miles • M55 Preston–Blackpool 18 miles

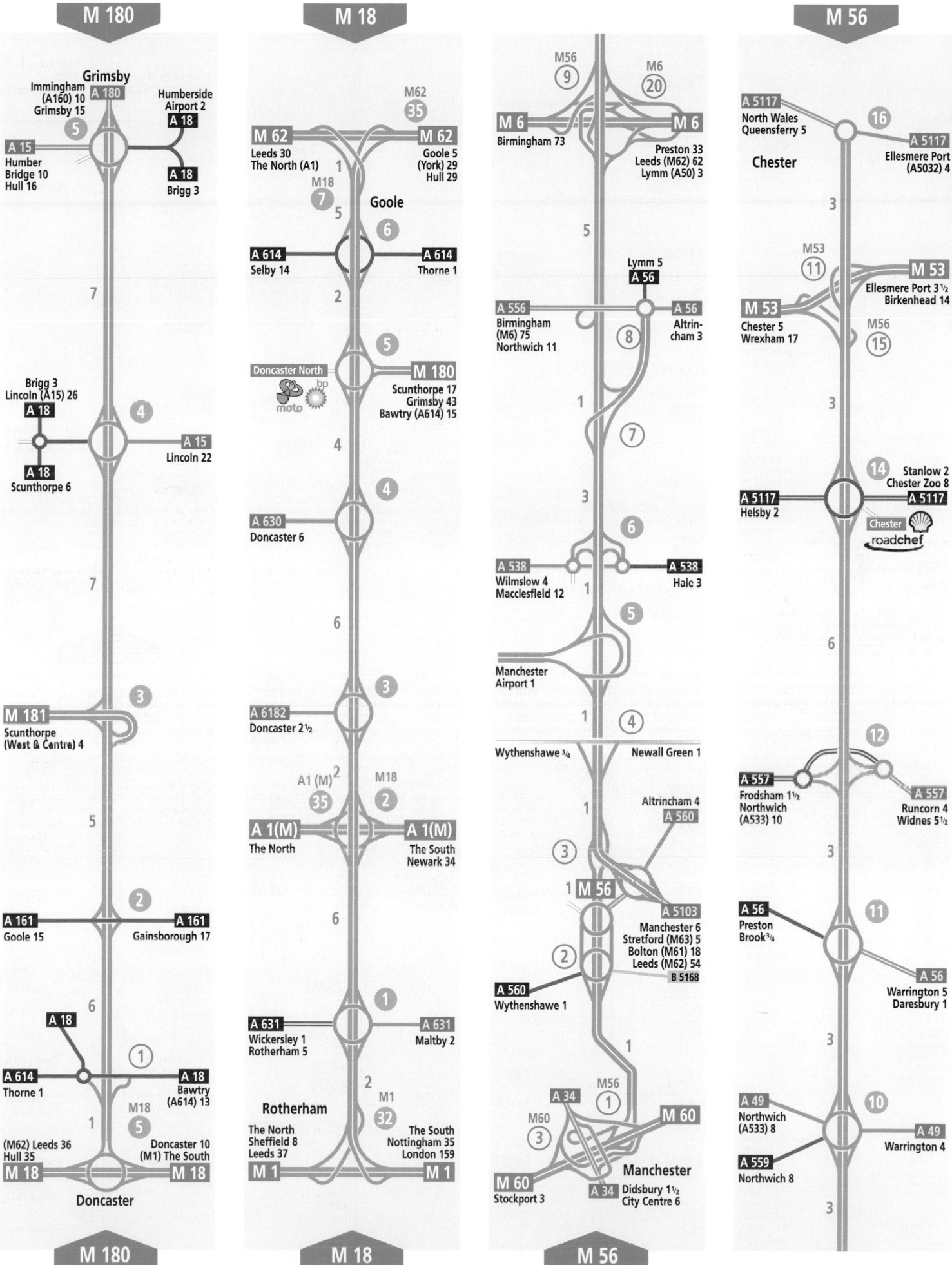

M 180

Grimsby

Immingham (A160) 10
Grimsby 15
A 180

Humberside Airport 2
A 18

⑤

A 15
Humber Bridge 10
Hull 16

A 18
Brigg 3

7

Brigg 3
Lincoln (A15) 26
A 18

④

A 15
Lincoln 22

A 18
Scunthorpe 6

7

③

M 181
Scunthorpe (West & Centre) 4

5

②

A 161
Goole 15

A 161
Gainsborough 17

6

A 18

①

A 614
Thorne 1

A 18
Bawtry (A614) 13

M18
⑤

(M62) Leeds 36
Hull 35

Doncaster 10
(M1) The South

M 18

M 18

Doncaster

M 180

M 18

M62
㉟

M 62
Leeds 30
The North (A1)

M 62
Goole 5
(York) 29
Hull 29

M18
⑦

5

Goole

⑥

A 614
Selby 14

A 614
Thorne 1

2

⑤

M 180
Scunthorpe 17
Grimsby 43
Bawtry (A614) 15

Doncaster North
moto   bp

④

4

A 630
Doncaster 6

6

③

A 6182
Doncaster 2½

A1 (M)   M18
㉟   ②

2

A 1(M)
The North

A 1(M)
The South
Newark 34

6

①

A 631
Wickersley 1
Rotherham 5

A 631
Maltby 2

2

M1
㉜

Rotherham
The North
Sheffield 8
Leeds 37

The South
Nottingham 35
London 159

M 1

M 1

M 18

M 56

M56
⑨

M6
⑳

M 6
Birmingham 73

M 6
Preston 33
Leeds (M62) 62
Lymm (A50) 3

5

Lymm 5
A 56

A 556
Birmingham (M6) 75
Northwich 11

A 56
Altrincham 3

⑧

1

⑦

3

⑥

A 538
Wilmslow 4
Macclesfield 12

A 538
Hale 3

1

⑤

Manchester Airport 1

1

④

Wythenshawe ¾

Newall Green 1

1

Altrincham 4
A 560

③

1   M 56

②

A 5103
Manchester 6
Stretford (M63) 5
Bolton (M61) 18
Leeds (M62) 54
B 5168

A 560
Wythenshawe 1

1

M56
①

A 34

M60
③

M 60

M 60
Stockport 3

A 34   Didsbury 1½
City Centre 6

Manchester

M 56

M 56

A 5117
North Wales
Queensferry 5

16

A 5117
Ellesmere Port (A5032) 4

Chester

3

M53
⑪

M 53
Ellesmere Port 3½
Birkenhead 14

M 53
Chester 5
Wrexham 17

M56
⑮

3

14
Stanlow 2
Chester Zoo 8

A 5117
Helsby 2

A 5117

Chester
roadchef

6

A 557
Frodsham 1½
Northwich (A533) 10

⑫

A 557
Runcorn 4
Widnes 5½

3

A 56
Preston Brook ¾

⑪

A 56
Warrington 5
Daresbury 1

3

A 49
Northwich (A533) 8

⑩

A 49
Warrington 4

A 559
Northwich 8

3

M 56

M180 Doncaster–Grimsby 51 miles • M18 Rotherham–Goole 35 miles • M56 Manchester–Chester 35 miles

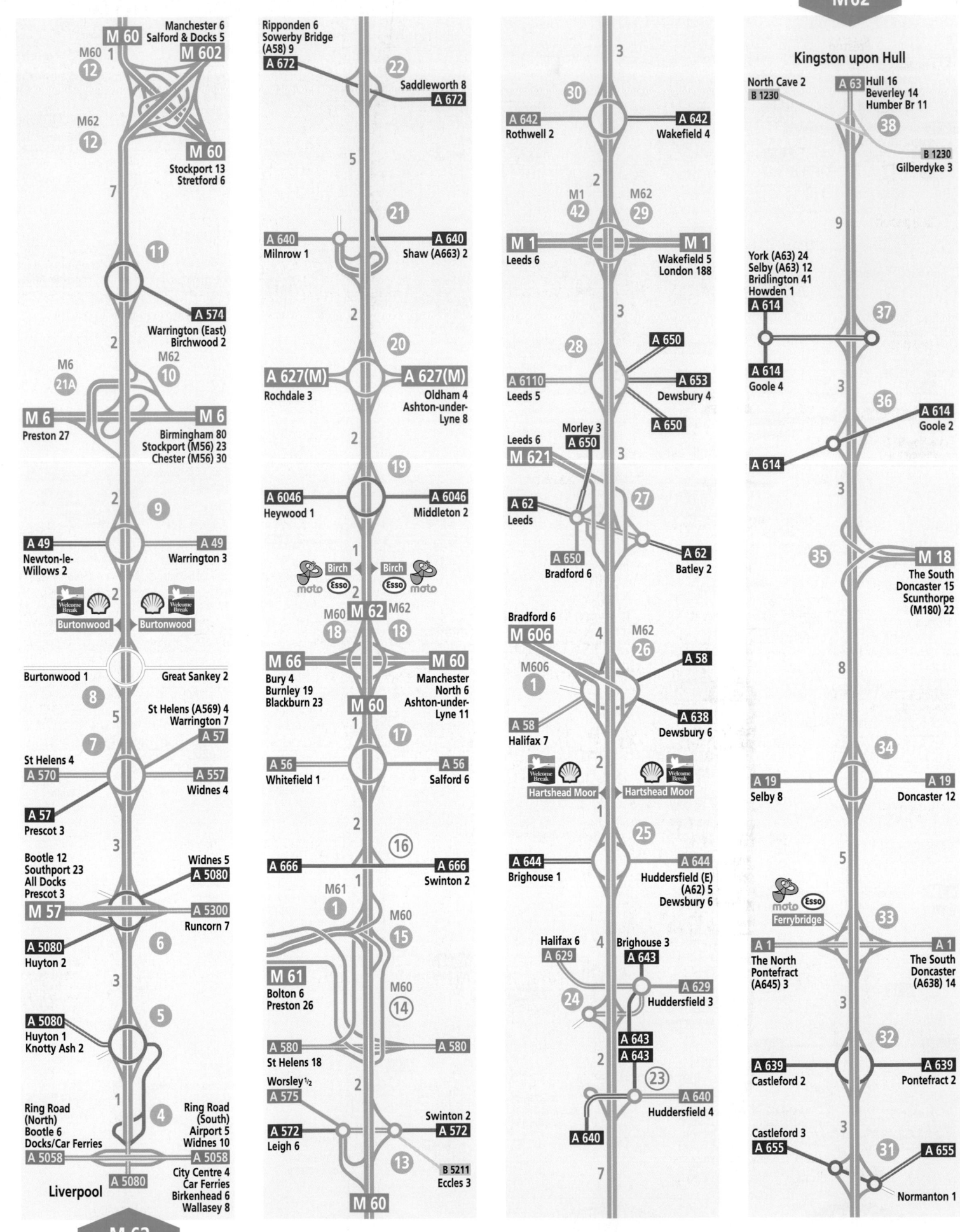

M62 M60 M62 Liverpool–Kingston upon Hull 128 miles

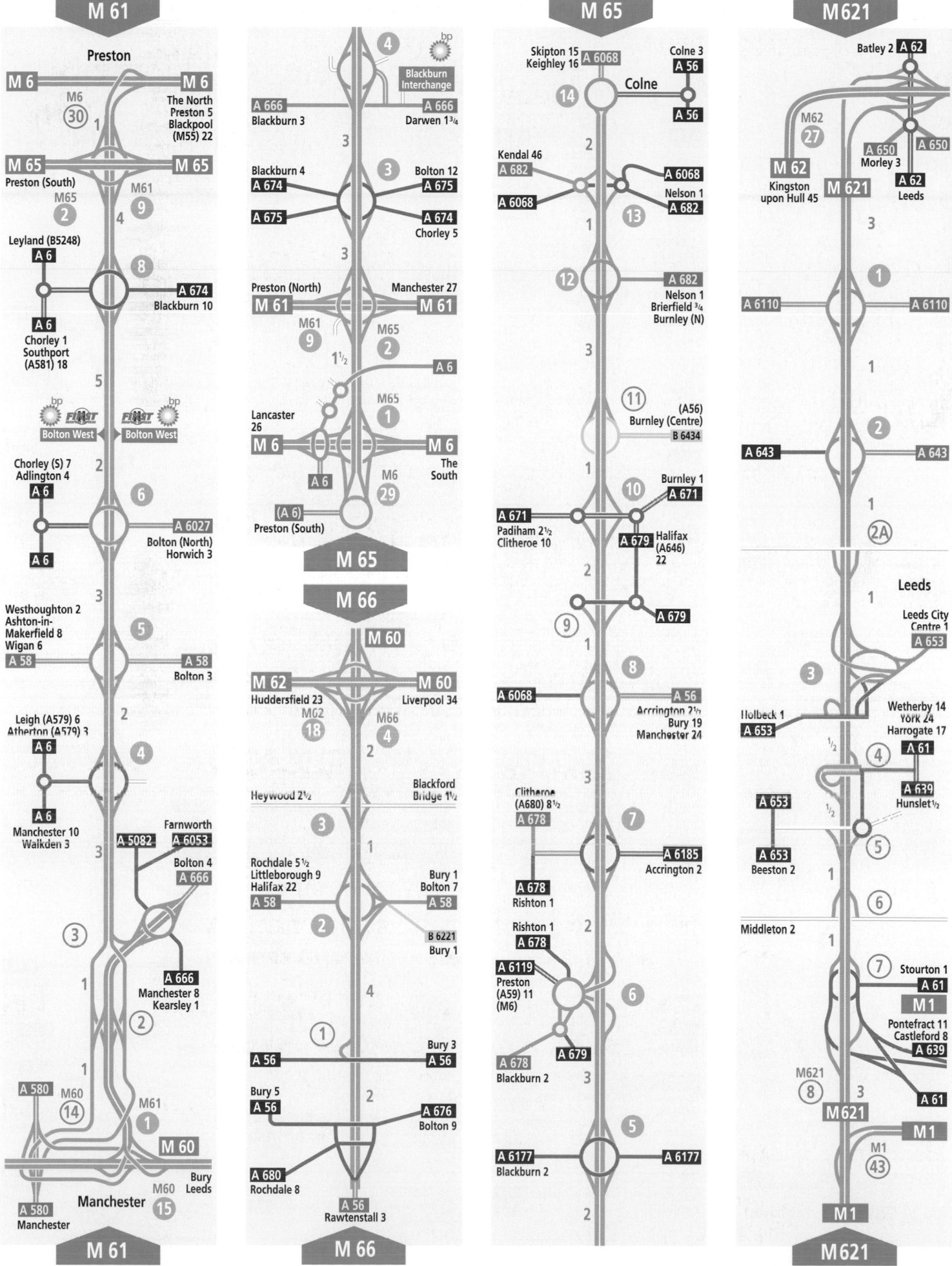

**M61 Manchester–Preston 31 miles • M66 Ramsbottom–Manchester 9 miles • M65 Bamber Bridge–Colne 28 miles
M621 Morley–Leeds 11 miles**

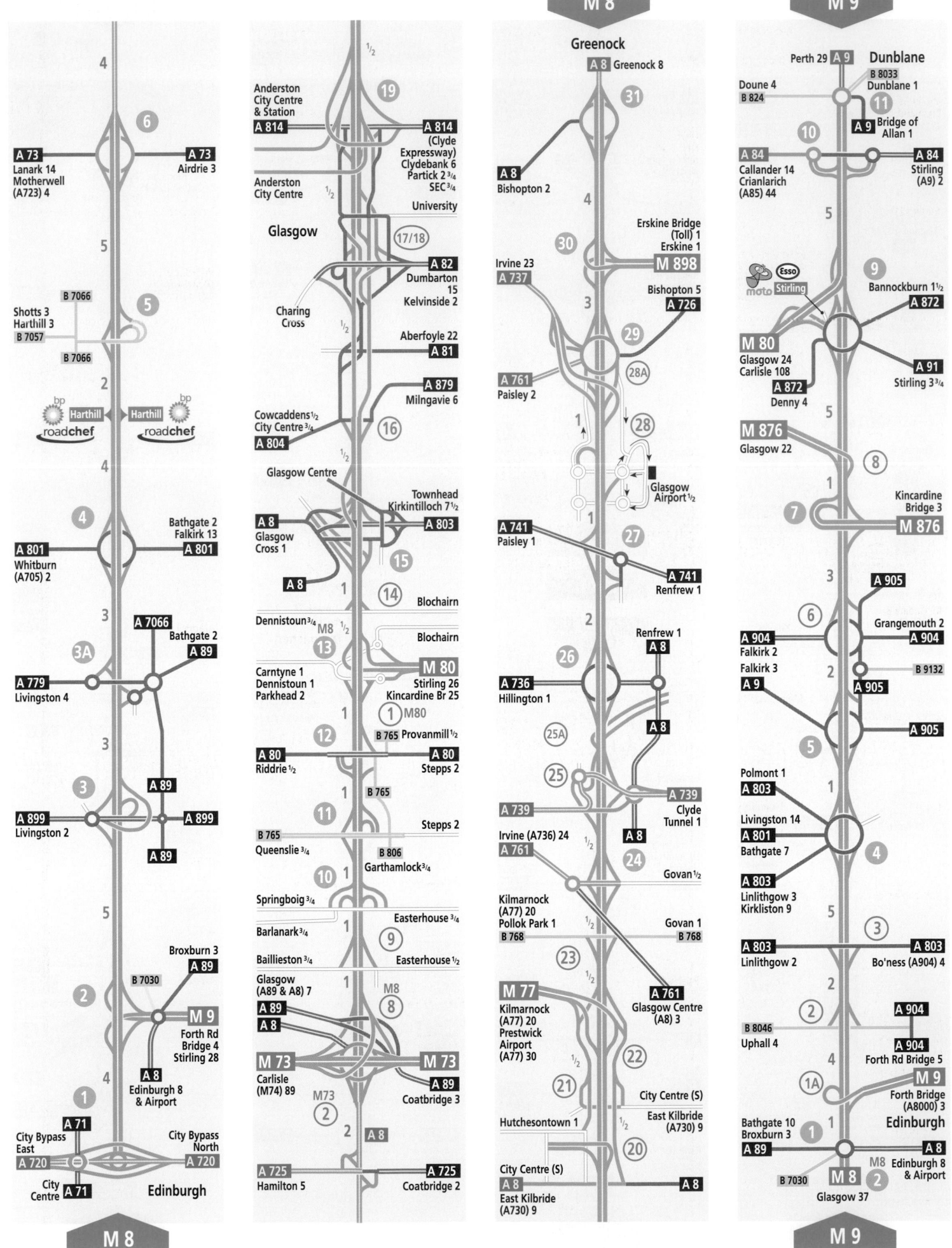

M8 Edinburgh Greenock 68 miles • M9 Edinburgh–Dunblane 40 miles

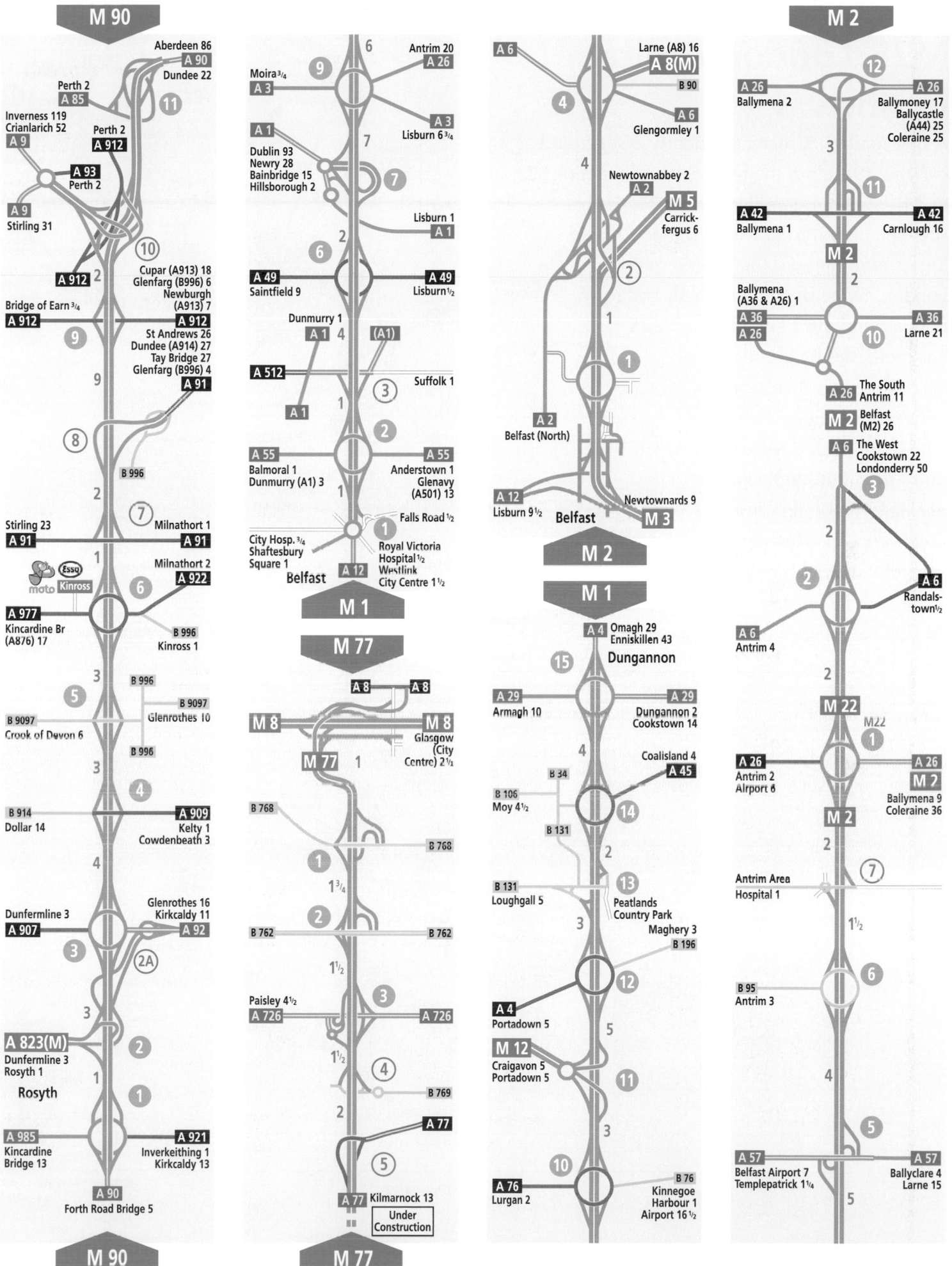

M90 Rosyth–Perth 30 miles • M1 Belfast–Dungannon 41 miles • M77 Kilmarnock–Glasgow 24 miles
M2 Belfast–Ballymena 26 miles

M25 London orbital motorway

A ring road for Greater London was suggested as early as 1905, but the first section – junctions 23 to 24 – was not completed until 1975. This strategic orbital road was designed to keep lorries and long distance traffic out of London. Since opening in 1986, traffic flow around the 117 mile long M25 has increased by around 60 per cent. **The busiest section is between junctions 13 and 14 which, on peak days, carries more than 200,000 vehicles per day.** The section from junctions 4 to 5 has the least traffic, with a daily average of fewer than 90,000 vehicles.

GOING WEST
• The M3 and M4 are the fastest routes from London to **the West Country** and into **Wales**.
• The M4 also provides central London with a vital link to **Heathrow airport**.
• If you are travelling to **Gatwick airport,** leave the M25 at junction 7 and join the M23 – the airport is a 10-minute drive from the M25.

CONGESTION BLACKSPOTS
• At Monday to Friday peak times, Saturday shopping times and on Sunday evenings, traffic can build up in both directions on the western sector between **junction 10** and **junction 21A**.
• This section can also be busy in late November, early December and during holiday periods.
• Congestion occurs between **junctions 23 and 27** on Monday to Friday peaks and Sunday evenings.
• **Junctions 10 to 7** can also be slow in Monday to Friday peaks, especially during summer because of airport traffic.
• Shopping traffic can halt the progress of traffic between **junctions 30 and 1B** in November and early December.

THE MIDLANDS
• At junction 16 you can leave the M25 for the M40 and travel towards the university town of **Oxford**, or the busy city of **Birmingham**.
• If **central London** is your destination, take the M40 eastbound, which links with the A40 – one of the faster standard routes into the capital.

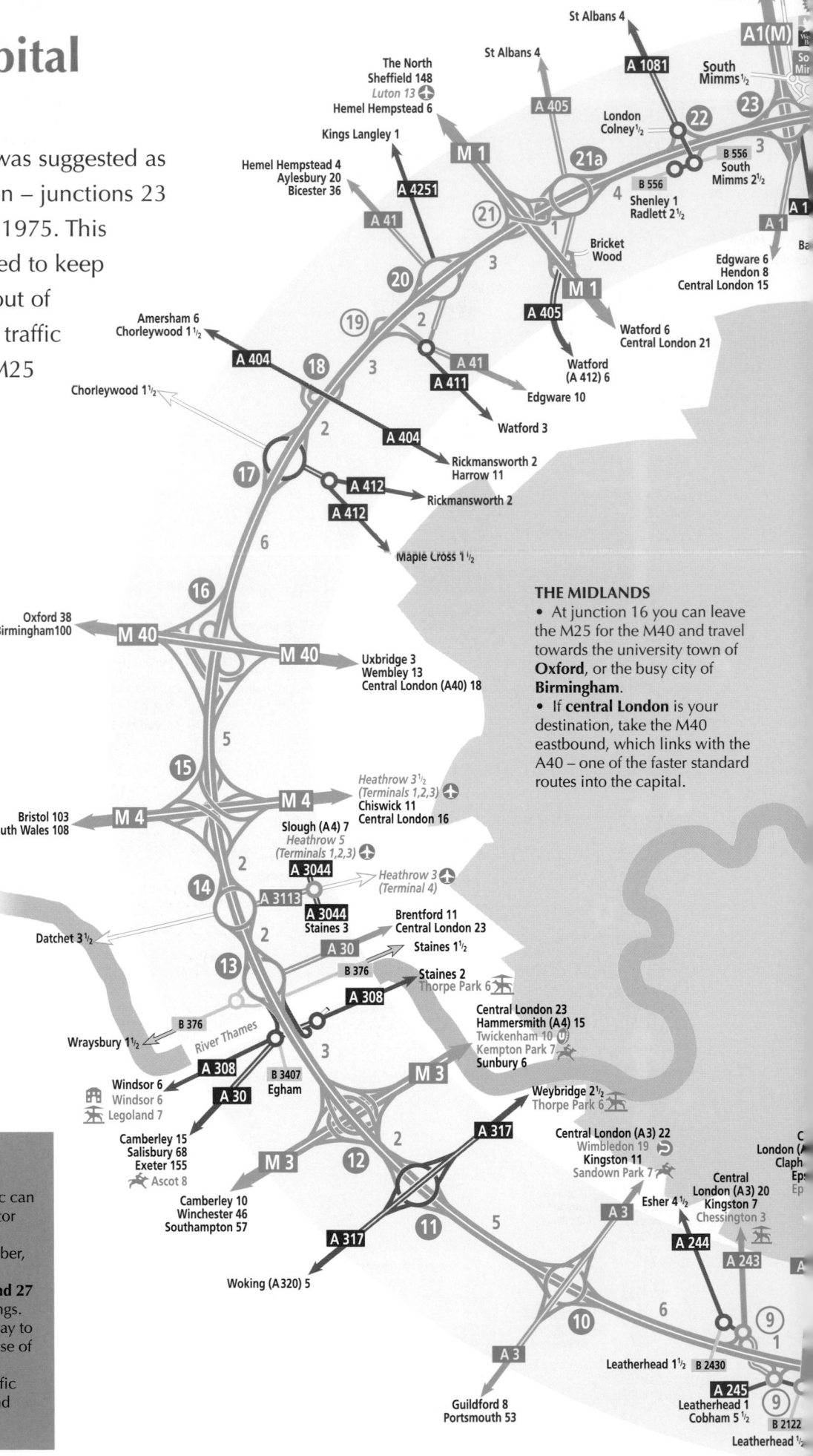

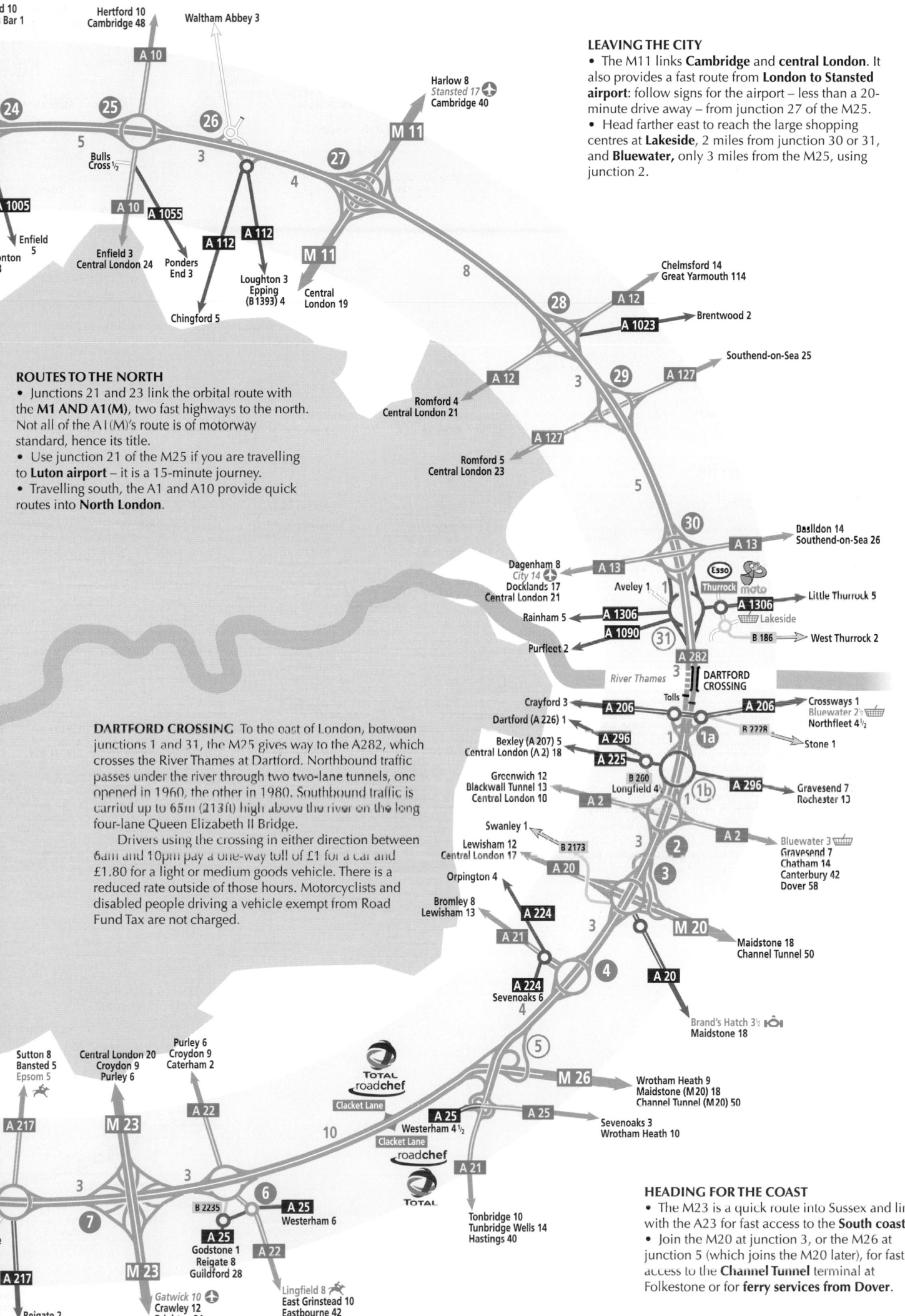

LEAVING THE CITY

- The M11 links **Cambridge** and **central London**. It also provides a fast route from **London to Stansted airport**: follow signs for the airport – less than a 20-minute drive away – from junction 27 of the M25.
- Head farther east to reach the large shopping centres at **Lakeside**, 2 miles from junction 30 or 31, and **Bluewater**, only 3 miles from the M25, using junction 2.

ROUTES TO THE NORTH

- Junctions 21 and 23 link the orbital route with the **M1 AND A1(M)**, two fast highways to the north. Not all of the A1(M)'s route is of motorway standard, hence its title.
- Use junction 21 of the M25 if you are travelling to **Luton airport** – it is a 15-minute journey.
- Travelling south, the A1 and A10 provide quick routes into **North London**.

DARTFORD CROSSING

To the east of London, between junctions 1 and 31, the M25 gives way to the A282, which crosses the River Thames at Dartford. Northbound traffic passes under the river through two two-lane tunnels, one opened in 1960, the other in 1980. Southbound traffic is carried up to 65m (213ft) high above the river on the long four-lane Queen Elizabeth II Bridge.

Drivers using the crossing in either direction between 6am and 10pm pay a one-way toll of £1 for a car and £1.80 for a light or medium goods vehicle. There is a reduced rate outside of those hours. Motorcyclists and disabled people driving a vehicle exempt from Road Fund Tax are not charged.

HEADING FOR THE COAST

- The M23 is a quick route into Sussex and links with the A23 for fast access to the **South coast**.
- Join the M20 at junction 3, or the M26 at junction 5 (which joins the M20 later), for fast access to the **Channel Tunnel** terminal at Folkestone or for **ferry services from Dover**.

M42 Birmingham orbital motorway

Birmingham is at the heart of the national motorway network: the M42, M5 and M6 form a complete orbital route around the city, as well as providing links with the M1, M40 and M69. The M6 is one of Britain's busiest roads, carrying – at some peak times – double the amount of traffic it was designed for. The new M6 Toll, which was opened in 2003, has improved traffic flows on its busiest section between junctions 4 and 11.

HEADING FOR THE NORTH
• The M6 provides a fast route to the **North West** – to join it from the west side of the city follow the M5 past junction 1 and it merges with the M6. If you are travelling on the M42, you can join the northbound M6 at junction 7.
• The M42 goes north to **Leicestershire** where it reverts to A42 and eventually meets the **M1** for routes towards Nottingham, Huddersfield and Leeds.

CONGESTION BLACKSPOTS
• Traffic builds up on the **M42 between junctions 3A and junction 1** during the Monday to Friday peak times (7–9am and 5–7pm).
• The stretch between **junction 3A and junction 6** becomes congested at the same peak times and after events held at the National Exhibition Centre.
• **The A38 and A38(M) – the Tyburn Road and Aston Expressway** – can be busy in Monday to Friday peak times as well as during weekly (10am–12 noon and 2–5pm) and Saturday shopping times (10am–5pm).

TO THE CITY CENTRE The fastest route into central Birmingham is to take the A38(M) Aston Express from junction 6, although the other A-roads provide quick routes from other junctions.
• If you are travelling to **Birmingham University** use the A38 – the main campus is situated between Edgbaston and Selly Oak.

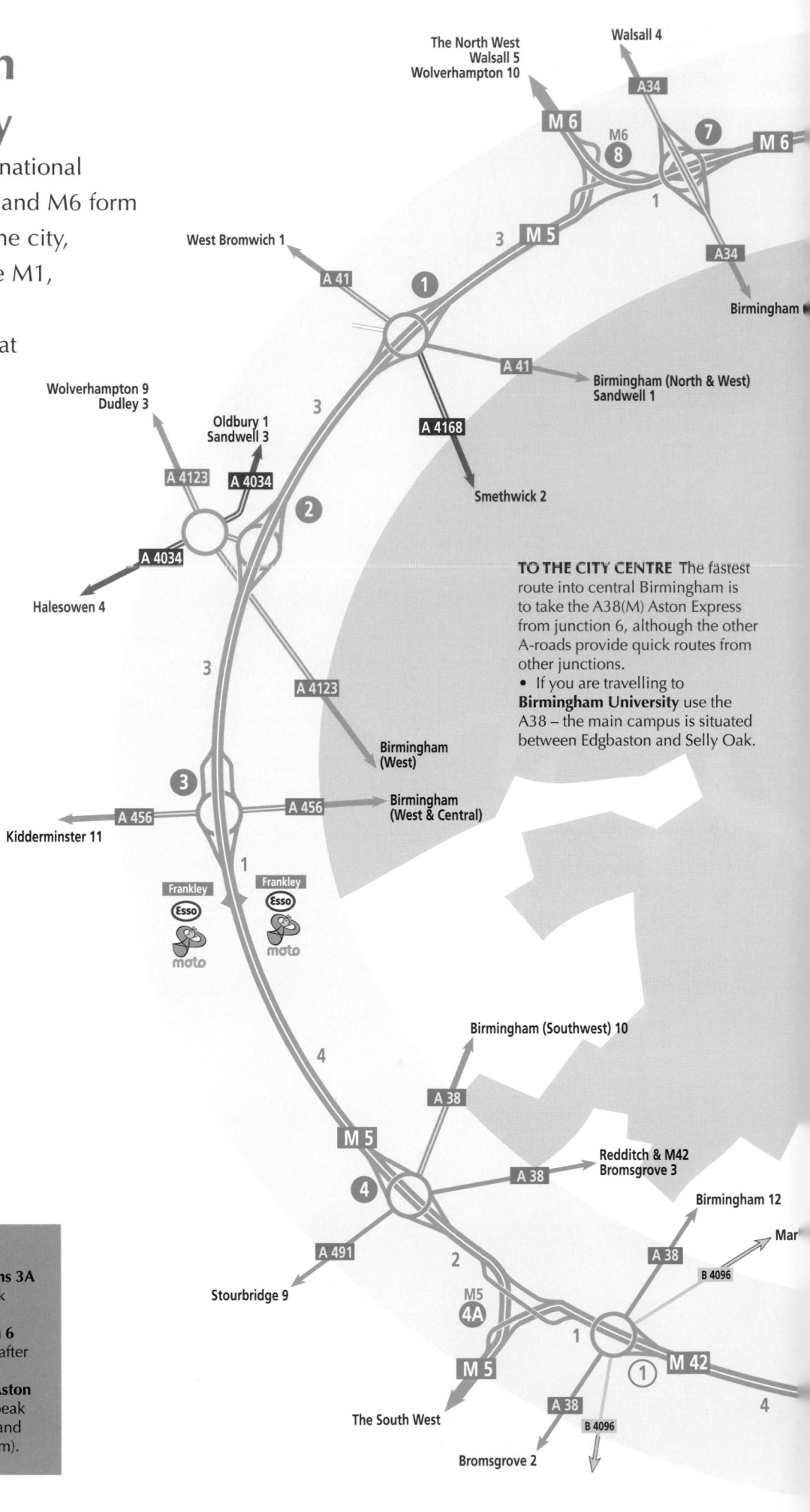

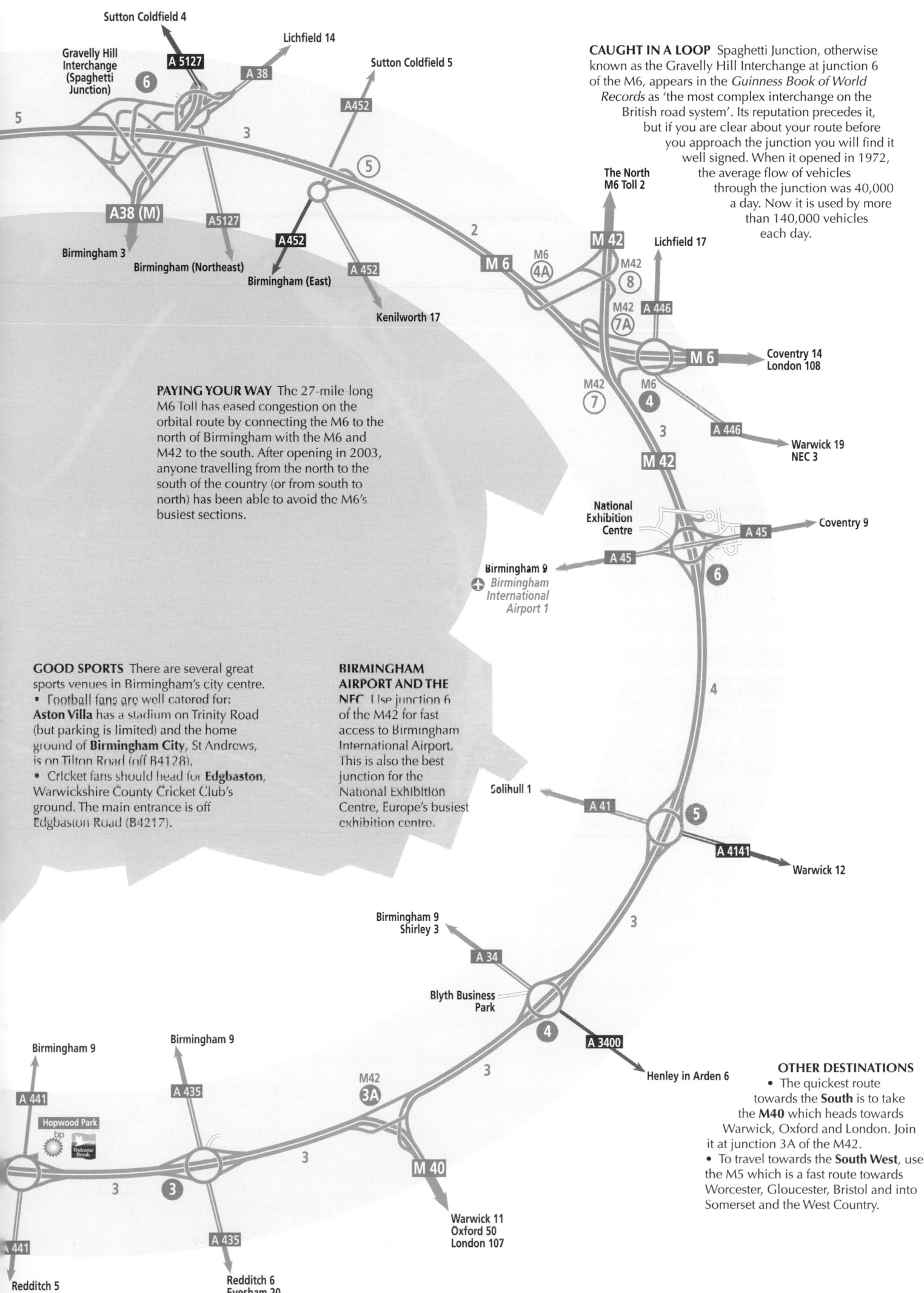

Sutton Coldfield 4

Gravelly Hill Interchange (Spaghetti Junction)

A 5127

Lichfield 14

A 38

Sutton Coldfield 5

A452

6

5

3

A38 (M)

A5127

A452

A452

A 452

5

Birmingham 3

Birmingham (Northeast)

Birmingham (East)

Kenilworth 17

CAUGHT IN A LOOP Spaghetti Junction, otherwise known as the Gravelly Hill Interchange at junction 6 of the M6, appears in the *Guinness Book of World Records* as 'the most complex interchange on the British road system'. Its reputation precedes it, but if you are clear about your route before you approach the junction you will find it well signed. When it opened in 1972, the average flow of vehicles through the junction was 40,000 a day. Now it is used by more than 140,000 vehicles each day.

The North
M6 Toll 2

M 42

Lichfield 17

M 6

M6 (4A)

M42 (8)

M42 (7A)

A 446

M 6

Coventry 14
London 108

M42 (7)

M6 (4)

2

3

A 446

Warwick 19
NEC 3

M 42

PAYING YOUR WAY The 27-mile long M6 Toll has eased congestion on the orbital route by connecting the M6 to the north of Birmingham with the M6 and M42 to the south. After opening in 2003, anyone travelling from the north to the south of the country (or from south to north) has been able to avoid the M6's busiest sections.

National Exhibition Centre

A 45

Coventry 9

A 45

Birmingham 9
✈ Birmingham International Airport 1

6

GOOD SPORTS There are several great sports venues in Birmingham's city centre.
• Football fans are well catered for: **Aston Villa** has a stadium on Trinity Road (but parking is limited) and the home ground of **Birmingham City**, St Andrews, is on Tilton Road (off B4128).
• Cricket fans should head for **Edgbaston**, Warwickshire County Cricket Club's ground. The main entrance is off Edgbaston Road (B4217).

BIRMINGHAM AIRPORT AND THE NEC Use junction 6 of the M42 for fast access to Birmingham International Airport. This is also the best junction for the National Exhibition Centre, Europe's busiest exhibition centre.

Solihull 1

A 41

5

4

A 4141

Warwick 12

3

Birmingham 9
Shirley 3

A 34

Blyth Business Park

4

A 3400

Henley in Arden 6

OTHER DESTINATIONS
• The quickest route towards the **South** is to take the **M40** which heads towards Warwick, Oxford and London. Join it at junction 3A of the M42.
• To travel towards the **South West**, use the M5 which is a fast route towards Worcester, Gloucester, Bristol and into Somerset and the West Country.

Birmingham 9

Birmingham 9

A 441

Hopwood Park
bp
Welcome Break

A 435

M42 (3A)

3

3

3

3

M 40

A 441

A 435

Redditch 5

Redditch 6
Evesham 20

Warwick 11
Oxford 50
London 107

M60 Manchester orbital motorway

After 40 years of planning, the final section of the M60 opened to traffic in October 2000. The orbital, which combines the old M62, M63 and M66 motorways, serves the busy Greater Manchester area with its population of more than 2.5 million. It also provides quick access for travel to some of Britain's most breathtaking landscapes including the Peak District, the Lake District and the Cheshire Plains. With 60 per cent of the British population (over 33 million people) living within a two-hour drive of the city, routes in and around Manchester can be busy, but the motorway has eased some of the pressure on local roads.

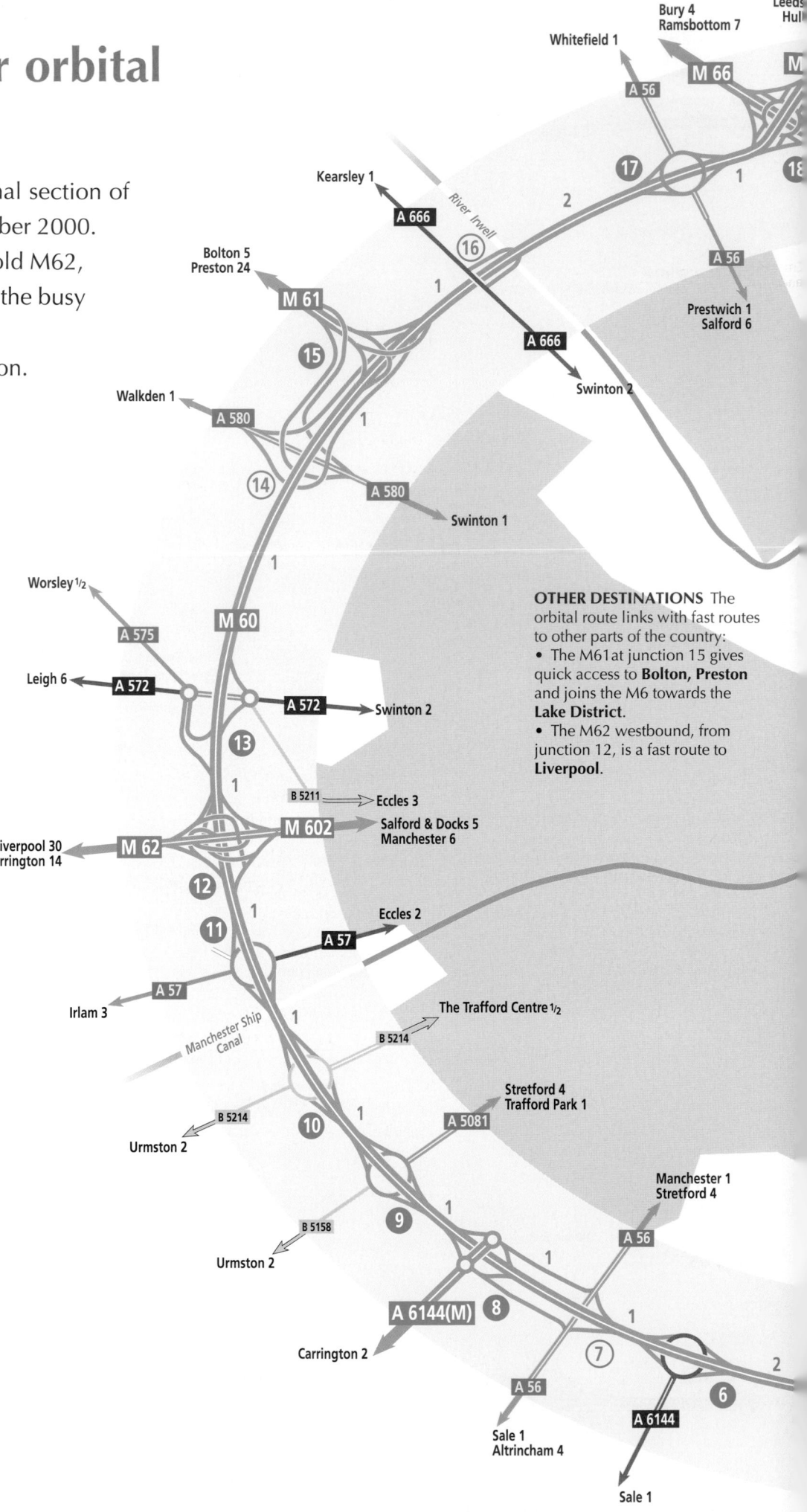

OTHER DESTINATIONS The orbital route links with fast routes to other parts of the country:
• The M61 at junction 15 gives quick access to **Bolton, Preston** and joins the M6 towards the **Lake District**.
• The M62 westbound, from junction 12, is a fast route to **Liverpool**.

CONGESTION BLACKSPOTS
• At peak times (from 7–9am and 5–7pm), traffic can become congested between **junctions 12 and 18**, especially in an anti-clockwise direction in the morning peak.
• In the **Trafford Park** area, between junctions 7 and 10, traffic builds up during the same morning and evening peaks, and sometimes at shopping times (10am–12noon and 2–5pm). The junctions are close together and traffic patterns can change quickly.

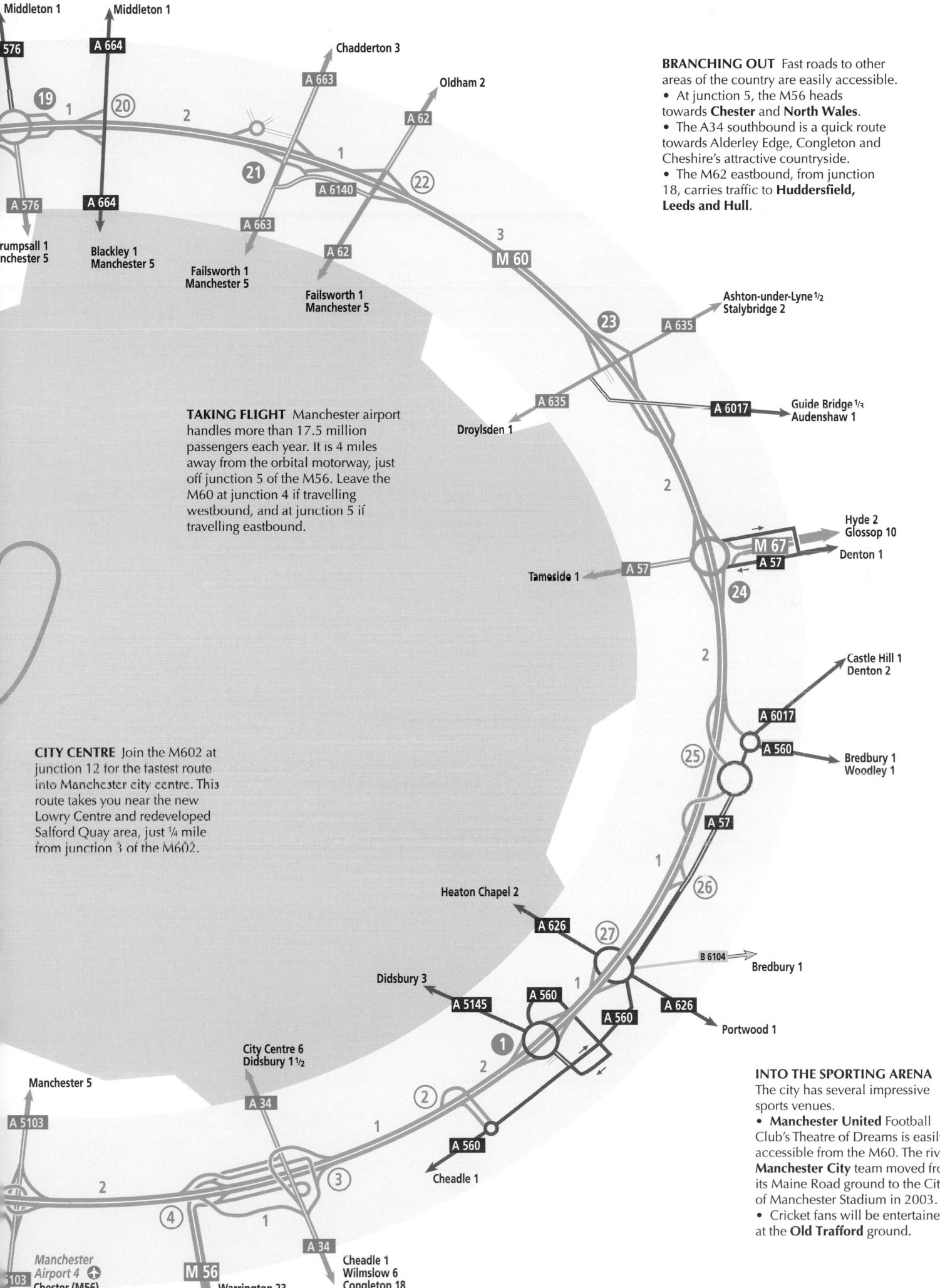

Middleton 1

A 576

Middleton 1

A 664

Chadderton 3

A 663

Oldham 2

(19) 1 (20) 2

A 62

(21)

A 576

(22)

A 664

A 6140

Crumpsall 1
Manchester 5

A 663

3

Blackley 1
Manchester 5

A 62

M 60

Failsworth 1
Manchester 5

Failsworth 1
Manchester 5

BRANCHING OUT Fast roads to other areas of the country are easily accessible.
• At junction 5, the M56 heads towards **Chester** and **North Wales**.
• The A34 southbound is a quick route towards Alderley Edge, Congleton and Cheshire's attractive countryside.
• The M62 eastbound, from junction 18, carries traffic to **Huddersfield, Leeds and Hull**.

(23)

A 635

Ashton-under-Lyne ½
Stalybridge 2

A 635

A 6017

Guide Bridge ⅓
Audenshaw 1

TAKING FLIGHT Manchester airport handles more than 17.5 million passengers each year. It is 4 miles away from the orbital motorway, just off junction 5 of the M56. Leave the M60 at junction 4 if travelling westbound, and at junction 5 if travelling eastbound.

Droylsden 1

2

Hyde 2
Glossop 10

M 67

A 57

Tameside 1

A 57

Denton 1

(24)

2

Castle Hill 1
Denton 2

CITY CENTRE Join the M602 at junction 12 for the fastest route into Manchester city centre. This route takes you near the new Lowry Centre and redeveloped Salford Quay area, just ¼ mile from junction 3 of the M602.

A 6017

A 560

Bredbury 1
Woodley 1

(25)

A 57

1

(26)

Heaton Chapel 2

B 6104

Bredbury 1

A 626

(27)

Didsbury 3

A 5145

A 560

A 560

A 626

Portwood 1

City Centre 6
Didsbury 1½

1

Manchester 5

A 34

INTO THE SPORTING ARENA
The city has several impressive sports venues.
• **Manchester United** Football Club's Theatre of Dreams is easily accessible from the M60. The rival **Manchester City** team moved from its Maine Road ground to the City of Manchester Stadium in 2003.
• Cricket fans will be entertained at the **Old Trafford** ground.

A 5103

(1)

2

A 560

2

(2)

Cheadle 1

3

(3)

2

(4)

1

A 34

Manchester
Airport 4

M 56

Chester (M56)
Birmingham (M6)
Wythenshawe 3

5103

Warrington 23
Chester 38
Birmingham (M6)

Cheadle 1
Wilmslow 6
Congleton 18

Railways, airports & ferry ports

The location of major rail routes, airports which carry passenger traffic and car ferry ports in Great Britain and Ireland are shown on the maps below. Also included are the main rail operators, the regions they serve and their telephone numbers. Contact information for the airports and ferry ports is also included.

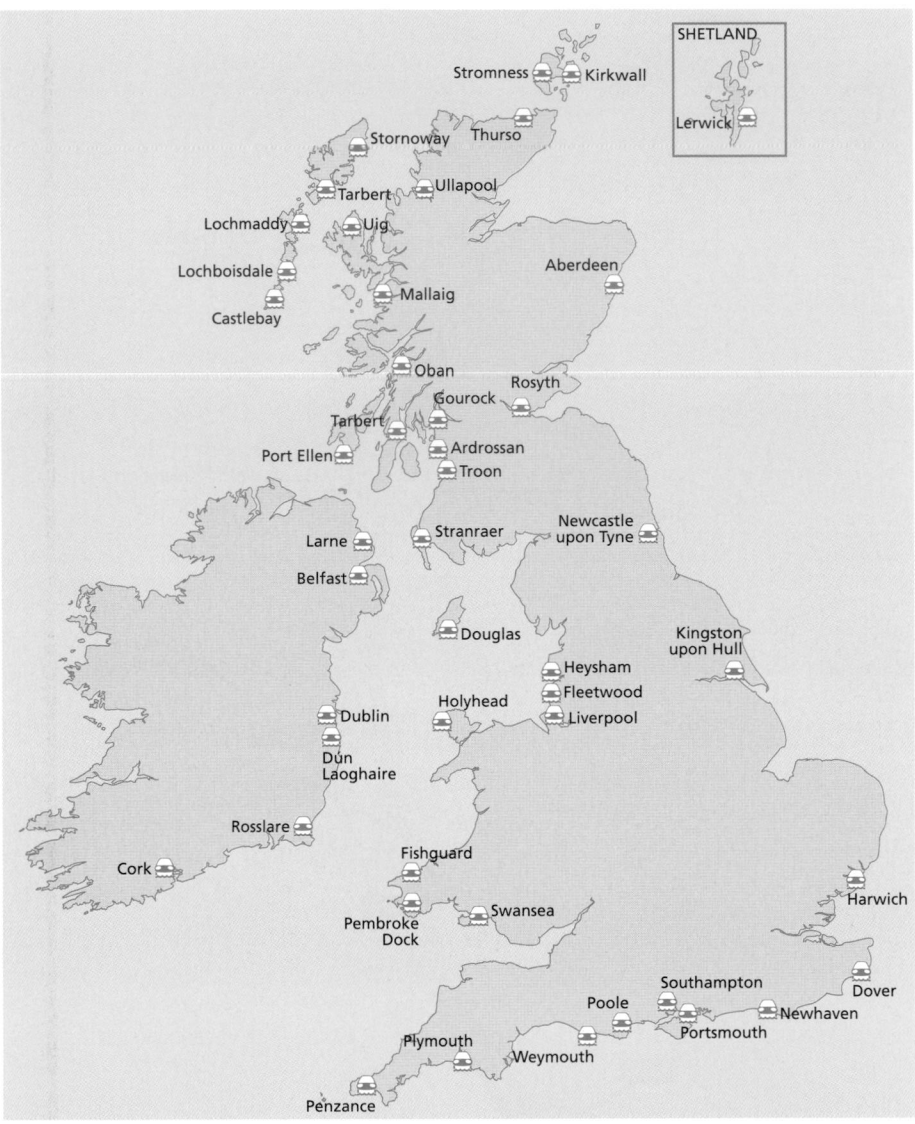

FERRY COMPANIES

Brittany Ferries 0870 3665 333
Routes from Portsmouth, Poole & Plymouth
Caledonian MacBrayne Ltd 08705 650000
Serves 22 islands off the West Coast of Scotland
Condor Ferries 0845 3452000
Sails from Weymouth, Portsmouth & Poole to Channel Islands
DFDS Seaways 08705 333000
Routes from Newcastle & Harwich
Fjordline (0191) 296 1313
Sails from Newcastle to Holland
Hoverspeed Ltd 0870 240 8070
Dover–Calais; Newhaven–Dieppe
Irish Ferries 08705 171717
Serves Dublin, Rosslare, Holyhead, Pembroke
Norfolkline (0304) 218400
Sails from Dover to Dunkerque
Northlink Ferries 0845 600 0449
Sails from Scotland to the Orkneys & Shetlands

Orkney Ferries (01856) 872044
Serves the mainland and islands in the Orkneys
P&O Ferries 08705 202020
Routes to Ireland and the Continent from Dover, Portsmouth & Hull
Red Funnel Ferries 0870 4448898
Sails from Southampton &Gosport to the Isle of Wight
Seacat (see Hoverspeed)
Sea France Ltd 08705 711711
Sails from Dover to Calais
Stena Line 0870 400 6798
Routes to Ireland from Fishguard, Holyhead, Fleetwood & Stranraer; and to Holland from Harwich
Swansea Cork Ferries (01792) 456116
Ferries operate between Swansea & Cork
Wightlink Ltd 0870 5827744
Serves Portsmouth, Fishbourne, Ryde, Lymington & Yarmouth

RAILWAY COMPANIES

Anglia Railways 08700 409 090
Trains serving London, Norfolk, Suffolk, Essex, Cambridgeshire
Arriva Trains Northern 0870 602 3322
Trains serving Yorkshire, Lancashire, Durham, Cumbria, Northumberland
Arriva Trains Wales (0845) 061660
Trains to Wales and the border counties
c2c (Cambridge) 0845 601 4873
Commuter trains from London Liverpool Street and Fenchurch Street to Essex
Central Trains 0870 609 6060
Serves central England including Liverpool, Birmingham, Leicester, Manchester, Sheffield, Nottingham, Cardiff, Norwich, Derby, Cambridge
Chiltern Railways 08456 005 165
From London Marylebone to High Wycombe, Banbury, Leamington Spa, Birmingham
Eurostar 08705 186 186
Trains from London Waterloo to Brussels, Paris & Disneyland Paris via Eurotunnel
First Great Eastern 08459 505 000
Suburban and mainline services to Southend, Ipswich, Romford, Manningtree and other Essex stations
First Great Western 08457 000 125
Trains between London, South Wales, the Cotswolds and the west of England
First North Western 0845 600 1159
Serves the north-west of England: Birmingham, Manchester, Liverpool, Stoke-on-Trent, Newcastle West Yorkshire and the Lake District
Gatwick Express 0845 850 1530
Fast service from London Victoria to Gatwick Airport
Great North Eastern Railway (GNER)
0845 722 5225
Services from London King's Cross to Leeds, York, Newcastle, Edinburgh, Glasgow, Aberdeen, Inverness
Island Line Ltd (01983) 812591
Train operator for the Isle of Wight, serving Ryde, Brading, Sandown, Lake and Shanklin
Merseyrail (0151) 702 2071
Suburban services serving the Mersey area including Liverpool, Chester, Ormskirk, Southport
Midland Mainline 08457 221 125
Operates out of London St Pancras, serving Yorkshire and the East Midlands
ScotRail 0845 755 0033
Runs trains throughout Scotland, including connecting ferry services to the islands
Silverlink 0845 601 4867 (metro)
(0845) 601 4868 (country)
London, Milton Keynes, Birmingham, Watford
South Eastern 0870 603 0405
Trains serve the south-east of London and Kent area
Southern 0870 830 6000
Trains to Surrey and Sussex, including Croydon, Haywards Heath and Brighton
South West Trains 0845 600 0650
Trains run out of London Waterloo to south-west London and suburbs and the West country
Thameslink (020) 7620 6333
Services from Bedford to London King's Cross Thameslink, Farringdon, City Thameslink, Blackfriars and London Bridge
Thames Trains (see First Great Western)
Virgin Trains 0870 789 1234
Trains go all over Britain including Birmingham, Liverpool, northern England and Scotland
Wessex Trains 0845 6000 880
The west country, the south coast and Birmingham
WAGN (West Anglia & Great Northern)
0870 850 8822
Trains to Cambridge, Ely, King's Lynn, London, Peterborough

National Rail Enquiries 08457 484950

AIRPORTS
(All numbers listed are for enquiry desks.)

Aberdeen Airport 0870 040 0006
Belfast City Airport (028) 9093 9093
Belfast International Airport (028) 9448 4848
Birmingham International Airport 0870 733 5511
Bristol International Airport 0870 121 2747
Cardiff International Airport (01446) 711111
Cork International Airport 00 353(0) 21 4313 131
Dublin Airport 00 353 (0) 1 8141 111
Durham Tees Valley Airport (01325) 332811
Edinburgh Airport 0870 040 0007
Glasgow Airport 0870 040 0008
Glasgow Prestwick International Airport
  0871 223 0700
Humberside International Airport
  (01652) 688456
Leeds/Bradford International Airport
  (0113) 250 9696
Liverpool John Lennon Airport
  0870 750 8484
London City Airport (020) 7646 0088
London Gatwick Airport 0870 000 2468
London Heathrow Airport 0870 000 0123
London Luton Airport (01582) 405100
London Stansted Airport 0870 000 0303
Manchester Airport (0161) 489 3000
Newcastle Airport 0870 122 1488
Nottingham East Midlands Airport (01332) 852852
Shannon Airport 00 353 (0) 61 712 000
Southampton International Airport 0870 040 0009

**National rail network
and airports**

—— Major routes
—— Other routes
✈ Airport

Scenic Britain & Ireland

Despite the density of its population, much of Great Britain remains wild and unspoiled. Remnants of ancient forest, rugged moorland, coast and mountain areas, many providing a habitat for unique and sometimes endangered birds, plants and animals, are the perfect escape for nature-lovers, climbers, ramblers and simply those seeking a change of scenery.

Large stretches of the most spectacular scenery in the British Isles and Ireland are protected for public use within National Parks or other designated areas. Walkers, and in many cases cyclists and horse-riders, can enjoy the views from the waymarked long-distance paths.

National Parks

The aims of National Parks are to conserve the landscape and to promote the quiet enjoyment and understanding of these areas by the public. Ten parks have been set in England and Wales under the National Parks and Access to the Countryside Act 1949. The Broads and the New Forest have equivalent status. Ireland has six areas designated as National Parks and Scotland has two. Because most of the land is privately owned, access is generally along footpaths and roads, with a more general right to roam over some open areas.

National Trails

National Trails are officially designated routes. There are 15 Trails in England and Wales and four routes in Scotland, providing over 3000 miles of maintained paths which cover beautiful countryside and offer spectacular views. There is more information on the website: **www.nationaltrail.co.uk** which gives detailed guidance on a number of walks. The Ramblers' Association also has useful information on **www.ramblers.org.uk.**

Following a path In England and Wales, National Trails are marked with an acorn, in Scotland with a thistle and in Ireland, the 'walking man' denotes a Waymarked Way. The Ridgeway (below) is part of a continuous trail from the Dorset coast to the Wash.

Waymarked Ways

Ireland has greatly expanded its network of Waymarked Ways since the opening of the Wicklow Way in 1982 and the number is increasing every year. Find out more on **www.walkireland.ie** (for the Irish Republic) and **www.waymarkedways.com** (for Northern Ireland).

Areas of Outstanding Natural Beauty

There are more than 50 areas of Outstanding Natural Beauty in England, Wales and Northern Ireland, and 40 similar National Scenic Areas in Scotland. AONBs enjoy limited protection under planning laws but there is no statutory provision for overall public access.

Forest Parks

The Forestry Commission manages a range of open expanses and forests in the United Kingdom. Many have picnic sites, visitor centres and waymarked walks.

World Heritage Sites

A few remarkable natural features of exceptional interest and importance are designated as World Heritage Sites. In Britain, the Dorset and East Devon Coast, the Giant's Causeway in Northern Ireland and the island of St Kilda have this rating.

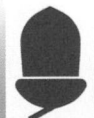  

NATIONAL PARKS

Brecon Beacons Dramatic hill country separating mid and south Wales. (01874) 624437

The Broads Shallow lakes, rivers, reed beds, wet woodlands and marshes. (01603) 610734

Cairngorms Swathes of high, wild land, including 46 Munros. (01479) 873535

Dartmoor High boggy plateau, with rocky tors, cut by the River Dart. (01626) 832093

Exmoor Moorland scored by wooded valleys and bordered by coastal cliffs. (01398) 323665

Lake District England's highest mountains loom over a score of lakes. (01539) 724555

Loch Lomond & The Trossachs Untamed glens and freshwater lochs. 0845 345 4978

New Forest Ancient forest and heath. (023) 802 8144

North York Moors A plateau dissected by valleys and bordered by cliffs. (01439) 770657

Northumberland Wild border country of moor and forest. (01434) 605555

Peak District Peat moorlands, a millstone grit escarpment and limestone plateaus. (01629) 816200

Pembrokeshire Coast Coastal cliffs, islands, estuaries and a high moorland plateau. 0845 345 7275

Snowdonia High mountains with glaciated valleys and lakes, a coast of dunes and sandy bays. (01766) 770274

Yorkshire Dales Upland limestone country with screes and pavement. (01969) 650456

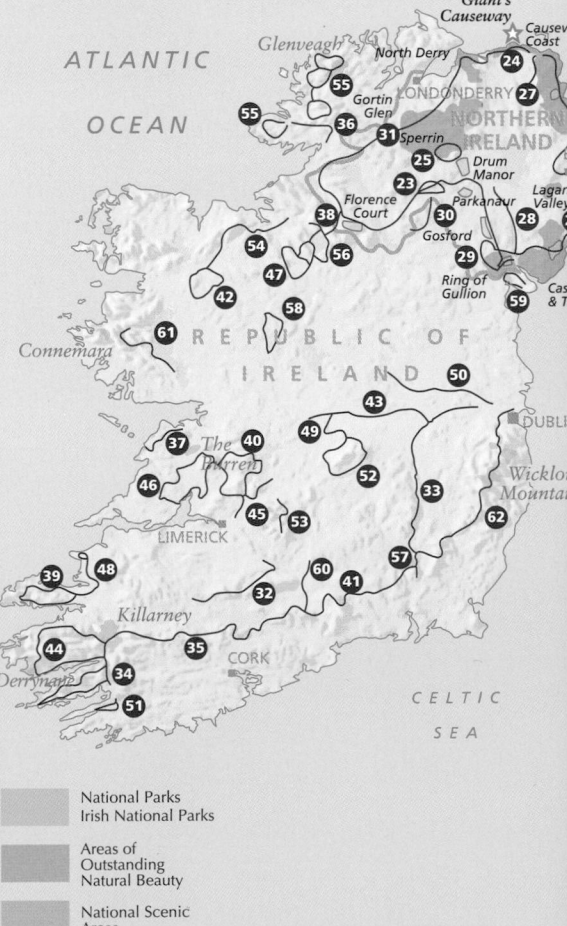

Legend:
- National Parks / Irish National Parks
- Areas of Outstanding Natural Beauty
- National Scenic Areas
- Forest Parks
- ☆ World Heritage Sites
- ⬤1 Long Distance Paths / National Trails / Waymarked Ways

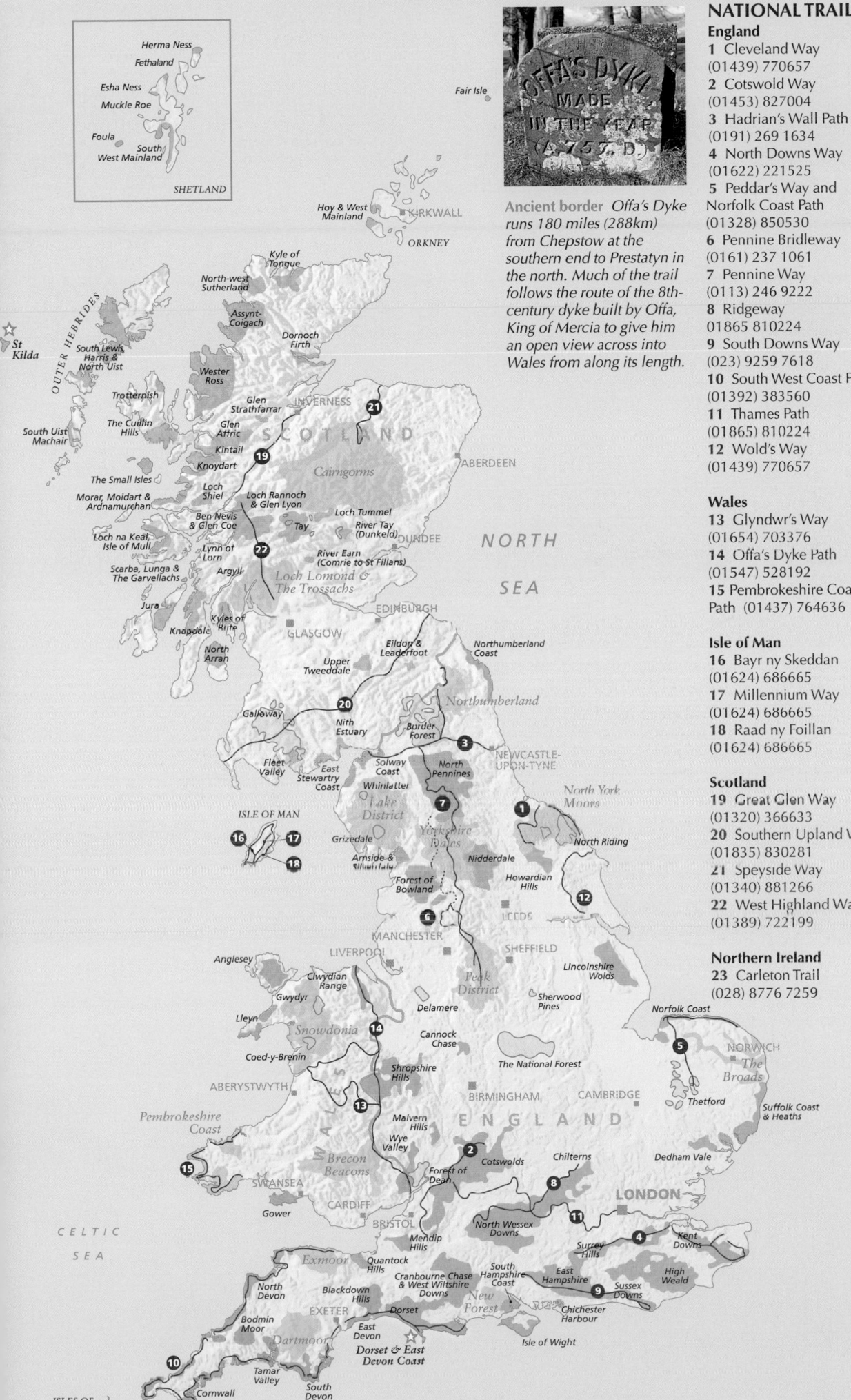

NATIONAL TRAILS

England

1 Cleveland Way
(01439) 770657
2 Cotswold Way
(01453) 827004
3 Hadrian's Wall Path
(0191) 269 1634
4 North Downs Way
(01622) 221525
5 Peddar's Way and
Norfolk Coast Path
(01328) 850530
6 Pennine Bridleway
(0161) 237 1061
7 Pennine Way
(0113) 246 9222
8 Ridgeway
01865 810224
9 South Downs Way
(023) 9259 7618
10 South West Coast Path
(01392) 383560
11 Thames Path
(01865) 810224
12 Wold's Way
(01439) 770657

Wales

13 Glyndwr's Way
(01654) 703376
14 Offa's Dyke Path
(01547) 528192
15 Pembrokeshire Coast
Path (01437) 764636

Isle of Man

16 Bayr ny Skeddan
(01624) 686665
17 Millennium Way
(01624) 686665
18 Raad ny Foillan
(01624) 686665

Scotland

19 Great Glen Way
(01320) 366633
20 Southern Upland Way
(01835) 830281
21 Speyside Way
(01340) 881266
22 West Highland Way
(01389) 722199

Northern Ireland

23 Carleton Trail
(028) 8776 7259

24 Causeway Coast Way
(028) 3026 8877
25 Central Sperrins Way
(028) 8224 7831
26 Lecale Way
(028) 4461 2233
27 Moyle Way
(028) 2076 2024
28 Newry Canal Way
(028) 3752 1800
29 Ring of Gullion
(028) 3026 8877
30 Sliabh Beagh Way
(028) 8776 7259
31 Ulster Way
(028) 9024 6609

Ireland

32 Ballyhoura Way
00 353 (0) 63 91300
33 Barrow Way
00 353 (0) 1 647 2557
34 Beara Way
00 353 (0) 1 27 70054
35 Blackwater Way
00 353 (0) 58 50007
36 Bluestack Way
00 353 (0) 74 21160
37 Burren Way
00 353 (0) 65 6828366
38 Cavan Way
00 353 (0) 49 4331799
39 Dingle Way
00 353 (0) 64 31633
40 East Clare Way
00 353 (0) 65 6835912
41 East Munster Way
00 353 (0) 51 875823
42 Foxford Way
00 353 (0) 94 56488
43 Grand Canal Way
00 353 (0) 1 6472557
44 Kerry Way
00 353 (0) 64 31633
45 Lough Derg Way
00 353 (0) 61 317522
46 Mid Clare Way
00 353 (0) 65 6835912
47 Miners' Way and
Historical Trail
00 353 (0) 78 20005
48 North Kerry Way
00 353 (0) 66 7121288
49 Offaly Way
00 353 (0) 506 25015
50 Royal Canal Way
00 353 (0) 1 647 2577
51 Sheep's Head Way
00 353 (0) 21 4273251
52 Slieve Bloom Way
00 353 (0) 506 25015
53 Slieve Felim Way
00 353 (0) 61 361555
54 Sligo Way
00 353 (0) 71 56666
55 Sli Dhun na nGall
(UK) 0800 7835708
(Ireland) 1800 621 600
56 Sli Liatroma
00 353 (0) 71 9620170
57 South Leinster Way
00 353 (0) 56 51500
58 Suck Valley Way
00 353 (0) 903 63602
59 Táin Way
00 353 (0) 42 9335484
60 Tipperary Heritage
Trail 00 353 (0) 62 55467
61 Western Way Galway
00 353 (0) 91 537700
62 Wicklow Way
00 353 (0) 404 20070

Ancient border *Offa's Dyke runs 180 miles (288km) from Chepstow at the southern end to Prestatyn in the north. Much of the trail follows the route of the 8th-century dyke built by Offa, King of Mercia to give him an open view across into Wales from along its length.*

Britain & Ireland by road

The following maps cover the United Kingdom and the Republic of Ireland. Most of Great Britain is shown at a scale of 1:200,000. Ireland and some of the less populated parts of Scotland are shown at slightly smaller scales. Every map has its own scale bar. The map pages are numbered consecutively throughout the section.

The maps have a simple alpha-numeric grid reference system – the same for each map and not related to scale – which is linked to the index of place names.

How to use the maps

A full key to the road maps is given opposite, and on the inside front cover. A number of other useful features are also included in the margin to each map.

Key to the road maps on pages 64–248

1 *Continuity arrows north, south, east and west to the next map.*

2 *Continuity arrows for all motorways, dual carriageways or A-roads with distances to the nearest principal destinations.*

3 *Details of local radio stations.*

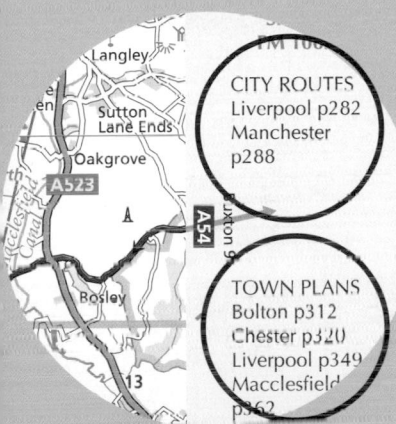

4 *A list of destinations which have a town plan or city route map.*

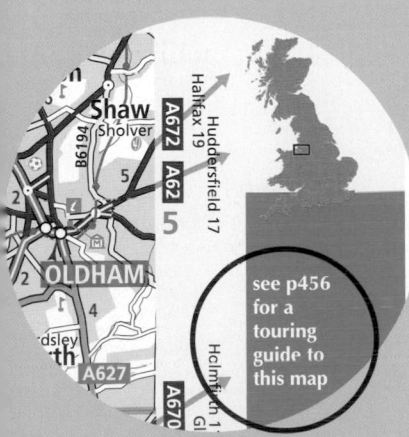

5 *A cross-reference to the pages in the Touring Guide that describe the area covered in the map.*

Symbols used on the road maps

ROADS

Motorway
═══	Motorway
▬ ▬ ▬	Under construction/projected

Primary route
═══	Dual carriageway
═══	Single carriageway
▪ ▪ ▪	Under construction
▪▪▪▪	Narrow with passing places

A road (non-primary)
═══	Dual carriageway
═══	Single carriageway
▪ ▪ ▪	Under construction
▪▪▪▪	Narrow with passing places

B road
═══	Dual carriageway
═══	Single carriageway
	Narrow with passing places
═══	Minor road

ROAD NUMBERING

M40	Motorway
A41	Primary route
N3	National primary road (Rep of Ireland)
A683	A road (non-primary)
N54	National secondary road (Rep of Ireland)
B6254	B road
R579	Regional road (Rep of Ireland)

ROAD INFORMATION

Motorway junction
14	Full access
8	Limited access (see strip plans on pages 34–57 for details)
Gordano	Motorway services
9	Motorway distances in miles between junctions and services
7	Road distances (miles) on main roads
	Multi-level junction
	Roundabout
	Primary route services
⇒ ⇐	Tunnel
	Level crossing
	Vehicle ferry
Toll	Toll

Gradients
⇐	Steeper than 1 in 7 (14%)

Telephones and parking
☎	Public telephones in rural areas
Ⓟ	Lay-by or parking with toilets

SETTLEMENTS
	City, town, village or other built-up area
LIVERPOOL	Primary route destination

BOUNDARIES
─ ─ ─	National or international
═══	National park

RAILWAYS AND AIRPORTS
─╫─	Normal gauge railway and station
	Narrow gauge railway or 'preserved' line

Road crossings
	Road over
	Road under
	Tunnel
✈	Airport/aerodrome with scheduled services
⊕	Other aerodromes

PHYSICAL FEATURES
Snowdon 3560	Height in feet
	Woodland or forest
	River
	Lake
	Canal
	Coastline
	Sandy foreshore
	Other tidal foreshore
☆	Natural feature

LANDMARKS
⚲	Lighthouse
⌂	Observatory
⋏	Radio/TV mast
⊤	Wind generator
✳	Windmill

ANTIQUITIES
⊓	Ancient monument
✳	Hill–fort
---	Roman road, ancient trackway
⚔	Site of battle

RECREATION AND LEISURE
⊕	Abbey, priory, etc
+	Air show
	Aquarium
⊤	Cathedral
𝕐	Country park
⚒	Craft centre
	Factory shopping village
✻	Garden

House or castle
⌂	Interesting interior
	In ruins
✿	Industrial attraction
†	Interesting parish church
🏛	Museum or gallery
-----	National Trail, Long Distance Path, Waymarked Way
	Nature reserve or bird sanctuary
	Picnic site
	Steam railway
	Theme park

Tourist information centre
ℹ	Tourist information centre
	View point
	Wildlife park
▲	Youth Hostel
	Zoo

CAMPSITES
	Caravans only
	Caravans and tents
▲	Tents only

SPORTING VENUES
⚽	Association Football
⚹	Athletics
	Championship lawn tennis
⊚	County cricket (first class)
	Flat racing and steeplechasing
⊗	Gaelic football and hurling

Golf courses
	18 holes
	Less than 18 holes
	Greyhound racing
	Highland games
	Motorsport
	Rugby League
	Rugby Union
	Showjumping and horse trials
	Skiing
	Speedway
	Stadium (venue for more than one sport)

E   F   G   H

Bideford 47
Bude 20
A39

Okehampton 26
Launceston 9
A30

70

B O D M I N

M O O R

Garrow
Tor

Lynher

5

New
Polzeath
Polzeath
Trebetherick
Tredrizzick

Longcross
St Endellion
B3314

Trelights
Pendoggett

Michaelstow

Codda
Jamaica
Inn
18
Bolventor

Trebartha
St Torney
North Hill
Coad's
Green

stow
Bay

B3267
Trelill
13

De Lank River
St Breward

Kilmar Tor
1280
Henwood

Bathpool
Rilla
Mill
Upton
Cross

B3254

Rock
Padstow

dstow
eaux Place
Splatt
Pityme

St Minver
Chapel
Amble
St Kew
St Kew
Highway

St Tudy

Row
Wentfordbridge

Keybridge

Dozmary
Pool

Fowey

Cheesewring
Minions
Hurlers
Stone Circles

Caradon Hill
1216

Darite
Middlehill

Pensilva

see p411
for a
touring
guide to
this map

Wadebridge

Bodieve

A39

Little
Petherick

Edmonton

Trevanson
St Breock
Egloshayle
Bodmin & Wenford
Railway

Blisland
Waterloo

A30
Temple

Colliford
Lake

Siblyback
Lake

Common
Moor

Golitha
Falls

Trethevy
Quoit
Tremar

A390
Merrymeet
Tavistock 15

Tredinnick
St Breock
Downs
Longstone
9
Spirit of
the West

A39
Rosenannon

Burlawn
Washaway

Pencarrow House
and Gardens
Longstone
7

Helland
SS Protus
and Hyacinth

BODMIN
Millpool
Maidenwell

Warleggan
Mount
St
Neot
Ley

Dobwalls
Adventure Park

Doublebois
12
Dobwalls

St
Cleer
Darite

St
Cleer

Pengover
Green
A390

Liskeard

Ruthernbridge

St Lawrence

Cardinham
St Petroc

Slate Cavern

Menheniot
A38

68

of
rey
tre
ddy
Withiel
St Wenn

A389
Nanstallon
2
2
4
Bodmin
A389
Lanivet

Trebyan
Lanhydrock
Sweetshouse
Restormel
Castle

13

East
Taphouse

St Pinnock

Herodsfoot
St Keyne

Trewidland

Music
Museum

Horningtops

A38

St Columb
Major

Tregonetha

4
B3268

B3269

Braddock
Boconnoc

Duloe

Trewidland

Plymouth 18
Saltash 11
Torpoint 18
A387

Castle-
an-Dinas

B3274
7
Victoria
Lockengate
Redmoor

Couchs Mill

Lostwithiel
1644

Bocaddon

Stone
Circle
Tredinnick

A387
9
Widegates

Ruthvoes
Toldish
Queens

Belowda
Roche
Bilberry
Bugle

Lanlivery
Luxulyan
8

Lostwithiel

St Winnow

Lerryn

Lanreath

Muchlarnick

Morval
Sandplace

B3253

A30
B3279

St
Dennis
Whitemoor
Stenalees
Bridges
B3314

A390
Penwithick

Penpillick

Lescrow
Pelynt

St Veep
Penpoll
Highway

Trenewan

St Martin

Woolly Monkey
Sanctuary

hale
Retew
Treviscoe

Hensbarrow
Downs
Nanpean
Carthew

Wheal
Martyn

Trethurgy

Eden
Project

Tywardreath
Highway

Golant
B3269

East Looe

19
Scarcewater
nton
Menna
A3058

Stepaside
Automobilia
High
Street

Foxhole
Hornick

Trethowel
Trewoon

St Blazey

St Austell

Tywardreath

Par
A3082

Bodinnick
Ferry

Fowey

6

Looe
West
Looe

Looe
Bay

Grampound
Road

Hewas
Water
Sticker

St Mewan
Telowth
Polgooth

Charlestown

Polkerris
Menabilly

9
Fowey

Polruan

Lansallos

Crumplehorn
Polperro

Carey
Park

Talland

Talland
Bay

St Georges or
Looe Island

Coombe
Lanjeth
Grampound

London
Apprentice

Porthpean
St Austell Bay

St Catherine's
Castle

South West
Coast Path

Trewithen
Creed
B3287

Trenarren

Black Head

Gribbin
Head

A3078

St Ewe
Pentewan

The Lost Gardens
of Heligan

Mevagissey
Bay

Veryan
Green

St Michael
Caerhays

Caerhays
Castle

Polmassick
Mevagissey

Portmellon

Chapel
Point

Tregony
thenick

Trevarrick

Gorran
Haven

South West
Coast Path

Veryan

Portholland

Boswinger

Penare

Dodman
Point

Veryan Bay

Portloe

are
ead

Carne

BODMIN

A   B   C

3

Scarletts
Well
Road

Camel Trail

Bodmin
Jail

Wallace Road

Cross Lane
East
Cornwall
Hospital

Camp
Site

3

2

Berrycoombe Hill
Tanwood

Hillside Park

Cardell Rd

Berrycoombe Road

Berry
Lane

Wadebridge 7
A389

Sherwood Dr
Alexandra Rd
Sandra Wy

Hillside Pk

Pool St
Rhind St

Castle St

DENNISON RD

St Petroc
Church

Midway Road

HIGHER BORE
St Leonards
PO

Lower Bore St
Fore St

Turf St

PRIORY RD
POL
A389

A30 Launceston 30

DUNMERE RD
WESTHEATH AVE
A389

St Leonards
HIGHER BORE

Barn Lane

Robartes Road
Beacon Hill

Courtroom
Experience

Meadow Pl
Northey Road

Crinnick's Hill

St Nicholas Street
Council
Offices

Haxleigh Rd

A391 St Austell 12

St Mary's
Cres
Rock Lane

Trelawney Rd

The Beacon
Nature
Reserve

Monument

Beacon Road

Beacon Lanes

Bodmin &
Wenford
Steam
Railway

Dragon
Leisure
Centre

Military
Museum
B3268

1

0   100   200yds
0   100   200m

A   B   C

BBC Radio Devon
FM 92.8/95.8/103.4

BBC
Radio Cornwall
FM 95.2

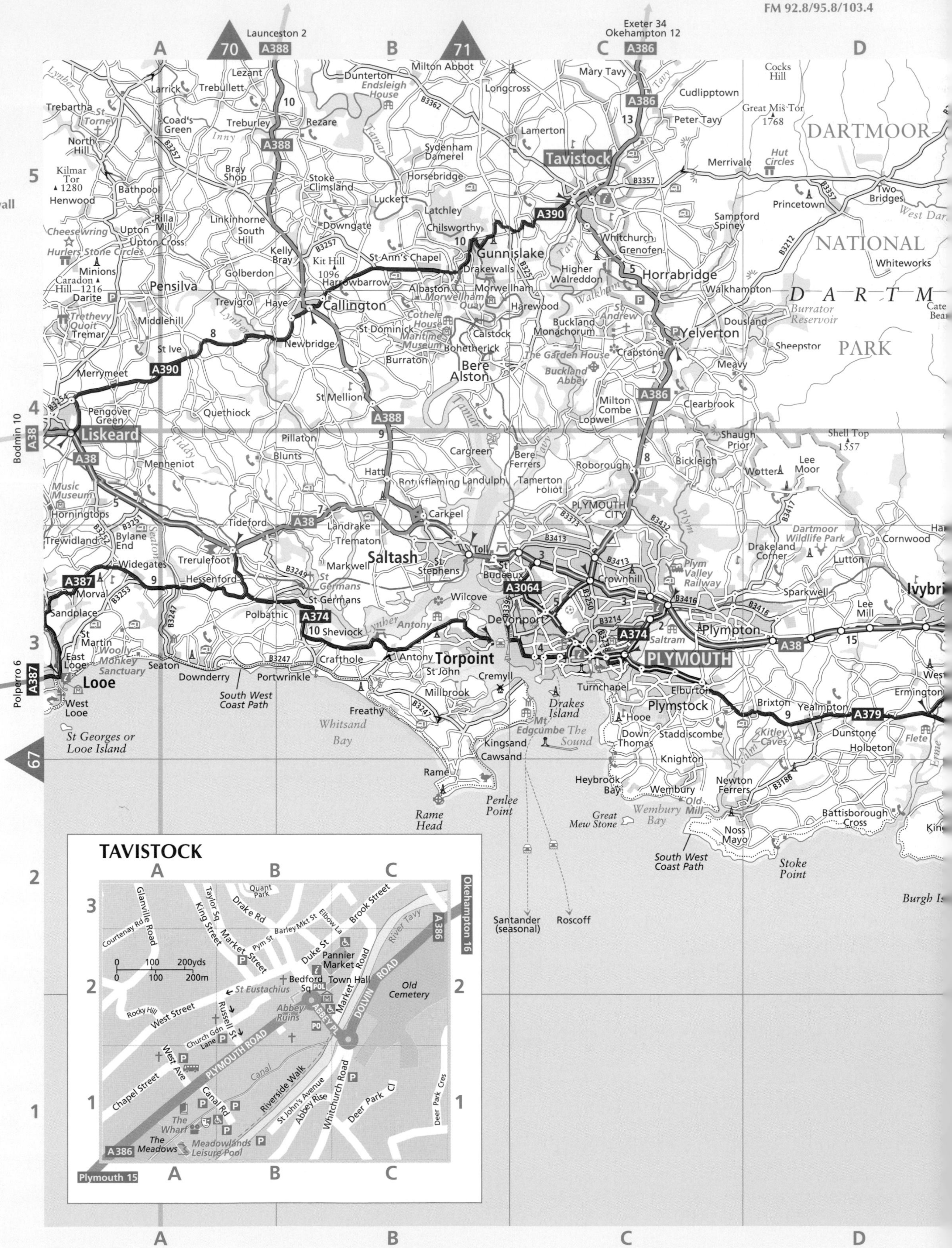
A
B
C
D
70
71
Launceston 2
A388
Exeter 34
Okehampton 12
A386
5
4
3
2
1
Bodmin 10
A38
Polperro 6
A387
67
Milton Abbot
Mary Tavy
Cocks Hill
Lezant
Dunterton
Endsleigh House
Larrick
Trebullett
Longcross
Cudlipptown
Great Mis Tor
1768
Trebartha
St Torney
Coad's Green
Treburley
Rezare
Lamerton
Peter Tavy
DARTMOOR
North Hill
Inny
Tamar
B3362
B3257
Sydenham Damerel
Tavistock
Merrivale
Hut Circles
Kilmar Tor
1280
Henwood
Bathpool
Bray Shop
Stoke Climsland
Horsebridge
B3357
Princetown
Two Bridges
Luckett
Latchley
Chilsworthy
A390
Sampford Spiney
West Dart
Rilla Mill
Linkinhorne
South Hill
Downgate
Whitchurch
Grenofen
NATIONAL
Cheesewring
Upton
Upton Cross
Hurlers Stone Circles
Kelly Bray
St Ann's Chapel
Gunnislake
Tavy
Whiteworks
Minions
Caradon Hill
1216
Kit Hill
1096
Golberdon
Drakewalls
Higher Walreddon
Horrabridge
Darite
Pensilva
Harrowbarrow
Albaston
Morwellham
Morwellham Quay
Walkham
Walkhampton
D A R T M
Trevigro
Haye
Callington
Harewood
St Andrew
Burrator Reservoir
Cate Bea
Trethevy Quoit
Tremar
Middlehill
Lynher
Cothele House
Maritime Museum
Calstock
Buckland Monachorum
Dousland
Yelverton
St Ive
Newbridge
St Dominick
Bohetherick
The Garden House
Crapstone
Sheepstor
PARK
Merrymeet
Burraton
Bere Alston
Buckland Abbey
Meavy
B3254
A386
Pengover Green
Quethiock
St Mellion
Milton Combe
Clearbrook
Lopwell
Liskeard
A388
Shaugh Prior
Shell Top
1557
Pillaton
Cargreen
Bere Ferrers
Bickleigh
Menheniot
Blunts
Roborough
Wotter
Lee Moor
Music Museum
Hatt
Botusfleming
Landulph
Tamerton Foliot
Plym
Horningtops
PLYMOUTH CITY
B3373
B3432
B3417
Carkeel
B3251
B3252
Tideford
Landrake
Dartmoor Wildlife Park
Trewidland
Bylane End
Seaton
Trematon
Saltash
Toll
B3413
Drakeland Corner
Cornwood
Widegates
Trerulefoot
Markwell
St Stephens
St Budeaux
Crownhill
Plym Valley Railway
Lutton
A387
Hessenford
B3249
St Germans
A3064
Morval
B3253
Sparkwell
Ivybri
St Germans
Wilcove
B3396
B3250
B3416
Lee Mill
Sandplace
B3247
Polbathic
A374
Devonport
B3214
Plympton
Sheviock
Lynher
Antony
Saltram
St Martin
Woolly Monkey Sanctuary
Torpoint
PLYMOUTH
East Looe
Seaton
Crafthole
Antony
St John
West
Downderry
Portwrinkle
Cremyll
Turnchapel
Elburton
Ermington
Looe
Millbrook
Drakes Island
Plymstock
Brixton
Yealmpton
A379
West Looe
South West Coast Path
Freathy
Mt Edgcumbe
The Sound
Hooe
Dunstone
Flete
St Georges or Looe Island
Whitsand Bay
Down Thomas
Staddiscombe
Kitley Caves
Holbeton
Kingsand
Cawsand
Knighton
Rame
Heybrook Bay
Wembury
Newton Ferrers
B3186
Penlee Point
Rame Head
Great Mew Stone
Wembury Bay
Old Mill
Noss Mayo
Battisborough Cross
Kin
South West Coast Path
Stoke Point
Burgh Is
Santander (seasonal)
Roscoff
TAVISTOCK
Quant Park
Glanville Road
Courtenay Rd
Taylor Sq
King Street
Drake Rd
Market Street
Pym St
Barley Mkt St
Elbow La
Brook Street
River Tavy
A386
Okehampton 16
0
100
200yds
200m
Duke St
Pannier Market Road
Bedford Sq
Town Hall
St Eustachius
Old Cemetery
Rocky Hill
West Street
Russell St
Abbey Ruins
ABBEY PL
DOLVIN ROAD
Church Gdn Lane
PLYMOUTH ROAD
West Ave
Canal
Chapel Street
Canal Rd
Riverside Walk
St John's Avenue
Abbey Rise
Whitchurch Road
Deer Park Cl
Deer Park Cres
The Wharf
The Meadows
Meadowlands Leisure Pool
Plymouth 15
miles
kms

Plymouth Sound FM
FM 96.6/97

Classic Gold 1152
AM 1152

see p412 for a touring guide to this map

Gemini FM
FM 96.4/
97/103

Classic Gold
AM 666/954

South Hams Radio
FM 100.5/100.8/101.2/101.9

TOWN PLANS
Plymouth p376
Tavistock p68
Torquay p398

Lantern FM
FM 96.2

see p413 for a touring guide to this map

TOWN PLANS
Bodmin p67
Launceston p343
Tavistock p68

BBC
Radio Devon
FM 92.8/95.8
103.4

Bideford 11
A388

81

Barnstaple 22
Bideford 14
A386

Great Torrington 7
A3124

81

Barnstaple 17
A377

E   F   G   H

Abbots Bickington
Newton St Petrock
Peters Marland
Winswell
Woollaton
Merton
Huish
Dolton
B3217
Riddlecombe
Ashreigney
Copy Lake
St Mary
Cheldon
16
Milton DamErel
Shebbear
Thornbury
Bradford
Buckland Filleigh
Petrockstowe
Ash Barton
Meeth
Dowland
Iddesleigh
13
Ashley
Hollocombe
Wembworthy
Bridge Reeve
Eggesford Forest
B3042
Chawleigh
Filleigh
5
A388
Isworthy
acon
Cookbury
Holemoor
Black Torrington
Sheepwash
St Lawrence
Monkokehampton
Hatherleigh
Broadwoodkelly
Winkleigh
Brushford
Coldridge
St Thomas of Canterbury
Eastington
Lapford
Lapford Cross
A377
Anvil Corner
Brandis Corner
Highampton
A3072
Monument
B3216
Honeychurch
Exbourne
North Tawton
Bondleigh
Zeal Monachorum
Down St Mary
A377
4
9
Graddon Moor
B3217
Jacobstowe
Sampford Courtenay
15
A3072
Broadnymett
Clannaborough Barton
A3072
Hollacombe
Halwill Junction
Beaworthy
5
Inwardleigh
Folly Gate
B3215
Itton
Yeo
Nymet Tracey
Bow
Nymet Rowland
Crediton 7
Exeter 15
4
Claw
Broadbury
Halwill
Quoditch
Northlew
Ashbury
Oak Cross
6
A386
Dartmoor Railway
Taw Green
A3124
Hillerton
Spreyton
St Michael
Hittisleigh
Crediton 6
A3079
Higher Prestacott
Ashwater
Eworthy
Germansweek
Boasley Cross
Thorndon Cross
Okehampton
B3260
A30
South Tawton
Sticklepath
Finch Foundry
Belstone
South Zeal
Whiddon Down
A30
Drewsteignton
Castle Drogo
Exeter 13
15
Henford
chapmans Vell
East Panson
Virginstow
Roadford Reservoir
Bratton Clovelly
Meldon
Meldon Reservoir
Okehampton Camp
Okehampton Common
Yes Tor 2030
Cosdon Hill
Throwleigh
Wonson
8
Teign
Easton
A382
A30
72
Broadwoodwidger
Stowford
Thrushelton
Lewdown
14
Bridestowe
Combebow
Shortacombe
Sourton
West Okement
High Willhays 2038
Bridestowe and Sourton Common
Hangingstone Hill 1983
Gidleigh
Murchington
Frenchbeer
Chagford
B3206
A382
Newton Abbot 12
3
Lifton
Tinhay
Portgate
Allerford
St Petrock
Lewtrenchard
Lydford
Amicombe Hill
DARTMOOR
Fernworthy Reservoir
Lettaford
A352
Marystow
Kelly
Greystone Bridge
Bradstone
Coryton
Lydford Gorge
Black Down
13
North Brentor
A386
Lane End
Gut Hill 1980
Sittaford Tor 1763
B3212
Grimspound
North Bovey
Chillaton
Brent Tor
Thorndon
NATIONAL
Hameldown Tor 1737
Milton Abbot
Longcross
Mary Tavy
Cudlipptown
Cocks Hill
Great Mis Tor 1768
Rough Tor
Postbridge
Bellever
Cator Court
Widecombe in the Moor
Hound Tor
2
Endsleigh House
B3362
Lamerton
Peter Tavy
P
B3387
Rippon Tor 1560
Rezare
Inny
Sydenham Damerel
Horsebridge
Merrivale
Hut Circles
PARK
DARTMOOR
B3357
Babeny
Dart Valley
Ponsworthy
The Church House
Stoke Climsland
Luckett
Latchley
Tavistock
A390
B3357
Two Bridges
Buckland in the Moor
B3257
Downgate
Chilsworthy
10
St Ann's Chapel
Whitchurch
Grenofen
Sampford Spiney
Princetown
West Dart
Hexworthy
Dartmeet
Poundsgate
1
Kelly Bray
Kit Hill 1096
Drakewalls
Gunnislake
Higher Walreddon
5
Horrabridge
Huckworthy Bridge
B3212
Whiteworks
Venford Reservoir
Holne
Harrowbarrow
Albaston
Morwellham
Morwellham Quay
Harewood
Walkham
A386
Walkhampton
Burrato Reservoir
Cater's Beam
Ryder's Hill 1691
Scorriton
Abbey
Exeter 18
Callington
St Dominick
Cotehele House
Maritime Museum
Calstock
Buckland Monachorum
St Andrew
Dousland
Yelverton
Meavy
Plym
Avon
Buckfast
A38
9
Burraton
Bohetherick
The Garden House
Crapstone
Milton Combe
Lopwell
Clearbrook
Avon Dam Reservoir
Dean
5
ridge
A388
laton
St Mellion
Bere Alston
Buckland Abbey
Buckfastleigh

E   F   G   H
A388   A386   A38

68

Saltash 4
Plymouth 8

Plymouth 5

Plymouth 19

Orchard FM
FM 96.5/97.1/102.6

82

Barnstaple 29   Minehead 28   Taunton 18   Taunton 15
A361 A396   A361   M5

Sampford Peverell

Uffculme
Coldh...
Smithincott   Mill

Cheldon   West Worlington   East Worlington   Nomansland
Chawleigh   Thelbridge Barton   Washford Pyne   Templeton   Withleigh
B3042   B3137   Halberton   B3181   B3440
Filleigh   Hele Barton   Puddington   Pennymoor   Crwys Morchard   Tiverton   Ash Thomas   Willand   Diggerland   Bradfield
Barnstaple 21   A377   Eastington   Black Dog   Way Village   A396   Butterleigh   Cullompton   Kentisbea...
Chawleigh   Morchard Bishop   Woolfardisworthy   Poughill   Upham   Bickleigh Mill   Cadeleigh   Bickleigh   Colebrook   A38
Lapford   St Thomas of Canterbury   Kennerleigh   Well Town   Bickleigh Castle   St Andre...   Cullompton   28   Dulford
Nymet Rowland   Lapford Cross   Oldborough   Stockleigh English   Cheriton Fitzpaine 12   Cadbury   Fursdon House   Ravenshayes   Bradninch   Mutterton   Kers...
B3220   Down St Mary   Ash Bullayne   East Village   A3072   Stockleigh Pomeroy   A396   Silverton   Westcott   Norman's Green   A3...
Zeal Monachorum   Newbuildings   Upton Hellions   Thorverton   Up Exe   Hele   Langford   Plymtree   Payhe...
Bude 42   A3072   Clannaborough Barton   Sandford   Little Silver   Nether Exe   Rewe   Budlake   Clyst Hydon   Higher Tale   Cole...
Bow   Coleford   Knowle   Creedy Park   Shobrooke   Efford   Stoke Canon   Killerton   Clyst St Lawrence   Talaton
Nymet Tracey   Colebrooke   Crediton   Fordton Mill   Brampford Speke   Upton Pyne   Poltimore   Broadclyst   Westwood   Whimple
Hillerton   Yeoford   Uton   Hookway   Newton St Cyres   Cowley   Exeter   Dog Village   Clyst   A30
Spreyton   Venny Tedburn   EXETER   Pinhoe   Rockbeare EXETER   14
Hittisleigh   Tedburn St Mary   Whitestone   Whipton   Clyst Honiton   Marsh Green   West Hill
BBC Radio Devon   Pathfinder Village   A30   Sowton   Exeter   Farringdon   Aylesbeare   Metcom...
FM 92.8/95.8   Cheriton Bishop   15   A30   Longdown   Ide   Alphington   Countess Wear   Clyst St Mary   B3184   Venn Ottery   Southerton
103.4   Crockernwell   B3212   Shillingford St George   Exminster   Topsham   A3052   11   Aylesbeare Common
Launceston 25   Drewsteignton   Dunsford   Dunchideock   Clyst St George   Woodbury Salterton   Hawkerland   Ne... Popp...
Okehampton 7   A382   Castle Drogo   Teign   Doddiscombsleigh   Kennford   A379   Exton   B3179   Woodbury   B3180   B3178
Okehampton 9   Easton   B3206   Chagford   Christow   Higher Ashton   Kenn   A376   Ebford   Bicton Park   Yettington
A382   Moretonhampstead   Doccombe   Bridford   Coombe   Powderham   Kenton   Lympstone   Black Hill   East Budleigh   Ott...
71   Lettaford   North Bovey   Lustleigh   Lower Ashton   Haldon   Powderham Castle   A la Ronde   Otter...
Grimspound   Manaton   Becka or Becky Falls   Hennock   Trusham   A38   Starcross   B3179   Knowle   Budleigh Salterton
1737   Hameldown Tor   Bovey Tracey   Chudleigh   Forest   12   Cockwood   Littleham   South West Coast Path
Widecombe in the Moor   Hound Tor   Yarner Wood   Chudleigh Knighton   Ashcombe   Exmouth
Haytor Rocks   Brimley   Heathfield   Ugbrooke House   Luton   Little Haldon   Dawlish Warren
Haytor Vale   Ilsington   Chudleigh Knighton   Sandygate   Dawlish
The Church House   Rippon Tor 1560   Liverton   Exeter Cross   Preston   Bishopsteignton   A379   Holcombe
Ponsworthy   Buckland in the Moor   Sigford   Coldeast   Kingsteignton   Combeinteignhead   A381   Teignmouth
A38   Caton   19   Bickington   Teigngrace   Shaldon   Wildlife Trust
Ashburton   A383   Newton Abbot   West Ogwell   East Ogwell   Stokeinteignhead
Holne   St Andrew   Woodland   Denbury   Abbotskerswell   A380   Haccombe   Babbacombe Bay
Scorriton   Buckfast   Forder Green   Torbryan   Ipplepen   Coffinswell   Daccombe   13   Maidencombe
Buckfastleigh   Abbey   Landscove   Broadhempston   Holy Trinity   North Whilborough   Kingskerswell   South West Coast Path
Dean   South Devon Railway   Woolston Green   Compton   Compton Castle   Shiphay   Model Village   Babbacombe
A38   A384   69   A381   A380   TORQUAY
Plymouth 20   Totnes 3   Paignton 8   Totnes 3   Paignton 3   Brixham 7

Gemini FM
FM 96.4/97/103

Classic Gold
AM 666/954

A   B   C   D

Andover 75
Ilminster 1   Ilminster 1
A303   A358

see p414
for a
touring
guide to
this map

83

Shaftesbury 23
Yeovil 1   A30

West
Chinnock

East
Chinnock
Haselbury
Plucknett
3

North
Perrott

A356

74   A356
Dorchester 15

Hemyock   Stapley
Churchinford   Buckland St Mary
Bishopswood
Crock
Street
Kingstone   Dinnington   Merriott

Bolham
Water   Madford
Abbey   Smeatharpe   Combe St
Nicholas   Cricket
Malherbie   Dowlish
Wake   Hinton
St George   Lower
Severalls
Garden

Newcott   Marsh   Whitestaunton   Wadeford   Chaffcombe   Cudworth   Crewkerne
Chard   St Bartholomews   A30

A30   Howley   A30   9
Yarcombe   Wambrook   Chard   B3167   Cricket
St Thomas   Cricket St
Thomas
Wildlife Park   Hewish   Misterton
Forton   Wayford   Clapton   A356
Tatworth   Winsham   Seaborough   South
Perrott   Chedington

Stockland   Furley   South
Chard   Forde Abbey   Clapton
Court   Mosterton
Drimpton

Monkton   Chardstock   Thorncombe   Burstock
Membury   Tytherleigh   Blackdown   A3066   12
Churchill   Holditch   Pilsdon
Pen   Broadwindsor

A358   Hawkchurch   B3163
Birdsmoorgate   B3162
Smallridge   Marshalsea   Bettiscombe   Beaminster
Dalwood   Loughwood
Meeting House   Axminster   Marshwood   Stoke
Abbott
Netherbury   12

Honiton   Ottery   Widworthy   Shute   Sector   Fishpond
Bottom   Pilsdon   South
Bowood   Melplash
Waytown

Gittisham   Kilmington   St Candida
and Holy Cross   Salway
Ash   Loders
Alfington   Shute
Barton   Broadoak
Whitchurch
Canonicorum   Dottery   Bradpole

Ottery
St Mary   Northleigh   Whitford   Wootton   Ryall   Symondsbury   Bridport
Farway   Musbury   Wootton
Fitzpaine   Morcombelake   North
Chideock   Waldich   A35
A375   Southleigh   Colyton   A35   Chideock   Shipton
Gorge
Broad
Down   Blackbury   Colyford   Uplyme   Charmouth   Seatown   Bothenhampton
Sidbury   Camp   Combpyne   A3052   St Michael
the Archangel   Golden   West
Bay   Burton
Bradstock
Harcombe   A3052   Lyme Regis   Cap

Salcombe
Regis   Branscombe   Axmouth
Seaton and District
Electric Tramway   Rousdon   The Cobb   South West
Coast Path
Sidmouth   Beer
Vicarage   Seaton   Pinhay
Dowlands   Lyme Bay
Branscombe   Beer
Head   Seaton Bay   South West
Coast Path

TOWN PLANS
Exeter p73
Tiverton p397
Torquay p398

EXETER

Park & Ride

A377   HONITON
ROAD
SOWTON   M5   29   A30

A30   MATFORD   A376
A38   31   A379

Wessex FM
FM 96/97.2

A B C D

Sherborne 9
Yeovil 4
A30

Shepton Mallet 22
Yeovil 2
A37

Sherborne 2
A352

84

Wincanton 12
A357

Newton 11
Fiddleford

West Chinnock
Lower Severalls Garden
East Chinnock
West Coker
North Coker
Barwick Stoford
Thornford
Lillington
Folke
Bishop's Caundle
Lydlinch
A3030
Broad Oak
Okeford Fitzpaine
A357
Shillingstone

East Chinnock
Hardington Mandeville
East Coker
Ryme Intrinseca
Beer Hackett
Yetminster
Longburton
Holwell
King's Stag
Fifehead Neville
Turnwo

Chard 9
Crewkerne 1
A356 A30

Haselbury Plucknett
Sutton Bingham Reservoir
Pendomer
Closworth
Hermitage
Holnest
Glanvilles Wootton
Middlemarsh
Pulham
Wonston
Hazelbury Bryan
Ibberton

North Perrott
Hardington Marsh
Halstock
Melbury Osmond
Chetnole
Leigh
Lyon's Gate
Mappowder
Droop
Woolland

Misterton
South Perrott
Corscombe
Melbury Sampford
Melbury Bubb
Hilfield
Minterne Magna
Alton Pancras
Duntish
Buckland Newton
Bulbarrow Hill
Higher Ansty
Winterborne Stickland

Chedington
West Chelborough
Batcombe
Giant St Mary
Lower Ansty
Ansty Cross
Melcombe Bingham
Hilton
Milton Abbey
Winterborne Houghton
Winterborne Clenston

Axe
Benville
Holywell
Minterne
Up Cerne
Plush
Whatcomb

A3066
A356
Rampisham
Frome St Quintin
Up Sydling
Cerne Abbas
A352
B3143
Piddletrenthide
Cheselbourne
Dewlish
Milton Abbas
St James the G
Winterborne Whitechurch
16

Stoke Abbott
B3163
Beaminster
B3163
Toller Whelme
Hooke
20
Higher Kingcombe
Wraxall
Chalmington
Cattistock
Sydling St Nicholas
White Lackington
Piddlehinton
A354
Low Stre

Netherbury
Mapperton
House
Lower Kingcombe
Chilfrome
Maiden Newton
A37
Nether Cerne
Godmanstone
Milborne St Andrew

73
Waytown
Melplash
Poorton
Toller Porcorum
Toller Fratrum
Forston
B3142
B3143
Puddletown
Athelhampton
A35
11

Salway Ash
West Milton
Powerstock
Wynford Eagle
Frampton
Grimstone
Charminster
Wolfeton House
A35
St Mary the Virgin
Tolpuddle
Turners Puddle

Honiton 20
Lyme Regis 8
A35
Dottery
B3163
Bradpole
Nettlecombe
West Compton
Compton Valence
Stratton
Bradford Peverell
Higher Bockhampton
Burleston
Affpuddle
Briantspudd

Bridport
Loders
Uploders
ROMAN ROAD
Askerswell
Kingston Russell
14
Bradford Peverell
Dorchester
Burton
Stinsford
Lower Bockhampton
Hardy's Cottage
Tincleton
Clouds Hill
Moreton
Bovingt Camp

Eype
Bothenhampton
Walditch
Shipton Gorge
Chilcombe
Litton Cheney
Long Bredy
A35
Winterbourne Abbas
Max Gate
West Stafford
Woodsford

West Bay
Burton Bradstock
Nine Stones
Barrows
Winterbourne Steepleton
Dinosaur Museum
Maiden Castle
Winterborne Came
Whitcombe
West Knighton
Crossways
Tank Museum

South West Coast Path
Swyre
Puncknowle
Littlebredy
Black Down
Martinstown or Winterborne St Martin
Winterborne Monkton
Winterborne Herringston
Broadmayne
5
Warmwell
East Burton
12

West Bexington
Hardy Monument
Portesham
South West Coast Path
A354
Bincombe
White Horse
Poxwell
Owermoigne
East Knighton
Coor Keyr
Winfrith Newburgh
A352

Abbotsbury
B3157
Sub-tropical Gardens
Swannery
Rodden
Upwey
B3159
Broadwey
Preston
Osmington
7
Holworth
Chaldon Down
584
Chaldon Herring or East Chaldon
Lulworth Camp

Langton Herring
Nottington
Coldharbour
A353
Temple
Osmington Mills
Ringstead Bay
South West Coast Path
Durdle Door
Lulw Cove

Chesil Beach
Chickerell
Lodmoor
Overcombe
Sea Life Park
Weymouth Bay

Fleet
Charlestown
Weymouth
Guernsey & Jersey

South West Coast Path
Wyke Regis
Portland Harbour
B3156

PORTLAND
A354
Portland Castle

West Bay
Fortuneswell
Grove
Easton
Isle of Portland

Weston
Southwell

Bill of Portland

miles kms
6 10
5 9
  8
4 7
  6
3 5
  4
2 3
1 2
  1

sminster 22
ftesbury 6

Salisbury 13

Andover 30
Salisbury 9

Winchester 20
Southampton 14

E   F   85   G   H

A350

A354

A338

A31

Stubhampton

Chettle

Monkton Up
Wimborne

Stuckton   Blissford

Fritham

Iwerne Courtney
or Shroton

Chettle
House

Cashmoor

Cranborne

Alderholt

Bickton

Hyde

Frogham

Tarrant
Gunville

Gussage
St Michael

Manor Gardens

B3078

North Gorley

Tarrant
Hinton

Gussage
All Saints

St Giles

Edmondsham
House

Harbridge

Mockbeggar

South Gorley

Deer
Sanctuary

5

Pimperne
Down

A354

Tarrant
Launceston

Long
Crichel

Church

Knowlton

Edmondsham

Ringwood
Forest

Ibsley

Linwood

11

Pimperne

Tarrant
Monkton

Sutton
Holms

Romford

Moyles
Court

Stourpaine

Moor
Crichel

Woodlands

Verwood

Ellingham

Blashford
Linford

A31

ston

Blandford
Camp

Manswood

Horton

Hangersley

Picket
Post

Blandford
St Mary

SS Peter
& Paul

Blandford Forum

Langton
Long Blandford

Tarrant
Rawston

Witchampton

Uppington

Chalbury
Common

Moors River

Ringwood

Blashford

Burley
Street

Tarrant
Keyneston

Hinton
Martell

Gaunt's
Common

Mannington

Three
Legged Cross

Moors Valley
Railway

Avon Castle

Kingston

Burley

Bisterne
Close

Charlton
Marshall

Tarrant
Rushton

Stanbridge

Holt

Holt
Heath

West
Moors

St Leonards

Bisterne

15

Thornicombe

Tarrant
Crawford

Shapwick

Holt

Broom
Hill

Clapgate

6

Ashley
Heath

A31

Thorney
Hill

Spetisbury

Kingston Lacy
House

Badbury
Ring

Highbury

Avon

Burley

Charlton
Down

A350

Stour

Walford
Mill

Colehill

Stapehill

Trickett's
Cross

Motor
House

Kingston

Ripley

Bisterne

A31

Pamphill

Deans Court

Ferndown

Parley
Common

Bransgore

Wootton

Winterborne
Kingston

White
Mill

Sturminster
Marshall

Wimborne
Minster

Oakley

Stapehill
Knoll

Hampreston

A348

West
Parley

A338

Avon

Wootton

Bashley

Anderson

A31

East End

Canford
Magna

Longham

BOURNEMOUTH

Branksome

B3058

New
Milton

Winterborne
Zelston

11

Corfe
Mullen

Merley Tropical
Bird Gardens

Merley

A341

Bearwood

Ensbury

Parley
Cross

B3073

Hurn

Sopley

Neacroft

A35

Almer

15

A350

Broadstone

Canford
Heath

9

Kinson

Moordown

Throop

Winkton

Hinton

B3055

Highcliffe

A337

Morden

Beacon
Hill

A347

A3060

Burton

Highcliffe

Barton
on Sea

loxworth

A35

East
Morden

Waterloo

A349

A3049

Newtown

Winton

Christchurch

Mudeford

9

Slepe

Creekmoor

A3040

A35

Pokesdown

Priory

Christchurch
Bay

Wareham
Forest

Upton

2

Branksome

Southbourne

Christchurch
Harbour

Organford

Lytchett
Minster

A350

Boscombe

Wick

Hengistbury
Head

Holton
Heath

Lytchett
Matravers

Hamworthy

A35

Parkstone

B3059

Westbourne

Holton
Heath

A351

Parkstone

6

Branksome
Park

Poole
Harbour

i

POOLE

Westbourne

BOURNEMOUTH

Trigon
Hill

Sandford

Frome

Brownsea
Island

Canford
Cliffs

Compton
Acres

Wareham

Stokeford

Arne

Ferry

Sandbanks

POOLE

Ridge

Arne

B3369

BAY

East
Stoke

Stoborough

Toll

3

West
Holme

Stoborough
Green

Studland
Heath

South West
Coast Path

Cherbourg
Guernsey & Jersey
St Malo (seasonal)

B3070

Wytch
Heath

Newton
Heath

TOWN PLANS
Bournemouth
p313
Poole p378
Swanage p394
Weymouth
p401

Grange
Heath

11

Norden

Studland Bay

Studland

Furzebrook

East Creech

Blue Pool
Church
Knowle

B3351

St Nicholas

The Foreland or
Handfast Point

East
Lulworth

ISLE

Nine
Barrow Down

Ulwell

Ballard Point

Corfe
Castle

A351

Harman's
Cross

OF

Steeple

Kimmeridge

B3069

Kingston

Langton Matravers

Swanage
Railway

Swanage Bay

Swanage

2

Purbeck Hills

Tyneham

Smedmore

PURBECK

Worth
Matravers

Peveril Point

Durlston Bay

Broad
Bench

South West
Coast Path

St Aldhelm's
or
St Alban's Head

Seacombe
Cliff

Durlston Head

Tilly
Whim Caves

see p415
for a
touring
guide to
this map

Lyndhurst 4

A35

4

76

Lyndhurst 14
Lymington 6

A337

Channel 103FM
FM 103.7

CHANNEL ISLANDS

0 miles   2   4   6
0 kms 2 4 6 8 10

Channel
Islands

Poole
Portsmouth
Weymouth

Grosnes
Point

JERSEY

1

L'Ancress

St John

Rozel

GUERNSEY

St Sampson

HERM

Mont du
Vallet

JERSEY

Guernsey, Jersey
(seasonal)

St Peter
Port

Jethou

St Helier

Gorey

Braye

Fort
Grey

GUERNSEY

Sausmarez
Manor

Brechou

La Ville
Roussel

St Brelade's

St
Aubin

Grouville

Mount
Orgueil
Castle

ALDERNEY
St Anne

St Martin

SARK

Portelet

Elizabeth
Castle

Le Bourg

ALDERNEY

Pleinmont

German
Occupation
Museum

Jersey, St Malo
Alderney (seasonal)

Guernsey, Poole
Portsmouth, Weymouth

St Malo
Alderney (seasonal)

E   F   G   H

South City FM
FM 107.8

103.2 Power FM
FM 103.2

Capital Gold
AM 1170/1557

Wave 105 FM
FM 105.2/105.8

BBC
Radio Solent
FM 96.1/103.8

Ocean FM
FM 96.7/97.5

107.4 The Quay
FM 107.4

Spirit FM
FM 96.6/102.3

see p416
for a
touring
guide to
this map

CITY ROUTES
Southampton
& Portsmouth
p296

TOWN PLANS
Chichester
p321
Cowes p77
Portsmouth
p378
Southampton
p388

COWES

Southampton

Cowes
Roads

EAST
COWES

Newport 5
Osborne House 1

Newport 4

Spirit FM
FM 96.6/102.3

Juice 107.2
FM 107.2

Southern FM
FM 96.9/102/102.4/16

A29 Dorking 29

A24 Horsham 14

88

A2037 Horsham 14

A23 Reigate 25 Crawley 15

A **B** **C** **D**

STANE STREET
South Downs Way
Madehurst
Houghton
North Stoke
South Stoke
Burpham
Bury
Amberley
B2139
Sullington
Washington
Wiston Park
Castle
Steyning
Bramber
Upper Beeding
Small Dole
Edburton
Fulking
Poynings
Westme
Pyecombe
813
Di

Chalk Pits Museum
Kithurst Hill
Harrow Hill
North End
Findon
Chanctonbury Ring
St Mary
Botolphs
Coombes
Upper Beeding
St Mary
Devil's Dyke
Patcham
Coldean

Chichester 6 A27

Slindon
B2134
Arundel Park
Wildfowl Trust
Warningcamp
Clapham
High Salvington
Cissbury Ring
Blessed Virgin
North Lancing
Southwick
Mile Oak
Kingston by Sea
Portslade
Preston
Moulseco
Beve

A29 A284 A27 A280 A24 A283 A27

Walberton
Binstead
Castle
Crossbush
Patching
Durrington
Upper Cokeham
Sompting
SHOREHAM Lancing
Arundel
Tortington
Eastgate
Lyminster
Poling
A284 A280 A259
Shoreham-by-Sea
Portslade-by-Sea
Royal Kemp Town

77 Barnham
Ford
Toddington
Angmering
A259
South Lancing
WORTHING
BRIGHTON AND HOVE
Volks E Rail

Flansham
Yapton
B2233
Climping
Wick
East Preston
Kingston
Ferring
Goring-by-Sea

Chichester 7 A259
Ancton
Rustington
Kingston Gorse
B2132
Littlehampton
Middleton-on-Sea

miles / kms
6 10
5 9
8
4 7
6
3 5
4
2 3
2
1 1

BRIGHTON

A **B** **C** **D**

A23 A27 Lewes 5

A270

Preston Park
London Road Station
Springfield Rd
Ditchling Rd
Prince's Rd
Richmond Rd
Hartington Road

Highcroft Villas
Dyke Road Drive
Ditchling Rise
Vere Rd
Prince's Cr
Crescent Road
Wakefield Road
Roundhill Cres
Franklin Road
Bonchurch Rd

Booth Museum of Natural History
Stanford Rd
Hamilton Road
Shaftesbury Rd
Gerard St
Prince's Rd
St Paul's Street
UPPER LEWES ROAD
LEWES ROAD
Wellington Road
Racecourse

Port Hall Rd
Exeter Street
Dyke Road
VIADUCT ROAD
Rose Hill
Park Crescent
Elm
Grove
Islingword
Howard
Cobden Rd
Bentham Rd

A27 Chichester 31
A270
OLD SHOREHAM RD
NEW ENGLAND RD
NEW ENGLAND ST
LONDON RD
Union Road
The Level
Hanover Ter
Southover
Washington St
Grant St
Finsbury Road

Highdown Rd
DYKE ROAD
Prestonville Rd
York Villas
Baker St
DITCHLING ROAD
LEWES ROAD
Belgrave Road
Grove St
Montreal Road
Queen's Park Rd

Addison Road
Chatham Pl
Howard Pl
Bath St
Compton Avenue
BUCKINGHAM PL
Central Station
Ann St
Albion St
Grove Hill
Albion
West Drive

B2120 Davigdor Road
Goldsmid Road
Vernon Ter
Clifton Road
Buckingham Road
Guildford Rd
Toy & Model Museum
RICHMOND PL
Ivory Pl
John St
Tarner Rd
Windmill Street
Queens Park

Nizells Avenue
Clifton Road
Albert Rd
Royal Alexandra Hospital
Trafalgar Street
Tidy St
GRAND PDE
Market (Wholesale)
St John's Place
West Av
South Av

Temple G
Norfolk Terrace
Denmark Ter
Powis Road
Victoria Rd
Clifton Hill
Nicholas Road
Gloucester Road
North Road
Brighton University
Carlton Hill
Freshfield Place

Norfolk Road
Montpelier Road
Clifton Terrace
Upper North St
QUEEN'S ROAD
Spring Gdns
Gardner St
Church St
Corn Exchange & Dome
Egremont Place
Park Street

B2066
PO
Western Road
WEST ST
A2010
Portland
Bond St
New Rd
Royal Pavilion
Courts
White Street
Edward Street

Castle St
Oriental Pl
Regency
Churchill Square
Duke St
Middle St
North St
The Lanes
George Street
Dorset Gardens
Chapel St
Hereford Street

B2122
Exhibition Halls
Cannon Pl
Russell Rd
Brighton Centre
Ship Street
Town Hall
Seal
Centre
St James's Street
B2066

Worthing 12 A259
KING'S ROAD
GRAND JUNCTION ROAD
A259
MARINE PARADE
Madeira Drive
A259 Newhaven 9 Marine 1

West Pier
Fishing Museum
West Pier
Palace Pier
Volk's Electric Railway

0 100 200 yds
0 100 200 m

A23 A27
WITHDEAN
A27 A259 A259

Park & Ride

BBC Southern Counties Radio
FM 95-95.3/104-104.8

Uckfield 5   A26   Uckfield 6   A22   89   Heathfield 6   A267   Battle 4   A271

Plumpton
Cooksbridge
Offham   Hamsey
South Malling
A26
Mount Harry
A275
Broyle Side
B2124
Whitesmith
Laughton
Muddles Green
Golden Cross
Lealands
Hellingly
Stunts Green
Herstmonceux
Windmill Hill
A271
Catsfield
B2204
Henley's Down

Lewes 1264
B2192
Ringmer
Cliffe Hill
Glyndebourne
Lower Dicker
Upper Dicker
Ripe
Chalvington
Lower Horsebridge
A295
Magham Down
A271
Ninfield
Lower Street
A269
Lunsford's Cross

Lewes
A27
Mount Caburn
Glynde Place
Glynde
11
Selmeston
Arlington
A22
Hailsham
Herstmonceux Castle
Wartling
Boreham Street
Hooe
Hooe Common
Little Common
Sidley

Kingston near Lewes
Iford
Beddingham
A27
Firle Place
Firle
Alciston
Wilmington
B2104
Polegate
A27
Hankham
12
Pevensey Levels
Cooden
BEXHILL
Hastings 4
A259

South Downs Way
Rodmell
Southease
Firle Beacon
South Downs Way
Berwick
Drusillas Zoo Park
Folkington
Stone Cross
Westham
Castle
Pevensey Bay
Pevensey Bay

Telscombe
Tarring Neville
South Heighton
Alfriston
Long Man of Wilmington
Filching
Wannock
Willingdon
Friday Street
Langney

Saltdean
Piddinghoe
Denton
Paradise Park
Bishopstone
Litlington
Westdean Forest
Jevington
Willingdon Hill
Hampden Park
A2270
Langney Point

Peacehaven
A259
Fort
Rookery Hill
East Blatchington
Friston
East Dean
EASTBOURNE

Newhaven
Seaford
13
A259
Friston
Seaford
B2103

Seaford Head
Seven Sisters
Birling Gap
South Downs Way
Beachy Head

Dieppe

see p417 for a touring guide to this map

EASTBOURNE

A22 London 64   A   B   C   Hastings 16   D

A2021
KING'S DRIVE
Burton Road
King's Avenue
Prideaux Road
Mill Road
Ashburnham Road
Carew Road
Selwyn Road
Watts Lane
PRIDEAUX ROAD
Gorringe Road
Ringwood Road
Courtlands Rd
Moy Avenue
St Philip's Avenue
Woodgate Rd
A259
SEASIDE
Latimer Rd
Whitley Rd View Rd
The Oval
Princes Park

A2270
UPPERTON
A2040
UPPER AVE
Firle Rd
Avondale Rd
A2021
WHITLEY ROAD
B2106
Royal Parade
Musgrave Collection

Brighton 25
A259
THE GOFFS
Towner Gallery
Gildredge Park
ROAD
THE AVENUE
Eastbourne Station
Commercial Rd
Cavendish
Langney
Bourne Rd
Dursley Rd
Belmore Rd
Cainbridge Road
Latimer Parade
Royal Parade
SEASIDE
Treasure Island
Redoubt Museum
Redoubt Gardens

Compton Place
Dittons Road
Saffrons Road
Southfields Rd
Ashford Rd
ASHFORD RD
Arndale Shopping Centre
SUSAN'S RD
Cavendish
Terminus Road
SEASIDE ROAD
Royal Hippodrome

Paradise Drive
The Saffrons
Grove Rd
GILDREDGE RD
SOUTH ST
Lismore Rd
TRINITY TREES
Grand Parade
B2106 Marine Pde

Compton Place
Meads Road
Granville Road
Furness Rd
College Rd
Hardwick Rd
Blackwater
Devonshire Pl
B2106
Compton
B2103
Pier
Devonshire Park Winter Gardens & Theatre
Devonshire Park
Heritage Centre
RNLI Museum

0 100 200 300yds
0 100 200 300m

A   B   C   D

E   F   G   H

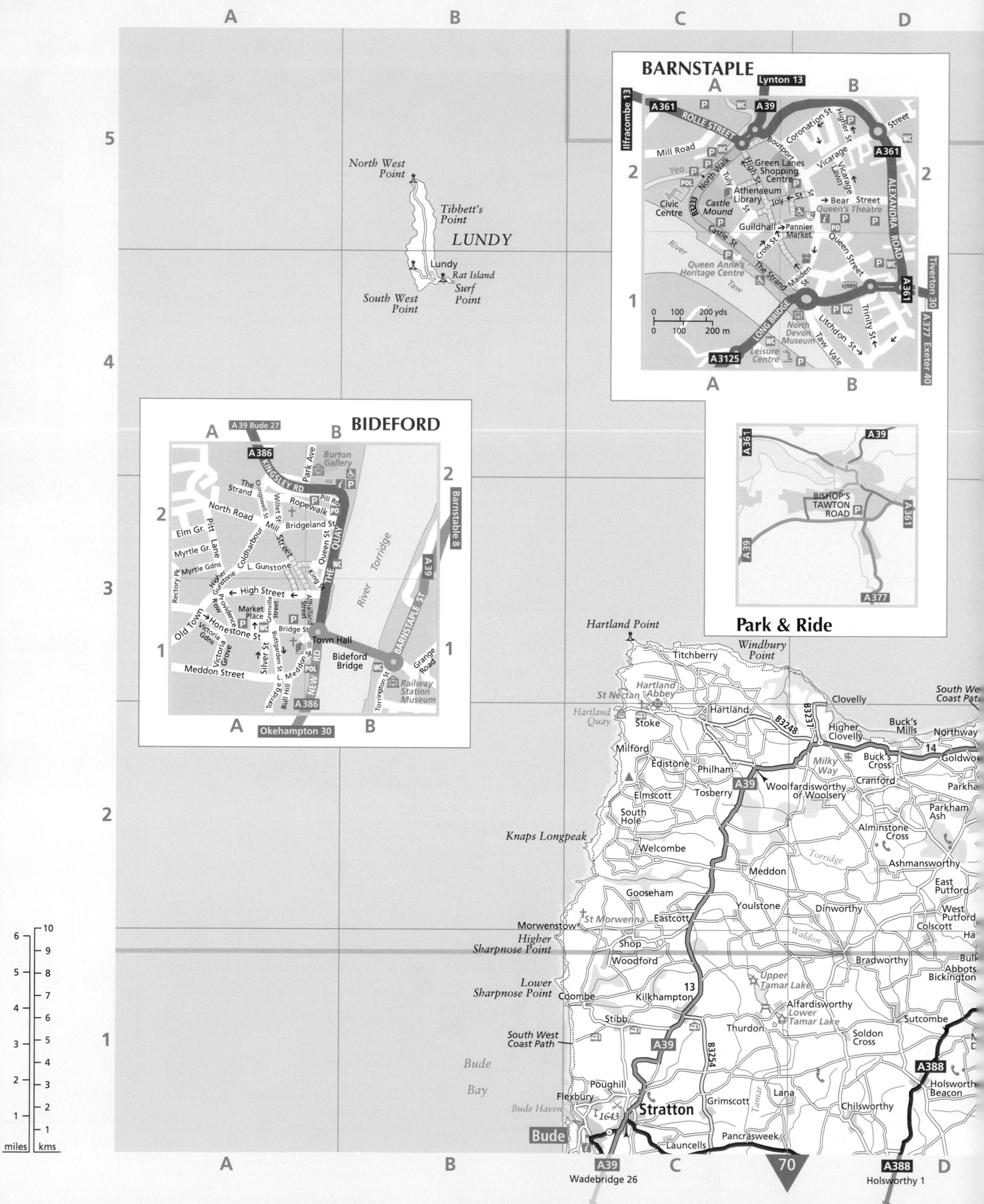

A B C D

BARNSTAPLE

Lynton 13

Ilfracombe 13
A361
ROLLE STREET
A39
A361

P
WC
Higher St
Coronation St
Street
WC

Mill Road
P
Vicarage
Lawn
2
Yeo
P
North Walk
Green Lanes
Shopping
Centre
Bear Street
P
PO
Tuly
High St
Queen's Theatre
POL
B3233
Athenaeum
Library
Joy St
ALEXANDRA ROAD
Civic
Centre
Castle
Mound
Guildhall
Pannier
Market
Queen Street
P

Castle St
Cross St
P
Tiverton 30
A361
River
Queen Anne's
Heritage Centre
The Strand
Maiden
A377 Exeter 40

Taw
WC

LONG BRIDGE
North
Devon
Museum
Litchdon St
Trinity St

0   100   200 yds
0   100   200 m
Leisure
Centre
Taw Vale
P

A3125

A B

BIDEFORD

A39 Bude 27
A
B

A386
KINGSLEY RD
Park Ave
Burton
Gallery

The
Strand
Willet St
Chingwell St
Ropewalk
Pill Rd
P
PO
2

North Road
Bridgeland St
Queen St
THE QUAY
Barnstable 8

Elm Gr.
Pitt Lane
Mill Street
King St
A39

Myrtle Gr.
Higher
Gunstone
L. Gunstone
BARNSTAPLE ST

Rectory Pk
Myrtle Gdns
Coldharbour

High Street
3

Old Town
Providence
Row
Market
Place
Grenville Street
P
WC
Bridge St

Victoria
Gdns
Silver St
Buzgarton St
Allhalland
Street
Town Hall
Bideford
Bridge
Grange
Road
1

Meddon Street
Torridge
Bull Hill
L. Meddon St
NEW RD
WC
POL

A386
Okehampton 30

A
B

A361   A39

BISHOP'S
TAWTON
ROAD
P
A361

A39

A377

Park & Ride

LUNDY

North West
Point

Tibbett's
Point

Lundy
Rat Island
South West
Point
Surf
Point

Hartland Point

Windbury
Point
Titchberry

South West
Coast Path
St Nectan
Hartland
Abbey
Clovelly
Buck's
Mills
Higher
Clovelly
B3237
B3248
Northway
Hartland
Hartland
Quay
Stoke
14
Goldwor

Milford
Edistone
Philham
Milky
Way
Buck
Cross
Parka

Elmscott
Tosberry
A39
Woolfardisworthy
or Woolsery
Cranford
Parkham
Ash

Knaps Longpeak
South
Hole
Alminstone
Cross
Ashmansworthy

Welcombe
Meddon
Torridge
East
Putford

St Morwenna
Gooseham
Youlstone
Dinworthy
West
Putford

Morwenstow
Eastcott
Waldon
Colscott

Higher
Sharpnose Point
Shop
Woodford
Bradworthy
Bulk
Abbots
Bickington

Lower
Sharpnose Point
Coombe
13
Kilkhampton
Upper
Tamar Lake
B3254

South West
Coast Path
Stibb
Thurdon
Alfardisworthy
Lower
Tamar Lake
Soldon
Cross
Sutcombe

Bude
Bay
Poughill
A39
Lana
A388

Bude Haven
Flexbury
Grimscott
Tamar
Chilsworthy
Holsworth
Beacon

1643
Stratton
Pancrasweek

Bude
Launcells

A39
Wadebridge 26

70

A388
Holsworthy 1

A B C D

miles   kms
6 — 10
       9
5 — 8
       7
4 — 6
       5
3 — 4
2 — 3
       2
1 — 1

South West Coast Path
Foreland Point
South West Coast Path

Lynton
Lynmouth
Watersmeet
Brendon
Malmsmead

Heddon's Mouth
Woody Bay
Valley of Rocks

Trentishoe
Martinhoe
Toll
West Lyn
East Ilkerton
Barbrook
Cheriton
Furzehill

A39
11

Heale
Kemacott
Lynton and Barnstaple Steam Railway

Ilfracombe
Hele
Berrynarbor
St Peter
Combe Martin
Combe Martin Bay
Coombe Martin Bay

Bull Point
Lee
Holy Trinity
Slade
Mill

Parracombe
St Petrock
Shallowford

EXMOOR

Brendon Common

B3223

Morte Point
Mortehoe
Lincombe
A361

A3123
10

West Down

B3229
Patchole
Kentisbury

A399
Blackmoor Gate

EXMOOR
Pinkery Pond
Barle

B3358
Challacombe
Shoulsbarrow Common

NATIONAL PARK

Burcombe

Woolacombe
Morte Bay

Trimstone
Bittadon

Kentisbury Ford
East Down
Clifton
Arlington Beccott

Wellandpound Reservoir
Exmoor Zoo

Knightacott
Leworthy

Simonsbath
B3223

Putsborough Sand
Pickwell
North Buckland
Georgeham
6

Milltown
Muddiford
A39
12
Loxhore
Arlington
Arlington Court

Bratton Fleming
Exmoor Steam Railway

Hangley Cleave 1585
Long Holcombe

Croyde Bay
Croyde
Saunton
B3231
Lobb
Knowle
Halsinger
Marwood
Guineaford
Kingsheanton
Shirwell

Lydcott
11
A399
Brayford

North Radworthy
Longstone Wells

Pippacott
Prixford
Marwood Hill

Stoke Rivers
Benton
High Bray

North Heasley
Heasley Mill
South Radworthy

Braunton
Wrafton
Toll
Heanton Punchardon
Ashford
A361
8
Goodleigh
Gunn
Charles
East Buckland

Twitchen

Braunton Burrows
CHIVENOR
Taw

Barnstaple
Sticklepath
Newport
Westacott

South West Coast Path

Mole

Fremington
Bickington
Lake
Landkey
Little Pill
West Buckland

Charles

North Molton

Appledore
Yelland
Instow
Bickleton
St Johns Chapel
Bishop's Tawton

Swimbridge Newland
Swimbridge
St James
A361
9
Filleigh

South Molton

B3227
B3227

A386
Tapeley Park
A39
7
Westleigh
Tawstock
Horwood

Fremington

Northam
Eastleigh
Newton Tracey
Hiscott
Horner
Cobbaton
Chittlehampton

Bishops Nympton

Bideford
Woodtown
Chapelton
Clapworthy

George Nympton
Alswear
Mariansleigh

20
A361
M5 20
Tiverton 12
Ash Mill

East-the-Water
Gammaton
Alverdiscott
Ensis
Fishleigh Barton
A377
St Mary
Umberleigh
Warkleigh

Satterleigh
Chittlehamholt
B3226

Rose Ash

Littleham
Landcross
4
Weare Giffard
Huntshaw
Yarnscombe
Langridgeford
Atherington

Romansleigh
Rowley
Meshaw

Buckland Brewer
Monkleigh
A386
Dartington Crystal
High Bullen
Sherwood Green
B3217
26
High Bickington

King's Nympton
B3137

Frithelstock Stone
Frithelstock
Great Torrington
St Giles in the Wood
Kingscott

Northcote Manor

Cadbury Barton
Week

A388
B3327
RHS Rosemoor

Roborough

Burrington
Elstone

Lutworthy

Langtree
Little Torrington
Villavin
EAGLESCOTT

16
Stibb Cross
Peters Marland
Winswell
Beaford
A3124
Ashreigney
B3096
Chulmleigh
Cheldon
West Worlington
East Worlington

Woollaton
Merton
Dolton
B3217
Riddlecombe
Copy Lake
St Mary
A377
Chawleigh
Thelbridge Barton

Shebbear
Buckland Filleigh
Huish
13
Ashley
Bridge Reeve
Eggesford Forest
B3042
Filleigh
Hele Barton

Ash Barton
A386
Hollocombe
Wembworthy
Yeo

Meeth
Iddesleigh
Dowland
Winkleigh
Nymet Rowland
St Thomas of Canterbury
Eastington
Lapford

St Lawrence
Petrockstowe
Torridge

Coldridge
Lapford Cross
Morchard Bishop

Black Torrington
Sheepwash
Okement
Broadwoodkelly
Monkokehampton
A3124
Brushford
B3220
East Leigh
Oldborough

Holemoor
Torridge

see p418 for a touring guide to this map

A39
Minehead 11

82

TOWN PLANS
Barnstaple p80
Bideford p80

71

A3072
Crediton 5

A396
Exeter 10

72

M5
Exeter 12

A373
Honiton 6

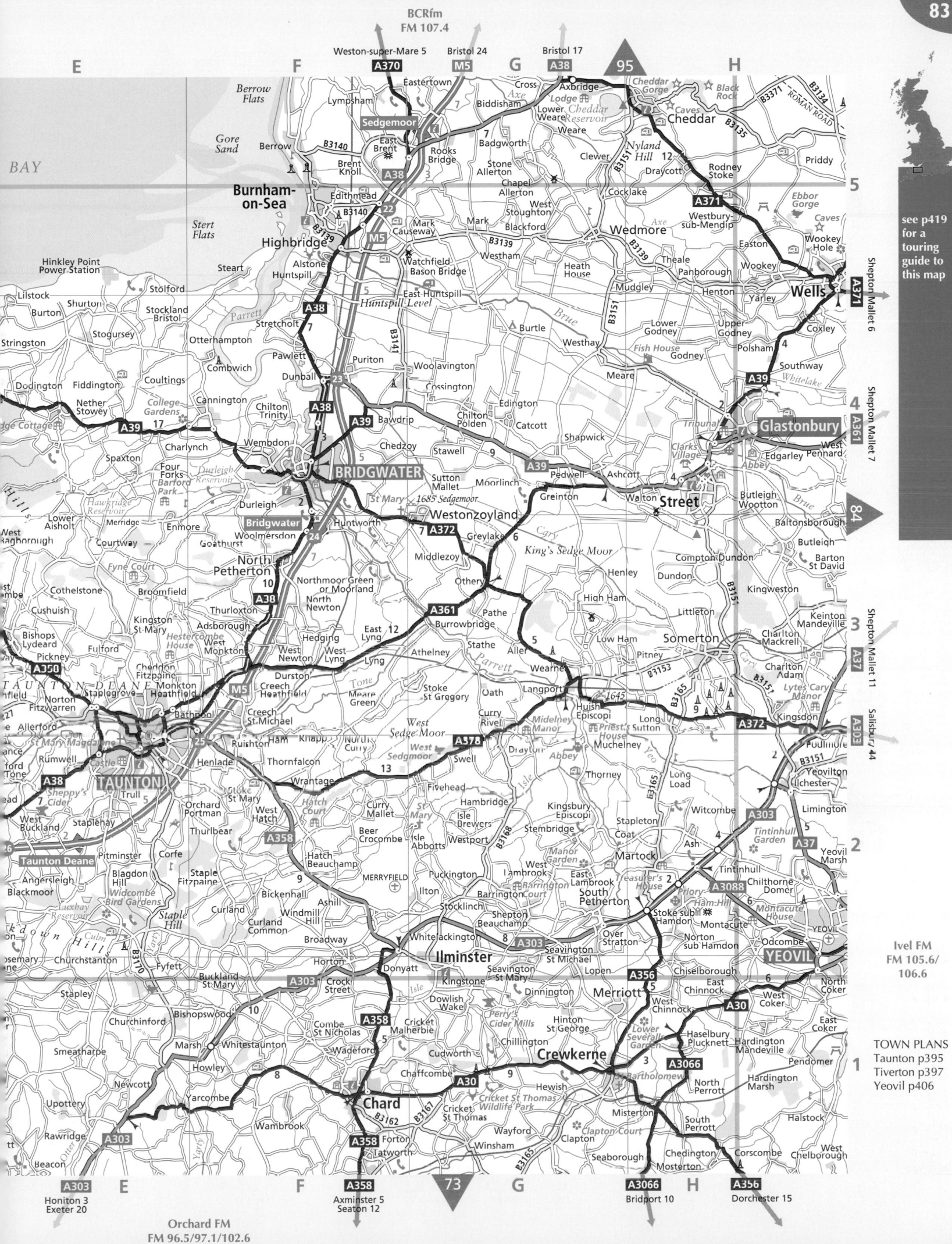

3TR FM
FM 107.5

BBC Wiltshire Sound
FM 103.5/103.6/104.3

Spire FM
FM 102

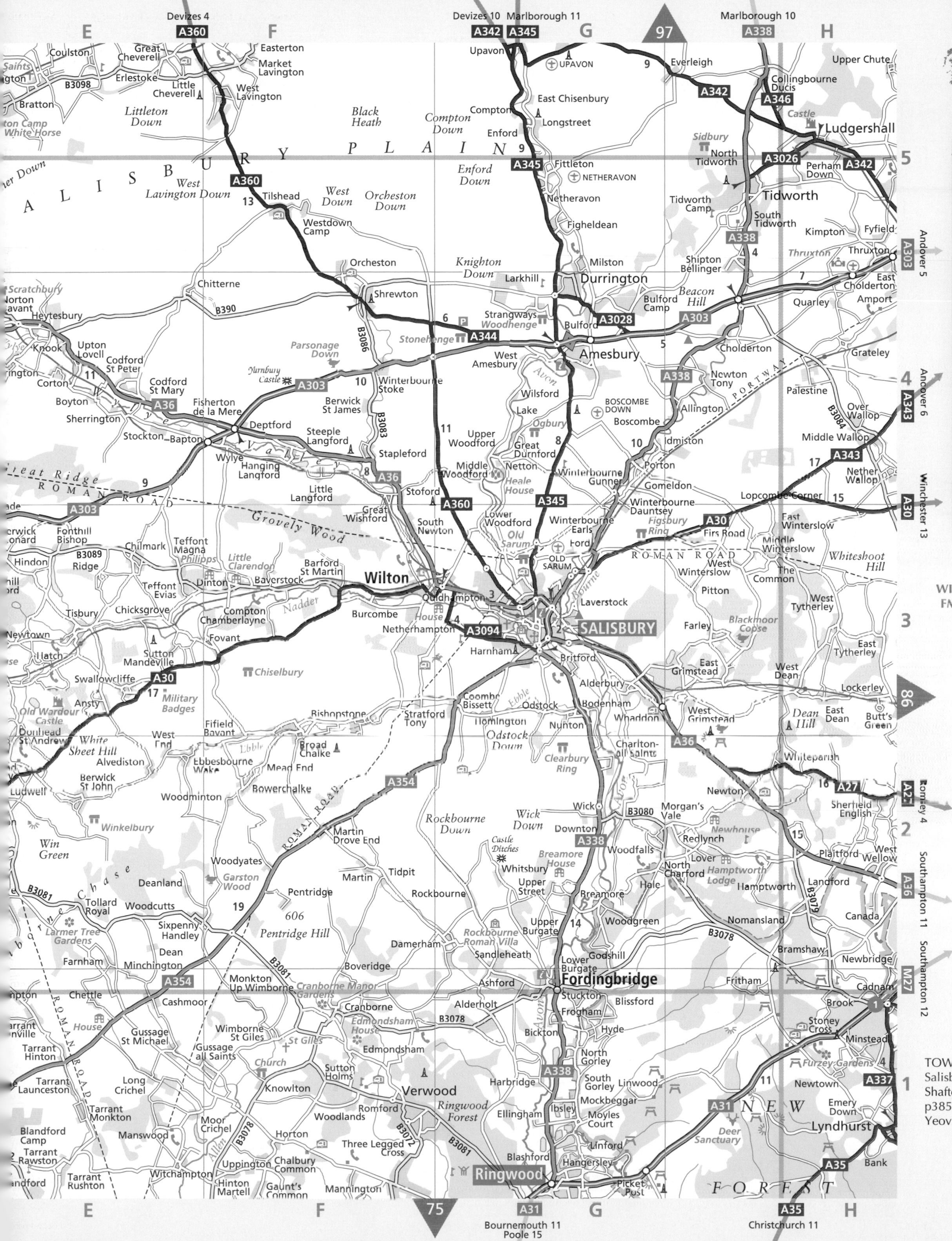

85

see p420
for a
touring
guide to
this map

SALISBURY PLAIN

SALISBURY

Amesbury

Durrington

Ludgershall

Tidworth

Wilton

Fordingbridge

Ringwood

Lyndhurst

Stonehenge

Old Sarum

NEW FOREST

WIN 107.2
FM 107.2

TOWN PLANS
Salisbury p384
Shaftesbury p385
Yeovil p406

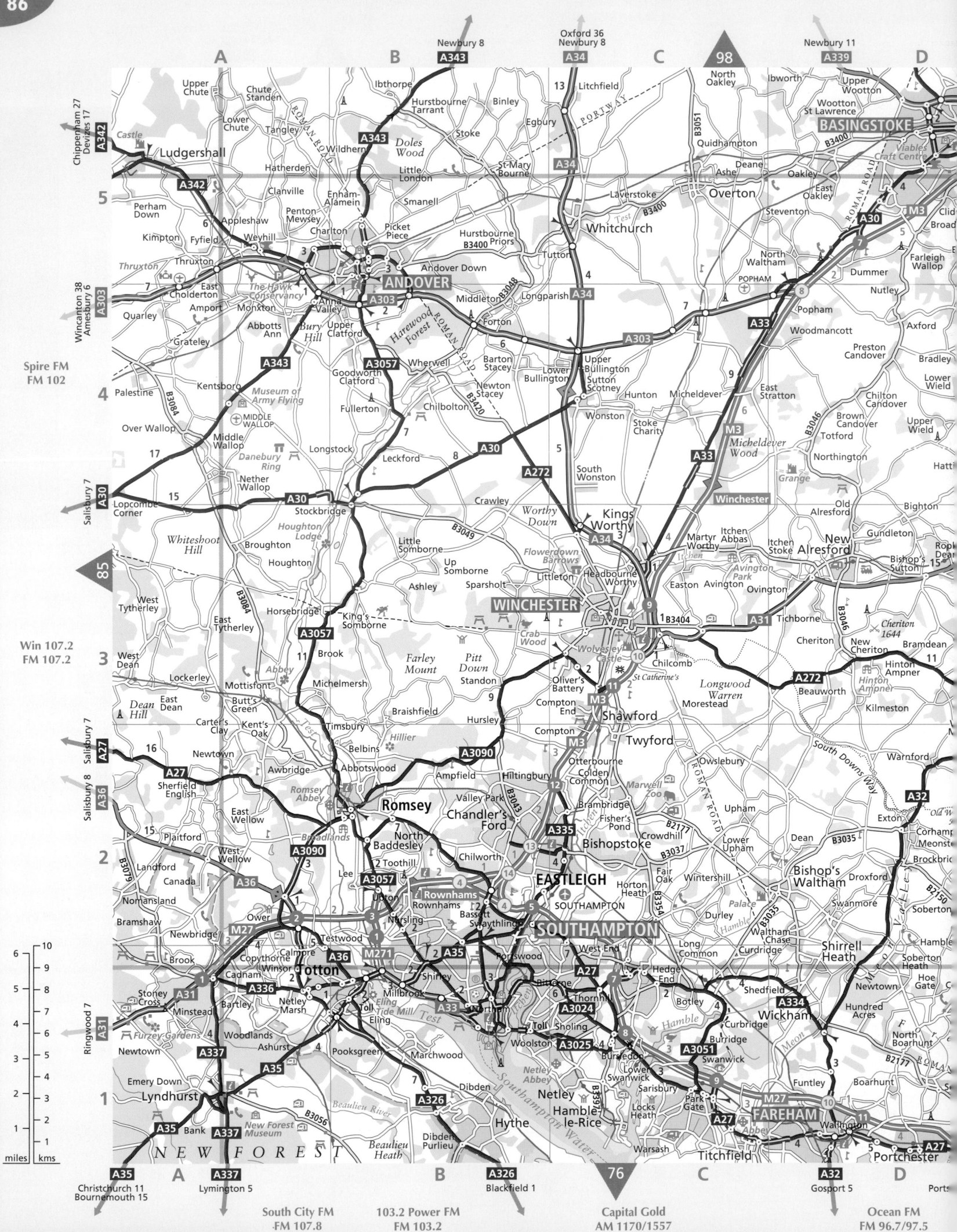

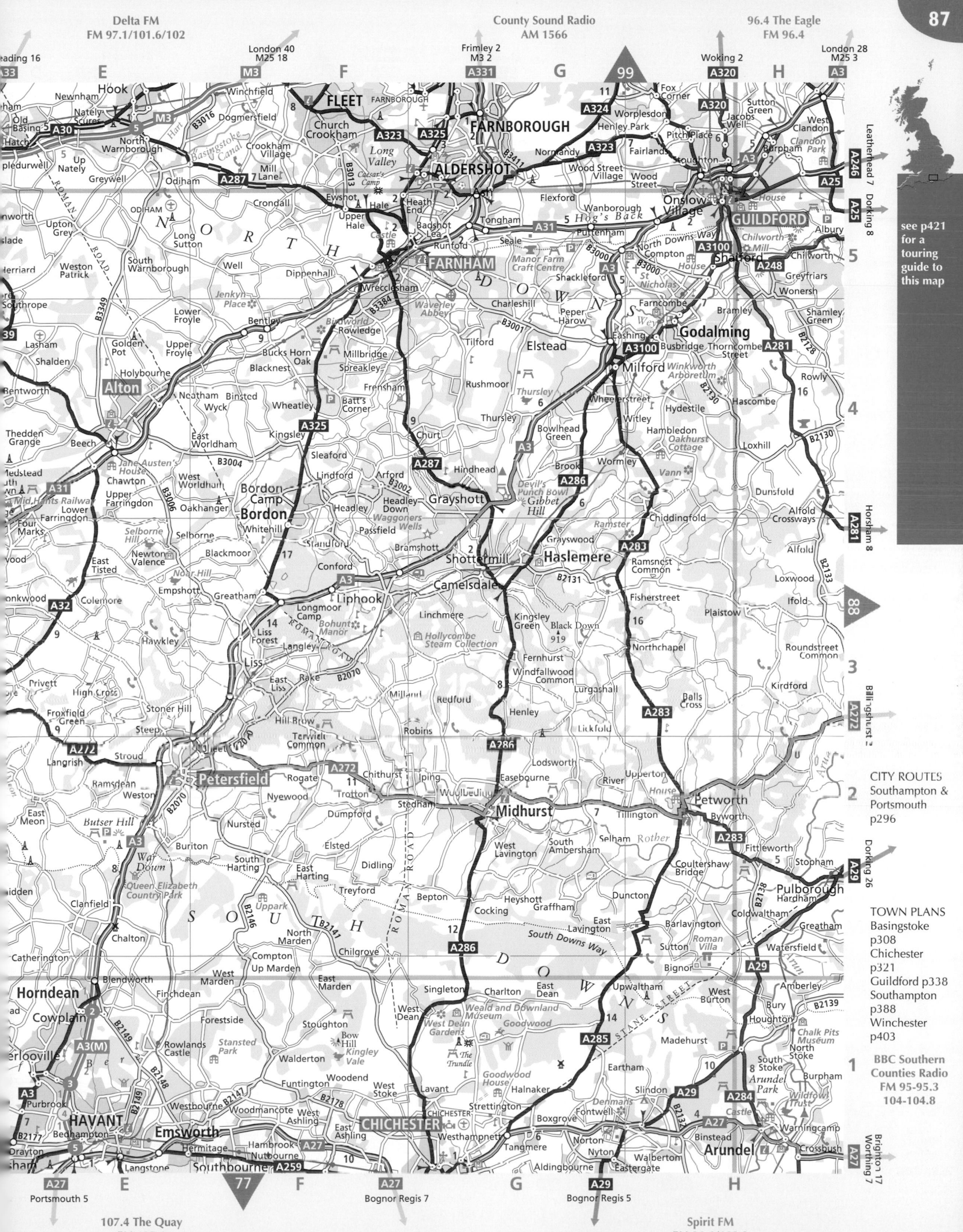

Delta FM
FM 97.1/101.6/102

County Sound Radio
AM 1566

96.4 The Eagle
FM 96.4

Reading 16
London 40
M25 18

Frimley 2
M3 2

Woking 2
London 28
M25 3

Leatherhead 7   Dorking 8

see p421
for a
touring
guide to
this map

E   F   G   99   H

33

Hook   FLEET   FARNBOROUGH   Woods Corner
Newnham
Natley
Scures
Old
Basing   A30
North
Warnborough   ALDERSHOT   Onslow
Village   GUILDFORD
A287
Odiham   FARNHAM   Shalford

Alton   Godalming   Milford

A287   Hindhead   A286   Haslemere   A283

Liphook   Liss

A3   Petersfield   Midhurst   Petworth

A272   Pulborough

Horndean
Cowplain   CHICHESTER   Arundel

HAVANT   Emsworth   Southbourne   A259

A27

BBC Southern
Counties Radio
FM 95-95.3
104-104.8

E   F   77   G   H

Portsmouth 5   Bognor Regis 5

County Sound
Radio
AM 1566

Mercury FM
FM 97.5/102.7

Bright 106.4
FM 106.4

GUILDFORD DORKING REIGATE Caterham Merstham Redhill Horley CRAWLEY East Grinstead

HORSHAM Haywards Heath Burgess Hill Hurstpierpoint Hassocks Keymer

Billingshurst Pulborough Storrington Steyning Arundel Southwick BRIGHTON Preston

Spirit FM
FM 96.6/102.3

Juice 107.2
FM 107.2

Southern FM
FM 96.9/102.4

Dartford Crossing 17 M25 1 Eynsford 7 A225 Gravesend 15 A227 101 M20 3 A228 Maidstone 1 A26 Maidstone 1 A229

E M25 A21 F G H

Clacket Lane A25 Westerham Brasted Sevenoaks Stone Street Knole House Ivy Hatch Mereworth East-Barming Wateringbury A26 Teston West Farleigh East Farleigh Shepway A274

Squerryes Court Brasted Chart B2042 Whitley Row A225 Underriver Plaxtol Dunk's Green Shipbourne Nettlestead Nettlestead Green Coxheath Boughton Monchelsea Chart Sutton 5

Goodley Stock Emmetts Sevenoaks Weald Ightham Mote West Peckham Yalding Hunton Linton Boughton Monchelsea Place

Crockham Hill B269 Chartwell Toy's Hill Four Elms Hildenborough Higham Wood A26 Hadlow East Peckham Laddingford Chainhurst Milebush Cross-at-Hand 12

Marlpit Hill Bough Beech Reservoir Chiddingstone Causeway Leigh Castle Medway Golden Green Whitbread Hop Farm Beltring Collier Street Marden A229

Edenbridge Hever Bough Beech Penshurst Place Bidborough TONBRIDGE A228 Queen Street Staplehurst

Haxted Eden Hever Castle Chiddingstone Castle Penshurst Tudeley Five Oak Green Paddock Wood Claygate Marden Thorn

Marsh Green B2026 Markbeech Southborough Crockhurst Street Capel 10 Brenchley Winchet Hill Curtisden Green

Cowden Fordcombe Speldhurst A26 A21 Pembury Matfield Horsmonden Cranbrook Common

A264 Blackham 14 Ashurst Langton Green Castle Hill Tudely Woods Kipping's Cross Spivers Goudhurst A262

Hammerwood Park Groombridge Eridge Green ROYAL TUNBRIDGE WELLS Frant Owl House 13 Iden Green Wisley Green Sissinghurst A262 Ashford 15

Forest Row Hartfield Withyham Spa Valley Railway Bells Yew Green Bayham Abbey Lamberhurst Finchcocks Scotney Castle Cranbrook 90

Ashurst Wood Upper Hartfield B2110 WEALD The Down Kilndown Bedgebury National Pinetum Hartley Golford

Coleman's Hatch Friar's Gate Boarshead A26 B2099 Cousley Wood Wadhurst Bewl Water Bedgebury Forest A229 Gill's Green

Ashdown Llama Farm Steel Cross Town Row Mark Cross Best Beech Hill Three Leg Cross Flimwell High Street Hawkhurst

A22 Forest Crowborough Rotherfield Tidebrook B2099 Ticehurst A268 The Moor Four Throws 3

Chelwood Gate King's Standing 12 Greenhill Jarvis Brook B2101 Argos Hill Stonegate Pashley Manor Hurst Green Sandhurst A268 Rye 11

Nutley Duddleswell Poundgate 6 Coggins Mill Merriments Silver Hill Bodiam Castle

Fairwarp High Hurstwood Butchers Cross Mayfield Rother Witherenden Hill Etchingham Bodiam

Maresfield A272 6 Hadlow Down Five Ashes Burwash Runwash Northbridge Street Darvell Rother Valley Railway Ewhurst Green

Fletching Buxted Wilderness Wood Cross in Hand Broad Oak A265 Darvell Burwash Weald Robertsbridge Salehurst Staplecross

Uckfield Ringles Cross New Town B2102 Heathfield Cade Street Brightling Oxley's Green John's Cross A21 Vinehall Street Cripp's Corner

A26 B2102 Blackboys Waldron Punnett's Town Three Cups Corner Mountfield Darwell Reservoir

Framfield Little London Maynard's Green Chapel Cross Netherfield 8 14 Sedlescombe

Little Horsted B2192 Foxhunt Green Horam Rushlake Green Dallington A2100 Whatlington

Isfield Halland Vines Cross Warbleton Penhurst Battle

Barcombe Cross 9 Bentley Wildfowl Collection Shortgate 11 East Hoathly Burlow Foul Mile Ponts Green Abbey Hastings 1066 Telham Beauport Park

A26 Chiddingly Cowbeech Bodle Street Green A271 Catsfield B2095 7

Broyle Side B2124 Whitesmith Lealands Stunts Green 13 Henley's Down Crowhurst Hollington

Ringmer Muddles Green Hellingly Herstmonceux Windmill Hill A271 Ninfield Lower Street A21 Hastings 2

Glyndebourne Golden Cross Lower Horsebridge A271 Hooe Common Sidley B2092

Cliffe Hill Laughton Lower Dicker Magham Down 12 Boreham Street A269 Lunsford's Cross Bulverhythe A259 Hastings 2

Mount Caburn Glynde Place Ripe Upper Dicker A295 Herstmonceux Castle Wartling Hooe Little Common Cooden Sidley

Glynde Chalvington Michelham Priory 4 Hailsham Pevensey Levels BEXHILL

Beddingham Firle Firle Place A27 11 Arlington Reservoir Waller's Haven B2182

Monk's House Charleston Farmhouse A22 Arlington B2104 Hankham Cooden

Firle Beacon Selmeston Alciston Berwick Polegate

A26 Newhaven 3 E F A27 A22 Eastbourne 8 79 Eastbourne 5 G H A259

see p422 for a touring guide to this map

TOWN PLANS
Crawley p324
Guildford p338
Horsham p340
Lewes p348
Royal Tunbridge Wells p398

107.8 Arrow FM
FM 107.8

107.5 Sovereign Radio
FM 107.5

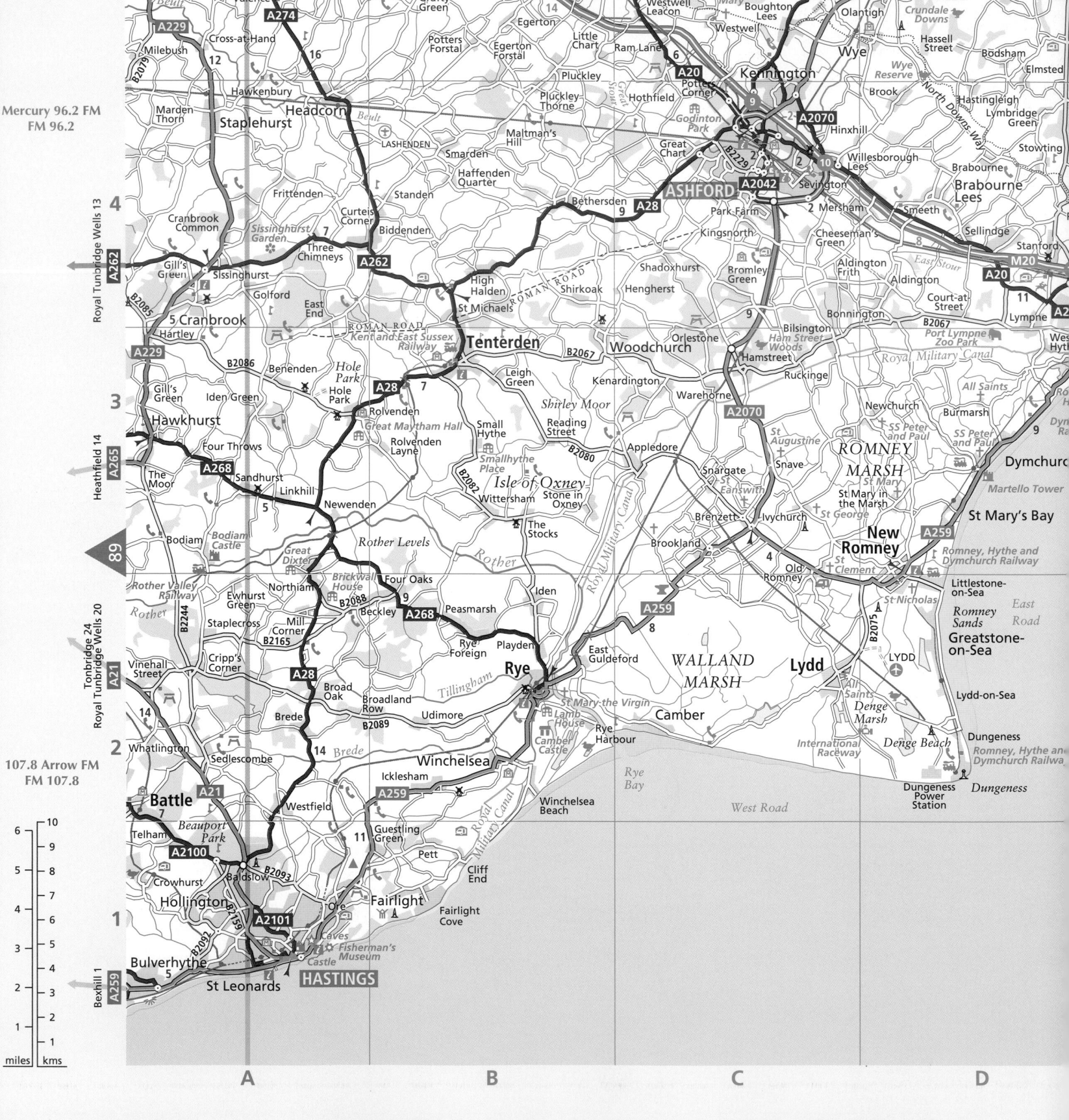

Neptune Radio
FM 96.4/106.8

103

Canterbury 3 A2

Ramsgate 11
Sandwich 2

A256

A258

DEAL
Deal Castle

Walmer
Walmer Castle

The Downs

see p423
for a
touring
guide to
this map

Kingsdown

St Margaret's
at Cliffe

Pines Gardens
St Margaret's Bay
South Foreland

Langdon Cliffs

DOVER

→ Dunkirk

CHANNEL TUNNEL
→ Calais

Boulogne

FOLKESTONE

A259 Sandgate

TOWN PLANS
Ashford p306
Dover p91
Folkestone
p333
Hastings p340

DOVER

Deal 8   Canterbury 16   Terminal Bldg

A258   Boulogne, Calais, Dunkirk

Connaught Park   Castle Walls   Dover Castle   Eastern Docks

St Mary's Church & The Pharos

Connaught Road

Castle Avenue   Monastery Ave   East Cliff

Castlemount Rd   Victoria Park

Salisbury Road   Leyburne Road   MARINE PARADE

Harold Street   Laureston Pl

MAISON DIEU ROAD

Sandwich 11 / Margate 20   A256

Dour Street   WOOLCOMBER STREET

Pencester Gardens   Russell St   Castle street

HIGH ST   Biggin Street   St James St   Marine Parade

Priory Hill   Cannon St

PRIORY RD   White Cliffs Experience   YORK ST   Queen St

Lanc Rd   Durham Hill   Albany Pl   De Bradelei Wharf   Outer Harbour

Priory Station   Cowgate Cemetery   TOWN WALL STREET   Cambridge Rd   Waterloo Crescent   Esplanade

Folkestone Road   North Military Road   SNARGATE   Wellington Basin

Clarendon Rd   Drop Redoubt   Prince of Wales Pier

B2011   Malvern Road   Grand Shaft   Granville Basin   Terminal Building

Clarendon street   Centre Road   STREET   Union Street   Hovercraft Terminal   North Pier   Calais

Clarendon Place   Knights Templars   Tidal Basin   Western Docks

Walls   Citadel Rd   Western Close   South Military Road   Channel View Road   THE VIADUCT   LORD WARDEN SQUARE   South Pier

A20   Cruise Terminal

0 100 200 300yds
0 100 200 300m

A   B   C   D
Folkestone 7

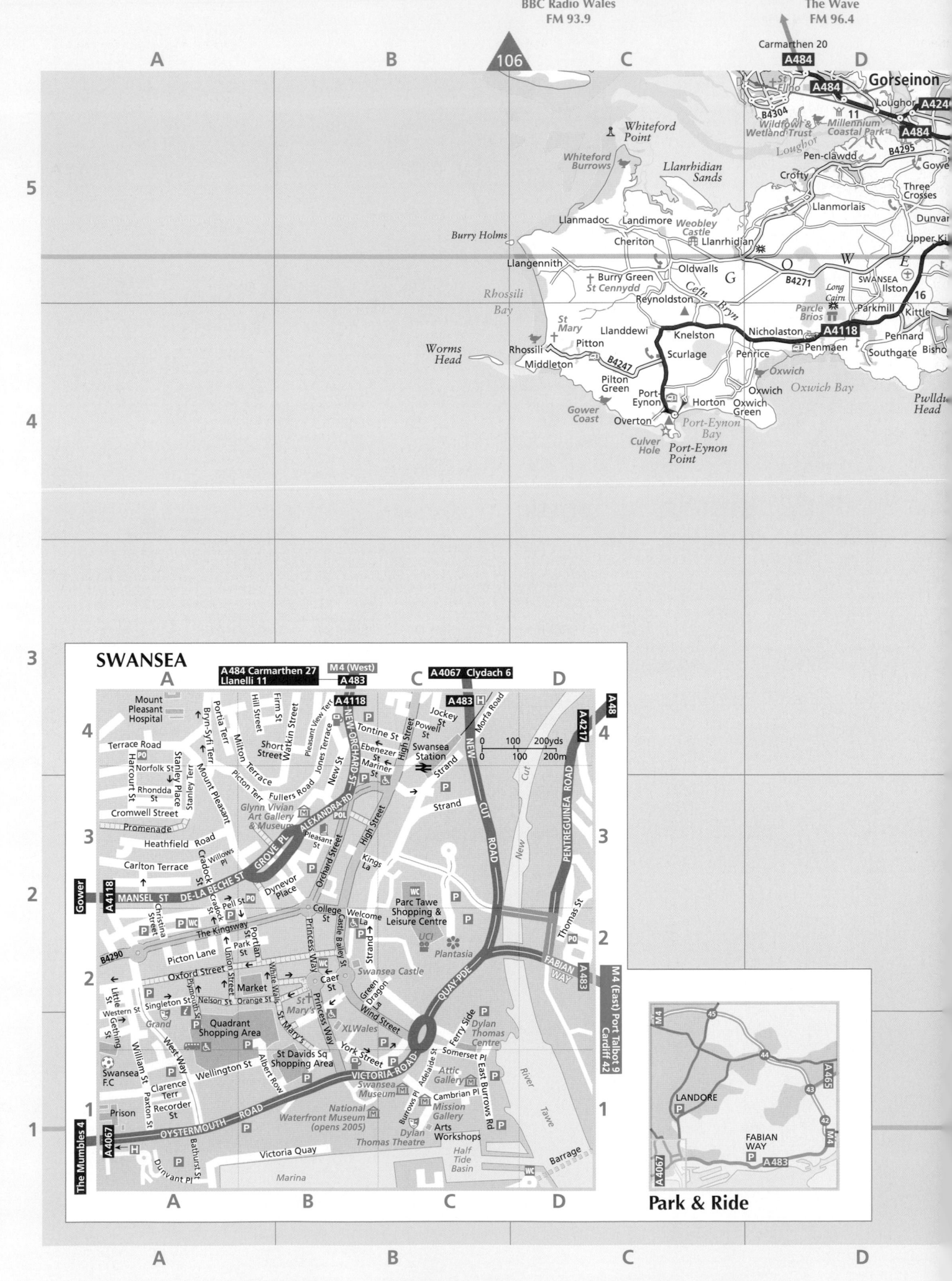

Swansea Sound
AM 1170

Pontardawe 5 A4067   Glyn-neath 8 A465   107   Hirwaun 8 A4061   Aberdare 4 A4233

then 19

E   F   G   H

Glyncorrwg   Blaenrhondda   Tynewydd   11

NEATH/   Aberdulais   Treherbert   Maerdy   A4233

CASTELL-NEDD   Tonna   B4434   Cymer   Blaengwynfi   RHONDDA   Treorchy

Rhydding   Duffryn   A4107   Abergwynfi   6   Cwmparc   3   RHONDDA

M4 45   B4291   Birchgrove   Tonmawr   Caerau   Croeserw   Ystrad

47   46   Skewen   A474   Briton   A4063   Mynydd   2   B4223

M4 A48   44   Ferry   Dyffryn   Caerau   Nant-   Clydach

Swansea   Llansamlet   43   Pontrhydyfen   Afan   Nantyffyllon   y-moel   Llwynypia   Vale

Llangyfelach   Morriston   Landore   A474   Argoed   Price   Tonypandy

Llandarcy   B4286   Miners'   Blaengarw   Town   5

A4067   Pentre-   Museum   Bryn   Blaengarw   Wyndham   A4058

A4217   dwr   Llandarcy   Pwll-y-glaw   A4064   Penygraig

A4216   42   Baglan   Cwmafan   Pontycymer   10   Mynydd   A4058

Sketty   A483   6   Mynydd   Garth   Ogmore   Maes-teg

A4483   5   Dinas   MAESTEG   Vale   Gilfach   B4564

Black Pill   846   A4061   Goch   Hendreforgan

West Cross   41   Taibach   Llangynwyd   Pont Rhyd-   7   Lewistown

Oystermouth   40   y-cyff   13   A4093

The   SWANSEA/   M4   Mynydd   Llangeinor   Glynllan   Glynogwr

Mumbles   ABERTAWE   Margam   Margam   12   Bettws   Blackmill

Swansea   PORT TALBOT   Abbey   1129   Mynydd   Lewistown

Bay   Groes   Moel   Baedon   Brynmenyn

Mumbles   39   Ton-mawr   Coytrahen   Bryncethin   Heol-   A473

Head   1048   Tondu   y-Cyw   Brynna

ingaskiddy (Cork)   38   Margam Park   Aberkenfig   Sarn   Brynnay   Brynna

Margam   Sarn Park   Gwynion   B4280

Eglwys Nunydd   A48   Kenfig   36   Pencoed   A473

Reservoir   Hill   Cefn   Cefn   Pen-y-Fai   Brynnau   Llanilid   M4   35

Margam   Cribwr   Cross   Castle   Gwynion

Sands   Mawdlam   Pyle   B4281   BRIDGEND/   St Mary   Coychurch   A473

North   PEN-Y-BONT   B4181

Kenfig   Cornelly   AR OGWR   2   St Mary Hill   Newport 27

Burrows   37   3   Laleston   Graig   Cardiff 14

Kenfig   A48   A4229   A4106   3   Treoes   Penllyn

South Cornelly   3   Ewenny   Llangan   Llansannor

Nottage   Tythegston   Ewenny   6   Penllyn   A48

Merthyr Mawr   Priory   A48   Colwinston   Cardiff 13

Newton   Castle   Cowbridge   B4270

Ogmore   Llanblethian   94

Porthcawl   Ogmore-by-Sea   St Bride's   Llandough

Major   Llysworney   Llanmihangel   106.3 Bridge FM

Tusker Rock   Southerndown   Llandow   FM 106.3

Wick   B4265

Broughton   Sigingstone

Monknash   Llanmaes

Marcross   Llantwit   2

Nash   Major   Boverton

Point   St Donat's

BRISTOL   Castle   CITY ROUTES

Ditches   Swansea p298

CHANNEL

Foreland   TOWN PLANS

Point   Swansea p92

E   F   G   H

see p424
for a
touring
guide to
this map

Ynyshir Cymmer 4   A4233

Cardiff 17   A4058

Llantrisant 4   A4093

Llantrisant 3   A473

Red Radio
FM 105.4/105.9/106

Galaxy 101
FM 97.2/101

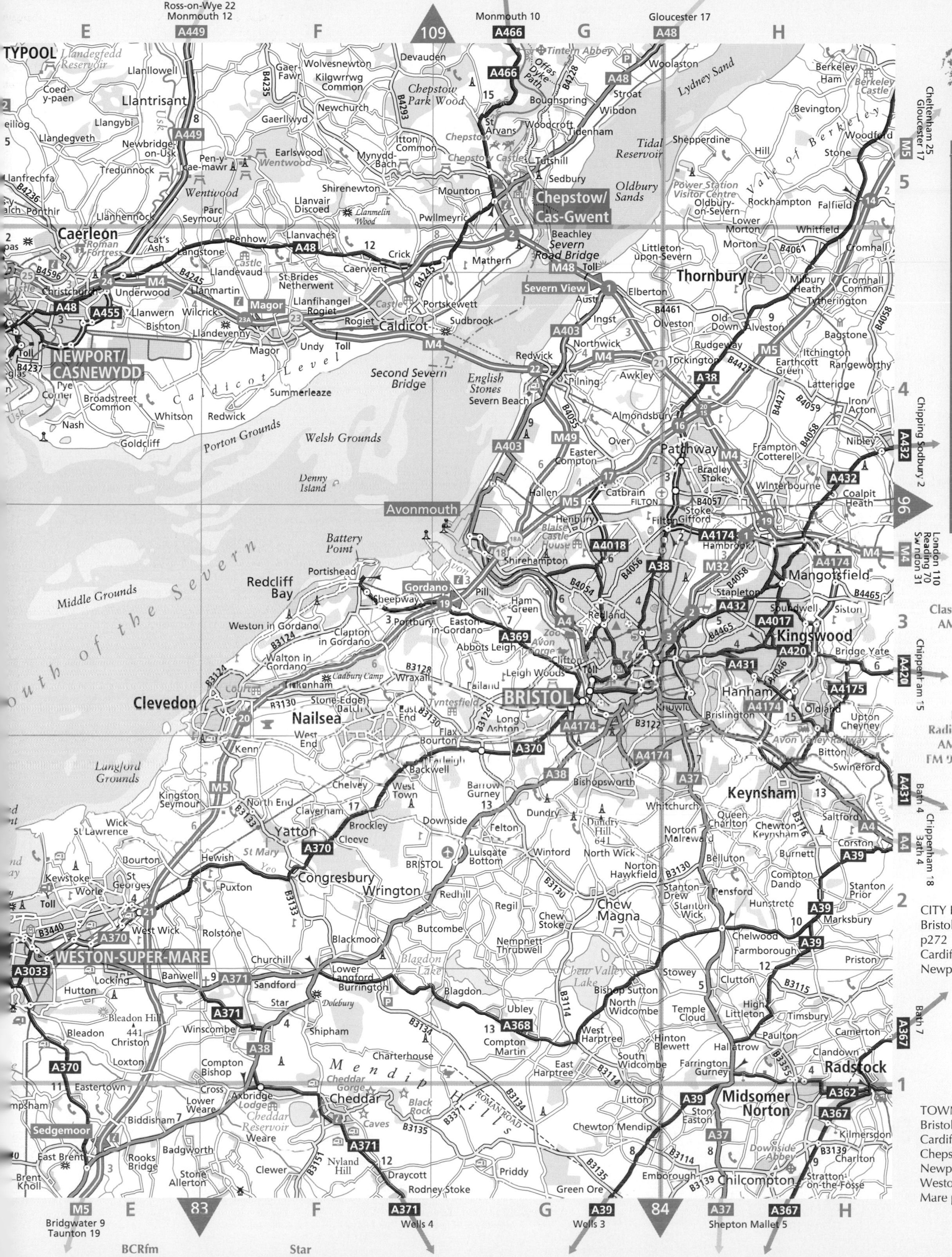

109

A466 Monmouth 10

Gloucester 17
A48

see p425 for a touring guide to this map

Chepstow/Cas-Gwent

Thornbury

Severn View

M48 Toll

Severn Road Bridge

Caldicot

NEWPORT/CASNEWYDD

Caerleon

M4

A48

A449

Llantrisant

Second Severn Bridge

English Stones
Severn Beach

Caldicot Level

Welsh Grounds

Denny Island

Avonmouth

Patchway

M49

M5

FILTON

Mangotsfield

Chipping Sodbury 2
A432

96

London 110
Reading 70
Swindon 31
M4

Classic Gold
AM 1260

Portishead

Redcliff Bay

Gordano

BRISTOL

Kingswood

Chippenham 15
A420

Middle Grounds

Mouth of the Severn

Clevedon

Nailsea

Hanham

Keynsham

Bath 4
Chippenham 18
Bath 4

BBC
Radio Bristol
AM 1548
FM 94.9/95.5

M5

WESTON-SUPER-MARE

Congresbury
Wrington

Chew Magna

Chew Valley Lake

A39

Bath 7
A367

CITY ROUTES
Bristol & Bath
p272
Cardiff & Newport p274

A3033

Sedgemoor

Cheddar

Blagdon Lake

Midsomer Norton

Radstock

A362
A367

TOWN PLANS
Bristol p315
Cardiff p317
Chepstow p320
Newport p370
Weston-super-Mare p402

M5
Bridgwater 9
Taunton 19

83

A371
Wells 4

Star
FM 107.3/107.7

A39
Wells 3

84

A37
A367
Shepton Mallet 5

BCRfm
FM 107.4

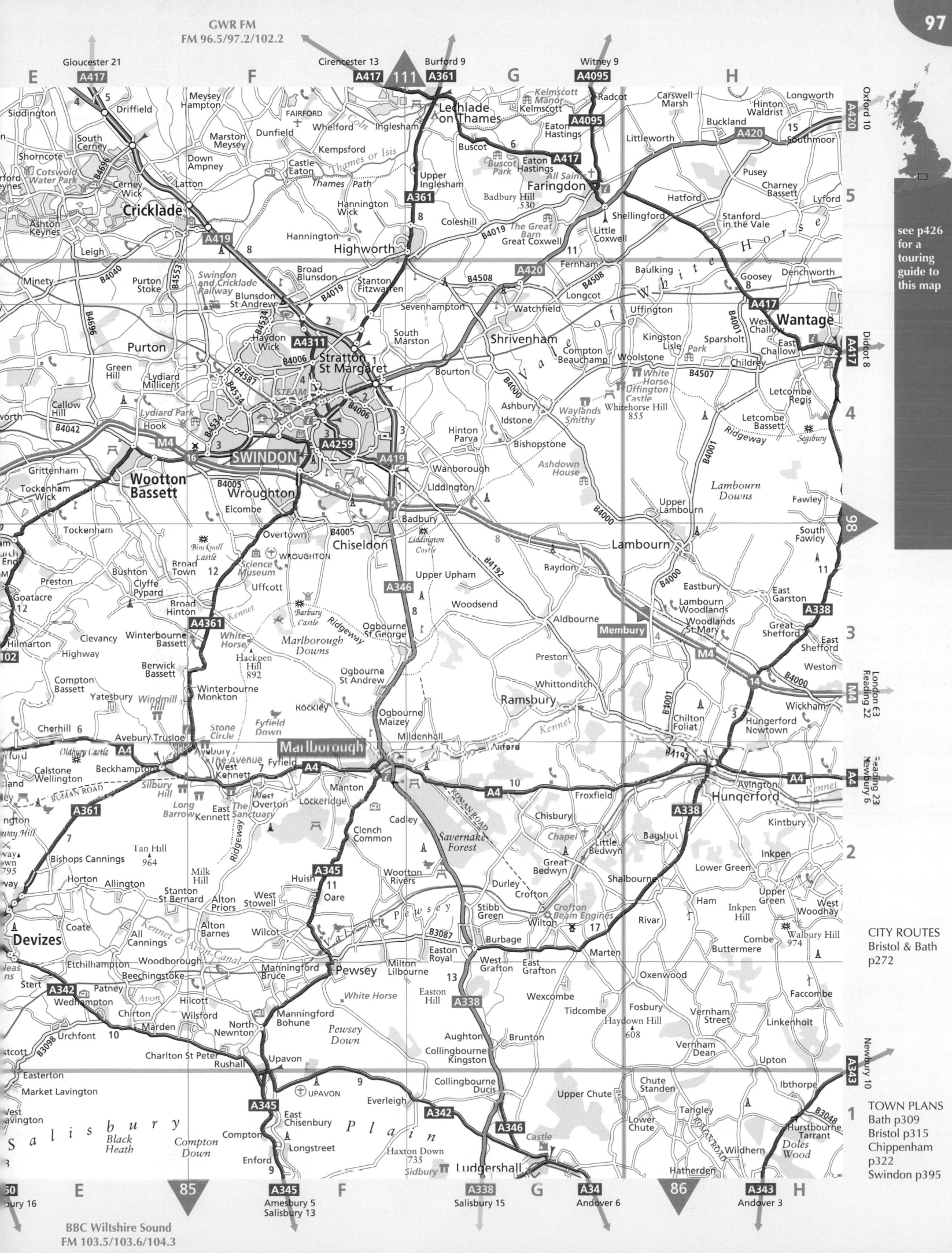

Gloucester 21
A417
Cirencester 13
A417 111
Burford 9
A361
Witney 9
A4095

Oxford 10
A420

see p426 for a touring guide to this map

Siddington
Driffield
Meysey Hampton
FAIRFORD
Lechlade on Thames
Kelmscott Manor Kelmscott
Radcot
A4095
Carswell Marsh
Hinton Waldrist
Longworth

South Cerney
Marston Meysey
Dunfield
Whelford
Inglesham
Buscot
Eaton Hastings
A4095
Buckland
Littleworth
A420
Southmoor 15

Shorncote
Cotswold Water Park
Down Ampney
Kempsford
Castle Eaton
Upper Inglesham
Thames or Isis
Buscot Park
Eaton Hastings
A417
Faringdon
Pusey
Charney Bassett
Lyford

Ashton Keynes
Cerney Wick
Latton
Thames Path
Hannington Wick
Badbury Hill 530
All Saints
Coleshill
Shellingford
Hatford
Stanford in the Vale
Denchworth

Cricklade
A419
Highworth
A361
Hannington
B4019
The Great Barn Great Coxwell
Little Coxwell
Fernham
Baulking
Goosey
A417
Wantage

Minety
Purton Stoke
Broad Blunsdon
Stanton Fitzwarren
Sevenhampton
B4508
A420
Longcot
Watchfield
B4508
Uffington
B4001
West Challow
East Challow
Didcot 8

Leigh
B4040
B4553
Swindon and Cricklade Railway
Blunsdon St Andrew
B4019
Shrivenham
Compton Beauchamp
Woolstone
White Horse
Kingston Lisle
Sparsholt
Childrey
A417

Purton
Haydon Wick
A4311
Stratton St Margaret
South Marston
Bourton
A4000
Ashbury
Idstone
White Horse Uffington Castle
Whitehorse Hill 855
B4507
Letcombe Regis
Letcombe Bassett

Green Hill
Lydiard Millicent
B4006
STEAM
Hinton Parva
Bishopstone
Waylands Smithy
Ridgeway
Segsbury

Callow Hill
Lydiard Park
Hook
B4534
A4259
SWINDON
A419
Wanborough
Ashdown House
Upper Lambourn
Lambourn Downs
Fawley

Wootton Bassett
B4005
Wroughton
Elcombe
Liddington
Badbury
15
Ashdown House
Lambourn
South Fawley

Grittenham
M4 16
Tockenham Wick
Overton
B4005
Chiseldon
Liddington Castle
8
B4192
Baydon
Eastbury
Lambourn Woodlands
East Garston
Great Shefford
A338

Tockenham
Bushton
Clyffe Pypard
Broad Town 12
Science Museum WROUGHTON
Upper Upham
Woodsend
Aldbourne
Woodlands St Mary
East Shefford
Weston

Preston
Broad Hinton
A4361
Uffcott
Barbury Castle
Ogbourne St George
Preston
Whittonditch
Membury
M4
A338

Goatacre
Hilmarton
Clevancy
Highway
Winterbourne Bassett
White Horse
Hackpen Hill 892
Ridgeway
Ogbourne St Andrew
Ramsbury
Chilton Foliat
Hungerford Newtown
M4 14
B4000
Wickham

Berwick Bassett
Winterbourne Monkton
Marlborough Downs
Rockley
Ogbourne Maizey
Kennet
London £3 Reading 22

Compton Bassett
Yatesbury
Windmill Hill
Stone Circle
Fyfield Down
Mildenhall
Axford
B4192
Avington
A4
Reading 23 Newbury 6

Cherhill 6
Avebury Trusloe
Avebury The Avenue
Marlborough
A4
10
Froxfield
A338
Hungerford
Kintbury
A4

Oldbury Castle
A4
Beckhampton
West Kennett
Fyfield
A4
Manton
ROMAN ROAD
Chisbury
Bagshot
Inkpen

Silbury Hill
ROMAN ROAD
West Overton
Lockeridge
Savernake Forest
Little Bedwyn
Lower Green
Upper Green
West Woodhay

A361
Long Barrow
East Kennett
The Sanctuary
Ridgeway
Cadley
Clench Common
Great Bedwyn
Shalbourne
Ham
Inkpen Hill
Combe
Walbury Hill 974

Tan Hill 964
Milk Hill
Huish
Wootton Rivers
Durley
Crofton
Crofton Beam Engines
Rivar
Buttermere

Bishops Cannings
Horton
Allington
Stanton St Bernard
Alton Priors
Oare 11
A345
Stibb Green
Wilton 17
Marten

Devizes
Coate
All Cannings
Alton Barnes
Wilcot
West Stowell
Vale of Pewsey
Burbage
West Grafton
Oxenwood

Etchilhampton
Woodborough
Beechingstoke
Manningford Bruce
Hilcott
White Horse
Milton Lilbourne
Easton Royal
East Grafton
Wexcombe
Tidcombe
Fosbury
Vernham Street
Vernham Dean
Linkenholt

A342
Patney
Wedhampton
Chirton
Wilsford
Manningford Bohune
North Newnton
Pewsey
Easton Hill
A338
Haydown Hill 608
Faccombe

Stert
Marden
Rushall
Upavon
Pewsey Down
Aughton
Brunton
Upton

B3098
Urchfont 10
Charlton St Peter
A345
UPAVON
Everleigh
Collingbourne Kingston
Upper Chute
Chute Standen
Ibthorpe
Newbury 10
A343

Easterton
Market Lavington
East Chisenbury
Longstreet
A342
Collingbourne Ducis
A346
Castle
Lower Chute
Tangley
B3048
Wildhern
Doles Wood
Hurstbourne Tarrant

Black Heath
Compton Down
Compton
Enford 9
Haxton Down 735
Sidbury
Ludgershall
Upper Chute
Hatherden

A345
85
E
A345 F
A338 G
A34
86
A343 H

Amesbury 5
Salisbury 13
Salisbury 15
Andover 6
Andover 3

CITY ROUTES
Bristol & Bath
p272

TOWN PLANS
Bath p309
Bristol p315
Chippenham p322
Swindon p395

A   B   A420   112   A34   C   A329   D

5

Carswell Marsh
Littleworth
Buckland
Hinton Waldrist
Longworth
Fyfield
Tubney
Cothill
ABINGDON
Oxford 7
Oxford 4
Thame 7
M40 3
Stoke Talmage
A420
15
Southmoor
Kingston Bagpuize
Fulford
Shippon
A4183
Radley
Nuneham Courtenay
Harcourt Arboretum
Marsh Baldon
Chiselhampton
Stadhampton
Swindon 14
Hatford
Pusey
Kingston Bagpuize House
Garford
Marcham
Abingdon
A4015
Drayton St Leonard
Berinsfield
A329
Chalgrove
Newington
Easington
1643
A480
Shellingford
A338
Charney Bassett
Lyford
A415
Thames Path
A34
Culham
Clifton Hampden
Wittenham St Peter and St Paul
Dorchester
Brightwell Baldwin
Cuxham
Pyrton
Watling
Stanford in the Vale
West Hanney
East Hanney
Steventon
B4016
Drayton
Sutton Courtenay
Appleford
Little Wittenham
Shillingford
Benson
Britwell Salome
Roke
BENSON
Ewelme

Baulking
Goosey
Denchworth
A417
Milton Hill
Manor
Milton
Thames Path
Didcot Railway Centre
Brightwell-cum-Sotwell
Benson
A4074
Ewelme

Uffington
Grove
A417
West Hendred
5
Harwell
Didcot
East Hagbourne
North Moreton
A4130
Wallingford
Crowmarsh Gifford
Ridgeway

4

Whitehorse Hill 855
West Challow
East Challow
Wantage
A417
Ardington
East Hendred
A4185
West Hagbourne
Upton
Aston Upthorpe
South Moreton
Cholsey
North Stoke
Ipsden
Wellplace Zoo
Stoke Row
Kingston Lisle
Park
Sparsholt
Childrey
B4507
Lockinge
West Ginge
East Ginge
Chilton
Blewbury
Aston Tirrold
A417
A329
Cholsey and Wallingford Railway
South Stoke
Woodcote
Checkendon
Nuffield
White Horse
Letcombe Regis
Letcombe Bassett
Ridgeway
Segsbury
Moulsford
Streatley
Goring
B4526
Cray's Pond
Exlade Street
A4074

97

Upper Lambourn
Lambourn Downs
Fawley
11
Farnborough
East Ilsley
Ridgeway
Compton
Aldworth
Lower Basildon
Beale Wildlife Gardens
Whitchurch Hill
Whitchurch-on-Thames
Cane End
B4000
Lambourn
South Fawley
Lilley
Brightwalton
Catmore
Stanmore
A34
Beedon
Living Rainforest
Basildon Park
B4526
Mapledurham
Purley on Tha

3

Membury
M4
Swindon 11
Bristol 51
Eastbury
Lambourn Woodlands
Woodlands St Mary
East Garston
Great Shefford
East Shefford
B4000
Leckhampstead
Weston
Welford
Chieveley
M4
14
Winterbourne
13
Chieveley
Hermitage
Longlane
Peasemore
World's End
Downend
B4009
Hampstead Norreys
Ashampstead
Upper Basildon
Yattendon
Frilsham
Stanford Dingley
Bradfield
North Street
Englefield
Theale
Tidmarsh
Pangbourne
A329
A340
Sulham
Tilehurst
A4
Calcot
12
Reading
Burghfield

Kick FM
FM 105.6/107.4

Chippenham 27
Marlborough 7
A4
Chilton Foliat
3
Hungerford Newtown
Wickham
Boxford
Curridge
Ashmore Green
Cold Ash
Bucklebury
Chapel Row
Beenham
Sheffield Bottom
Sulhamstead
Aldermaston Wharf
Burghfield Common
B4192
Wickham Heath
B4000
Bagnor
Donnington
5
Shaw
Upper Bucklebury
Midgham
Upper Woolhampton
Woolhampton
8
A4
Ufton Nervet
Burghfield Hill

2

Hungerford
A4
Avington
Halfway
Stockcross
Speen
Donnington Castle
1643
Thatcham
Kennet
Colthrop
Padworth
Aldermaston
Mortimer
Kennet & Avon Canal
Kintbury
Enborne
Newbury
Greenham
Brimpton
Stratfield Mortimer
Bagshot
A338
Hamstead Marshall
1643
Greenham Common
Goldfinch Bottom
Crookham
Brimpton Common
Wasing
A340
Aldermaston Soke
Pamber Heath
Mortimer West End
Calleva Museum

Lower Green
Inkpen
Ham
Shalbourne
Inkpen Hill
Upper Green
West Woodhay
North End
Ball Hill
Broad Layings
Newtown
Headley
B4640
Plastow Green
Ashford Hill
Browninghill Green
Heath End
Tadley
Baughurst
Pamber Green
Little London
Silchester
West End Green
Fair Oak Green
Bramley
Stra

Salisbury 27
A338
Rivar
Buttermere
Combe
Walbury Hill
East Woodhay
Woolton Hill
East End
Highclere
Burghclere
Whitway
Ecchinswell
Sandham Memorial Chapel
Highclere Castle
A339
Kingsclere
Wolverton
Charter Alley
The Vyne
Pamber End
Bramley Green
Sherfield on Loddon
Church End
A33

1

Oxenwood
Fosbury
Haydown Hill 608
Vernham Street
Vernham Dean
Upton
Faccombe
Ashmansworth
17
Crux Easton
Beacon Hill
Highclere Castle
Old Burghclere
Sydmonton
Kingsclere
17
West Heath
Ramsdell
Monk Sherborne
Sherborne St John
Chineham
A33

Chute Standen
Lower Chute
Tangley
A343
Ibthorpe
Doles Wood
Stoke
A34
Litchfield
13
Binley
Egbury
St Mary Bourne
Quidhampton
North Oakley
Ibworth
Hannington
A339
Upper Wootton
Wootton St Lawrence
Deane
East Oakley
Oakley
B3400
BASINGSTOKE
Viables Craft Centre
M3
Maple

Hurstbourne Tarrant
B3048
Wildhern
Hatherden

A343   A34   M3
Andover 3   Winchester 13   Winchester 16
Southampton 31   Southampton 28
86

miles kms
10 9 8 7 6 5 4 3 2 1
6 5 4 3 2 1

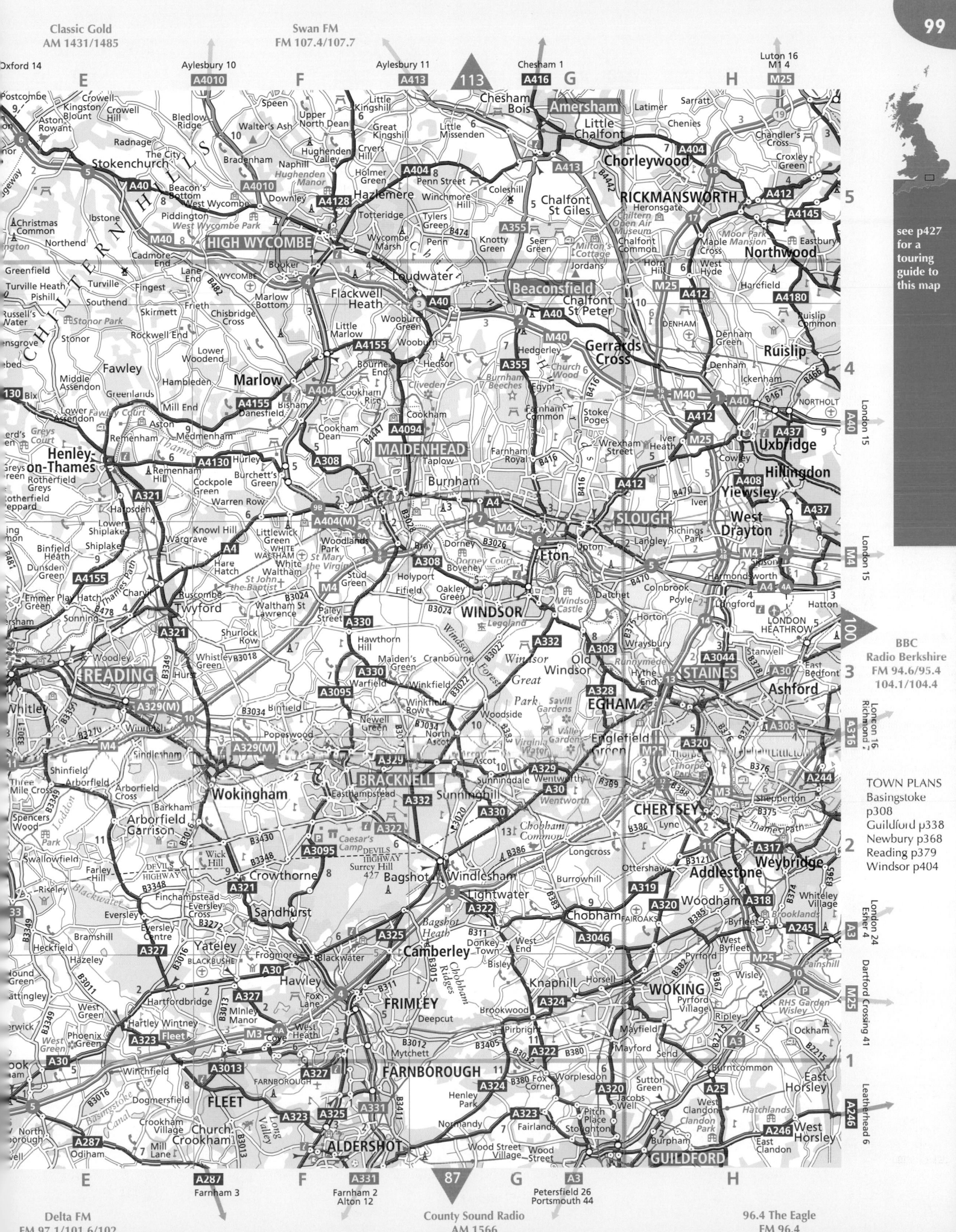

Grid references (top): A M25 A405 M1 B A5183 A1(M) C 114 A10 D

Directions (top margin): M1 4 · St Albans 6 · Luton 14 · St Albans 5 · Stevenage 17 Hatfield 6 · Royston 26 Ware 9

Left margin directions: Amersham 3 A404 · Amersham 4 A413 · High Wycombe 11 M40 · Maidenhead 8 Slough 1 A4 · Bristol 98 Swindon 58 Reading 21 M4 · Southampton 55 Winchester 43 M3 · (A27) Portsmouth 50 Petersfield 28 A3

Major place names:
Chorleywood, WATFORD, BUSHEY, Radlett, Borehamwood, ELSTREE, Barnet, East Barnet, Southgate, Enfield, Edmonton, RICKMANSWORTH, Croxley Green, Northwood, Stanmore, Edgware, Finchley, Friern Barnet, Wood Green, Tottenham, Pinner, Kenton, Hendon, Hornsey, Stoke Newington, Hackney, Ruislip, Harrow, Harrow on the Hill, Hampstead, Camden Town, Islington, Bethnal Green, Uxbridge, Northolt, Wembley, Greenford, Willesden, Marylebone, Finsbury, Shoreditch, Stepney, Bow, Hillingdon, Yiewsley, Hayes, Southall, Ealing, Acton, Paddington, CITY OF LONDON, West Drayton, Heston, Brentford, Hammersmith, Kensington, WESTMINSTER, Bermondsey, LONDON HEATHROW, Hounslow, Isleworth, Chiswick, Chelsea, Lambeth, Camberwell, Greenwich, Deptford, STAINES, Twickenham, RICHMOND, Barnes, Fulham, Battersea, Clapham, Brixton, Lewisham, EGHAM, Ashford, Feltham, Putney, Wandsworth, Streatham, Hanworth, Teddington, KINGSTON UPON THAMES, Merton, Wimbledon, Upper Tooting, West Norwood, Penge, Sunbury, East Molesey, Surbiton, New Malden, Mitcham, Beckenham, CHERTSEY, WALTON-ON-THAMES, Thames Ditton, Long Ditton, Worcester Park, Morden, Carshalton, CROYDON, Weybridge, Addlestone, Woodham, Hersham, Claygate, Chessington, Hook, ESHER, Cheam, SUTTON, Wallington, Purley, WOKING, Cobham, Oxshott, EPSOM, EWELL, Banstead, Coulsdon, Warlingham, Whyteleafe, Pyrford, Stoke D'Abernon, Ashtead, Tadworth, Kingswood, Burgh Heath, Chaldon, Caterham, Fetcham, Great Bookham, LEATHERHEAD, Walton on the Hill, East Horsley, West Horsley, Effingham, Mickleham, Headley, Merstham, GUILDFORD, REIGATE, Redhill, Buckland

Scale bar: miles / kms (1–6 miles, 1–10 kms)

Bottom margin grid: A A24 B 114/88 C A23 M23 D A22

Bottom directions: Dorking 1 Horsham 14 · Gatwick Airport 6 Crawley 9 · Gatwick Airport 6 (A23) Brighton 32 · East Grinstead 8 Eastbourne 40

Virgin 105.8
FM 105.8

BBC Radio Essex
FM 95.3/103.5

see p428 for a touring guide to this map

TOWN PLANS
Croydon p325
Kingston upon Thames p343
Central London p352
London West End p356
London Docklands & Greenwich p360
Maidstone p363
Rochester p381
Watford p400

CITY ROUTES
Outer London: North p284
Outer London: South p286

CTR 105.6 FM
FM 105.6

ITN News Direct
FM 97.3

Southend-on-Sea 7
Southend-on-Sea 6
Canterbury 26 (A2)
Dover 42
Dover 40
Canterbury 24
Ashford 18

Cambridge 42
Stansted Airport 17
Chipping Ongar 3
Chelmsford 6
Chelmsford 6

Tonbridge 5
Hastings 37
Tonbridge 2
Tonbridge 3
Royal Tunbridge Wells 9
Cranbrook 10
Hawkhurst 14

Map of the London and Kent/Essex region including London, Brentwood, Basildon, Southend, Dartford, Gravesend, Rochester, Chatham, Maidstone, Sevenoaks, Orpington and surrounding areas.

RAMSGATE

St Luke's Avenue
Winstanley Cres
Alexandra Rd
Percy Road
Hollicondane Rd
Upper Dumpton Park Rd
Ann's Rd
Denmark Rd

Margate 4
A254
MARGATE ROAD
BOUNDARY ROAD
A255
Broadstairs 2
B2054
WC

Station Approach Rd
PARK ROAD
Chatham Street
Church Road
Hardres Street
Turner Street
Bright's Pl
Artillery Rd
Victoria Road
Truro Road
Victoria Parade
Marina Rd
Granville Theatre & Cinema

Ramsgate Station
A255
M2
A299
A28 Canterbury 16

High Street
Broad Street
High St
Council Offices
Plains of Waterloo
Bellevue
Augusta Road
Wellington Cres
Marina Esplanade

South Eastern Road
Cannon Road
Chapel Place
George St
King St
Queen St
Albion
Madeira Walk
Harbour Parade
Amusement Centre
Royal Victoria Pavilion
PO
POL

Ellington Road
Grove Rd
North Ave
Elms
Ramsgate Museum
Argyle Centre
Maritime Museum
Yacht Marina

Picton Road
Duncan Road
Codrington Road
Marlborough Rd
Avenue
Queen Street
Queen
Parade
Royal
Royal Harbour

Dundonald Rd
Grange Road
South Eastern Road
Vale Road
Willson's Rd
Vale Sq
Vale Sq
Addington Street
Spencer
Nelson Cr
Paragon
Military Road
West Pier
East Pier

St Mildred's Road
Grange Road
Cannonbury Rd
West Cliff
Royal Rd
Square

St Augustine's Pk
London Rd
Grange Rd
Augustine's Road
Nes Cliff Promenade
Motor Museum
Royal Harbour
B2054
WC

0 100 200 300yds
0 100 200 300m

N

see p429 for a touring guide to this map

TLR
FM 107.2

South Channel
Long Nose Spit
Foreness Point
MARGATE
Caves
B2051
White Ness
North Foreland
Westgate on Sea
B2052
Bleak House
HERNE BAY
Reculver
Birchington
A28
Isle of Thanet
A255
A254
St Peter's
BROADSTAIRS
TSTABLE
Beltinge
Towers
Queen House Aroll
B2052
A256
RAMSGATE
Swalecliffe
B2205
Eddington
Hillborough
Broomfield
St Nicholas at Wade
MANSTON
Manston
A299
Greenhill
Hunters Forstal Herne
Boyden Gate
Sarre
A253
A253
Cliffs End
Pegwell Bay
Chestfield
A2990
Maypole
Chislet
Monkton
Minster
Richborough Port
Herne Common
Hoath
Upstreet
West Stourmouth
Richborough Castle
Sandwich Flats
A299
Wildwood
Sturry
A291
Hersden
A28
East Stourmouth
Sandwich Bay
Tyler Hill
Broad Oak
Westbere
Preston
Westmarsh
Great Stonar
St Clement
Blean
Hales Place
Stodmarsh
Ware
Elmstone
Hoaden
Toll
Royal St George
Fordwich
Augustine's Abbey
Wickhambreaux
Ickham
Shatterling
Ash
Marshborough
A256
Sandwich
The Small Downs
Howletts Zoo Park
A257
Littlebourne
Wingham
Woodnesborough
Worth
Goodwin Sands
CANTERBURY
Bramling
Staple
Goodnestone
Eastry
Ham
The Downs
Bekesbourne
Patrixbourne
Goodnestone Park
Knowlton
Finglesham
Betteshanger
DEAL
Deal Castle
Adisham
Higham Park
Chillenden
Nonington
Sholden
Northbourne
Nackington
Bridge
B2046
Walmer
Walmer Castle
Bishopsbourne
Kingston
Aylesham
Easole Street
Tilmanstone
Great Mongeham
A258
Lower Hardres
Snowdown
Elvington
Womenswold
A2
A256
A258
Upper Hardres Court
Barham
St Nicholas
91
Dover 10
Dover 6
Dover 6

106 CTFM Radio
FM 106

Neptune Radio
FM 96.4/106.8

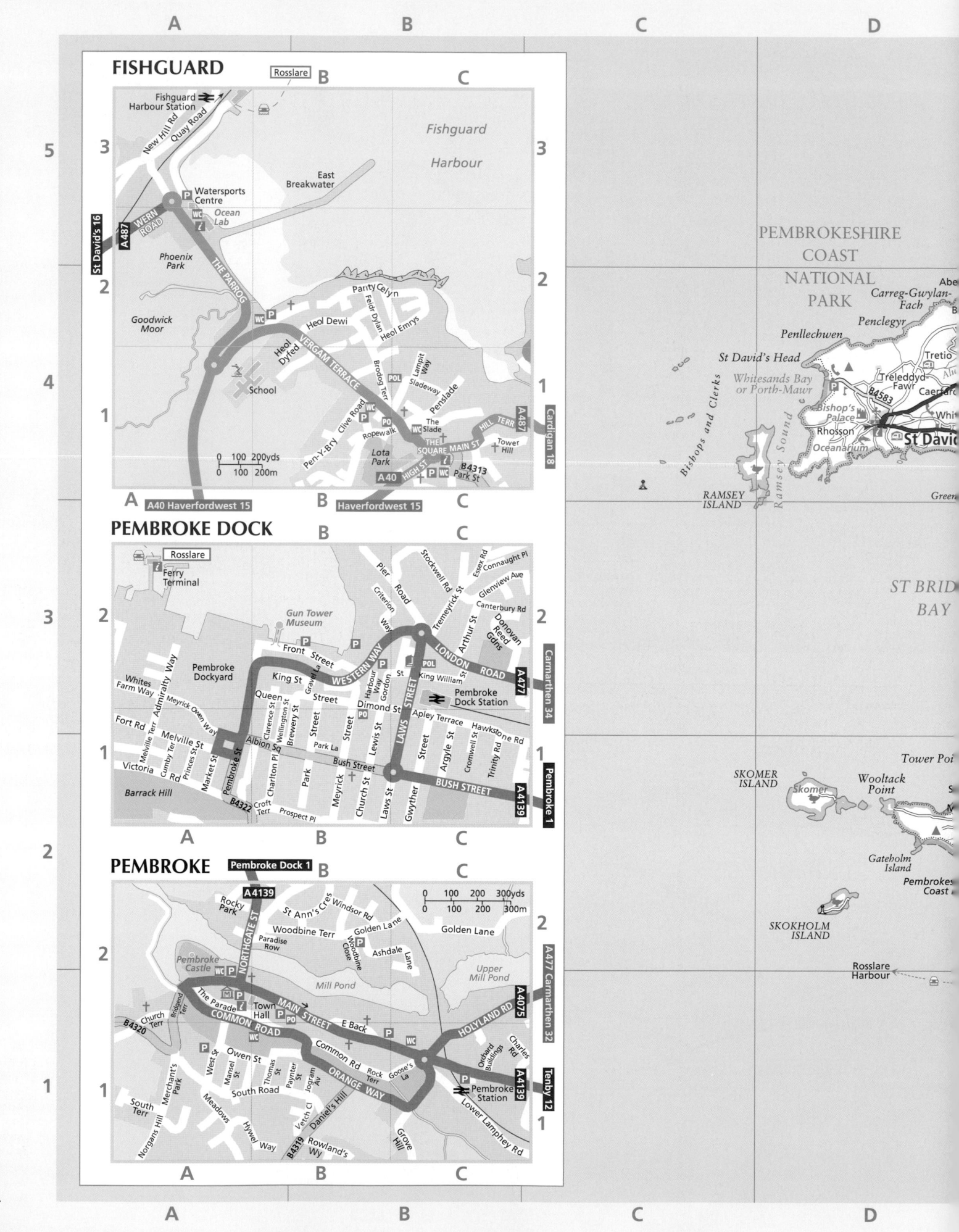

TOWN PLANS
Fishguard p104
Pembroke
p104
Pembroke
Dock p104
Tenby p396

see p430
for a
touring
guide to
this map

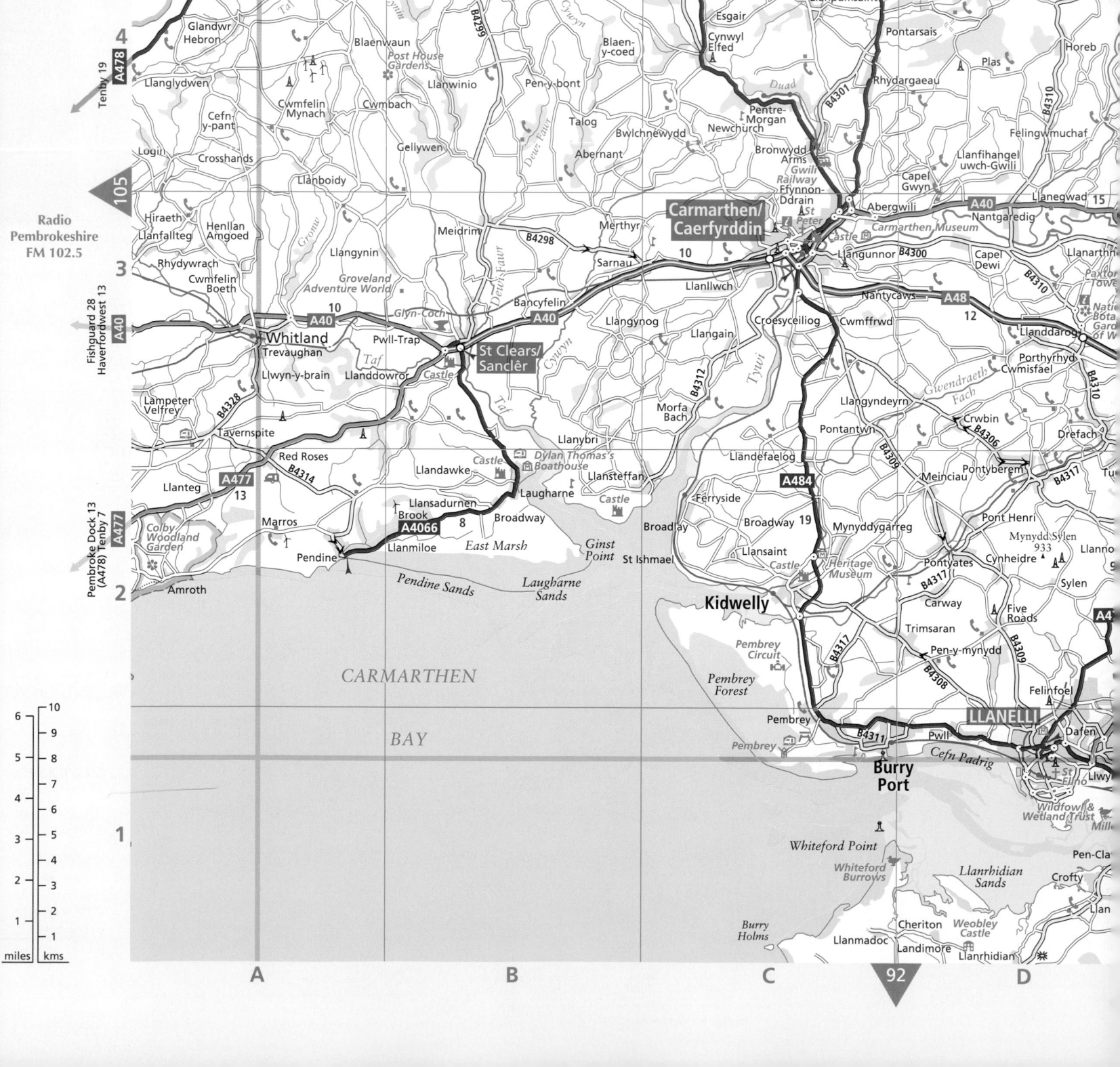

Cardigan 3 | A487

Cardigan 5 | A484

Lampeter 13 | A475

Lampeter 6 | A485

118

105

92

St David's 29
Fishguard 13 | A487

Tenby 19 | A478

Radio
Pembrokeshire
FM 102.5

Fishguard 28
Haverfordwest 13 | A40

Pembroke Dock 13
(A478) Tenby 7 | A477

Llantood
Bridell
Rhos-hill
Bro Meiban
Llanfair-Nant-Gwyn-Eglwyswen
Blaenffos
Frenni Fawr 1295
A478
Crymych
Hermon
Pentre Galar
Glandwr
Hebron
Llanglydwen
Cefn-y-pant
Login
Crosshands
Hiraeth
Henllan Amgoed
Rhydwrach
Cwmfelin Boeth
Lampeter Velfrey
Tavernspite
Red Roses
Llanteg
Marros
Colby Woodland Garden
Amroth

Cenarth
Abercych
Newchapel
Boncath
Bwlchygroes
Star
Tegryn
Llanfyrnach
Dinas
Trelech
Blaenwaun
Post House Gardens
Cwmfelin Mynach
Cwmbach
Gellywen
Llanboidy
Llanfallteg
Rhydywrach
Groveland Adventure World
Llangynin
Meidrim
Whitland
Trevaughan
Llwyn-y-brain
Llanddowror
Pwll-Trap
Glyn-Coch
Castle
St Clears/Sanclêr
B4328
B4314
Red Roses
Llansadurnen Brook
A4066
Llandawke
Laugharne
Dylan Thomas's Boathouse
Llanybri
Llansteffan
Broadway
Castle
Pendine
Llanmiloe
East Marsh
Pendine Sands

Newcastle Emlyn
Holy Trinity
Pentrecagal 6
Felindre
Penrherber
Capel Iwan
Cilrhedyn
Moelfre 1100
Cwmorgan
Bryn Iwan
B4333
Cwmfelin
Pen-y-bont
Llanwinio
Talog
Abernant
Bancyfelin
A40
Morfa Bach
Ginst Point
St Ishmael
Laugharne Sands

Llandyfríog
Teifi Valley Railway
Penrhiw-llan
Henllan
Llangeler
Drefach
Saron
Drefelin
Cwmpengraig
Rhos
Hermon 14
A484
Blaen-y-coed
Cynwyl Elfed
Esgair
Pentre-Morgan
Newchurch
Bwlchnewydd
Merthyr
Sarnau
B4298
Llangynog
Llangain
Llanllwch
Llandefaelog
Ferryside
Broadlay
Broadway

Penrhiw-llan
Llandysul
Llanfihangel-ar-arth
Llangeler
Drefach 6
A486
Pentre-cwrt
Bancyffordd
Dolgran
Pencader
Alltwalis
Llanpumsaint
Llanllawddog
Pontarsais
Rhydargaeau
Bronwydd Arms
Gwili Railway
Ffynnon-Ddrain
Abergwili
St Peter
Carmarthen/Caerfyrddin
Castle
Carmarthen Museum
Llangunnor
Croesyceiliog
Nantycaws
Cwmffrwd
Llanddarog
Nantgaredig
Capel Dewi
A48
A40

Maesycrugiau
St Tyssul
Teifi
Llanfihangel-ar-arth
Llanllwni
Gwarallt
New Inn
Gwyddgrug
Gwernogle
Brechfa
Horeb
Plas
Felingwmuchaf
Llanfihangel uwch-Gwili
Capel Gwyn
Llanegwad
A485
A485
23
B4336
B4459
1319
A40
15

Llangyndeyrn
Pontantwn
Meinciau
Llansaint
Castle
Heritage Museum
Kidwelly
Mynyddygarreg
Trimsaran
Carway
Pembrey Circuit
Pembrey Forest
Pembrey
Burry Port
Whiteford Point
Whiteford Burrows
Burry Holms
CARMARTHEN

BAY

Cheriton
Weobley Castle
Llanmadoc
Landimore
Llanrhidian

Pont Henri
Mynydd Sylen 933
Pontyberem
Pontyates
Five Roads
Cynheidre
Sylen
Pen-y-mynydd
Felinfoel
LLANELLI
Dafen
Cefn Padrig
St Elli
Wildfowl & Wetland Trust
Llanrhidian Sands
Pen-Clawdd
Crofty

Tywi
Gwendraeth Fach
B4309
B4306
Drefach
Porthyrhyd
Cwmisfael
B4310
B4312
B4317
B4308
B4311
B4317

10
6
9
8
7
6
5
4
3
2
1
miles | kms

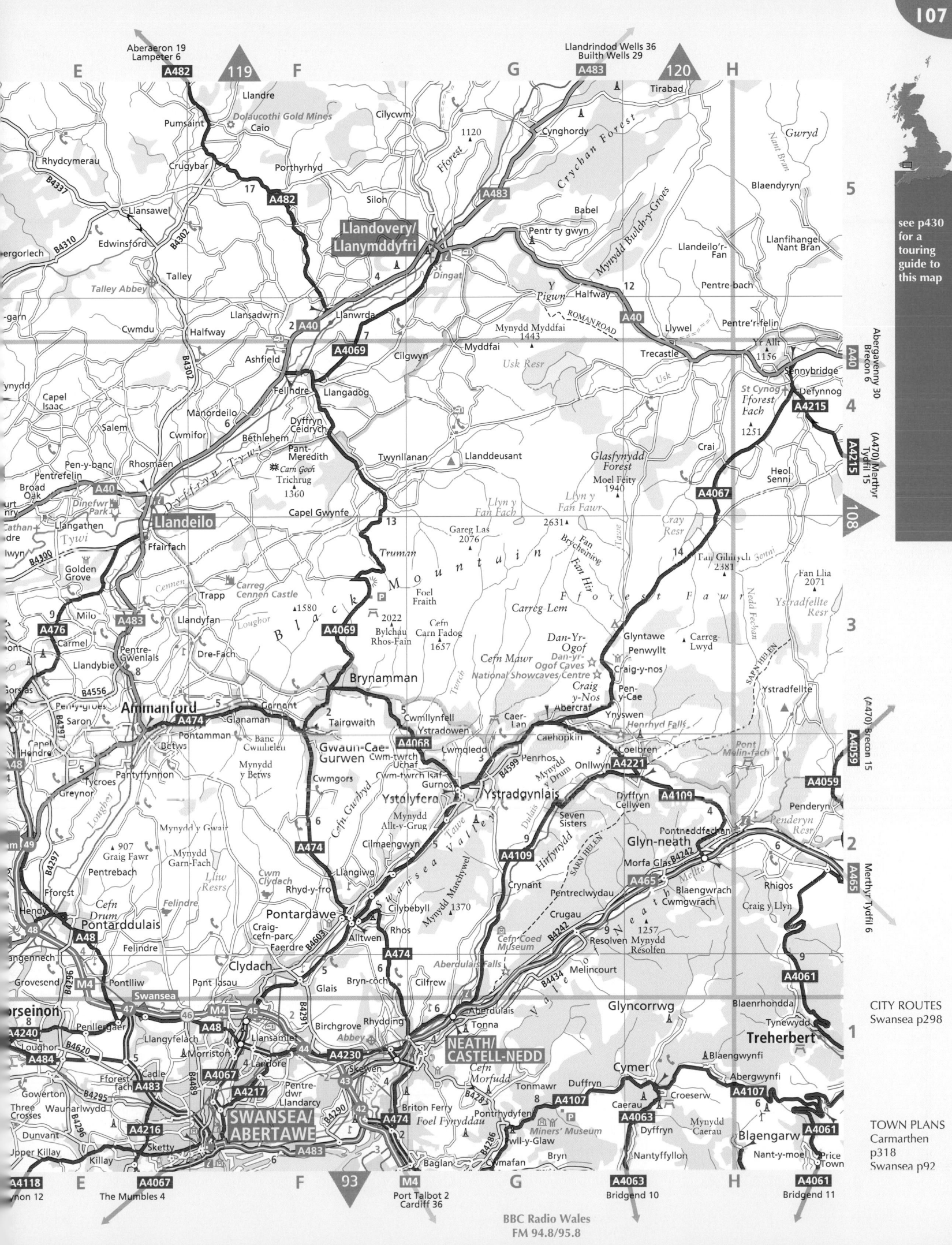

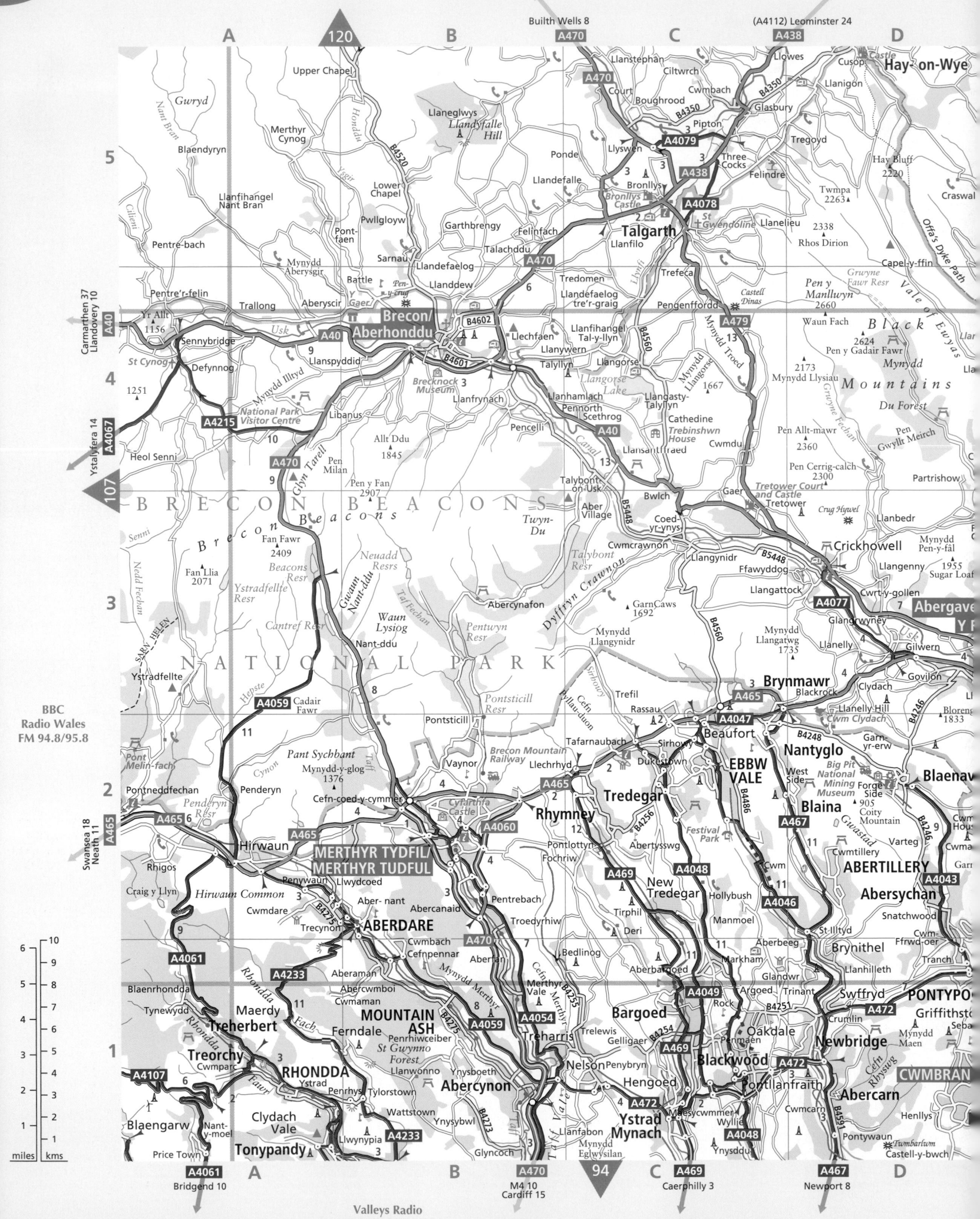

see p431 for a touring guide to this map

102.4 Severn
Valley Sound
FM 102.4/103

TOWN PLANS
Brecon p314
Chepstow p320
Hereford p339
Monmouth
p366
Ross-on-Wye
p382

BBC Radio Wales
FM 95.1/95.2/95.9

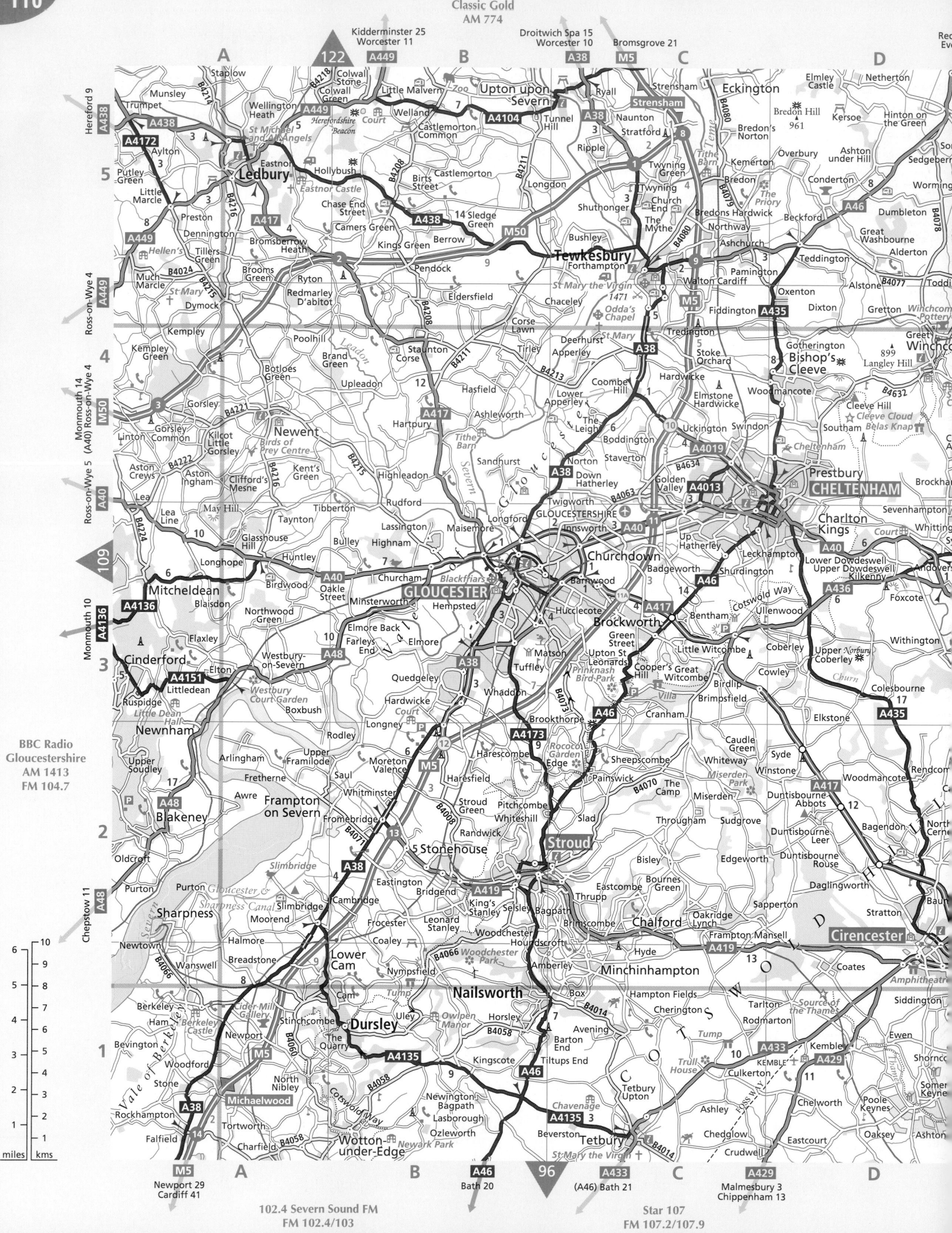

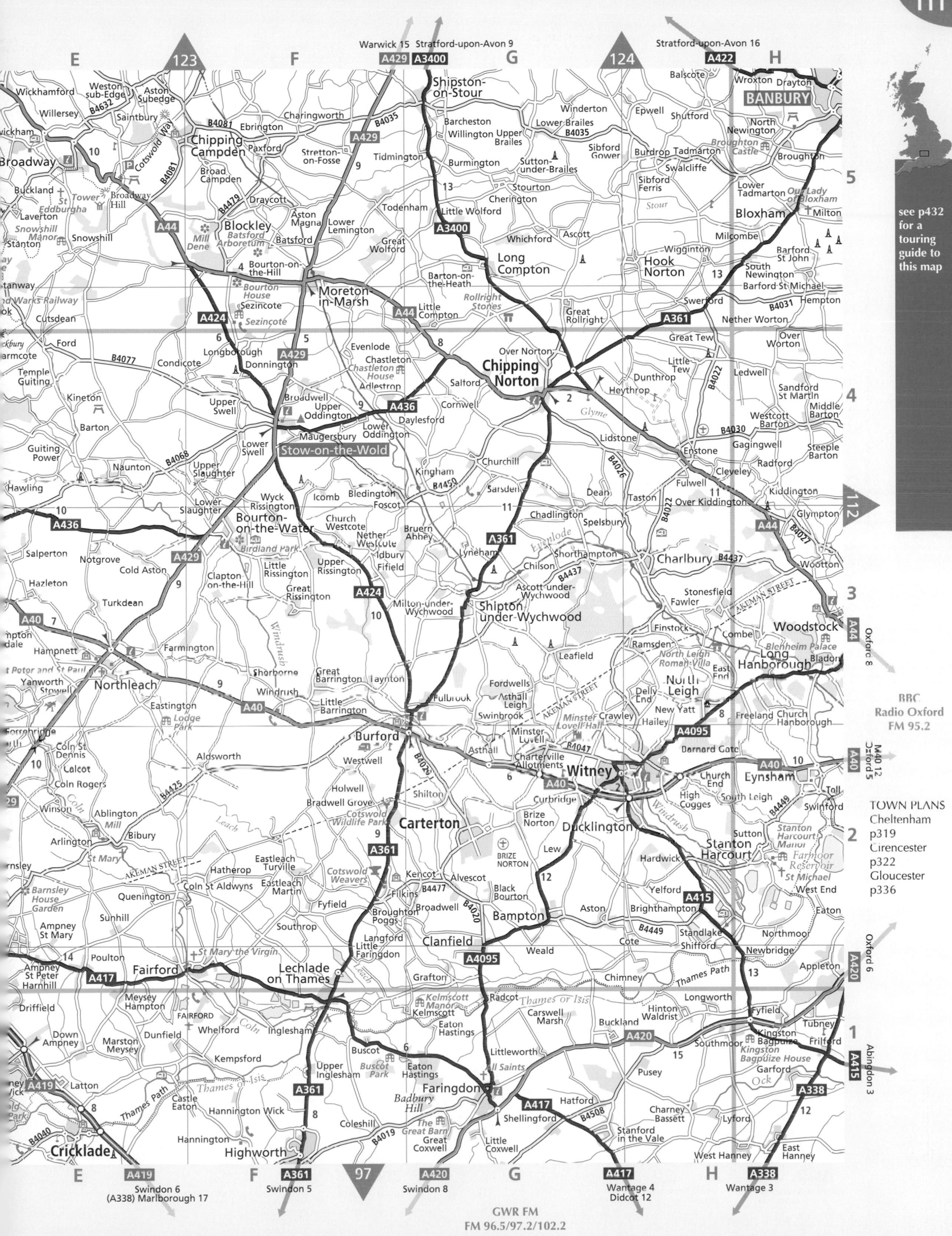

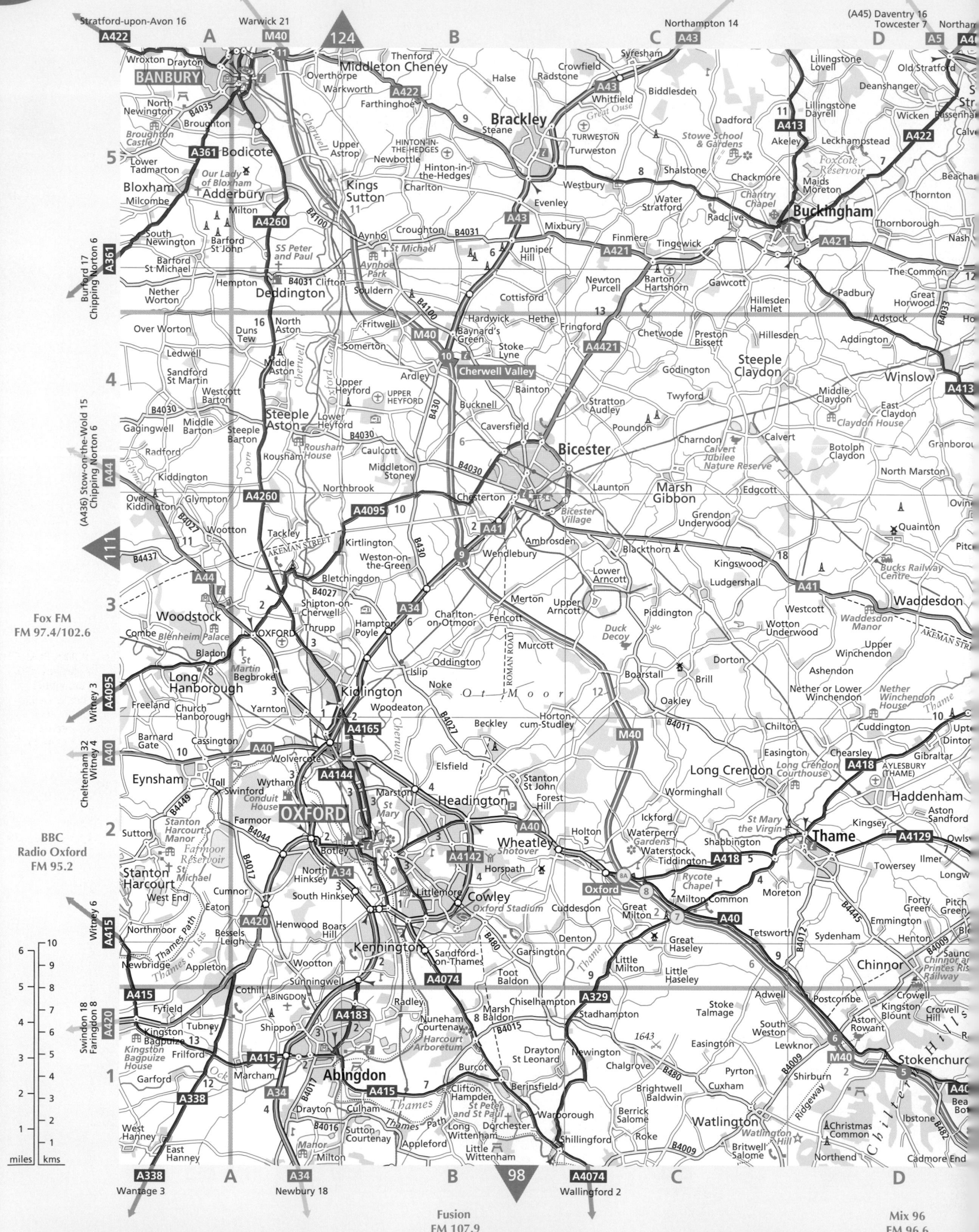

Fox FM
FM 97.4/102.6

BBC
Radio Oxford
FM 95.2

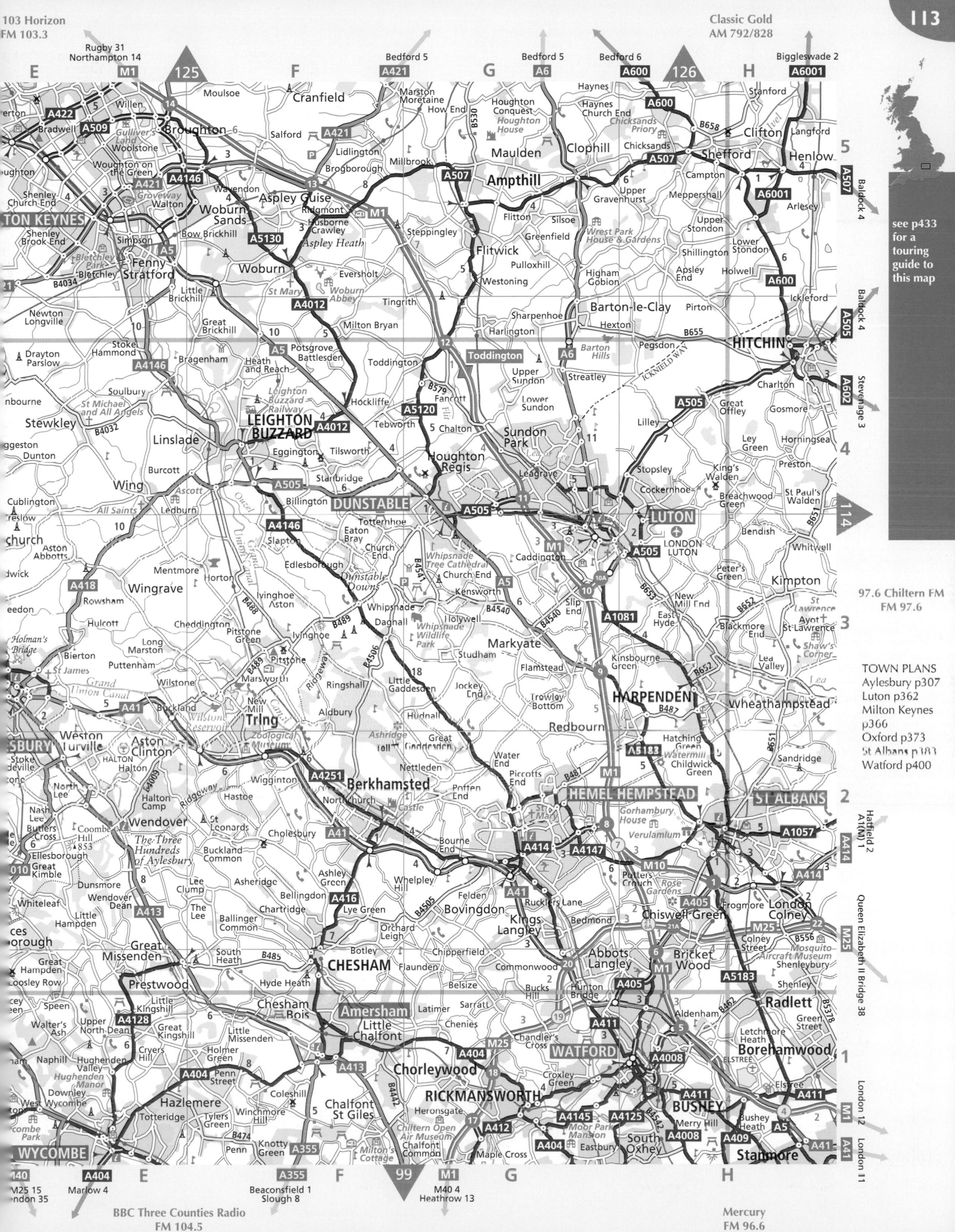

BBC
Three Counties
Radio
FM 103.8

BBC Radio Essex
FM 95.3/103.5

see p434 for a touring guide to this map

SGR Colchester
FM 96.1

Dream 107.7
FM 107.7

TOWN PLANS
Chelmsford
p319
St Albans p383
Stevenage
p390

Colchester 9

Ipswich 18
Colchester 3

Haverhill 5

Bury St Edmunds 17

Elizabeth II Bridge 11

Basildon 4

Basildon 2

Basildon 3
(A13) Tilbury 17

Major towns and places:

Sudbury
Great Cornard
Halstead
Earls Colne
Coggeshall
Braintree
Bocking
Great Dunmow
Thaxted
Chelmsford
Witham
Kelvedon
Tiptree
Heybridge
Maldon
Great Baddow
Galleywood
Writtle
Danbury
Ingatestone
Billericay
Brentwood
Wickford
Runwell
Hockley
Ashingdon
Burnham-on-Crouch
South Woodham Ferrers
Hullbridge
Battlesbridge
Rawreth
Maylandsea
Mayland
Steeple
Mundon
Purleigh
Latchingdon
Althorne
Stow Maries
Cold Norton
Great Canney
Woodham Ferrers
Rettendon
South Hanningfield
West Hanningfield
East Hanningfield
Bicknacre
Sandon
Little Baddow
Woodham Walter
Woodham Mortimer
Hazeleigh
Langford
Heybridge Basin
Northey Island
Osea Island
Blackwater
Goldhanger
Tollesbury
Tolleshunt Major
Tolleshunt Knights
Tolleshunt D'Arcy
Salcott
Great Wigborough
Layer Marney
Layer Breton
Layer de la Haye
Birch
Messing
Inworth
Feering
Marks Tey
Great Tey
Little Tey
Aldham
Stanway
Eight Ash Green
Fordstreet
Chappel
Wakes Colne
White Colne
Colne Engaine
Greenstead Green
Gosfield
Sible Hedingham
Castle Hedingham
Great Yeldham
Little Yeldham
Toppesfield
Stambourne
Ridgewell
Tilbury Juxta Clare
Birdbrook
Steeple Bumpstead
Helions Bumpstead
Red Oaks Hill
Hempstead
Radwinter
Wimbish
Debden Green
Cutlers Green
Cherry Green
Monk Street
Duton Hill
Lindsell
Great Easton
Little Easton
Bamber's Green
Great Dunmow
Little Dunmow
Felsted
Barnston
Great Waltham
Little Waltham
Howe Street
Pleshey
High Easter
Good Easter
Mashbury
Chignall Smealy
Chignall St James
Broomfield
Writtle
Roxwell
Willingale
Fyfield
Norton Mandeville
Blackmore
Doddinghurst
Mountnessing
Shenfield
Hutton
Ingrave
Brook Street
Herongate
East Horndon
Stock
Buttsbury
Margaretting
Fryerning
Mill Green

Colne Valley Railway
Castle
Gosfield Hall
Leez Priory
Saling Hall
Andrewsfield
Hanningfield Reservoir
Danbury Common
Hyde Hall
Hatfield Peverel
Chipping Hill
East Anglian Railway Museum
Prestons
Countess Cross
Paycocke's
Coggeshall Abbey
Brookes Nature Reserve
All Saints

A-roads: A1017, A1124, A131, A134, A130, A120, A12, A414, A1060, A1114, A132, A129, A176, A1245, A12, A1245

B-roads: B1054, B1057, B1053, B1051, B1184, B1008, B1002, B1007, B1009, B1010, B1012, B1018, B1019, B1022, B1023, B1026, B1024, B1137, B1389, B1508

Dream 100 FM
FM 100.2

BBC Radio Suffolk
FM 95.5/103.9/104.6

Southwold 36
Woodbridge 6

(A1214) Ipswich 3

Hadleigh 2

128 A1071

SGR Colchester
FM 96.1

Halstead 5

BBC
Radio Essex
FM 95.3/103.5

Sudbury 2 · A134

Key map towns and labels (north section):

Groton, Newton, Boxford, Bower House Tye, Hadleigh Heath, Lower Layham, Upper Layham, Copdock, IPSWICH, Nacton, Bucklesham, Levington, Trimley St Martin, Trimley St Mary, Shotley, Shotley Gate, Harwich, Dovercourt, Parkeston, Ramsey, Little Oakley, Great Oakley, Wix, Horsleycross Street, Horsley Cross, Beaumont, Tendring, Weeley, Weeley Heath, Thorpe-le-Soken, Kirby-le-Soken, Kirby Cross, Walton-the-Naze, Frinton-on-Sea, Great Holland, Holland-on-Sea, CLACTON-ON-SEA, Great Clacton, Little Clacton, Jaywick, Seawick, St Osyth, St Osyth Marsh, Point Clear, East Mersea, West Mersea, Mersea Island, Brightlingsea, Wivenhoe, Rowhedge, Fingringhoe, Abberton, Langenhoe, Peldon, Great Wigborough, Salcott, Tollesbury, Tolleshunt D'arcy, Tolleshunt Knights, Goldhanger, Maylandsea, Mayland, Steeple, Tillingham, Bradwell on Sea, Bradwell Waterside, St Lawrence, Ramsey Island, Southminster, Burnham-on-Crouch, Althorne, Ostend, Stoneyhills, Montsale, Ridgemarsh, Courtsend, Churchend, Paglesham Churchend, Paglesham Eastend, Wallasea Island, Foulness Island, COLCHESTER, Stanway, Marks Tey, Copford Green, Easthorpe, Birch, Layer Breton, Layer Marney, Layer-de-la-Haye, Shrub End, Heckfordbridge, Blackheath, Alresford, Thorrington, Aingers Green, Great Bentley, Frating Green, Elmstead Market, Crockleford Heath, Ardleigh, Dedham, Langham, Stratford St Mary, East Bergholt, Brantham, Cattawade, Manningtree, Mistley, Lawford, Bradfield, Wrabness, Holbrook, Stutton, Harkstead, Erwarton, Chelmondiston, Pin Mill, Woolverstone, Freston, Wherstead, Belstead, Capel St Mary, Raydon, Higham, Polstead, Stoke-by-Nayland, Nayland, Bures, West Bergholt, Fordham, Aldham, Ford Street, Fox Street, Mile End

Roads: A134, A1071, A12, A14, A137, A1232, A120, A133, A1124, A1408, B1070, B1068, B1081, B1029, B1080, B1035, B1352, B1414, B1456, B1033, B1441, B1442, B1032, B1027, B1025, B1022, B1023, B1026, B1021, B1018, B1010, B1508, B1028

Colne, Stour, Brett, Orwell, Blackwater, Crouch, Roman River, Abberton Reservoir, Ardleigh Reservoir, Alton Water Reservoir, Hamford Water, Horsey Island, Hamford Water, The Naze, Gunfleet, Colne Point, Mersea Flats, The Nass, Osea Island, Dengie Flat, Ray Sand, Foulness Sands, Holliwell Point, Foulness Point, Sales Point, St Peter's Chapel, St Peter's Flat

miles / kms scale

CLACTON-ON-SEA (inset)

Colchester 15 · A133

Clacton Station, Skelmersdale Road, Beaconsfield Road, Granville Road, High Street, Holland Road, Chapman Road, Carnarvon Road, Dudley Rd, Warwick Rd, Herbert Rd, Page Road, St Osyth Road, Meredith Road, Market, Wellesley Road, Alexandra Rd, Princes Theatre, Anchor Road, Pier Avenue, Hayes Road, The Grove, Station Road, Multi-Storey, Waterglade Retail Park, Rosemary Rd W, Rosemary Road, Superstore, Ellis Road, Jackson Road, Agate Road, Pier Avenue, West Avenue, Colne Road, Pallister Rd, Orwell Rd, Beach Rd, Marine Parade East, Blenheim Rd, Park Road, Leas Rd, Alton Park Road, Wash Lane, Penfold Road, Edith Rd, Alton Road, Vicarage Gdns, Beatrice Road, St. James's, West Cliff Theatre, Clacton & District Hospital, Arnold Road, Marine Parade West, Pier Gap, Pier, Aquarium

FELIXSTOWE

A 14 Ipswich 12

A 154 · GROVE RD · Colneis Road
Recreation La
High Road West · Exeter Road · Glenfield Ave · Dellwood Avenue
Graham Rd · Fairfield Ave · Fleetwood Rd
Seaton Rd · Kensley Rd · Chester Road · High Road West · High Road East
Cornwall Road · Town Station · A 1021 · Croute Rd · Road
Bridge Rd · St · Andrew's · Gainsborough Rd
Valley Walk · A 154 · Cowley Rd · Penfold Rd · York Road · Felix Rd
Cobbold Ave · Princes Road · Queen's Road · B1082 · Rd · Renelagh
Newry Rd · Surrey Rd · Crescent · Tomline Road · Victoria St · Hamilton Gdns
Goyfield Avenue · Mill Lane · Leopold Rd · Highfield Rd · Hamilton Road
Mill Lane · Chaucer Rd · ORWELL ROAD · Wolsey Gdns · West · Spa Pavilion
GARRISON LANE · A 1021 · Martello Tower · Town Hall · Road
Lincoln Ter · Bacton Road · North Sea
B1082 Undercliff · Leisure Centre · Pier (no public access)
LANGER RD · Manning Rd · Sea Road
A 154 · Children's Railway

0 100 200 300yds
0 100 200 300m

A 14 Felixstowe Docks 1

see p435 for a touring guide to this map

HARWICH

0 200 400 600 800 yds
0 200 400 600 800 m

Cuxhaven, Esbjerg, Hook of Holland

Parkeston Quay
Passenger Terminal
Car Ferry Terminal · Harwich International Station
Coller Rd · River Stour
Una Rd · Station Road · Garland Road · Ramsey Creek
Europa Wy · Superstore
A 120 · Navyard Wharf
Parkeston Road · New Pier · THE QUAY · Electric Palace
Clarke's Rd · Fryatt Ave · The Vineway · Deepdale Road · King's Head St · West · Church St · Guildhall
Shaftesbury Ave · The Ridgeway · Bath Side · Harwich Town Stn · Radio Museum
Ashley Road · King George's Avenue · A 120 · Maritime Museum · The Redoubt
Colchester 19 · A 120 · Main Road · Football Ground · Fernlea Rd · Main Road · Lifeboat Museum
Highfield Ave · Hill Rd · Dovercourt Bay Station · Grafton Road · Barrack Lane · Beacon Hill
Harwich & District Hospital · B1352 · High Street · Cliff Park · Kingsway
B1414 · Marine Pde · Dovercourt Bay
Fronk's Rd · Minesweeper Memorial

(left map)
129
Alderton
Bawdsey
B1083
Deben
Old Felixstowe
FELIXSTOWE
Esbjerg
Cuxhaven
Hook of Holland

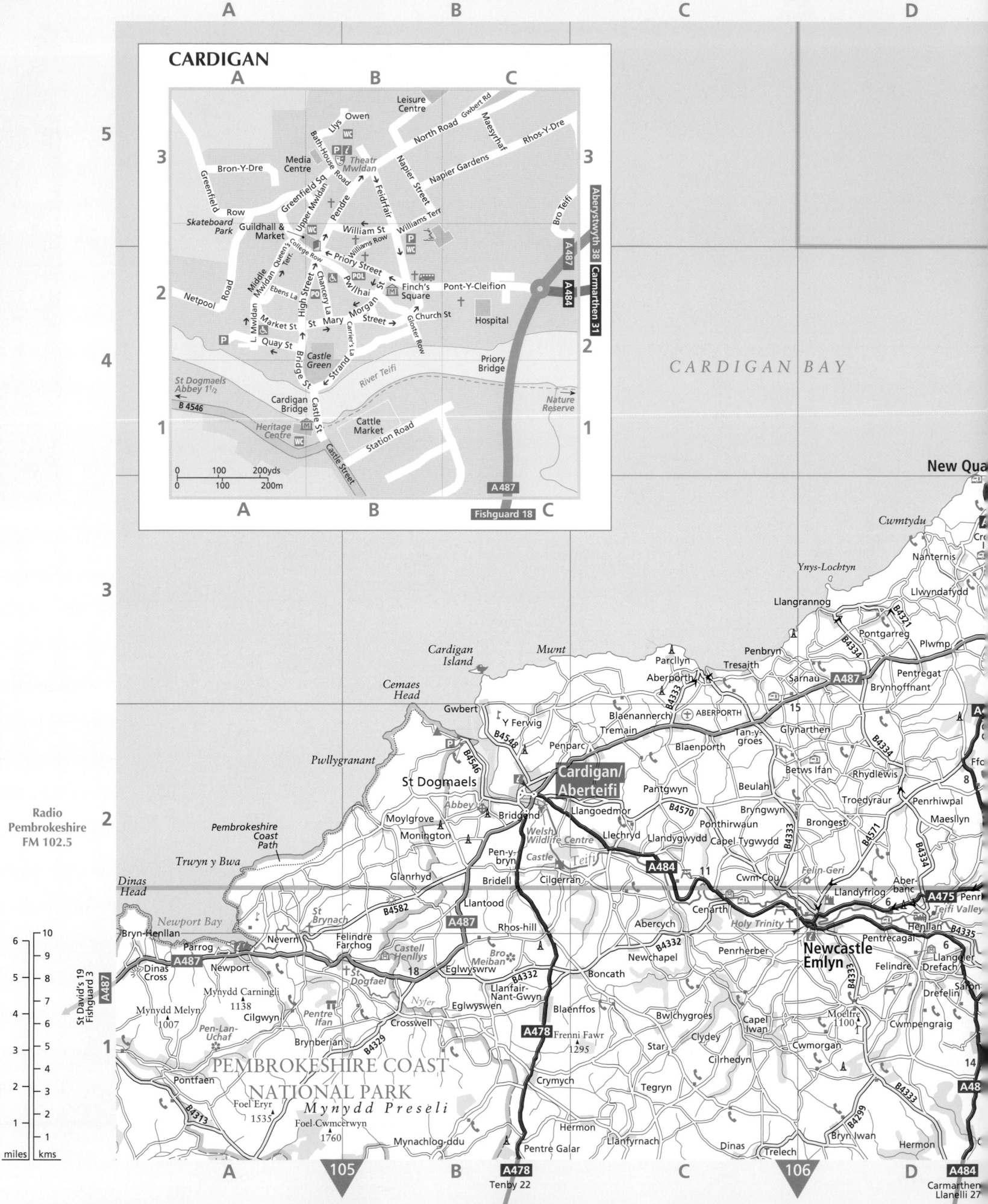

CARDIGAN

Leisure Centre
Owen
Llys
Media Centre
Bron-Y-Dre
Theatr Mwldan
North Road
Gwbert Rd
Maesyrhaf
Rhos-Y-Dre
Greenfield Row
Skateboard Park
Greenfield Sq
Upper Mwldan
Pendre
Napier Street
Napier Gardens
Bro Teifi
Bath-House Road
Feldrfair
Williams Terr
Guildhall & Market
William St
Williams Row
Priory Street
Middle Mwldan
Queen's College Row
Tan
Ebens La
High Street
Chancery La
Pwllhai
Morgan Street
Finch's Square
Pont-Y-Cleifion
Netpool Road
St Mary
Carrier's La
Gloster Row
Church St
Hospital
Market St
L. Mwldan
Quay St
Bridge St
Castle Green
Strand
River Teifi
Priory Bridge
St Dogmaels Abbey 1½
B 4546
Cardigan Bridge
Heritage Centre
Castle St
Cattle Market
Station Road
Nature Reserve
Aberystwyth 38
Carmarthen 31
A 487
A 484
A 487
Fishguard 18

0   100   200yds
0   100   200m

CARDIGAN BAY

New Qua

Cwmtydu
Ynys-Lochtyn
Llangrannog
Llwyndafydd
B4321
Pontgarreg
Plwmp
Parcllyn
Penbryn
Pentregat
Aberporth
Tresaith
Sarnau
A487
Brynhoffnant
B4333
ABERPORTH
Cardigan Island
Mwnt
15
Cemaes Head
Blaenannerch
Glynarthen
Gwbert
Y Ferwig
Tremain
Tan-y-groes
Betws Ifan
Rhydlewis
8
B4548
Penparc
Blaenporth
B4334
Pwllygranant
B4546
Cardigan/ Aberteifi
Pantgwyn
Bryngwyn
Troedyraur
Penrhiwpal
St Dogmaels
B4570
Ponthirwaun
B4571
Maesllyn
Pembrokeshire Coast Path
Abbey
Moylgrove
Bridgend
Llangoedmor
Welsh Wildlife Centre
Llechryd
Llandygwydd
Capel Tygwydd
B4333
Brongest
Monington
Trwyn y Bwa
Pen-y-bryn
Castle
Teifi
A484
Felin-Geri
Aber-banc
Dinas Head
Glanrhyd
Bridell
Cilgerran
11
Cwm-Cou
Llandyfriog
A475
Penr
Newport Bay
St Brynach
B4582
Llantood
Cenarth
6
Teifi Valley
Bryn-Henllan
Parrog
Nevern
Felindre Farchog
Rhos-hill
Abercych
Holy Trinity
Henllan
B4335
Dinas Cross
Newport
Castell Henllys
Bro Meiban
Newchapel
Penrherber
Newcastle Emlyn
Pentrecagal
Llangeler Drefach
6
A487
St Dogfael
18
Eglwyswrw
B4332
Boncath
Felindre
Salem
Drefelin
Mynydd Carningli 1138
Llanfair-Nant-Gwyn
Blaenffos
Capel Iwan
Moelfre 1100
Cwmpengraig
Cilgwyn
Eglwyswen
Bwlchygroes
14
Mynydd Melyn 1007
Pentre Ifan
Crosswell
A478
Clydey
Cwmorgan
Pen-Lan-Uchaf
Brynberian
B4329
Frenni Fawr 1295
Star
Cilrhedyn
Foel Eryr 1535
Pontfaen
Crymych
Tegryn
Bryn Iwan
Hermon
B4313
Foel-Cwmcerwyn 1760
Mynachlog-ddu
Pentre Galar
Hermon
Dinas
B4333
Trelech
A48

PEMBROKESHIRE COAST NATIONAL PARK
Mynydd Preseli

Radio Pembrokeshire FM 102.5

St David's 19 Fishguard 3
A487

105
B
A478
Tenby 22
106
A484
Carmarthen
Llanelli 27

miles   kms
6   10
5   9
     8
4   7
     6
3   5
     4
2   3
1   2
     1

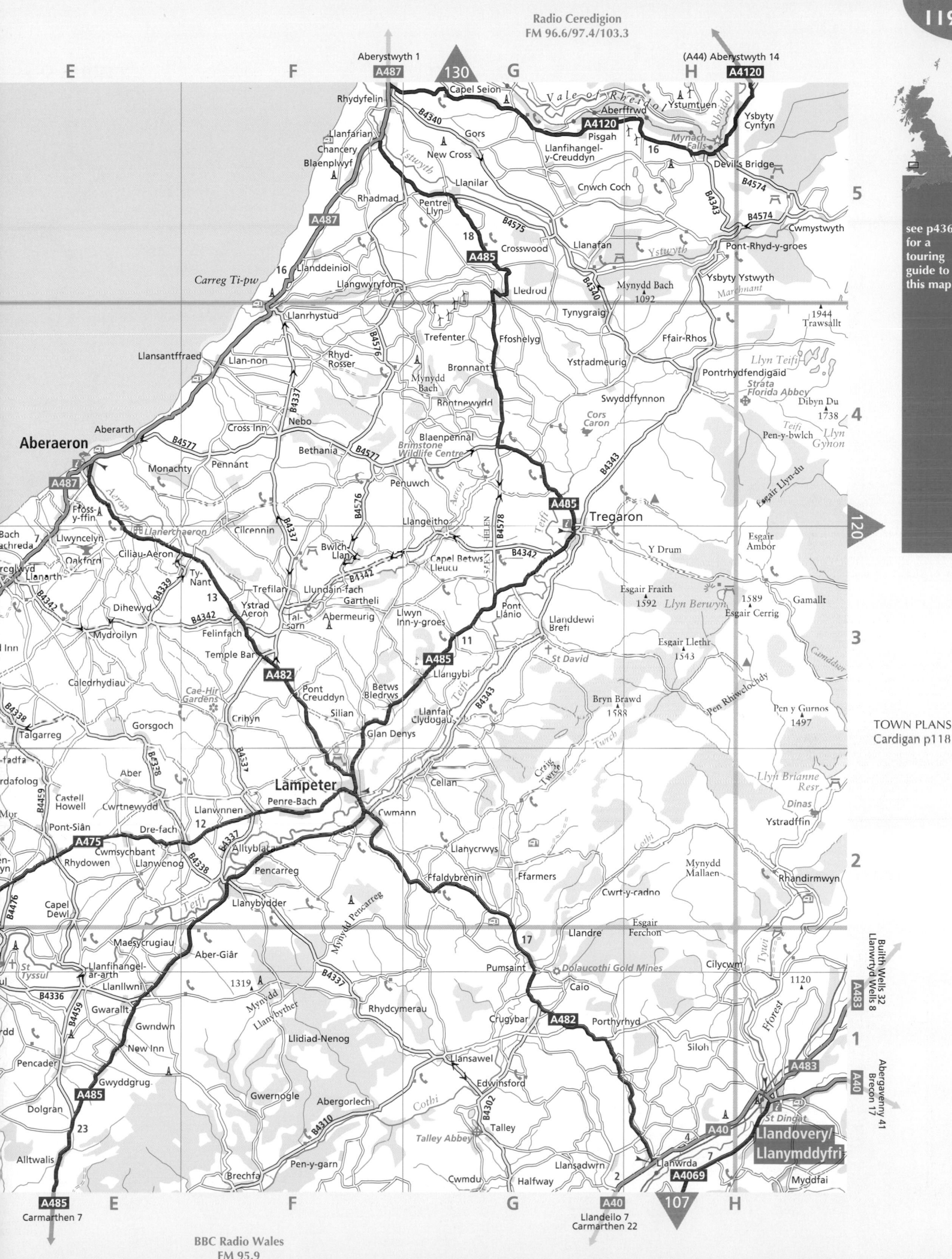

Radio Ceredigion
FM 96.6/97.4/103.3

Aberystwyth 1

(A44) Aberystwyth 14

A4120

Vale of Rheidol

Rhydyfelin   Capel Seion
B4340   Gors   Aberffrwd   Ystumtuen
Llanfarian   A4120   Pisgah   Ysbyty
Chancery   New Cross   Llanfihangel-   16   Mynach   Cynfyn
Blaenplwyf   y-Creuddyn   Falls
Rhadmad   Pentre-   Devil's Bridge
Llyn   Llanilar   B4574

A487   18   Cnwch Coch
                                         A485   Crosswood   Llanafan   B4343   Cwmystwyth
Carreg Ti-pw   Llandeiniol   B4575   Ystwyth   Pont-Rhyd-y-groes
16   Llangwyryfon   Lledrod   B4340   B4574
                                         Mynydd Bach
                                         1092   Ysbyty Ystwyth
Llanrhystud   Marchnant
                      Trefenter   Ffoshelyg   Trawsallt
Llansantffraed   Llan-non   Rhyd-   Bronnant   Tynygraig   Ffair-Rhos   1944
            Rosser   B4576   Ystradmeurig
Aberarth   B4577   Cross Inn   Mynydd   Bontnewydd   Pontrhydfendigaid   Strata
                   Bach   Swyddffynnon   Florida Abbey
Aberaeron   Nebo   Bethania   B4577   Blaenpennal   Cors   Llyn Teifi   Dibyn Du
            Monachty   Pennant   Brimstone   Caron   Teifi   1738
A487   Ciliau-Aeron   Wildlife Centre   Penuwch   Pen-y-bwlch   Llyn
Ffos-   Llwyncelyn   Cilcennin   Llangeitho   Esgair   Gynon
y-ffin   Llanerchaeron   B4337   Bwlch-   B4578   Tregaron   Ambor
Bach   Oakford   Trefilan   Llan   Capel Betws   Y Drum   Esgair Cerrig
Tachreda   Llanarth   Ty-   Llundain-fach   Lleucu   B4342   Gamallt
B4342   Nant   13   Ystrad   Gartheli   Esgair Fraith   Llyn Berwyn   1589
Dihewyd   Aeron   Abermeurig   Llwyn   1592   Esgair   Pen y Gurnos
Mydroilyn   B4342   Tal-   Inn-y-groes   Pont   Llanddewi   Esgair Llethr   1543   1497
            Felinfach   sarn   11   Llanio   Brefi   Pen Rhiwclochdy
Temple Bar   A485   Llangybi   St David   Bryn Brawd
Caledrhydiau   A482   Llanfair   1588
            Pont   Betws   Clydogau   B4343   Craig
B4338   Cae-Hir   Creuddyn   Bledrws   Twrce
Talgarreg   Gardens   Crihyn   Silian   Glan Denys   Llyn Brianne
                                                                Resr
                   Gorsgoch   Cellan   Dinas
Lampeter   Ystradffin
A475   Castell   Llanwnnen   Penre-Bach
       Howell   Cwrtnewydd   Cwmann
Pont-Siân   Dre-fach   12   Llanycrwys   Mynydd
       Cwmsychbant   Llanwenog   B4337   Mallaen   Rhandirmwyn
Rhydowen   Ffaldybrenin   Ffarmers
Capel   Pencarreg   Cwrt-y-cadno
Dewl   Llanybydder   Esgair
                                         Ferchon
Maesycrugiau   Aber-Giâr   Llandre
St   B4337   17   Pumsaint   Dolaucothi Gold Mines   Cilycwm
Tyssul   Llanfihangel-   1319   Caio   A482
        ar-arth   Rhydcymerau   Crugybar   Porthyrhyd
B4336   Llanllwni   A482
Gwarallt   Gwndwn   Llidiad-Nenog
Pencader   New Inn   Llansawel   Siloh
        Gwyddgrug   Llansawel   Edwinsford
Dolgran   A485   Gwernogle   Abergorlech
        23   B4302   Talley
Alltwalis   Pen-y-garn   Talley Abbey   Talley

see p436
for a
touring
guide to
this map

TOWN PLANS
Cardigan p118

Builth Wells 32
Llanwrtyd Wells 8
Abergavenny 41
Brecon 17
A483
A40

1120
A483
Llanwrda
A4069   Llandovery/
        Llanymddyfri
St Dingat
A40
Myddfai

A485   A40   107   H
Carmarthen 7   Llandeilo 7
            Carmarthen 22

BBC Radio Wales
FM 95.9

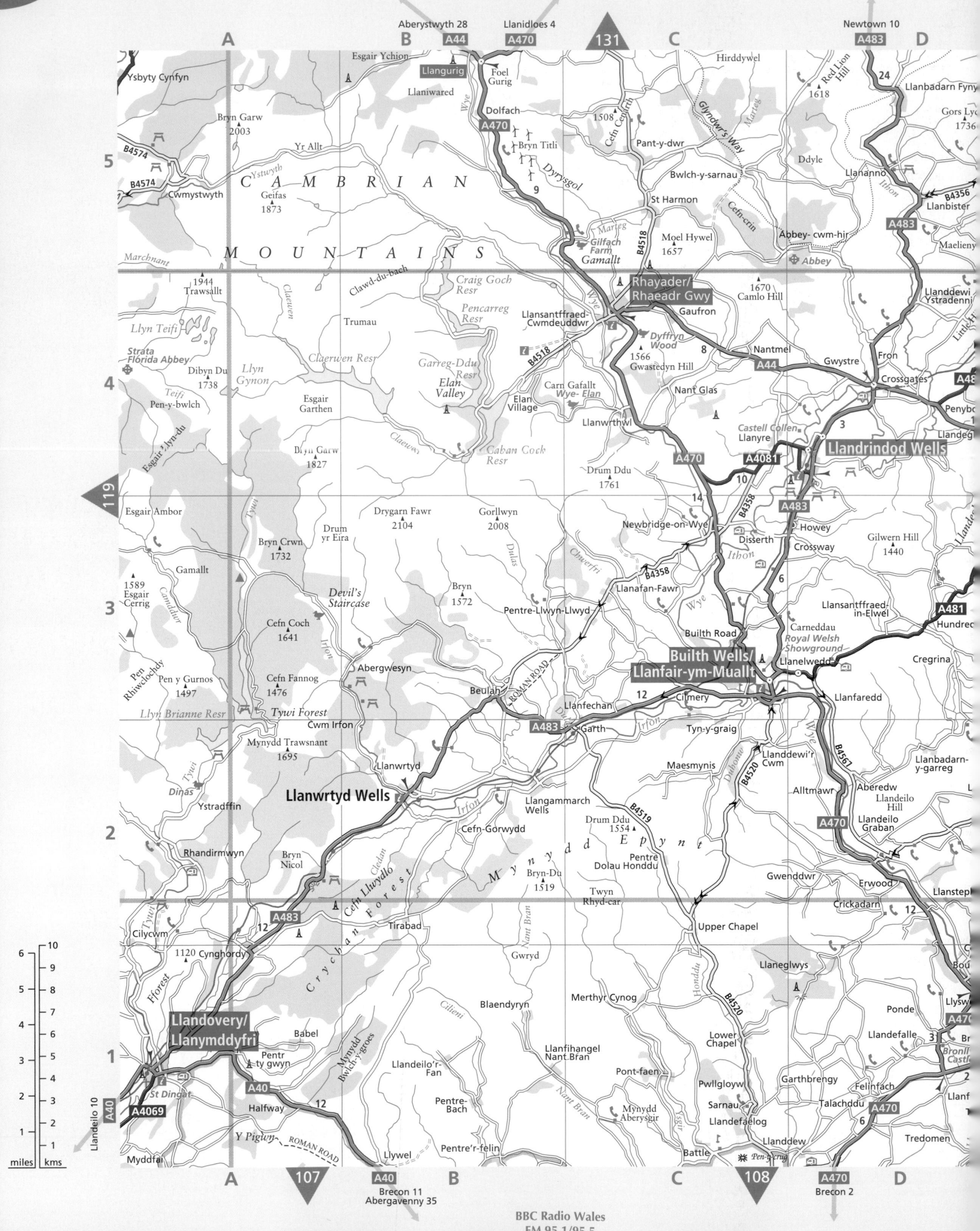

Sunshine 855
AM 855

BBC Hereford & Worcester
FM 94.7/104/104.6

see p437
for a
touring
guide to
this map

TOWN PLANS
Hereford p339
Ludlow p348

Classic Gold
AM 954/1530

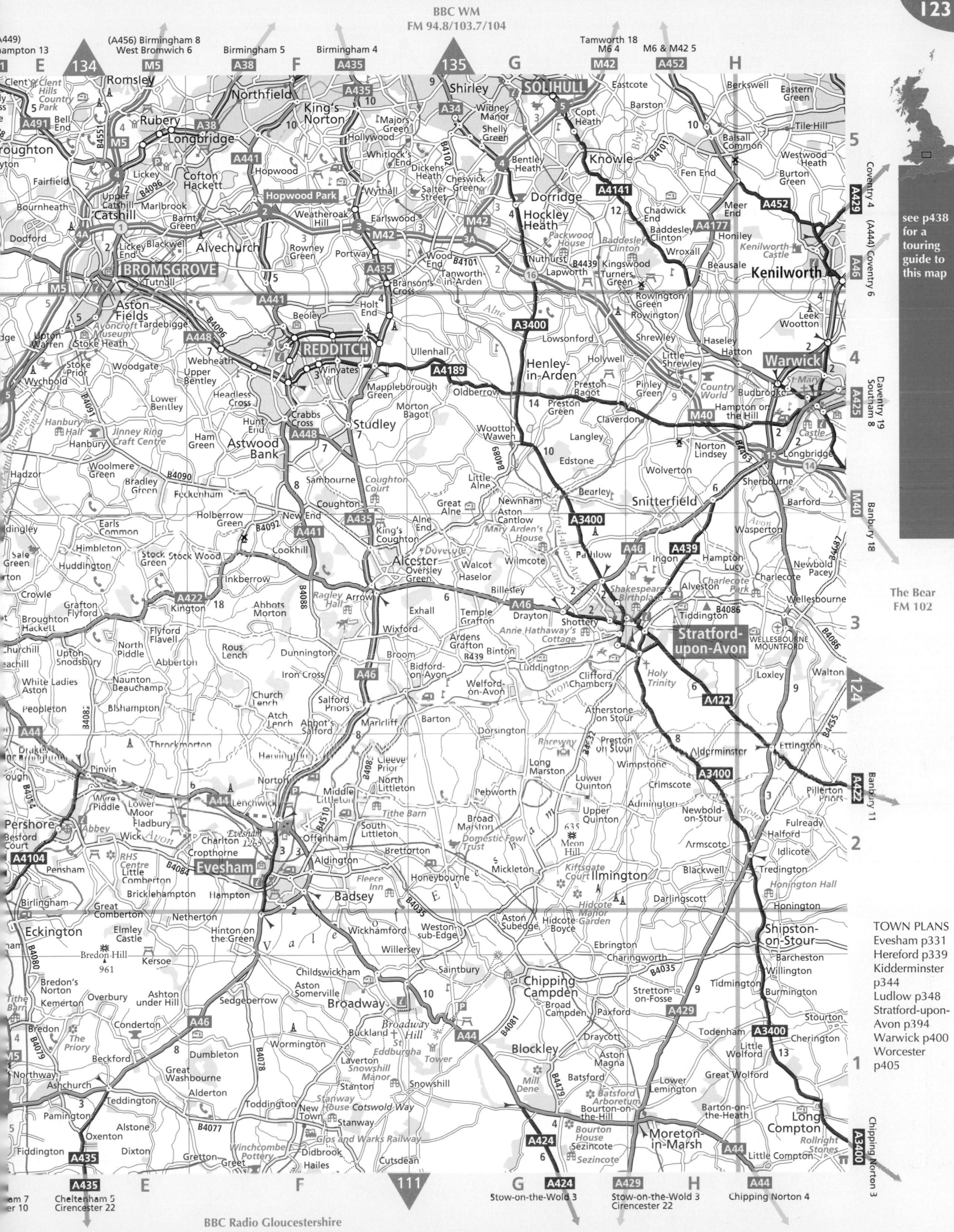

see p438 for a touring guide to this map

TOWN PLANS
Evesham p331
Hereford p339
Kidderminster p344
Ludlow p348
Stratford-upon-Avon p394
Warwick p400
Worcester p405

Mercia FM
FM 97/102.9

Rugby FM
FM 107.1

Birmingham 16
M42 7

(M69) Leicester 21
M6 & M69 1

Birmingham 29
M42 19

Leicester 17

BBC WM
FM 94.8/
103.7/104

The Bear
FM 102

COVENTRY
Eastern Green
Tile Hill B4101
Westwood Heath
Burton Green
A452
Earlsdon
Stivichall
A45
A429
Baginton
Lunt Roman Fort
Ryton-on-Dunsmore
Stoneleigh
Bubbenhall
A46
A445
Ashow
Kenilworth Castle
Kenilworth
Leek Wootton
Hill Wootton
Old Milverton
A452
Budbrooke
Hampton on the Hill
A46
St Mary
Warwick
Longbridge
A425
Sherbourne
Barford
Wasperton
Hampton Lucy
Newbold Pacey
Charlecote
Charlecote Park
B4086
WELLESBOURNE MOUNTFORD
Loxley
A429
A422
Walton
B4086
Combrook
Little Kineton
Ettington
Pillerton Hersey
Pillerton Priors
Fulready
Halford
Idlicote
Tredington
Honington Hall
Honington
Shipston-on-Stour
A3400
Barcheston
Willington
Tidmington
Burmington
Cherington
Little Wolford
Barton-on-the-Heath
Long Compton
Little Compton
Rollright Stones

Willenhall
A444
A4082
Binley
Binley Woods
Brandon
Wolston
Ryton Gardens
Ryton Pools
National Agricultural Museum
Stareton
Stretton-on-Dunsmore
Princethorpe
Frankton
Wappenbury
Weston under Wetherley
Eathorpe
Cubbington
Hunningham
ROYAL LEAMINGTON SPA
Offchurch
Leamington Hastings
Radford Semele
Whitnash
A452
Bishop's Tachbrook
Harbury
Chesterton
Bishop's Itchington
A425
Bascote
Bascote Heath
Ufton
Ashorne
Moreton Morrell
Warwick
M40
Lighthorne
Gaydon
B4451
Knightcote
Chadshunt
Compton Verney
Kineton
Temple Herdewyke
Butlers Marston
Radway
Edgehill 1642
Ratley
Edge Hill
Edgehill
Oxhill
Whatcote
Lower Tysoe
Upton House
Middle Tysoe
Upper Tysoe
Shenington
Alkerton
Brook Cottage
Winderton
Upper Brailes
Lower Brailes
Epwell
B4035
Burdrop
Sibford Gower
Sibford Ferris
Swalcliffe
Lower Tadmarton
Whichford
Ascott
Hook Norton
Wigginton
Swerford
Nether Worton

Brinklow
B4021
Bretford
Binley
King's Newnham
Church Lawford
A428
Long Lawford
Easenhall
Harborough Magna
Newbold on Avon
A4071
Bilton
Dunchurch
Bourton on Dunsmore
Thurlaston
Draycote
Draycote Water
Birdingbury
Marton
Hill
A426
Grandborough
Sawbridge
Long Itchington
Broadwell
Stockton
Lower Shuckburgh
Southam
Napton on the Hill
A425
Ladbroke
Marston Doles
Catesby
Hellidon
Priors Marston
Priors Hardwick
Upper Boddington
Charwelton
A361
Woodford Halse
Byfield
Wormleighton
Lower Boddington
Northend
Fenny Compton
Aston le Walls
Claydon
Chipping Warden
Edgcote
Farnborough
Avon Dassett
Mollington
Cropredy
1644 Cropredy
1469 Edgcote
Warmington
Shotteswell
Upper Wardington
Wardington
Williamscot
Great Bourton
Horley
Hornton
Hanwell
Wroxton
Drayton
Balscote
BANBURY
A422
North Newington
Broughton Castle
Tadmarton
Broughton
Bodicote
Our Lady of Bloxham
A4260
Bloxham
Adderbury
Milcombe
South Newington
Barford St John
Barford St Michael
Milton
SS Peter & Paul Clifton
A361
Deddington
Hempton

Cosford
Newton
A426
Clifton upon Dunsmore
RUGBY
Hillmorton
B4429
Barby
Kilsby
M45
Braunston
A45
Willoughby
Welton
Nethercote
Staverton
Daventry
Daventry Reservoir
Norton
Dodford
A45
Newnham
Badby
Everdon
Preston Capes
Canons Ashby
Eydon
Culworth
Weston
Moreton Pinkney
Wardington
Sulgrave Manor
Sulgrave
Chacombe
Thorpe Mandeville
Marston St Lawrence
Middleton Cheney
Greatworth
Warkworth
A422
Farthinghoe
Overthorpe
Thenford
Halse
Radstone
Upper Astrop
Newbottle
HINTON-IN-THE-HEDGES
Hinton-in-the-Hedges
Charlton
Kings Sutton
Aynho
Aynhoe Park
Souldern
St Michael
B4031
Croughton
Juniper Hill

Stanford Hall
Swinford
Stanford on Avon
Catthorpe
A14
Lilbourne
Claycoton
M1
A5
A4038
Yelvertoft
Crick
West Haddon
Watford
Grand Union Canal
Ashby St Ledgers
A45
Watford Gap
Long Buckby
A5
Weedon Bec
Upper Weedon
Arbury Hill 734
A43
Brackley
Whitfield
Steane
TURWESTON
Turweston
Westbury
Evenley
Mixbury
A421
Cottisford
Newton Purcell

Stratford-upon-Avon 6
Stratford-upon-Avon 7
Stratford-upon-Avon 4
Stow-on-the-Wold 13
Stow-on-the-Wold 13
(A439) Stratford-upon-Avon 6

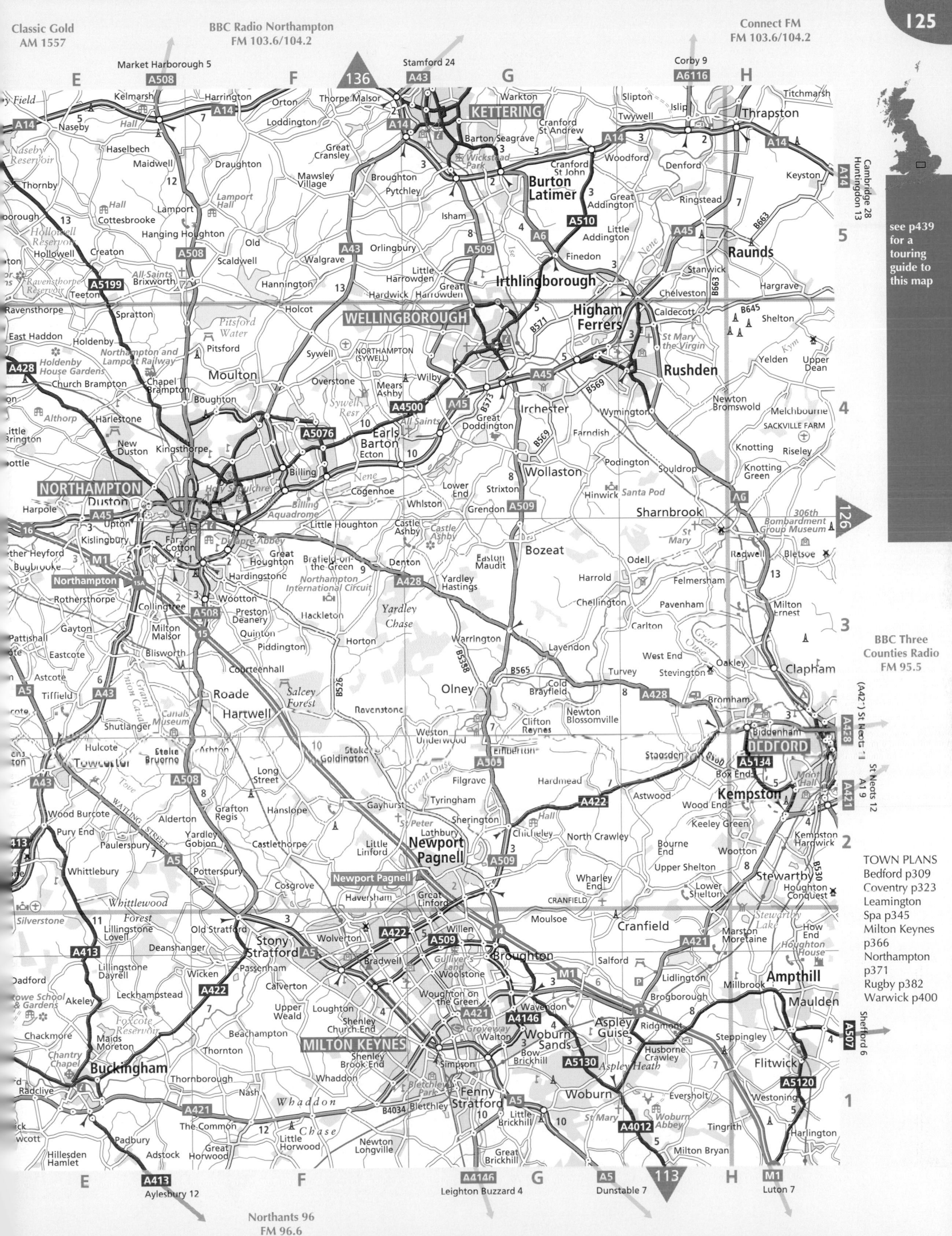

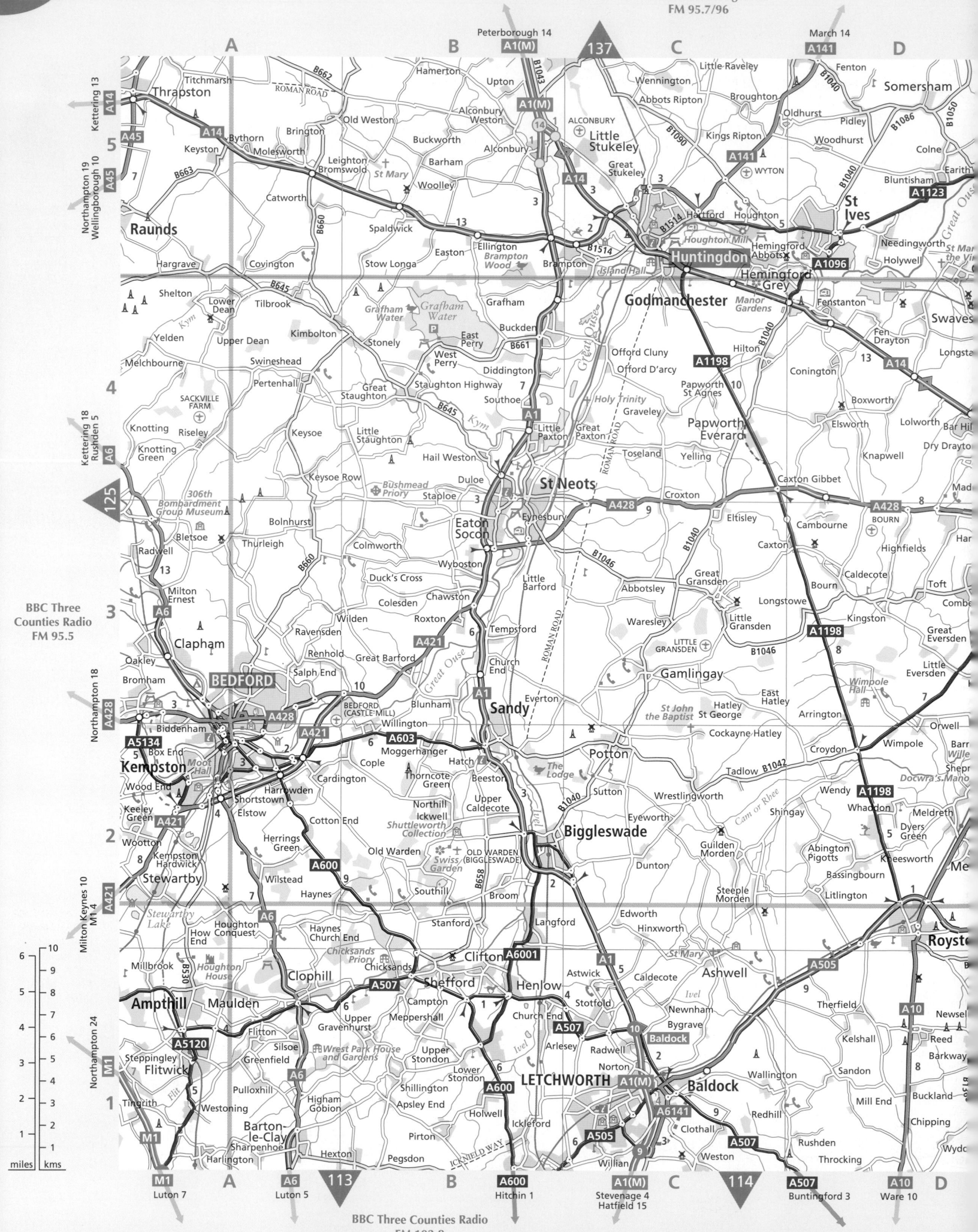

BBC Three
Counties Radio
FM 95.5

(A141) March 13
Chatteris 6
Downham Market 18
Littleport 8 A1101
Swaffham 21 A1065
Thetford 4 A11

138

see p440 for a touring guide to this map

E A142 F A10 G A1101 H A1065

5

A142 St Andrew Witchford Ely Middle Fen Great Fen Kenny Hill Beck Row Eriswell
B1381 Sutton Wentworth Little Thetford Stuntney Isleham Fen Mildenhall Fen Holywell Row
A1421 Haddenham A10 Barway Broad Hill Isleham Marina Thistley Green West Row MILDENHALL A1101 A1065 Icklingham 10 A11
Hill Row Doles North Hill Wilburton Stretham Padney Soham Isleham St Andrew Mildenhall Worlington Barton Mills 11 Lark
15 Aldreth A1123 Soham Mere B1104 B1102 Freckenham A11 Tuddenham Herringswell

Smithey Fen Upware Wicken Fen Wicken Fordham B1102 Red Lodge Cavenham Lackford A1101
Dullingham A10 Chittering North Fen Bank Adventurers' Fen Little Fen Landwade B1085 Kennett Herringswell Risby Bury St Edmunds 4
Rampton Denny Abbey Cottenham Cant Reach Burwell B1103 Exning A142 Chippenham Snailwell Kentford A14 12 Higham Burthorpe Bury St Edmunds 4

4

Westwick Landbeach Waterbeach Swaffham Prior B1102 A142 Newmarket Heath Newmarket A14 Moulton Gazeley Denham A14
Histon Impington Horningsea Anglesey Abbey Lode Commercial End Holy Trinity B1063 Ashley Cheveley Dunstall Green Hargrave Chevington Bury St Edmunds 6
Girton Milton Stow cum Quy Swaffham Bulbeck Bottisham Holy Trinity A1303 Wooddit ton Broad Green Ousden Genesis Green Lady's Green Chedburgh A143
A14 Chesterton Fen Ditton Little Wilbraham A1304 Stetchworth Saxon Street Upend Lidgate Kirtling Thorns Wickhambrook Depden Green Depden

CAMBRIDGE Teversham Great Wilbraham Six Mile Bottom Dullingham Ditton Green Kirtling Kirtling Green Cowlinge Wickham Street Clopton Green Hawkedon Denston 19 128

3

A603 A1134 Cherry Hinton Fulbourn Westley Waterless Burrough Green B1061 Great Bradley Little Bradley Stradishall Stansfield Thurston End
University Botanic Garden Grantchester Gog Magog Hills Wandlebury Brinkley Weston Colville Carlton Little Thurlow A143 Thurston End
Trumpington Stapleford A1307 West Wratting Weston Green Stour Little Thurlow Great Thurlow Barnardiston Poslingford
M11 A1201 Great Shelford Granta Babraham FLEAM DYKE B1052 Balsham ROMAN ROAD West Wickham Great Wratting Hundon Chilton Street

2

Newton Sawston Little Abington Hildersham Withersfield Little Wratting Kedington Clare A1092 (A134) Sudbury 10
Whittlesford Pampisford Great Abington A1307 Linton Horseheath Hanchett End A1307 Haverhill A1092 Stour
Thriplow Duxford A11 Linton Zoo Bartlow Shudy Camps A1017 15 Sturmer Stoke by Clare Belchamp St Paul
Imperial War Museum DUXFORD Hinxton Ickleton Stump Cross Hadstock Castle Camps Wixoe Baythorne End Ashen Ovington
A505 Rivenhall Great Chesterford Ashdon Camps End B1057 Ridgewell Knowl Green

1

9 B1052 Church End Helions Bumpstead Steeple Bumpstead Birdbrook Colne Tilbury Juxta Clare Little Yeldham
Elmdon Little Chesterford Little Walden Red Oaks Hill B1054 Stambourne Green Great Yeldham
Chrishall B1039 Strethall Littlebury Green St Mary's Audley End Sewards End B1053 Radwinter Hempstead Cornish Hall End Robinhood End Toppesfield 8 A1017 Colne Valley Railway Castle
Pond Street Bridge Green M11 AUDLEY END Saffron Walden Wimbish Great Sampford Stambourne Delvin End Castle Hedingham
Duddenhoe End Wendens Ambo Shortgrove Wimbish Green Howe Street B1057 Gainsford End Sible Hedingham
Langley Newport Howlett End Pant Great Sampford Wethersfield Forry's Green
Lower Green Arkesden North End Debden Debden Green Thaxted Bardfield End Green Little Sampford Great Bardfield Blackmore End Whiteash Green
B1038 Ford End Clavering Rickling Prior's Hall Barn Mole Hall Widdington Hamperden End Cutlers Green Finchingfield Little Bardfield Southey Green A1124 Halstead 1
Brent Pelham Starlings Green Quendon WETHERSFIELD

E M11 F G 115 H A1017
Bishop's Stortford 6 Stansted Airport 6 Braintree 4

TOWN PLANS
Bedford p309
Cambridge p316
Ely p331
Huntingdon p341

Thetford 4   Thetford 2   A11   A134   Thetford 15   A1066

139

Diss

A11   10   Elveden   Barnham   Euston   Hopton   Blo Norton   Palgrave
Tank Museum   Euston Hall   Coney Weston   Thelnetham   Redgrave   Wortham   Thrandeston
B1112   12   Fakenham Magna   Sapiston   Barningham   Market Weston   Hinderclay   A143   Burgate   Mellis   Yaxley
B1106   12   HONINGTON   Honington   Hepworth   Rickinghall   Botesdale   Candle Street
A134   A1088   Ixworth Thorpe   Bardwell   Stanton   Upthorpe   Wattisfield   Allwood Green   Thornham Parva   A140
Icklingham   Wordwell   Brockley Corner   Ingham   Ampton   Great Livermere   Ixworth   Walsham le Willows   Four Ashes   Gislingham   Thornham Magna   Stoke Ash
Lark   Cavenham   Lackford   West Stow   Culford   Timworth Green   A143   Langham   Badwell Ash   Crownland   Finningham   Wickham Street   Wickham Skeith   Thwaite

Cambridge 25 Newmarket 11   A11
Cambridge 22 Newmarket 8   A14

A1101   Flempton   Hengrave   Fornham St Genevieve   Fornham All Saints   Fornham St Martin   B1106   Great Barton   Pakenham   Hunston   Long Thurlow   Great Ashfield   Wyverstone Street   Wyverstone   Westhorpe   Brockford Street   Wether
A14   12   Risby   Westley   BURY ST EDMUNDS   A1088   Norton   Stanton Street   Earl's Green   Bacton   Cotton
Burthorpe   A1302   Abbey   Thurston   10   Elmswell   Haughley Green   Bacton Green   Mechanical Music Museum   Mid Light
Barrow   Little Saxham   Manor House   Blackthorpe   Beyton   Tostock   A14   Wetherden   Ward Green   Mendlesham   Mendlesham Green
Great Saxham   Horringer   St Mary   Rushbrooke   Rougham   Kingshall Street   Drinkstone   Woolpit   Haughley   Old Newton   Gipping   A140

Vibe FM
FM 105.6/107.7

127   A143   Denham   Chevington   Nowton   Great Welnetham   Sicklesmere   Rougham Green   Hessett   Drinkstone Green   Borley Green   Haughley Park   Onehouse   Stowupland   A1120
Hargrave   Lady's Green   Ickworth   Hawstead   Little Welnetham   Bradfield St George   Gedding   Poystreet Green   Buxhall   Combs Ford   Stowmarket   Earl Stonham   Stonham Aspal
Depden Green   Chedburgh   Whepstead   Bradfield Combust   Felsham   Hightown Green   High Street Green   Great Finborough   Combs   Creeting St Mary   Sanctu

3   19   Rede   A134   Stanningfield   Brett   Little Finborough   Battisford   Needham Market   Codde
Clopton Green   Brockley Green   Somerton   Lawshall   Great Green   Cockfield   Thorpe Green   Brettenham   Battisford Tye   Ringshall   Barking Tye   Barking   Baylham
Wickham Street   Hawkedon   Hartest   Shimpling Street   11   Thorpe Morieux   Cross Green   Charles Tye   Ringshall Stocks   Willisham Tye   Great Blakenham
A143   Denston   Stansfield   Thurston End   Fenstead End   Boxted   Shimpling   Alpheton   20   Kettlebaston   Hitcham   WATTISHAM   Nedging Tye   Great Bricett   Offton   Willisham   Woodland Gardens

Haverhill 7   A143   Poslingford   Glemsford   Stanstead   Kentwell Hall   Preston St Mary   Bildeston   Chelsworth   Naughton   Somersham   Little Blakenham   Flowton   Bramford
B1063   Chilton Street   Cavendish   A1092   Pentlow   Holy Trinity   Bridge Street   Lavenham   A1141   Monks Eleigh   Ash Street   Aldham   Burstallhill   Sproughton
Clare   11   Melford Hall   Long Melford   A134   Brent Eleigh   Milden   Lindsey Tye   Whatfield   Elmsett
Nether Hall   Stour   Liston   4   Acton   Little Waldingfield   St James Chapel   Semer   B1113

Cambridge 28 Haverhill 7   A1017
(A1307)   Ovington   Belchamp St Paul   Foxearth   Great Waldingfield   Upsher Green   Lindsey   Priory   Kersey   A1071   Burstall   Hintlesham
Temple End   Borley   B1064   Sudbury   Edwardstone   Wolves Wood   Aldham
Tilbury Juxta Clare   Knowl Green   Bulmer   Belchamp Walter   Belchamp Otten   St Gregory   Gainsborough's House   Groton   Bower House Tye   Hadleigh   Chattisham   Washbrook
Little Yeldham   Puttock End   Bulmer Tye   Ballingdon   Great Cornard   A134   Newton   Boxford   A1071   Hadleigh Heath   Lower Layham   Upper Layham   Copdock   Belste
Great Yeldham   Middleton   Little Henny   Sackers Green   Assington   3   Polstead Heath   Raydon   Capel St Mary   A12
A1017   Colne Valley Railway   Gestingthorpe   Henny Street   Little Cornard   Leavenheath   Polstead   Lower Raydon   Great Wenham   12   Bentley
Castle Hedingham   Wickham St Paul   Great Henny   Twinstead   Lamarsh   Dorking Tye   Leavenheath   Stoke-by-Nayland   Higham   Holton St Mary   East Bergholt   A137
Delvin End   8   Great Maplestead   A131   Alphamstone   Bures Green   Honey Tye   A134   Thorington Street   Stratford St Mary   A12   East End
Sible Hedingham   Little Maplestead   Bures   Wissington   Nayland   Stour   Boxted   Langham   Flatford Mill   Brantham
Forry's Green   Southey Green   Countess Cross   Mount Bures   Little Horkesley   Boxted Cross   Dedham Heath   Castle House   Cattawade
A1124   Whiteash Green   Colne Engaine   Wormingford   Great Horkesley   Lamb Corner   Foxash Estate   Manningtree
Halstead   Prestons Lake   Pebmarsh   Lawford   Mistle

A1017   A131   Braintree 4   Braintree 5   115   A134   Colchester 3   A12   Colchester 3 Chelmsford 25   116

miles   kms

Great Yarmouth 34
Beccles 18

Great Yarmouth 20
Lowestoft 10

see p441
for a
touring
guide to
this map

Halesworth

Southwold

Walberswick

Framlingham

Saxmundham

Leiston
Aldringham
Thorpeness

Wickham Market

Aldeburgh
Moot Hall

Woodbridge

IPSWICH

Shingle Street

Harwich

Esbjerg
Cuxhaven
Hook of Holland

FELIXSTOWE

Great Yarmouth 20

Colchester 15

TOWN PLANS
Bury St
Edmunds p314
Felixstowe
p117
Harwich p117
Ipswich p342

ABERYSTWYTH

CARDIGAN

BAY

CARDIGAN

BAY

to Cliff Railway & Camera Obscura

Albert Pl

Castell Brychan

Pen-Y-Graig

North Beach

Recreation Ground

Lisburne Terr

Town Hall

Marine Terrace

Bath St

Ceredigion Museum

Portland St

Queen's Road

Loveden Road

North Road

Trefor Road

Infirmary Road

University of Wales National Library of Wales

Arts Centre

Machynlleth 18

A487

Pier Pavilion

B4346

Corporation St

Terrace Road

Portland Rd

Vaenor St

NORTHGATE ST

A44

Llangurig 22

Eastgate

Baker Street

NORTH PARADE

Cambrian St

Moor La

Poplar Row

LLANBADARN RD

University of Wales

Pier Street

GREAT DARKGATE ST

Chalybeate

TERRACE RD

THESPIAN ST

Stanley Road

Edge-Hill Road

Banadl Road

Plascrug Leisure Centre

War Memorial

Laura Pl

New St

Mkt St

PO

Union St

ALEXANDRA ROAD

Elm Tree Ave

Trinity Road

Buarth

New Promenade

Castle

Sea View Pl

Vulcan St

Prospect St

High Street

Gray's Inn Rd

George St

STREET

MILL

Park Avenue

Aberystwyth Station

South Rd

Quay Rd

Powell St

BRIDGE STREET

Glyndwr Road

Vale of Rheidol Narrow Gauge Steam Railway

South Beach

New Promenade

A487

Park & Ride 300yds

POL

Cardigan 38

Queen's St

0   100   200 yds
0   100   200 m

A487 Porthmadog 24
Blaenau Ffestiniog 21

A496

143

Uwch-Mynydd

Coed Garth Ge

Bontddu

Caerdeon

A496

10

Penm

Llanaber

Cutiau

A493

Islaw

RNLI

Barmouth

Barmouth Bay

The Bar

Arthog Bog

Arthog

Fairbourne & Barmouth Steam Railway

Fairbourne

20

Mynydd Pennant

Llwyngwril

Esgair Berfa

Castell y Bere

Llanf y-per

Llangelynnin

Dysynni

Abergynolwyn

B4405

Rhoslefain

Llanfendigaid

Llanegryn

Dolgoch

Myny Tan-y-
2076

Tonfanau

Bryncrug

Dolgoch Falls

Pen Trum-gwr

A493

St Cadfan

Rhyd-yr-onen

Trum Gelli

Tywyn

Talyllyn Railway

Caethle

Cw

Aberdovey (Aberdyfi)

15

Aberdovey Bar

Dovey (Dyfi)

Ynys-hir

Furnace

Cors Fochno

18

Dyfi

B4353

Tre'r-ddol

Ynyslas

Llancynfelyn

Tre Taliesin

Yr Hen Ga

Borth

Animalarium

Cwm

Upper Borth

Tal-y-bont

Afon Ler

B4353

Dol-y-Bont

B4572

Llandre

Bont-Goch or Elrich

A487

Bow Street

Penrhyn-coch

Salem

Cwm

Llangorwen

Comins Coch

Plas Gogerddan

Capel Dewi

Pen-bor Rhydybed

Aberystwyth

A4159

Castle

Llanbadarn Fawr

Capel Bangor

A44

The Bar

Pen Dinas

Vale of Rheidol Railway

Rheidol

Penparcau

Rhydyfelin

Capel Seion

A4120

Llanfarian

B4340

Gors

Chancery

New Cross

Llanfihan y-Creudd

Blaenplwyf

Ystwyth

Pentre-Llyn

Cnv Coe

Llanilar

A487

Rhadmad

A485

B4575

18

Crosswood

B4576

Carreg Ti-pw

16

Llanddeinio

A487

B4340

Lledrod

119

Llangwyryfon

A487

A485

Aberaeron 7
Cardigan 29

Lampeter 19

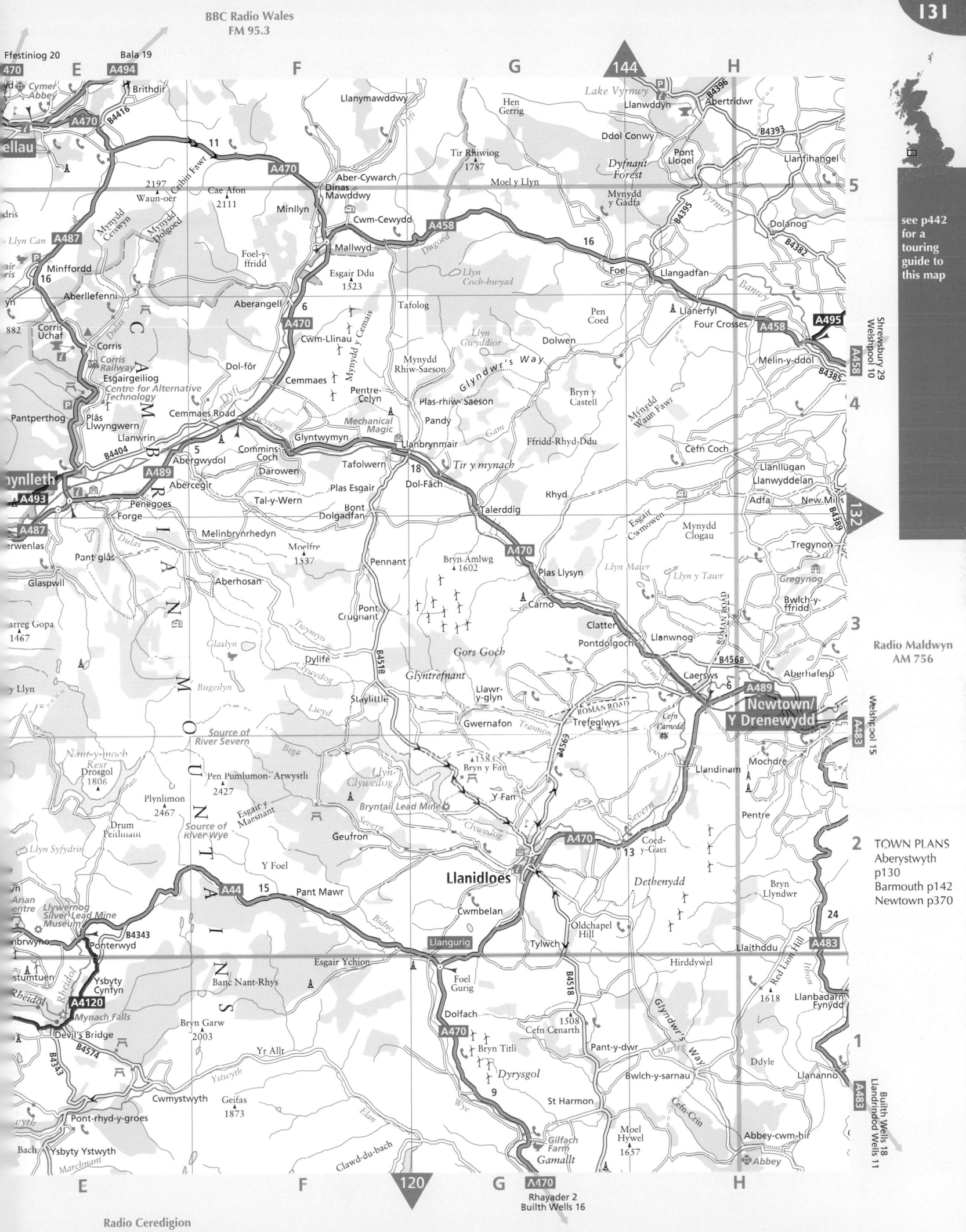

144

see p442
for a
touring
guide to
this map

Shrewsbury 29
Welshpool 10

132

Radio Maldwyn
AM 756

Welshpool 15

TOWN PLANS
Aberystwyth
p130
Barmouth p142
Newtown p370

Builith Wells 18
Llandrindod Wells 11

120

G A470

Beacon FM
FM 97.2/103.1

107.4 Telford FM
FM 107.4

Classic Gold WABC
AM 990/1017

Ellesmere 15 Whitchurch 19 Market Drayton 13 (A41) Whitchurch 16 Whitchurch 19 Stafford 12

E A528 A49 A53 **F** A442 **G** 146 A41 **H** A518

see p443
for a
touring
guide to
this map

Preston
Gubbals
Albrighton
Astley
13
Great
Wytheford
Rowton
Waters
Upton
Summerhill
Edgmond
Longford
Aqualate
Hall
Newport
Church
Eaton
Moreton
High
Onn

Shrewsbury
1403
Poynton
Green
Walton
Crudgington
B5062
Cherrington
Adeney
Church Aston
Kynnersley
Chetwynd
Aston
Outwoods
Orslow
Great
Chatwell

Battlefield
Haughton
Roden
B5062
High
Ercall
Longdon
on Tern
Sleapford
Eyton upon
the Weald Moors
Preston upon
the Weald Moors
8
Lilleshall
Woodcote
Heath
Hill
Weston
Heath
Brineton
Marston

A528
A5112
Uffington
Withington
Upton
Magna
Walcot
Wrockwardine
Admaston
A5223
Hadley
Trench
Donnington
Lilyhurst
Lilleshall
Abbey
A518
Sheriffhales
Blymhill

SHREWSBURY
Attingham
Park
Sunnycroft
Wellington
Arleston
Oakengates
A5
Crackleybank
Weston-
under-Lizard
Weston
Park
Bishop's
Wood
Boscobel
House

Meole Brace
Bayston
Hill
Atcham
Cronkhill
Hall
Viroconium
Rushton
Aston
Old
Park
TELFORD
Lawley
M54
A5
Tong
Shackerley
White
Ladies
Priory

Wroxeter
Cross
Houses
Donnington
Upper
Longwood
The Wrekin
1335
Telford
Steam Railway
Dawley
A442
Shifnal
The
Wyke
A464
Cosford
Cousall
Wood

Berrington
11
Dryton
Eaton
Constantine
Little Wenlock
A5223
Stirchley
A4169
Kemberton
Brockton
Aerospace
Museum
Albrighton
9

Condover
Cantlop
Great
Ryton
Pitchford
Golding
Cound
Leighton
Sheinton
Coalbrookdale
Buildwas
Abbey
Sutton
Hill
Coalport
Grindle
Ryton
Beckbury
Boningale
16

Little Ryton
Dorrington
Acton
Pigott
Benthall
Hall
Ironbridge
Wyke
Benthall
Sutton
Maddock
Burnhill Green
Badger
Pattingham

A49
Frodesley
Longnor
Acton
Burnell
A458
A4169
Homer
Broseley
Norton
Stockton
A442
Ackleton
Chesterton
The
Walls
Trescott

Leebotwood
Stretton
Westwood
Harley
Kenley
Wenlock
Priory
Barrow
Willey
Severn
9
Worfield
Shipley
14
A454

Church
Preen
Hughley
Presthope
**Much
Wenlock**
Nordley
Astley
Abbotts
Allscot
Roughton
Wyken
Hilton
Upper Ludstone
Upper
Aston
Seisdon

Enchmarsh
Plaish
9
Acton
Round
Haughton
Cross
Head Lane
A454
Ludstone
A176

Cardington
Caer Caradoc
B4371
Bourton
Easthope
Brockton
Aston Eyre
Morville
Bridgnorth
Swancote
All
Saints
Claverley
Heathton

**Church
Stretton**
Wall Bank
Longville
in the Dale
East
Wall
Wilderhope
Manor
Shipton Hall
Weston
Monkhopton
Upton
Cressett
Tasley
Castle
Oldbury
Eardington
Motor
Museum
Bobbington
HALFPENNY
GREEN

Wall under
Heywood
Rushbury
Shipton
Stanton Long
Middleton
Priors
Chetton
Glazeley
Dudmaston
Quatford
Halfpenny
Green

Ticklerton
Eaton
Broadstone
Huldgate
Ditton Priors
Middleton
Scriven
Neenton
Sidbury
Chelmarsh
Resr
A442
Tuckhill
15
Enville

Harton
Middlehope
Munslow
Tugford
Cleobury
North
Burwarton
Upper
Heath
Abdon
Middleton
Scriven
Chelmarsh
Sutton
Hampton
Birdsgreen
Kinver
St Peter

Westhope
Diddlebury
Aston
Munslow
Peaton
Bouldon
Clee
St Margaret
Loughton
Billingsley
Alveley
Woodhill
Highley
14
Romsley
Kinver
Edge

Seifton
Corfton
Great
Sutton
Stoke
St Milborough
Wheathill
Chorley
Stottesdon
Arley
Arboretum
Kingsford
Blakeshall

Culmington
1052
Weston Hill
Clee
Hill
Cleedownton
Farlow
Oreton
Kinlet
Severn
Upper
Arley
Shatterford
Caunsall
Cookley

Stanton
Lacy
Middleton
Titterstone
Clee Hill
1750
Silvington
Catherton
Baveney
Wood
Buttonoak
Trimpley
Trimpley
Resr
Wolverley
Fairfield
Franche

Henley
Farden
Bitterley
Cleeton
St Mary
Hopton
Wafers
Neen Savage
Wyre Forest
Habberley
KIDDERMINSTER

A49
Ludlow
Snitton
Cleehill
Hints
Knowle
A4117
**Cleobury
Mortimer**
Lem Hill
Far Forest
Bewdley
Wribbenhall
Blakebrook
West
Midland
Safari Park

Knowbury
Hope
Bagot
Coreley
Milson
Bayton
Pound
Bank
Callow Hill
Ribbesford
A449

Caynham
Whitton
Neen Sollars
Nash
Mamble
Clows
Top
Rock
A456
**Stourport-
on-Severn**
Hartlebury

E A49 **F** 122 A456 **G** A449 **H**

Leominster 7 Tenbury Wells 5 Worcester 10
Great Malvern 17

147
133
123

Classic Gold WABC AM 990/1017

Beacon FM FM 97.2/103.1

107.7 The Wolf FM 107.7

BBC WM FM 95.6

Heart FM FM 100.7

Saga FM FM 105.7

96.4 FM BRMB FM 96.4

Galaxy 102.2 FM 102.2

Grid columns: A B C D
Grid rows: 5 4 3 2 1

Edge references:
Stoke-on-Trent 18 — Stafford 2 — Stone 14 — Ashbourne 18
Telford 7 — (A5) Shrewsbury 22 / Telford 7 — Shifnal 4
Bridgnorth 5 — Bridgnorth 6 — Bridgnorth 9 — Tenbury Wells 15
Worcester 10 / Great Malvern 18 — Droitwich Spa 5 — Worcester 14 — Redditch 5 — Redditch 2 — (A46) Evesham 19

Scale: miles / kms — 10, 6, 9, 5, 8, 7, 4, 6, 5, 3, 4, 2, 3, 1, 2, 1

Major places:
Rugeley, Cannock, Lichfield, Wolverhampton, Walsall, Sutton Coldfield, Wednesfield, Bloxwich, Brownhills, Aldridge, Sedgley, Dudley, West Bromwich, Smethwick, Birmingham, Stourbridge, Halesowen, Solihull, Kidderminster, Bromsgrove, Stourport-on-Severn, Hartlebury

Selected roads: M6, M6 Toll, M54, M5, M42, A5, A34, A38, A51, A449, A454, A460, A461, A452, A453, A41, A47, A4040, A4123, A4124, A435, A441, A450, A451, A456, A458, A464, A463, A491, A459, A4036, A4100, A4101, A4031, A457, A446, A5127, A5192, A5190, A513, A515, A3400

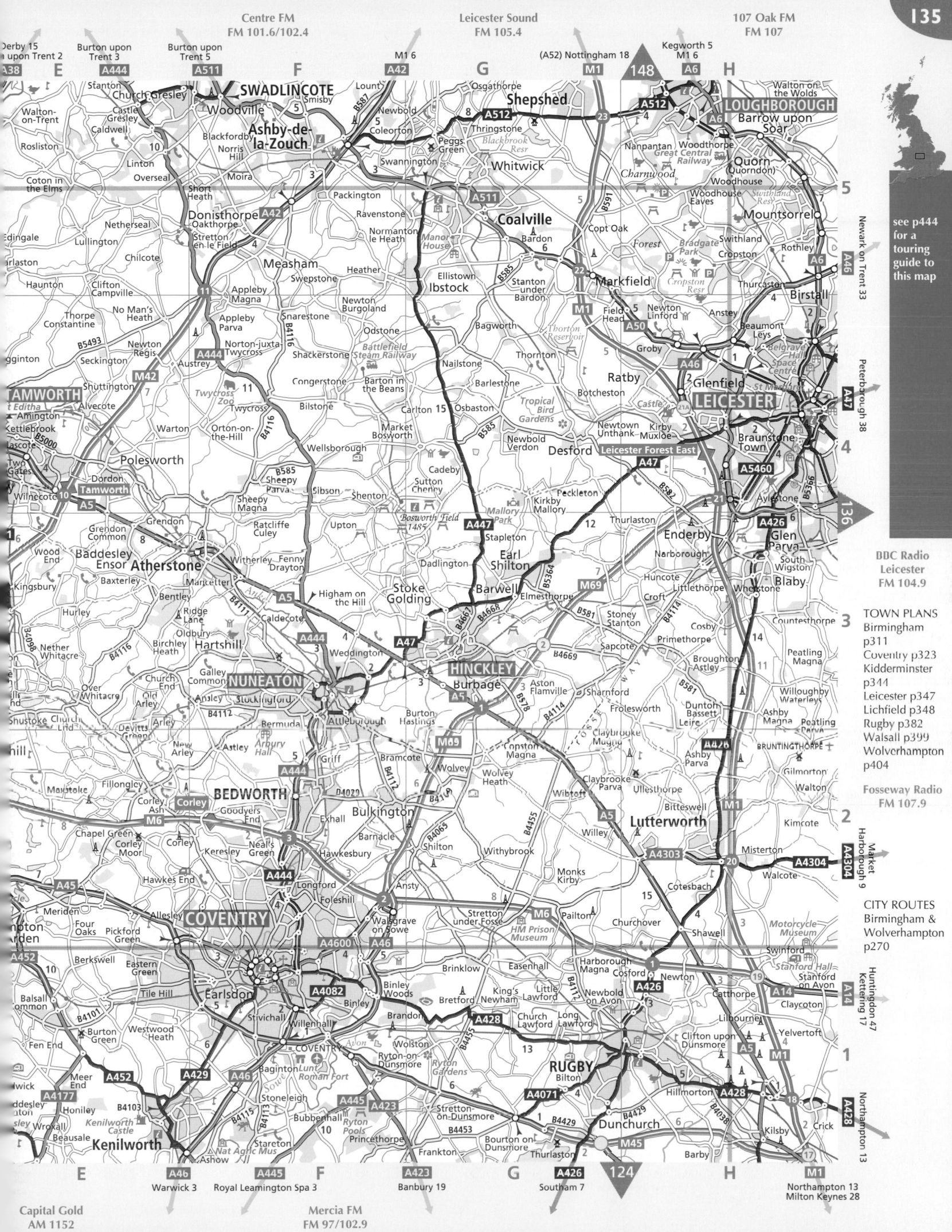

Rutland Radio
FM 97.4/107.2

Leicester Sound
FM 105.4

BBC
Radio Leicester
FM 104.9

BBC Radio Northampton
FM 103.6/104.2

Sleaford 17

Boston 16
Spalding 3

Weston
Hills

Whaplode
St Catherine
Holbeach St Johns

Cowbit

Moulton
Chapel

FENLAND

Castle
Bytham

Lound

Thurlby

Tongue
End

BOURNE

Deeping
Fen

Deeping
St Nicholas

Little
Bytham

Toft

Northorpe

Witham on
the Hill

Careby

CROWLAND
(SPALDING)

Whaplode
Drove

Manthorpe

Shepeau
Stow

Holbeach
Drove

Carlby

Wilsthorpe

Hop Pole

Great
Postland

Braceborough

Baston

Gedney Hill

Pickworth

Essendine

Langtoft

Dowsdale

Greatford

Market Deeping

Deeping
St James

Crowland

North Fen

Tickencote

Belmesthorpe

Barholm

Abbey
Church

Great
Casterton

Little
Casterton

West
Deeping

Deeping
Gate

Stamford

Uffington

Tallington

Northborough

Morris
Fen

Wryde Croft

Tinwell

Bainton

Maxey

Peakirk Wildfowl
& Wetlands Centre

BEDFORD LEVEL
North Level

Burghley House

Barnack

Etton

Peakirk

Ashton

Glinton

Newborough

Helpston

Eye Green

Thorney

SS Mary
& Botolph

Priest's
House

Easton on
the Hill

Pilsgate

St John
the Baptist

Ufford

Marholm

Werrington

Thorney Toll

Wittering

Southorpe

Eye

Collyweston

Wittering

Newark

Duddington

Thornhaugh

Upton

PETERBOROUGH

North Side

Nene

Tixover

Wansford

Ailsworth

Longthorpe

Whittlesey

Eldernell

Sutton

Castor

Stibbington

Nene
Valley
Railway

Coates

King's Cliffe

Yarwell

Water
Newton

Orton
Longueville

Eastrea

Sibson

Alwalton

Turves

Blatherwycke

PETERBOROUGH
(SIBSON)

Farcet

King's
Delph

Flag Fen

Apethorpe

Nassington

Chesterton

Nene (Old Course)

Bulwick

Woodnewton

Peterborough

Farcet
Fen

St Mary &
All-Saints

Hampton

Elton

Haddon

White
Fen

Southwick

Fotheringhay

Castle
Hall

Pondersbridge

Benwick

Morborne

Yaxley

Oundle

Lyveden
New Bield

Warmington

Whittlesey Mere

The
Herne

Ramsey Mereside

Benefield

Lower
Benefield

Cotterstock

Tansor

Folksworth

Stilton

Ramsey St Mary's

Middle
Moor

Ramsey Hollow

Glapthorn

Norman Cross

Holme
Fen

Ramsey

Tick
Fen

Ashton

Lutton

Holme

Ramsey Forty Foot

Stoke
Doyle

Polebrook

Caldecote

Denton

PETERBOROUGH

Ramsey
Heights

Abbey
Gatehouse

Armston

Barnwell

Glatton

Conington

Upwood

Bury

Pilton

Hemington

Wadenhoe

Luddington
in the Brook

Sawtry

Wood
Walton

Great Raveley

Warboys

Pidley
Fen

Wigsthorpe

Thurning

Great
Gidding

Little
Gidding

Little Raveley

Wistow

Fenton

Sudborough

Thorpe
Waterville

Steeple
Gidding

Wennington

Broughton

Oldhurst

Pidley

Aldwincle

Clopton

Winwick

Coppingford

Woodhurst

Lowick

Titchmarsh

Hamerton

Upton

Kings Ripton

Islip

Old
Weston

Alconbury
Weston

Abbots Ripton

WYTON

Thrapston

Brington

Buckworth

ALCONBURY

Little
Stukeley

Denford

Bythorn

Molesworth

Barham

Alconbury

Great
Stukeley

Hartford

St Ives

Keyston

Leighton
Bromswold

St Mary

Woolley

Huntingdon

Needingworth

Ringstead

Raunds

Catworth

Spaldwick

Stow Longa

Easton

Ellington

Godmanchester

Houghton
Mill

Houghton

Hemingford
Abbots

Holywell

Hargrave

Covington

Brampton
Wood

Brampton

Island Hall

Hemingford
Grey

Stanwick

St Neots 7
Biggleswade 18

Cambridge 14

Haddenham 8

see p445
for a
touring
guide to
this map

Lite FM
FM 106.8

TOWN PLANS
Huntingdon
p341
Leicester p347
Peterborough
p376
Stamford p391

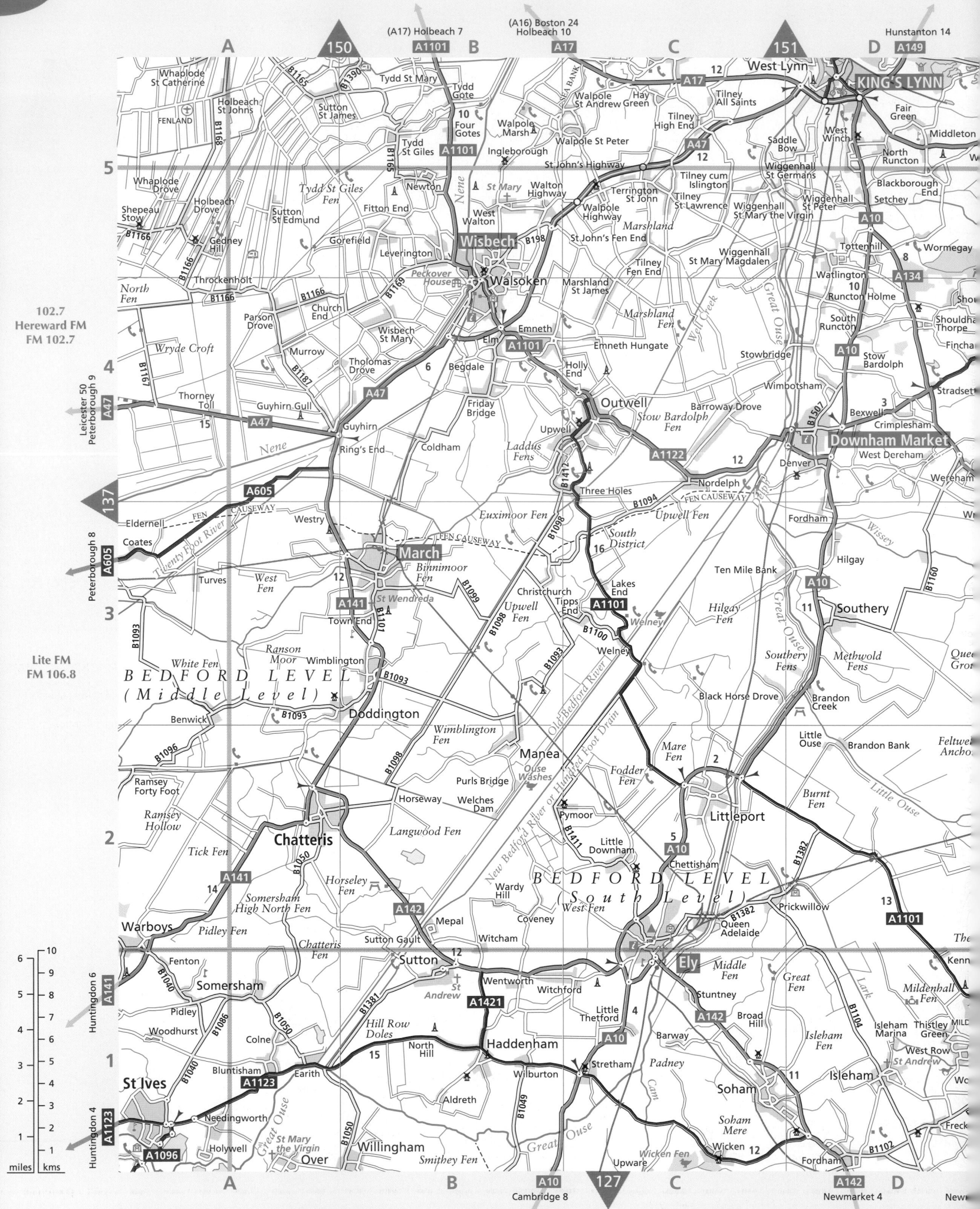

(A17) Holbeach 7

(A16) Boston 24
Holbeach 10

Hunstanton 14

150   A1101   B   A17   C   151   D   A149

A17   12   West Lynn   KING'S LYNN

Whaplode
St Catherine

Holbeach
St Johns

FENLAND

B1168

B1165

B1390

Tydd St Mary

Tydd
Gote

Walpole
St Andrew Green   Hay

Tilney
All Saints

West
Winch

Fair
Green

Middleton

Sutton
St James

10
Four
Gotes

Walpole
Marsh

Tilney
High End

Saddle
Bow

North
Runcton

A47   12

Tydd
St Giles   A1101   Walpole St Peter

Ingleborough   St John's Highway

Tilney cum
Islington

Wiggenhall
St Germans

Blackborough
End   Setchey

Whaplode Drove

Newton   Walton
Highway   Terrington
St John   Tilney
St Lawrence   Wiggenhall
St Mary the Virgin   Wiggenhall
St Peter   A10

Shepeau
Stow

Holbeach
Drove   Sutton
St Edmund   Fitton End   West
Walton   Walpole
Highway   St John's Fen End   Marshland
Fen   Wiggenhall
St Mary Magdalen   A134

B1166

Gedney
Hill   Gorefield   Wisbech   B198   Wisbech   Tottenhill   Wormegay

Throckenholt   Leverington   Peckover
House   Walsoken   Marshland
St James   Watlington   10   South
Runcton   Shouldham
Thorpe   Fincha

North
Fen   B1166   Parson
Drove   Church
End   Wisbech
St Mary   Emneth   Marshland
Fen   Stowbridge   Stow
Bardolph   A10

B1166   Murrow   Tholomas
Drove   Begdale   Elm   A1101   Emneth Hungate   Wimbotsham   Bexwell

Wryde Croft   B1187   6   Holly
End   Barroway Drove   B1507   Crimplesham   Downham Market

Thorney
Toll   Guyhirn Gull   Friday
Bridge   Outwell   Stow Bardolph
Fen   A1122   12   Denver   West Dereham   Wereham

A47   15   Guyhirn   Upwell   A1122   Nordelph   Fordham   Wissey

Ring's End   Coldham   Laddus
Fens   B1412   Three Holes   B1094   FEN CAUSEWAY   Upwell Fen   Hilgay   B1160

Nene   Euximoor Fen   B1098   South
District   16   Ten Mile Bank   Southery

Eldernell   Westry   FEN CAUSEWAY   March   Christchurch   Tipps
End   A1101   Hilgay
Fen   11

Coates   Turves   West
Fen   A141   Binnimoor
Fen   St Wendreda   B1099   Upwell
Fen   Lakes
End   B1100   Welney   Southery
Fens   Methwold
Fens

BEDFORD LEVEL
(Middle Level)

White Fen   Ranson
Moor   Wimblington   Town End   B1101   Welney   Black Horse Drove   Brandon
Creek

Benwick   B1093   B1093   Doddington   B1098   B1093   Little
Ouse   Brandon Bank

Ramsey
Forty Foot   B1096   Wimblington
Fen   Mare
Fen   Brandon
Creek

Ramsey
Hollow   Manea   Fodder
Fen   2   Littleport   Burnt
Fen   Little Ouse

Tick Fen   Chatteris   Purls Bridge   Ouse
Washes   Pymoor   B1411   5   A10   Chettisham   B1382

A141   14   Somersham
High North Fen   B1050   Horseway   Welches
Dam   Little
Downham   Wardy
Hill   BEDFORD LEVEL
(South Level)   B1382   Prickwillow   13   A1101

Warboys   Pidley Fen   A142   Horseley
Fen   Langwood Fen   Coveney   West Fen   Queen
Adelaide

Fenton   Sutton Gault   Mepal   Witcham   Ely   Middle
Fen   Great
Fen   Mildenhall

Somersham   B1040   Sutton   12   Wentworth   Witchford   A142   Stuntney   Isleham
Fen   Isleham
Marina   Thistley
Green

Pidley   B1086   St Andrew   A1421   A10   4   Barway   Broad
Hill   Isleham   West Row

Woodhurst   Colne   Hill Row
Doles   North
Hill   Haddenham   Little
Thetford   B1104   Soham   St Andrew

St Ives   Bluntisham   Earith   Wilburton   Stretham   Soham   11   Isleham

A1123   Needingworth   Aldreth   B1049   Padney   Wicken Fen   Freck

Holywell   St Mary
the Virgin   Willingham   Smithey Fen   Upware   Wicken   12   B1102

A1096   Over   Great Ouse

102.7
Hereward FM
FM 102.7

Lite FM
FM 106.8

BBC Radio Cambridgeshire
FM 95.7/96

Star
FM 107.1/107.5

A10   Cambridge 8   127   Newmarket 4

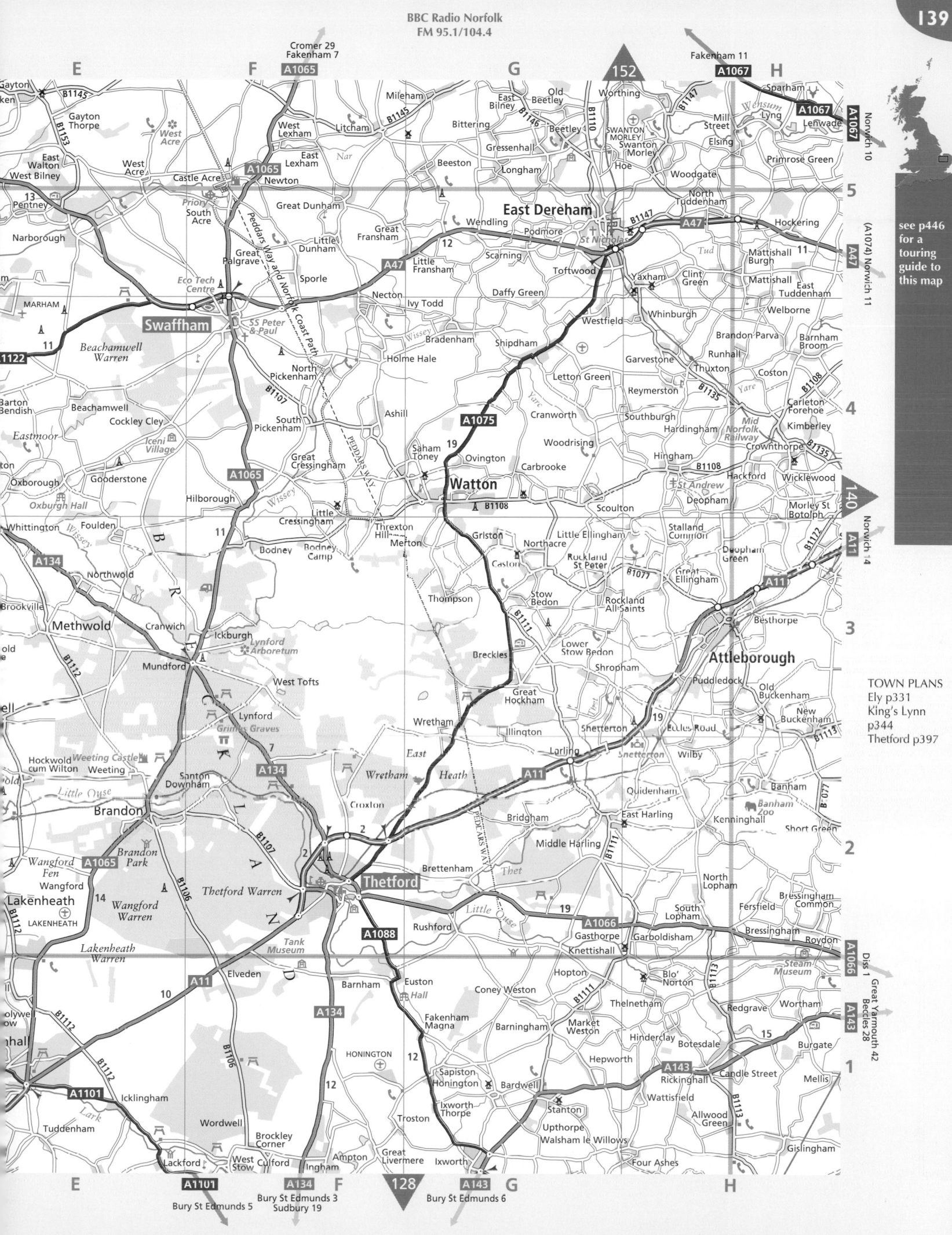

BBC Radio Norfolk
FM 95.1/104.4

see p446
for a
touring
guide to
this map

TOWN PLANS
Ely p331
King's Lynn
p344
Thetford p397

Fakenham 11 A1067

Cromer 16 A140

(A149) North Walsham 9 A1151

Cromer 21 A149

A / B / C / D

152
153

BBC Radio Norfolk FM 95.1/104.4

139

NORWICH

Norfolk Wildlife Park
Sparham · Lenwade · Swanningham · Haveringland · Waterloo · Horstead · Coltishall · Belaugh · Ludham · Potter He
Mill Street · Lyng · Alderford · Felthorpe · Hainford · Frettenham · Hoveton · Wroxham · Horning · Bastw
Elsing · Morton · Weston Longville · Thorpe Marriot · Horsford · Newton St Faith · Spixworth · Crostwick · Woodbastwick · St Helen · Upper Street · Repps
Primrose Green · Taverham · Horsham St Faith · Rackheath · Salhouse · Ranworth · Thurne · Clippesby
Hockering · Weston Green · Ringland · Drayton · Hellesdon · Catton · New Rackheath · Little Plumstead · Panxworth · South Walsham · Upton
Mattishall Burgh · Honingham · Costessey · Easton · New Costessey · Sprowston · Thorpe End · Blofield Heath · Great Plumstead · Hemblington · North Burlingham · Acle
Mattishall · East Tuddenham · Colton · Marlingford · Bowthorpe · Colney · Earlham · Thorpe St Andrew · Brundall · Blofield · Lingwood · Beighton · Moulton St Mary · Tunstall
Welborne · Bawburgh · Eaton · Postwick · Surlingham · Bramerton · Strumpshaw · South Burlingham · Freethorpe · Halverg
Brandon Parva · Barford · Little Melton · Lakenham · Trowse Newton · Kirby Bedon · Surlingham Marsh · Buckenham · Southwood · Wickhar
Runhall · Coston · Barnham Broom · Wramplingham · Hethersett · Cringleford · Keswick · Armingall · Framingham Pigot · Rockland St Mary · Hassingham · Cantley · Limpenhoe
Hackford · Carleton Forehoe · High Green · Ketteringham · Swardeston · Caistor St Edmund · Dunston · Upper Stoke · Framingham Earl · Hellington · Claxton · Langley Street
Wymondham · Kimberley · Crownthorpe · East Carleton · Stoke Holy Cross · Yelverton · Ashby St Mary · Thurton · Hardley Street · Ferry
Wicklewood · Abbey Church · Swainsthorpe · Poringland · Howe · Bergh Apton · Chedgrave · Norton Subcourse
Morley St Botolph · Hethel · Mulbarton · Bracon Ash · Newton Flotman · Saxlingham Nethergate · Brooke · Mundham · Seething · Loddon · Thurlton
Suton · Silfield · Wreningham · Flordon · Lower Tasburgh · Saxlingham Thorpe · Saxlingham Green · Kirstead Green · Hales · Ravingham · Three Cocked Hat
Besthorpe · Spooner Row · Ashwellthorpe · Fundenhall · Hapton · Tasburgh · Hempnall · Maypole Green
Puddledock · Bunwell · Tacolneston · Forncett End · Forncett St Mary · Tharston · Stratton St Michael · Lundy Green · Fritton · Silver Green · Topcroft · Hedenham · Kirby Cane · Stockton
Old Buckenham · Carleton Rode · Forncett St Peter · Wacton · Long Stratton · Morningthorpe · Hempnall Green · Topcroft Street · Broome · Kirby Row · Geldeston · Gillingham
New Buckenham · Hargate · Bunwell Hill · Aslacton · Shelton · Shelton Green · Ditchingham · Mettingham · Shipmeadow · Beccles · Barsham
Banham · Tibenham · Sneath Common · Great Moulton · Hardwick · North Green · Earsham · Bungay · Ringsfield
Banham Zoo · Goose Green · Tivetshall St Margaret · Bush Green · Pulham Market · Denton · Alburgh · Ilketshall St Andrew · Ringsfield Corner
Short Green · Winfarthing · Gissing · Tivetshall St Mary · Piccadilly Corner · Flixton · Ilketshall St Margaret · Redisham
Shelfanger · Shimpling · Dickleburgh Moor · Pulham St Mary · Homersford · Ilketshall St Lawrence · High Street · Cox Common
Fersfield · Burston · Rushall · Wortwell · St Cross South Elmham · St Michael South Elmham · Stone Street · Shadin
Bressingham Common · Dickleburgh · Harleston · Mendham · St Margaret South Elmham · All Saints South Elmham · Spexhall · Bra
Bressingham · Roydon · Thelveton · Needham · Withersdale Street · Rumburgh · Brampton
Diss · Scole · Thorpe Abbotts · Weybread · Metfield · St James South Elmham · Westhall
Steam Museum · Upper Street · Brockdish · Metfield Common · Wissett · Broadway
Palgrave · Billingford · Syleham · Wingfield · Cheiston · Sotherton Corner
Wortham · Stuston · Brome Street · Oakley · Wingfield Old College · Little Whittingham Green · Linstead Parva · Holton · Halesworth
Burgate · Thrandeston · Brome · Hoxne · Fressingfield · Cratfield · Silverley's Green · Cookley · Mells
Mellis · Yaxley · Denham · Pixey Green · Huntingfield · Walpole
Gislingham · Eye · Stradbroke · Ashfield Green · Ubbeston · Bramfield · Blackheath · Thorington
Thornham Parva · Braiseworth · Horham · Wilby · Laxfield · Ubbeston Green · Heveningham
Thornham Magna · Stoke Ash · Redlingfield · Athelington · Crown Corner · Brundish Street

A47 · A11 · A140 · A143 · A144 · A146 · A1062 · A1064 · A1074 · A1042 · A1151 · A1066 · A1067 · A12

miles / kms

Swaffham 17 A47
Thetford 18 A11
Thetford 15 A1066
Bury St Edmunds 15 A143

A140 (A14) Ipswich 18

A12 Ipswich 28 (A14) Felixstowe 33

see p447
for a
touring
guide to
this map

E · F · G · H

East Somerton
Winterton-on-Sea
Hemsby
Hemsby Hole
Newport
Scratby
Ormesby
St Margaret
California
Ormesby
St Michael
Filby
A149
Mautby
Roman Site
Holy Trinity
Castle
Caister-on-Sea
West Caister
West End
GREAT YARMOUTH
HELIPORT
Bure
GREAT YARMOUTH
Halvergate Marshes
Breydon Water
Yarmouth Roads
Pleasure Beach
Burgh Castle
Bradwell
Burgh Castle
Belton
Gorleston-on-Sea
A143
A12
Hopton on Sea
Fritton Lake
St Olaves
Lound
Herringfleet
Hall
Corton
Blundeston
Somerleyton
B1074
Pleasurewood Hills
Waveney
Oulton
Camps Heath
A1117
B1375
B1385
Burgh St Peter
THE ROADS
Oulton Broad
LOWESTOFT
Kirkley
A146
Pakefield
Barnby
Carlton Colville
Mutford
Gisleham
Hulver Street
Rushmere
Kessingland
Henstead
Wildlife Park
Benacre
B1127
A12
Ikold's Green
Wrentham
Benacre
Covehithe
South Cove
B1127
Barnaby Green
Wangford
B1126
St Edmund
Reydon
Sole Bay
095
Southwold
Walberswick
Walberswick
Dunwich

LOWESTOFT

A · B · C

0   200   400yds
0   200   400m

Great Yarmouth 10
Lowestoft Denes
WC TH
North Beach
A12
Whapload Road
Lowestoft Ness
HIGH ST
JUBILEE WAY
Park Road
Town Hall
High Street
Gas Works Road
Whapload Road
Rant Score
Wilde Street
Newcombe Rd
Trinity Rd
Coastguard Station
Oulton Broad 2
A1144
ST PETER'S ST
ARTILLERY W
OLD NELSON ST
POL
Tennyson Rd
Alexandra
Raglan
Hospital
Milton Rd East
Hamilton Road
Hamilton Dock
Love Road
Mitton Rd
London Road
Regent Rd
WC
BATTERY GREEN RD
Waveney Dock
Seago St
Wollaston Road
Gordon Road
WC
Britten Shopping Centre
Marina Theatre
North
Beach Rd
Roman Rd
Smoke House
Clapham Rd S
Surrey St
PO
North Pier
Bevan St W
Tonning St
WAVENEY RD
Trawl Basin
Outer Harbour
South Pier
Maidstone Road
Hervey Street
Denmark Road
Central Station
Custom House
STATION SQUARE
ROYAL TERR
South Basin
WC
East Point Pavilion
South Beach
North Sea
Commercial Road
Inner Harbour
A146
A12
A1118
PIER TERR

Beccles 10   A12 Ipswich 43

A · B · C

KATWIK WAY

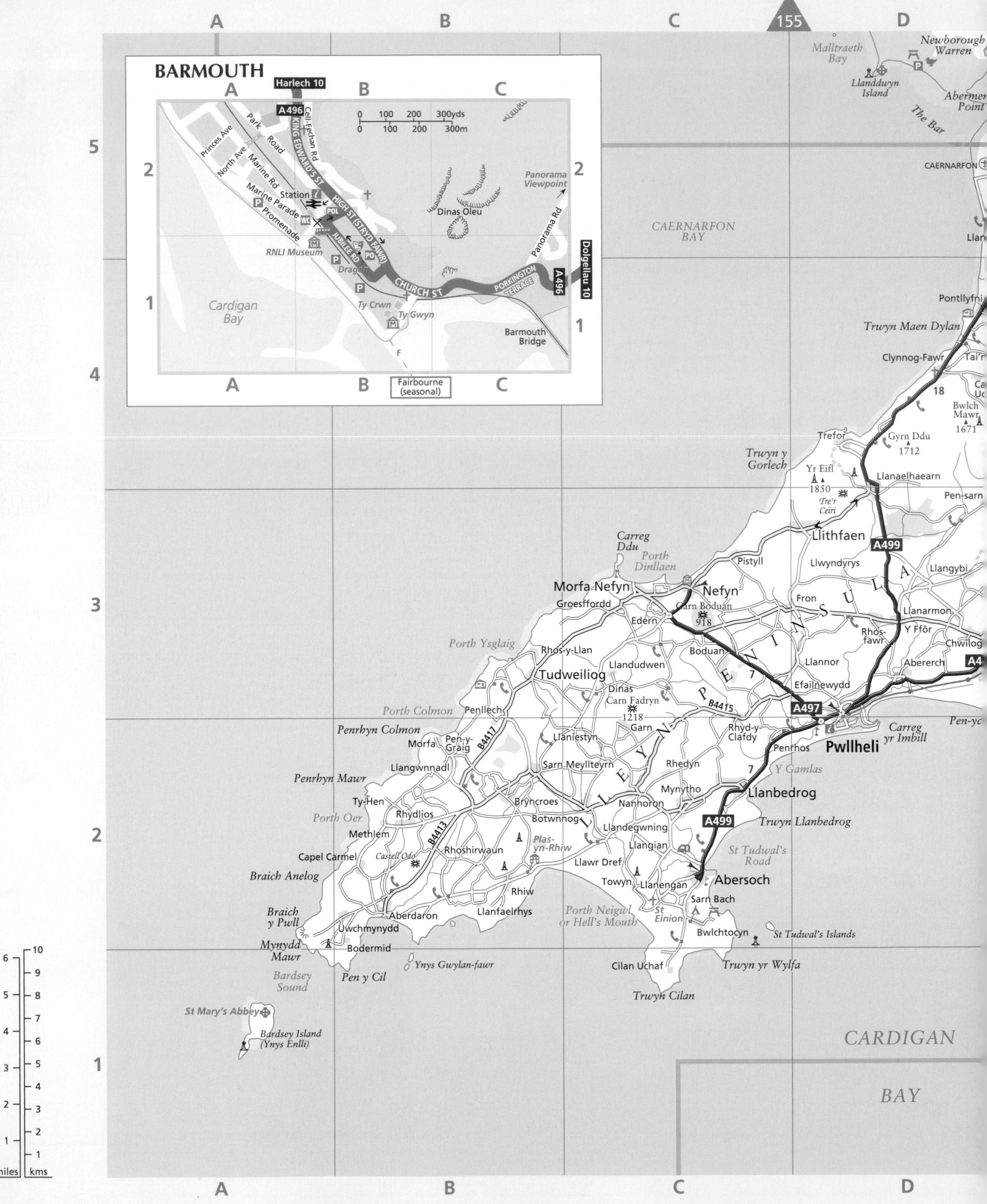

155

BARMOUTH

Harlech 10

A496

Ceir-Fechan Rd

Princes Ave

North Ave

Park Road

Marine Rd

KING EDWARD'S ST

Marine Parade

Station

Promenade

HIGH ST (STRYD FAWR)

POL

JUBILEE RD

PO

RNLI Museum

Dragon

CHURCH ST

PORKINGTON TERRACE

Ty Crwn

Ty Gwyn

Cardigan Bay

Dinas Oleu

Panorama Viewpoint

Panorama Rd

Dolgellau 10

A496

Barmouth Bridge

Fairbourne (seasonal)

0 100 200 300yds
0 100 200 300m

Malltraeth Bay

Newborough Warren

Llanddwyn Island

Abermen-Point

The Bar

CAERNARFON

CAERNARFON BAY

Llan

Pontllyfni

Trwyn Maen Dylan

Clynnog-Fawr

Tai'r

Uc

Trefor

18

Bwlch Mawr 1671

Gyrn Ddu 1712

Trwyn y Gorlech

Yr Eifl 1850

Tre'r Ceiri

Llanaelhaearn

Pen-sarn

Carreg Ddu

Porth Dinllaen

Llithfaen

A499

Pistyll

Llwyndyrys

Llangybi

Morfa Nefyn

Nefyn

Carn Boduan 918

Fron

Llanarmon

Groesffordd

Edern

Y Ffôr

Chwilog

Porth Ysglaig

Rhos-y-Llan

Llandudwen

Boduan

Rhosfawr

Llannor

Abererch

A4

Tudweiliog

Dinas Carn Fadryn 1218

B4415

Efailnewydd

A497

7

Porth Colmon

Penllech

Garn

Rhyd-y-Clafdy

Carreg yr Imbill

Pen-yc

Penrhyn Colmon

Llaniestyn

Penrhos

Pwllheli

Morfa

Pen-y-Graig

B4417

Rhedyn

7

Y Gamlas

Penrhyn Mawr

Llangwnnadl

Sarn-Meyllteyrn

Mynytho

Llanbedrog

Ty-Hen

Rhydlios

Bryncroes

Nanhoron

Trwyn Llanbedrog

A499

Porth Oer

Methlem

Botwnnog

Llandegwning

St Tudwal's Road

Capel Carmel

Castell Odo

Rhoshirwaun

Plas-yn-Rhiw

Llangian

Llanengan

Abersoch

Braich Anelog

Rhiw

Llawr Dref

Towyn

Sarn Bach

St Einion

Braich y Pwll

Aberdaron

Llanfaelrhys

Porth Neigwl or Hell's Mouth

Bwlchtocyn

St Tudwal's Islands

Mynydd Mawr

Uwchmynydd

Bodermid

Cilan Uchaf

Trwyn yr Wylfa

Ynys Gwylan-fawr

Trwyn Cilan

Bardsey Sound

Pen y Cil

St Mary's Abbey

Bardsey Island (Ynys Enlli)

CARDIGAN

BAY

miles / kms

Champion FM
FM 103

BBC Radio Wales
FM 94.8

Bangor 7
A487

Bangor 7
A4244

(A55) Holyhead 28
Bangor 6
A5

156

Llandudno 12
Conwy 10
A470

see p448
for a
touring
guide to
this map

Penisa'r Waun
Llanrug
Deiniolen
A4244
Clwt-y-Bont

CARNEDD LLEWELYN
3485

CARNEDD
DAFYDD
3423

Pen Llithrig
y-Wrâch

Llyn Eigiau
Resr

Llyn
Cowlyd
Resr

Trefriw

A548

Llanddoged

Pentre-tafarn-
y-fedw

rnarfon
B4366
Castle
glan

Segontium
Roman Fort
Caeathro

Pont-rug
Cwm-
y-Glo

Bryn Bras
Castle

Dinorwig
Welsh Slate
Museum
Llanberis
Lake Railway
Llanberis

Mynydd
Perfedd

Ffynnon
Llugwy

Pont Pen-
y-Benglog

13
A5

SNOWDONIA

Swallow
Falls

Ty-hyll

Capel Curig

Gwydyr
Forest

Melin-
y-coed

Llanrwst

A470

B5113

B5106

Oaklands

Betws-
y-Coed

5

Bontnewydd
Waunfawr

Dolbadarn
Castle

Nant Peris

GLYDER
FAWR
3279

Cwm Idwal

Pont Cyfyng

Mynydd Cribau
1132

St
Michael

Nebo

Dinas
Rhostryfan
Rhosgadfan
Penffridd

Betws Garmon
14

Snowdon
Mountain Railway
14

Llyn
Peris

A4086

Y Wyddfa
Snowdon

Carnedd Moel-siabod
2861

Pont-y-pant

A470

A5
Fairy Glen
6

Llanwnda
Groeslon

Carmel
Nantlle
Talysarn

Llyn
Cwellyn

Llyn
Nantle
Uchaf
B 4418

Rhyd-
Ddu

SNOWDON
3560

NATIONAL

A498
Llyn
Llydaw

PARK

Dolwyddelan
Dolwyddelan
Castle

Pentre-Bont

Conwy
Falls

Ty'n-y-
Coed
Uchaf

Glan Conwy

gaol
87
Nebo

Llanllyfni

Garneddgoch
2408

Ffridd Uchaf

Yr Aran
2451

Llyn
Gwynant
8

Bethania

Plas Gwynant

Yr Arddu

A470
10

Moel Penamnen
1978

Ty
Mawr

Penmachno

Pen y Bedw
1727

B4406

Ysbyty Ifan

4

Nasareth
Llwyn Cwm
Dulyn

Pant Glâs

Llanfihangel-
y-pennant

Bryncir

Garndolbenmaen

Moel Hebog
2566

Beddgelert

Pont
Aberglaslyn
Nantmor

Sygun
Copper
Mine

Nantgwynant

Pass of
Aberglaslyn

Bwthyn Llywelyn

Croesor

Cnicht
2265

Rhiwbryfdir

Llechwedd
Slate Caverns

Cwm
Penmachno

Llyn
Conwy

B4407

Blaenau
Ffestiniog

Ffestiniog
Railway

144

Rhoslan
Golan
A487

Llyn
Cwmystradllyn

Moel-ddu
1811

A498
A4085
8

Garreg

B4410

Plas
Brondanw

Moelwyn Mawr
2527

Tanygrisiau
Tanygrisiau
Resr

Congl-y-wal

A496

Migneint

Arenig Fâch
2259

A4212
Bala 6

Dolbenmaen

Penmorfa
Tremadog

Prenteg

Llanfrothen

Rhyd

Ffestiniog
Railway
5

Maentwrog

2

A470

Llan Ffestiniog

Rhaeadr
Cynfal

Rhaeadr
y Cwm

Carnedd
Iago

18

Porthmadog

Welsh Highland
Railway

Penrhyndeudraeth
Toll

Minffordd
Bryn Glas

Borth,
Y-Gest
Portmeirion

Gellilydan

Craig
Gyfynys

A470

6

5
Graig Wen
1823

B4391

Craig y
Hyrddod

3

Criccieth

Castle

Morfa Bychan

Penrhyndeudraeth
3

Talsarnau

Tomen-y-Mur

Llyn
Trawsfynydd

Trawsfynydd

Clem Prysor

A4212

Arenig Fawr
2801

TOWN PLANS
Barmouth p142
Caernarfon
p156

Llanystumdwy
14

Traeth Bach

Llanfihangel-y-Traethau

Morfa
Harlech

Eisingrug

Moel Y'sgyfarnogod
2044

Moel Llyfnant
2461

Llafar

Harlech

Morfa
Harlech

A496

B4573

Harlech
Castle

Craig
Ddrwg

Roman Steps

Bronaber

A470

13

Moel y
Feidiog

Mynydd
Bryn-llech

SNOWDONIA

2

NATIONAL

Llandanwg

Pen-Sarn

Llanfair

Pentre Gwynfryn

Rhinog Fawr
2362

SARN HELEN

Pistyll
Cain

Rhaeadr
Mawddach

Rhobell Fawr
2409

18

Bala 10
A494

Shell Island

Llanbedr

LLANBEDR

Y Llethr
2475

Llyn
Hywel

Rhinog

Rhaeadr
Du

Coed-y-
Brenin Forest

Dyrysgol

A494

PARK

Morfa
Dyffryn
20

Moelfre
1932

Llyn
Bodlyn

Craig-
Garn y-Cae

Y Garn
2063

Ganllwyd

Arboretum

Llanfachreth

Rhydymain

Llanenddwyn
Llanddwywe

Coed Ystumgwern

Dyffryn Ardudwy

Diffwys
2462

Llawlech

A470

A470

Tal-y-Bont

Coed
Garth Gell

Cymer Abbey

Llanelltyd

Brithdir

Y Gribin

Uwch-Mynydd

Bontddu
10

Pen-y-
Bryn

Toll

Penmaenpool

B4416

Dolgellau

A470

11

Cribin Fawr

Llanaber

Caerdeon
Cutiau

A496
A493

Abergwynant

A487

A470

(A4458) Welshpool 29

Barmouth

RNLI

Islaw'r-dref

Dyfi

E
A493
Tywyn 13

F

131

G
A487
Machynlleth 11

H
A470

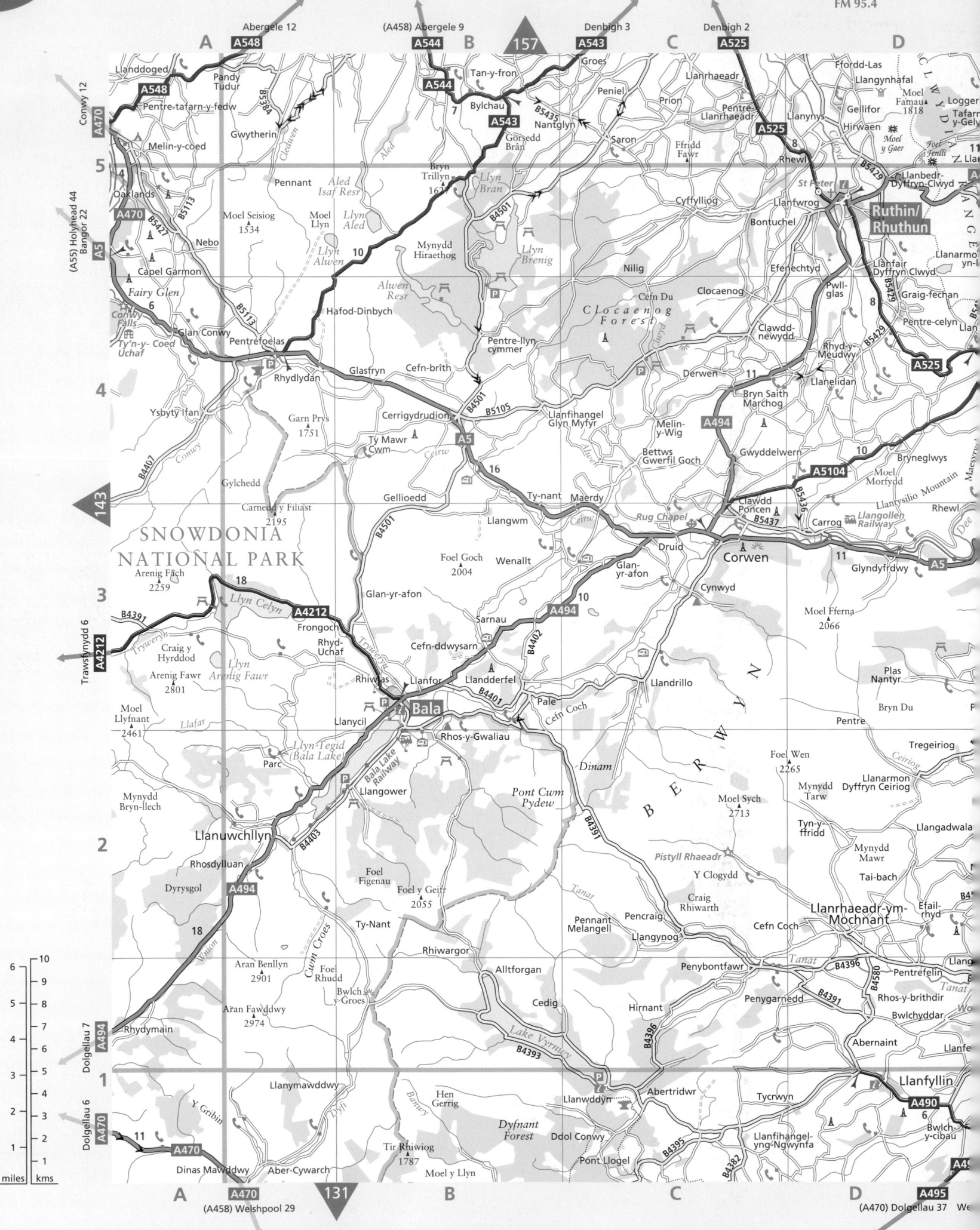

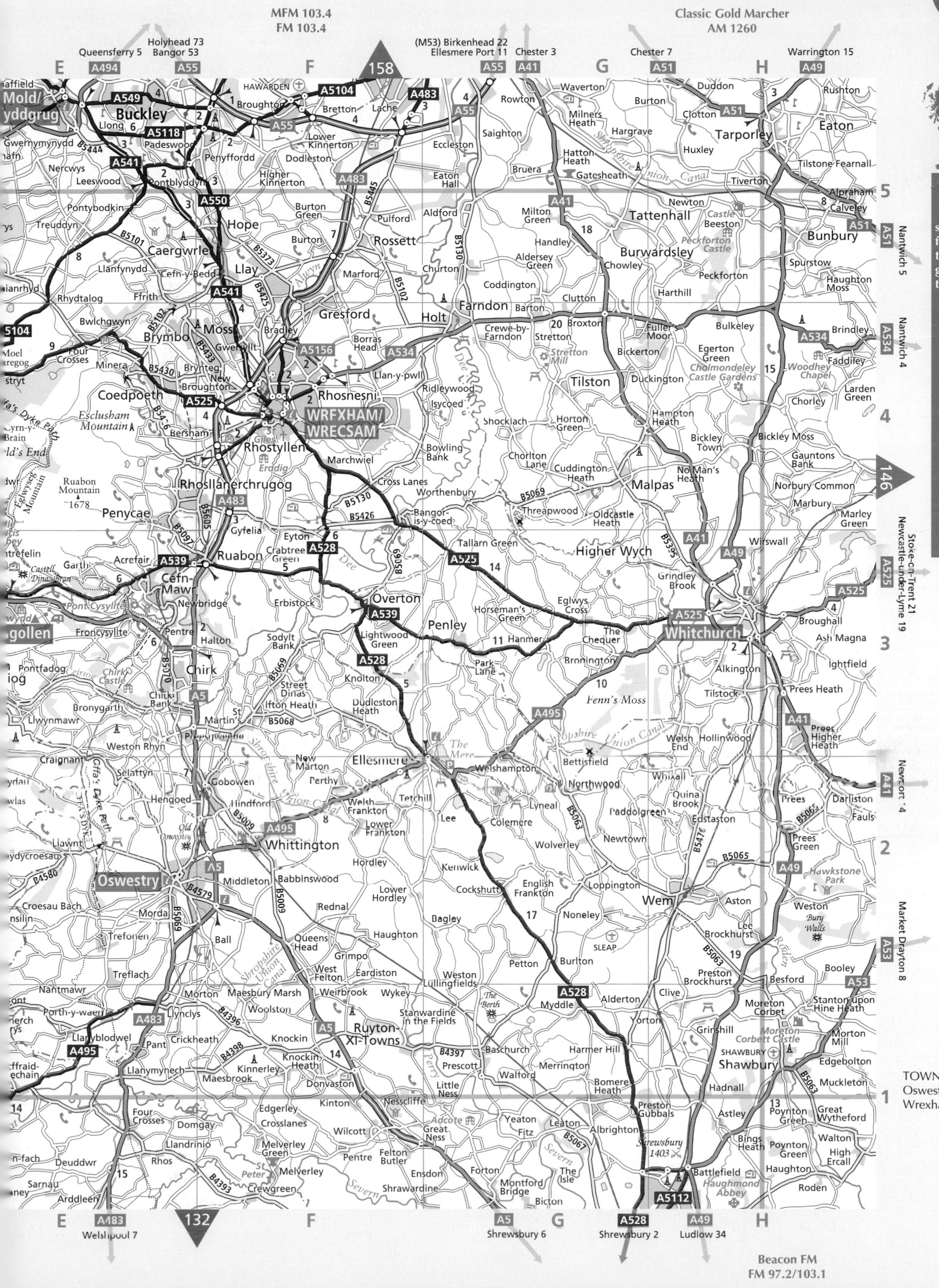

Holyhead 73
Queensferry 5 Bangor 53
(M53) Birkenhead 22 Chester 3
Ellesmere Port 11
Chester 7
Warrington 15

158

see p449 for a touring guide to this map

146

132

Welshpool 7
Shrewsbury 6
Shrewsbury 2 Ludlow 34

TOWN PLANS
Oswestry p375
Wrexham p406

Mold/yddgrug
Buckley
Broughton
Bretton
Lache
Hawarden
Rowton
Waverton
Milners Heath
Burton
Clotton
Tarporley
Duddon
Rushton
Eaton

Llong
Padeswood
Penyffordd
Lower Kinnerton
Dodleston
Higher Kinnerton
Eccleston
Saighton
Hatton Heath
Hargrave
Huxley
Tilstone Fearnall

Nercwys
Treuddyn
Pontybodkin
Pontblyddyn
Hope
Burton Green
Pulford
Aldford
Eaton Hall
Gatesheath
Bruera
Milton Green
Newton
Tattenhall
Alpraham
Calveley

Leeswood
Caergwrle
Llanfynydd
Cefn-y-Bedd
Llay
Burton
Rossett
Handley
Aldersey Green
Burwardsley
Chowley
Peckforton
Bunbury
Spurstow

Rhydtalog
Bwlchgwyn
Ffrith
Brymbo
Mossy
Bradley
Marford
Gresford
Churton
Coddington
Clutton
Harthill
Peckforton
Haughton Moss

Four Crosses
Minera
Bersham
New Broughton
Borras Head
Holt
Farndon
Barton
Broxton
Fuller's Moor
Bulkeley
Bickerton
Egerton Green
Cholmondeley Castle Gardens
Brindley
Faddiley

Coedpoeth
WREXHAM/WRECSAM
Rhosnesni
Ridleywood
Isycoed
Crewe-by-Farndon
Stretton
Tilston
Duckington
Hampton Heath
Woodhey Chapel
Larden Green
Chorley

Rhostyllen
Marchwiel
Bowling Bank
Worthenbury
Horton Green
Chorlton Lane
Cuddington Heath
Bickley Town
Bickley Moss
Gauntons Bank

Rhosllanerchrugog
Cross Lanes
Bangor-is-y-coed
Threapwood
Oldcastle Heath
Malpas
No Man's Heath
Norbury Common
Marbury
Marley Green

Penycae
Gyfelia
Eyton
Crabtree Green
Tallarn Green
Higher Wych
Wirswall

Acrefair
Ruabon
Overton
Horseman's Green
Eglwys Cross
Grindley Brook
Broughall
Ash Magna

Cefn-Mawr
Newbridge
Erbistock
Penley
The Chequer
Whitchurch
Alkington
Prees Heath

Froncysyllte
Pentre
Halton
Lightwood Green
Hanmer
Bronington
Tilstock

Chirk
Knolton
Dudleston Heath
Park Lane
Fenn's Moss
Welsh Hollinwood End
Prees Higher Heath

Oswestry
Gobowen
Whittington
Ellesmere
Welshampton
Bettisfield
Whixall
Quina Brook
Prees
Darliston
Fauls

Whitchurch

Ruyton XI-Towns
Baschurch
Shawbury

Shrewsbury 1403

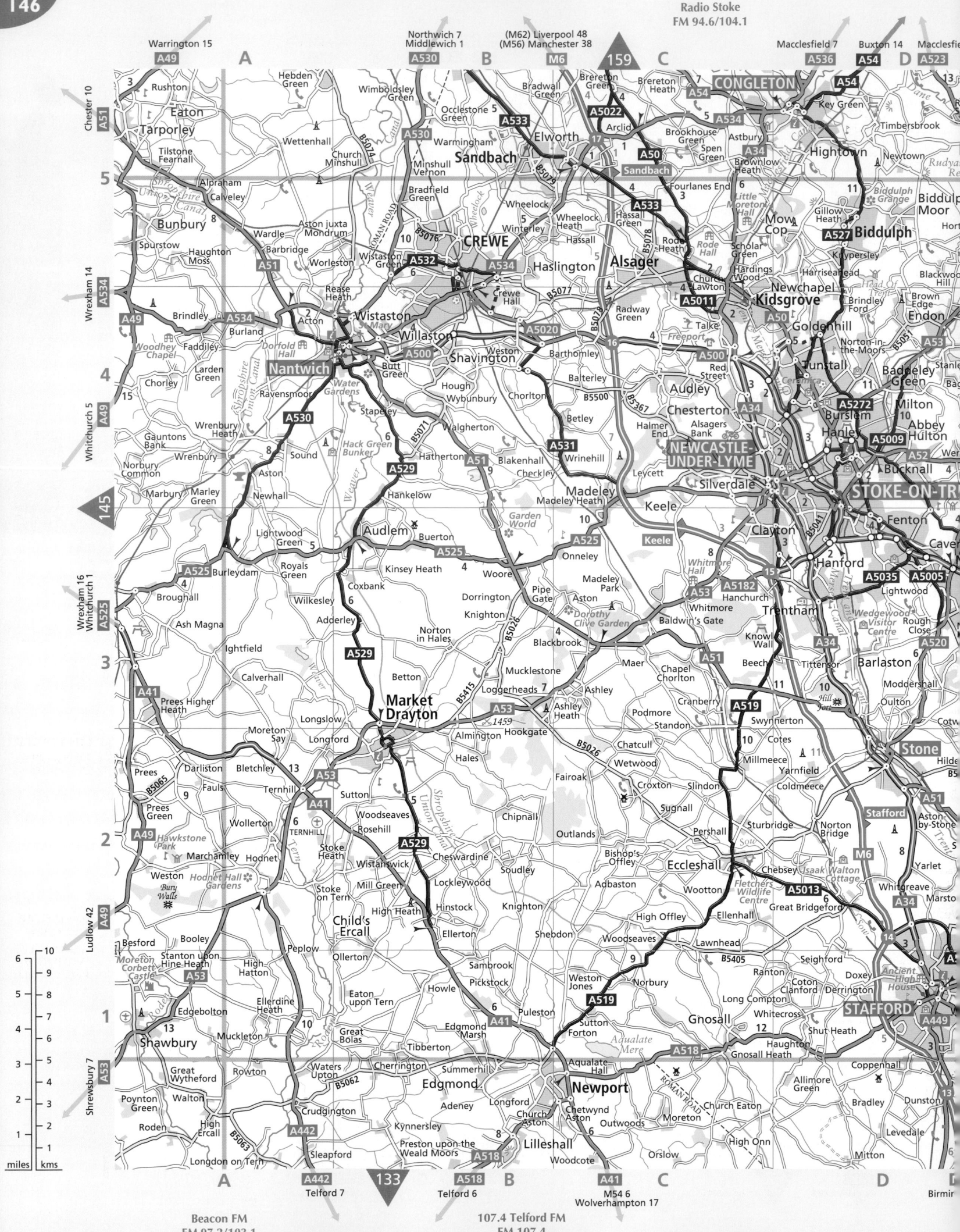

Radio Stoke
FM 94.6/104.1

Beacon FM
FM 97.2/103.1

107.4 Telford FM
FM 107.4

Buxton 7 · A53 · **160** · Buxton 8 · A515 · Buxton 16 · Bakewell 4 · A6 · Chesterfield 6 · A632

E · **F** · **G** · **H**

The Roaches · Fawfieldhead · Longnor · Pilsbury · Parsley Hay · Arbor Low · Youlgreave · Northwood · Peak Rail · B5057 · Darley Dale · Kelstedge · 9 · B6036

Hen Cloud · 13 · Newtown · Brund · Sheen · Roman Road · Middleton · Stanton in Peak · Nine Ladies · Birchover · Darley Bridge · Two Dales · Upper Hackney · A632 · Tansley

Upper Hulme · Meerbrook · Hartington · Heathcote · Biggin · Newhaven · Elton · Winster · Wensley · Market House · Brightgate · **Matlock** · Bonsall · Matlock Bath · Riber · A615 · B6014

Blackshaw Moor · A53 · Upper Elkstone · Hulme End · B5054 · **PEAK** · **DISTRICT** · A515 · Pikehall · 10 · A5012 · Grangemill · Bonsall · Lea · Lea Gardens

Leek · Thorncliffe · Warslow · **NATIONAL** · **PARK** · Aldwark · Ible · Cromford · Cromford Mill · Holloway

Mixon · Butterton · Wetton · Alstonefield · Alsop en le Dale · Ballidon · Longcliffe · Middleton · Leawood Pumphouse · Tramway Museum

Bradnop · A523 · Onecote · Ford · Grindon · Hopedale · Milldale · 10 · Parwich · Brassington · Wirksworth · Whatstandwell

Basford Green · B5053 · Blackbrook · Winkhill · 15 · Waterfall · Ilam Park · Ilam · Tissington · Bradbourne · Hopton · Carsington · Aldwarsley · 8 · A6

Ipstones · Waterhouses · Cauldon · Calton · Blore · Thorpe · Fenny Bentley · Carsington Water · Ecclesbourne Valley

Consall · Froghall · Foxt · 11 · Swinscoe · Mapleton · Kniveton · Hognaston · Kirk Ireton · Belper Lane End · Shottle

A52 · Whiston · Cotton · A52 · **Ashbourne** · Atlow · Biggin · Idridgehay · Shottlegate · Blackbrook

Kingsley · Weaver Hills 1217 · Stanton · Mayfield · A517 · Hulland Ward · Hulland · 12 · Turnditch · Cross o'th'hands · Cowers Lane · Hazelwood

Cheadle · Oakamoor · Ramshaw · Wootton · Clifton · St Oswald · Osmaston · Mercaston · Muggington · Windley · Duffield

Dilhorne · Alton Towers · Farley · Ellastone · Norbury · Shelston · Wyaston · Commonside · Weston Underwood · Kedleston · Quarndon

A521 · Forsbrook · Bradley in the Moors · Alton · B5032 · Roston · Darley Moor · Shirley · Rodsley · Ednaston · Brailsford · Kedleston Hall · A38 · Allestree

Draycott in the Moors · Great Gate · Croxden Abbey · Denstone · Rocester · A515 · Yeaveley · Hollington · Kirk Langley · Longlane · **DERBY** · Mackworth

A50 · Upper Tean · Hollington · Checkley · B5030 · Great Cubley · Alkmonton · Roman Road · Thurvaston · Lees · Mickleover · A5111

Lower Tean · Fole · Beamhurst · Stramshall · Waldley · Little Cubley · Longford · Radbourne · A38 · Littleover

Church Leigh · Withington · Somersal Herbert · Boylestone · Trusley · Dalbury · Sutton on the Hill · A516 · Burnaston · Stenson Fields

Garshall Green · A522 · Fradswell · **Uttoxeter** · Doveridge · Church Broughton · Etwall · Findern · A50 · M1 9

Field · Bramshall · Blounts Green · Sudbury · Foston · Hilton · Works · Twyford

Coton · Gratwich · A518 · Marchington · Scropton · A50 · Marston on Dove · Stenson · Willington · St Wystan · Foremark

Grindley · Kingstone · Marchington Woodlands · Draycott in the Clay · Tutbury · Rolleston on Dove · Egginton · Repton · Milton

Chartley Castle · Amerton Light Railway · The Blythe · Hanbury · Marston on Dove · A38 · B5008 · Newton Solney · Bretby

Stowe-by-Chartley · Drointon · Newton · Abbots Bromley · Newborough · Needwood Forest · Anslow Gate · Horninglow · Anslow · Winshill · Foremark Resr

Hixon · Lea Heath · Blithfield Resr · B5234 · Hanbury Woodend · TATENHILL · A5121 · Stretton · Newhall · B5353 · A514

Ingestre · A51 · Admaston · Hoar Cross · A515 · Rangemore · Tatenhill · A5189 · **BURTON UPON TRENT** · Stapenhill · Hartshorne

Great Haywood · Colwich · Colton · Blithbury · Hadley End · B5018 · Branston · Newhall · **SWADLINCOTE** · Woodville

A513 · Little Haywood · Dunstall · Stanton · A444 · Church Gresley · Blackfordby

Rugeley · Hill Ridware · Pipe Ridware · Hamstall Ridware · B5016 · Barton-under-Needwood · Walton-on-Trent · Caldwell · Castle Gresley · Norris Hill · A511

CANNOCK CHASE · Etchinghill · Mavesyn Ridware · Morrey · Woodhouses · Yoxall · Linton · Overseal · Moira

A460 · Brereton · Handsacre · King's Bromley · Orgreave · A38 · Coton in the Elms · Rosliston · M42 4 · Nuneaton 18

Brindley Heath · Armitage · A513 · **134** · A51 · A515 · A38 · A444

Cannock 5 · Lichfield 6 · Lichfield 5 · Lichfield 6

see p450 for a touring guide to this map

148

102.8 RAM FM
FM 102.8

CITY ROUTES
Nottingham & Derby p292

TOWN PLANS
Crewe p324
Derby p326
Stafford p390
Stoke-on-Trent p393

Mansfield 21 · A38 · A50 · M1 9 · Ashby-de-la-Zouch 1 · Alfreton 5 · A615

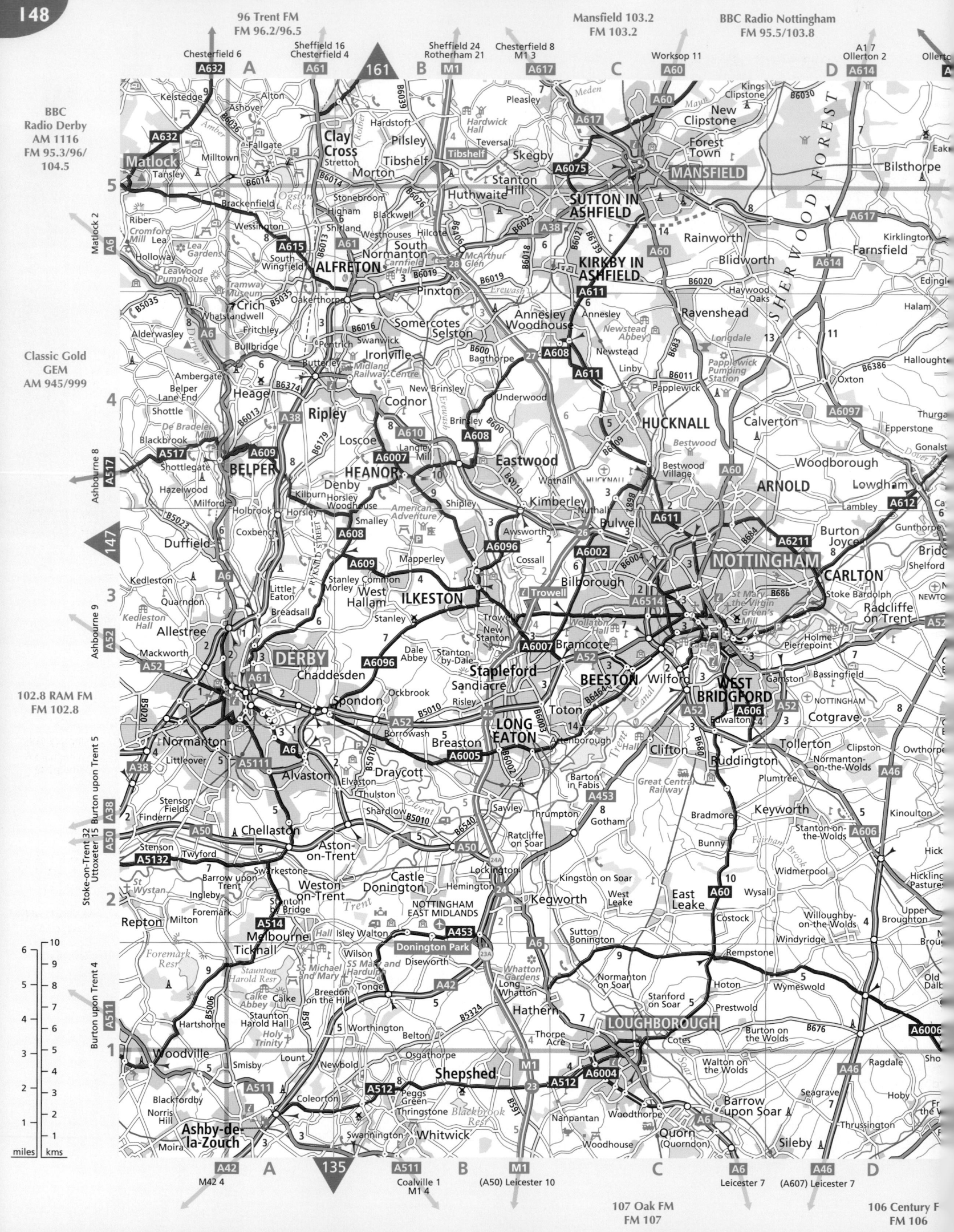

BBC Radio Lincolnshire
AM 1368/FM 94.9/104.7

see p451
for a
touring
guide to
this map

CITY ROUTES
Nottingham &
Derby p292

TOWN PLANS
Derby p326
Grantham
p336
Mansfield p363
Newark on
Trent p367
Nottingham
p372

Radio Rutland
FM 97.4/107.2

Lincs FM
FM 96.7/97.6/102.2

BBC Radio
Lincolnshire
AM 1368
FM 94.9/104.7

Louth 18
Horncastle 3
A153

Louth 16
A16

Woodhall Spa

Nocton
Dunston
Sots Hole
Roughton
Wood Enderby
Old Bolingbroke
Toynton All Saints
Greaves

Metheringham
Blankney
Martin Dales
Kirkby on Bain
Mareham le Fen
Haltham
Moorby
Miningsby
West Keal
East Keal
Toynton Fen Side
Toynton St Peter
Little Steeping

Scopwick
Martin
Timberland Delph
Tattershall Thorpe
A155
East Kirkby
Keal Cotes
Revesby
Stickford

B1189
B1191
Timberland
Tumby
Tumby Woodside
Midville
New Leake
Eastville

Kirkby Green
Rowston
Walcott
Tattershall
Coningsby
New Bolingbroke
Stickney
Carrington
Northlands
Lade Bank
Wrangle Bank

Scopwick Heath
Ashby de la Launde
Digby
Tattershall Bridge
Dogdyke
CONINGSBY SCRUB Hill
Hawthorn Hill
New York
Medlam
Bunker's Hill
West Fen
Sibsey Fen Side
Frithville
B1184
Sibsey
Wrangle
Leake Commonside

Bloxholm
Dorrington
Billinghay
North Kyme
Chapel Hill
Wildmore Fen
Gipsey Bridge
Langrick
Fishtoft Drove
Frith Bank
High Ferry
Hilldyke
Leverton Highgate
Leverton Lucasgate
Old Leake

Ruskington
A153
Anwick
Holland Fen
Amber Hill
Hedgehog Bridge
Hubbert's Bridge
Anton's Gowt
Brothertoft
St Botolph
A52
Bennington

Lincoln 16
A15
Newark on Trent 17
A17
Leasingham
B1209
Evedon
Ewerby Thorpe
Ewerby
South Kyme
South Kyme Fen
Car Dyke Roman Canal
Holdingham
Kirkby La Thorpe
Howell
BOSTON
Haltoft End
Butterwick

Sleaford
Quarrington
Heckington
Asgarby
St Andrew
East Heckington
A1121
Kirton Holme
Wyberton
Fishtoft
Freiston
Freiston Shore
Scrane End

Silk Willoughby
Burton Pedwardine
Great Hale
Swineshead Bridge
A17
Fenhouses
Frampton West End
Frampton
Sandholme

A15
Aswarby
Little Hale
Helpringham
Swineshead
Blackjack
Kirton End
Kirton
Skeldyke

Osbournby
Spanby
Scredington
Bicker
Northorpe
Hoffleet Stow
Wigtoft
Sutterton
Algarkirk
Black Buoy Sand

Walcot
Threekingham
Swaton
Bridge End
Horbling
Donington
Church End
Quadring Eaudike
Sutterton Dowdyke
Fosdyke
Fosdyke Bridge

Billingborough
Donington South Ing
A152
Quadring
Gosberton
Holbeach St Marks
Holbeach St Matthew

Folkingham
Pointon
Millthorpe
Westhorpe
Risegate
Surfleet Seas End
A17
Holbeach Bank
Holbeach Marsh

Aslackby
Graby
Dowsby
Gosberton Clough
B1397
Surfleet
Crossgate
Pinchbeck Engine
Moulton Seas End
Saracen's Head
Holbeach Hurn
Gedney Dyke

Rippingale
Dunsby
Northgate
Pinchbeck
Holbeach Clough
Fleet Hargate
Chapelgate

Kirkby Underwood
Bulby
Stainfield
Haconby
Pinchbeck West
B1180
Weston
Moulton
Whaplode
Gedney
Long Sutton

Hanthorpe
Elsthorpe
Northgate
Spalding
Springfields
All Saints
St Mary
Holbeach
Butterfly & Wildlife Park

Morton
Dyke
Cawthorpe
A151
Guthram Gowt
Pode Hole
Little London
Weston Hills
Gedney Broadgate

Bourne
Edenham
Bourne Wood
Twenty
Tongue End
Cowbit
Moulton Chapel
Whaplode St Catherine
Holbeach St Johns
Sutton St James
Tydd St Giles

Lound
Toft
Witham on the Hill
Northorpe
Thurlby
Deeping Fen
Deeping St Nicholas
A1073
Fenland
Tydd St Giles

A6121
Stamford 5
A15
Peterborough 11
A16
Stamford 14
A1073
Peterborough 11

see p452 for a touring guide to this map

BOSTON

Grimsby 47
A 16

Maud Foster Windmill

Superstore

County Court

Central Park

Tattershall Rd

NORFOLK ST

FYDELL ST

Tunnard St

Thorold St

Tawney Street

Norman Av

Red Lion

Park St

Bargate

Wide

Bargate

Pen St

Queen's Rd

Tower Road

Freiston Road

Maud Foster Drain

Union St

Witham St

Witham Pl

Irby Street

Witham PL

Worngate

The Haven

Silver St

Thread-needle St

Mitre La

Main Ridge W

PUMP Sq

Artillery Row

Field St

Main Ridge

Grantham 29

Boston Station

Station App

Station St

Trinity St

James St

Tower St

Irby St

Lincoln Lane

Bank St

St Botolph

County Hall

Assembly Rooms

Town Bridge

West Street

Council Offices

Paddock Grove

George St

Trafalgar Pl

Fydell Crescent

High St

Blackfriars

Guildhall

Sam Newsom Centre

Fydell House

Spayne Road

Football Ground

York Street

Manor Gardens

Pilgrim Road

Rowley Road

Windsor Cr

ADAMS WAY

LIQUORPOND ST

HAVEN BRIDGE RD

Docks

A 16 Spalding 15

0 100 200yds
0 100 200m

THE WASH

Roger Sand

Gat Sand

South

Boston Deeps

Long Sand

Lynn Deeps

Peddars Way and Norfolk Coast Path

Brancaster Bay

Scolt Head Island

Holme next the Sea

Titchwell Marsh

Burnham Deepdale

Burnham Overy Staithe

Cromer 25
Sheringham 21
A149

Thornham

Titchwell

18

Brancaster

Brancaster Staithe

Burnham Norton

Burnham Market

Old Hunstanton

Ringstead

Burnham Market

B1161

Sea Life Centre

Hunstanton

Norfolk Lavender

Summerfield

B1454

B1153

B1155

B1355

North Norfolk Radio
FM 96.2/103.2

Heacham

A149

Sedgeford

Docking

Stanhoe

Seal Sand

Snettisham

Snettisham Southgate

Ingoldisthorpe

Fring

Bircham Newton

Barmer

Syderstone

Peter Black Sand

12

B1440

Shernborne

Great Bircham

Bircham Tofts

Bagthorpe

B1155

B1454

Wicken Green

152

Dersingham

Fakenham 5
A148

Gedney Drove End

Bull Dog Sand

Sandringham

Anmer

New Houghton

Houghton Hall

Tallersell
Coxford

Bircham Newton

Breast Sand

Wolferton

House

B1440

West Newton

B1439

Flitcham

B1153

West Rudham

East Rudham

Pockthorpe

Harpley

BBC Radio Norfolk
FM 95.1/104.4

Guy's Head

Trinity Hospital

Babingley River

Hillington

A148

17

Castle Rising

Congham

Little Massingham

Great Massingham

Weasenham St Peter

Rougham

Cromer 29
Fakenham 7
A1065

North Wootton

KING'S LYNN

South Wootton

4

Roydon

Grimston

Herb Garden

Pott Row

Massingham Heath

B1145

Terrington Marsh

Ongar Hill

Gaywood

A149

4

Bawsey

Gayton

Gayton Thorpe

West Acre

West Lexham

A1065

Terrington St Clement

Clenchwarton

A1078

West Lynn

2

Ashwicken

B1145

A17

Walpole Cross Keys

12

Hay Green

Tilney All Saints

Fair Green

West Winch

Middleton

East Winch

13

East Walton
West Bilney

West Acre

Castle Acre

Newton

TOWN PLANS
Boston p151
King's Lynn p344
Skegness p165

Saddle Bow

North Runcton

A10

A47

Downham Market 7

Swaffham 7

Swaffham 3

A1065

E   F   G   H

A47

Wisbech 5
Peterborough 26

138

KL.FM 96.7
FM 96.7

A158

Lincoln 38
Horncastle 17

A52

Mablethorpe 16

164

Natureland

SKEGNESS

Burgh le Marsh 7

Seacroft

Croft

A52

Wainfleet All Saints

Gibraltar

Gibraltar Point

Wainfleet St Mary

Wainfleet Tofts

Friskney Eaudyke

22

Friskney Tofts

Wainfleet Sand

Croft Marsh

Thorp St Peter

Bratoft

Irby in the Marsh

Friskney Flats

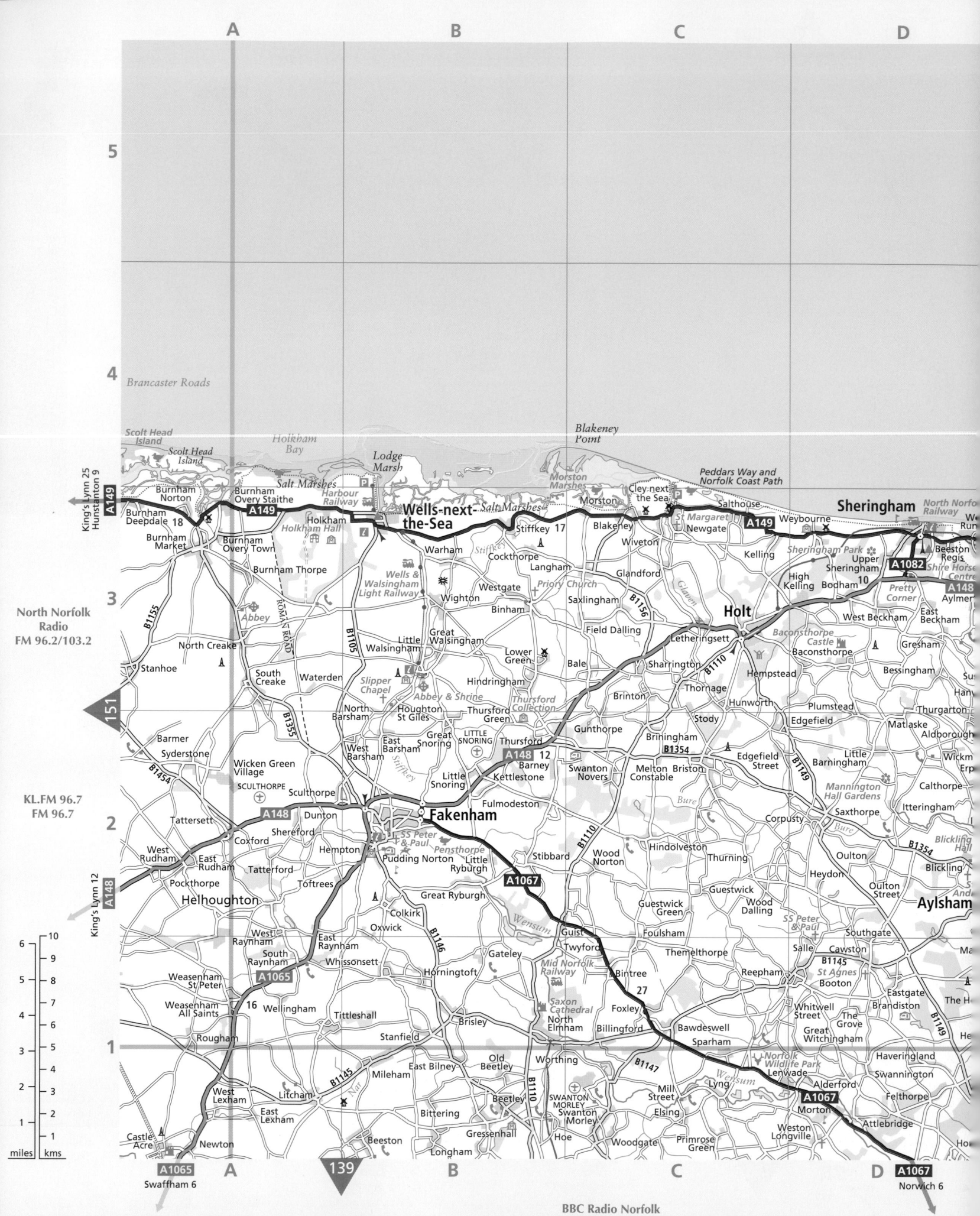

see p453
for a
touring
guide to
this map

NORTH

SEA

E F G H

5

4

3

2

1

Cromer
Foulness
Overstrand
Crossdale
Street
Sidestrand
Trimingham
Northrepps
Mundesley
Southrepps Gimingham
Upper Tower
Street Street
Paston
Thorpe
Market
Bacton
Green
Trunch
Bacton
Antingham
Knapton
Keswick
Suffield
Edingthorpe
Walcott
Bradfield
Ostend
Swafield
Witton
Bridge
Happisburgh
Colby
North
Walsham
Spa
Common
Ridlington
Whimpwell
Green
Crostwight
B1145 Felmingham
A149
Happisburgh
Common
Eccles on Sea
Tuttington
East Ruston Lessingham
Hempstead
Sea
Palling
Waxham
Valley
way
Skeyton Westwick
Worstead
7
Honing
Ingham B1151
Stalham
B1159
Swanton
Abbot
Sloley
Dilham
Smallburgh
Hickling
Lamas
COLTISHALL
Scottow
Sco
Ruston
Pennygate
Barton
Turf
Stalham
Green
Museum of
the Broads
Hickling Green
Hickling Broad
Sutton
Horsey
Little
Hautbois
7
Catfield
Hickling
Heath
Horsey
Windpump
Great
Hautbois
Tunstead A1151
Neatishead
A149
THE
BROADS
East
Somerton
Waterloo B1354
Horstead
Coltishall B1354
Ashmanhaugh
Irstead
Potter
Heigham
West
Somerton
Winterton-on-Sea
Hainford
Frettenham
Belaugh
Ludham
B1152
Hemsby
B1159
Newton
St Faith
Hoveton
Wroxham
Horning
A1062
7
St Benet's
Abbey
Bastwick
Martham
*Hemsby
Hole*
Spixworth
Crostwick
Upper
Street
Woodbastwick
Thurne
Repps
11
Rollesby
Newport
Scratby

E F G H
A1151 140 A149
Norwich 5 Great Yarmouth 6

Broadland 102
FM 102.4

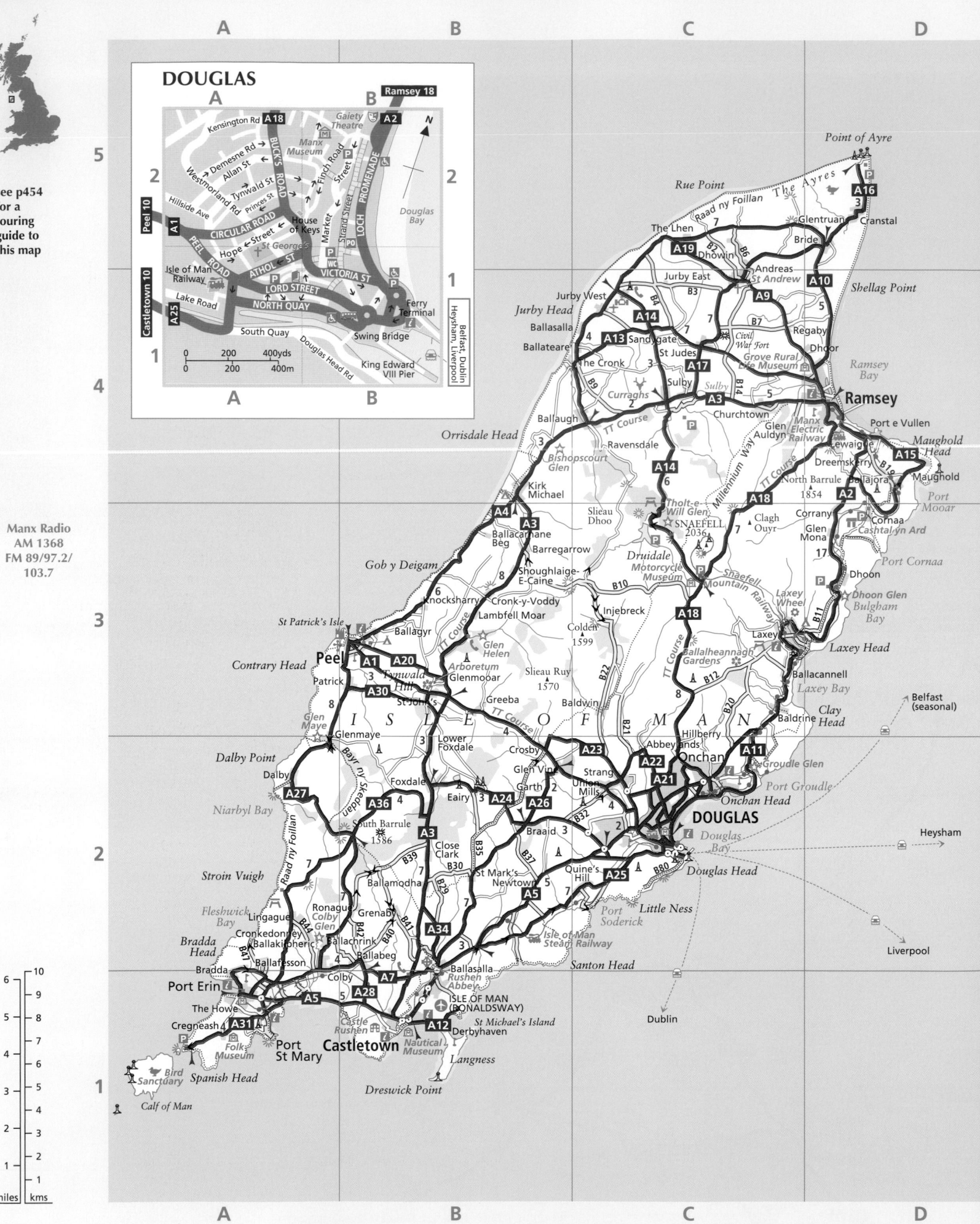

see p454 for a touring guide to this map

Manx Radio
AM 1368
FM 89/97.2/
103.7

DOUGLAS

Ramsey 18

Kensington Rd **A18**
Demesne Rd
Allan St
Westmorland Rd
Tynwald St
Princes St
BUCK'S ROAD
Finch Road
Strand Street
Market
Hillside Ave
CIRCULAR ROAD
House of Keys
A1
Hope Street
St George's
PEEL ROAD
ATHOL ST
Victoria St
Isle of Man Railway
LORD STREET
NORTH QUAY
Lake Road
A25
South Quay
Swing Bridge
King Edward VIII Pier

Gaiety Theatre
A2
Manx Museum
PROMENADE
LOCH
Douglas Bay
Ferry Terminal
Douglas Head Rd

Belfast, Dublin, Heysham, Liverpool

Peel 10
Castletown 10

0   200   400yds
0   200   400m

THE ISLE OF MAN

Point of Ayre
Rue Point
The Ayres
Raad ny Foillan
A16
The Lhen
Glentruan   Cranstal
A19 Dhowin   **B7** B6 Bride
Jurby East   St Andrew   **A10**   Shellag Point
Jurby West   **A14**   B4 B3 Andreas   **A9**   B7   Regaby
Jurby Head   **A13** Sandygate   St Judes   Civil War Fort   Dhoor
Ballasalla   4   The Cronk   3   **A17**   Sulby   Grove Rural Life Museum   Ramsey Bay
Ballateare   B9   Curraghs   Sulby   **A3**   5   Ramsey
Ballaugh   **A14**   TT Course   Churchtown   Manx Electric Railway
Orrisdale Head   3   Bishopscourt Glen   Glen Auldyn   Lewaigue   **A15**   Maughold Head
Ravensdale   **A14**   6   Tholt-e-Will Glen   North Barrule 1854   Dreemskerry   B18   Maughold
Kirk Michael   Slieau Dhoo   SNAEFELL 2036   **A18**   Ballajora   **A2**   Cornaa   Port Mooar
A4   Druidale   Clagh Ouyr   Corrany   Cashtal yn Ard
A3   Ballacarnane Beg   Motorcycle Museum   Glen Mona   17   Port Cornaa
Gob y Deigam   Barregarrow   B10   Snaefell Mountain   Dhoon
Shoughlaige-E-Caine   Injebreck   Laxey Wheel   Dhoon Glen   Bulgham Bay
Knocksharry   6   Cronk-y-Voddy   Colden 1599   Ballaheannagh Gardens   Laxey
St Patrick's Isle   8   Lambfell Moar   Ballalheannagh   B11   Laxey Head
Contrary Head   Ballagyr   Glen Helen   Slieau Ruy 1570   B12   Ballacannell   Belfast (seasonal)
Peel   **A1**   **A20**   Arboretum   Baldwin   Laxey Bay   Baldrine   Clay Head
Patrick   3   Tynwald Hill   Glenmoar   B22   Hillberry   **A11**   Groudle Glen
A30   St John's   Greeba   B21   Abbeylands   **A22**   Onchan   Port Groudle
Glen Maye   ISLE   OF   MAN   **A23**   Strang   **A21**   Onchan Head
Glenmaye   3   Lower Foxdale   Crosby   Union Mills   **DOUGLAS**
Dalby Point   4   Glen Vine   B32   Douglas Bay
Dalby   Foxdale   Eairy   Garth   2   4   Douglas Head
A27   **A36**   4   **A24**   **A26**   B37   Heysham
Niarbyl Bay   South Barrule 1586   Braaid   3   Quine's Hill   B80
Raad ny Foillan   **A3**   B39   B35   St Mark's   5   **A25**   Little Ness
Stroin Vuigh   Close Clark   B30   Newtown   **A5**   Port Soderick
Ballamodha   B9   Quine's Hill   Isle of Man Steam Railway   Liverpool
Fleshwick Bay   Ronague   Grenaby   B41   **A34**   Santon Head
Lingague   Colby Glen   B42   B40   3
Cronkedonney   B44   Ballachrink   Ballabeg
Bradda Head   Ballakilpheric   4   Ballasalla   Rusheen Abbey
Bradda   Ballafesson   Colby   Rushen Abbey
Port Erin   **A5**   5   **A28**   **A7**   ISLE OF MAN (RONALDSWAY)   St Michael's Island
The Howe   Castle Rushen   **A12**   Derbyhaven
Cregneash   4   **A31**   Folk Museum   **Castletown**   Nautical Museum   Langness
Bird Sanctuary   Spanish Head   Port St Mary
Calf of Man   Dreswick Point
Dublin

miles | kms
6 | 10
5 | 9
| 8
| 7
4 | 6
3 | 5
| 4
2 | 3
| 2
1 | 1

CAERNARFON

Bangor 9

Victoria Dock

Maritime Museum

Creative Enterprise Centre

Balaclava Road

Bangor Street

B4419

A487

St David's Road

Twthill

Twthill Monument

Seilo Theatre

Twthill East

Bank Quay

Church Street

Crown St

Market St

Old Town

Council Offices

High St

INNER

Twthill West

Council Offices

North Penrallt

South Penrallt

RELIEF

Llanberis 7

A4086

Castle Ditch

PENLLYN

PO

Pool St

Pool Street

Hill

ROAD

Beddgelert 13

A4085

Castle

Foot-bridge

Castle Hill

Chapel St

Segontium Terr

Helen's Rd

New St

Welsh Highland Railway

A487

Foreshore Road

River Seiont

Slate Quay

Porthmadog 19

0 100 200 yds
0 100 200 m

Amlwch 1
Holyhead 21

A5025

Point Lynas

Pengorffwysfa

Penysarn

Gadfa

Dulas

Ynys Dulas

Dulas Bay

City Dulas

Brynrefail

8

Din Nigwy

Moelfre

Mynydd Bodafon

Llanallgo

Champion FM
FM 103

Marian-Glas

Maenaddwyn

Capel Coch

Brynteg

Tynygongl

B5108

Benllech

Red Wharf Bay

Great Ormes Head
(Pen-y-Gogarth)

Toll

Llandudno

Little Ormes

Llanbedrgoch

Red Wharf Bay

Puffin Island

Gogarth

B5115

Penrhyn-Side

Penrhyn Bay

Priory

Penmon

St Seiriol

Conwy Bay

Conwy Sands

A546

A470

Llandrillo yn Rhos

155

B5110

B5109

Llanddyfnan
Stone Science

8

Pentraeth

Pen-y-Garnedd

Llanddona

Llangoed

B5109

Llanfaes

Dutchman Bank

Deganwy

Welsh Mountain Zoo

4

Tywyn

Llandudno Junction

Mo

A547

Talwrn

Rhoscefnhir

A5025

Llansadwrn

Castle

Beaumaris

Conwy

Dwygyfylchi

Castle

Gyffin

Bryn y-Mae

Llangefni

Ceint

Penmynydd

B5420

Butterfly Palace

Llandegfan

Menai Bridge

SS Mary & Nicholas

A545

Lavan Sands
(Traeth Lafan)

A55

15

Cefn Coch

Penmaenmawr

Capelulo

Llansanffraid
Glan Conwy

Holyhead 14

A55

A5

Llanfair Pwllgwyngyll

A55

1

2

Penrhyn Castle

Bangor

A55

Llanfairfechan

Abergwyngregyn

Tal-y-fan
2000

ROMAN ROAD

Rowen

Henryd

Ty'n-y-Groes

B5106

15

Tal-y-cafn

Bodnant Garden

Graig

Pentre Berw

Gaerwen

A5

3

Llandegai

Tal-y-Bont

Crymlyn

Moel Wnion
1902

Aber Valley Reserve

Aber Falls

Caerhun

A470

Eglwysbach

Rhosneigr 12

A4080

Pentre Berw

Llanddaniel Fab

Bryncir Ddu

Plas Newydd

Vaynol Hall

A487

1

Glasinfryn

3

Tal-y-Bont

Llanllechid

Drosgl
2484

Drum
2528

Llanbedr-y-cennin

FOEL FRAS
3091

Dolgarrog

Mwdw
12

Brynsiencyn

A4080

Llanedwen

Bethel

y-Felinheli

6

Seion

Pentir Rhiwlas

B4547

Tregarth

A4244

Rachub

Bethesda

B4409

Dulyn Resr

Afon Dulyn

CARNEDD LLEWELYN

Llyn Eigiau

Sea Zoo

B4419

Menai Strait

Llanddeiniolen

Dinas Dinorwig

Mynydd Llandegai

3485

Ffynnon Llugwy Resr

Llanddoged

Trefriw

Caernarfon

A4086

Llanrug

Pont-Rug

Perisa'r Waun

Deiniolen

14

Clwt-y-Bont

Cwm-y-Glo

Mynydd Perfedd
2665

CARNEDD DAFYDD
3423

Pen Llithrig
y-Wrâch

Llyn Cowlyd Resr

Llyn Crafnant Resr

Llanrwst

Segontium Roman Fort

Caeathro

Bryn Bras Castle

Llanberis Lake Railway

Dinorwig

Llanberis

Nant Ffrancon

Llyn Ogwen

13

A470

Llanfaglan

Welsh Highland Light Railway

Welsh Slate Museum

Pont Pen-y-benglog

143

A5

Gwydir Castle

Melin-y-coed

A487
Porthmadog 20

A4085
Beddgelert 10

A4086
(A498) Capel Curig 11

A5

A5
Capel Curig 2
Betws-y-coed 8

BBC Radio Wales
FM 94.8

A470
Betws-y-coed 2
Blaenau Ffestiniog 13

miles | kms

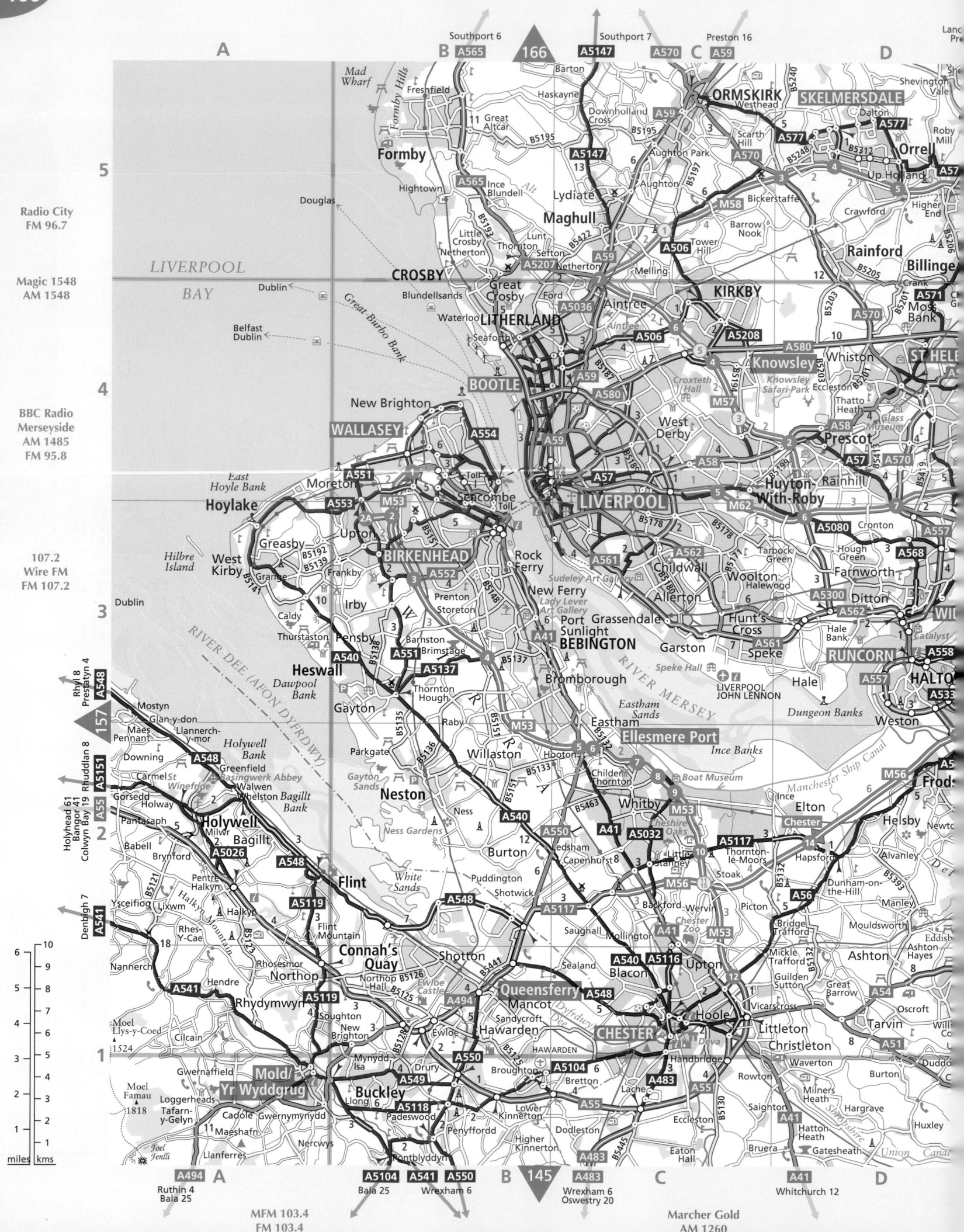

A   B   166   C   D

5

Radio City
FM 96.7

Magic 1548
AM 1548

BBC Radio
Merseyside
AM 1485
FM 95.8

107.2
Wire FM
FM 107.2

4

LIVERPOOL
BAY

Douglas

Dublin ←

Belfast →
Dublin

Mad
Wharf

Formby Hills

Freshfield

Formby

Hightown

Great
Burbo Bank

New Brighton

WALLASEY

East
Hoyle Bank

Hoylake

West
Kirby

Greasby

Moreton

Upton

BIRKENHEAD

3

Dublin

Hilbre
Island

Caldy

Thurstaston

Pensby

Irby

Frankby

Grange

Heswall

Dawpool
Bank

Gayton

2

Rhyl 8   Prestatyn 4   A548

157

Mostyn
Glan-y-don
Maes
Pennant   Llannerch-
y-mor

Downing

Carmel St
Gorsedd
Pantasaph   Holway

Holywell   Milwr
Babell   Bagillt
Brynford

A5026

Holyhead 61   A55   A5151   Rhuddlan 8   Bangor 41   Colwyn Bay 19

Holywell
Bank

Greenfield
Basingwerk Abbey
Winefride   Walwen
Whelston   Bagillt
Bank

Parkgate

Gayton
Sands

Neston

Ness

Ness Gardens

Burton

1

Denbigh 7   A541

Nannerch

Moel
Llys-y-Coed
1524

Cilcain

Gwernaffield
Loggerheads
Tafarny-
y-Gelyn

Moel
Famau
1818

Foel
Fenlli

Cadole
Maeshafn

Gwernymynydd

Nercwys

Llanferres

MFM 103.4
FM 103.4

A494   A
Ruthin 4
Bala 25

Mold/
Yr Wyddgrug

Buckley

A5104   A541   A550   B
Bala 25   Wrexham 6

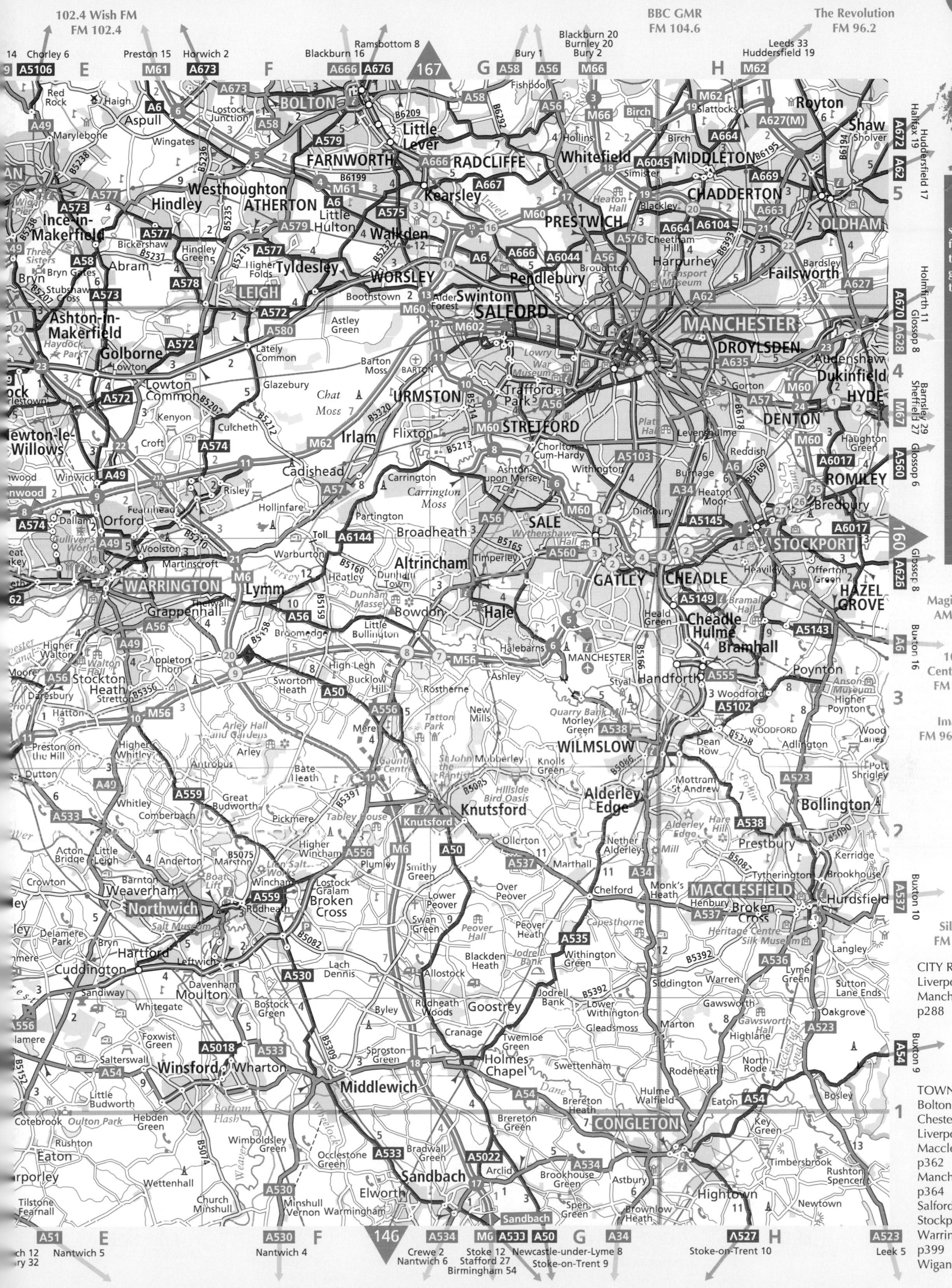

see p456 for a touring guide to this map

Magic 1152
AM 1152

105.4
Century FM
FM 105.4

Imagine
FM 96.4/104.9

Silk FM
FM 106.9

CITY ROUTES
Liverpool p282
Manchester p288

TOWN PLANS
Bolton p312
Chester p320
Liverpool p349
Macclesfield p362
Manchester p364
Salford p383
Stockport p392
Warrington p399
Wigan p402

102.4 Wish FM
FM 102.4

BBC GMR
FM 104.6

The Revolution
FM 96.2

MANCHESTER
OLDHAM
CHADDERTON
Royton
Shaw
Failsworth
ASHTON-UNDER-LYNE
STALYBRIDGE
DROYLSDEN
Audenshaw
Dukinfield
DENTON
HYDE
Mossley
Tintwistle
Hollingworth
Hadfield
Glossop
ROMILEY
Bredbury
MARPLE
STOCKPORT
HAZEL GROVE
Bramhall
Cheadle Hulme
Woodford
Poynton
New Mills
Newtown
Disley
Hayfield
Chinley
Whaley Bridge
Chapel-en-le-Frith
Dove Holes
Bollington
Prestbury
Hurdsfield
Broken Cross
MACCLESSFIELD
Buxton
Burbage
Chelmorton
Bakewell
Ashford in the Water
Hathersage
Hope
Castleton
Bradwell
Brough
Thornhill
Bamford
Eyam
Tideswell
Youlgreave
Monyash
Hartington
Longnor
Crowdecote
CONGLETON
Hightown

PEAK DISTRICT NATIONAL PARK
HIGH PEAK
Snake Pass
Kinder Scout 2088
Black Hill 1908
Bleaklow Hill 2077
Edale
Lose Hill
Holmfirth
Penistone

miles | kms

(A15) Kingston upon Hull 18
(A15) Humber Bridge 9
Humberside Airport 4
Humberside Airport 1
Stallingborough 1
(A180) Immingham 8

E M180 A18
F A18
G 171
H

M180 A18
Wrawby
B1206
Barnetby le Wold
Bigby
Keelby
Riby
Aylesby
GRIMSBY
CLEETHORPES
A46 Scartho
A1098
Discovery Centre
Pleasure Island

Brigg
Searby
Grasby
A1173
Irby upon Humber
Swallow
Laceby
Waltham
Bradley
New Waltham
Humberston
B1219

B1208
Howsham
Cadney
A1084
Cabourne
Beelsby
Barnoldby le Beck
Brigsley
Ashby Cum Fenby
Holton le Clay
Tetney
Humberston
A1031
Tetney Lock
North Cotes
Water Gardens

Hibaldstow
North Kelsey
SS Peter & Paul
Caistor
B1205
Cuxwold
Hatcliffe
East Ravendale
Grainsby
North Thoresby
A1031

Redbourne
Moortown
Nettleton
Rothwell
Croxby
Thorganby
Swinhope
Wold Newton
Brookenby
Ludborough
B1201
Great Northern Railway
Fulstow
Covenham St Bartholomew
Covenham St Mary
Utterby

South Kelsey
Brandy Wharf
Waddingham
Holton le Moor
Thornton le Moor
North Owersby
Normanby le Wold
Claxby
BINBROOK
Thoresway
Stainton le Vale
Binbrook
Kirmond le Mire
North Ormsby
Fotherby

Snitterby
Atterby
Bishop Norton
Usselby
Osgodby
Kirkby
Kingerby
Bishopbridge
Walesby
B1203
Kelstern
North Elkington

A1103
Spital in the Street
A631
Glentham
Caenby Corner
Normanby-by-Spital
Owmby-by-Spital
Saxby
Middle Rasen
West Rasen
Tott next Newton
A46
Market Rasen
North Willingham
Tealby
Ludford
A631
Welton le Wold
South Elkington
Louth
St James
A157

Spridlington
Cold Hanworth
Newton by Toft
B1202
Linwood
Legsby
Sixhills
Burgh on Bain
Hallington
Raithby
Maltby
Withcall
Dovendale
Tathwell
Haugham
A16

Hackthorn
Welton
Faldingworth
Lissington
Friesthorpe
Snarford
Hainton
East Torrington
A157
South Willingham
Benniworth
Donington on Bain
Stenigot
Cadwell Park
Cawkwell
Scamblesby
Farforth
Ruckland
Oxcombe

WICKENBY
Wickenby
Snelland
Holton cum Beckering
West Torrington
East Barkwith
West Barkwith
Market Stainton
Asterby
Goulceby
Ranby
A16

Dunholme
Scothern
A46
Sudbrooke
Stainton by Langworth
Rand
A158
Wragby
Panton
Hatton
Langton by Wragby
Kingthorpe
Great Sturton
ROMAN ROAD
A153
Belchford
Tetford

Nettleham
North Greetwell
Reepham
Apley
Chamber's Farm Wood
Baumber
Minting
Hemingby
Fulletby
Salmonby
Somersby
Ashby Puerorum

LINCOLN
Bishop's Palace
B1273
North Greetwell
Cherry Willingham
Stainfield
Gautby
Wispington
West Ashby
Greetham
Hagworthingham
A158

Washingborough
Witham
Barlings Abbey
Fiskerton
Bardney Abbey
Bardney
Bucknall
Edlington
Horncastle
Mareham on the Hill
Snipe Dales
B1195
Lusby
Asgarby
Hareby

Canwick
Heighington
Branston
Branston Booths
Potterhanworth Booths
Horsington
Thimbleby
Langton
Thornton
St Mary the Virgin
Dalderby
Hameringham

Bracebridge Heath
A15
B1188
B1178
Potterhanworth
Southrey
Tupholme Abbey
Stixwould
B1191
Wood Enderby
Moorby
Miningsby
A155

Waddington
WADDINGTON
ERMINE STREET
Metheringham
Nocton
Dunston
Sots Hole
Martin Dales
Woodhall Spa
Kirkby on Bain
Haltham
Mareham le Fen
Revesby
A155
East Kirkby

A607
B1178
B1202
Blankney
B1189
B1192
A153
150
Spilsby 4

A607 E A15
Grantham 16 Sleaford 9
F G
Sleaford 15
H

see p458 for a touring guide to this map

TOWN PLANS
Doncaster p327
Grimsby p337
Lincoln p347
Louth p165

Skegness 33 Mablethorpe 18
(A1104) Mablethorpe 14
(A1028) Skegness 18
Boston 27
Skegness 16
Spilsby 4

A B C D

CLEETHORPES

Grimsby 1
A16
A180
Discovery Centre
Lincoln 36
A46
A1098
Pleasure Island
A1243
B1219
5 Scartho New Waltham Humberston
B1203 Waltham
Holton le Clay
Brigsley A1031
Ashby cum Fenby Tetney Lock
Tetney Tetney Marshes
North Cotes
Water Gardens
Grainsby Marshchapel
Laceby 5 A18 A16 B1201 Eskham
North Thoresby North Somercotes Donna Nook
Great Northern Railway Fulstow Grainthorpe
A18 27 Ludney
BBC Radio Lincolnshire Ludborough Covenham Reservoir Conisholme Church End Skidbrooke North End
AM 1368 15 14 Covenham St Bartholomew Saltfleet
FM 94.9/104.7 North Ormsby Covenham St Mary South Somercotes A1031
Utterby Yarburgh Skidbrooke Saltfleetby
163 North Elkington Fotherby Alvingham North Cockerington St Clement Saltfleetby-Theddlethorpe Dunes
Market Rasen 10 Kelstern Saltfleetby St Peter Theddlethorpe St Helen
Wragby 10 A631 South Elkington Keddington B1200 Saltfleetby All Saints
Lincoln 21 A157 Welton le Wold Grimoldby Theddlethorpe All Saints
Hallington **Louth** Stewton Three Bridges Animal Gardens
3 Raithby Manby **Mablethorpe**
Maltby Legbourne Little Carlton
Withcall South Reston Great Carlton Great Eau Gayton le Marsh A1104 3 Trusthorpe
Dovendale Tathwell Little Cawthorpe North Reston A157 12 Withern Strubby Thorpe Sutton on Sea
Stenigot Haugham Muckton Authorpe Tothill Maltby le Marsh
Cadwell Park Burwell B1373 Beesby Sandilands
Asterby Belleau Aby A111 Hannah
Goulceby Cawkwell Farforth Ruckland 10 Saleby 6 Markby
14 Scamblesby A16 White Pit Thoresthorpe Asserby
A153 Oxcombe South Ormsby South Thoresby St Wilfrid Huttoft Anderby Creek
ROMAN ROAD Belchford Calceby Bilsby B1449 Anderby
Lincs FM Tetford Driby **Alford** Thurlby On Your Marques
FM 96.7/97.6/ Salmonby Brinkhill Ulceby Cross Farlesthorpe Mumby Authorpe Row
102.2 Fulletby Ulceby Well Cumberworth A52
West Ashby St Margaret Bag Enderby Mawthorpe Willoughby **Hogsthorpe** **Chapel St Leonards**
Lincoln 20 Somersby Harrington A1104 Fordington Claxby Sloothby 15 Hardy's Animal Farm
Low Toynton Ashby Harrington Hall 4 Dalby A1028 Welton le Marsh Addlethorpe Ingoldmells Point
A158 Puerorum 5 B1196 Funcoast World
Greetham Langton **Ingoldmells**
1 High Toynton A158 Aswardby 10 Sausthorpe Skendleby A158 Orby Winthorpe Seathorne
Horncastle Mary the Virgin Snipe Dales Hagworthingham Partney Scremby Orby Marsh
Mareham on Lusby Raithby Candlesby Gunby Hall Burgh Naturelend
the Hill B1195 by Spilsby 2 Ashby by Partney 4 Bratoft le Marsh **SKEGNESS**
Hameringham Asgarby **Spilsby** Halton Holegate A158 7
Hareby Mavis **Hundleby** St Andrew Great Irby in A52
A153 Old Bolingbroke Enderby A16 Toynton Steeping the Marsh
8 Miningsby West Keal St Peter B1195 Croft Seacroft
Sleaford 18 Wood Moorby East Keal Toynton All Saints Firsby Thorpe Croft Marsh
Mareham Enderby West Keal Toynton Fen Side Little St Peter A52
miles kms le Fen Revesby A155 East Kirkby Keal Cotes Steeping
Sleaford 15 B1183 13 Stickford Thorpe Fendykes Thorpe Culvert
A155 Boston 10 150 Boston 17
A16 Grantham 46

A B C D

LOUTH

A 16 Grimsby 16

B 1520

Hospital
High Holme Road
Mount Olvet
Hawthorne Avenue
Charles Street
Wellington St

5

St Mary's Park
St Mary's Park
Grimsby Road
Union St
Cisterngate
Temple Terr
Cedar Cl
Broadbank
Kiln La
Eve St
James Street
Ramsgate

3

Gray's Ct
Spout Yard
P
Northgate
P
Pleasant Pl

St Mary's Lane
Bridge St
Chequergate
Cannon St
Town Hall
Vickers Lane
Market Pl
Eastgate
Albion Pl

River Lud
Westgate Pl
St James's
Upgate
New St
Cornmarket
Mercer Row
Burnt Hill La
Spring Gardens
Queen St

2

Westgate
Schoolhouse
Church Cl
Gospelgate
Aswell Street
Kidgate
Kidgate
Church St

A 16
B 1200
Breakneck Lane
Edward Street
George St
Little S Street
Lee St
Cinder Lane
Ashby Rd

Irish Hill
Crowtree Lane
The Paddock
South St
Spital Hill
Ungate
St Michael's Rd

4

Newmarket B 1200

Livestock Market
Quarry Rd

1

0   100   200yds
0   100   200m

Linda Cres
Subury
Meridian View
St James View
B 1520

A

B
A 16 Boston 32

C

see p458 for a touring guide to this map

3

SKEGNESS

A
Lincoln 42
A 158
B
A 52
Maltby Rd
Council Offices
C

0   150   300yds
0   150   300m

BURGH RD
B1451
Castleton Blvd
Park Avenue
North Parade
POL
Court
Natureland

3

Playing Fields
Brunswick Dr
Cavendish Road
Lumley Cr
Lumley Av
Park Avenue

Grosvenor Road
ROMAN BANK
Scarbrough
Lumley Av
North Parade
Prince Edward Walk

Lincoln Road
Dorothy Ave
Cecil Ave
St Matthew's
Avenue
Pier

2

Grantham Dr
Ida St
Lumley Av Road
Scarbrough Esp
Pleasure Beach

Boston 22
A 52
WAINFLEET ROAD
Algitha
Road
Prince George Street
Tower Gardens
Rutland Road
Grand Parade
Embassy Centre
(indoor)

Alexandra Road
Robin Hood Rd
Super-store
Skegness Station
High Street
Lumley Road
(outdoor)
North Bracing

2

Cricket Ground
Arcadia Rd
Hildreds Centre
Clock Tower
Clock Tower Esp
Lifeboat Stn

Richmond Drive
Sandbeck Avenue
Lawn Av
Avenue
Drummond Road
South Parade
South Bracing
Lagoon Walk

1

William Way
Briar Way
Beresford
Saxby Avenue
Princes Pde

A

B

C

TOWN PLANS
Louth p165
Skegness p165

173
158

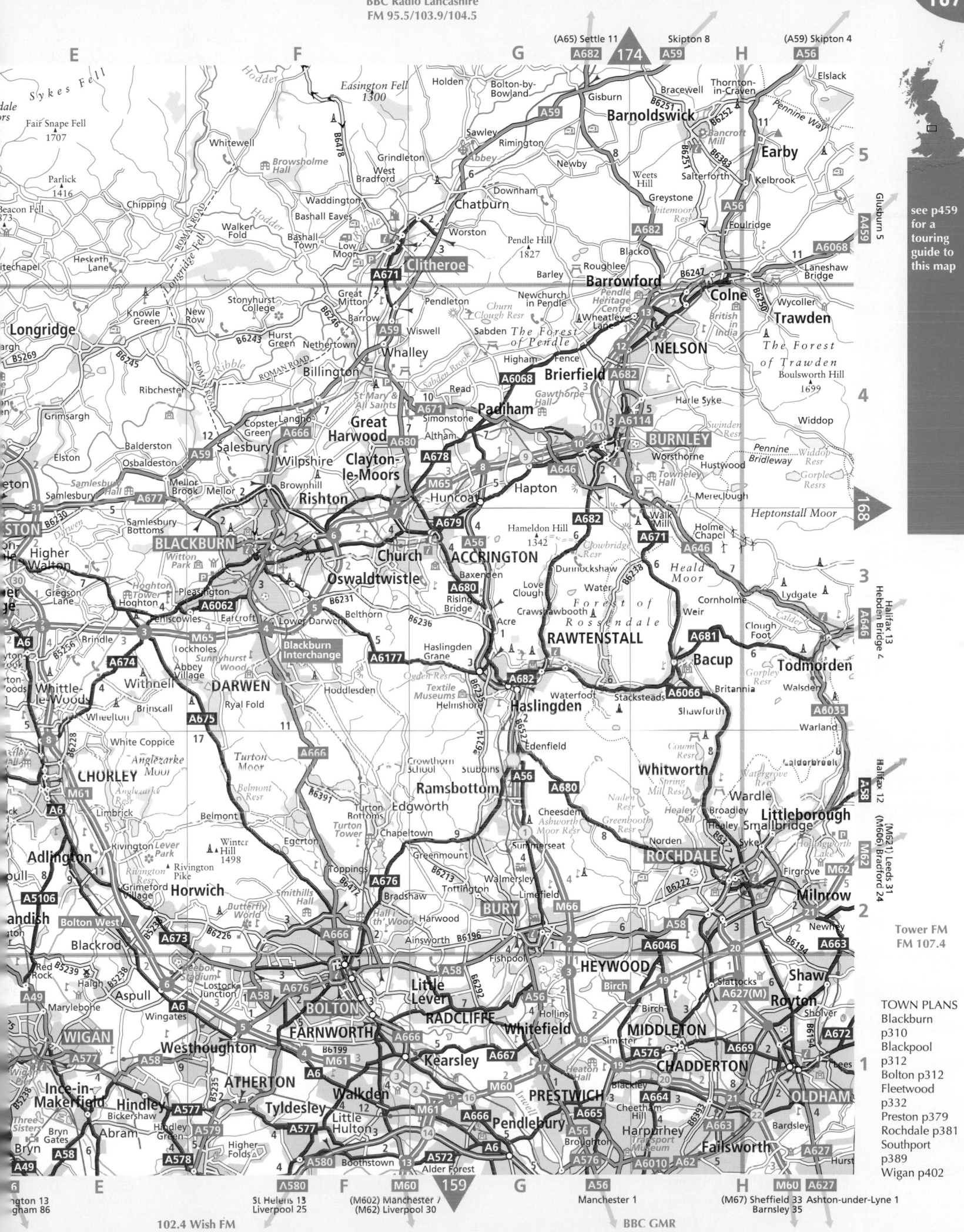

BBC Radio Lancashire
FM 95.5/103.9/104.5

see p459
for a
touring
guide to
this map

TOWN PLANS
Blackburn
p310
Blackpool
p312
Bolton p312
Fleetwood
p332
Preston p379
Rochdale p381
Southport
p389
Wigan p402

Tower FM
FM 107.4

102.4 Wish FM
FM 102.4

BBC GMR
FM 104.6

(A59) Skipton 4 (A65) Settle 16 Skipton 6
A56 A629 174 A65 175

Carleton-in-Craven
Elslack Ravenshaw
Thornton-in-Craven
Earby
Kelbrook Cononley Kildwick
Lothersdale Glusburn
A6068 Cross Hills Steeton
Lane Ends Sutton-in-Craven
Cowling
Trawden Wycoller Cliffe Castle Utley
A6086 Laneshaw Bridge 11
B6250

Addingham Middleton
Manor House All Saints Denton
ILKLEY B6382 Askwith Farnley Stainburn Huby
White Wells Cow and Calf Rocks Weston **Otley** Leathley
1320 Menston Burley in Wharfedale A659
A65 Pool Arthing Bramhope
Guiseley A660 Golden Acre

Classic Gold
AM 1278/1530

Nelson 5 Colne 3
(M65) Burnley 8 Colne 1

Keighley Moor
Oakworth Harden
Oldfield Cross Roads Wilsden
Stanbury **Haworth** Cullingworth
Bronte Parsonage Oxenhope Leeming Denholme
The Forest of Trawden
Boulsworth Hill 1699
Widdop Haworth Moor
Walshaw Dean Resrs
A6033 Thornton Moor Reservoir
Wadsworth Moor Denholme Clough Thornton
Pennine Bridleway Warley Moor Reservoir Ogden Clayton
Gorple Resrs Pecket Well A644 Queensbury
Hardcastle Crags Wainstalls Illingworth Ovenden

KEIGHLEY
Laycock Riddlesden Stockbridge East Riddlesden Hall
Goose Eye Keighley & Worth Valley Railway Crossflatts Eldwick
East Morton Hawksworth
BINGLEY Saltaire Cottingley
A650 **SHIPLEY** Calverley A6120 Farsley
A6038 Frizinghall Cartwright Hall
BRADFORD Clayton
A647 A6177 A6110 **PUDSEY**
A58

LEEDS/BRADFORD Rawdon **Yeadon** Cookridge
Baildon A65 **Horsforth** Tinshill A65
Esholt New Farnley A58

167

Heptonstall Moor
Blackshaw Head Slack **Heptonstall**
Mytholm Midgley
Hebden Bridge Luddenden
Lydgate Eastwood **Mytholmroyd** Mount Tabot
A646 A646
Cragg Vale Sowerby
Todmorden A646 **Sowerby Bridge** A6026
A681 Mankinholes Triangle
A6033 Cotton Stones **HALIFAX** Shibden Hall
Walsden Withens Clough Resr Mill Bank Greetland
Warland Warland Resr Ripponden Holywell Green **BRIGHOUSE**
Gorpley Resr B6138 Soyland Moor Barkisland A6025 Elland Rastrick
Watergrove Resr Summit Stainland A6107
Calderbrook A58 Rishworth Outlane A629
Wardle Rishworth Moor Booth Wood A641 Mirfield
Smallbridge B6114 Moss Moor Moselden Height 23 A640 **HUDDERSFIELD**
B6225 **Littleborough** M62 22 **Slaithwaite**
Hollingworth Lake A672 Linthwaite Golcar
Rochdale 1 A58 Firgrove Castleshaw Moor A62
Milnrow 21 A663 Newhey 13 Marsden Meltham Honley
A664 Denshaw Holt Head Netherthong Brockholes
B6194 A6052 B6197 A635 Thurstonland
Shaw Moorside Belph Diggle Upperthong Holmfirth
Royton Artisan Delph **Uppermill** Flush House Holme Hepworth
Sholver B6194 Grasscroft A635 Saddleworth Moor Holme A616
OLDHAM Lees Greenfield Dovestone Reservoir Black Hill 1908 Hade Edge
A669 A6050 A669 Crow Edge Carlecotes
22 Bardsley B6175 Winscar Reservoir
Failsworth **Mossley** Chew Reservoir A6024 Dunford Bridge **Penistone**
M60 A627 Hurst Buckton Vale Langsett A616

Oakenshaw Wyke Northowram A641
Hipperholme Shelf Butterstraw M606 A650 Birkenshaw M621
Southowram A58 26 Gomersal Oakwell Birstall Smithies MOR
Hartshead Moor **Cleckheaton** A643 27 28 **BATLEY**
Liversedge **Heckmondwike** A638 B6124 A653
Roberttown A652 B6123 Kirkhe **DEWSBURY**
Ravensthorpe A644 Thornhill Edge Oss
M62 A641 A62 Upper Hopton Ho
24 A640 Kirkheaton Whitley Lower **Middlestown**
Fenay Bridge Cowmes Mining Museum B6118 14 B6
Almondbury Lepton Highburton Grange Moor A642 A637
Castle Hill Farnley Tyas **Kirkburton** Flockton Midgley
Emley Moor Emley 12 Clayton
Brockholes Shelley Kirklees Light Railway Sculp Pa
Thurstonland **Skelmanthorpe**
New Mill Lane Head **Denby Dale**
Scholes A616 Upper Denby High Hoy
Hepworth Ingbirchworth Resr A635 **Cawthorne**
Crow Edge Carlecotes B6175 Ingbirchworth Hoylandswaine Silks
A6106 **Thurstone** A629 Com
Penistone B6462 Oxs

160

BBC GMR
FM 104.6

Rochdale 4
Rochdale 1 M60 6 M62 A627(M)

miles kms

M60 A627 A635 A628 A616
Stockport 8 Ashton-under-Lyne 1 Stalybridge 1 M60 15 (M67) Manchester 21 Stockbridge 4

The Revolution
FM 96.2

Home 107.9
FM 107.9

BBC Radio Leeds
AM 744/FM 92.4/95.3

Galaxy 105
FM 105/105.6/105.8

E 661   F   G   H

Harrogate 6   (A1(M)) Boroughbridge 10
(A64) Scarborough 44   York 1   York 1   Scarborough 31
(A64) Malton 22   Malton 18

A661   A1   A1237   A1237   A1036   A19   176   A64

Kirkby Overblow
Sicklinghall
Clap Gate
Netherby
Collingham
East Keswick
Bardsey
Scarcroft
Thorner
Shadwell

Wetherby
Linton
Walton
Boston Spa
Clifford
Thorp Arch
Bramham
Stutton
Newton Kyme
Wighill
Catterton
Bilbrough
Healaugh
Askham Richard
Angram

Askham Bryan
Copmanthorpe
Bishopthorpe
McArthur Glen
Naburn
Acaster Malbis
Fulford
Elvington
Air Museum

Tadcaster
Kirby Wharfe
Roman Road
Colton
Appleton Roebuck
Holme Green
Acaster Selby
York (Acaster Malbis)

Crockey Hill
Deighton
Escrick
Wheldrake
Thorganby

Wharfe

A659   A58   A659   A162   A64   A19   A163

Roundhay
Aberford
Scholes
Barwick in Elmet
Kiddal Lane End
Pondas Fields
Lotherton Hall
Bird Garden

Towton 1461
Saxton
Barkston Ash
Church Fenton
Little Fenton
Biggin
Wistow
Cawood
Ryther
Kelfield

Ulleskelf
Sherburn in Elmet
Towton
Riccall
North Duffield
Skipwith

A6120   A64   A1(M)   M1-47   A63

LEEDS
Temple Newsam
Garforth
Micklefield
Old Micklefield
New Micklefield
South Milford
Monk Fryston
Hambleton
Brayton
Selby
Abbey
Barlby
Osgodby
Lund
Cliffe
South Duffield

A63   A642   A656   A1   A63   A1238   A19   A63   A163

Woodlesford
Oulton
Swillington
Great Preston
Allerton Bywater
Kippax
Ledsham
Ledston
Fairburn
Lumby
Brotherton
Burton Salmon
Birkin
Beal
Kellington
Gateforth
West Haddlesey
Chapel Haddlesey
Camblesforth
Drax
Long Drax
Barmby on the Marsh
Carlton
Newland

ROTHWELL
Carlton
Lofthouse
Methley
Mickletown
New Fryston
Castleford
Whitwood
Ferrybridge
Knottingley
Kellingley
Eggborough
Hensall
Snaith
Rawcliffe
East Cowick
West Cowick

A639   A61   M62   A645   A614

Lofthouse Gate
Stanley
Altofts
Normanton
Xscape
Freeport
Castle
Ferrybridge
Cridling Stubbs
Whitley
Gowdall
Pollington
Southfield Reservoir
Balne
Great Heck
Womersley
Walden Stubbs
Moss
Fenwick
Sykehouse
Fishlake

WAKEFIELD
Warmfield
Ackton
Pontefract
Darrington
Featherstone
Purston Jaglin
Sharlston
Crofton
East Hardwick
West Hardwick
High Ackworth
Low Ackworth
Ackworth Moor Top
Fitzwilliam
Wentbridge
Thorpe Audlin
Kirk Smeaton
Little Smeaton
Norton
Campsall
Askern
Braithwaite
Kirk Bramwith
Thorpe in Balne
Stainforth
Thorne
Moorends

A655   A645   A628   A1   A19   A638   A18   A614   A180

Normanton
Walton
Crofton
Wragby
Nostell Priory
Wintersett
South Hiendley
Ryhill
Notton
Kinsley
Badsworth
Upton
South Elmsall
North Elmsall
Skelbrooke
Burghwallis
Sutton
Owston
Carcroft
Doncaster North

HEMSWORTH
Royston
Shafton
Brierley
South Kirkby
Hampole
Hooton Pagnell
Clayton
Brodsworth
Highfields
Hatfield
Dunscroft
Dunsville
Kirk Sandall
Hatfield Woodhouse

A61   A628   A635   A638   A18   A614

Cudworth
Grimethorpe
Monk Bretton Priory
Great Houghton
Billingley
Hickleton
Marr
Adwick le Street
Toll Bar
Brodsworth Hall
Roman Road
Edenthorpe
Armthorpe
Sandall Beat Wood
Nutwell
Arksey
Barnby Dun
Bentley

BARNSLEY
Ardsley
Darfield
Wombwell
Worsbrough
Thurnscoe
Thurnscoe East
Goldthorpe
Bolton upon Dearne
Barnburgh
Sprotbrough
Melton
High Melton
Cadeby
Conisbrough
Warmsworth
DONCASTER
Bessacarr
Cantley
Branton
Auckley
Blaxton

A61   A633   A6195   A633   A6023   A60   A6182   A638   A614

Birdwell
Hoyland
Jump
Brampton
Elsecar
Adwick upon Dearne
Harlington
Dearne Valley

M1   E   F   161   G   A1(M)   M18   H   A614

Sheffield 10   Rotherham 9   Rotherham 5   Conisbrough 2   M18 2   M1 12   Bawtry 5
Sheffield 10   Blyth 10

Ridings FM
FM 106.8

Magic 828
AM 828

see p460 for a touring guide to this map

Holme-on-Spalding-Moor 8   A163
170   A63
(M62) Kingston-upon-Hull 31   Howden 4
Goole 3 (A63; Kingston-upon-Hull 29   A614   M62
Goole 3   A645
Grimsby 34; Scunthorpe 14   Immingham 34
Grimsby 39; Scunthorpe 14
M180

CITY ROUTES
Leeds & Bradford p280

TOWN PLANS
Barnsley p308
Bradford p313
Doncaster p327
Halifax p338
Huddersfield p341
Leeds p346

York 10

96.9 Viking FM
FM 96.9

Bridlington 19
Driffield 8

Driffield 5

A1079 | 176 | A1079 | B1246 | 177 | A614 | A164

A | **B** | **C** | **D**

ELVINGTON
Air Museum
Elvington
Newton upon Derwent
Barmby Moor
Pocklington
Nunburnholme
Middleton on-the-Wolds
Kilnwick
B1248
Lund
Beswick

Sutton upon Derwent
15
Allerthorpe
Burnby Hall
Kipling Cotes
Holme on the Wolds
Lockington
A164

Wheldrake
Thornton
Melbourne
Bielby
Hayton
Burnby
Londesborough
A614
Shiptonthorpe
South Dalton
Scorborough

5

East Cottingwith
Thorganby
Seaton Ross
Everingham
Thorpe le Street
All Hallows
Goodmanham
Etton
Leconfield
LECONF
BEVERLEY

Ellerton
Laytham
Holme-on-Spalding-Moor
Market Weighton
Sancton
A1079
Molescroft

Skipwith
Aughton
Foggathorpe
All Saints Moor End
9
Cherry Burton
Bishop Burton
A1035

North Duffield
A163
Harlthorpe
Highfield
Sand Hole
North Cliffe
A1034
North Newbald
Walkington
Bentley

4

Bubwith
Gunby
Gribthorpe
Willitoft
South Cliffe
South Newbald
High Hunsley
B1230
Skidby

South Duffield
Breighton
Spaldington
Bursea
Hotham
Little Weighton

Lund
Cliffe
Wressle
Brind
Portington
Sandholme
North Cave
B1230
South Cave
Riplingham
A1164
KIRK ELLA

Hemingbrough
A63
Newsholme
Eastrington
B1230
Newport
Walling Fen
Everthorpe
West End
Ellerker
Elloughton
Brantingham
Welton
Swanland

169

Long Drax
Barmby on the Marsh
Asselby
Knedlington
Howden
Gilberdyke
Staddlethorpe
Brough
North Ferriby
Humber Bridge Country Park

Drax
B1228
Airmyn
A614
Hook
Balkholme
Kilpin
Skelton
Laxton
Blacktoft
Faxfleet
Whitton
BROUGH
Hull

Newland
M62
Goole
Saltmarshe
Yokefleet
Reedness
Blacktoft Sands
Ousefleet
Winteringham
Reads Island
South Channel
Barton-upon-Humber
South Ferriby

3

Rawcliffe
A614
East Cowick
Rawcliffe Bridge
Waterways Museum
Dutch River
Swinefleet
Whitgift
Adlingfleet
Alkborough
West Halton
Ferriby Sluice

M62 Leeds 30 A1 12

Southfield Resr
Goole Fields
Marshland
Fockerby
Garthorpe
A161
Eastoft
Coleby
Thealby
Winterton
Horkstow
Saxby All Saints

2

Moorends
Thorne Waste or Moors
Luddington
A1077
Normanby
Normanby Hall
Roxby
Appleby
Bonby
Worlaby

Fishlake
6
Old R Don
Amcotts
Flixborough
Flixborough Stather
High Risby
Low Risby

Thorne
Doncaster North
Crowle
Ealand
Keadby
Gunness
Crosby
A1029
Santon
Elsham Hall

A18
Hatfield Chase
Althorpe
Burringham
SCUNTHORPE
Brumby
Broughton
Wressle
Wrawby

1

Hatfield
Hatfield Woodhouse
Sandtoft
SANDTOFT
Westgate
A161
M180
Derrythorpe
Beltoft
M181
B1450
Ashby
Bottesford
A18
A1084

A18
M18
A614
Belton
Isle of Axholme
West Butterwick
East Butterwick
Yaddlethorpe
Messingham
Brigg
B1206

Hatfield Moors
Epworth
Wroot
Low Burnham
The Old Rectory
Susworth
A159
Manton
Scawby

Auckley
Blaxton
B1396
Owston Ferry
Scotterthorpe
Scotter
B1398
Hibaldstow
North Ke

A614 | A161 | A159 | A15

Bawtry 5 | Bawtry 5 A1 9 | Gainsborough 9 | Lincoln 19

BBC Radio Humberside FM 95.9

BBC Radio Lincolnshire AM 1368/FM 94.9/104.

miles | kms

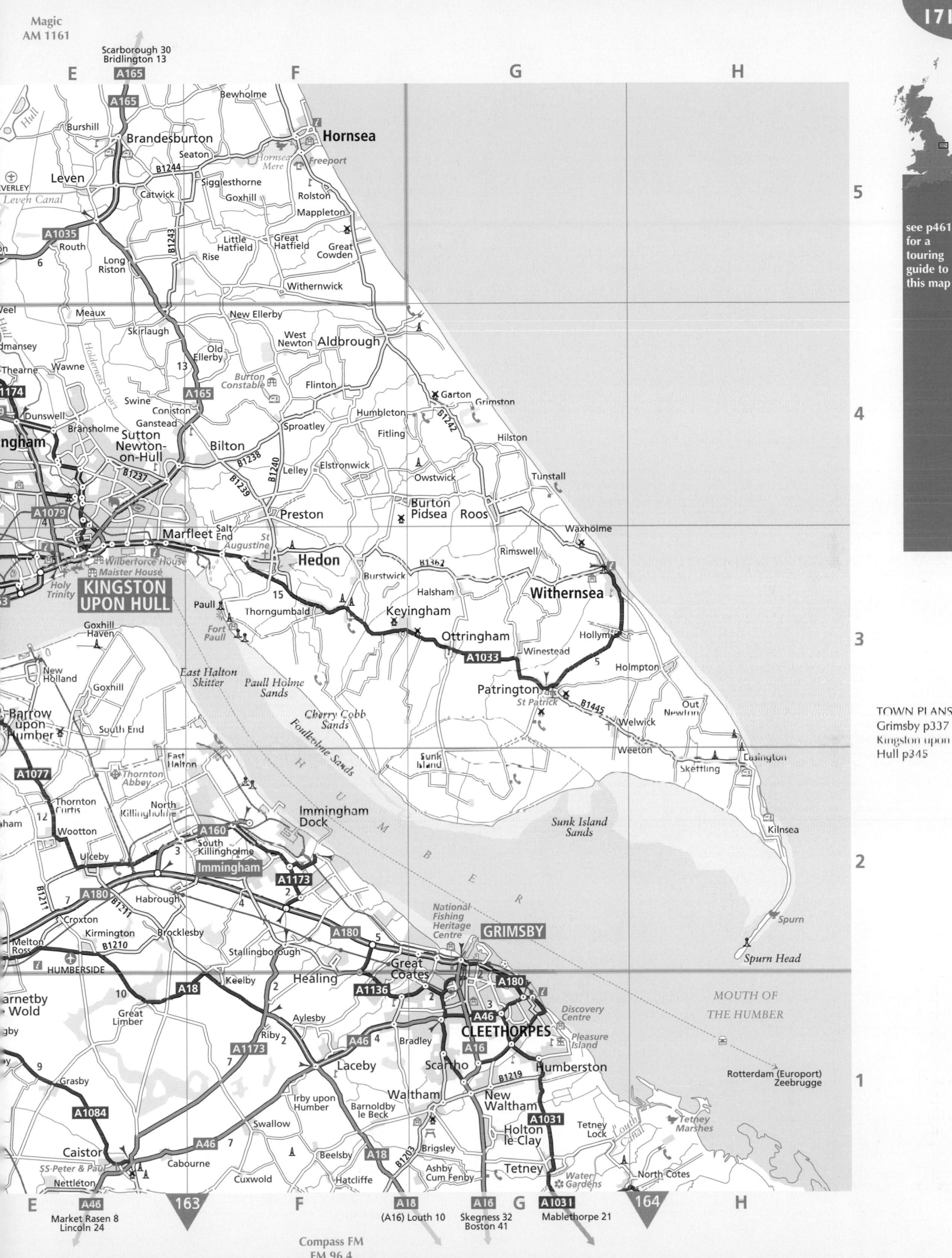

Magic
AM 1161

Scarborough 30
Bridlington 13

E   A165   F   G   H

A165

Hull   Burshill   Bewholme

Brandesburton   Hornsea
Leven   Seaton   Hornsea   Freeport
EVERLEY   B1244   Sigglesthorne   Mere
Leven Canal   Catwick   Goxhill   Rolston

A1035   Route   Little   Great   Mappleton
B1243   Hatfield   Hatfield
Long   Rise   Great
Riston   Cowden

Withernwick

Veel   Meaux   New Ellerby
dmansey   Skirlaugh   West   Aldbrough
Thearne   Wawne   Old   Newton
Ellerby   Garton
1174   Burton   Flinton   Grimston
Dunswell   Constable   Humbleton   Hilston
Bransholme   Swine   Sproatley   Fitling
ingham   Sutton   Coniston   Lelley   Owstwick
Newton-   Ganstead   Elstronwick   Tunstall
on-Hull   Bilton   B1238   Burton
B1237   B1240   Preston   Pidsea   Roos
A1079   B1239   Waxholme
4   Marfleet   Salt   St   Rimswell
End   Augustine   Hedon   B1362
Wilberforce House   15   Burstwick   Halsham   Withernsea
Maister House   Paull   Thorngumbald   Keyingham
KINGSTON   Fort   Ottringham   Hollym
UPON HULL   Paull   A1033   Winestead
Holy   Trinity   Patrington   5   Holmpton
Goxhill   St Patrick   Welwick   B1445   Out
Haven   East Halton   Newton
New   Skitter   Paull Holme   Weeton
Holland   Goxhill   Sands   Easington
Barrow   South End   Cherry Cobb   Sketling
upon   Sands   Skettling
Humber   Foulholme Sands   Kilnsea
A1077   East   Sunk
Thornton   Halton   Island
Abbey   H   Sunk Island
Thornton   North   U   Sands
Curtis   Killingholme   Immingham   M
12   Wootton   Dock   B
Ulceby   A160   E
South   R
Killingholme   Immingham
Immingham   A1173
A180   2   Spurn
Habrough   Spurn Head
B1211   Croxton   National
7   A180   B1211   Fishing   MOUTH OF
Melton   Kirmington   Brocklesby   Heritage   GRIMSBY   THE HUMBER
Ross   B1210   Centre
HUMBERSIDE   Stallingborough   A180
Barnetby   A18   Keelby   Great   Rotterdam (Europort)
le Wold   10   Healing   Coates   Zeebrugge
gsby   Great   A1136   A46   A180
Limber   Aylesby   3   Discovery
A1173   Riby   2   Bradley   A46   CLEETHORPES   Centre
7   A46   4   Pleasure
Laceby   Scartho   A16   Island
9   Grasby   Irby upon   Humberston
Humber   B1219
A1084   Waltham   New   Humberston
Barnoldby   Waltham
Caistor   le Beck   A1031
SS Peter & Paul   Swallow   Holton   Tetney   Tetney
Nettleton   Cabourne   Beelsby   le-Clay   Lock   Marshes
Cuxwold   Hatcliffe   Brigsley   Tetney   North Cotes
A46   Ashby   B1203   Water
163   Cum Fenby   A18   Gardens
A1031   164

Market Rasen 8   (A16) Louth 10   Skegness 32   Mablethorpe 21
Lincoln 24   Boston 41

Compass FM
FM 96.4

see p461
for a
touring
guide to
this map

TOWN PLANS
Grimsby p337
Kingston upon
Hull p345

178

Workington 33
Whitehaven 24
A595

Ambleside 20
Coniston 12

(A593) Coniston 5
A593
A5084

Selker Bay
Hycemoor
Stoneside Hill
Bootle
Bootle Fell
Annaside
Lower Hawthwaite
Duddon Bridge
A593
Broughton in Furness
Woodland Fell
Water Yeat
Blawith
Ruslan
Oxen Park
Colton Spark Bridge
Bouth
A5084
Black Combe
Hallthwaites
Foxfield
Grizebeck
Lowick
A5092

11
Whitbeck
The Green
10
Gawthwaite
A5092
Greenod
Whicham
7
The Hill
Kirkby-in-Furness
Beck Side
1088
Broughton Beck
B5287
Penny Bridge
5
Haver
Silecroft
8
A5093
Souter gate
Shooting House Hill
Mansriggs
Arrad Foot
3
Kirksanton
10
A590
Folk Museum
Ireleth
A595
Laurel & Hardy Museum
Ulverston
Haverigg
Millom
Marton
Pennington
Canal Foot
Cartme Sands

Hodbarrow Reserve
Askam in Furness
Lindal in Furness
Hall
Swarthmoor
Conishead Pr
Duddon Sands
Dalton Castle
South Lakes
5
Great Urswick
Bardsea

Little Urswick
Scales
Bardsea Park

Dalton-in-Furness
Newton
Baycliff
A590
Stainton with Adgarley
Barrow-In-Furness
BARROW (WALNEY ISLAND)
Furness Abbey
Dendron
Gleaston
14
Aldingham

North Scale
Roosecote
Leece
Newbiggin
A590
A5087

Vickerstown
Roosebeck

Biggar
Rampside
WALNEY ISLAND
Roa Island
Foulney Island
MORECAMB

South End
Piel Island
Piel Bar

LANCASTER

Kendal 22
A6
M6 Kendal 22

Morecambe 3
A589
Salt Ayre Sports Centre
MORECAMBE ROAD
PO
OWEN ROAD
Mainway
A683
5
MORECAMBE RD
Skerton Bridge
St George's Quay
River Lune
Lune Street
Derby Road
Skateboard Park
KINGWAY
CATON ROAD
Bulk Road
4
Maritime Museum
Sports Ground
GREYHOUND BRIDGE ROAD
Greyhound Bridge
Green Ayre Park
PARLIAMENT STREET
A589
Millennium Foot/Cycle Bridge
Cyclepath
Vicarage Field
Roman Bath House (Remains)
Damside St
North Road
De Vitre St
Lancaster Canal
Lancaster Priory Church
Judges' Lodgings
BRIDGE LA
CABLE STREET
Chapel St
St Leonard's Gate
3
Castle & Shire Hall
Cottage Museum
YMCA
Damside St
ROSEMARY LA
WC Grand
Church Street
Dukes Theatre & Cinema
Music Room
City Mus
West Road
Castle Pk
CHINA ST
Market Square
St Nicholas Arcade
Moor
Palatine Hall
Edward St
Lancaster Station
Friends Meeting House
Market
Cheapside
Sulyard St
Lane
Station Rd
Meeting House Lane
PO
Marketgate
Mary St
WC
Bulk St
Nelson St
East Road
2
Wheatfield Street
Fenton St
KING STREET
Common Gdn St
Brock St
St Peter's Road
St Peter's RC Cathedral
Sibsey Street
Bladen Street
Dallas
Regent
POL
George St
Marton Street
THURNHAM STREET
Town Hall
Street
Magistrates Courthouse
Balmoral Rd
High St
Penny Street
Quarry Road
Lindow St
White Cross Education Centre
A6
Queen Street
Playing Fields
Carr House La
Portland St
Regent St
Road
SOUTH ROAD
H
Royal Lancaster Infirmary
Ashton Road
White Cross Trading Estate
Meadowside
Dale Street
Prospect Street
1
Aldcliffe
Lancaster Canal
Brook St
Bowerham Rd
A588
A6
University of Lancaster
M6
Blackpool 24
Preston 21

Larne

North Wharf

FLEETWOOD
A587

A585
Cleveleys
Tho

A584
Blackpool 2
Lytham St Anne's 6

0 100 200 300yds
0 100 200 300m

6 — 10
5 — 9
4 — 8
— 7
3 — 6
— 5
2 — 4
— 3
1 — 2
— 1
miles kms

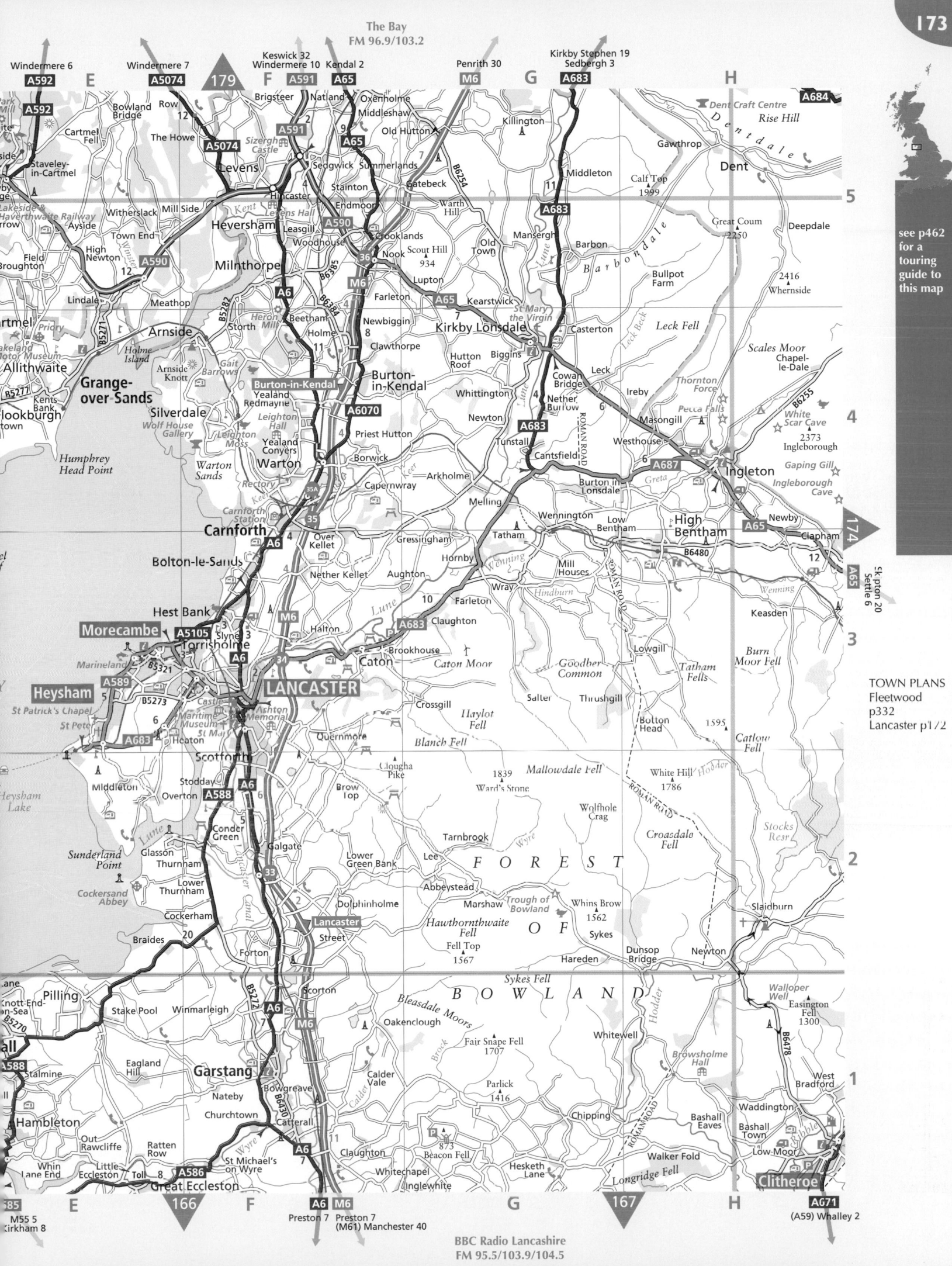

The Bay
FM 96.9/103.2

Keswick 32
Windermere 10 Kendal 2

Kirkby Stephen 19
Sedbergh 3

see p462
for a
touring
guide to
this map

BBC Radio Lancashire
FM 95.5/103.9/104.5

Preston 7   Preston 7
(M61) Manchester 40

Hawes 25 Leyburn 9   A1(M) Darlington 20 Catterick 6   Darlington 19 Northallerton 2   Northallerton 3   Middlesbrough 20

E   181   A684   **F**   A1   **G**   A167   A168   A19   **H**

Finghall
Spennithorne
Newton-le-Willows
St Gregory
Aiskew
Leeming
LEEMING
North Otterington
Thornton-le-Moor
Cowesby
Kirby Knowle
Borrowby
Knayton
Upsall
Boltby

Middleham
Cowling
Bedale
Londonderry
Gatenby
Newby Wiske
South Otterington
Thornton-le-Street
North Kilvington

Castle
Burrill
Exelby
B6285
Theakston
Maunby
Kirby Wiske
South Kilvington B144B
Felixkirk
Thirlby

Thornton Steward
Thornton Watlass
Burneston
10
Sinderby
Pickhill
Sandhutton
A167
12
St Mary the Virgin
6
Thirsk
Sowerby
Sutton-under-Whitestonecliffe
A170

East Witton
Jervaulx Abbey
Thirn
Snape
Carthorpe
Howe
Carlton Miniott
A611
TOPCLIFFE
4
Bagby
Great Thirkleby
Little Thirkleby

Ellingstring
Low Ellington
Well
Nosterfield
B6267
Baldersby
Skipton-on-Swale
Catton
A168
Topcliffe
Dalton
Carlton Husthwaite

High Ellington
19
Low Burton
Thornborough
West Tanfield
Sutton Howgrave
Wath
Melmerby
Rainton
Asenby
Hutton Sessay

Masham
A6108
Mickley
North Stainley
Norton Conyers
Catton
49
Dishforth
Cundall
Crakehill
Fawdington
Thormanby

Fearby
Swinton
Ilton
Grewelthorpe
Lightwater Valley
DISHFORTH
A168
Sessay

Healey
Druid's Circle
Leighton Resr
Roundhill Resr
KIRKBY MALZEARD
Sutton Grange
Hutton Conyers
5
2
3
Marton-le-Moor
Norton-le-Clay
Brafferton
Raskelf

Dallowgill Moor
Hambleton Hill 1331
Greygarth
Laverton
Galphay
Sharow
Copt Hewick
B6265
Helperby
Thormanby

Ramsgill
High Grantley
Winksley
RIPON
Holy Trinity
Bridge Hewick
Kirby Hill
Langthorpe

Gouthwaite Resr
Dallowgill Moor
Risplith
Aldfield
St Mary
Studley Roger
Studley Royal
Littlethorpe
Skelton on Ure
Newby Hall
Roman Town
Aldborough
Myton-on-Swale
Flawith
Alne

Wath
Pateley Moor
Sawley
Fountains Abbey
Markenfield Hall
Bishop Monkton
Devil's Arrows
St Andrew
Boroughbridge
Lower Dunsforth
Aldwark
Tholthorpe

Pateley Bridge
Bewerley
B6265
Markington
11
Roecliffe
Minskip
48
Grafton
Upper Dunsforth
Youlton
LINTON-ON-OUSE

Glasshouses
Wilsill
Brimham Rocks
Bishop Thornton
South Stainley
Burton Leonard
Staveley
A1(M)
A6055
Marton
Arkendale
5
Great Ouseburn
Linton-on-Ouse

B6265
Low Laithe
Summerbridge
Shaw Mills
Ripley
Nidd
Drearton
Farnham
6
Little Ouseburn
Toll

Dacre Banks
Dacre
Burnt Yates
Castle
Clint
Scotton
Ferrensby
Thorpe Underwood

Padside
Darley Head
Low Green
Birstwith
All Saints
B6165
Scriven
Coneythorpe
A168
Allerton Park
Whixley
Green Hammerton

Thornthwaite
Darley
Staupes
Hampsthwaite
Killinghall
Nidd
Knaresborough
Flaxby
47
A59
Kirk Hammerton

Bank Head
West End
Thruscross Resr
Kettlesing Bottom
Forest Moor
A59
Castle
Goldsborough
York 7
A59

Blubberhouses
Fewston Resr
19
Kettlesing
Royal Pump Room Museum
Cave
B6163
A658
Walshford
Nidd
Cattal
Marston Moor
1644

A59
ROMAN ROAD
Fewston
Scargill Resr
Beckwithshaw
RHS Harlow Carr
B6162
A59
Little Ribston
Goldsborough
3
Hunsingore
Marston Moor

Timble
Swinsty Resr
Bland Hill
HARROGATE
3
Plumpton Rocks
North Deighton
4
Cowthorpe
Tockwith

March Ghyll Resr
Jack Hill
Lindley Wood Resr
Pannal
Follifoot
A661
Castle
Kirk Deighton
Due open Spring 2005
A1
Bickerton
B1224

Middleton
All Saints
Denton
B6451
Stainburn
Kirkby Overblow
Sicklinghall
A658
Wetherby
Walton
Bilton in Ainsty

Cow and Call Rocks
Askwith
Weston
Farnley
North Rigton
Huby
Spofforth
Netherby
Clap Gate
Linton
Thorp Arch
Wighill
Healaugh

Burley in Wharfedale
A65
Otley
Leathley
Weeton
A658
Netherby
Clap Gate
Collingham
6
Boston Spa
Clifford
Newton Kyme
Malton 29 York 9

A659
Pool
Arthington
Harewood House
A659
East Keswick
Harewood
A58
A659
Tadcaster
A64

Menston
A65
Guiseley
A660
Bramhope
Golden Acre
Eccup Resr
A61
Bardsey
Bramham
Bramham Park
A1
A64
Stutton
A162

Hawksworth
Esholt
Yeadon
A658
LEEDS/BRADFORD
Cookridge
Eccup
Scarcroft
Thorner
A1(M)

Eldwick
E   A658   **F**   A660   **G**   A61   A58   **H**
Bradford 5   Leeds 5   Leeds 5   Leeds 5   (M1) Leeds 13

169

see p463 for a touring guide to this map

176

BBC Radio York
AM 666/1260
FM 95.5/103.7/ 104.3

TOWN PLANS
Harrogate p339
Hawes p340
Ripon p380
Settle p384
Skipton p387
Thirsk p397

Fresh AM
AM 936/1413

97.2 Stray FM
FM 97.2

see p464
for a
touring
guide to
this map

TOWN PLANS
Scarborough
p385
York p407

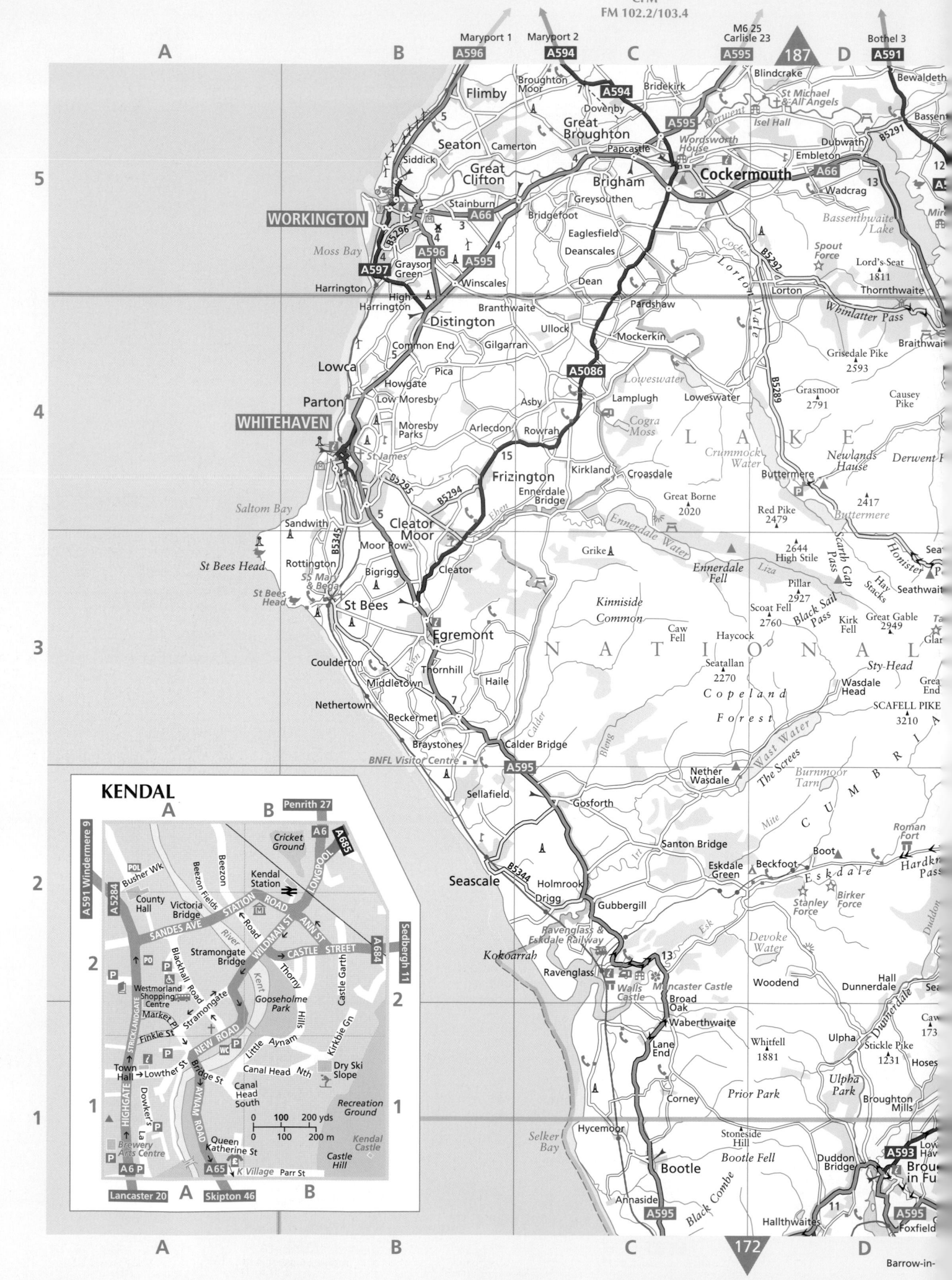

CFM
FM 102.2/103.4

187

172

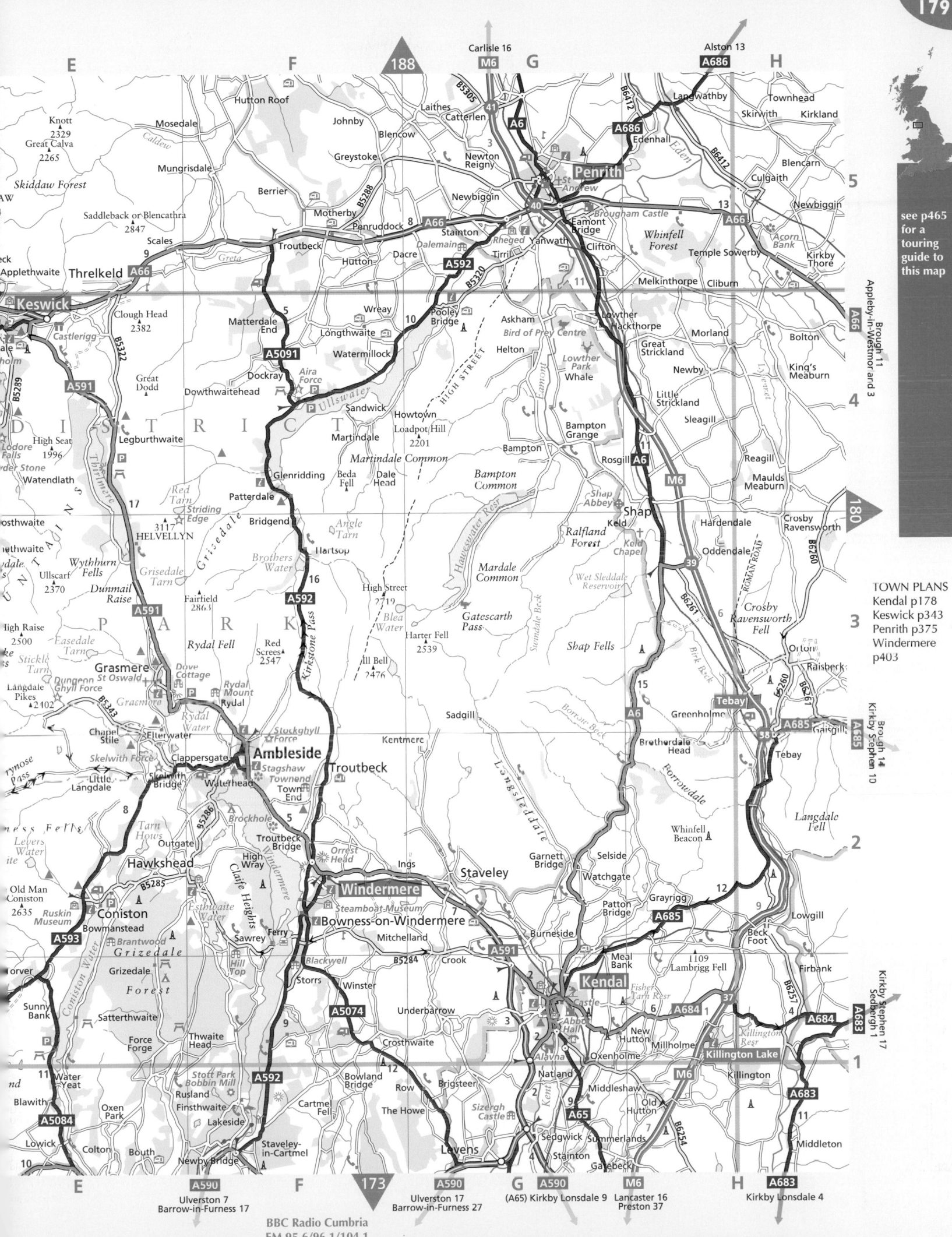

Carlisle 16

M6

Alston 13   A686

B5305

Townhead

Skirwith   Kirkland

B6412   Langwathby

A6   A686   Edenhall

Laithes
Catterlen   41

Johnby   3

Blencow   Newton
Reigny

Greystoke   Penrith

Berrier   Newbiggin   St
Andrew   40

Blencarn

Culgaith

Newbiggin

Knott
2329   Mosedale   Hutton Roof

Great Calva
2265

Skiddaw Forest

AW

Saddleback or Blencathra
2847

Scales   9   Troutbeck

B5288   Penruddock   8   A66   Stainton

Motherby   Dacre   Dalemain

Hutton   A592   Tirril

Rheged   Yanwath

Brougham Castle

Whinfell
Forest   13   A66   Temple Sowerby

Acorn
Bank   Kirkby
Thore

Threlkeld   A66

Greta

Applethwaite

Keswick

Castlerigg   B5322

B5289

A591

Matterdale
End   5

A5091

Wreay   10

Longthwaite

Watermillock

Pooley
Bridge

Askham

Bird of Prey Centre   Eamont
Bridge   Clifton

Melkinthorpe   Cliburn

11   Lowther
Hackthorpe

Morland

Bolton

High Seat
1996   Legburthwaite

Great
Dodd

Dowthwaitehead

Dockray

Aira
Force   Ullswater   Sandwick

Helton

Lowther
Park
Whale

Great
Strickland

King's
Meaburn

DISTRICT

Lodore
Falls   Watendlath

High Seat   17

Red
Tarn   Striding
Edge   3117
HELVELLYN

Glenridding

Patterdale

Beda
Fell   Dale
Head

Howtown
Loadpot Hill
2201   Bampton

Bampton
Grange

Newby

Little
Strickland

Sleagill

Ralphall
Forest   Rosgill   A6   Reagill

Maulds
Meaburn

crosthwaite

Ullscarf
2370   Wythburn
Fells   Dunmail
Raise   Grisedale
Tarn   Fairfield
2863   Bridgend   Angle
Tarn   Hartsop   Brothers
Water   16   A592   High Street
2719   Blea
Water   Harter Fell
2539

Martindale
Common

Bampton
Common

Shap
Abbey   Shap
Keld

Keld
Chapel

Hardendale   Crosby
Ravensworth

Oddendale   39

MOUNTAINS

High Raise
2500   Easedale
Tarn   Red
Screes
2547   Ill Bell
2476

Stickle
Tarn   Langdale
Pikes   2402

PARK

Rydal Fell

Kirkstone Pass

Sadgill

Mardale
Common   Gatescarth
Pass

Wet Sleddale
Reservoir   Shap Fells

B6261   6   Crosby
Ravensworth
Fell   Orton

Raisbeck

TOWN PLANS
Kendal p178
Keswick p343
Penrith p375
Windermere
p403

Grasmere   Dove
Cottage   Rydal
Mount
Rydal

Dungeon
Ghyll Force   St Oswald

Grasmere

B5343

Chapel
Stile   Elterwater   Rydal
Water

Skelwith Force   Clappersgate   Stockghyll
Force

Skelwith
Bridge

Little
Langdale

Brockhole

AMBLESIDE

Stagshaw   Townend
Waterhead   Troutbeck

Town
End

Kentmere

Garnett
Bridge   Selside

Watchgate

Borrowdale   A6   Greenholme

Brethordale
Head

Tebay   A685   Gaisgill   A685

Tebay   38

Whinfell
Beacon   Langdale
Fell

B5286

Tarn
Hows

Outgate   Troutbeck
Bridge   5

Orrest
Head

Ings

Staveley

High
Wray   WINDERMERE

Grayrigg   12   9   Lowgill

Beck
Foot

Leathes
Water   Levers
Water

Old Man
Coniston
2635

Ruskin
Museum   Coniston

Hawkshead

B5285

Claife Heights   Esthwaite
Water

Steamboat Museum

Bowness-on-Windermere

Patton
Bridge   A685

A593

Bowmanstead

Brantwood

Grizedale
Forest

Hill Top   Sawrey   Ferry

Blackwell   Mitchelland   B5284   Crook   A591   Burneside

Meal
Bank   1109
Lambrigg Fell

Firbank

B6257

orver

Sunny
Bank   Satterthwaite

Grizedale

Winster

A5074   Underbarrow

Crosthwaite   KENDAL

New
Hutton   A684   37   A684

Killington
Resr

A5084

Water
Yeat   11   Stott Park
Bobbin Mill   A592   Thwaite
Head   9   Bowland
Bridge   Row   Brigsteer   Natland   Oxenholme   M6   Killington

Blawith   Oxen
Park   Rusland   Finsthwaite   Cartmel
Fell   The Howe   Sizergh
Castle   Old
Hutton   B6254

A683   11   Middleton

Lowick   Colton   Bouth   Staveley-
in-Cartmel   Lakeside   Newby Bridge   173   Levens   Sedgwick   Stainton   Summerlands   Middleshaw   Gatebeck

A590   A590   A590   A65   M6   A683

Ulverston 7
Barrow-in-Furness 17   Ulverston 17
Barrow-in-Furness 27   (A65) Kirkby Lonsdale 9   Lancaster 16
Preston 37   Kirkby Lonsdale 4

BBC Radio Cumbria
FM 95.6/96.1/104.1

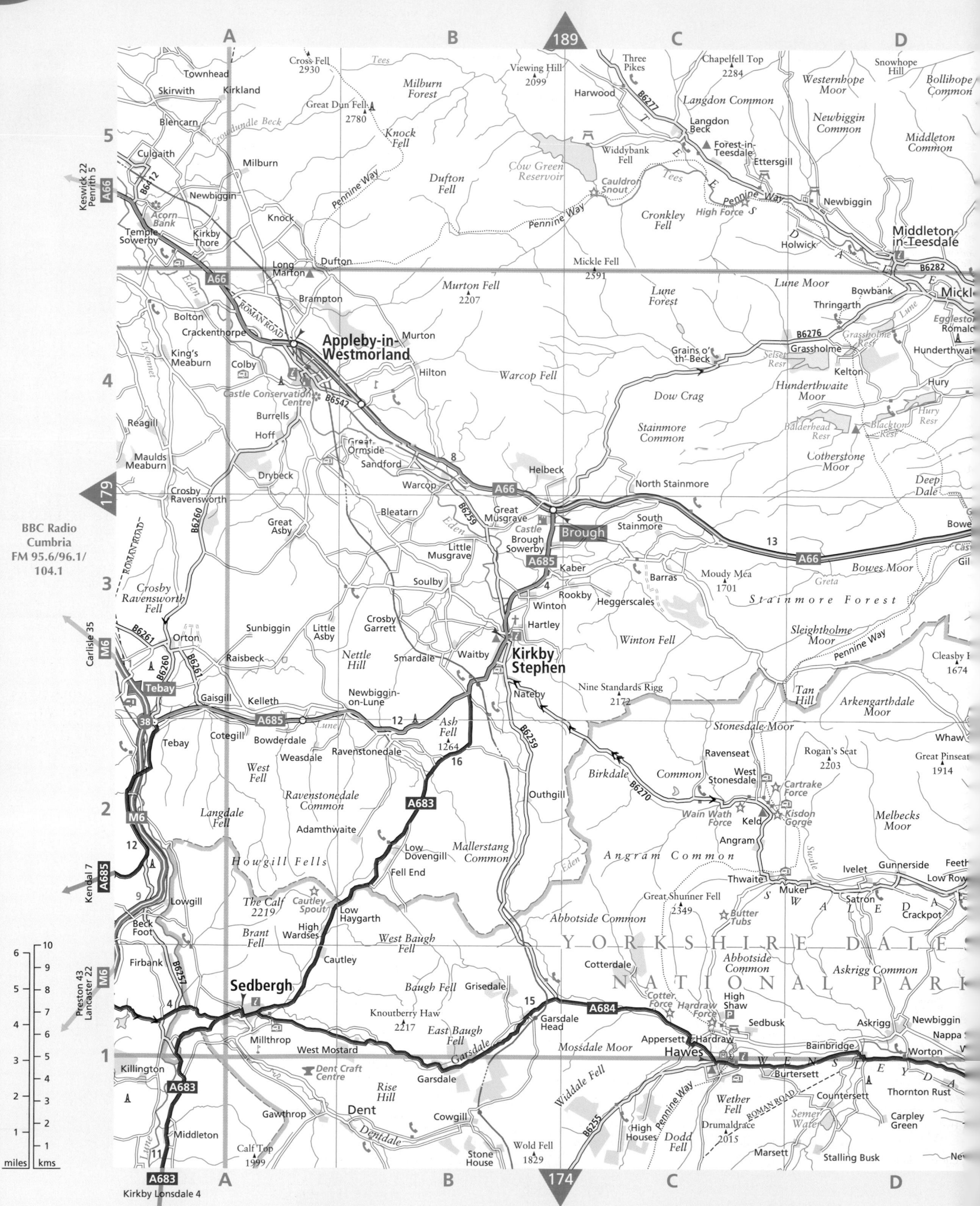

BBC Radio
Cumbria
FM 95.6/96.1/
104.1

miles | kms

Magic 1170
AM 1170

TFM
FM 96.6

Chester-le-Street 11   Newcastle-upon-Tyne 23
Durham 6   Durham 9

Corbridge 24   Crook 1   A689   190   Spennymoor   Cornforth   Trimdon
A68   F   G   Ferryhill   Fishburn

see p466
for a
touring
guide to
this map

BBC Radio
Cleveland
FM 95

TOWN PLANS
Darlington
p325
Hawes p340
Richmond
p380

E   F   A6108   175   G   A1   H   A167
Ripon 13   Wetherby 24   Topcliffe 6

Alpha 103.2
FM 103.2

Sunderland 16
Peterlee 6

△191

Trimdon
Fishburn
Sedgefield
Bishop Auckland 8
St Edmund
A689
A177
Thorpe Larches
Foxton
Stillington
Whitton
Bishopton
Elton
Longnewton
Urlay Nook
Aislaby
Eaglescliffe
DURHAM TEES VALLEY
Yarm
Low Worsall
Kirklevington
Girsby
Picton
Hornby
Appleton Wiske
Welbury
Deighton
Lovesome Hill
West Rounton
East Harlsey
Brompton
Kirby Sigston
Ellerbeck
Northallerton
Romanby
Crosby Court
North Otterington
Thornton-le-Beans
Thornton-le-Moor
Newby Wiske
Maunby
South Otterington
Thornton-le-Street
North Kilvington

Hunworth
Burn Resr
Crookfoot
Reservoir
Elwick
Dalton Piercy
Brierton
Owton Manor
Greatham
Newton Bewley
Wynyard Village
Thorpe Thewles
Redmarshall
Carlton
Norton
Wolviston
Cowpen Bewley
Billingham
Toll Bar
Stockton-on-Tees
Thornaby-on-Tees
Acklam
Ingleby Barwick
Maltby
Thornton
Hilton
Stainton
Hemlington
Newby
Tanton
Seamer
Middleton-le-Leven
Crathorne
Rounton
Swainby
Ingleby Arncliffe
Mount Grace Priory
Osmotherley
Over Silton
Nether Silton
Kepwick
Cowesby
Borrowby
Knayton
Upsall
Kirby Knowle
Boltby
Thirsk 2
York 24

HARTLEPOOL
The Headland
Quayside
Hartlepool Bay
Seaton Carew
Teesmouth
Tees Bay
Graythorp
Steel Works
Oil Refinery
South Bank
Grangetown
Eston
Dormanstown
Coatham
Redcar
West Scar
Salt Scar
The Flashes
Marske-by-the-Sea
Saltburn-by-the-Sea
Brotton
Skinningrove
New Marske
Wilton
Lazenby
Dunsdale
Kirkleatham
St Cuthbert
Yearby
Upleatham
New Skelton
North Skelton
Skelton
Boosbeck
Carlin How
Loftus
Lingdale
Stanghow
Liverton
Moorsholm
MIDDLESBROUGH
Ormesby
Guisborough
Marton
Coulby Newham
Nunthorpe
Great Ayton
Little Ayton
Stokesley
Newton under Roseberry
Roseberry Topping 1050
Highcliff Nab
Captain Cook's Monument
Kildale
Easby
Battersby
Great Broughton
Kirkby
Great Busby
Ingleby Greenhow
Westerdale
Carlton in Cleveland
Potto
Faceby
Whorlton
Ura
Cleveland Way
Round Hill 1490
Commondale
Danby Low Moor
Danby
Moors Centre
Castleton
Ainthorpe
Danby Rigg
Westerdale Moor
CLEVELAND HILLS
Seave Green
Chop Gate
Cockayne Ridge
Farndale Moor
Glaisdale Moor
Botton
Whorlton Moor
Snilesworth Moor
Cow Ridge
The Grange
Fangdale Beck
Helmsley Moor
Cockayne
Church Houses
Low Mill
Thorgill
Rosedale Abbey
Rudland Rigg
Spaunton Moor
NORTH YORK MOORS
Arden Great Moor
Hawnby
Old Byland
Rievaulx
Carlton
Pockley
Kirkbymoorside
Fadmoor
Gillamoor
Hutton-le-Hole
Ryedale Folk Museum
Appleton-le-Moors
Keldholme
Kirkby Mills
Nawton
Helmsley 3
Thirsk 16

A19
A179
B1280
B1086
A1185
A178
A689
B1276
A1046
A66
A67
A135
A1044
A19
A67
A172
A173
A171
A174
A171
A1032
A1053
A1042
A1085
A174
A173
A168
A167
A684
A170
A1043
B1278
B1274
B1275
B1264
B1365
B1380
B1257
B1269
B1268
B1366
B1333
A1(M)
Darlington 4
Darlington 9
Leeming Bar 5
Topcliffe 6

181
176

miles kms

A B C D
5
4
3
2
1

WHITBY

see p467 for a touring guide to this map

CITY ROUTES
Teesside p300

TOWN PLANS
Middlesbrough
p365
Scarborough
p385
Whitby p183

Yorkshire Coast Radio
FM 96.2/103.1

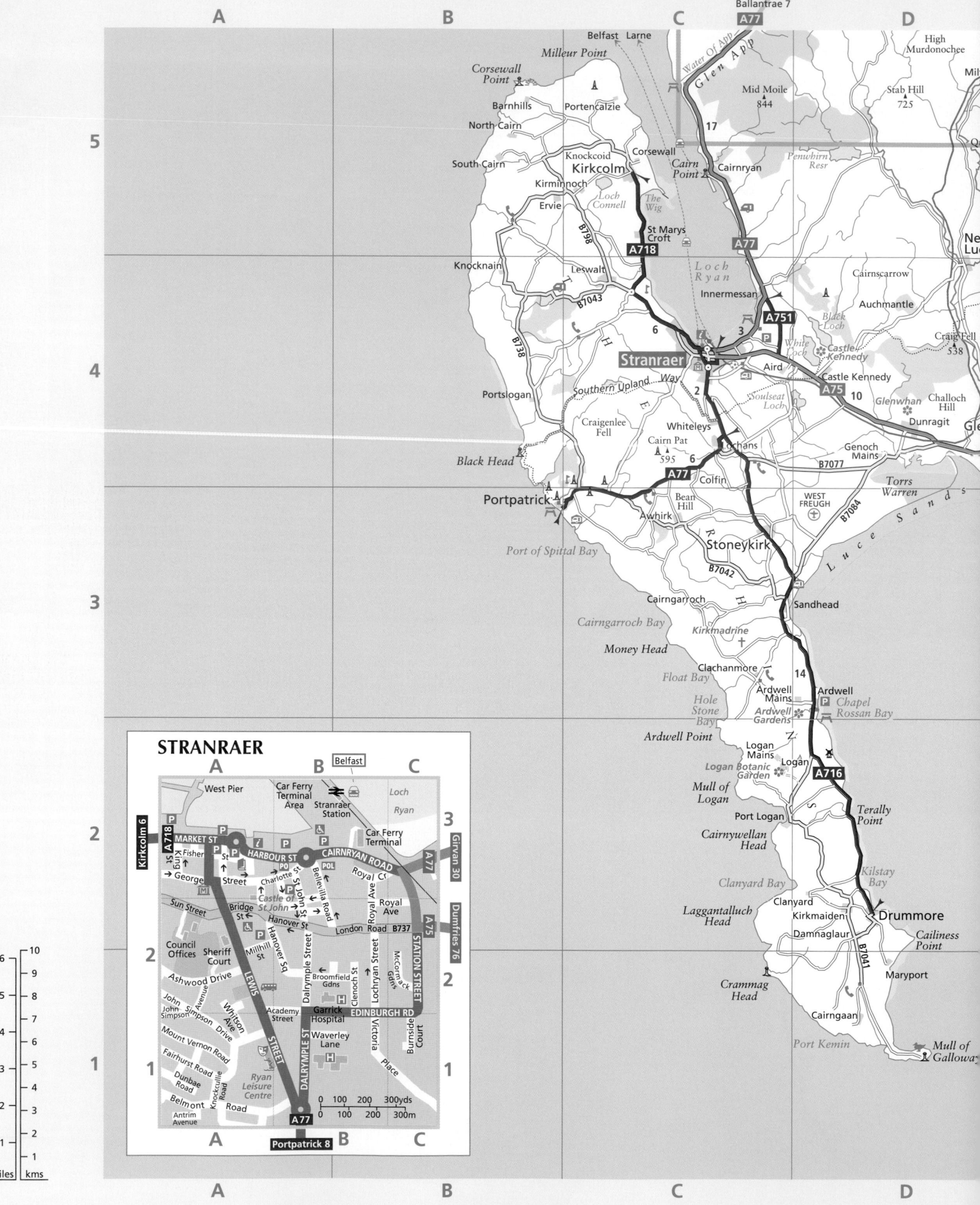

STRANRAER

BBC Radio Scotland
AM 810/FM 92-95

192

Girvan 18
A714
22

New Galloway 6
A712

Brockloch
Hill
19
Knocknevis

GALLOWAY
FOREST
PARK

Loch
Derry
Loch
Maberry

Craig
Airie Fell
Polbae

Loch
Ochiltree

Garlick
Hill

Penkiln Burn

Round
Fell
Loch
Grannoch

Shaw Hill
1255

Knowe

Wood
of Cree

Auchinleck

Fell of Fleet
1544

Urrall Fell
605

E   F   G   H

5

Eldrig Fell
742

A714

Glenrazie

B7027

Boreland

Cumloden

A712

Craiglowrie

Cree

Carscreugh

Artfield Fell
888

Carseriggan

Challoch

Minnigaff

G A L L O W A Y

Cairnsmore of Fleet

see p468
for a
touring
guide to
this map

nurrie

Newton
Stewart

Calgow
Stronord

Palnure Burn

Drumphail

Shennanton

Benfield

Palnure

Clints of Dromore

Loch
Heron

Loch
Ronald

Bladnoch

A75

Culcronchie

Fell

A75

14

B735

Barraer Fell
403

Barraer

Pibble Hill

Stey Fell

B796

4

Carscreugh

Barlae

Kirkcowan

Causeway
End   6

Craiglaw
Mains

High Moor of
Killiemore

A714

Carsegowan

Culsharg

186

Dergoals

itecairn

Dernaglar
Loch

Knock Moss

Spittal

B733

Torhousemuir

Wigtown
Sands

Creetown

18

Cairnharrow
1496

Gatehouse
of Fleet

Anwoth
Cardoness
Castle

A75

Castle Douglas 13
(A755) Kirkcudbright 8

Castle
Loch

Stone
Circle

B7052

Wigtown

Cairn
Holy

Carsluith

Glen

Ravenshall Point

Sandgreen

haven

Auchenmalg

The Machars

Bladnoch

Baldoon
Castle

Baldoon
Sands

Fleet
Bay

Craignarget
Hill

Doon
of May

Culshabbin

B7005

Brachead

Knockbrex

Islands
of Fleet

3

13

Mochrum Fell
646

Loch
Head

Barrachan

Kirkinner

Whauphill

B7004

Wigtown   Bay

TOWN PLANS
Stranraer p104

Alticry

A747

Elrig

B7085

B7052

11

Garlieston

Eggerness Point

Airyhassen

Sorbie

Milton
Point

Mochrum

Galloway
House

Port William

Drumtroddan

Big Balcraig

A746

Cults

B7052

Castlewigg

U C E   B A Y

Monreith
Mains

Port Allen

2

Barsalloch
Fort

Fell of
Barhullion

B7021

Barsalloch Point

Monreith

Monreith
Animal
World

Priory

Whithorn

Portyerrock Bay

Monreith Bay

Memorial

9

Glasserton

B7004

Cairn Head

Point of Cairndoon

Fell of Carleton
480

St Ninian's
Chapel

Isle of Whithorn

St Ninian's
Cave

Tonderghie

Port Castle Bay

Cutcloy

Scares

Burrow
Head

1

E   F   G   H

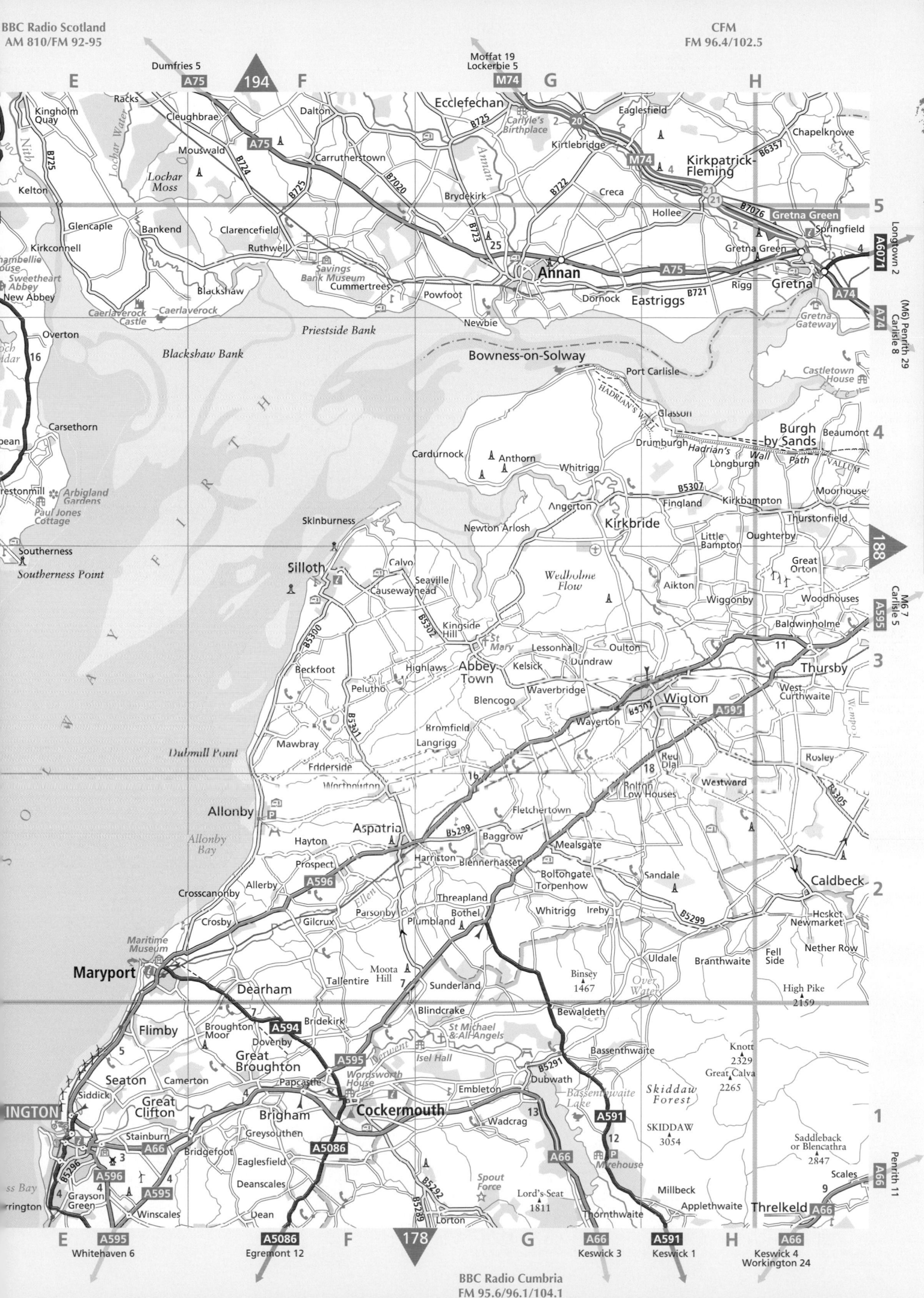

see p468
for a
touring
guide to
this map

Dumfries 5   A75   194

Moffat 19
Lockerbie 5   M74

E   F   G   H

Kingholm
Quay
Racks
Cleughbrae
Dalton
Ecclefechan
B725
Carlyle's
Birthplace
Eaglesfield
Chapelknowe
B6357

Mouswald
Carrutherstown
Kirtlebridge
M74
Kirkpatrick-
Fleming

Kelton
Lochar
Moss
Clarencefield
B725
Brydekirk
B722
Creca
Hollee
B7076
21
Gretna Green
Springfield

Glencaple
Bankend
Ruthwell
B723
25
A75
Gretna Green
Gretna
A74

Kirkconnell
ambellie
ouse
Sweetheart
Abbey
New Abbey
Blackshaw
Savings
Bank Museum
Cummertrees
Annan
Eastriggs
Powfoot
Dornock
B721
Rigg
Gretna
Gateway

Longtown 2   A6071
(M6) Penrith 29
Carlisle 8   A74

Overton
16
Caerlaverock
Castle
Caerlaverock
Priestside Bank
Newbie

Bowness-on-Solway
Port Carlisle
Castletown
House

M6 7
Carlisle 5   A595

Carsethorn
Blackshaw Bank
Cardurnock
Anthorn
Drumburgh
Hadrian's
Wall
Burgh
-by Sands
Beaumont

restonmill
Arbigland
Gardens
Paul Jones
Cottage
Whitrigg
Longburgh
VALLUM
Moorhouse

ean
Southerness
Skinburness
Newton Arlosh
Angerton
B5307
Finglard
Kirkbampton
Thurstonfield

Southerness Point
Silloth
Calvo
Seaville
Causewayhead
Wedholme
Flow
Kirkbride
Little
Bampton
Oughterby
Great
Orton
Woodhouses
188

Aikton
Wiggonby
Baldwinholme

Beckfoot
B5300
B5302
Kingside
Hill
St Mary
Highlaws
Abbey
Town
Lessonhall
Dundraw
Oulton
11
Thursby
A595
West
Curthwaite

Peutho
Kelsick
Waverbridge
Wigton
A595
Rosley

Mawbray
B5301
Blencogo
Bromfield
Langrigg
Waverton
Red
Dial
Westward
B5305

Dubmill Point
Edderside
Wortholton
16
18
Bolton
Low Houses

Allonby
Fletchertown
Caldbeck

Aspatria
B5299
Baggrow
Mealsgate
Sandale
Hesket
Newmarket

Allonby
Bay
Hayton
Harriston
Blennerhasset
Boltongate
Torpenhow
Whitrigg
Ireby
B5299
Nether Row

Prospect
A596
Crosscanonby
Allerby
Threapland
Bothel
Uldale
Branthwaite
Fell
Side

Crosby
Gilcrux
Parsonby
Plumbland
Binsey
1467
Over
Water
High Pike
2159

Maritime
Museum
Maryport
Dearham
Moota
Hill
7
Sunderland
Bewaldeth
Knott
2329

Flimby
Broughton
Moor
7
A594
Bridekirk
Blindcrake
Bassenthwaite
Great Calva
2265

Seaton
Dovenby
A595
St Michael
& All-Angels
Isel Hall
B5291
Dubwath
Skiddaw
Forest

Siddick
Great
Broughton
Papcastle
Wordsworth
House
Embleton
Bassenthwaite
Lake
SKIDDAW
3054

INGTON
Great
Clifton
Brigham
Cockermouth
Wadcrag
13
A591
12
Saddleback
or Blencathra
2847

Stainburn
A66
Bridgefoot
Greysouthen
A5086
Mirehouse
Penrith 11   A66

ss Bay
B5296
A596
Eaglesfield
Deanscales
B5292
Spout
Force
Lord's Seat
1811
Millbeck
Applethwaite
Scales
9

rrington
Grayson
Green
Winscales
Dean
Lorton
Thornthwaite
Threlkeld
A66

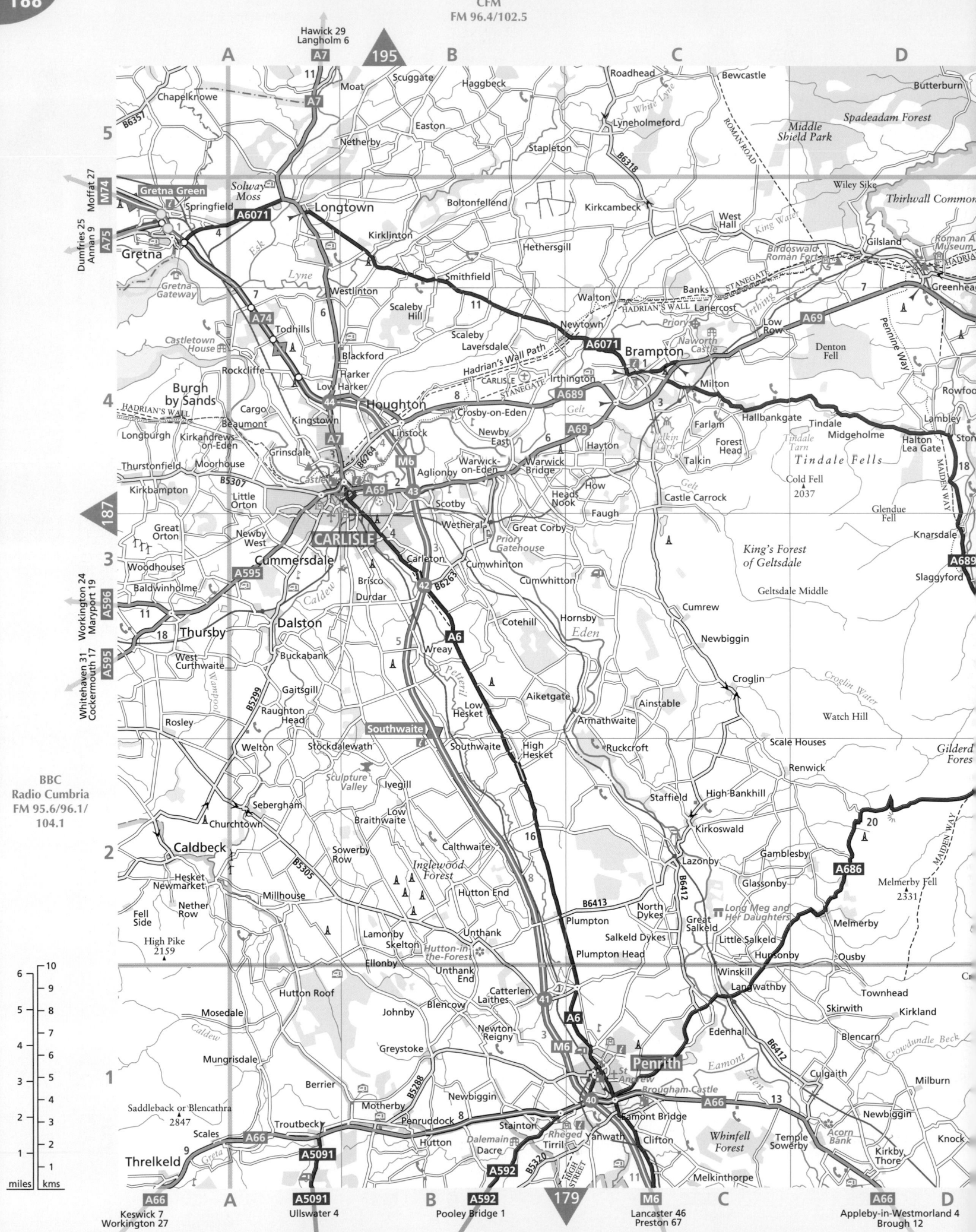

BBC
Radio Cumbria
FM 95.6/96.1/
104.1

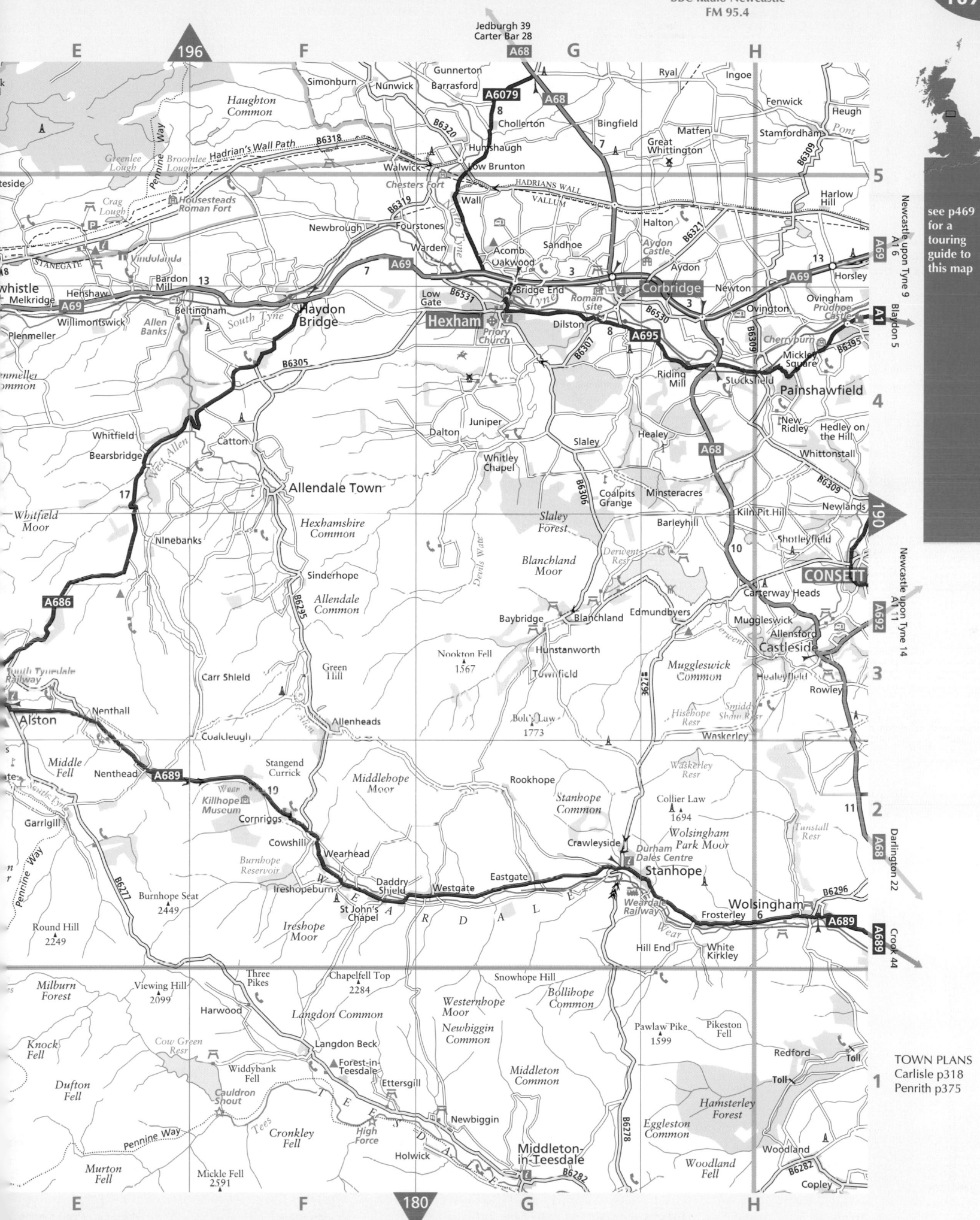

BBC Radio Newcastle
FM 95.4

see p469
for a
touring
guide to
this map

TOWN PLANS
Carlisle p318
Penrith p375

Galaxy 105-106
FM 105.3/105.6/105.8/106.4

Metro Radio
FM 97.1/102.6/103/103.2

Magic 1152
AM 1152

BBC Radio
Newcastle
FM 95.4

Century FM
FM 96.2/96.4/
100.7/101.8

(A68) Jedburgh 46
Otterburn 20

197

Alnwick 26
Morpeth 7

Blyth 4

WHITLEY BAY

Cullercoats

TYNEMOUTH

**SOUTH
SHIELDS**

Ferry

Stava
Haug
Berge

Goth
Kristi

IJmui
(Ams

Fenwick
Heugh
Dalton
Stamfordham
Medburn
Harlow
Hill
Hadrian's Wall Path
George Stephenson's
Cottage
Heddon-on-
the-Wall
Horsley
Wylam
Ovington
Ovingham
Castle
Cherryburn
Mickley
Square
Crawcrook
Prudhoe
Stocksfield
Painshawfield
New
Ridley
Hedley on
the Hill
Whittonstall
Newlands
Shotleyfield
Shotley
Bridge
CONSETT
Allensford
Castleside
Healeyfield
Rowley
Waskerley
Satley
Knitsley
Delves
Iveston
Leadgate
Butsfield
Cornsay
Quebec
Esh
Satley

Ponteland
Prestwick
Dinnington
Darras
Hall
Woolsington
Black
Callerton
High
Callerton
NEWCASTLE
Throckley
Newburn
Ryton
BLAYDON
WHICKHAM
Greenside
Barlow
High
Spen
Highfield
**Rowlands
Gill**
Chopwell
Hamsterley
Blackhall
Mill
Burnopfield
Hobson
Medomsley
Dipton
Tantobie
**Annfield
Plain**
Tantobie
Tanfield Moor
STANLEY
**South
Moor**
Maiden
Law
The
Middles
Craghead
Holmside
Burnhope
Lanchester
Langley
Park
Bearpark
Esh
Winning
Waterhouses
Ushaw
Moor
New
Brancepeth
Brandon

Seaton
Burn
Wide
Open
Dudley
Burradon
Killingworth
Backworth
Earsdon
Shiremoor
New York
LONGBENTON
WALLSEND
Willington
Jesmond
Heaton
Byker
GATESHEAD
Walker
JARROW
HEBBURN
Monkton
Felling
Pelaw
Fellgate
Wrekenton
Felling
Lamesley
Sunniside
Marley
Hill
Gibside
Chapel
Crookgate
Bank
Tanfield
Railway
Causey
Arch
Kibblesworth
Beamish
Open Air
Museum
Beamish
Pelton
Grange
Villa
**Chester-
le-Street**
Waldridge
Edmondsley
Sacriston
Witton
Gilbert
Witton
Priory
Framwellgate
Moor
DURHAM
Carrville
Castle
High Shincliffe
Shincliffe

Boldon
Colliery
West
Boldon
East
Boldon
Cleadon
Whitburn
Harton
Marsden Bay
Souter
Lighthouse
Fulwell
Roker
Southwick
Castletown
Washington
South
Hylton
SUNDERL
Hendon
New
Silksworth
Ryhope
Coll
Ryhop
Doxford
Park
Penshaw
Shiney Row
Bournmoor
New
Herrington
**HOUGHTON-
LE-SPRING**
Colliery
Row
Great
Lumley
Plawsworth
Kimblesworth
Fence
Houses
East
Rainton
West
Rainton
**Hetton-
le-Hole**
Murton
Easington
Lane
South
Hetton
Pittington
Littletown
Haswell
Plough
Haswell
SEAH
Seaton
Dalton
Park
Cold Hes
Easing
Coll
Easington
Sherburn
Shadforth
Ludworth
Shotton
Colliery
PETE
Thornley
Wheatley Hill
Shotton
Castle
Eden
Wingate
Station
Cassop
Quarrington
Hill
Kelloe
Coxhoe
Dear Hill
Trimdon
Colliery
Hutton
Henry
Trimdon Grange
Trimdon
Fishburn
Crookfoot
Reservoir
Sedgefield
**BISHOP
AUCKLAND**
Shildon
St Helen
Auckland
West
Auckland
Middridge
Mordon
Bradbury
Wynyard Village
Thorpe Larches

181

Barnard Castle 11   Darlington 9

Darlington 7

Stockton-on-Tees 5   Middle

SUNDERLAND

see p470
for a
touring
guide to
this map

CITY ROUTES
Newcastle upon
Tyne &
Gateshead
p290

TOWN PLANS
Durham p329
Newcastle
upon Tyne
p369
Sunderland
p191

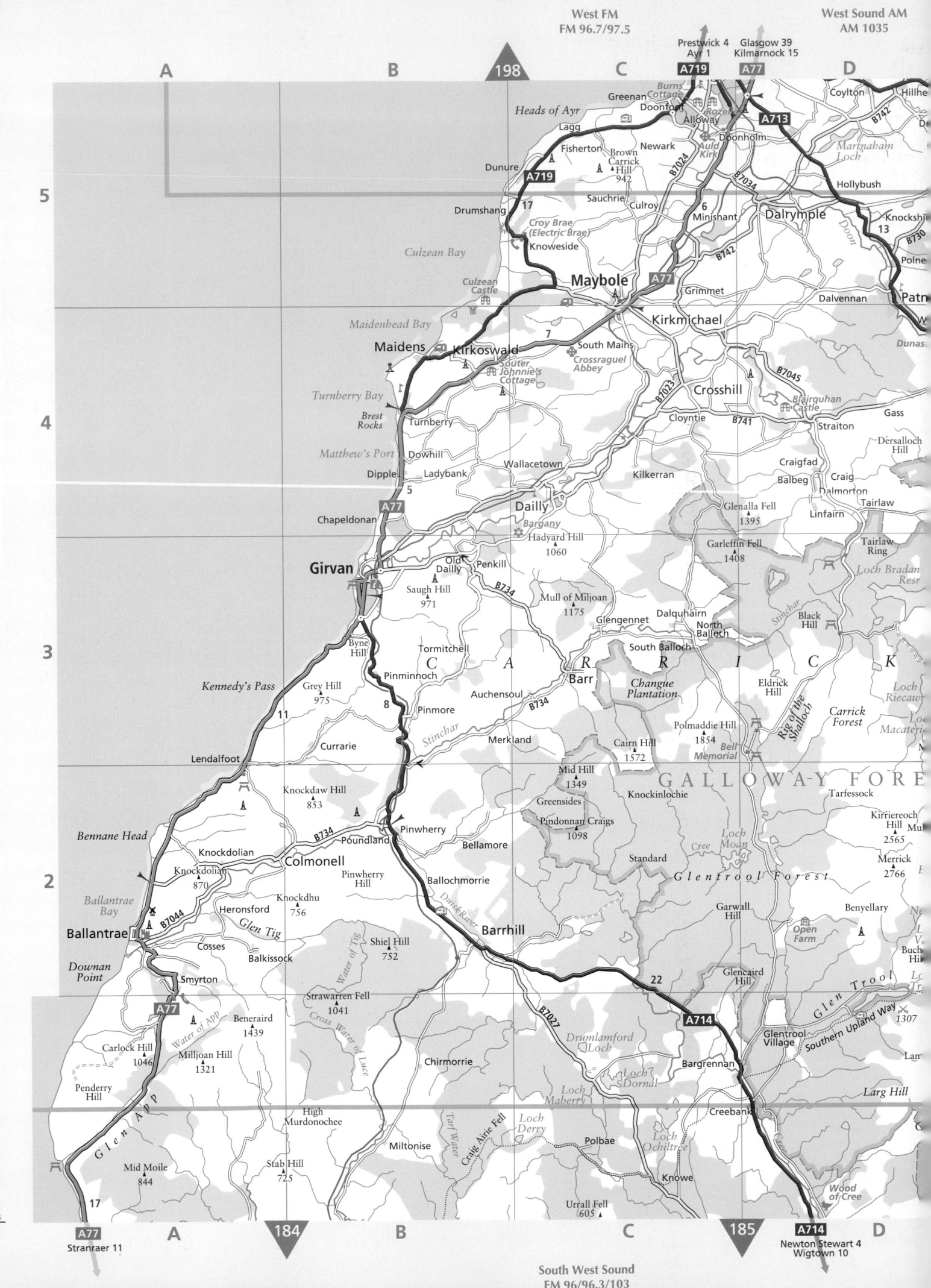

198

Prestwick 4
Ayr 1

Glasgow 39
Kilmarnock 15

A719

A77

D

Burns'
Cottage
Greenan
Doonfoot
Rozelle
Alloway

Coylton

Hillhe

Heads of Ayr
Lagg

Newark

Auld
Kirk
Doonholm

A713

Fisherton
Brown
Carrick
Hill
942

B7024

B7034

*Martnaham
Loch*

Dunure

A719

Newark

5

Drumshang

17

Sauchrie

Culroy

6

Minishant

Dalrymple

Knockshi

Croy Brae
(Electric Brae)
Knoweside

Culzean Bay

Maybole

A77

Grimmet

Dalvennan

13

B730
Polne

Culzean
Castle

Kirkmichael

7

South Mains

Doon

Patn

Maidenhead Bay

South Mains

Crossraguel
Abbey

B7045

B7023

Dunas

Maidens

Kirkoswald

Crosshill

Souter
Johnnie's
Cottage

Blairquhan
Castle

Gass

Turnberry Bay

Cloyntie

B741

Straiton

4

*Brest
Rocks*

Turnberry

Wallacetown

Kilkerran

Craigfad

Balbeg

Craig

Dersalloch
Hill

Matthew's Port

Dowhill

Dipple

Ladybank

Dailly

Glenalla Fell
1395

Dalmorton

Tairlaw

A77

5

Garleffin Fell
1408

Tairlaw
Ring

Chapeldonan

Bargany

Hadyard Hill
1060

Linfairn

*Loch Bradan
Resr*

Girvan

Old
Daily

Penkill

B734

Mull of Miljoan
1175

Glengennet

Dalquhairn

North
Balloch

Black
Hill

Stinchar

Saugh Hill
971

South Balloch

*Rig of the
Shalloch*

*Loch
Riecaw*

Byne
Hill

C

A

R

R

I

C

K

*Loch
Macater*

3

Kennedy's Pass

Grey Hill
975

Pinminnoch

Barr

*Changue
Plantation*

Eldrick
Hill

*Carrick
Forest*

11

8

Tormitchell

Polmaddie Hill
1854

Bell
Memorial

Pinmore

Auchensoul

B734

Cairn Hill
1572

Kirriereoch
Hill
2565

Mul

Stinchar

Currarie

Merkland

Mid Hill
1349

Knockinlochie

G A L L O W A Y   F O R E

Tarfessock

Lendalfoot

Knockdaw Hill
853

Greensides

Pindonnan Craigs
1098

Standard

Merrick
2766

Bennane Head

B734

Pinwherry

Bellamore

*Cree
Moan*

Glentrool   Forest

Knockdolian

Poundland

Knockdolian
870

Colmonell

Ballochmorrie

Garwall
Hill

Benyellary

2

*Ballantrae
Bay*

Pinwherry
Hill

Duisk River

Open
Farm

B7044

Heronsford

Knockdhu
756

B7027

Glen   *Trool*

Tr

Ballantrae

Cosses

Glen Tig

Shiel Hill
752

Barrhill

Glencaird
Hill

*Downan
Point*

Balkissock

22

Glencairn
Hill

1307

Smyrton

Water of Tig

A714

A77

Carlock Hill
1046

Water of App

Beneraird
1439

Glentrool
Village

Southern Upland Way

Bargrennan

Larg Hill

Milljoan Hill
1321

Chirmorrie

*Drumlamford
Loch*

Penderry
Hill

Strawarren Fell
1041

Cross Water of Luce

*Loch
S Dornal*

Creebank

3

High
Murdonochee

*Loch
Maberry*

Mid Moile
844

Stab Hill
725

Miltonise

Tarf Water

*Loch
Derry*

Polbae

*Loch
Ochiltree*

Knowe

*Wood
of Cree*

17

Urrall Fell
605

Craig Airie Fell

Glen App

A77

184

185

A714

miles | kms
10
9
8
7
6
5
4
3
2
1
6
5
4
3
2
1

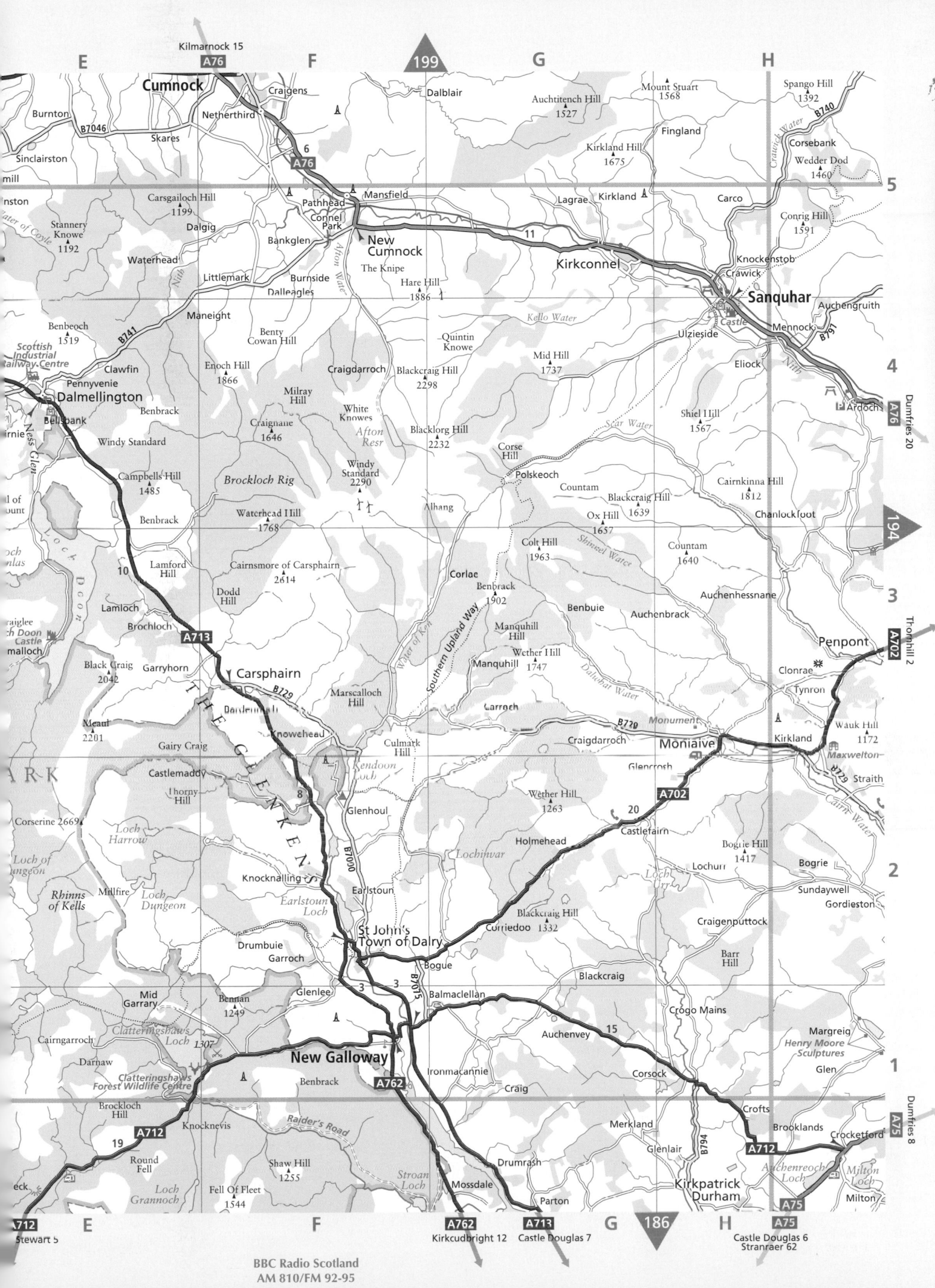

see p471 for a touring guide to this map

Kilmarnock 15
A76

Cumnock
Craigens
Dalblair
Auchtitench Hill
1527
Mount Stuart
1568
Spango Hill
1392
B740

Burnton
Netherthird
Fingland
Corsebank
Wedder Dod
1460

B7046
Skares
Kirkland Hill
1675
Kirkland
Carco
Conrig Hill
1591

Sinclairston
6
A76
Lagrae

Water of Coyle
Carsgailoch Hill
1199
Pathhead
Connel Park
Mansfield
Knockenstob

Stannery Knowe
1192
Dalgig
Bankglen
New Cumnock
11
Kirkconnel
Crawick
Knockenstob

Dalmellington
Maneight
Burnside
Dalleagles
The Knipe
Hare Hill
1886
Kello Water
Sanquhar
Castle
Mennock
Auchengruith
B797

Benbeoch
1519
B741
Benty Cowan Hill
Quintin Knowe
Ulzieside
Eliock
Nith

Scottish Industrial Railway Centre
Clawfin
Enoch Hill
1866
Milray Hill
Craigdarroch
Blackcraig Hill
2298
Mid Hill
1737
Shiel Hill
1567
Ardoch
A76
Dumfries 20

Dalmellington
Benbrack
White Knowes
Scar Water
Cairnkinna Hill
1812

Bellsbank
Windy Standard
Craignane
1646
Afton Resr
Blacklorg Hill
2232
Corse Hill
Polskeoch
Countam
Blackcraig Hill
1639
Chanlockfoot
194

Ness Glen
Campbells Hill
1485
Brockloch Rig
Windy Standard
2290
Alhang
Ox Hill
1657
Countam
1640

Loch Doon
Benbrack
Waterhead Hill
1768
Colt Hill
1963
Shinnel Water
Auchenhessnane

Cairnsmore of Carsphairn
2614
Corlae
Benbrack
1902
Benbuie
Auchenbrack

Craiglee
Loch Doon Castle
malloch
Lamford Hill
Dodd Hill
Manquhill Hill
Manquhill
1747
Wether Hill
1747
Penpont
A702
Thornhill 2

Black Craig
2042
Garryhorn
A713
Carsphairn
B729
Marscalloch Hill
Southern Upland Way
Garroch
B729
Clonrae
Tynron
Wauk Hill
1172

Meaul
2201
Dardarroch
Knowehead
Culmark Hill
Monument
B729
Straith

Gairy Craig
THE GLENKENS
Kendoon Loch
Craigdarroch
Moniaive
Kirkland
Maxwelton

Castlemaddy
Thorny Hill
8
Glenhoul
Wether Hill
1263
Glencrosh
A702
Bogtie Hill
1417
Bogrie

Corserine 2669
Loch Harrow
20
A702
Castlefairn
Lochurr
Bogrie

Loch Dungeon
Knocknalling
B7000
Lochinvar
Holmehead
Loch Urr
Sundaywell
Gordieston

Rhinns of Kells
Millfire
Earlstoun
Loch
Wether Hill
Craigenputtock

Loch of Dungeon
Earlstoun Loch
Blackcraig Hill
1332
Barr Hill

Drumbuie
Garroch
St John's Town of Dalry
Corriedoo
Blackcraig

Bennan
1249
Glenlee
Bogue
B7075
Crogo Mains
Margreig
Henry Moore Sculptures

Mid Garrary
3
3
Balmaclellan
15
Auchenvey
Corsock
Glen

Cairngarroch
Clatteringshaws Loch
1307
Benbrack
A762
Ironmacannie
Craig
Crocketford

Darnaw
Clatteringshaws Forest Wildlife Centre
New Galloway
A762
Crofts
Brooklands
A75
Dumfries 8

Brockloch Hill
Knocknevis
Raider's Road
Merkland
Glenlair
B794
A712
Auchenreoch Loch
Milton Loch

19
A712
Round Fell
Shaw Hill
1255
Stroan Loch
Drumrash
Glenlair
Kirkpatrick Durham
Milton

Loch Grannoch
Fell Of Fleet
1544
Mossdale
Parton
A75

A712
E
F
Kirkcudbright 12
A762
A713
Castle Douglas 7
186
G
Castle Douglas 6
Stranraer 62
H
A75

Stewart 5

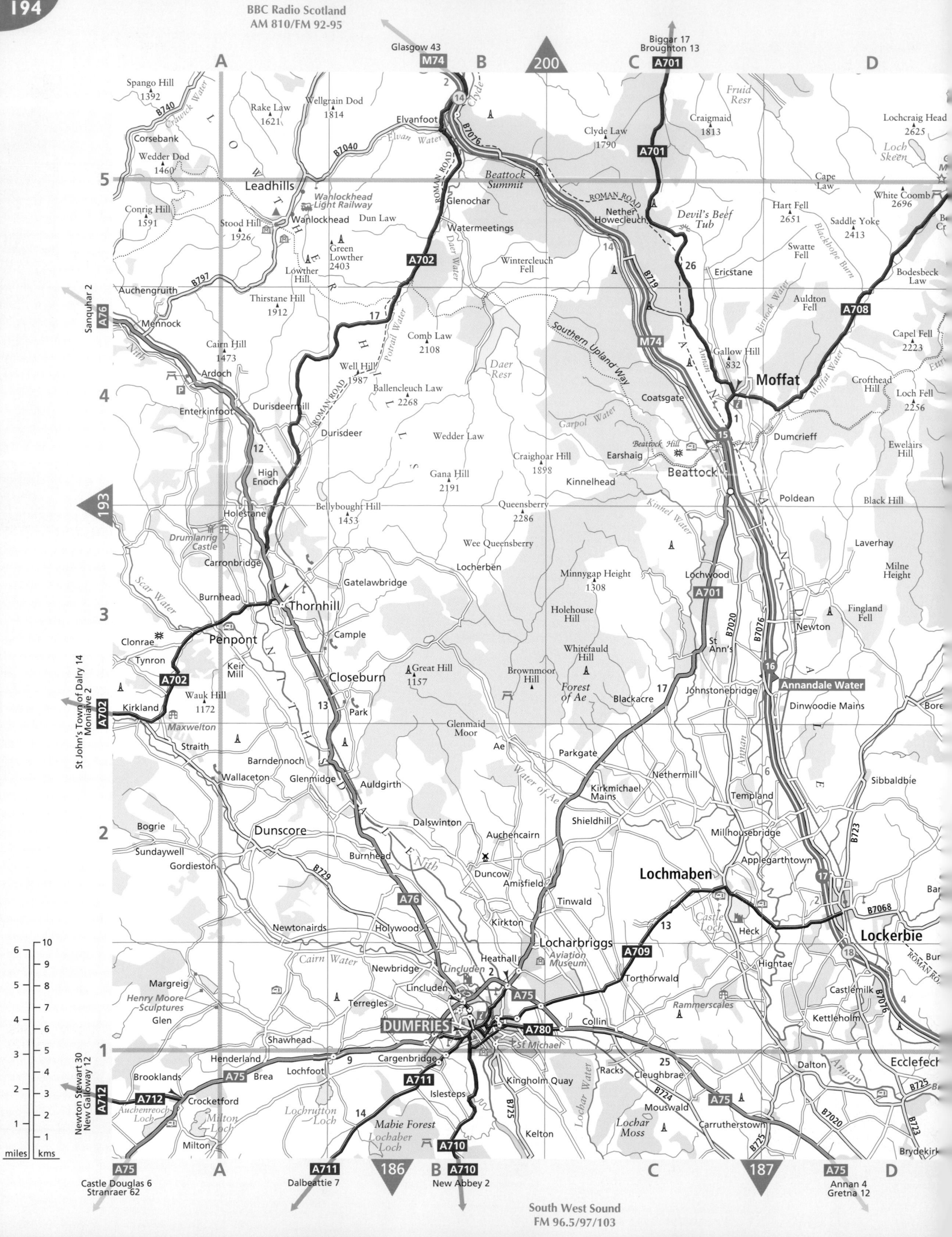

Selkirk 19
A708

Galashiels 13
Selkirk 7
A7

Glasgow 43
(A68) Jedburgh 6
A698

201

188

196

see p471 for a touring guide to this map

(A68) Corbridge 42
Carter Bar 7
A6088

TOWN PLANS
Dumfries p326

Southern Upland Way

Tushielaw Inn
Crosslee
Cacrabank
B7009
Dun Knowe
Redfordgreen
Shaws under-Loch
Hellmoor Loch
Ale Water
Smasha Hill 1056
Drinkstone Hill

Horsleyhill
Knowetownhead
Clarilaw
A698
Appletreehall
Denholm
Ashybank
Cavers
Rubers Law 1391
Hallrule

Ramsey Knowe
Wardlaw
Ettrick
Ramseycleuch
Ettrickhill
Monument
Law Kneis 1634
B709
B711
Buccleuch
Borthwickshiels
Borthwickbrae
Roberton
Burnfoot
Alemoor Resr

Burnfoot
Hawick
A7
White Hill 987
Kirkton
A6088
Bonchester Bridge
Hobkirk
Cleuch Head
B6357
A6088

Black Knowe 1804
Glenkerry
Sauchie Law
Gair
Black Knowe
Craik
Craik Forest
Borthwick Water
Redcleuch Edge 1278
Deanburnhaugh
Hott Hill
Branxholme
Newmill
Broadhaugh
Dryden Fell 1321
Teviot
Dodburn

Hyndlee

Cross Hill
Craik Cross Hill
Nether Cassock
Howpasley
Pike Hill 1369
Teviothead
Castleweary
Skelfhill Pen 1746
The Pike 1516
Fanna Hill 1688
B6357

Pen
Shank
dalemuir Forest
Davington
Blaeberry Hill
Eweslees Knowe
23
Comb Hill
Millstone Edge
Cauldcleuch Head 1996
Greatmoor Hill 1966
Maiden Paps
Leap Hill
B6399
Singdean
Lamblair Hill

ROMAN ROAD
aldwaterfoot
White Esk
B709
Eskdalemuir
Causeway Grain Head
Wisp Hill 1953
Mosspaul Hotel
Geordie's Hill
Tudhope Hill
Hermitage Castle
Saughtree Fell

nings Hill 1088
B723
Loupin Stanes
Jamestown
White Hope Edge
Faw Side 1722
A7
Din Fell 1737
Hermitage
Arnton Fell 1464
Saughtree
Foulmire Heights

ck Esk
Castle O'er Fort
Girdle Stanes
Castle O'er Forest
Broad Head 1614
Pike Fell
Roan Fell 1840
Newlands
North Birny Fell 902
Steele Road
Larriston
Larriston Fells 1678
Black Knowe

Castle O'er
Esk
Crumpton Hill 1373
Ewes
Watch Hill
Dinlabyre
Glendhu Hill 1684

The Knock
Bentpath
Hog Fell
Black Edge 1464
Old Castleton
Caplestone Fell

Hart Fell 1107
The Shin
Telford Memorial
Ewes Water
Tarras Water
Liddel Water
Newcastleton or Copshaw Holm
Black Knowe

Calkin Rig 1478
Craigcleuch
Glentenmont Height
Tinnis Hill 1326
Kershope Burn

Langholm

rrie mmon
Raes Knowes
B7068
Winterhope Reservoir
Earshaw Hill 921
Bruntshiel Hill
Kershopefoot
Kershope Forest
Bewcastle Fells

Grange Fell 1047
B7068
Caulside
Blackpool Gate
The Flatt
White Preston 1384

wat's Hill
Waterbeck
B7068
B6318
Nook
Arthur Seat
Crossings
Black Lyne
Roughsike
Roadhead

B725
Middlebie
Springkell
Evertown
Milltown
B720
Rowanburn
Canonbie
Catlowdy
Lyneholmeford
Bewcastle

20
Eaglesfield
Chapelknowe
11
Tower-of-Sark
Moat
Scuggate
Haggbeck
ROMAN ROAD

M74
Creca
Kirkpatrick-Fleming
(21)
Netherby
Easton
Stapleton

E F G H

M74
Gretna 3
Carlisle 13
Longton 1
Carlisle 10
A7
188

Radio Borders
FM 96.8/97.5/103.1/103.4

BBC
Radio Scotland
AM 810
FM 92-95

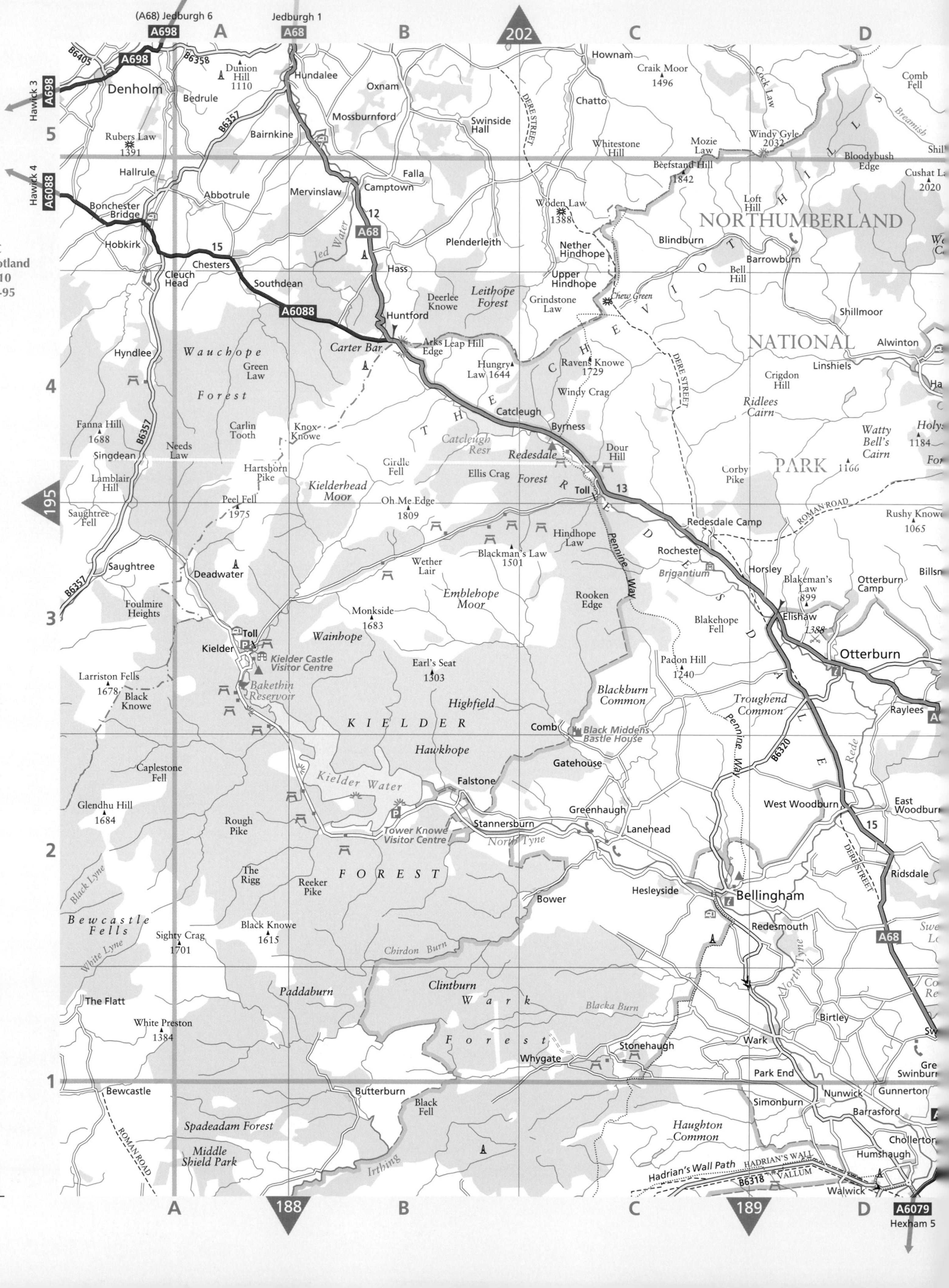

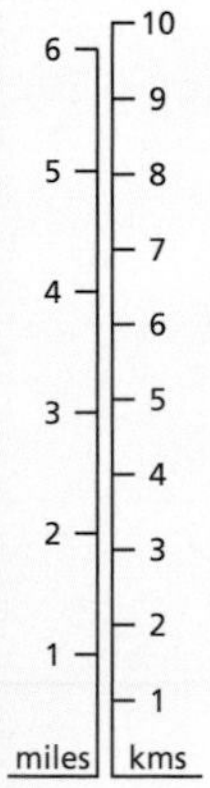

(A68) Jedburgh 6
A698
Jedburgh 1
A68
202
A
B
C
D
Hawick 3
A698
Hawick 4
A6088
B6405
B6358
Denholm
Bedrule
Dunion Hill 1110
Hundalee
Oxnam
Hownam
Craik Moor 1496
Comb Fell
Cock Law
Chatto
DERE STREET
Mossburnford
Bairnkine
B6357
Rubers Law 1391
Swinside Hall
Whitestone Hill
Mozie Law
Windy Gyle 2032
Breamish
Bloodybush Edge
Cushat Law 2020
Hallrule
Falla
Camptown
Beefstand Hill 1842
Loft Hill
Abbotrule
Mervinslaw
Bonchester Bridge
Woden Law 1388
NORTHUMBERLAND
12
A68
Jed Water
Hobkirk
15
Chesters
Cleuch Head
Southdean
Plenderleith
Nether Hindhope
Upper Hindhope
Blindburn
Barrowburn
Bell Hill
Hass
Leithope Forest
Deerlee Knowe
Grindstone Law
Chew Green
CHEVIOT HILLS
Shillmoor
A6088
Huntford
Carter Bar
Arks Edge
Leap Hill
Hungry Law 1644
Ravens Knowe 1729
NATIONAL
Alwinton
Linshiels
Crigdon Hill
Hyndlee
Wauchope Forest
Green Law
Windy Crag
Ridlees Cairn
Catcleugh
Fanna Hill 1688
B6357
Carlin Tooth
Knox Knowe
Catcleugh Resr
Byrness
Watty Bell's Cairn
Holystone
1184
Singdean
Needs Law
Redesdale
Dour Hill
Lamblair Hill
Hartshorn Pike
Girdle Fell
Kielderhead Moor
Ellis Crag
Forest
Corby Pike
PARK
1166
195
Toll
13
Saughtree Fell
Peel Fell 1975
Oh Me Edge 1809
ROMAN ROAD
Rushy Knowe 1065
Redesdale Camp
Hindhope Law
Blackman's Law 1501
Rochester
Saughtree
Deadwater
Wether Lair
Pennine Way
Brigantium
Horsley
Billsmoor
B6357
Foulmire Heights
Emblehope Moor
Rooken Edge
Blakeman's Law 899
Otterburn Camp
Monkside 1683
Elishaw
Blakehope Fell
1388
Toll
Kielder
Wainhope
Otterburn
Kielder Castle Visitor Centre
Earl's Seat 1303
Padon Hill 1240
Larriston Fells 1678
Black Knowe
Bakethin Reservoir
Highfield
Blackburn Common
Troughend Common
Raylees
KIELDER
Comb
Black Middens Bastle House
Hawkhope
Pennine Way
B6320
Caplestone Fell
Gatehouse
Rede
Kielder Water
Falstone
Glendhu Hill 1684
West Woodburn
East Woodburn
Rough Pike
Greenhaugh
Stannersburn
15
Tower Knowe Visitor Centre
North Tyne
Lanehead
DERE STREET
Black Lyne
The Rigg
Reeker Pike
FOREST
Ridsdale
Bower
Hesleyside
Bellingham
Bewcastle Fells
Sighty Crag 1701
Black Knowe 1615
Redesmouth
A68
White Lyne
Chirdon Burn
North Tyne
Clintburn
Paddaburn
Wark
The Flatt
Blacka Burn
White Preston 1384
Forest
Birtley
Stonehaugh
Wark
Whygate
Park End
Bewcastle
Butterburn
Black Fell
Simonburn
Nunwick
Gunnerton
Barrasford
Spadeadam Forest
Haughton Common
Chollerton
Humshaugh
ROMAN ROAD
Middle Shield Park
Irthing
Hadrian's Wall Path
HADRIAN'S WALL
VALLUM
B6318
Walwick
188
189
A6079
Hexham 5
5
4
3
2
1

6
5
4
3
2
1
10
9
8
7
6
5
4
3
2
1
miles
kms

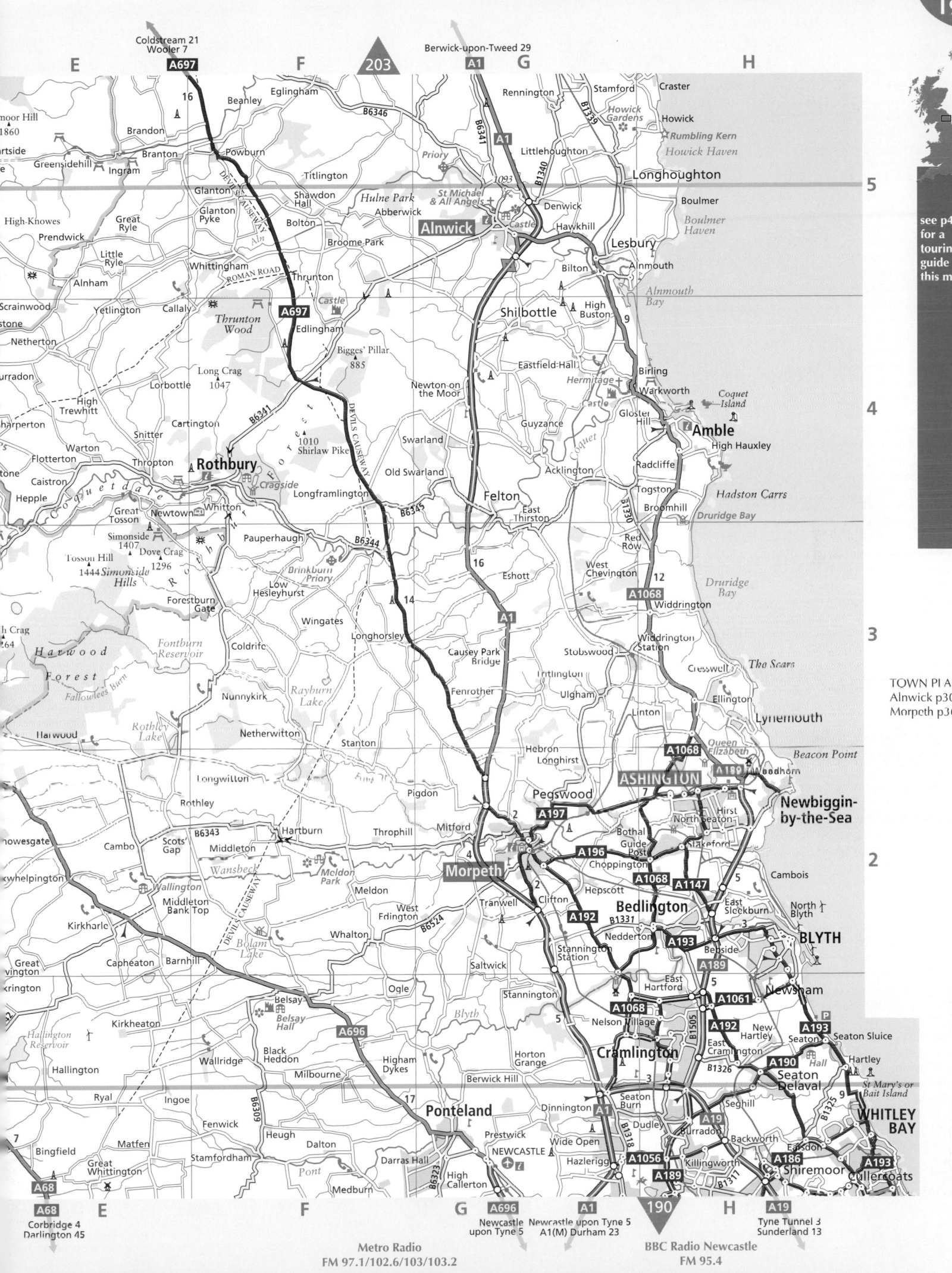

Coldstream 21
Wooler 7

A697

16

Berwick-upon-Tweed 29

A1

203

see p472
for a
touring
guide to
this map

TOWN PLANS
Alnwick p307
Morpeth p367

moor Hill
1860

Brandon

Greensidehill
Ingram

High-Knowes
Prendwick

Little Ryle
Alnham

Scrainwood

Netherton

urradon

High
Trewhitt

harperton

Warton
Flotterton

Caistron

Hepple

Eglingham

Beanley

B6346

Powburn

Titlington

Glanton
Glanton
Pyke

Shawdon
Hall

Bolton

Hulne Park
Abberwick

St Michael
& All Angels

Alnwick

Castle

Denwick

Hawkhill

Rennington

Stamford

Craster

Littlehoughton

Howick
Gardens

Howick

Rumbling Kern
Howick Haven

Longhoughton

Boulmer

Boulmer
Haven

5

Whittingham

ROMAN ROAD

Thrunton

Great Ryle

Broome Park

Lesbury

Alnmouth

Thrunton
Wood

A697

Castle

Edlingham

Bigges' Pillar
885

Shilbottle

High
Buston

Bilton

Alnmouth
Bay

4

Long Crag
1047

B6341

Cartington

Snitter

Throp ton

Rothbury

Cragside

Newton-on
the Moor

Eastfield Hall

Hermitage

Birling

Warkworth

Castle

Gloster
Hill

Coquet
Island

Amble

High Hauxley

Swarland

Guyzance

Radcliffe

Togston

Hadston Carrs

Druridge Bay

Great
Tosson

Newtown

Whitton

Longframlington

B6345

Felton

East
Thirston

Old Swarland

Acklington

Broomhill

Red
Row

Druridge
Bay

Simonside
1407

Dove Crag
1296

Tosson Hill
1444

Simonside
Hills

Pauperhaugh

B6344

Brinkburn
Priory

Forestburn
Gate

Low
Hesleyhurst

Fontburn
Reservoir

Wingates

16

14

Eshott

West
Chevington

12

A1068

Widdrington

3

h Crag
264

Harwood

Forest

Fallowlees burn

Rothley
Lake

Nunnykirk

Rayburn
Lake

Coldrife

Longhorsley

Causey Park
Bridge

Fenrother

Stobswood

Tritlington

Ulgham

Widdrington
Station

Cresswell

Ellington

The Scars

A1

Harwood

Netherwitton

Stanton

Hebron
Longhirst

Linton

Lynemouth

Longwitton

Rothley

Pigdon

A1068

Queen
Elizabeth

Beacon Point

ASHINGTON

A189

Woodhorn

howesgate

Cambo

Scots'
Gap

B6343

Middleton

Hartburn

Throphill

Middleton
Bank Top

Wansbeck

Mitford

Meldon
Park

Morpeth

Pegswood

2

A197

North
Seaton

Hirst

Newbiggin-
by-the-Sea

kwhelpington

Kirkharle

Cambo

Wallington

Meldon

Tranwell

4

2

A196

Clifton

Bothal
Guide
Post

Choppington

A1068

A1147

Slakeford

Cambois

North
Blyth

Great
vington

Capheaton

Barnhill

Bolam
Lake

West
Edington

Whalton

Hepscott

Bedlington

Nedderton

B1331

A192

A193

East
Sleekburn

Bebside

A189

5

BLYTH

Kirkharle

DEVILS CAUSEWAY

Saltwick

Stannington
Station

Stannington

East
Hartford

A1061

5

Newsham

Hallington
Reservoir

Kirkheaton

Belsay

Belsay
Hall

Ogle

A696

A1068

Nelson Village

B1505

New
Hartford

A192

East
Cramlington

A193

Seaton

Seaton Sluice

Hallington

Wallridge

Black
Heddon

Higham
Dykes

Horton
Grange

Cramlington

3

A190

Seaton
Delaval

Hartley

St Mary's or
Bait Island

Ryal

Ingoe

Milbourne

Berwick Hill

Dinnington

Seaton
Burn

Seghill

Dudley

A19

Burradon

Backworth

B1325

WHITLEY
BAY

7

Bingfield

Matfen

Stamfordham

B6309

Fenwick

Heugh

Dalton

Prestwick

A1

Wide Open

NEWCASTLE

Hazlerigg

A1056

High
Callerton

Darras Hall

B6323

Pont

Medburn

A68

E

Corbridge 4
Darlington 45

E

A68

F

A696

Newcastle
upon Tyne 5

G

A1

Newcastle upon Tyne 5
A1(M) Durham 23

190

BBC Radio Newcastle
FM 95.4

Killingworth

B1318

A189

B1311

A186

Shiremoor

A19

Tyne Tunnel 3
Sunderland 13

A193

Cullercoats

H

Metro Radio
FM 97.1/102.6/103/103.2

Port Glasgow 7

(M8) Glasgow 8
Paisley 2

A761

Greenock 9

A78

204

205

A737

ISLE
OF
BUTE

A844

Ascog

Kerrycroy

Scoulag Point

Mount
Stuart

Piperhall

Bruchag
Point

Torr Mór
485

Kilchattan
Bay

Little
Cumbrae
Island

Gull Point

Farland Head

Portencross

Ardneil Bay

Blackhouse
Moor

Middleton

Routenburn

Vikingar

Largs

A760

Tomont
End

Portrye

GREAT
CUMBRAE
ISLAND

B896

Millport

B889

Fairlie
Roads

Power
Station

Campbelton

West
Kilbride

B7047

B7048

B781

Queenside
Muir

Hill of Stake
1712

Girtley Hill
1254

Waterhead
Moor

Irish Law
1587

Blairpark

Waterfalls

Kelburn Country
Centre

Routaneburn

Fairlie

Camphill
Resr

Kaim Hill
1272

Knockendon
Resr

Baidland Hill
1097

South Hourat

Caaf
Resr

Gill

Giffordland

Mistylaw
Muir

Kaim
Dam

Ladyland
Moor

Burnt Hill
1084

Glengarnock

Rye Water

Drakemyre

Dalry

Highfield

A737

Dalgarven

Munnoch
Reservoir

Muirhead
Resr

Carruthmuir

Heathfield

Millikenpark

Kilbarchan

Weaver's
Cottage

A737

B789

Brookfield

Johnstone

Elderslie

Howwood

B786

Lochwinnoch

Reserve

Kilbirnie

A760

Beith

B777

Gateside

Longbar

The
Den

B706

Barrmill

Burnhouse

B780

B778

B760

Garnock

B775

Glenffe
Braes
Harelaw
Resr

Gatesid

Neilston

Uplawmoor

Halket

Lugton

Gabroc
Hill

Fullwood

Windy-
Yett

Corsehouse
Resr

Dunlop

Kingsford

Barcraigs
Resr

Paisley

Glenb

Long
Loch

Neilstor
Pad

Due op
2005

14

8

11

11

CUNNINGHAM

A736

A735

Stewarton

Burnfoot
Resr

B778

17

Wat

Horse Isle

Arran (Brodick)

230

Kilwinning

Abbey

Montgreenan

Cunninghamhead

B769

A735

Fenwick

Moscov

Stevenston

A738

Ardrossan

Saltcoats

3

Perceton

Kilmaurs

Knockentiber

Springside

B751

B7064

KILMARNOCK

Crookedholm

Arran (Brodick)

Irvine

The Big Idea

Maritime Museum

Irvine
Bay

Dreghorn

Crosshouse

Riccarton

Hurlford

Ga

A71

A71

A78 Greenock 26

North
Shore

0 200 400yds
0 200 400m

Caledonia Ct

Kilmahew St

Glasgow La

Winton St

Hill Lane

Anderson Terr

A78 Irvine 7

Montgomerie Pier Road

Montgomerie Street

Glasgow Street

Hill Place

Civic
Centre

Castle
Hill

Ruin

PO

Marina

Ferry
Terminal

Princes
St

Hill St

Monument

Crathie
Drive

A738

Arran La

ARRAN PLACE

Ardrossan
Harbour Station

Dock Rd

Town
Station

PRINCES ST

HARBOUR RD

WC

Promenade

South
Beach

Ardrossan Harbour

Springside

Dybridge

Gatehead

Earlston

A78

A759

Dundonald

Castle

Shortlees

B730

B751

Craigie

Crosshan

Mosside

Carnel

Barassie

B746

Loans

Symington

Rosemount

Troon

Royal
Troon

Meikle
Craigs

Larne
Belfast (seasonal)

Monkton

B739

PRESTWICK

Prestwick

A79

Mossblown

Adamhill

Millburn

A77

Bogend

Bachelors'
Club

Mossgie

11

Tarbolton

Failford

B743

Trabboch

Trabbo

St Quivox

Whitletts

AYR

Wallacetown

Annbank

B744

Ayr

B730

Belston

Hillhead

Heads of Ayr

Burns
Cottage

Doonfoot

Greenan

Rozelle
Alloway

Newark

Auld Kirk

Doonholm

Coylton

Drongan

Martnham
Loch

Fisherton

A719

Lagg

Doonham

B742

B7024

A77

Dunure

Brown Carrick Hill
942

A719

192

A77

A713

Maidens 9
Girvan 15

Maybole 4
Girvan 16

St John's Town of Dalry 28

miles kms

206

Clyde 1
FM 97/102.5/103.3

Clyde 2
AM 1152

see p473 for a touring guide to this map

200

193

BBC Radio Scotland
AM 810/FM 92-95

CITY ROUTES
Glasgow p278

TOWN PLANS
Ardrossan p198
Ayr p307
Glasgow p335
Paisley p374

Clyde 2
AM 1152

Edinburgh 24

M8

Edinburgh 14

207

A71

Edinburgh 10

A70

C

Edinburgh

D

Woodhouse
Castlelaw

Clyde 1
FM 97/102.5/
103.3

M8

M8

(A8) Glasgow 19

5

Forestburn
Resr

Harthill

Eastfield

B7066

Almond

B717

Whitburn

Stoneyburn

Addiewell

B7015

Polbeth

Freeport

5

Bellsquarry

Murieston

Morton
Resr

Threipmuir
Resr

Harperrig
Resr

Water of Leith

Loganlea
Resr

Glencorse
Resr

Black Hill
1636

Scald Law
1898

Bore Stane
1570

Silverburn

Penicuik

8

Shotts

Dykehead
Stane

Longridge

B192

Loganlee

West
Calder

4

B7008

26

The Mount
1763

North
Usk Resr

Nine
Mile
Burn

A766

4

Fauldhouse

Greenburn

Breich

A704

Crosswood
Resr

Baddingsill
Resr

A7

Wishaw 5
A71

Allanton

B7010

9

A71

1

A704

Hendry's Corse

Woolfords
Cottages

Carlops

Auchencorth
Moss

Leadburn

Clan FM
FM 107.5/107.9

Auchter Water

B715

Climpy

Wilsontown

Tarbrax

White
Craig

Byrehope Mount
1752

West Water
Resr

11

Lamancha

Greenac

199

Motherwell 9
Wishaw 6

A721

Yieldshields

Roadmeetings

B7056

Netherton
Braehead

Springfield
Resr

Mouse Water

Forth

8

Rootpark

Stobwood

Braehead
Moss

Auchengray

North Medwin

Bleak Law
1461

Mendick Hill
1481

West Linton

B7059

Romannobridge

9

Wether Law
1570

Waterhe

Halmyre
Mains

5

Kilncadzow

A706

A721

Harelaw

West
Mains

B7016

Dunsyre

Weston

South Medwin

Dolphinton

Mountain
Cross

Crailzie Hill
1562

Eddles

5

Cartland

Cleghorn

1

3

Carnwath

Newbigging

Black Mount
1692

Walston

Blyth Bridge

A721

3

Castlecraig

Black
Meldon
1334

White
Meldon
1402

Hamilton 12
A72

A743

4

Lanark

Carstairs

West
End

Ravenstruther

Carstairs
Junction

Pettinain

4

Libberton

Whitecastle

Elsrickle

8

A72

Broughton Heights
1874

10

A70

New
Lanark

P

Hynford Bridge

3

B7016

Shieldhill

Quothquan

Candy
Mill

Ewe Hill
1177

5

Skirling

5

Hallyne

Neidpath
Cast

St Kentigern

Falls
of Clyde

Hawksland

Covington

Carmichael

6

Thankerton

Gladstone
Court

St Mary

Greenhill
Covenanter's House

Biggar

A701

John Buchan
Centre

Broughton

Trahenna Hill
1792

Stobo

Whitelaw Hill
1563

Dawyck House
Gardens

Kirkt
Man

Douglas
Water

7

A70

B7016

Wolfclyde

4

A72

Symington

Goseland Hill
1427

Bellspool

Drumelzier

Tweed

Hunc
He

Rigside

Glasgow 31

M74

Happendon

Cairn Lodge

12

Uddington

A70

Cumnock 24

Scaur Hill
1331

B7055

Howgate Hill
1456

Tinto
2320

Newton

Wiston

Marchlands

8

Coulter

Snaip
Hill

12

Lamington

Common
Law

Holms Water

26

Finglen
Rig

Blakehope Head
1783

Stanhope

Pykestone Hill
2417

Stob Law
2218

Horse
Hope Hill

Roberton Law
1238

Dungavel Hill
1673

A73

Startup
Hill

Broad
Hill

Culter Water

Glenlood
Hill

Taberon Law
2089

Dollar Law
2682

Black Law
2285

M74

7

Backstane
Hill

Roberton

Culter Fell
2455

Culter
Waterhead
Resr

Hearthstane

Manor Water

Auchensaugh
Hill
1286

B7078

Glenwhappen Rig
2263

Oliver

Tweedsmuir

Deer Law

Middle
Muir

A702

Abington

13

Crawfordjohn

B740

Drake Law
1586

Abington

Kirkton

Crawford

Tewsgill Hill
1868

Culter Cleuch
Shank

Glenmuck
Height

Broad
Law
2756

Megget
Resr

St
Capperclo

St Ma
Lo

White
Hill

B797

3

14

Camps Water

Camps
Resr

Talla
Resr

Monument
Tibbie Shie

Rake Law
1621

Wellgrain Dod
1814

2

A702

14

Clyde Law
1790

Meggethead

Talla Linnfoots

Megget
Stone

Craigmaid
1813

Lochcraig Head
2625

A70

B7040

Elvanfoot

ROMANROAD

Fruid
Resr

Loch
Skeen

Grey Mare's
Tail

22

Leadhills

Beattock
Summit

Glenbreck

Cape
Law

A708

Birkhill

miles | kms

A702

Carronbridge 14

M74

Moffat 11
Carlisle 48

A701

Moffat 8
Dumfries 27

194

A708

Moffat 11

BBC
Radio Scotland
AM 810
FM 92-95

see p474
for a
touring
guide to
this map

TOWN PLANS
Peebles p375

Edinburgh 6
Edinburgh 7
Edinburgh 11
Dalkeith 5

E **F** **G** **H**

208

Bonnyrigg
Chapel
Roslin
Rosewell
Gorebridge
Carrington
Newtongrange
Newlandrig
Arniston
North Middleton
Borthwick
Middleton
Temple
Dewartown
Pathhead
Crichton
Chrichton Castle
Fala Dam
Fala
Humbie
Leaston
Stobshiel
Blegbie
Lammer Law 1730
Meikle Says Law 1755
Whiteadder Resr

Tynehead
Falahill
Gilston
Oxton
Crib Law 1670
Hunt Law 1625
Hogs Law 1470
Blythe Edge

Edgelaw Reservoir
Rosebery Resr
Gladhouse Resr

Torfichen Hill 1510
Heriot
Fountainhall
Dun Law 1691
Torquhan
Collie Law 1251
Thirlestane Castle
Lauder
Westruther
Blythe
Thirlestane
Whiteburn
Houndslow

Dewar
Blackhope Scar 2137
Ladyside Height
Lauder Common
Legerwood
Huntlywood

Dunslair Heights 1975
Whitehope Law 2038
Windlestraw Law 2163
Killochyett
Stow
Torsonce
Nether Blainslie
Fans
Mellerstain

Glentress Forest
Black Law 1764
Colquhar
Priesthope Hill 1802
Great Law 1666
Bowland
William Law 1314
Langshaw
Earlston
Smailholm

Peebles
Glentress
Kirkburn
Cardrona
Lee Pen 1648
Innerleithen
Walkerburn
Museum of Woollen Textiles
Blackhaugh
Knowes Hill 1222
Buckholm
Old Gala House
Galashiels
Gattonside
Priorwood Gardens
Smailholm Tower

Wallace's Hill 1507
Kail's Print Works
Traquair House
Elibank and Traquair Forest
Clovenfords
Meigle Hill 1387
Langlee
Abbotsford
Darnick
Newstead
Gomrnslie
Clintmains

Kirkhouse
Traquair
Mingh Moor 1859
Ashiestiel Hill
Caddonfoot
Boleside
Melrose
Eildon Hills
Abbey
Dryburgh Abbey
Mertoun Gardens

Blake Muir
Yair Hill Forest
Broomy Law
Lindean
Cauldshiels Hill
Newtown St Boswells
St Boswells

Deuchar Law 1779
Yarrowford
Sunderland
Lingle Hill
White Law 1059
Bowden
Maxton
Rutherford

Yarrow
Fastheugh Hill 1645
Bowhill
Philiphaugh
Selkirk
Charlesfield
Longnewton

Mountbenger
Yarrow Feus
Broadmeadows
Midlem
New Belses

Sundhope
Ettrickbridge
Kirkhope
Clerklands
Lilliesleaf
Old Belses
Greenhouse
Chesters
Ancrum
Lanton

Ettrick Forest
Riddell
B6400
Ashkirk
Woll
Hassendean
Minto Hills 905
Minto
Newton

Black Knowe Head 1805
Gilmanscleuch
Caver's Hill 1209
Akemoor Loch
Newburgh
Crosslee
Cacrabank
Wardlaw
Redfordgreen
Shaws under Loch
Dun Knowe
Hellmoor Loch
Smasha Hill 1056
Horsleyhill
Clariliaw
Knowetownhead
Appletreehall
Ashybank
Denholm
Bedrule
Rubers Law 1391
Dunion Hill 1110

Burnfoot
Hawick
Cavers

195

Longholm 23
Carlisle 43
Carter Bar 13

A7, A68, A697, A698, A699, A708, A6088, A6089, A6091, A6094, A6105
B709, B710, B7060, B7062, B6355, B6357, B6358, B6359, B6360, B6362, B6367, B6368, B6371, B6374, B6397, B6398, B6400, B6404, B6405, B6453, B6456, B6457, B6458, B7009, B7011

DERE STREET
LAMMERMUIR HILLS
MOORFOOT HILLS
Southern Upland Way
Lauderdale
Gala Water
Tweed
Teviot
Ettrick Water
Yarrow Water

Coldstream 14 / Greenlaw 4
Duns 11 / Greenlaw 4 / Kelso 8
Coldstream 15 / Kelso 6
Jedburgh 2

Radio Borders
FM 96.8/97.5/
103.1/103.4

Edinburgh 42
Dunbar 14

Eyemouth

Duns

Kelso

Coldstream

Jedburgh

Wooler

Ayton

Burnmouth

Lamberton

Chirnside

Houndwood

Cairncross

Auchencrow

Horseley Hill 859

Marygold

Lintlaw

Chirnsidebridge

Edrom

Allanton

Hutton

Paxton

Foulden

Clappers

Halidon Hill 1333

Tweedmo...

Preston

Ellemford

Longformacus

Cranshaws

Cranshaws Hill 1245

Whiteadder Reservoir

Fasenly Water

Dye Water

Blythe Edge

Watch Water Resr

Dirrington Great Law 1307

Dirrington Little Law

Westruther

Halliburton

Houndslow

Gavinton

Choicelee

Polwarth

Hule Moss

Fogo

Fogorig

Swinton

Swintonmill

Simprim

Leitholm

Orange Lane

Manderston

Blackadder

Whitsome

New Horndean

Horncliffe

Horndean

Ladykirk

Norham Castle

Norham

Upsettlington

Grindon

Felkington

Duddo

Thornton Park

Thornton

Shoresdean

Shoreswood

West Allerde...

Greenlaw

Gordon

Huntlywood

Fans

Mellerstain

Viewfield

Lambden

Humehall

Eccles

Legars

Hume Castle

Sweethope Hill 730

Stichill

Nenthorn

Smailholm

Smailholm Tower

Clintmains

Makerstoun

Mertoun Gardens

Maxton

Rutherford

Fairnington

Peniel Heugh 777

Ancrum

Chesters

Lanton

Queen Mary's House

Abbey

Dunion Hill 1110

Hundalee

Bedrule

Bairnkine

Mossburnford

Oxnam

The Hirsel Grounds

Lennel

Dundock Wood

Birgham

Carham

Wark

West Learmouth

East Learmouth

Cornhill on Tweed

Crookham

Branxton

Flodden 1513

Kimmerston

Flodden

Milfield

Ford

Fenton

Hendersyde Park

Floors Castle

Turret House

Maxwellheugh

Sprouston

Hadden

Pressen

Downham

Howtel

Houseldon Hill 877

Lanton

Coupland

Ewart Newtown

Akeld

Ednam

Heiton

Trows

Roxburgh

Blakelaw

Lempitlaw

Mindrum

Pawston

Kilham

Westnewton

Kirknewton

Yeavering Bell

Humbleton

Crookhouse

Linton

Morebattle

Linton Hill 926

Town Yetholm

Kirk Yetholm

Shotton

Coldsmouth Hill

Hethpool

White Law

Newton Tors 1761

Fredden Hill

Middlet...

Nisbet

Eckford

Crailing

Crailinghall

Cessford

Whitton

Howgate

Hownam

Hownam Law 1471

Mowhaugh

Sourhope

Steer Rig

White Law

Crookedshaws Hill

The Curr

The Schil 1985

Preston Hill

Cold Law 1485

Langleeford

Bonjedward

Chatto

Craik Moor 1496

Cock Law

Windy Gyle 2032

Mozie Law

Whitestone Hill

Auchope Cairn

THE CHEVIOT 2674

Comb Fell

Hedgehope Hill

Dunmoor Hi... 1860

Linhope

Shill Moor

Swinside Hall

Carter Bar 6
Corbridge 42

Hawick 7
Denholm 2

Lauder 13

Lauder 4

(A68) Newtown St Boswells 7
Earlston 2

A1
A1107
A6112
A6105
A6089
A697
A698
A699
A68
B6355
B6365
B6456
B6460
B6461
B6470
B6437
B6438
B6364
B6350
B6396
B6397
B6404
B6400
B6401
B6436
B6352
B6357
B6358
B6351
B6354
B6355

Pennine Way
DERE STREET

BERWICK-UPON-TWEED

Duns 16   A1 Edinburgh 57

A6105
A1167

Berwick-upon-Tweed Station

Castle Remains

Markworth Terr
Northumberland Ave
Bell Tower Pl
High Greens   Low Greens

Magdalene Fields

Royal Border Bridge

Castle Dene Park

Brucegate
Berwick Infirmary
Well Close Square
Violet Terr
Municipal Buildings
Elizabethan Walls
Huly Trinity

Coxons Lane
Walkergate Lane
Chapel St
Church St
Parade

Berwick Barracks

Riverside Gdns
Riverside Road
Blakewell Gdns

West St
Marygate
Eastern Lane
Town Hall
POL
Wool Mkt
Flagstaff Park

West End Rd
Union Park Rd
West End
Blakewell Road

Royal Tweed Bridge

The Maltings
Bridge St
Hide Hill
Silver St
Ness St

Coldstream 15
A698
ORD DR
Osborne Crescent

PRINCE EDWARD ROAD
Union Brae

Berwick Bridge
Quay
Sandgate
Palace St
Palace St E

Pier Road

Dock Road

Palace Gr

A1167
A1 Alnwick 30

Tweed Dock

River

Tweed

0   100   200 yds
0   100   200 m

see p475 for a touring guide to this map

TOWN PLANS
Berwick-upon-
Tweed p203

Berwick-upon-Tweed

Redshin Cove

Cheswick Black Rocks

Cheswick
Goswick
Haggerston

Beal
West Mains

Emmanuel Head

Lindisfarne
Holy Island
HOLY ISLAND
Lindisfarne Castle
Castle Point
Lindisfarne Priory
Holy Island Sands

Guile Point

Lowick
West Kyloe
East Kyloe
Fenwick
Buckton

Kyloe Hills

Elwick
Ross
Budle Bay

Farne Islands

Detchant
Holburn
Middleton

Easington
Budle
St Aidan
Castle

Staple Sound

Belford
Waren Mill
Bamburgh
Red Barns

Inner Sound

North Hazelrigg
B1342
Glororum
St Aidan's Dunes

Hazelrigg
Spindlestone
Burton

Mousen
Bradford
Seahouses

Warenton
Bellshill
Lucker
Elford
North Sunderland
B1340

Adderstone

Beadnell

B6348
Warenford
Newham
West Fleetham
Swinhoe
Beadnell Bay

Greendykes
Newstead
Chatton
Chathill
Ellingham
Snook Point
High Newton-by-the-Sea

Chillingham
Rosebrough
Preston
Low Newton-by-the-Sea
Newton Pool

Ros Castle
Brunton
Embleton Bay

Newtown
Lilburn Tower
Middle Moor   28
Embleton
Dunstanburgh Castle

East Lilburn
Hepburn
Cateran Hill 876
Brownieside
North Charlton
Christon Bank
Rock
Dunstan

Wooperton
16
Old Bewick
West Ditchburn
South Charlton
Stamford
Craster

New Bewick
Harehope
Rennington
Howick Gardens

Brandon
Powburn
Beanley
Eglingham
B6341
Littlehoughton
Howick
Rumbling Kern
Howick Haven

A697
Breamish
Branton
Priory
Titlington

Longhoughton
197
A1

A697
Morpeth 22

A1
Alnwick 2
Morpeth 19

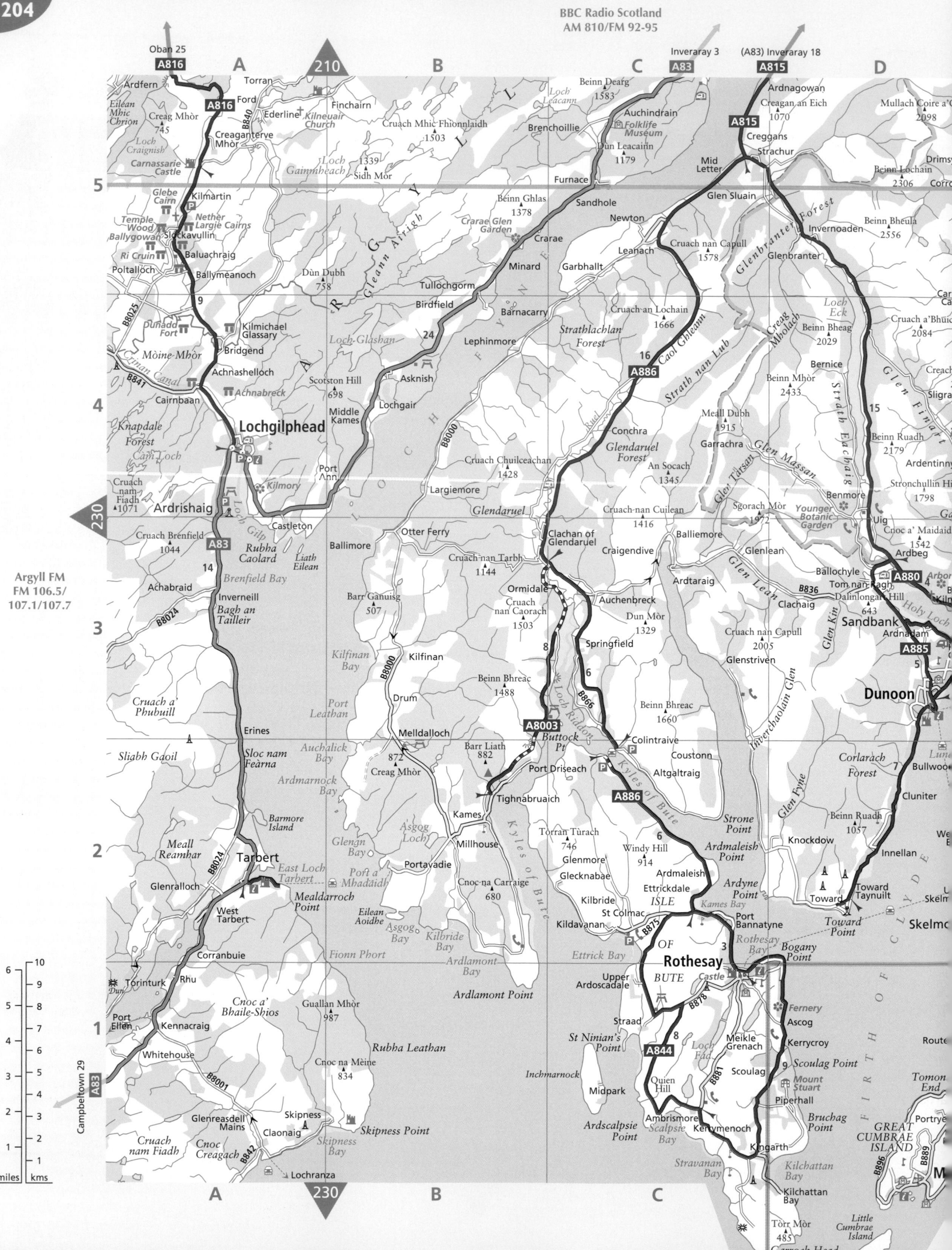

Oban 25
A816
Inveraray 3
(A83) Inveraray 18
A815

Ardfern
Torran
Ford
Finchairn
Cruach Mhic Fhionnlaidh
1503
Beinn Dearg
1583
Auchindrain
Folklife Museum
Ardnagowan
Creagan an Eich
1070
Mullach Coire a'C
2098
Eilean Mhic Chrion
Creag Mhòr
745
Ederline
Kilneuair Church
A816
A840
Creaganterve Mhòr
Brenchoillie
Dun Leacainn
1179
Creggans
Strachur
Drimsy

Loch Craignish
Loch Gainmheach
Sidh Mòr
1339
Mid Letter
Glen Sluain
Beinn Lochain
2306
Corr

Glebe Cairn
Kilmartin
Beinn Ghlas
1378
Sandhole
Newton
Invernoaden
Beinn Bheula
2556

Temple Wood
Nether Largie Cairns
Crarae Glen Garden
Crarae
Furnace
Leanach
Cruach nan Capull
1578
Glenbranter
Cruach a'Bhuic
2084

Ballygowan
Slockavullin
Minard
Garbhallt
A886

Ri Cruin
Baluachraig
Dùn Dubh
758
Tullochgorm
Barnacarry
Cruach an Lochain
1666
Beinn Mhòr
2433
Bernice
Cruach a'Bhuic
2084

Poltalloch
Ballymeanoch
Birdfield
Lephinmore
Strathlachlan Forest
Caol Gleann
Strath nan Lub
Beinn Bheag
2029
Carr
Cas

B8025
9
Kilmichael Glassary
Scotston Hill
698
Asknish
16
Meall Dubh
1915
Garrachra
15

Dunadd Fort
Bridgend
Loch Glashan
Lochgair
A886
Conchra
Glendaruel Forest
Sgorach Mòr
1972
Beinn Ruadh
2179

Mòine Mhòr
Achnashelloch
Middle Kames
Cruach Chuilceachan
1428
An Socach
1345
Ardentinny

B8024
Achnabreck
B8000
Largiemore
Cruach-nan Cuilean
1416
Balliemore
Younger Botanic Garden
Stronchullin Hi
1798

B841
Cairnbaan
Glendaruel
Craigendive
Glenlean
Uig

Knapdale Forest
Cam Loch
Lochgilphead
Port Ann
Otter Ferry
Clachan of Glendaruel
Cnoc a' Maidain
1542
Ardbeg

Cruach nam Fiadh
1071
Kilmory
Ballimore
Cruach-nan Tarbh
1144
Ormidale
Auchenbreck
Ardtaraig
Ballochyle
Tom nan Ragh
A880

Ardrishaig
Castleton
Liath Eilean
Cruach nan Caorach
1503
Dun Mòr
1329
Cruach nan Capull
2005
Clachaig
Dalinlongart
Sandbank
Ardnadam

Cruach Brénfield
1044
A83
Rubha Caolard
14
Barr Ganuisg
507
8
Springfield
6
Glenstriven
A885

Achabraid
Inverneill
Bagh an Tailleir
Kilfinan Bay
Kilfinan
Beinn Bhreac
1488
Loch Riddon
B866
Beinn Bhreac
1660
Dunoon

Erines
Port Leathan
Drum
Melldalloch
Barr Liath
882
A8003
Buttock Pt
Colintraive
Coustonn
Corlarach Forest

Sliabh Gaoil
Sloc nam Feàrna
Auchalick Bay
872
Creag Mhòr
Port Driseach
Altgaltraig
Clunier

Ardmarnock Bay
Tighnabruaich
A886
Kyles of Bute
Beinn Ruadh
1057
Innellan

Cruach a' Phubuill
Barmore Island
Kames
Millhouse
Torran Tùrach
746
Windy Hill
914
Ardmaleish Point
Knockdow

Meall Reamhar
B8024
Tarbert
Glengn Bay
Portavadie
Glenmore
Ardmaleish
Ardyne Point
Toward Taynuilt
Skelm

Glenralloch
East Loch Tarbert
Mealldarroch Point
Port a' Mhadaidh
Eilean Aoidhe
Asgog Bay
Glecknabae
Ettrickdale
ISLE
Toward Point
Skelmo

West Tarbert
Corranbuie
Fionn Phort
Ardlamont Bay
Kilbride
St Colmac
Kildavanan
Port Bannatyne
Rothesay Bay
Bogany Point

Torinturk
Rhu
Cnoc a' Bhaile-Shios
Guallan Mhòr
987
Ardlamont Point
Upper Ardoscadale
OF
Rothesay
Castle
Fernery

Port Ellen
Kennacraig
Rubha Leathan
Straad
BUTE
Meikle Grenach
Ascog

Whitehouse
B8001
Cnoc na Mèine
834
St Ninian's Point
A844
Loch Fad
Scoulag
Kerrycroy
Scoulag Point

Campbeltown 29
A83
Glenreasdell Mains
Skipness
Skipness Point
Inchmarnock
Midpark
Quien Hill
Mount Stuart
Piperhall
Tomon End

Cruach nam Fiadh
Cnoc Creagach
Claonaig
Skipness Bay
Ambrismore
Ardscalpsie Point
Scalpsie Bay
Kerrymenoch
Bruchag Point
GREAT CUMBRAE ISLAND

B842
Lochranza
Stravanan Bay
Kingarth
Kilchattan Bay
Little Cumbrae Island

Tòrr Mòr
485
Garroch Head

Argyll FM
FM 106.5/
107.1/107.7

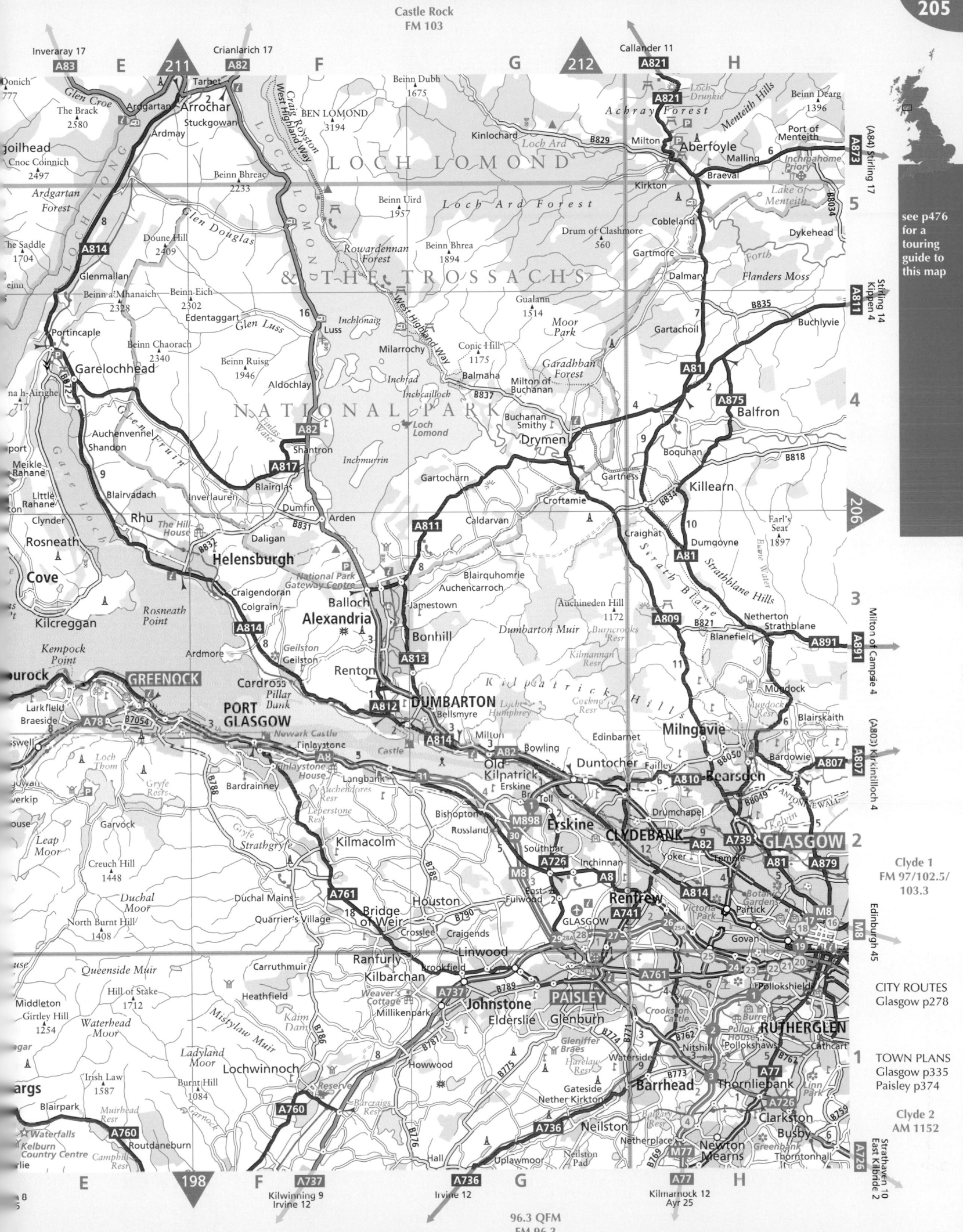

Castle Rock
FM 103

Inveraray 17 **A83** **E** **211** Crianlarich 17 **A82** **F** **G** **212** Callander 11 **A821** **H**

A821

Glen Croe
The Brack
2580
Ardmay

Arrochar
Stuckgowan

Achray Forest
Loch Drunkie
Beinn Dearg
1396

Menteith Hills

Ardgartan
Forest

Beinn Bhreac
2233

BEN LOMOND
3194

Kinlochard

Milton
Aberfoyle
Malling

Port of
Menteith

A873

Cnoc Coinnich
2497

Ardgartan
Forest

Beinn Uird
1957

B829

Loch Ard

Braeval

Kirkton

Inchmahome
Priory

5

The Saddle
1704

A814

Glenmallan

Doune Hill
2409

Glen Douglas

L O C H   L O M O N D

Cobleland

Lake of
Menteith

Forth

B8034

see p476
for a
touring
guide to
this map

Beinn a'Mhanaich
2328

Beinn Eich
2302

L O C H   L O M O N D

&   T H E   T R O S S A C H S

Rowardennan
Forest

Beinn Bhrea
1894

Drum of Clashmore
560

Gartmore

Dalmary

Flanders Moss

Stirling 14
Kippen 4

A811

Portincaple

Edentaggart

Glen Luss

16

Inchlonaig

Luss

West Highland Way

Gualann
1514

Moor
Park

Gartachoil

B835

Buchlyvie

Garelochhead

Beinn Chaorach
2340

Beinn Ruisg
1946

Milarrochy

Conic Hill
1175

Garadhban
Forest

7

A81

na h-Airighe

Auchenvennel
Shandon

Aldochlay

B837

Inchfad

Balmaha

Milton of
Buchanan

A875

Balfron

A82

N A T I O N A L   P A R K

Inchmurrin

Inchcailloch

Buchanan
Smithy

Drymen

Boquhan

Dumgoyne

B818

Earl's
Seat
1897

Meikle
Rahane

Little
Rahane

A817

Blairglas

Dumfin

Arden

Gartocharn

Caldarvan

Garth ess

Killearn

B834

A881

206

Clynder

Rhu

The Hill
House

B832

Daligan

B831

Croftamie

A81

10

Craighat

Dumgoyne

Strathblane Hills

Milton of Campsie 4

Rosneath

Blairvadach

Inverlauren

Helensburgh

Auchenq homrie

Auchencarroch

11

Netherton
Strathblane

A891

A891

Cove

A814

Craigendoran
Colgrain

National Park
Gateway Centre

Balloch

Jamestown

Auchineden Hill
1172

Burncrooks
Resr

Blanefield

Blairskaith

(A803) Kirkintilloch 4

Kilcreggan

Rosneath
Point

Ardmore

Geilston

Alexandria

Bonhill

Dumbarton Muir

Kilmannan
Resr

Mugdock

A807

Kempock
Point

Cardross

Renton

A813

K i l p a t r i c k   H i l l s

Cockno
Resr

Milngavie

Mugdock

A807

GREENOCK

Pillar
Bank

A812

DUMBARTON

Bellsmyre

Lyoch
Humphrey

Edinbarnet

B8049

Bardowie

Larkfield

**PORT
GLASGOW**

Newark Castle

Finlaystone

Castle

A814

Milton

Bowling

Duntocher

Failley

B8050

A810

Bearsden

Braeside

A78

B7054

Finlaystone
House

Langbank

31

Old
Kilpatrick

Erskine

Toll

Drumchapel

A810

6

Loch
Thom

Bardrainney

Auchendores
Resr

4

Erskine
Br

2

Gryfe
Resr

Leperstone
Resr

Bishopton

Rossland

M898

30

Southbar

M8

Yoker

Temple

A81

A879

Clyde 1
FM 97/102.5/
103.3

Garvock

Gryfe
Strathgryfe

Kilmacolm

B789

Erskine

CLYDEBANK

A82

A739

GLASGOW

Creuch Hill
1448

Duchal
Moor

B788

Houston

A726

Inchinnan

12

A814

Botanic
Gardens

Partick

M8

Edinburgh 45

North Burnt Hill
1408

Duchal Mains

A761

18

Bridge
of Weir

B790

M8

A8

East d

Fulwood

Renfrew

A741

GLASGOW

2

Victoria
Park

26

Govan

M8

Queenside Muir

Carruthmuir

Ranfurly

Brookfield

Crosslee

Craigends

Linwood

28

27

25

24

CITY ROUTES
Glasgow p278

Middleton

Hill of Stake
1712

Waterhead
Moor

Heathfield

Kilbarchan

A737

B789

Weaver's
Cottage

PAISLEY

A761

23

22

21

20

Girtley Hill
1254

Ladyland
Moor

Mistylaw Muir

Kaim
Dam

Millikenpark

Johnstone

Eldcrslie

Glenburn

Crookston
Castle

Pollokshields

1

Pollok
House

RUTHERGLEN

Irish Law
1587

Muirhead
Resr

Burnt Hill
1084

B786

Howwood

A737

B781

Gleniffer
Braes

Harelaw
Resr

Nitshill

Pollokshaws

B762

Cathcart

TOWN PLANS
Glasgow p335
Paisley p374

A760

Lochwinnoch

Reserve

Barcraigs
Resr

B775

Gateside

Waterside

9

B773

A77

Thornliebank

Clarkston
Busby

Clyde 2
AM 1152

Waterfalls

Kelburn
Country Centre

Routdaneburn

A760

Barcraigs
Resr

Hall

Uplawmoor

Nether Kirkton

Neilston
Pad

A736

Neilston

Netherplace

M77

Newton
Mearns

Greenbank

Thorntonhall

A726

Strathaven 10
East Kilbride 2

A725

E **198** **F** **A737** **G** **A736** **H** **A77**

Kilwinning 9
Irvine 12

Irvine 12

Kilmarnock 12
Ayr 25

96.3 QFM
FM 96.3

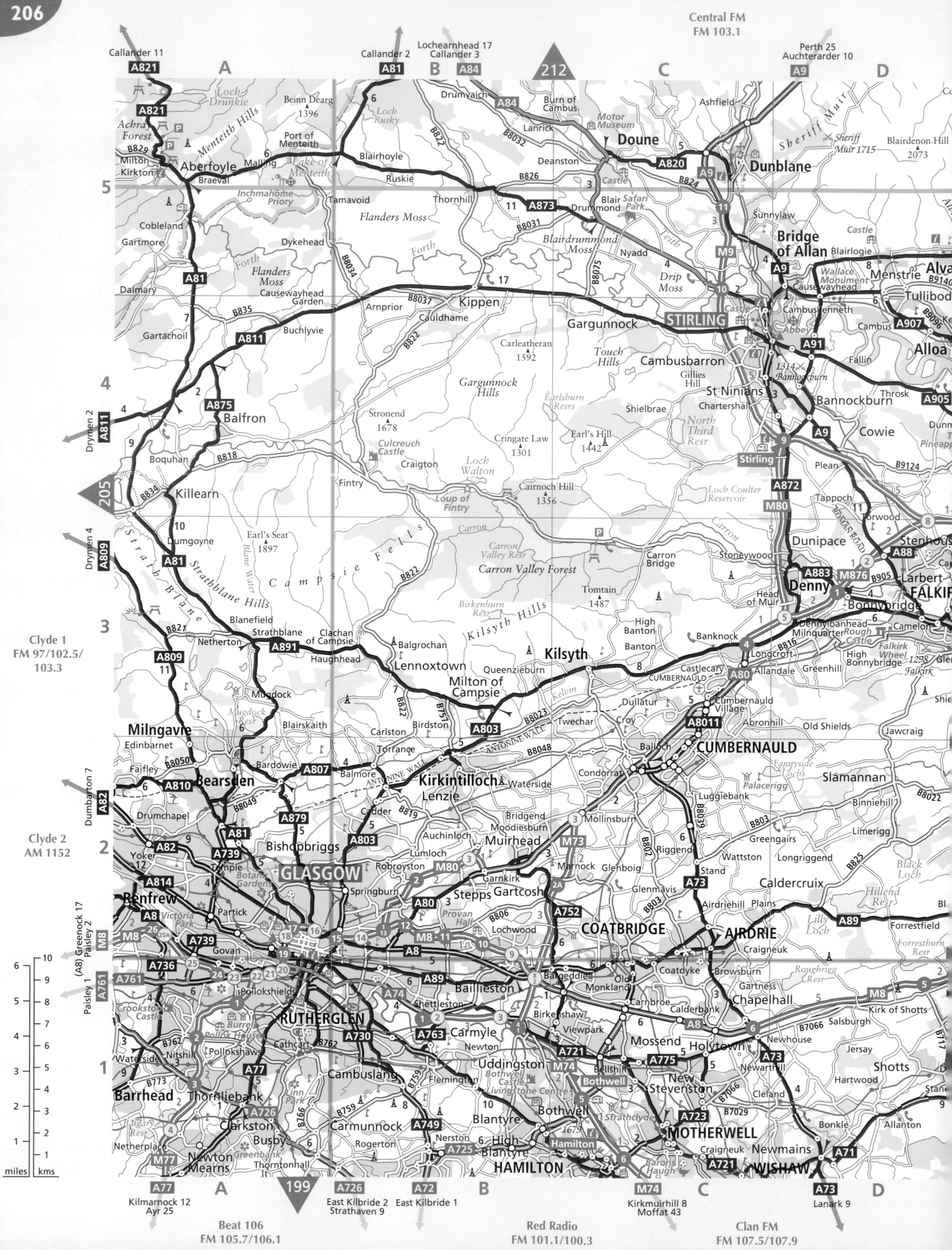

BBC Radio Scotland
AM 810/FM 92-95

(A822) Crieff 16   Perth 15   Dundee 24

E   F   213   G   H

A823 **A92**

Glen Devon   Dalqueich   M90   Milnathort   Wester Balgedie   Ballo Resr   A92
Glendevon   Kinross   7   Easter   Bishop   Pitkevy
Burnfoot   Lendrick Hill   Carnbo   7   B918   Balgedie   Hill   Arnot   Holl Resr   Balfarg
1496   7   6   Kinnesswood   A911   Hall Resr   Cadham
A823   Yetts o'   Drum   South Queich   Loch   12   Scotlandwell   **A911**
Commonedge   Muckhart   Kinross   Leven   Leslie
Hill   2   Coldrain   Castle   Auchmuirbridge   **GLENROTHES**   A911
1539   Loch   St Serf's   B920   Methil 5
Kings Seat Hill   Crook of Devon   Leven   Island   FIFE   Kinglassie   Cadham
2126   Castle   Dollar   B9097   Gairney Bank   B922   Thornton   A92   4   5
Campbell   Glen   **A91**   Rumbling Bridge   P   Vane   B921
Tillicoultry   Dollar   7   Powmill   Cleish   B9097   Farm   Ballingry   B9097   Auchterderran
Waterfall   Benarty Hill   Woodend   Ore   B9130
Sterling Mills   Blairingone   Cult   Cleish Hills   1168   Lochore   Cardenden   Cluny   3
Devonside   Coalsnaughton   Hill   1243   Meadows   Crosshill   B981   Gallatown
B9140   866   Hill   Loch   Glencraig   B981   Chapel   McDouall Stuart   A92   2
Gartmorn   Forest   End   Ore   Kelty   Lochgelly   Museum   Ravenscraig
Dam   Mill   B913   Knockhill   9   Lumphinnans   **KIRKCALDY**   A910   4
Clackmannan   Balgonar   Knock Hill   4   Loch   Pathhead
A977   Saline   1194   Loch   A92   Gelly
Cowstrandburn   B914   Fitty   Cowdenbeath   Auchtertool   Linktown   A921   4
Craigluscar Hill   Bowershall   B925   B9157   A921
11   B913   744   Kingseat   Hill of Beath   Donibristle   5
Blairhall   Carnock   A02J   Townhill   Crossgates   A909   Stenhouse
Devilla   Gowkhall   Wellwood   Fordell   B9157   Resr   B923   Kinghorn
Forest   Oakley   Milesmark   3   2A   A909   Pettycur
A985   Valleyfield   Cairneyhill   Abbey &   **DUNFERMLINE**   Castle   Burntisland   208
Kincardine   Culross   Low   Palace   A994   A823   Aberdour   Dalgety
Bridge   Palace   Torry   Torryburn   Crossford   13   Carnegie   A916   Bay   Abbey
Longannet   Crombie   A985   Museum   Hillend   Inchkeith
Point   Charlestown   Rosyth   FIRTH
Limekilns   Inverkeithing   OF   FORTH
Grangemouth   Bo'ness &   St Margaret's Hope   North Queensferry   Inchcolm   Oxcars   3
Bo'ness   Kinneil Railway   Hopetoun   Forth   Inchmickery   CITY ROUTES
A993   Grangepans   Castle   House   Road   Queensferry   Cramond   Edinburgh
Nether   Muirhouses   Blackness   Bridge   Inch Garvie   Island   Dalmeny   p276
Kinneil   A904   Dalmeny   House   Glasgow p278
Champany   A8000   Newton   Cramond   **EDINBURGH**   HELIPORT   Royal Yacht
A706   The   Lauriston   Britannia
Linlithgow   A803   Old   Granton   A901   Leith   A199
Bridge   Palace   Philpstoun   Kingscavil   Turnhouse   A90   Royal Botanic   Lamb's House
Linlithgow   Bridgend   B9080   Cramond   Gardens   A199
A706   Belsyde   Winchburgh   Kirkliston   A902   Murrayfield   A8
Cockleroy   Ecclesmachan   M9   Edinburgh   Corstorphine   Arthur's
Beecraigs   Newbridge   EDINBURGH   Seat   A7
Torphichen   Uphall   Burnside   A8   822
A800   Dechmont   A899   Broxbrum   Ratho   Ingliston   Morningside   A702   6
Wester   Station   M8   Suntrap   A71   Craiglockhart   Royal   A772
Bathgate   Dechmont   M8   Ratho   Hermiston   Colinton   Observatory   2
Boghall   Deans   East   Bonnington   Juniper Green   Fairmilehead   Liberton
A801   B7002   Calder   Almondell   Wilkieston   A720   Currie   Kaimes   A720
Whiteside   Livingston   Mid   Mallen   Hillend
A779   Calder   Garden   Allermuir Hill   A703   Straiton
Blackburn   Seafield   McArthur   Kirknewton   1618   Loanhead   A6094
Whitburn   Glen   Dedridge   Oakbank   Balerno   Woodhouselee   Bilston
Bellsquarry   Easter Howgate   A701   Chapel   Roslin
Stoneyburn   Addiewell   Murieston   Black Hill   Glencorse   Milton   Auchendinny
Loganlee   Polbeth   Morton   1636   Castlelaw   Bridge   Forth 2
West   Reservoir   A70   Reservoir   A702   AM 1548
Greenburn   Breich   Calder   Harperrig   Scald Law   Silverburn   Penicuik
Reservoir   1898   A6094   10
Longridge   A704   26   Bore Stane   Nine   B7026   Edgelaw
1570   Mile Burn   A766   Howgate   Reservoir
A706   The Mount   North Usk   TOWN PLANS
Wilsontown   Cobbinshaw   1763   Reservoir   Dunfermline
Woolfords   Reservoir   PENTLAND   HILLS   A701   p327
Cottages   Crosswood   Baddinsgill   Carlops   Auchencorth   Edinburgh
A706   Reservoir   Reservoir   Moss   Leadburn   p330
Tarbrax   Glasgow p335
Lanark 8   200   A70   F   A702   G   A701   H   Stirling p392
Carnwath 6   Biggar 13   Biggar 17
Carstairs 9

see p477 for a touring guide to this map

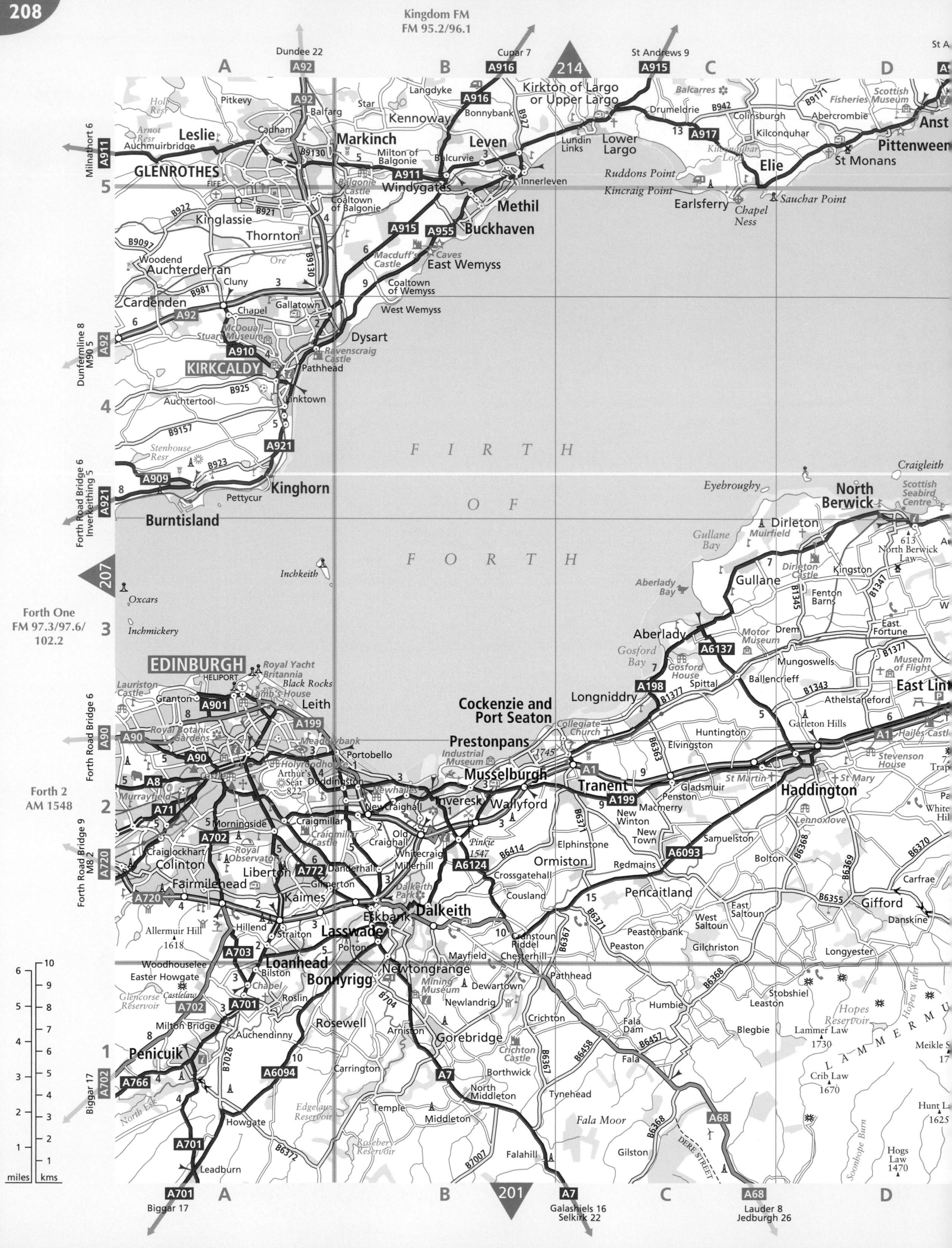

5

N O R T H

S E A

4

Isle of May

see p478
for a
touring
guide to
this map

aldred's Boat

Scoughall

3

*St Baldred's
Cradle*
Tyne Mouth

ninghame   **Dunbar**
                  West Barns   2   **A1087**
A199   2   Broxburn   *Barns Ness*
     B6370   3   *Doon
Pitcox   Spott   Hill Hall*   Skateraw   *Torness Nuclear
                  Brunt Hill   **A1**   Power Station
Stenton   737   Visitor Centre*
                                  Thorntonloch

CITY ROUTES
Edinburgh
p276

Halls   Innerwick   8

Dry Burn   Reed
          Cocklaw Hill   Point
Bransly Hill   1046   Cockburnspath   Siccar   *Wheat Stack*
1301   Point   Telegraph
nbar-Common   Oldhamstocks   *Dunglass Burn*   Hill   *St Abb's Head*
                                                    Lumsdaine

TOWN PLANS
Edinburgh
p330

2

          Ecclaw   Meikle Black Law   Cross Law   Northfield
                                     803   744   St Abbs
Monynut Edge   Heart Law   *Coldingham   *Coldingham Bay*
Spartleton Edge   1283   Blackburn   **A1**   Moor*   12
Bothwell Water   Rig   Grantshouse   Coldingham
LLS   *Buss Craig*
Whiteadder   **Eyemouth**
Reservoir   **B6355**   Houndwood
Cranshaws Hill   Abbey St   *Eye Water*   Cairncross   19
1245   Cranshaws   Bathans   **A1**   Ayton   Burnmouth
                              12   Horseley Hill   **B6438**   Reston
Ellemford   859   Auchencrow   *Ayton
Dye Water   **B6437**   Castle*
                                   Marygold   *Lamberton
                    A6112   Lintlaw   Beach*   1
Longformacus   Chirnsidebridge   **B6355**
Watch Water   Preston   **B6385**   15   Lamberton
Resr   Southern Upland Way   *Whiteadder Water*   Edrom   Foulden   Clappers
L   **Chirnside**   Halidon Hill   **A1**

                              Duns 1   Duns 3   Berwick-   Berwick-upon-Tweed 1
                              Coldstream 13   upon-Tweed 3 Alnwick 32

BBC Radio Scotland
AM 810/FM 92-95

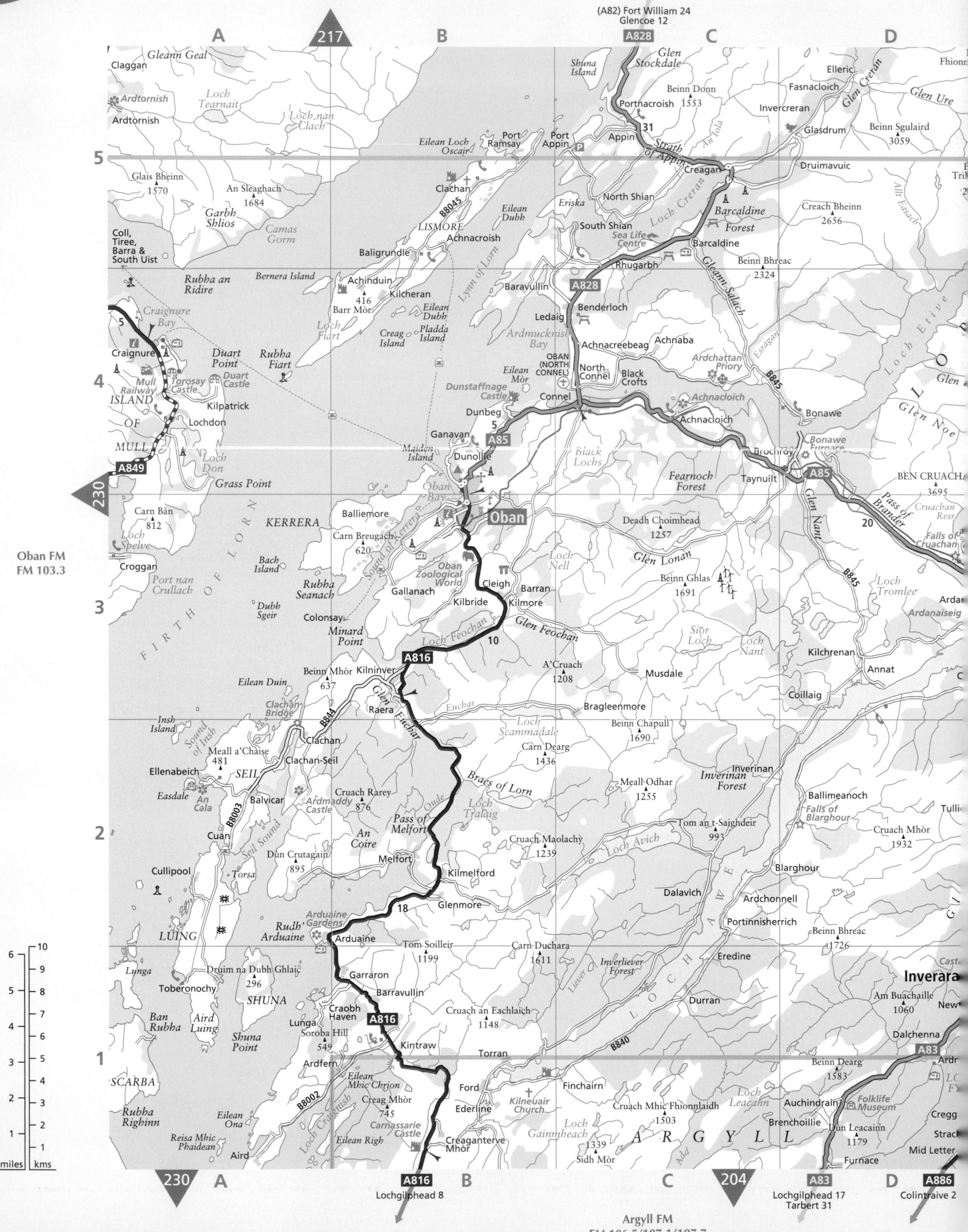

A   217   B   (A82) Fort William 24   C   Glencoe 12   A828   D

5

Oban FM
FM 103.3

230

3

A816

A816

A816
Lochgilphead 8

4

2

1

6 10
5 9
   8
4 7
   6
3 5
   4
2 3
   2
1 1
miles kms

230   A   A816
Lochgilphead 8   B   204   C   A83
Lochgilphead 17
Tarbert 31   A83   D   A886
Colintraive 2

Argyll FM
FM 106.5/107.1/107.7

Claggan   Gleann Geal   Loch Tearnait   Loch nan Clach   Shuna Island   Glen Stockdale   Beinn Donn   Elleric   Fasnacloich   Fhionn
Ardtornish   Porthacroish   Appin   131   Invercreran   Glasdrum   Glen Creran   Glen Ure
Ardtornish   Port Ramsay   Port Appin   Strath of Appin   Beinn Sgulaird 3059
Glais Bheinn 1570   An Sleaghach 1684   Eilean Loch Oscair   Creagan   Druimavuic   An Iola
Garbh Shlios   Clachan   Eilean Dubh   Eriska   North Shian   Loch Creran   Barcaldine Forest   Creach Bheinn 2656
LISMORE   Achnacroish   South Shian   Sea Life Centre   Barcaldine   Beinn Bhreac 2324   Alli Easach
Coll, Tiree, Barra & South Uist   Baligrundle   Rhugarbh   A828   Gleann-Salach
Rubha an Ridire   Bernera Island   Achinduin   Kilcheran   Baravullin   Ledaig   Benderloch   Esragan   B845
Craignure Bay   416   Barr Mòr   Eilean Dubh   Ardmucknish Bay   Achnacreebeag   Achnaba   Ardchattan Priory   Glen
Craignure   Duart Point   Loch Fiart   Creag Island   Pladda Island   Oban (North Connel)   North Connel   Black Crofts   Achnacloich   Bonawe   Glen Noe
Mull Railway   Torosay Castle   Duart Castle   Dunbeg   Connel   Achnacloich   Brochroy   Bonawe Furnace
ISLAND   Kilpatrick   Maiden Island   Ganavan   5   A85   Black Lochs   Taynuilt   A85   BEN CRUACHAN
OF   Lochdon   Dunollie   Deadh Choimhead 1257   Cruachan Resr   3695   Pass of Brander
MULL   A849   Loch Don   Oban Bay   Oban   Fearnoch Forest   Falls of Cruachan
Grass Point   Balliemore   Loch Nell   Glen Lonan   20   B845
Carn Bàn 812   KERRERA   Carn Breugach 620   Glen Feochan   Beinn Ghlas 1691   Loch Tromlee   Ardan
Loch Spelve   FIRTH OF LORN   Bach Island   Oban Zoological World   Cleigh   Barran   Ardanaiseig
Croggan   Rubha Seanach   Gallanach   Kilbride   Kilmore   Siar Loch   Loch Nant   Kilchrenan
Dubh Sgeir   Colonsay   Minard Point   Loch Feochan   10   A'Cruach 1208   Musdale   Annat
Port nan Crullach   A816   Kilninver   Glen Euchar   Coillaig
Eilean Duin   Beinn Mhòr 637   Raera   Euchar   Loch Scammadale   Bragleenmore   Beinn Chapull 1690   Inverinan Forest
Insh Island   Clachan Bridge   B844   Braes of Lorn   Càrn Dearg 1436   Meall Odhar 1255   Inverinan   Ballimeanoch   Falls of Blarghour
Sound of Insh   Meall a'Chaise 481   Clachan   Oude   Loch Tralaig   Cruach Maolachy 1239   Tom an t-Saighdeir 993   Cruach Mhòr 1932
Ellenabeich   SEIL   Clachan-Seil   Pass of Melfort   Loch Avich   Blarghour   Tulli
Easdale   An Cala   Balvicar   Cruach Rarey 876   An Coire   Dalavich   Ardchonnell   Beinn Bhreac 1726
Cuan   B8003   Ardmaddy Castle   Melfort   Kilmelford   Portinnisherrich
Cullipool   Dùn Crutagain 895   Glenmore   18   Inverliever Forest   Eredine   Inverara
LUING   Torsa   Arduaine Gardens   Rudh'Arduaine   Arduaine   Tom Soilleir 1199   Carn Duchara 1611   Am Buachaille 1060   New
Lunga   Druim na Dubh Ghlaic 296   SHUNA   Garraron   Barravullin   Cruach an Eachlaich 1148   Durran   Dalchenna
Toberonochy   Craobh Haven   Soroba Hill 549   Beinn Dearg 1583   A83   Ardr
Ban Rubha   Aird Luing   Shuna Point   Lunga   Kintraw   Torran   B840   Loch
SCARBA   Ardfern   Ford   Finchairn   Auchindrain   Cregg   Strac
Rubha Righinn   B8002   Eilean Mhic Chrion   Creag Mhòr 745   Ederline   Kilneuair Church   ARGYLL   Folklife Museum   Mid Letter
Reisa Mhic Phaidean   Creaganterve Mhòr   Carnassarie Castle   Cruach Mhic Fhionnlaidh 1503   Auchindrain   Dùn Leacainn 1179   Furnace
Aird   Eilean Righ   1339   Loch Gainmheach   Sidh Mòr   Brenchoillie

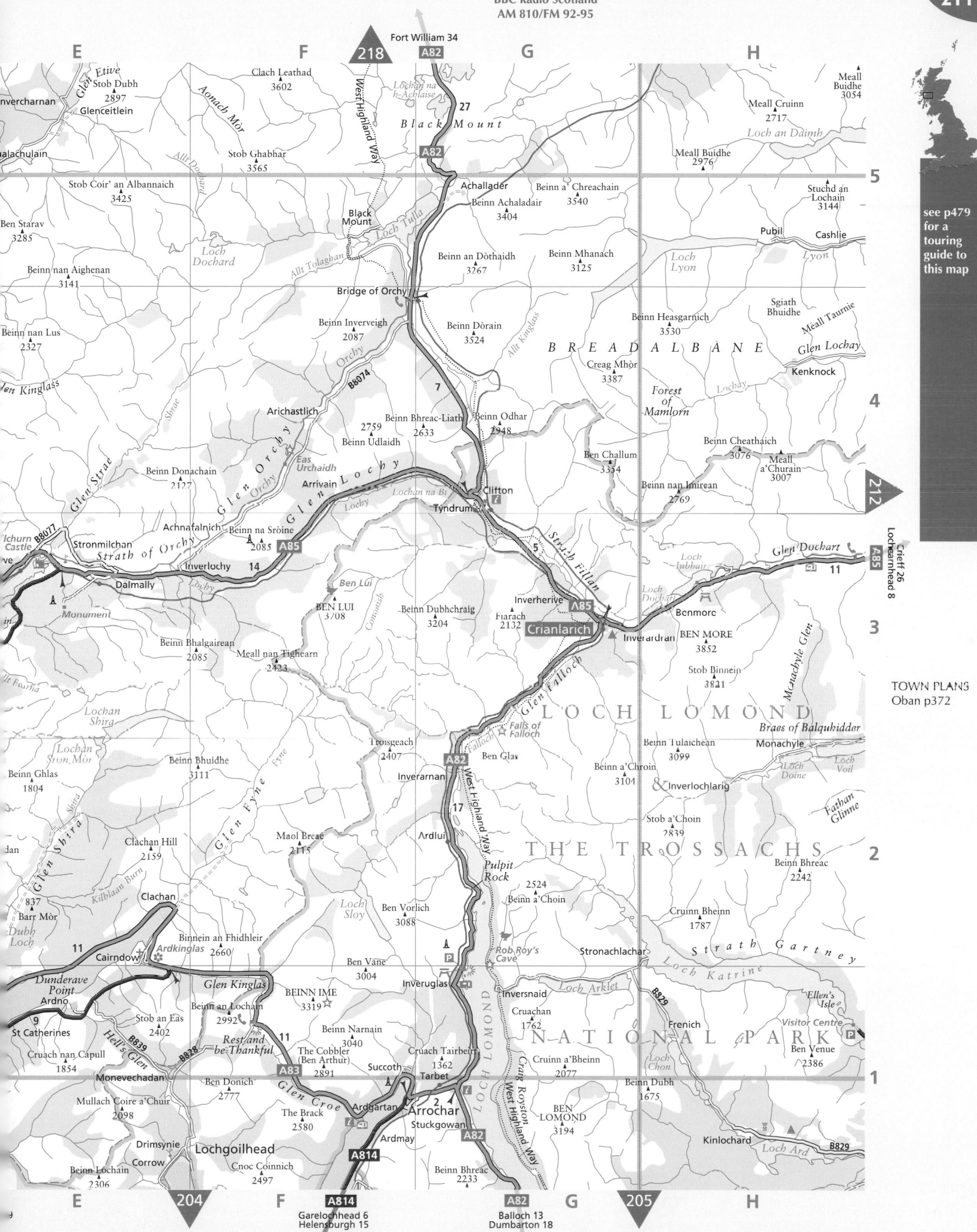

BBC Radio Scotland
AM 810/FM 92-95

see p479 for a touring guide to this map

TOWN PLANS
Oban p372

E   F   G   H

Fort William 34
A82
218

27

Glen Etive
Stob Dubh
2897
Glenceitlein

Clach Leathad
3602

Aonach Mòr

West Highland Way

Lochan na h-Achlaise

B L A C K M O U N T

Invercharnan

alachulain

Stob Coir' an Albannaich
3425

Stob Ghabhar
3565

Allt Dochard

Achallader

Beinn a' Chreachain
3540

Meall Cruinn
2717

Meall Buidhe
3054

5

Black Mount

Loch Tulla

Beinn Achaladair
3404

Meall Buidhe
2976

Loch an Daimh

Ben Starav
3285

Loch Dochard

Beinn an Dòthaidh
3267

Beinn Mhanach
3125

Pubil

Cashlie

Stuchd an Lochain
3144

Beinn nan Aighenan
3141

Allt Tolaghan

Bridge of Orchy

Loch Lyon

Lyon

len Kinglass

Beinn nan Lus
2327

Beinn Inverveigh
2087

Orchy

Beinn Dòrain
3524

Allt Kinglass

B R E A D A L B A N E

Beinn Heasgarnich
3530

Sgiath Bhuidhe

Meall Taurnie

Glen Lochay

4

B8074

Creag Mhòr
3387

Forest of Mamlorn

Lochay

Kenknock

Glen Strae

Shira

Arichastlich

Glen Orchy

Beinn Bhreac-Liath
2759
2633

Beinn Odhar
2948

Ben Challum
3354

Beinn Cheathaich
3076

Meall a'Churain
3007

Beinn Donachain
2127

Eas Urchaidh

Beinn Udlaidh

Beinn nan Imirean
2769

lchurn Castle

B8077

Stronmilchan

Achnafalnich

Arrivain

Glen Lochy

Beinn na Sròine
2085

Lochan na Bi

Clifton

A85

Strath Fillan

Glen Dochart

A85

Chrieff 26
Lochearnhead 8

212

Strath of Orchy

Inverlochy
14

A85

Lochy

Tyndrum

Loch Iubhair

11

ve

Dalmally

Lochy

5

Loch Dochart

Benmore

Monument

Ben Lui

Ben Dubhchraig
3204

Inverherive
A85

A

Lochan Shira

BEN LUI
3708

Convinish

Fiarach
2132

Crianlarich

Inverardran

BEN MORE
3852

3

Beinn Bhalgairean
2085

Meall nan Tighearn
2423

Glen Falloch

L O C H L O M O N D

Stob Binnein
3821

Monachyle Glen

Lochan Sron Mòr

Beinn Bhuidhe
3111

Glen Fyne

Fyne

Troisgeach
2407

Falls of Falloch

Braes of Balquhidder

Beinn Tulaichean
3099

Monachyle

Loch Doine

Loch Voil

Fathan Glinne

Beinn Ghlas
1804

Shira

Glen Shira

Inverarnan

West Highland Way

Ben Glas

Beinn a'Chroin
3104

Inverlochlarig

Clachan Hill
2159

Maol Breac
2115

A82

17

Ardlui

T H E T R O S S A C H S

Stob a'Choin
2839

Beinn Bhreac
2242

2

dan

837

Barr Mòr

Dubh Loch

Clachan

Kilblaan Burn

Loch Sloy

Ben Vorlich
3088

Pulpit Rock

2524

Beinn a'Choin

Rob Roy's Cave

Cruinn Bheinn
1787

Stronachlachar

Strath Gartney

Loch Katrine

Binnein an Fhidhleir
2660

Ardkinglas

Ben Vane
3004

Inveruglas

Inversnaid

Loch Arklet

B829

Ellen's Isle

11

Cairndow

Dunderave Point
Ardno

Glen Kinglas

Beinn an Lochain
2992

BEINN IME
3319

Beinn Narnain
3040

Cruachan
1762

Frenich

Visitor Centre

Ben Venue
2386

9

St Catherines

Stob an Eas
2402

Rest and be Thankful

The Cobbler
(Ben Arthur)
2891

Cruach Tairbeirt
1362

Craig Royston

West Highland Way

N A T I O N A L P A R K

Cruinn a'Bheinn
2077

Loch Chon

Beinn Dubh
1675

Cruach nan Capull
1854

Hell's Glen

B839

B828

11

Monevechadan

Ben Donich
2777

Glen Croe

Succoth

Tarbet

BEN LOMOND
3194

Kinlochard

Loch Ard

B829

Mullach Coire a'Chuir
2098

The Brack
2580

Ardgartan

Arrochar

A83

A82

2

Drimsynie

Corrow

Lochgoilhead

Cnoc Coinnich
2497

Ardmay

Stuckgowan

L O C H L O M O N D

Beinn Lochain
2306

Beinn Bhreac
2233

A814

A82

1

E   F   G   H

204

A814

205

Garelochhead 6
Helensburgh 15

Balloch 13
Dumbarton 18

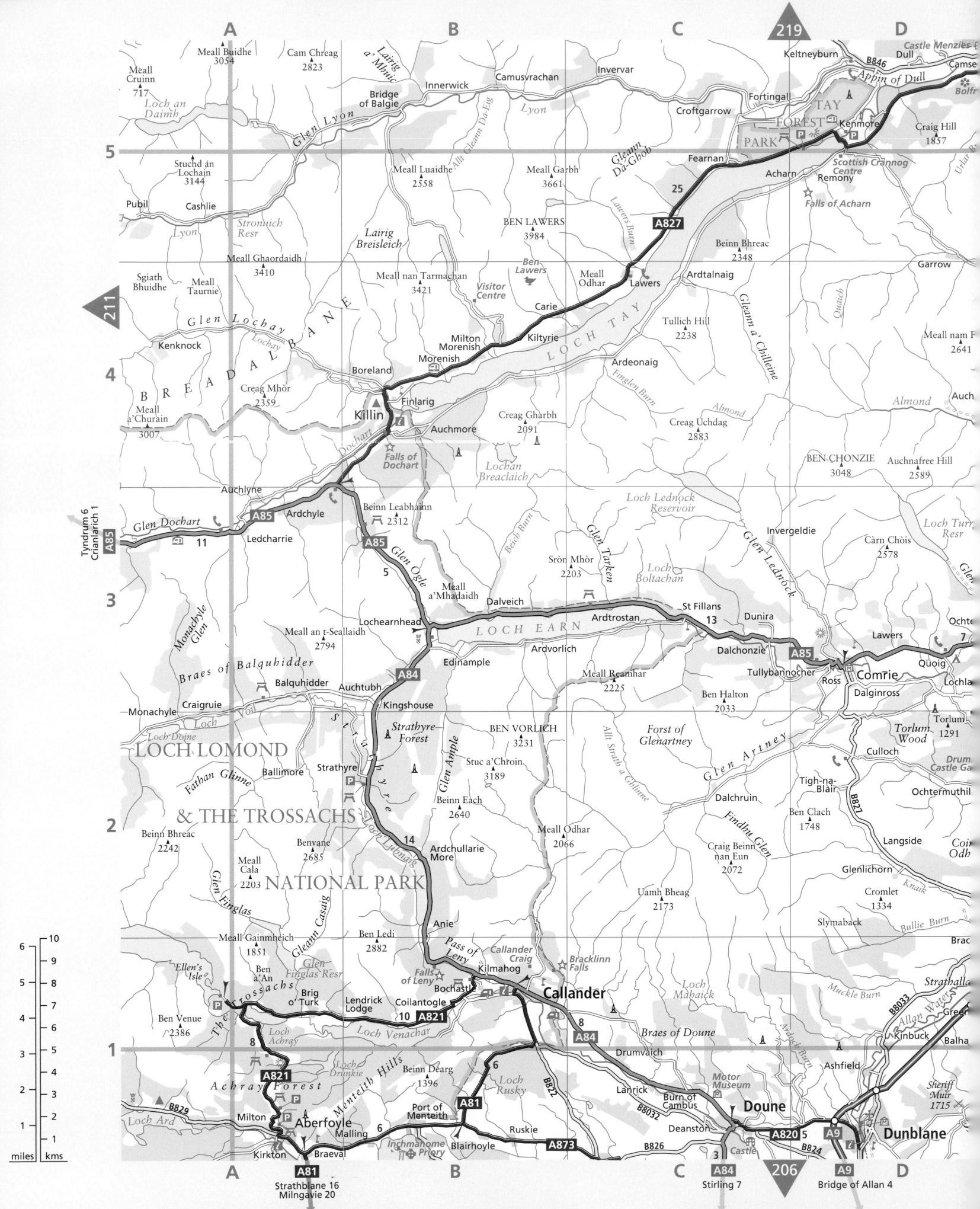

Tay AM
AM 1161/1548

Tay FM
FM 96.4/102.8

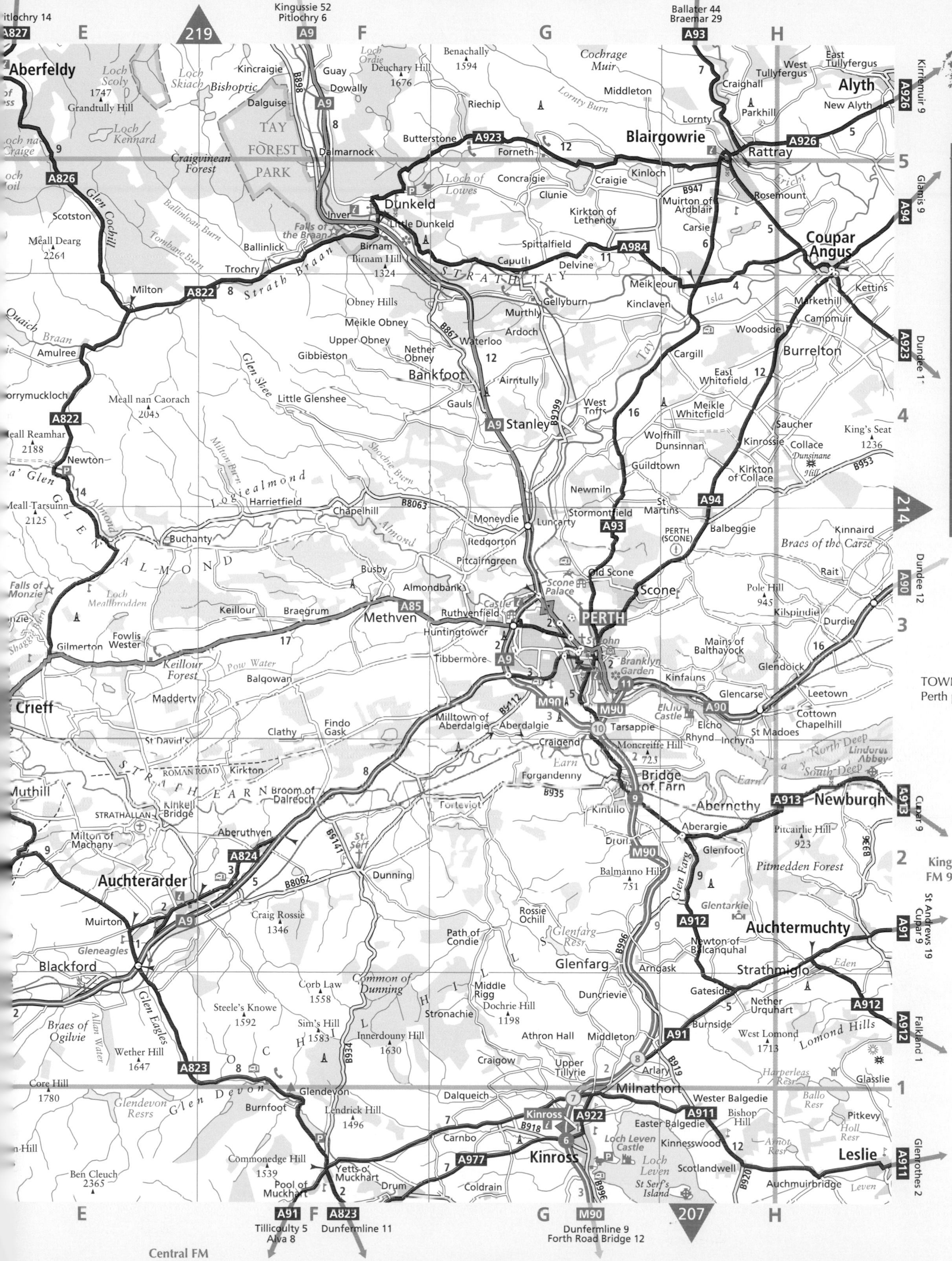

Central FM
FM 103.1

Kingdom FM
FM 95.2/96.1

TOWN PLANS
Perth p374

see p479
for a
touring
guide to
this map

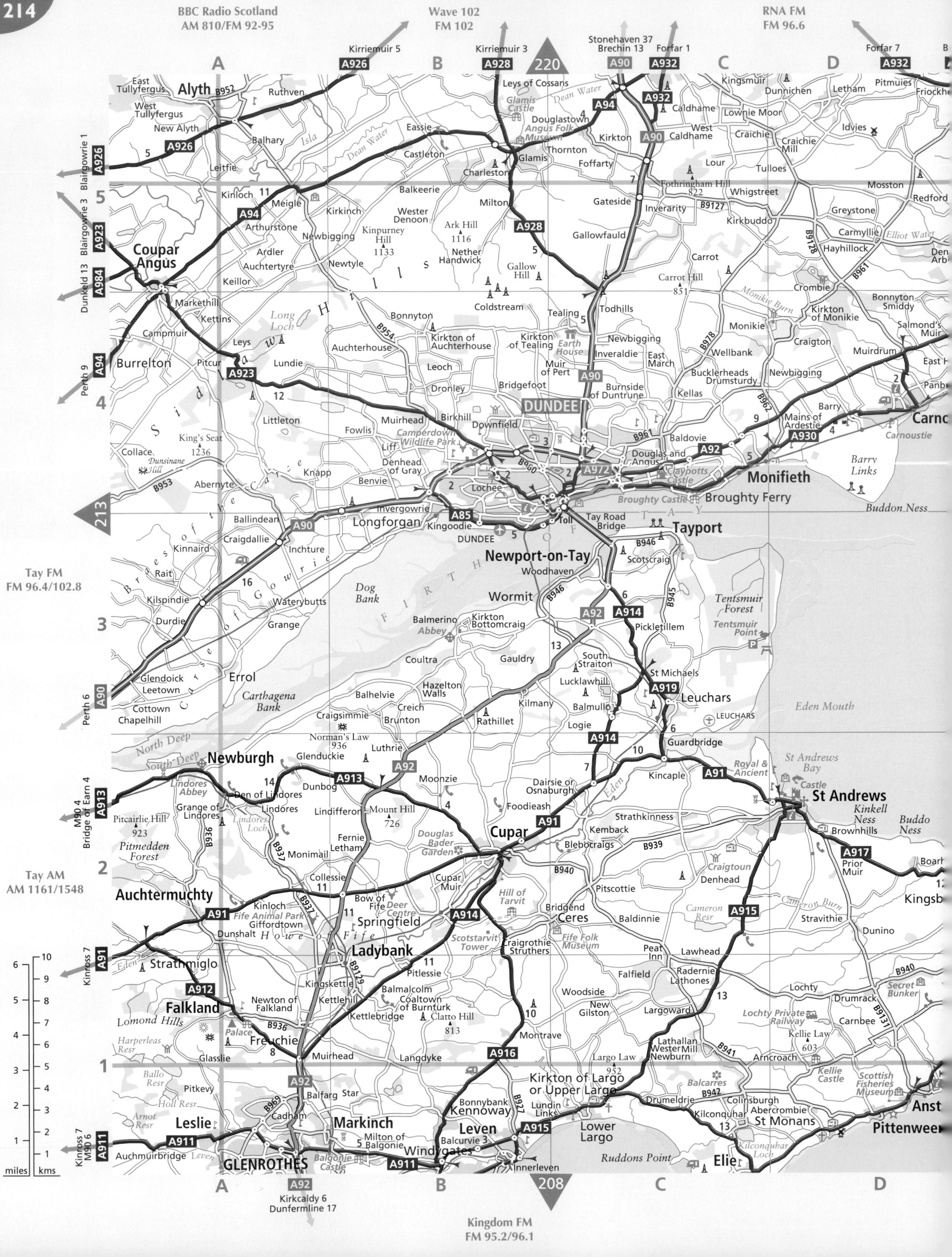

Tay FM
FM 96.4/102.8

Tay AM
AM 1161/1548

Kirkcaldy 6
Dunfermline 17

Map labels (grid reference A–D, 1–5):

220

213

208

Alyth, East Tullyfergus, West Tullyfergus, New Alyth, Leitfie, Ruthven, Balhary, Kirriemuir 5, A926, A928, Kirriemuir 3, Leys of Cossans, Glamis Castle, Dean Water, Stonehaven 37, Brechin 13, Forfar 1, A90, A932, A94, Forfar 7, A932, Kingsmuir, Dunnichen, Letham, Pitmuies, Friockhe

Coupar Angus, Markethill, Kettins, Campmuir, Burrelton, Pitcur, Leys, A923, Kinloch 11, Meigle, Arthurstone, Ardler, Auchtertyre, Keillor, Newbigging, Newtyle, Kirkinch, Wester Denoon, Kinpurney Hill 1133, Ark Hill 1116, Nether Handwick, Milton, A928, Gallow Hill, Gallowfauld, Tealing, Todhills, Gateside, Inverarity, Kirkbuddo, Carrot, Carrot Hill 851, Fothringham Hill 822, Whigstreet, Lour, Tulloes, Mosston, Greystone, Redford, Carmyllie, Hayhillock, B9127, B9128

Long Loch, Balkeerie, Eassie, Castleton, Charleston, Glamis, Foffarty, Thornton, Kirkton, Douglastown, Angus Folk Museum, A94, A90, Caldhame, West Caldhame, Craichie, Craichie Mill, Idvies, Den Arb, Elliot Water, B9361, Crombie

Collace, Dunsinane Hill, Abernyte, King's Seat 1236, Littleton, Muirhead, Birkhill, Fowlis, Liff, Denhead of Gray, Knapp, Benvie, Camperdown Wildlife Park, Downfield, DUNDEE, Douglas and Angus, A972, Claypotts Castle, Monifieth, Broughty Castle, Broughty Ferry, Buddon Ness, A92, A930, Baldovie, Kellas, Burnside of Duntrune, Muir of Pert, Inveraldie, Newbigging, Wellbank, Monikie, Kirkton of Monikie, Bonnyton Smiddy, Salmond's Muir, Muirdrum, East H, Carn, Carnoustie, Barry, Mains of Ardestie, Barry Links

Ballindean, Craigdallie, Kinnaird, Rait, Kilspindie, Durdie, A90, Inchture, Waterybutts, Grange, Invergowrie, Longforgan, Kingoodie, A85, Toll, Tay Road Bridge, Newport-on-Tay, Woodhaven, Wormit, B946, Tayport, Scotscraig, B946, B945, Tentsmuir Forest, Tentsmuir Point, DUNDEE, FIRTH OF TAY

Glendoick, Leetown, Errol, Cottown, Chapelhill, A90, Carthagena Bank, Dog Bank, North Deep, South Deep, Balmerino Abbey, Kirkton Bottomcraig, Coultra, Hazelton Walls, Gauldry, A92, A914, Pickletillem, St Michaels, A919, Leuchars, LEUCHARS, Eden Mouth, Perth 6

Newburgh, Lindores Abbey, Glenduckie, Norman's Law 936, Luthrie, Craigsimmie, Brunton, Creich, Balhelvie, Rathillet, Kilmany, Logie, Balmullo, A914, Guardbridge, Kincaple, A91, Royal & Ancient, St Andrews Bay, St Andrews, Castle, Kinkell Ness, Brownhills, Buddo Ness, A913, A92, Dunbog, Den of Lindores, Grange of Lindores, Lindores, Moonzie, Dairsie or Osnaburgh, Foodieash, A914, Strathkinness, Kemback, Blebocraigs, B939, Craigtoun, Denhead, Prior Muir, A917, Kingsb, M90 4, Bridge of Earn 4

Pitcairlie Hill 923, Pitmedden Forest, B936, Lindores Loch, B937, Lindifferon, Mount Hill 726, Fernie, Letham, Monimail, Collessie, Auchtermuchty, Kinloch, Giffordtown, Dunshalt, Bow of Fife, Deer Centre, Fife Animal Park, Springfield, A914, Cupar, Cupar Muir, Hill of Tarvit, Bridgend, Ceres, Baldinnie, Douglas Bader Garden, Scotstarvit Tower, Craigrothie, Struthers, Fife Folk Museum, Pitscottie, B940, B939, Cameron Resr, Stravithie, Dunino, A915, Cameron Burn, Kinross 7, A91, A91

Strathmiglo, A912, Falkland, Lomond Hills, Harperleas Resr, Palace, Freuchie, Glassie, Newton of Falkland, Kettlehill, Kettlebridge, Kingskettle, B9129, Pitlessie, Balmalcolm, Coaltown of Burnturk, Clatto Hill 813, Ladybank, A916, Montrave, Peat Inn, Falfield, Woodside, New Gilston, Largoward, Lawhead, Radernie, Lathones, Lochty, Lochty Private Railway, Carnbee, Kellie Law 603, B931, B940, Secret Bunker, Drumrack, Kinross 7, M90 6

Ballo Resr, Pitkevy, Holl Resr, Arnot Resr, Leslie, A911, Auchmuirbridge, B969, Cadham, Balfarg, Star, GLENROTHES, Markinch, Milton of Balgonie, Balgonie Castle, Balcurvie 3, Windygates, A92, A911, Kennoway, B921, Bonnybank, Langdyke, Muirhead, Leven, A915, Lower Largo, Largo Law 952, Kirkton of Largo or Upper Largo, Lundin Links, Innerleven, Ruddons Point, Drumeldrie, Colinsburgh, Kilconquhar, Abercrombie, St Monans, Elie, Anst, Pittenwee, Balcarres, Kellie Castle, Scottish Fisheries Museum, Kilconquhar Loch, B942, B941, Arncroach, Lathallan Wester Mill Newburn, Largo Bay, A916

miles / kms scale (10, 9, 8, 7, 6, 5, 4, 3, 2, 1)

DUNDEE

Stonehaven 29
Montrose 7

A92

Boysack
Inverkeilor
Lang Craig
Chapelton
14
Cauldcots
Ethie Mains
Red Head
Letham Grange
Drunkendub
Auchmithie
Marywell
Meg's Craig
Woodville
St Vigeans
Seaton
The Deil's Heid
Arbroath
Wormiehills

Panmure Terrace
Dudhope Terrace
Constitution Street
Don's Road
Rosebank
Hilltown
James St
Alexander Street
Ann Street
0 100 200 300yds
0 100 200 300m
Cotton Road
Infirmary Brae
Union Terrace
Rosebank Road
Ann Street
Nelson Street
Sth George St
William Street
Prospect Pl
Arthur St
McDonald St
Hilltown
Forebank Road
Bonnybank Road
Wellington St
Laurel Bank
DENS ROAD
B960
A90 Forfar 14
Barrack Road
Dudhope Street
Little Theatre
VICTORIA ROAD
B959
CouparAngus 14
A923
LOCHEE ROAD
NORTH MARKETGAIT
State Theatre
A991
Ladywell Ave
KING STREET
A929
Douglas Street
Brown Street
WEST MARKETGAIT
POL
Abertay University
Meadowside
St Andrew's St
MARKETGAIT
Cowgate Port (Gate)
Cowgate
Dens St
Miln Street
Blinshall Street
Bell Street
Wellgate Shopping Centre
Lower Princes St
Foundry Lane
Verdant Works Museum
West Bell St
Constitution Rd
Euclid
Cowgate
East Whale Lane
Bus Depot
Guthrie Street
Barrack St Museum
Meadowside
Commercial St
Murraygate
Seagate
Mary Ann Lane
Trades Lane
Hunter Street
Ward Road
The Howff
Reform Street
Candle Lane
Gellatly St
EAST DOCK ST
A92
Arbroath 16
Hawkhill
South Ward St North
Willison St
Bank St
High Street
Castle St
St Paul's Cath
Exchange St
Camperdown Street
West Port
WC
Crichton St
City Quay
HM Frigate Unicorn
Victoria Dock
Small's Wynd
Small's La
Dental Hospital
Park Place
Overgate Shopping Centre
St Mary's Tower
Nethergate
Union St
Whitehall Cres
Caird Hall
Tayside House
King William Street
South Victoria Dock Road
Airlie Pl
University of Dundee
South Tay Street
Dundee Repertory Theatre
St Andrew's Cathedral
A991
Greenmarket
S MARKETGAIT
Earl Grey Pl
Toll Booths & Viewpoints
Marine Parade
Nethergate
Dundee Contemporary Arts
Inland Revenue
Customs & Excise
Discovery Point
Olympia Leisure Centre
Sensation Science Centre
Dundee Station
Discovery Quay
RRS Discovery
Firth of Tay
A85
RIVERSIDE DRIVE
Craig Pier
A92
Perth 21 A90
St Andrews 13

ST ANDREWS

The Royal & Ancient Golf Club
Old Course
Grannie Clar's Wynd
Golf Place
British Golf Museum
Sea Life Centre
Stirling 51
A919 Tay Br 10
A91
LINKS CRES
The Links
The Scores
Murray Place
Murray Park
Crawford Art Centre
Visitor Centre
Castle (ruins)
Windmill Road
Abbotsford
Hope Street
NORTH ST
St Salvator's College
E Scores
North Castle St
WC
POL
Station Rd
City Road
Greyfriars Gdn
College St
Union St
Kinburn Park
Kinburn Museum
Bell Street
Market Street
Church St
WC
South Castle St
Gregory Place
Doubledykes Road
PO
Logie's Lane
St Mary's College
Cathedral (ruins)
Queen's Gardens
Town Hall
Byre Theatre
The Pends
The Pends
B939
Argyle Street
SOUTH STREET
Queen Mary's House
West Port
Rose La
A915
Kirkcaldy 25
Forth Bridge 38
A917
Crail 10

see p480 for a touring guide to this map

TOWN PLANS
Dundee p215
St Andrews p215

FIFE NESS
Craighead
Kirklands
Crail
st Ness

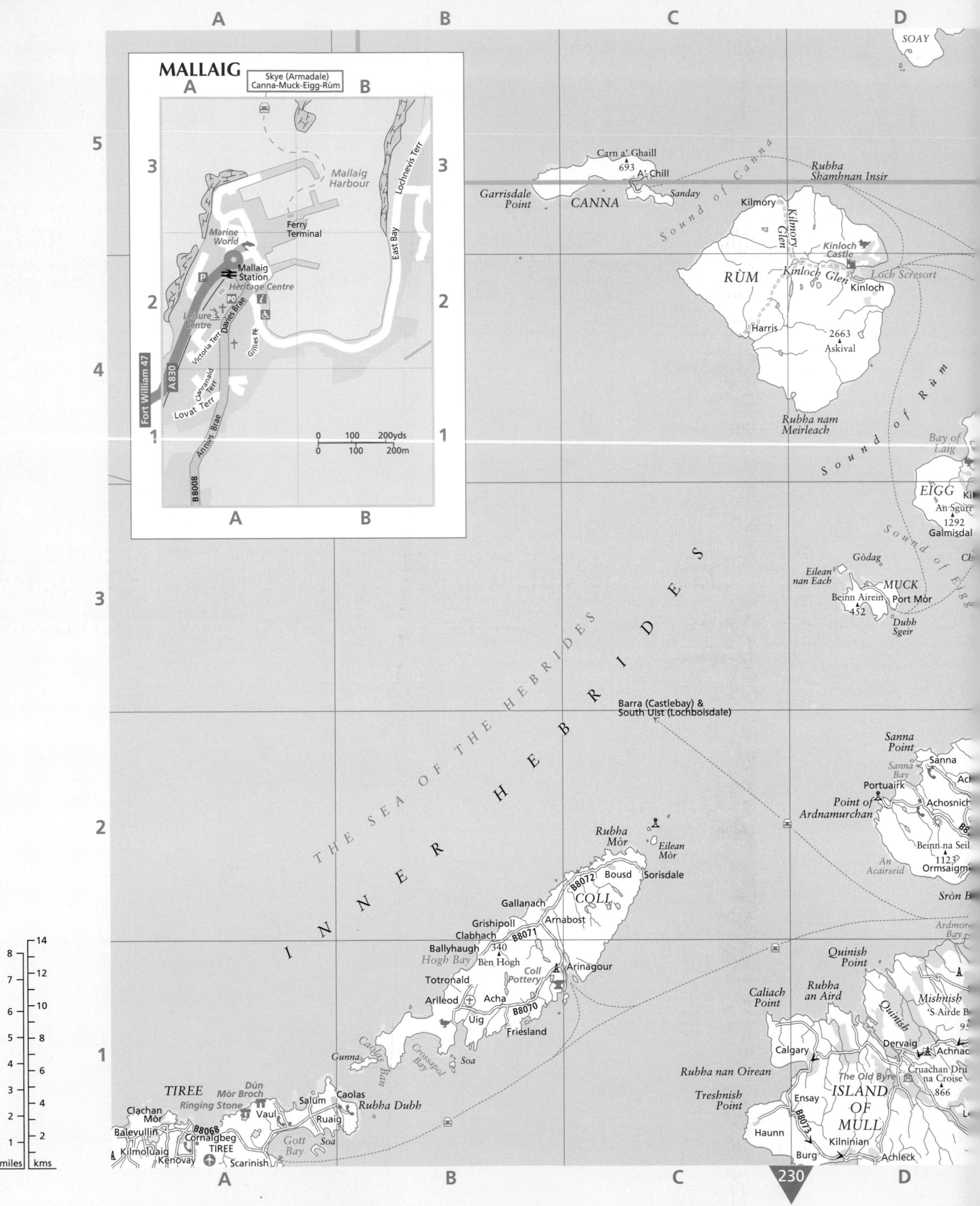

MALLAIG

Skye (Armadale)
Canna-Muck-Eigg-Rùm

Mallaig Harbour

Ferry Terminal

Marine World

Mallaig Station
Heritage Centre

Leisure Centre

East Bay

Fort William 47

A830

Victoria Terr
Carranald Terr
Lovat Terr
Annie's Brae
Davies Brae
Gilles Pk
Lochnevis Terr

B8008

0   100   200yds
0   100   200m

SOAY

Carn a' Ghaill
693
A'-Chill
Sanday

Garrisdale
Point

CANNA

Sound of Canna

Rubha
Shamhnan Insir

Kilmory

Kilmory Glen

Kinloch
Castle

RÙM

Kinloch Glen

Loch Scresort

Kinloch

Harris

2663
Askival

Rubha nam
Meirleach

Sound of Rùm

Bay of
Laig

EIGG

Ki
An Sgurr
1292
Galmisdal

Sound of Eigg

Gòdag

Eilean
nan Each

MUCK

Beinn Airein
452
Port Mòr

Dubh
Sgeir

T H E   S E A   O F   T H E   H E B R I D E S

I N N E R   H E B R I D E S

Barra (Castlebay) &
South Uist (Lochboisdale)

Sanna
Point

Sanna

Sanna
Bay

Ac

Portuairk

Point of
Ardnamurchan

Achosnich

B8

Beinn na Seil
1123
Ormsaigm

An
Acairseid

Sròn B

Rubha
Mòr

Eilean
Mòr

Ardmore
Bay

B8072
Bousd
Sorisdale

Gallanach

COLL

Grishipoll
Clabhach

Arnabost

B8071

Quinish
Point

Rubha
an Aird

Ballyhaugh

Hogh Bay

340
Ben Hogh

Arinagour

Caliach
Point

Mishnish
'S-Airde B
9

Totronald

Coll
Pottery

Quinish

Arileod

Acha

B8070

Uig

Friesland

Calgary

Dervaig

Achnac

Cruachan Dru
na Croise
866

Gunna

Caolas Gunna

Crossapol
Bay

Soa

Rubha nan Oirean

The Old Byre

ISLAND
OF
MULL

Treshnish
Point

Ensay

B8073

Le

TIREE

Dún
Mòr Broch

Ringing Stone

Salum

Caolas

Rubha Dubh

Haunn

Kilninian

Burg

Achleck

Clachan
Mòr

Vaul

Ruaig

Balevullin

B8068

Soa

Kilmoluaig

Cornaigbeg
TIREE

Gott
Bay

Kenovay

Scarinish

14
8   12
7   12
6   10
5   8
4   6
3   4
2   2
1

miles | kms

A   B   C   D

Portree 31
Broadford 9
A851

Kyle of Lochalsh 19
A87

F 223 G H

Invergarry 24
A87

see p481
for a
touring
guide to
this map

Glasnakille
Dunsgaith Castle
Ord
Duisdalemore
Isleornsay or
Eilean Iarmain
Ornsay
Camus Croise
Sandaig Islands
Màm an Staing
Beinn Sgritheall 3194
Beinn nan Caorach 2536
The Saddle 3319
Sgurr na Sgine 3098
Glenshiel 1719
Glen Shiel
34

Tokavaig
Achnacloich
Tarskavaig
Saasaig
Teangue
A851
Rubha Buidhe
Rubha Ruadh
Eilean Ràrsaidh
Arnisdale
Glen Arnisdale
Corran
Druim Fada 2327
Buidhe Bheinn 2884
Kinloch Hourn
Sgurr a' Mhaoraich 3365
Aonach Air Chrith 3342
Maol Chinn-Dearg
Gleouraich 3394

ISLAND
Ferindonald
Kilmore
Kilbeg
Inverguseran
Beinn na Caillich 2573
Loch Hourn
Barrisdale Bay
Ladhar Bheinn 3343
Glen Barrisdale
Barrisdale Forest
Gleann Cosaidh
Loch Quoich

OF
Armadale Castle
Ardvasar
Calligarry
Airor
Sandaig
KNOYDART
Barrisdale
Gairich 3015

SKYE
Aird of Sleat
Point of Sleat
Inverie Bay
Scottas
Aultvoulin
Inverie
Sgurr Coire Choinnichean 2612
Meall Buidhe 3107
Sgurr na Ciche 3412
Sgurr Mòr 3290
Glen Kingie
Loch Blàir

Mallaig
Sgurr an Eilein Ghiubhais 1796
Mallaig Bheag
Beinn Bhuidhe 2805
Kingie
4

Beoraidbeg
Morar
Bracara
Bracorina
NORTH MORAR
Loch Nevis
Tarbet
Sgurr Breac 2387
Carn Mòr 2718
Murlaggan

Glenancross
B8008
Loch Morar
Swordland
An Stac 2350
Sgurr Thuilm 3164
Strathan

Portnaluchaig
Bunacaimb
A830
SOUTH MORAR
Meoble
Meith Bheinn 2328
Streap 2988
Gaor Bheinn or Gulvain 3238
218

Eilean Ighe
Back of Keppoch
ARISAIG
Sidhean Mòr 1970
Beinn nan Cabar 1888
Loch Beoraid
Dessarry
Mallie

Luinga Bheag
Arisaig
19
Creag Bhàn 1675
Slios Garbh 2076
Sgurr an Utha 2610
Pean
Beinn an t-Sneachda 2175

Rubh' Arisaig
Druimindarroch
The Prince's Cairn
Arieniskill
Ranochan
14
Loch Eilt
Visitor Centre
Gleann Dubh Lighe
Dubh Lighe
Fionn Lighe
Gleann Fionnlighe
3

Eilean a Ghaill
Lochailort
Inverailort
Beinn Odhar Mhòr 2855
Glenfinnan
Monuments
A830
Kinlocheil
Fassfern 14
Fort William 11
A830

Eilean an t-Snidhe
Loch Ailort
Ardnish
Eilean nan Gobhar
Druim Fiaclach 2852
Beinn Odhar Bheag 2895
Drumsallie
Loch Eil
Duisky
Blaich

Sound of Arisaig
Samalaman Island
Roshven
Rois-Bheinn 2895
Croit Bheinn 2178
A861
South Garvan
A830

Ruhha na Faing Mòire
Glenuig
A861
20
MOIDART
Moidart
Beinn Gàire 2179
Sgurr Ghuibhsachain 2784
A861

Rubh' Aird an Fheidh
Baramore
Turquhar's Point
Invermoidart
Eilean Shona
Kinlochmoidart
Sgorr Craobh a' Chaorainn 2543
Glen Garvan
Stob Coire a' Chearcaill 2528

Rubha Aird Druimnich
Castle Tioram
Cùl Doirlinn
Ardmolich
Sgorr an Tarmachain 2474
Cona Glen
Nevis Radio
FM 96.6/97/102.3/102.4

Ockle Point
Newton of Ardtoe
Shielfoot
Dalnabreck
Dalelia
Sgorr an Tarmachain
Glen Hurich
Beinn Mheadhoin 2579
Druim-Leathad nam Fias 1893
Aryhoulan
Inverscaddle Bay
A82

Ardtoe
B80
Kentra
Mingarrypark
Muss
Pulloch
Loch Doilet
Sgurr Dhomhnuill 2914
Glen Scaddle
Spean Bridge 17
Fort William 7

ARDNAMURCHAN
Leac Shoilleir
Beinn Bhreac 1171
Acharacle
Ardshealach
SUNART
Beinn Resipol 2775
ARDGOUR
Sgurr na h-Eanchainne 2398
Corran
Clovullin
A82
9

nan Logann 1026
Loch Mudle
Meall nan Each 1607
Salen
Resipole
Scotstown
Anaheilt
Garbh Bheinn 2093
Ferry
Inchree
Keppanach
Onich
A82

Ben Hiant 1731
Glenbeg
Ben Laga 1679
Ardery
Strontian
Glen Gour
Glen Tarbert
A861
Sallachan Point
North Ballachulish
5

B8007
Glenborrodale
Ardslignish
Laga
Ceol na Mara
12
Ardnastang
13
Tarbert
Inversanda Bay

aclean's Nose
Oronsay
Risga
Carna
Meall an Damhain 1693
Liddesdale
Achleek
Creach Bheinn 2798
Rubha Mòr
Cuil Bay
South Ballachulish
Kentallen

uliston Point na Ball
bermory
Calve Island
Drimnin
Beinn Iadain 1873
Beinn nam Beathrach 1869
Lòchuisge
19
Fuar Bheinn 2511
Kilmalieu
Eilean Balnagowan
A828

Beinn Bhuidhe 1481
B849
Rhemore
MORVERN
Beinn na h-Uamha 1521
Beinn Chlaonleud 1569
B8043
Beinn na Cille 2136
Camasnacroise
Glen Duror
Fraochaidh 2883
1

Sithean na Raplaich 1806
Gleann Dubh
A884
Ceanna Mòr
Shuna Island
Portnacroish
Glen Stockdale
Beinn Donn 1553
Elleric

nacross
Aros 11
Killundine
Acharn
Claggan
Gleann Geal
Loch Tearnait
Loch nan Clach
Port Ramsay
Port Appin
Appin
Strath of Appin
Fasnacloich
Invercreran
Beinn Sgulaird 3059

Salen Forest
A848
Fiunary
Kinlochaline Castle
Larachbeg
Ardtornish
Ardtornish

Castle
Aros Mains
Savary
A848
E 230 F A884 G 210 H A828

Craignure 12
Lochaline 1
Oban 22

TOWN PLANS
Mallaig p216

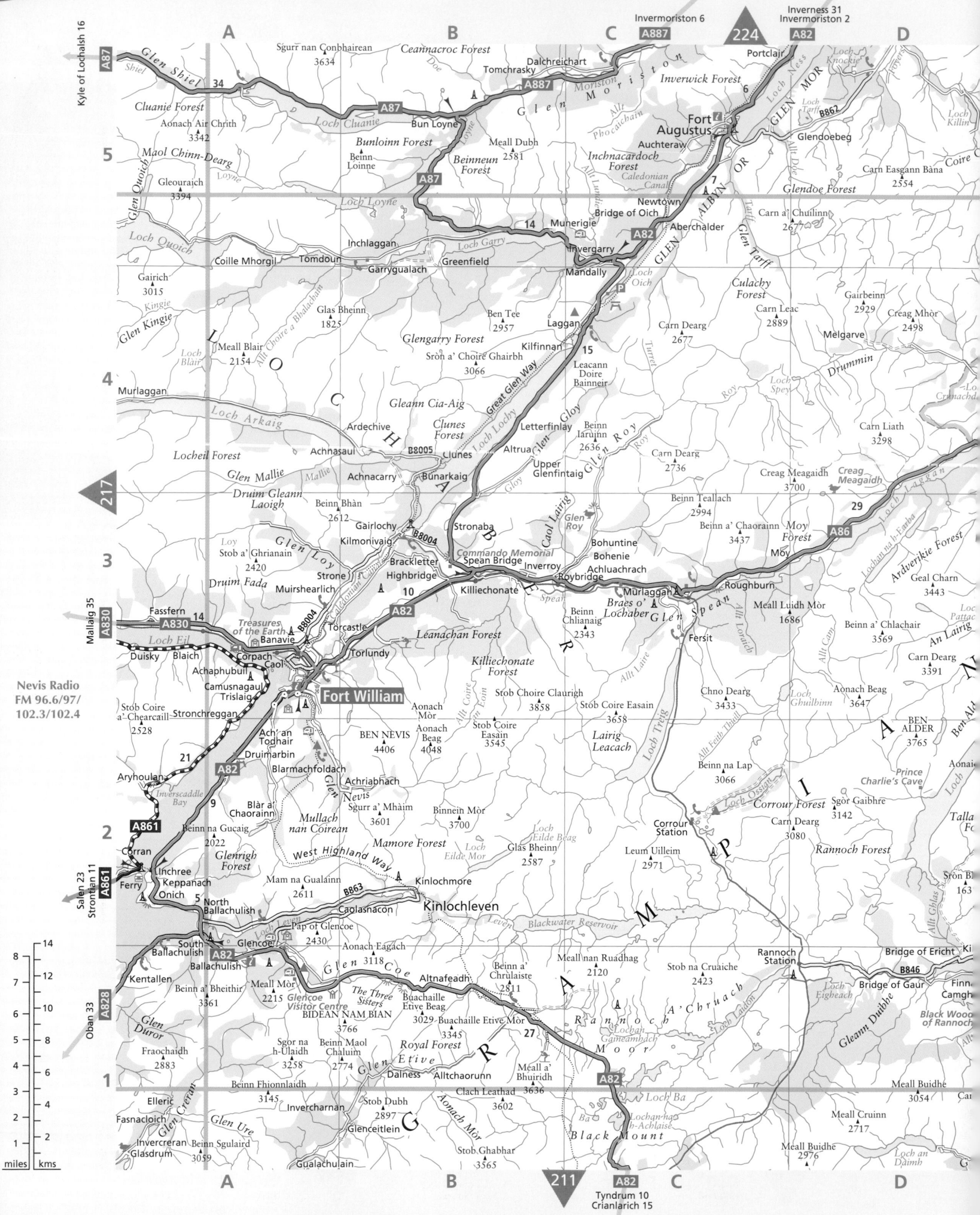

BBC Radio Scotland
AM 810/FM 92-95

Nevis Radio
FM 96.6/97/
102.3/102.4

Fort William

BEN NEVIS
4406

BIDEAN NAM BIAN
3766

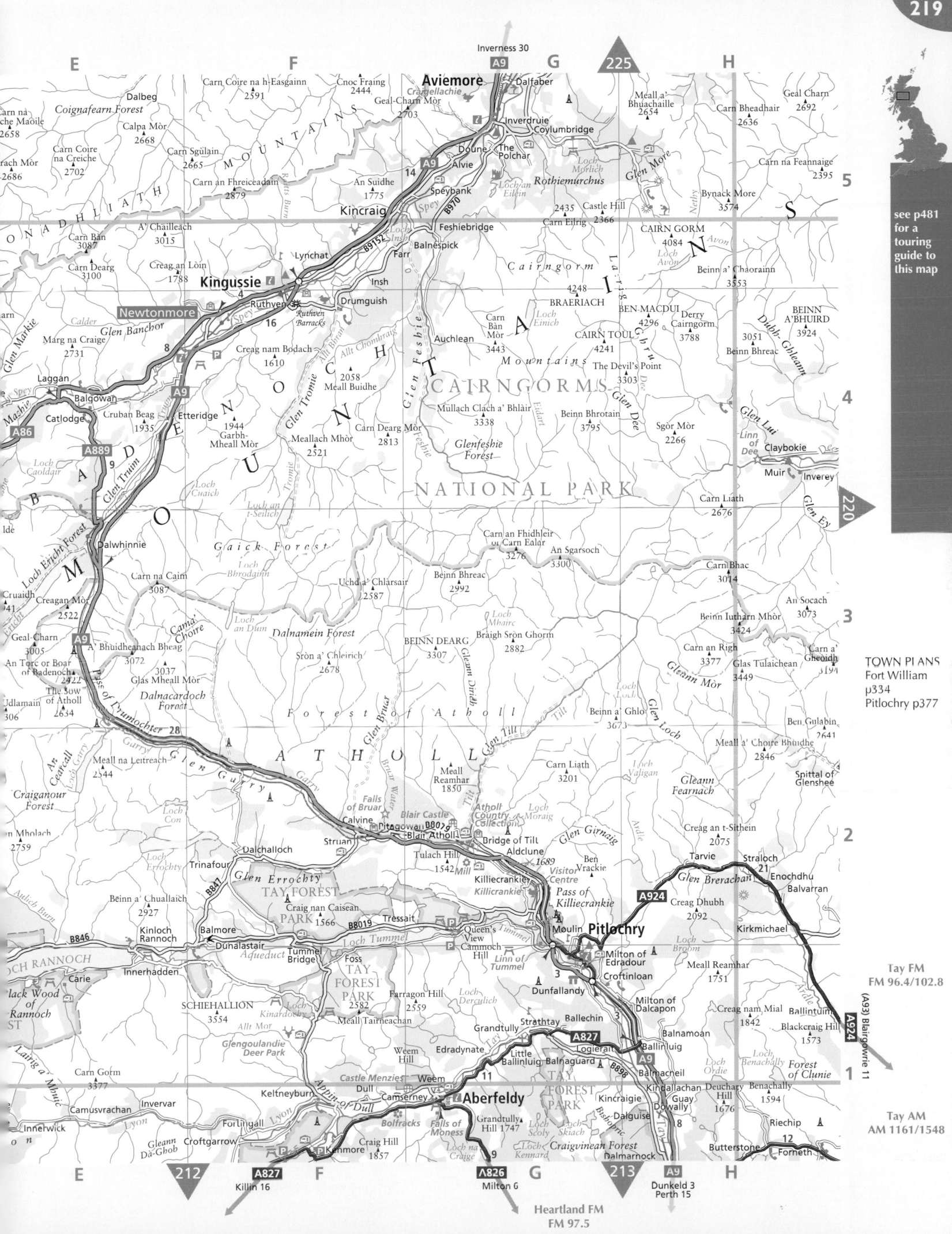

see p481 for a touring guide to this map

TOWN PLANS
Fort William
p334
Pitlochry p377

Tay FM
FM 96.4/102.8

Tay AM
AM 1161/1548

Heartland FM
FM 97.5

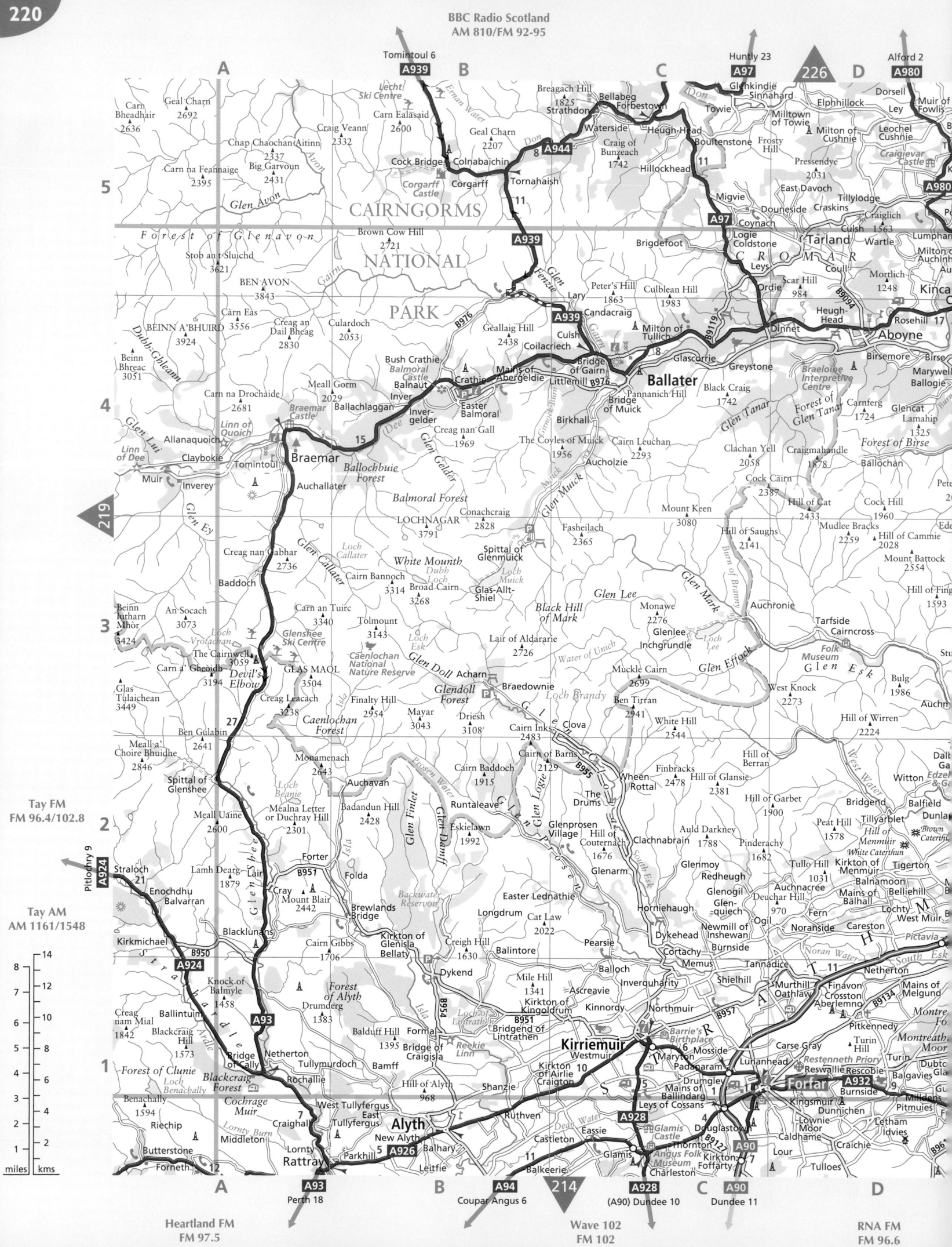

see p482 for a touring guide to this map

Northsound Two
AM 1035

Huntly 28
Inverurie 4

A96

Oldmeldrum 11
A947

Northsound One
FM 96.9/97.6/103

Fraserburgh 44
Peterhead 26

A90

Blackdog

227

Bergen (via Lerwick) (seasonal)
Orkney (Kirkwall)
Shetland (Lerwick)
Tórshavn

E F G H

Moor of Balvack
Craigearn
Leschangie
Leylodge
Lauchintilly
B997
Blackburn
Munduno
11
ld 4
Kirkton Tough
lyfourie
Causeyton
Black Hill
608
Castle Fraser
Muir of Kinellar
Blackchambers
ABERDEEN
Chapel of
Stoneywood
Clinterty
Stoneywood
Dyce
Denmore
ennie
orest
Ordhead
27
Sauchen
Achath
Lyne of Skene
B9126
East Auchronie
Bankhead
Bucksburn
Stoneywood
Bridge of Don
Milton of Corsindae
Old A944 Dunecht
Kirkton of Skene
Northfield
Mastrick
Old Aberdeen
Kinnernie
Corsindae
Tillybirloch
B979
Westhill
Kingswells
ABERDEEN
5
Bankhead
Comers
Drumlassie
South Garlogie
Echt
Kirkton
Elrick
Carnie
Torry
Nigg Bay

Midmar Forest
B9119
Easter Culfosie
Landerberry
Redhill
Easter Ord
Wester Ord
Blacktop
Ruthrieston
Mannofield
A956
Nigg
Souter Head
Cove Bay

Torphins
Hill of Fare
1545
B9125
Schoolhill
Benthoul
Contlaw
Bieldside
Cults
Kincorth
Banchory-Devenick
Hare Ness

Milton of Campfield
B977
The Blackdams
Birks Hardgate
Craigton
Milltimber
A93
Milton of Murtle
Heathcot
Charlestown
Marywell
Findon Ness

A980
Hirn
Peterculter
Kirkton of Maryculter
Auchlunies
Findon
Schoolhill
Portlethen
Portlethen Village

Upper Lochton
Drum Castle
Mains of Drum
Drumoak
Hillside
Downies
Cammachmore Bay

Mid Beltie
Brathens
The Neuk
West Park
Craiglug
Auchlee
16
Cammachmore
Portlethen

Bridge of Canny
East Mains
3
Crathes
Crathes Castle
B9077
Woodlands
Muirskie
Denside
Auchlee
Newtonhill

rch of Trustach
Blackhall
Kirkton of Durris
Upper Burnhaugh
Cookney
Muchalls

Banchory
Auchattie
Bridge of Feugh
Craft Village
Crossroads
Borrowfield
Netherley
Backburn
Muchalls Castle
Bridge of Muchalls
Doonie Point

Strachan
Blackness
13
Darnford
Cairn-Mon-Earn
1241
B979

B976
Blairydryne
Lochton
Mongour
1232
Rickarton
Garron Point

Craig of Dalfro
1042
Mergie
A957
A90
Redcloak
Cowie

Bridge of Dye
Kerloch
1754
Fetteresso Forest
Kirktown of Fetteresso
Tewel
Stonehaven

Dye
Carmont
Castle Haven
Dunnottar Castle
Thornyhive Bay

Goyle Hill
1526
Mains of Dellavaird
Drumlithie
Glenbervie
Carmont
Tannachie
Newmill
Fiddes
Barras
Mill of Uras
Crawton
Fowlsheugh
Crawton Bay

eluncart
1725
Cairn Mount
Glensaugh
Mondynes
Monboddo
Auchenblae
Pitforthie
Roadside of Catterline
Catterline
Braidon Bay

Clatterin Brig
Strathfinella Hill
East Cairnbeg
Brownmuir
Fordoun
Grassic Gibbon Visitor Centre
Fawsyde
Roadside of Kinneff
Todhead Point

Fasque
Nether Howe o' the Mearns
Arbuthnott
Allardice
Kinneff
Little Johns Haven

tercairn
Bent
Scotston
Bervie Bay
Knox Hill
Gourdon
Inverbervie
Doolie Ness

Laurencekirk
Mains of Thornton
Tulloch
Garvock
Benholm

Dryplaid
Meikle Strath
B974
Sauchieburn
10
A90
Dykelands
13
Johnshaven

Luthermuir
A937
Mains of Kirktonhill
Marykirk
Ecclesgreig
North Water Bridge
Pert
Lochside
Morphie
St Cyrus
Milton Ness

Logie Pert
Craigo
Logie
A92
St Cyrus

chin
Muirton of Ballochy
10
Hillside
Kirkhill

House of Dun
9
A935
Montrose Basin
Ferryden
Montrose

Bonnyton
Maryton
Scurdie Ness

Carcary
Westerton
11
Kirkton of Craig
Usan
Boddin Point

Braehead
Lunan
Lunan Bay
Redcastle

Inverkeilor
Lang Craig
Ethie Mains
Red Head

Chapelton
14
Cauldcots
Drunkendub

A92
Letham Grange

Arbroath 2
Dundee 19

STONEHAVEN

A90 Aberdeen 15

A B C

Barchory 16
A957
W Glebe
East Glebe
East Glebe
Football Ground
Leisure Centre
(Outdoor)
3

Westfield Rd
Westfield Avenue
Fetteresso Terr
Stonehaven Station
Arduthie
Princes Rd
Kirk Rd
St Leonard Terr
Bath Street
Urie Crescent
Gurney
Robert
Belmont
Ann
Brae
Beach Rd
Bowling & Tennis
Helen Road
B979
David St
Ironfield La

Christie
Queen's Rd
Man's Hill Av
Duke St
Hudson St
Mary
Street
Rodney St
Allardice
Cowie
Beachgate La
2

King's Road
Evan Street
EVAN ST
Margaret St
Market Sq
Town Hall
Salmon La

Low Wood Road
Cameron Ct
Carronhall
Ardmore St
Carron Terr
Cameron St
Arbuthnott St
Bridgefield
Bervie High St
Keith Pl
Old Pier
1

Dunnottar Woods
Carron Gdns
A957
Victoria Street
Old Town

A90 Dundee 50

A B C

E F G H

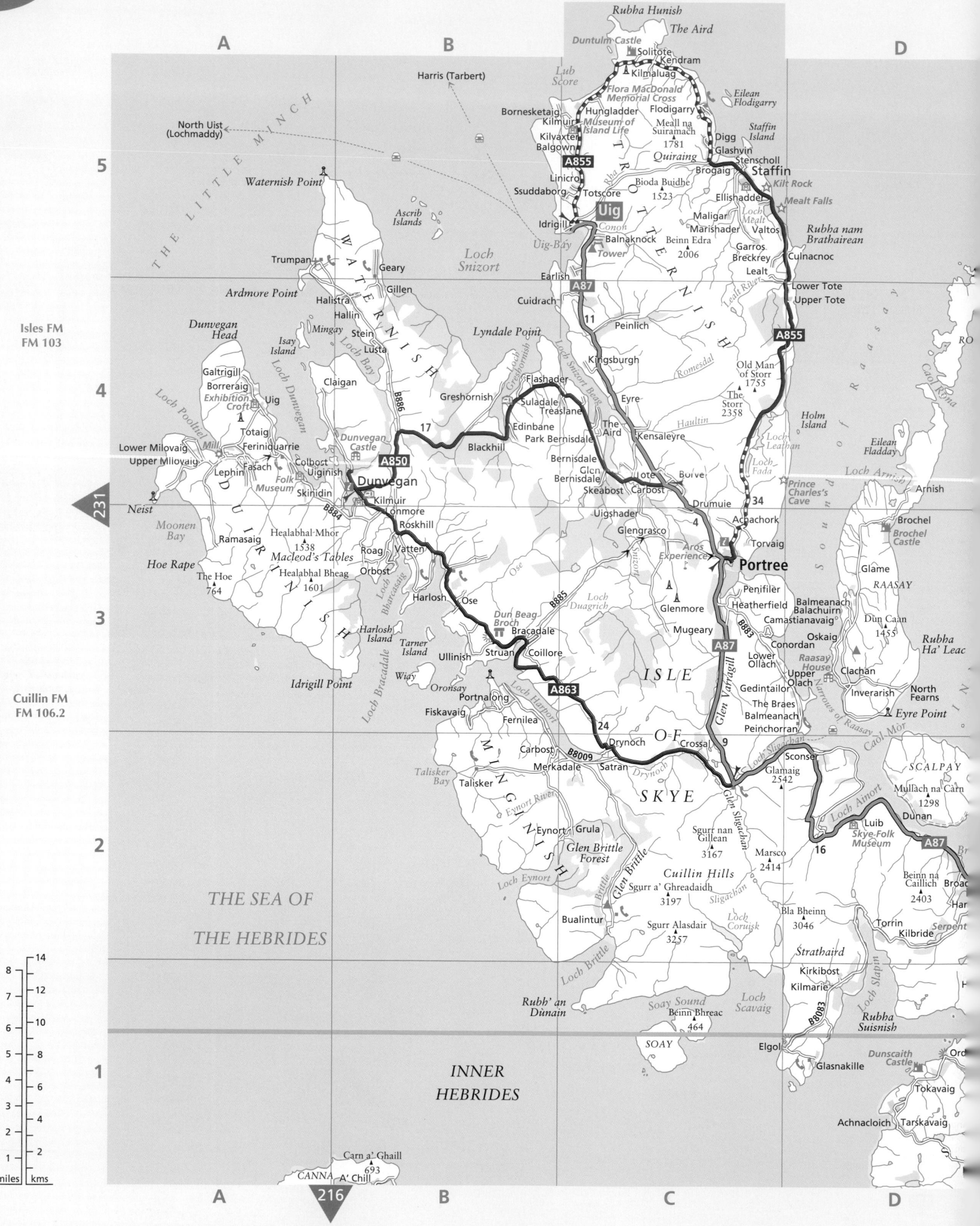

Rubha Hunish
The Aird
Duntulm Castle
Solitote
Kendram
Kilmaluag
Flora MacDonald
Memorial Cross
Borneskeitag
Hungladder
Flodigarry
Eilean
Flodigarry
Kilmuir
Museum of
Island Life
Meall na
Suiramach
1781
Digg
Staffin
Island
Kilvaxter
Balgown
Quiraing
Glashvin
Stenscholl

A855

Linicro
Brogaig
Staffin

Ssuddaborg
Bioda Buidhe
1523
Ellishadder

Uig
Totscore
Maligar
Marishader
Valtos
Kilt Rock

Idrigill
Loch
Conon
Mealt Falls

Balnaknock
Beinn Edra
2006
Garros
Breckrey
Lealt
Rubha nam
Brathairean

Tower
Earlish
A87
Culnacnoc

Harris (Tarbert)

North Uist
(Lochmaddy)

THE LITTLE MINCH

Waternish Point

Ascrib
Islands

Loch
Snizort

Cuidrach
Lyndale Point
Peinlich
Lower Tote
Upper Tote

A855

Trumpan
Geary
Gillen

Ardmore Point
Halistra
Hallin
Kingsburgh
Romesdal

Dunvegan
Head
Isay
Island
Mingay
Stein
Lusta

Greshornish
Eyre
Old Man
of Storr
1755

Galtrigill
Borreraig
Exhibition
Croft
Uig
Claigan
Flashader
Suladale
Treaslane
The
Aird
Kensaleyre
The
Storr
2358
Holm
Island

Edinbane
Park Bernisdale
Haultin
Eilean
Fladday

Lower Milovaig
Upper Milovaig
Mill
Feriniquarrie
Fasach
Colbost
Uiginish
Blackhill
Bernisdale
Skeabost
Glen
Bernisdale
Tote
Borve
Loch
Fada
Prince
Charles's
Cave
Arnish

Neist
Lephin
Folk
Museum
Skinidin
A850
Dunvegan Castle
Dunvegan
Uigshader
Drumuie
34
Achachork
Torvaig

Moonen
Bay
Ramasaig
Healabhal Mhor
1538
Kilmuir
Lonmore
Roskhill
Glengrasco
Aros
Experience
Portree
Brochel
Brochel
Castle

Hoe Rape
The Hoe
764
Healabhal Bheag
1601
Roag
Orbost
Vatten
Ose
Dun Beag
Broch
Penifiler
Heatherfield
Glame
RAASAY

Harlosh
Island
Harlosh
Bracadale
Coillore
Glenmore
Mugeary
Balmeanach
Balachuirn
Camastianavaig
Dun Caan
1455
Rubha
Ha' Leac

Idrigill Point
Tarner
Island
Ullinish
Struan
Conordan
Oskaig
Clachan

A863
Wiay
Oronsay
Portnalong
Fiskavaig
24
Drynoch
Crossa
9
Gedintailor
The Braes
Balmeanach
Peinchorran
Raasay
House
Lower
Ollach
Upper
Olach
Inverarish
North
Fearns
Eyre Point

Fernilea
Carbost
Merkadale
Satran
Drynoch
ISLE
Sconser
Glamaig
2542
SCALPAY
Mullach na Càrn
1298

Talisker
Bay
Talisker
B8009
OF
Luib
Skye-Folk
Museum
16
A87
Loch Ainort
Dunan

MINGINISH
Eynort
Grula
Glen Brittle
Forest
SKYE
Sgurr nan
Gillean
3167
Marsco
2414
Beinn na
Caillich
2403
Broad
Har

Eynort River
Glen Brittle
Cuillin Hills
Sgurr a' Ghreadaidh
3197
Sligachan
Bla Bheinn
3046
Torrin
Kilbride
Serpent

Bualintur
Sgurr Alasdair
3257
Loch
Coruisk
Strathaird
Kirkibost
Kilmarie

Rubh' an
Dunain
Loch Brittle
Beinn Bhreac
464
Loch Scavaig
Loch Slapin
Rubha
Suisnish

THE SEA OF
THE HEBRIDES
SOAY
Elgol
Glasnakille
Dunscaith
Castle
Ord

INNER
HEBRIDES
Achnacloich
Tarskavaig
Tokavaig

Carn a' Ghaill
693
CANNA
A' Chill

231

Isles FM
FM 103

Cuillin FM
FM 106.2

miles | kms

228

see p483
for a
touring
guide to
this map

TOWN PLANS
Portree p377

see p483 for a touring guide to this map

Placenames and features (north to south, west to east):

Poolewe 4
Gairloch 1
A832

Sròn na Carra
Bádachro
Opinan
Port Henderson
South Erradale
Shieldaig
Redpoint
B8056
Loch Clair
Kerry
Kerrysdale

Eilean Ruairidh Mòr
Eilean Subhainn
Victoria Falls
Talladale
21
A832
Letterewe
Letterewe Forest
Loch Fada
Loch Maree

Beinn Làir 2817
Mullach Coire Mhic Fhearchair 3326
A' Chailleach 3276
Sgurr Mòr 3637
Loch a Bhraoin
Groban 2424
Loch a' Choire Mhòir
Loch Fannich

Sgeir Ghlas
Flowerdale Forest
Loch na h-Oidhche
Beinn an h Eòin 2805
Shieldaig Forest
Loch a Bhealaich
SLIOCH 3217
Kinlochewe Forest
Beinn a' Mhùinidh 2231
Beinn nan Ramh 2333
Leckie

Rubha na Fearn
Fearnmore
Fearnbeg
Arinacrinachd
Cuaig
Kenmore
Ardheslaig
Alligin Shuas
Lower Diabaig
Beinn Alligin 3232
Rechullin
Inveralligin
Torridon Forest
LIATHACH 3456

Beinn Eighe National Nature Reserve
Visitor Centre
Kinlochewe
Táagan
Anancaun
Incheril
BEINN EIGHE 3313
A896
Heights of Kinlochewe
Carn a' Ghlinne 1768
Glen Docherty
Badavanich
Fionn Bheinn 3062
Meall a' Chaorainn 2313

ROSS

A832
Conon Bridge 25
Garve 13
(A835)

Achnasheen
9
Loch a Chroisg
Ledgowan Forest
Carn Beag 1804
Carn Mhàrtuin 1765
Loch Gowan
Loch Bran

Croic-na Bheinn 1619
Upper Loch Torridon
Balgy
Shieldaig
36
Torridon
Annat
Torridon Countryside Centre
Ben-damph Forest
Loch Damh
Sgurr Dubh 2566
Coulin Forest
Loch Clair
Loch Coulin
Carn Breac 2221
Glen Carron
Moruisg 3026
Carn Gorm 2866
Creag na h-Iolaire
Loch Sgamhain
Meig

W E S T E R

Loch Torridon
Abhainn Chuaig
Loch Shieldaig
Loch Lundie
Glenshieldaig Forest
A896
Maol Chean-Dearg 3060
Sgorr Ruadh 3142
Lair
Craig
18
A890
Glencarron and Glenuig Forest
Gleann Fhiodhaig
Maoile Lunndaidh 3304
Sgùrr na Feartaig 2830
Sgurr a' Chaorachain 3455

Applecross Forest
Beinn Bhàn 2938
Sgurr a' Gharaidh 2396
Glas Bheinn 2332
Coulags
Balnacra
Loch Dughaill
Achnashellach Forest
West Monar Forest
East Monar Forest

Applecross
Bealach na Ba
Camusteel
amusterrach
rd-Dhubh
Culduie
Meall Gorm 2328
Tornapress
Rassal Ashwood
Allt nan Carnan
Strathcarron
Kirkton
New Kelso
Achintee
Carn Geuradainn 1950
Loch an Laoigh
Lurg Mhòr 3234
An Gead Loch
Meallan Buidhe

Toscaig
Ardarroch
Sanachan
Lochcarron
Attadale
Attadale Forest
Loch Calavie
An Cruachan 2312
Beinn Dronaig
An Riabhachan 3508
Sgurr na Lapaich 3775

Loch Kishorn
Achintraid
15
Loch Carron
Strome Castle
Kishorn Island
Stromemore
Archarff
Carn nan Iomairean 1590
Loch an lasaich
Ling
Loch Cròisbhe
Killilan Forest
Aonach Buidhe 2949

Ardaneaskan
Stromeferry
Plockton
PLOCKTON
Achmore
Craig Highland Farm
A890
Sallachy
Allt-nan-Sùgh
Killilan
Sguman Còinntich 2883
Camas Luinie
Loch Monar

Port-an-eorna
Port Càm
Black Islands
Duirinish
Drumbuie
Erbusaig
Badicaul
Duirinish Lodge
Balmacara Square
7
Auchtertyre
Conchra
Camas Lunie
Glen Elchaig
Glen Cannich
Toll Creagach 3475
Tom a' Chòinich 3646

Kyle of Lochalsh
Toll
Kyleakin
Caisteal Maol
Balmacara
Kirkton
Nostie
Dornie
Ardelve
Eilean Donan Castle
Keppoch
Bundalloch
Carnach
Loch na Leitreach
Abhainn Sìthidh
Carn Elge 3880
Gleann-nam-Fiadh
Màm Sodhail 3862
Sgurr na Lapaich 3401

5
Drochaid Lusa
lamus
Glen Arroch
Sgurr na Coinnich 2424
Kylerhea (seasonal)
Loch Alsh
Glas Eilean
Totaig
Letterfearn
Loch Duich
Inverinate
Sgurr an Airgid 2759
Visitor Centre
Dorusduain
Morvich
A' Ghlas-Bheinn 3006
Falls of Glomach
Sgurr nan Ceathreamhnan 3771
Loch Affric
Glen Affric
Affric
Allt Garbh

Ben Aslak 1839 1984
Bernera
Galltair
Glenelg
Bernera Barracks
Eilanreach
Dùn Troddan
Dun Telve
Ratagan
Shiel Bridge
Invershiel
Ault a' Chruinn
Carn-Gorm
Kintail Forest
BEINN FHADA 3385
Ciste Dhubh 3218
Mullach Fraoch-Choire 3614
Aonach Shasuinn 2901

17
Beinn na Seamraig
Sandaig
Beinn a' Chapuill 2421
Beinn a' Chaoinich 1340
Sgurr Mhic Bharraich 2553
Torrlaoighseach
Sgurr Fhuaran 3505
FIVE SISTERS
A' Chràlaig 3673
Sgurr nan Conbhairean 3634
Ceannacroc Forest

Camus Croise
Sandaig Islands
Màm an Staing
Beinn Sgritheall 3194
Beinn nan Caorach 2536
The Saddle 3319
Sgurr na-Sgine 3098
A87
Glenshiel 1719
34
Glen Shiel
Loch Cluanie
Invermoriston 16
A87

Rubha Buidhe
Eilean Rarsaidh
Rubha Ruadh
Arnisdale
Glen Arnisdale
Corran
Buidhe Bheinn 2884
Sgurr na-Sgine
Cluanie Forest
Aonach Air Chrith 3342
Maol Chinn-Dearg
Bunloinn Forest
Beinn Loinne

Inverguseran
Beinn na Caillich 2573
Druim Fada 2327
Kinloch Hourn
Sgurr a' Mhaoraich 3365
Gleouraich 3394
Loch Quoich
Loch Loyne

Airor
Loch Hourn
Barrisdale Bay

217
A87
Invergarry 14

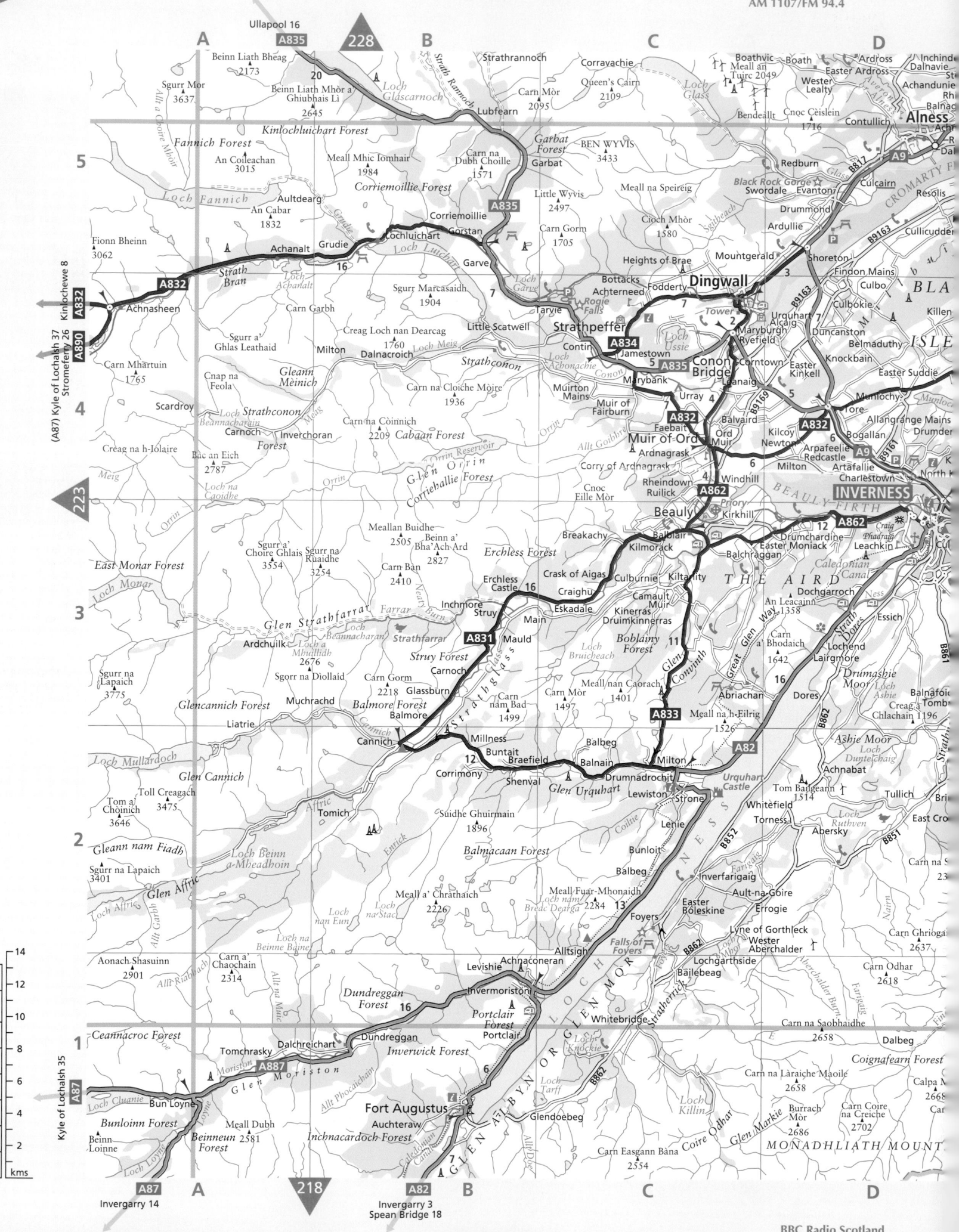

Moray Firth Radio
AM 1107/FM 94.4

Ullapool 16

228

A835

20

Beinn Liath Bheag
2173

Strathrannoch

Corravachie

Boathvic
Meall an
Tuirc 2049

Boath

Ardross
Inchindel
Dalnavie

Easter Ardross

Wester
Lealty

Achandunie
Cnoc
Balnao

Contullich

Alness

Sgurr Mor
3637

Beinn Liath Mhòr a
Ghiubhais Lì
2645

Loch
Glascarnoch

Strath Rannoch

Carn Mòr
2095

Queen's Cairn
2109

Loch
Glass

Bendeallt

Cnoc Ceislein

1716

Redburn

B817

A9

Culcairn

Resolis

Fannich Forest

Kinlochluichart Forest

Lubfearn

Carn na
Dubh Choille
1571

Garbat
Forest

BEN WYVIS
3433

Garbat

Meall na Speireig

Black Rock Gorge
Swordale

Evanton

Findon Mains

Culbo

5

An Coileachan
3015

Meall Mhic Iomhair
1984

Little Wyvis
2497

Drummond

Ardullie

Mountgerald

Shoreton

3

B9163

Culcudden

An Cabar
1832

Corriemoillie

Corriemoillie Forest

Aultdearg

Gorstan

Carn Gorm
1705

Cìoch Mhòr
1580

Heights of Brae

Dingwall

Urquhart
Alcaig

7

Culbokie

ISLE

BLA

Loch Fannich

Fionn Bheinn
3062

Loch
Luichart

A835

Garve

Bottacks
Achterneed

Foddertы

i

Tower

2

Maryburgh
Ryefield

Belmaduthy

Knockbain

Easter Suddie

A832

Achanalt

Grudie

Lochluichart

Garbat

Loch Garve

Tarvie

Rogie
Falls

Strathpeffer

Contin

A834

Jamestown

Conon
Bridge

Corntown

Easter
Kinkell

Duncanston

Strath
Bran

Achnasheen

Loch
Achanalt

16

Sgurr Marcasaidh
1904

7

Loch
Achonachie

Marybank

A835

Leanaig

Kilcoy

(A87) Kyle of Lochalsh 37
Stromeferry 26
Kinlochewe 8

A890

A832

Carn Garbh

Creag Loch nan Dearcag
1760

Little Scatwell

Strathconon

Contin

Loch
Ussie

5

Muirton
Mains

Urray

4

Marybank

B9169

Tore

Newton

Munlochy

Allangrange Mains

Drumder

Carn Mhartuin
1765

Sgurr a'
Ghlas Leathaid

Milton

Dalnacroich

Loch Meig

Gleann
Mèinich

Carn na Cloiche Mòire
1936

Muir of
Fairburn

7

A832

Balvaird
Ord
Muir

Faebait

Kilcoy

A832

Bogallan

A9

4

Scardroy

Carnoch

Inverchoran

Loch Strathconon

Meig

Carn na Còinnich
2209

Cabaan Forest

Ardnagrask

Muir of Ord

6

Milton

Redcastle

Arpafeelie

Artafallie
Charlestown

Beannacharan

Forest

Bùc an Eich
2787

Corry of Ardnagrask

Windhill

A862

North

223

Creag na h-Iolaire

Orrin Reservoir

Glen Orrin

Cnoc
Eille Mòr

Rheindown
Ruilick

Priory

Beauly

Kirkhill

INVERNESS

Loch na
Caoidhe

Orrin

Corriehallie Forest

BEAULY FIRTH

East Monar Forest

Meallan Buidhe
2505

Beinn a'
Bha'Ach Ard
2827

Erchless Forest

Breakachy

Balblair

Kilmorack

Drumchardine

Easter Moniack
Balchraggan

12

A862

Craig
Phadrig

Leachkin

Cu

Loch Monar

Sgurr a'
Choire Ghlais
3554

Sgurr na
Ruaidhe
3254

Carn Bàn
2410

Erchless
Castle

16

Craighù

Crask of Aigas

Culburnie

Camault
Muir

Kiltarlity

THE AIRD

An Leacainn
1358

Essich

Sgurr na
Lapaich
3775

Glen Strathfarrar

Farrar

Neaty Burn

Inchmore

Struy

Main

Eskadale

Kinerras
Druimkinnerras

Dochgarroch

Carn
Bhodaich
1642

Lairgmore

Drumashie
Moor

Loch
Ashie

3

Ardchuilk

Loch a
Mhuillidh

Loch
Beannacharan

Strathfarrar

Mauld

A831

Struy Forest

Carnoch

Boblainy
Forest

11

Glen
Convinth

Abriachan

16

Dores

Balnafoich

Creag a'
Tomb
Chlachain 1196

Sgurr na
Lapaich
3401

Glencannich Forest

Muchrachd

Càrn Gorm
2218

Glassburn

Balmore Forest

Carn
nam Bad
1499

Carn Mòr
1497

Meall nan Caorach
1401

A833

Meall na h-Eilrig
1526

Liatrie

Balmore

Cannich

Millness

Buntait

Balbeg

Balnain

Milton

A82

Urquhart
Castle

Tom Bailgeann
1514

Whitefield

Ashie Moor

Loch
Duntelchaig

Achnabat

Tullich

Bri

Loch Mullardoch

Glen Cannich

12

Braefield

Corrimony

Shenval

Glen Urquhart

Drumnadrochit

Lewiston

Strone

Torness

Abersky

East Cro

Toll Creagach
3475

Tom a'
Choinich
3646

Tomich

Suidhe Ghuirmain
1896

Balmacaan Forest

Lenie

Bunloit

B852

Carn na S

B851

2

Gleann nam Fiadh

Sgurr na Lapaich
3401

Loch Beinn
a-Mheadhoin

Glen Affric

Allt Garbh

Entrick

Meall a' Chrathaich
2226

Loch
nan Eun

Loch
na Stac

Meall Fuar-Mhonaidh
2284

Carn nam
Breac Dearga

13

Balbeg

Inverfarigaig

Fariga...

Ault-na-Goire

Errogie

Carn Ghrioga
2637

Carn na S

Aonach Shasuinn
2901

Carn a'
Chaochain
2314

Loch na
Beinne Bàine

Alltsigh

Achnaconeran

Levishie

Falls of
Foyers

Foyers

Easter
Boleskine

Lyne of Gorthleck
Wester
Aberchalder

B862

Lochgarthside

Bailebeg

Carn Odhar
2618

Dundreggan
Forest

16

Invermoriston

Portclair
Forest

Portclair

Whitebridge

Straherrick

Carn na Saobhaidhe

E

Ceannacroc Forest

Tomchrasky

Dalchreichart

Dundreggan

A887

Inverwick Forest

6

GLEN ALBYN OR GLEN MOR

Loch
Knockie

B862

Carn na Làraiche Maoile
2658

Carn na
Odhar

Dalbeg

Coignafearn Forest

1

Kyle of Lochalsh 35

A87

Loch Cluanie

Bun Loyne

Glen Moriston

Loch
Tarff

Fort Augustus

Auchteraw

Coire Odhar

Carn Easgann Bàna
2554

Loch Killin

MONADHLIATH MOUNT

Bunloinn Forest

Beinn
Loinne

Meall Dubh

Beinneun 2581
Forest

Inchnacardoch Forest

Caledonian Canal

Glendoebeg

Allt Dee

7

Carn Coire
na Creiche
2702

Carn Coire
Mòr
2686

Calpa M

2668

A87

218

A82

Invergarry 14

Invergarry 3
Spean Bridge 18

see p484 for a touring guide to this map

TOWN PLANS
Elgin p329
Inverness p342

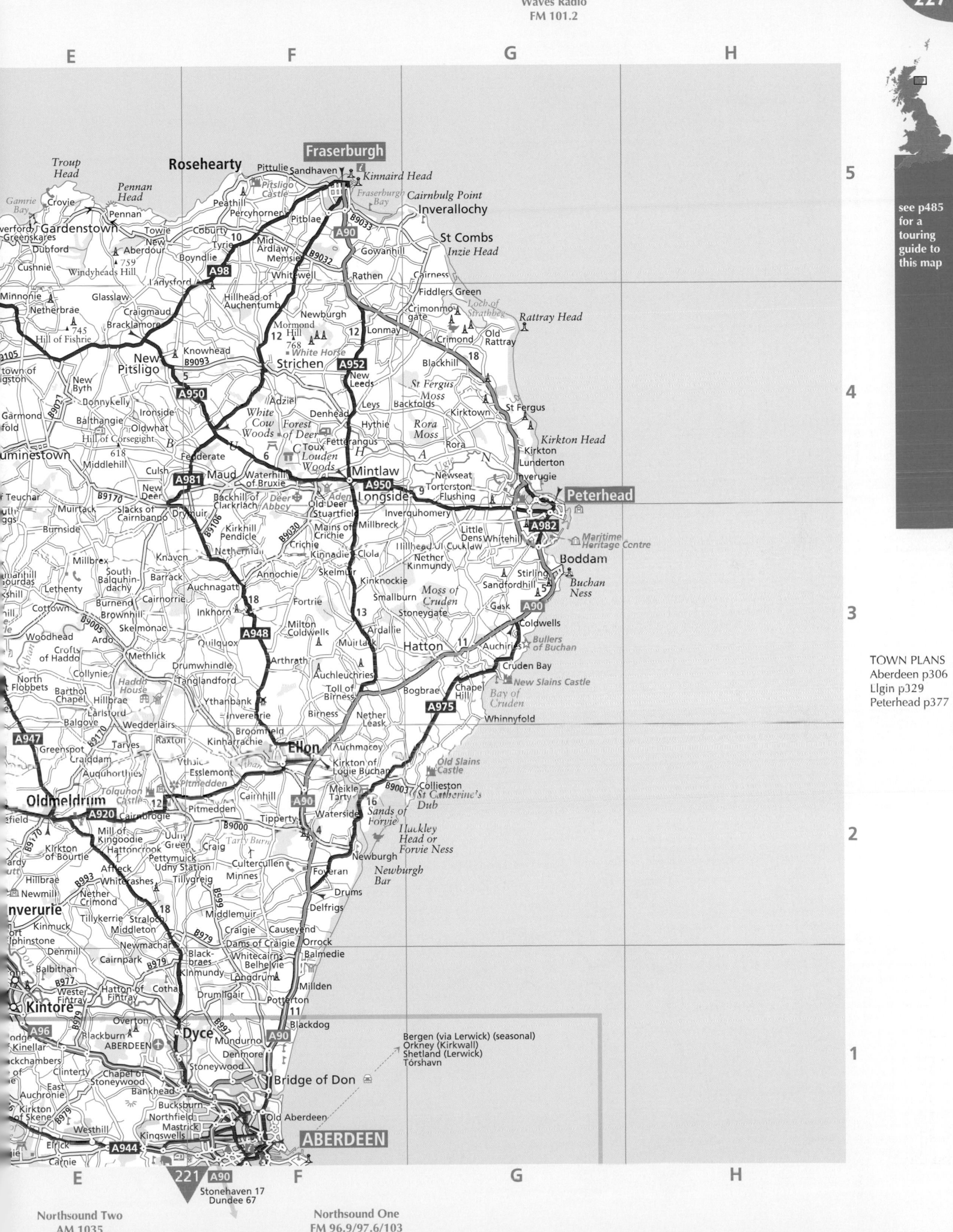

see p485
for a
touring
guide to
this map

TOWN PLANS
Aberdeen p306
Llgin p329
Peterhead p377

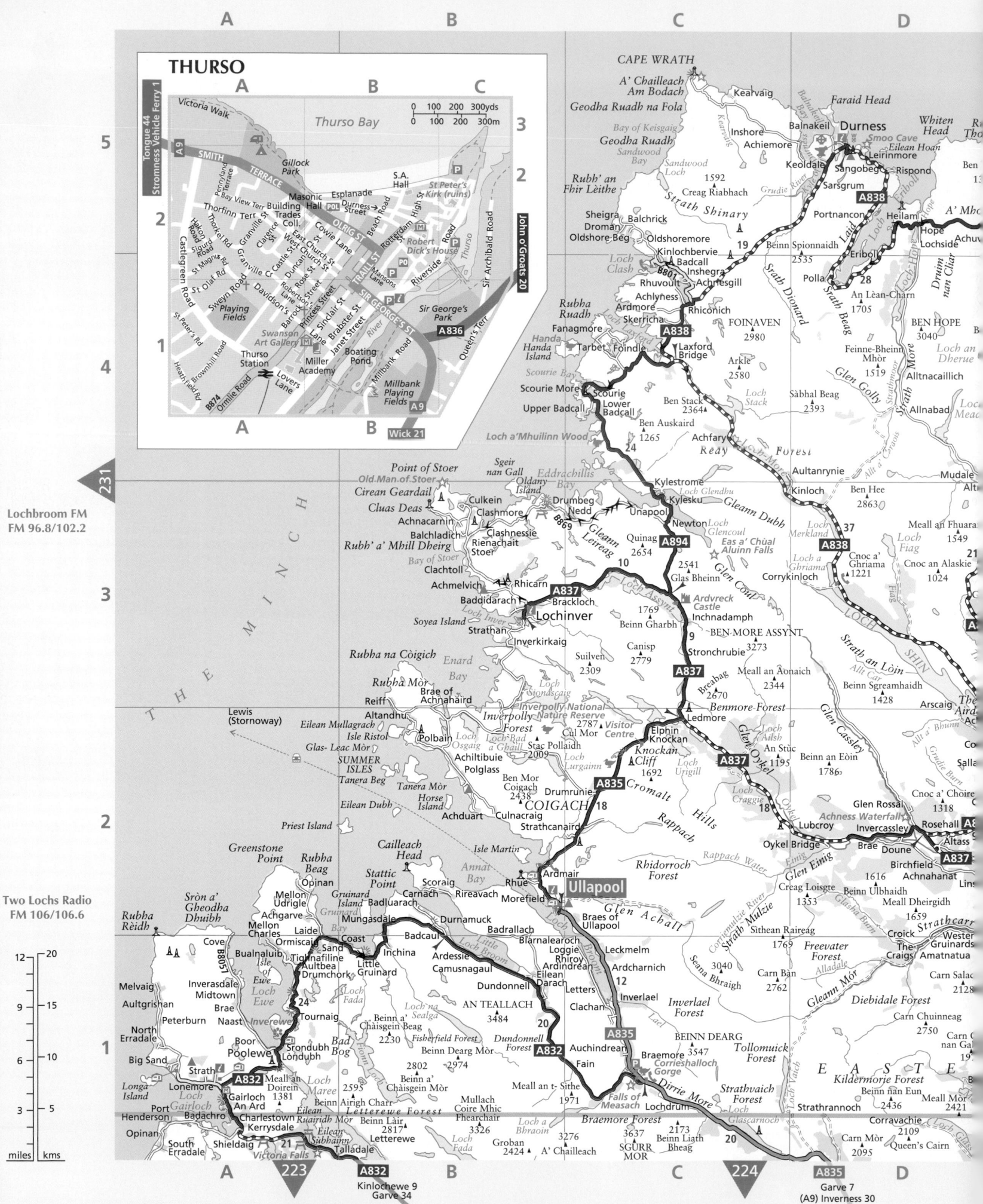

231

Lochbroom FM
FM 96.8/102.2

Two Lochs Radio
FM 106/106.6

THURSO

Thurso Bay

Tongue 44
Stromness Vehicle Ferry 1

John o'Groats 20

A836

Victoria Walk

SMITH TERRACE

Gillock Park
Pennyland Terrace
Bay View Terr
Thorfinn Terr
Hakoin Road
Thorkel Rd
Sigurd Road
St Magnus Rd
Granville Cr
Clarence St
East Church St
West Church St
Castle St
Duncan St
Robertson St
Rose St
Davidson's Lane
Barrock St
Princes Street
Sinclair St
Janet Street
Brabster St
Swanson Art Gallery
Castlegreen Road
St Olaf Rd
Sweyn Road
St Peter's Rd
Heathfield Rd
Brownhill Road
Ormlie Road

Masonic Hall
Building Hall
Trades Coll.
Cowie Lane
Esplanade
Beach Road
OLRIG ST
Durness Street
Rotterdam Street
TRAILL ST
SIR GEORGE'S ST
High St
Riverside Road
Sir Archibald Road
Queen's Terr

S.A. Hall
St Peter's Kirk (ruins)
Duncan St
POL
PO
Mansons Lane
Robert Dick's House
Sir George's Park
Miller Academy
Thurso Station
Lovers Lane
Boating Pond
Millbank Road
Millbank Playing Fields
Playing Fields
River Thurso

B874
B9

0 100 200 300yds
0 100 200 300m

Wick 21
A9

CAPE WRATH

A' Chailleach
Am Bodach
Geodha Ruadh na Fola
Bay of Keisgaig
Geodha Ruadh
Sandwood Bay
Sandwood Loch
Rubh' an Fhir Lèithe
Sheigra
Droman
Oldshoremore
Oldshore Beg
Kinlochbervie
Badcall
Rhuvoult
Ardmore
Skerricha
Rubha Ruadh
Fanagmore
Handa Island
Handa Tarbet
Foindle
Scourie Bay
Scourie More
Scourie
Lower Badcall
Upper Badcall
Loch a'Mhuilinn Wood

Kearvaig
Inshore
Achiemore
Balnakeil
Keoldale
Sangobeg
Leirinmore
Sangomore
Rispond
Portnancon
Heilam
Hope
Lochside
Eriboll
Polla
An Lèan-Charn 1705
28

Creag Riabhach 1592
Strath Shinary
Beinn Spionnaidh 2535
19
Strath Dionard
Loch Laxford
B801
Inshegra
Achresgill
Achlyness
Rhiconich
A838
Laxford Bridge
FOINAVEN 2980
BEN HOPE 3040
Arkle 2580
Feinne-Bheinn Mhòr 1519
Sàbhal Beag 2393
Ben Stack 2364
Ben Auskaird 1265
24
Reay Forest
Achfary

Faraid Head
Durness
Smoo Cave
Eilean Hoan
Whiten Head
A' Mho
Druim nan Cliar
Alltnacaillich
Loch an Dherue
Strathmore

Point of Stoer
Old-Man-of-Stoer
Cirean Geardail
Cluas Deas
Achnacarnin
Balchladich
Rubh' a' Mhill Dheirg
Bay of Stoer
Clachtoll
Achmelvich
Baddidarach
Soyea Island
Rubha na Còigich
Rubha Mòr
Reiff
Brae of Achnahaird
Eddrachillis Bay
Oldany Island
Culkein
Clashmore
Drumbeg
Nedd
Clashnessie
Rienachait Stoer
Rhicarn
Bracloch
Lochinver
Strathan
Inverkirkaig
Kylestrome
Kylesku
Unapool
Newton
A894
Quinag 2654
Glen Dubh
Gleann Leireag
10
Loch Glendhu
B869
Eas a' Chùal Aluinn Falls
2541
Glas Bheinn
Ardvreck Castle
Inchnadamph
A837
1769
Beinn Gharbh
Loch Assynt
Glen Coul
Kinloch
Ben Hee 2863
A838
37
Cnoc a' Ghriama 1221
Corrykinloch
BEN-MORE ASSYNT 3273
Meall an Fhuarain 1549
Loch Fiag
Cnoc an Alaskie 1024

Kylestrome
Stronchrubie
Suilven 2309
Canisp 2779
9
Breabag 2670
Meall an Aonaich 2344
Beinn Sgreamhaidh 1428
Strath an Lòin
Arscaig
The Aird

Lewis (Stornoway)
Altandhu
Eilean Mullagrach
Isle Ristol
Glas-Leac Mòr
SUMMER ISLES
Tanera Beg
Horse Island
Tanera Mòr
Eilean Dubh
Priest Island
Greenstone Point
Rubha Beag
Opinan
Stattic Point
Cailleach Head
Polbain
Achiltibuie
Polglass
Ben Mor Coigach 2438
Achduart
Culnacraig
Strathcanaird
Inverpolly National Nature Reserve
Inverpolly Forest
2787
Cùl Mòr
Stac Pollaidh 2009
Cùl Beag 2523
Knockan
Elphin
Ledmore
A837
Knockan Cliff 1692
Loch Urigill
An Stùc 1195
Benmore Forest
Glen Cassley
Beinn an Eòin 1786
Loch Craggie
Glen Oykel
A837
Glen Rossal 1318
Cnoc a' Choire
Achness Waterfall
Lubcroy
Oykel Bridge
Brae Doune
Rosehall
Invercassley
A837
Birchfield
Achnahanat
1616
Altass
A8

Rubha Rèidh
Sròn a' Gheodha Dhuibh
Mellon Udrigle
Achgarve
Mellon Charles
Ormiscaig
Bualnaluib
Tighnafiline
Aultbea
Laide
Sand
Drumchork
Cove
B8051
Isle of Ewe
Inverasdale
Midtown
Brae
Naast
Inverewe
Melvaig
Aultgrishan
Peterburn
North Erradale
Boor
Poolewe
Big Sand
Strath
Longa Island
Lonemore
Port Henderson
Badachro
Opinan
South Erradale
Shieldaig
Gairloch
An Ard
Charlestown
Kerrysdale
Victoria Falls
Eilean Ruairidh Mòr
Eilean Subhainn
Talladale
Gruinard Island
Gruinard Bay
Laide
Little Gruinard
Inchina
Badcaul
Ardessie
Camusnagaul
Dundonnell
Mungasdale
Durnamuck
Badralloch
Blarnalearoch
Loggie
Rhiroy
Ardindrean
Eilean Darach
Letters
Clachan
Inverlael
AN TEALLACH 3484
Dundonnell Forest
Loch na Sealga
Fisherfield Forest
Beinn a' Chaisgein Beag 2230
Beinn Dearg Mòr 2974
Letterewe Forest
Beinn a' Chaisgein Mòr 2817
Beinn Lair 2817
Letterewe
Loch Maree
Meall an Doirein 1381
Beinn Airigh Charr 2595
Mullach Coire Mhic Fhearchair 3326
Loch a Bhraoin
Groban 2424
A' Chailleach 3276
SGURR MOR
Bad Bog
Loch Fada
Sròndubh
Lòndubh
Bad Bog
2802
Isle Martin
Ardmair
Rhue
Morefield
Ullapool
Braes of Ullapool
Rhidorroch Forest
Rappach Hills
Glen Achall
Loch Broom
Leckmelm
Ardcharnich
Loggie
12
BEINN DEARG 3547
Braemore
Corrieshalloch Gorge
Auchindrean
Fain
A832
20
Falls of Measach
Dirrie More
Lochdrum
A835
24
Rireavach
Carnach
Annat Bay
Corrieulzie River
Strath Mulzie
Sithean Raireag
Seana Bhraigh 3040
Carn Bàn 2762
Freevater Forest
Croick
The Craigs
Amatnatua
1769
Creag Loisgte 1353
Beinn Ulbhaidh 1659
Meall Dheirgidh
Strathcarr
Croic
Western Gruinards
1616
Linsi
Glasha Burn
Gleann Mòr
Diebidale Forest
Carn Chuinneag 2750
Carn nan Gad
Carn Salach 2128
Carn Mòr 19
EASTE
Kildermorie Forest
Tollomuick Forest
Strathvaich Forest
Inverlael Forest
Braemore Forest
Beinn Liath Bheag 2173
Beinn nan Eun 2436
Strathrannoch
Corravachie
Carn Mòr 2109
Queen's Cairn
Loch Glass
20
2095

A832
223
Kinlochewe 9
Garve 34

A832

224
A835
Garve 7
(A9) Inverness 30

miles / kms
12 — 20
9 — 15
6 — 10
3 — 5

ATLANTIC OCEAN

232

Orkney
(Stromness)

Dunnet Head
Island of Stroma
Netherton
St Margaret's
Hope
Uppertown
DUNCANSBY
HEAD

see p486
for a
touring
guide to
this map

Brims
Ness
Spear
Head
Holborn
Head
Castle
of Mey
Mell
Head
Scarfskerry
Brough
Rattar
Huna
John
o' Groats
Stacks of
Duncansby

Dounreay
Exhibition
Centre
Crosskirk
Scrabster
Thurso
Hunspow
Ham
Mey
Gills
Warse
Canisbay
Skirza
Ness Head

A836
Bridge
of Forss
St Peter
Dunnet
Bay
Clardon
Murkle
Inkstack
Greenland
Lochend
Brabster
Freswick
A99
Auckengill

Red
Point
Buldoo
Fresgoe
Achreamie
Glengolly
Newlands
of Geise
Westfield
Weydale
Castletown
Tain
Reaster
Slickly
Alterwall

Strathy Point
Totegan
Brawl
Portskerra
Melvich
Bighouse
Isauld
Achvarasdal
Shebster
Geise
Buckies
Durran
Stemster
Bower-
madden
Hastigrow
Howe
Sortat
Nybster

Farr
Point
Aultiphurst
Armadale
Baligill
Strathy
Golval
Drum
Hollistan
608
Loch
Calder
Broubster
Shurrery
Calder
Mains
Sordale
Knockdee
Clayock
North
Watten
Kirk
Killimster
Brough Head
Noss
Head

Skerray
Torrisdale
Bettyhill
Achina
Invernaver
Leckfurin
Lednagullin
Wordly
Farr
28
Strathy
Forest
Beinn Ruadh
834
Achiemore
Craigtown
Dalhalvaig
Trantlemore
Brawlbin
Harpsdale
Olgrinmore
A9
Spittal
Watten
Bilbster
Winless
Ackergill
Castle
Sinclair
Castle Girnigoe
Caithness Glass
Staxigoe
Heritage Centre

Tongue
A836
Borgie
Forest
Skelpick
Achargary
Upper Bighouse
751
Beinn nam Bò
Cnoc Badaireach
na Gaoithe
698
797
Cnoc an
Fhuarain Bhàin
Loch na
Seilge
Loch
Shurrery
Dorrery
A882
Westerdale
B870
Backlass
Mybster
15
WICK
Milton
Newton
Wick
Whiterow

Loch
Craggie
Beinn
Stumanadh
1728
Rhifail
Rough
Haugh
Skail
B871
21
Cnoc Preas a' Mhadaidh
665
Quarry
17
Badlipster
Tannach
Grey Cairns
of Camster
Thrumster

Loch
Loyal
Syre
Sletill Hill
918
Forsinard
Loch
More
Loch
Ruard
Achavanich
Cnoc an
Earrannaiche
Upper
Camster
Hill o'
Many Stones
A99
Sarclet

Pole Hill
965
Loch Druim
a Chliabhain
Forsinard
A897
Ben Alisky
1144
Loch
Thulachan
Rumster
Forest
692
Roster
Ulbster
Whaligoe
Bruan
Halberry Head

Loch
Truderscaig
Ben Griam
Mòr
1936
Loch an
Ruathair
Knockfin
Heights
Lochside
1437
Achentoul
Glutt
Crofts of Benacheilt
Lybster
Swiney
Clyth

Loch
Rimsdale
Cnoc an
Liath-Bhaid Mhòir
1423
Kinbrace
Morven
2313
Cnoc an Eireannaich
1699
Meall na Caorach
Dunbeath Water
Smerral
Badnagie
Forse
Latheron
Latheronwheel
Laidhay Croft
Museum

Loch
Choire
1907
Meall a' Bhata
Borrobol Forest
1194
Altanduin
Creag Scalabsdale
1819
Wag
Langwell Forest
Braemore
Balnabruich
Knockally
Inver
Dunbeath
Heritage Centre

Ben Armine Forest
2338
Creag Mhòr
Cnoc na
Breun-Choille
Cnoc na Maoile
1315
Scaraben
2055
Ramscraigs
Borgue
Newport
Berriedale
20

Srath na Seilge
Black Water
Meall a' Phiobaire
1230
Cnoc Meadhonach
1134
17
Craggie
Torrish
Kilphedir
Strath of Kildonan or Strath Ullie
Ousdale
Ord Point
A9

NORTH SEA

Sidhean
nan Eun
1040
Achnaluachrath
961
Cnoc Leathnachd
Balnacoil
Glen Sletdale
Gartymore
Helmsdale
East Helmsdale
West
Helmsdale
Timespan
Visitor Centre

West
Langwell
East
Langwell
Muie
14
Dalreavoch
Rhilochan
Ben Horn
1706
Gordonbush
Clynelish
Distillery
20
Lothbeg
A9
Portgower
Culgower
Lothmore
Sron Rubha na Gaoithe
Lothbeg
Point

Ardachu
Morvich
Rogart
Farlary
West Clyne
Clynelish
Dalchalm
Achrimsdale

Pittentrail
Duke of
Sutherland
Monument
Rackies
Doll
Brora

Ardchlas
Creagan
Glas
1028
Little
Torboll
A839
Culmaily
Kirkton
Golspie
Dunrobin Castle

Bonar
Bridge
Spinningdale
A949
9
Whiteface
Little
Creich
Clashmore
Lonemore
A836
Ardshave
Badninish
Rearquhar
Astle
Proncy
Evelix
Poles
Embo
Littleferry
Skelbo
Fourpenny
Pitgrudy
Dornoch

Easter
Fearn
13
A836
Edderton
Balleigh
Tarlogie
Quarryhill
Morangie
Ardmore
A9
Dornoch
Firth
Tain
Morangie
Forest
Balcherry
Inver
Arboll
Tarrel
Tarbat
Ness
Wilkhaven
Whiteness
Sands
Portmahomack
Rockfield

B9176
Tolbooth
Aldie
24
Rhynie
Logie
Hill
Lamington
Scotsburn
Newfield
Hill of Fearn
Kildary
Arabella
Fearn
Abbey
Hilton of Cadboll
Balintore
Shandwick
Lochslin

Easter
Ardross
Dalnavie
Achandunie
Balnaguisich
Rhicullen
Kilmuir
Tomich
Delny
Milton
Kilmuir
Chapelhill
Pitcalnie
Port an Righ
Nigg
Nigg
Bay

Covesea
Skerries
Halliman Skerries
Covesea
Lossiemouth

WICK (town plan)

A John o'Groats 17 B

A99
Green Rd
Government
Building
HIGH STREET
Louisburgh St
St Fergus Rd
Willowbank
Whitehouse Park
High St
Bay View
The Shore

Wick
Station
High Street
Town Hall
River
BRIDGE ST
Wick
Burn St
Telford St
Concert
Hall
Heritage
Centre

Thurso 21
A882
Hospital
River St
Union St
Sinclair Terr
Bank Row
Fish
Market
B9159

Newton Road
Newton
Ave
THURSO ST
A99
Dempster St

A9 Helmsdale 37
Inverness 108

A F B

0 200yds
0 200m

Inverness 23
Avlemore 54

217　218

Inverness 43

see p487 for a touring guide to this map

Oban FM
FM 103.3

TOWN PLANS
Ardrossan p198
Ayr p307
Fort William
p334
Oban p372

Argyll FM
FM 106.5/107.1/
107.7

THE SEA OF
THE HEBRIDES

I N N E R　H E B R I D E S

RÙM
EIGG
Sound of Rùm
MUCK
COLL
TIREE
COLONSAY
ISLAND OF MULL
IONA
ROSS OF MULL
JURA
Paps of Jura
ISLAY
KINTYRE
ISLE OF ARRAN
Goat Fell
2868

Harris
Askival 2663
Cleadale
Galmisdale
Port Mòr

Mallaig
Beoraidbeg
Portnaluchaig
Arisaig
Druimindarroch
SOUTH MORAR
LOCH MORAR
Glenfinnan
MOIDART
Eilean Shona
Ardtoe
Shielfoot
Kentra
Salen
SUNART
Anaheilt
Strontian
Scotstown
ARDGOUR
Corpach
Fort William
BEN NEVIS 4406
Corran
Kinlochleven
Ballachulish
Duror

Tobermory
Drimnin
MORVERN
Lochuisge
Acharn
Ardtornish
Fiunary
Claggan
Salen
BEN MORE 3171
Gruline
Ulva
Derryguaig
Balnahard
Ardmeanach
Pennycross
Baile Mòr
Fionnphort
Bunessan
Uisken

Torosay Castle
Duart Castle
Lochdon
Croggan
Lochbuie
Grass Point
KERRERA
LISMORE
Dunstaffnage Castle
Appin
Port Ramsay
Portnacroish

Oban
Connel
Taynuilt
BEN CRUACHAN 3695
Dalmally
Crianlarich
Tyndrum
BEN LUI
LORN
ARGYLL
BEN STARAV 3285
Bridge of Orchy
Black Mount

Kilninver
Melfort
Kilmelford
Arduaine
Ford
Ardfern
Inveraray
BEN VORLICH 3088
Cairndow
BEINN IME 3319
Arrochar
Lochgoilhead
Garelochhead
Crinan
Crarae Glen
Minard
Lochgilphead
Ardrishaig
Tarbert
Kilfinan
Otter Ferry
Dunoon
ISLE OF BUTE
Rothesay
GREENOCK
PORT GLASKOW
Skelmorlie
Largs
Millport
GREAT CUMBRAE

Tayvallich
Keillmore
Lagg
Craighouse
Jura Forest
Jura House
Feolin Ferry
Bunnahabhain
Port Askaig
Ballygrant
Bridgend
Bowmore
Bruichladdich
Port Charlotte
Portnahaven
Orsay
Port Wemyss
ISLAY
Laphroaig
Lagavulin
Ardbeg
Port Ellen
Mull of Oa
Lower Killeyan

GIGHA ISLAND
Achamore Gardens
Tarbert
West Loch Tarbert
Skipness
Claonaig
Clachan
Crossaig
Carradale
Saddell
Ugadale
Kilchenzie
CAMPBELTOWN
Machrihanish
Southend
Mull of Kintyre

Lochranza
Pirnmill
Imachar
High Dougarie
Auchagallon
Blackwaterfoot
Bennecarrigan
Sliddery
Kilmory
ISLE OF ARRAN
Sannox
Corrie
Brodick
Lamlash
Holy Island
Whiting Bay
Dippen

Ardrossan
Saltcoats
Irvine
Troon
Prestwick
AYR
KILMARNOCK
Stevenston
West Kilbride
Dalry
Maybole
Kirkoswald
Maidens
Dunure
Heads of Ayr
Lady Isle

RATHLIN ISLAND
Giant's Causeway
Benbane Head
Portballintrae
NORTH CHANNEL
Belfast
Larne

Stranraer 41

miles / kms

192

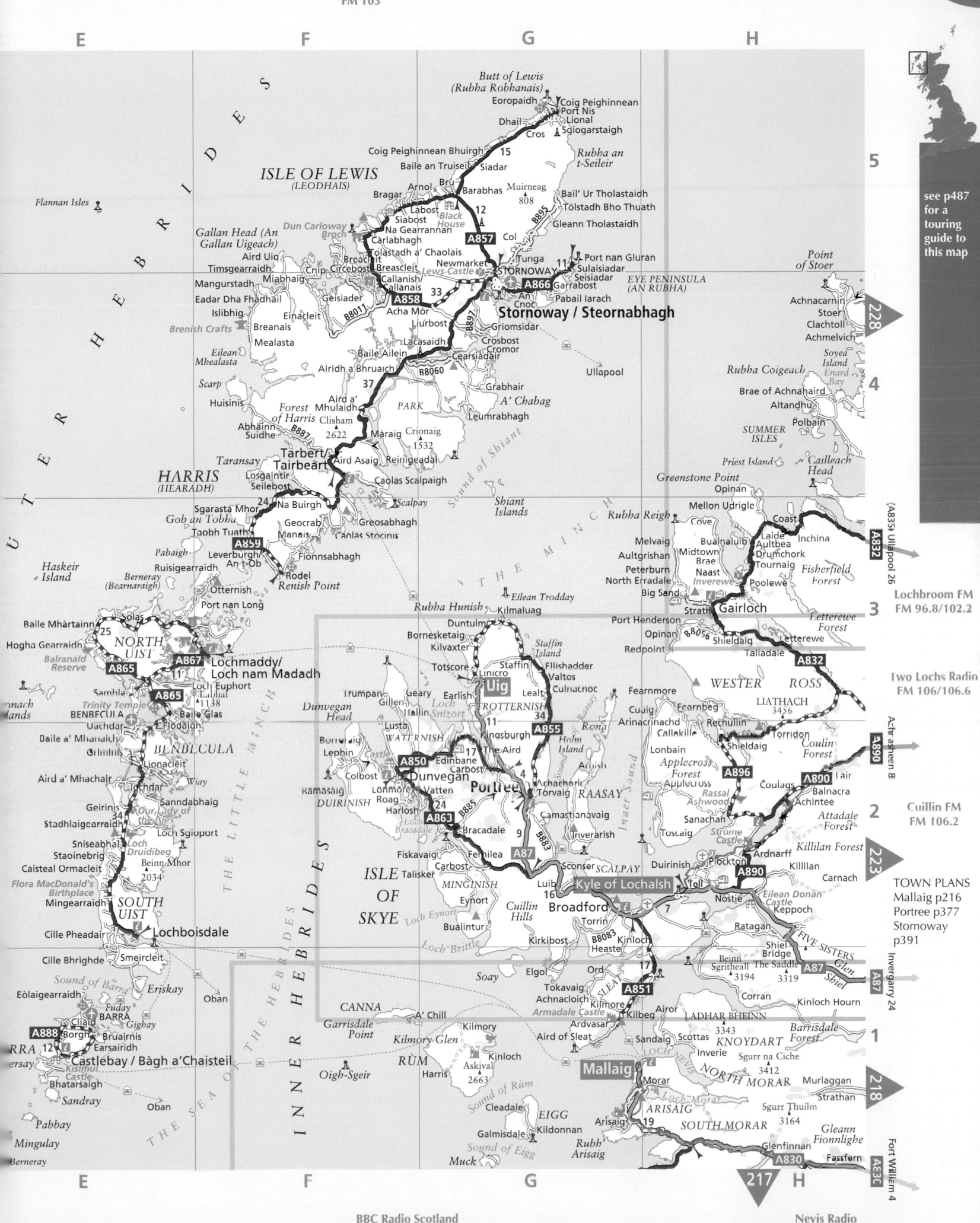

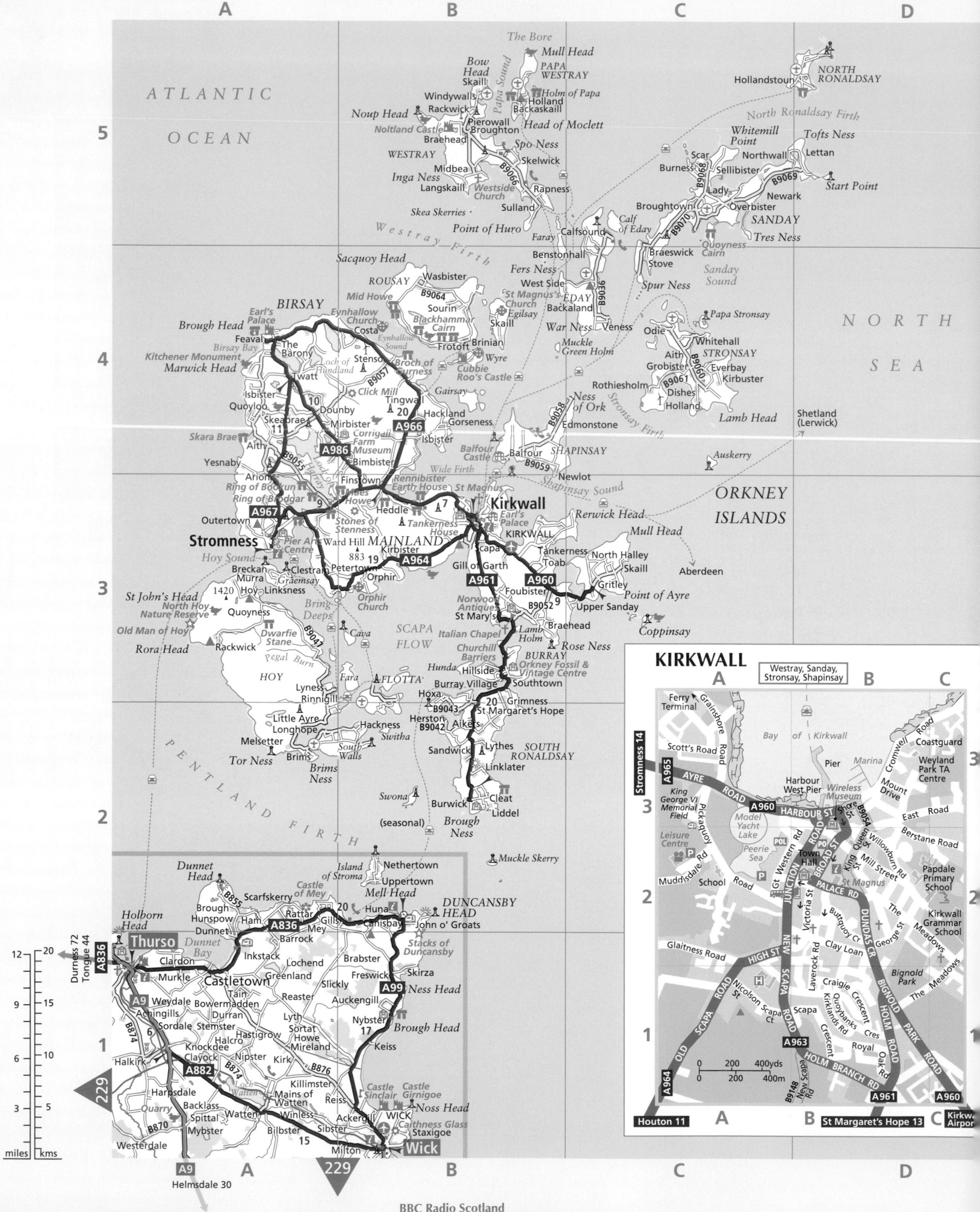

ATLANTIC
OCEAN

The Bore
Bow Head
Skaill
Mull Head
PAPA WESTRAY
Windywalls
Holm of Papa
Holland
Noup Head
Rackwick
Backaskaill
Noltland Castle
Pierowall
Braehead
Broughton
Head of Moclett
WESTRAY
Spo Ness
Skelwick
Hollandstoun
NORTH RONALDSAY
Midbea
Inga Ness
Rapness
Langskaill
Westside Church
Whitemill Point
Tofts Ness
Scar
Northwall
Lettan
Burness
Sellibister
Lady
Newark
Start Point

Skea Skerries
Sulland
Point of Huro
Faray
Calfsound
Calf of Eday
Broughtown
Overbister
Quoyness Cairn
SANDAY
Tres Ness

Westray Firth
Benstonhall
Stove
Braeswick
Spur Ness
Sanday Sound

Sacquoy Head
Fers Ness
ROUSAY
Wasbister
St Magnus's Church
EDAY
War Ness
Veness
Odie
Papa Stronsay
Whitehall
STRONSAY
Everbay
Kirbuster

BIRSAY
Earl's Palace
Brough Head
Feaval
Eynhallow Church
Mid Howe
Sourin
Blackhammar Cairn
Egilsay
Backaland
Muckle Green Holm
Aith
Grobister
Rothiesholm
Dishes
Holland

NORTH SEA

Kitchener Monument
Marwick Head
Birsay Bay
The Barony
Twatt
Loch of Hundland
Eynhallow Sound
Frotoft
Brinian
Wyre
Ness of Ork
Edmonstone
Lamb Head
Shetland (Lerwick)

Isbister
Quoyloo
Skara Brae
Skeabrae
Aith
Yesnaby
10
Dounby
Mirbister
Corrigall Farm Museum
Bimbister
20
A966
A986
Click Mill
Tingwall
Hackland
Gorseness
Isbister
Gairsay
Broch of Burness
Cubbie Roo's Castle
Balfour
B9058
SHAPINSAY
Auskerry

ORKNEY ISLANDS

Arion
Ring of Bookun
Ring of Brodgar
Outertown
A967
Finstown
Maes Howe
Heddle
9
Rennibister Earth House
St Magnus
7
Kirkwall
Earl's Palace
KIRKWALL
Rerwick Head
Mull Head

Stromness
Stones of Stenness
Pier Arts Centre
Ward Hill
MAINLAND
Tankerness House
883
19
Kirbister
Orphir
A964
Gill of Garth
Scapa
Tankerness
Toab
North Halley
Skaill
Gritly
Point of Ayre
Aberdeen

Hoy Sound
Breckan
Murra
Graemsay
Clestran
Linksness
Petertown
Orphir Church
A961
Foubister
B9052
9
Upper Sanday

St John's Head
North Hoy Nature Reserve
Old Man of Hoy
1420
Quoyness
Dwarfie Stane
Cava
Bring Deeps
SCAPA FLOW
Norwood Antiques
St Mary's
Italian Chapel
Lamb Holm
Braehead
Rose Ness
Coppinsay

Rora Head
Rackwick
Pegal Burn
HOY
Lyness
Rinnigill
Fara
FLOTTA
Hunda
Hillside
Churchill Barriers
Orkney Fossil & Vintage Centre
Southtown

Little Ayre
Longhope
Melsetter
Hackness
Herston
B9043
B9042
Aikers
20
Grimness
St Margaret's Hope
Burray Village
Hoxa
Swithia
Lythes
Linklater
SOUTH RONALDSAY

Tor Ness
Brims
Brims Ness
South Walls
Swona
(seasonal)
Sandwick
Burwick
Cleat
Liddel
Brough Ness

PENTLAND FIRTH

Dunnet Head
Island of Stroma
Nethertown
Uppertown
Mell Head
DUNCANSBY HEAD
Muckle Skerry

Holborn Head
Scarfskerry
Castle of Mey
Brough
Hunspow
Ham
20
Huna
Canisbay
John o' Groats
Stacks of Duncansby

Thurso
A836
Clardon
Murkle
Dunnet
A836
Mey
Gills
Barrock
Brabster
Freswick
Skirza
Ness Head

Dunnet Bay
Inkstack
Lochend
Slickly
A99

A9
Castletown
Weydale
Bowermadden
Greenland
Reaster
Auckengill
Brough Head

Durness 72
Tongue 44
Tain
Achingills
Durran
Lyth
Sortat
Howe
Nybster
17
Keiss

B874
Sordale
Stemster
Hastigrow
Mireland

Knockdee
Halcro
Kirk
B876
Castle Sinclair
Castle Girnigoe
Noss Head

Halkirk
A882
Clayock
Nipster
Loch Watten
Killimster
Mains of Watten
Reiss
WICK

Harpsdale
Backlass
Spittal
Watten
Winless
Ackergill
Caithness Glass
Staxigoe

B870
Mybster
Bilbister
15
Sibster
Milton
Wick

Westerdale

A9
Helmsdale 30
229

KIRKWALL

Westray, Sanday, Stronsay, Shapinsay

Ferry Terminal
Grainshore Road
Scott's Road
Bay of Kirkwall
Cromwell Road
Coastguard
Weyland Park TA Centre

Stromness 14
A965
AYRE ROAD
A960
HARBOUR ST
Pier
Marina
Mount Drive
East Road

King George VI Memorial Field
Pickaquoy Road
Harbour West Pier
Wireless Museum
B9054
Willowburn Rd
Berstane Road

Leisure Centre
Model Yacht Lake
Peerie Sea
POL
Town Hall
Gt Western Road
King St
Victoria St
Buttquoy Cr
St Magnus
Papdale Primary School

Muddisdale
School
Road
Glaitness Road
JUNCTION ROAD
NEW ROAD
BROAD ST
Nicolson St
PALACE RD
SCAPA ROAD
Clay Loan
Laverock Rd
DUNDAS CR
George St
Kirkwall Grammar School
The Meadows

OLD SCAPA ROAD
HIGH ST
Scapa Court
Quoybanks Cres
Kirklands Rd
Craigie Crescent
BIGNOLD PARK ROAD
Bignold Park
The Meadows

A963
A964
New Scapa Rd
B9148
New Scapa Rd
Royal
Oak Rd
HOLM BRANCH RD
A961
A960

Houton 11
St Margaret's Hope 13
Kirkwall Airport

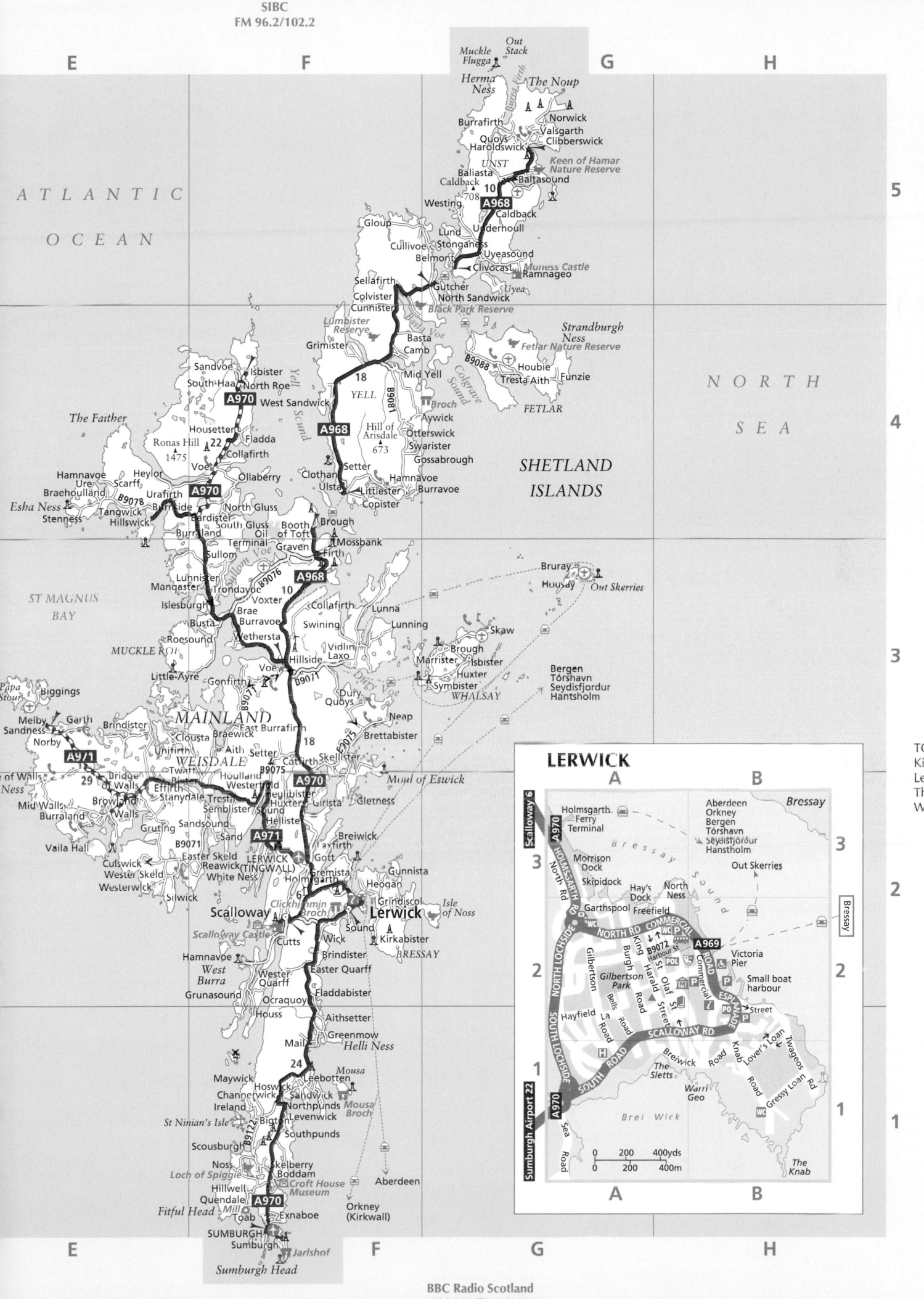

see p488 for a touring guide to this map

SIBC
FM 96.2/102.2

ATLANTIC
OCEAN

Muckle Flugga
Out Stack
Herma Ness
The Noup
Burrafirth
Norwick
Quoys Haroldswick Valsgarth Clibberswick
UNST
Keen of Hamar Nature Reserve
Baliasta
Caldback
Baltasound
Westing
708
A968
Caldback
Gloup
Lund
Underhoull
Cullivoe
Stonganess
Uyeasound
Belmont
Clivocast
Muness Castle
Sellafirth
Gutcher
Ramnageo
Colvister
North Sandwick
Cunnister
Uyea
Black Park Reserve
Lumbister Reserve
Basta Voe
Strandburgh Ness
Fetlar Nature Reserve
Grimister
Basta
B9088
Houbie
Camb
Tresta Aith
Funzie
YELL
Mid Yell
18
B9081
FETLAR
West Sandwick
The Father
Yell Sound
Housetter
Fladda
22
Hill of Arisdale
Aywick
Collafirth
673
Otterswick
Swarister
Gossabrough
Voe
Ollaberry
Hamnavoe
Heylor
Scarff
Ure
A970
Setter
Littlester
Burravoe
Hamnavoe
Braehoulland
Clothan
Ura firth
B9078
Urafirth
Ulsta
Copister
Stenness Tangwick Hillswick
Burnside
North Gluss
Esha Ness
Bardister
Brough
A970
South Gluss
Booth of Toft
Burraland
Oil
Terminal
Graven
Mossbank
Sullom
Sullom Voe
Firth
Lunnister
Manqaster
B9076
A968
ST MAGNUS BAY
Islesburgh
Trondavoe
10
Bruray
Voxter
Collafirth
Lunna
Housay
Out Skerries
Busta
Brae
Lunning
MUCKLE ROE
Roesound
Burravoe
Wetherta
Swining
Skaw
Bergen
Tórshavn
Seydisfjordur
Hantsholm
Papa Stour
Biggings
Little-Ayre
Hillside
Vidlin
Laxo
Brough
Marrister
Isbister
Huxter
WHALSAY
B9071
Gonfirth
Voe
Symbister
Melby
Sandness
Garth
MAINLAND
Clousta
Dury Quoys
Neap
Norby
Brindister
Braewick
Brettabister
B9075
of Walls
Unifirth
Setter
18
A971
29
Twatt
WEISDALE
Aith
Catfirth
Skellister
Bixter
B9075
Mou of Eswick
Bridge of Walls
Houlland
Westerfield
A970
Browland
Stanydale
Tresta
Heglibister
Huxter
Girsta
Gletness
Mid Walls
Walls
Sandsound
Semblister
Hellister
Burraland
Sand
Sandsound
Breiwick
Vaila Hall
B9071
Gott
Culswick
Easter Skeld
A971
TINGWALL
Gremista
Gunnista
Wester Skeld
Reawick
LERWICK
Heogan
Westerwick
White Ness
Holmsgarth
Grindiscol
Isle of Noss
Silwick
61
Clickhimin Broch
Lerwick
Scalloway
Cutts
Sound
Kirkabister
Scalloway Castle
Wick
BRESSAY
Hamnavoe
Brindister
West Burra
Wester Quarff
Easter Quarff
Fladdabister
Grunasound
Ocraquoy
Houss
Aithsetter
Silwick
Mail
Greenmow
Helli Ness
24
Maywick
Leebotten
Mousa
Channerwick
Sandwick
Hoswick
Ireland
Northpunds
Mousa Broch
Bigton
Levenwick
B9122
Southpunds
St Ninian's Isle
Scousburgh
Noss
Skelberry
Loch of Spiggie
Boddam
Hillwell
Croft House Museum
Quendale
Aberdeen
Mill
A970
Toab
Exnaboe
Fitful Head
Orkney (Kirkwall)
SUMBURGH
Sumburgh
Jarlshof
Sumburgh Head

SHETLAND ISLANDS

NORTH SEA

TOWN PLANS
Kirkwall p232
Lerwick p233
Thurso p228
Wick p229

LERWICK

Bressay

Holmsgarth Ferry Terminal
A970
Aberdeen
Orkney
Bergen
Tórshavn
Seydisfjordur
Hantsholm
Bressay Sound
Morrison Dock
Out Skerries
Skipidock
NORTH RD
Hay's Dock
North Ness
Bressay
Garthspool
Freefield
WC
B9072
Harbour St
A969
Victoria Pier
NORTH RD
COMMERCIAL ROAD
King
Burgh St
POL
Small boat harbour
Gilbertson
Gilbertson Park
Harald
Commercial
ESPLANADE
Bells
Olaf Street
Street
NORTH LOCHSIDE
Hayfield
La Road
Road
PO
SOUTH LOCHSIDE
SCALLOWAY RD
SOUTH ROAD
Knab
Breiwick
Road
Lover's Loan
Twageos Rd
H
Road
The Sletts
Warri Geo
Gressy Loan
A970
Brei Wick
Sea Road
WC
The Knab

Scalloway 6
Sumburgh Airport 22

0   200   400yds
0   200   400m

BBC Radio Scotland
AM 810/FM 92-95

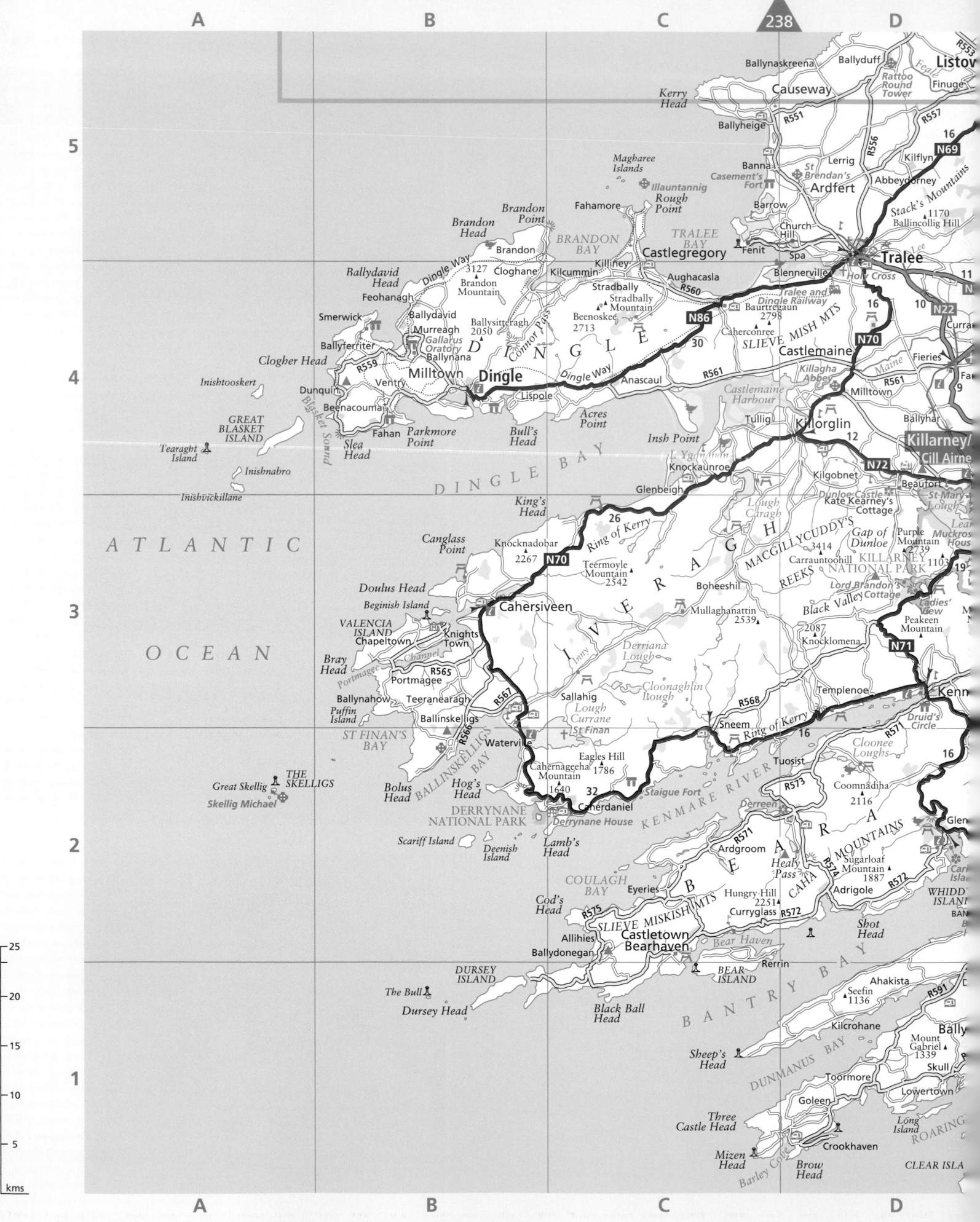

ATLANTIC OCEAN

DINGLE BAY

KENMARE RIVER

BANTRY BAY

COULAGH BAY

DUNMANUS BAY

see p489 for a touring guide to this map

TOWN PLANS
Cork p236

WLR FM
FM 95.1/97.5

South East Radio
FM 95.6/96.2/96.4

Carlow 30
13

Dublin 75
Wicklow 47
Enniscorthy 2

Enniscorthy 5

N9

E

F

N30

N11

G

241

H

Ballyhale
Mullennakill

Ballygub

R731

Clonroche

Castleellis
Castleellis

Blackwater

Donard

12

Redgate

N30

N11

Oilgate

Screen

R741

R744

Market
Ballyhale
stown

Tullagher

R100

R705

Clonroche

R730

CASTLEBRIDGE
(WEXFORD)

Castlebridge

Curracloe

5

South Leinster Way

Lukeswell

New
Ross

Adamstown

Galbally

Crossabeg

WEXFORD
OR
NORTH BAY

16

Mullinavat

Glenmore

Old
Ross

Raheen

Killurin

N9

Dunganstown

Ballynabola

N25

Newbawn

Taghmon

Selskar
Abbey

WEXFORD/
LOCH GARMAN

The Raven Point

Ballincrea

Cassagh

Foulkesmill

N25

Johnstown
Castle

Wexford
Harbour

Rosslare Point

ncoin

Whitechurch

R733

Clongeen

Gusserane

Hilltown R733

Piercetown

Drinagh

ROSSLARE
OR
SOUTH BAY

Fishguard
Pembroke Dock

Slieveroe

Priesthaggard

Campile

Tullycanna

Murntown
Rathmacknee
Castle

11

Killinick

Rosslare

Rosslare
Harbour

Cherbourg
Roscoff (seasonal)

allygorey
cketstown

Dunbrody
Abbey

Passage
East

Ramsgrange

Wellingtonbridge

Mayglass

Tagoat

Kilrane

N25

Greenore
Point

WATERFORD/
PORT LAIRGE

Arthurstown

Saltmills

Bridgetown

Horetown

Broadway

Kilrane

Tuskar Rock

ss

Halfway
House

Ferry

Duncannon

Tomhaggard

Churchtown

orris

R682

R685

WATERFORD

Woodstown

Keeragh
Islands

Killag

Duncormick

Tacumshin
Lake

Lady's
Island
Lake

Carnsore
Point

nor

Clohernagh

Killea

Tramore

Dunmore
East

Fethard

Kilmore
Quay

BALLYTEIGE
BAY

Crossfarnoge or
Forlorn Point

Ballymacaw

Templetown

Baginbun
Head

4

TRAMORE
BAY

Brownstown

Brownstown
Head

Churchtown

Hook
Head

Saltee
Islands

see p490
for a
touring
guide to
this map

3

TOWN PLANS
Cork p236
Waterford
p237

WATERFORD

Kilkenny 19

A

B

C

Wexford 39

Plunkett
Station

N9

N25

Bilberry Road

Grattan Quay

Rice
Bridge

DOCK ROAD

FOUNTAIN S

Abbey Rd

3

Waterford
Museum
of Treasures

3

100

200yds

Gracedieu Road

0

100

200m

MERCHANTS QUAY

Clock
Tower

River Suir

O'Connell St

Anne
St

COAL QUAY

Reginald's
Tower

Ozanam Street

Arts
Centre

Morgan St

Blackfriars
Abbey

Congress

POL

Patrick St

Christ
Church
Cathedral

City Hall

2

Upper Yellow Road

Lower Yellow Road

Green St

City
Walls

John's St

Courthouse

2

Place

Morrison's Avenue

Barrack Street

PARNELL ST

Catherine St

People's
Park

Newtown Road

Griffith Place

Morrison's Road

Doyle's Street

Mayors
Walk

Bath St

John's St

Water Street

R683

Slievekeale Road

MANOR STREET

John's Hill

Lower Newtown

Cannon
Street

Connolly Place

Road

Passage Road

1

Vincent White Rd

Hennessy's

CORK ROAD

John's River

Ballytruckle Road

Upper
Grange
Road

St Patrick's
Hospital

1

Waterford
Glass
Factory

N25

R686

R675

Polberry St

Inner
Ring Road

A

Dungarvan 27

B

C

E

F

G

H

E   **F**   **G**   **H**

Castlebar 31
Ballinrobe 14
N84

Claremorris 21
Tuam 4
N17

Longford 43
Roscommon 24
N63

243

Roscommon 15
N61

Edgeworthstown 23
N55

Headford

Corrofin

14

N17

23

Caltra

Ballyforan

Brideswell
Kiltoom

Castle
Williamstown

Ballykeeran
Ballybornia
Bealin

5

moreknock

Aucloggeen

Skehanagh

Menlough

Castleblakeney

Thomas
Street
R363

R357

Bellanamullia

Athlone
Fardrum
Killogeenaghan

N6

16

Cloonboo

N63

Ryehill

Glentane

Ahascragh

R358

Cornafulla

N62

ycullen
gh Cuilinn
Ballycuirke L

R347

Monivea

Gorteen

Ballymacward

R359

Friary

R348

Ballinasloe

N6

Ballydangan

Clonmacnoise

Ballynahown

5

Claregalway
Baile Chláir

R339

Newcastle

Kilconnell

Garbally
Old Town

Shannonbridge

R444

Highstreet

17

N84

6

5

GALWAY
(CARNMORE)

R348

Esker

Aughrim

1691

Clontuskert
Abbey

Bellmount

Ferbane

Menlough

Oranmore

R348

Kiltullagh

Cappataggle

Laurencetown

Clonfert

Clonony

Cloghan

R357

GALWAY
GAILLIMH

N6

Kilcaimin

R349

Turoe Stone

Bullaun

Kilreekill

Kiltormer

Clonfert

Eyrecourt

R356

Banagher

Shannon
Harbour

R438

Tawin
Island

Clarinbridge

Killeeneenmore

Craughwell

18

Kilmacduagh

Kilcolgan

R350

Ballydavid

Mullagh

Meelick

R433

Silver

Aughinish

Kilcreest

Killimor

Gortavoran

Newtown

9

Fiveallev

N52

Newtownlynch

N67

Ardrahan

N66

Loughrea

Lough
Rea

18

Tynagh

Garraun

R355

Ballycrossaun
Derryhivenny
Castle

Rathcabban

Rapemills

N52

Rath

Burren

R347

12

14

Kilchreest

R351

Duniry
Abbey

R352

Portumna

Portland

Lorrha
Pike

R489

Birr

Killyon

comroe Abbey

Kinvarra

Slieve

Aughty

Power's
Cross

Priory

Carrigahorig

Riverstown

Carrig

Castle
Gardens

Clareen

llyvaghan
Aillwee
Cave

Bealaclugga
Slievecarran
1075

Thoo
Ballylee

Cashlaundrumlahan
1207

Derrybrien

R353

Woodford

Ballinderry

Terryglass

9

Carrig

BIRR

Sharavogue

240

Poulnabrone
Dolmen

Kiltartan Castle

Gort

Ballingarry

Borrisokane

The
Pike

R439

12

Coolderry

THE BURREN
NATIONAL PARK

Coole Park

Coole
Lough

Bostory

R460

Lough
Cutra

Gorteeny

Coolbaun

R490

Modreeny

Kilcomin

Shinrone

R492

Lomaneigh
Castle

Kilmacduagh

Ballyeighter
Loughs

Maghera
1312

Caher

Whitegate

Ardcrony

12

Cloghjordan

Roscrea

N7

Dublin 77
Portlaoise 77

Killinaboy

Corrofin

R462

Feakle

R461

Mountshannon

Puckaun

Dromineer

Barna

9

Dunkerrin

Clare
Centre
O'Dea
nd Cross

R476

Crusheen

Inchicronan
Lough

Scarriff

LOUGH
DERG

Youghal
Bay

N52

Clash

Clonakenny

1318
Mauricesmills

N18

Barefield

Bodyke

Tuamgraney

Holy
Island

Portroe

Youghal

Ballymackey

13

Moneygall

Killea

12

Kilnamona

Tulla

R466

Callaghansmills

Slieve
Bernagh
1748

Nenagh

Toomyvara

Ennis

R469

R465

Glennagalliagh

Broadford

Killaloe

Ballina

11

R499

Sallypark

Templemore

R501

Clare
Abbey

Quin

Knappogue
Castle

Kilbane

R496

Dolla

Silvermines

Templederry

Drom
Loughmoe

N68

Claracastle

Kilkishen

Craggaunowen
Project

Kilmurry

Kilmore

Montpelier

Birdhill

Ballynahinch

Silvermine Mts
Slievekimalta
or
Keeper Hill
2279

Borrisoleigh

R498

N62

Limerick's Live
FM 95.0/95.3

Newmarket-
on-Fergus
Hurlers
Cross

Sixmilebridge
Woodcock Hill
1010

Cloonlara

Newport

Mauherslieve or
Mother Mountain
1783

Curreeny

Upperchurch

Bouladuff

Annfield
Ballycahill

SHANNON

N19

Bunratty

N18

Castleconnell

R503

Rear Cross

Inch

Rosmult

Thurles

Bunratty Castle

LIMERICK
(COONAGH)

Annacotty

Slievefelim Mountains
1524
Cullaun
1467

Kilcommon

Milestone

R660

Carrigogunnell
Castle

Coonagh
Mungret

Moroe

Ring Hill
1398

Holycross
Abbey

Pallaskenry

New
Kildimo

Clarina

R512

Abington

Cappamore

Cappagh
White

Clonoulty

Ballysteen

17

Old
Kildimo

R526

LIMERICK/
LUIMNEACH

Roher

Doon

Annacarty

Dundrum

R505

Askeaton

Patrickswell

N20

Caherconlish

N24

Kilmurry

Pallas
Green (New)

Toem

Rock of Cashel

Barrigone
Desmond
Castle
Creeves

Curraghchase

Cappagh

Adare

R511

Crecora

26

Pallas
Green

Oola

Donaskeagh

Cashel

Golden

Ballingarrane

Manor
House

Croom

Fedamore

Ballybrood

Barna
Cullen

R661

Dually

Newbridge

12

Monaster

R514

Kilteely

Herbertstown

Limerick
Junction

Ballagh
Boherlahan

R691

R692

Kilcolman
Castle
Matrix

Rathkeale

Kilfinny

R516

Monaster
Abbey

Holycross

Kilfeakle

12

N74

Thomastown

R688

Ardagh

8

Morenane

N20

Bruff

Knockainy

R515

Bansha

14

Rosegreen

11

N21

R518

Ballingarry

12

Hospital

Emly

Tipperary
Tiobraid Arann

Newcastle West

R520
Kilmeedy

Castletown

Athlacca
De Valera
Museum

Dromin

Bruree

Lattin

Kilross

R662

R663

Newinn

E   235   **F**   **G**   **H**

N24   N8

see p491
for a
touring
guide to
this map

TOWN PLANS
Galway p234
Limerick p238

Caher 5   Caher 4
Cork 54

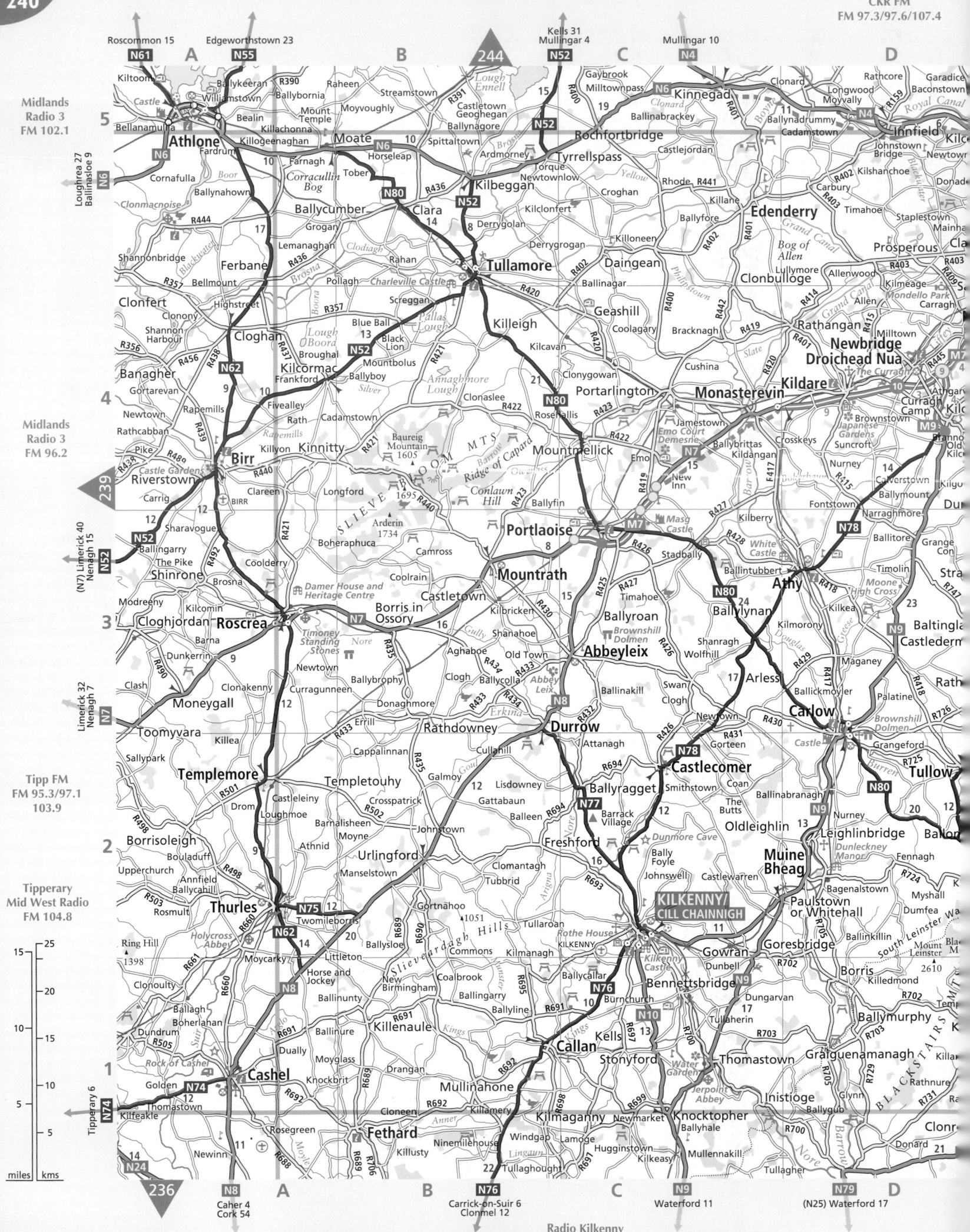

Midlands
Radio 3
FM 102.1

Midlands
Radio 3
FM 96.2

Tipp FM
FM 95.3/97.1
103.9

Tipperary
Mid West Radio
FM 104.8

98 FM
FM 98.1

FM104
FM 104.4

Spin 103.8
FM 103.8

Lite 102.2 FM
FM 102.2

Kells 27
Navan 17

Monaghan 69
Ardee 33

Dundalk 38
Drogheda 22

E N3 **E** N2 **M1** **F** 245 **G** **H**

R754
Dunboyne
Clonee
R157
Blanchardstown
Castleknock
Glasnevin
M50 Toll
Leixlip
R148
ynooth
M4
Castleknock
Lucan
Chapelizod
bridge
DUBLIN (WESTON)
CASEMENT (BALDONNEL)
Clondalkin
Crumlin
Rathgar
Newcastle
Straffan
Canal
Saggart
Rathfarnham
Dundrum
Tallaght
Stillorgan
Newcastle
R120
Kilteel
Kill
Brittas
Kilbride
N7
N81
Rathmore
Kilbride
R114
use
Roads
21
Blessington
WICKLOW
R759
2476
Kippure
2788
Mullaghcleevaun
R758
MOUNTAINS
R756
NATIONAL PARK
Donard
2302
Table Mountain
Glendalough
Lugnaquilla Mountain
3039
Valleymount
Hollywood
Ballyknockan
Dargle
Djouce Mountain
2385
L Tay
L Dan
Roundwood
Togher
Laragh
R763
R764
Vartry Reservoir
2146
Keadeen Mountain
R755
Rathdangan
2181
Greenan
Croaghanmoira Mountain
Rathdrum
Ballinaclash
R753
Avoca
Askanagap
Moyne
Aughrim
Annacurragh
R147
Woodenbridge
Croaghan Mountain 1993
Tinahely
Curraghlawn
Johnstown
R149
Coolboy
Crosspatrick
Coolgreany
nillelagh
R748
Killinierin
Inch
Coolattin
Monaseed
R725
Hollyfort
Carnew
Askamore
N11
Craanford
Gorey
Ballyroebuck
Clohamon
Camolin
yshall
Strahart
N80
18
Ballyoughter
Ballycanew
Ferns
Ballycarney
The Harrow
Monamolin
Killenagh
Ballygarrett
daggan
Crane
R741
R742
Enniscorthy
R744
Clondaw
Kilnamanagh
N11
12
Kilcotty
Ballaghkeen
Castleellis
Killincooly
Oilgate
Redgate
R741
Screen
Blackwater
R730
237

St Margaret's
Ward
Swords
DUBLIN
Kinsaley
Malahide
Malahide Castle
Portmarnock
Ireland's Eye
Raheny
Howth Castle
Drumcondra
Dollymount
Howth
Clontarf
Toll Toll
Merrion
DUBLIN/
BAILE ATHA CLIATH
Blackrock
DUN LAOGHAIRE
Stillorgan
James Joyce Tower
Dalkey
Carrickmines
Killiney
Stepaside
Golden Ball
Kiltiernan
M11
Bray
Dargle Glen
Enniskerry
Kilruddery House
Kilmacanoge
Powerscourt
Waterfall
Greystones
28
Delgany
Kilpedder
Kilcoole
Newtownmountkennedy
NEWCASTLE
Newcastle
R761
Killiskey
Vartry
Mount Usher Gardens
Ashford
Annamoe
Carrick Mountain
Rathnew
Black Castle
1256
Glenealy
R752
R751
Wicklow
Wicklow Head
Kilbride
16
R750
Avondale Forest Park
R754
BRITTAS BAY
Mizen Head
Arklow
Arklow Head
Kilmichael Point
Castletown
Glassnorman Banks
Courtown
Riverchapel
Cahore Point
Kilmuckridge

DUBLIN BAY

Douglas (seasonal)
Liverpool
Holyhead

Holyhead

IRISH

SEA

5

4

3

2

1

see p492 for a touring guide to this map

East Coast FM
FM 94.9/96.2
102.9/104.4

TOWN PLANS
Dublin p328
Dún Laoghaire p241

DÚN LAOGHAIRE

A **B** Holyhead

DART Suburban Station
West Pier
0   200   400yds
0   200   400m
Dún Laoghaire Harbour
Commissioners of Irish Lights
St Michael's Pier
Ferry Terminal
East Pier
N11 Dublin 7
A31
Harbour Rd
CROFTON RD
George's Pl
Dún Laoghaire Station
Town Hall
Queen's Rd
Scotsman's Bay
Hospital
George's St Lwr
Library
George's St
Royal Marine Rd
Pavilion
Royal Marine Museum
Bloomfields Centre
Shopping Centre
National Maritime Museum
Cross Ave
Windsor Terrace
Patrick Street
George's St Upper
Northumberland Ave
Corrig Ave
Clarinda Park
Link Rd
Summerhill Rd
Tivoli Road
POL
Corrig Road
Sandycove Station
Orphanage
Royal Terr W
Royal Terr E
Corrig Road
Glenageary Road Lower
Eden Road
A N11 Wicklow 27 **B**

E **F** **G** **H**

Wexford 7
Rosslare 17

South East Radio
FM 95.6/96.2/96.4

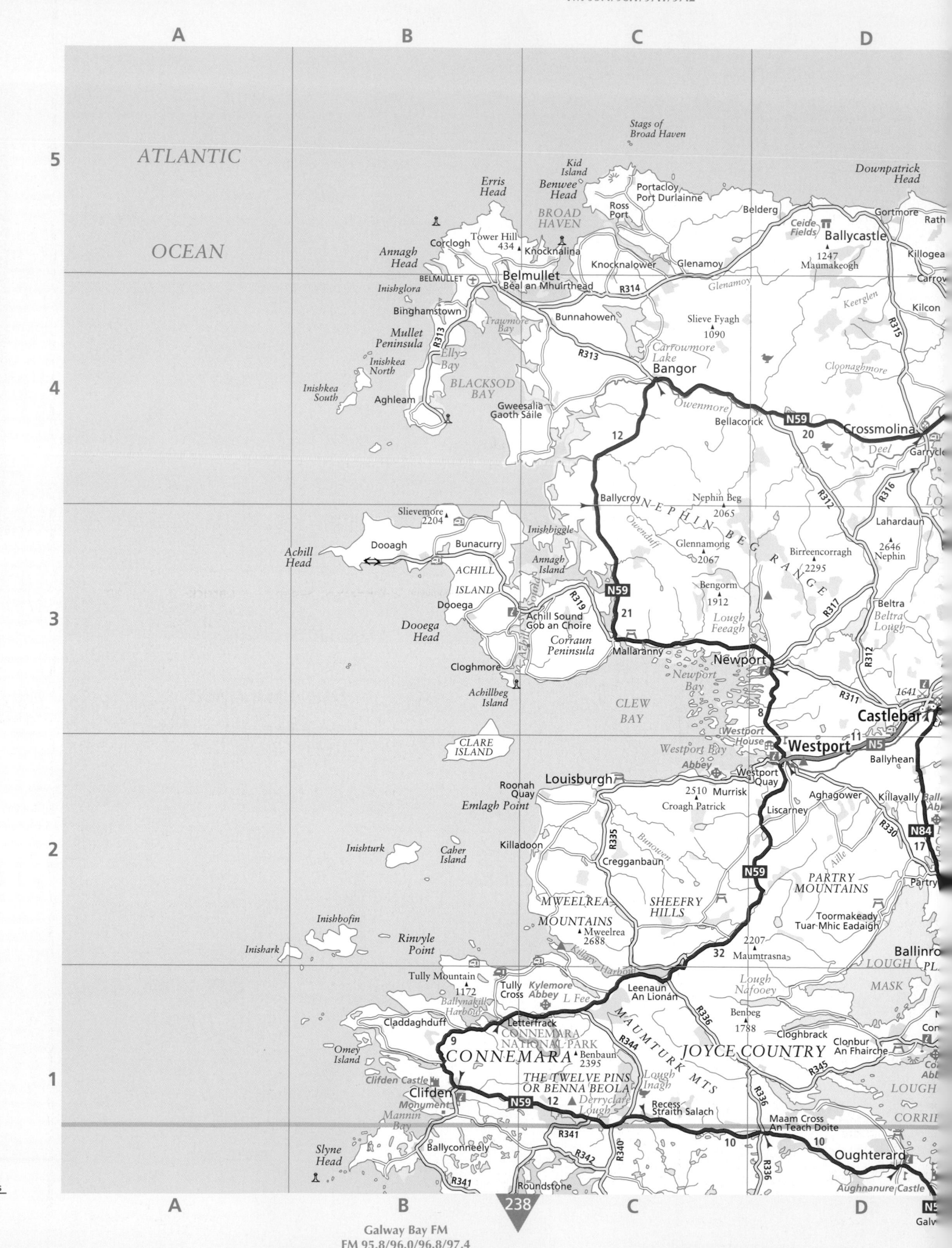

ATLANTIC

OCEAN

Stags of Broad Haven

Kid Island
Benwee Head
Portacloy
Port Durlainne
Downpatrick Head

Erris Head
Ross Port
Belderg
Gortmore
Rath

BROAD HAVEN

Ceide Fields
Ballycastle
Killogea
Carrow

Annagh Head
Corclogh
Tower Hill 434
Knocknalina
Knocknalower
Glenamoy
1247 Maumakeogh

Belmullet
BELMULLET
Béal an Mhuirhead
R314

Inishglora
Bunnahowen
Slieve Fyagh 1090
R315
Kilcon

Binghamstown
R313
Carrowmore Lake
Keerglen

Mullet Peninsula
Elly Bay
Glenamoy
Cloonaghmore

Inishkea North
BLACKSOD BAY
Bangor
N59
Crossmolina

Inishkea South
Aghleam
Gweesalia Gaoth Sáile
Owenmore
N59 20
Deel
Garry

12
Bellacorick

Slievemore 2204
Ballycroy
Nephin Beg 2065
R312
Lahardaun

Dooagh
Bunacurry
Inishbiggle
Owenduff
Glennamong 2067
Birreencorragh 2295
2646 Nephin

Achill Head
ACHILL ISLAND
Annagh Island
N59
Bengorm 1912
R317
Beltra

Dooega
R319
21
Lough Feeagh
Beltra Lough

Dooega Head
Achill Sound
Gob an Choire
Corraun Peninsula
Mallaranny
Newport
R311
1641

Cloghmore
Mallaranny
8
Castlebar

Achillbeg Island
Newport Bay

CLEW BAY
Westport House
11
N5

Clare Island
CLARE ISLAND
Westport Bay
Westport
Ballyhean

Abbey
Westport Quay
N84

Roonah Quay
Louisburgh
2510 Murrisk
Aghagower
Killavally
Ball

Emlagh Point
Croagh Patrick
Liscarney
R330
17

Inishturk
Killadoon
R335
Burrowen
Partry

Caher Island
Cregganbaun
N59
PARTRY MOUNTAINS

Inishbofin
MWEELREA MOUNTAINS
SHEEFRY HILLS
2207 Maumtrasna
Toormakeady Tuar-Mhic Eadaigh
Ballinro

Rinvyle Point
Mweelrea 2688
32
Lough Nafooey
LOUGH MASK

Inishark
Killary Harbour
Leenaun An Lionán
R336
Benbeg 1788

Tully Mountain 1172
Tully Cross
Kylemore Abbey
L Fee
MAUMTURK MTS
Cloghbrack
Clonbur An Fhairche

Ballynakill Harbour
Letterfrack
CONNEMARA NATIONAL PARK
Benbaun 2395
R344
JOYCE COUNTRY
R345

Claddaghduff
9
CONNEMARA
Lough Inagh
R336
LOUGH CORRIB

Omey Island
THE TWELVE PINS OR BENNA BEOLA
Recess Straith Salach
Maam Cross An Teach Doite

Clifden Castle
Clifden Monument
N59 12
Derryclare Lough
10
10
Oughterard

Mannin Bay
R341

Slyne Head
Ballyconneely
R342
R340
Aughnanure Castle

Roundstone
N5
Galw

miles | kms
25
15
20
10
15
5
10
5

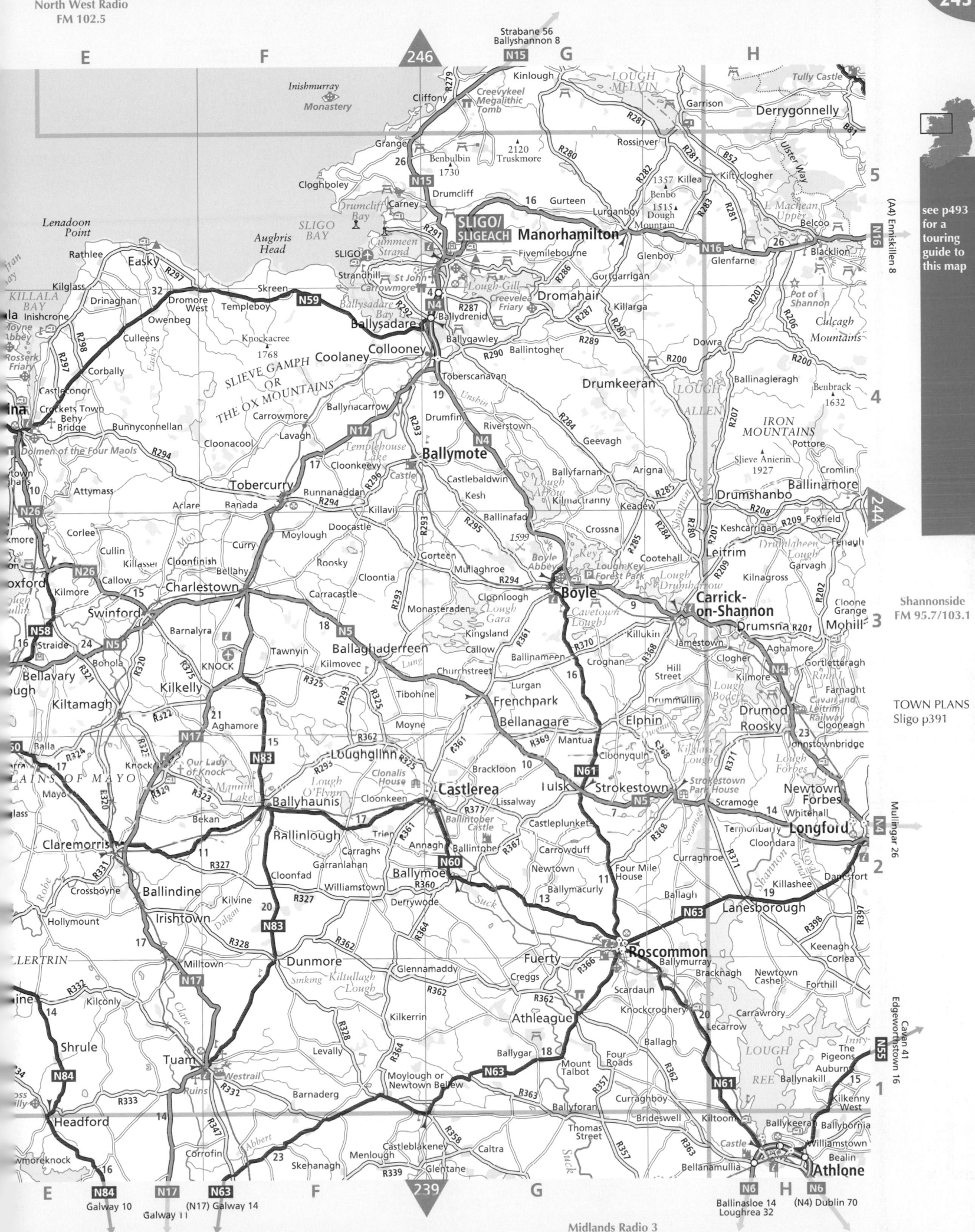

North West Radio
FM 102.5

see p493 for a touring guide to this map

(A4) Enniskillen 8

Shannonside
FM 95.7/103.1

TOWN PLANS
Sligo p391

Mullingar 26

Edgeworthstown 16
Cavan 41

Midlands Radio 3
FM 102.1

Galway 10
(N17) Galway 14
Galway 11

Ballinasloe 14
Loughrea 32
(N4) Dublin 70

247

(N15) Donegal 32
Ballyshannon 17

Omagh 18

Strabane 34
Omagh 18

Dungannon 13

Dungannon

A46

A32

A5 A4

A29

Tully Castle

LOWER
LOUGH
ERNE

Trillick

Tomb 5

Augher

Lisdoart

Eglish
Charlemont

Blacktown

Derrygonnelly

A46

A32

Kilskeery

B80

Clogher

A28 6

Carnteel

Benburb

B81

ST ANGELO

Ballinamallard

Clabby

Aughnacloy

Crilly

Dyan

Allistragh

Springfield

Monea
Castle

Tempo

Creagh

Fivemiletown

Ulster Way

Minterburn

ARMAGH

Kiltyclogher

Enniskillen

Castle
Coole

B80

Emyvale

Castle
Leslie

Caledon
Navan
Fort

Killylea

Belcoo

Lisbellaw

Brookeborough

Glaslough

Tynan

Milford

Letterbreen

Tamlaght

A4

Scotstown

Middletown

Sligo 22

N16

26

A4

9

Bellanode

N16

Glenfarne

Blacklion

Lough
Macnean
Lower

Arney

Bellanaleck

B514

A34

Lisnaskea

Rosslea

Monaghan

Castleshane

Keady

Mackan

Maguiresbridge

15

Clontibret

Florence
Court

Kinawley

UPPER
LOUGH ERNE

B36

Smithborough

Dowra

Swanlinbar

N87

Derrylin

22

Donagh

B143

Stone Bridge

12

Pot of
Shannon

B108

Newtownbutler

Clones

Killeevan

Cuilcagh
Mountains

A509

Teemore

N54

Anlore

Newbliss

R183

Annayalla

Benbrack
1632

Slieve Rushen
1331

1689

Scotshouse

Rockcorry

Ballybay

Castleblayney

LOUGH
ALLEN

Bawnboy

Ballyconnell

Belturbet

Redhills

Drum

Aghnamullen

IRON
MOUNTAINS

Cromlin

Milltown

18

Ballyhaise

Cootehill

Pottore

Derradda

Ardlougher

Butlers
Bridge

Tullyvin

Shantonagh

Slieve Anierin
1927

Ballinamore

R199

Derrycassan
Lough

Annalee

Kill

Drumshanbo

243

Garadice
Lough

Newtown
Gore

Killygar

Killykeen

Cavan

Canningstown

Knockbride

Northlands

Keshcarrigan

Foxfield

Fenagh

Killashandra

Lough
Oughter

Stradone

Cliferna

Glasleck

Carrickmac

Leitrim

Kilnagross

Garvagh

Carrigallen

Crossdoney

Cross
Keys

New
Inn

Bailieborough

Kingscourt

Drumsna

Mohill

Cloone
Grange

Gart L

Bellanagh

Carrickaboy

Killinkere

Teevurcher

Drumce

Jamestown
Clogher

Aghamore

Gortletteragh

Ballinmuck

Lock Gowna

Carrigan

Crosserlough

Ballyjamesduff

Nobber

Kilmore

N4

Leggah

Aghnacliff

Kilnaleck

Virginia

Mullagh

Drumod

Farnaght

17

Ballynarry

Castlerahan

Lough
Ramor

29

Lisduff

Moynalty

Roosky

Drumlish

Corn Hill
916

Dring
Bunlahy

Ballyheelan

Ballymachugh

Kilcogy

Oldcastle

Carnaross

Johnstownbridge

Esker
South

Clooneen

Ross

Ballinlough

Lough
Forbes

Newtown
Forbes

Granard

N55

Kilnaleck

Finnea

911

Drumone

Kells

Whitehall

Ballinalee

Abbeylara

R396

Castletown

Slieve na Calliagh
644

Crossakeel

Oristown

N5

14

N5

Carriglas
Manor

8

Lisryan

Coole

Fore

Killallon

Clonmellon

14

Fordstown

Longford

Corbay
Upper

Boherquill

Tullynally
Castle

St-Fechin

Donaghpatr

Lanesborough

N63

19

Danesfort

Ardagh

Edgeworthstown

Street

Kiltoom

Castlepollard

N52

Navan

Killashee

Moydow

12

Crossea

N4

Rathowen

Lough
Derravaragh

Collinstown

Drumcree

Athboy

19 N51

Corlea

Keenagh

Rathaspick

Lackan

18

Multyfarnham

Delvin

Dunderry

Newtown
Cashel

Barry

Colehill

Legan

Ballinalack

Bunbrosna

Crookedwood

Bracklin

Kildalkey

TRIM

Carrawrory

Forthill

ABBEYSHRULE

Inny

Ballynafid
Portnashangan

Fennor

Monilea

13

Clonlost

Kilbride

R154

Abbeyderg

Royal
Canal

Lough
Iron

Ballynacarrigy

Crazy
Corner

Trim

Ballymahon

Milltown

Lough
Owell

Mullingar

Cloghan

Killucan

Raharney

Laracor

N55

Auburn

Moyvore

Rathconrath

The
Downs

12

Rathwire

Rathmoylon

The Pigeons

15

Skeagh R392

Killare

Gainestown

N61

Ballynakill

Ballymore

Loughanavally

Coralstown

N4

LOUGH
REE

Kilkenny
West

Drumraney

Lough
Ennell

Gaybrook

Clonard

Kinnegad

Rathcore

N61

20

Kiltoom

Ballykeeran

Moyvoughly

Raheen

Castletown
Geoghegan

15

N6

Milltownpass

Longwood
Moyvally

Innfield

Castle

Williamstown

Ballybornia

Streamstown

Rochfortbridge

Ballinabrackey

N4

Bellanamulla

Athlone

Bealin

Mount
Temple

Killachonna

Spittaltown

Ballynagore

Ballynadrummy

6

N6

N6

N52

N6

240

Ballinasloe 14
Loughrea 32

(N4) Dublin 70

Tullamore 12 Athlone 28

Shannonside
FM 95.7/104.1

see p494 for a touring guide to this map

Downtown Radio
FM 103.1/103.4

(M1) Belfast 25
Lurgan 3 Lurgan 1

Belfast 16
Lisburn 6

Belfast 11   Belfast 14

Donaghadee 16
Newtownards 14

E M12 A3 A26 **F** A1 A24 A7 **G** 248 A20 A2 **H**

B28
Scotch
Street

CRAIGAVON
PORTADOWN
Wells Cross   9 Donaghcloney
Dunbarton
Laurelvale
Milltown

Dromore
Kilntown   1689   14

Waringstown
Lurgan

Annahilt
Lough
Agher

B177

Ballynahinch   1798

B6   Derryboye   Ardkeen   Cloghy
Shrigley   B7   Killyleagh   Audley's   Kearney
The   Castle   Point
Cock
Crossgar   Castle   Portaferry
Ward
Strangford

A50 B3 A26
Lawrencetown
Gilford 10
Banbridge

A1 Mound
Waringstown
Dromara
The Spa

Ballykeel   B2
Kilmore

Drumaness   B2   Annacloy
Loughinisland   Inch   Churchtown
Loughisla.   Abbey   Saul
Annadorn   Church
Ballee

A25 Downpatrick
Struell
Wells

Kilclief
Bishops
Court   Ballyquintin Point

5

Tandragee
Scarva

Loughbrickland
Acton

Karesbridge   Lowtown
Annaclone   Moneyslane

Leganany
Dolmen
Seaforde   A25 6   Church   Guns Island

Ballynoe   8
Stone Circle   Chapeltown
Ardglass

Clare
B2

Poyntz
Pass   13

Ballyward   Clough
Castlewellan   Dundrum

Ringfad Point
Killough

Bessbrook
Camlough

Mountnorris
Whitecross   B133

A28 A27
Jerrettspass

McGaffins
Corner   B10
Barnmeen   Ballyroney

A50 Annsborough
Castlewellan
Maghera   10   Minerstown
A2   Church

Rathfriland   Bryansford   4   St John's
Point

DUNDRUM
BAY

Murlough

Goward
Dolmen
Tollymore

Newcastle

Hilltown
Mayobridge

NEWRY
A2   Burren
Milltown

Warrenpoint
Rostrevor

MOURNE   MOUNTAINS
2796
Slieve
Donard
13   Dunmore Head

A2   Annalong

Lisnacree   18
Attical

Ballymartin

Greencastle
Point   Lee Stone Point

Kilkeel

Carlingford
Peninsula

Cranfield Point

IRISH

SEA

DUNDALK
DÚN DEALGAN
The
Bush

Cooley
Point

DUNDALK
BAY

3

Castlebellingham
Annagassan

Dunany
Point
Dunany

Ardee

Dunleer

Clogher Head

Clogherhead
Termonfeckin

DROGHEDA
DROICHEAD ÁTHA

2   LM FM
FM 95.5/97.8
104.7/104.9

Balbriggan

Skerries

Rush
Lusk

1

Donabate

Lambay
Island

Swords   DUBLIN
Malahide

E N3 N2 M1 **F** 241 **G** **H**

Dublin 6

98 FM   FM 104   Spin 103.8   Lite 102.2 FM
FM 98.1   FM 104.4   FM 103.8   FM 102.2

LONDONDERRY

ATLANTIC

OCEAN

TORY SOUND

DONEGAL BAY

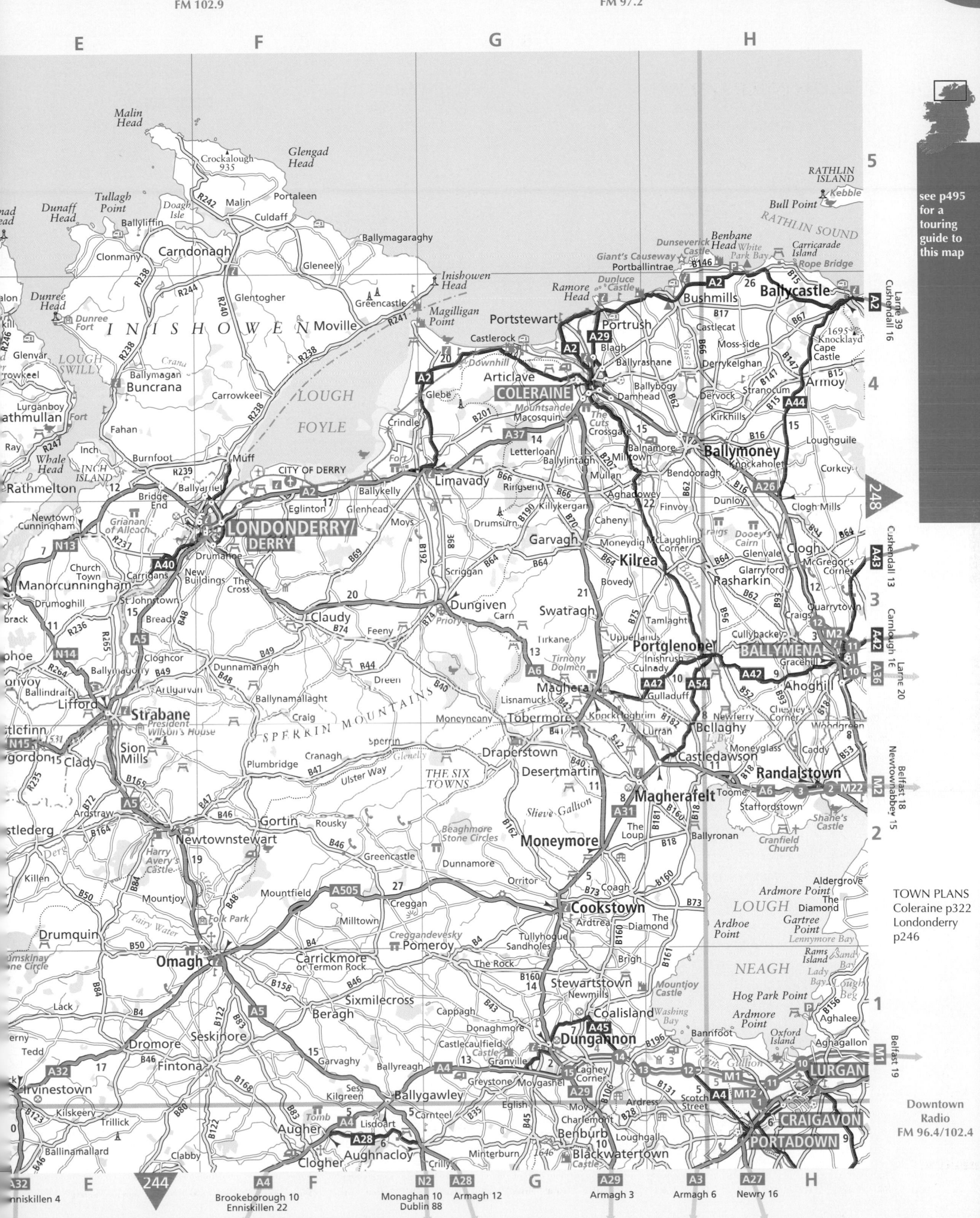

see p495
for a
touring
guide to
this map

TOWN PLANS
Coleraine p322
Londonderry
p246

Downtown
Radio
FM 96.4/102.4

Q97.2 Causeway Coast Radio
FM 97.2

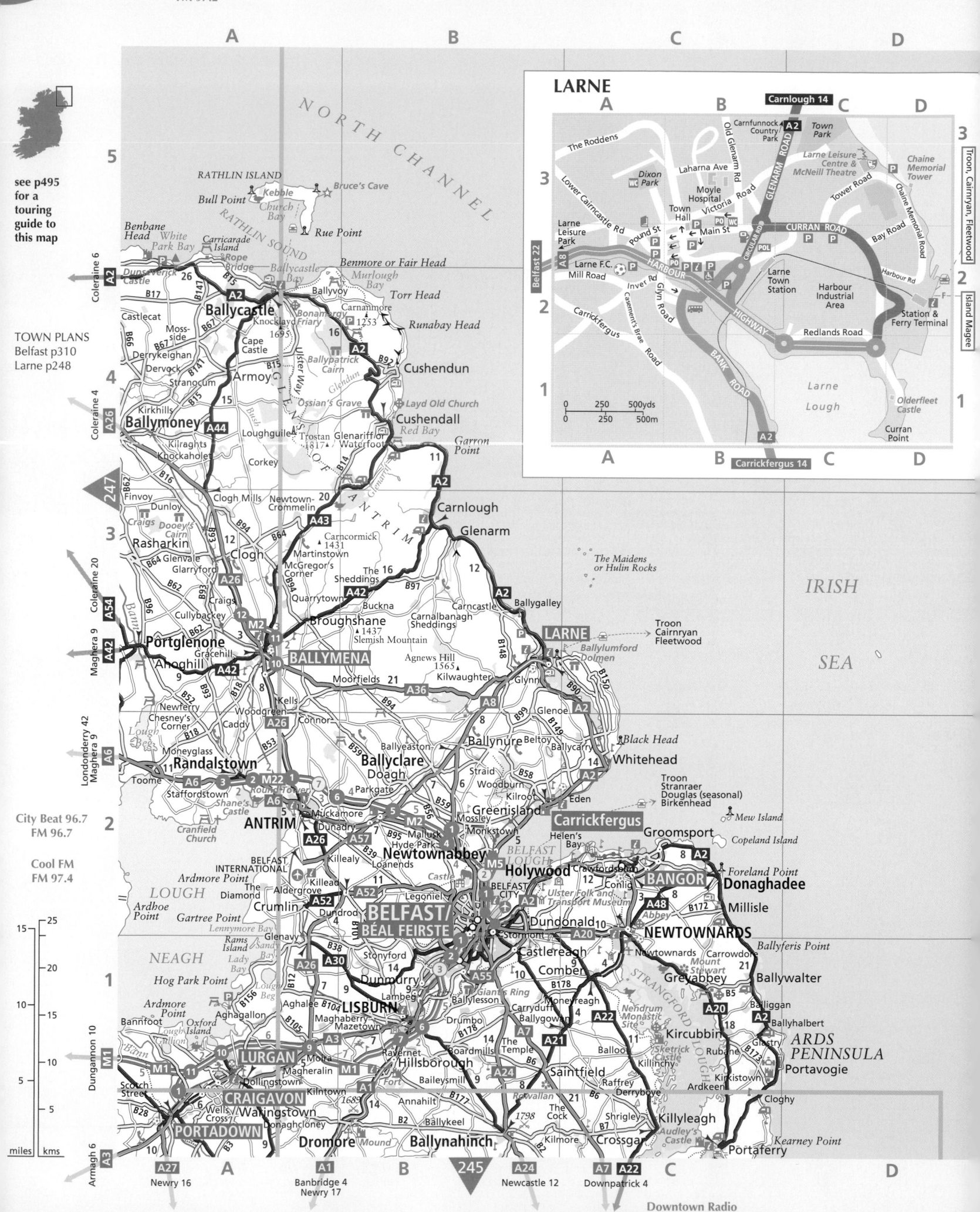

see p495
for a
touring
guide to
this map

TOWN PLANS
Belfast p310
Larne p248

City Beat 96.7
FM 96.7

Cool FM
FM 97.4

LARNE

Carnlough 14

Carrickfergus 14

IRISH

SEA

Town plans &
city routes

The comprehensive selection of town plans, city routes, airport maps and ferry ports has been chosen to reflect the widest possible range of holiday, touring and business destinations easily accessible by car both in Britain and Ireland, and in parts of continental Europe.

Channel Tunnel 252–253
Detailed maps of the Channel Tunnel terminals at Calais and Folkestone are shown along with the main routes to each terminal and destinations on the northern coast of France.

Calais and Boulogne 254–255
Shoppers' maps of two favourite cross-Channel towns show the main shopping streets and out-of-town superstores.

Ferry ports 256–261
Plans of 22 North Sea, Baltic and Channel Island ports focus on the major road and rail routes to the ferry and jetfoil terminals as well as tourist information and nearby car parks.

Airports 262–269
Comprehensive maps of 23 airports in Britain and Ireland which carry commercial passengers, include details of long-term and short-term parking, hotel accommodation, terminals and rail, bus and road links to and from each airport.

City routes 270–301
Clear maps of 15 of Britain's most populous urban areas give the main rail, motorway, dual carriageway and A-road links along with hospitals, sporting venues and places of interest in the local area. Each map is accompanied by a touring guide for the region, highlighting places of interest to visitors.

Town plans 302–407
There are plans of 230 towns in this book. They are listed alphabetically in the index overleaf. Some appear in the main road mapping pages close to where they are shown on the map. The rest are organised alphabetically and include a selective index. Each map shows major road links to and through the town, car parks, places of interest, tourist information, police and hospitals, and bus and train stations.

Park and Ride *The historic university city of Oxford can be a nightmare for the unwary driver. Follow the guide to the city's Park and Ride schemes on p373 to make the most of your visit.*

Contents

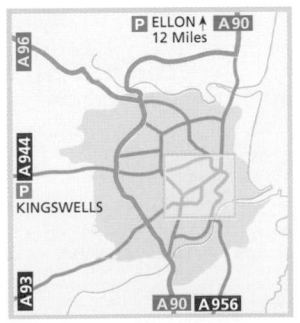

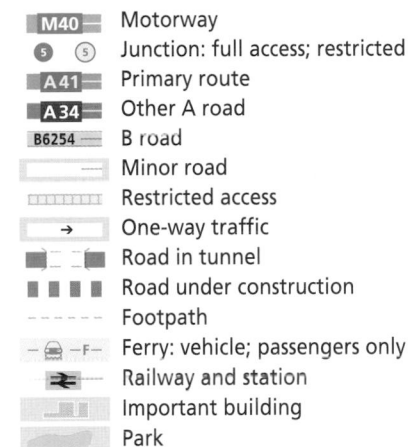

Understanding the town plans

Symbols used on ferry ports, airports, city routes and town plans

One-way street *Short red arrows indicate the permitted traffic direction on one-way streets.*

Pedestrian areas *Streets only accessible to those on foot are shown by a series of short vertical grey lines.*

M40	Motorway
5 5	Junction: full access; restricted
A41	Primary route
A34	Other A road
B6254	B road
	Minor road
	Restricted access
→	One-way traffic
	Road in tunnel
	Road under construction
	Footpath
F	Ferry: vehicle; passengers only
	Railway and station
	Important building
	Park

ABERDEEN

Places to see *Sights and places of special interest to visitors are displayed with a symbol – see panel opposite – and in blue italic type.*

Bus and train *Stations for buses and coaches are marked with a coach symbol. The railway symbol designates train stations.*

Park and Ride *Small inset maps show the full urban area of each town, the town centre as shown in the town plan, major routes in and out of the centre and the name and location of the Park and Ride schemes.*

FACILITIES

- Bus station
- P Car park
- H Hospital with A&E department
- Library
- POL Police station
- PO Post office
- WC Public convenience
- Public convenience including facilities for the disabled
- Railway station
- 24hr petrol station

RECREATION & LEISURE

- Abbey, priory, etc
- Air show
- Aquarium
- † Church
- Cinema
- Country park
- Craft centre
- Factory shopping village
- Garden

House or castle

- Interesting interior
- In ruins
- Industrial attraction
- Museum or gallery
- Nature reserve or bird sanctuary
- Steam railway
- Theatre
- Theme park
- Tourist information centre
- Wildlife park
- ▲ Youth Hostel
- Zoo

SPORTING VENUES

- Association Football
- Athletics
- Championship lawn tennis
- County cricket (first class)
- Flat racing and steeplechasing

Golf courses

- 18 holes
- Less than 18 holes
- Greyhound racing
- Motorsport
- Rugby League
- Rugby Union
- Showjumping and horse trials
- Skiing
- Speedway
- Stadium (venue for more than one sport)
- Swimming pool

LANDMARKS

- Lighthouse
- Observatory

TRANSPORT

- Airport with scheduled services
- Other aerodrome
- Railway station
- × Level crossing

CAMPSITES

- Caravans only
- Caravans and tents
- Tents only

Using the Channel Tunnel

More than 7 million people and 3 million vehicles travel through the Channel Tunnel each year. Passengers can use the Eurostar rail link, or take the car or a coach on the service operated by Euro Tunnel. The high speed link takes a little over half an hour to complete the journey between England and France.

To reach the Folkestone terminal, leave the M20 eastbound at junction 11A, westbound at junction 12. Passengers from the United Kingdom must have a valid passport; there are passport controls and random Customs checks. Your passport will be checked at the departure terminal but not rechecked on arrival, you will also need vehicle documentation (see Driving Abroad pp510–11). Tickets can be bought just before the journey or booked in advance. You should check-in at least 35 minutes before your booked departure time. When you have shown your ticket you can drive straight onto Le Shuttle or make a stop in the terminal building, which has a duty-free shop, bureau de change, automatic cash dispensers, restaurants and shops. Drivers and passengers travel inside their vehicles, but you can get out to walk around. The French terminal is at Coquelles, just outside Calais, and is well signposted from the A16 (E402) and A26 (E15) motorways.

For enquiries about Euro Tunnel services, telephone 08705 353535. Passengers on foot can travel on the Eurostar rail link from London Waterloo. For ticket and timetable information telephone 08705 186186.

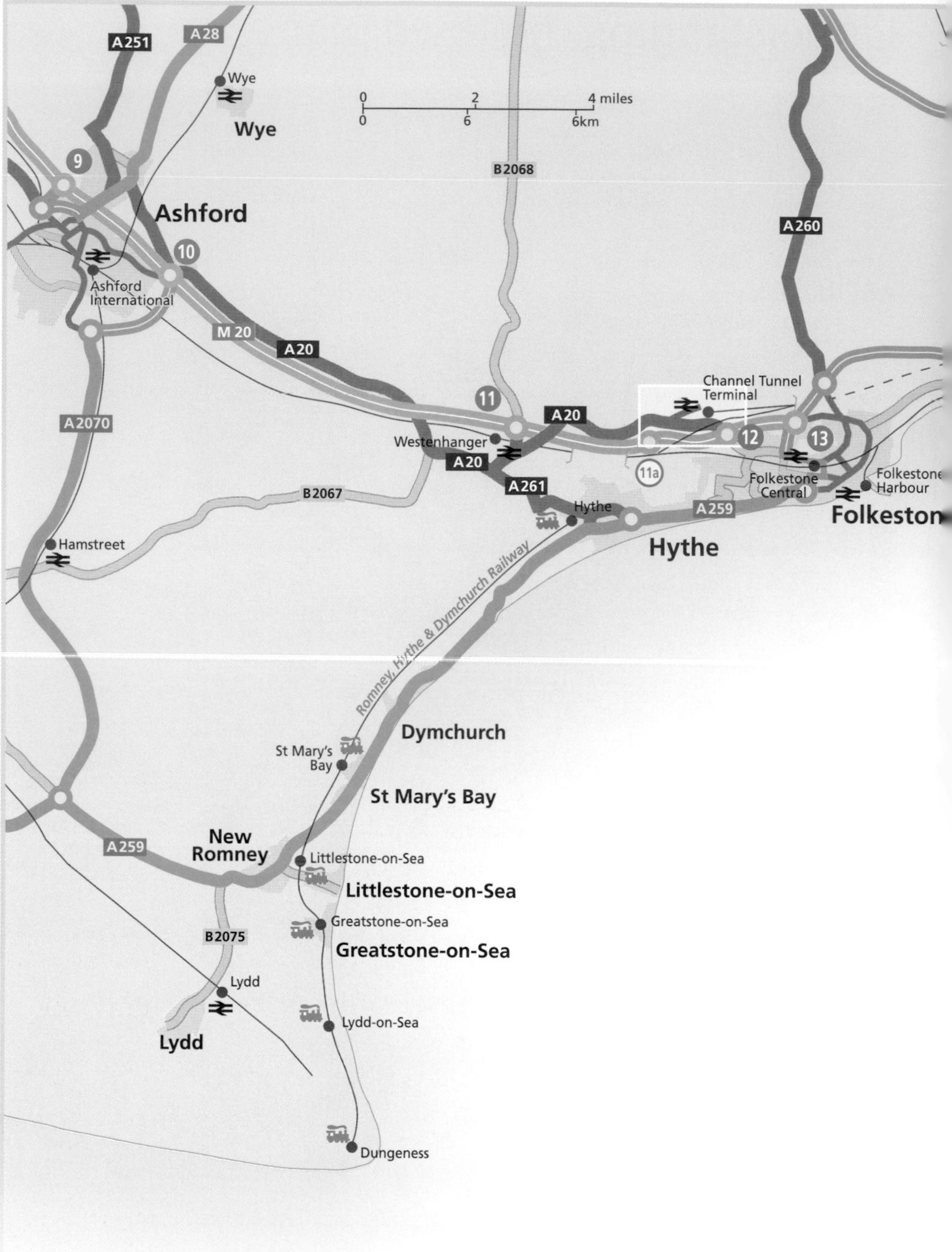

Wye

Ashford

Ashford International

Channel Tunnel Terminal

Westenhanger

Folkestone Central

Folkestone Harbour

Folkeston

Hythe

Hamstreet

Romney, Hythe & Dymchurch Railway

Dymchurch

St Mary's Bay

St Mary's Bay

New Romney

Littlestone-on-Sea

Littlestone-on-Sea

Greatstone-on-Sea

Greatstone-on-Sea

Lydd

Lydd-on-Sea

Lydd

Dungeness

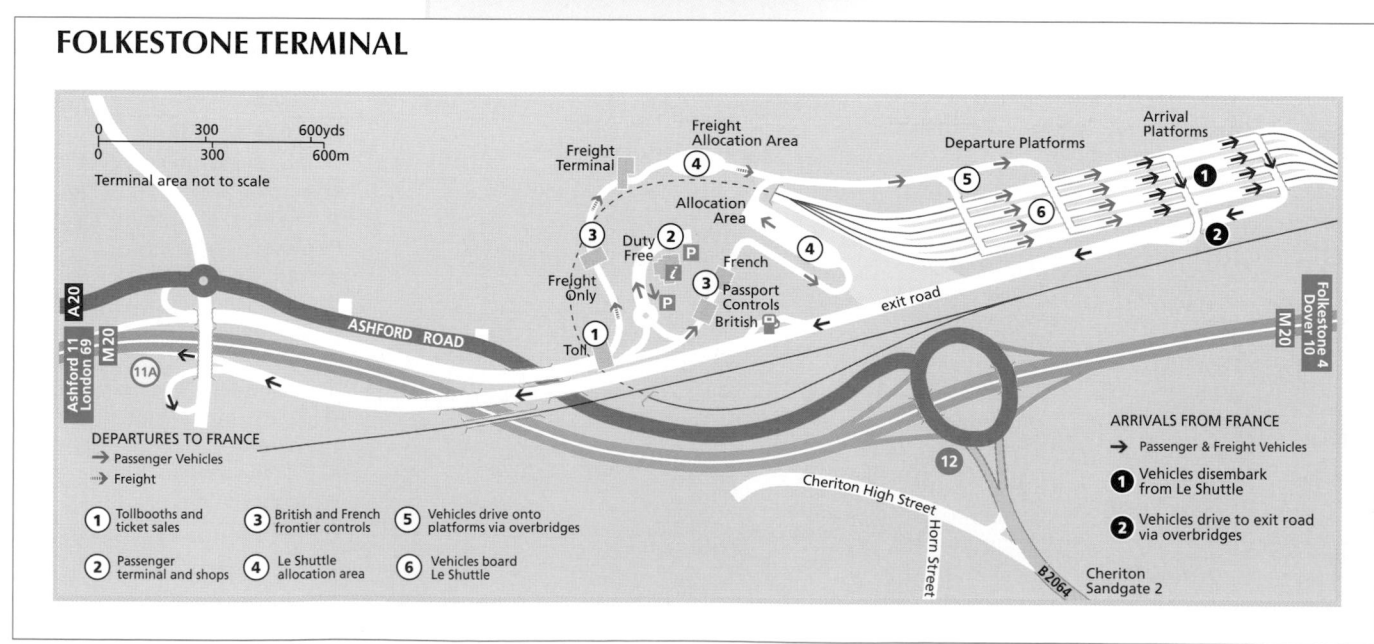

FOLKESTONE TERMINAL

Terminal area not to scale

Freight Terminal

Freight Allocation Area

Departure Platforms

Arrival Platforms

Allocation Area

Duty Free

French

Freight Only

Passport Controls British

exit road

Toll

Ashford 11 London 69

Folkestone 4 Dover 10

ASHFORD ROAD

Cheriton High Street

Horn Street

Cheriton Sandgate 2

DEPARTURES TO FRANCE
→ Passenger Vehicles
→ Freight

① Tollbooths and ticket sales
② Passenger terminal and shops
③ British and French frontier controls
④ Le Shuttle allocation area
⑤ Vehicles drive onto platforms via overbridges
⑥ Vehicles board Le Shuttle

ARRIVALS FROM FRANCE
→ Passenger & Freight Vehicles
❶ Vehicles disembark from Le Shuttle
❷ Vehicles drive to exit road via overbridges

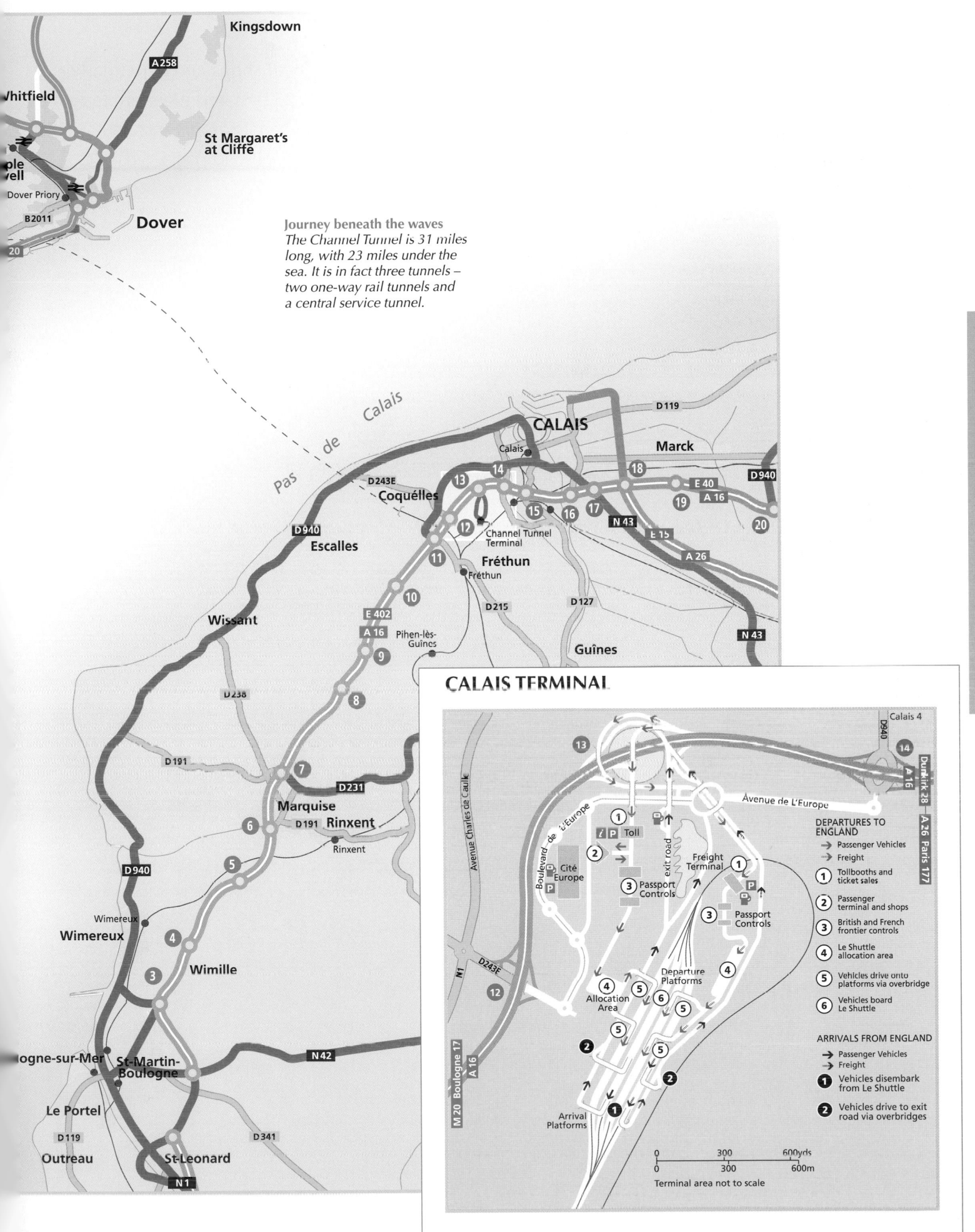

Kingsdown

A 258

Whitfield

St Margaret's at Cliffe

ole vell

Dover Priory

B2011

20

Dover

Journey beneath the waves
The Channel Tunnel is 31 miles long, with 23 miles under the sea. It is in fact three tunnels – two one-way rail tunnels and a central service tunnel.

Pas de Calais

D 119

CALAIS

Calais

Marck

13 14

18

D 940

D243E

Coquélles

E 40

A 16

19

20

D 940

12

15 16 17

N 43

E 15

Escalles

11

Channel Tunnel Terminal

Fréthun

Fréthun

A 26

10

D 215

D 127

Guînes

N 43

E 402

A 16

9

Pihen-lès-Guînes

Wissant

D 238

8

D 191

7

D 231

Marquise

6

D 191 Rinxent

Rinxent

5

D 940

Wimereux

4

Wimereux

3

Wimille

ogne-sur-Mer

St-Martin-Boulogne

N 42

Le Portel

D 119

D 341

Outreau

St-Leonard

N 1

CALAIS TERMINAL

13

Calais 4

D 940

14

Dunkirk 28 — A 26 Paris 177

A 16

Avenue de L'Europe

Avenue Charles de Gaulle

Boulevard de l'Europe

1

i P Toll

2

exit road

Freight Terminal

1

DEPARTURES TO ENGLAND

→ Passenger Vehicles

⇢ Freight

① Tollbooths and ticket sales

Cité Europe

P

3 Passport Controls

P

Passport Controls

3

② Passenger terminal and shops

③ British and French frontier controls

N1

D243E

4

Departure Platforms

4

④ Le Shuttle allocation area

12

4 5

6

5

⑤ Vehicles drive onto platforms via overbridge

Allocation Area

5

⑥ Vehicles board Le Shuttle

M 20 Boulogne 17

A 16

2

5

ARRIVALS FROM ENGLAND

→ Passenger Vehicles

⇢ Freight

2

① Vehicles disembark from Le Shuttle

1

② Vehicles drive to exit road via overbridges

Arrival Platforms

0   300   600yds

0   300   600m

Terminal area not to scale

Shopping in Boulogne and Calais

A trip to Boulogne or Calais makes a good day out, with many bargains at local shops and hypermarkets. Both towns are within easy reach of the Channel Tunnel terminal (see pages 252–3) and there are ferry services to Calais. Most shops open from 8am until 6pm, but may close between 12 noon and 2pm – remember that French time is one hour ahead of British time. See also Driving Abroad pages 510–11.

BOULOGNE The attractive town of Boulogne is just a 30 minute drive from Calais and only 20 miles from the Channel Tunnel terminal. Keen shoppers will delight in the wonderful patisseries, cheese shops, bakeries, beer and spirit merchants and department stores found in the town. On Wednesday and Saturday mornings a market is held at **Place Dalton [B2]** and there is a fish market at **Quai Gambetta [A3]** every morning except Sunday. The town's many cafés, restaurants and bars offer welcome refreshment after a busy shopping expedition. To discover more about Boulogne's history, wander into the old town. The medieval **castle** within its 13th-century walls is now the town's museum and has a large collection of Greek and Etruscan vases as well as an Egyptian collection. **Nausicaa [A3]**, Europe's largest sea life centre, with a sea-lion pool, tropical aquarium and coral reef, is just off the Boulevard Sainte Beuve. For more information, the tourist office is found at 24 Quai Gambetta, telephone 00 33 3 21 10 88 10.

BOULOGNE

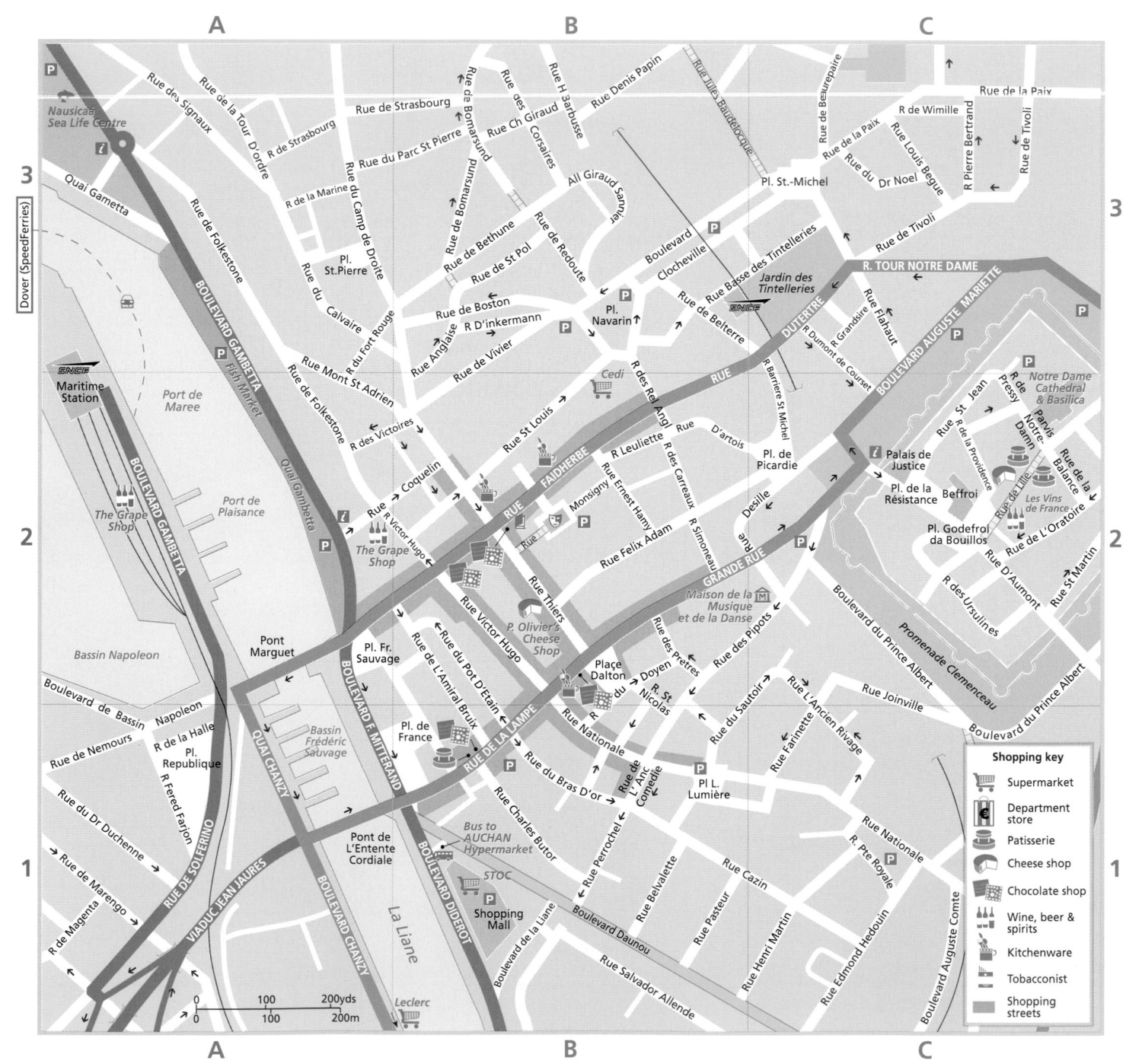

Shopping key

🛒 Supermarket
🏬 Department store
🧁 Patisserie
🧀 Cheese shop
🍫 Chocolate shop
🍷 Wine, beer & spirits
🍳 Kitchenware
🚬 Tobacconist
▊ Shopping streets

CALAIS With crossings from Britain each day and only a short drive from the Channel Tunnel terminal (see pages 252–3), Calais is a convenient choice for day shoppers. Cité Europe, near the terminal and only a short distance from the town, has 150 shops including Carrefour, Tesco Vin Plus and Oddbins. Sainsbury's and Auchan are also found nearby, just off the Route de Boulogne. If you prefer to avoid the large outlets, you can shop very well in central Calais. The **Boulevard Lafayette [B1]** and **Jacquard [A2]** are the main shopping areas in the south of town with delicious breads and pastries available from Fred and Au Bon Pain de France (Boulevard Jacquard). In the north of Calais, most shops are on the **Rue Royale [A2]** and **Place d'Armes [A2]** – the Calais Nord (Rue Royale) is good for food, and La Maison du Fromage et des Vins (off the Place d'Armes) sells fine cheeses and wines. Markets are held on Wednesday and Saturday mornings at the Place d' Armes and on Thursday and Saturday mornings at the **Place Crevecoeur [B1]**. The Tourist Office is open from Monday to Saturday and on Sundays during summer. It is at 12 Boulevard Clemenceau, telephone + 33 (0) 3 21 96 62 40.

CALAIS

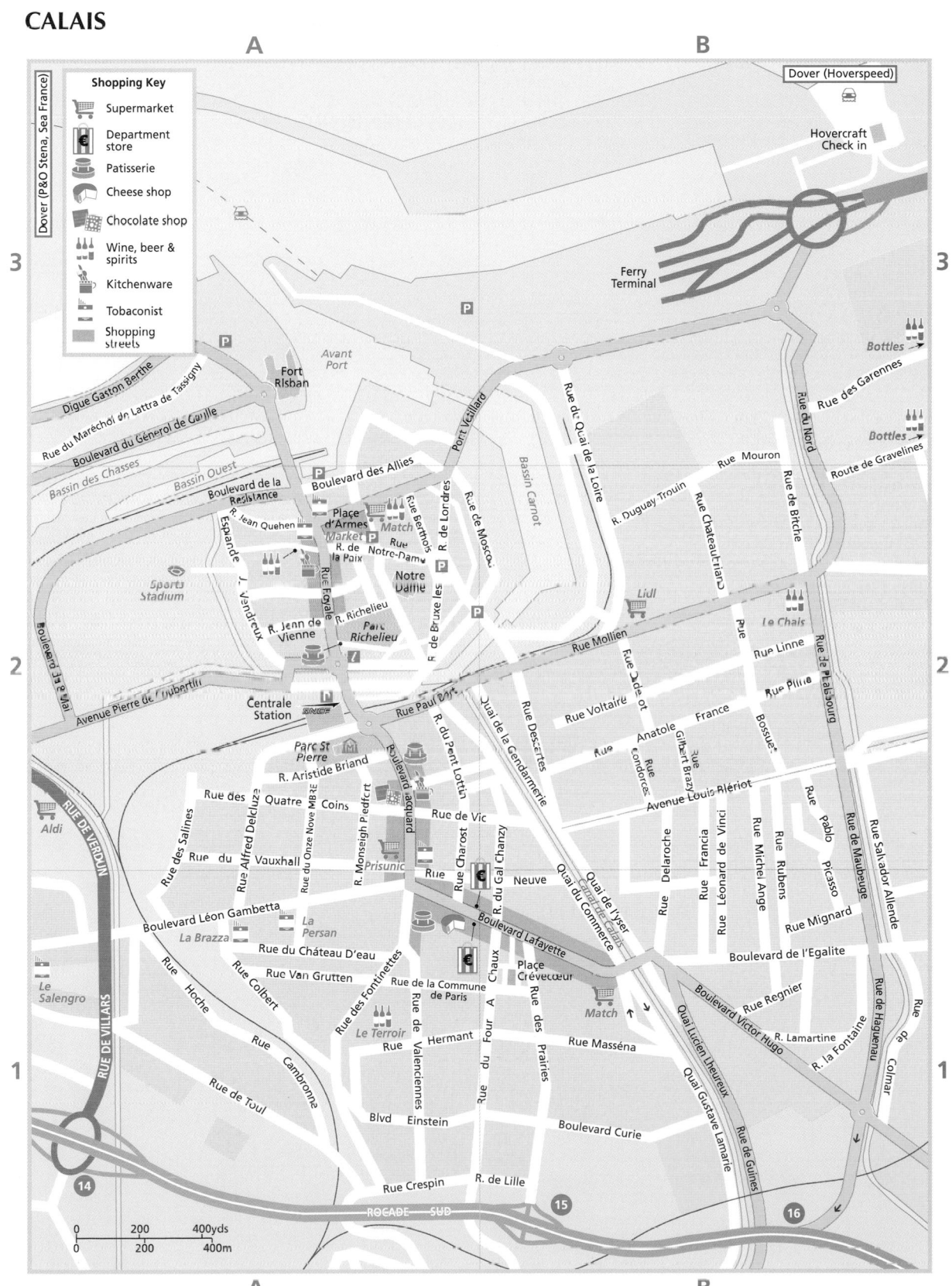

Continental & Channel Isles ferry ports

More than 45 million journeys are made by ferry between Britain and the Continent, the Republic of Ireland and on domestic British routes. For many drivers, the convenience of taking as much luggage as your vehicle can carry is an attractive prospect – but check its maximum load in your manufacturer's handbook, especially if you intend to bring anything back from your trip. Traffic regulations vary from country to country – see Driving Abroad, pages 510–511.

SWEDEN, DENMARK, GERMANY
DFDS Seaways run ferry services to these ports. For details of sailings and fares, telephone 08705 333000, for information about holidays and mini cruises call 08705 333111. The route from Newcastle to **Gothenburg** takes 22 hours and runs throughout the year. Ferries sail from Harwich to **Esbjerg** all year, and the journey takes approximately 20 hours. The service to **Cuxhaven** also leaves from Harwich, is available all year, and takes 18 hours.

GOTHENBURG

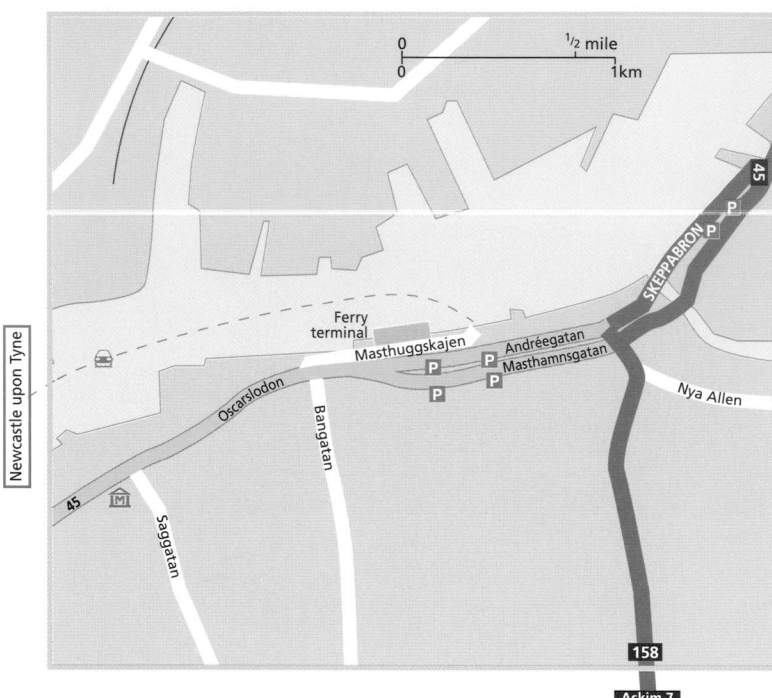

ESBJERG

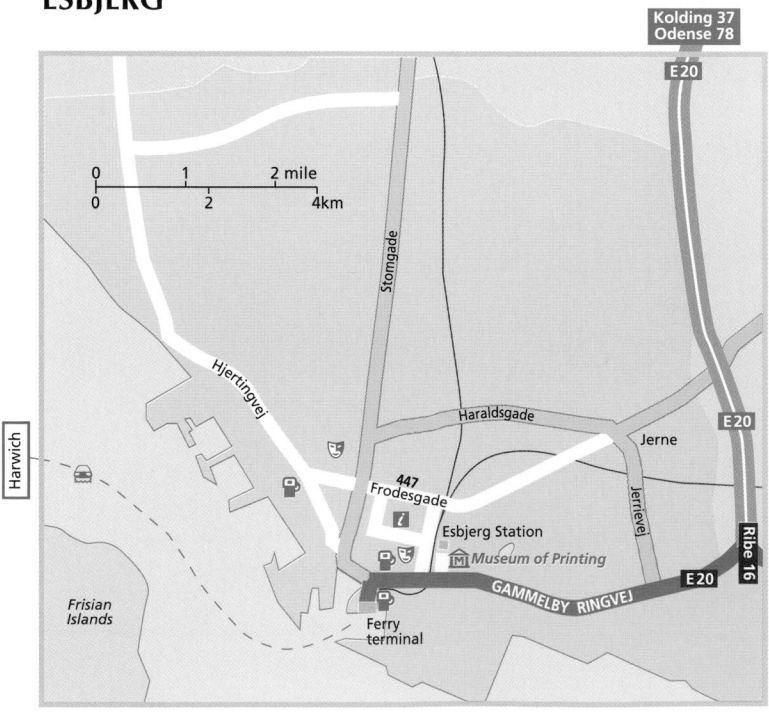

CUXHAVEN

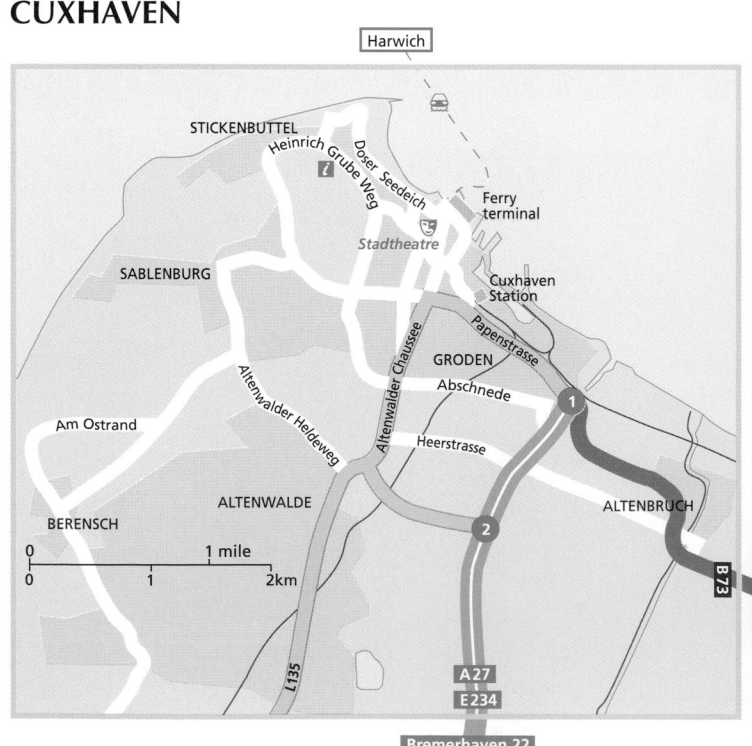

NORWAY

Ferry services to Norway sail from Newcastle and Aberdeen. A service from Newcastle to **Bergen** via **Stavanger** and **Haugesund** is run by the Fjord Line all year. The trip to **Stavanger** takes 19 hours and the entire journey to **Bergen** takes 26 hours. For enquiries and reservations, call the Fjord Line on (0191) 296 1313. The crossing from Newcastle to **Kristiansand** takes approximately 18 hours, depending on the time of year you travel, and is operated by DFDS Seaways (call 0870 533 3000 for information). The route from Aberdeen to **Bergen** via Lerwick is run by two companies. Northlink Ferries, telephone 0845 6000449, run between Aberdeen and Lerwick all year – the journey takes up to 14 hours. The Smyril Line operates from Lerwick to **Bergen**, telephone (01595) 690845 for crossing times and fares.

BERGEN

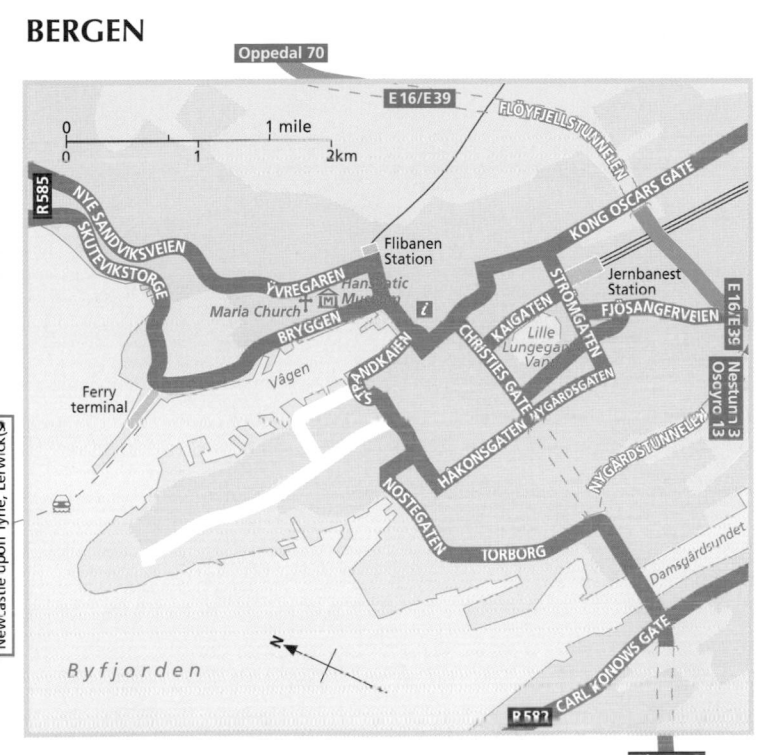

HAUGESUND

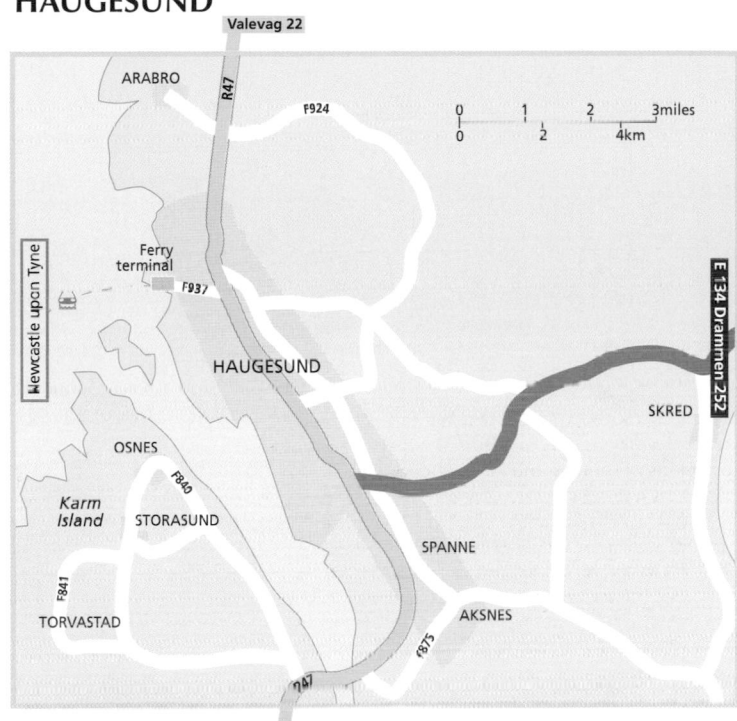

STAVANGER

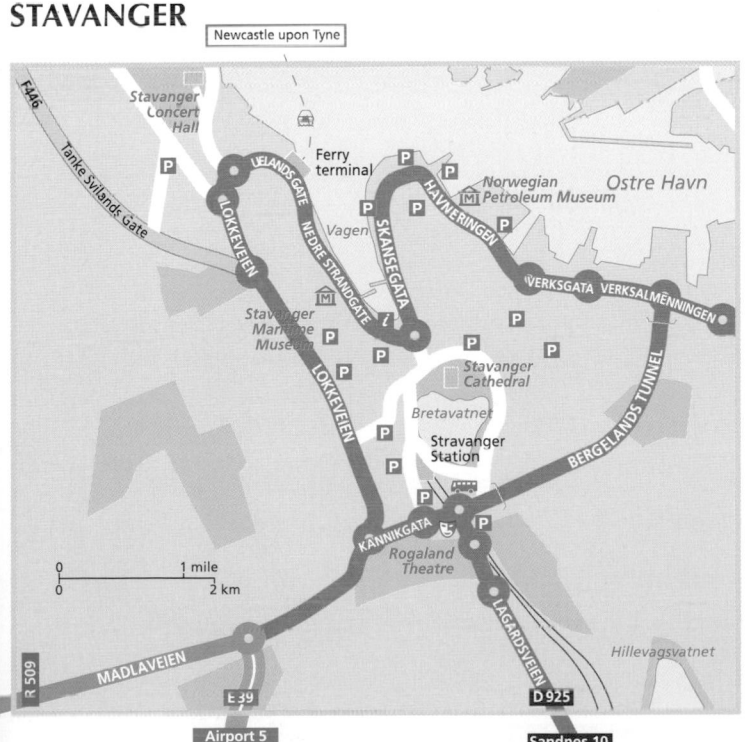

KRISTIANSAND

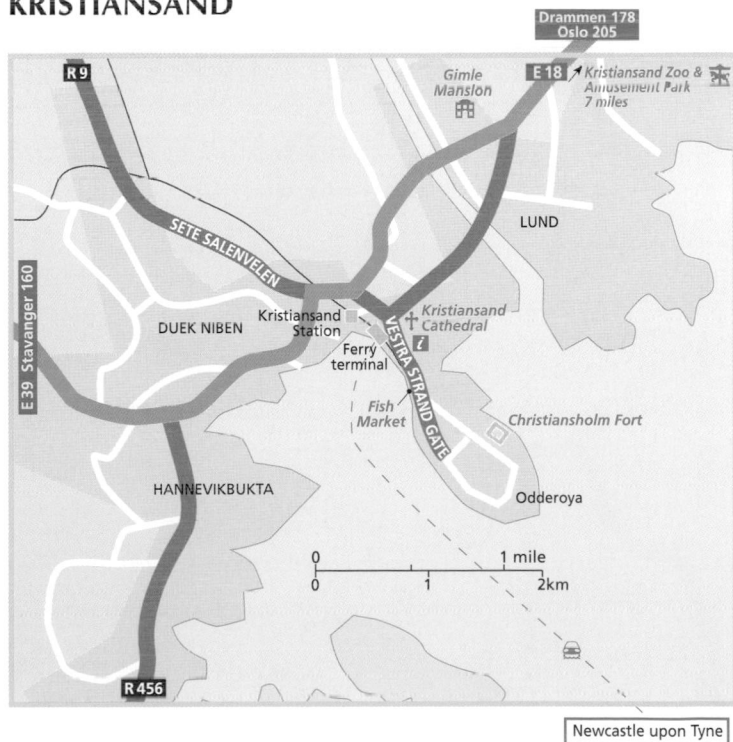

NETHERLANDS, BELGIUM

DFDS Seaways operates a service through the year from Newcastle to **Ijmuiden** – it takes around 14 hours. For details of sailings and fares, telephone 0870 533 3000. Ferries from Harwich to the **Hook of Holland** are run by the Stena Line throughout the year. Crossings take between 6½ and 8½ hours by superferry or just under 4 hours by the Stena Line's high speed ferry, telephone 0870 400 6798 for information. P&O North Sea ferries run a service between Hull and **Rotterdam**. It operates all year round and takes 11 hours, call 08705 202020 for information. They also operate ferries from Hull to **Zeebrugge**, a journey that takes just under 14 hours and is available all year.

IJMUIDEN

HOOK

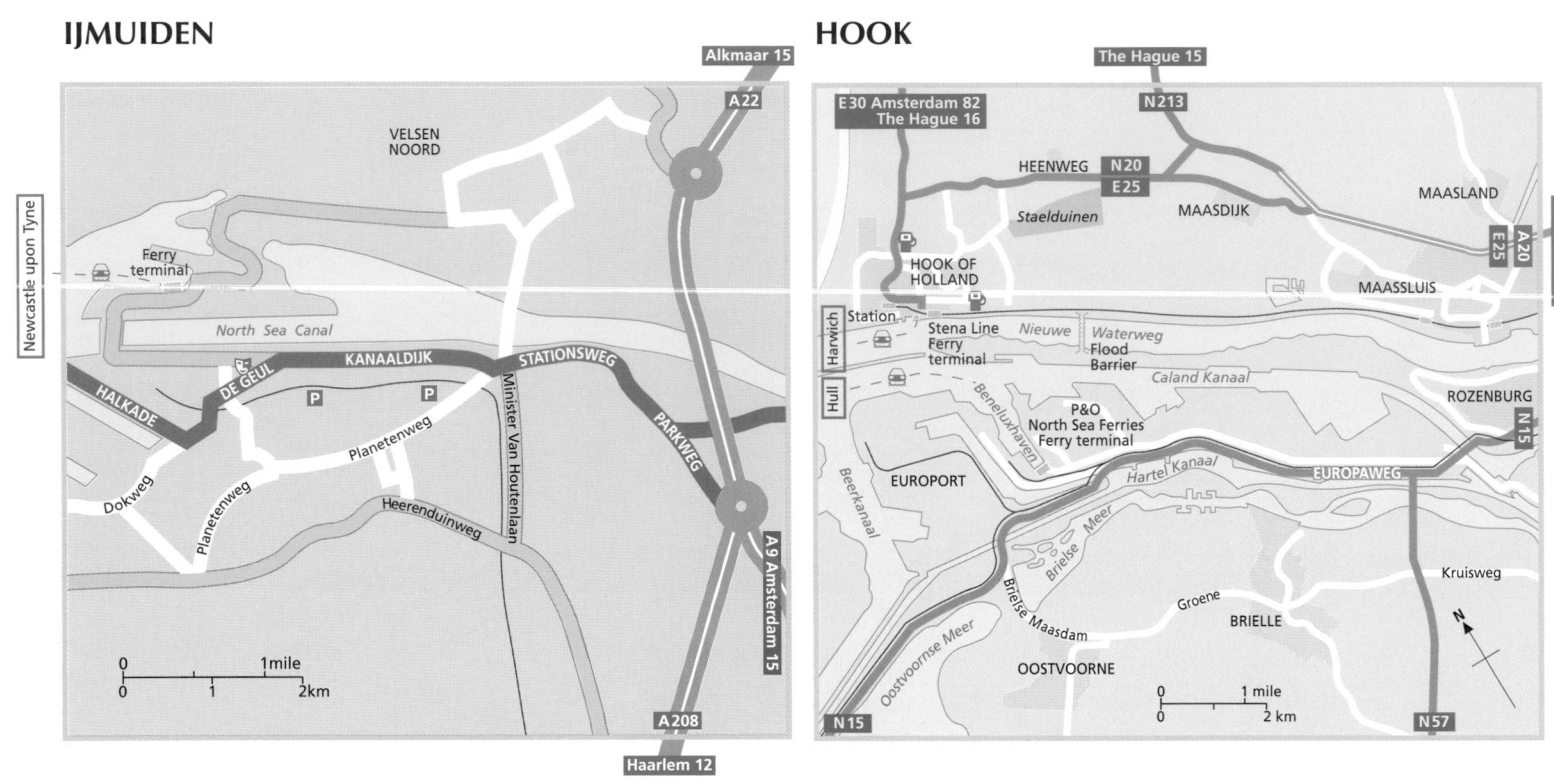

ROTTERDAM

ZEEBRUGGE

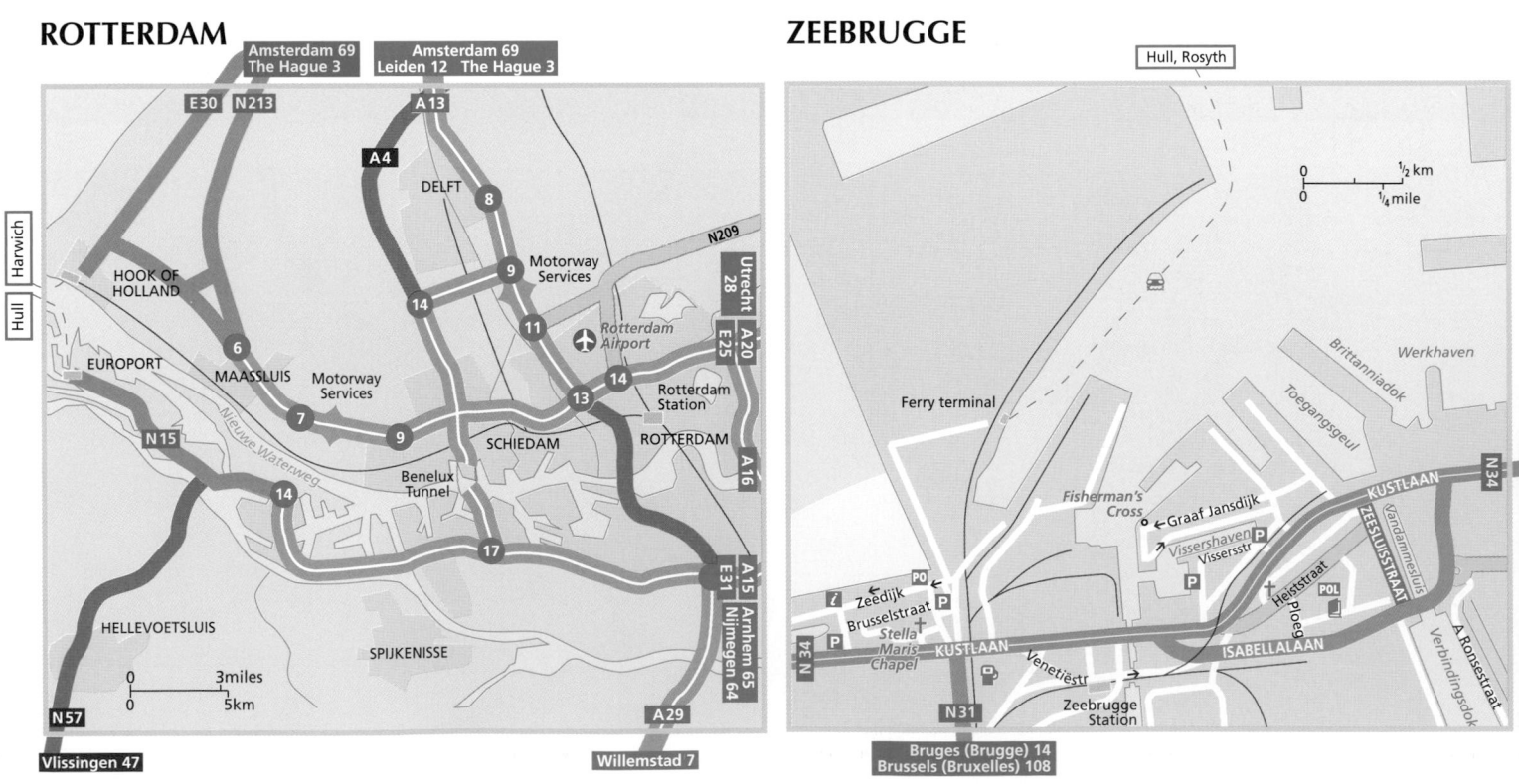

FERRY PORTS

FRANCE

Norfolkline operate a service from Dover to **Dunkirk** all year round. For information about crossings and fares telephone (01304) 218400. Hoverspeed also operates Seacat ferries between Newhaven and **Dieppe** from April to September. The journey takes 2 hours – call 0870 240 8070 for information. Ferries between Portsmouth and **Le Havre** are run by P&O Portsmouth, call 08705 202020 for details. The service operates all year and takes 5½ hours during the day and 7½ hours at night.

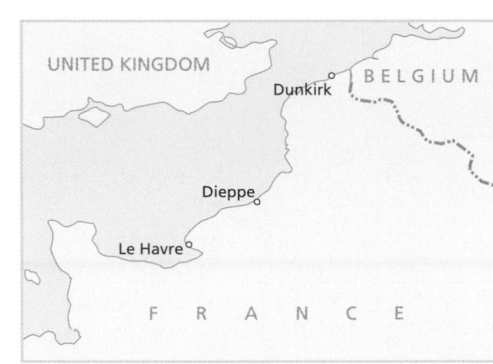

DUNKIRK

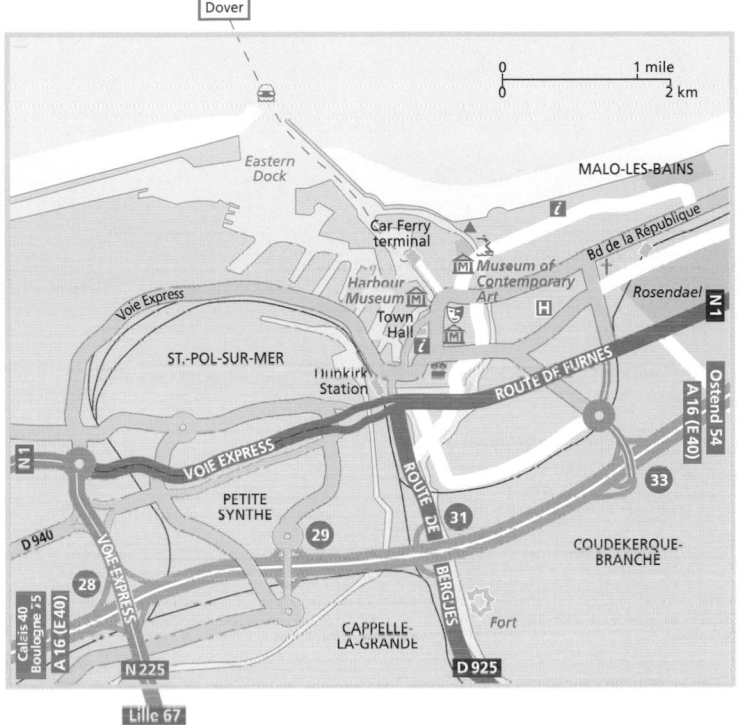

DIEPPE

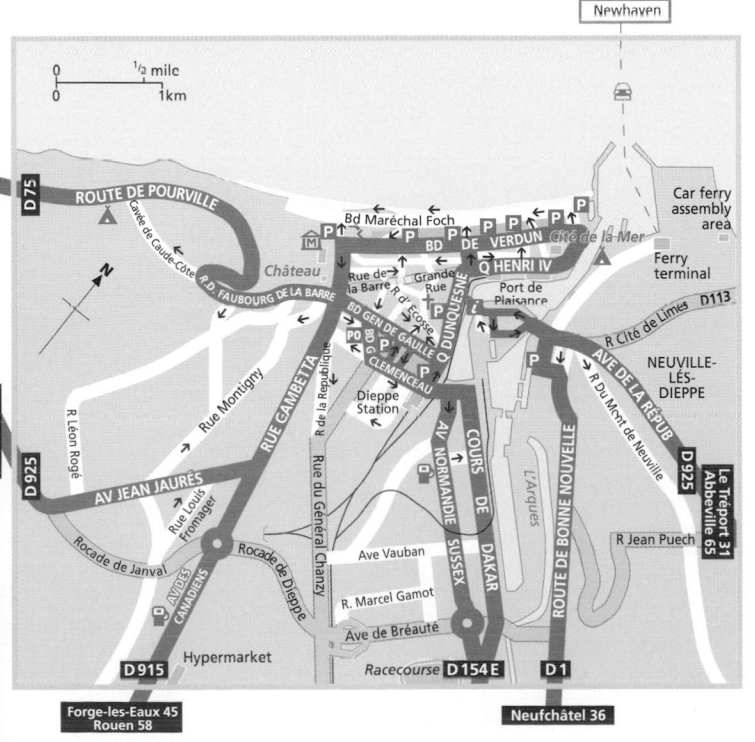

LE HAVRE

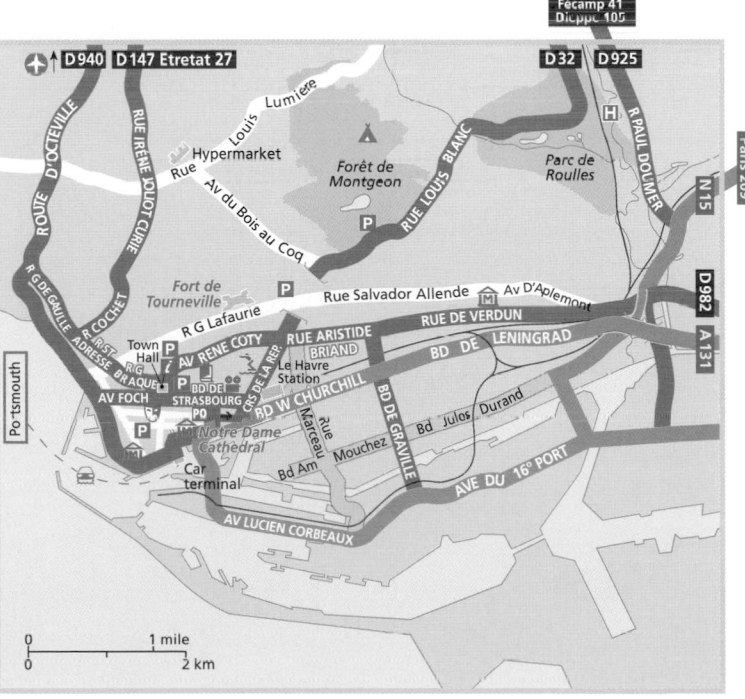

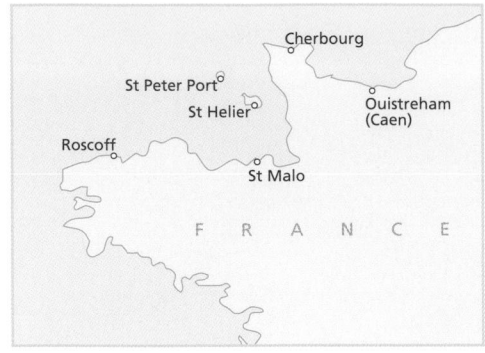

FRANCE, CHANNEL ISLES

Brittany Ferries operate services from Portsmouth to **Caen** throughout the year. Crossings take 6 hours during the day and just under 7 hours at night. For information call 0870 366 5333. Services to **Cherbourg** operate from Portsmouth, Poole and Rosslare in Ireland. P&O Portsmouth operate the service from Portsmouth all year, telephone 08705 202020 for information. The crossing takes 5 hours during the day and 7 hours at night. Brittany Ferries (number as above) sail between Poole and **Cherbourg** – the journey is just over 4 hours long. Irish Ferries operate between Rosslare and **Cherbourg** all year, call 0870 517 1717 for details

– the crossing takes 17 hours. Ferries to **St Malo** sail from Portsmouth and are run by Brittany Ferries, the journey lasts just under 9 hours during the day and just under 11 hours at night. Condor Ferries also run a service from Weymouth and Poole to **St Malo** via the Channel Islands, telephone 0845 345 2000 for more information. Brittany Ferries also cover the route from Plymouth to **Roscoff**, which runs all year and takes 6 hours. Irish Ferries (number as above) sail from Rosslare to **Roscoff** during the summer and the crossing takes just over 14 hours. Contact Condor Ferries (number as above) for details of crossings to **St Helier**, Jersey and **St Peter Port**, Guernsey.

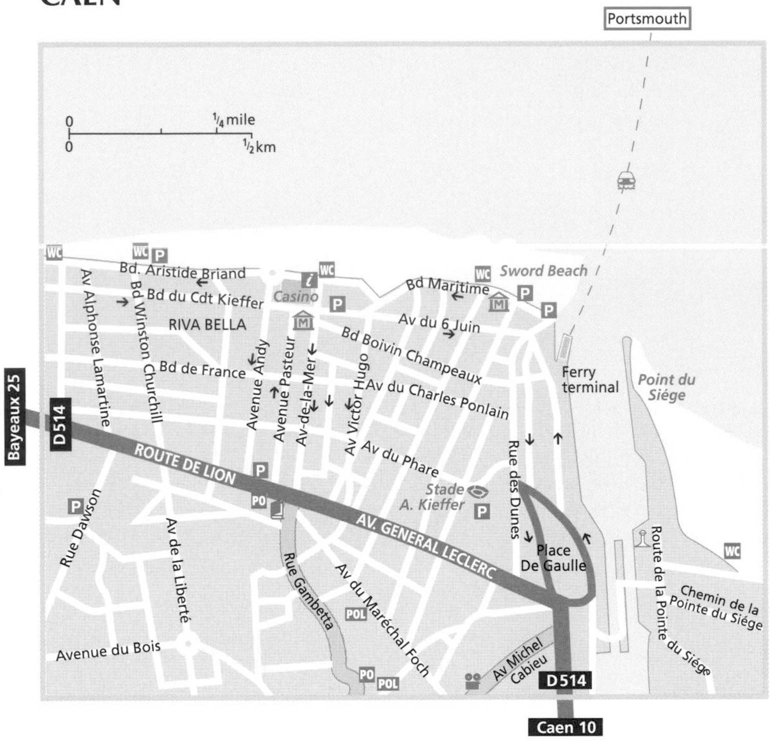

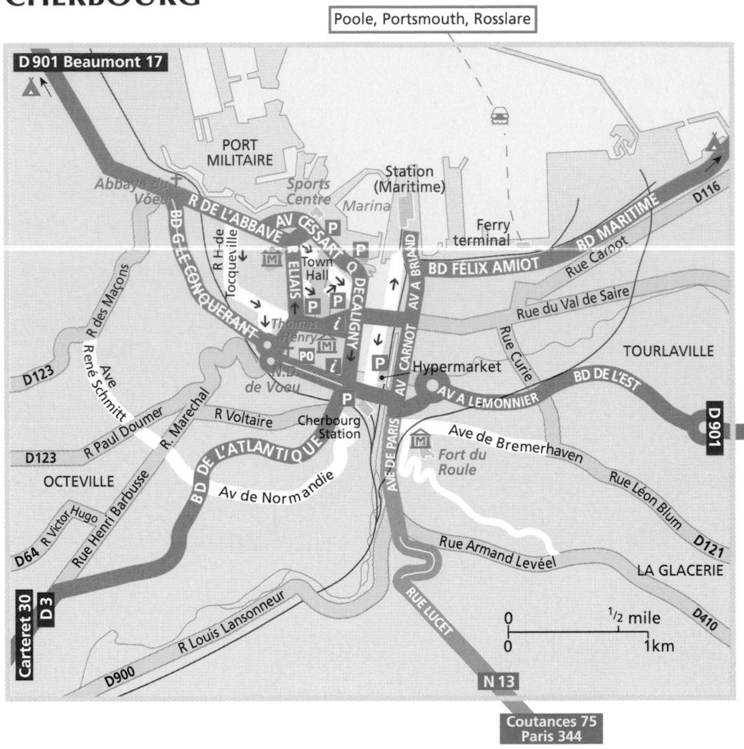

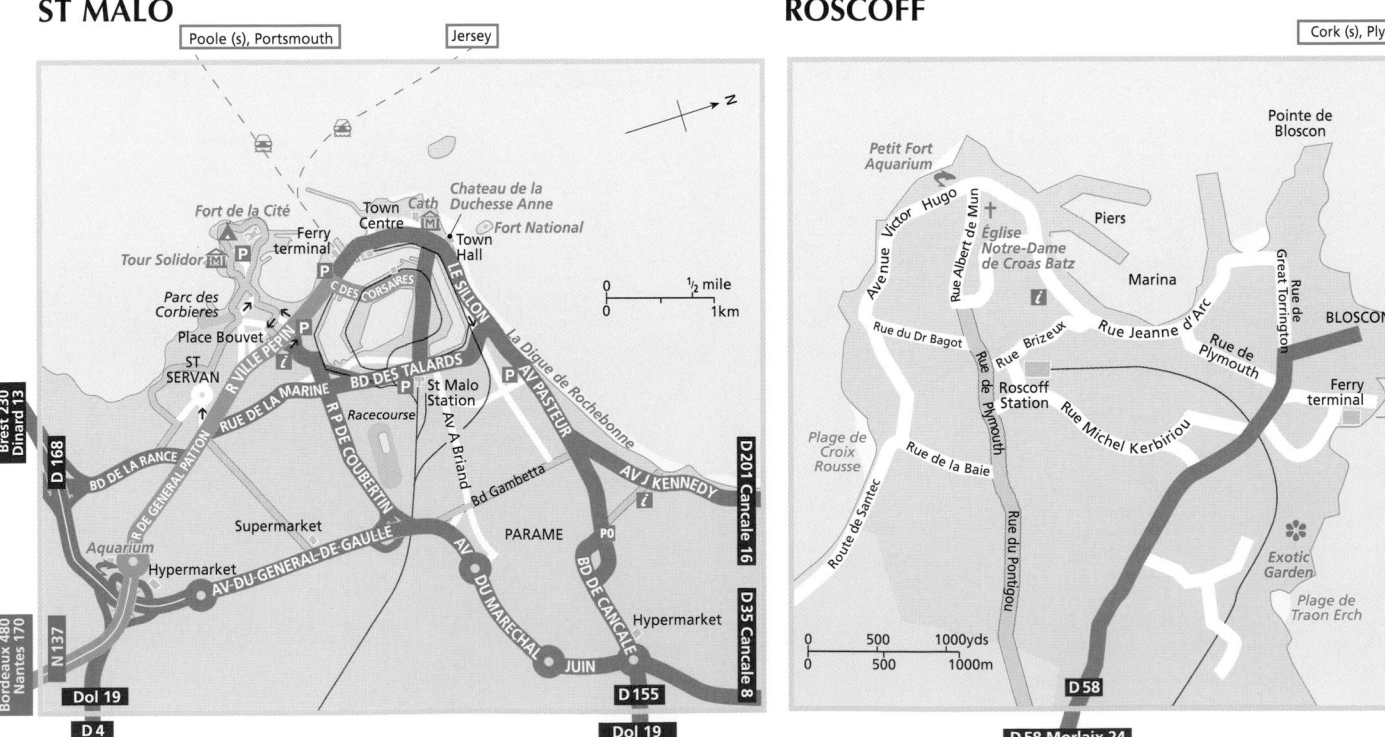

ST HELIER

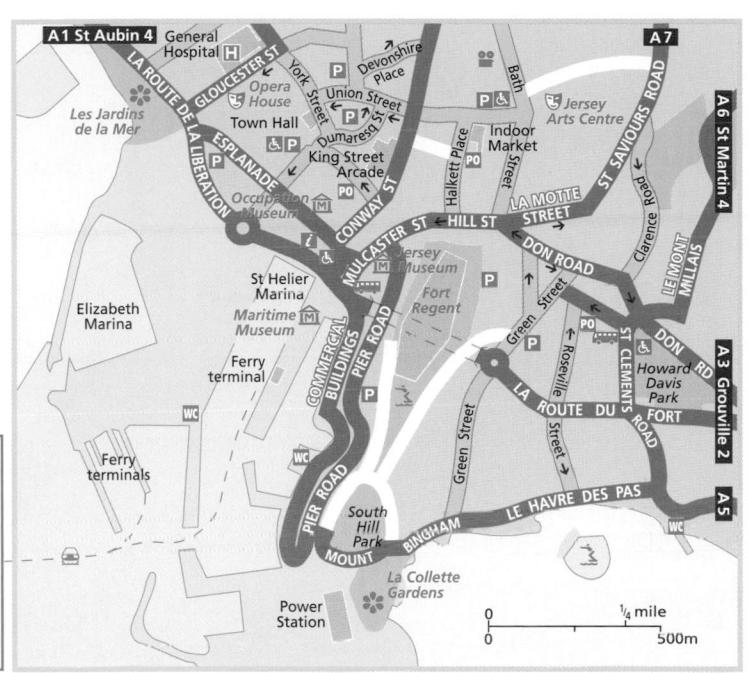

ST PETER PORT

Poole, Portsmouth, Weymouth

SPAIN

Brittany Ferries operate services to **Santander** from Plymouth during the summer – telephone 0870 366 5333 for crossing times and fares. The journey takes 24 hours. P&O Portsmouth run crossings between Portsmouth and **Bilbao** throughout the year. Call 08705 202020 for more information about the journey, which takes around 35 hours.

SANTANDER

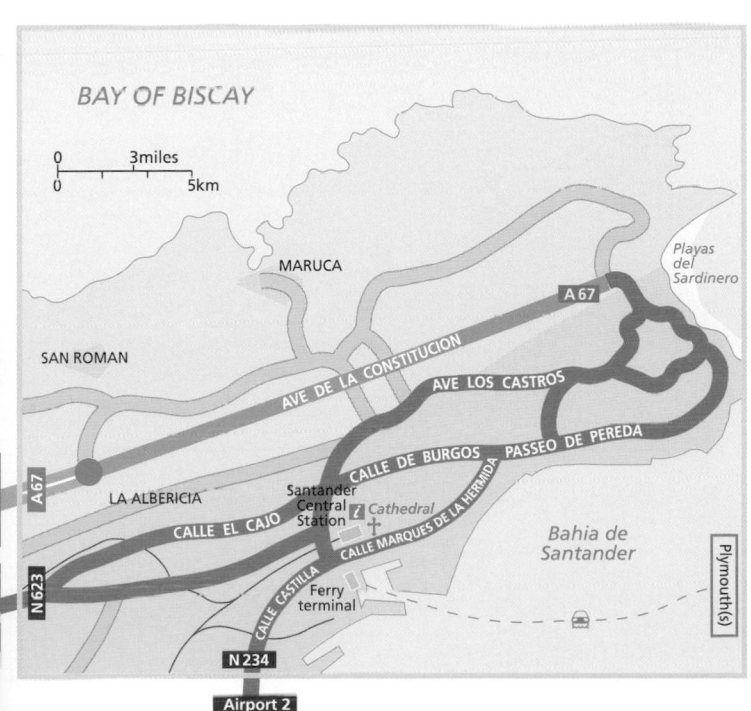

BILBAO

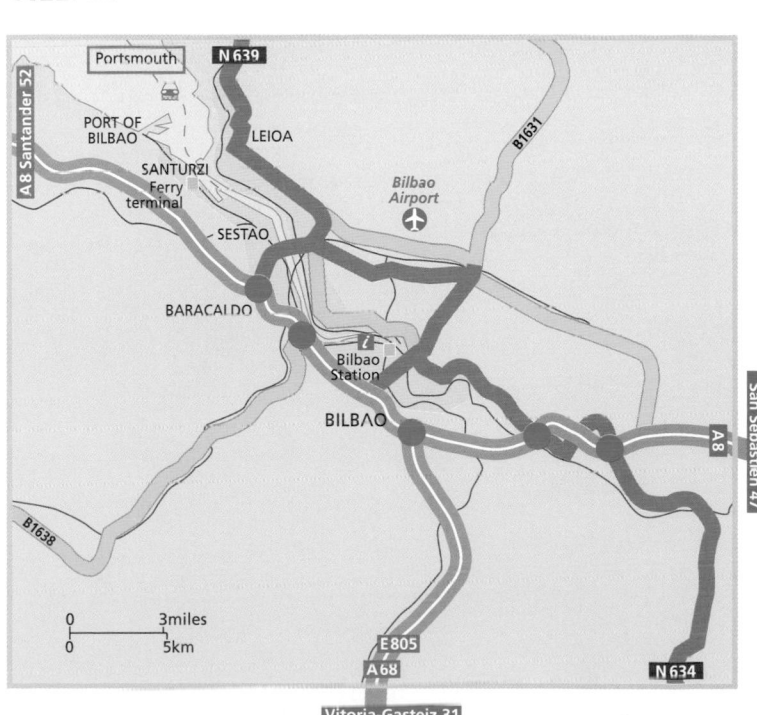

FERRY PORTS

Local airports

Plans of 23 airports in Britain and Ireland which carry passenger traffic are shown, in alphabetical order, on these pages. Each plan shows the closest motorway junctions and main routes around and within the airport as well as distances to nearby towns and cities in miles. The location of short and long stay car parks in relation to terminal buildings is clearly shown. Bus, railway and coach links are indicated, and where applicable, airport hotels are also given.

ABERDEEN

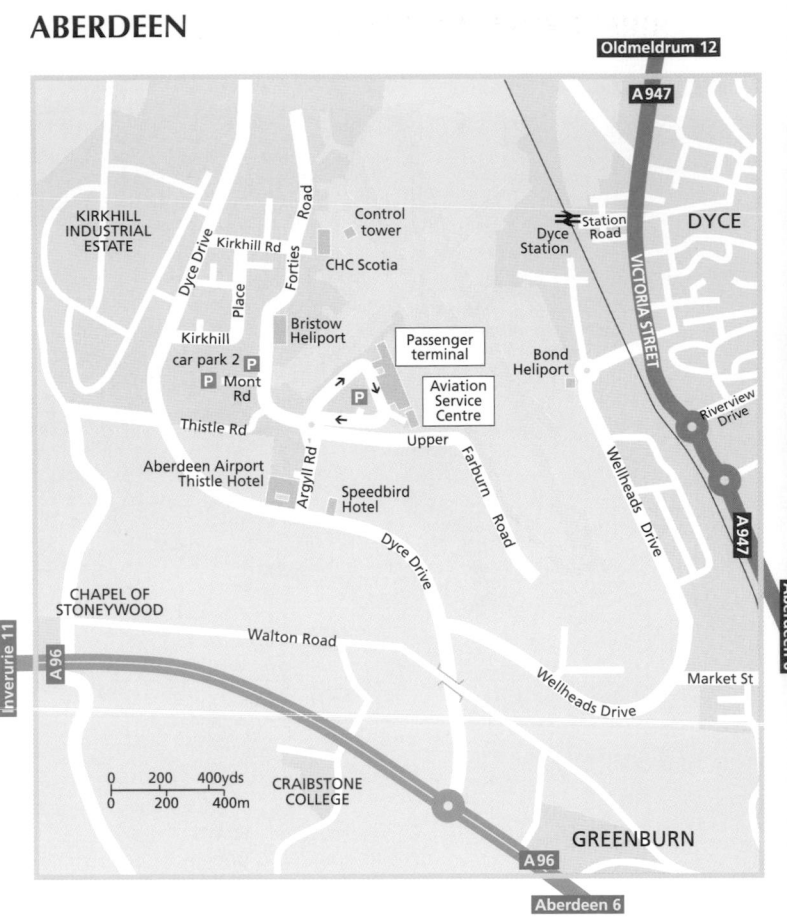

BELFAST CITY

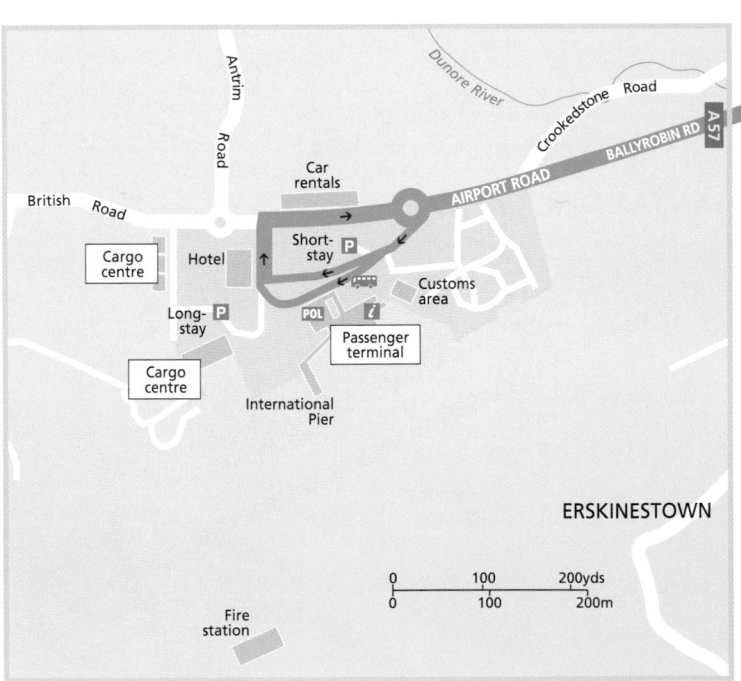

BELFAST INTERNATIONAL

BIRMINGHAM INTERNATIONAL

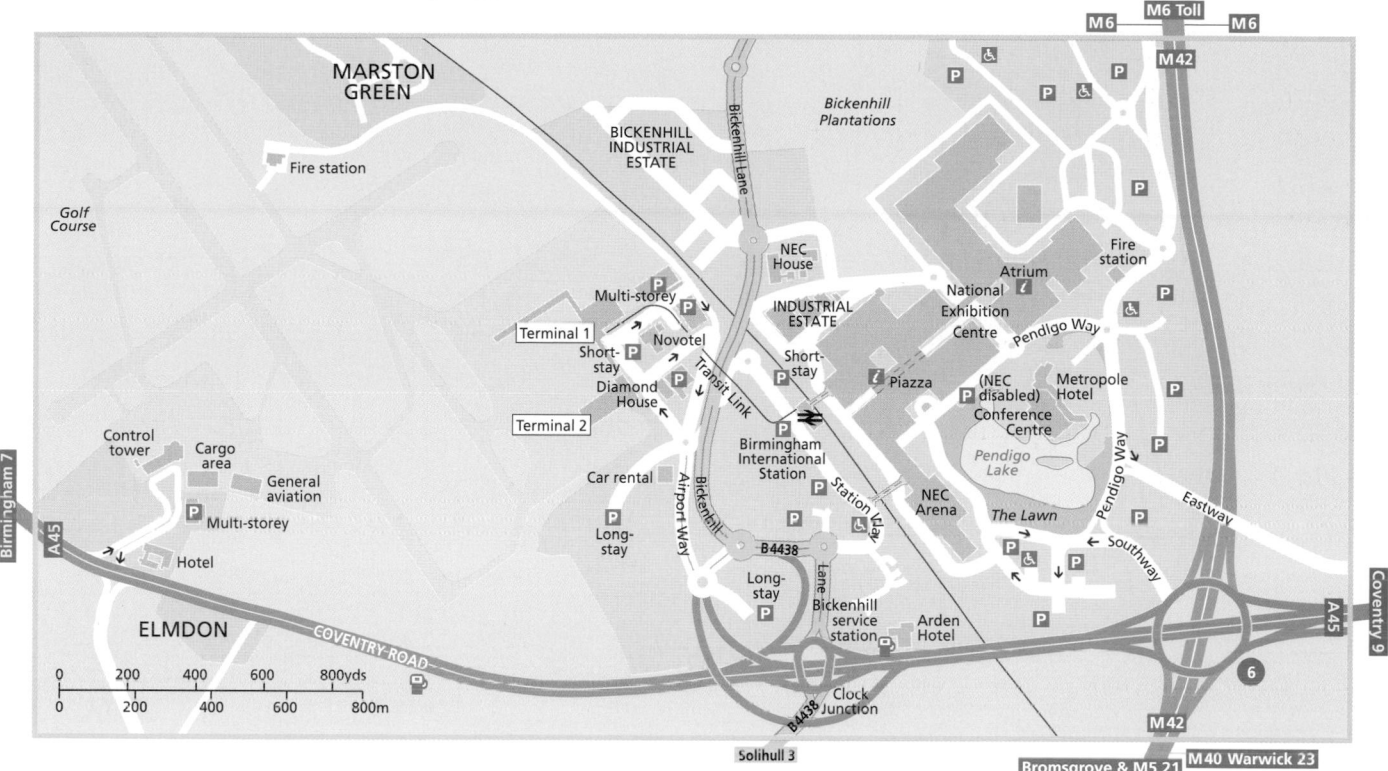

MARSTON GREEN

Bickenhill Plantations

M6   M6 Toll   M6

M42

BICKENHILL INDUSTRIAL ESTATE

Bickenhill Lane

Fire station

Golf Course

NEC House

Fire station

Atrium

Multi-storey

Terminal 1

National Exhibition Centre

Pendigo Way

Short-stay

Novotel

INDUSTRIAL ESTATE

Short-stay

Piazza

Transit Link

Diamond House

Terminal 2

(NEC disabled)

Conference Centre

Metropole Hotel

Pendigo Way

Control tower

Cargo area

General aviation

Car rental

Birmingham International Station

Pendigo Lake

Station Way

Eastway

Birmingham 7

A45

Multi-storey

Hotel

Airport Way

Bickenhill Lane

B4438

NEC Arena

The Lawn

Southway

Coventry 9

A45

ELMDON

COVENTRY ROAD

Long-stay

Long-stay

Bickenhill service station

Arden Hotel

6

0   200   400   600   800yds
0   200   400   600   800m

B4438

Clock Junction

M42

Solihull 3

Bromsgrove & M5 21   M40 Warwick 23

AIRPORTS

BRISTOL

The Batch

Oatfield

A38 Bristol 8

DOWNSIDE

Downside Road

LULSGATE BOTTOM

Coombe Dale

Golf Course

Cooks Bridge Path

Car hire parking

Short stay

Long-stay

North Side Road

Passenger terminal

Fire station

Winters Lane

Administration building

P

Winter Lane

New Road

REDHILL

0   200   400yds
0   200   400m

A38

Row of Ashes Lane

Taunton 35

CARDIFF

B4265

Dragonfly Dr

M4 10 A4226 Cardiff 12

British Airways maintenance buildings

Long-stay

Short-stay

Passenger terminal   Cargo terminal

Fire station

Maintenance area

Rhoose Road

0   200   400yds
0   200   400m

Readers Way

RHOOSE

Porthkerry Road

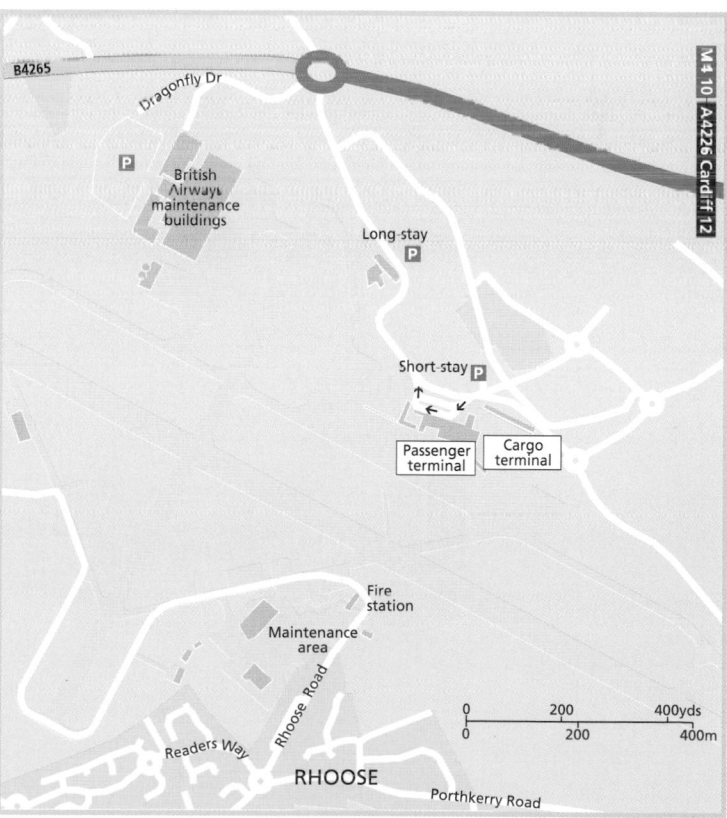

CORK

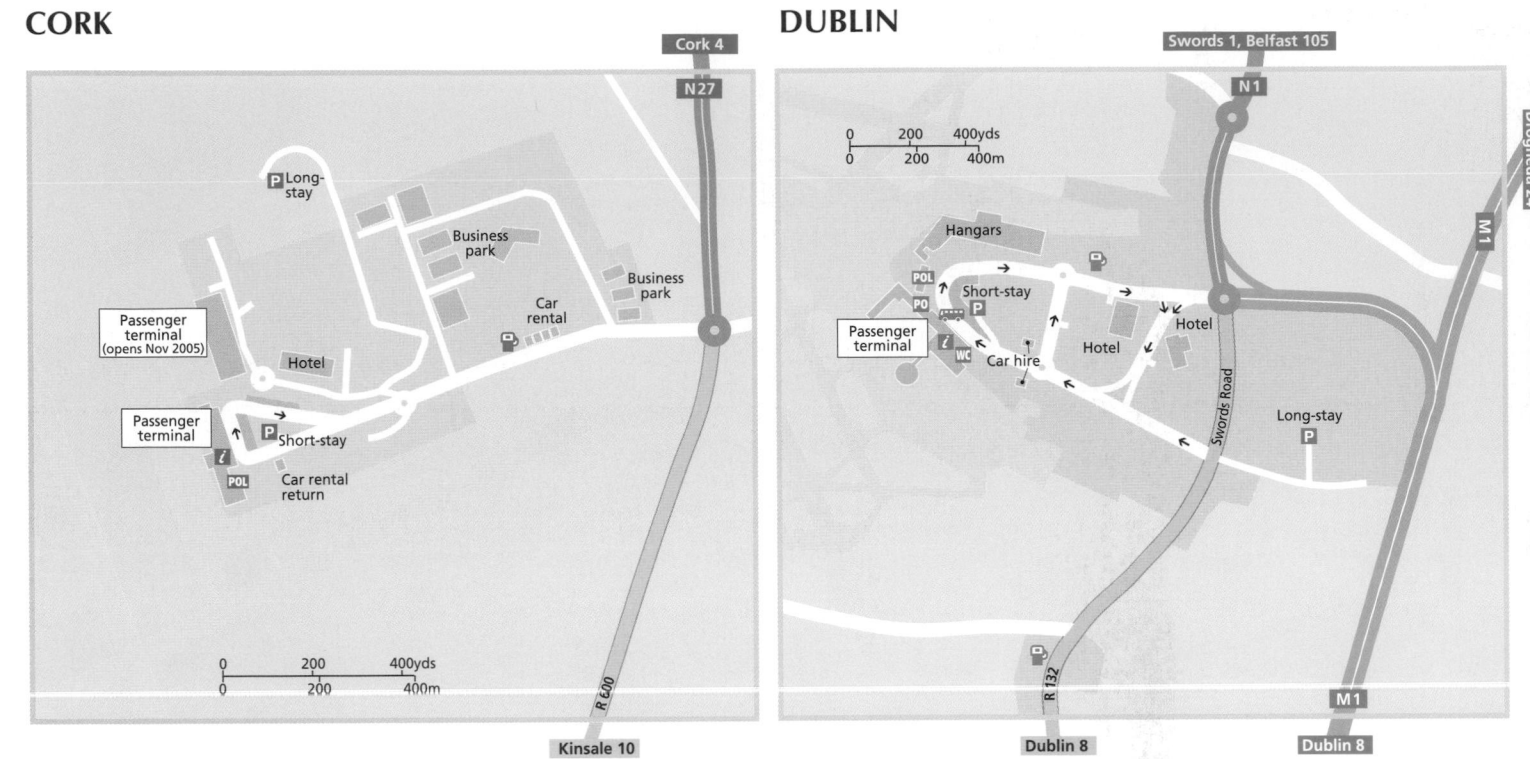

Cork 4

N27

Long-stay

Business park

Business park

Car rental

Passenger terminal (opens Nov 2005)

Hotel

Passenger terminal

Short-stay

Car rental return

POL

0 200 400yds
0 200 400m

R 600

Kinsale 10

DUBLIN

Swords 1, Belfast 105

N1

Drogheda 24

M1

0 200 400yds
0 200 400m

Hangars

POL
PO
Short-stay

Passenger terminal

WC
Car hire

Hotel

Hotel

Long-stay

Swords Road

R 132

Dublin 8

M1

Dublin 8

NOTTINGHAM EAST MIDLANDS

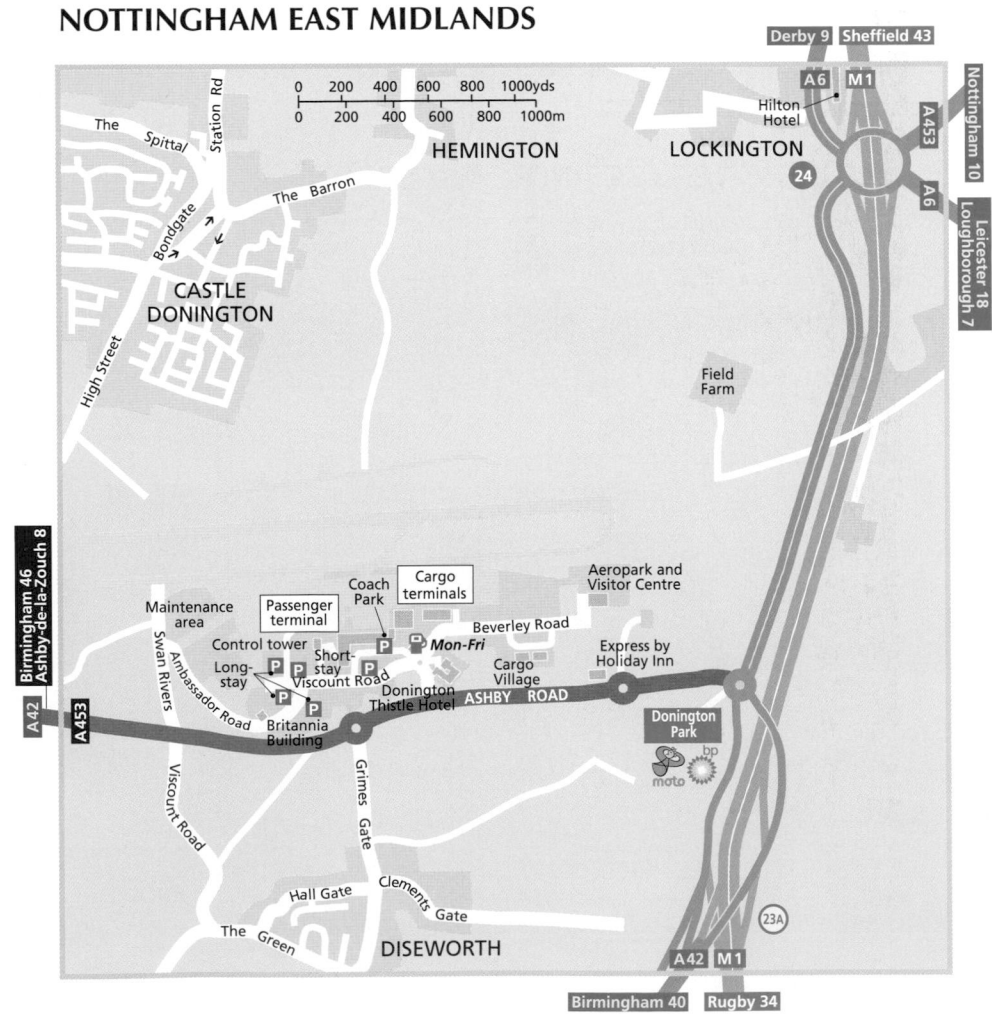

Derby 9 Sheffield 43

A6 M1

Hilton Hotel

Nottingham 10

A453

A6

Leicester 18
Loughborough 7

Station Rd

0 200 400 600 800 1000yds
0 200 400 600 800 1000m

HEMINGTON

LOCKINGTON

The Spittal

The Barron

Bondgate

24

CASTLE DONINGTON

High Street

Field Farm

Birmingham 46
Ashby-de-la-Zouch 8

Maintenance area

Ambassador Road

Swan Rivers

Coach Park

Cargo terminals

Aeropark and Visitor Centre

Passenger terminal

Control tower
Short-stay
Long-stay
Viscount Road

Mon-Fri

Beverley Road

Cargo Village

Express by Holiday Inn

A42

A453

Britannia Building

Donington Thistle Hotel

ASHBY ROAD

Donington Park

bp
moto

Viscount Road

Grimes Gate

Hall Gate

Clements Gate

The Green

DISEWORTH

23A

A42 M1

Birmingham 40 Rugby 34

EDINBURGH

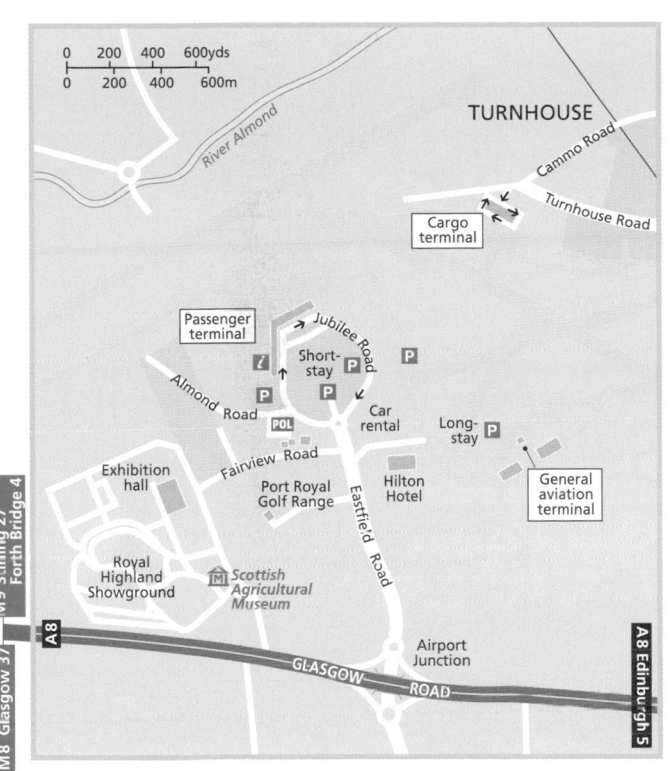

TURNHOUSE

Cargo terminal

Cammo Road

Turnhouse Road

River Almond

Passenger terminal

Jubilee Road

Short-stay

Car rental

Almond Road

Fairview Road

POL

Port Royal Golf Range

Eastfield Road

Hilton Hotel

Long-stay

General aviation terminal

Exhibition hall

Royal Highland Showground

M Scottish Agricultural Museum

M9 Stirling 27 / Forth Bridge 4

M8 Glasgow 37

A8

GLASGOW ROAD

Airport Junction

A8 Edinburgh 5

0 200 400 600yds
0 200 400 600m

GLASGOW

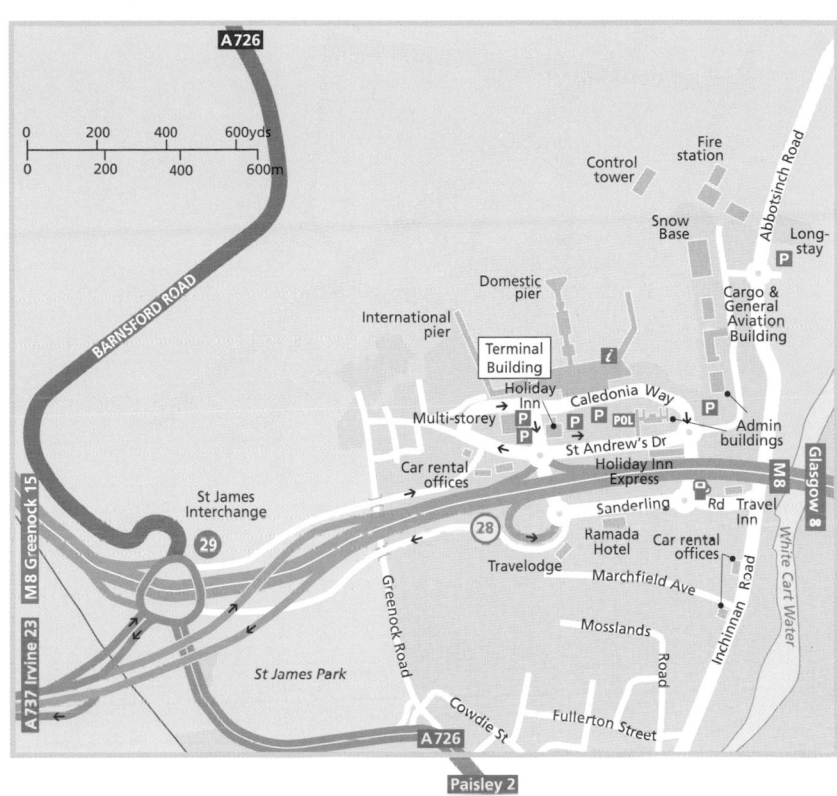

A726

BARNSFORD ROAD

Control tower

Fire station

Abbotsinch Road

Snow Base

Long-stay

Domestic pier

International pier

Terminal Building

Cargo & General Aviation Building

Holiday Inn

Caledonia Way

Multi-storey

POL

St Andrew's Dr

Admin buildings

Car rental offices

Holiday Inn Express

M8

Glasgow 8

St James Interchange

29

28

Sanderling

Rd

Travel Inn

Ramada Hotel

Car rental offices

Travelodge

Marchfield Ave

Inchinnan Road

White Cart Water

Mosslands Road

Greenock Road

St James Park

Cowdie St

Fullerton Street

M8 Greenock 15

A737 Irvine 23

A726

Paisley 2

0 200 400 600yds
0 200 400 600m

HUMBERSIDE

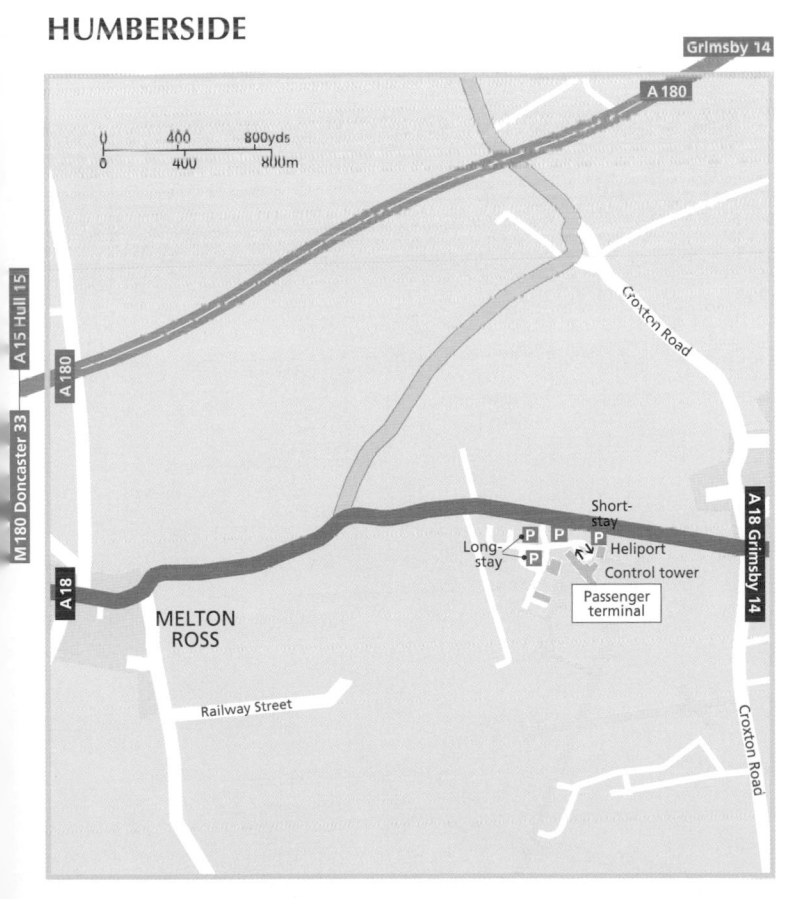

Grimsby 14

A180

Croxton Road

A15 Hull 15

A180

M180 Doncaster 33

A18

MELTON ROSS

Short-stay

Long-stay

Heliport

Control tower

Passenger terminal

A18 Grimsby 14

Railway Street

Croxton Road

0 400 800yds
0 400 800m

LEEDS/BRADFORD

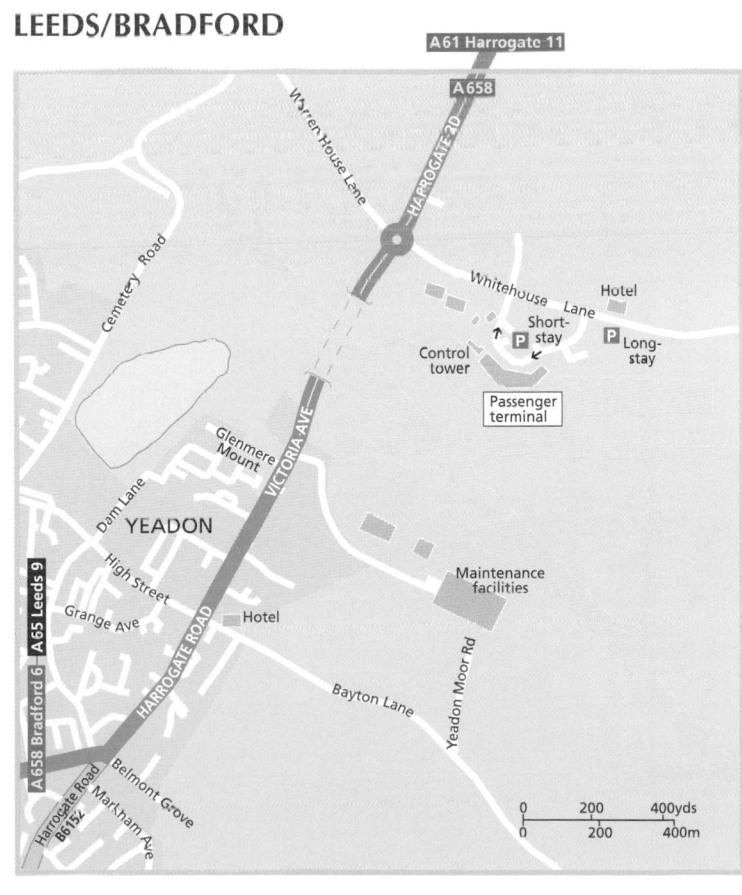

A61 Harrogate 11

A658

Wyren House Lane

HARROGATE RD

Cemetery Road

Whitehouse Lane

Hotel

Short-stay

Long-stay

Control tower

Passenger terminal

Glenmere Mount

Dam Lane

VICTORIA AVE

YEADON

High Street

Grange Ave

HARROGATE ROAD

Hotel

Maintenance facilities

Bayton Lane

Yeadon Moor Rd

A658 Bradford 6

A65 Leeds 9

Belmont Grove

Harrogate Road

Markham Ave

B6152

0 200 400yds
0 200 400m

AIRPORTS

LIVERPOOL JOHN LENNON

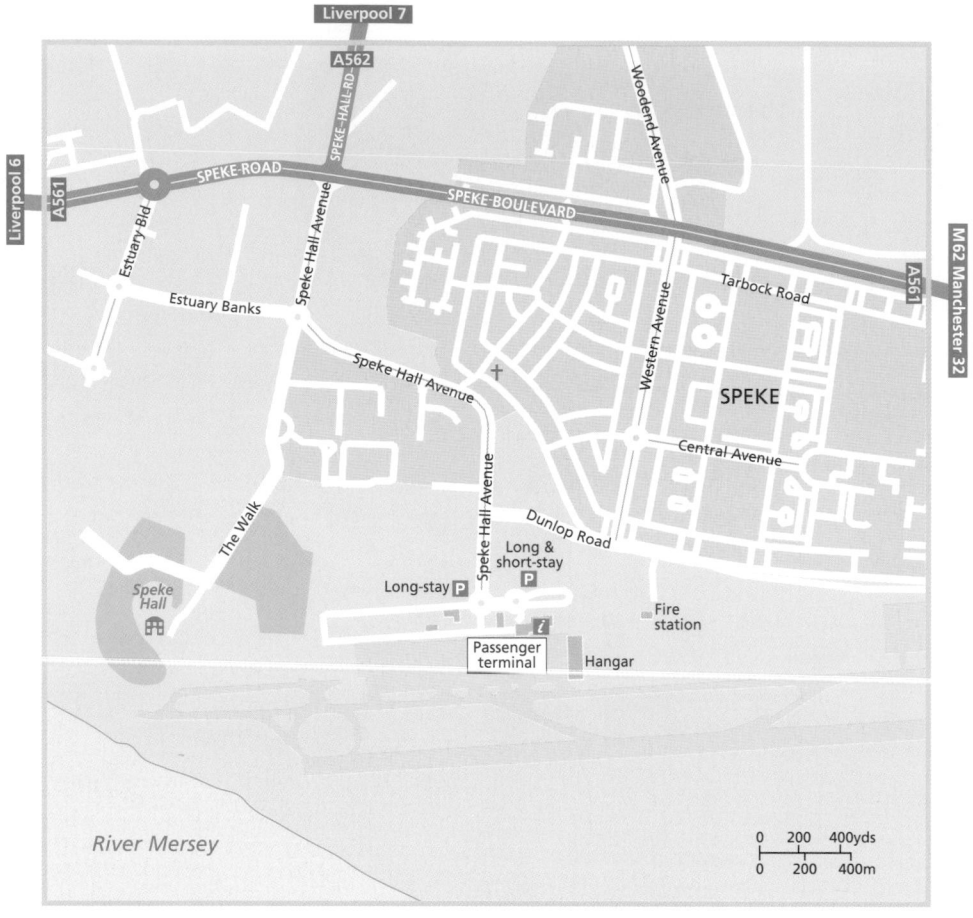

Liverpool 7

A562

SPEKE-HALL-RD

Woodend Avenue

Liverpool 6

A561

SPEKE ROAD

SPEKE BOULEVARD

M62 Manchester 32

A561

Estuary Bld

Estuary Banks

Speke Hall Avenue

Tarbock Road

Western Avenue

Speke Hall Avenue

SPEKE

Central Avenue

The Walk

Speke Hall Avenue

Dunlop Road

Long & short-stay

Speke Hall

Long-stay

Fire station

Passenger terminal

Hangar

River Mersey

0   200   400yds
0   200   400m

LONDON GATWICK

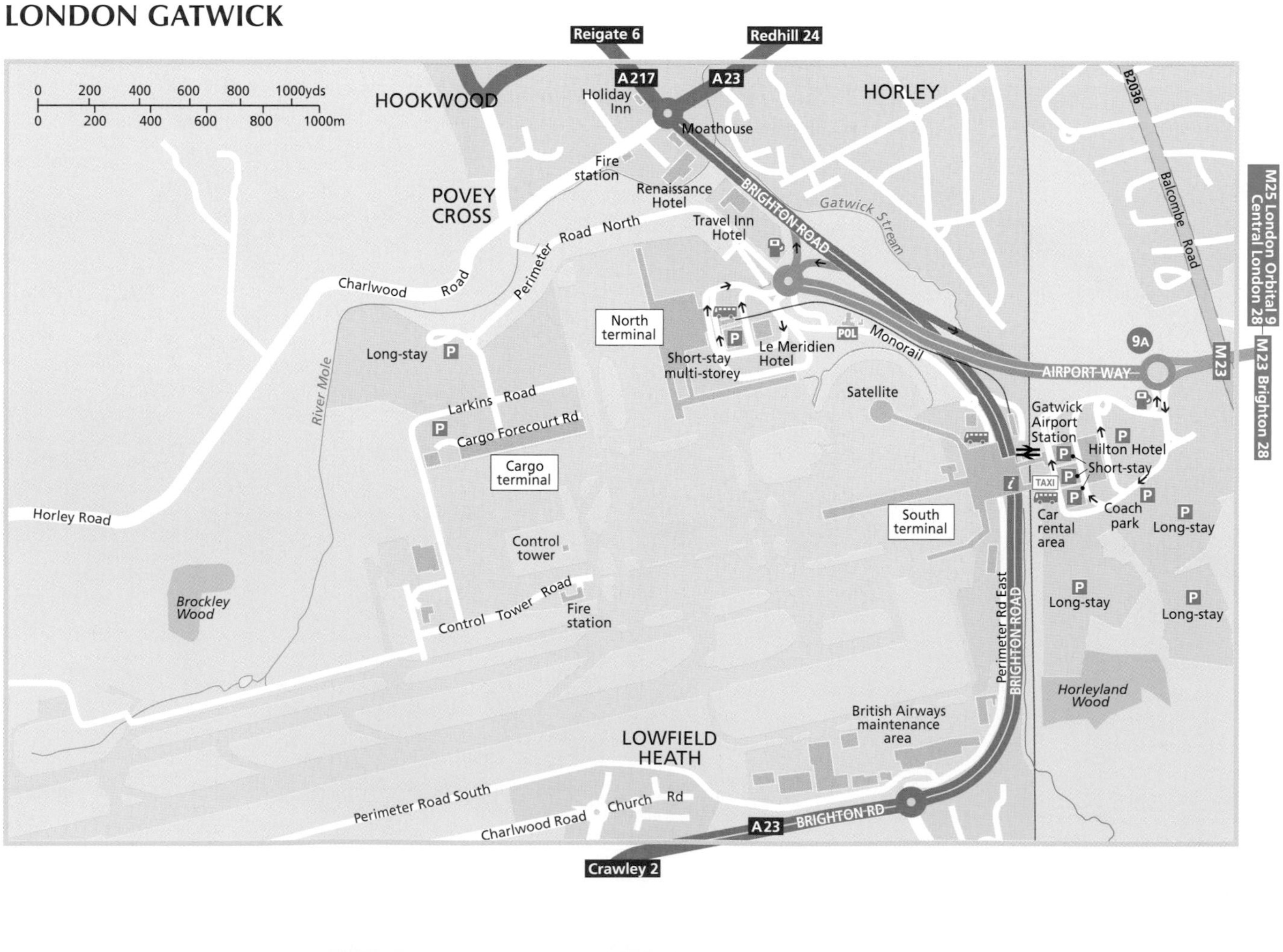

0   200   400   600   800   1000yds
0   200   400   600   800   1000m

Reigate 6

Redhill 24

HOOKWOOD

A217

Holiday Inn

A23

HORLEY

Moathouse

B2036

POVEY CROSS

Fire station

Renaissance Hotel

Travel Inn Hotel

BRIGHTON ROAD

Gatwick Stream

Balcombe Road

Charlwood Road

Perimeter Road North

North terminal

Short-stay multi-storey

Le Meridien Hotel

POL

Monorail

AIRPORT WAY

M25 London Orbital 9
Central London 28

M23 Brighton 28

9A

M23

Long-stay

River Mole

Larkins Road

Cargo Forecourt Rd

Satellite

Gatwick Airport Station

Hilton Hotel

Short-stay

Horley Road

Cargo terminal

TAXI

Car rental area

Coach park

Long-stay

Control tower

South terminal

Brockley Wood

Control Tower Road

Fire station

Perimeter Rd East

BRIGHTON ROAD

Long-stay

Long-stay

Horleyland Wood

LOWFIELD HEATH

British Airways maintenance area

Perimeter Road South

Charlwood Road

Church Rd

A23

BRIGHTON RD

Crawley 2

LONDON HEATHROW

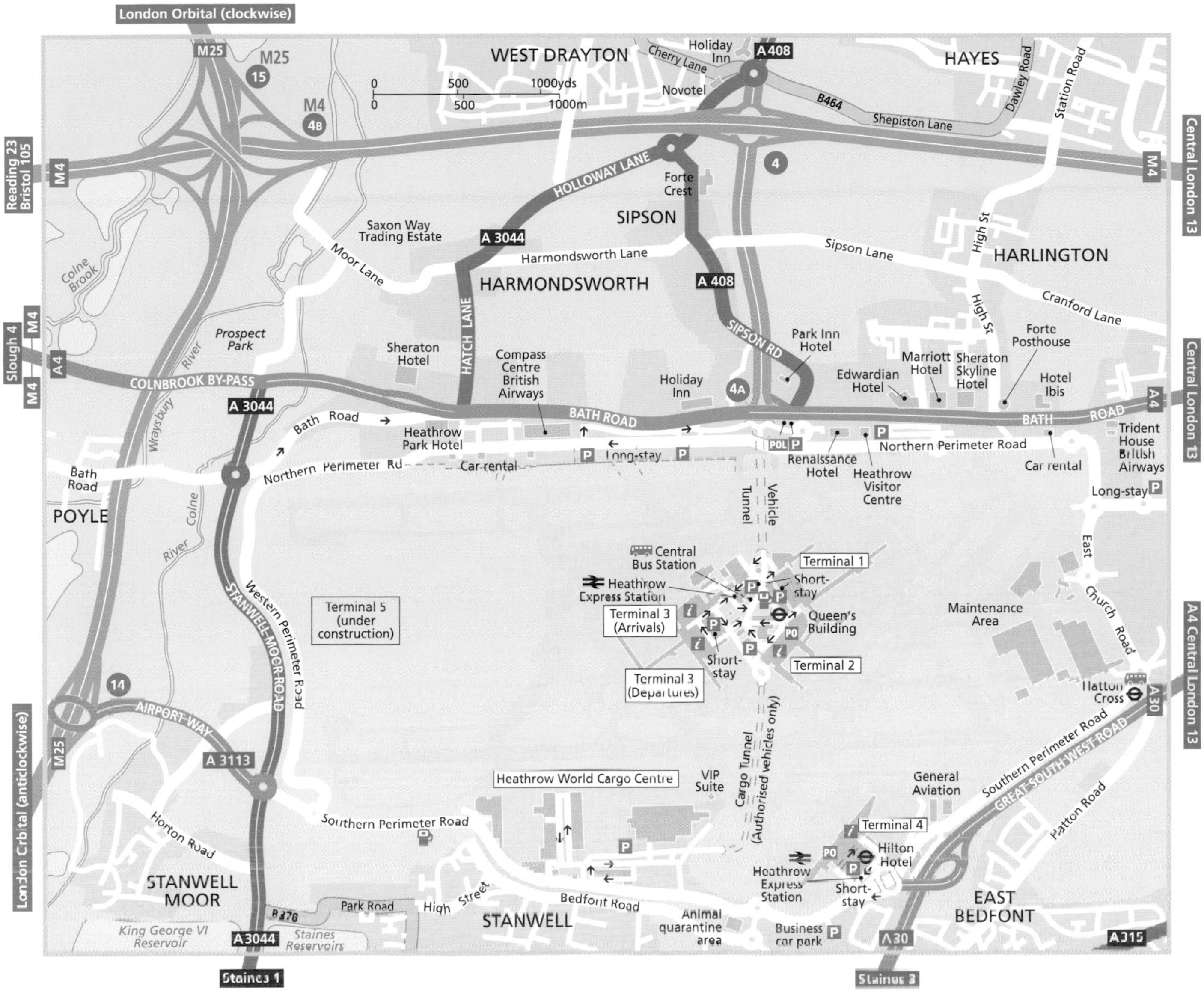

LONDON LUTON

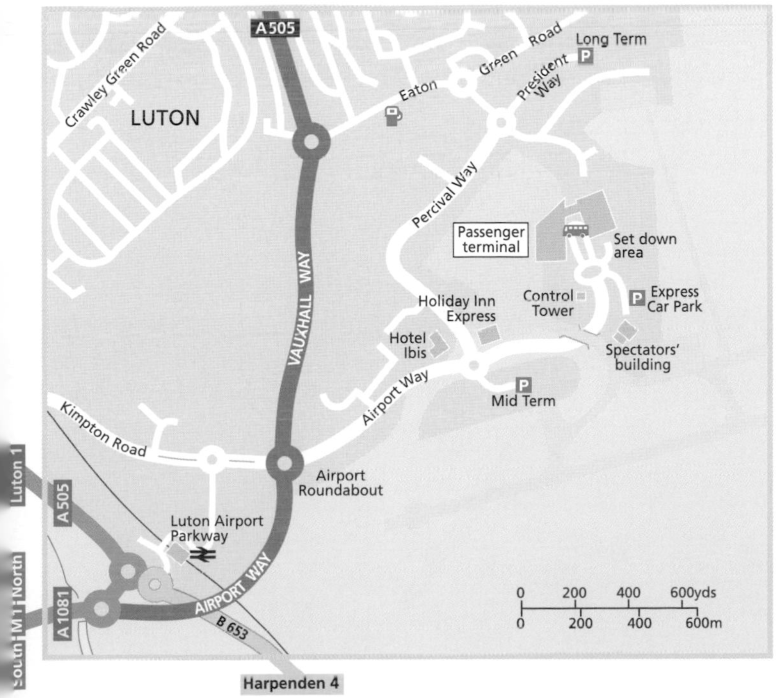

LONDON CITY

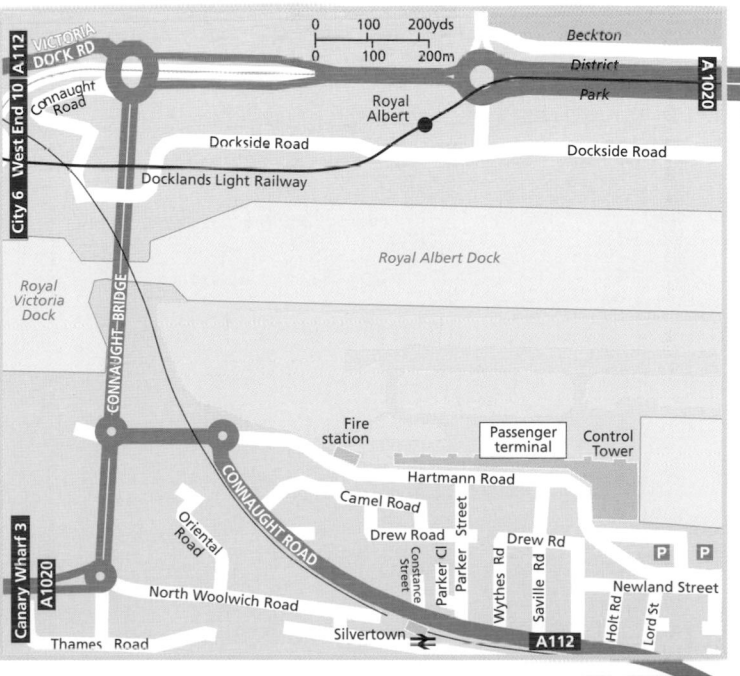

LONDON STANSTED

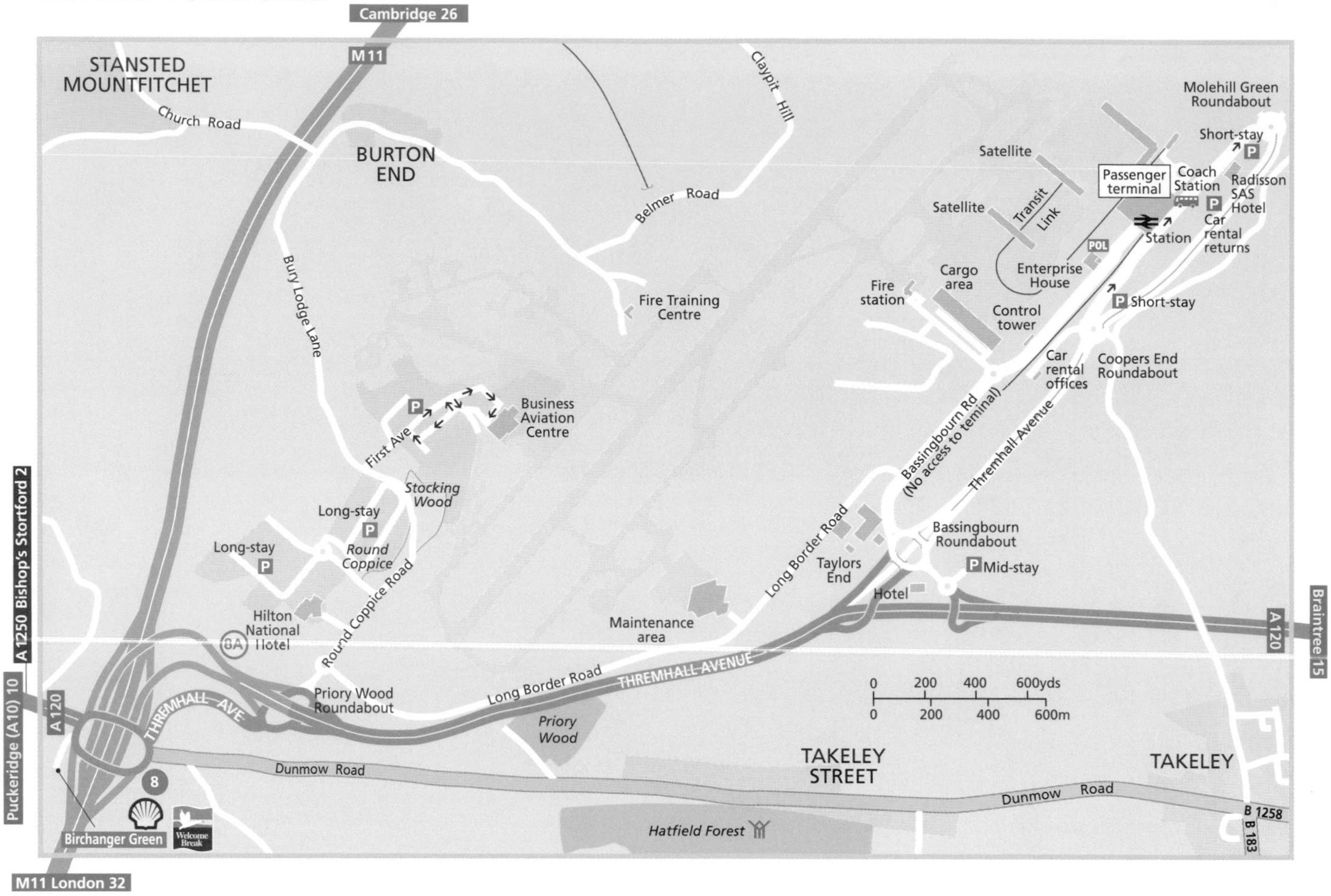

Cambridge 26
M11

STANSTED MOUNTFITCHET

Church Road

BURTON END

Claypit Hill

Belmer Road

Molehill Green Roundabout

Satellite

Short-stay

Passenger terminal

Coach Station

Transit Link

Radisson SAS Hotel

Satellite

POL

Station

Car rental returns

Fire Training Centre

Fire station

Cargo area

Enterprise House

Control tower

Short-stay

Bury Lodge Lane

First Ave

Business Aviation Centre

Car rental offices

Coopers End Roundabout

Stocking Wood

Bassingbourn Rd (No access to terminal)

Thremhall Avenue

Long-stay

Round Coppice

Long Border Road

Bassingbourn Roundabout

Long-stay

Taylors End

Mid-stay

Round Coppice Road

Hilton National Hotel

Maintenance area

Hotel

A120

Braintree 15

A 1250 Bishop's Stortford 2

Priory Wood Roundabout

Long Border Road

THREMHALL AVENUE

0   200   400   600yds
0   200   400   600m

Puckeridge (A10) 10

A120

THREMHALL AVE.

Priory Wood

TAKELEY STREET

TAKELEY

Dunmow Road

8

Birchanger Green

Welcome Break

Hatfield Forest

Dunmow Road

B 1258
B 183

M11 London 32

MANCHESTER (RINGWAY)

Manchester 7
M56

0   200   400   600yds
0   200   400   600m

5

Portway

Portway

Bailey Lane

WOODHOUSE PARK

Hasty Lane

M56

M6

Runger Lane

Long-stay

Short-stay multi-storey

i

Terminal 2

Hilton Hotel

Chester 33

M6

Station

Bewley's Hotel

Ringway Rd West

Skyport self-service station

Posthouse Hotel

Short-stay multi-storey

TAXI

POL

Long-stay

Ringway Road

P

Altrincham 4

A538

International flights

i

Terminal 1

Terminal 3

General Aviation

Maintenance area

Wilmslow Old Road

Fire station

Moss Lane

Viewing area

River Bollin

Styal Country Park

A538 Macclesfield 10

NEWCASTLE

0   100   200yds
0   100   200m

A 696 Jedburgh 52

Long-stay

Britannia Hotel

Short-stay

Passenger terminal

i

M

Control tower

Travel Inn

Cargo terminal

Airport Freightway

Level crossing

Callerton Parkway (Park & Ride)

P   M

B6918

A696

A1 3   A 167 Newcastle Upon Tyne 7

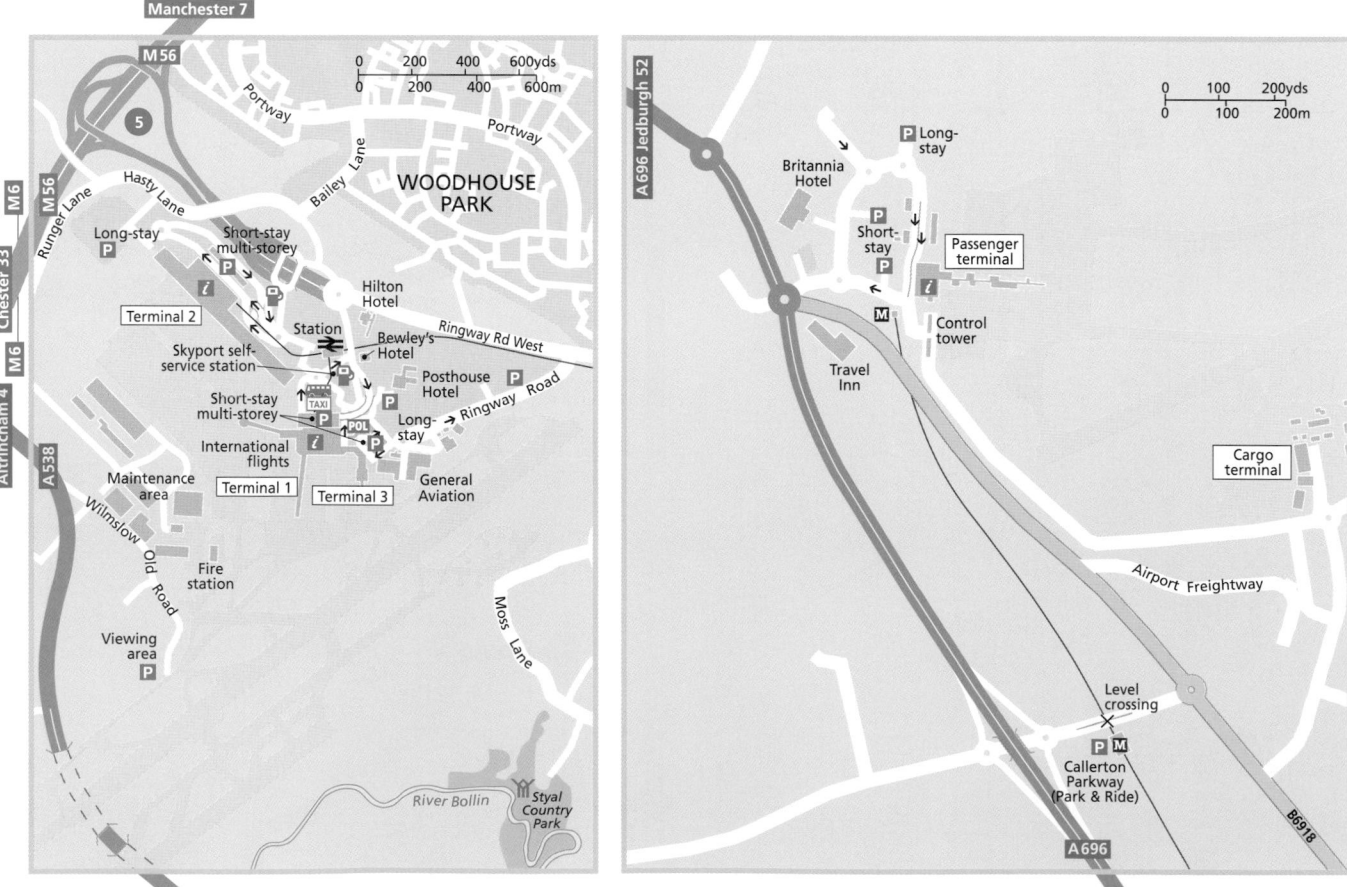

PRESTWICK

A77 Glasgow 36
A79
B739
Station Road
Main Street
MONKTON
Tarbolton Road
B739
Main Street
INDUSTRIAL AREA
Tay Road
Passenger terminal
Moffat Rd
Prestwick International Airport
McNee Rd
i
P2 Short-stay
P1 Short-stay
Welsh Rd
P4 Long-stay
Monkton Rd
P3 Long-stay
Powmill Rd
A79
Ayrpark
P5
Ayr 3

0   100   200   300yds
0   100   200   300m

SHANNON

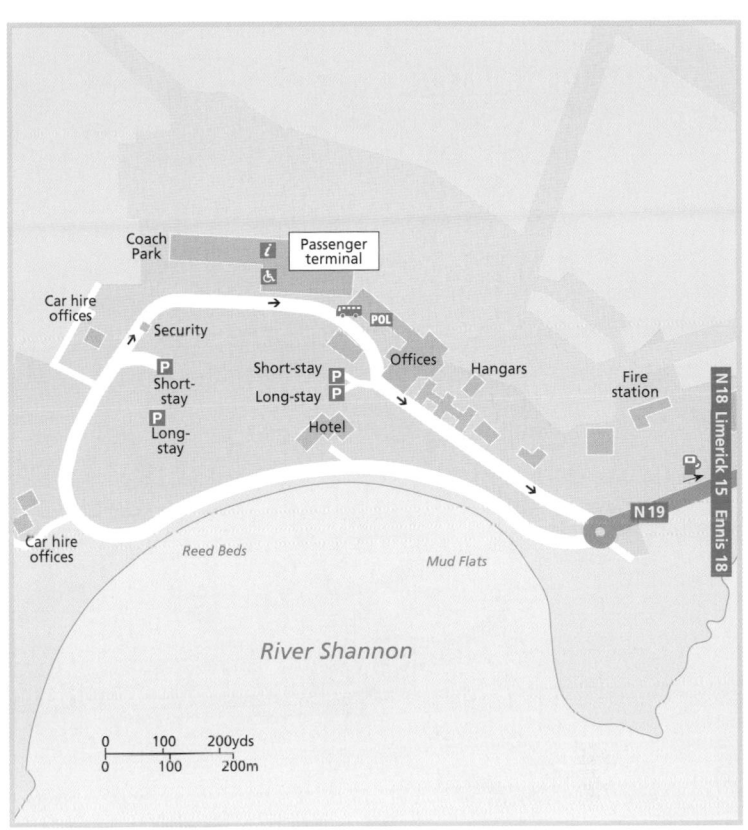

Coach Park
i
Passenger terminal
Car hire offices
Security
POL
Short-stay
Offices
Hangars
Fire station
N18 Limerick 15 Ennis 18
P Short-stay
P Long-stay
P Long-stay
Hotel
N19
Car hire offices
Reed Beds
Mud Flats
River Shannon

0   100   200yds
0   100   200m

SOUTHAMPTON

M3 Winchester 9
A335
P Long-stay
StonehamLane
Tinker Alley
Fire station
WIDE LANE
Control tower
P Short-stay
M27
5
Spitfire Loop
Southampton Airport (Parkway) Station
Mitchell Way
Wide La
Passenger terminal
STONEHAM WAY
Royal Mail
Premier Lodge Hotel
George Curl Way
A335
INDUSTRIAL AREA
Wide Lane
M27
Portsmouth 21

0   200   400yds
0   200   400m

Southampton 5

DURHAM TEES VALLEY

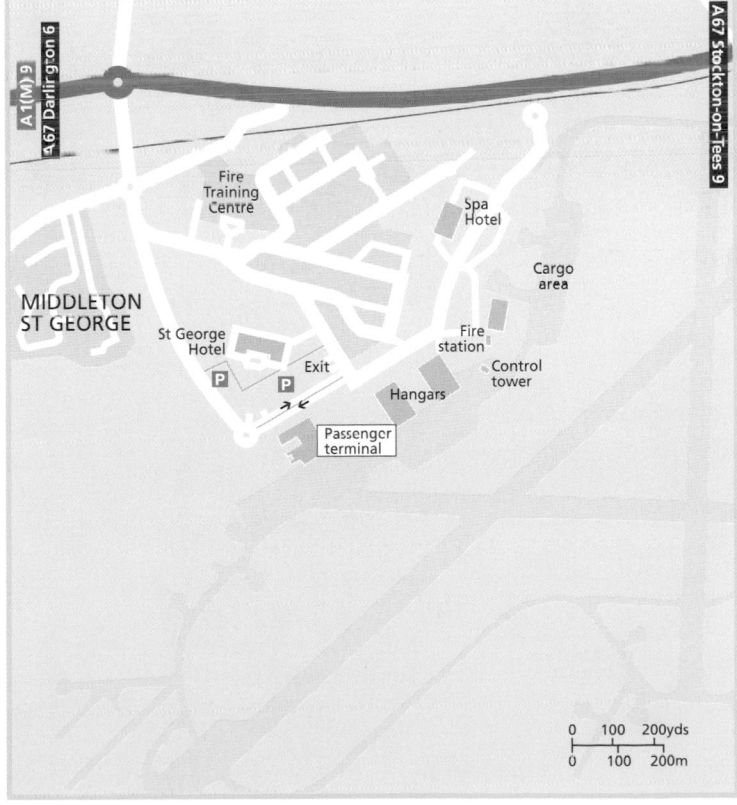

A1(M) 9 Darlington 6
A67 Stockton-on-Tees 9
A67 Stockton-on-Tees 9
Fire Training Centre
Spa Hotel
MIDDLETON ST GEORGE
Cargo area
St George Hotel
Fire station
P
Exit
P
Control tower
Hangars
Passenger terminal

0   100   200yds
0   100   200m

AIRPORTS

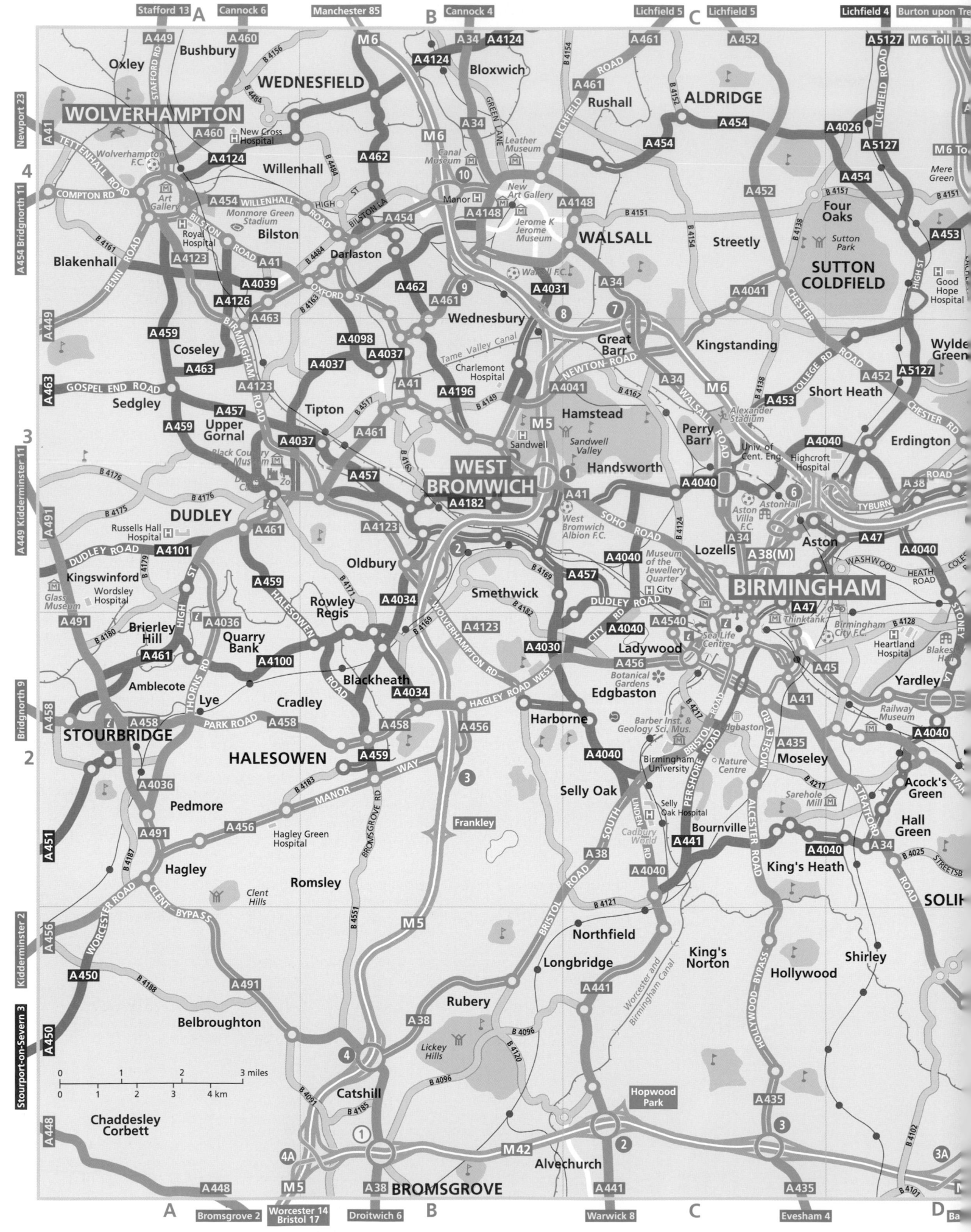

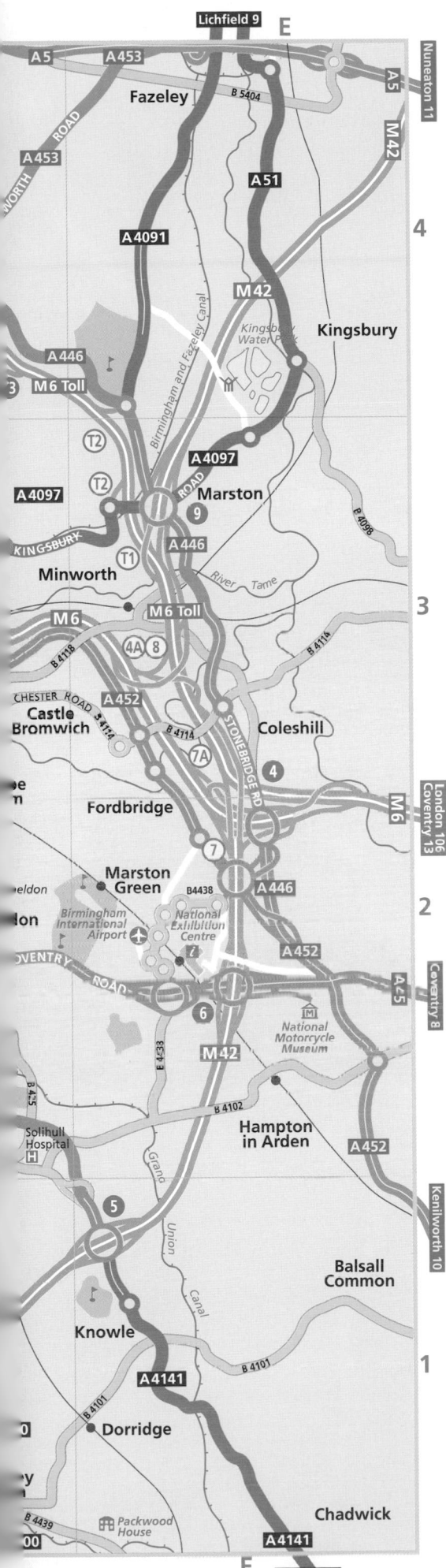

SEE TOWN PLANS PP311 & 404 AND TOURING GUIDE P444

Birmingham & Wolverhampton

Birmingham, at the heart of England, is one of Britain's foremost convention and exhibition centres and a major regional focus for art and music. Legacies of the city's industrial and commercial past include the fascinating Jewellery Quarter, an extensive network of canals which offer scenic towpath walks and some splendid examples of civic architecture. Birmingham's latest addition, the stunning new interactive discovery centre, Thinktank, is a symbol of the city's innovation and modernity.

Wolverhampton lies at the heart of what was once the Black Country – a sprawl of towns, including Dudley, Stourbridge and Walsall, that developed into large industrial centres during the 19th century. The area's heritage is today recalled in the many popular tourist attractions such as Walsall's Leather Museum and the Black Country Museum.

TOURIST OFFICES

Birmingham
(0121) 202 5099
Wolverhampton
(01902) 556110

WHERE TO PARK

Birmingham (p311):
Dale End **D3**
Dudley Street **C2**
Livery Street **B4**

Wolverhampton (p404):
Wulfrun Centre **C2**
Piper's Row **C3**

CITY ROUTES

ASTON HALL [C3] A riot of turrets, gables and octagonal chimneys surmount the ornate Jacobean country house of 1618–35. Its elaborate interior includes a 41m (135ft) oak-panelled gallery, a cantilevered oak staircase and fine plasterwork ceilings.

BIRMINGHAM MUSEUM AND ART GALLERY [p311 B3] An impressive collection of Pre-Raphaelite works as well as archaeological and natural history exhibits are on show in the city's principal museum and gallery.

BIRMINGHAM TOWN HALL [p311 B3] Joseph Hansom, designer of the Hansom cab, is said to have modelled the city's neoclassical town hall of 1834–49 on the Temple of Castor and Pollux in Rome. Opposite is the Renaissance-style Council House of 1879.

BLACK COUNTRY MUSEUM [A3] Victorian workshops, homes, a pub, a chapel and a small colliery recreate life from the region's industrial past. Nearby, there are canal trips through **Dudley Tunnel**'s spectacular limestone caverns.

BLAKESLEY HALL [D2] A half-timbered house of 1590, the hall is furnished according to an inventory of 1684. The Painted Chamber has 16th-century wall paintings.

BOTANICAL GARDENS [C2] Filled with rhododendrons and azaleas, the gardens also house tropical plants in greenhouses.

BOURNVILLE [C2] George and Richard Cadbury built the village in 1894 for workers at their chocolate factory. **Cadbury World** tells the history of the Quaker firm.

DUDLEY ZOO [A3] On Castle Hill stands a partly medieval but mainly 16th-century castle with a well-preserved great hall. The zoo, begun in the 1930s, is set in the wooded grounds of the castle.

JEROME K. JEROME MUSEUM [B4] The author of *Three Men In A Boat*, Jerome was born in Walsall in 1859; his birthplace in Bradford Street is now a museum on his life and work.

LEATHER MUSEUM [B4] Saddles, bridles, belts and satchels are among the variety of leather goods on display at this museum in Walsall, an important leather centre for nearly two centuries. Demonstrations show skilled workers crafting leather goods.

MUSEUM OF THE JEWELLERY QUARTER [C3] An award-winning museum built around the perfectly preserved workshops of Smith & Pepper jewellers offers a fascinating insight into Birmingham's historic jewellery trade.

NATIONAL SEA LIFE CENTRE [C2] Designed by Norman Foster, the centre houses over 3,000 British freshwater and marine creatures, ranging from shrimps to sharks, and includes a transparent walk-through underwater tunnel.

ST CHAD'S CATHEDRAL [p311 B5] Augustus Pugin designed the red-brick, twin-spired building of 1841 – the first Roman Catholic cathedral to be built in Britain since the 16th-century Reformation.

ST PHILIP'S CATHEDRAL [p311 C3] Four 1890s stained-glass windows by Edward Burne-Jones, who was born in the city, adorn the elegant 18th-century baroque building.

SAREHOLE MILL [D2] Birmingham's only surviving water mill, the 18th-century building inspired J R R Tolkien, who spent his boyhood in the area, to write *The Hobbit*.

SUTTON PARK [D4] An old royal hunting ground, Sutton has been a public park since Henry VIII's time. It includes a 2km (1½ mile) stretch of the Roman Ryknild Street.

THINKTANK [C2] This new interactive science centre at **Millennium Point** has ten galleries of exhibits ranging from the world's oldest working steam engine to an innovative car welding robot.

WALSALL NEW ART GALLERY [B4] Costing £21 million, the gallery has a 4500m (14763ft) facade and a 100m (328ft) high tower, and contains a modern art collection, including works by the sculptor Jacob Epstein, donated by his widow.

WOLVERHAMPTON ART GALLERY [A4] The imposing Italianate building of 1883 displays mainly British 18th–20th-century art.

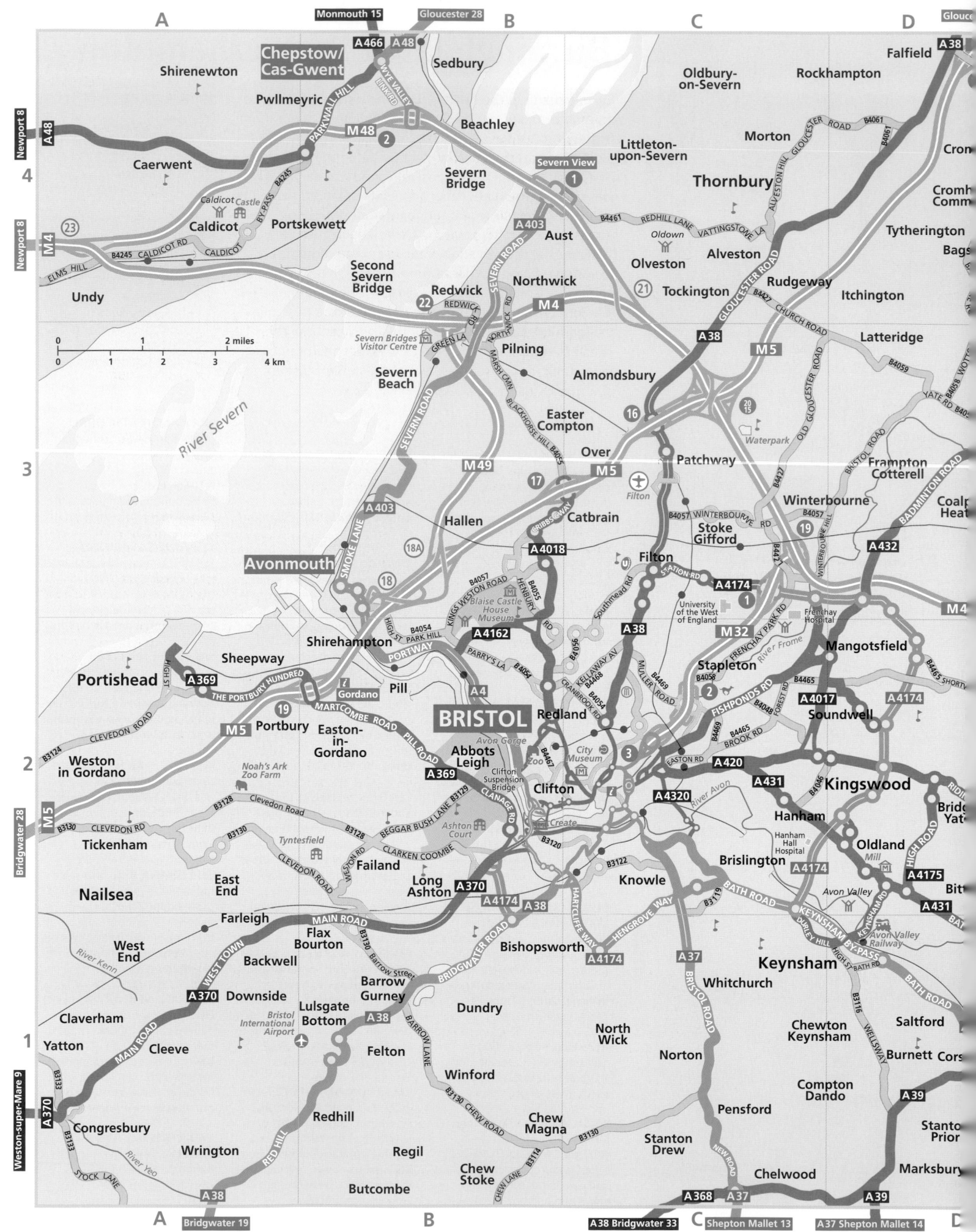

Chepstow/
Cas-Gwent

Shirenewton
Pwllmeyric
Sedbury
Beachley
Severn View
Oldbury-on-Severn
Rockhampton
Falfield
Caerwent
Littleton-upon-Severn
Morton
Thornbury
Cromh Comm
Caldicot Castle
Portskewett
Caldicot
Severn Bridge
Aust
Oldown
Alveston
Tytherington
Bags
Undy
Second Severn Bridge
Redwick
Northwick
Olveston
Tockington
Rudgeway
Itchington
Severn Bridges Visitor Centre
Pilning
Almondsbury
Latteridge
Severn Beach
Easter Compton
Over
Patchway
Winterbourne
Frampton Cotterell
Coalp Heat
Hallen
Catbrain
Stoke Gifford
Avonmouth
Blaise Castle House Museum
Filton
University of the West of England
Frenchay Hospital
Shirehampton
Henbury
Mangotsfield
Portishead
Sheepway
Pill
Redland
Stapleton
Soundwell
Gordano
BRISTOL
Abbots Leigh
Zoo
City Museum
Kingswood
Weston in Gordano
Portbury
Easton-in-Gordano
Clifton Suspension Bridge
Clifton
Hanham
Oldland
Bridg Yate
Tickenham
Tyntesfield
Ashton Court
Knowle
Hanham Hall Hospital
Brislington
Bit
Nailsea
East End
Failand
Long Ashton
Keynsham
Avon Valley Railway
Farleigh
Flax Bourton
Bishopsworth
Whitchurch
Chewton Keynsham
Saltford
West End
Backwell
Barrow Gurney
Dundry
North Wick
Norton
Keynsham
Downside
Lulsgate Bottom
Bristol International Airport
Felton
Winford
Pensford
Compton Dando
Claverham
Cleeve
Redhill
Chew Magna
Stanton Drew
Chelwood
Stanton Prior
Yatton
Wrington
Regil
Chew Stoke
Marksbury
Congresbury
Butcombe

Bristol & Bath

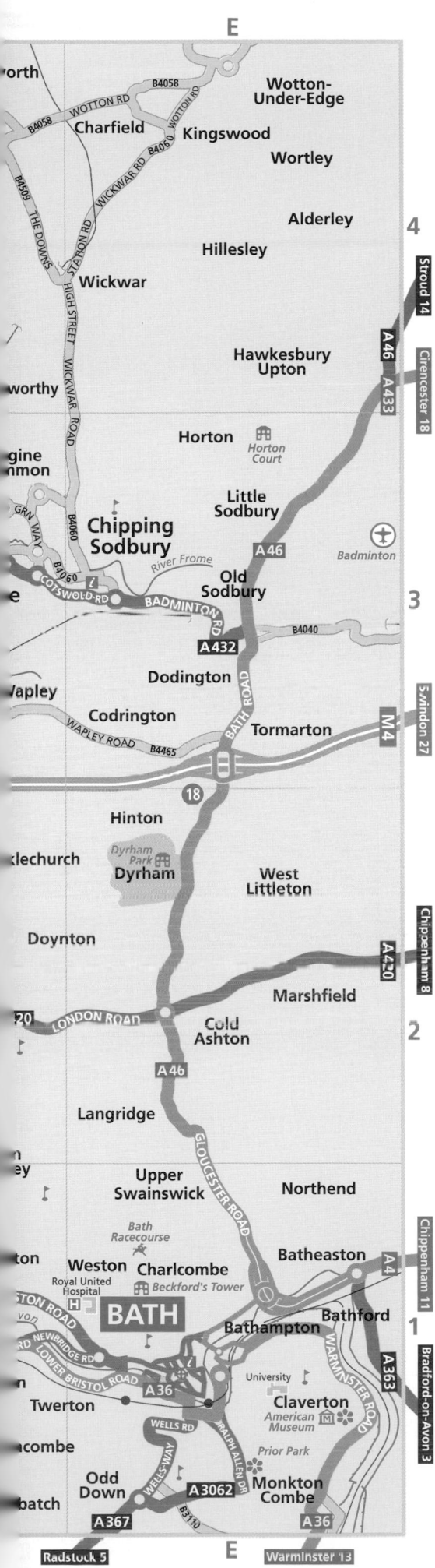

Even before John Cabot sailed from Bristol in 1497 and opened up trade with the New World, Bristol was a busy port. Vestiges of its maritime days can be seen along the waterfront where Isambard Kingdom Brunel's *SS Great Britain* and a replica of Cabot's *The Matthew* are docked. The leafy suburb of Clifton and dramatic Avon Gorge, with Brunel's fine suspension bridge, offer a quiet get-away from the bustle of the city centre.

One of Britain's oldest and best preserved cities, historic Bath dates back to Roman times when the Aquae Sulis temple and baths were built around natural hot springs. Their rediscovery in the 18th century transformed Bath into a popular resort, with the help of John Wood and his son John, who planned the city's elegant Georgian terraces, and Richard 'Beau' Nash who made Bath a hub of fashionable society.

TOURIST OFFICES

Bath (0906) 711 2000
Bristol (0906) 711 2191

WHERE TO PARK

Park & Ride: Bath p309 and Bristol p315.

Bath (p309):
Avon Street **A3**
Broad Street **B4**
Charlotte Street **A3**
Manvers Street **C2**

Bristol (p315):
Lower Castle Street **C4**
Prince Street **B2**
Queen Charlotte Street **B3**
Rupert Street **B4**

CITY ROUTES

ASSEMBLY ROOMS [p309 B4] These elegant rooms were the focal point of evening entertainment in 18th-century Bath. Restored after wartime bombing, they now house the **Museum of Costume**.

AT-BRISTOL [p315 A2] Funded by the Millennium Commission, the centre has a multimedia exhibition of the natural world and an interactive science centre with a futuristic planetarium.

BATH ABBEY [p309 C3] Built on the site of a Saxon monastery, the imposing 16th-century abbey has fine fan vaulting and stained glass windows. In the vaults below, a museum relates its history.

BATH POSTAL MUSEUM [p309 B4] The first stamp, 'the Penny Black', was posted from here in 1840. The museum has displays on the postal system.

BLAISE CASTLE HOUSE MUSEUM [B3] A Gothic folly of 1766 within the ramparts of an Iron Age hill fort, the house now has displays on everyday life in Bristol.

BRISTOL CATHEDRAL [p315 A2] Founded in 1140 as a monastery, the cathedral has a fine Norman chapter house and ornate carvings.

BRISTOL INDUSTRIAL MUSEUM [p315 B1] In a converted dockside shed are exhibits from Bristol's industrial past, including a working crane and steam locomotives.

BRISTOL ZOO GARDENS [B2] Over 300 species of wildlife can be seen in landscaped grounds which include an underwater walkway.

BRITISH EMPIRE AND COMMONWEALTH MUSEUM [p315 D2] Housed in a former railway station, the museum charts Britain's imperial past and includes old manuscripts, photographs and costumes.

CITY MUSEUM AND ART GALLERY [C2] A collection of fine art as well as exhibits on natural history, Egyptology and archaeology are on show.

THE CLIFTON SUSPENSION BRIDGE [B2] Spanning the Avon Gorge, this world famous bridge was designed by Brunel for a competition in 1836.

JANE AUSTEN CENTRE [p309 B4] The centre has displays on the author's life and Georgian Bath, the setting for *Northanger Abbey* and *Persuasion*.

NO 1. ROYAL CRESCENT [P309 A4] The first house on Bath's most prestigious terrace has been furnished in late 18th-century style.

PRIOR PARK LANDSCAPE GARDEN [E1] This striking garden 🌿 was created in the 18th century by philanthropist Ralph Allen, with advice from the poet Alexander Pope and 'Capability' Brown. It has magnificent views of the City of Bath and its wealth of features includes a Palladian bridge, a series of three lakes and a

recently restored Serpentine lake, grotto, grass cabinet and Gothic temple.

RED LODGE [p315 A3] A suite of 16th-century rooms, a carved stone chimney piece and fine oak panelling are on view in the red stone house.

THE ROMAN BATHS MUSEUM AND PUMP ROOM [p309 B2] The remarkable Roman temple and bathing complex is still flowing with natural hot water. The museum holds treasures found when the baths were uncovered in 1880. Overlooking the springs, the **Grand Pump Room** was the heart of Bath and visitors can still taste the famous waters.

ST MARY REDCLIFFE CHURCH [P315 C1] Described by Elizabeth I as 'the goodliest, fairest and most famous parish church in England', the 13th-century church has a hexagonal outer porch and a window depicting scenes from Handel's 'Messiah'.

SALLY LUNN'S REFRESHMENT HOUSE AND MUSEUM [p309 C2] Bath's oldest house is home to the famous Sally Lunn bun, which is still made using the original secret recipe.

SS GREAT BRITAIN [p315 A1] The first iron-built, propellor-driven ocean liner, launched in Bristol in 1843, is now moored in the docks and can be toured.

WILLIAM HERSCHEL MUSEUM [p309 A3] Scientist and astronomer William Herschel discovered Uranus from his home, now a museum.

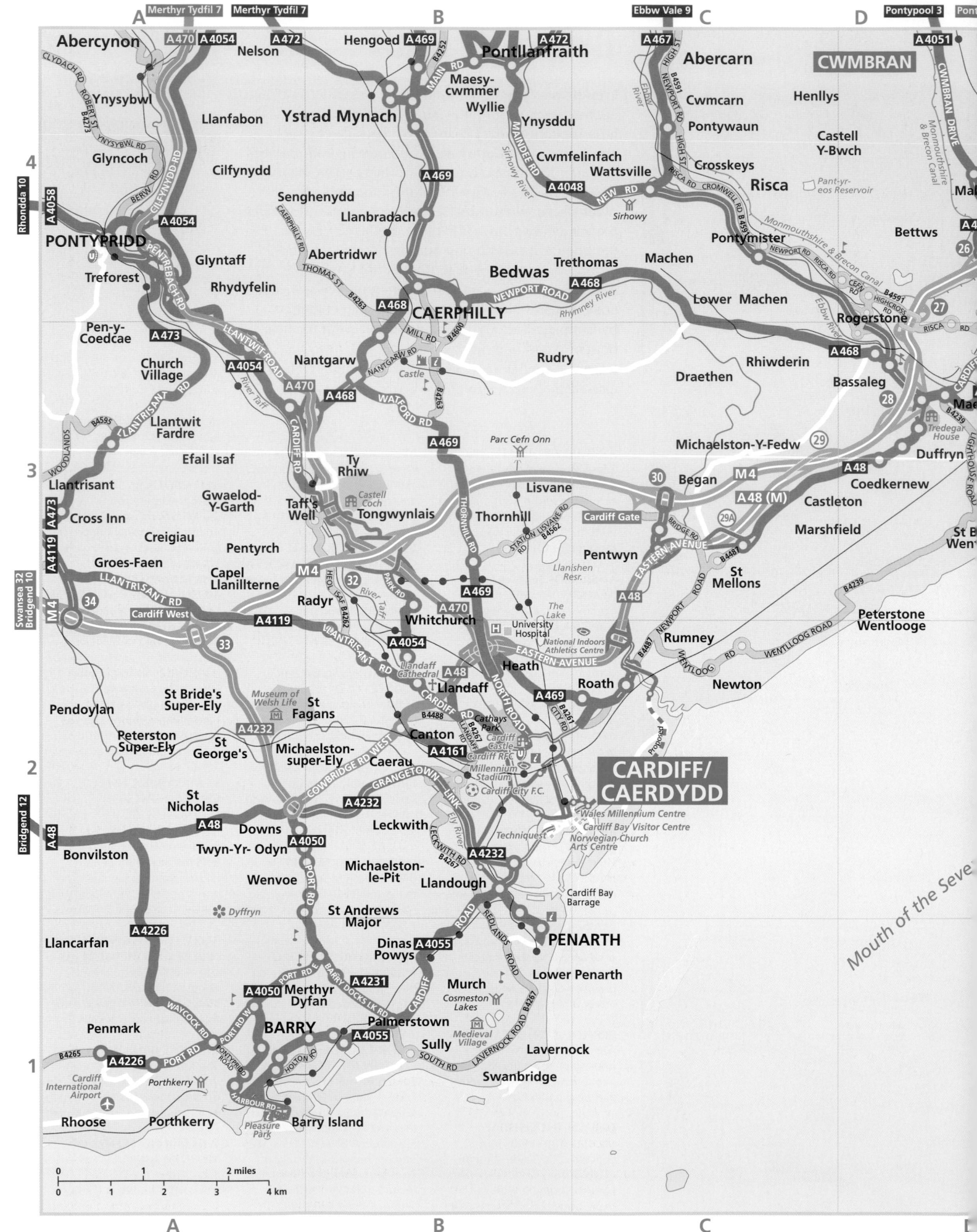

Merthyr Tydfil 7
Merthyr Tydfil 7
Ebbw Vale 9
Pontypool 3

CWMBRAN

Abercynon
Nelson
Hengoed
Pontllanfraith
Maesy-cwmmer
Wyllie
Abercarn
Cwmcarn
Henllys
Ynysybwl
Llanfabon
Ystrad Mynach
Ynysddu
Pontywaun
Castell Y-Bwch
Glyncoch
Cilfynydd
Cwmfelinfach
Wattsville
Crosskeys
Risca
Senghenydd
Llanbradach
Pant-yr-eos Reservoir
Sirhowy
Pontymister
Bettws

PONTYPRIDD
Abertridwr
Trethomas
Machen
Treforest
Glyntaff
Bedwas
Lower Machen
Rogerstone
Rhydyfelin
CAERPHILLY
Newport Road
Rhymney River
Pen-y-Coedcae
Nantgarw
Castle
Rudry
Draethen
Rhiwderin
Bassaleg
Church Village
Watford Rd
Michaelston-Y-Fedw
Duffryn
Llantwit Fardre
Parc Cefn Onn
Tredegar House

Efail Isaf
Ty Rhiw
Lisvane
Beg, an
Coedkernew
Llantrisant
Taff's Well
Castell Coch
Thornhill
Cardiff Gate
Castleton
Cross Inn
Tongwynlais
Marshfield
Creigiau
Pentyrch
Pentwyn
St Mellons
Groes-Faen
Capel Llanillterne
Llanishen Resr.
St B Wen
Radyr
Peterstone Wentlooge
Cardiff West
Whitchurch
Rumney
Newton
St Bride's Super-Ely
Llandaff Cathedral
University Hospital
National Indoors Athletics Centre
Roath
Pendoylan
Museum of Welsh Life
St Fagans
Llandaff
Heath
Peterston Super-Ely
Michaelston-super-Ely
Canton
St George's
Caerau
Cathays Park
Cardiff Castle
CARDIFF/CAERDYDD
Grangetown
Cardiff RFC
Millennium Stadium
Cardiff City F.C.
Wales Millennium Centre
Leckwith
Cardiff Bay Visitor Centre
St Nicholas
Norwegian Church Arts Centre
Downs
Techniquest
Bonvilston
Twyn-Yr-Odyn
Michaelston-le-Pit
Llandough
Cardiff Bay Barrage
Wenvoe
Dyffryn
St Andrews Major
Mouth of the Seve
Llancarfan
Dinas Powys
Murch
Cosmeston Lakes
PENARTH
Lower Penarth
Merthyr Dyfan
Palmerstown
Medieval Village
Penmark
BARRY
Sully
Lavernock
Cardiff International Airport
Porthkerry
Swanbridge
Rhoose
Porthkerry
Barry Island
Pleasure Park

0   1   2 miles
0 1 2 3 4 km

SEE TOWN PLANS PP317 & 370 AND TOURING GUIDE P425

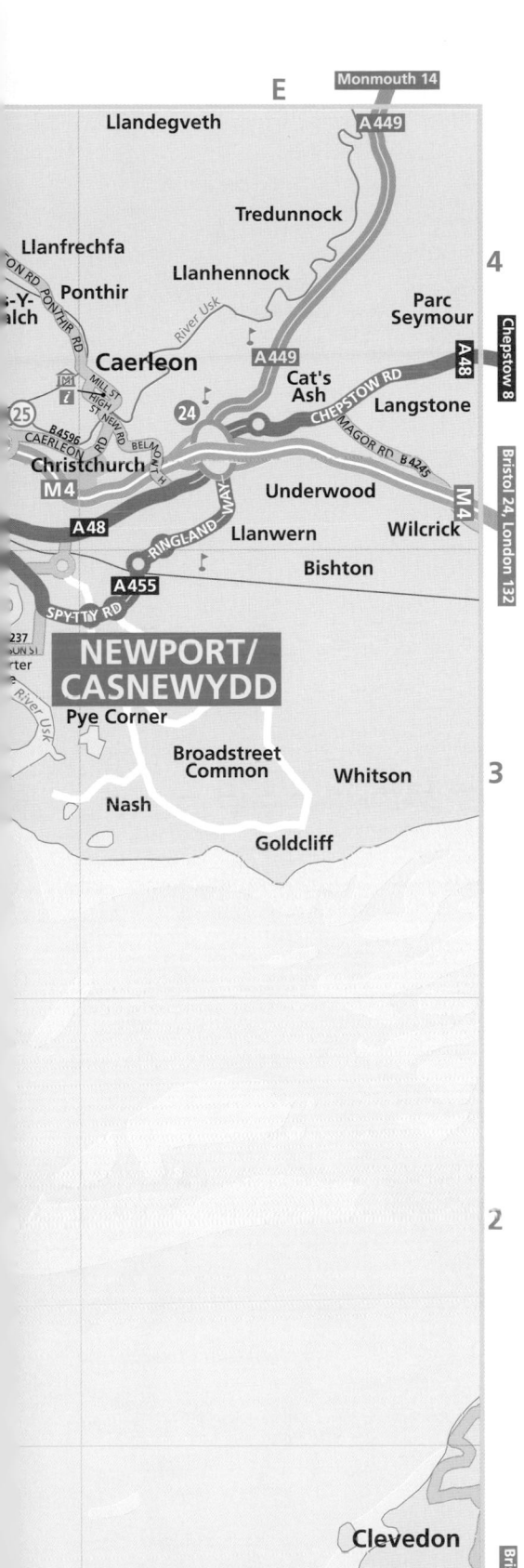

Cardiff & Newport

Cardiff was one of the world's busiest seaports in the 19th century, with a prosperous coal trade. The wealth amassed by local mine owners, in particular the Bute family, is reflected in the city's elegant Victorian and Edwardian architecture. Cardiff Bay, the previously derelict waterfront, has undergone regeneration and other developments include the Millennium Stadium, the Welsh Assembly, and the Wales Millennium Centre, the home of the new opera house.

An industrial town at the mouth of the River Usk, Newport's growth in the 19th century was based on its coal and iron exports. Newport was the scene of riots by Chartist reformers in 1839 and bullet marks can still be seen on pillars at the Westgate Inn. Dominating the town's skyline is a transporter bridge, which once carried vehicles over the river on a moving platform.

TOURIST OFFICES

Cardiff (029) 2022 7281
Newport (01633) 842962

WHERE TO PARK

Cardiff (p317):
Bridge Street **D2**
Dumfries Place **D3**
Greyfriars Road **C3**
Westgate Street **B2**

Newport (p370):
Cambrian Centre **B2**
North Street **B2**
Hill Street **C1**
Capital **C2**

CARDIFF BAY VISITOR CENTRE [C2] A space-age silvery building contains displays on the regeneration projects in Cardiff Bay, including a model of the bay and a video wall with 15 screens. The centre affords visitors fine views over the harbour.

CARDIFF CASTLE [p317 B2] Although founded in Roman times, most of the castle today dates back only to the 1860s when the 3rd Marquis of Bute had it restored as a fairytale mansion, with mock medieval turrets and lavishly decorated interiors in Gothic, Arab and classical Greek styles. However, the Norman keep and moat still remain, as does a 13th-century tower and a section of Roman wall. Surrounding the castle and stretching down to the river is a fine landscaped park, designed by 'Capability' Brown in the 18th century.

CITY HALL [p317 C3] Built of Portland stone in 1905, the neoclassical building is crowned by an ornate clock tower and dome bearing a fierce dragon, the national emblem of Wales. The spectacular **Marble Hall** houses life-size statues of Welsh heroes such as St David, the patron saint of Wales, and the **Assembly Hall** has an impressive decorated ceiling.

LLANDAFF CATHEDRAL [B2] Llandaff became part of Cardiff in 1922. Its 12th–13th-century cathedral is on the site of a 6th-century wooden church. Bombed in the Second World War, the cathedral was restored in 1957–60. It has fine stained glass windows and panels by Gabriel Rossetti and Edward Burne-Jones. Sir Jacob Epstein's 5m (16ft)-high figure of Christ, made of aluminium, graces the nave.

THE MILLENNIUM STADIUM [P317 B1] Dominating the city's skyline, Cardiff's new stadium was built for the Rugby World Cup in 1999 on the site of the former stadium, Cardiff Arms Park. It seats over 72,000 people and is the only stadium in Britain with a retractable roof. Visitors can tour the stadium.

NATIONAL MUSEUM & GALLERY, CARDIFF [p317 C3] Featuring a remarkable range of art and science displays, with collections on subjects from archaeology to zoology and including interactive exhibits, this museum also has a fine collection of Impressionist and Post-Impressionist paintings.

NEWPORT MUSEUM AND ART GALLERY [p370 C2] The museum's collections range from Roman archaeological finds to natural history exhibits. Most notable are the displays on the Chartist uprising and the Roman mosaics found at Caerwent.

NORWEGIAN CHURCH [C2] A timbered church, dating from 1868, was built for the many Norwegian sailors that could be found in Cardiff in the 19th century when the city was a busy port. The church is now an art gallery and exhibition centre. The popular children's author Roald Dahl was baptised here in 1916.

ST WOOLOS' CATHEDRAL [p370 B1] Dating from 500 AD, the church became a cathedral in 1949. With a Norman nave and doorways, and a 15th-century tower, it perches on top of **Stow Hill** affording wonderful views over the town of Newport.

TECHNIQUEST [B2] A high-tech science centre with 160 interactive exhibits, activities and experiments, Techniquest also includes a planetarium, a science theatre and a discovery room. It is one of Britain's biggest science centres

TREDEGAR HOUSE [D3] Set within 90 acres of landscaped parkland, the magnificent 17th-century mansion house on the edge of Newport has been the home of the Morgan family for five centuries. It is one of the finest surviving Restoration houses in Wales.

WELCH REGIMENT MUSEUM [p317 B2] The Black and Barbican towers of Cardiff Castle are now home to a museum with displays on the history of the Welch regiment. Exhibits include relics from the Crimean War, a Japanese machine gun captured in Burma during the Second World War, Welsh insignia and many other objects that bring into focus the life and work of the regiment over the years.

CITY ROUTES

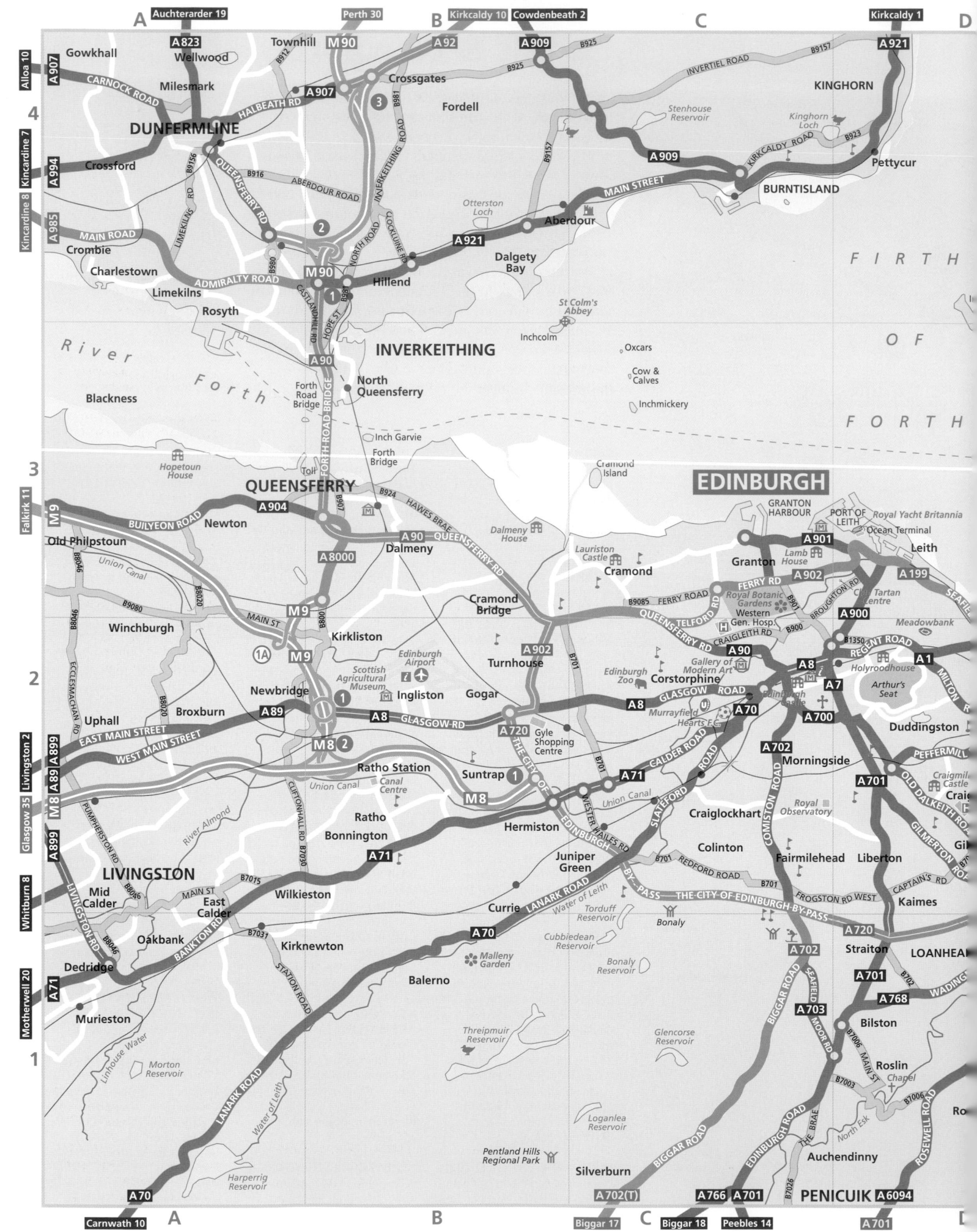

SEE TOWN PLANS p330 AND TOURING GUIDE p477

Edinburgh

One of Europe's most beautiful cities and the proud capital of Scotland, Edinburgh lies amid craggy heights. Arthur's Seat, a striking volcanic mountain, provides breathtaking vistas over Edinburgh and the Firth of Forth. Towering over the city is the dramatic silhouette of the Castle with the lofty buildings of the medieval Old Town stretching down below it along the Royal Mile in a labyrinth of dark, narrow streets and alleys. North of the castle, the New Town's elegant streets and crescents are lined with Georgian houses and the classical buildings which give it its nickname, 'the Athens of the North'. A lively city with a diverse cultural identity, Edinburgh boasts an impressive selection of museums and the annual summer Edinburgh International Festival of Arts, which has helped to spread the city's fame world wide.

TOURIST OFFICES

Edinburgh
0845 2255 121
Edinburgh Airport
0870 040 0007

WHERE TO PARK

Park & Ride: see p330.

Calton Road **p330 D4**
Castle Terrace **p330 A3**
Chalmers Street **p330 C2**
Morrison Street **p330 A2**
New Street **p330 E4**
St James' Centre **p330 D5**

CANONGATE TOLBOOTH [p330 E4] A former tollhouse is home to the social history exhibition, **The People's Story.**

CLAN TARTAN CENTRE [D3] An extensive collection of clans is shown here and visitors can trace their Scottish heritage.

EDINBURGH CASTLE [p330 B3] Perched on Castle Rock is Edinburgh Castle. The oldest part is St Margaret's Chapel, of the 12th century. Highlights include the Mons Meg cannon, the Scottish Crown Jewels and The Stone of Destiny.

EDINBURGH ZOO [C2] Set in beautiful hillside parkland, Edinburgh Zoo has over 1,000 species of animals.

GEORGIAN HOUSE [p330 A4] An elegant Charlotte Square house dating from the late 18th century is lavishly furnished in period style.

GLADSTONE'S LAND [p330 C3] This six-storey merchant's house of 1620 has an arcaded ground floor. The interior has been furnished in period style.

GREYFRIARS KIRK [p330 C3] Outside the church, named after a medieval friary that once stood on the site, is a statue of Greyfriars Bobby, a Skye terrier who guarded his owner's grave for 14 years.

JOHN KNOX HOUSE [p330 D4] Knox was the father of Scottish Presbyterianism and his home, on the Royal Mile, is dedicated to his life and work.

LADY STAIR'S HOUSE [p330 C3] The home of an 18th-century socialite is now the **Writer's Museum** which commemorates Sir Walter Scott, Robert Burns and Robert Louis Stevenson.

MUSEUM OF CHILDHOOD [p330 D3] The museum has a vast collection of historic toys, dolls and games.

MUSEUM OF EDINBURGH [p330 E4] The city's principal museum on local history contains Edinburgh silver and Scottish pottery.

NATIONAL GALLERY OF SCOTLAND [p330 C4] A neoclassical building has a large collection of notable Scottish art and works by Monet and Turner.

OUR DYNAMIC EARTH [p330 F4] Special effects and the latest technology tell the story of the planet.

OUTLOOK TOWER [p330 C3] The observation tower, commonly known as Camera Obscura, uses revolving mirrors to create panoramic city views.

PALACE OF HOLYROODHOUSE [p330 F4] The 1498 palace is linked with Mary, Queen of Scots, whose secretary was murdered here. It is the official Scottish residence of Queen Elizabeth II.

ROYAL BOTANIC GARDEN [C3] Started as a physic garden at Holyrood Palace in 1670, it later moved and now

holds over 2000 species, with a collection of rhododendrons and tropical greenhouses.

ROYAL MUSEUM/MUSEUM OF SCOTLAND [p330 D3] A grand Victorian mansion and its modern neighbour house displays on archaeology, the arts and Scotland's history.

ROYAL OBSERVATORY [C2] The interactive science displays include one of Scotland's largest telescopes.

ROYAL SCOTTISH ACADEMY [p330 C4] Originally opened in 1826 and now refurbished. The building is linked by an underground mall to the National Gallery.

ROYAL YACHT BRITANNIA [D3] After 44 years of service, the ship is now moored in the port of Leith. There are tours and displays on its history.

ST GILES CATHEDRAL [p330 D3] The **High Kirk** is noted for its famous spire, fine stained glass and **Thistle Chapel.**

SCOTCH WHISKY HERITAGE CENTRE [p330 C3] Tours in barrel cars tell the history of Scotland's most famous drink.

SCOTTISH NATIONAL GALLERY OF MODERN ART [C2] A neo-classical building houses 20th-century art, with works by Picasso and Hockney.

SCOTTISH NATIONAL PORTRAIT GALLERY [p330 C5] The gallery has portraits of famous Scottish figures, from Robert Burns to Sean Connery.

SCOTT MONUMENT [p330 C4] The ornate 1884 spire depicts characters from Scott's novels and historical figures.

CITY ROUTES

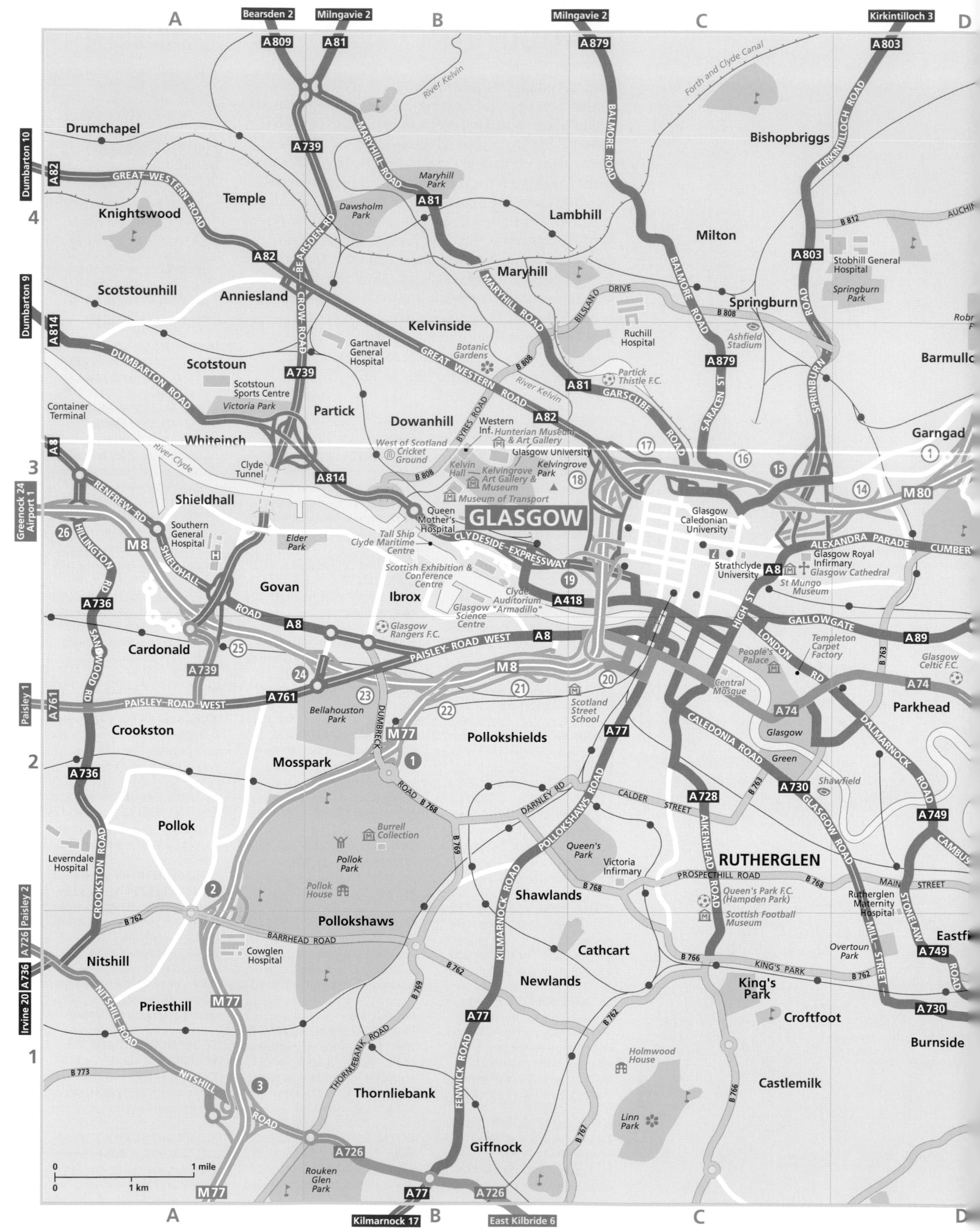

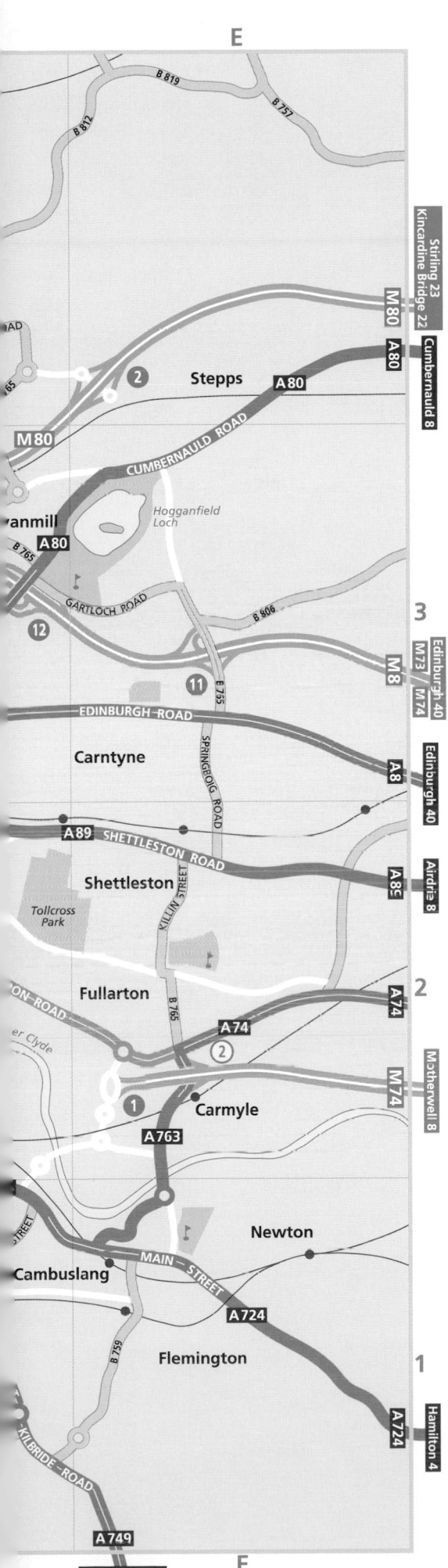

SEE TOWN PLANS p335 AND TOURING GUIDE p477

Glasgow

A lively, cosmopolitan city and Scotland's largest, Glasgow has seen a rebirth in recent years as a centre of style and culture. Music, art and architecture play a large part in Glasgow life. The Royal Scottish National Orchestra, the Scottish Opera and the Scottish Ballet are based there, and it is home to an impressive selection of world-famous art collections and museums. Provand's Lordship, Glasgow's oldest house, is a tiny surviving reminder of the medieval city. Glasgow's centre is now farther west in a grid of streets developed in the 18th–19th centuries, with a magnificent mix of Victorian and Art Nouveau architecture. The late 20th century has added St Enoch's Square shopping centre, with Europe's largest glass roof, and the revitalised riverside boasts Glasgow's most recent attraction, the titanium-clad Glasgow Science Centre.

TOURIST OFFICES

Glasgow
(0141) 204 4400

WHERE TO PARK

Candleriggs **p335 E1**
Cambridge Street
p335 C3
George Street **p335 E2**
High Street **p335 F2**
Mitchell Street **p335 C2**

BOTANIC GARDENS [B3]
Noted for their orchids and begonias, the gardens are dominated by **Kibble Palace**, a Victorian conservatory where white statues stand out amid the luxuriant tree ferns. Skirting the gardens is the **Kelvin Walkway**, leading through a wooded gorge.

THE BURRELL COLLECTION [B2] In the grounds of **Pollok Park**, this prodigious collection of art and artefacts was donated by Sir William Burrell to Glasgow and includes Egyptian, Greek and Roman earthenware and sculpture, oriental rugs, medieval doorways and paintings by Degas, Sisley and Manet.

CITY CHAMBERS [p335 D2]
A symbol of the city's former wealth, the spectacular Italianate building of 1888 stands on the east side of George Square. Its interior reveals marble staircases, lavish mosaics, granite columns and an opulent banqueting hall.

GALLERY OF MODERN ART [p335 D2] The **Royal Exchange** of 1780, once a tobacco lord's mansion, is now home to Glasgow's biggest gallery. It is divided into four themed spaces – earth, air, fire and water – and includes art by David Hockney, Andy Warhol and Scottish artists Ken Curry and John Bellany.

GLASGOW CATHEDRAL [p335 F2] The Gothic cathedral dates mainly from the 13th century. It is believed to stand on the site of a church built by Glasgow's founder, St Mungo, in the 6th century, and has the saint's tomb in the crypt. Close by are the **St Mungo Museum of Religious Life and Art**, and Glasgow's **Necropolis**, with imposing tombs of city magnates.

GLASGOW SCIENCE CENTRE [B3] Britain's biggest science centre boasts an interactive science mall and the unique 100m (328ft) rotating **Glasgow Tower**, which gives fantastic views over the Clyde valley.

HUNTERIAN MUSEUM AND ART GALLERY [B3] Within the vast neo-Gothic buildings of Glasgow University, Scotland's oldest museum was opened in 1807, and includes one of the world's finest collections of coins and medals. The art gallery contains many paintings by James McNeill Whistler, and works by Scottish artists.

KELVINGROVE ART GALLERY AND MUSEUM [B3] A red sandstone building of 1902 houses the city's principal art gallery and museum, which has a fine collection of British and European paintings, including works by the Pre-Raphaelites and French Impressionists. The building stands in **Kelvingrove Park**, laid out in 1852 by Sir Joseph Paxton, who designed London's Crystal Palace.

MUSEUM OF TRANSPORT [B3] Glasgow trams, Scottish locomotives, models of Clyde ships and a reconstruction of a 1938 Glasgow street, with a cinema and underground station, can be seen in this museum in Kelvin Hall.

PEOPLE'S PALACE [C2]
Opened in 1898 as a cultural centre for Glasgow's East End, the 'palace' museum tells the city's history from 1175 and includes Winter Gardens and a fine Victorian conservatory. Nearby, the former **Templeton Carpet Factory** of 1889 was modelled in bricks and tiles on the Doge's Palace in Venice.

PROVAND'S LORDSHIP [p335 F2] Glasgow's oldest house dates from 1471 and was used by the Prebend of Provan, a canon of the Cathedral. Mary Queen of Scots is thought to have stayed here in 1566. Furnished in period style, the house is now a museum.

SCOTLAND STREET SCHOOL [C2] Designed in 1904 by Charles Rennie Mackintosh, the school houses a museum of education from Victorian times to the late 1960s.

SCOTTISH MUSEUM OF FOOTBALL [C1] The museum's fantastic collection of memorabilia includes objects belonging to the Greats of Scottish football such as Dennis Law, Kenny Dalglish and Jimmy McGrory, and the reconstructed changing room and press box from the original Hampden Park stadium.

TALL SHIP [B3] One of only five Clyde-built sailing boats still afloat, the 1896 *Glenlee* is now moored in Glasgow's harbour and an interactive exhibition relates her history.

TENEMENT HOUSE [p335 A4] Life in a gaslit Glasgow tenement in the early 20th century is evoked in the former home (**NTS**) of Miss Agnes Toward, a typist who lived here from 1911 to 1965.

CITY ROUTES

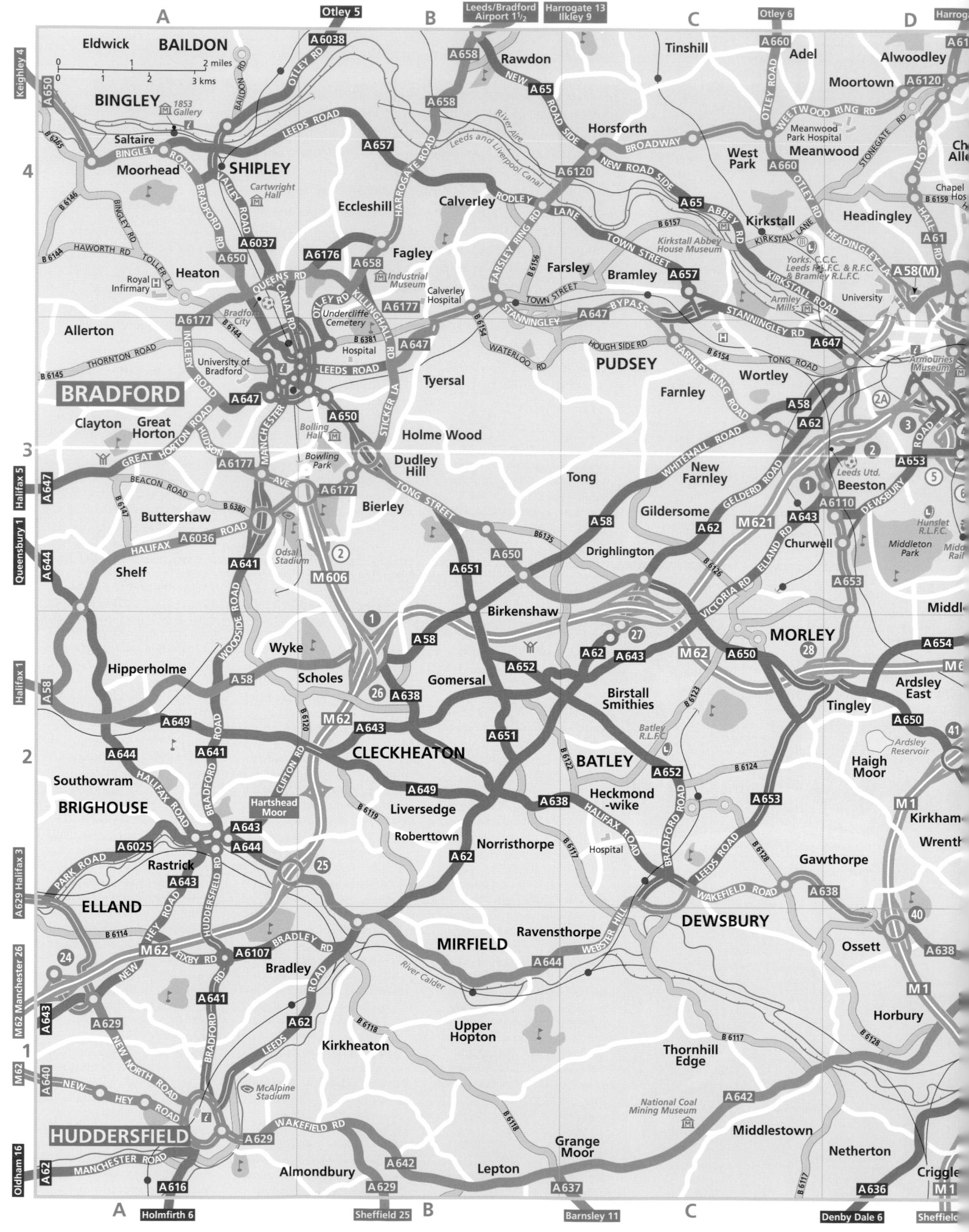

Otley 5
Leeds/Bradford Airport 1½
Harrogate 13 Ilkley 9
Otley 6
Keighley 4
Halifax 5
Queensbury 1
Halifax 1
A 629 Halifax 3
M 62 Manchester 26
M 62
Oldham 16
Holmfirth 6
Sheffield 25
Barnsley 11
Denby Dale 6

Eldwick BAILDON
Bingley
Saltaire
Moorhead
1853 Gallery
SHIPLEY
Eccleshill
Calverley
Rawdon
Tinshill
Adel
Alwoodley
Moortown
Horsforth
West Park
Meanwood Park Hospital
Meanwood
Heaton
Fagley
Farsley
Bramley
Kirkstall
Headingley
Royal Infirmary
Kirkstall Abbey House Museum
Yorks. C.C.C. Leeds R.L.F.C. & R.F.C. & Bramley R.L.F.C.
Armley Mills
University
Allerton
Industrial Museum
Calverley Hospital
Bradford City
Uncliffe Cemetery
Farsley
Town Street
Stanningley
Pudsey
Wortley
Armouries Museum
BRADFORD
Clayton Great Horton
University of Bradford
Hospital
Tyersal
Farnley
Buttershaw
Bolling Hall
Bowling Park
Holme Wood
Dudley Hill
Tong
New Farnley
Leeds Utd.
Beeston
Shelf
Odsal Stadium
Bierley
Gildersome
Churwell
Hunslet R.L.F.C.
Middleton Park
Wyke
Birkenshaw
Drighlington
Morley
Hipperholme
Scholes
Gomersal
Birstall Smithies
Ardsley East
Tingley
Southowram
Hartshead Moor
Liversedge
CLECKHEATON
BATLEY
Batley R.L.F.C.
Haigh Moor
BRIGHOUSE
Robertown
Norristhorpe
Heckmond-wike
Hospital
Gawthorpe
Rastrick
ELLAND
MIRFIELD
Ravensthorpe
DEWSBURY
Ossett
Bradley
River Calder
Kirkheaton
Upper Hopton
Thornhill Edge
Horbury
HUDDERSFIELD
McAlpine Stadium
Almondbury
Lepton
Grange Moor
National Coal Mining Museum
Middlestown
Netherton

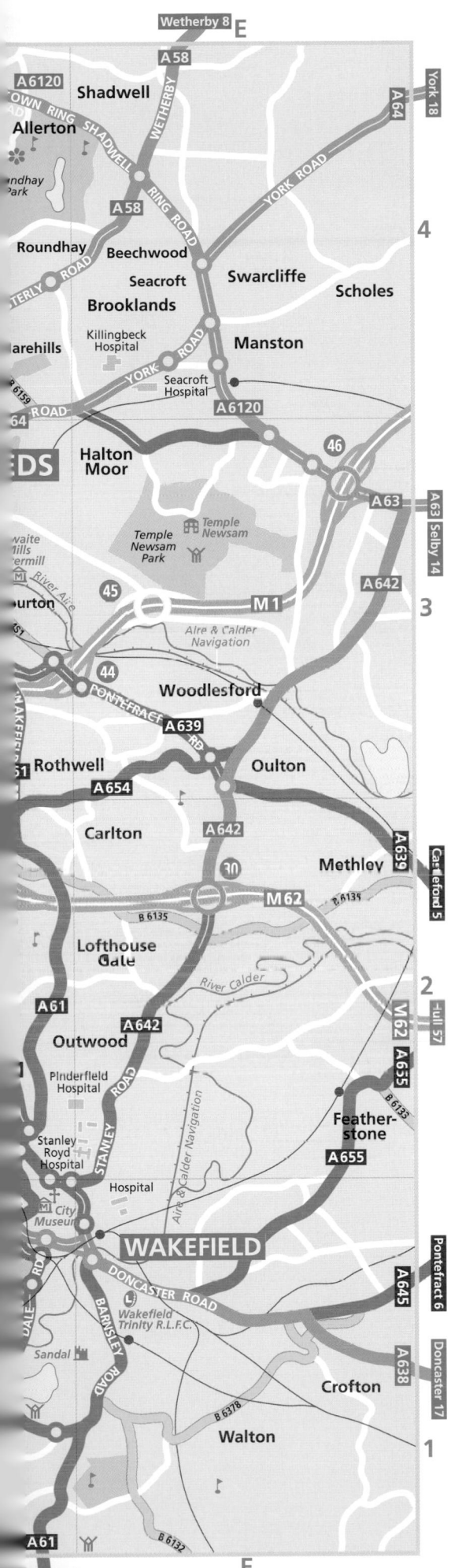

Leeds & Bradford

Both Leeds and Bradford have emerged as business and cultural centres, making new use of the industrial and civic buildings that date from their heyday as giant textile producers in the 19th century. Leeds has restored the Edwardian Kirkgate Market and its ornate Victorian shopping arcades and converted riverside grain mills into offices and restaurants. The City Varieties Theatre has Britain's oldest music hall, the Grand Theatre is home to Opera North and the Town Hall hosts an international piano competition every three years.

Once a centre of the worsted trade, Bradford has fine 19th-century honey-coloured buildings. The Venetian-style Wool Exchange is now a shopping centre, and the Alhambra Theatre has been restored to its former splendour. The large Asian population brings a zest and flavour to the city, enhancing its character.

TOURIST OFFICES
Bradford (01274) 433678
Leeds (0113) 242 5242

WHERE TO PARK
Bradford (p313):
Charles Street **D2**
Hall Ings **C2**
Kirkgate Centre **B3**
Westgate **B3**
Leeds (p346):
Albion Street **D3**
St John's Centre **D4**
Portland Crescent **C4**
Templar Street **E4**

ARMLEY MILLS INDUSTRIAL MUSEUM [C4] A former woollen mill on an island in the River Aire, Armley Mills was once the world's largest mill. It is now a museum on Leeds's industrial history.

BOLLING HALL MUSEUM [B3] Formerly a country residence, the hall was built onto a medieval pele tower in the 16th–18th centuries. It boasts fine panelling, oak furniture and a stained-glass window with 24 coats of arms.

BRADFORD CATHEDRAL [p313 D3] Until 1919, the 14th–15th century cathedral was a parish church. Its Chapter House and Lady Chapel, with stained glass from the studios of William Morris, were added in 1951–63. The nearby merchant quarter of **Little Germany** has 19th-century warehouses.

BRADFORD INDUSTRIAL MUSEUM [B4] Moorside Mills, where raw wool was converted into cloth, has been restored and visitors can view the former homes of the mill owner and his workers. There are horse-drawn tram and bus rides round the site.

CARTWRIGHT HALL ART GALLERY [A4] A Bradford mill owner, Samuel Cunliffe Lister, financed the building of this baroque-revival art gallery in 1904. Its collections of 19th–20th-century British paintings include works by Dante Gabriel Rossetti and David Hockney.

COLOUR MUSEUM [p313 A3] Britain's only museum devoted to colour includes an exhibit showing the world as seen through the eyes of a dog and a demonstration of the making of dyes.

KIRKSTALL ABBEY HOUSE MUSEUM [C4] This former manor was converted from the gatehouse of a 12th-century Cistercian abbey, the remains of which include the abbey church, with a finely carved west doorway. Today the gatehouse has reconstructions of Victorian streets with cottages, shops and an inn.

LEEDS CITY ART GALLERY [p346 C3] Sculptors Henry Moore and Barbara Hepworth both studied at Leeds College of Art, and some of their works are on display. The gallery has a fine collection of Victorian paintings and early English watercolours. Nearby, the **City Museum** has displays including natural history and coins.

MIDDLETON RAILWAY [D3] The world's oldest running railway was also the first railway to run steam locomotives. There are diesel and steam trains on show.

NATIONAL MUSEUM OF PHOTOGRAPHY, FILM AND TELEVISION [p313 B1] The museum's lively exhibits enable visitors to read the news on camera and to 'ride' on a flying carpet. There are also vintage televisions, cameras and photographs on display, as well as a magic lantern show.

ROYAL ARMOURIES MUSEUM [p346 F1] Opened in 1996 as the new home for the national collection of arms and armour, the museum has five themed galleries which tell the story of arms and armour using interactive, hi-tech displays and costumed demonstrations. In the summer there are skilled demonstrations of jousting, fencing, horsemanship and falconry in a recreated tiltyard.

TETLEY'S BREWERY WHARF [p346 E2] Displays on English pub life through the ages can be seen at this theme museum, which celebrates Leeds's place as a brewing centre. There are tours round Tetley's brewery.

THACKRAY MEDICAL MUSEUM [D4] Housed in St James' Hospital, the museum contains over 35,000 medical objects, including a surgical chainsaw, a 17th-century correction frame and Prince Albert's medical chest, as well as interactive displays on how the body works.

THWAITE MILLS WATERMILL [D3] There are tours of this working water-powered mill on the River Aire. The restored Georgian mill owner's house provides information on the history of the mill.

TROPICAL WORLD [D4] From Amazon rainforest to arid desert, a wide range of natural habitats have been recreated in a huge conservatory and are filled with colourful butterflies, birds, fish and reptiles.

UNDERCLIFFE CEMETERY [B4] The ornate tombs of many of Bradford's wealthy Victorians can be viewed in this hillside cemetery of 1854.

CITY ROUTES

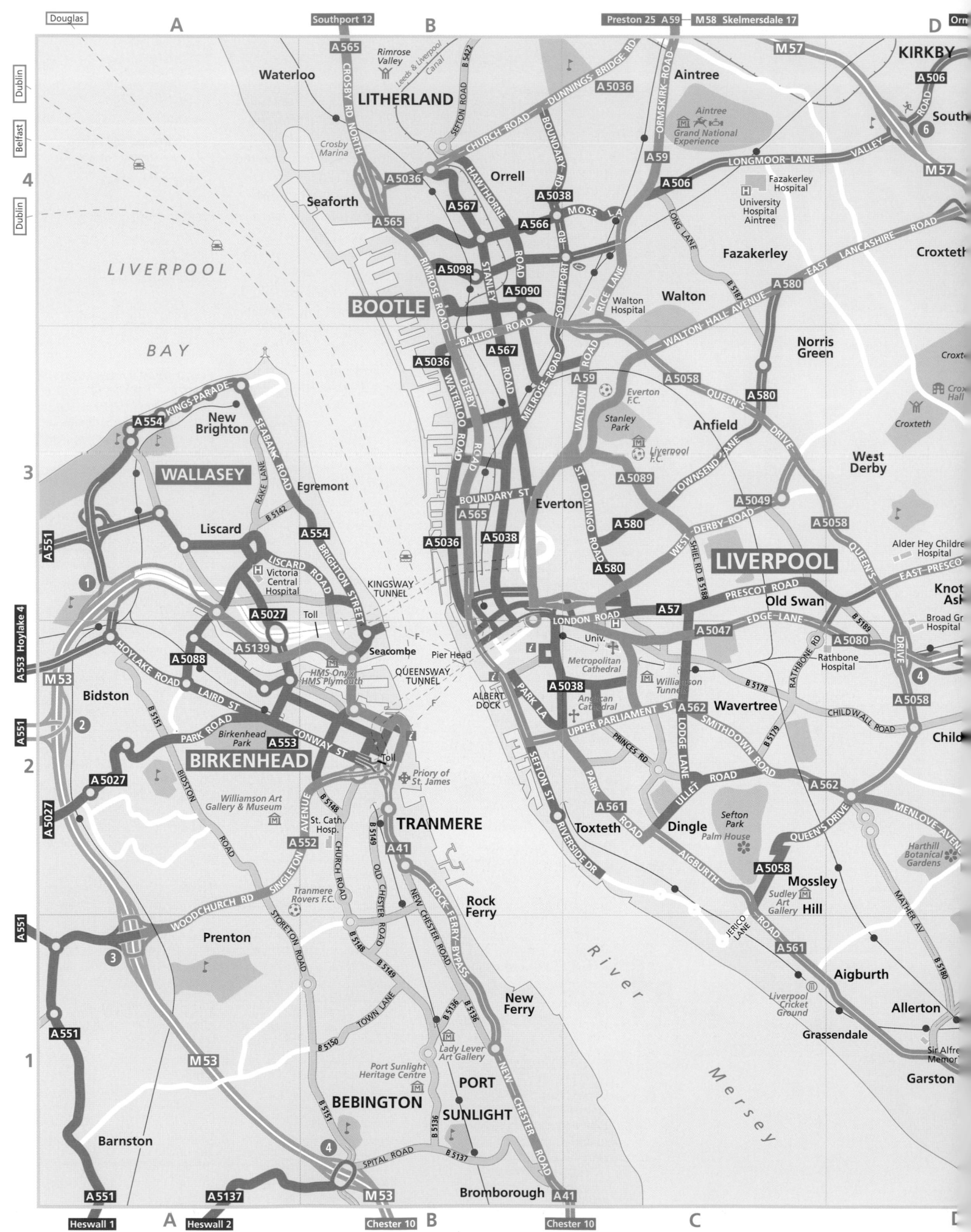

Liverpool & Birkenhead

By the late 19th century Liverpool had become one of the world's greatest ports and millions of emigrants used its docks as a gateway to America. The city's grand buildings include the Walker Art Gallery and neoclassical St George's Hall, while the Royal Liver Building, the Cunard Building and the Port of Liverpool Building are well-known landmarks. Although passenger liners no longer enliven the waterfront, the Victorian Albert Dock has a new lease of life as a family entertainment centre.

Also a 19th-century port, Birkenhead now harbours two Falklands War ships, the submarine *HMS Onyx* and the frigate *HMS Plymouth*. Hamilton Square has fine Victorian architecture and Birkenhead Park – laid out in 1847 by Sir Joseph Paxton – was Britain's first public park and the model for Central Park in New York.

TOURIST OFFICES

Birkenhead
(0151) 647 6780
Liverpool
(0906) 680 6886

WHERE TO PARK

Liverpool (p349):
Albert Dock **B1**
Brunswick Street **B2**
Dale Street **C3**
Mount Pleasant **D2**
Seel Street **C1**

CITY ROUTES

ANGLICAN CATHEDRAL [C2]
Britain's largest cathedral, 194m (636ft) long, this red sandstone Gothic Revival building was designed by Giles Gilbert Scott at the age of 21. Begun in 1904, it was not completed until 1978. From the central tower, Blackpool and the Welsh hills can be seen.

BEATLES STORY [p349 B1]
The visitor attraction recreates the experience of Beatlemania with a reconstruction of the Cavern Club where the Liverpool-born pop group played in the 1960s.

BIRKENHEAD PRIORY [B2]
Founded by Benedictine monks in 1150, the **Priory of St James** is now a ruin. The Benedictines ran the very first Mersey ferry some 800 years ago.

CROXTETH HALL AND COUNTRY PARK [D3] Once part of the country estate of the Earl of Sefton, the Jacobean hall has Edwardian furnishings and costumes, a Victorian walled garden, and extensive woods and parkland.

GRAND NATIONAL EXPERIENCE [C4] The visitor centre charts the history of the world's most famous steeplechase, with plenty of memorabilia on past winners, a simulator ride and guided tours of the Aintree race course.

KNOWSLEY SAFARI PARK [E3]
In the early 1800s, the 13th Earl of Derby set up a fine private menagerie here. Today, lions, zebras and tigers are among the animals to be seen in the park, which has sea lion shows and a miniature railway.

LIVERPOOL FOOTBALL CLUB MUSEUM [C3] In addition to trophies, match shirts and newspaper clippings, the museum also boasts a perfectly recreated dressing room, an interactive penalty gallery and tours of the Anfield pitch.

LIVERPOOL MUSEUM [p349 C3] The displays here range from dinosaurs to space exploration, and include an aquarium, planetarium and a natural history centre.

MERSEYSIDE MARITIME MUSEUM [p349 B1] Spread over six floors, the museum recalls Liverpool's heyday as a port, with displays on the slave trade, items seized by Customs and sniffer dog demonstrations.

METROPOLITAN CATHEDRAL [p349 E2] A spiked lantern tower tops the circular nave of the modern Roman Catholic cathedral of 1967, designed by Sir Frederick Gibberd. The crypt is the only completed part of Sir Edwin Lutyens's immense 1930s design.

MUSEUM OF LIVERPOOL LIFE [p349 A1] The story of Merseyside life, including the Grand National and the lives of cotton graders, shipbuilders and dockers, is told here.

NATIONAL WILDFLOWER CENTRE [D2] The former Gladstone family estate has been transformed into a conservation area with exhibitions to promote endangered British wildflowers.

PIER HEAD [p349 A2] The pier is dominated by the twin towers of the 1911 Royal Liver Building, topped by the mythical Liver Birds. Alongside are the 1916 Cunard Building and the green-domed Port of Liverpool Building of 1907.

ST GEORGE'S HALL [p349 C3] The fine neoclassical building dates from 1854 and has a portico of 18m (60ft) high Corinthian columns.

SUDLEY ART GALLERY [C2] The art collection of Victorian shipping magnate George Holt is displayed in his former home. It includes works by the Pre-Raphaelites and Landseer.

TATE GALLERY [p349 A1] In a converted warehouse in Albert Dock, the gallery has the largest collection of modern art outside London.

WALKER ART GALLERY [p349 C3] The gallery has renowned art collections ranging from the 14th century to the present day. Of particular note are the Italian, Dutch and Pre-Raphaelite works.

WESTERN APPROACHES [p349 B2] This underground command centre for the Second World War Battle of the Atlantic is open to the public.

WILLIAMSON ART GALLERY AND MUSEUM [A2] Liverpool porcelain and watercolours by Gainsborough and Turner are on view here, as well as displays on Birkenhead's maritime history.

SEE TOWN PLANS PP350-361 AND TOURING GUIDE P428

Outer London: North

Stand on top of Parliament Hill, on Hampstead Heath, to sense the extent of north London. Architects have been inspired in this part of the city, television programmes are still made here, and a cemetery's grand gothic memorials recall its past residents.

BBC BACKSTAGE TOURS [D1] Tours (pre-booked) change according to the day's schedule, but may include visits to the News and Weather Centre.

FIREPOWER [F1] The Royal Artillery Museum at Woolwich displays over 800 guns and military vehicles as well as medals, photos and uniforms.

THE GARDENS OF THE ROSE [B4] More than 30,000 roses bloom, and new species are trialled, at the Royal National Rose Society's gardens.

HIGHGATE CEMETERY [D2] Statues, spires and spectral figures rise from the undergrowth of this cemetery. The East Side is open daily.

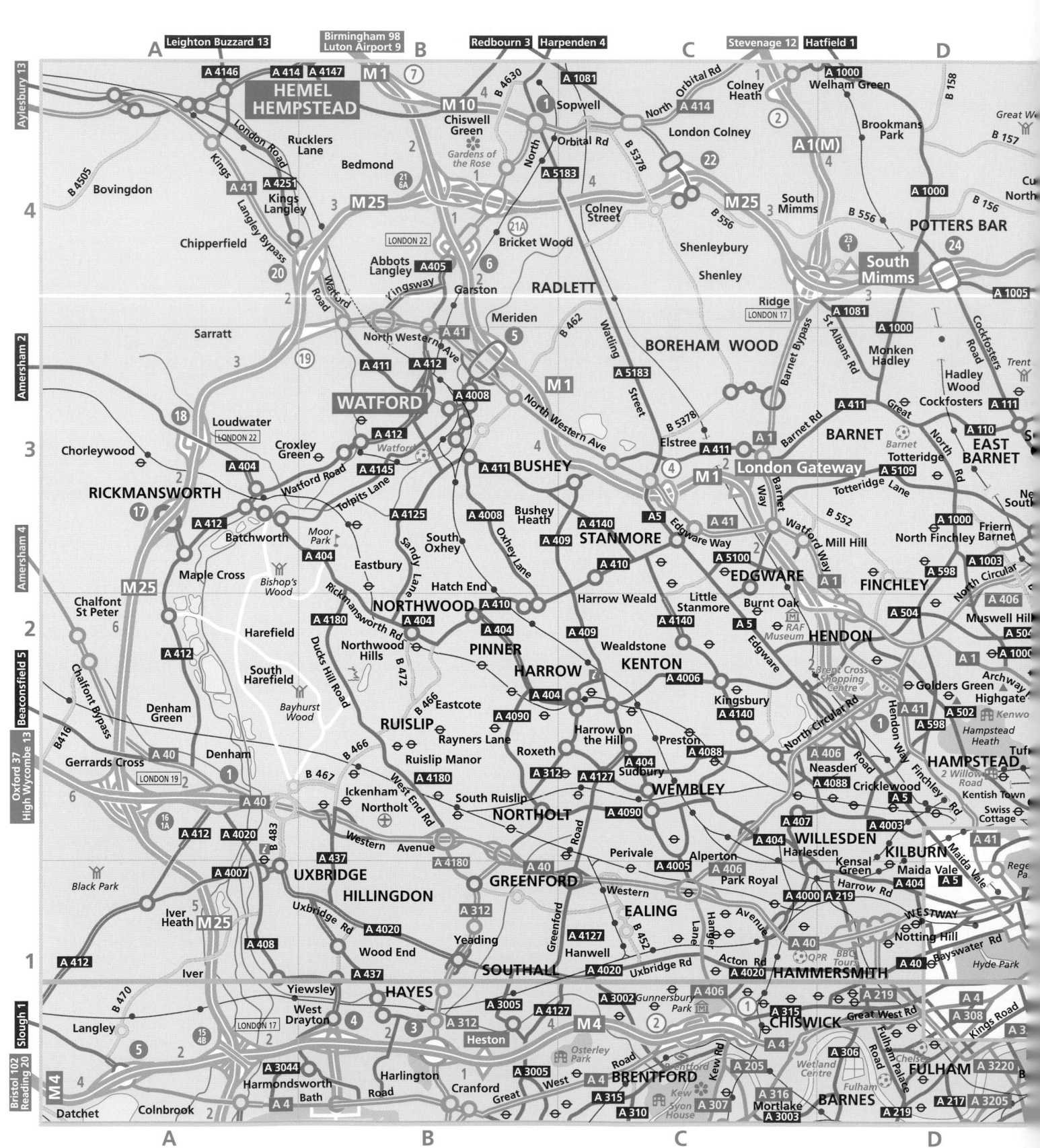

Continues on pages 286–287

KENWOOD HOUSE [D2] Paintings by Rembrandt and Turner hang in the cream and gold light-filled interiors of this neo-classical villa ⌗.

OSTERLEY PARK [C1] A classical villa ❦ was created from the original Tudor mansion and many of the rich Georgian furnishings remain.

RAF MUSEUM [C2] The National Museum of Aviation at Hendon records the history of flight – exhibits include aircraft and flight simulators.

ROYAL GUNPOWDER MILLS [E4] Displays at the site, in operation for over 300 years, explore the history of gunpowder and life in the mills.

SYON HOUSE [C1] The stunning interiors of this elegant mansion were created by Robert Adam. 'Capability' Brown landscaped the park.

THAMES BARRIER [F1] A visitor centre in Unity Way, Woolwich, explains why London's flood defence was needed and how it works.

WILLIAM MORRIS GALLERY [E2] Morris's fabrics, furniture, wallpaper and stained glass can be seen in the house where he lived from 1848–56.

2 WILLOW ROAD [D2] Erno Goldfinger, the architect, designed and built his modern style house ❦ and much of the furniture in 1939.

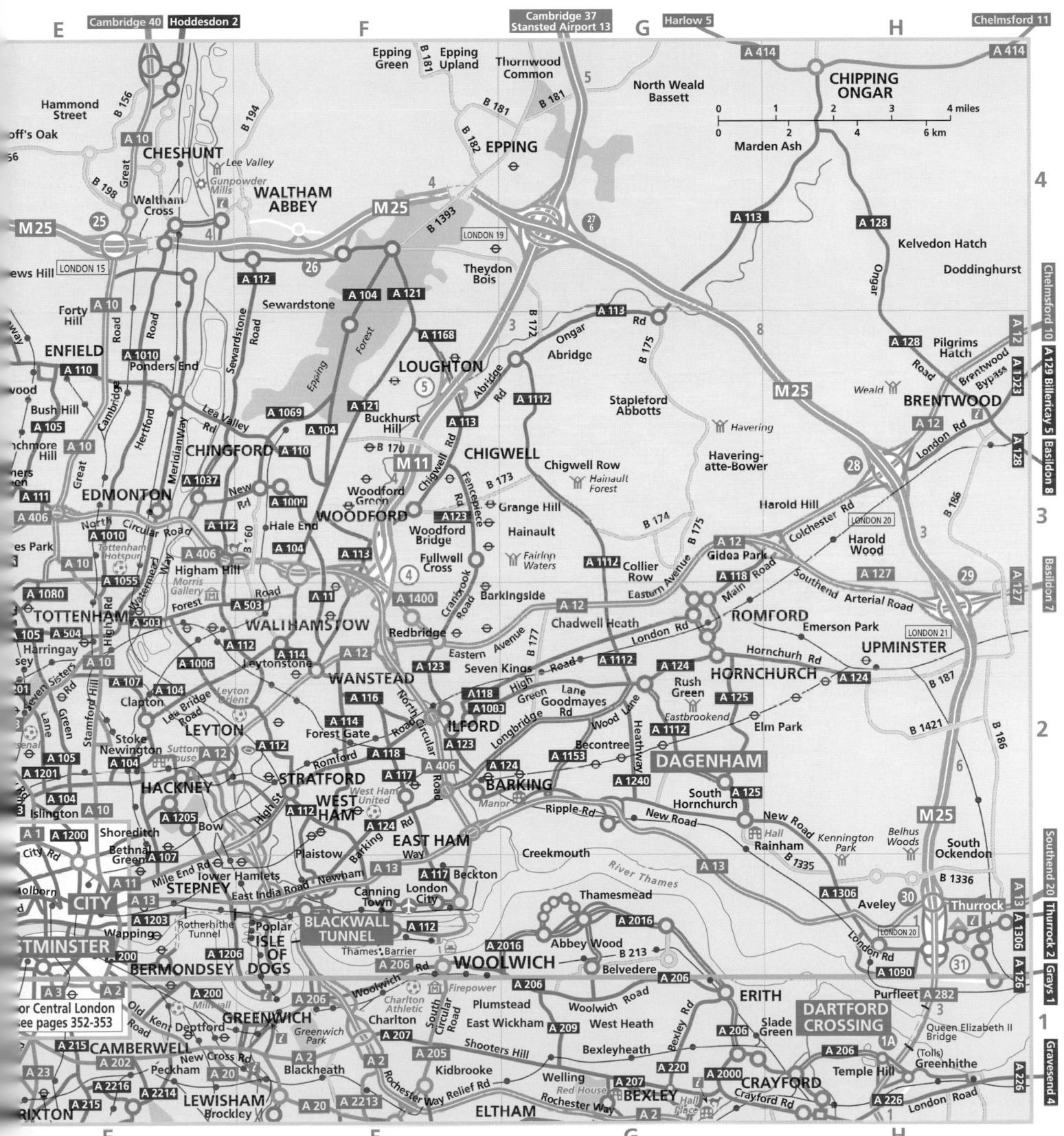

SEE TOWN PLANS PP350–361 AND TOURING GUIDE P428

Outer London: South

Watched over by the towers of the city, south London offers a fascinating mix of attractions as well as green space away from the city's sprawl. From grand houses and gardens to a wetland retreat and ancient caves, there is something here for everyone.

CHISLEHURST CAVES [G3] Tours guide visitors through a dark maze of mysterious passageways carved out over the past 8000 years.

CLAREMONT [B2] A spectacular turf amphitheatre, the only one in Europe, survives at this landscape garden ❧ which dates from 1715.

DOWN HOUSE [F2] For 40 years, naturalist Charles Darwin lived in the mainly 18th-century house ✠, set on the edge of the North Downs.

ELTHAM PALACE [F4] The palace's great hall ✠, with a medieval oak hammerbeam roof, is surrounded by a 1930s art deco country house.

Continues from pages 284–285

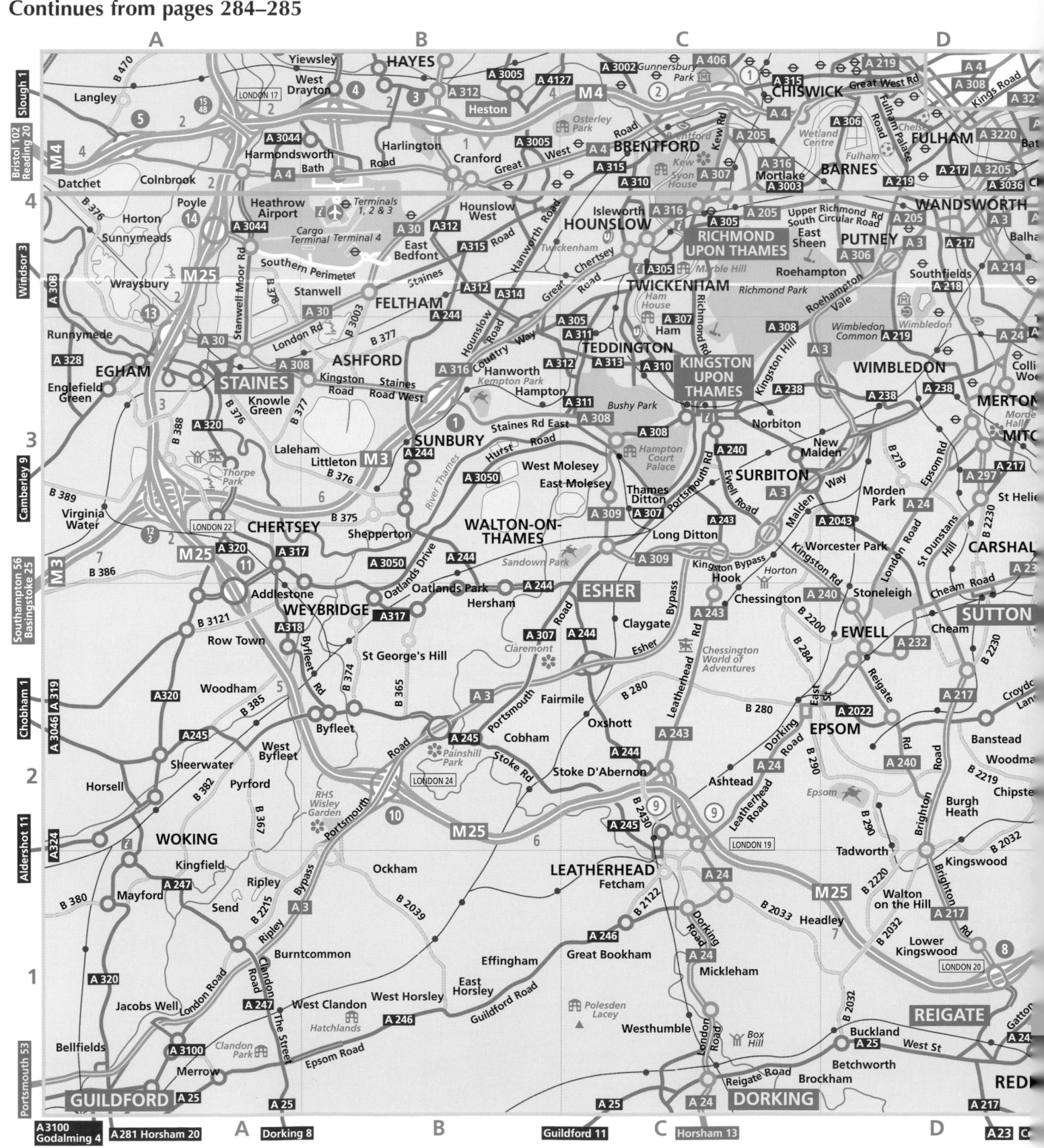

HAM HOUSE [C4] Beautiful formal gardens, which feature an orangery, surround the impressive 17th-century mansion ❧ set on the River Thames.

HAMPTON COURT PALACE [C3] Splendid state apartments, Tudor kitchens and an indoor real tennis court can be seen at the vast palace.

LONDON WETLAND CENTRE [D4] Created from Victorian reservoirs, the centre's lakes and ponds attract water birds from around the globe.

MARBLE HILL HOUSE [C4] The magnificent Palladian villa ⌗ was built for Henrietta Howard, mistress of George II, in 1724–9.

PAINSHILL [B2] A gothic temple, Turkish tent, ruined abbey and a bath house are among the follies at this 18th-century landscaped garden.

THORPE PARK [A3] The leisure park covers 500 acres (202ha) and has a variety of rides – including the Zodiac (a fast, spinning ride).

WIMBLEDON LAWN TENNIS MUSEUM [D3] Displays chart the development of the sport, its greatest players and this famous tournament.

WISLEY GARDEN [B2] Just off the busy A3 is the showpiece of the Royal Horticultural Society. It has a mix of formal and informal planting.

CITY ROUTES

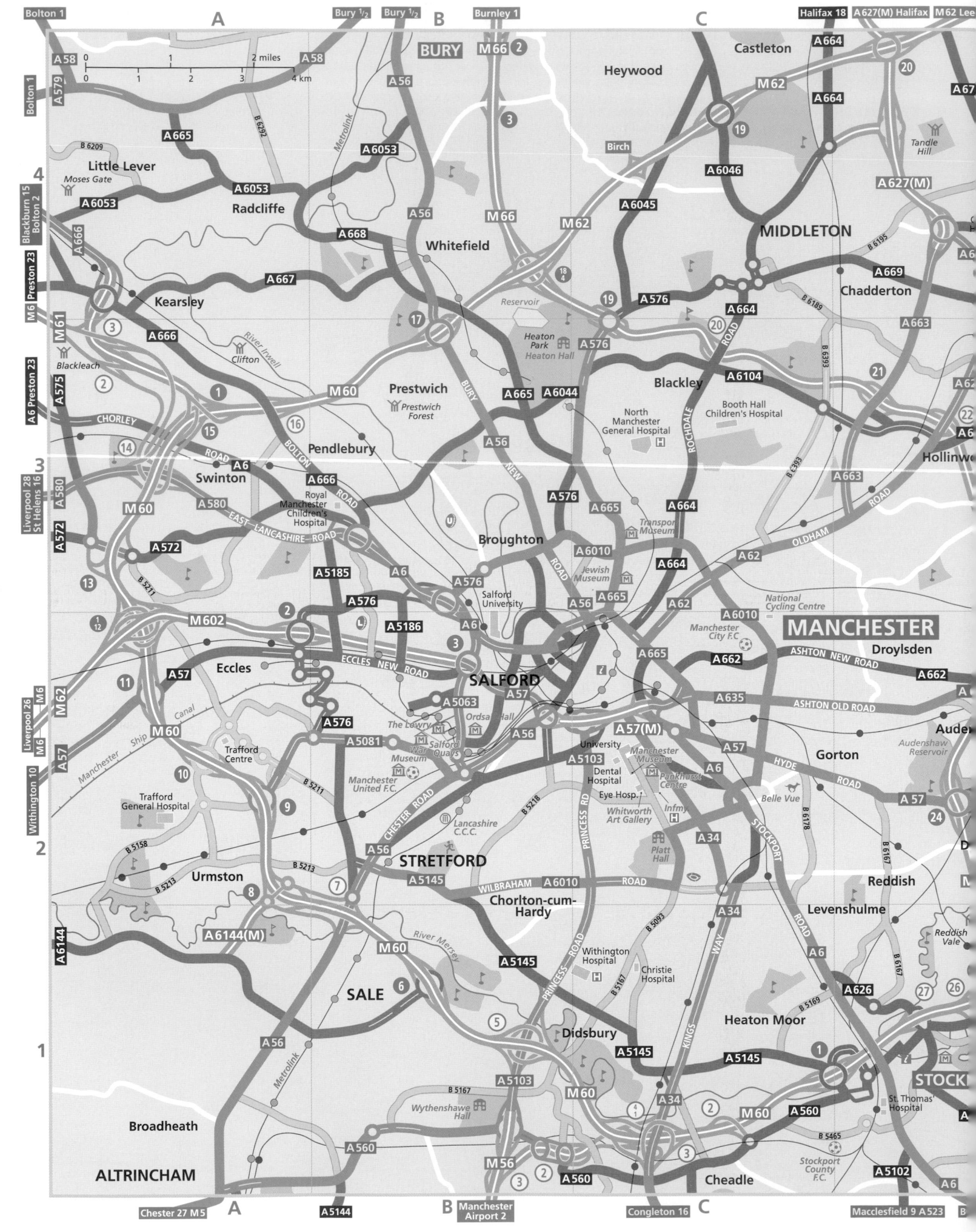

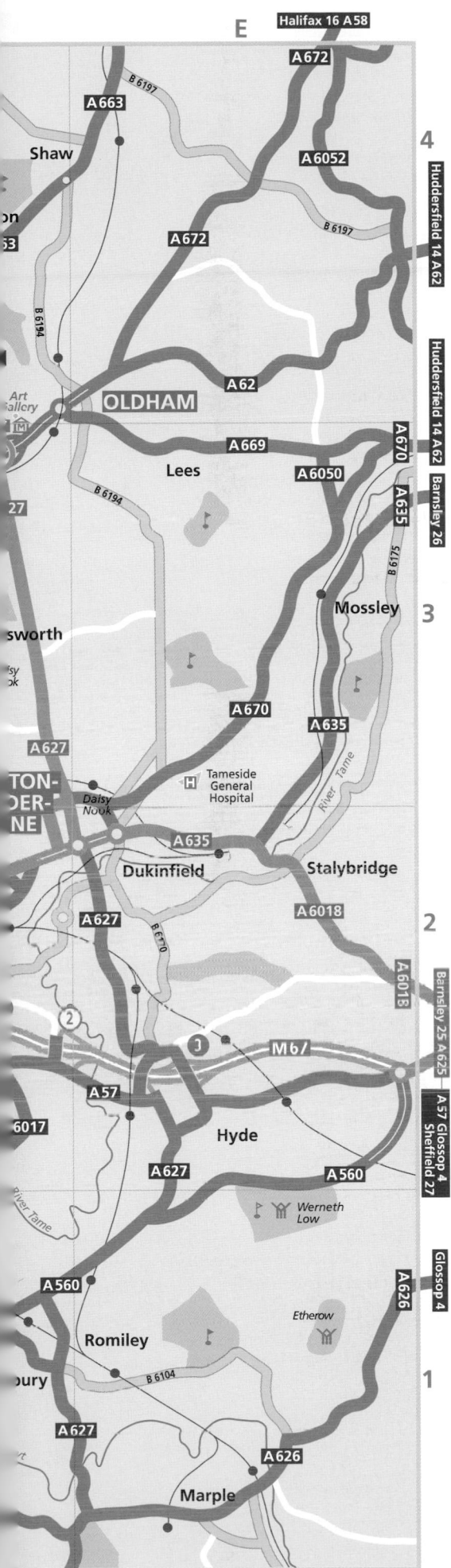

SEE TOWN PLANS P364 AND TOURING GUIDE P456

Manchester

England's earliest working canal, built for the Duke of Bridgewater in 1761, brought coal and raw cotton to the heart of Manchester and helped to make it a boom town at the forefront of the Industrial Revolution. The city has many impressive 19th-century monuments from its days as a major centre for the Lancashire cotton industry, such as the galleried, glass-domed Barton Arcade, the grandiose town hall and the neo-Gothic John Rylands Library. Castlefield, an area near the city centre, is now a heritage park linking the city's past and future with restored warehouses and lively redevelopments. The city's new Millennium Quarter boasts the Urbis museum, housed in an impressive glass building, as part of the plans to regenerate the centre of Manchester after the devastation wrought by the 1996 IRA bomb attack.

TOURIST OFFICES

Manchester
(0161) 234 3157/8
Manchester Airport
(0161) 436 3344

WHERE TO PARK

Church Street **p364 E4**
Blackfriars Street **p364 D4**
Oxford Street **p364 D2**
G-MEX Centre, Lower
   Mosley Street **p364 D2**
Whitworth Street **p364 E2**

ALBERT SQUARE [p364 D3]
Overlooking the pedestrianised square is the **neo-Gothic town hall** of 1877, with an 86m (281ft) clock tower; its great hall has murals by Ford Madox Brown recounting Manchester's history. In the square, mosaics surround the **Albert Memorial** of 1862, depicting roses, thistles, leeks and shamrocks.

CITY ART GALLERY [p364 D3]
An impressive collection of Pre-Raphaelite paintings is on display in Sir Charles Barry's classical building of 1829.

HEATON HALL [B3] Set amid parkland, the classical mansion of 1772 has a domed central block flanked by colonnaded wings. The Cupola Room is styled on Pompeii. In the park, a boulder marks the spot where the Pope celebrated Mass when he visited Manchester in 1982.

IMPERIAL WAR MUSEUM NORTH [B2] The striking aluminium-clad building displays 20th-century wartime objects which include a Harrier jump-jet and a Russian tank.

THE LOWRY [B2] Providing a permanent purpose-built home for the paintings of L.S. Lowry, this modern gallery plays host to musical entertainment at night, with operas, concerts and popular music shows.

MANCHESTER CATHEDRAL [p364 D4] Dark red stone distinguishes this Perpendicular 15th–16th-century church, made a cathedral in 1847. Carved misericords of animals

grace the choir. To the north is **Chetham's Hospital** of 1421. Nearby, **Chetham's Library** of 1653 is one of England's oldest public libraries. It is open by appointment only.

MANCHESTER JEWISH MUSEUM [C3] A former Spanish and Portuguese synagogue of 1874 tells of 250 years of local Jewish history in its Ladies' Gallery. The lower floor has been restored to its original condition.

MANCHESTER MUSEUM [C2] Displays at the museum include a renowned collection of Egyptian mummies, a Japanese section and an interactive science gallery.

MANCHESTER UNITED MUSEUM AND TOUR CENTRE [B2] Covering three floors of the North Stand of Old Trafford, the museum traces the football club's history. Exhibits include an awe-inspiring trophy room, team kits and displays on the club legends, past and present. There are virtual reality and real-life tours of the stadium.

MUSEUM OF SCIENCE AND INDUSTRY [p364 B3] Housed in Liverpool Road Station of 1830, the museum has working exhibits and includes a Power Hall, and Air and Space, Gas, and Electricity galleries, as well as a reconstruction of a Victorian sewer.

PANKHURST CENTRE [C2] Emmeline Pankhurst, the founder of the Suffragette Movement, lived in this

Georgian town house. It is now a museum on her life and the work of the suffragettes.

PEOPLE'S HISTORY MUSEUM [p364 C3] The museum's galleries are sited in the Pump House, a former Edwardian pumping station. The exhibition traces the lives of working people in the city over the last 200 years and includes displays on working class dissent, the suffragettes and trade unionism.

PLATT HALL [C2] Fashionable and everyday clothes from Tudor times until the 20th century are on view by appointment only in this hall of 1762, built for a wealthy textile merchant.

SHAMBLES SQUARE [p364 D4] In the medieval square stands the Old Wellington Inn of about 1550, the home of John Byrom, who wrote the hymn 'Christians Awake' as a Christmas present for his daughter.

THE TRANSPORT MUSEUM [C3] A collection of over 80 beautifully restored vintage buses together with plenty of memorabilia can be viewed in the museum.

URBIS [p364 D5] A striking glass building at the centre of the city's new **Millennium Quarter** uses high-tech, interactive displays to recreate the experience of city life.

WHITWORTH ART GALLERY [C2] The gallery holds collections of watercolours and European prints as well as textiles and historic wallpaper.

WYTHENSHAWE HALL [B1] A half-timbered 16th-century manor house with Georgian additions, the hall has 16th–17th-century paintings and furniture on display.

CITY ROUTES

SEE TOWN PLANS P369 AND TOURING GUIDE P470

Newcastle upon Tyne & Gateshead

A coal port and shipbuilding centre for centuries, Newcastle upon Tyne is today a lively industrial metropolis, overlooked by the majestic arch of the Tyne bridge. Alleys slope down from the 12th-century castle keep and its Black Gate to the rejuvenated quayside, where old warehouses have been converted into stylish hotels, restaurants and bars.

Across the river, Gateshead has undertaken some impressive regeneration projects. Recent architectural feats include the striking Millennium Bridge and the monumental Baltic Centre for Contemporary Arts, as well as the magnificent Sage Gateshead Music Centre, designed by Norman Foster, due to open in 2005.

ANGEL OF THE NORTH [B1]
Rising 20m (66ft) from the ground, with a wing span of 54m (177ft), Britain's largest and most impressive sculpture greets around 90,000 motorists each day as they drive past Gateshead.

BALTIC CENTRE FOR CONTEMPORARY ARTS [B2]
The disused 1940s Baltic Flour Mills warehouse on Gatehead's quayside has been transformed into one of Europe's biggest temporary art spaces. The centre provides the space and resources for artists to create art as well as an impressively large exhibition room, lit by natural light from above.

BESSIE SURTEES' HOUSE
[p369 C2] Bessie Surtees was a well-known figure in 17th-century Newcastle; she is said to have eloped through a window of this house to marry local landowner John Scott, who later became Lord Eldon. The house is a good example of fine Jacobean architecture, with plastered ceilings and carved panelling.

THE BISCUIT FACTORY [B2]
Despite its name, this is an art gallery – the biggest single commercial art space in the UK. It houses an extensive array of paintings and sculpture in a former biscuit-maker's Victorian building.

DISCOVERY MUSEUM [p369 A2]
Themed galleries in the museum house exhibitions on the city's military history, maritime heritage and Victorian heyday. Also to be found are

an interactive Science Factory and the 33m (100ft) Turbinia, once the world's fastest vessel.

HANCOCK MUSEUM [p369 C5]
An excellent natural history museum first opened in 1884, it is named after celebrated local naturalists. The permanent galleries contain exhibits ranging from stuffed birds to fossils and include displays on ancient Egypt, natural history and geology.

LAING ART GALLERY [p369 C4]
The renowned gallery has an excellent collection of British art, a children's gallery and an award-winning 'Art on Tyneside' exhibition which traces the development of the region's art and craft tradition.

LIFE INTERACTIVE WORLD [P369 A2]
An innovative interactive science centre explores the origins of life with audio visual exhibits and includes a simulator ride.

MILLENNIUM BRIDGE [p369 D2]
Built for pedestrians and cyclists, the breathtaking bridge connecting Gateshead with Newcastle upon Tyne operates like the lid of a giant eye, opening to form an arch under which ships can pass. It was lifted into place by one of the world's largest floating cranes.

MUSEUM OF ANTIQUITIES [p369 B5]
A notable collection of artefacts, models and diagrams relating to Hadrian's Wall is found here, as are other Roman remains, prehistoric rock art, Stone Age axes, Bronze Age tools and pottery.

NEWCASTLE CASTLE [p369 C2]
The 'New Castle', from which the city derives its name, was founded by Robert Curthose, the son of William the Conqueror, in 1080. Originally built of wood and earth, it was rebuilt in stone in the 12th century. **The Keep** has survived as has the **Black Gate**, which was cut off from the keep by the construction of a railway line in Victorian times.

NEWCASTLE CATHEDRAL [p369 C2]
Built in the 13th–14th century on the site of an earlier Norman church, the cathedral is dedicated to St Nicholas. It has the oldest surviving and most ornate lantern tower, of which there are only three others in the country, and the Chapel of the Incarnation contains a dramatic stone sculpture.

NEWCASTLE MILITARY VEHICLE MUSEUM [p369 C6]
Over 50 historic military vehicles, from bicycles to armoured tanks, and a World War I trench and Anderson air raid shelter, have been painstakingly restored and are now on display in the last surviving pavilion of the 1929 North East Coast Exhibition.

SHIPLEY ART GALLERY [B2]
This is one of the largest collections of contemporary craft in the North, including Old Master paintings and the 'Made in Gateshead' exhibition on the town's history.

THE TYNE BRIDGE [p369 D2]
A prominent landmark, the bridge was built by Dorman Long of Middlesbrough and was the largest single-span bridge in Britain when it was opened in 1928 by King George V.

TOURIST OFFICES

Gateshead
(0191) 478 4222
Newcastle upon Tyne
(0191) 227 8000

WHERE TO PARK

Park & Ride: see p369.

Newcastle (p369):
Dean Street C2
New Bridge Street C3
Newgate Street B3
Percy Street B4

CITY ROUTES

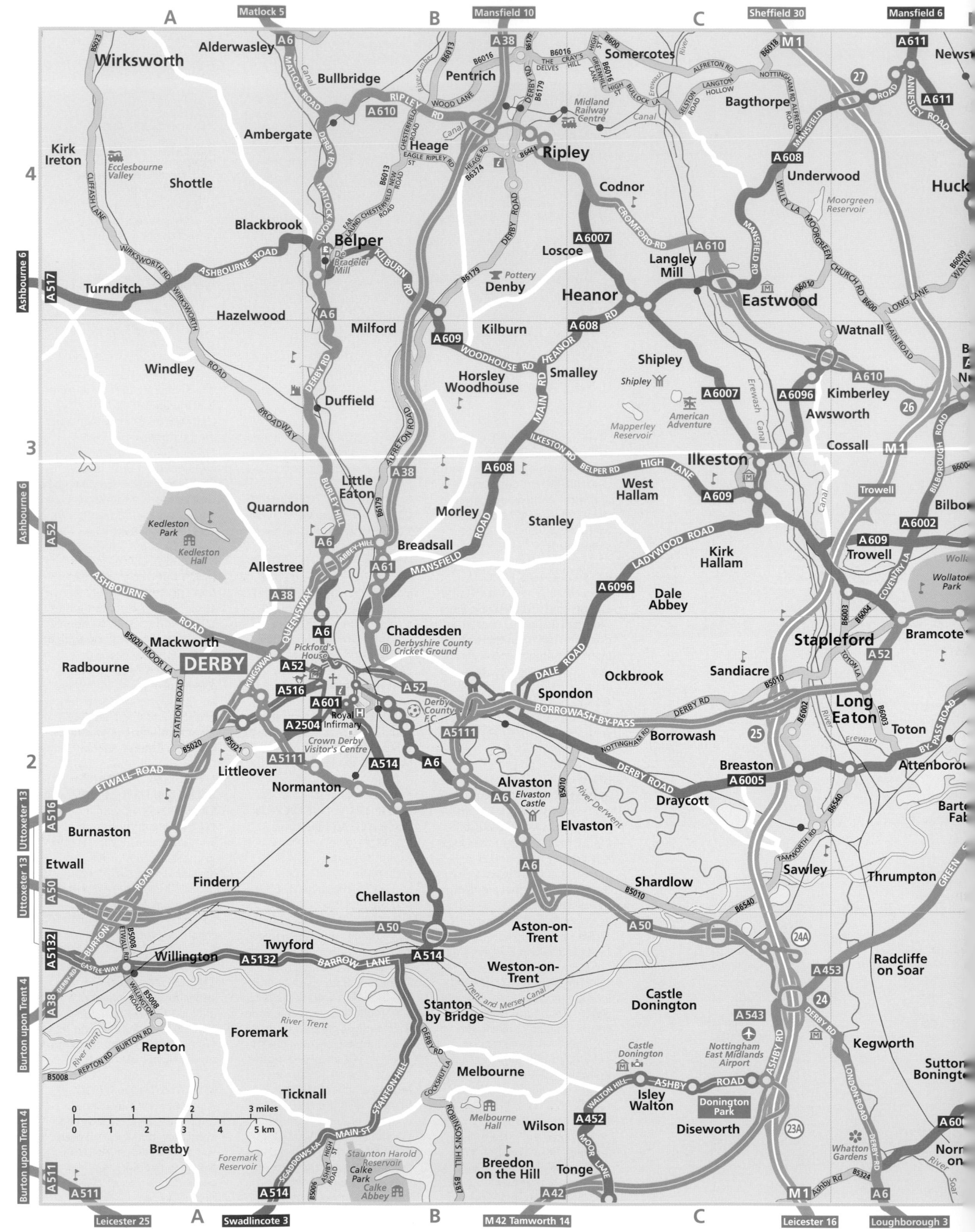

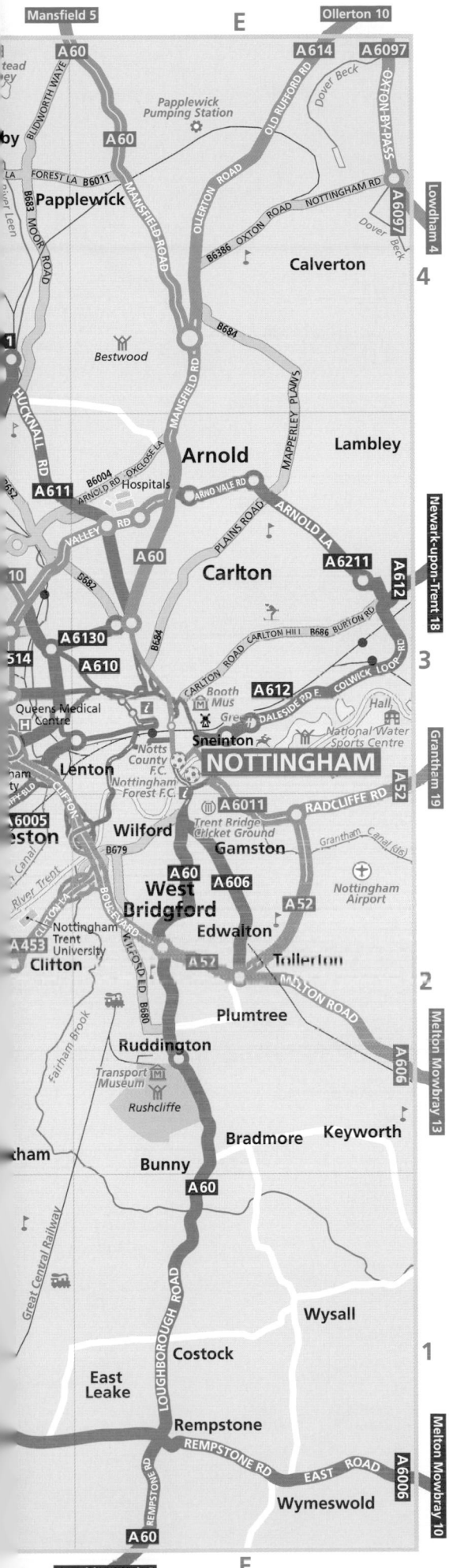

Nottingham & Derby

Known worldwide as the home of Robin Hood, the city of Nottingham is steeped in legend and history. On a rock high above the city is the 17th-century castle, built on the site of a Norman keep, and beneath Nottingham's bustling streets is a unique labyrinth of caves once used for dwellings and stores. The city's industrial heritage is founded on lace and the Lace Market Centre relates the story of its former days.

Some of England's earliest factories and spinning mills were established in Derby during the Industrial Revolution, and Rolls Royce aero engines have been in production here since 1908. The city is perhaps best known for its fine Royal Crown Derby porcelain, which was first made in the town in the 1750s. The company was the first to be granted a royal warrant to use the words 'Royal' and 'Crown'.

TOURIST OFFICES

Derby (01332) 255802
Nottingham
(0115) 915 5330

WHERE TO PARK

Park & Ride: Derby **p326** and Nottingham **p372**.

Derby (p326):
Colyear Street **B3**
Cockpitt **D3**
Full Street **C4**

Nottingham (p372):
Fletcher Gate **C2**
Broadmarsh **C1**
Victoria Centre **C3**

CITY ROUTES

BREWHOUSE YARD MUSEUM [p372 B1] Housed in a row of cottages beneath Castle Rock, the museum has displays on local life in Nottingham over the last 300 years, including reconstructed rooms and shops.

CITY OF CAVES [p372 C2] A labyrinth of 13th-century hand-carved caves offers a glimpse of Nottingham's past, with tours through reconstructed Victorian slums, a tannery and an air-raid shelter.

DERBY CATHEDRAL [p326 B4] The 16th-century church tower of the cathedral is the second highest in England at 63m (212ft), with the oldest ring of ten bells in the world. The interior is renowned for its intricate wrought iron screens and the tomb of Bess of Hardwick in the vault. There is a new visitor centre which houses an education centre, library and a display of the cathedral's many treasures.

DERBY MUSEUM AND ART GALLERY [p326 B3] Displays cover fine art, archaeology, military history, geology and wildlife, and include fine displays of Derby porcelain. The Art Gallery holds a large collection of works by the celebrated 18th-century local artist Joseph Wright.

GALLERIES OF JUSTICE [p372 C2] Set in a Victorian courthouse, the museum has impressive displays on 19th-century justice. The highlight is the re-enactment of a trial and prison life using

reconstructed cave cells, a prisoner's exercise yard and an Edwardian police station.

GREEN'S MILL AND SCIENCE CENTRE [E3] A restored working flour mill, once owned by the mathematician and physicist George Green, is now a hands-on science centre with displays on milling and Green's contribution to science.

LACE MARKET CENTRE [p372 C2] Across the road from **Lace Hall**, once the hub of the world's lace industry, this visitor centre has examples of exquisite lace and working lace machines on display and holds bobbin lace demonstrations.

LACE CENTRE [p372 B2] A 15th-century medieval house holds a fine collection of Nottingham lace which is mostly for sale.

NOTTINGHAM CASTLE MUSEUM AND ART GALLERY [p372 A1] The original Norman fortress was destroyed by Cromwell in 1651. It was replaced by a ducal mansion in the 17th century which now holds collections of fine and decorative arts, as well as exhibitions on the history of the city. Outside the castle is a statue of Robin Hood, the 13th-century folk hero who is said to have robbed the rich to help the poor.

PICKFORD'S HOUSE [B2] The Georgian house, built by architect Joseph Pickford in 1770, is now a museum, with rooms recreated in period style.

ROYAL CROWN DERBY VISITOR'S CENTRE [B2] Derby's famous fine bone china, dating back to 1752, can be seen here. There is also plenty of information on the history of the company, demonstrations by craftsmen and tours of the factory.

ST MARY'S BRIDGE CHAPEL [p326 C4] For many years, the 13th-century bridge chapel, one of only a few left in the UK, levied tolls for all people and livestock using the bridge. The 'martyrs of Padley', three Roman Catholic priests, were executed here.

THE SILK MILL [p326 C4] One of Britain's first factories, John and Thomas Lombe's silk mill was built in 1717. It is now a museum called **Derby's Museum of Industry and History** and has displays on railway engineering and Rolls Royce aero engines.

THE TALES OF ROBIN HOOD [p372 B2] Using audio-visual technology, the museum recreates everyday life in medieval Nottingham and Robin Hood's Sherwood Forest.

THE WILLIAM BOOTH BIRTHPLACE MUSEUM [E3] William Booth, founder of the Salvation Army, was born here. His home is now open to the public by appointment.

WOLLATON HALL [D3] A magnificent Tudor house set in parkland is the home of the city's **Natural History Museum**. The neighbouring **Industrial Museum** includes a working steam pump and displays on lace making.

CITY ROUTES

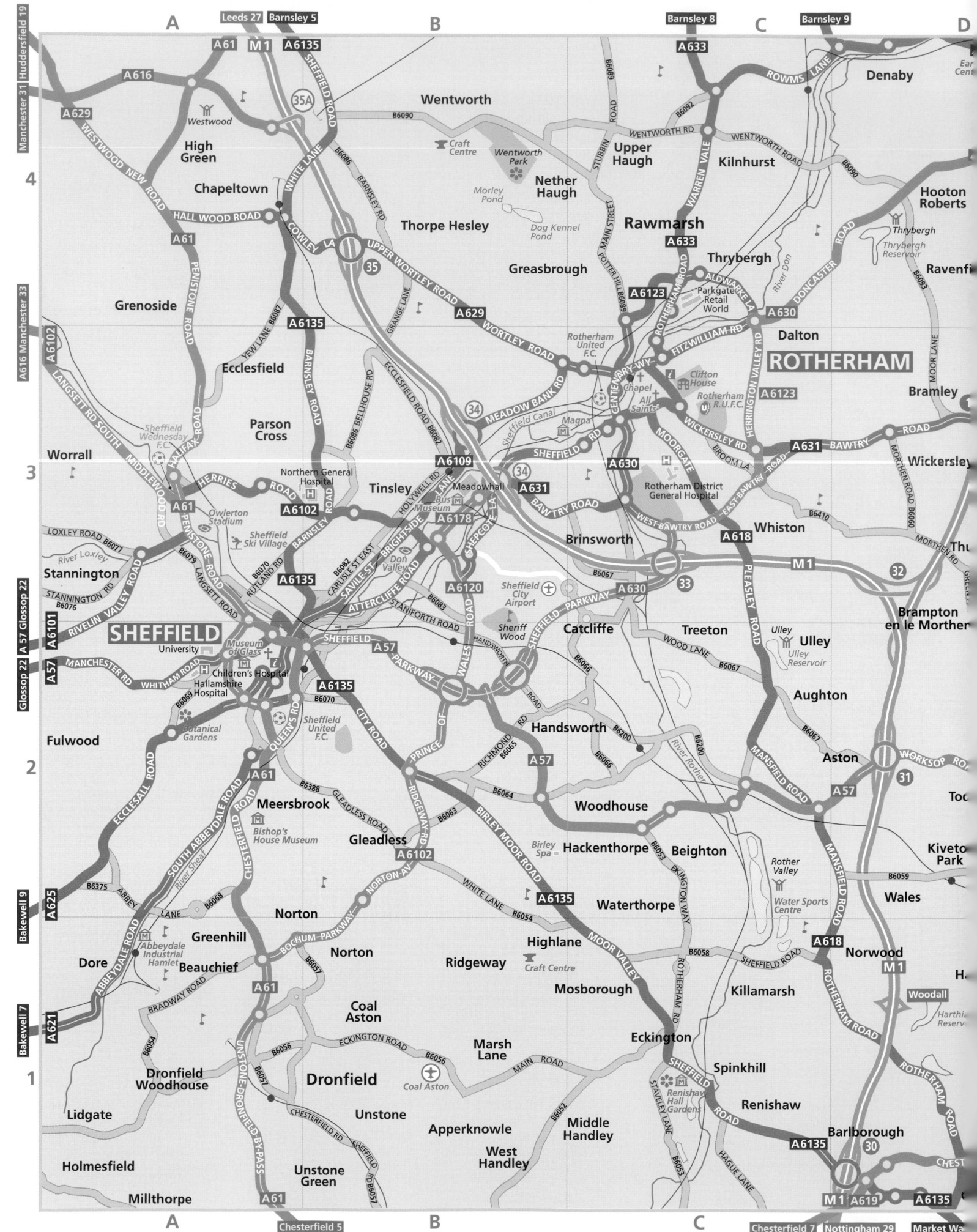

SEE TOWN PLANS **p386** AND TOURING GUIDE **p457**

Sheffield & Rotherham

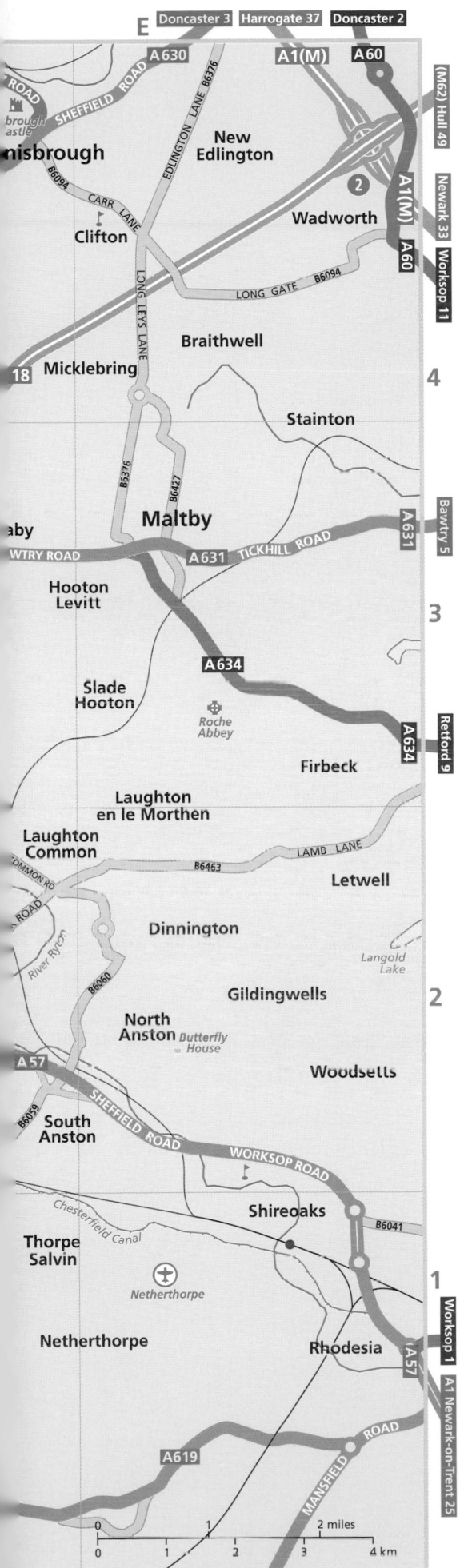

A statue of the Roman god of metalworking, Vulcan, perches on top of Sheffield's town hall, a symbol of the city's main industry. Cutlery has been made here since medieval days, and steel since the 18th century. Today, this industrial city has the most modern urban tramway system in the country and a palatial indoor shopping centre, Meadow Hall; the formerly derelict canal basin has been redeveloped as Victoria Quays; and the Winter Gardens, an urban greenhouse adjoining the stunning new Millennium Galleries, have revitalised the centre.

Coal, iron and steel transformed 19th-century Rotherham into an industrial town. Little of the medieval town remains today but Rotherham has capitalised on its industrial heritage by transforming a former steelworks into the hugely popular tourist attraction Magna.

TOURIST OFFICES

Sheffield
(0114) 221 1900
Rotherham
(01709) 835 904

WHERE TO PARK

Park & Ride: See p386.

Sheffield (p386):
Arundel Gate **D3**
Campo Lane **C4**
Charles Street **C2**
Charter Row **B2**

CITY ROUTES

ABBEYDALE INDUSTRIAL HAMLET [A1]
A former industrial complex is home to a museum which recreates the local steelmaking industries of the 18th and 19th centuries. On display are working water wheels, forging hammers and grindstones, and the only surviving Huntsman crucible furnace. A new gallery equipped with audioguides and interactive displays brings the experience to life.

ALL SAINTS' CHURCH [C3]
Most of the church dates from the 15th century. Interesting features include fan vaulting, a Saxon coffin lid, and finely carved bench ends.

BISHOP'S HOUSE [A2]
The oldest surviving timber-framed house in Sheffield was built around 1500 and retains many original features. It is now a museum of domestic life with furnishings recreating the style of the home of a prosperous 17th-century yeoman.

BOTANICAL GARDENS [A2]
A fine example of the Victorian informal 'Gardenesque' style, the recently restored gardens display a wide variety of trees and shrubs and are noted for their grand promenade and some of the earliest curvilinear glass pavilions, built by Joseph Paxton, architect of the fabled Crystal Palace.

CITY MUSEUM AND MAPPIN ART GALLERY [P386 A3]
The **City Museum** has displays of Sheffield plate, antique cutlery, archaeology, natural history and decorative arts. The adjoining **Mappin Gallery** has some splendid landscapes, portraits and still-lifes, dating from between the 16th and 19th centuries, and includes the works of artists such as Turner and Constable. In 2005, the complex will reopen as **Weston Park Museum**.

THE CHAPEL OF OUR LADY [C3]
Perching on top of the four-arched old Don bridge in Rotherham, the restored 1483 chapel is one of very few remaining bridge chapels in Britain. In the 18th century it became the town gaol and two tiny cells in the crypt are vestiges from these days.

CLIFTON HOUSE [C3]
Built in 1783 as a home for the Walkers, a family of Rotherham iron manufacturers, it is now the town museum. On view is an extensive collection of Rockingham porcelain as well as glass and archaeological exhibits and the ruins of a Roman fort at Templeborough.

THE FIRE POLICE MUSEUM [P386 C4]
A collection of old fire engines, equipment and uniforms are displayed in a Victorian police and fire station. The exhibits include reconstructions of cells and the scene of a road traffic accident.

GRAVES ART GALLERY [P386 D3]
In the heart of the city centre, the gallery has an impressive collection of late 19th–20th-century British and European art including works by Matisse and Picasso.

KELHAM ISLAND INDUSTRIAL MUSEUM [p386 C5]
Sheffield's industrial heritage is recreated in this museum, with demonstrations by craftsmen using traditional steelmaking techniques. Among the exhibits are a steam engine and a Bessemer converter, a giant steel producing piece of machinery.

MAGNA [B3]
Set within a vast former steelworks, the innovative science adventure centre has superb interactive displays in four themed pavilions on the main elements used in steelmaking: air, earth, water and fire. The building won the 2001 RIBA Stirling prize for architecture.

MILLENNIUM GALLERIES [P386 D3]
The inspiring new venue for visual arts, craft and design includes a collection of paintings, drawings, minerals and prints brought together by 19th-century social reformer John Ruskin. The galleries also contain displays on Sheffield's metalworking heritage and works on loan from museums such as the Tate and the Victoria and Albert Museum.

SHEFFIELD BUS MUSEUM [B3]
The former tram depot at Tinsley is home to a collection of old buses as well as bus timetables, tickets and models.

SHEFFIELD CATHEDRAL [p386 C4]
Built in the Perpendicular Gothic style, the cathedral's oldest parts date from the 15th century. Notable features include the Shrewsbury Chapel and Chapter House with fine stained glass depicting scenes from Sheffield's history.

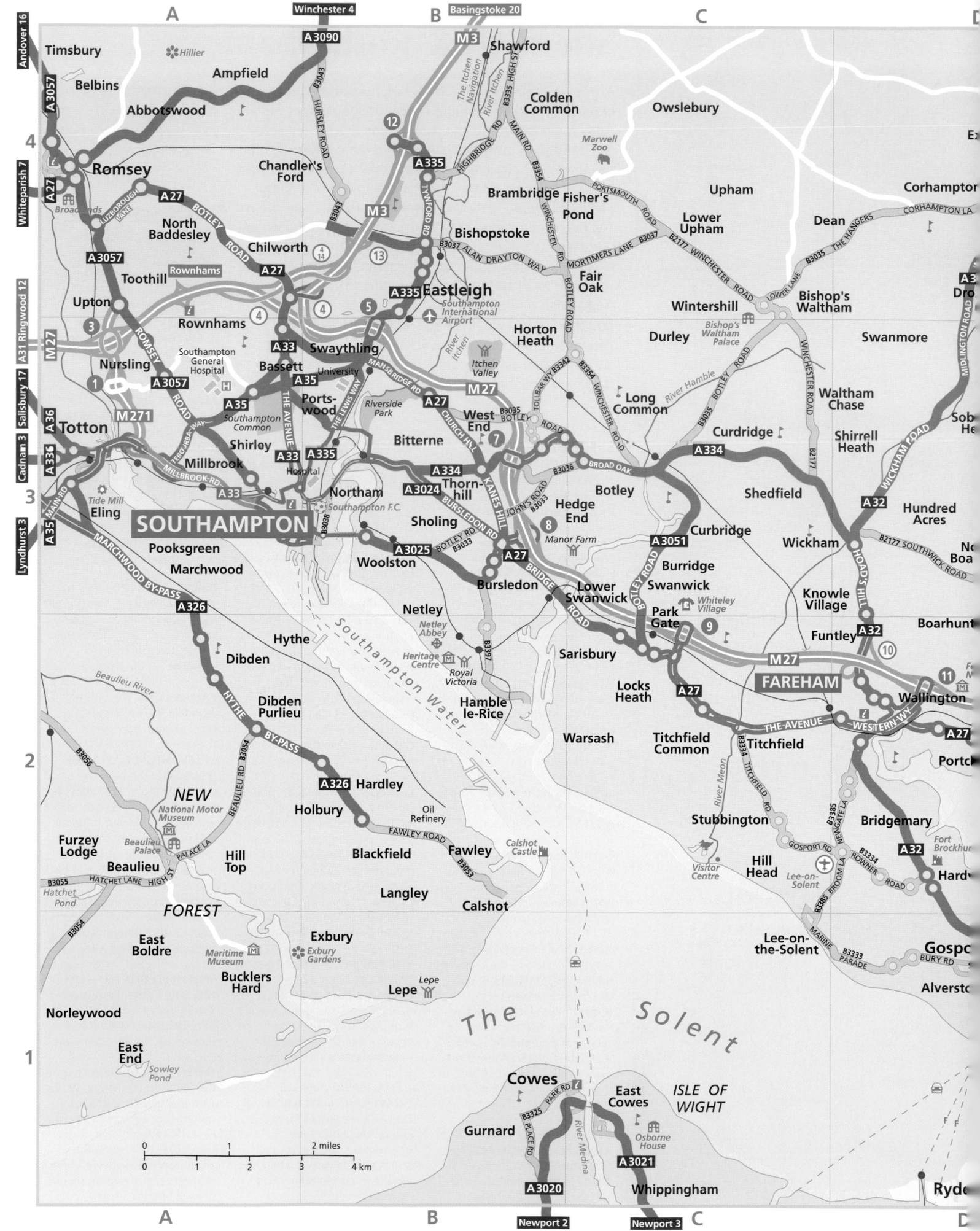

Southampton & Portsmouth

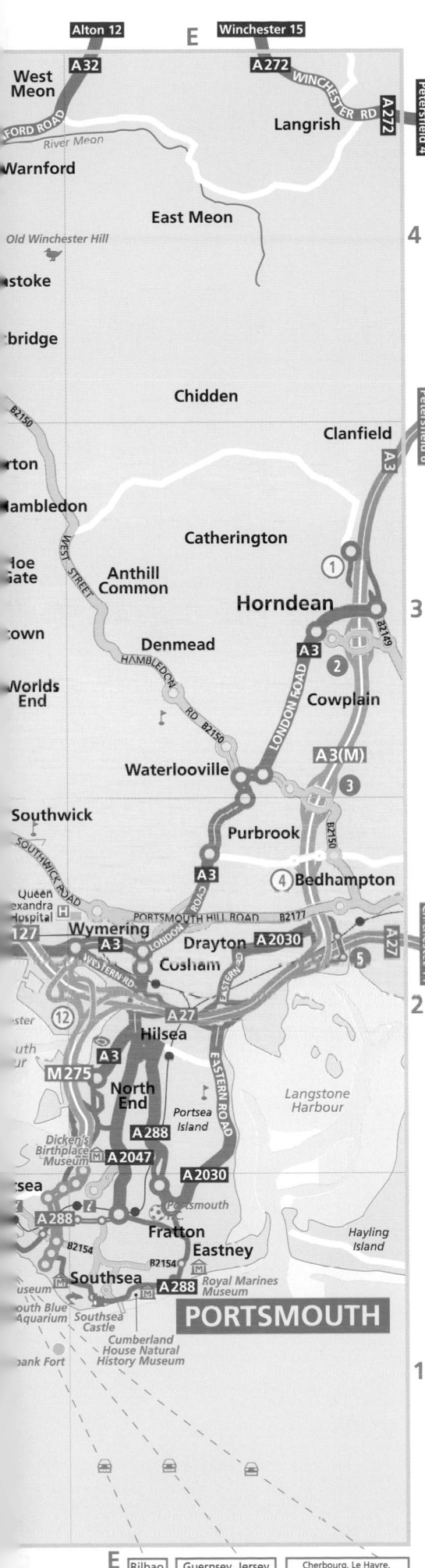

A seaport in Norman times and a popular 18th-century spa, Southampton became a leading port for passenger liners in the 19th century. Among the millions of ships that have sailed from its harbour are the *Mayflower* and the ill-fated *Titanic*. The city was badly destroyed by World War II bombing but the well-preserved Norman walls and Bargate, and a handful of other surviving historic buildings, offer a glimpse into the city's past.

Since Henry VII made Portsmouth a royal dockyard some 500 years ago, it has become Britain's foremost naval port. Today its many museums help to preserve the maritime atmosphere and traditions of the past. The city centre has been regenerated with the Millennium Parade, linking the historic dockside with the Old Town, and the 165m (541ft) high Spinnaker Tower at the entrance to the harbour.

TOURIST OFFICES

Portsmouth
 (023) 9282 6722
Southampton
 (023) 8083 3333

WHERE TO PARK

Portsmouth (p378):
Cascades Centre **C4**
Station Street **D3**
Winston Churchill Ave **C2**

Southampton (p388):
Bargate Centre **B3**
Lime Street **C2**
Mayflower Park **A2**
Portland Terrace **B3**

CUMBERLAND HOUSE NATURAL HISTORY MUSEUM [E1] Natural history displays include a freshwater aquarium and a butterfly house with a wide range of British and European butterflies.

D-DAY MUSEUM [D1] Located in Southsea, the museum's centrepiece is the 83m (272ft) long Overlord Embroidery commemorating the Allied invasion of France in 1944. It also has archive film footage and a reconstruction of the events of D-Day itself.

DICKENS' BIRTHPLACE MUSEUM [E2] Writer Charles Dickens was born here in 1812. The museum is furnished in Regency style and its exhibits include the couch on which he died in 1870.

GOD'S HOUSE TOWER [p388 B1] Once a 15th-century gun battery, these stone towers now house Southampton's **Museum of Archaeology**, with displays on the city's Roman, Saxon and medieval past.

HALL OF AVIATION [p388 D1] The designer of the Spitfire, Reginald J. Mitchell, lived in Southampton and the history of the legendary aircraft is recounted here. Visitors can also board a Sandringham Flying Boat and sit at the controls of a supersonic jet.

HISTORIC DOCKYARD [p378 A3-B4] Three famous ships are berthed here: Henry VIII's *Mary Rose* which was raised from the bed of the Solent in 1982;

Nelson's 1805 flagship *HMS Victory*; and the Victorian ironclad warship *HMS Warrior*. A large hall holds items found on the *Mary Rose* whilst its hull can be viewed nearby. Tours onboard *HMS Victory* and the restored *HMS Warrior* relive their eventful past days.

MARITIME MUSEUM [p388 B1] Set in the **Wool House**, a medieval warehouse, the museum covers the history of Southampton's port and the doomed *Titanic* which set off on its maiden voyage from Southampton in 1912.

MEDIEVAL MERCHANT'S HOUSE [p388 B2] A restored 13th century timber-framed house ⌗ has been furnished in period style to recreate its original appearance.

PORTSMOUTH BLUE REEF AQUARIUM [D1] Open-top tanks, glass tunnels, tide pools, and crashing surf displays featuring both local Solent life and tropical species reveal the magic of the underwater world.

PORTSMOUTH CITY MUSEUM [p378 C1] Displays on local history, fine art and room settings depict Portsmouth life between the 17th century and the 1950s.

ROYAL MARINES MUSEUM [E1] Video displays on the Falklands War and D-Day, and a collection of medals including Victoria Crosses awarded to the Royal Marines, are just some of the exhibits on show here.

ROYAL NAVAL MUSEUM [p378 A3] Georgian dockside warehouses are home to lively displays of models, paintings and medals, and include interactive exhibitions on the Battle of Trafalgar, Horatio Nelson and *HMS Victory*.

ROYAL GARRISON CHURCH [p378 B1] Once a hospice for pilgrims, Charles II was married here in 1662. The church was badly damaged by bombing in 1941 and remains roofless.

SOUTHAMPTON CITY ART GALLERY [p388 B4] Among a notable collection of 20th-century British art are works by Sir Stanley Spencer and Philip Wilson Steer, as well as European art and sculpture.

SOUTHSEA CASTLE [E1] Built by Henry VIII in 1545 to ward off a French invasion, the castle has a revolutionary design using angled rather than rounded bastions to make the firing of artillery more effective. Today it contains a museum on Portsmouth's military history.

SPITBANK FORT [D1] Accessed by boat from the Naval Base, the seafort has guarded Portsmouth's harbour for over 120 years. It consists of a maze of passages and rooms, and has replicas of huge 38-ton guns and a 130m (420ft) working well.

TUDOR HOUSE MUSEUM AND GARDEN [p388 B2] A restored Tudor house with a knot garden gives a fascinating glimpse into 15th-century life.

CITY ROUTES

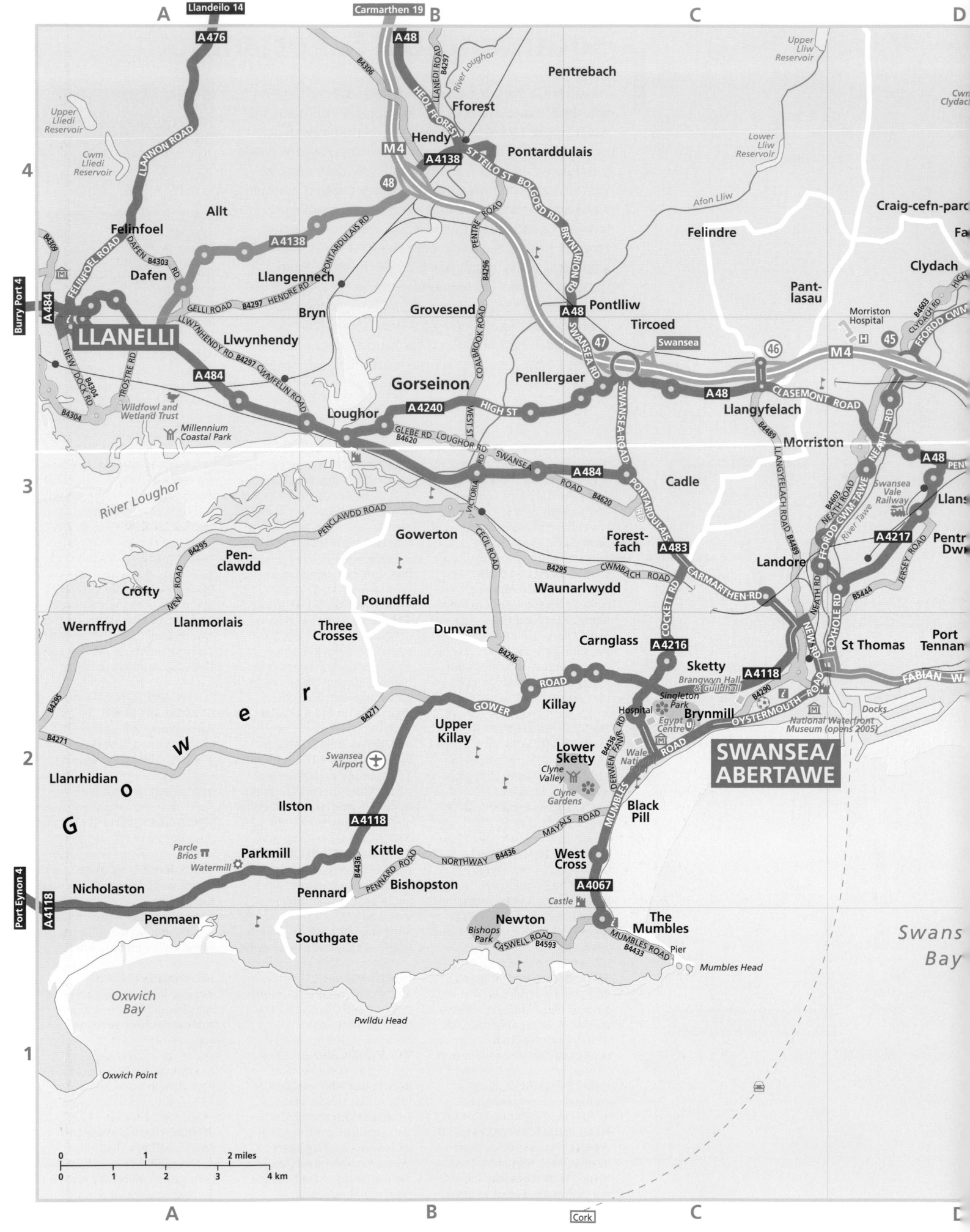

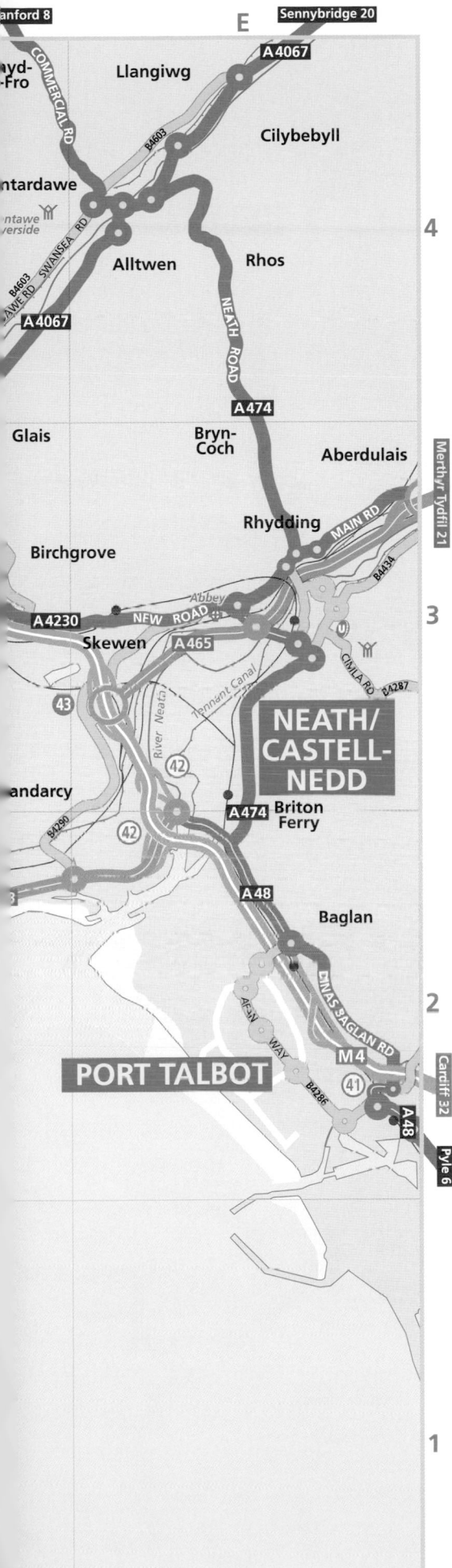

Swansea

Situated on the wide sweeping sands of Swansea Bay, and the gateway to the spectacular Gower Peninsula, Swansea grew from a fishing village into a huge port after the mid 19th century. It was the copper-smelting capital of the world during the Industrial Revolution and boasted the world's first passenger railway in 1807. Described by one of Swansea's most famous sons, the poet Dylan Thomas, as an 'ugly, lovely town', much of the city has been rebuilt since the Second World War, including the large market where laver bread and cockles from the Pen-clawdd beds off the north Gower coast are on sale. Swansea and the surrounding landscape suffered greatly from industry and pollution but recent efforts to amend the damage have resulted in the transformation of the city's derelict docks into the award-winning Maritime Quarter.

ATTIC GALLERY [p92 C1]
Founded in 1962, this is the longest established gallery in Wales. Changing exhibitions highlight the work of contemporary artists working in Wales, and display work of the pricipality's most important artists.

BRANGWYN HALL [C2]
Situated in the 1934 **Guildhall**, the grand concert hall is graced with 16 baroque wall panels depicting the British Empire, which were painted by Sir Frank Brangwyn at the turn of the 20th century for the House of Lords. They remained in Wales because they were considered controversial.

CLYNE GARDENS [C2]
Overlooking Swansea Bay, the gardens have an outstanding collection of rhododendrons and azaleas and include a bog garden and lovely woodland walks.

DYLAN THOMAS CENTRE [p92 C2]
Devoted to Welsh literature, the highlight is the permanent 'I, In My Intricate Image' exhibition, which contains memorabilia on the life and works of Swansea-born poet and author Dylan Thomas, including original manuscripts. The centre also holds an annual Dylan Thomas Festival.

EGYPT CENTRE [C2]
Many of the items in this notable collection of Egyptian artefacts were donated to the museum by the pharmacist Sir Henry Wellcome. There are more than 3500 pieces including the painted coffin of a female musician, beautiful intricately-beaded necklaces dating from the reign of Tutankhamun and everyday objects used by the ancient Egyptians.

GLYNN VIVIAN ART GALLERY & MUSEUM [p92 B3]
The museum has important displays of rare Swansea porcelain, which was produced locally between 1814 and 1824, as well as British and European art and sculpture. There are also fine collections of stained glass commemorating Swansea's worldwide reputation in the craft. The gallery places much emphasis on the work of Welsh artists, in particular the celebrated local artist Cerl Richards.

GRAND THEATRE ARTS WING [p92 A2]
A new wing in the Victorian theatre has been refurbished in Art Deco style and houses temporary exhibitions of fine art, photography and sculpture.

MISSION GALLERY [p92 C1]
Sited in a converted seaman's chapel dating from 1858, the independent public art gallery has changing exhibitions of art by Welsh, British and international artists.

PLANTASIA [p92 C2]
This futuristic pyramid-shaped glasshouse has climatically controlled areas and contains over 5000 tropical and desert plants, and creatures ranging from monkeys to piranha. Several of the species growing here are now extinct in their natural habitats.

TOURIST OFFICES

Swansea
(01792) 468321

WHERE TO PARK

The Kingsway **p92 A2**
Orchard Street **p92 B3**
Oystermouth Road **p92 B1**
The Quadrant Shopping Centre **p92 B2**
Strand **p92 B2**

SINGLETON PARK AND BOTANIC GARDENS [C2]
The Botanical Gardens are based in the old walled gardens in the grounds of Singleton Park and are renowned for their splendid displays of bedding plants. The temperate and tropical glasshouses contain a large collection of rare and unusual species including orchids and bromeliads.

SWANSEA CASTLE [p92 B2]
The rugged ruins of 13th–14th-century Swansea Castle, built by Bishop Henry de Gower, tower above the Strand. The castle had a turbulent history and was mostly destroyed during Civil War. The remains include a striking 14th-century first-floor arcade but can only be viewed from outside.

SWANSEA MARKET [p92 B2]
The vibrant and colourful covered market, one of the largest in the UK, teams with life. An annual Swansea Food Festival is held here in early October – the area has been famous for its cockle beds since Roman times.

SWANSEA MUSEUM [p92 C1]
The oldest museum in Wales was described by Dylan Thomas as 'the museum that should have been in a museum'. The neoclassical building dates from 1841 and contains collections ranging from local history to Egyptology. Exhibits include a traditional Welsh kitchen, replicas of the oldest human bones found in Wales and the mummy of a 4000-year-old Egyptian priest called Hor.

WALES NATIONAL POOL [C2]
The only Olympic-size swimming pool to be found in Wales, this recent addition to Swansea's burgeoning leisure facilities is state-of-the-art.

CITY ROUTES

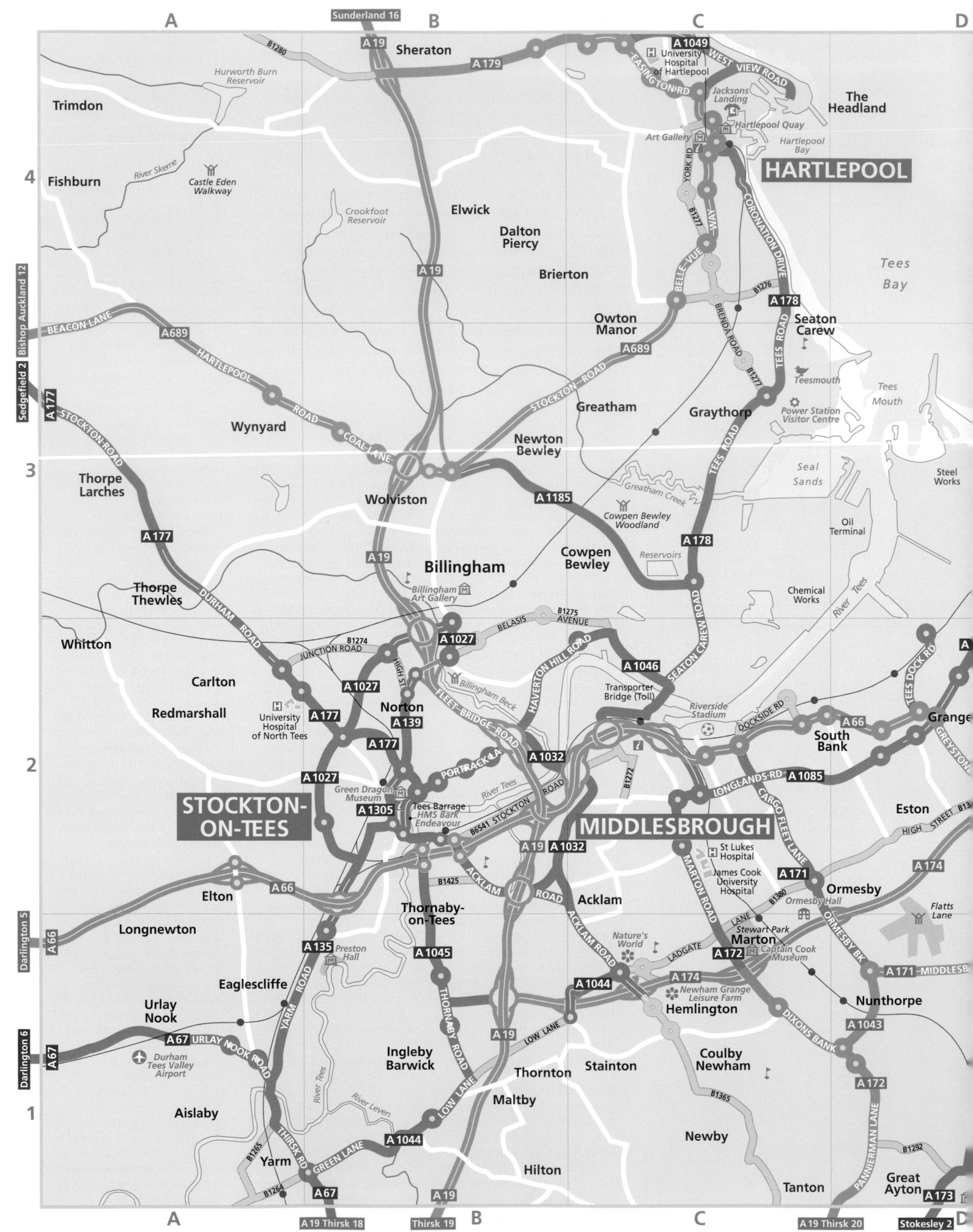

A **B** **C** **D**

Sunderland 16

B1280

A 19 Sheraton

A 179

A 1049

University Hospital of Hartlepool

Jacksons Landing

WEST VIEW ROAD

Hartlepool Quay

The Headland

Trimdon

Hurworth Burn Reservoir

EASINGTON RD

Art Gallery

HARTLEPOOL

4

Fishburn

River Skerne

Castle Eden Walkway

Crookfoot Reservoir

Elwick

Dalton Piercy

Brierton

A 19

YORK RD

BELLE VUE WAY

B1277

CORONATION DRIVE

Hartlepool Bay

Tees Bay

Owton Manor

B1276

A 178

Seaton Carew

BEACON LANE

A 689

Bishop Auckland 12

STOCKTON ROAD

HARTLEPOOL ROAD

Wynyard

COAL LANE

Greatham

BRENDA ROAD

B1271

Graythorp

Teesmouth

Power Station Visitor Centre

Tees Mouth

Sedgefield 2

A 177

Newton Bewley

A 1185

TEES ROAD

Greatham Creek

Seal Sands

Steel Works

3

Thorpe Larches

Wolviston

Cowpen Bewley Woodland

SEATON CAREW ROAD

A 178

Oil Terminal

A 177

A 19

Billingham

Cowpen Bewley

Reservoirs

Chemical Works

River Tees

Thorpe Thewles

DURHAM ROAD

Billingham Art Gallery

BELASIS AVENUE

B1275

A 1046

Whitton

JUNCTION ROAD

B1274

A 1027

Billingham Beck

HAVERTON HILL ROAD

Transporter Bridge (Toll)

Riverside Stadium

DOCKSIDE RD

TEES DOCK RD

Carlton

A 1027

HIGH ST

Dockside Rd

A 66

Grange

Redmarshall

A 177

University Hospital of North Tees

Norton

A 139

A 1032

B1272

LONGLANDS RD

A 1085

South Bank

GREYSTONE

2

A 1027

A 177

PORTRACK LA.

FLEET BRIDGE ROAD

MIDDLESBROUGH

CARGO FLEET LANE

Eston

HIGH STREET B13

Green Dragon Museum

STOCKTON ROAD

A 19 A 1032

A 174

STOCKTON-ON-TEES

A 1305

Tees Barrage HMS Bark Endeavour

B6541 STOCKTON

River Tees

St Lukes Hospital

A 171

ORMESBY ROAD

Darlington 5

A 66

Elton

A 66

B1425

ACKLAM

Acklam

James Cook University Hospital

B1380

Ormesby Hall

Ormesby

A 174

Flatts Lane

A 171 MIDDLESB

Longnewton

MARTON ROAD

Stewart Park

LANE

ORMESBY BK

A 135

Preston Hall

Thornaby-on-Tees

ACKLAM ROAD

Nature's World

Marton

Captain Cook Museum

Eaglescliffe

YARM ROAD

A 1045

LADGATE

A 172

Coulby Newham

A 171

Darlington 6

Urlay Nook

A 67

URLAY NOOK ROAD

THORNABY ROAD

A 1044

A 174

Newham Grange Leisure Farm

Hemlington

DIXONS BANK

A 1043

Nunthorpe

1

Aislaby

Durham Tees Valley Airport

THIRSK RD

GREEN LANE

Ingleby Barwick

A 19

LOW LANE

LOW LANE

Thornton

Stainton

B1365

A 172

Coulby Newham

B1365

Yarm

B1265

A 67

Maltby

Hilton

Newby

Tanton

Great Ayton

A 173

B1266

A 67

A 19

A 19 Thirsk 18

Thirsk 19

A 19 Thirsk 20

Stokesley 2

A **B** **C** **D**

Teesside

The steel chimneys and tanks of oil refineries and chemical plants dominate the flat landscape of the Tees valley and its urban conurbation of Middlesbrough, Stockton-on-Tees and Hartlepool. Teesside rapidly evolved from a cluster of small market towns and ports into a thriving area of coal works and iron foundries in the 19th century, boosted by the opening of the world's first railway in 1835 from Stockton to Darlington. Hartlepool was one of England's busiest ports in the 1880s and shipbuilding had long been a prosperous industry in the area. The maritime explorer Captain James Cook was born in Middlesbrough and his legacy lives on in museums, statues and a replica of his ship, the *HMS Bark Endeavour*, in Stockton's Castlegate Quay. Today, developments such as the Tees Barrage have brought a new focus to the river.

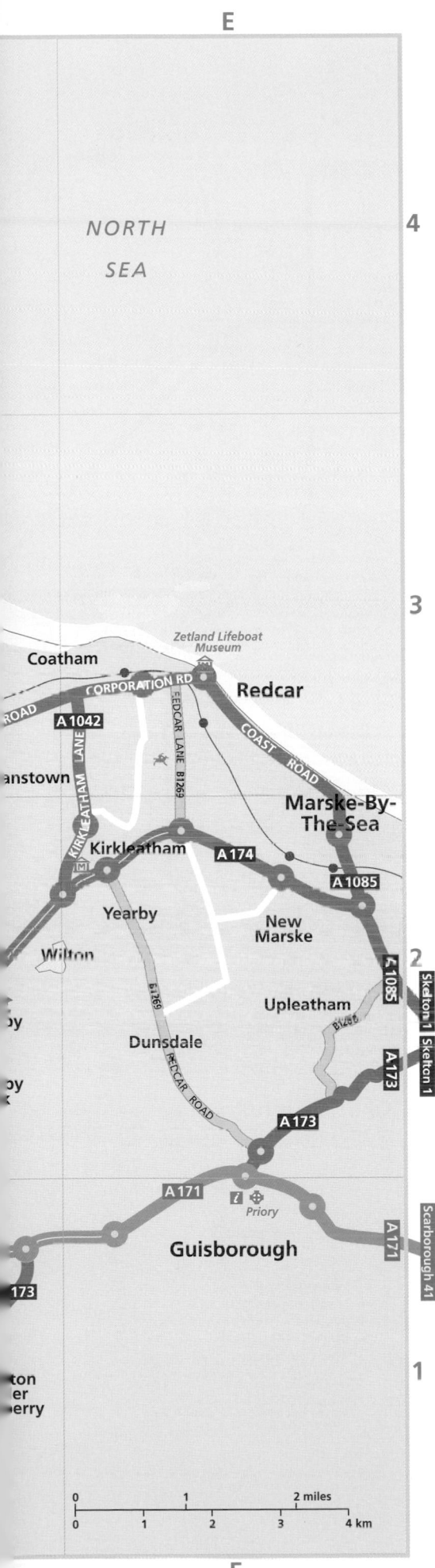

TOURIST OFFICES

Middlesbrough
(01642) 729700
Hartlepool
(01429) 869706
Stockon-on-Tees
(01642) 393936

WHERE TO PARK

Middlesbrough (p365):
Captain Cook Square **C3**
Cleveland Shopping
Centre **C3**
Dundas Arcade, Wilson
Street **C4**
Zetland Road **C4**

CAPTAIN COOK BIRTHPLACE MUSEUM [C1] The 18th-century explorer Captain James Cook was born at Marton in Middlesborough. His birthplace museum is situated in the landscaped grounds of **Stewart Park**, with hands-on displays and interactive computer simulations detailing his life and voyages.

DORMAN MUSEUM [p365 C1] Newly refurbished, the museum boasts a fine collection of locally produced Linthorpe pottery, displays on local history, geology and zoology, and an interactive natural science centre.

GREEN DRAGON MUSEUM [B2] Sited in a former sweet factory, the museum houses two galleries – the Upper Gallery where there is an exhibition of local history, made up of both art and photography, and the Focus Gallery on the ground floor, which displays contemporary photography.

HARTLEPOOL ART GALLERY [C4] A restored Victorian church is home to an art gallery with contemporary art, ceramics, photography and the work of local artists on display.

HARTLEPOOL MUSEUM [C4] There are good displays on local history with a maritime slant at this museum. Exhibits include a Celtic 'round house' building, the first lighthouse to be illuminated by gas and the restored 1934 paddle steamer *Wingfield Castle*.

HARTLEPOOL QUAY [C4] Reconstructed houses, shops, a market and a jail line the historic quayside, offering visitors a glimpse into life in a Napoleonic seaport. There is an exhibition on fighting ships, a maritime adventure centre and virtual reality exhibits.

HMS BARK ENDEAVOUR [B2] A full-size replica of Captain Cook's vessel graces Stockton's **Castlegate Quay**. It contains exhibits ranging from surgeons' knives to telescopes.

HMS TRINCOMALEE [C4] One of Britain's oldest surviving warships, the *HMS Trincomalee* dates from 1817. Fully restored, she is moored in Hartlepool's historic quayside.

NATURE'S WORLD [C1] Recreated habitats and organic gardens can be seen at this environmental demonstration centre. An innovative 'ecostructure' contains displays on environmental technology, and there is a 'hydroponicum' – a soil-less garden.

NEWHAM GRANGE LEISURE FARM [C1] A working farm since the 17th century, it has rare breeds, an agricultural museum and reconstructions of a veterinary surgery and saddler's shop.

ORMESBY HALL [C2] The elegant 18th-century mansion is set in 270 acres of parkland. The hall contains elaborate plasterwork and there is also a restored Victorian kitchen and laundry, and a model railway.

PRESTON HALL MUSEUM AND PARK [B1] A reconstructed Victorian high street with authentic period-room sets shows traditional craftsmen at work. The museum also has collections of toys, games and armoury. In the surrounding parkland are an aviary, miniature railway and peaceful woodland and riverside walks. Also in the grounds is the nature centre **Butterfly World**, in which hundreds of species of butterfly flitter about against the exotic backdrop of a recreated jungle.

TEES BARRAGE [B2] An impressive construction, the barrage was completed in 1995 and involved diverting the Tees from its course. A viewing point affords good vistas over the surrounding landscaped area and fish can be seen negotiating a 'fish ladder', a series of weirs which enables fish to swim upstream.

TRANSPORTER BRIDGE [C2] Spanning the River Tees, this toll bridge, built in 1911 as a clever alternative to a drawbridge, still shuttles pedestrians and cars across the river in a suspended gondola. A visitor centre provides information on the history of the bridge and Middlesbrough's industrial heritage.

THE ZETLAND LIFEBOAT MUSEUM [E3] Home to the world's oldest lifeboat, the *Zetland*, the museum also contains a replica fisherman's cottage and displays on local maritime history.

CITY ROUTES

The London Underground

London's underground railway is the world's oldest, dating from 1863 with the opening of the Metropolitan Railway between Paddington and Farringdon Street. The Tube now has 12 separate lines, more than 243 miles of track and 275 stations.

Every day, more than 3 million passenger journeys are made on the Tube, with over 900 million journeys in an average year. At peak times (7.30–9.30am and 4.30–7pm), overcrowding can be intense. During the day, the Tube is an excellent alternative to the car for travelling in London.

Using the Tube

The Tube system is divided into six zones with fares priced according to the number of zones. All trips taking in central zone 1 are more expensive than the outer zones.
• Unless you have to get to early morning meetings, avoid travelling before 9.30am – discount fares generally apply after this time.
• Travelcards, offering unlimited travel on the Tube, bus and trains can be good value, especially if you have a number of places to visit during the day. They can be purchased for the day, week or even month, from tube stations and newsagents.
• A number of more modern tube stations now have lifts for those unable to manage escalators and stairs.

Tube lines

Bakerloo Runs above and below ground serving central and north London.
Central Runs above and below ground serving west, central and east London.
Circle Runs above and below ground serving central London.
District Runs above and below ground serving west, central and east London.
East London Overground line serving south-east London
Hammersmith and City Overground line serving central and west London.
Jubilee Runs under and overground serving east, central and north London.
Metropolitan Overground line serving central and north-west London.
Northern Runs above and below ground serving south-west, central and north London.
Piccadilly Runs above and below ground serving west, central and north London.
Victoria Runs above and below ground serving south, central and north-east London.
Waterloo and City Weekday underground line between Waterloo and Bank stations.

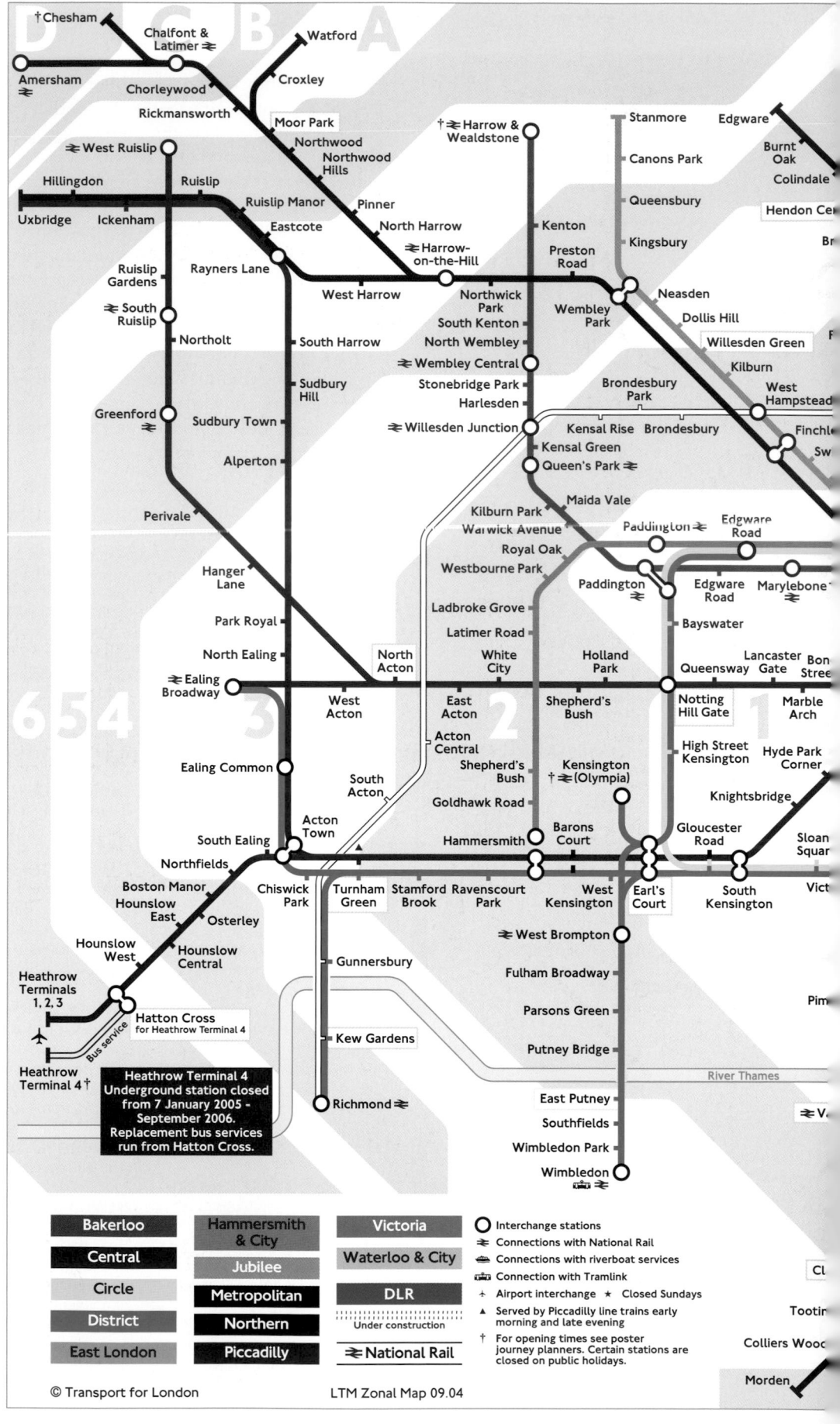

24 hour travel information
i 020 7222 1234

Textphone
020 7918 3015

Website
www.tfl.gov.uk

UNDERGROUND

Reg. user No. 04/4240   Version 9.04

SEE ALSO PAGES 58–59

Central & suburban London rail routes

Beyond the Underground, suburban and central London is linked by a comprehensive range of rail services.

A zonal pricing scheme for travelcards applies to the rail routes shown here. For further information and timetables, contact numbers are given on pages 58–59.

Euston

Silverlink metro trains operate out of Euston serving North-West London stations such as Cricklewood and Hendon on the way to Watford Junction, and with routes through East London to Barking and North Woolwich, and to Richmond in the south.

King's Cross

Trains on the **Thameslink** line to Luton travel through North-West London and a commuter line serving the city's southern suburbs stops at Streatham, Wimbledon and Sutton. **WAGN** trains run to Welwyn Garden City and Stevenage via Finsbury Park. The **South Central** network operates trains to Brighton via East Croydon and to Guildford via Sutton and Wimbledon.

Liverpool Street

Services from Liverpool Street cover London's eastern and north-eastern suburbs, running to Chingford via Walthamstow, Southend via Stratford, and to Stansted via Enfield. Operators include **Anglia Railways**, **c2c** and **WAGN**. The **Stansted Express** runs a fast service to Stansted Airport.

Paddington

Thames Trains run services along the Thames Valley to Oxford, Reading and Slough, stopping at Acton and Ealing in west London. The **Heathrow Express** operates a direct service to Heathrow Airport.

Victoria

Trains on the **South Central** routes serve Croydon and Beckenham via Forest Hill, Crystal Palace and Norbury in south London. The **Gatwick Express** runs a fast service to Gatwick Airport.

Waterloo

South West Trains run services through Richmond, Kingston and Wimbledon in south-west London to Staines and Windsor, Guildford and Woking. From Charing Cross, Waterloo East and London Bridge, **South Eastern** trains go to south-east London and Kent, via East Croydon.

Travelcard Zones

Explanation of Zones

	Station outside the zones
D	Station in Zone D
C	Station in Zone C
B	Station in Zone B
A	Station in Zone A
	Station in Zone 6 and Zone A
6	Station in Zone 6
5	Station in Zone 5
4	Station in Zone 4
3	Station in Zone 3
	Station in both zones
2	Station in Zone 2
	Station in both zones
1	Station in Zone 1

7.04

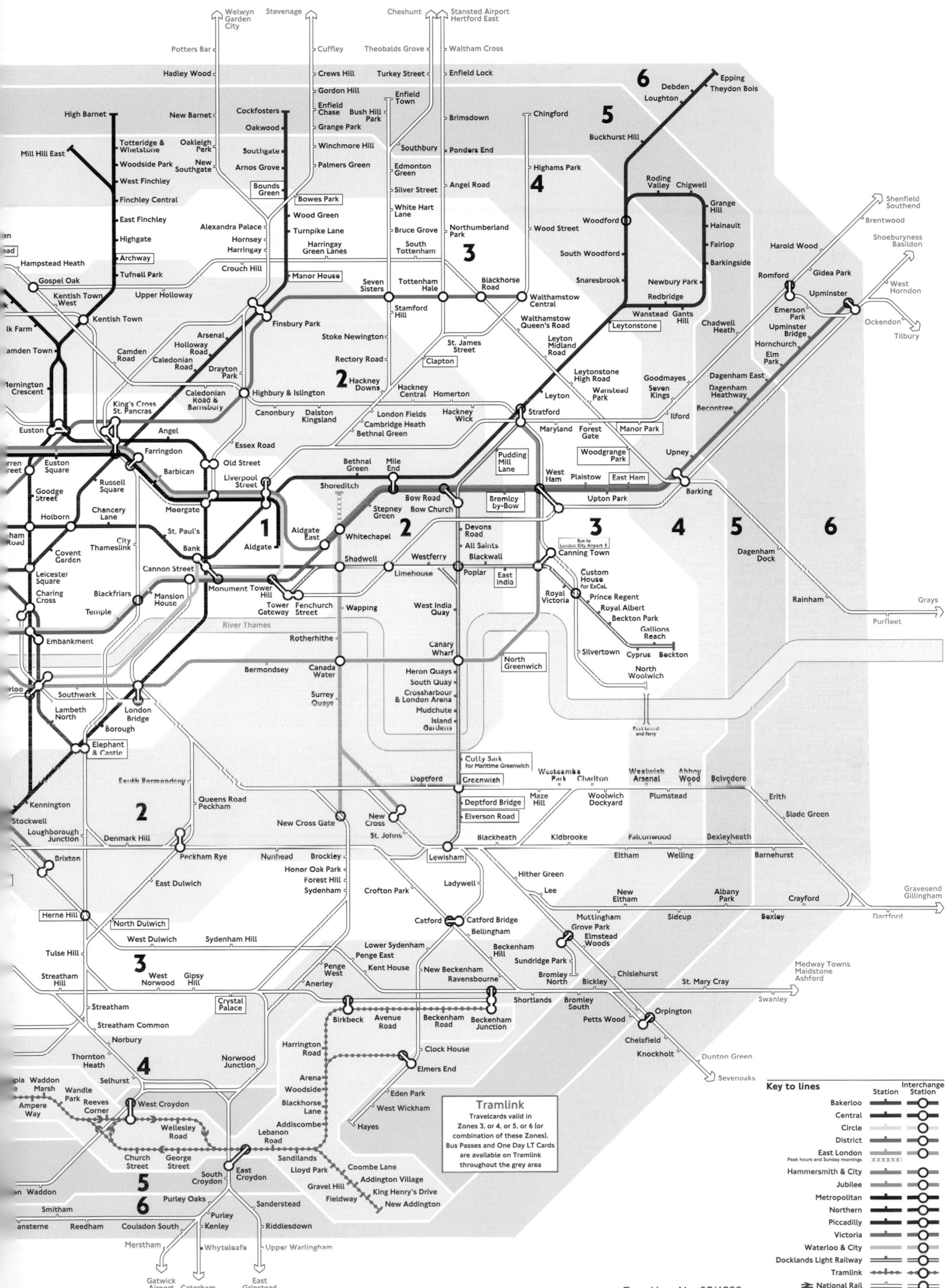

Reg. User No. 05/4233

ABERDEEN

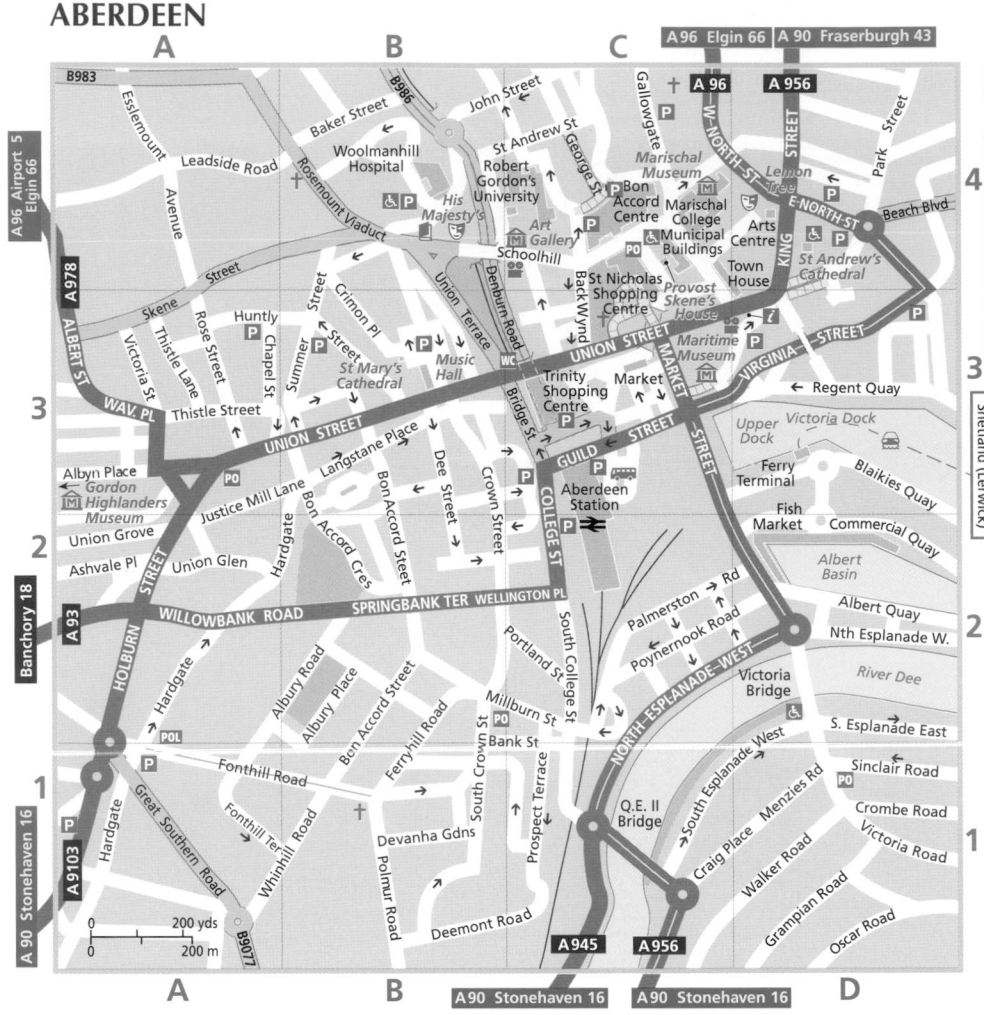

ASHFORD

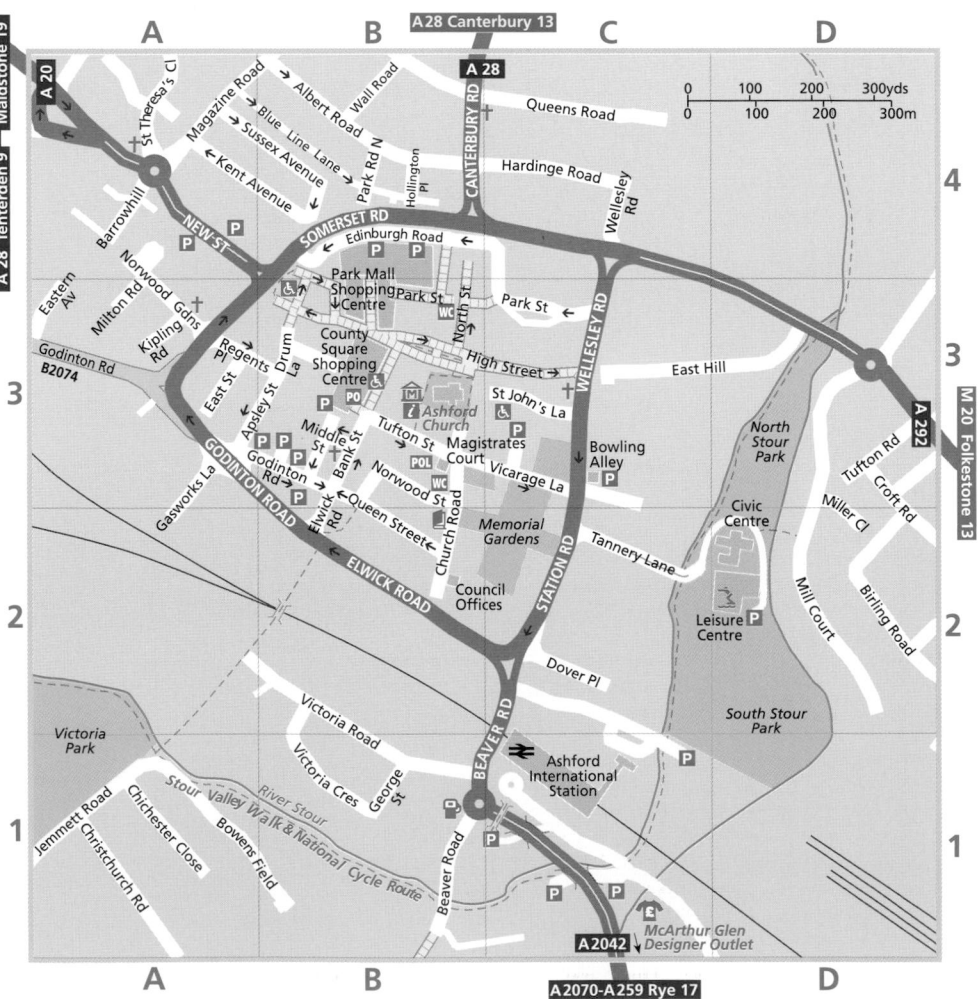

ALNWICK

STREET INDEX

Bailiffgate B3
Bondgate Within C2
Bondgate Without C2
Clayport Square B2
Clayport Street A1
Dispensary Street A2
Dovecote Road C1
Fenkle Street B2
Green Batt B1
Greenwell Road C2
Grey Place C1
Hotspur Place C1
Hotspur Street C1
Howick Street B1
King Street A1
Lagny Street B2
Lisburn Street B1
Lisburn Terrace A1
Market Street B2
Narrowgate B3
New Row A2
Northumberland
   Street A3
Paikes Street B2
Percy Street B1
Percy Terrace B1
Pottergate A3
Prudhoe Street C1
St Michael's Lane B2
The Avenue C1
The Peth B3
Tower Lane B1
Windsor Gardens
   A1–A2

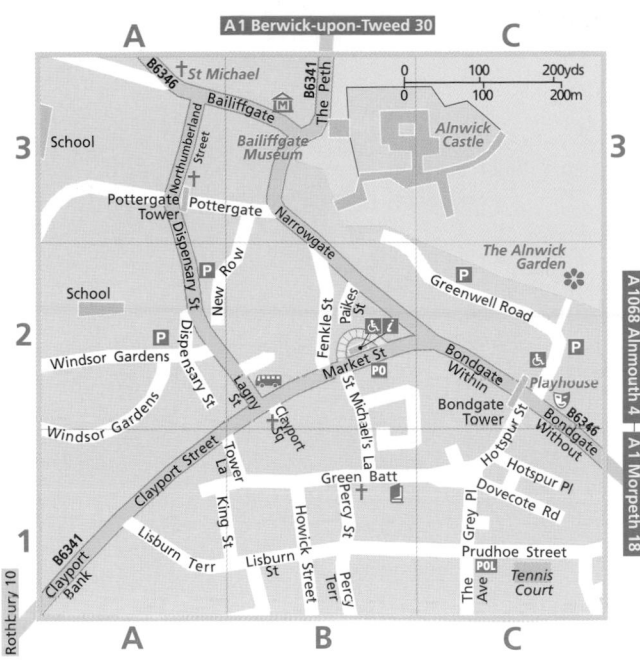

AYLESBURY

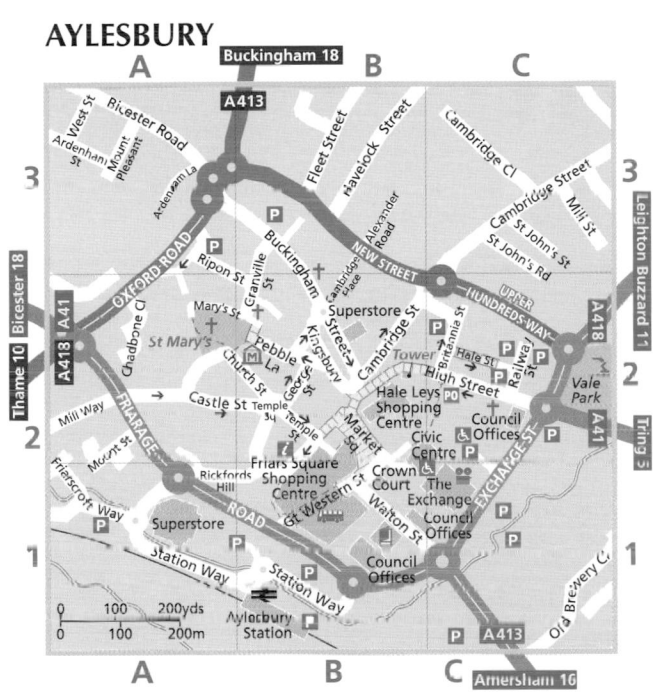

STREET INDEX

Alexander Road B3
Ardenham Street A3
Ardenham Lane A3
Bicester Road A3
Britannia Street C2
Buckingham Street B3
Cambridge Close C3
Cambridge Place B2
Cambridge Street B2–C3
Castle Street A2
Chadbone Close A2
Church Street B2
Exchange Street C1
Fleet Street B3
Friarage Road A2 B1
Friarscroft Way A1
George Street B2
Granville Street B2
Great Western Street B1
Hale Street C2
Havelock Street B3
High Street C2
Kingsbury B2
Market Square B2
Mary's Street A2
Mill Street C3
Mill Way A2
Mount Pleasant A3
Mount Street A2
New Street B3
Old Brewery Close C1
Oxford Road A2
Pebble Lane B2
Railway Street C2
Rickfords Hill A1
Ripon Street A3
St John's Road C3
St John's Street C3
Station Way A1–B1
Temple Square B2
Temple Street B2
Upper Hundreds
   Way C2
Walton Street B1
West Street A3

AYR

STREET INDEX

Alloway Place B1
Alloway Street B1
Arran Terrace A2
Ashgrove Street C1
Barns Street B1
Bath Place A1
Charlotte Street A2
Citadel Place A2
Craigie Avenue C2
Craigie Road C2
Craigie Way C2
Cromwell Road A2
Dalblair Road B1
Eglinton Terrace A2
Elba Street B2
Esplanade A1
Fairfield Road A1
Fort Street B2
George Street B2
High Street B2
Holmston Road C1
John Street B2
King Street B2
Kyle Street B1
Main Street B2
Mill Street B1
Miller Road B1
North Harbour Street B2
Park Circus B1
Park Terrace A1
Pavilion Road A1
Sandgate B2
Seabank Road A2
Smith Street B1
South Harbour Street A2
Station Road C1
Whitletts Road C2

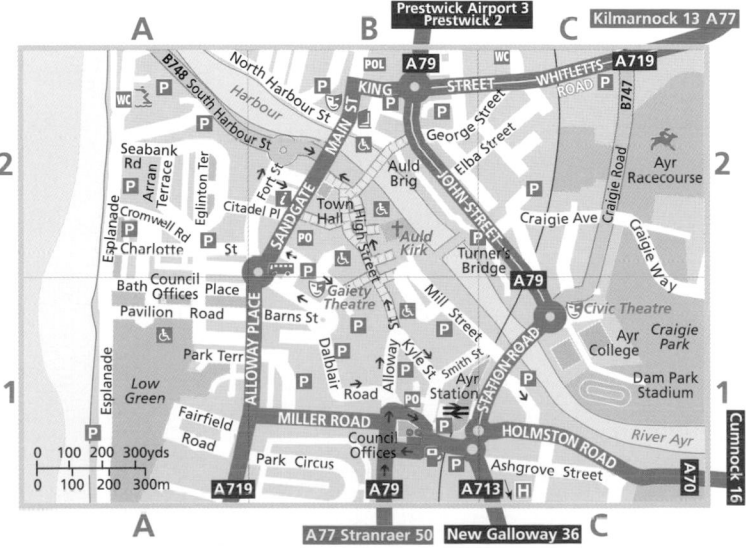

BARNSLEY

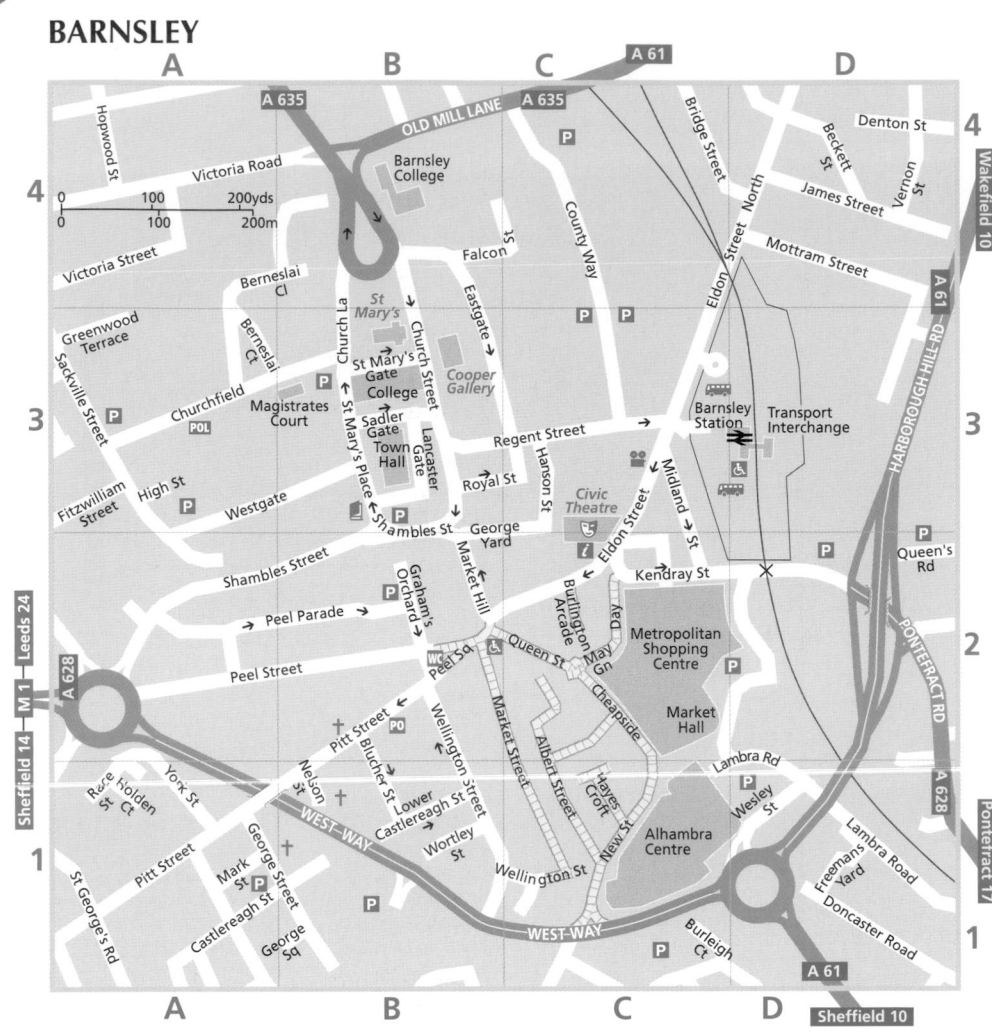

BASINGSTOKE

Park & Ride

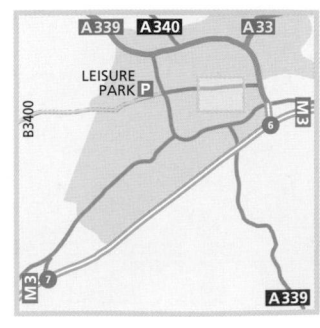

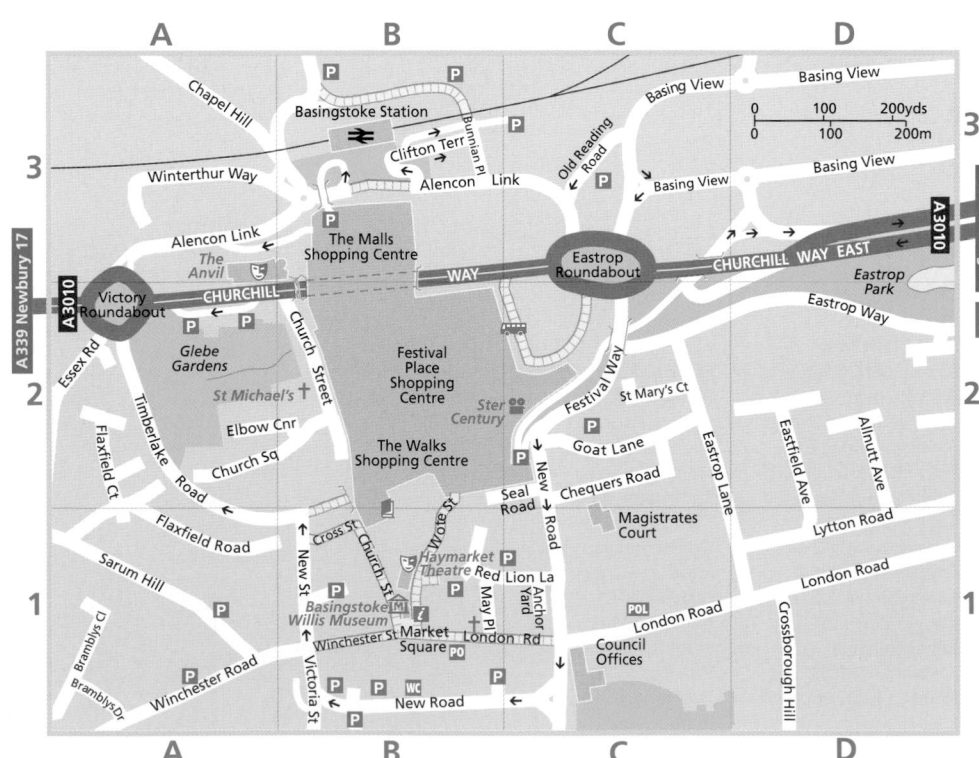

BATH

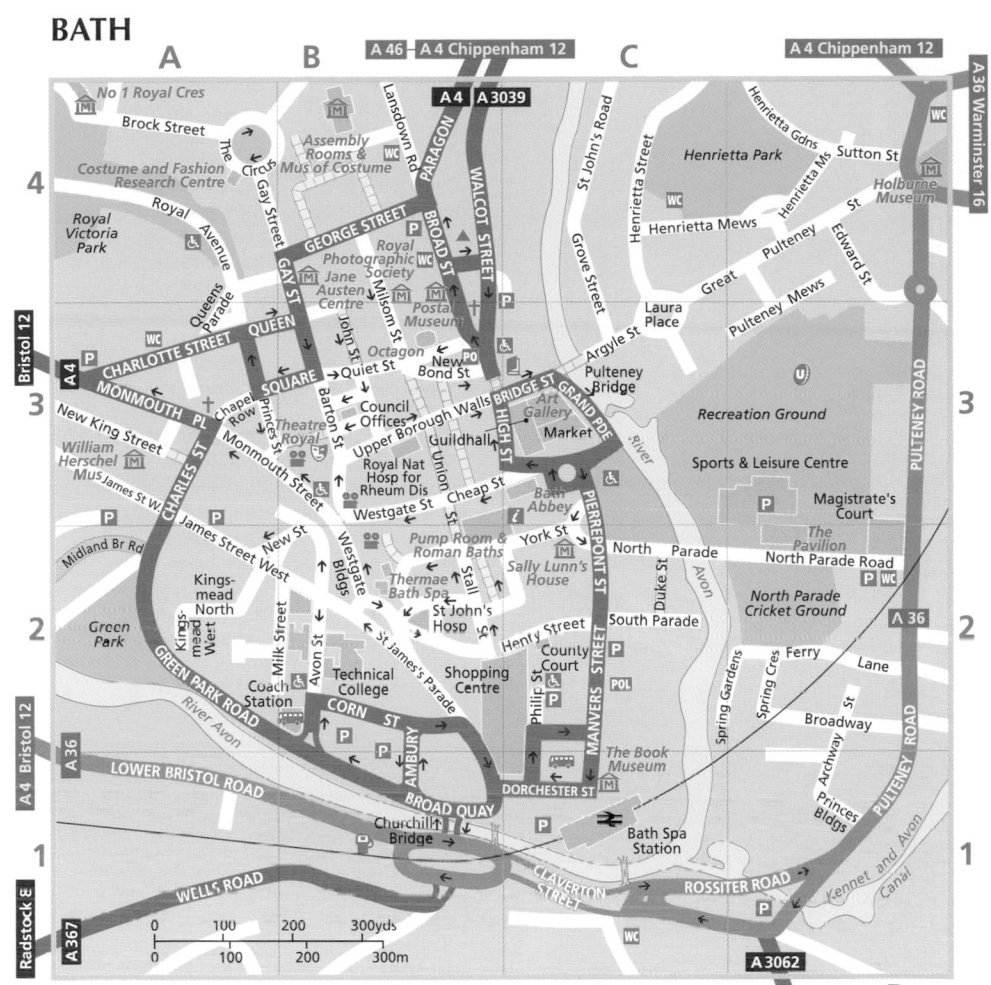

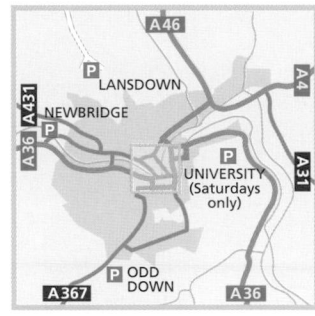

Park & Ride

STREET INDEX

Ambury B1–B2	Lower Bristol Road A1
Argyle Street C3	Manvers Street C2
Bridge Street C3	Milsom Street B4–B3
Broad Quay B1	Monmouth Place A3
Broad Street B4	Monmouth Street A3
Chapel Row A3	North Parade C2
Charles Street A3	Paragon B4
Charlotte Street A3	Philip Street C2
Cheap Street B3	Pierrepont Street C2
Claverton Street C1	Princes Street A3
Corn Street B2	Pulteney Road D1–D4
Dorchester Street C1	Queen Square A3–B3
Gay Street A4–B3	Rossiter Road C1–D2
George Street B4	St James's Parade B2
Grand Parade C3	St John's Road C4
Great Pulteney St D4	Sutton Street D4
Green Park Road A2	The Circus A4
High Street B3–C3	Upper Borough
James Street West A2	Walls B3
Lansdown Road B4	Walcot Street B4
Laura Place C3	Wells Road A1
	Westgate Street B3

BEDFORD

STREET INDEX

Adelaide Square B4	Lansdowne Road A4
Alexandra Road A3	Lurke Street C3
Allhallows B3	Maitland Street B2
Ampthill Road C1	Melbourne Street C1
Ashburnham Road A3	Midland Road B2
Battison Street B2	Mill Street C3
Brace Street B3	Newnham Street D3
Brereton Road B3	Prebend Street B2
Bromham Road B3	Priory Street B3
Burnaby Road C4	Queen Street B4
Cardington Road D1	River Street B2
Castle Lane C2	Roff Avenue B4
Castle Road D3	Roise Street B3
Cauldwell Street B1	Rope Walk D1
Chethams D2	Rothsay Road D3
Commercial Road B2	Rutland Road A3
Conduit Road A3	Silver Street C3
Costin Street B2	St Cuthbert's Street C3
Dame Alice Street B3	St John's Street C1
De Parys Avenue C4	St Loyes Street B3
Duck Mill Lane C2	St Mary's Street C2
Ford End Road A2	St Paul's Square C2
Foster Hill Road C4	St Peter's Street C3
Glebe Road D4	Tavistock Street B4
Grafton Road A3	The Broadway C4
Greyfriars A3	The Crescent B4
Grove Place D3	The Embankment D2
Harpur Street C3	The Grove D3
Hassett Street B3	Union Street A4
High Street C3	Warwick Avenue A4
Horne Lane B2	Waterloo Road D2
Kimbolton Road D4	Wellington Street C4
Kingsway C1	Western Street B2
	Woburn Road A3

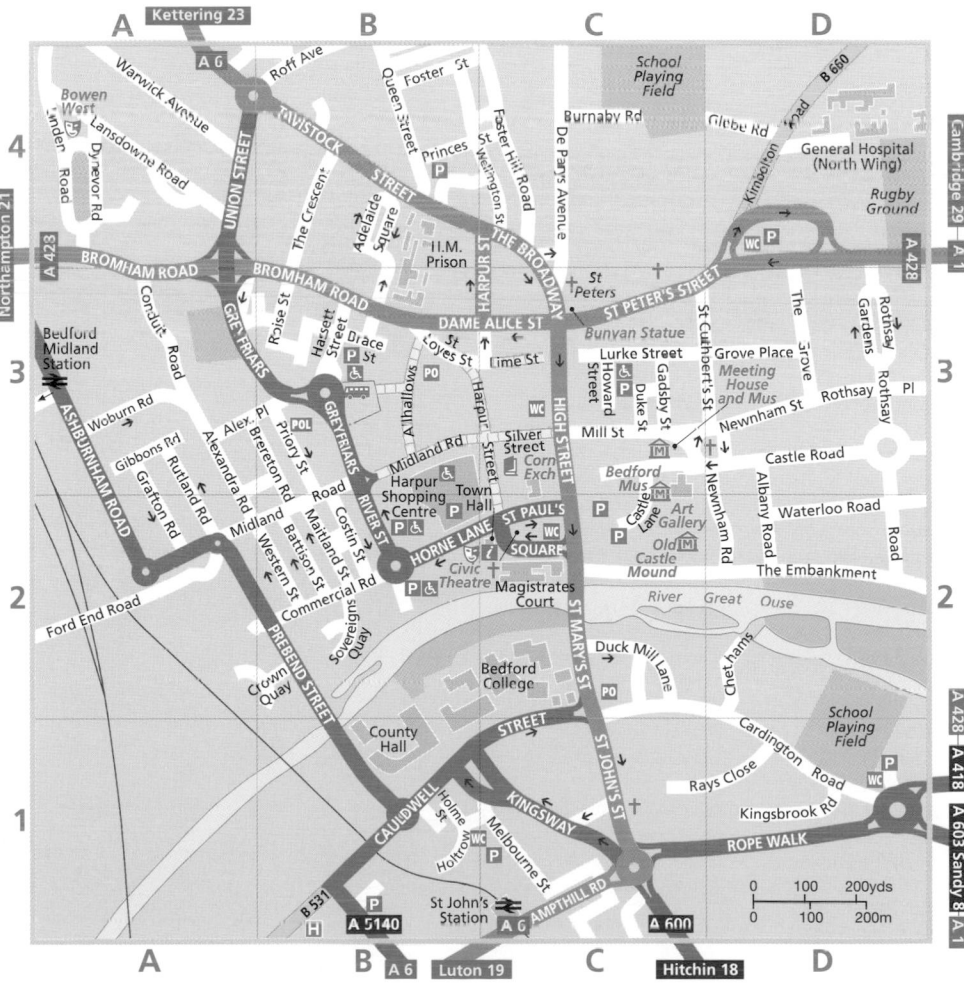

BELFAST

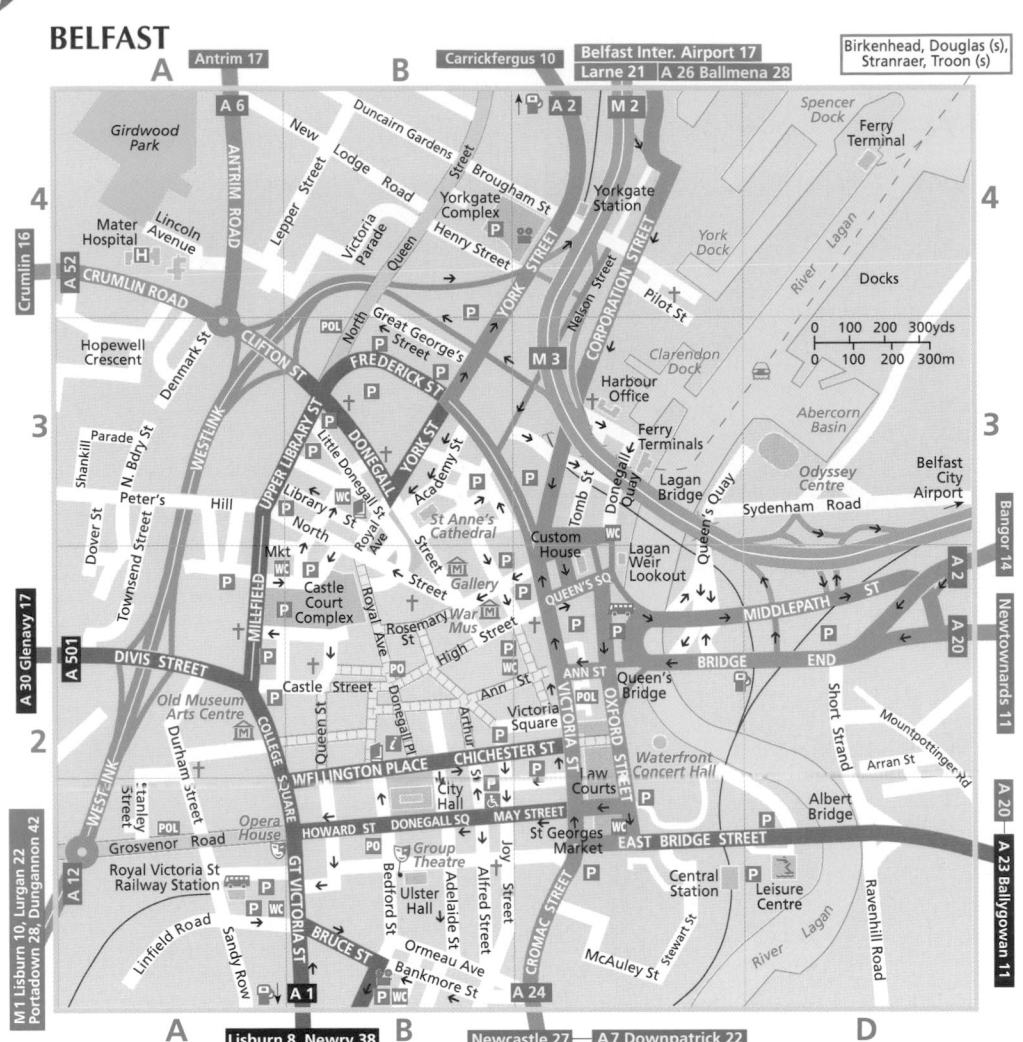

BLACKBURN

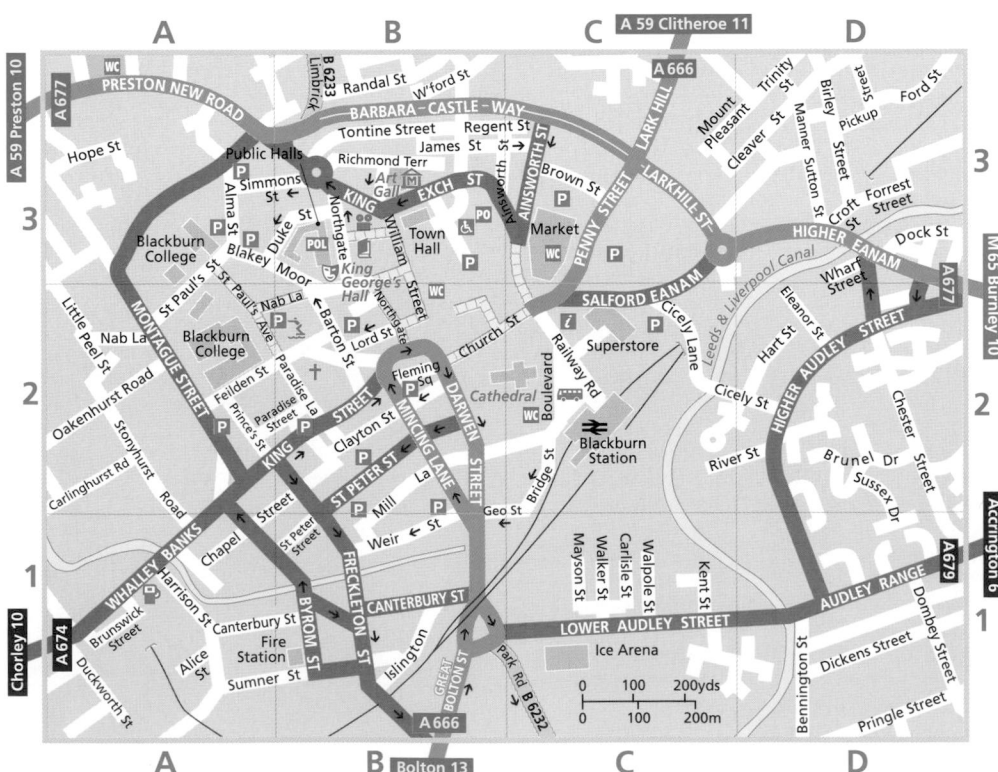

BIRMINGHAM

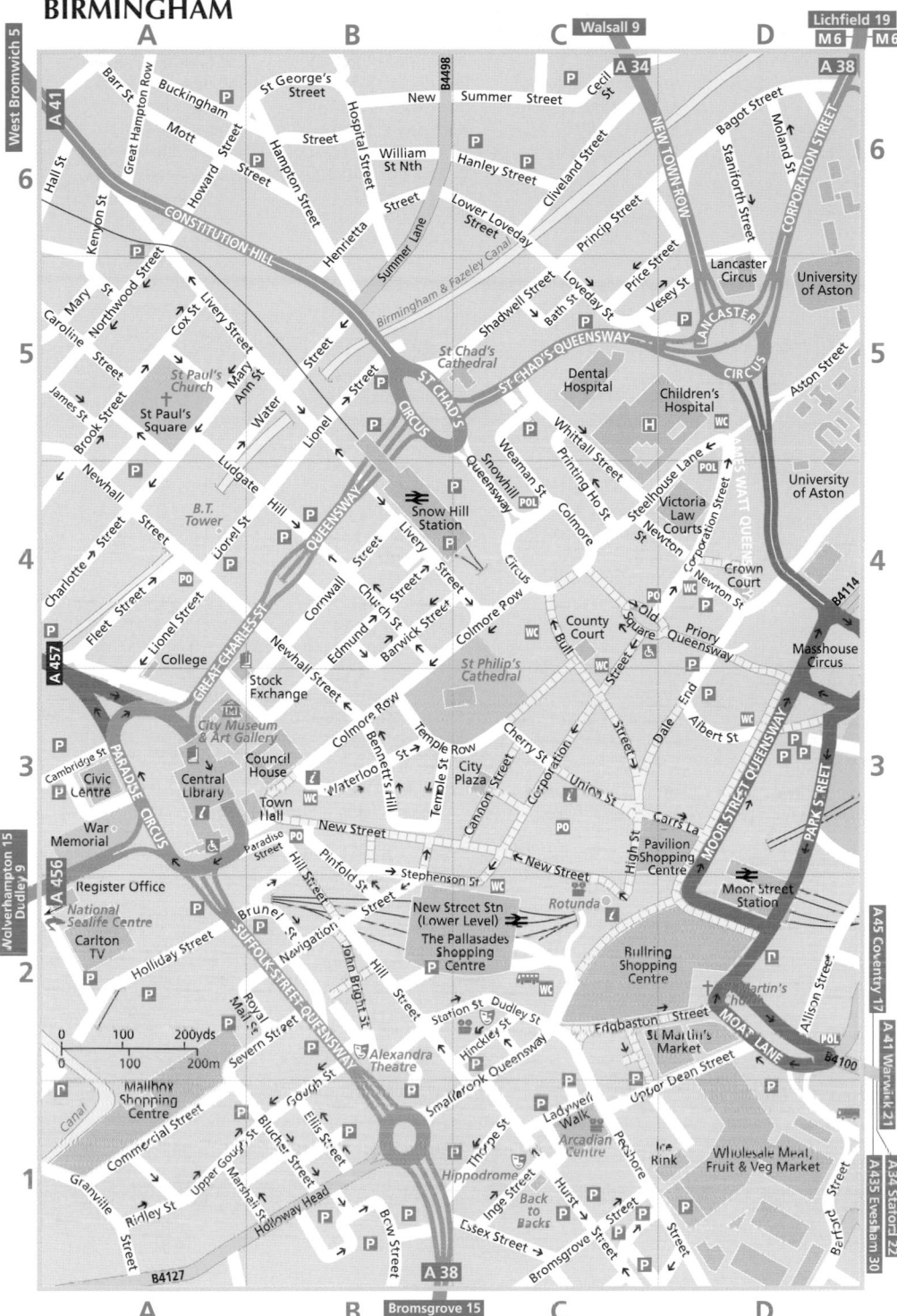

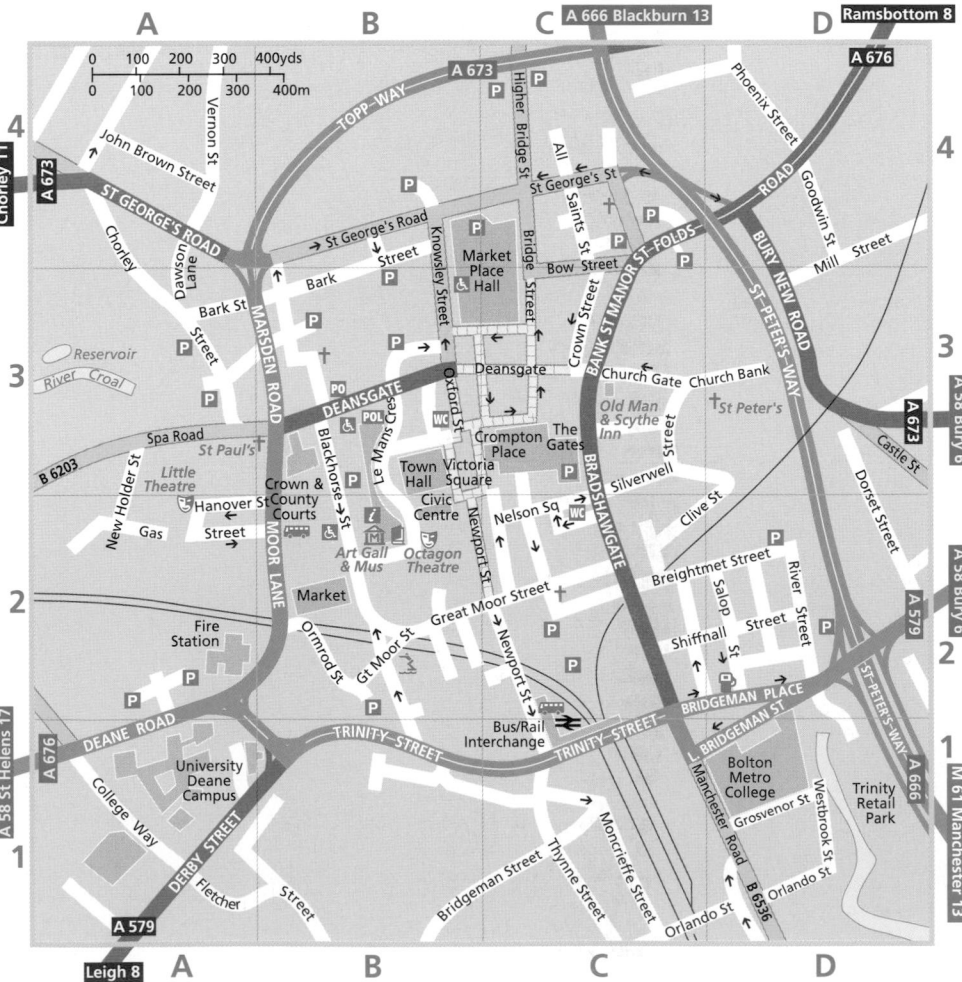

BLACKPOOL

Fleetwood 9   A   B   Lancaster 26   C

A 584   A 586

Lytham 8   A   B   A5073   C

A 584

STREET INDEX

BOLTON

STREET INDEX

A 666 Blackburn 13   Ramsbottom 8

Chorley 11   A 58 St Helens 17   Leigh 8   A 579

A 58 Bury 6   A 579   M 61 Manchester 13

BOURNEMOUTH

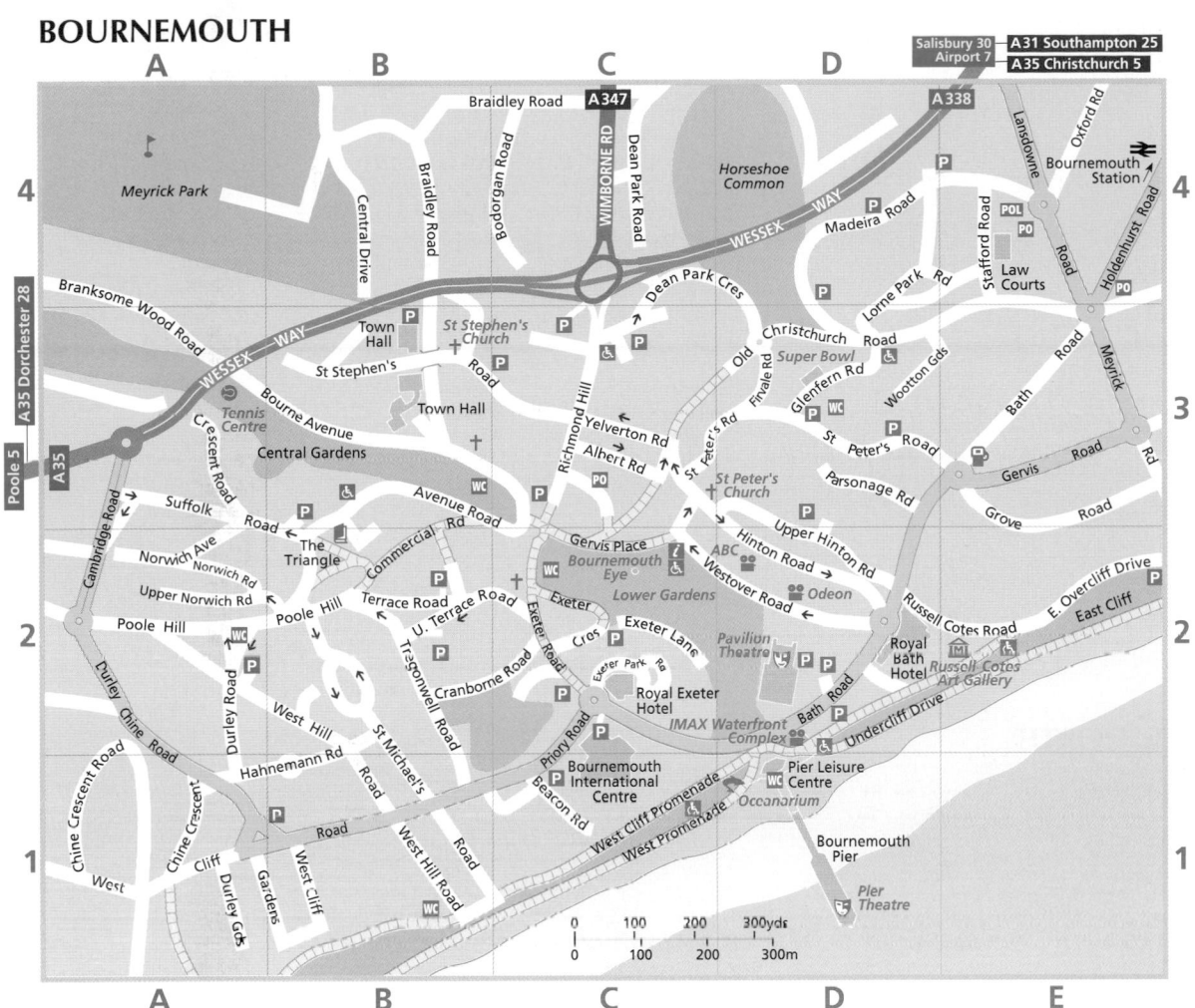

BRADFORD

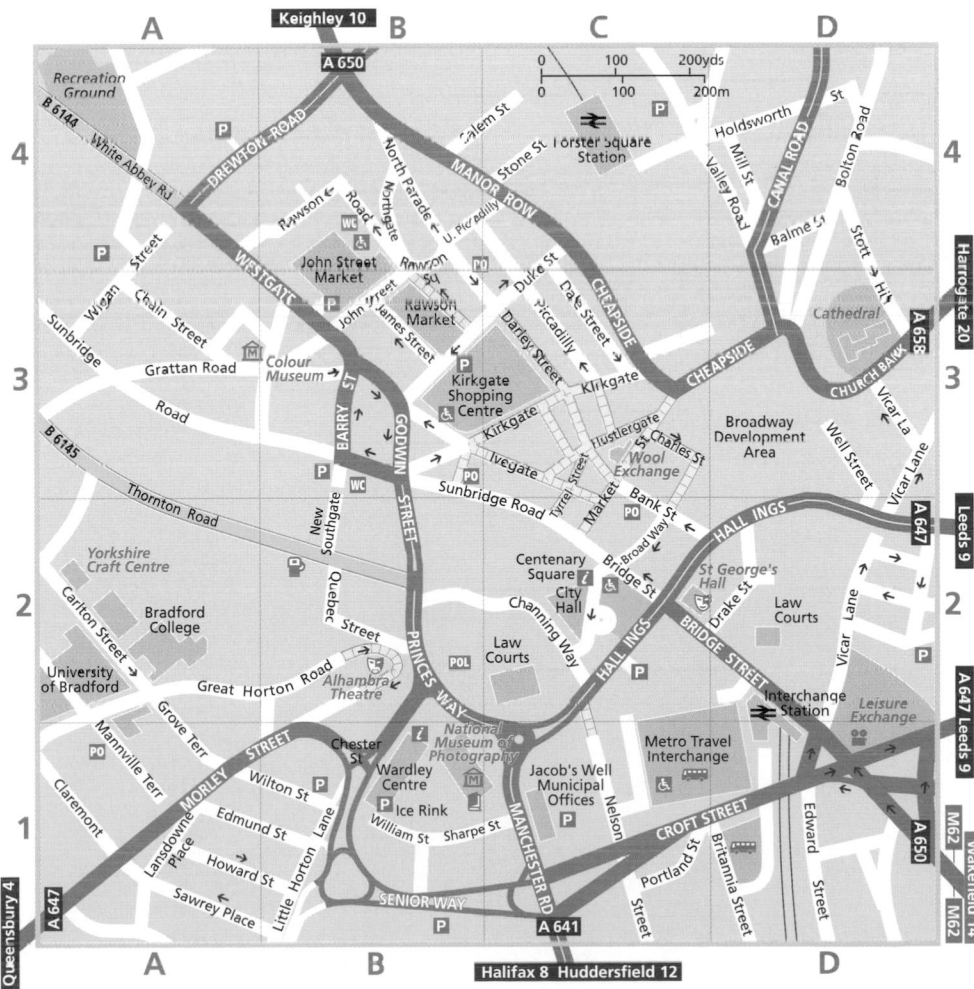

BRECON

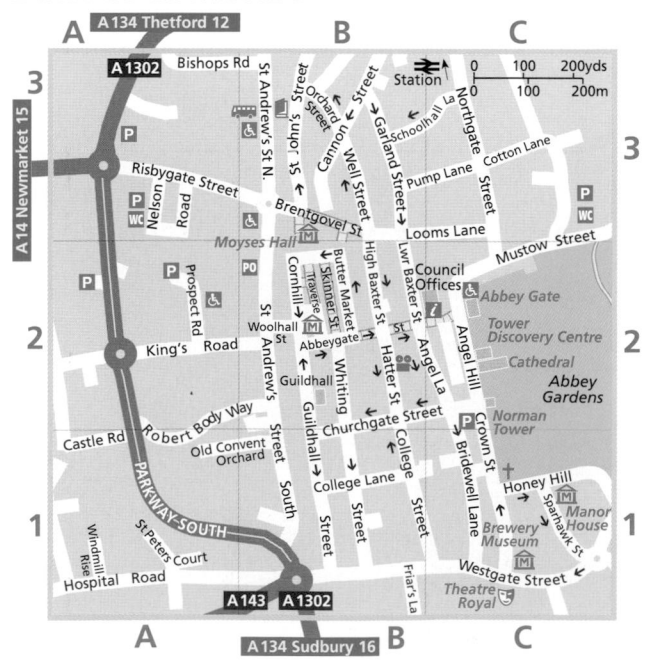

BRIDGNORTH

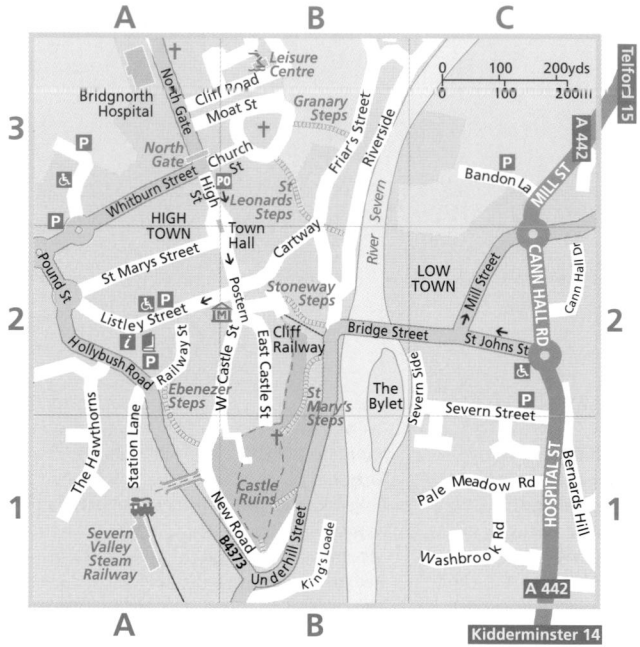

BURY ST EDMUNDS

BRISTOL

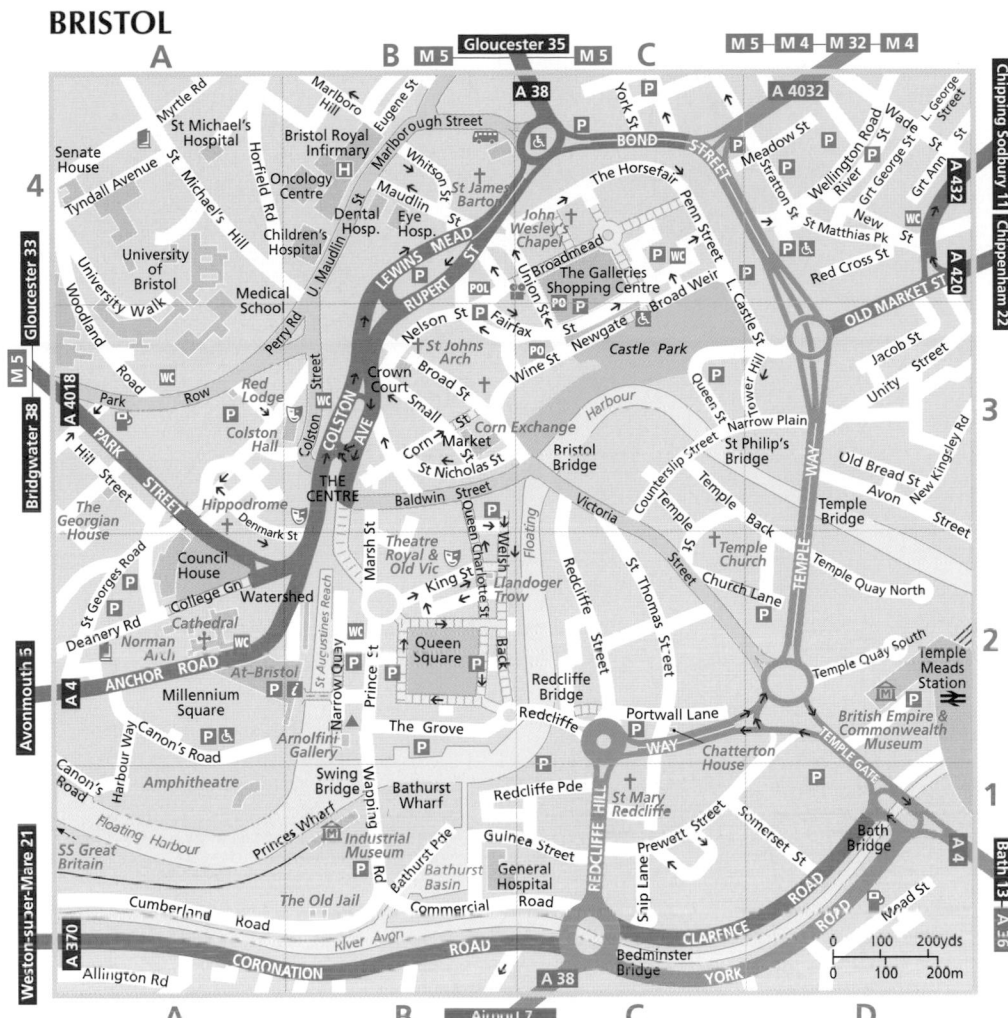

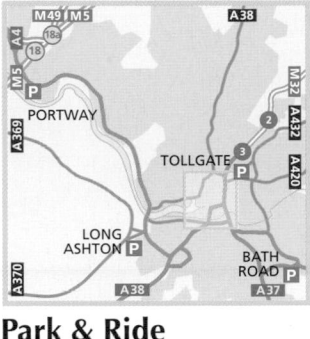

Park & Ride

Little Castle Street D3
Little George Street D4
Marlborough Hill B4
Marlborough Street B4
Marsh Street B2
Maudlin Street B4
Mead Street D1
Meadow Street D4
Myrtle Road A4
Narrow Plain D3
Narrow Quay B2
Nelson Street B3
New Kingley Road D3
New Street D4
Newgate C3
Old Bread Street D3
Old Market Street
   D3–D4
Park Row A3
Park Street A3
Penn Street C4
Perry Road A3
Portwall Lane C2
Prewett Street C1
Prince Street B2
Queen Charlotte
   Street B2
Queen Street C3
Red Cross Street D4
Redcliffe Hill C1
Redcliffe Parade C1
Redcliffe Street C2
Redcliffe Way C2

River Street D4
Rupert Street B4
Ship Lane C1
Small Street B3
Somerset Street D1
St Georges Road A2
St Matthias Park D4
St Michael's Hill A4
St Nicholas Street B3
St Thomas Street C2
Stratton Street D4
Temple Back C3–D2
Temple Gate D2
Temple Quay North D2
Temple Quay South D2
Temple Street C3–C2
Temple Way D2–D3
The Grove B2
The Horsefair C4
Tyndall Avenue A4
Union Street C4
Unity Street D3
University Walk A4
Victoria Street C3–C2
Wade Street D4
Wapping Road B1
Wellington Road D4
Welsh Back B2
Whitson Street B4
Wine Street C3
Woodland Road A3
York Road C1 D1
York Street C4

STREET INDEX

Allington Road A1
Anchor Road A2
Avon Street D3
Baldwin Street B3
Bathurst Parade B1
Bond Street C4
Broad Street B3
Broad Weir C3–C4

Broadmead C4
Canon's Road A2
Church Lane C2–D2
Clarence Road C1–D1
College Green A2
Colston Avenue B3
Colston Street B3
Commercial Road
   B1–C1

Corn Street B3
Coronation Road
   A1–B1
Countership Street C3
Cumberland Road
   A1–B1
Deanery Road A2
Eugene Street B4
Fairfax Street B3–C3

Great Ann Street D4
Great George Street D4
Guinea Street B1
Harbour Way A2
Hill Street A3
Horfield Road A4
Jacob Street D3
King Street B2
Lewins Mead B4

BUXTON

STREET INDEX

Ash Street B1
Bath Road A1
Bennett Street C1
Broad Walk A1
Burlington Road A1
Cliff Mill C2
Clifton Road C2
Clough Street B1
Crowestones C1
Curzon Road C2
Dale Road B1–C1
Darwin Avenue C2
Devonshire Road A3
Eagle Parade B2
Fountain Street A1
George Street B2
Grange Road C1
Hall Bank B2
Hardwick Square B2

Hardwick Square
   South B2–C2
Hardwick Street B2
Hartington Road A1
Heath Park Road C1
High Street B1
Holker Road C2
Hollins Street B1
Manchester Road A3
Market Street B1
New Market Street B1
New Wye Street C3
Palace Road B3
Park Road A2–A3
Peveril Road C1
Silverlands C2
South Avenue B1
South Street B1
Spring Gardens B3–C3
St James' Terrace A1

St John's Road A2
Station Road B3
Sylvan Cliff C2
Sylvan Park C3
Terrace Road B2
The Crescent B2
The Square B2

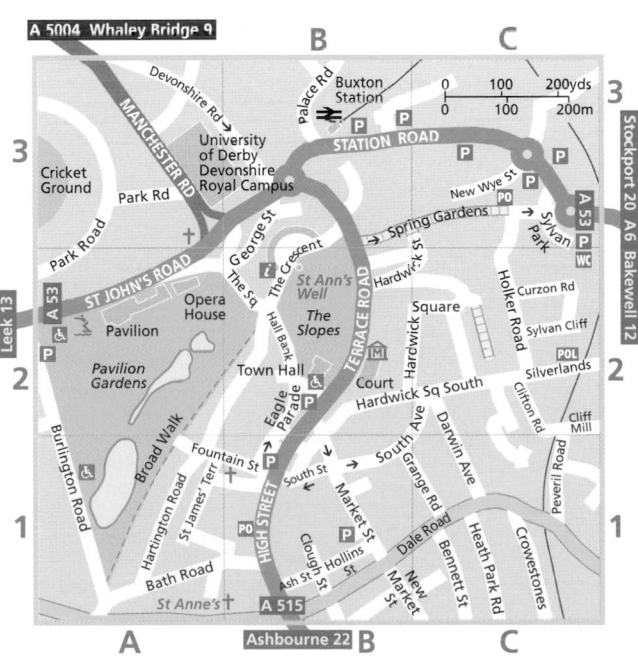

CAMBRIDGE

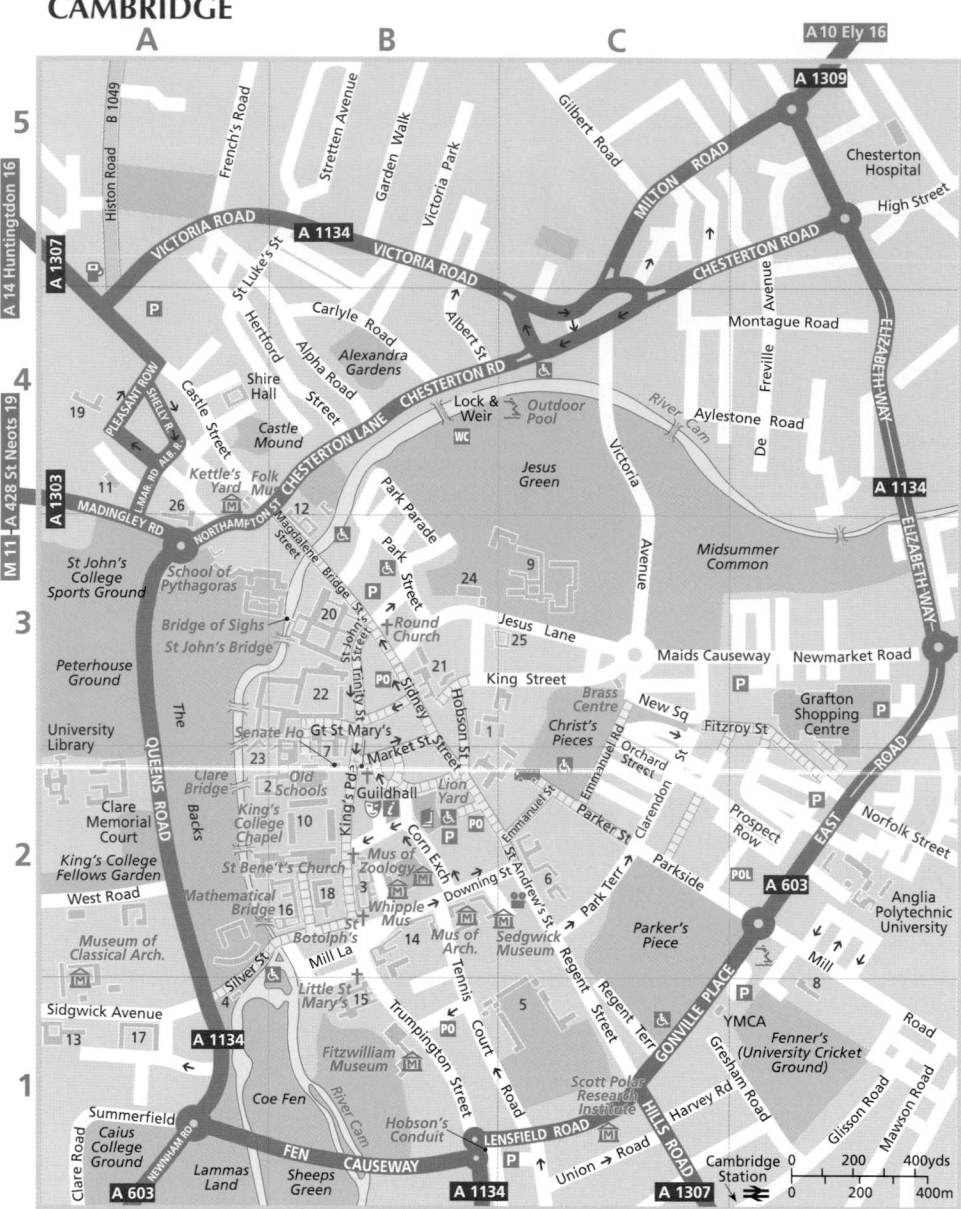

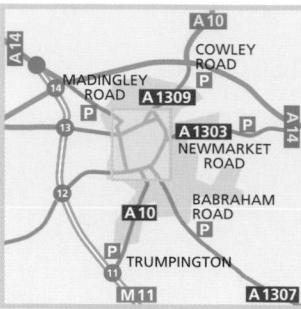

Park & Ride

CANTERBURY

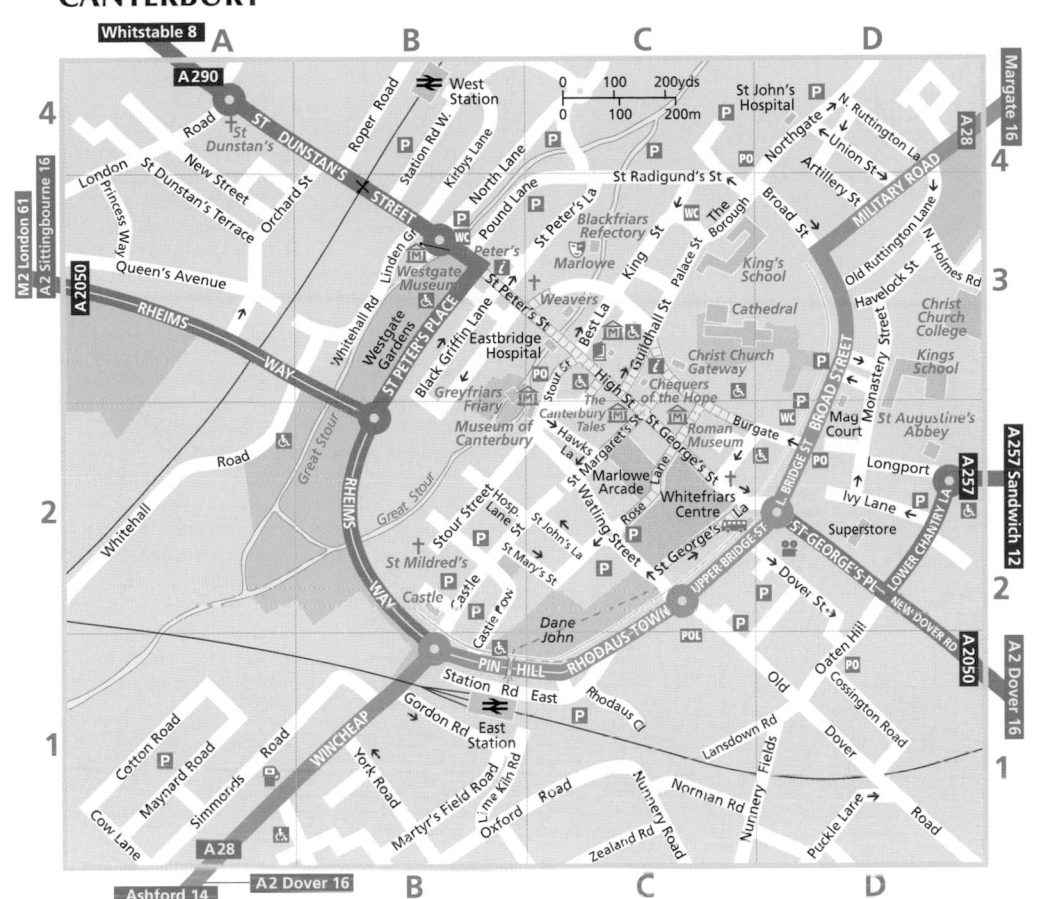

Whitstable 8

A 290

M2 London 61 / A2 Sittingbourne 16

A2050

Whitehall

Margate 16 / A28

A257 Sandwich 12

A2 Dover 16

A2050

Ashford 14 / A2 Dover 16

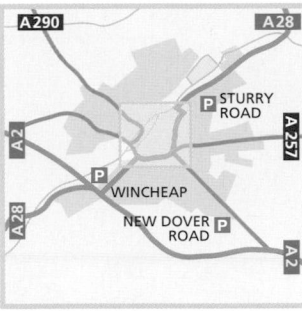

Park & Ride

STREET INDEX

Black Griffin Lane B3
Broad Street D2–D3
Castle Street B2
London Road A4
Longport D2
Lower Bridge
 Street D2
Lower Chantry
 Lane D2
Military Road D3
New Dover Road
 D2–D1
Northgate D4
North Lane B3–C4
Nunnery Fields D1
Old Dover Road D1
Pinhill B1
Pound Lane B3
Queen's Avenue A3
Rheims Way A3–B2
Rhodaus Town C1–C2

Roper Road B4
Rose Lane C2
St Dunstan's Street
 A4–B3
St George's Lane C2
St George's Place D2
St John's Lane C2
St Margaret's
 Street C2
St Mary's Street
 B2–C2
St Peter's Place B3
St Radigund's
 Street C3
Simmonds Road A1
Stour Street B2–C3
Union Street D4
Upper Bridge
 Street C2
Watling Street C2
Wincheap B1

CARDIFF

STREET INDEX

Boulevard de Nantes C3
Bridge Street D2
Brook Street A2
Bute Street D1
Bute Terrace D1
Callaghan Square
 C1–D1
Caroline Street C1
Castle Street B2
Charles Street D2
Churchill Way D2
City Hall Road B3
Clare Street A1
Coldstream Terrace A2
College Road B4
Cowbridge Road East A2
Custom House Street C1
Despenser Place A1
Despenser Street A1
Duke Street C2
Dumfries Place D3
Fitzhamon
 Embankment B1
Gloucester Street A1
Green Street A2
Greyfriars Road C3
Herbert Street D1
King Edward VII
 Avenue B4
Lower Cathedral
 Road A2
Mill Lane C1
Museum Avenue C4

Museum Place C4
Neville Street A2
Ninian Park Road A1
North Road B4–B3
Park Green D4
Park Lane D3
Park Place C4
Park Street B1
Plantagenet Street B1
Queen Street C2
Salisbury Road D4
Senghennyd Road D4
St Andrew's Place D3
St John Street C2
St Mary Street C1
Station Terrace D2
Stuttgarter Strasse D3
The Friary C3
The Hayes C2
Tudor Street B1
Westgate Street B2
Wharton Street C2
Windsor Place D3
Wood Street B1–C1
Working Street C2

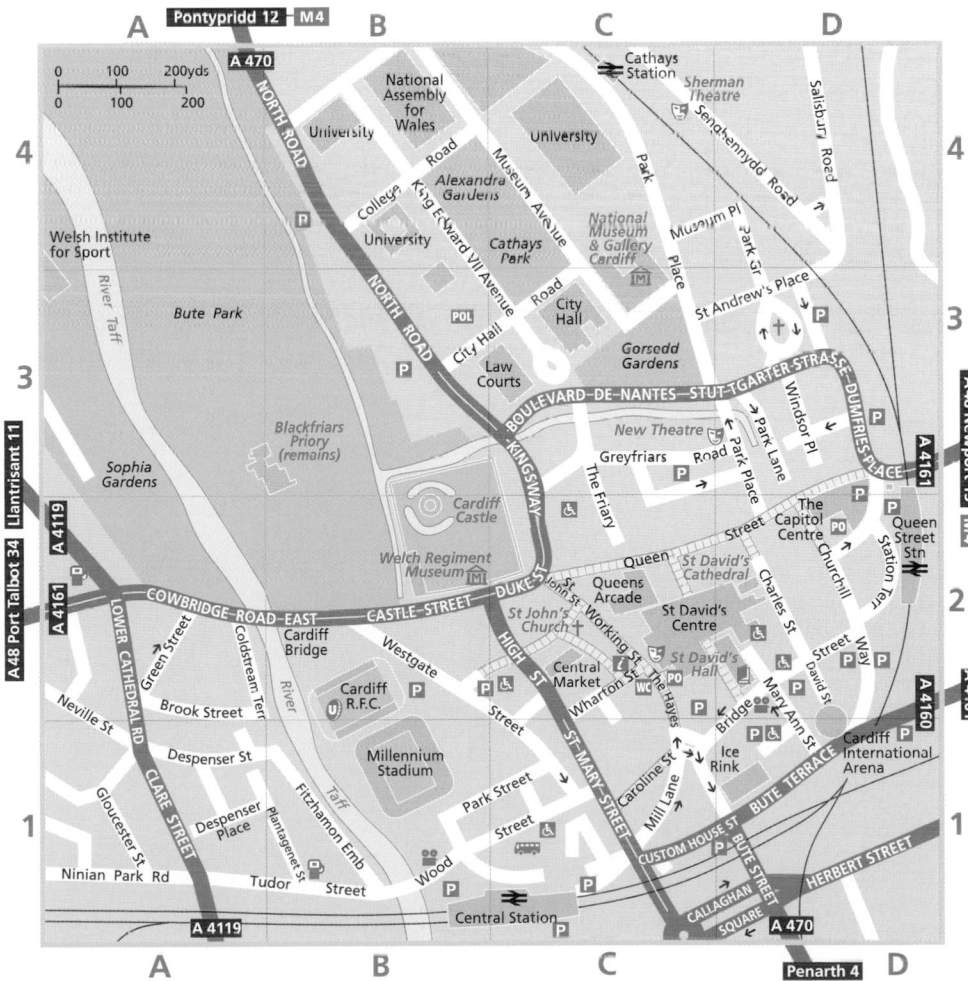

Pontypridd 12 — M4

A 470

Llantrisant 11

A 4119

A48 Port Talbot 34

A4161

A48 Newport 13 — M4

A 4161

A 4160

A 4161

A 4119

Penarth 4

A 470

CARLISLE

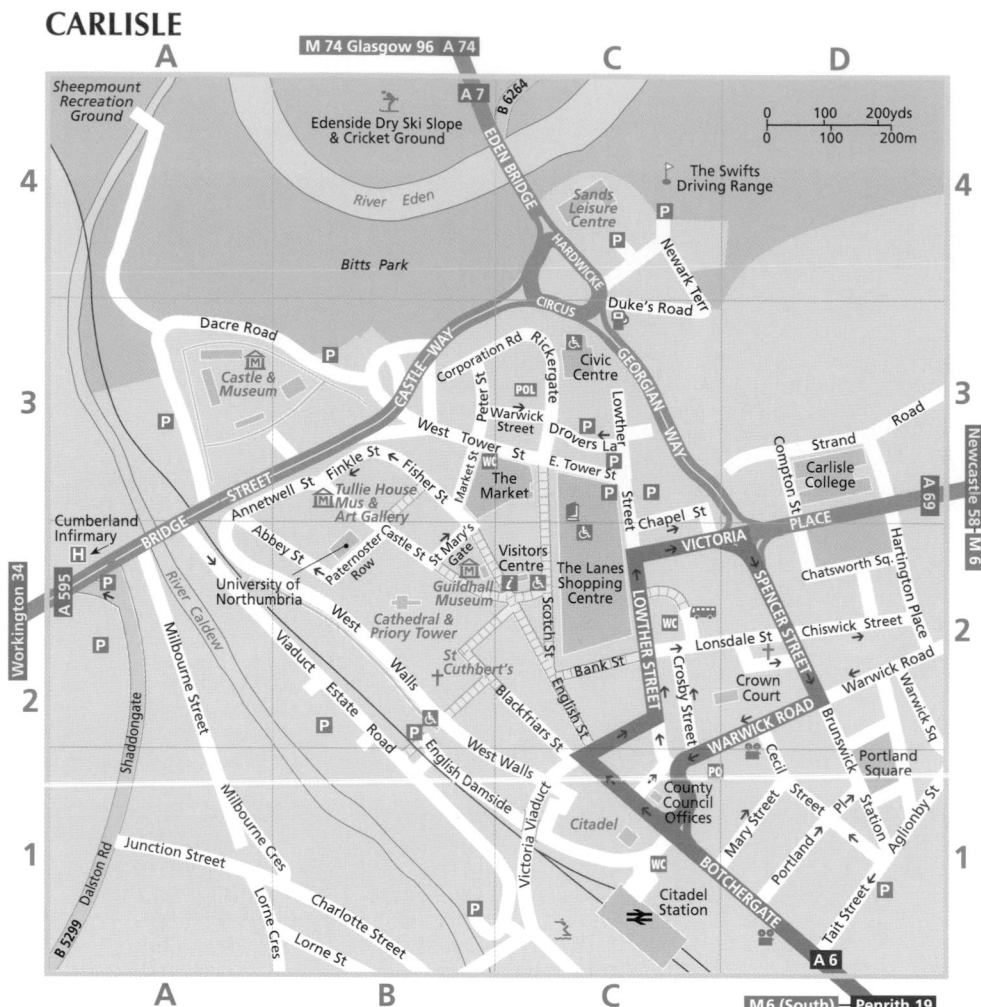

CARMARTHEN

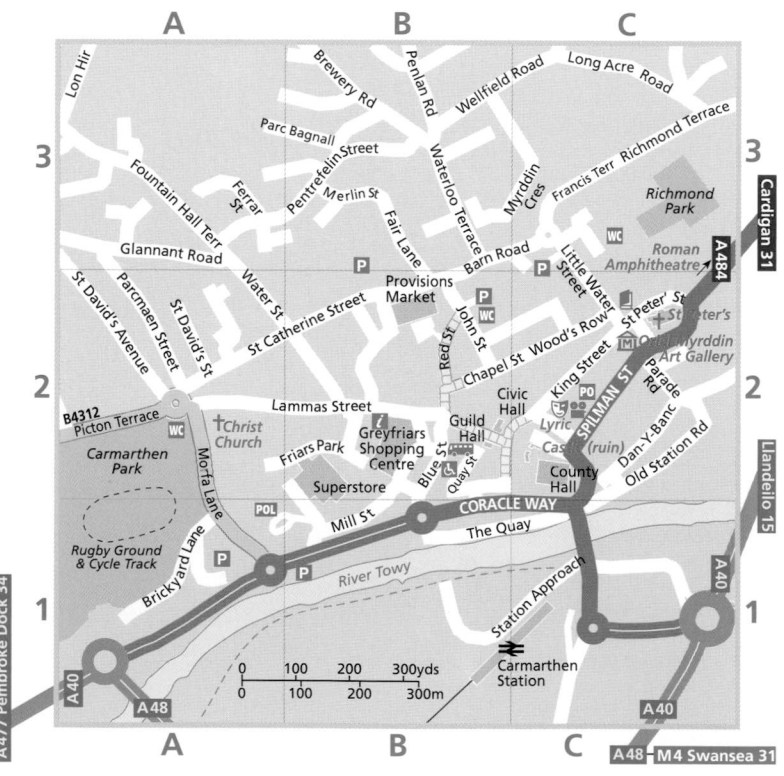

CHELMSFORD

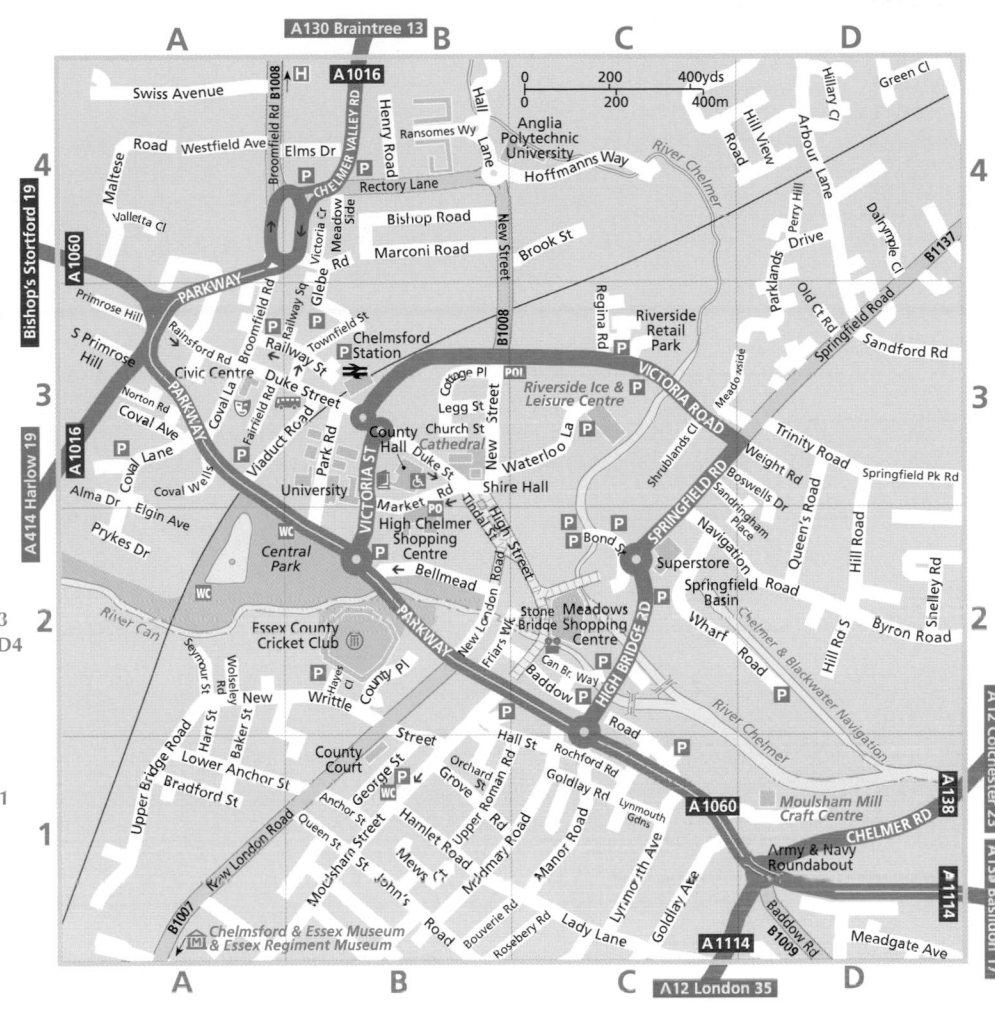

STREET INDEX

Anchor Street B1
Arbour Lane D4
Baddow Road C2–D1
Baker Street A1
Bellmead B2
Bishop Road B4
Bond Street C2
Broomfield Road A3–A4
Byron Road D2
Canal Bridge Way C2
Chelmer Road D1
Chelmer Valley Road B4
Cottage Place B3
County Place B2
Coval Avenue A3
Coval Lane A3
Dalrymple Close D4
Duke Street A3
Fairfield Road A3
Friars Walk B2
George Street B1
Glebe Road B3
Grove Road B1
Hall Lane B4
Hamlet Road B1
Henry Road B4
High Bridge Road C2
High Street B2
Hill Road D2
Hill View Road D4
Hoffmanns Way C4
Legg Street B3
Lower Anchor Street A1
Lynmouth Avenue C1

Maltese Road A4
Manor Road C1
Marconi Road B4
Market Road B3
Mildmay Road B1
Moulsham Street B1
Navigation Road C2
New London Road A1–B2
New Street B3–B4
New Writtle Street A2
Park Road B3
Parklands Drive D3
Parkway A4–B2
Queen Street B1
Queen's Road D2
Railway Street A3
Rainsford Road A3
Rectory Lane B4
Regina Road C3
Rochford Road C1
Sandford Road D3
Springfield Park Rd D3
Springfield Road C2–D4
St John's Road B1
Swiss Avenue A4
Tindal Street B3
Townfield Street B3
Trinity Road D3
Upper Bridge Road A1
Viaduct Road A3
Victoria Road C3
Victoria Street B2
Waterloo Lane C3
Wharf Road C2

CHELTENHAM

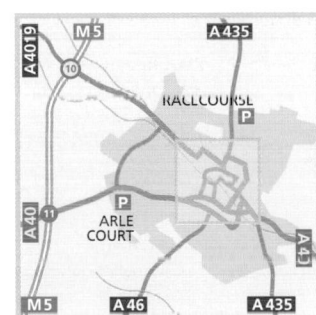

Park & Ride

STREET INDEX

Albion Street C3
All Saints Road D3
Andover Road A1
Bath Road C2
Berkeley Street D2
Clarence Square C4
College Road C2
Evesham Road C4
Gloucester Road A4
Hewlett Road D2
High Street C3
Lansdown Road A2
London Road D2
Montpellier Terrace B2
Montpellier Walk B2
North Place C4
North Street C3
Old Bath Road D1
Oriel Road C2
Park Place A1

Pittville Circus D4
Poole Way B4
Prestbury Road D4
Regent Street C3
Rodney Road C2
Royal Well Road B3
St George's Road A3
St John's Avenue D3
St Margaret's Road C4
St Paul's Road B4
Sandford Mill Road D1
Sandford Road C1
Suffolk Road B1
Swindon Road B4
Tewkesbury Road A4
Thirlestaine Road C1
Wellington Road C4
Winchcombe Street C3

CHEPSTOW

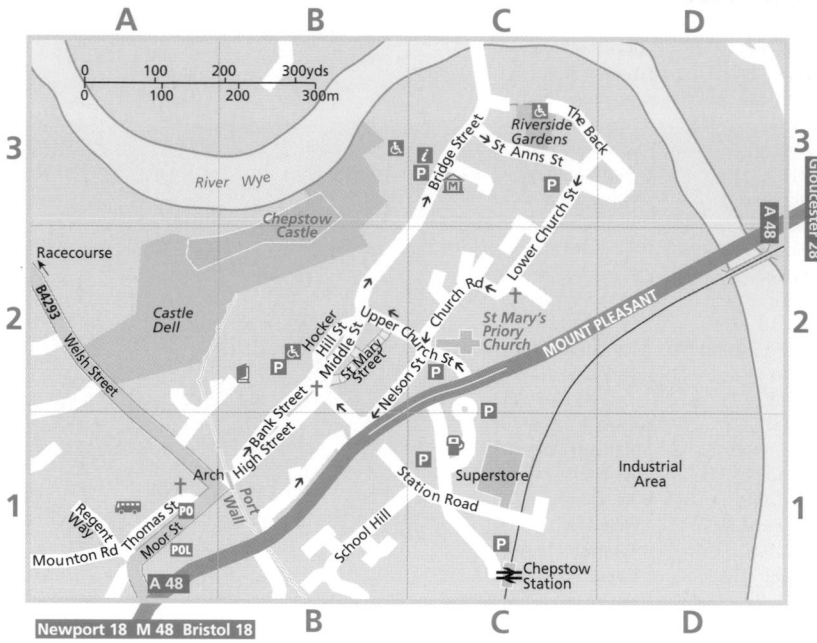

CHESTER

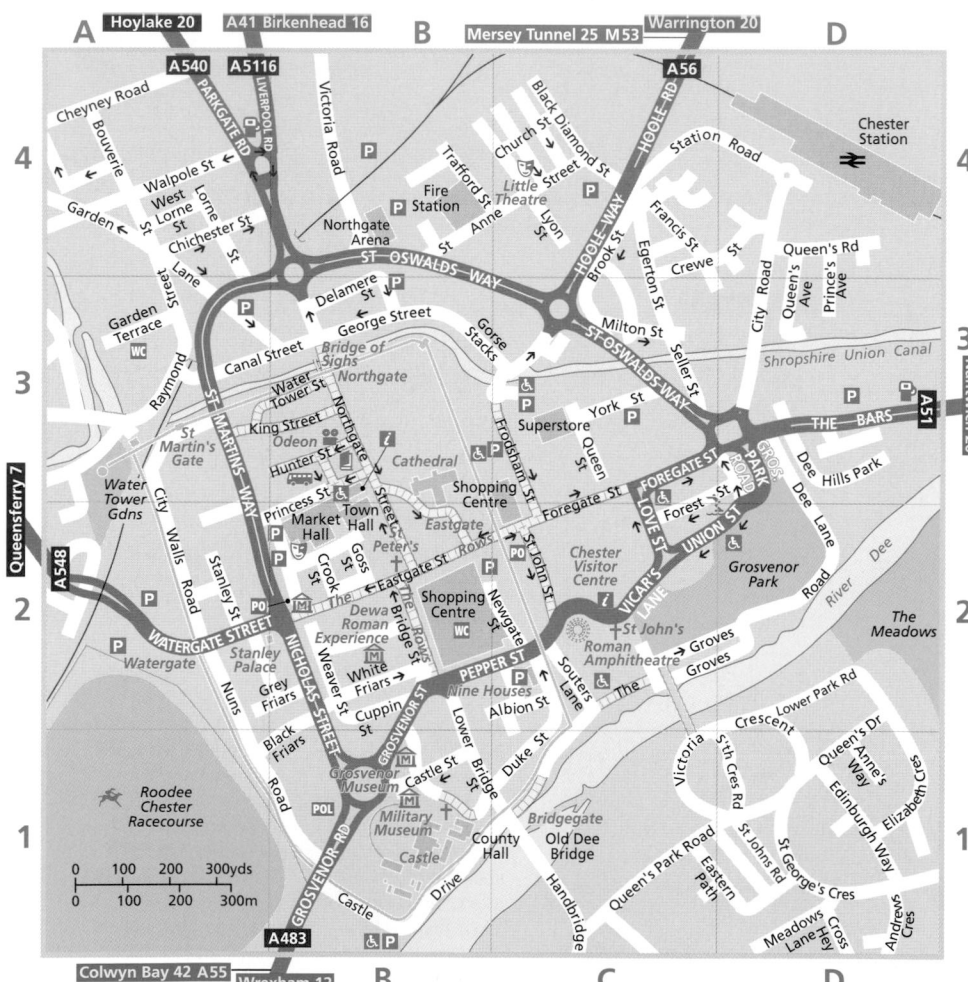

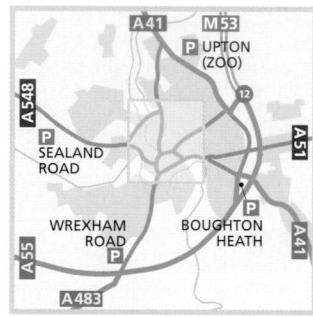

Park & Ride

CHESTERFIELD

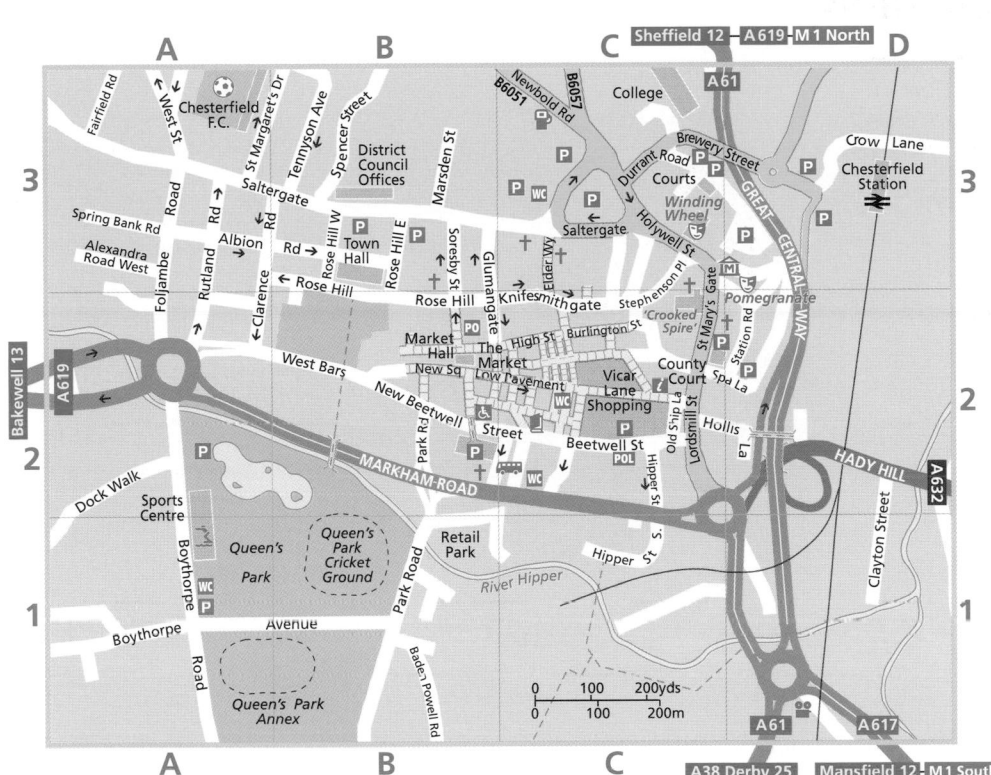

CHICHESTER

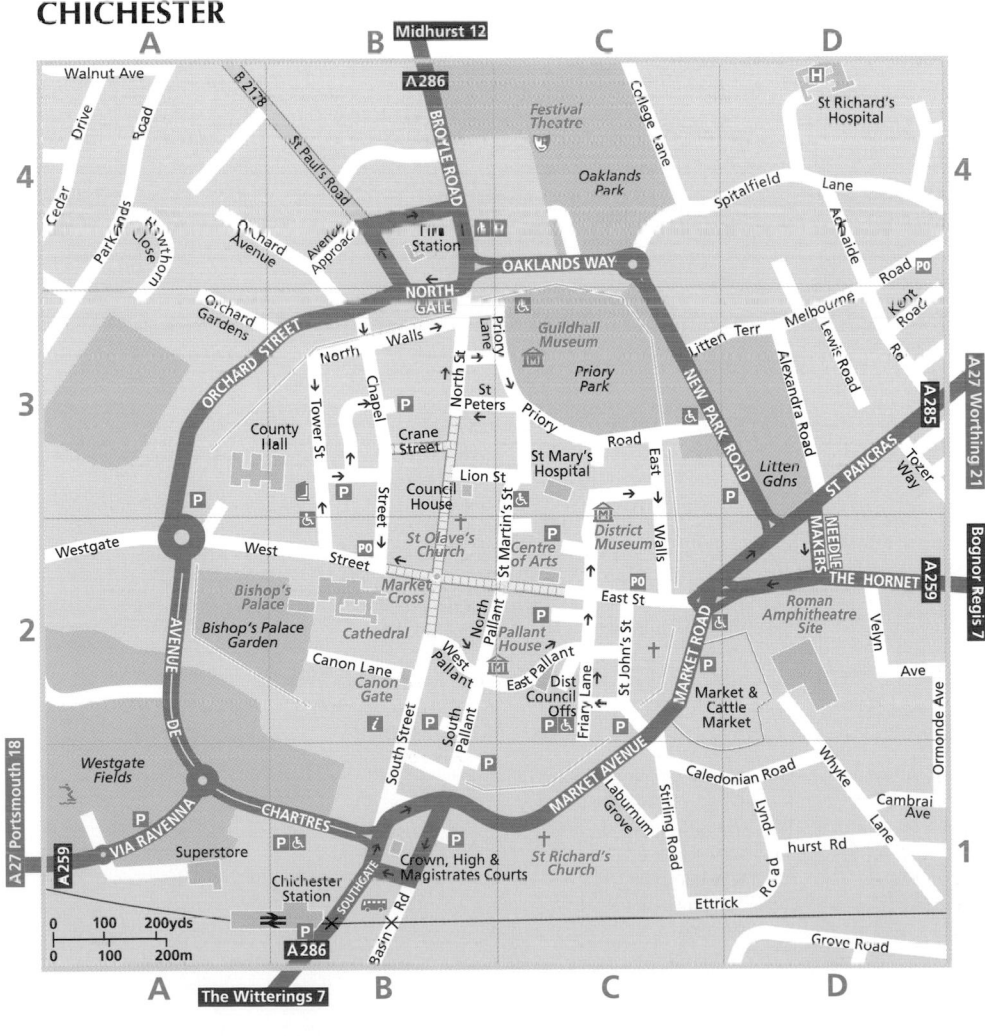

TOWN PLANS

CHIPPENHAM

CIRENCESTER

COLERAINE

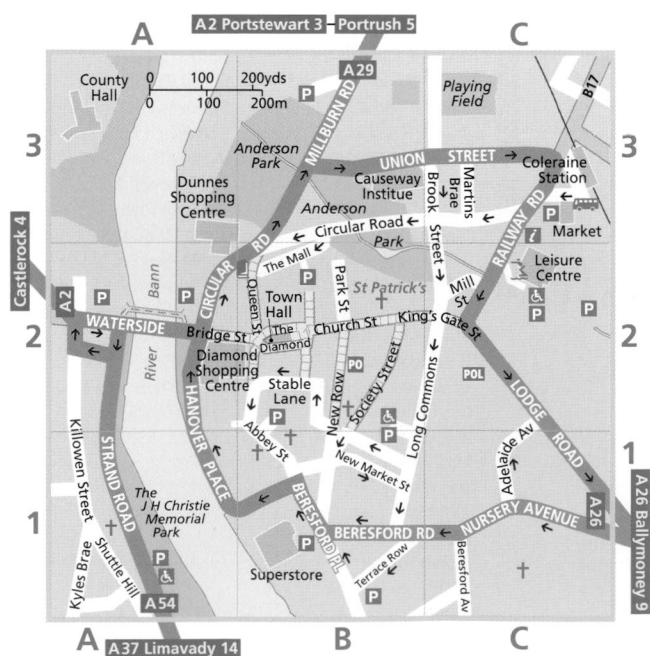

COLCHESTER

STREET INDEX

Balkerne Hill B2
Butt Road B1
Church Street B2
Crouch Street B2
Culver Street East C2
Culver Street West B2
East Hill D2
East Stockwell Street C3
Headgate B2
Head Street B2
High Street C2
Lexden Road A2
Long Wyre Street C2
Magdalen Street D1

Maldon Road A1
Mersea Road D1
Osborne Street C2
Priory Street D2
Queen Street D2
St Botoloph's St C2
St John's Street B2
Southway C1
West Way A3

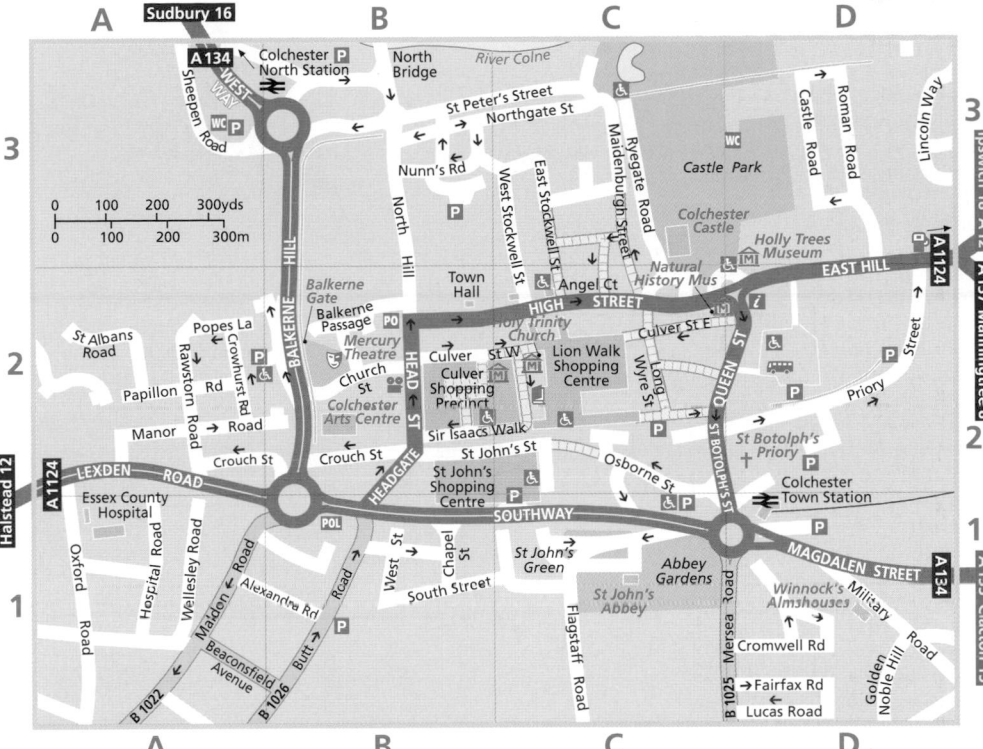

COVENTRY

STREET INDEX

Abbotts Lane A3
Acacia Avenue D1
Albert Street D4
Alma Street D3

Barras Lane A3
Bishop Street B3
Butts Road A2
Canterbury Street D3
Clifton Street D4

Corporation Street B3
Coundon Road A4
Cox Street C2
Croft Road A2
Earl Street C2

Eaton Road B1
Fairfax Street C3
Foleshill Road C4
Ford Street D3
Fowler Road A4

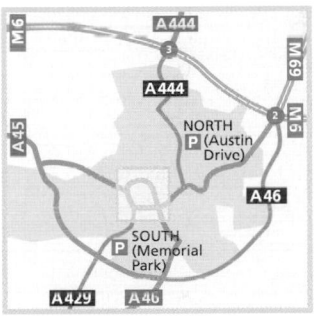

Park & Ride

Gloucester Street A3
Gordon Street A2
Gosford Street D2
Greyfriars Road B2
Grosvenor Road A1
Gulson Road D2
Harnall Lane East D4
Harper Road D2
Hewitt Avenue A4
Hill Street B3
Holyhead Road A3
Jordan Well C2
King William Street D4
Lamb Street B3
Leicester Row B4
Little Park Street C2
London Road D1
Lower Ford Street D3
Manor Road B1
Meadow Street A2
Meriden Street A3
Michaelmas Road B1
Middleborough Road A4
Mile Lane C1
New Union Street B2
Park Road B1
Parkside C1
Primrose Hill Street C4
Queen Victoria Road B2

Queens Road A2
Quinton Road C1
Radford Road B4
Raglan Street D3
Read Street D3
Regent Street A2
Ringway Hill Cross A3
Ringway Queens A2
Ringway Rudge A2
Ringway St Johns C2
Ringway St Nicholas B4
Ringway St Patricks B1
Ringway Swanswell C3
Ringway Whitefriars D2
Spencer Avenue A1
St Nicholas Street B4
Stoney Road B1
Stoney Stanton Road C4
Strathmore Avenue D1
Swans Well Street C4
Tomson Avenue A4
Upper Well Street B3
Upper York Street A2
Victoria Street D4
Vine Street D3
Warwick Road A1–B2
Westminster Road A1
Windsor Street A2
Yardley Street D4

CRAWLEY

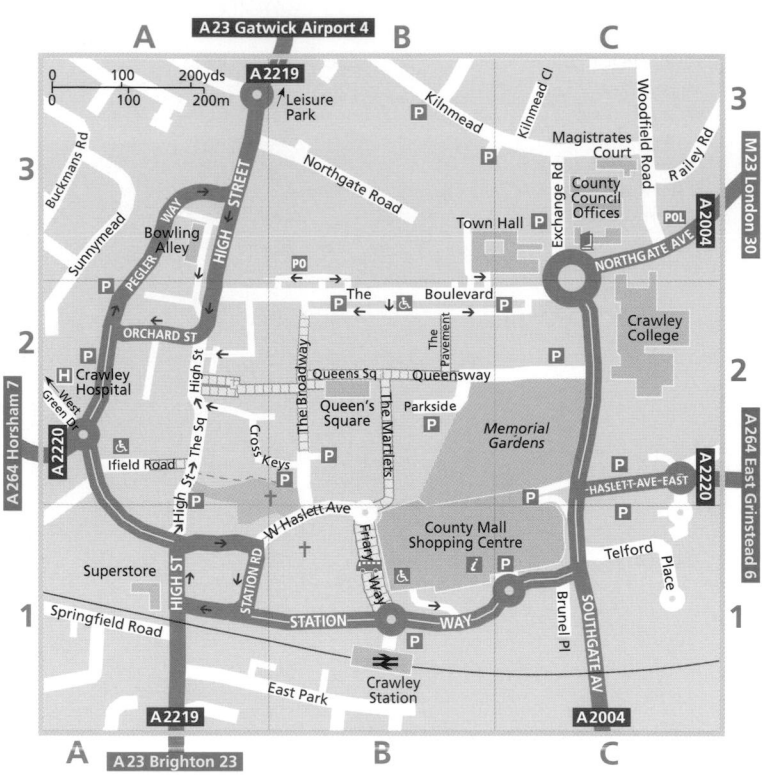

CREWE

CROYDON

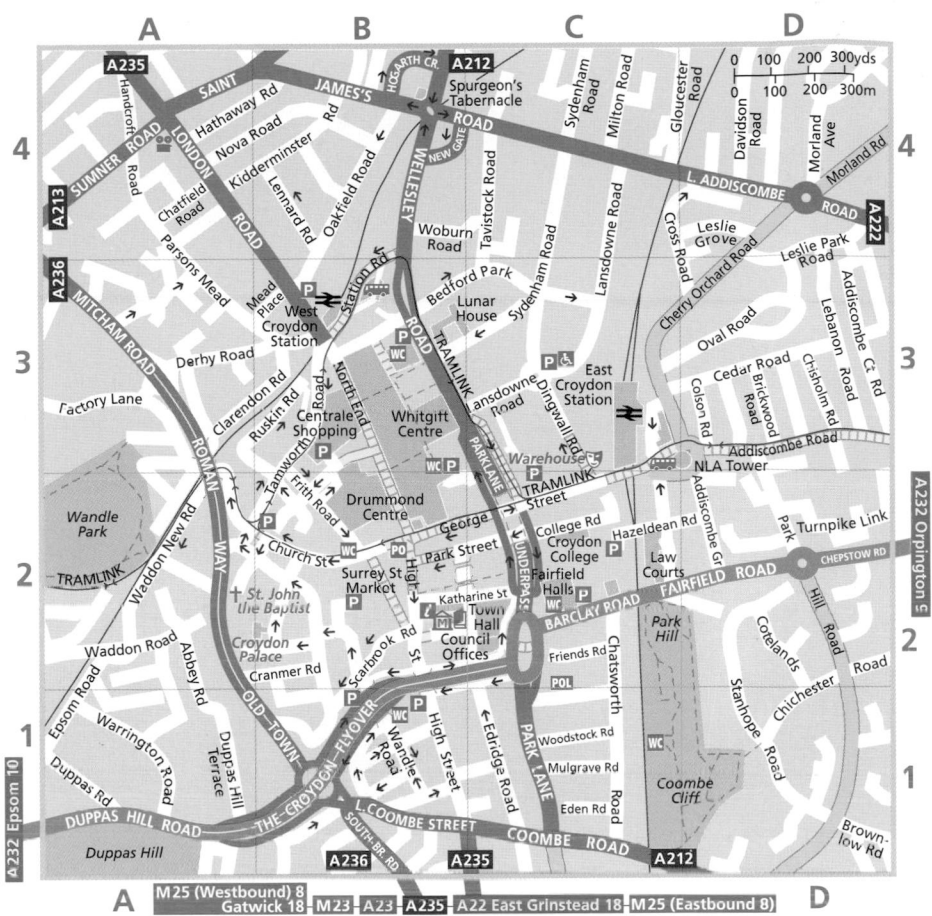

TOWN PLANS

DARLINGTON

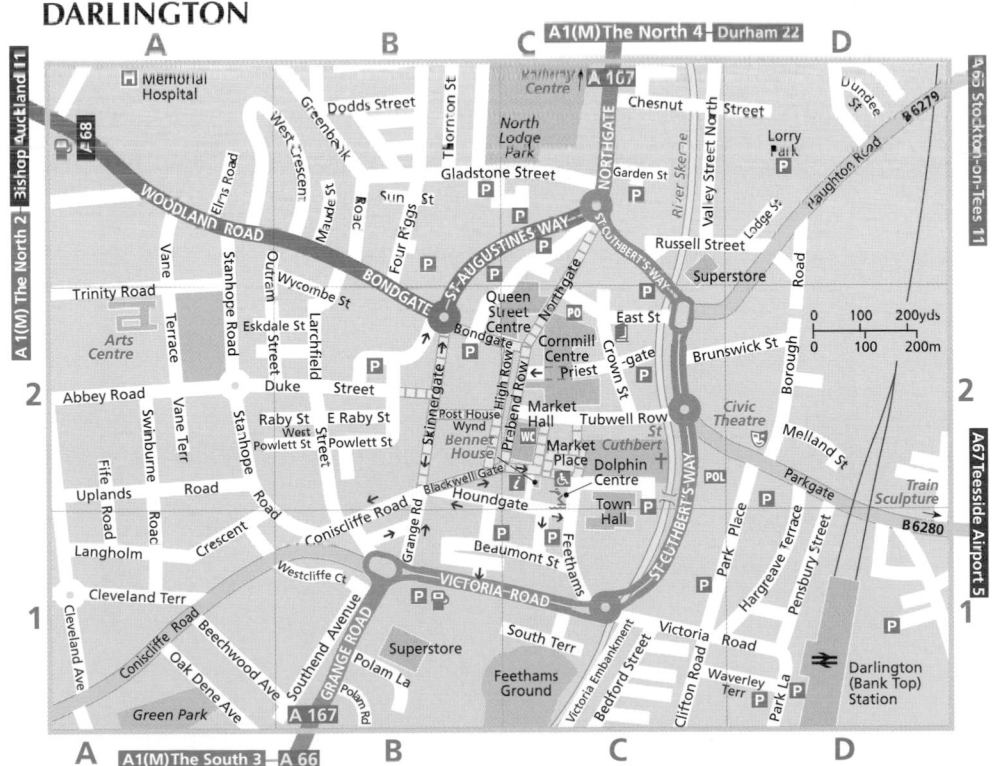

DERBY

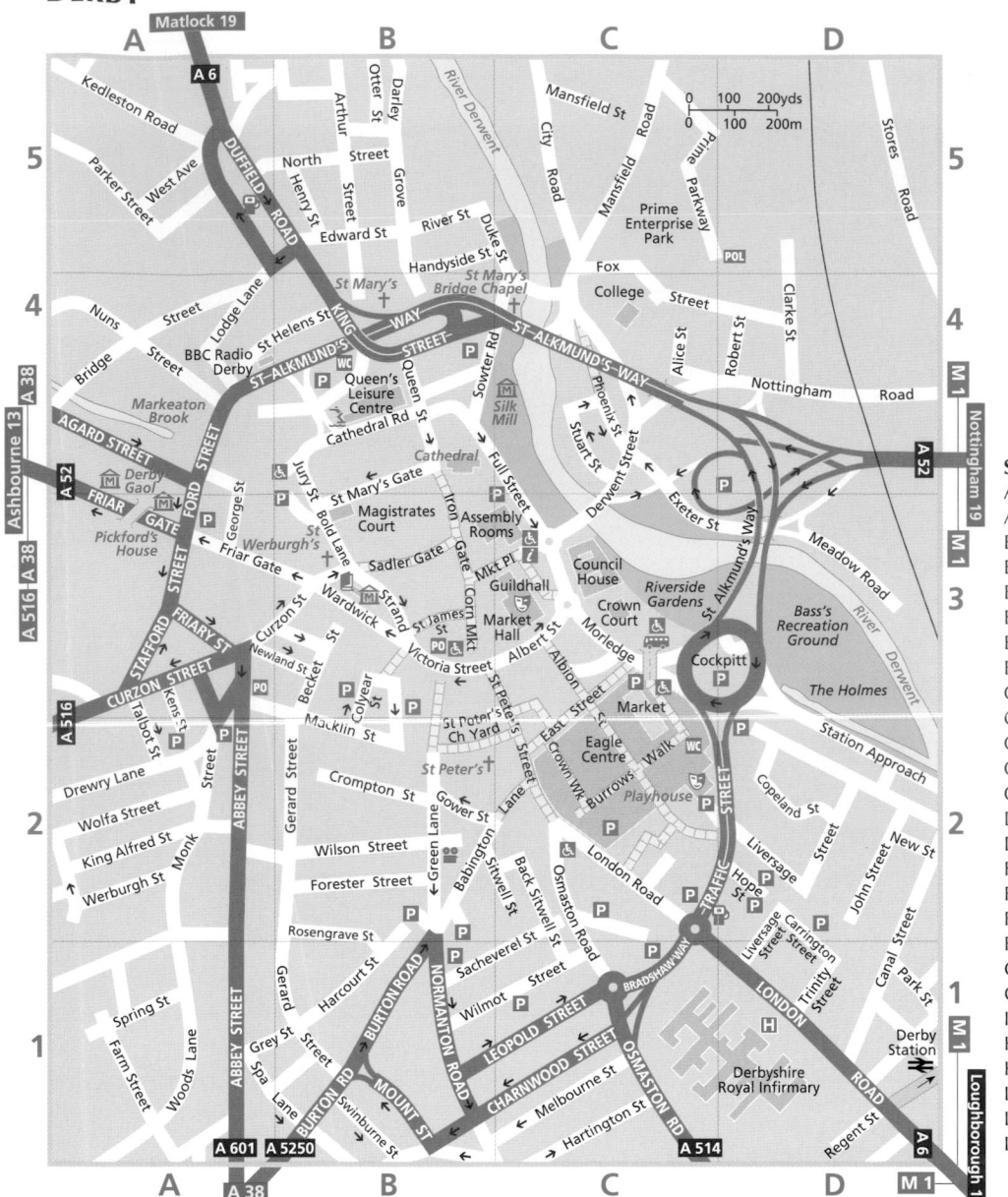

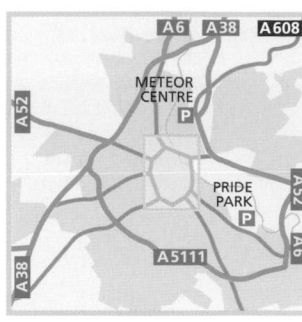

Park & Ride

DUMFRIES

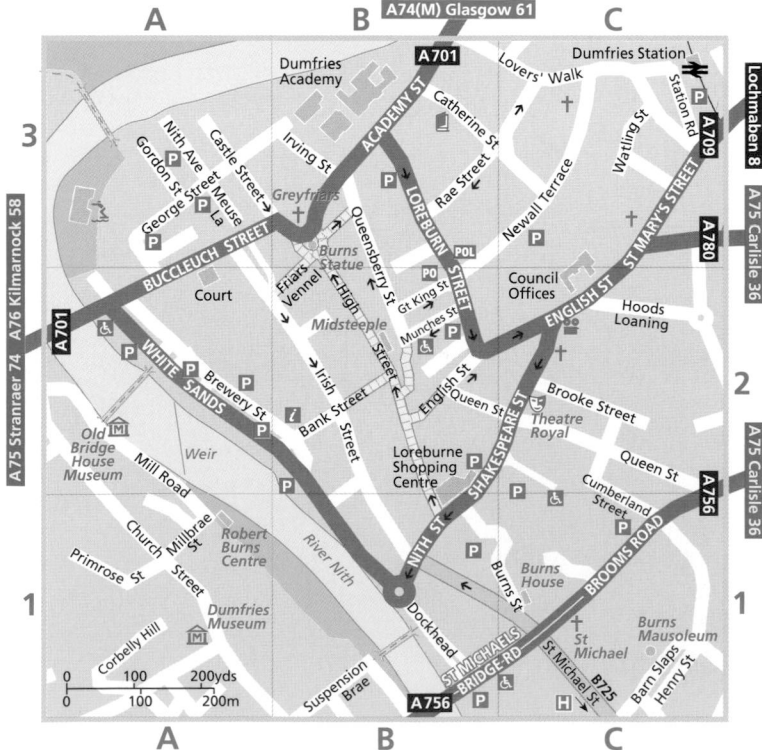

DONCASTER

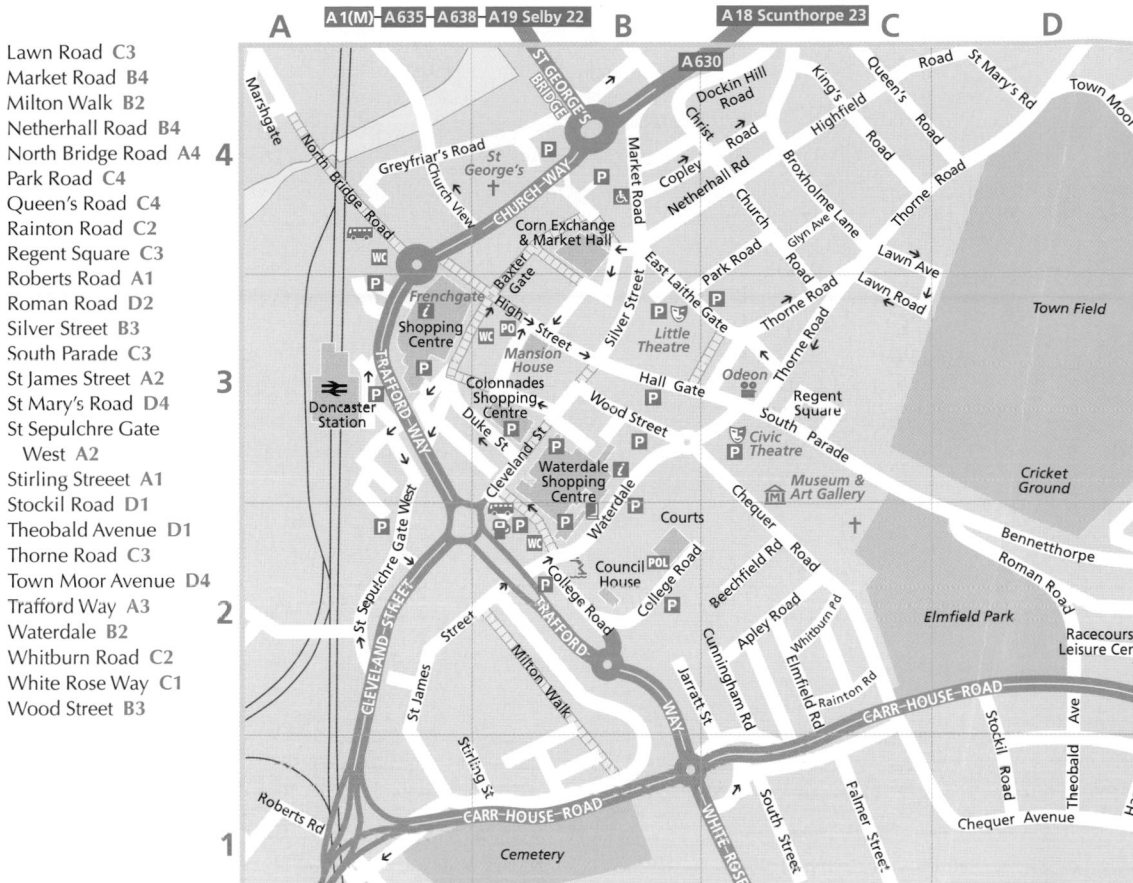

DUNFERMLINE

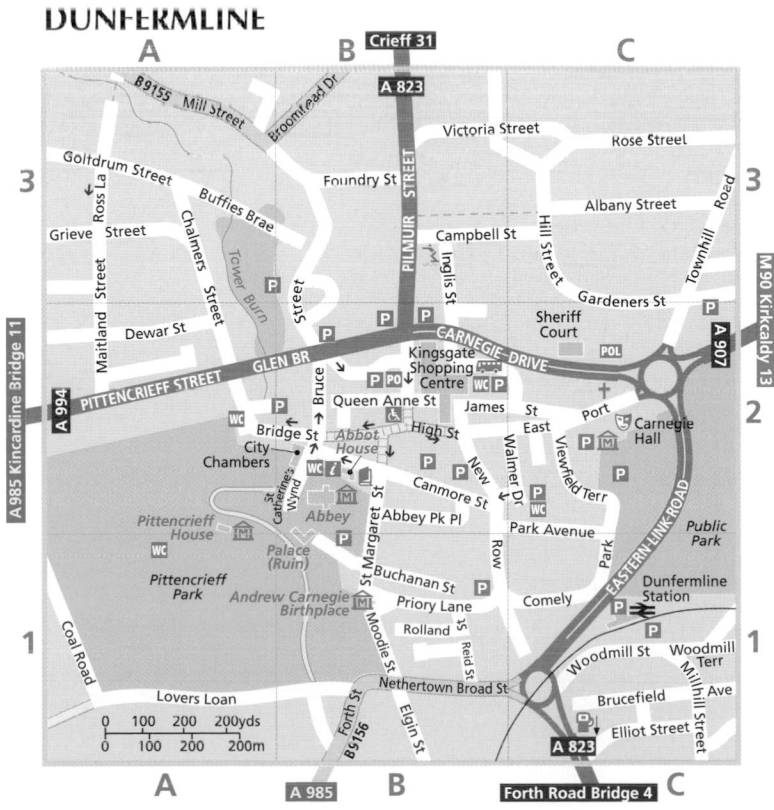

DUBLIN

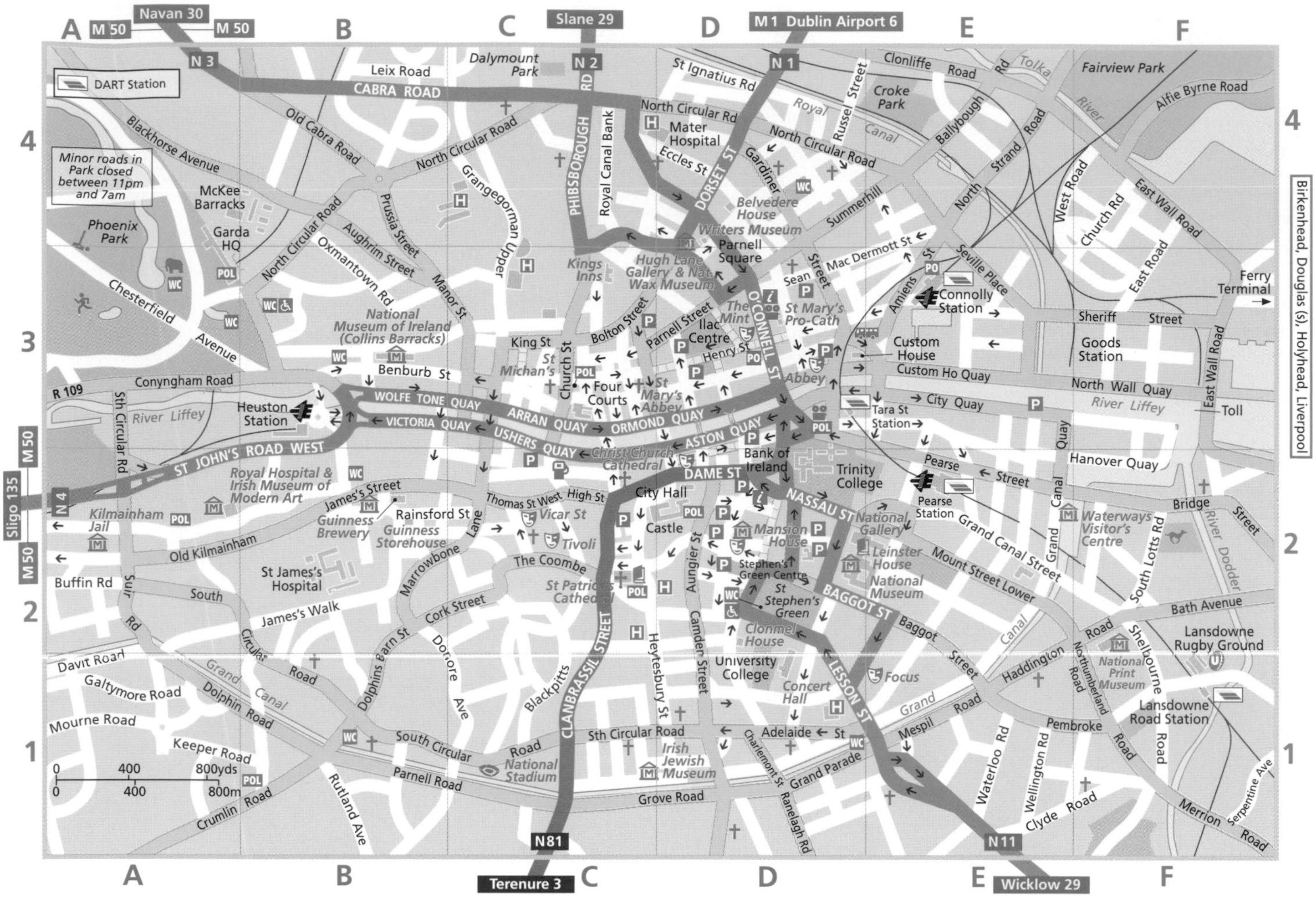

Map labels (roads, places, features):

Navan 30 · M 50 · M 50 · N 3 · Slane 29 · N 2 · M 1 Dublin Airport 6 · N 1 · Clonliffe Road · Rd · Tolka · River · Fairview Park · Alfie Byrne Road

DART Station · Leix Road · Dalymount Park · St Ignatius Rd · Russel Street · Croke Park · Ballybough

CABRA ROAD · North Circular Rd · Mater Hospital · Eccles St · North Circular Road · West Road · Church Rd · East Wall Road

Minor roads in Park closed between 11pm and 7am · Blackhorse Avenue · Old Cabra Road · North Circular Road · Grangegorman Upper · PHIBSBOROUGH · Royal Canal Bank · Dorset St · Gardiner · Belvedere House · Writers Museum · WC · North Strand Road

McKee Barracks · Garda HQ · POL · Prussia Street · Aughrim Street · Manor St · Kings Inns · Hugh Lane Gallery & Nat. Wax Museum · Parnell Square · Sean · Mac Dermott St · PO · Seville Place · Connolly Station · Sheriff · Street · Goods Station

Phoenix Park · Chesterfield · WC · North Circular Road · Oxmantown Rd · WC · National Museum of Ireland (Collins Barracks) · King St · St Michan's · Bolton St · Parnell Street · Ilac Centre · Henry · The Mint · St Mary's Pro-Cath · Amiens · Custom House · Custom Ho Quay · North Wall Quay

Chesterfield Avenue · WC · Benburb St · Four Courts · St Mary's Abbey · O'CONNELL ST · Abbey · Tara St Station · City Quay · River Liffey · Toll

Conyngham Road · R 109 · WOLFE TONE QUAY · ARRAN QUAY · ORMOND QUAY · ASTON QUAY · Bank of Ireland · Pearse · Street · Hanover Quay

River Liffey · Heuston Station · VICTORIA QUAY · USHERS QUAY · Christchurch Cathedral · DAME ST · Trinity College · Pearse Station · Grand Canal · Bridge · River Dodder

M 50 · Sligo 135 · N 4 · ST JOHN'S ROAD WEST · Royal Hospital & Irish Museum of Modern Art · WC · Thomas St West · High St · City Hall · NASSAU ST · National Gallery · Waterways Visitor's Centre

Kilmainham Jail · Suir Rd · Old Kilmainham · James's Street · Guinness Brewery · Rainsford St · Vicar St · Castle · Mansion House · Leinster House · National Museum · South Lotts Rd · Bath Avenue

Buffin Rd · St James's Hospital · James's Walk · Guinness Storehouse · Marrowbone Lane · The Coombe · Tivoli · St Stephen's Green Centre · St Stephen's Green · Baggot · Mount Street Lower · BAGGOT ST · National Print Museum · Lansdowne Rugby Ground

Davit Road · South · Circular · Road · Dolphins Barn St · Cork Street · Clanbrassil · Street · Clonmel House · University College · Concert Hall · Focus · Haddington · Shelbourne Rd · Lansdowne Road Station

Galtymore Road · Grand Canal · Dolphin Road · Blackpitts · Heytesbury Street · Camden Street · St Patrick's Cathedral · Mespil · Pembroke · Merrion · Serpentine Ave

Mourne Road · Keeper Road · 0 400 800yds · 0 400 800m · POL · South Circular · Road · National Stadium · 5th Circular Road · Adelaide · St · Irish Jewish Museum · Charlemont St · Grand Parade · Waterloo Rd · Wellington Road · Clyde Road · Merrion · Road

Parnell Road · Crumlin · Road · Rutland Ave · Dorore · Ave · Grove Road · N81 · Terenure 3 · N11 · Wicklow 29

Birkenhead, Douglas (s), Holyhead, Liverpool · Ferry Terminal

DURHAM

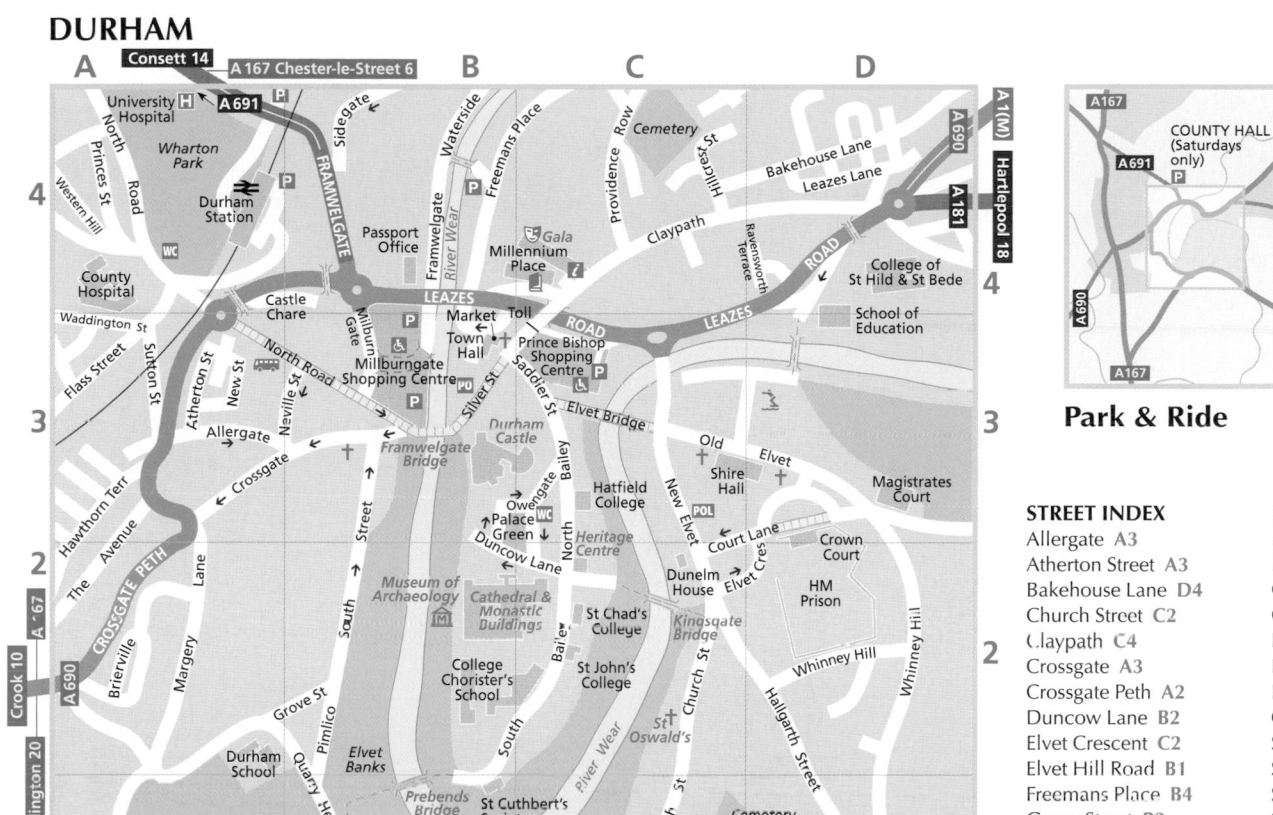

Park & Ride

COUNTY HALL (Saturdays only)

ELGIN

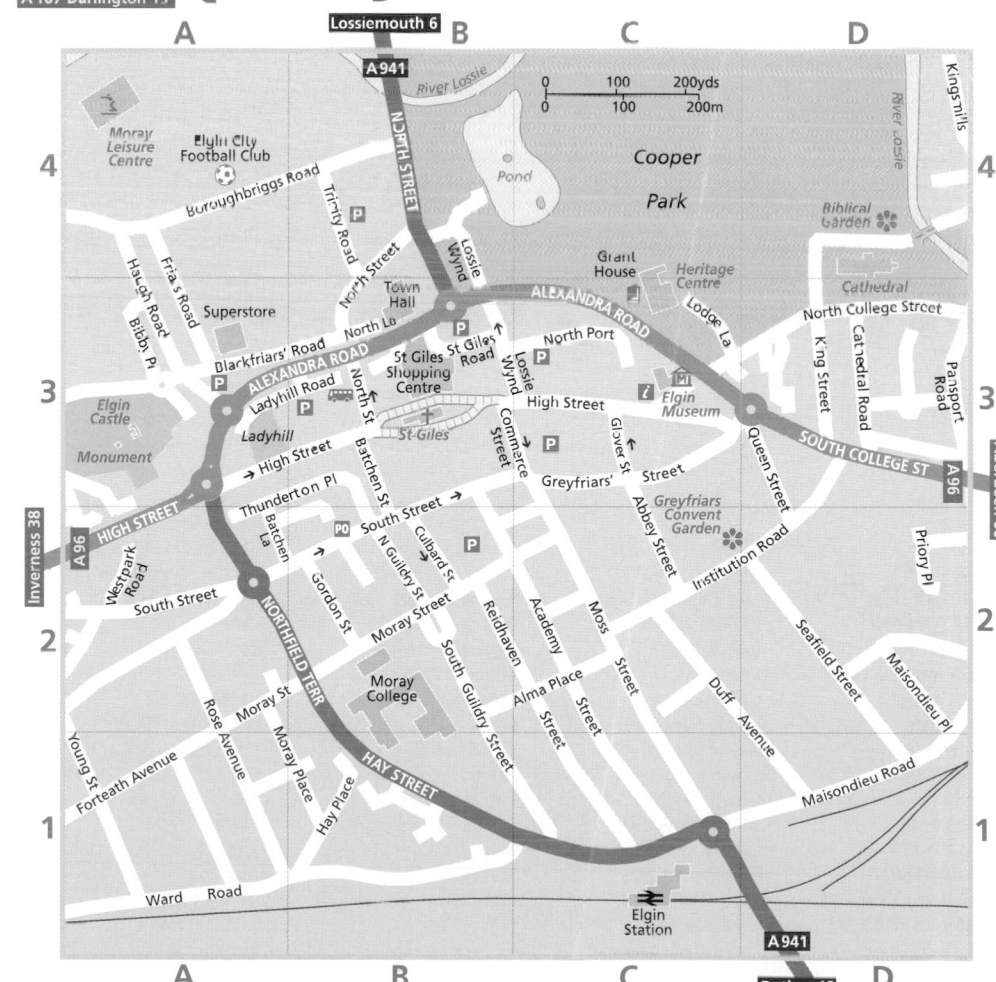

EDINBURGH

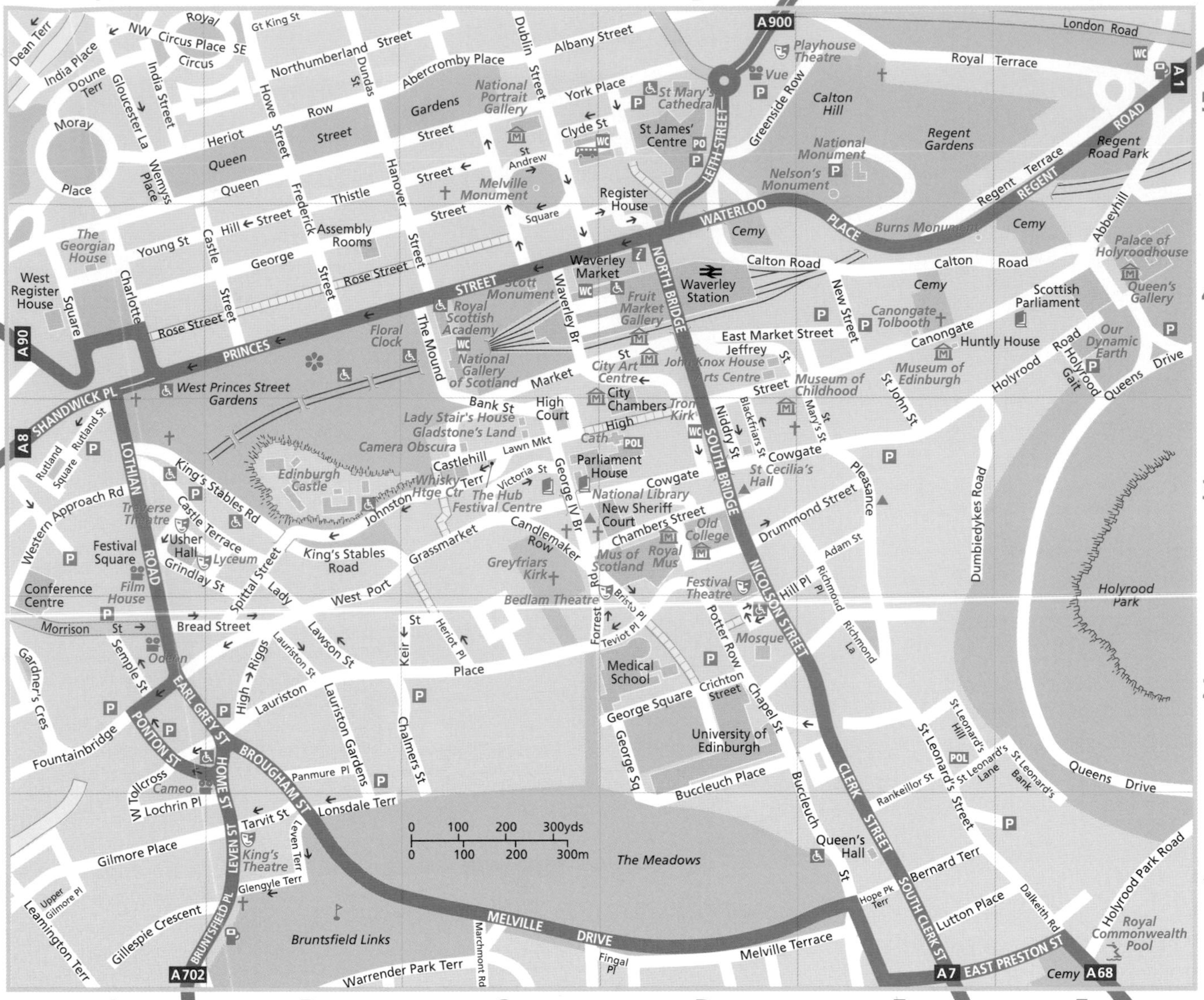

A900 Leith 1
A90 Forth Road Bridge 10
A8 Glasgow 45
A90 Shandwick Pl
A702 Carlisle 98
A7 East Preston St
Galashiels 33
F Dalkeith 7
A68
Berwick 57 A1

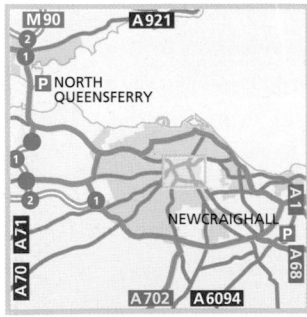

Park & Ride

M90 A921
NORTH QUEENSFERRY
NEWCRAIGHALL
A71 A70 A1 A68 A702 A6094

ELY

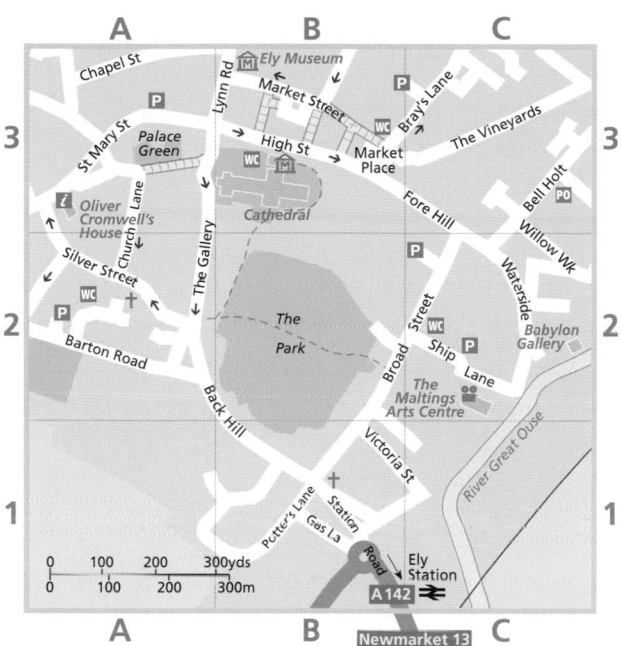

STREET INDEX

Back Hill A2–B1
Barton Road A2
Bell Holt C3
Bray's Lane C3
Broad Street B2–C2
Chapel Street A3
Church Lane A2
Fore Hill C3
Gas Lane B1
High Street B3
Lynn Road B3

Market Place B3
Market Street B3
Potter's Lane B1
St Mary Street A3
Ship Lane C2
Silver Street A2
Station Road B1
The Gallery A2
The Vineyards C3
Victoria Street B1
Waterside C2
Willow Walk C2

EVESHAM

STREET INDEX

Abbey Lane A2
Abbey Road A1
Avon Street B3
Bewdley Street A3
Blind Lane A3
Boat Lane A2
Briar Close B3
Brick-Kiln Street B3
Bridge Street B2
Castle Street C2
Common Road C3
Cooper's Lane C1
Cowl Street B2
Henry Street A3
High Street B3
Lower Leys C2
Mansion Gardens C1
Merstow Green A2
Mill Street C2
Oat Street B3
Overbrook C1
Owletts End C1
Rynal Place C3
Rynal Street C3
Swan Lane B3
Waterside B1–C2
West Street A3

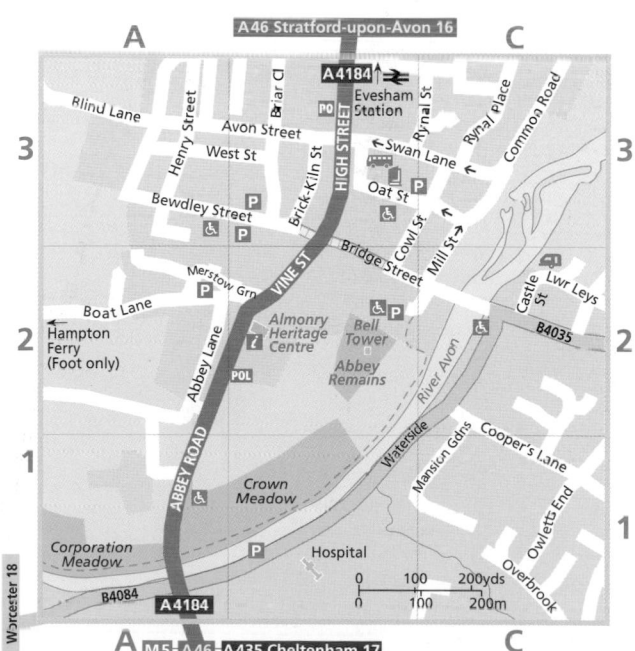

FALMOUTH

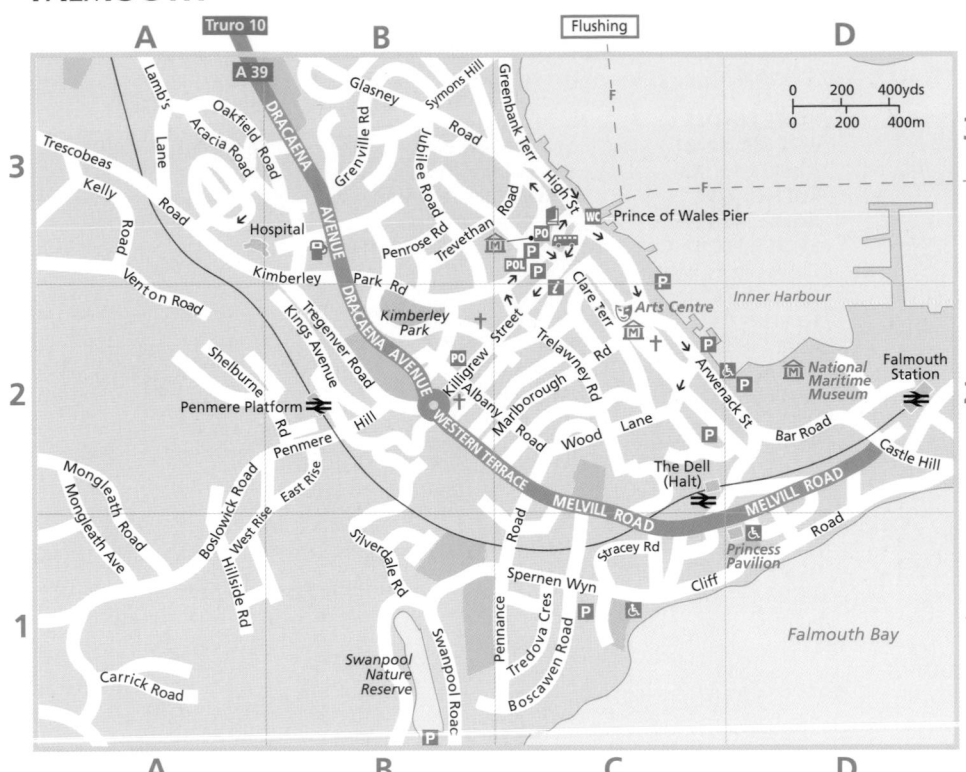

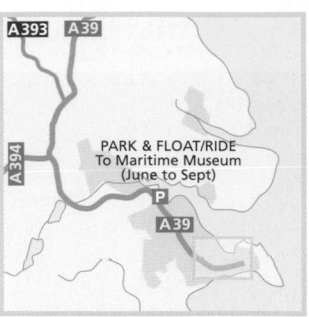

Park & Float/Ride

FLEETWOOD

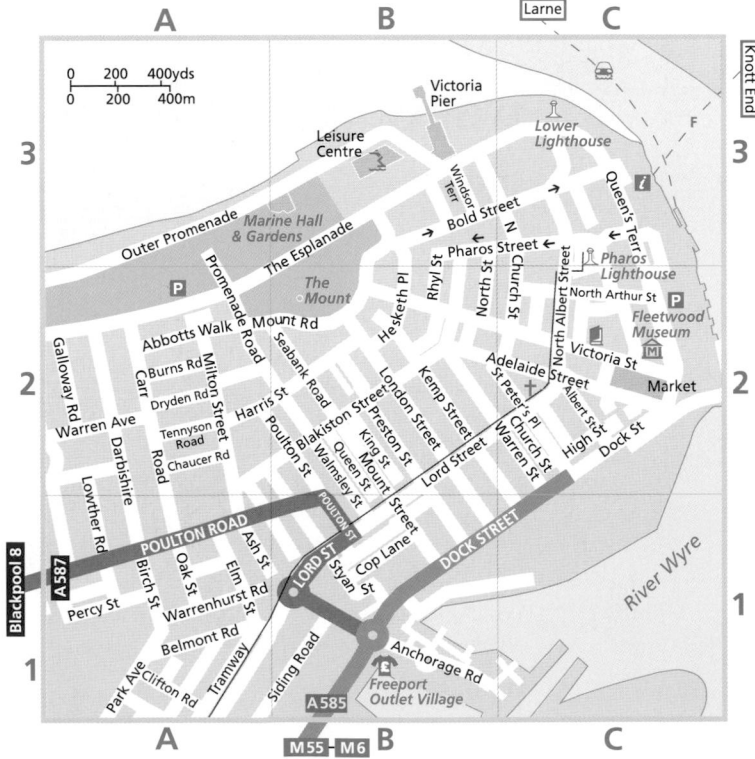

FOLKESTONE

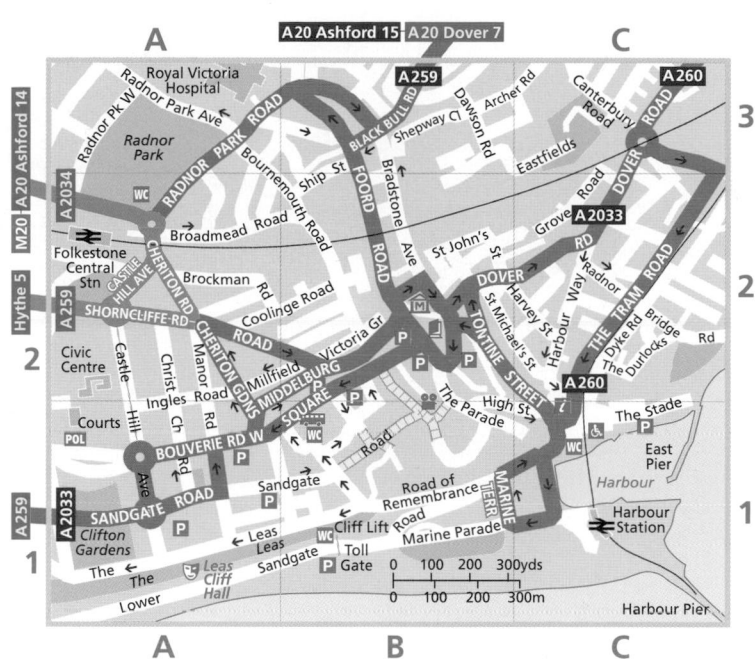

FORFAR

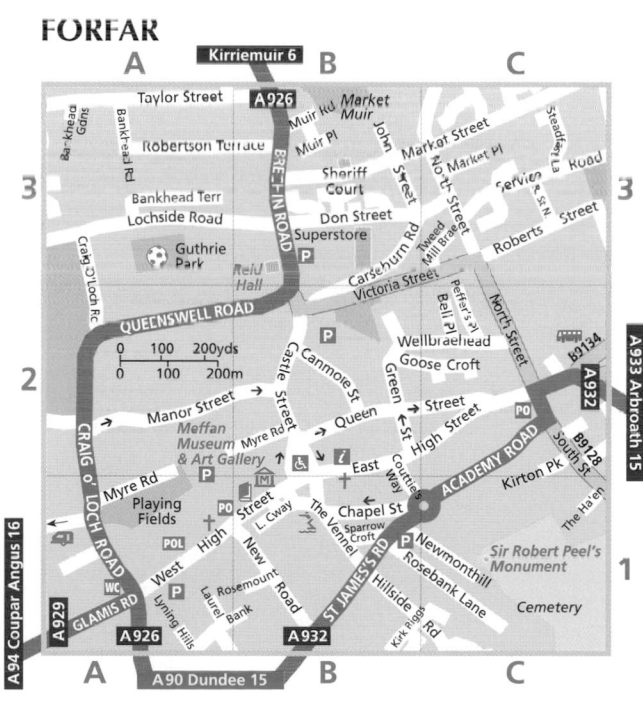

FORT WILLIAM

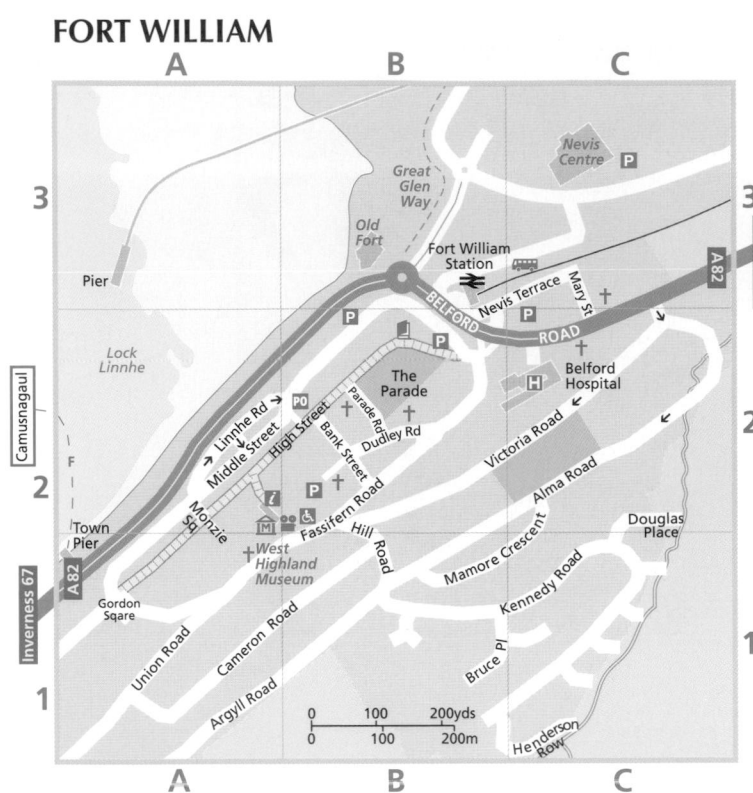

GALWAY

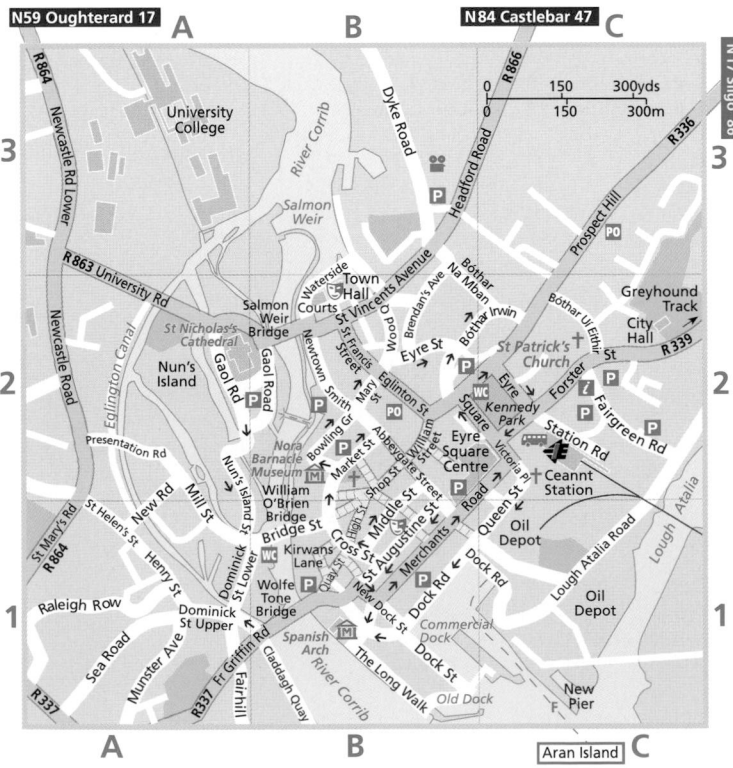

GLASGOW

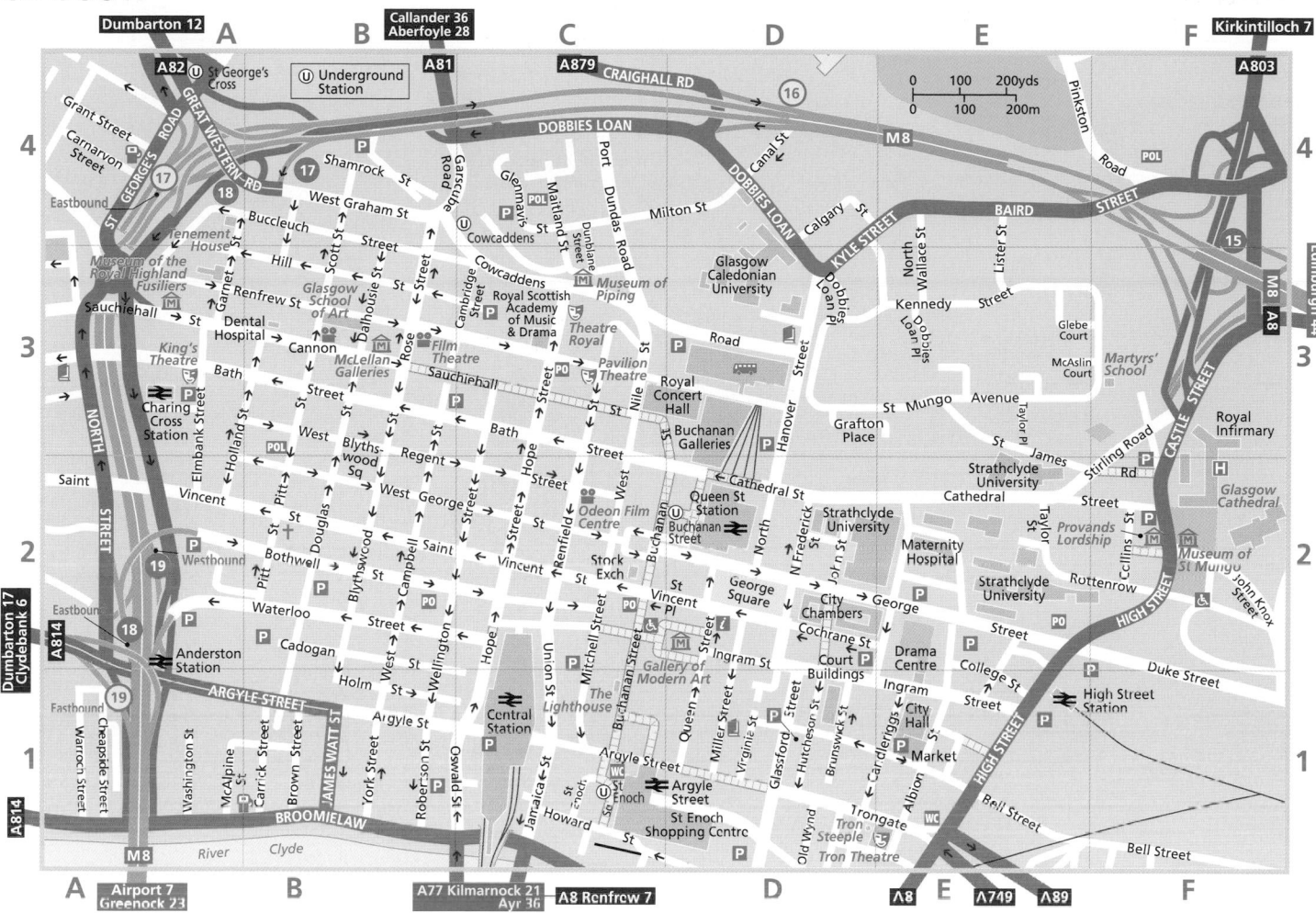

STREET INDEX

Albion Street **E1**
Argyle Street **A1–D1**
Baird Street **E4**
Bath Street **C3**
Bell Street **E1**
Blythswood Square **B3**
Blythswood Street **B2**
Bothwell Street **B2**
Broomielaw **B1**
Brown Street **B1**
Brunswick Street **D1**
Buccleuch Street **B4**
Buchanan Street **C3**
Cadogan Street **B2**
Calgary Street **D4**
Canal Street **D4**
Cambridge Street **C3**
Candleriggs **E1**
Carnarvon Street **A4**
Carrick Street **B1**
Castle Street **F3**
Cathedral Street **D**
Cheapside Street **A1**
Cochrane Street **D2**
College Street **E1**
Collins Street **F2**
Cowcaddens Road **C3**
Craighall Road **C4**
Dalhousie Street **B3**
Dobbies Loan **C4**
Dobbies Loan Place **E3**

Douglas Street **B3**
Duke Street **F1**
Dunblane Street **C4**
Elmbank Street **A3**
Garnet Street **A3**
Garscube Road **B4**
George Square **D2**
George Street **E2**
Glassford Street **D1**
Glebe Court **E3**
Glenmavis Street **C4**
Grafton Place **D3**
Grant Street **A4**
Great Western Road **A4**
High Street **E1**
Hill Street **B3**
Holland Street **A3**
Holm Street **B1**
Hope Street **C2**
Howard Street **C1**
Hutcheson Street **D1**
Ingram Street **D2**
Jamaica Street **C1**
James Watt Street **B1**
John Knox Street **F2**
John Street **D2**
Kennedy Street **E3**
Kyle Street **D3**
Lister Street **E3**
McAlpine Street **A1**
McAslin Court **E3**
Maitland Street **C4**

Miller Street **D1**
Milton Street **D4**
Mitchell Street **C2**
North Street **A3**
North Frederick
  Street **D2**
North Hanover
  Street **D3**
North Wallace Street **E3**
Old Wynd **D1**
Oswald Street **B1**
Pinkston Road **F4**
Pitt Street **B2**
Port Dundas Road **C4**
Queen Street **D1**
Renfield Street **C2**
Renfrew Street **B3**
Robertson Street **B1**
Rose Street **B3**
Rottenrow **F2**
St Enoch Square **C1**
St George's Road **A4**
St James Road **E3**
St Mungo Avenue **E3**
St Vincent Place **D2**
St Vincent Street **A2–C2**
Sauchiehall Street
  A3–C3
Scott Street **B3**
Shamrock Street **B4**
Stirling Road **F2**
Taylor Place **E3**

Taylor Street **E2**
Trongate **D1**
Union Street **C2**
Virginia Street **D1**
Warroch Street **A1**
Washington Street **A1**
Waterloo Street **A2**
Wellington Street **B2**
West Campbell
  Street **B2**
West George Street **B2**
West Graham Street **B4**
West Nile Street **C3**
West Regent Street **B3**
York Street **B1**

GLOUCESTER

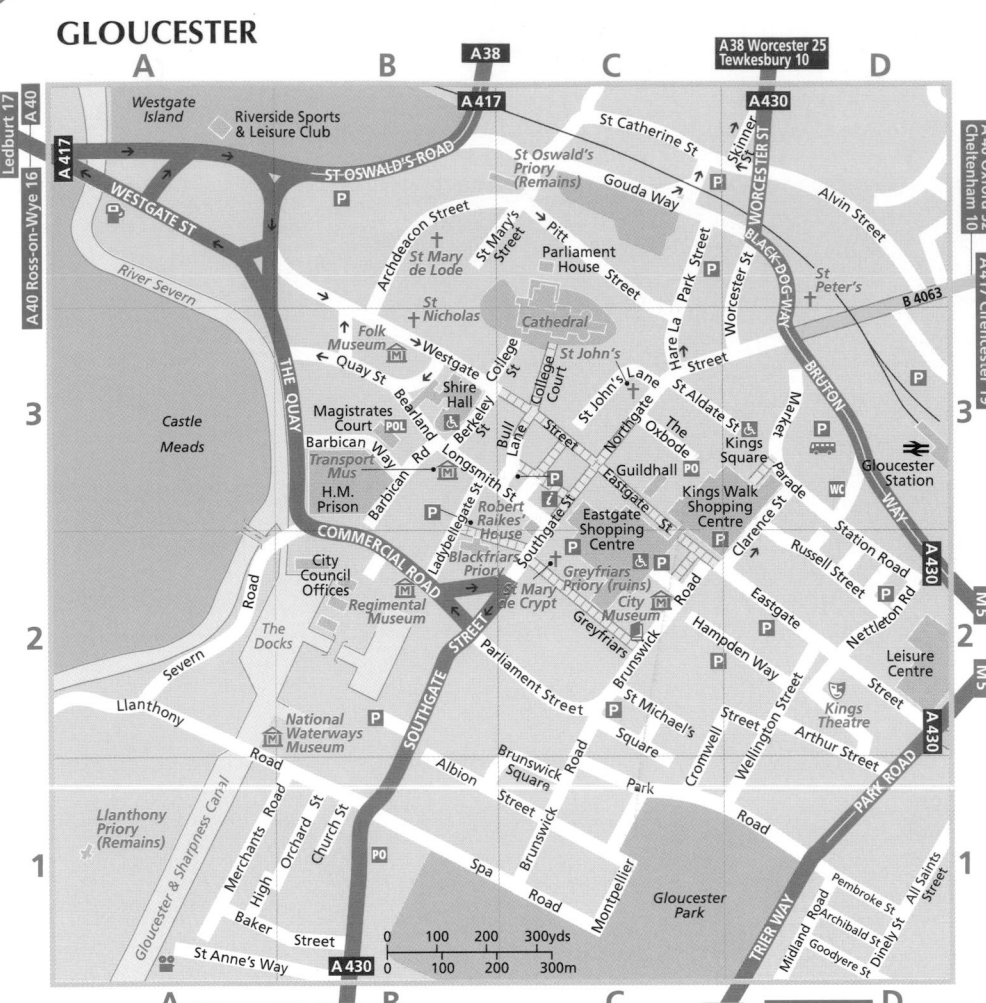

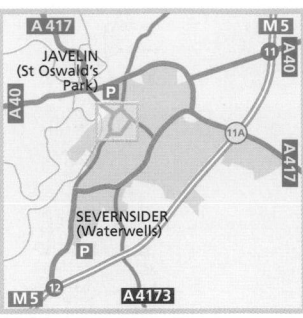

Park & Ride

STREET INDEX

Archdeacon Street **B4**
Barbican Road **B3**
Barbican Way **B3**
Bearland **B3**
Berkeley Street **B3**
Black Dog Way **D4**
Brunswick Road **C1**
Bruton Way **D3**
College Court **C3**
College Street **C3**
Commercial Road **B2**
Cromwell Street **C1–D2**
Eastgate Street **C3**
Greyfriars **C2**
Hampden Way **D2**
Ladybellegate Street **B2**
Llanthony Road **A2**
Longsmith Street **B3**

Merchants Road **A1**
Northgate Street **C3**
Park Road **C1**
Parliament Street **C2**
Pitt Street **C4**
Quay Street **B3**
Russell Street **D2**
St Aldate Street **C3**
St John's Lane **C3**
St Michael's Square **C2**
St Oswald's Road **B4**
Severn Road **A2**
Southgate Street **B2**
Spa Road **B1**
The Oxbode **C3**
The Quay **B3**
Trier Way **D1**
Westgate Street **A4–C3**
Worcester Street **D4**

GRANTHAM

STREET INDEX

Agnes Street **C3**
Alexandra Road **A1**
Alford Street **C4**
Barrowby Road **A4**
Brewery Hill **B2**
Broad Street **B4**
Brook Street **B4**
Cambridge Street **C2**
Campbell Close **A4**
Castlegate **B3**
Church Street **B4**
College Street **C2**
Commercial Road **B2**
Conduit Lane **B3**
Dudley Road **C2**
Dysart Road **A3**
East Street **C3**
Elmer Street North **B3**
Elmer Street South **B3**
Finkin Street **B3**
George Street **C3**
Gladstone Terrace **B4**
Grantley Street **B2**
Greenwood's Row **B3**
Guildhall Street **B3**
Harlaxton Road **A1**
Harrow Street **C2**
High Street **B3**
Huntingtower Road **A1**
Inner Street **C1**
Launder Terrace **B1**
London Road **C1**
Market Place **B3**

Middlemore Yard **B3**
New Street **B4**
North Parade **A4**
North Street **B4**
Norton Street **B2**
Old Wharf Road **A2**
Oxford Street **C2**
Queen Street **B2**
Redcross Street **B4**
Riverside **C3**
Rycroft Street **C2**
Saint Augustin Way **A3**
Spring Gardens **C1**
St Catherine's Road **C2**
St Peter's Hill **B3**
Station Road **B2**
Station Road East **B1**
Stonebridge Road **C3**
Swinegate **B4**
Tyndal Road **A4**
Union Street **B4**
Vine Street **B3**
Watergate **B4**
Welby Street **B3**
Welham Street **C3**
Westgate **B3**
Wharf Road **B2**

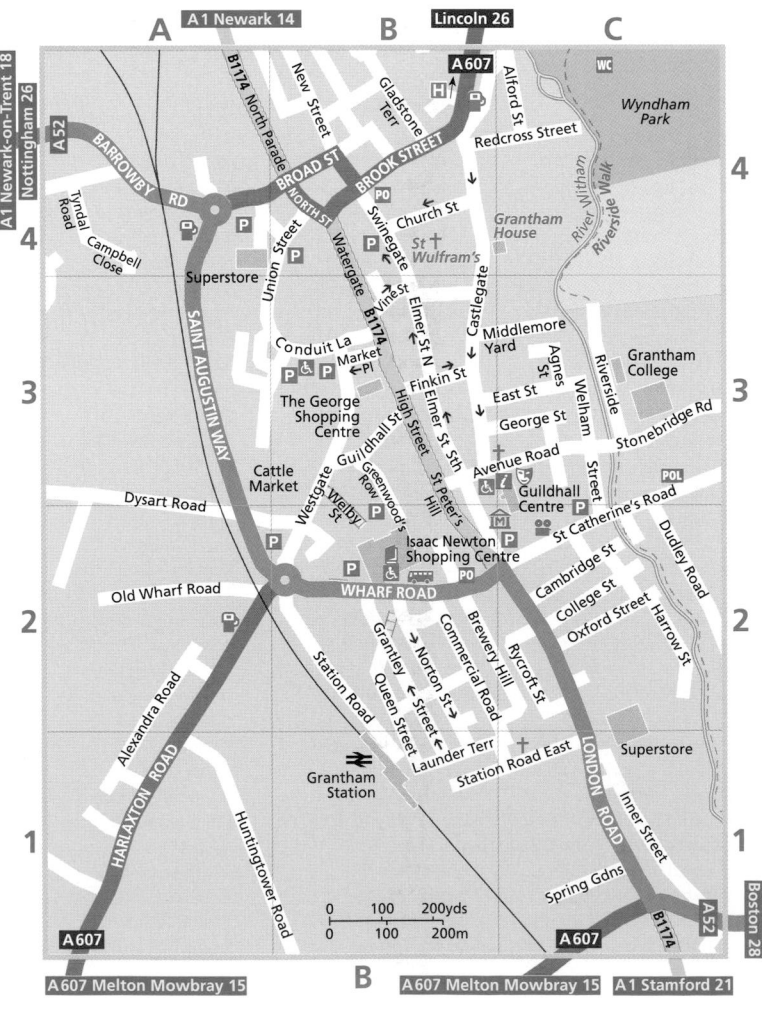

GREAT YARMOUTH

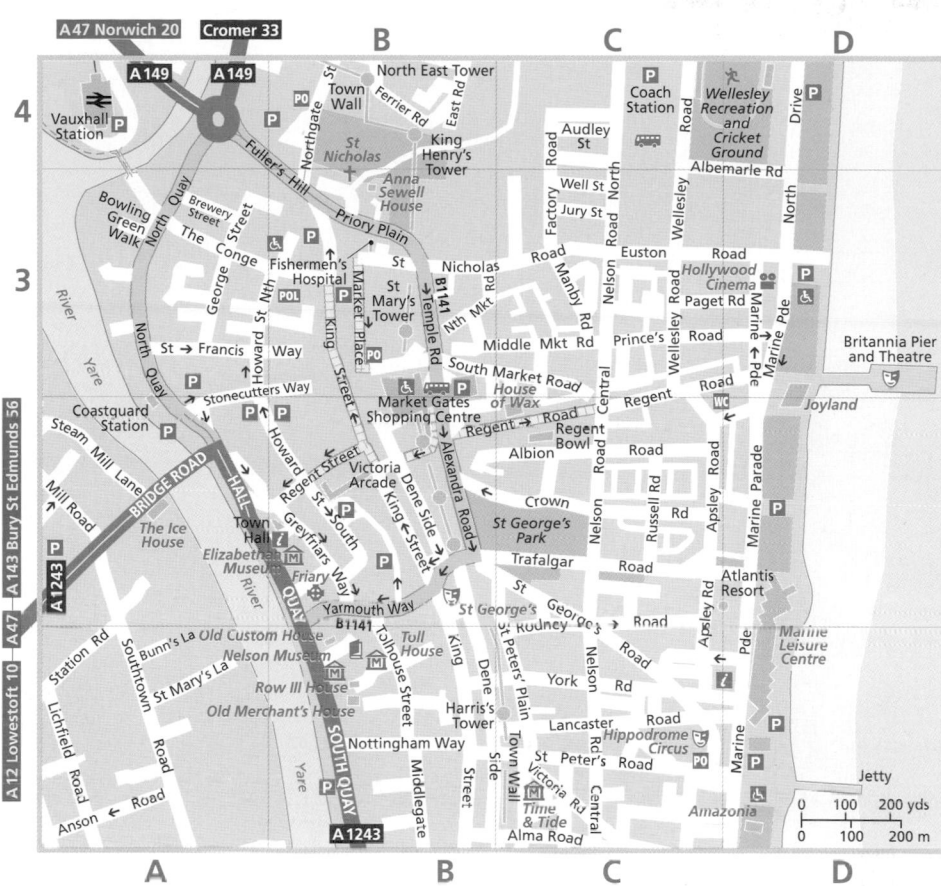

GRIMSBY

TOWN PLANS

GUILDFORD

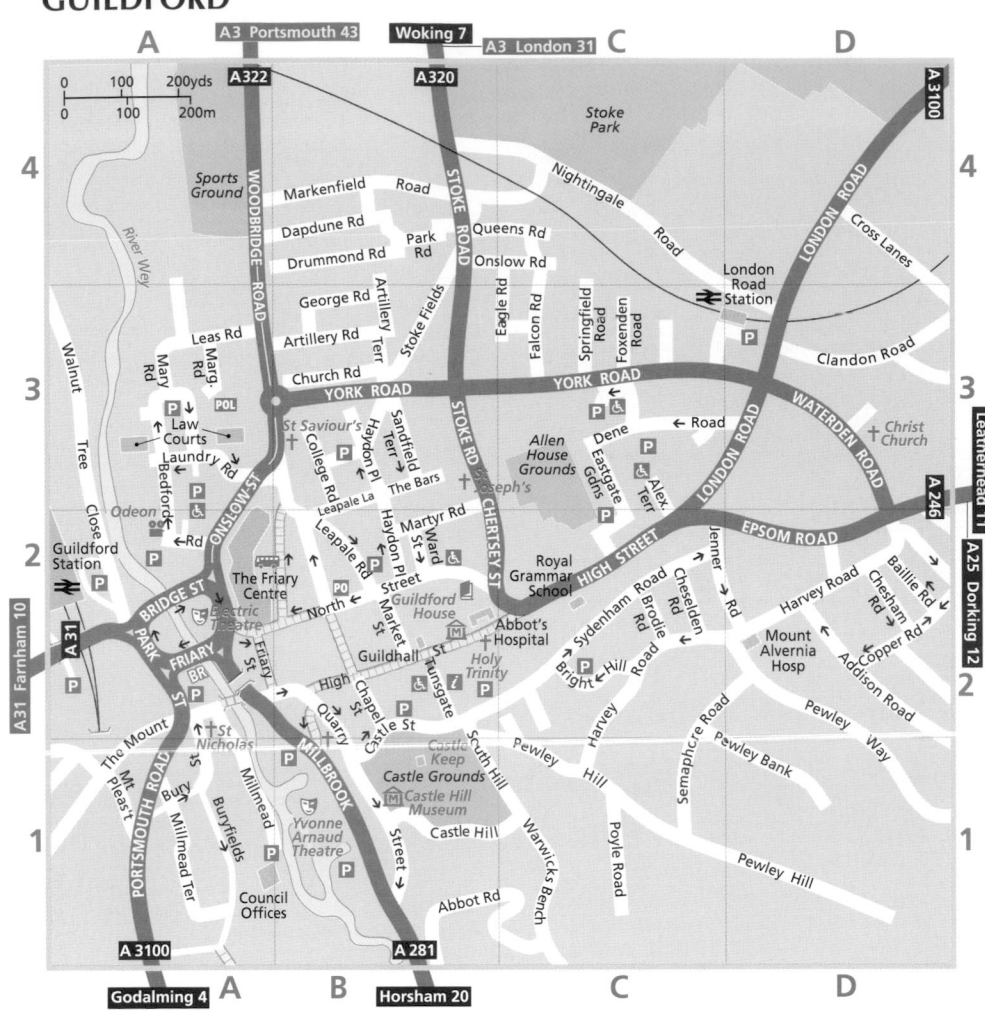

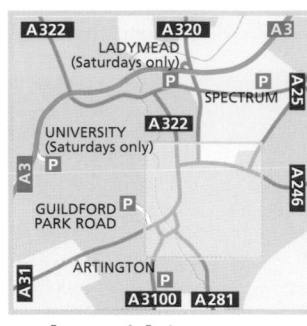

Park & Ride

HALIFAX

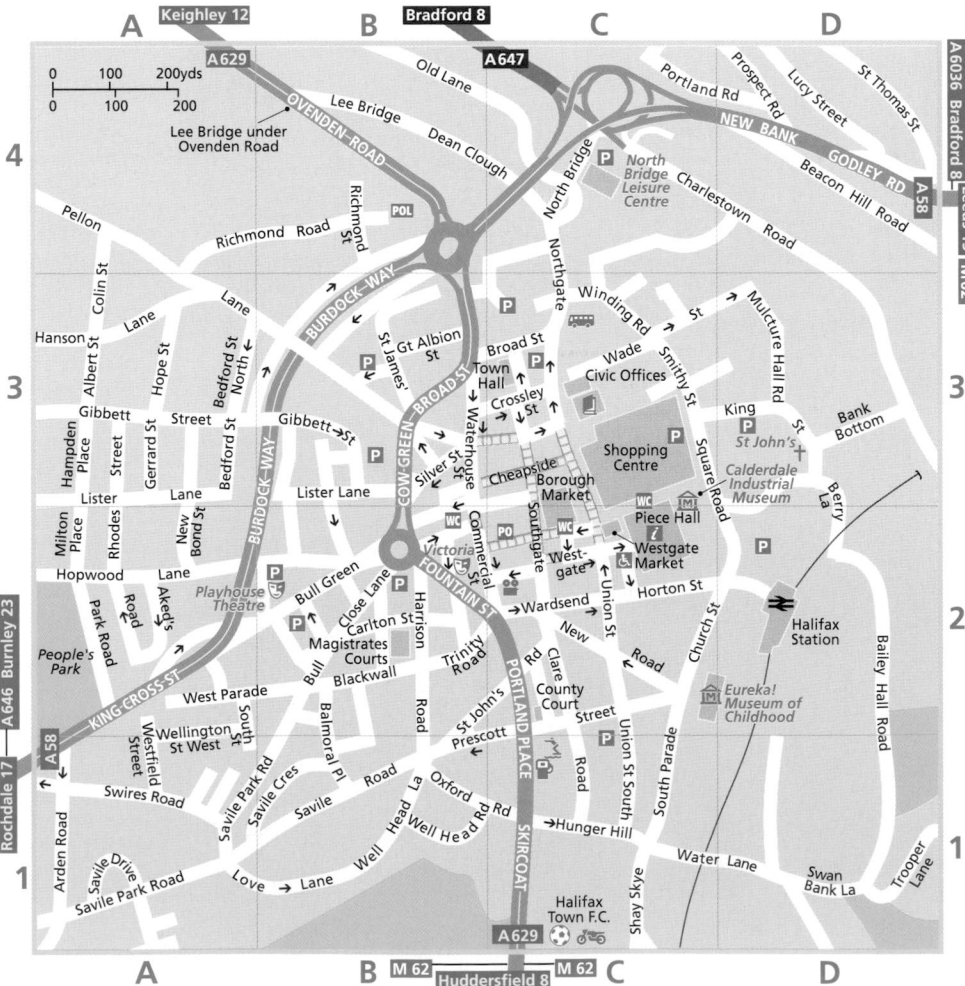

HARROGATE

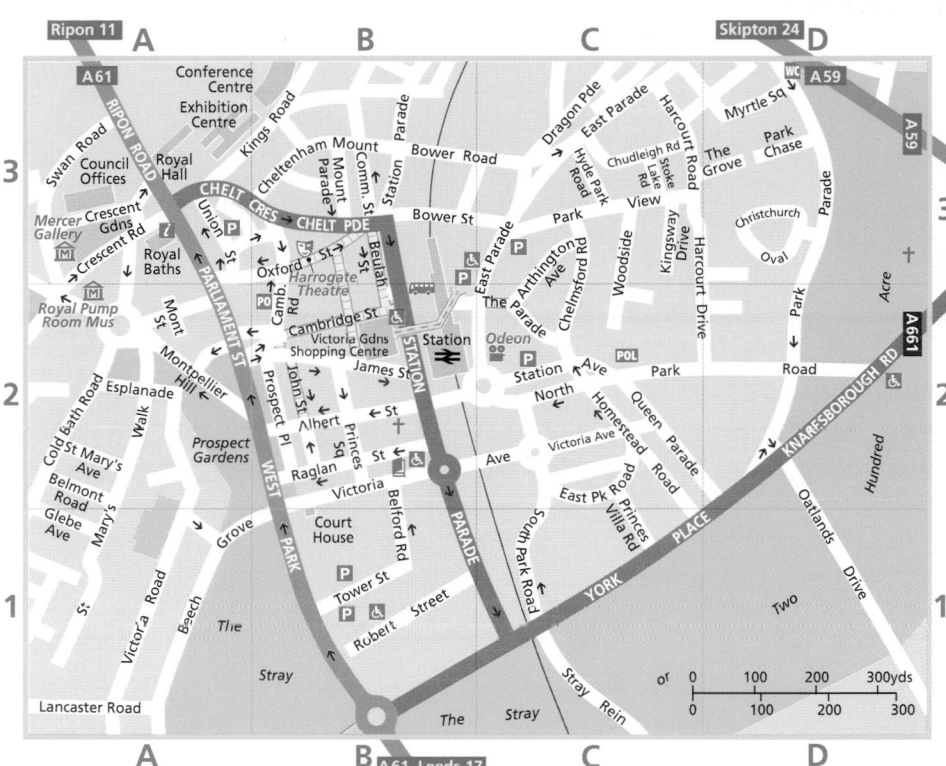

HEREFORD

TOWN PLANS

HASTINGS

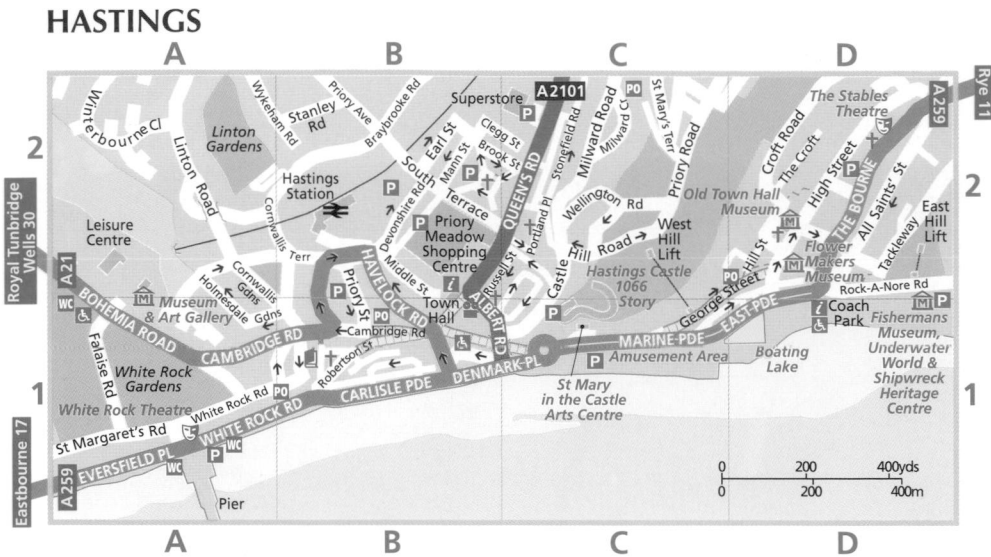

HAWES

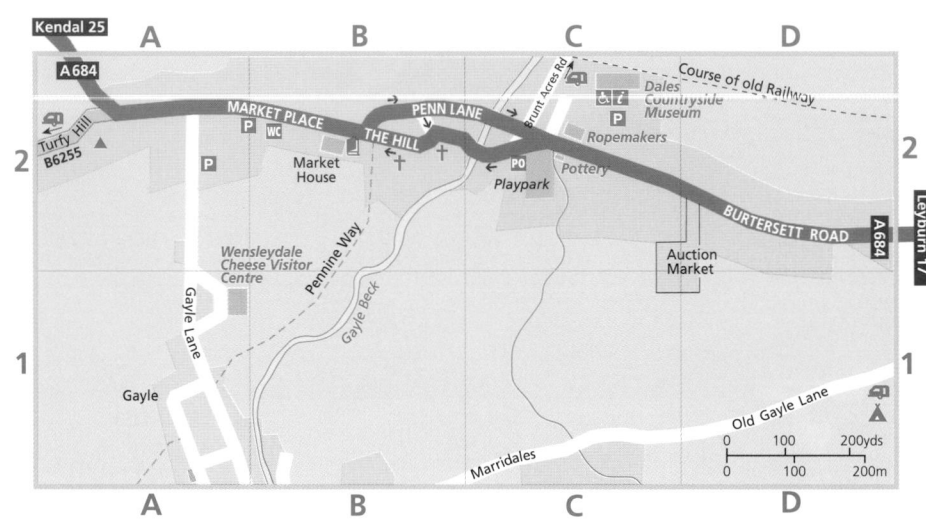

HORSHAM

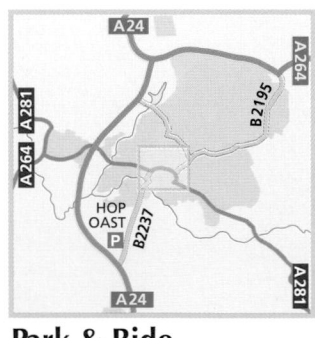

Park & Ride

HUDDERSFIELD

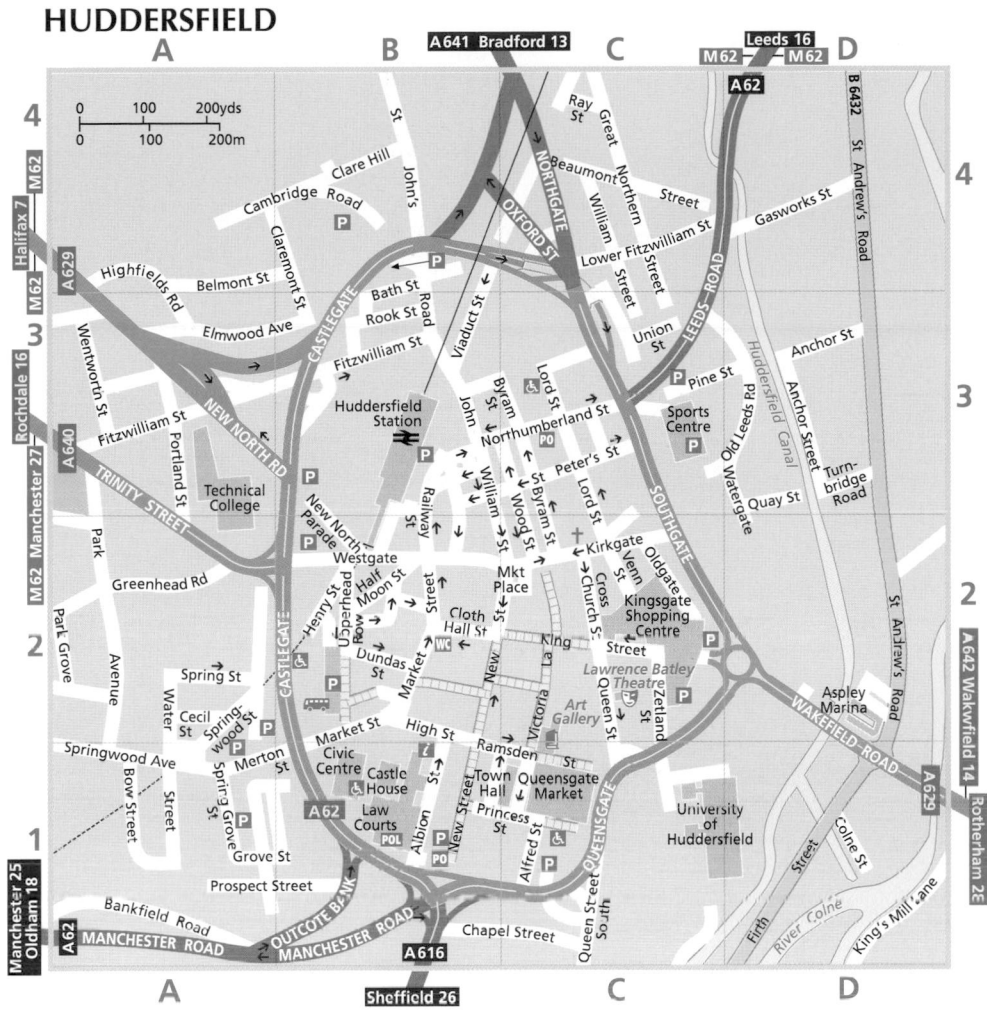

TOWN PLANS

HUNTINGDON

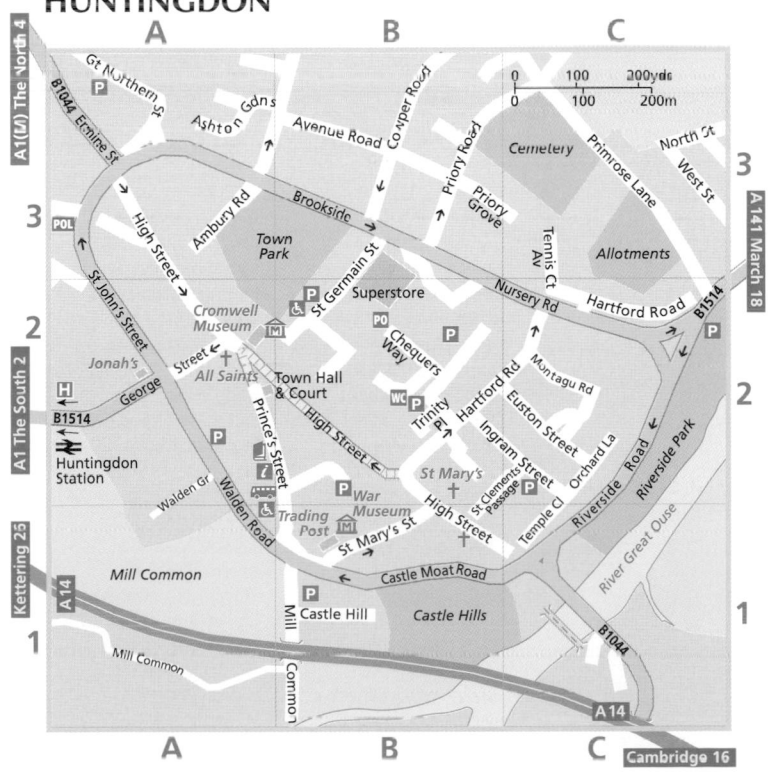

INVERNESS

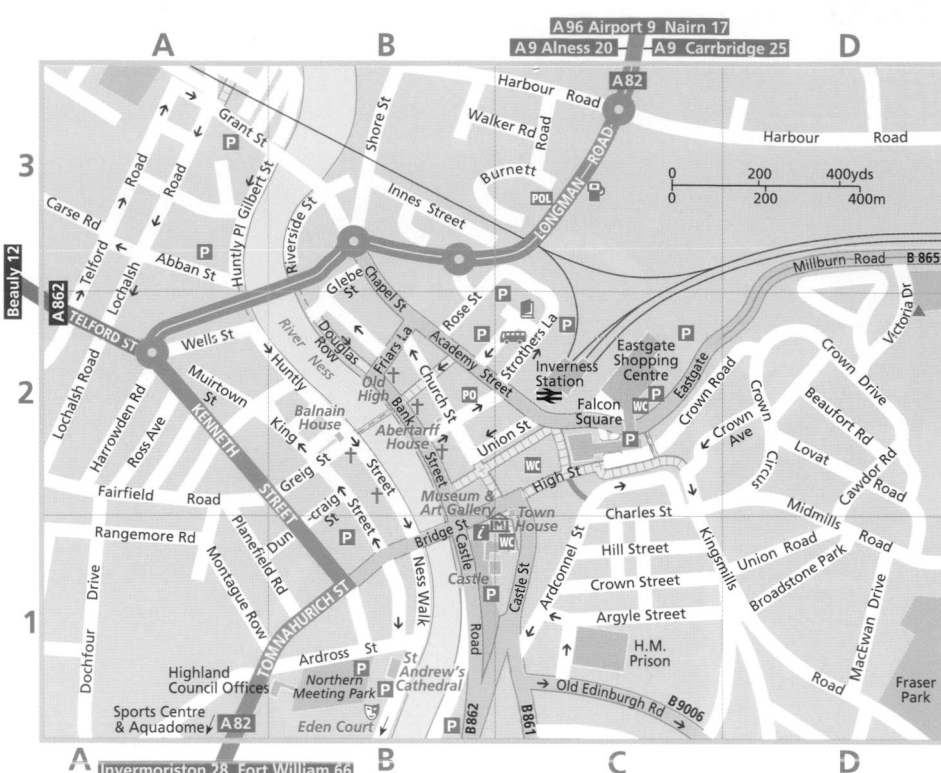

IPSWICH

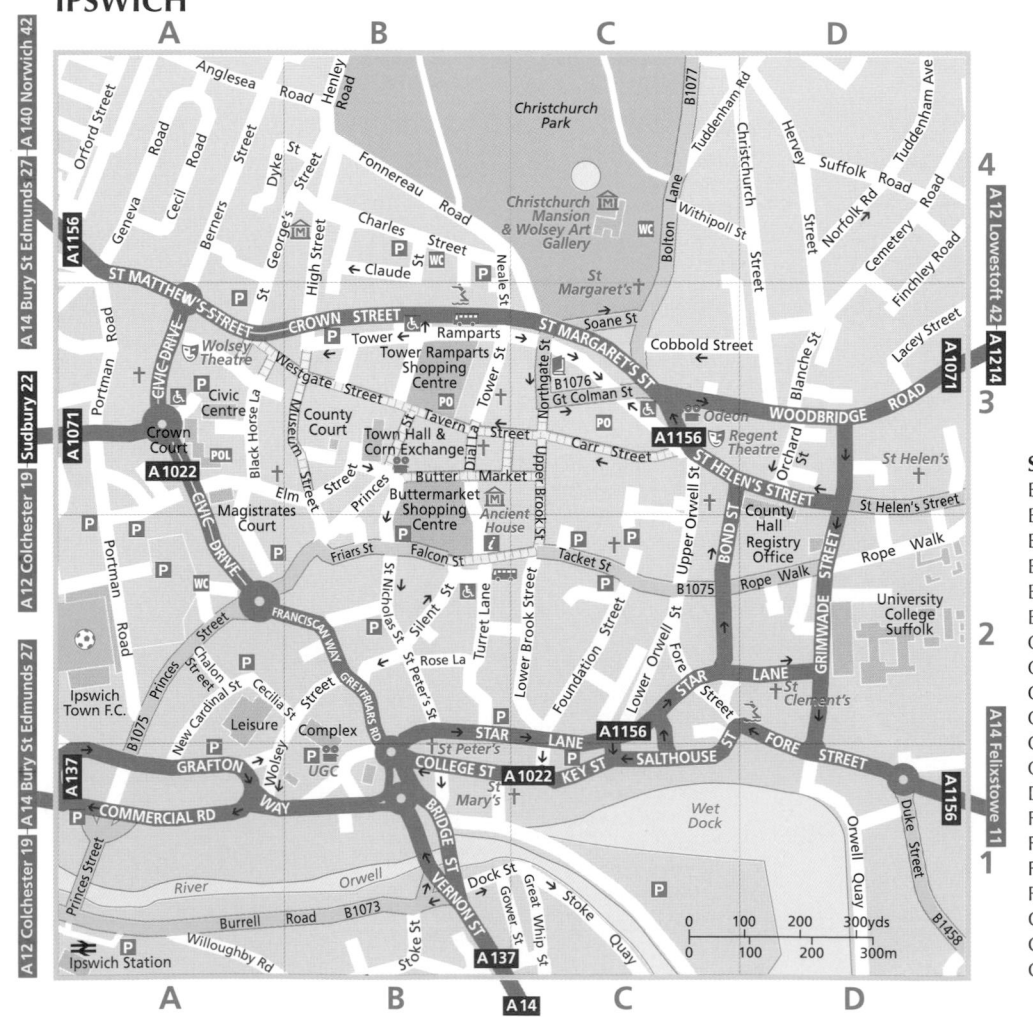

Park & Ride

KESWICK

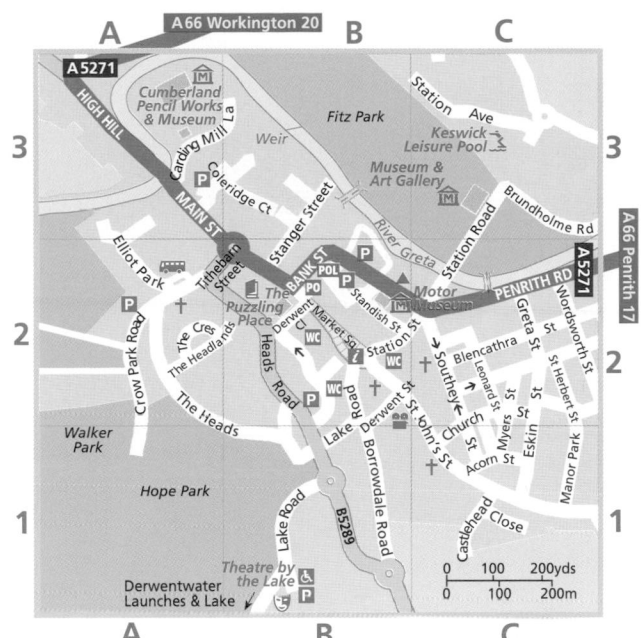

KINGSTON–UPON–THAMES

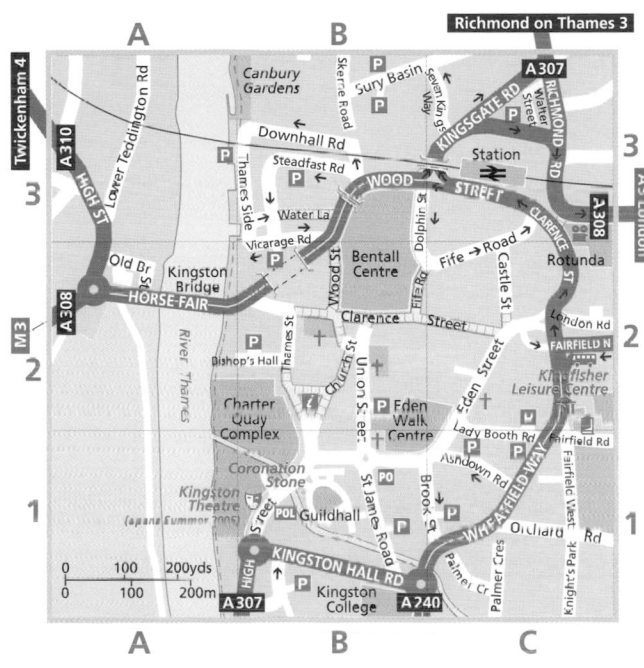

LAUNCESTON

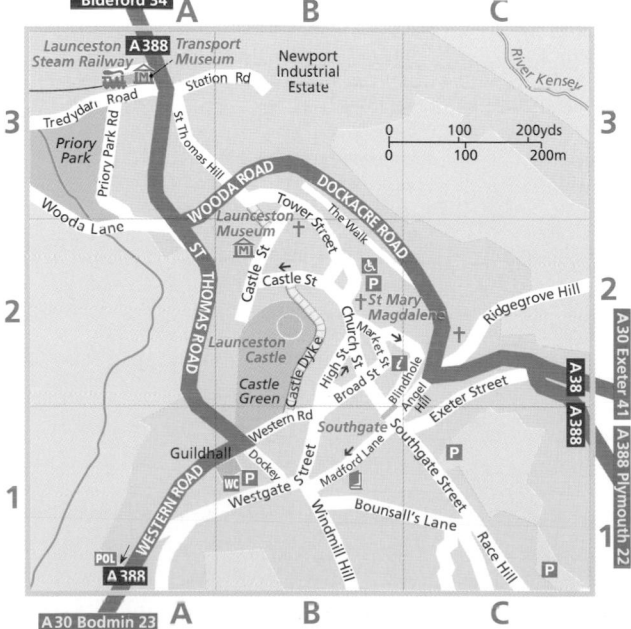

TOWN PLANS

KIDDERMINSTER

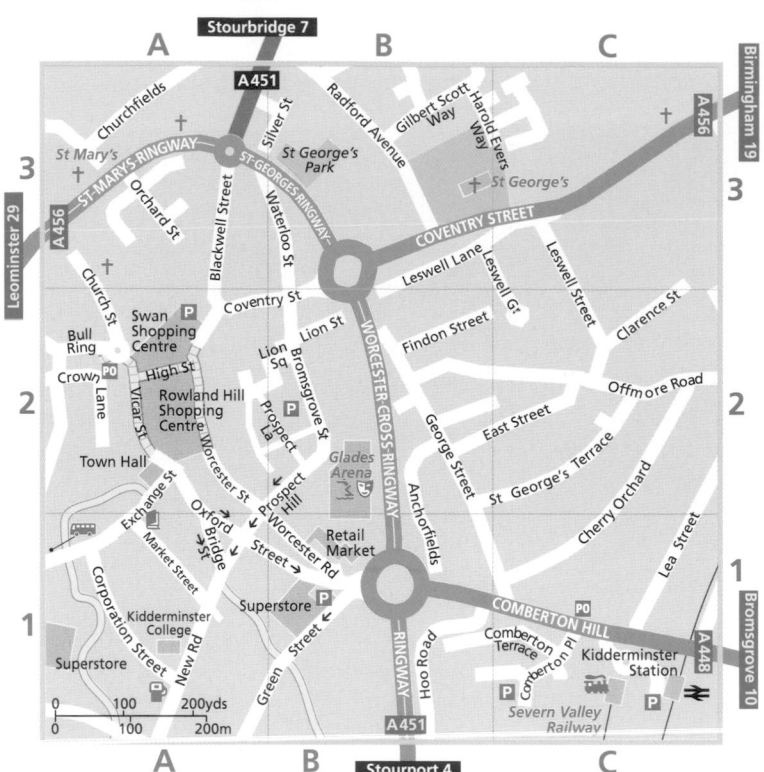

KINGS LYNN

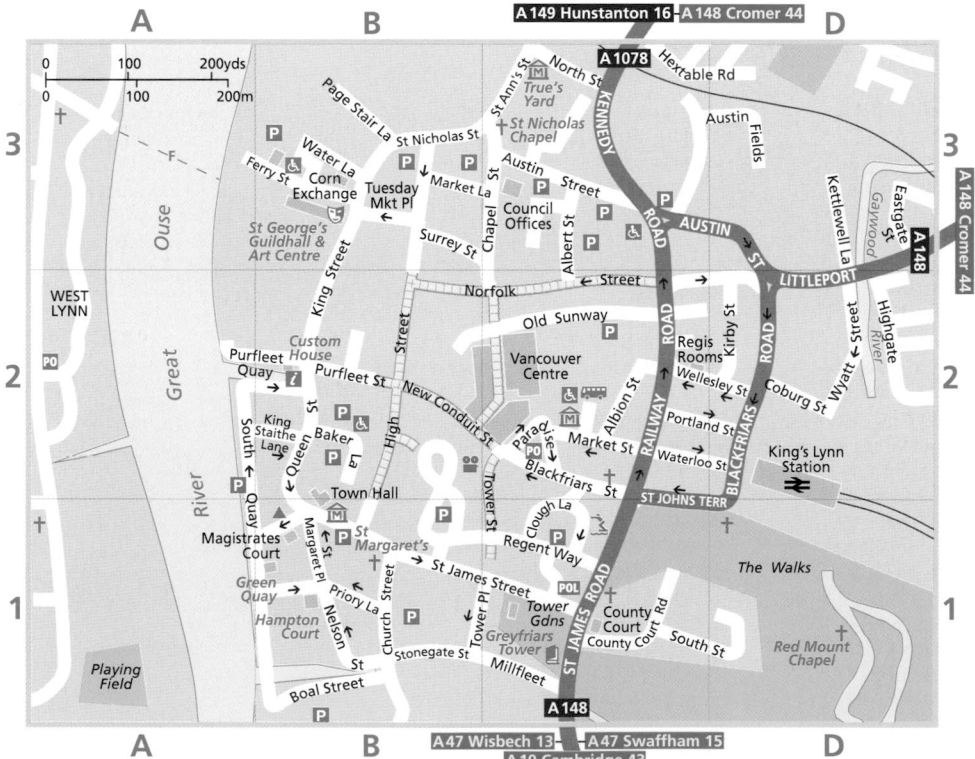

KINGSTON–UPON–HULL

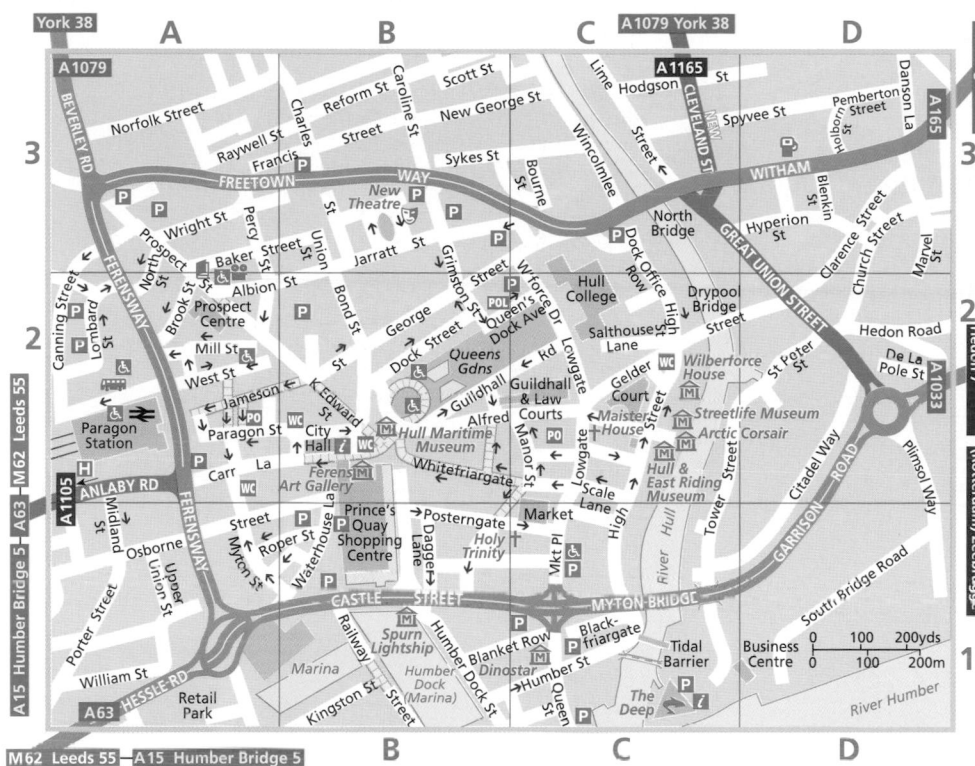

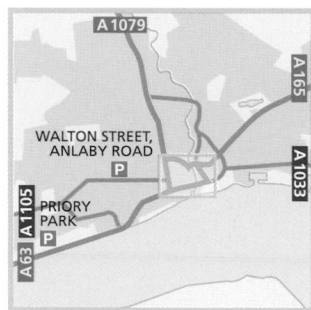

Park & Ride

Park & Ride index

Guildhall Road B2	Paragon Street A2
Hessle Road A1	Percy Street A3
High Street C1	Porter Street A1
Humber Dock Street B1	Posterngate B1
Humber Street C1	Prospect Street A3
Hyperion Street D3	Railway Street B1
Jameson Street A2	Reform Street B3
Jarratt Street B3	Salthouse Lane C2
King Edward Street B2	Spyvee Street D3
Lime Street C3	Sykes Street B3
Lombard Street A2	Tower Street C1–C2
Lowgate C2	Waterhouse Lane B1
Manor Street C2	West Street A2
Midland Street A1	Whitefriargate B2
Myton Bridge C1	Wincolmlee C3
New Cleveland	Witham D3
Street C3	Wright Street A3
Norfolk Street A3	
Osborne Street A1	

STREET INDEX

Alfred Gelder Street C2	Bond Street B2	Church Street D3	Ferensway A2
Anlaby Road A2	Canning Street A2	Citadel Way D1-D2	Freetown Way A3
Baker Street A3	Caroline Street B3	Clarence Street D3	Garrison Road D1
Beverley Road A3	Carr Lane A2	Dagger Lane B1	George Street B2
Blackfriargate C1	Castle Street B1	Dock Office Row C3	Great Union Street D2
	Charles Street B3	Dock Street B2	Grimston Street B3

ROYAL LEAMINGTON SPA

STREET INDEX

Abbotts Street C1	Grove Street A3	Priory Terrace C1
Adelaide Road B2	Guy Place East C3	Regent Grove C2
Albany Terrace A3	Guy Place West C3	Regent Place C1
Alveston Place C3	Guy Street C3	Regent Street A2–C2
Archery Road A1	Hall Road B3	Rosefield Place C2
Augusta Place B2	Hamilton Terrace C2	Rosefield Street C2
Avenue Road A1–B1	Holly Walk C2	Rugby Road A3
Bath Place C1	Hyde Place A2	Russell Street B3
Beauchamp Hill A3	John Street B2	Satchwell Court C2
Bedford Place B2	Kenilworth Road B3	Smith Street C1
Bedford Street B2	Kenilworth Street C3	Spencer Yard C1
Brandon Parade C2	Lansdowne Road C3	St Peter's Road B2
Chandos Street C3	Lansdowne Street C3	Station Approach B1
Chapel Street C1	Livery Street C2	Stratharn Road A3
Church Hill A2	Lower Avenue C1	Swan Street C3
Church Street C1	Mill Road C1	Tavistock Street B3
Church Terrace C1	Mill Street C1	Union Road A3
Clarendon Avenue	Milverton Hill A2	Upper Grove Street
B3–C3	Milverton Terrace A2	A3
Clarendon Crescent A3	Morton Street C3	Victoria Road A1
Clarendon Place B3	New Brook Street A2	Victoria Street A1
Clarendon Square B3	Newbold Street C2	Warwick Place A3
Clarendon Street C3	Newbold Terrace C2	Warwick Street B3
Clinton Street C1	Oxford Row C3	Warwick Terrace A3
Cross Street C3	Oxford Street C3	Windsor Place B3
Dale Street B3	Parade B2–C1	Windsor Street B3
Dormer Place B2	Park Drive A1	Wood Street C2
Euston Place C2	Park Street C3	Woodbine Street A2
George Street C1	Portland Place A2–B2	York Road B1
Gloucester Street C1	Portland Street B2	
	Powers Court B3	

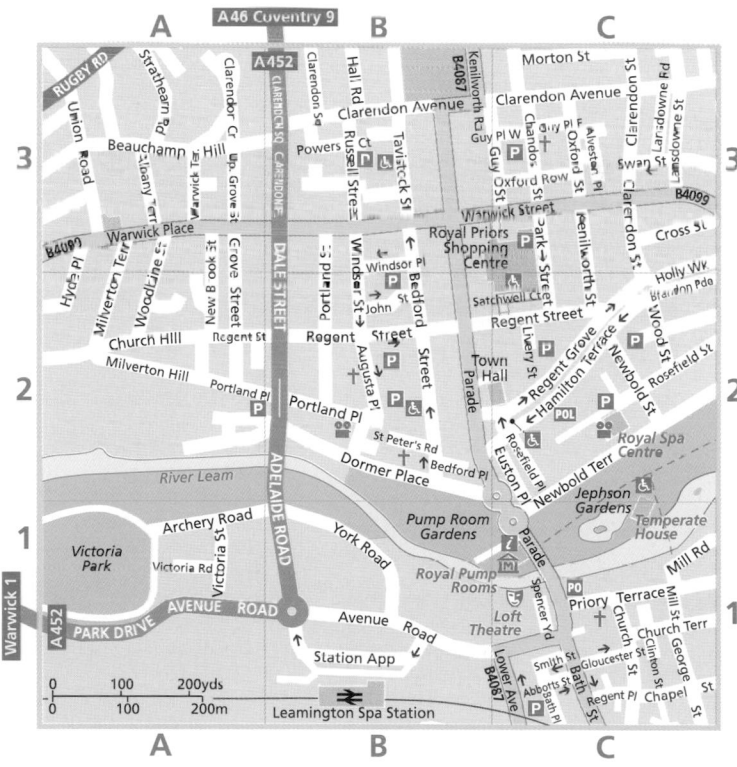

LEEDS

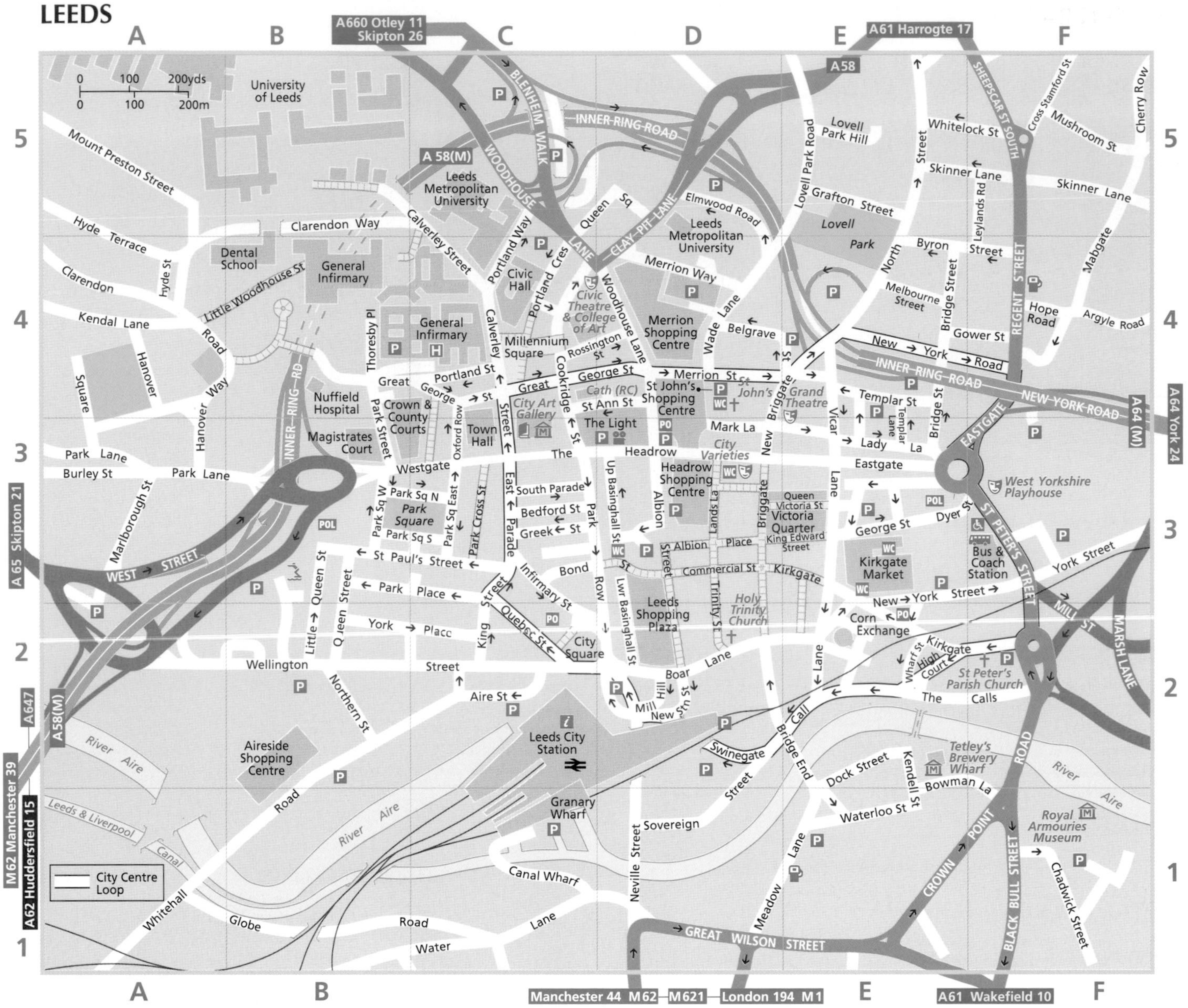

A660 Otley 11
Skipton 26

A61 Harrogte 17

A58

University of Leeds

INNER-RING-ROAD

0 100 200yds
0 100 200m

Mount Preston Street

Leeds Metropolitan University

BLENHEIM WALK

WOODHOUSE

A 58(M)

Whitelock St

Cross Stamford St

Mushroom St

Cherry Row

Hyde Terrace

Clarendon Way

Calverley Street

Portland Way

Queen Sq

Elmwood Road

Leeds Metropolitan University

Lovell Park Road

Lovell Park Hill

Skinner Lane

Leylands Rd

Skinner Lane

Mabgate

Clarendon

Dental School

General Infirmary

Little Woodhouse St

Portland pard Cres

Civic Hall

CLAY-PIT-LANE

Merrion Way

Lovell Park

North

Byron

Street

Melbourne Street

Bridge Street

Gower St

Regent Street

Hope Road

Argyle Road

Kendal Lane

Hanover Way

Thoresby Pl

General Infirmary

Calverley

Millennium Square

Rossington St

Merrion Shopping Centre

Wade Lane

Belgrave

New → York → Road

INNER-RING-ROAD

NEW-YORK-ROAD

A64 (M) York 24

Park Lane

Burley St

Park Lane

Nuffield Hospital

Great George St

Portland St

Great George St

Cookridge

George St

Cath (RC)

St Ann St

Merrion St

St John's Shopping Centre

John's

Mark La

Grand Theatre

Templar St

Templar La

City Art Gallery

Town Hall

Oxford Row

The

South Parade

The Headrow

Headrow

Headrow Shopping Centre

City Varieties

Eastgate

EASTGATE

West Yorkshire Playhouse

Marlborough Street

INNER-RING-RD

Magistrates Court

Crown & County Courts

Westgate

Park Sq W

Park Square

Park Sq N

East Parade

Park Cross St

Bedford St

Greek

Up Basinghall St

Albion

Lady

Lane

Briggate

Queen Victoria St

Victoria Quarter

George St

Dyer

POL

St Peter's Street

York Street

WEST STREET

Park Sq S

Greek

Park

King Edward Street

Kirkgate Market

Bus & Coach Station

A65 Skipton 21

St Paul's Street

Park Place

Infirmary St

Bond

Row

Lwr Basinghall St

Commercial St

Kirkgate

New → York Street

MILL ST

MARSH LANE

A647

A58(M)

Queen Street

York Place

King Street

Quebec St

PO

Leeds Shopping Plaza

Holy Trinity Church

Corn Exchange

High Court

Kirkgate

St Peter's Parish Church

The Calls

Wellington Street

Northern St

Aire St

City Square

Boar

Lane

Mill Hill

New

Wharf St

Swinegate

Bridge End

The Calls

Aireside Shopping Centre

River Aire

Leeds City Station

Leeds & Liverpool Canal

Granary Wharf

Neville Street

Sovereign

Swinegate

Bridge End

Call

Dock Street

Kendell St

Bowman La

Tetley's Brewery Wharf

River Aire

A62 Huddersfield 15

M62 Manchester 39

Whitehall Road

Globe Road

Water

Canal Wharf

Meadow Lane

Great Wilson Street

Waterloo St

CROWN POINT ROAD

BLACK BULL STREET

Royal Armouries Museum

Chadwick Street

City Centre Loop

Manchester 44 M62 — M621 — London 194 M1

A61 Wakefield 10

Park & Ride

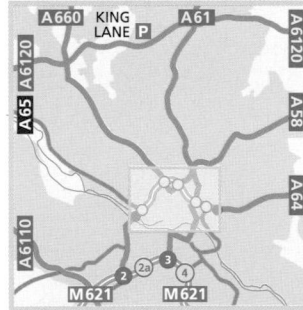

A660 KING LANE

A61

A6120

A65

A6120

A58

A64

A6110

M621 M621

STREET INDEX

Aire Street C2
Albion Place D3
Albion Street D3
Bedford Street C3
Belgrave Street D4
Black Bull Street F1
Blenheim Walk C5
Boar Lane D2
Bond Street C3
Bowman Lane E2
Bridge End E2
Bridge Street E4
Briggate D3

Byron Street E4
Call Lane E2
Calverley Street C4
Chadwick Street F1
City Square C2
Clarendon Road A4
Clarendon Way B5
Clay Pit Lane D5
Commercial Street D3
Cookridge Street C4
Cross Stamford Street F5
Crown Point Road E1
Dock Street E2
Dyer Street E3

East Parade C3
Eastgate E3
Elmwood Road D5
George Street E3
Globe Road B1
Gower Street F4
Grafton Street E5
Great George Street C4
Great Wilson Street D1
Greek Street C3
Hanover Square A4
Hanover Way A3
High Court E2
Hope Road F4
Hyde Terrace A5
Infirmary Street C3
Inner Ring Road B3–E4
Kendal Lane A4
Kendell Street E2
King Edward Street E3
King Street C2
Kirkgate E3
Lady Lane E3
Lands Lane D3
Leylands Road F5

Little Queen Street B2
Little Woodhouse Street B4
Lovell Park Road E5
Lower Basinghall Street D2
Mabgate F4
Mark Lane D3
Marlborough Street A3
Marsh Lane F2
Meadow Lane D1
Melbourne Street E4
Merrion Street D4
Merrion Way D4
Mill Hill D2
Mill Street F2
Mushroom Street F5
Neville Street D1
New Briggate D3
New Station Street D2
New York Road E4–F4
New York Street E3
North Street E5
Northern Street B2
Oxford Row C3

Park Cross Street C3
Park Lane A3
Park Place B3
Park Row C3
Park Square East C3
Park Square North B3
Park Square South B3
Park Square West B3
Park Street B3
Portland Crescent C4
Portland Street C4
Portland Way C4
Quebec Street C2
Queen Square D5
Queen Street B2
Queen Victoria Street E3
Regent Street F4
Rossington Street C4
St Ann Street D4
St Paul's Street B3
St Peter's Street F3
Sheepscar Street South F5
Skinner Lane E5
South Parade C3

Sovereign Street D1
Swinegate D2
Templar Lane E3
Templar Street E4
The Calls E2
The Headrow D3
Thoresby Place B4
Trinity Street D3
Upper Basinghall Street D3
Vicar Lane E3
Wade Lane D4
Water Lane C1
Waterloo Street E1
Wellington Street B2
Westgate C3
West Street A3
Wharf Street E2
Whitehall Road A1
Whitelock Street E5
Woodhouse Lane C5
York Place B2
York Street F3

LEICESTER

Park & Ride

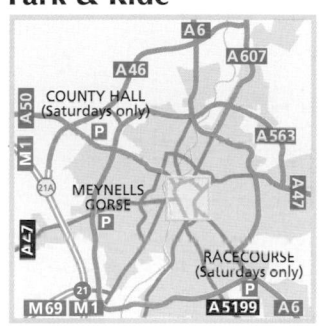

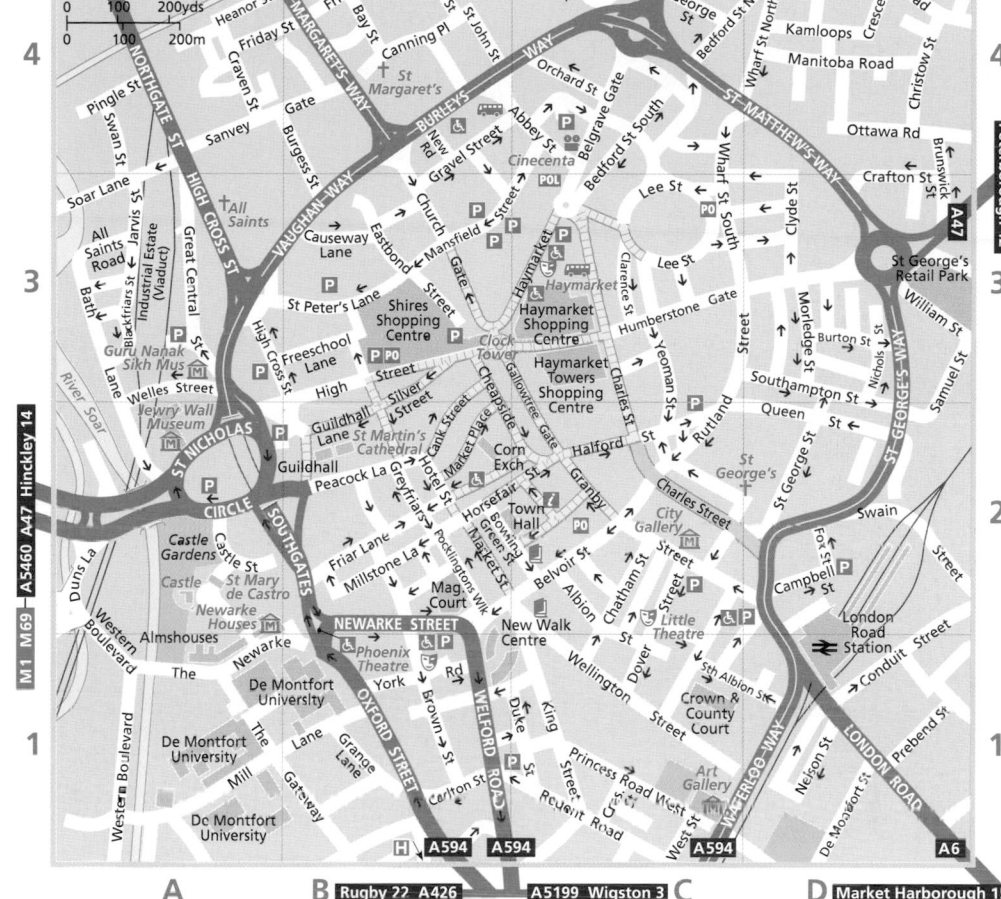

LINCOLN

TOWN PLANS

LEWES

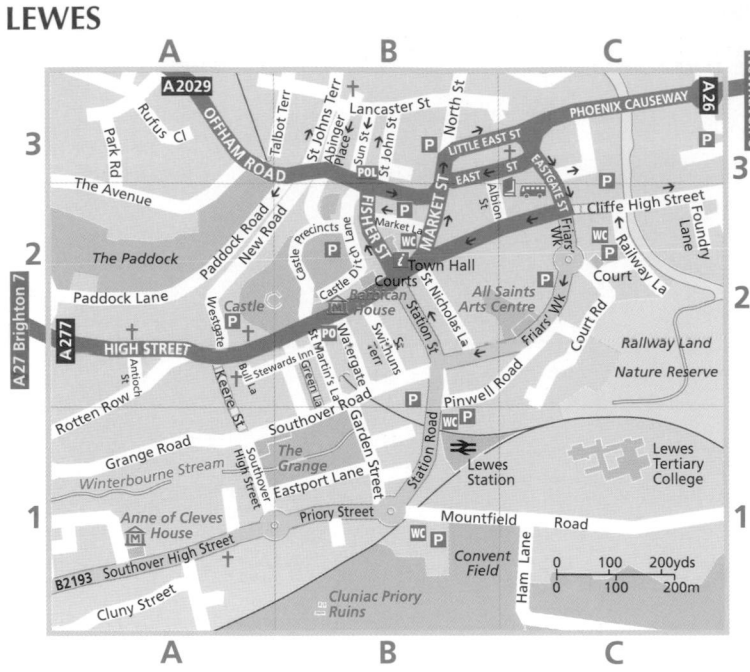

LICHFIELD

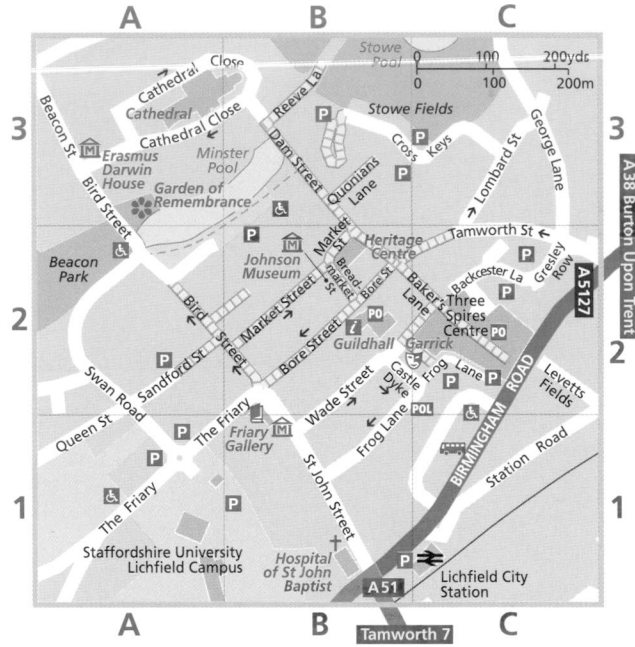

LUDLOW

LIVERPOOL

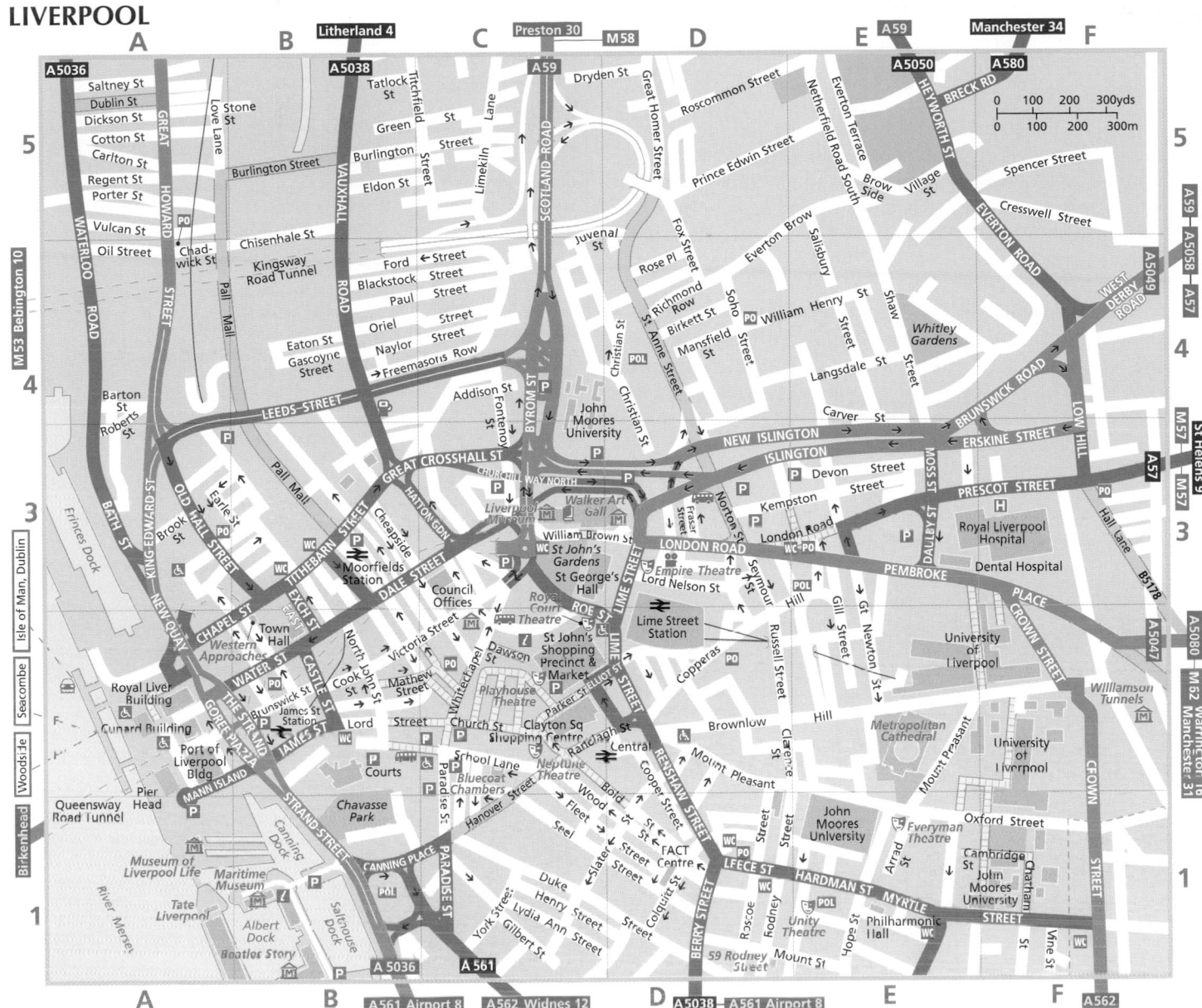

STREET INDEX

Addison Street C4
Arrad Street E1
Barton Street A4
Bath Street A3
Berry Street D1
Birkett Street D4
Blackstock Street B4
Bold Street D1
Breck Road E5
Brook Street A3
Brownlow Hill D2–E2
Brow Side E5
Brunswick Road E3–F4
Brunswick Street B2
Burlington Street B5
Byrom Street C4
Cambridge Street F1
Canning Place B1
Carlton Street A5
Carver Street E4
Castle Street B2
Chadwick Street A4
Chapel Street A2
Chatham Street F1
Cheapside B3
Chisenhale Street B5
Christian Street D4

Churchill Way North C3
Church Street C2
Clarence Street D2
Colquitt Street D1
Cook Street B2
Cooper Street D2
Copperas Hill D2
Cotton Street A5
Cresswell Street F5
Crown Street F1
Dale Street B3
Daulby Street E3
Dawson Street C2
Devon Street E3
Dickson Street A5
Dryden Street C5
Dublin Street A5
Duke Street C1
Earle Street A3
Eaton Street B4
Eldon Street B5
Elliot Street C2
Erskine Street F3
Everton Brow D4
Everton Road F4
Everton Terrace E5
Exchange Street East B3
Fleet Street C1

Fontenoy Street C4
Ford Street B4
Fox Street D5
Fraser Street D3
Freemasons Row B4
Gascoyne Street B4
Gilbert Street C1
Gill Street E2
Goree Piazza A2
Great Crosshall
  Street C3
Great Homer Street D5
Great Howard Street A4
Great Newton Street E2
Green Street B5
Hall Lane F3
Hanover Street C1
Hardman Street E1
Hatton Garden C3
Henry Street C1
Heyworth Street E5
Hope Street E1
Islington D3
James Street B2
Juvenal Street C5
Kempston Street E3
King Edward Street A3
Kingsway Rd Tunnel A4

Langsdale Street F4
Leece Street D1
Leeds Street B4
Limekiln Lane C5
Lime Street D2
London Road D3
Lord Nelson Street D3
Lord Street B2
Love Lane A5
Low Hill F4
Mann Island A2
Mansfield Street D4
Mathew Street B2
Moss Street E3
Mount Pleasant E2
Mount Street E1
Myrtle Street E1
Naylor Street B4
Netherfield Road South
  E5
New Islington D3
New Quay A2
North John Street B2
Norton Street D3
Oil Street A4
Old Hall Street A3
Oriel Street B4
Oxford Street F1

Pall Mall A5–B3
Paradise Street C1
Parker Street C2
Paul Street B4
Pembroke Place E3
Porter Street A5
Prescot Street F3
Prince Edwin Street D5
Queensway Road Tunnel
  A2
Ranelagh Street C2
Regent Street A5
Renshaw Street D2
Richmond Row D4
Roberts Street A3
Rodney Street D1
Roe Street C2
Roscoe Street D1
Roscommon Street D5
Rose Place D4
Russell Street D2
St Anne Street D4
Salisbury Street E4
Saltney Street A5
School Lane C2
Scotland Road C5
Seel Street C1
Seymour Street D3

Shaw Street E4
Slater Street C1
Soho Street D4
Spencer Street F5
Stone Street B5
Strand Street B1
Tatlock Street B5
The Strand B2
Titchfield Street C5
Tithebarn Street B3
Vauxhall Road B5
Victoria Street B2
Village Street E5
Vine Street F1
Vulcan Street A5
Waterloo Road A5
Water Street B2
West Derby Road F4
Whitechapel C2
William Brown
  Street C3
William Henry Street E4
Wood Street C1
York Street C1

Central London

Covering just 3km² (1sq mile) north of the river, the City of London is the capital's legal and commercial hub. It still has many streets that follow medieval courses, and Roman gateways live on in street names such as Moorgate and Ludgate. The City skyline is graced by the dome of St Paul's Cathedral and dozens of distinctive churches, such as Fleet Street's St Bride's. During the 18th and 19th centuries, elegant residential areas such as Bloomsbury, Belgravia and Marylebone spread north and west of the City. The green expanses of Hyde Park, Kensington Gardens and Regent's Park provide spacious playgrounds for Londoners; the more compact Primrose Hill has a fine view over the capital.

The map reference in bold after each entry identifies the grid square in which it appears on **pages 352–353**.

Art galleries & museums

Bramah Tea & Coffee Museum **E2**
(020) 7378 0222
Britain at War Museum **F2** (020) 7403 3171
British Museum **D3**
(020) 7636 1555
British Museum of Natural History **A1**
(020) 7938 9123
Geffrye Museum **F4**
(020) 7739 9893
Imperial War Museum **E2**
(020) 7416 5000
Museum of London **E3**
(020) 7600 3699
Museum of the Order of St John **E3**
(020) 7324 4005
National Army Museum **B1** (020) 7730 0717
National Gallery **D2**
(020) 7747 2885
National Portrait Gallery **D3** (020) 7306 0055

Science Museum **B2**
(020) 7938 8080
Serpentine Gallery **B2**
(020) 7402 6075
Tate Britain **D1**
(020) 7887 8000
Tate Modern **E2**
(020) 7887 8008
Victoria & Albert Museum **B1** (020) 7942 2000
Wallace Collection **C3**
(020) 7935 0687
White Cube Gallery **F4**
(020) 7930 5373

Cinemas

Barbican **E3**
(020) 7638 8891
Chelsea Cinema **B1**
(020) 7351 3742
Screen on Baker Street **B3**
(020) 7935 2772
UGC Chelsea **B1**
0870 907 0710

City of contrasts *The splendidly gothic Houses of Parliament lie opposite the modern grace of the London Eye. New attractions on the river include Tate Modern and the Millennium Bridge.*

UGC Fulham Road **B1**
0870 907 0711
Odeon Marble Arch **B3**
0870 505 0007
Renoir **D4**
(020) 7837 8402
(see West End pp.254–255 for more cinemas)

Shopping

Brompton Road **B1/2**
Columbia Road **F4**
Covent Garden **D3**
Fulham Road **B1**
Kensington High Street **A2**
Kings Road, Chelsea **B1**
Knightsbridge **B2**
Marylebone High Street **C3**
New Bond Street **C3**
Oxford Street **C3**
Regent Street **C3**
Tottenham Court Road **C3**
Upper Street **E4**

Theatres

Apollo Victoria **C1**
0870 400 0650
Barbican Centre **E3**
(020) 7638 8891
Cochrane **D3**
(020) 7269 1606
Globe **E2**
(020) 7401 9919

Mermaid **E3**
(020) 7236 1919
Open Air **C4**
(020) 7486 2431
Royal Court **C1**
(020) 7565 5000
Sadler's Wells **E4**
(020) 7863 8000
Shaw **D4**
(020) 7387 6864
Victoria Palace **C2**
(020) 7834 1317
(see West End pp.354–355 for more theatres)

Parks & gardens

Green Park **C2**
Hyde Park **B2**
Kensington Gardens **A2**
Regent's Park **B4–C4**
St James's Park **D2**

Other places of interest

Dickens House **D4**
(020) 7405 2127
London Eye **D2**
0870 500 0600
HMS Belfast **F2**
(020) 7940 6300
London Dungeon **F2**
(020) 7403 7221
London Zoo **B4–C4**
(020) 7722 3333
Madame Tussaud's **C3**
0870 400 3000
The Monument **F3**
(020) 7626 2717
The Oval **D1**
(020) 7582 6660
Royal Hospital, Chelsea **C1** (020) 7881 5204
St Paul's Cathedral **E3**
(020) 7236 4128
Southwark Cathedral **E2**
(020) 7367 6700
Wesley's House **E4**
(020) 7253 2262

Street index

WHERE TO PARK

Bayswater
Arthur Court,
    Queensway
    (020) 7229 9381
Porchester Terrace
    (020) 7221 8020
Bloomsbury
Adeline Place YMCA,
    Great Russell Street
    (020) 7637 0964
Brunswick Centre
    (020) 7278 9792
Museum Street
    (020) 7836 2039
Woburn Place
    (020) 7837 6101
City
Barbican Centre
    (020) 7382 7071
Bell Wharf Lane,
    Upper Thames Street
    (020) 7248 6089
Clere Street
    (020) 7490 2574
Finsbury Square
    (020) 7588 5545
Paul Street
    (020) 7613 3639
Tabernacle Street,
    0870 606 7050
Clerkenwell
Aldersgate
    0870 606 7050
Bowling Green Lane
    (020) 7278 1745
Hatton Garden
    0870 606 7050
Skinner Street
    (020) 7837 4645
Smithfield Market
    (020) 7236 4547
Holborn
Marchmont Street
    (020) 7278 9792
Museum Street
    (020) 72427577
Parker Street
    0870 242 7144
Kensington
Kensington Gardens
    (020) 7229 9381

Young Street
    (020) 7938 1101
Knightsbridge
Pavilion Road
    (020) 7589 0401
Cadogan Place
    (020) 7584 5667
Lancelot Place
    (020) 7584 1144
London Bridge
Kipling Street
    (020) 7378 1147
Maida Vale
Lanark Road
    (020) 7289 7729
Marylebone
Burwood Place
    (020) 7289 7729
Bryanston Street (020)
    7499 7050 ext 2313
Crawford Street
    (020) 7706 2273
Portman Square
    0870 544 8259
Shouldham Street
    0870 606 7050
Welbeck Street
    (020) 7486 2296
Weymouth Mews
    (020) 7636 6313
Mayfair
Carrington Street
    (020) 7491 4661
Chesterfield Gardens
    (020) 7499 5621
Newington
Elephant & Castle
    (020) 7703 9035
Regents Park
Cleveland Street
    0870 606 7050
Shoreditch
Great Eastern Street
    (020) 7739 2508
Southwark
Library Street
    (020) 7633 9445
Westminster
Semley Place, Victoria
    0870 242 7144

CENTRAL LONDON

A41 M1 The North · A1   M1 The North A1 Hatfield   Watford   A1(M) Hatfield · A1 · A400   A503 NE London   A503

A   B   C

A5

4

Kilburn High Road
Brondesbury Road
Brondesbury Villas
Kilburn Park
Greville Place
Carlton
Carlton Vale
KILBURN HIGH RD
Loudoun Road
Abbey Road
Hill
Barracks
St John's Wood
Acacia Road
Avenue Road
B425
ALBERT ROAD
A5205
Grand Union Canal
Regent's Park Zoo
Regent's Park
Outer Circle
A4201
Park Village East
Mornington Crescent
Crowndale Rd
REGENTS PARK
HAMPSTEAD
Carlton Vale
MAIDA VALE
Paddington Recreation Ground
MAIDA VALE
Randolph
Hamilton
FINCHLEY ROAD
Hospital of St John & St Elizabeth
St John's Wood Grounds
Circus Rd
St John's Wood Church
London Central Mosque
Open Air Theatre
Queen Mary's Gardens
PRINCE
Barracks
Robert St
Stanhope St
N Gower St
Euston Station
Cardington St
A4200
Ferhead Road
Elgin Avenue
Maida Vale
Hall Road
Terrace
Lord's
A5205
Regent's College
A41
Outer Circle
Outer Circle
Portland Street
Great
Warren St
EUSTON ROAD
A400

3

Westbourne Park Road
Chippenham
Elgin
Shirland
Warwick
Lauderdale Road
Avenue
Sutherland
HARROW ROAD
Grand Union Canal
WESTWAY
Blomfield Rd
Little Venice
PADDINGTON
Marylebone Station
MARYLEBONE ROAD
A41
BAKER
Madame Tussaud's & Planetarium
Baker Street
Regents Park
A501
Wallace Collection
MARYLEBONE
Devonshire St
Weymouth St
Great Portland Street
Cleveland Street
Telecom Tower
Middlesex Hosp
Pollock's Toy Museum
Goodge St
Eastcastle St
STREET
BBC
All Souls
Wells

Westbourne Park Road
Talbot Road
Ledbury Grove
A4206
WESTBOURNE GROVE
BAYSWATER
Gloucester Terr
Westbourne Terrace
Royal Oak
Porchester Rd
BISHOP'S
EASTBOURNE
Paddington Station
Paddington
St Mary's Hospital
PRAED ST
SUSSEX GARDENS
EDGWARE ROAD
George Street
Upper Berkeley St
SEYMOUR ST
PORTMAN SQUARE
WIGMORE STREET
OXFORD
Oxford Circus
REGENT STREET
New Bond St
Old Bond St
Broadwick

2

Westbourne Grove
Chepstow Villas
Hereford Road
Chepstow Road
Dawson Place
Bayswater
Queensway
PEMBRIDGE VILLAS
Inverness Terrace
Leinster Gdns
Craven Hill
Leinster Terr
BAYSWATER
A4209
Connaught Street
A402
Lancaster Gate
Marble Arch
Green St
Grosvenor Square
Brook Street
Grosvenor St
MAYFAIR
A4202
Mount Street
Charles St
PICCADILLY
ST JAMES
Kensington Park Rd
Notting Hill
NOTTING HILL GATE
A402
Palace Gardens Terrace
Kensington Palace Gardens
Kensington Palace
Kensington Gardens
Round Pond
Peter Pan's Statue
The Long Water
Hyde Park
PARK LANE
Curzon St
Green Park
St James's Palace
Pall Mall
Holland Park
Campden Hill Road
Hornton St
Kensington Church Street
A4204
Albert Memorial
Serpentine Gallery
Diana Memorial Fountain
The Serpentine
Queen Elizabeth Gate
Apsley House
Hyde Park Corner
Constitution Hill
Buckingham Palace
Royal Mews
Palace

2

Holland Park Theatre
Commonwealth Melbury Inst
Phillimore Gds
Kensington Town Hall
High St Kensington
KENSINGTON HIGH STREET
KENSINGTON
Allen Street
Victoria Road
Gloucester Road
Queens Gate
KENSINGTON ROAD
KENSINGTON GORE
KENSINGTON RD
Royal Albert Hall
Royal Geographical Society
Rutland Gate
KNIGHTSBRIDGE
A315
Knightsbridge
Hyde Park Barracks
Harrods
SLOANE STREET
Belgrave Square
GROSVENOR PL
A302
A4
Victoria
Victoria Palace
Apollo
Westminster Cathedral
A315
A3220
WARWICK GDS
Cornwall Gardens
Marloes Road
Royal College of Music
Science Museum
Natural History Museum
Victoria & Albert Museum
Brompton Oratory
BROMPTON ROAD
THURLOE PLACE
A4
A308
Walton Street
Pont Street
Cadogan Square
A3216
Cadogan La
Eaton Square
Eaton Place
BELGRAVIA
A3217
Victoria Station
Victoria Coach Stn
Passport Offices
BELGRAVE ROAD
A202

1

WARWICK ROAD
WEST CROMWELL ROAD
CROMWELL ROAD
EARL'S COURT
Earl's Court
Collingham Rd
Gloucester Road
Stanhope Gdns
Onslow Sq
South Kensington
SOUTH KENSINGTON
A4
Drayton
Sydney Street
Sloane Avenue
Michelin House
Sloane Square
A4
KING'S ROAD
Smith Street
LWR SLOANE ST
PIMLICO ROAD
Ebury
Eaton
Royal Court Theatre
S. Eaton Pl
St George's Drive
Alderney Street
Warwick Way
PIMLICO
M4 Hammersmith 1
A4
West Cromwell Road
WARWICK ROAD
Earl's Court Exhibition Centre
EARL'S COURT
The Boltons
Finborough Road
REDCLIFFE GARDENS
OLD BROMPTON ROAD
WEST CROMWELL ROAD
North End Road
Star Rd
West Brompton
Brompton Cemetery
A3218
WEST BROMPTON
A3220
A308
A3217
Chelsea & Westminster Hospital
Beaufort St
Church Street
Oakley Street
Flood Street
UGC
SOUTH KENSINGTON
Royal Marsden Hospital
Royal Brompton Hospital
CHELSEA
Fulham Road
Old Church Street
Physic Garden
Royal Hospital Chelsea
National Army Museum
CHELSEA EMBANKMENT
A3212
Chelsea Bridge
A3216
Ranelagh Gardens
Lupus Street
PIMLICO
Thames
GROSVEN
A3 G

A   B   C

A308   A308 Putney Br 2½   A24 Dorking

London Congestion Charges

Chargeable Area

For London route maps see pages 284–285 (North) and 286–287 (South)
For London West End map see pages 356–357
For London Docklands map see pages 360–361

Oxford Street where marked is closed,
except for buses and taxis, between 7am
and 7pm, Monday-Saturday

The West End

London's West End has several distinct areas. Piccadilly, home of the Ritz, is flanked by exclusive St James, with gentlemen's clubs and foreign embassies and elegant Mayfair. Soho lies north of Shaftesbury Avenue and Chinatown south; east are the shops, opera house and theatres of Covent Garden. From Admiralty Arch, The Mall leads to Buckingham Palace, the Queen's London home. Britain's Parliament building, the Palace of Westminster, with Big Ben, rises in majestic splendour by the Thames. Across the river at Waterloo is the South Bank Arts Centre, home to an entertainment complex including the Royal Festival Hall, the Royal National Theatre and the Hayward Gallery.

The map reference in bold after each entry identifies the grid square in which it appears on **pages 356–357.**

Art galleries & museums
Cabinet War Rooms **C1**
(020) 7930 6961
Courtauld Institute **E3**
(020) 7848 2777
Hayward Gallery **E2**
(020) 7960 5226
National Gallery **C3**
(020) 7747 2885
National Portrait Gallery
C3 (020) 7306 0055
Royal Academy of Arts **B3**
(020) 7300 8000

Cinemas
Curzon Soho **C4**
0871 871 0022
ICA **C2** (020) 7930 3647
IMAX **E2**
(020) 7902 1234
National Film Theatre **E2**
(020) 7928 3232
Odeon, Leicester Square
C3 0871 224 4007
Odeon Panton Street **C3**
0871 224 4007
Odeon, Wardour Street
C3 0871 224 4007
Odeon, West End **C3**
0871 224 4007
Other **C3**
(020) 7437 0757
Prince Charles **C3**
(020) 7437 7003
UCI Empire **C3**
0870 010 2030
UGC Haymarket **C3**
0871 200 2000
UGC Trocadero **C3**
(020) 7434 0032
Vue **C3** 0870 240 6020

Shopping
Charing Cross Road **C4**
Covent Garden **D4**
Gabriel's Wharf Market **F3**
Oxford Street **A4/B4**
Piccadilly **B3**
Regent Street **A4/B3**

Theatres
Adelphi **D3**
(020) 7344 0055
Albery **C3**
0870 060 6621
Aldwych **E4**
(020) 7379 3367
Apollo **C3**
(020) 7494 5070
Arts **C3** (020) 7836 3334
Cambridge **D4**
(020) 7494 5549
Comedy **C3**
(020) 7369 1731
Criterion **B3**
(020) 7413 1437
Donmar Warehouse **D4**
(020) 7369 1732
Duchess **D/E4**
(020) 7494 5075
Duke of York's **C3**
0870 060 6623
Fortune **D4**
(020) 7369 1737
Garrick **C3**
(020) 7494 5085
Gielgud **C3**
0870 890 1105
Her Majesty's **C3**
(020) 7494 5400
London Coliseum **C3**
(020) 7632 8300
Lyric, Shaftsbury Avenue
C3 (020) 7494 5045
Mayfair **A2**
(020) 7413 1415
New Ambassadors **C4**
0870 060 6627
New London **D4**
0870 890 0141
Old Vic **F1**
(020) 7369 1722
Palace **C4**
(020) 7494 5094
Palladium **A4**
(020) 7494 5020
Peacock **E4**
0870 737 0337
Phoenix **C4**
(020) 7369 1733
Piccadilly **B3**
(020) 7369 1734

Playhouse **D2**
(020) 7839 4401
Prince Edward **C4**
(020) 7447 5458
Prince of Wales **C3**
0870 850 0393
Queen Elizabeth Hall &
Purcell Room **E2**
0870 401 8181
Queen's **C3**
(020) 7494 5040
Royal Festival Hall **E2**
0870 401 8181
Royal National **E2**
(020) 7452 3000
Royal Opera House **D4**
(020) 7304 4000
St Martins **C4**
0870 162 8787
Savoy **D3**
0870 164 8787
Shaftesbury **D4**
0870 906 3798
Strand **E4**
0870 060 2335
Theatre Royal
Drury Lane **D4**
(020) 7494 5000
Theatre Royal
Haymarket **C3**
0870 901 3356
Vaudeville **D3**
0870 890 0511
Villiers **D2**
(020) 7976 1307
Whitehall **C2**
0870 060 6632
Wyndhams **C3**
(020) 7369 1736
Young Vic **F2**
(020) 7928 6363

Parks & gardens
Green Park **A1/A2**
St James' Park **B1/B2/C2**
Victoria Embankment
Gardens **D2/D3**

Other places of interest
Big Ben **D1** Not open to
general public
Buckingham Palace **A1**
(020) 77667300
Houses of Parliament **D1**

London Eye **E1**
0870 5000 600
Royal Courts of Justice **E4**

Street index
Adam and Eve Court **B4**
Adam Street **D3**
Adelaide Street **D3**
Adelphi Terrace **D3**
Addington Street **E1**
Agar Street **D3**
Air Street **B3**
Albemarle Street **A3**
Aldwych **E4**
Ame Street **D4**
Apple Tree Yard **B3**
Aquinas Street **F2**
Argyll Street **B4**
Arlington Street **B2**
Arundel Street **E3–E4**
Avery Row **A3**
Barge Street **F3**
Bateman Street **C4**
Baylis Road **F1**
Beak Street **B3–B4**
Bedfordbury **D3**
Bedford Street **D3**
Bell Yard **E4**
Belvedere Road **E2**
Bennett Street **B2**
Berkeley Square **A3**
Berkeley Street **A2–A3**
Berners Street **B4**
Berwick Street **B4**
Betterton Street **D4**
Birdcage Walk **B1–C1**
Blore Court **B4**
Bolton Street **A2**
Bourdon Street **A3**
Bouverie Street **F4**
Bow Street **D4**
Boyle Street **A3–B3**
Brad Street **F2**
Brewer Street **B3**
Brick Street **A2**
Bridge Street **D1**
Bridle Lane **B3**
Broad Court **D4**
Broad Sanctuary **C1**
Broadwall **F2**
Broadway **C1**
Broadwick Street **B4**
Brook Street **A4**
Bruton Lane **A3**
Bruton Place **A3**
Bruton Street **A3**
Buckingham Gate **B1**
Buckingham Street **D3**
Burlington Arcade **B3**
Burlington Gardens **B3**
Bury Street **B2**
Cambridge Circus **C4**
Cannon Row **D1**
Carey Street **E4**
Carlisle Lane **E1**
Carlisle Street **C4**
Carlton Gardens **C2**
Carlton House Terrace
C2
Carlton Street **C3**
Carmelite Street **F3–F4**
Carnaby Street **B3–B4**
Carteret Street **C1**
Carting Lane **D3**
Catherine Street **D4**
Cavendish Square **A4**

Chancery Lane **E4**
Chandos Place **D3**
Charing Cross Road **C4**
Charles II Street **B2–C2**
Charles Street **A2–A3**
Chicheley Street **E1**
Clare Market **E4**
Clarges Mews **A2**
Clarges Street **A2**
Clements Inn **E4**
Cleveland Place **B2**
Cleveland Row **B2**
Clifford Street **A3–B3**
Cockspur Street **C2**
Coin Street **F2**
Concert Hall Approach
E2
Conduit Street **A3**
Cons Street **F2**
Constitution Hill **A1**
Coral Street **F1**
Cork Street **A3–B3**
Cornwall Road **F2**
Coventry Street **C3**
Cranbourn Street **C3**
Craven Street **D2**
Curzon Street **A2**

D'Arblay Street **B4**
Dartmouth Street **C1**
Dean Farrar Street **C1**
Dean Street **B4–C4**
Denman Street **B3**
Denmark Street **C4**
Derby Gate **D1**
Doon Street **E2**
Dover Street **A3**
Downing Street **C1–D1**
Drury Lane **D4**
Dryden Street **D4**
Duchy Street **F2**
Duke of York Street **B2–B3**
Duke Street St James's **B2**
Duncannon Street **D3**
Earlham Street **C4**
Earnshaw Street **C4**
Eastcastle Street **B4**
Emery Street **F1**
Endell Street **D4**
Essex Street **E4**
Exeter Street **D3–D4**
Exton Street **F2**
Fetter Lane **F4**
Fleet Street **F4**
Floral Street **D3–D4**

London's theatreland *The West End is the heart of London's entertainment industry. Dozens of theatres, cinemas and restaurants are clustered just north and west from Trafalgar Square along Haymarket and Shaftsbury Avenue (right) and round Leicester Square and Piccadilly Circus.*

TOWN PLANS

LONDON: THE WEST END

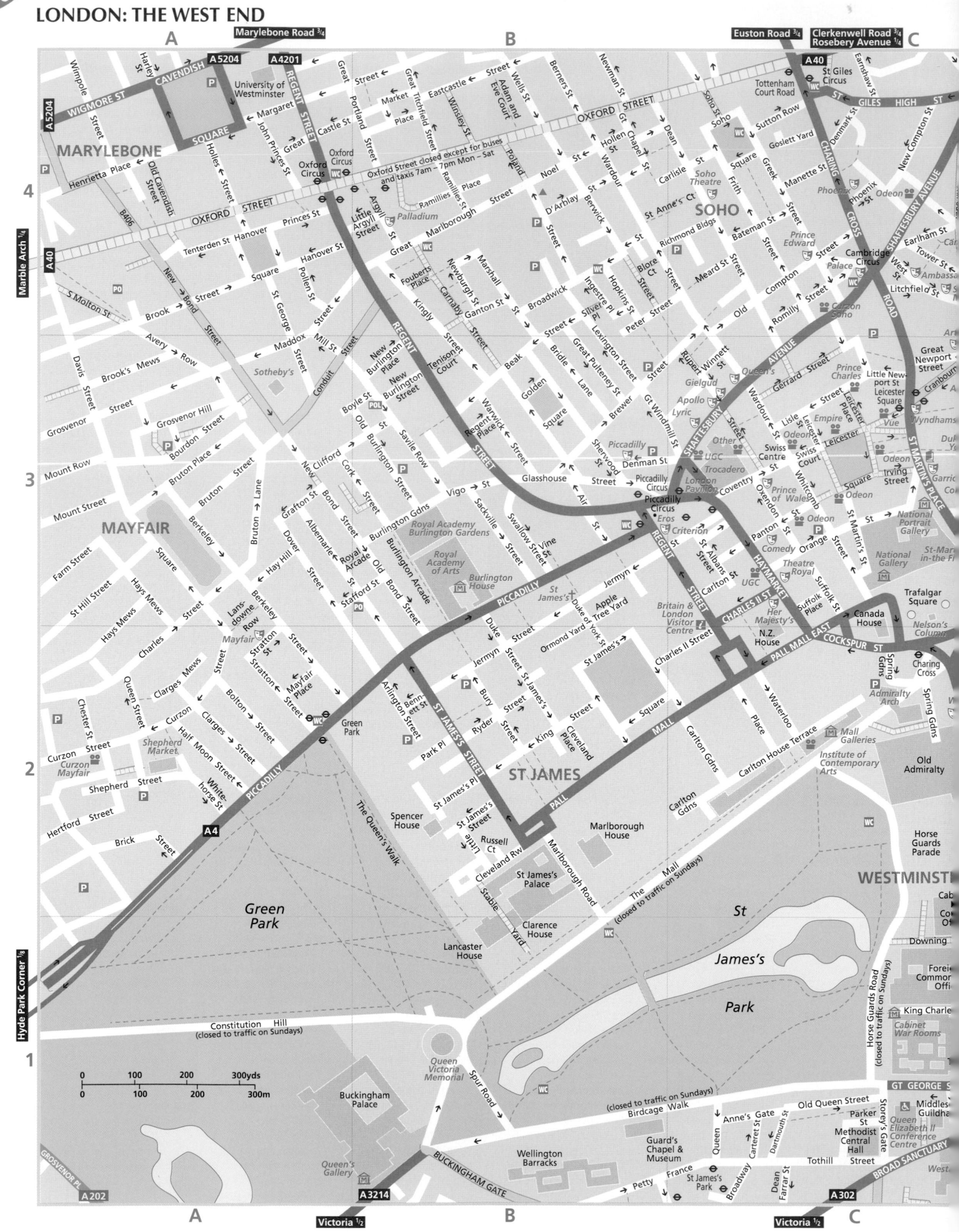

A   B   C

A5204

Wimpole St

Harley St

CAVENDISH

A4201

University of
Westminster

Great

Street

Great

Eastcastle

Titchfield

Street

Wells St

Adam and
Eve Court

Berners St

Newman St

OXFORD STREET

Soho St

St Giles
Circus

Tottenham
Court Road

ST GILES HIGH ST

A40

Margaret

St

Castle St

Portland

Market

Place

Street

Noel

Dean

Soho

Sutton Row

Goslett Yard

Denmark St

New Compton St

Earnshaw St

MARYLEBONE

Holles

Oxford
Circus

Poland

Hollen

Chapel

Wardour

St

Carlisle

St

St Anne's Ct

Greek

Manette St

Phoenix

Odeon

Henrietta Place

Old Cavendish
Street

Street

Street

OXFORD STREET closed except for buses
and taxis 7am – 7pm Mon – Sat

Ramillies St

Ramillies Place

Street

D'Arblay

Berwick

Richmond Bldgs

Bateman St

SOHO

Soho
Theatre

Frith

St

Square

Prince
Edward

CHARING

Cambridge
Circus

Palace

Litchfield
St

Earlham St

Tower St

West

CROSS

Ambassa

4

A5204

OXFORD   STREET

Tenterden St

Hanover

Princes St

Little
Argyll
Street

Great

Palladium

Marlborough

Street

Great

Marshall

Broadwick

Ingestre Pl

Blore
Ct

Meard St

Old

Romilly

Compton

Street

Curzon
Soho

B406

Hanover St

Foubert's
Place

Carnaby

Ganton St

St

Silver

Peter

St

Great

Newport
Street

Square

Pollen St

Kingly

Golden

Street

Lexington Street

Hopkins St

Winnett

Rupert

Queen's

Gerrard

Street

Prince
Charles

Little New-
port St

Cranbourn

S Molton St

New

Bond

Maddox

St George

Mill St

Conduit

New
Burlington
Place

Beak

Bridle

Great Pulteney St

Brewer

Gt Windmill St

Apollo
Lyric

Gielgud

Lisle

Leicester

Empire

Leicester
Square

Vue

Wyndham's

Brook

Street

Sotheby's

New
Burlington
Street

Boyle St

Warwick

Lane

Square

Sherwood

Denman St

Piccadilly

Other

UGC

Swiss
Centre

Swiss
Court

Odeon

Leicester

Square

Irving
Street

Garric

Davis

Street

Brook's   Mews

Avery   Row

Grosvenor Hill

Grosvenor

Bourdon

Street

Boyle St

Old

Cork

Savile Row

Regent

Street

Vigo

Glasshouse

Air

Street

Piccadilly
Circus

London
Pavilion

Coventry

Orendon

Panton

Prince
of Wales

Odeon

National
Portrait
Gallery

3

Mount Row

Bruton

Lane

Burlington Gdns

St

Glasshouse

Piccadilly
Circus

Eros

Trocadero

St

National
Gallery

St-Ma
in-the-Fi

Mount Street

MAYFAIR

Berkeley

Bruton

Grafton St

New

Bond

Burlington Gardens

Swallow Street

Vine
St

Criterion

St Albans

Comedy

St Martin's

Orange

Odeon

Farm Street

Square

Dover

Albemarle

Royal
Arcade

Old

Burlington Arcade

Royal
Academy
of Arts

Jermyn

St James's

Apple
Tree Yard

Panton

Carlton

UGC

Theatre
Royal

Trafalgar
Square

St Hill Street

Hays   Mews

Hay Hill

Bond

Stafford St

Burlington
House

PICCADILLY

Duke of
York St

Britain &
London
Visitor
Centre

Her
Majesty's

Suffolk
Place

Nelson's
Colum

Hays Mews

Charles

Berkeley

Street

PICCADILLY

Duke

Street

Jermyn

Ormond Yard

CHARLES II ST

N.Z.
House

Canada
House

Clarges   Mews

Lans-
downe
Row

Stratton

Street

Jermyn

Street

St James's

Charles II Street

PALL MALL EAST

COCKSPUR ST

Admiralty
Arch

Charing
Cross

Queen Street

Stratton

Mayfair

Bolton St

Bury

Street

Square

Carlton Gdns

Spring
Gdns

Chester St

Curzon

Clarges

Street

Arlington Street

Benn
ett St

Park Pl

Ryder

St

King

Cleveland
Place

MALL

Carlton

place

Mall
Galleries

Curzon
Mayfair

Half

Moon Street

Green
Park

ST JAMES

Square

Street

Institute of
Contemporary
Arts

Old
Admiralty

2

Curzon

Shepherd
Market

White-
horse St

Street

Street

PALL

Carlton
Gdns

Shepherd

Street

Hertford

Street

PICCADILLY

St James's
Street

Marlborough
House

WC

Horse
Guards
Parade

Brick

Street

A4

The Queen's Walk

Spencer
House

St James's
Street

Russell
Ct

Little

Marlborough Road

WESTMINSTE

Green
Park

Cleveland Rw

St James's
Palace

The Mall
(closed to traffic on Sundays)

St

James's

Cab

Co
Of

Downing

Stable
Yard

Clarence
House

James's

WC

Horse Guards Road
(closed to traffic on Sundays)

Foreig
Commo
Offi

Lancaster
House

Park

King Charle

1

Constitution   Hill
(closed to traffic on Sundays)

Queen
Victoria
Memorial

Spur Road

WC

Cabinet
War Rooms

GT GEORGE

0   100   200   300yds

0   100   200   300m

Buckingham
Palace

Birdcage Walk
(closed to traffic on Sundays)

Anne's Gate

Old Queen Street

Parker
St

Queen
Elizabeth II
Conference
Centre

Middlese
Guildha

GROSVENOR PL

A202

Queen's
Gallery

Wellington
Barracks

Guard's
Chapel &
Museum

Queen

Anne's Gate

Dartmouth St

Carteret St

France

Methodist
Central
Hall

Storey's
Gate

St James's Park

Petty

France

Broadway

Dean
Farrar St

Tothill

Street

BROAD SANCTUARY

West

A3214

A302

A   B   C

Euston Road 1¼
Bloomsbury ¼

Holborn Circus ¼

City Thameslink

A4

Gt New Street
Little New St

FETTER LANE

ST BRIDE STREET

FARRINGDON STREET

Gough Sq

Shoe Lane

Dr Johnsons's House

St Bride's

NEW BRIDGE STREET

Fleet Street

Pleydell St

Salisbury Court

Dorset Rise

4

tesbury

Drury Lane

Macklin St

Parker Street

New London

Wild Court

Lincoln's Inn Fields

New Square

Serle Street

Star Yd

Bell Yard

Chancery Lane

Bouverie Street

Whitefriars Street

Lombard Street

Carmelite Street

John Carpenter St

Brideswell

PO

Gardens St

Betterton St

Keeley St

Wild Street

Lincoln's Inn Fields

Royal College of Surgeons

Carey Street

Fleet Street

Inner Temple La

Temple Lane

Tudor Street

Unilever House

Endell

Arne Dryden St

Kemble

Kean Street

Old Curiosity Shop

Portugal Street

Carey Street

Temple La

Inns of Court

The Temple

Temple Avenue

Tallis St

Langley St

Bow St

Drury

Sheffield Street

St Clements
La
Clare Mkt
L.S.E

Houghton St

Clements
Inn

STRAND

Peacock

Royal Courts of Justice

Middle Temple La

Inner Temple

King's Bench Walk

Neal St

Hanover Place

Fortune

Theatre Royal

Lane

Aldwych

ALDWYCH

Melbourne Pl

Australia House

St Clement Danes

Essex St

Little Essex St

Middle Temple

Temple Church

mar Street

Covent Garden

Royal Opera House

Russell St

Tavistock St

Strand

India Pl

Montreal Place

St Mary-le-Strand

Mitford Lane

Arundel

Essex Street

Lane

Middle Temple

COVENT GARDEN

Theatre Mus

Wellington

Duchess St

Bush House

Surrey

Temple

3

Market

London Transport Mus

Street

Courtauld Institute Galleries

King's College

Temple Place

Victoria Embankment Gdns

The Thames Path

HMS President (1918)

Blackfriars Millennium Pier

CITY 1

King

St Paul's

Henrietta St

Exeter

STRAND

Somerset House

Temple

A321

BLACKFRIARS BRIDGE

Floral

Southampton St

Tavistock

Lyceum

LANCASTER PLACE

The Yacht St Katharine

HQS Wellington

Bedford Street

Maiden Lane

Savoy

Savoy Row

Savoy Street

EMBANKMENT

Thames Sailing Barge Wilfred

Vaudeville

Adelphi

Carting La

Savoy Hill

Thames

Chandos Pl

Adam Street

Savoy Place

VICTORIA

TS Queen Mary former Clyde Steamer

Agar St

POL

Robert St

Adelphi Terr

3

IV St

John Adam Street

WATERLOO BRIDGE

Cleopatra's Needle

London Bridge 1

A320

ON ST

York Bldgs

A301

The Jubilee Walkway

Oxo Tower Wharf

A201

Charing Cross

Villiers Street

Victoria Embankment Gardens

The Queen's Walk

Gabriel's Wharf

Bernie Spain Gardens

Barge St

Upper Ground

Rennie St

Charing Cross Station

Buckingham St

Charing Cross Pier

National Film Theatre

Riverside Walk

Royal National Theatre

Ground

Can

Duchy

Broadwall

Hatfields

Paris Garden

2

Villiers

Festival Pier

Queen Elizabeth Hall & Purcell Room

Upper

Cornwall

STAMFORD STREET

Street

UMBERLAND

AVE

Embankment

Charing Cross Pier

Festival Pier

Hayward Gallery

Doon Street

Aquinas Street

Hatfields

Colombo Street

Playhouse

Royal Festival Hall

Ground

Street

Meyott Street

Whitehall Place

Victoria Embankment Gardens

RS Hispaniola

Concert Hall Approach

IMAX

PO

Theed Street

Windmill Walk

Joan Street

BLACKFRIARS ROAD

2

Horseguards Ave

Tattershall Castle Paddle Steamer

Waterloo

Whittlesey St

Roupell St

PO

Banqueting House

Jubilee Gardens

Mepham Street

Exton

Cornwall

Brad

Waterloo (East) Station

Isabella St

Belvedere Road

Waterloo

Wootton Street

Cons St

Southwark

Richmond Ter

London Eye

York Road

Waterloo International

Sandell St

Young Vic

enotaph

VICTORIA EMBANKMENT

Riverside Path

Chicheley St

Waterloo Station

WATERLOO ROAD

The Cut

Short Street

1

Westminster Millennium Pier

Dali Universe

Old Vic

Mitre Road

Derby Row

Cannon Row

The London Aquarium

Old County Hall

LAMBETH

Leake Street

Marsh

Ufford Street

Webber Street

Westminster

Queen Boudicca

Saatchi Gallery

Coral St

Gray Street

Webber Row

BRIDGE ST

WESTMINSTER BRIDGE

WESTMINSTER BRIDGE RD

ADDINGTON ST

Lower Marsh

Murphy St

Frazier Street

Pearman

WATERLOO ROAD

Morley St

Dodson Street

A3212

Big Ben

Westminster Hall

Florence Nightingale Museum

LAMBETH PALACE RD

Upper Marsh

Baylis Road

Greenham Close

Emery St

Gerridge St

Houses of Parliament

St Thomas' Hospital

Royal Street

Carlisle Lane

WESTMINSTER BRIDGE RD

Lambeth North

A23

A302

A3036

hall Bridge 1

D

Vauxhall 1

E

Kennington 1

Elephant & Castle ½

F

Docklands & Greenwich

Britain's tallest building – the Canary Wharf tower – rises 244m (800ft) above part of a huge system of docks that made 19th-century London the world's largest port. The disused quays and wharves have been regenerated since the 1980s as a major new business and financial centre, along with housing and extensive leisure facilities, and are now linked to central London by the Jubilee Line extension and the Docklands Light Railway. Greenwich, London's historic maritime centre, is home to the Royal Naval College, the National Maritime Museum, the tea clipper Cutty Sark and the Old Royal Observatory. At weekends, antiques and arts and crafts markets add a lively bustle.

The map reference in bold after each entry identifies the grid square in which it appears on **pages 360–361**.

Art galleries & museums
Brunel's Engine House **B3**
(020) 7231 3840
Design Museum **A3**
(020) 7940 8790
Fan Museum **D1**
(020) 8305 1441
Livesey Museum **A1**
(020) 7639 5604
National Maritime
Museum **D1**
(020) 8858 4422
Old Royal Observatory
D1 (020) 8312 6608
Queen's House **D1**
(020) 8312 6565
Tower Bridge Museum **A3**
(020) 7403 3761
Whitechapel Art Gallery
A4 (020) 7522 7888

Cinemas
Filmworks **E2**
0870 010 2030
UCI Surrey Quays **B3**
0870 010 2030
UGC West India Quay **C4**
0870 907 0722

Theatres
Albany Theatre **C1**
(020) 8692 4446
Greenwich Playhouse **D1**
(020) 8858 9256
Greenwich Theatre **D1**
(020) 8858 4447

Shopping
Butler's Wharf **A3**
Canary Wharf **C3**
Greenwich Market **D1**
Isle of Dogs **D2**
Spitalfields Market **A4**
St Katharine Dock **A3**
Surrey Quays Shopping
Centre **B3**
West India Docks **C3**

Parks & gardens
Blackheath **D1–E1**
Greenwich Park **D1–E1**

Other places of interest
Billingsgate Fish
Market **D3** Open
5–8.30am Tues–Sat
Burrell's Wharf **C2**
Canary Wharf Tower **C3**
Not open to public but
can be viewed from

Canada Square
Charlton House **F1**
(020) 8856 3951
Cutty Sark **D2**
(020) 8858 3445
East London Mosque **A4**
(020) 7247 1357
Gypsy Moth **D2**
(020) 8858 3445
Isle of Dogs Pumping
Station **D3** Not open
to public
Millennium Dome **D3**
Can be viewed from
Greenwich Peninsula
or North Greenwich
station
Mudchute Farm **D2**
(020) 7515 5901
Ranger's House **D1**
(020) 8853 0035
Royal Naval College **D2**
(020) 8269 4747
Thames Barrier **F3**
(020) 8305 4188
The Grapes **C4**
(020) 7987 4396
Tower of London **A3**
(0870) 756 6060
Vanbrugh Castle **D1**
Not open to public but
there is a blue plaque

Street index
Abbey Street **A3**
Abbott Road **D4**
Albert Road **F3**
Aldgate East Station **A4**
Aldgate Station **A4**
Anchor and Hope
Lane **F2**
Angel Inn **A3**
Aspen Way **C4–D3**

New city in the east *The Canary Wharf tower was completed in 1991, one of the earliest and most impressive of a series of new structures to be built on the Isle of Dogs peninsula. In 2001 it was flanked by the Citicorp and HSBC towers and the area around Canada Square and Canary Wharf tube station is being swiftly colonised by a new generation of skyscrapers.*

TOWN PLANS

LONDON: DOCKLANDS & GREENWICH

A — B — C

M11 Cambridge

A 1202
Spitalfields Market
SPITALFIELDS
Whitechapel
A11
Mile End Road
B108
A13
B121 Stepney Green
Stepney Green Park
STEPNEY
Ben Jonson Rd
St Dunstan & All Saints
Mile End Park
A 1205
St Paul's Way
B140
B140
Canal (Regent's Canal)
BURDETT ROAD
Thomas Road

4

Whitechapel Road
East London Mosque
Royal London Hospital
Whitechapel Bell Foundry
Whitechapel Art Gallery
Aldgate East
Aldgate
A13 COMMERCIAL ROAD
Christian St
Cannon St B108
New Rd
Stepney Way
Sidney Street
Jubilee Street
Salmon La
COMMERCIAL ROAD
A13
LIMEHOUSE
Thomas Road
Limehouse Cut
Upper North St
EAST
A 1205
POPLAR
St Matthias
Pop Recre Gro

WHITECHAPEL
Cable St
Shadwell
B126
Shadwell
Docklands Light Railway
Limehouse Link Tunnel
Limehouse Basin
Limehouse
St Anne
A13
A1203
POL
WEST INDIA DOCK RD
Poplar

Tower Gateway
Tower Hill
Tower of London
MINORIES
LEMAN ST
EAST SMITHFIELD
THE HIGHWAY
St George-in-the-East
Wapping
A 101
Tobacco Dock
Shadwell Basin
SHADWELL
St Paul
Rotherhithe Tunnel
Narrow St
The Grapes
Limehouse Reach
Westferry
A 1203
Westferry
UGC
The Museum in Docklands
West India Quay
West

3

Tower Bridge
A 100
Tower Bridge Mus
TOWER BRIDGE RD
DRUID ST
A 100
A2207
A 200
Butler's Wharf
Design Museum
St Saviour's Dock
The Pool
Hermitage Basin
St Katharine Docks
WAPPING
St Peter
Prospect of Whitby
Wapping Lane
Wapping High Street
Town of Ramsgate
Wapping Old Stairs
Mayflower Inn
Lower Pool
Cherry Garden Pier
St Mary
Rotherhithe
Brunel's Engine House
Salter Rd
B205
Surrey Water
Stave Hill Nature Reserve
Russia Dock Woodland
Lavender Pond Pump House & Nature Park
Holy Trinity
Rotherhithe Street
West India Dock Pier
Marsh Wall
South
Canary Wharf Pier
Canary Wharf
Heron Quays
Canary Wharf Tow
India Dock

BERMONDSEY
Angel Inn
West Lane
Civic Centre
ROTHERHITHE
Surrey Docks Farm
Sir John McDougal Gardens
Alpha Grove
Millharbour
ISLE

2

A 2206
A2207
GRANGE ROAD
Abbey St
B202
JAMAICA ROAD
Bermondsey
Spa Road
Southwark Park
Lower Road
Canada Water
POL
Canada Water
UCI
B205
Redriff Road
Greenland Dock
South Dock
MILLWALL
Millwall Outer D

Seven Islands Leisure Centre
Southwark Park
Surrey Quays Shopping Centre
A2208
Surrey Quays
A2206
NEW ROAD
A2208
Plough Way
The Thames Path
A 1206
Burrell's Wharf

St James's
SOUTHWARK PARK ROAD
Silwood Street
A 200
Grove Street
Royal Naval Dock
Greenwich Reach
Thames

Dunton Rd B203
Rolls Road B204
Catlin St
ROTHERHITHE
South Bermondsey
Bolina Rd
Millwall F.C.
Zampa Rd
Trundley's Road
Deptford Park
EVELYN STREET
DEPTFORD
The Thames Path

A2
B214
Cobourg Rd
Trafalgar Ave
OLD KENT ROAD
A2208
Grinstead Road
Sayes Ct St
Prince St
CREEK RO
St Nicholas

Burgess Park
Neate St
St Georges Way
Peckham Park Rd
Willowbrook Road
Iderton Road
Surrey Canal Rd
Mercury Way
Juno Way
Blow Lane
Rolt Street
Childers St
Arklow Rd
Edward Street
CREEKSIDE
St Paul
Deptford
POL
A 2209

1

CAMBERWELL
Commercial
B217
A202
PECKHAM ROAD
Peckham Hill St
HIGH ST
Way
Livesey Museum
OLD KENT ROAD
Clifton Way
NEW CROSS
Pomeroy St
KENDER ST
B2227
Hunsdon Road
Brockiehurst St
Cold Blow Lane
Sanford Street
Pagnell St
New Cross
New Cross Gate
A2
A20
NEW CROSS ROAD
LEWISHAM WAY
Albany Theatre
Deptford High St
DEPTFORD CHURCH ST
A 2209
NEW CROSS
ST JOHN'S
GREENWICH
BLACKH
Deptford Bridge
A 2210

A 302 A 4202 A 5
A 202
A2215
Queens Road (Peckham)
QUEENS ROAD
PECKHAM
Queens Road
A2214
NEW CROSS GATE
A2210

A — B — C

LUTON

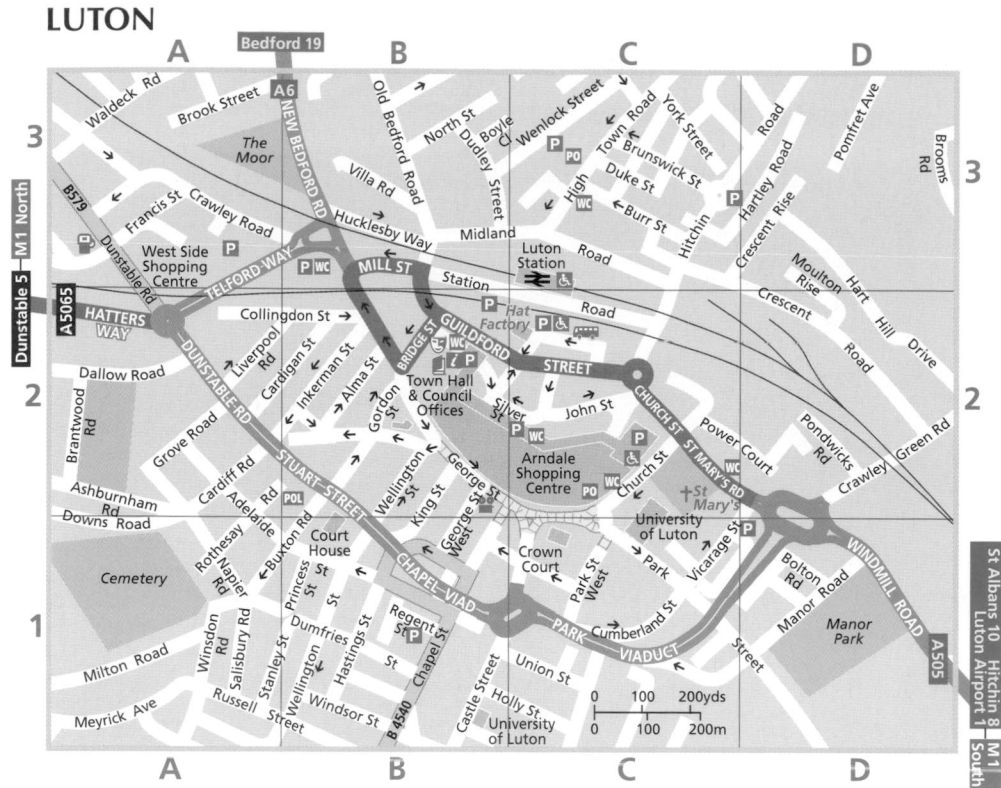

MACCLESFIELD

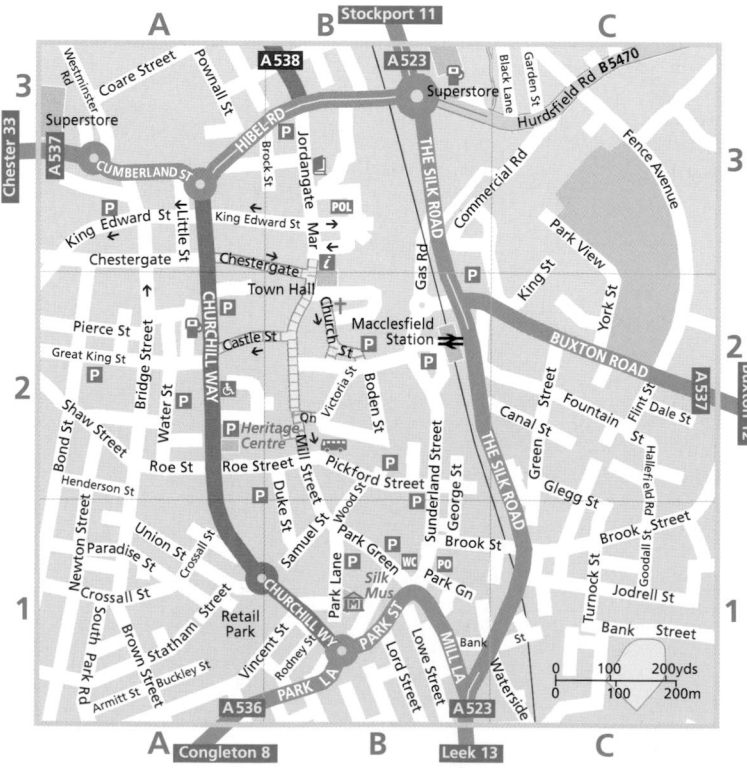

MAIDSTONE

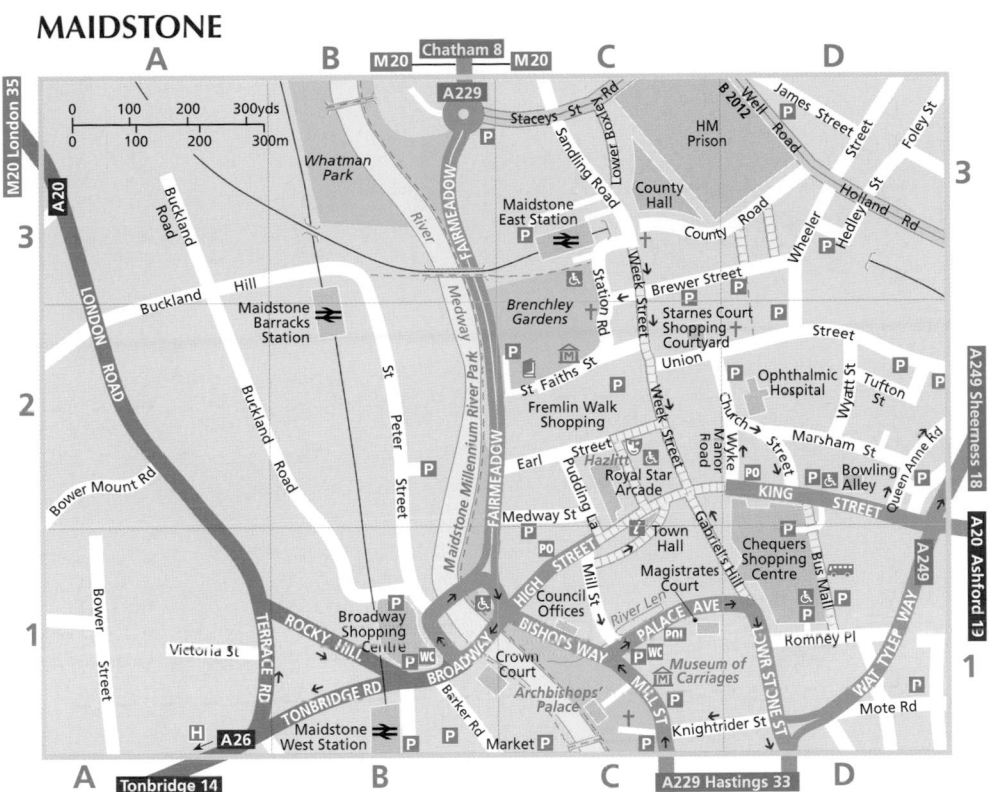

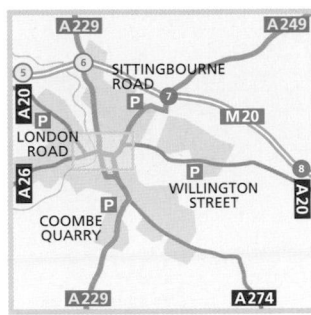

Park & Ride

STREET INDEX

Barker Road B1
Bishops Way C1
Bower Mount Road A2
Bower Street A1
Brewer Street C3
Broadway B1
Buckland Hill A3

Buckland Road A3
Church Street D2
County Road C3
Earl Street C2
Fairmeadow B3
Foley Street D3
Gabriel's Hill C1
Hedley Street D3

High Street C1
Holland Road D3
James Street D3
King Street D2
Knightrider Street C1
London Road A2
Lower Boxley
  Road C3

Lower Stone Street D1
Marsham Street D2
Medway Street C2
Mill Street C1
Mote Road D1
Palace Avenue C1
Pudding Lane C2
Queen Anne Road D2

Rocky Hill B1
Romney Place D1
St Peter Street B2
Sandling Road C3
Station Road C3
Terrace Road A1
Tonbridge Road B1
Tufton Street D2

Union Street C2
Victoria Street A1
Wat Tyler Way D1
Week Street C2
Well Road D3
Wheeler Street D3
Wyatt Street D2
Wyke Manor Road D2

MANSFIELD

STREET INDEX

Albert Street C2
Bancroft Lane A2
Bath Lane D3
Bath Street C1
Belvedere Street A2
Bridge Street C2
Chaucer Street A2
Chesterfield Road
  South B3
Church Lane C1
Church Side C2
Church Street C2
Clumber Street C3
Commercial Gate C1
Dallas Street A1
Garden Road B1
Goldsmith Street A2
Great Central
  Road D1
Grove Street B1
Grove Street C1
Hill Drive C3
Leeming Street C2–C3
Midworth Street C2
Nottingham Road C1
Padley Hill A2
Pelham Street D2

Portland Street B2
Quaker Way B2
Queen Street C2
Radford Street B2
Ratcliffe Gate D2
Regent Street C2
Rock Court D2
Rock Valley C2
Rooth Street B1
Rosemary Street A3
St John Street A3
St Peter's Way C2
Station Road B2
Station Street B1
Stockwell Gate
  A2–B2
Toothill Lane C2
Union Street B3
Victoria Street A1
Walkden Street A2
West Gate B3
Westfield Lane A3
White Hart Street C2
Wood Street A3

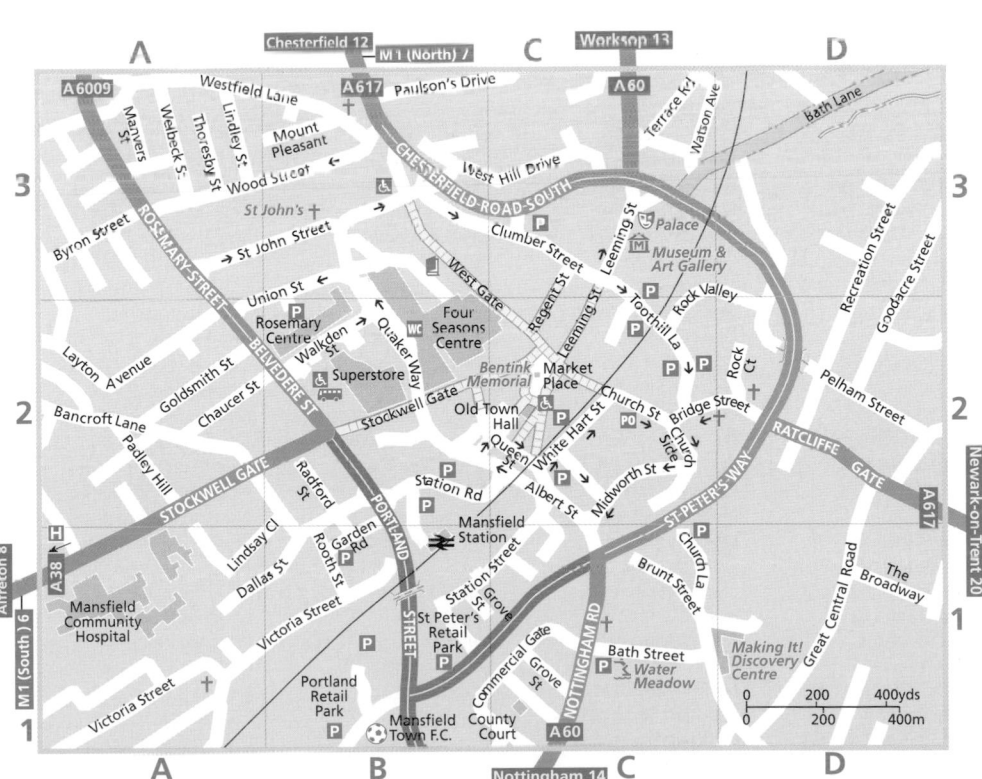

MANCHESTER

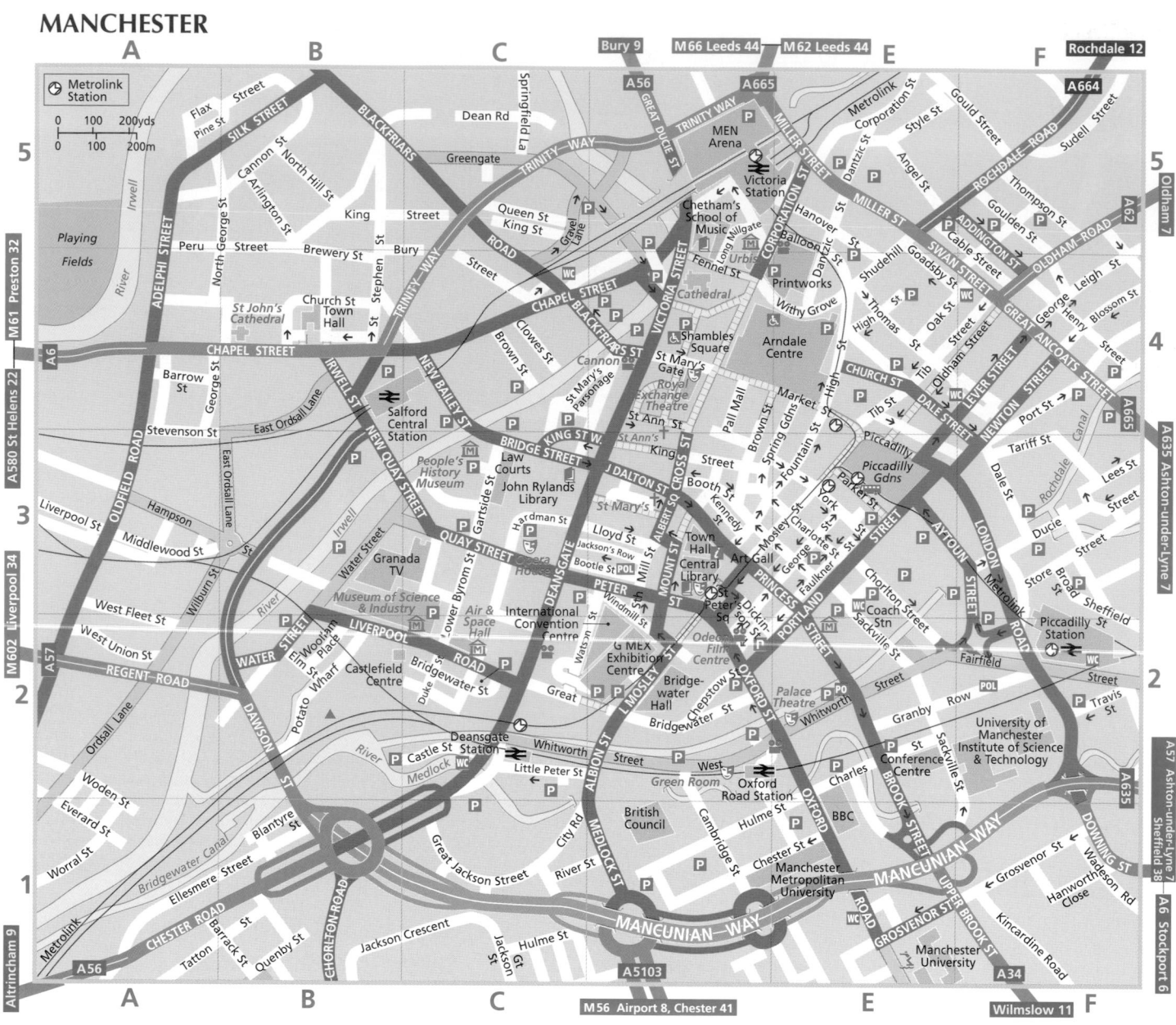

MARGATE

STREET INDEX

Addington Road C2
Addington Street C2
All Saints Avenue A1
Belgrave Road B2
Cecil Street C2
Char Square C1
Churchfields C1
Churchfields Place C2
Cowper Road C1
Dane Hill C3
Dane Road C2
Eaton Road B1
Fort Crescent C3
Fort Hill C3
Grosvenor Place B2
Hawley Street C2
High Street C1–B2

King Street C3
Marina Drive B2
Marine Terrace A2
Market Street B2
Mill Lane C1
Milton Avenue C1
New Street B2
Northdown Road C3
Queens Avenue C1
St Peter's Footpath C1
The Parade B3
Tivoli Park Avenue A1
Trinity Square C3
Union Crescent C2
Union Row C2
Victoria Road C1
Zion Place C3

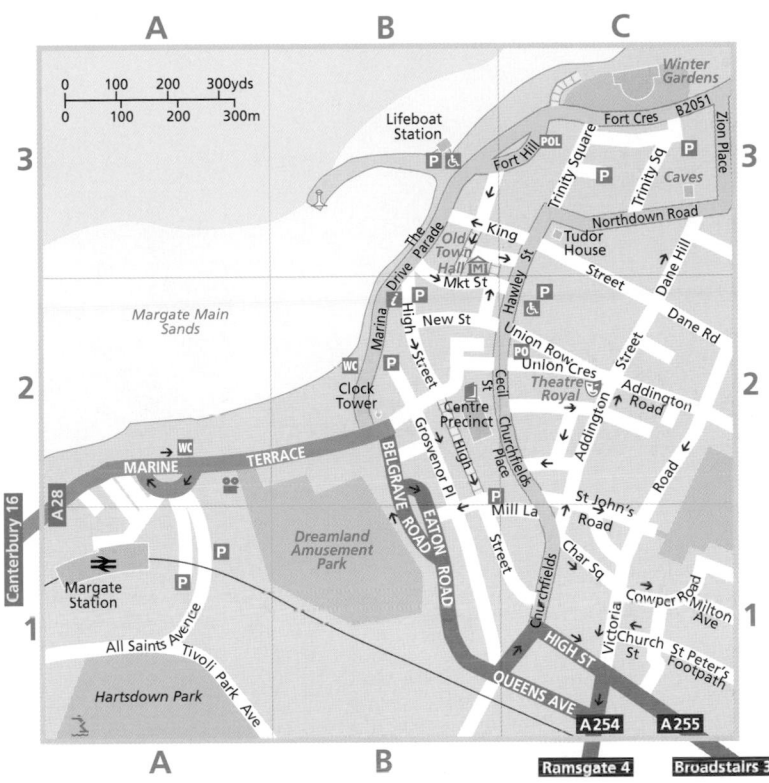

MIDDLESBROUGH

STREET INDEX

Acklam Road A1
Albert Road C3
Albert Terrace C2
Ayresome Green Lane A1
Ayresome Park Road B1
Ayresome Street A2
Borough Road C3
Bridge Street West C4
Chipchase Road B1
Clairville Road D2
Clarendon Road C3
Clive Road B1
Corporation Road C4
Crescent Road B2
Derwent Street B3
Diamond Road B3
Dock Street D4
Eden Road D1
Grange Road D3
Gresham Road B2
Hartington Road B3
Heywood Street A2
Linthorpe Road B1–C4
Marsh Street B3
Marton Road D1–D3
Newport Road A3
North Road B4
Park Lane C2
Park Road North C2
Park Road South C1
Park Vale Road D2
Parliament Road B2
Princess Road B2
Riverside Park Road A4
Roman Road B1
Southfield Road C3
The Boulevard C3
Union Street B3
West Lane A2
Westminster Road C1
Wilson Street C4
Woodlands Road C2
Worcester Street B2

MILTON KEYNES

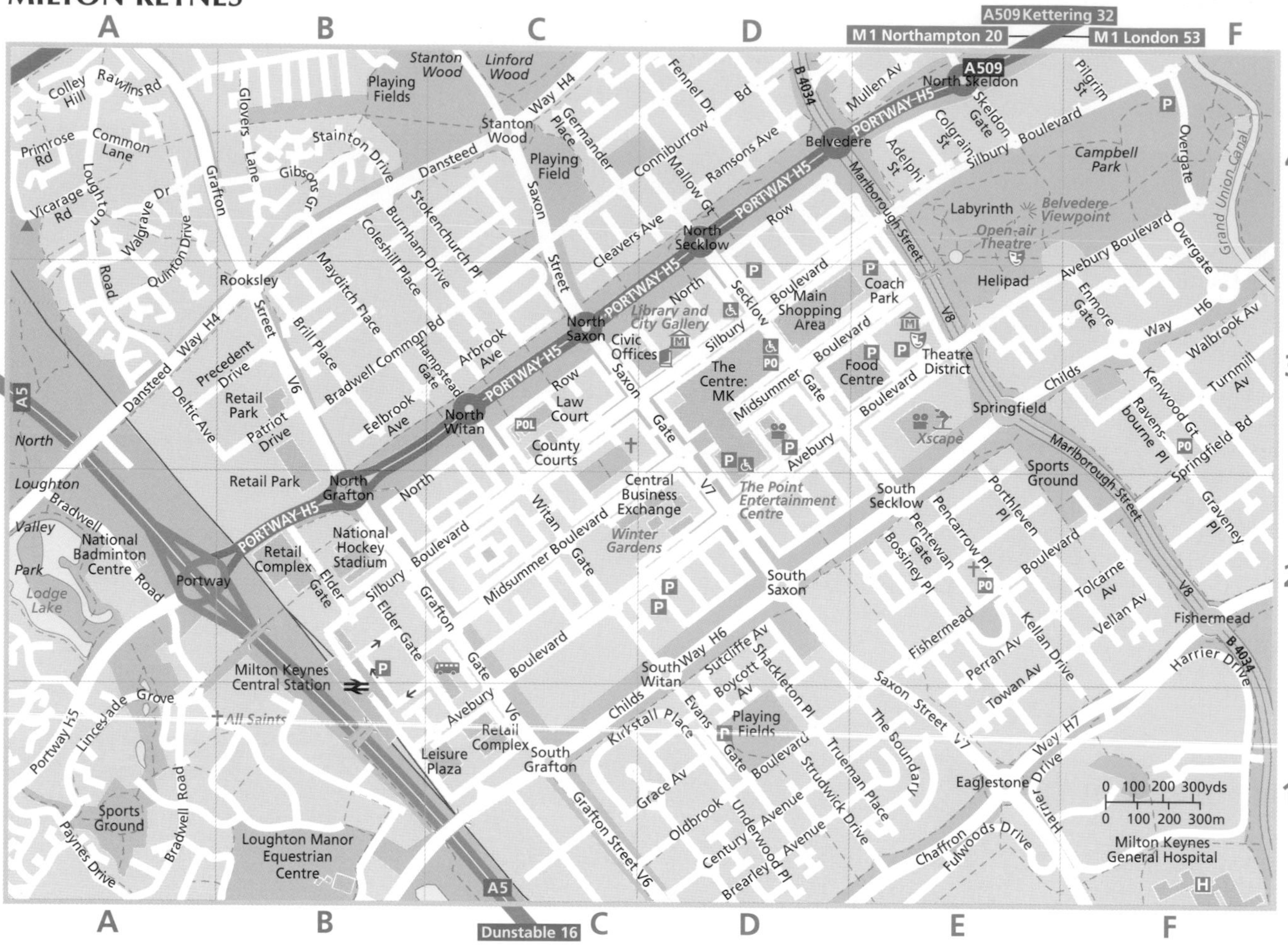

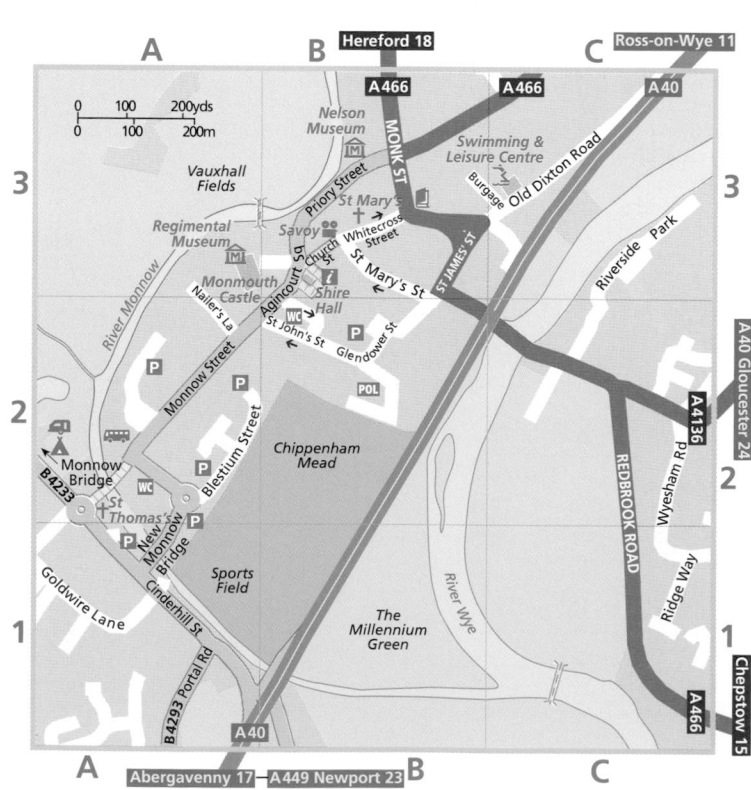

STREET INDEX

Avebury Boulevard
C1–F4
Bradwell Common
Boulevard **B3**
Chaffron Way **E1**
Childs Way **C1–F3**
Dansteed Way **A3–C4**

Elder Gate **B2**
Fishermead
Boulevard **E2**
Grafton Gate **C2**
Grafton Street **B4–B3**
Grafton Street **C1**
Hampstead Gate **C3**
Harrier Drive **F1–F2**

Marlborough Street
E4–F2
Midsummer Boulevard
C2–D3
North Row **B2–D4**
Pencarrow Place **E2**
Pentewan Gate **E2**
Portway **A1–E4**

Saxon Gate **C3–D3**
Saxon Street **C4**
Saxon Street **E2–E1**
Secklow Gate **D3**
Silbury Boulevard
B2–D3
Witan Gate **C2**

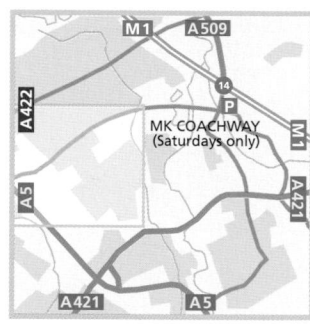

Park & Ride

MONMOUTH

STREET INDEX

Agincourt Square **B2**
Blestium Street **A2**
Burgage **B3**
Church Street **B3**
Cinderhill Street **A1**
Glendower Street **B2**
Goldwire Lane **A1**
Monk Street **B3**
Monnow Street **A2**
Nailer's Lane **A2**
New Monnow Bridge
A1
Old Dixton Road **C3**
Portal Road **A1**
Priory Street **B3**
Redbrook Road **C2**
Ridge Way **C1**
Riverside Park **C3**
St James' Street **B3**
St John's Street **B2**
St Mary's Street **B3**
Whitecross Street **B3**
Wyesham Road **C2**

MORPETH

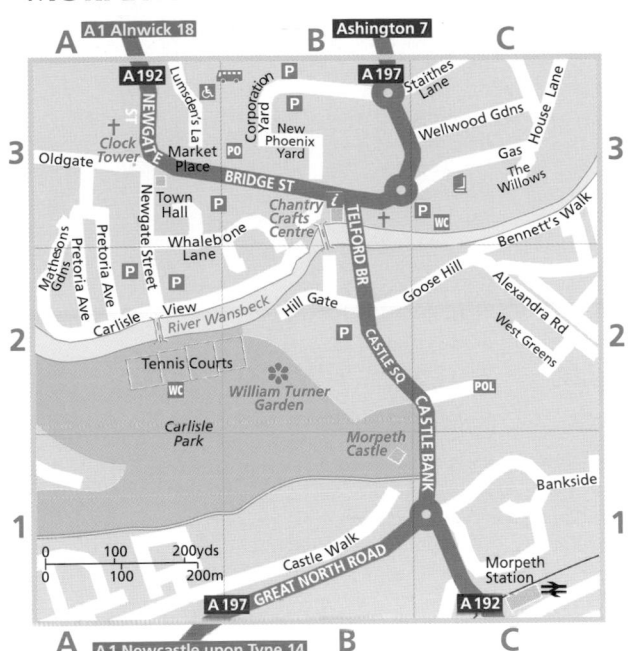

A1 Alnwick 18
A192
Ashington 7
A197

Lumsden's La
NEWGATE ST
Clock Tower
Oldgate
Market Place
BRIDGE ST
Corporation Yard
New Phoenix Yard
PO
Wellwood Gdns
House Lane
Staithes Lane
Gas
The Willows
Town Hall
Pretoria Ave
Newgate Street
Carlisle View
Whalebone Lane
Chantry Crafts Centre
Telford BR
Hill Gate
Goose Hill
Bennett's Walk
Alexandra Rd
West Greens
River Wansbeck
Tennis Courts
WC
William Turner Garden
CASTLE SQ
POL
Carlisle Park
Morpeth Castle
CASTLE BANK
Bankside
Castle Walk
GREAT NORTH ROAD
Morpeth Station
A197
A192
A1 Newcastle upon Tyne 14

0 100 200yds
0 100 200m

STREET INDEX

Alexandra Road C2
Bankside C1
Bennett's Walk C3
Bridge Street B3
Carlisle View A2
Castle Bank C2
Castle Square B2
Castle Walk B1
Corporation Yard B3
Gas House Lane C3
Goose Hill C2
Great North Road B1
Hill Gate B2
Lumsden's Lane A3
Mathesons Gardens A2
New Phoenix Yard B3
Newgate Street A3
Oldgate A3
Pretoria Avenue A3
Staithes Lane C3
Telford Bridge B3
The Willows C3

Wellwood Gardens C3
West Greens C2
Whalebone Lane A3

NEWARK-ON-TRENT

STREET INDEX

Albert Street B1
Appleton Gate D3
Balderton Gate C1
Bar Gate B3
Barnby Gate C2–D1
Beast Market Hill B3
Bede House Lane C2
Boar Lane B2
Bridge Street C2
Carter Gate C2
Castle Gate B2
Century Street D1
Chain Lane B2
Church Street C2
Cow Lane C4
Edward Avenue A1
Friary Road D2
George Street D4
Great North Road A4
Guildhall Street C2
Kelham Road A4
King Street A1
King's Road C3
Kirk Gate B3
Lawrence Street D3
Lombard Street B2
London Road C1
Lover's Lane D4
Magnus Street D2
Manners Road A3
Mather Road B4
Middle Gate B2
Mill Gate A1

North Gate C4
Ossington Way B3
Parliament Street A1
Pelham Street A1
Portland Street B1
Queen's Road C3
Sandhills Park A4
Sherwood Avenue D1
Slaughterhouse Lane B3
Sleaford Road D3
Stodman Street B2
Sydney Street D4
Tannery Wharf A1
Tolney Lane A2
Warburton Street D4
Water Lane C3
Wellington Road D2
Whitfield Street D1
William Street D1
Wilson Street C3

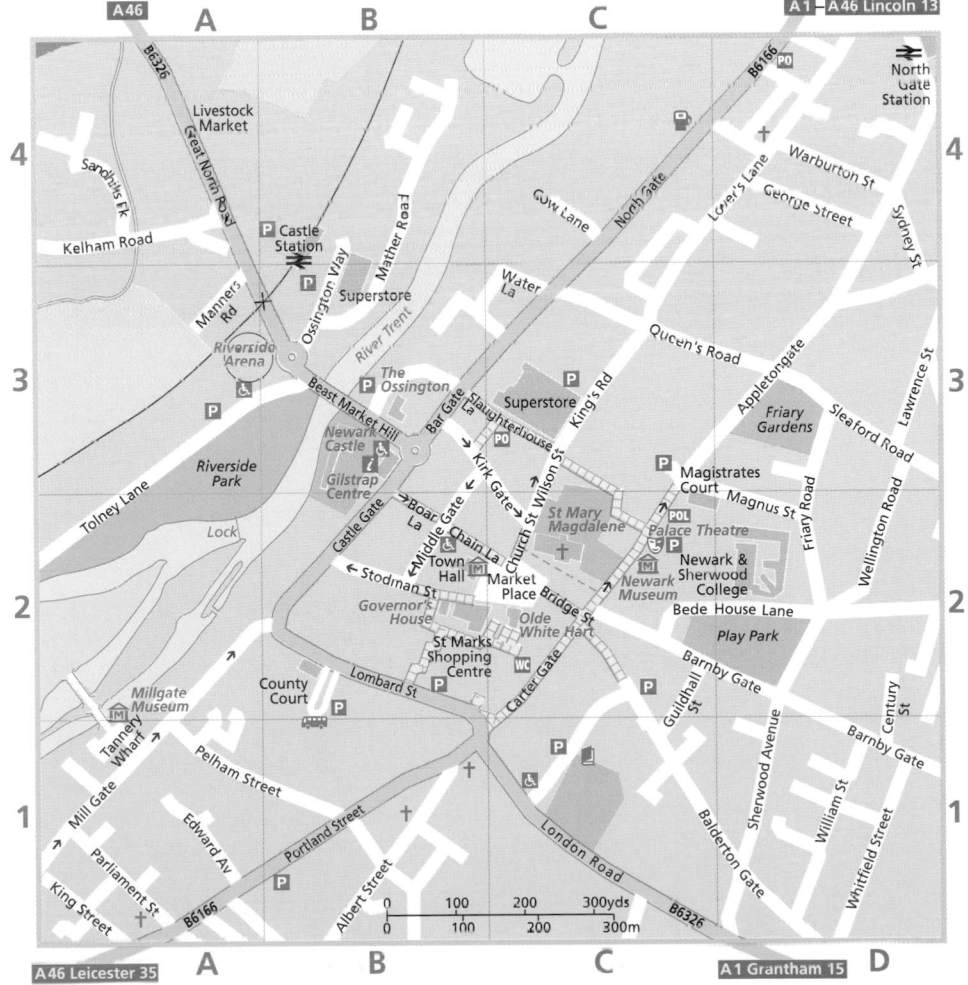

A46
A1 – A46 Lincoln 13
North Gate Station
B6326
Livestock Market
Sandhills Pk
Great North Road
Kelham Road
Manners Rd
Ossington Way
Mather Road
Cow Lane
North Gate
B6166
PO
Warburton St
George Street
Lover's Lane
Sydney St
Castle Station
Superstore
River Trent
Water La
Queen's Road
Riverside Arena
Beast Market Hill
The Ossington
Newark Castle
Superstore
King's Rd
Appletongate
Sleaford Road
Lawrence St
Friary Gardens
Riverside Park
Gilstrap Centre
Bar Gate
Slaughterhouse St
Kirk Gate
St Mary Magdalene
Magistrates Court
Magnus St
Palace Theatre
Tolney Lane
Lock
Castle Gate
Boar La
Wilson St
Chain La
Middle Gate
Church St
Newark Museum
Newark & Sherwood College
Town Hall
Market Place
Bridge St
Bede House Lane
Stodman St
Governor's House
Olde White Hart
Play Park
St Marks Shopping Centre
WC
Carter Gate
Barnby Gate
Guildhall St
County Court
Lombard St
Sherwood Avenue
Barnby Gate
Century St
Millgate Museum
Tannery Wharf
Mill Gate
Edward Av
Pelham Street
Portland Street
London Road
Balderton Gate
William St
Whitfield Street
Parliament St
King Street
B6166
Albert Street
B6326
A46 Leicester 35
A1 Grantham 15

0 100 200 300yds
0 100 200 300m

NEWBURY

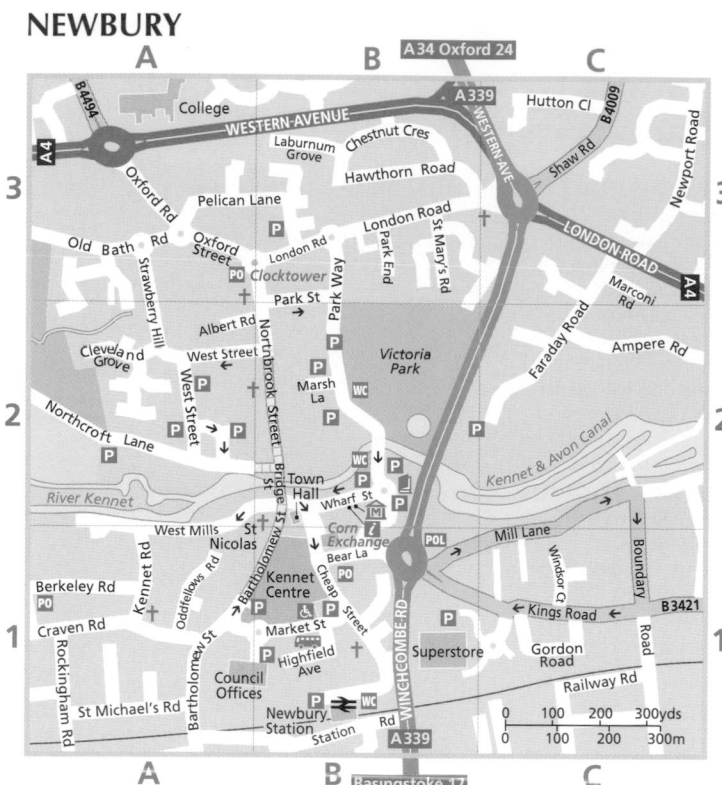

NEWHAVEN

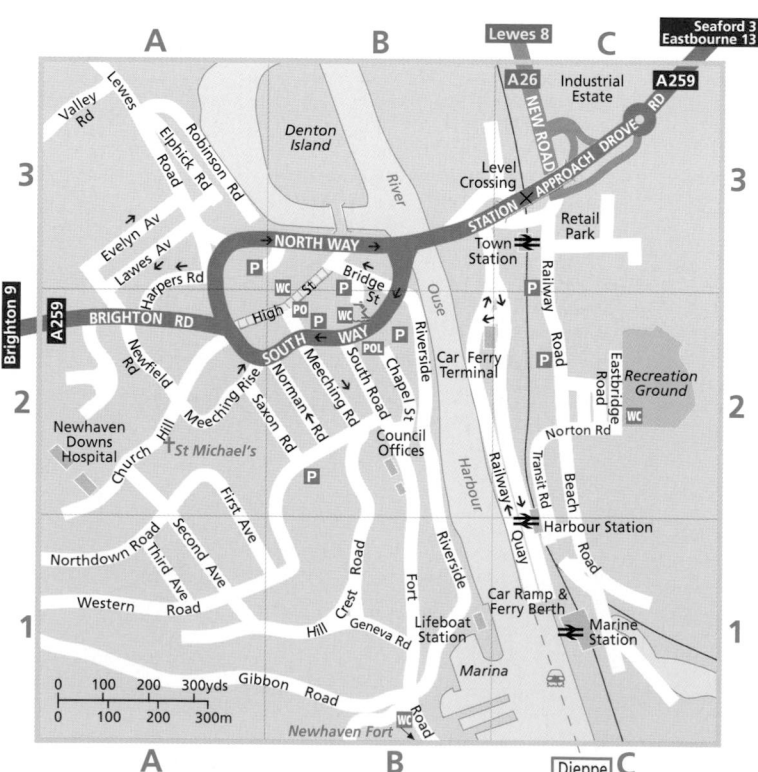

NEWCASTLE

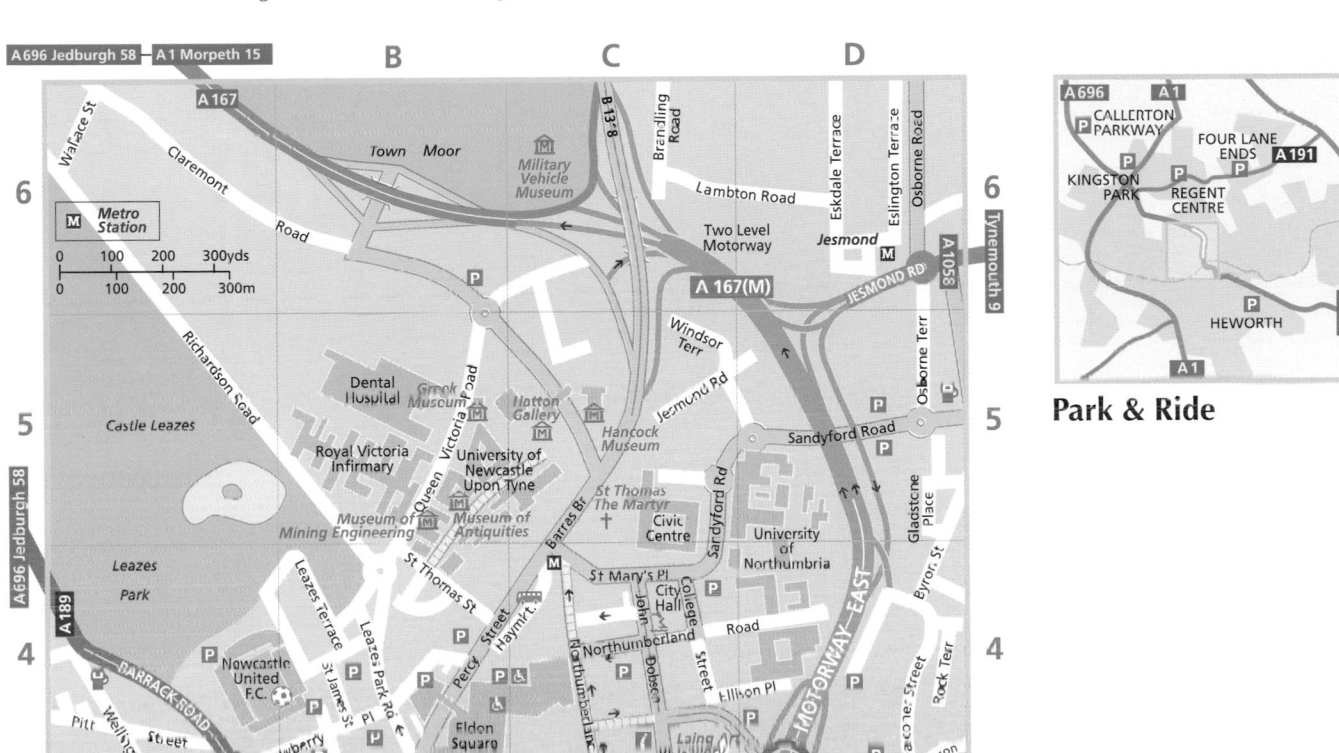

Park & Ride

TOWN PLANS

NEWPORT

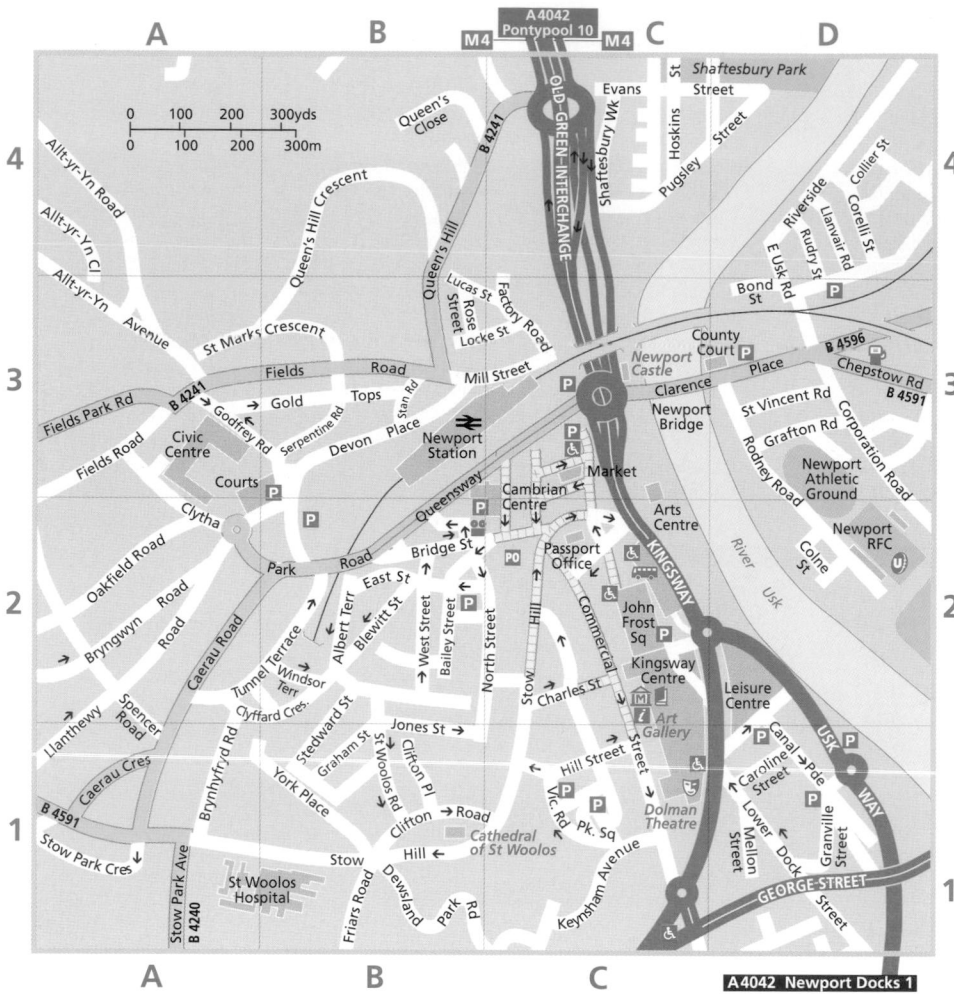

NEWTOWN

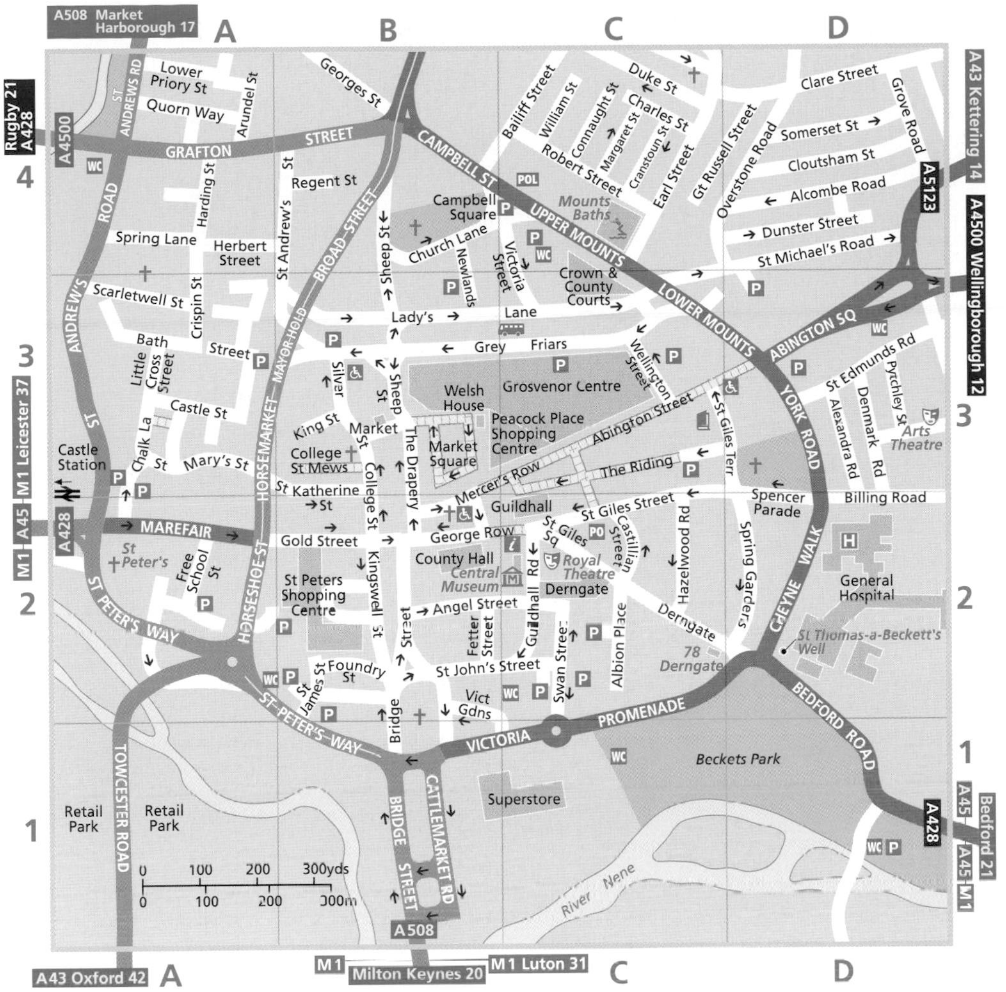

TOWN PLANS

NORTHAMPTON

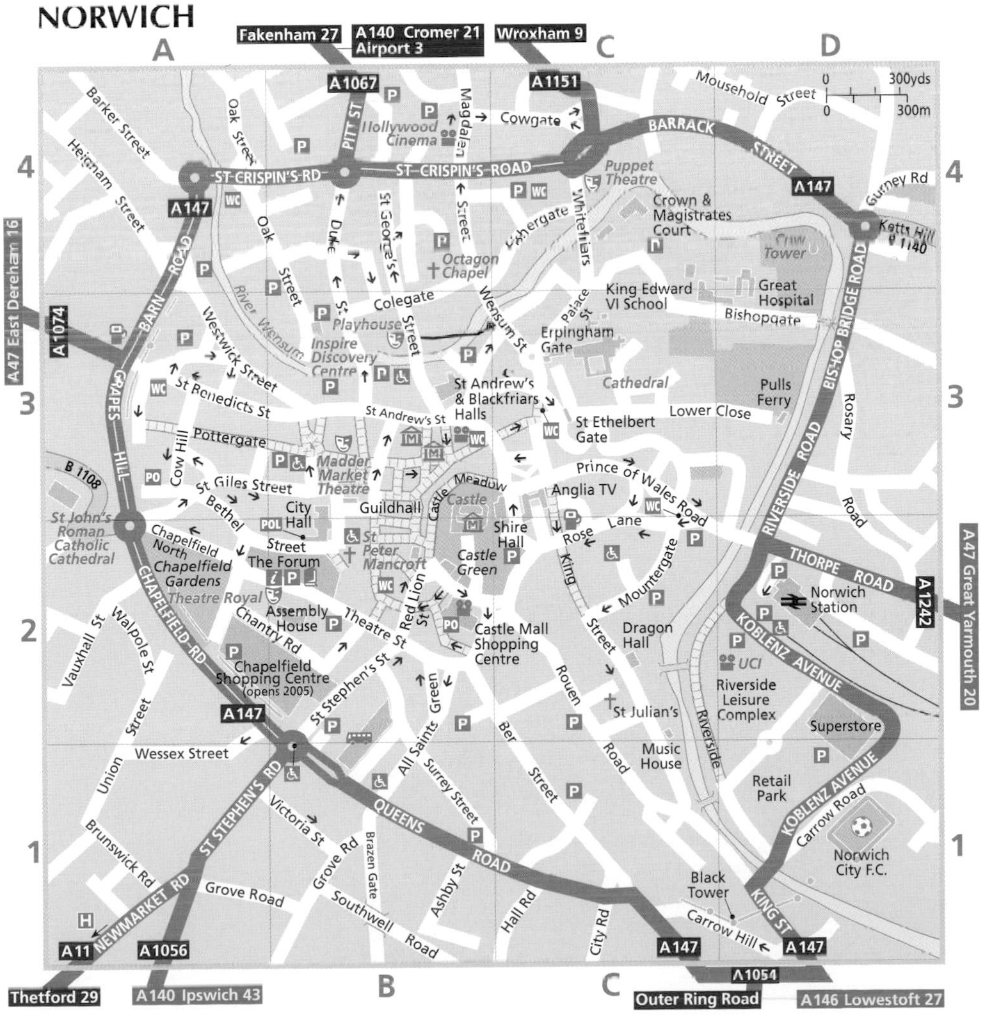

NORWICH

Park & Ride

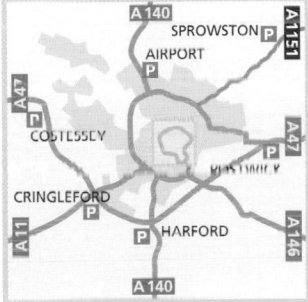

NOTTINGHAM

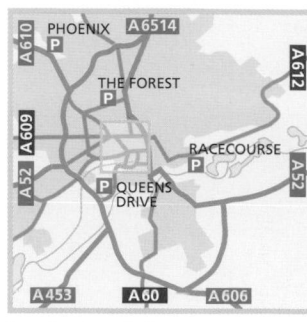

Park & Ride

OBAN

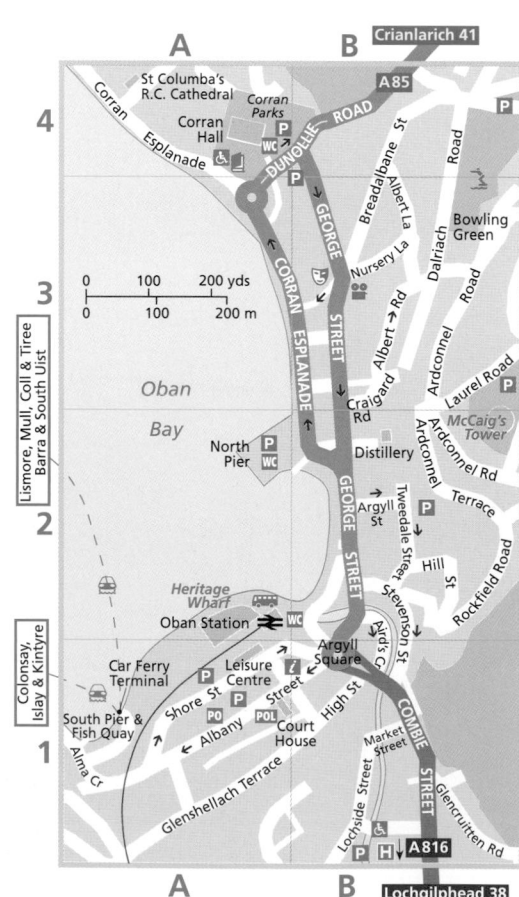

OXFORD

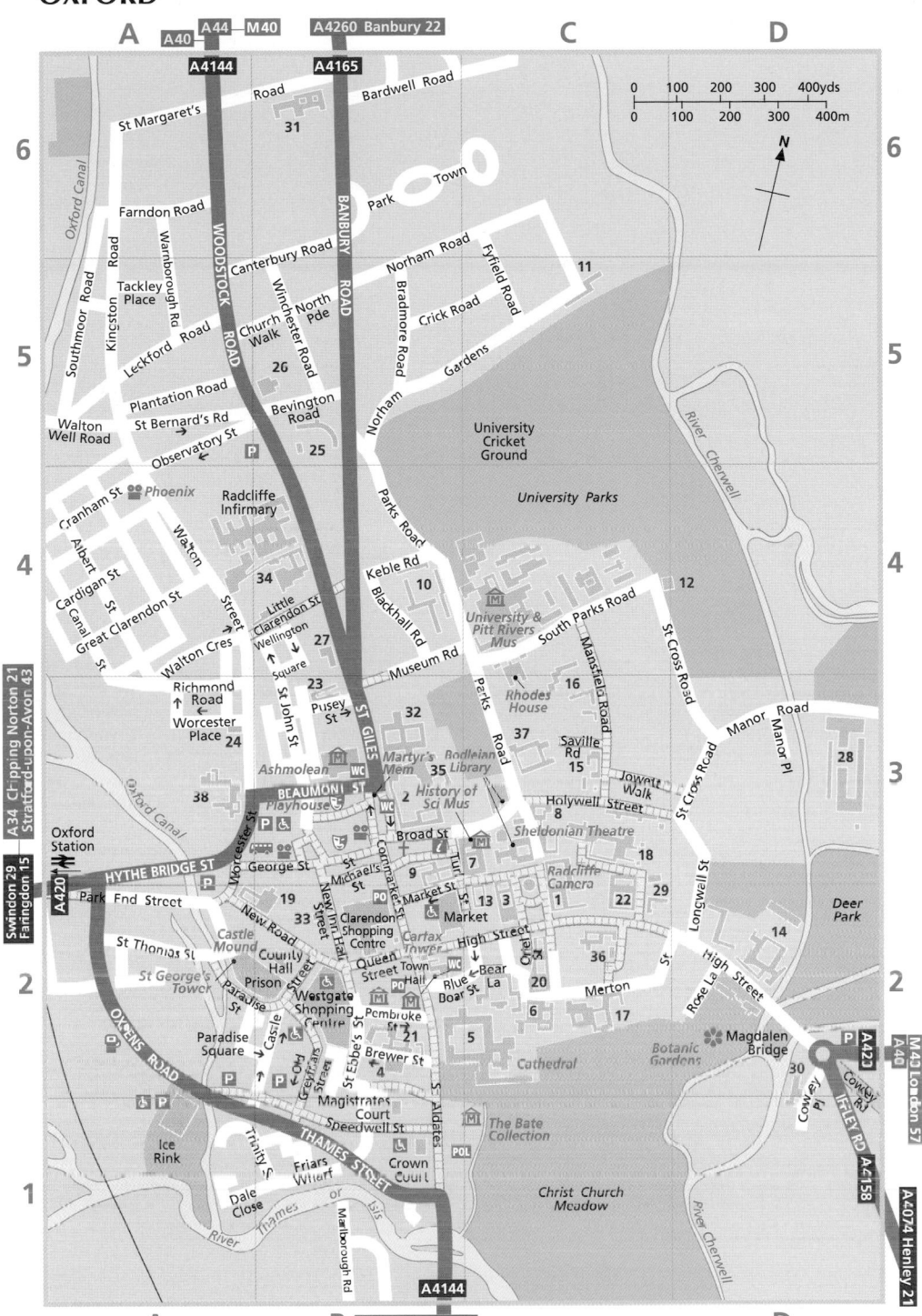

A44 M40
A40
A4260 Banbury 22
A4144
A4165

Park & Ride

WATER EATON
PEAR TREE
SEACOURT
THORNHILL
REDBRIDGE
A 44 A 34
A 40
A 40
A 420 A 34 A 4074

A34 Chipping Norton 21
Stratford-upon-Avon 43
Swindon 29
Faringdon 15
A420
A4144
A34 Abingdon 7
Newbury 28
A4074 Henley-on-Thames 21
M43 London 57
A40
A423
A4158
A4074 Henley 21
Cowley Rd
Iffley Rd

PLACES OF INTEREST

Ashmolean Musum B3
Bodleian Library C3
Botanic Gardens D2
Carfax Tower B2
Castle Mound A2
History of Science
  Musuem C3
Martyr's Memorial B3
Radcliffe Camera C3
Rhodes House C3
St George's Tower A2
Sheldonian Theatre C3
University Museum &
  Pitt Rivers Museum C4
University Parks C4

UNIVERSITY COLLEGES

 1 All Souls C2
 2 Balliol B3
 3 Brasenose C2
 4 Campion Hall B2
 5 Christ Church C2
 6 Corpus Christi C2
 7 Exeter C3
 8 Hertford C3
 9 Jesus B3
10 Keble B4
11 Lady Margaret
   Hall C5
12 Linacre D4
13 Lincoln C2
14 Magdalen D2
15 Manchester C3
16 Mansfield C3
17 Merton C2
18 New College C3
19 Nuffield B2
20 Oriel C2
21 Pembroke B2
22 Queen's C2
23 Regent's Park B3
24 Ruskin A3
25 St Anne's B5
26 St Antony's B5
27 St Bene't's Hall B4
28 St Catherine's D3
29 St Edmund Hall C2
30 St Hilda's D2
31 St Hugh's B6
32 St John's B3
33 St Peter's B2
34 Somerville B4
35 Trinity B3
36 University C2
37 Wadham C3
38 Worcester A3

TOWN PLANS

STREET INDEX

Albert Street A4
Banbury Road B6
Bardwell Road B6
Bear Lane C2
Beaumont Street B3
Bevington Road B5
Blackhall Road B4
Bradmore Road B5
Brewer Street B2
Broad Street B3
Canal Street A4
Canterbury Road B6
Cardigan Street A4
Castle Street B2
Church Walk B5
Cornmarket Street B3
Cowley Road D2
Cranham Street A4
Crick Road B5
Farndon Road A6
Fyfield Road C5
George Street B3
Great Clarendon
  Street A4
High Street C2
Holywell Street C3
Hythe Bridge
  Street A3
Iffley Road D1
Jowett Walk C3
Keble Road B4
Kingston Road A5
Leckford Road A5
Little Clarendon
  Street B4
Longwall Street D2
Manor Road D3
Mansfield Road C4
Marlborough Road B1
Merton Street C2
Museum Road B4
New Inn Hall B2
New Road B2
Norham Gardens B5
Norham Road B5
North Parade B5
Observatory Street A5
Old Greyfriars Street B2
Oriel Street C2
Oxpens Road A2
Paradise Square A2
Paradise Street A2
Park End Street A2
Park Town B6
Parks Road B4–C3
Pembroke Street B2
Plantation Road A5
Pusey Street B3
Queen Street B2
Richmond Road A3
St Aldates B1
St Bernard's Road A5
St Cross Road D4
St Ebbe's Street B2
St Giles B3
St Margaret's Road A6
St Michael's Street B3
St Thomas Street A2
Saville Road C3
South Parks Road C4
Southmoor Road A5
Speedwell St B1
Tackley Place A5
Thames Street B1
Turl Street B3
Walton Crescent A4
Walton Street A4
Walton Well Road A5
Warnborough Road A6
Wellington Square B4
Winchester Road B5
Woodstock Road A6
Worcester Place A3
Worcester Street A3

PAISLEY

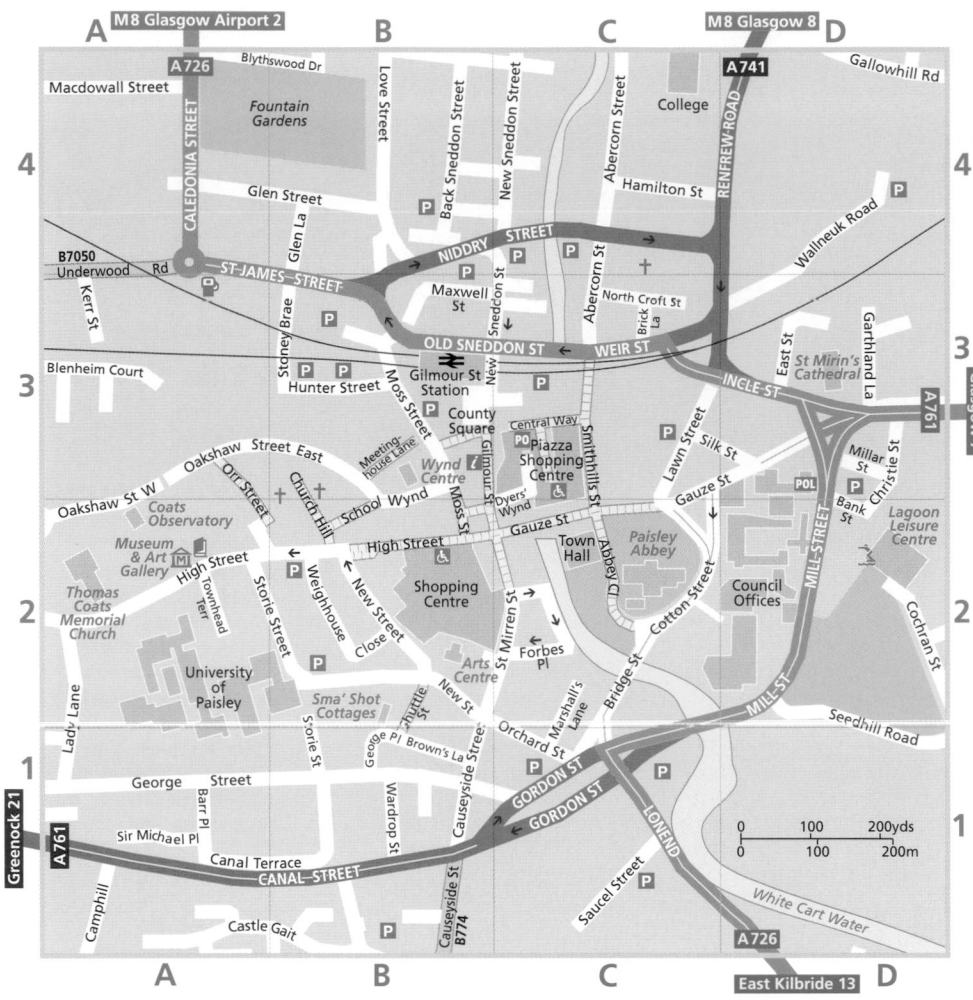

STREET INDEX

PERTH

STREET INDEX

Park & Ride

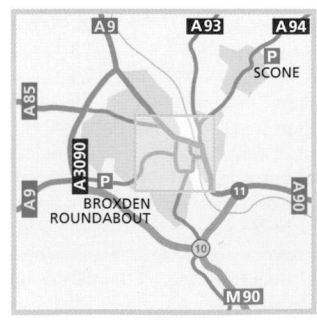

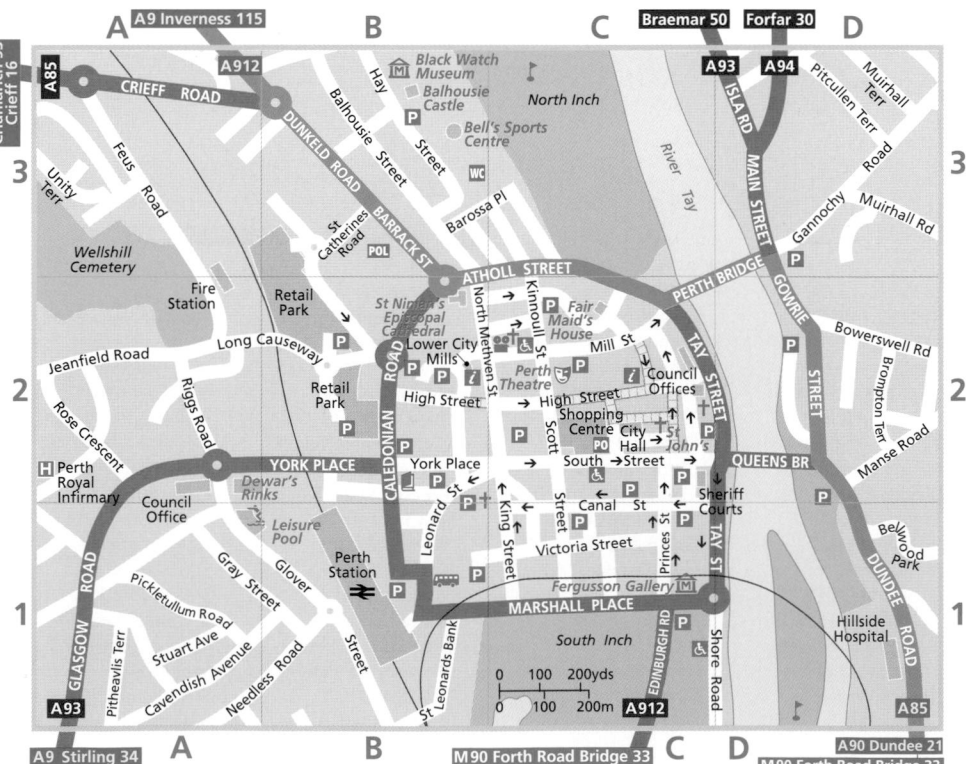

OSWESTRY

STREET INDEX

Albert Mews B3
Albert Road B3
Ambleside Road C2
Arthur Street A2
Ash Road B3
Bailey Street B2
Beatrice Street C3
Black Gate Street B2
Castle Street A3
Chapel Street A3
Church Street A1
Coney Green B2–C2
Cross Street B2
English Walls B1
King Street C3
Leg Street B2
Llys Lane C1
Lord Street A3
Madog Place B2
Middleton Road C1
New Street B2
Oak Street A3
Oswald Road C2
Powis Place B3
Prince Lorne Street B3
Prince Street B3
Roft Street B1
Salop Road C1
Smithfield Road B1
Smithfield Street A1
Station Road C3
Stewart Road C1
Swan Lane B3
Welsh Walls A1–A2
Willow Street A2
York Street A3

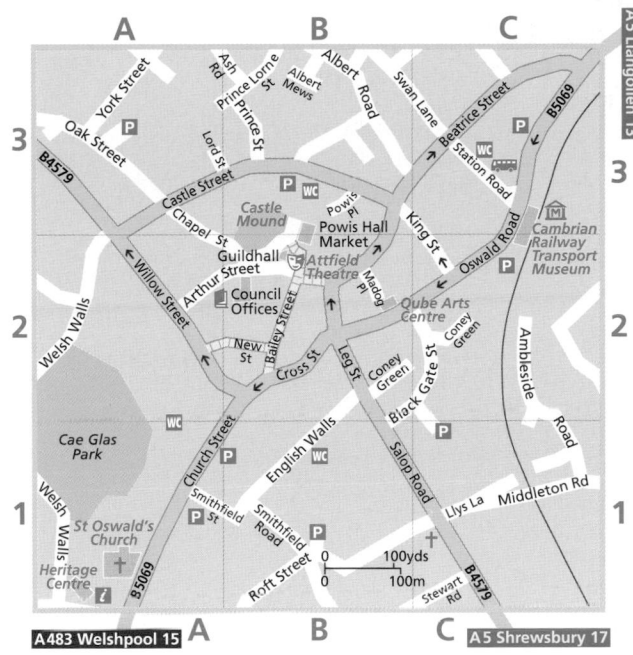

PEEBLES

STREET INDEX

Biggiesknowe A2
Bridgegate B2
Caledonian Road A1
Cross Road A3
Cross Street A3
Crossland Crescent A2
Cuddyside B3
Damdale B3
Dean Park B3
Dukehaugh A1
Eastgate C2
Edinburgh Road C2–B3
Elcho Street A2
Elcho Street Brae A2
Greenside A2
High Street B2
Kingsmeadows Road B1
March Street A3
Montgomery Place A3
Murray Place B3
Northgate B3
Old Church Street B2
Old Town A2
Rosetta Road A3
Springhill Road B1
St Michaels Bank B2
The Bridges C2
The Mount A1
Tweed Avenue C1
Tweed Brae C2
Tweed Bridge Court A1
Tweed Green B2
Venlaw High Road C3
Walkershaugh C2

PENRITH

STREET INDEX

Albert Street B3
Angel Lane B2
Arthur Street C3
Benson Row C3
Bluebell Lane B2
Brook Street B2
Brunswick Road A2
Brunswick Square A3
Brunswick Terrace A3
Burrowgate C2
Castle Terrace B1
Castle Hill Road B1
Castlegate B2
Corn Market B2
Corney Place B3
Duke Street B3
Elm Terrace B2
Friargate C2
Great Dockray B2
Hunter's Lane B3
King Street C1
Market Square C2
Meeting House Lane C3
Middlegate B3
Mill Street A2
Myers Lane A1
Neville Avenue B1
Norfolk Road A1
Portland Place B3
Princes Street B1
Queen Street B3
Rowcliffe Lane C2
Sandgate C3
Southend Road C1
Ullswater Road A1
Victoria Road C1
West Lane B1
William Street B3
Wilson Row B3
York Street A2

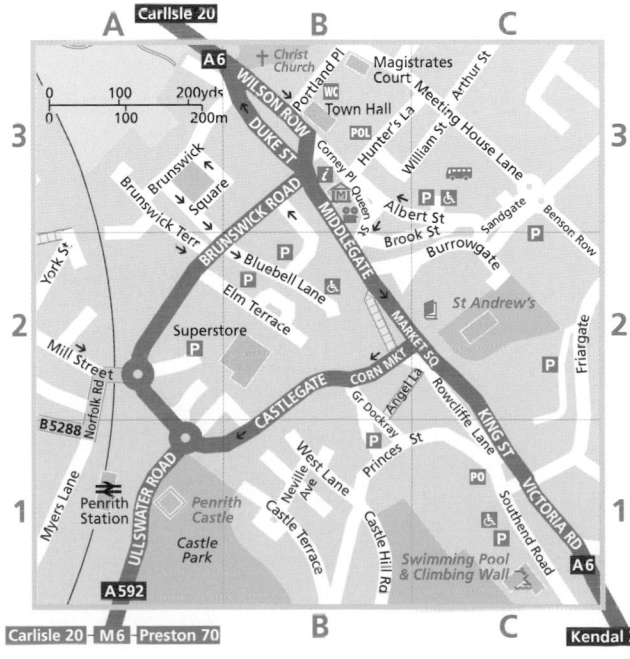

TOWN PLANS

PETERBOROUGH

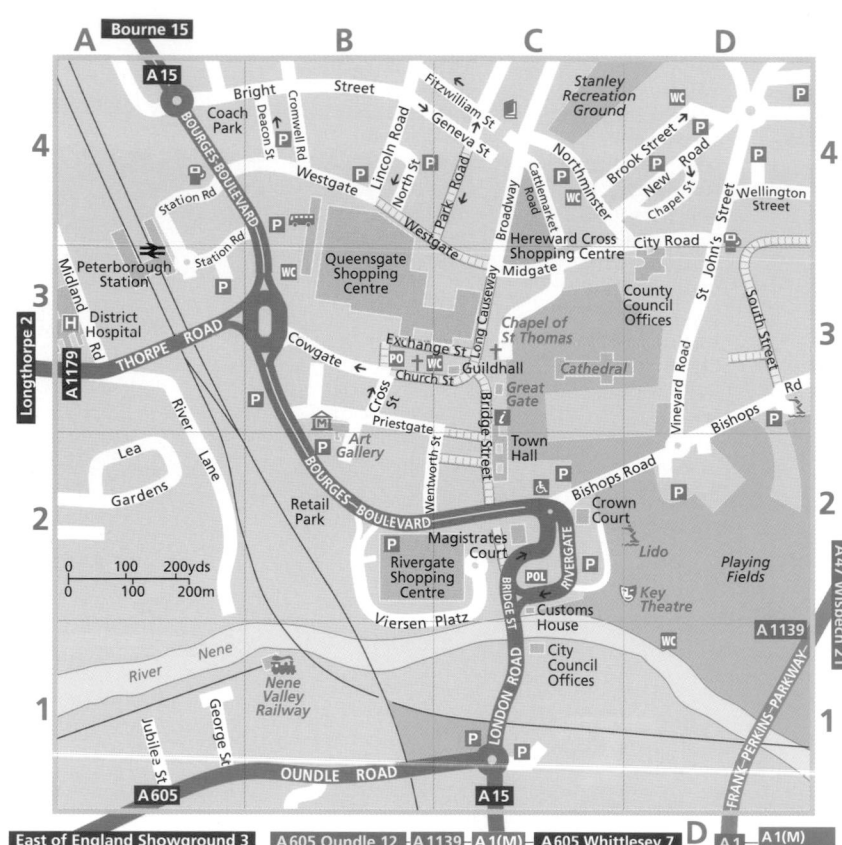

PLYMOUTH

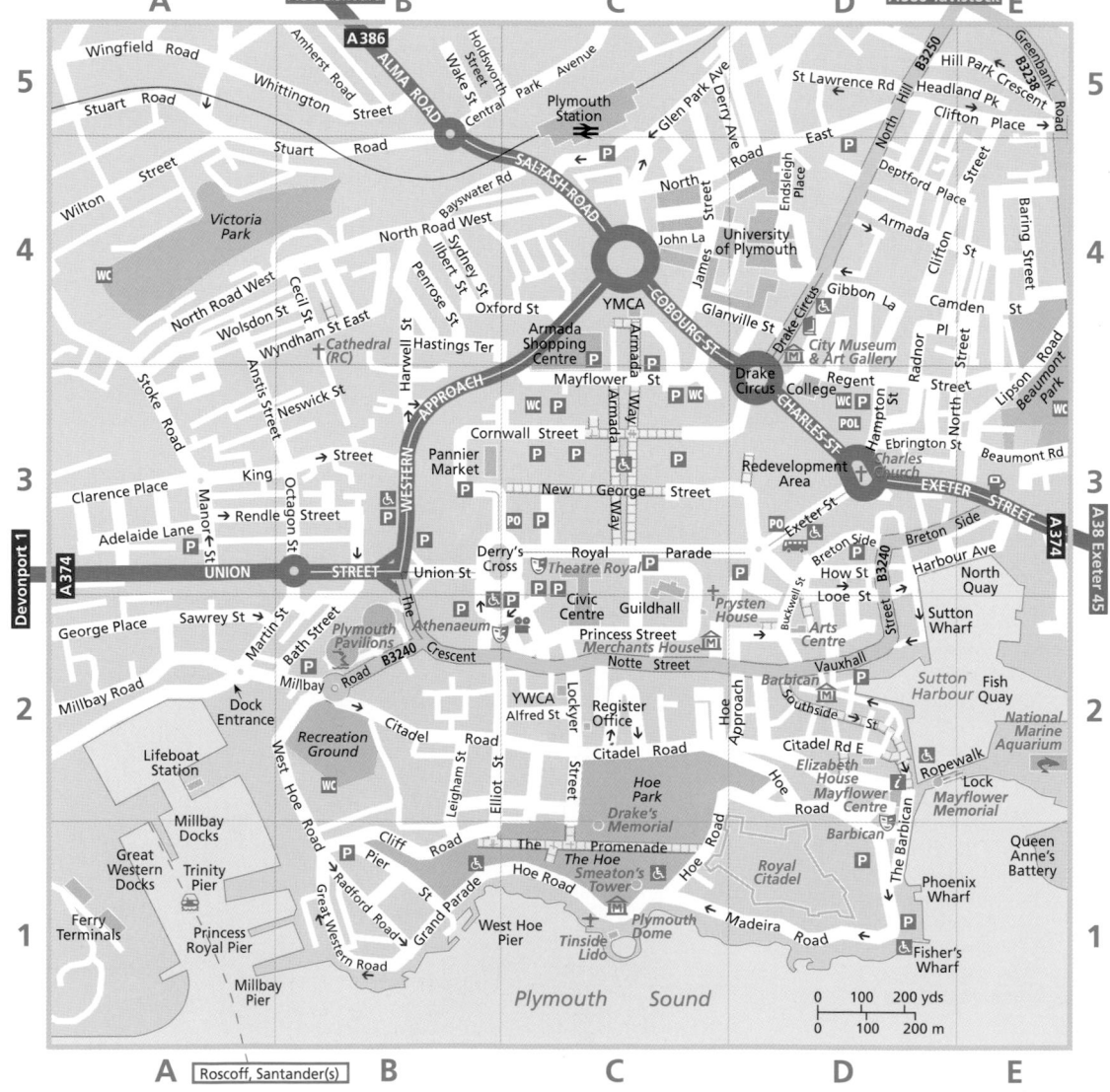

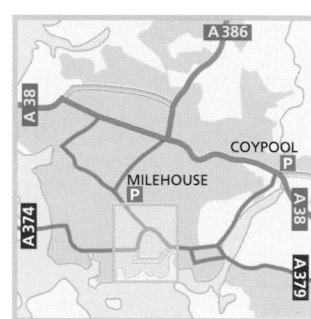

Park & Ride

PETERHEAD

STREET INDEX

Albert Street C2
Alexandra Parade C2
Almanythie Road B3
Back Street B2
Baltic Place C2
Bath Street B1
Battery Park B3
Bridge Street C1
Broad Street B2
Brook Lane B2
Castle Street C1
Chapel Street B2
Charlotte Street B1
East North Street B3
Ellis Street B2
Erroll Street A2
Farmers' Lane C1
Gadle Braes B3
Gladstone Road B3
Grant Court B2
Greenhill Road C1
Hanover Street A2
Harbour Street C1
Hay Crescent A3
Ives Road A3
Jamaica Street B1
James Street B1
Keith Street C1
King Street A2
Landale Road A2
Lodge Walk B1
Longate B2
Love Lane B2
Maiden Street B1
Marischal Street B2
Merchant Street B1
New Street B3
North Street B2
Park Lane B2
Pleasure Walk C1
Pool Lane C1
Port Henry Road B3
Prince Street A2
Queen Street A3–B2
Raemoss Road A3
Seagate B2
Ship Street C1
Shiprow C1
Skene Street B3
St Andrew Street B1
St Mary Street A2
St Peter Street A2
The Esplanade C3
Tolbooth Wynd B1
Ugie Street A3
Uphill Lane B1
Victoria Road A3
Volum Street C2
Wallace Street B1
Wilson Street B3
Windmill Street A3
York Street A2

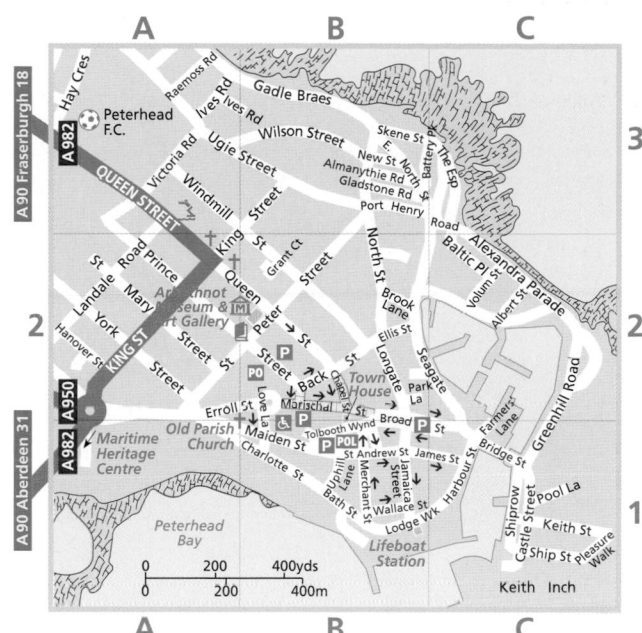

PITLOCHRY

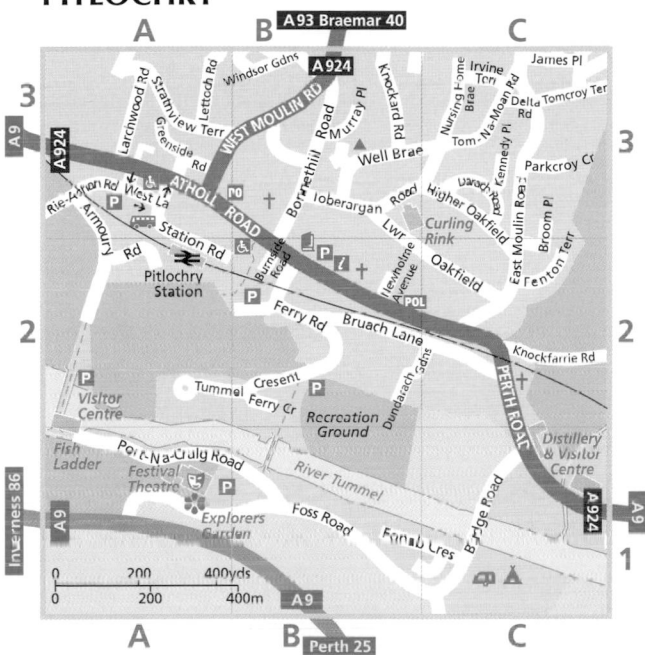

STREET INDEX

Armoury Road A3
Atholl Road A3
Bonnethill Road B3
Bridge Road C1
Broom Place C3
Bruach Lane B2
Burnside Road B2
Darach Road C3
Delta Road C3
Dundarach Gardens B2
East Moulin Road C2
Fenton Terrace C2
Ferry Crescent B2
Ferry Road B2
Fonab Crescent B1
Foss Road B1
Greenside Road A3
Higher Oakfield C3
Irvine Terrace C3
James Place C3
Kennedy Place C3
Knockard Road B3
Knockfarrie Road C2
Larchwood Road A3
Lettoch Road A3
Lower Oakfield B3
Murray Place B3
Newholme Avenue B2
Nursing Home Brae C3
Parkcroy Crescent C3
Perth Road C2
Port-Na-Craig Road A1
Rie-Achan Road A3
Station Road A3
Strathview Terrace A3
Toberargan Road B3
Tom–Na–Moan
    Road C3
Tomcroy Terrace C3
Tummel Cresent A2
Well Brae B3
West Lane A3
West Moulin Road B3
Windsor Gardens B3

PORTREE

STREET INDEX

Balmoral Road B3
Bank Street C1–C2
Bayfield Road B1
Beaumont Crescent C2
Blaven Road B3
Bosville Terrace C2
Bridge Road A2
Coolin Drive C2
Cruachan Place B3
Fraser Crescent C3
Home Farm Road A3
Kitson Crescent C3
Manse Lane A2
Marsco Place B3
Martin Crescent C2
Mill Road C2
Park Road B2
Quay Street C1
Rosebank Terrace A3
Seafield Place A2
Somerled Square B2
Staffin Road C3
Stormy Hill Road B3
The Green B2
Viewfield Road A2
Wentworth Street B2
Windsor Crescent B3
York Drive B2

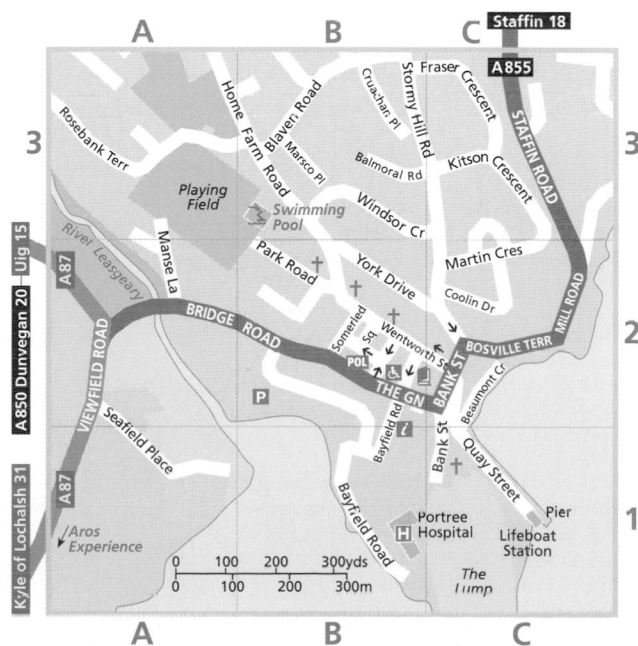

TOWN PLANS

POOLE

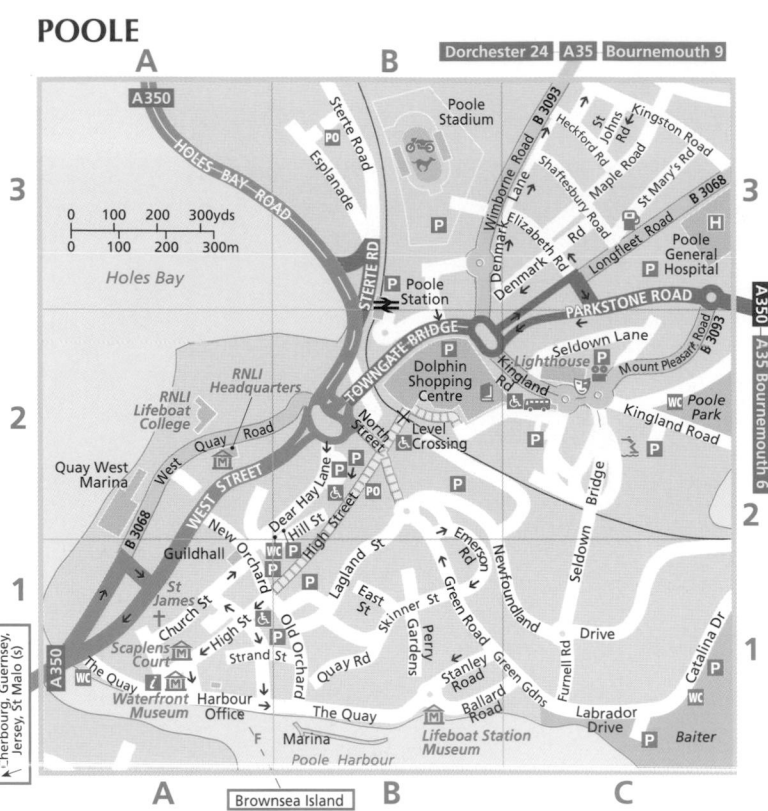

PORTSMOUTH

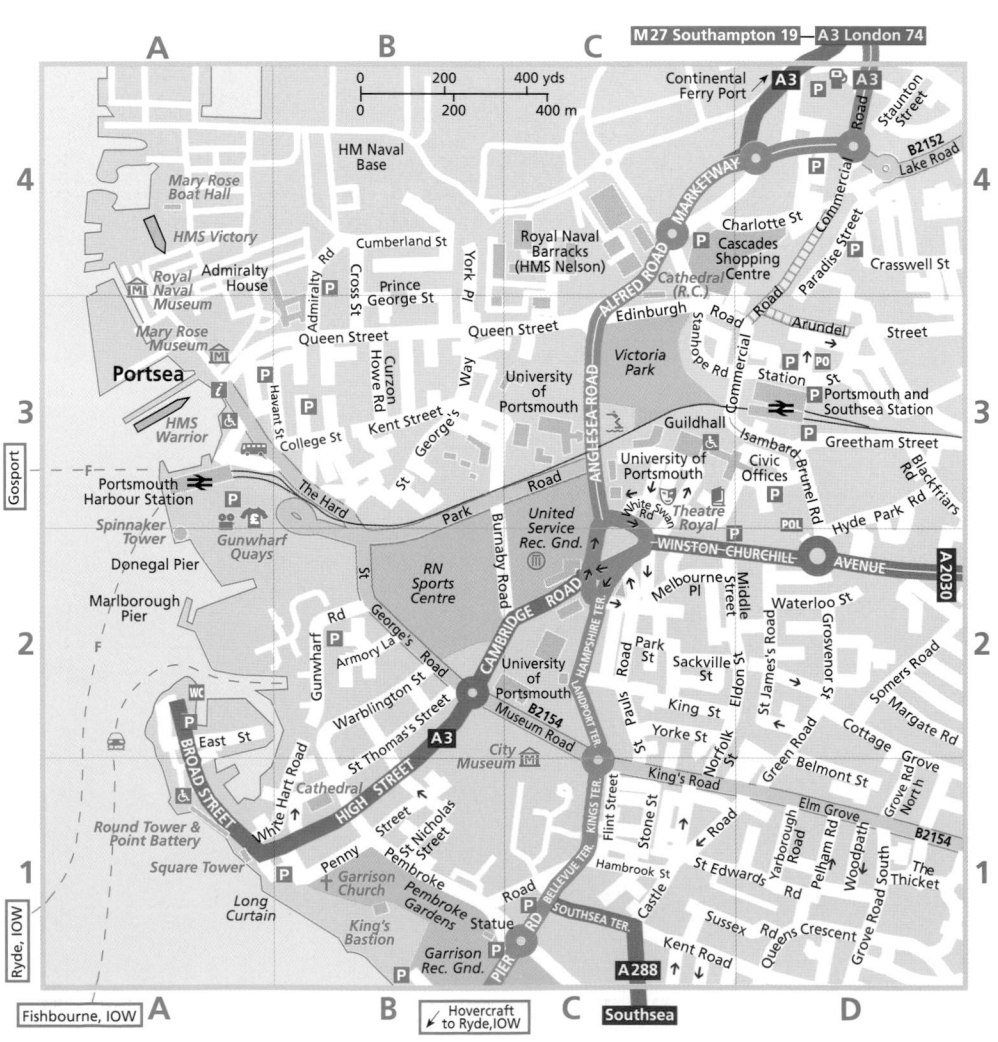

PRESTON

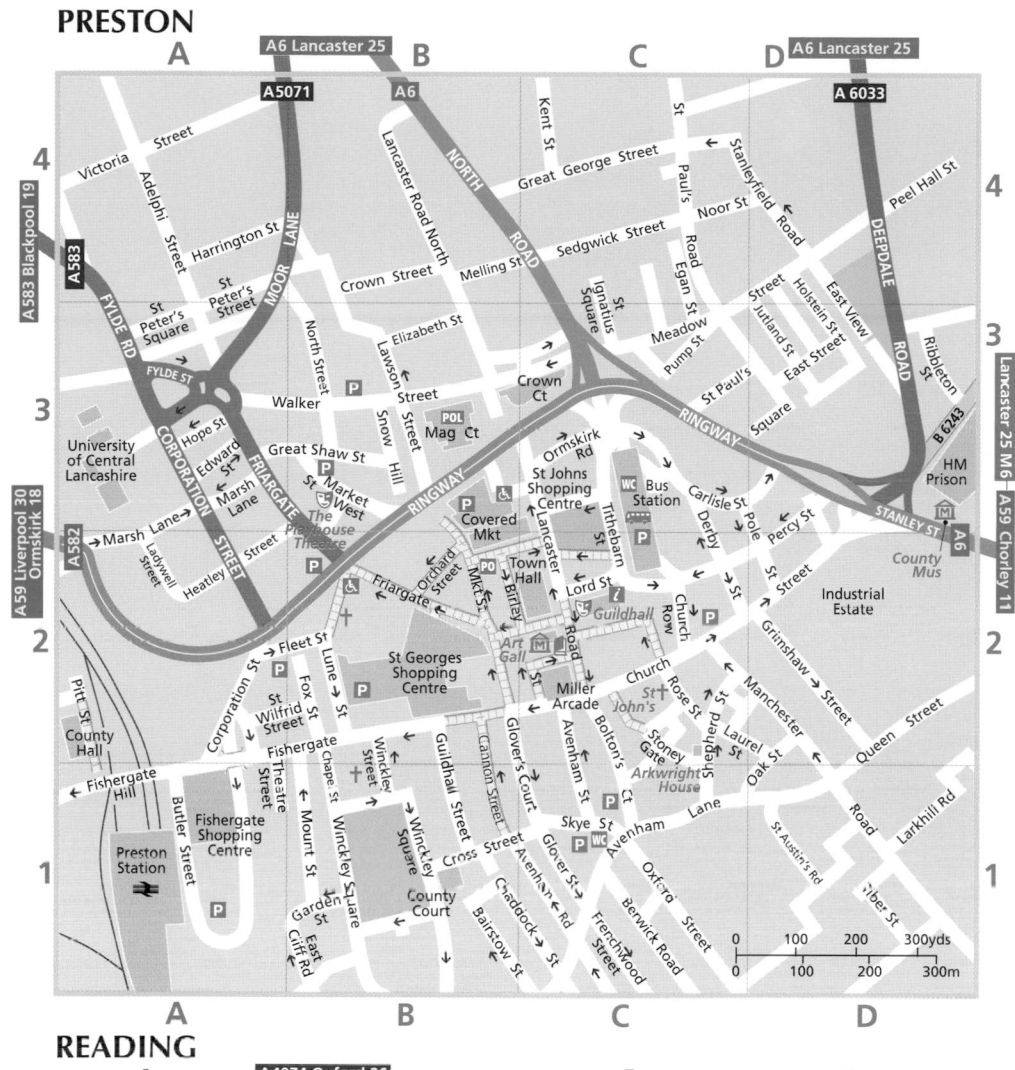

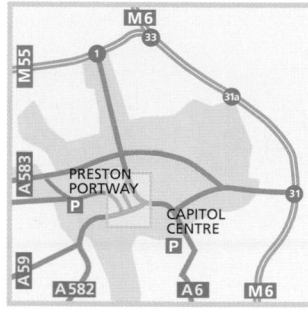

Park & Ride

STREET INDEX

Adelphi Street A4	Larkhill Road D1
Avenham Lane C1	Lawson Street B3
Birley Street B2	Lune Street B2
Bolton's Court C2–C1	Manchester Road
Butler Street A1	D2–D1
Carlisle Street C3	Market Street B2
Church Street C2–D2	Marsh Lane A3
Corporation Street	Mcadow Street C3–D4
A3–A2	North Road B4–C3
Deepdale Road D4–D3	Orchard Street B2
Derby Street C2	Ormskirk Road C3
Elizabeth Street B3	Oxford Street C1
Fishergate A2–B2	Pitt Street A2
Fleet Street B2	Pole Street D2
Friargate A3	Queen Street D2
Fylde Road A3	Ringway A2–D3
Fylde Street A3	St Paul's Road C4
Grimshaw Street D2	Sedgwick Street C4
Lancaster Road C2	Tithebarn Street C3–C2
Lancaster Road	Victoria Street A4
North B4	Walker Street A3–B3
	Winckley Square B1

READING

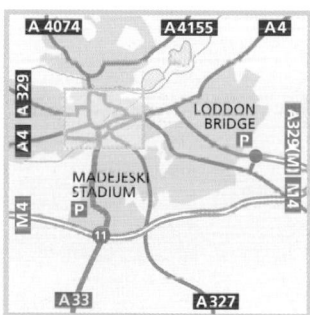

Park & Ride

STREET INDEX

Bath Road A2	Kendrick Road D1
Battle Street A3	Kings Road C3
Berkeley Avenue B1	London Road D2
Blagrave Street C3	London Street C2
Bridge Street C2	Mill Lane C2
Broad Street B3	Minster Street C3
Castle Hill A2	Oxford Road A3–B3
Castle Street B2	Pell Street C1
Caversham Rd B3	Queen's Road D2
Chatham Street A3	Russell Street A2
Coley Avenue A1	Silver Street C1
Crown Street C2	South Street D2
Duke Street C3	Southampton Street C2
Forbury Road C3	Station Hill B3
Friar Street B3	Tilehurst Road A2
George Street A3	Valpy Street C3
George Street C4	Vastern Road B4
Gun Street B2	Watlington Street D2
Inner Distribution	West Street B3
Road B2	Whitley Street C1
	Zinzan Street B2

RICHMOND

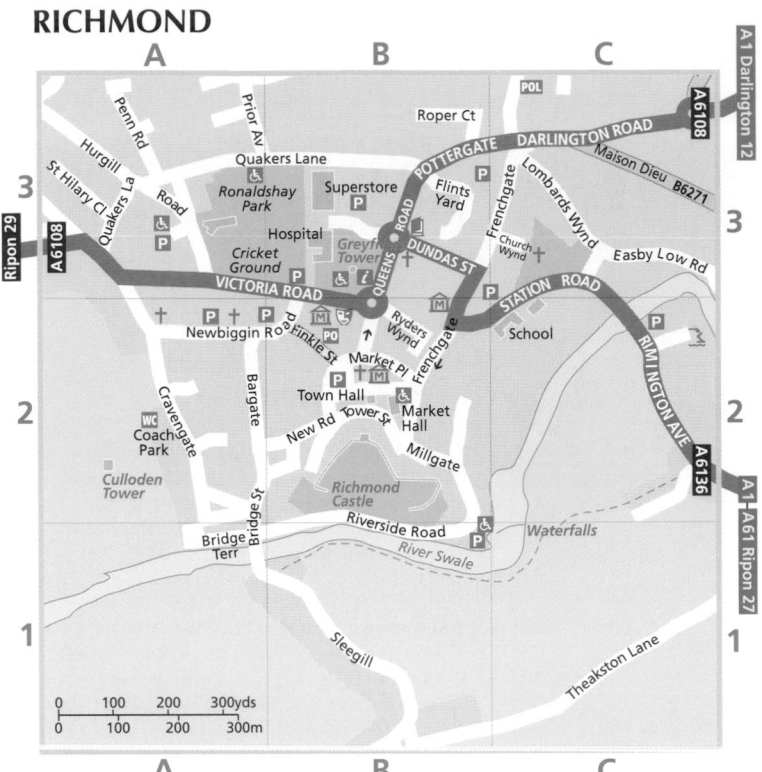

RIPON

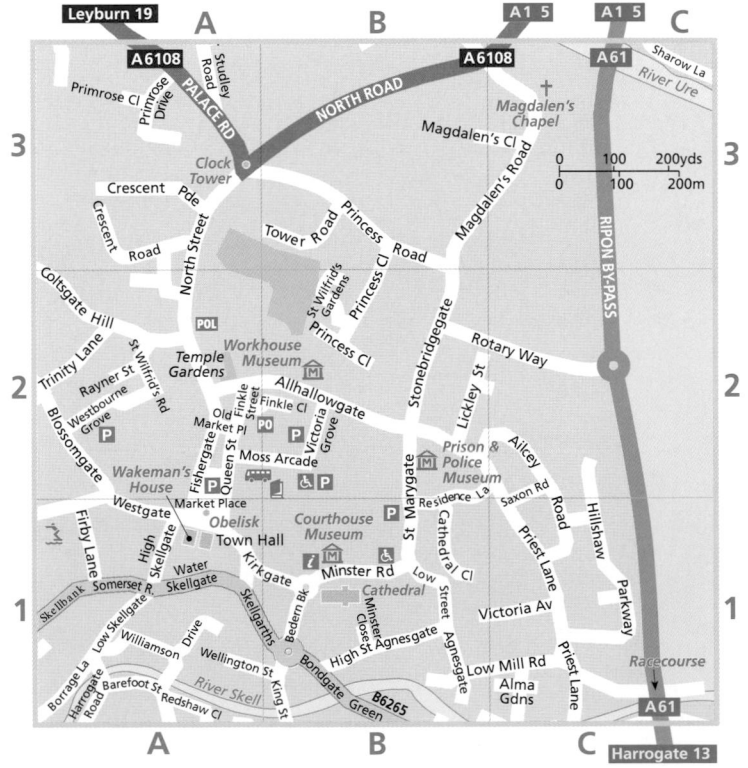

ROCHDALE

STREET INDEX

Ann Street C1
Ashworth Street A4
Back Drake Street C2
Baillie Street B3–D4
Baron Street C3
Bell Street B4
Blossom Place C4
Broadfield Street B1
Castlemere Street A1
Cheetham Street B4
Church Lane B2
Church Stile B2
College Road A3
Constantine Road C3
Crook Street C4
Dowling Street B1
Drake Street A1–C3
Entwisle Road D4
Faulkner Street C3
Fleece Street B3
George Street C4
Great George St C2
Henry Street B1
High Level Road C1
High Street B4
Hill Street D3
Holland Street A4
Howard Place B4
Hunter's Lane B4
John Street C4
Kelsall Street C4
Kenion Street C3
Lincoln Street D1
Livsey Street D2
Maclure Road C2

Manchester Road A1
Mere Street B1
Miall Street C1
Milkstone Road B1
Molesworth Street D2
Moore Street C2
Moss Lane D2
Nelson Street B3
Newgate B3
Oldham Road C2–D1
Packer Street B3
Penn Street C4
Richard Street C1
River Street C3
Robinson Street D3
St Mary's Gate B4
St Alban's St A1–B2
School Lane C2
Sheriff Street A4
Slack Street C3
Smith Street C3
Sparrow Hill B2
Station Road C1
Suffolk Street B1
Sussex Street B1
Tatham Street D2
The Avenue B3
The Butts B3
The Esplanade A3
Toad Lane B4
Tweedale Street B1
Union Street C4
Vicar's Drive B2
Vicar's Gate B3
Water Street C3
Yorkshire Street B4

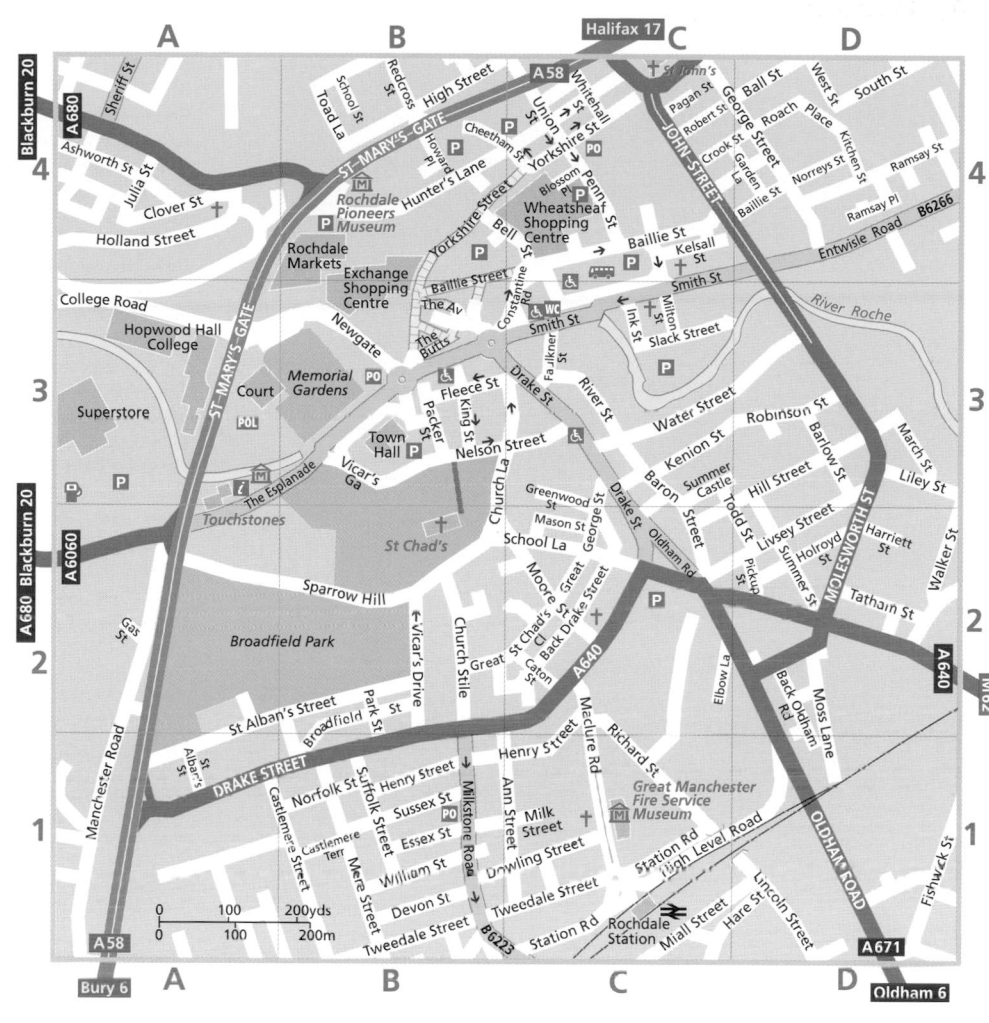

ROCHESTER

STREET INDEX

Bardell Terrace C2
Blue Boar Lane B3
Boley Hill A3
Castle Hill A3
Cazeneuve Street B2
City Way C1
Corporation Street B3
Crow Lane B2
East Row B2
Eastgate B2
Esplanade A3
Ethelbert Road A1
Foord Street B1
Furrells Road C2
Gashouse Road B4
Gordon Terrace A1
High Street A3–C2
Hoopers Road B1

James Street B1
John Street B1
King Edward Road A2
King Street B2
Lockington Grove A2
Longley Road A1
Love Lane A2
Maidstone Road A1
New Road C1
Rochester Avenue B1
Rochester Bridge A4
Roebuck Road A2
St Margaret's Street A2
Star Hill B2
The Close A1
The Terrace B2
Victoria Street B2
Vines Lane A2
Watts Avenue A1

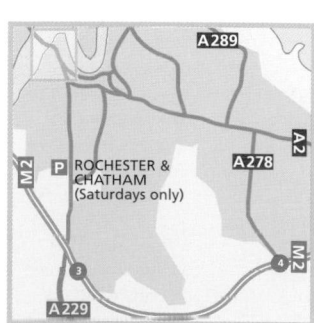

Park & Ride

TOWN PLANS

ROSS–ON–WYE

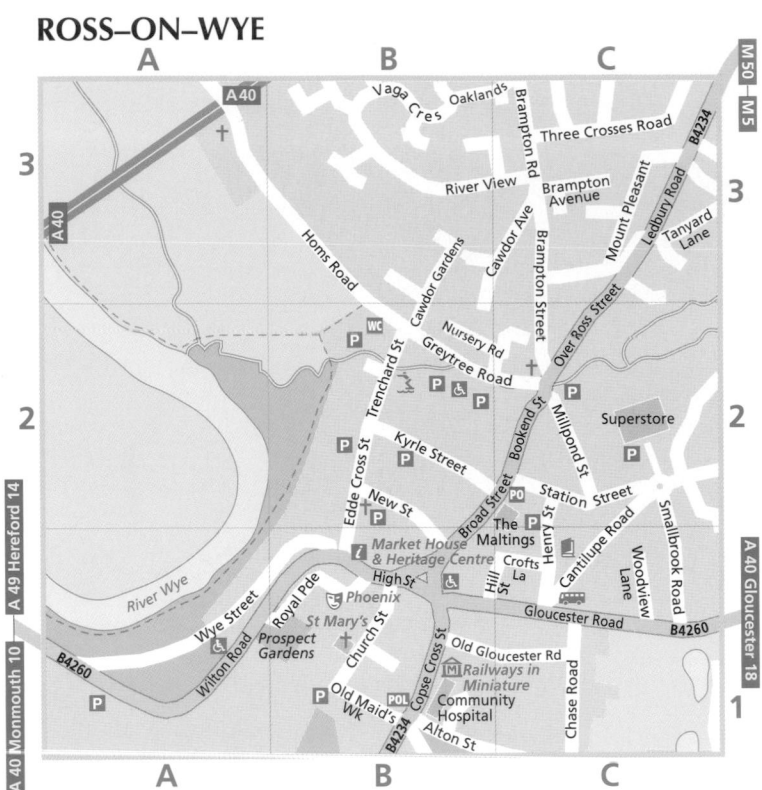

RUGBY

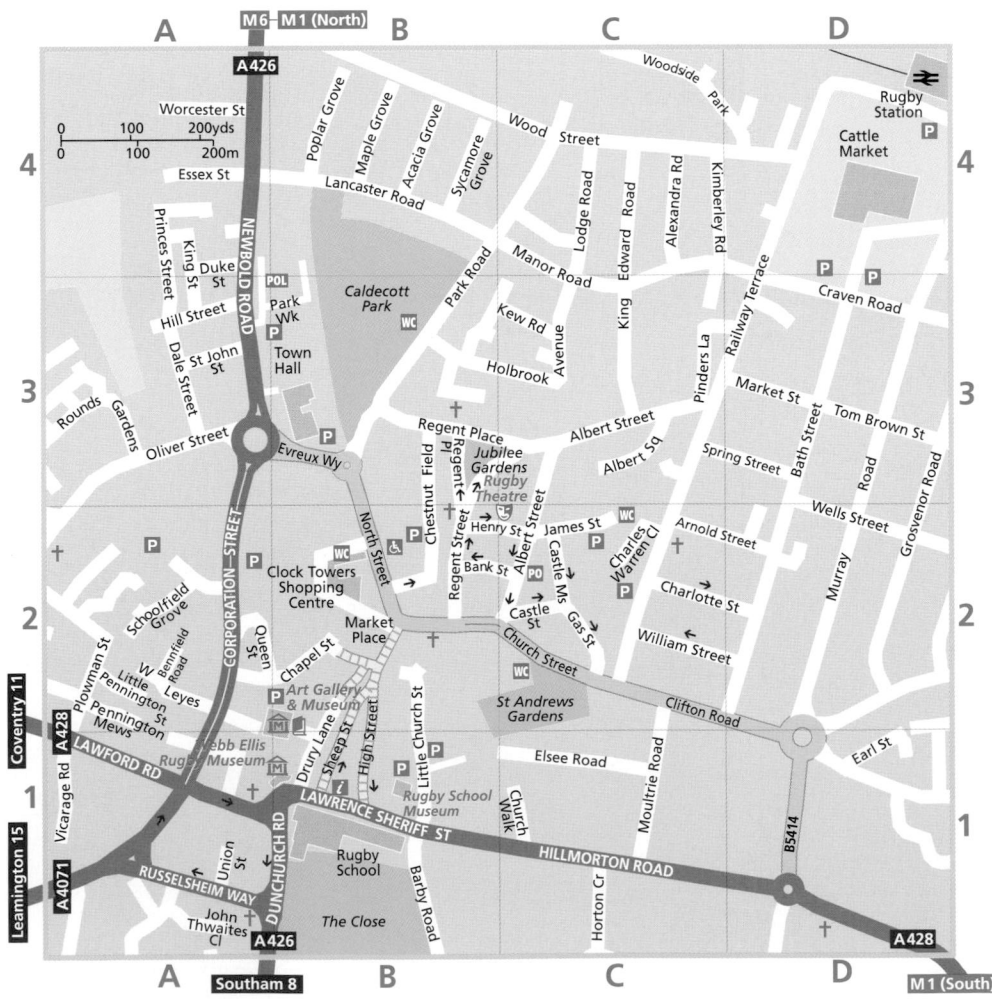

ST ALBANS

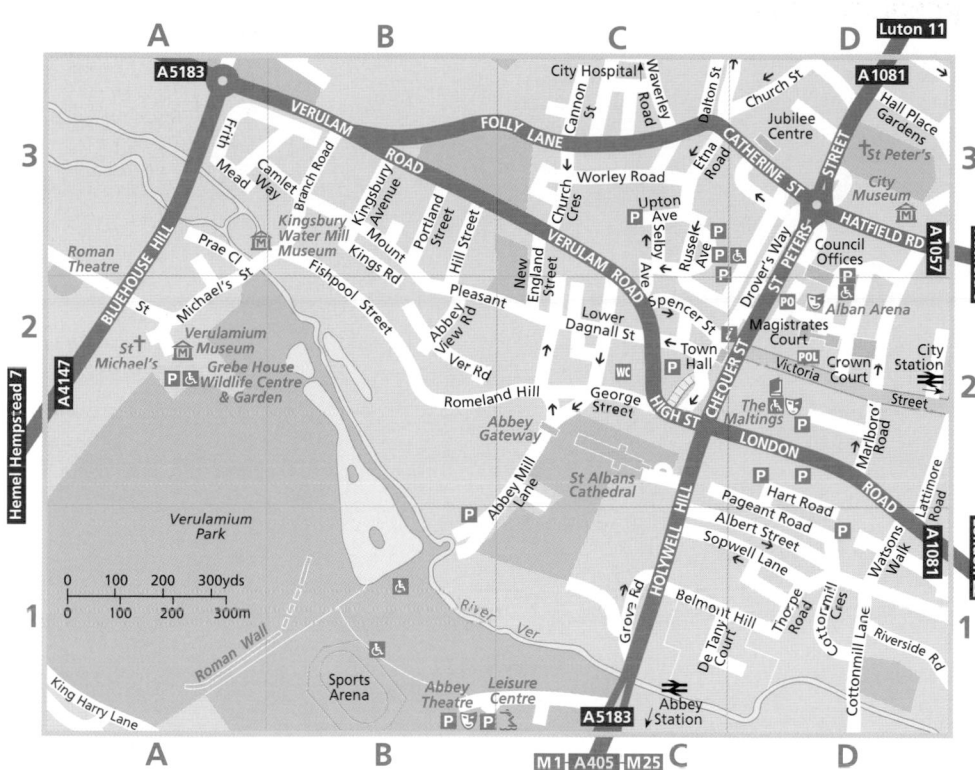

TOWN PLANS

SALFORD

SALISBURY

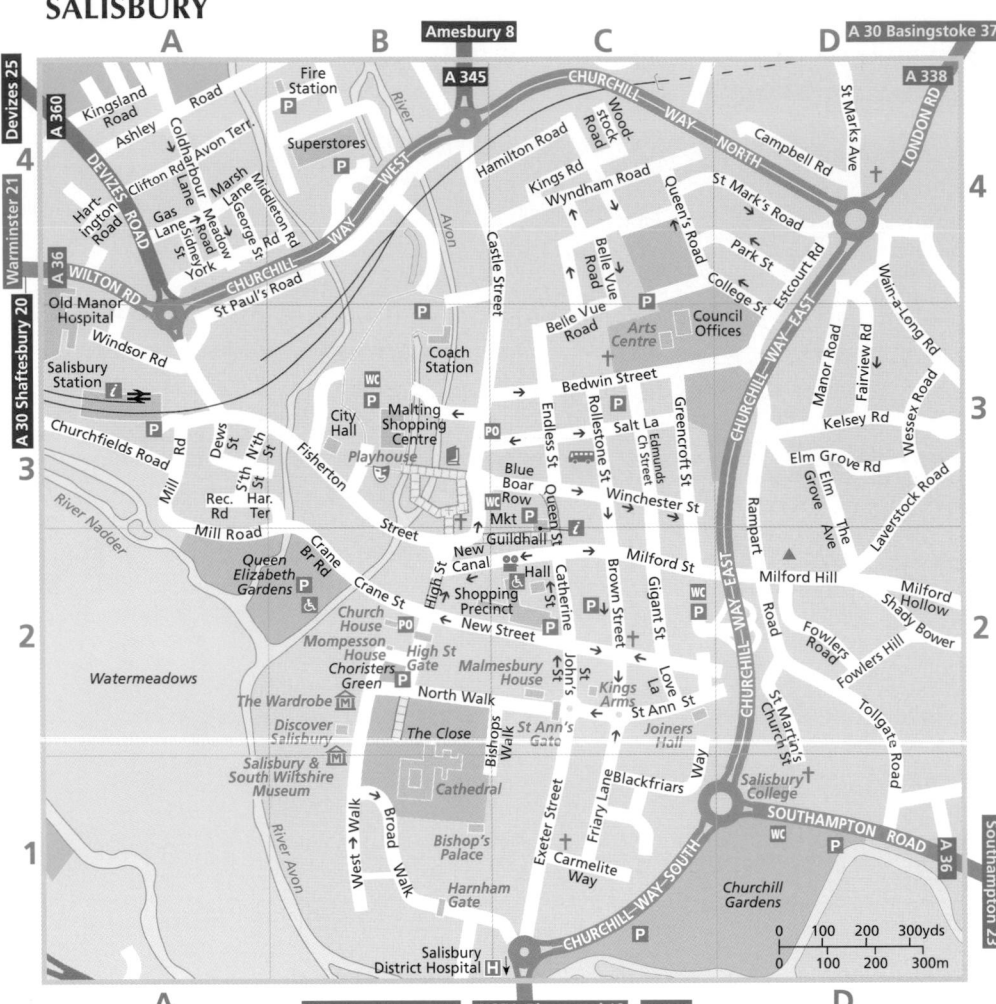

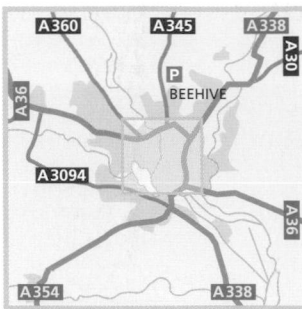

Park & Ride

SETTLE

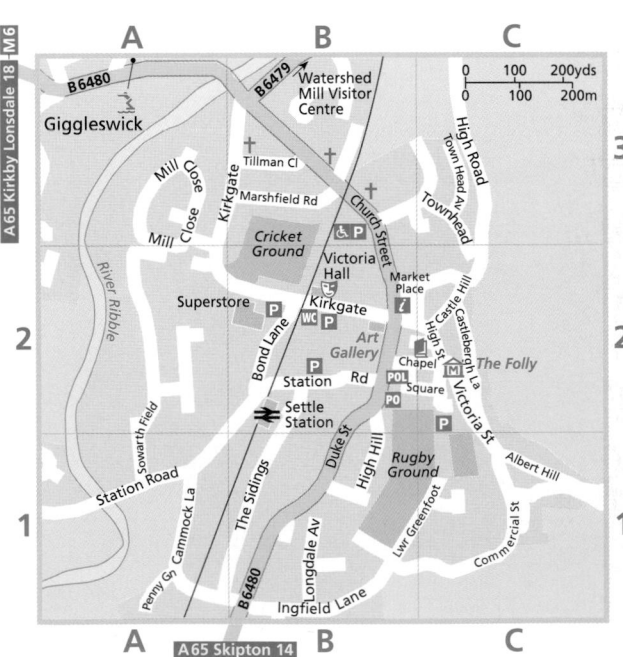

SCARBOROUGH

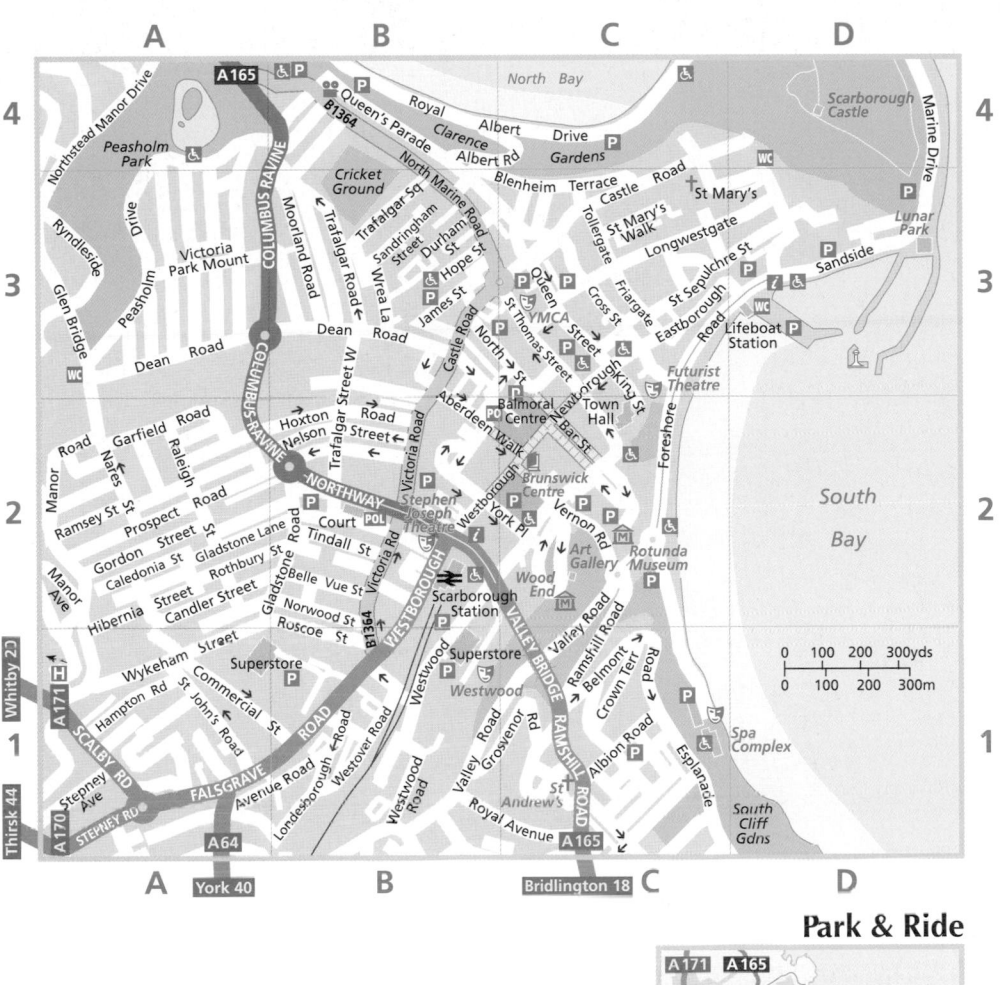

Park & Ride

SHAFTESBURY

TOWN PLANS

SHEFFIELD

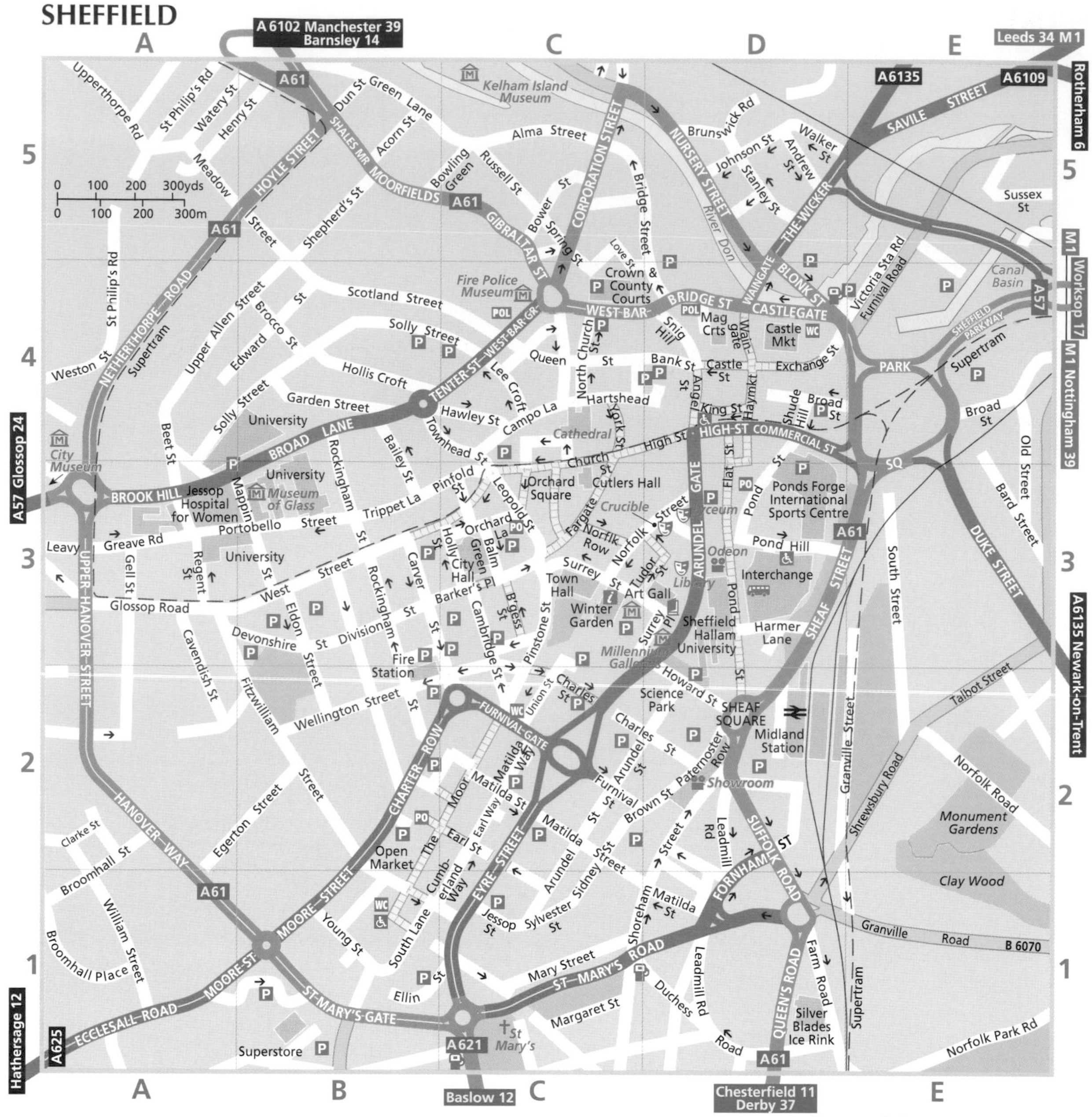

Park & Ride
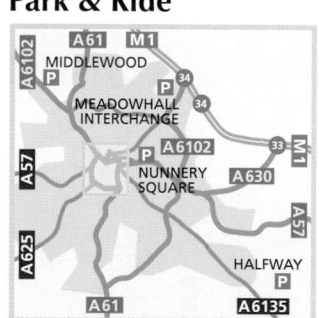

SHREWSBURY

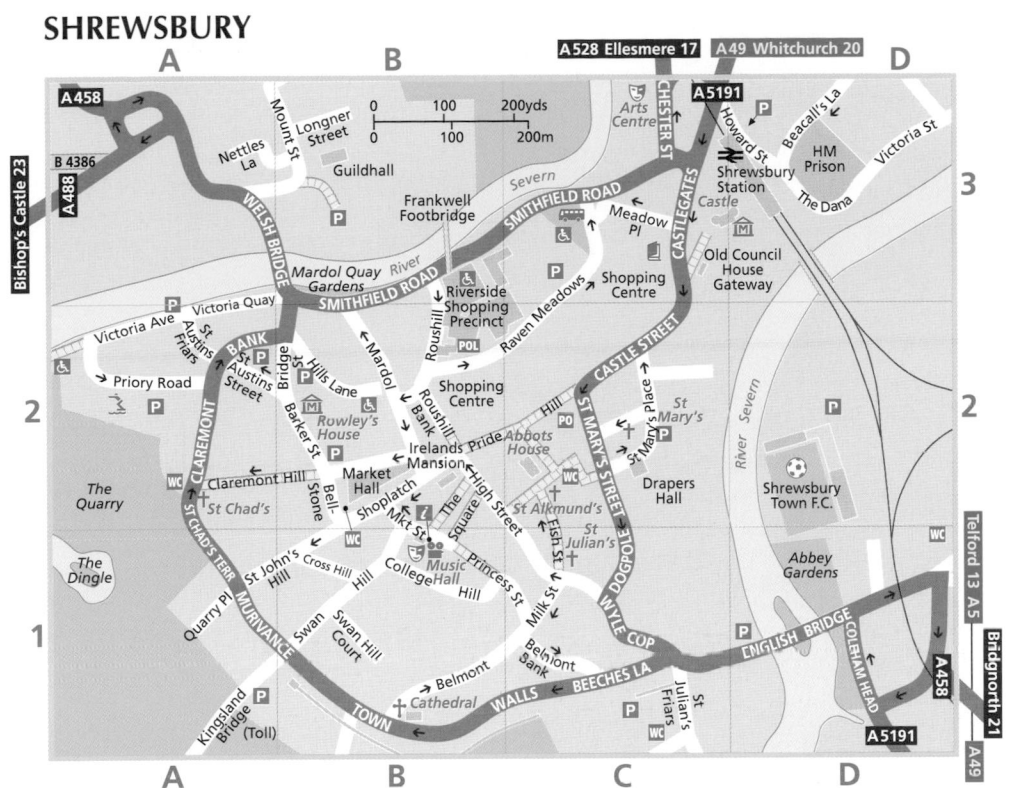
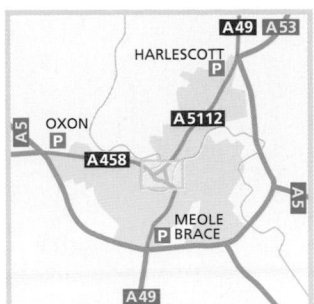

Park & Ride

TOWN PLANS

SKIPTON

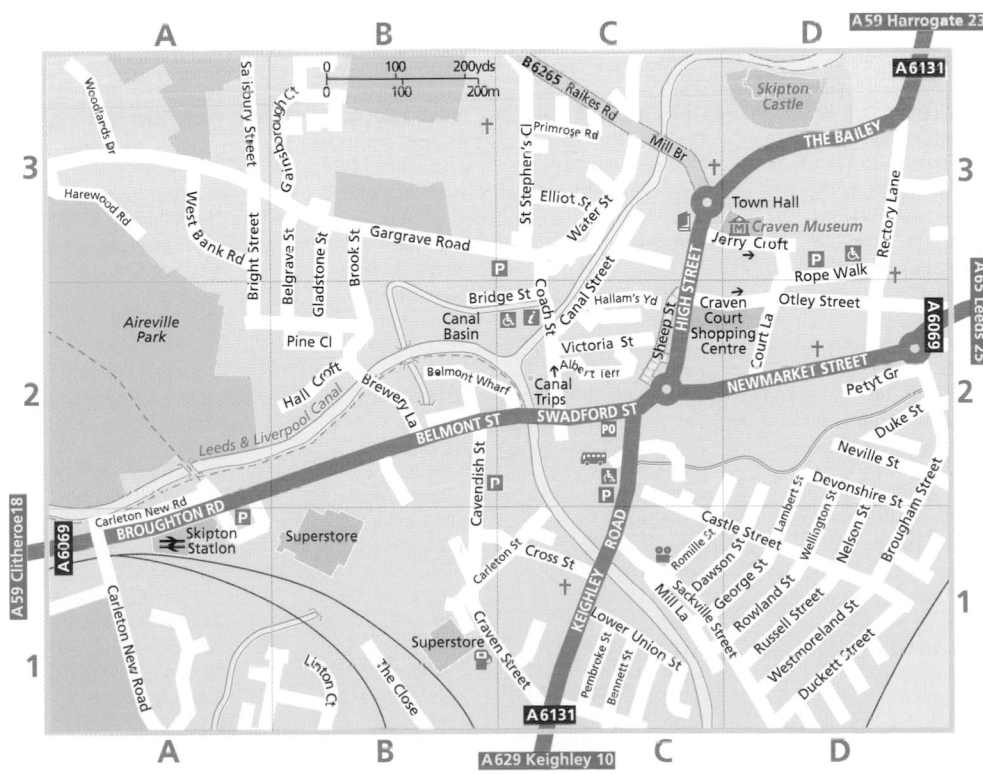

SOUTHAMPTON

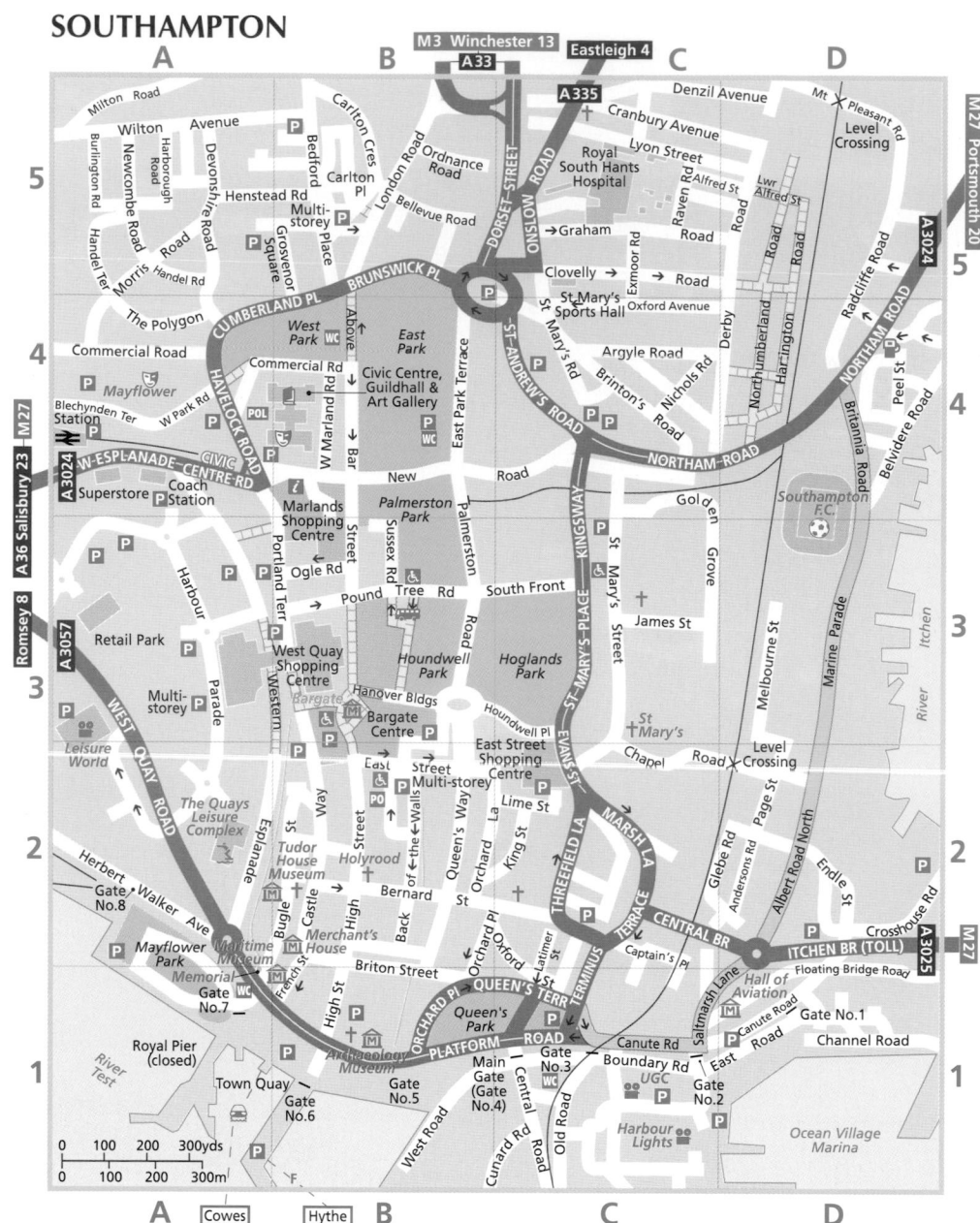

SOUTHEND-ON-SEA

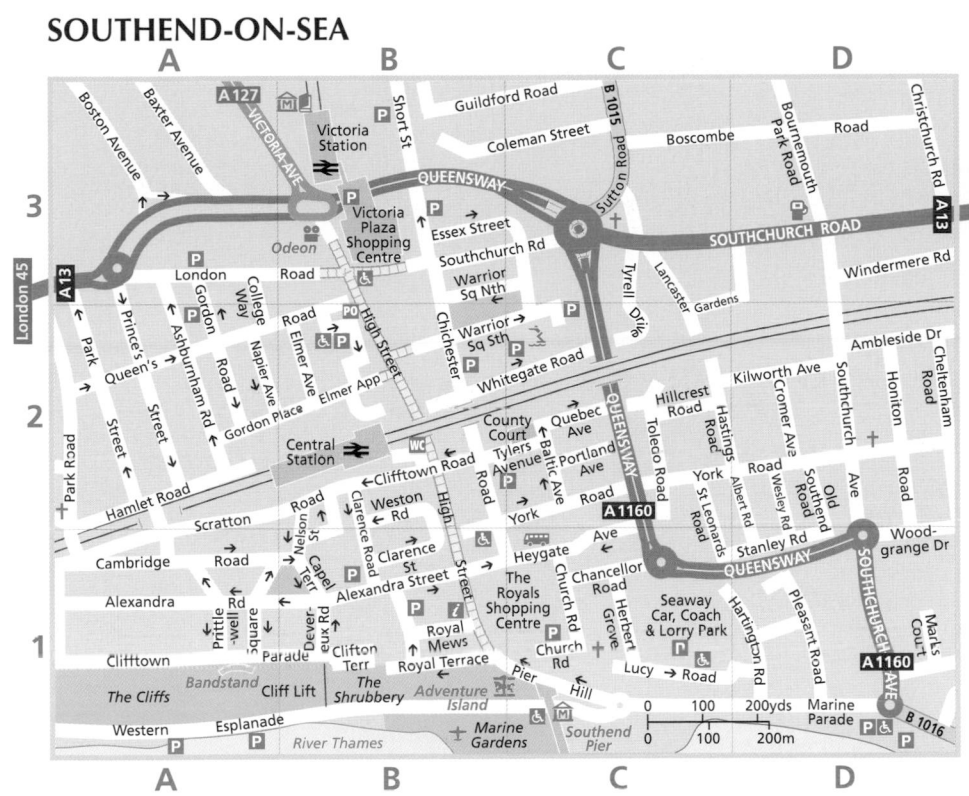

TOWN PLANS

SOUTHPORT

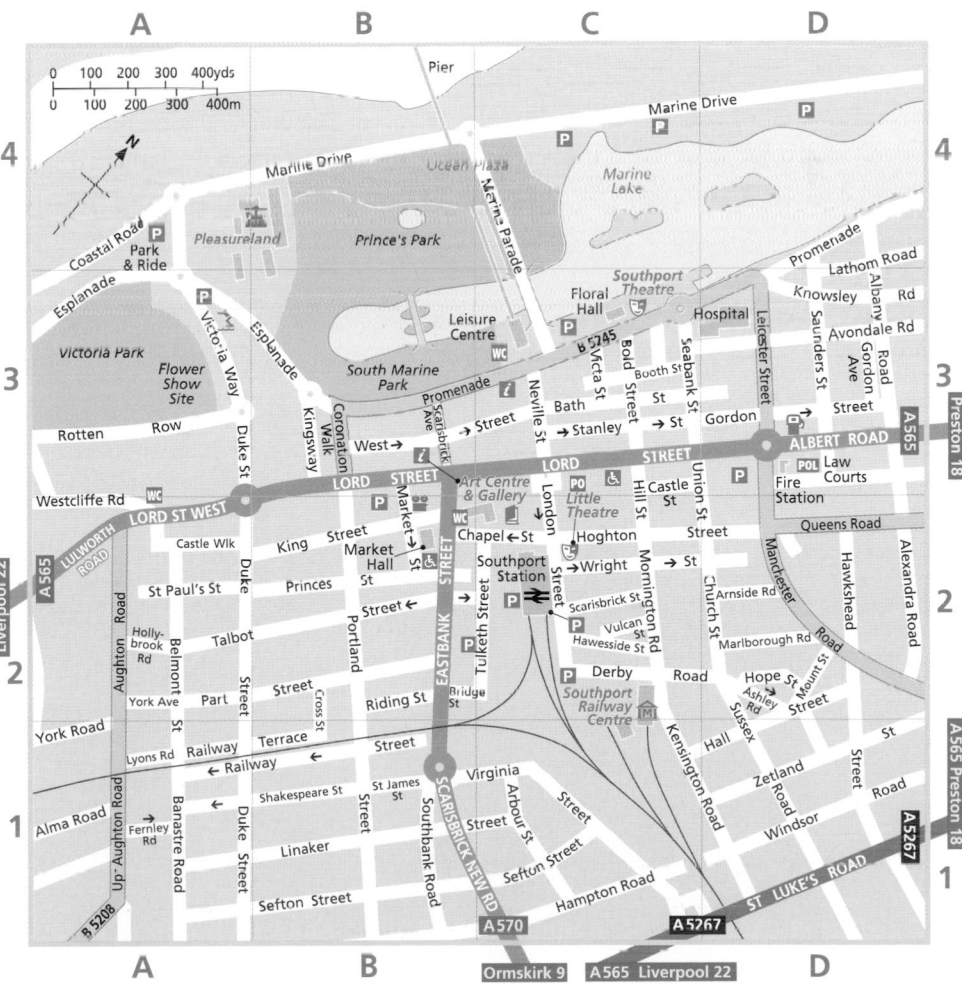

STAFFORD

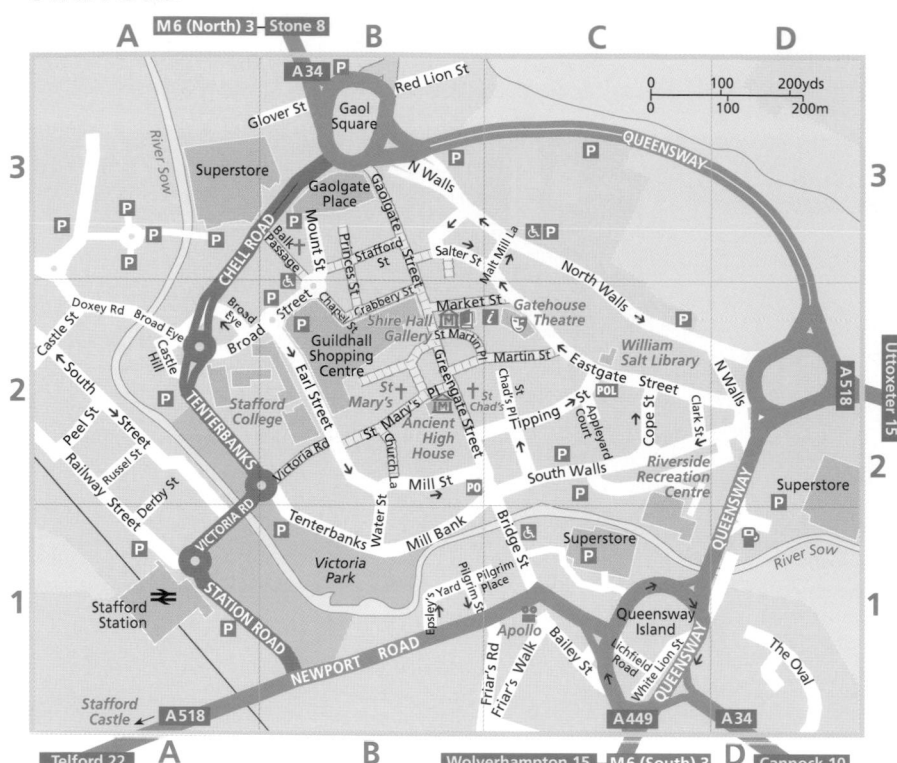

STEVENAGE

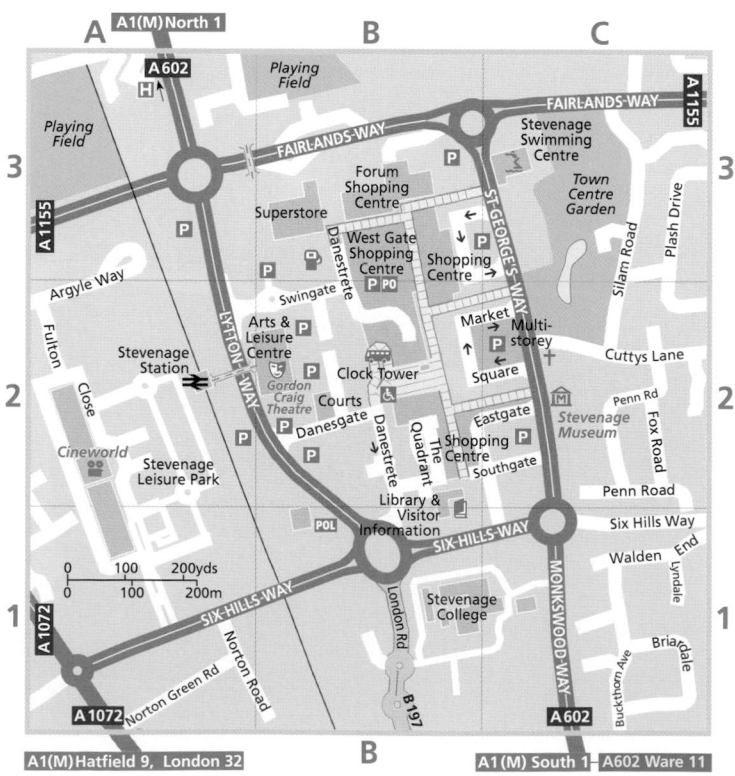

SLIGO

STREET INDEX

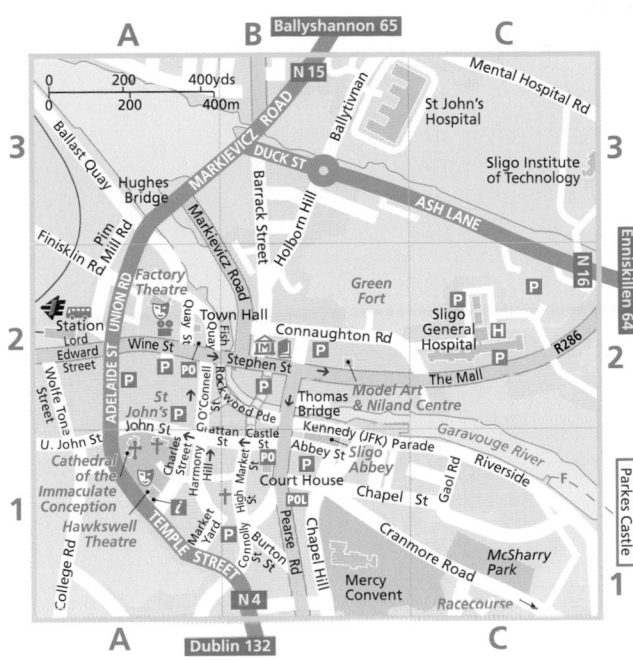

STAMFORD

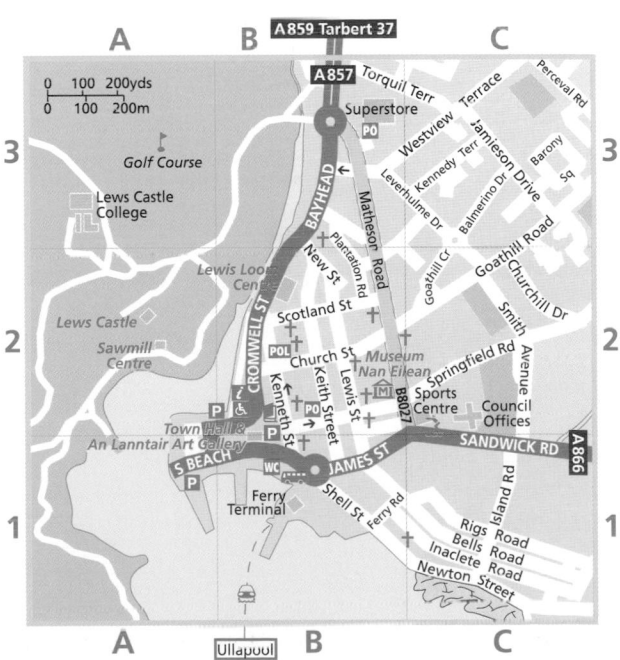

STREET INDEX

STORNOWAY

STREET INDEX

TOWN PLANS

STIRLING

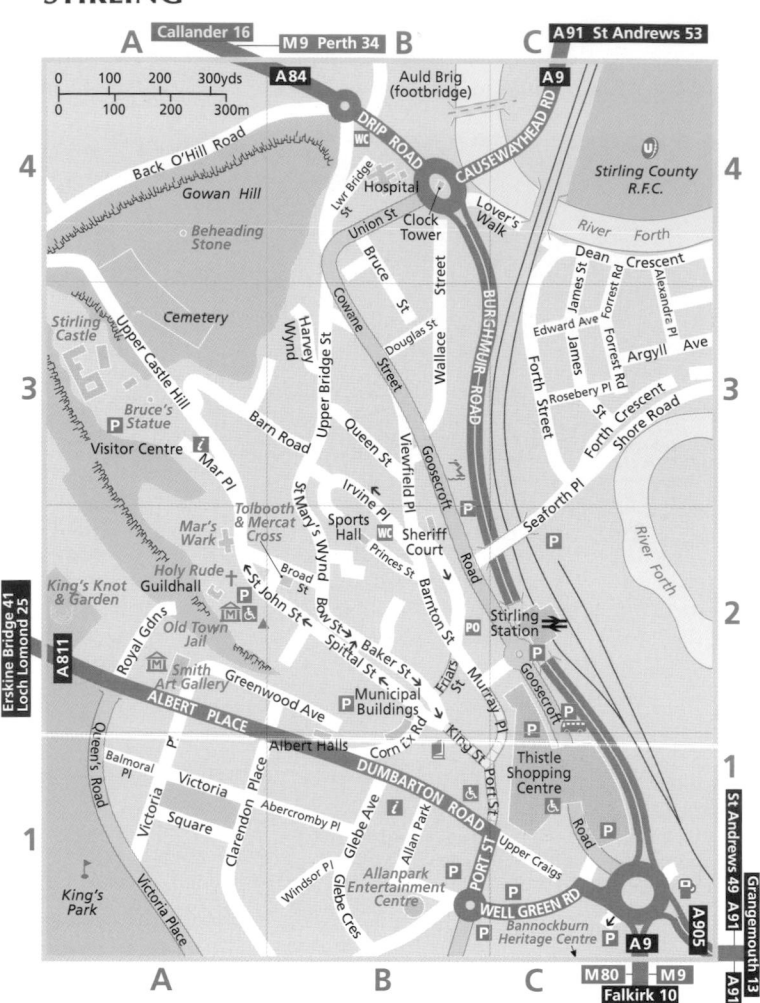

Callander 16 · M9 Perth 34 · A91 St Andrews 53

A84 · A9 · A811 · Erskine Bridge 41 · Loch Lomond 25

St Andrews 49 · A91 · Grangemouth 13 · M80 · M9 · Falkirk 10 · A905 · A9

Auld Brig (footbridge)

Stirling County R.F.C.

Back O'Hill Road · Gowan Hill · Beheading Stone · Cemetery · Stirling Castle · Bruce's Statue · Visitor Centre · Mar's Wark · Tolbooth & Mercat Cross · Holy Rude · King's Knot & Garden · Old Town Jail · Smith Art Gallery · Royal Gdns · Guildhall · Municipal Buildings · Albert Halls · King's Park · Allanpark Entertainment Centre · Bannockburn Heritage Centre · Thistle Shopping Centre · Stirling Station · Hospital · Clock Tower · Sheriff Court · Sports Hall

River Forth · Lover's Walk · Dean Crescent

STOCKPORT

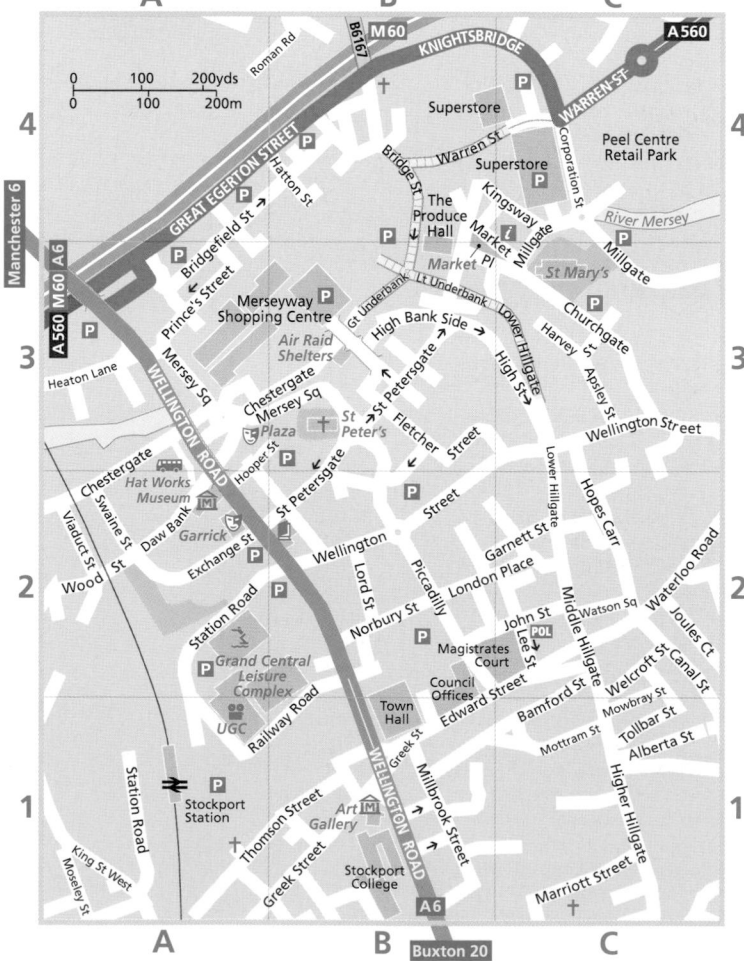

Manchester 6 · B6167 · M60 · Roman Rd · KNIGHTSBRIDGE · A560 · WARREN ST · M60 A6 · A560 · Buxton 20 · A6

Superstore · Peel Centre Retail Park · River Mersey · St Mary's · The Produce Hall · Market Pl · Merseyway Shopping Centre · Air Raid Shelters · Chestergate · Mersey Sq · St Peter's · Plaza · Hat Works Museum · Daw Bank · Garrick · Grand Central Leisure Complex · UGC · Station Road · Stockport Station · Magistrates Court · Council Offices · Town Hall · Art Gallery · Stockport College

GREAT EGERTON STREET · WELLINGTON ROAD · Bridgefield St · Prince's Street · Great Underbank · Lt Underbank · High Bank Side · St Petersgate · High St · Lower Hillgate · Harvey St · Churchgate · Apsley St · Wellington Street · Hopes Carr · Waterloo Road · Middle Hillgate · Welcroft St · Canal St · Joules Ct · Mowbray St · Tollbar St · Alberta St · Higher Hillgate · Marriott Street · Mottram St · Bamford St · Edward Street · Lord St · Norbury St · Piccadilly · London Place · John St · Lee St · Watson Sq · Garnett St · Fletcher Street · Wellington · Hooper St · Exchange St · Swaine St · Viaduct St · Wood St · Thomson Street · Greek Street · King St West · Moseley St · Railway Road · Millbrook Street · Hatton St · Bridge St · Kingsway · Warren St · Corporation St · Millgate · Heaton Lane

STOKE-ON-TRENT (HANLEY)

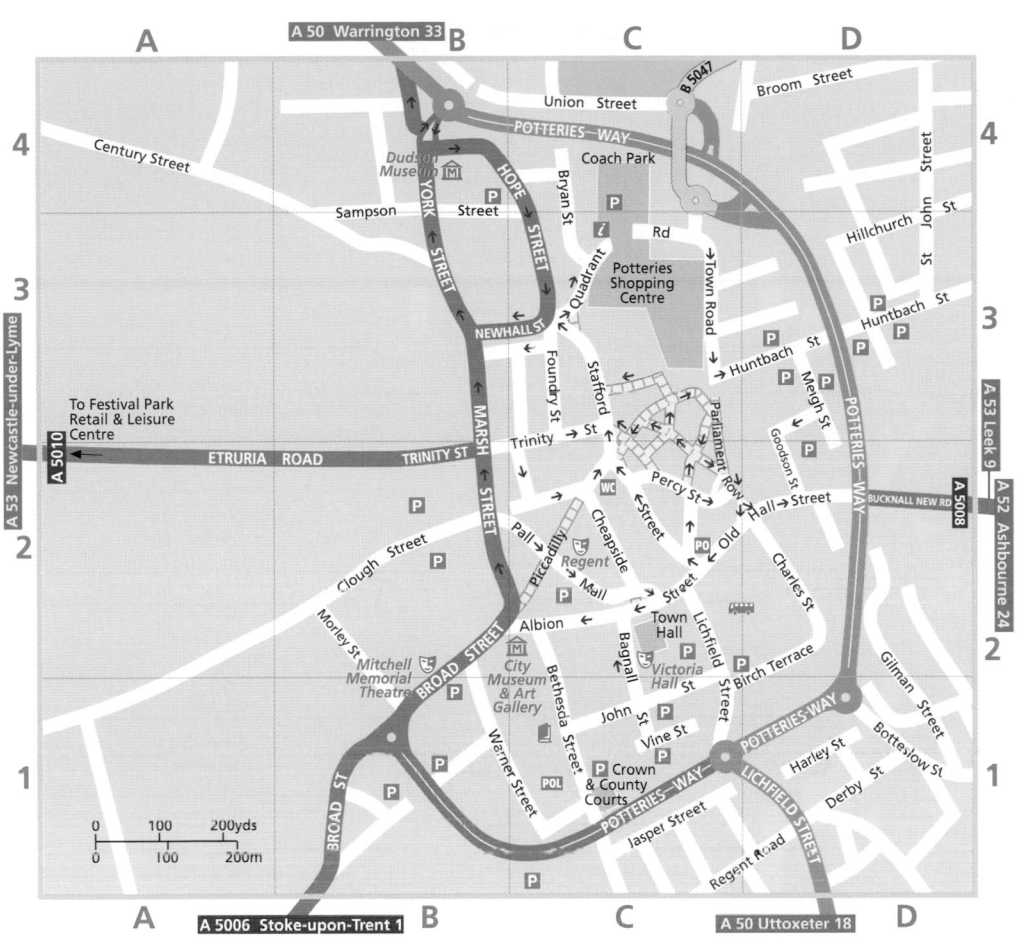

TOWN PLANS

STOKE-ON-TRENT

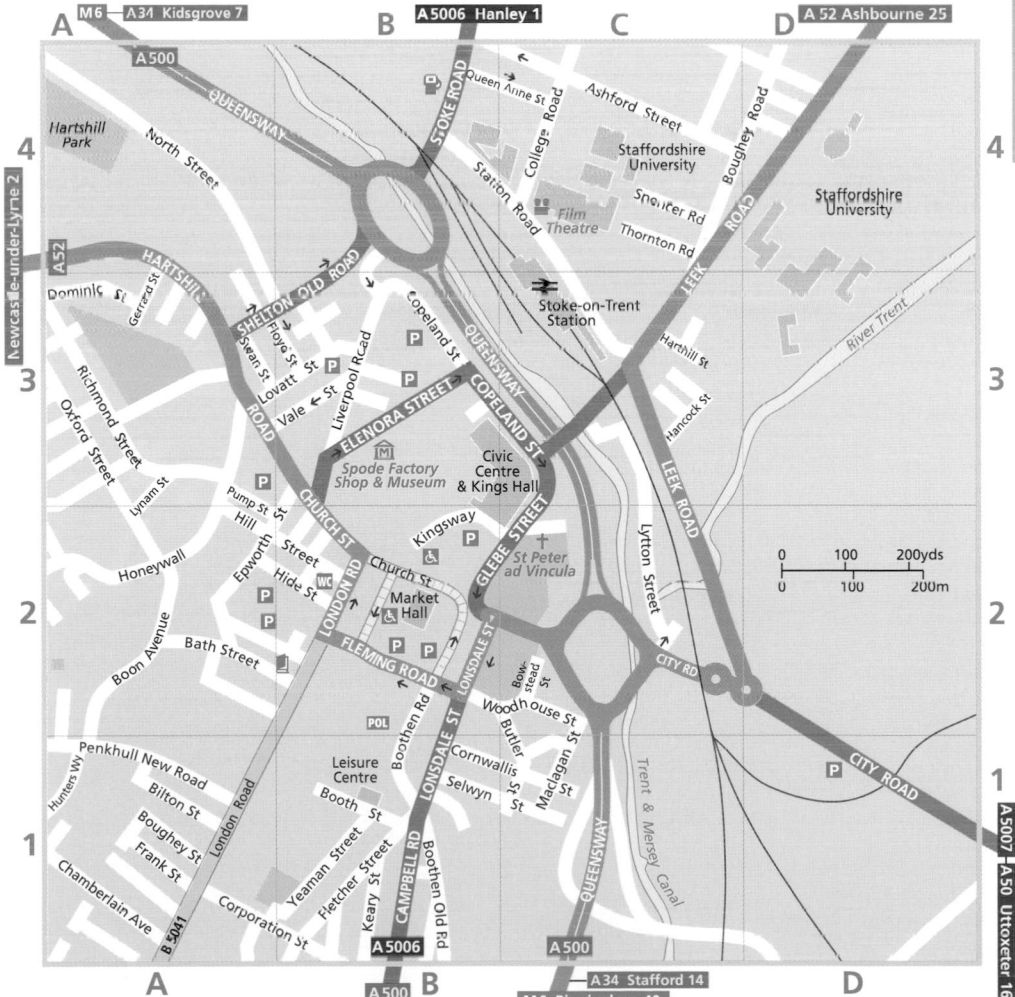

STRATFORD-UPON-AVON

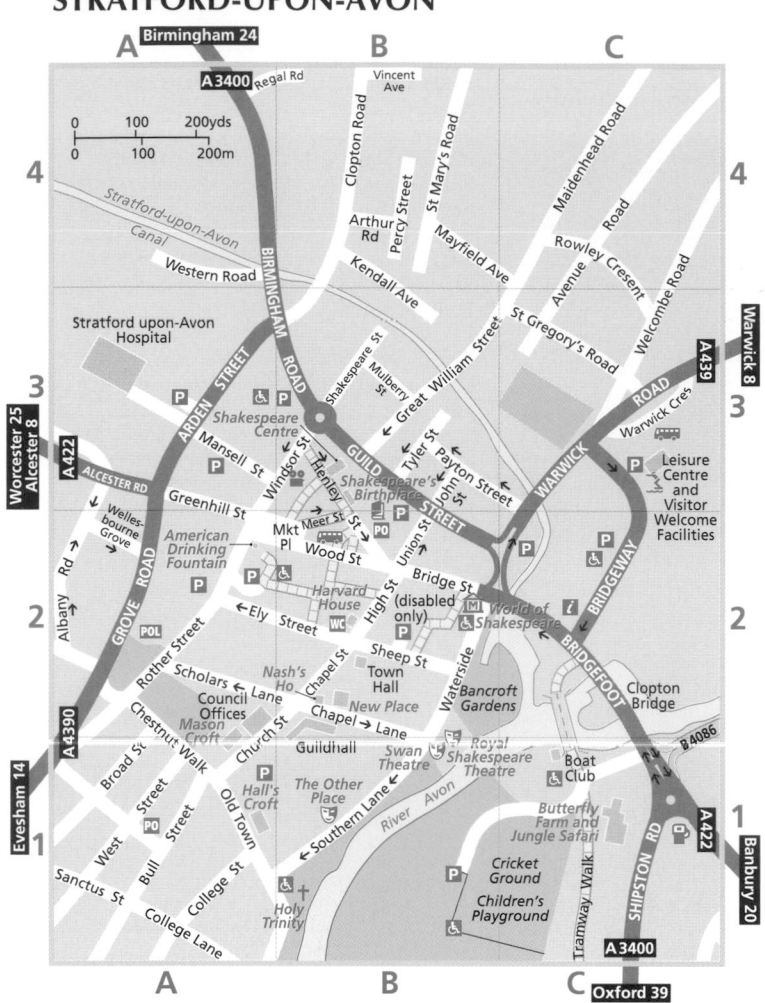

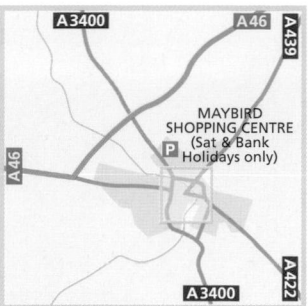

Park & Ride

SWANAGE

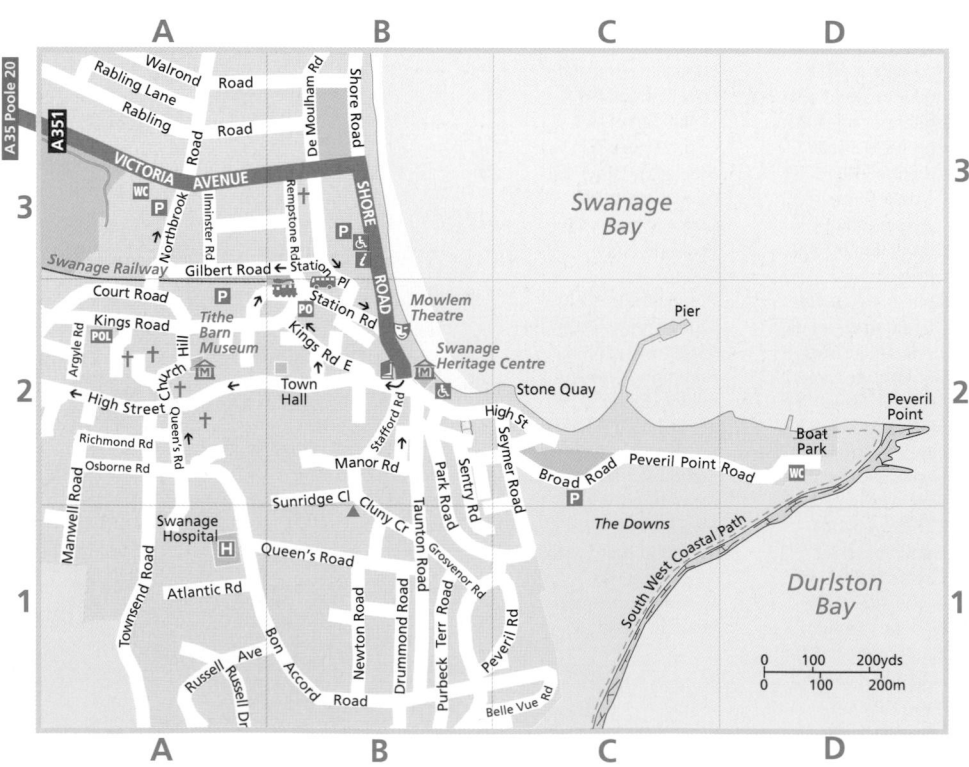

SWINDON

STREET INDEX

Bath Road C1
Broad Street C3
Cheney Manor Road A4
Cirencester Way D4
Commercial Road C2
County Road D3
Cricklade Street D1
Cricklade Road C4
Crombey Street C2
Deacon Street B2
Devizes Road C1
Drakes Way E3
Drove Road D2
Faringdon Road B2
Fleet Street B2–B3
Fleming Way C3–D3
Graham Street C3–D3
Great Western Way B4
Gypsy Lane D4
High Street D1
Kemble Drive A3
Kingshill Road A1–B1
London Street B2–B3
Manchester Road C3
Marlborough Road D1
Newport Street D1
Ocotal Way D4–E3
Prince's Street C2
Queens Drive D3–E1
Rodbourne Road A3
Shrivenham Road D3
Station Road C3
Victoria Road C2–C1
William Street B2
Wootton Bassett Road A1

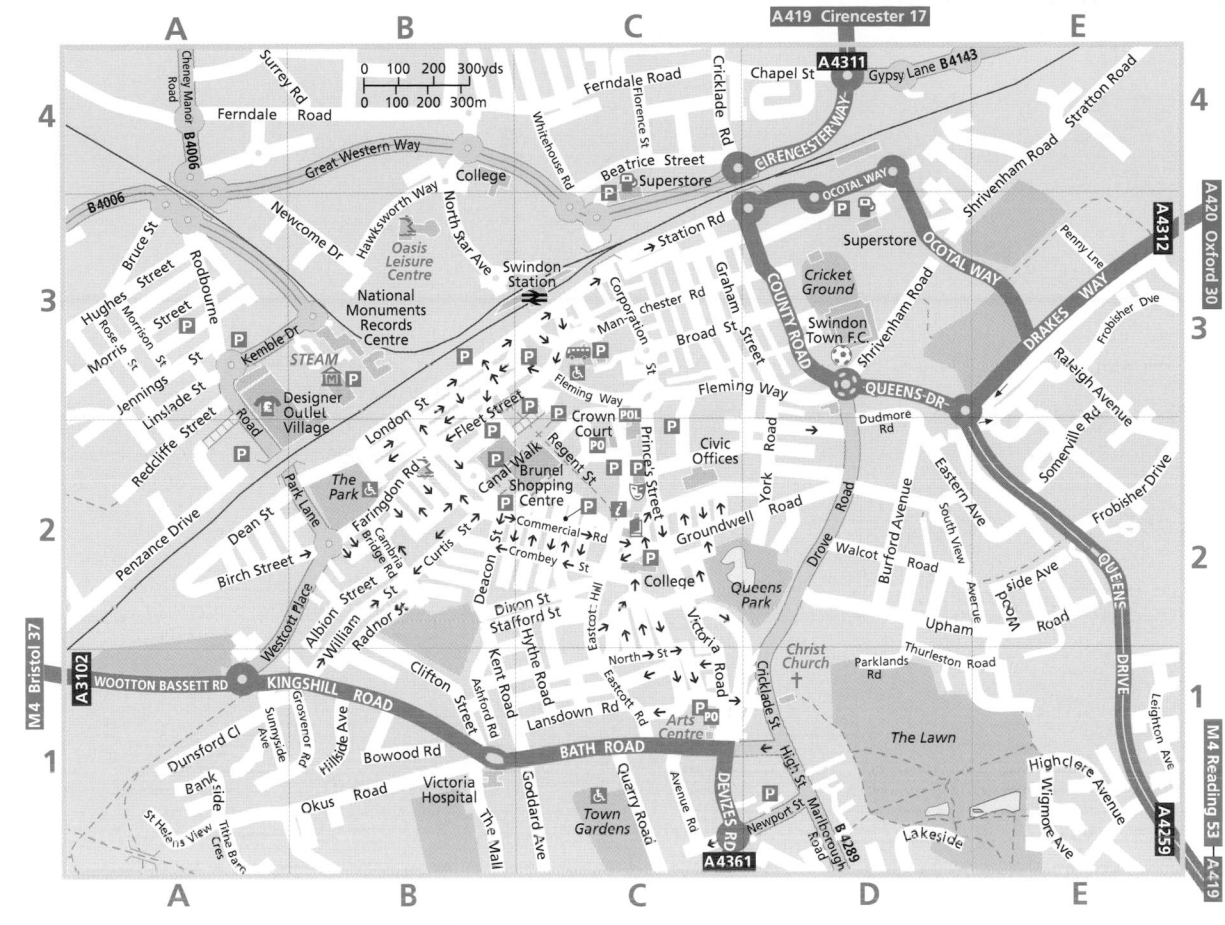

Park & Ride

TAUNTON

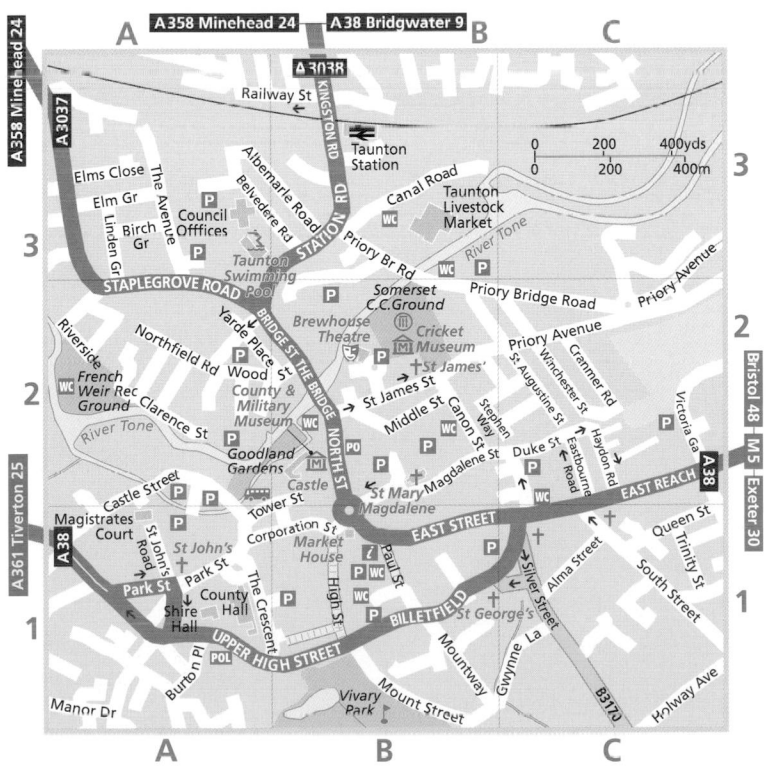

STREET INDEX

Albemarle Road A3
Alma Street C1
Belvedere Road A3
Billetfield B1
Birch Grove A3
Bridge Street A2
Burton Place A1
Canal Road B3
Canon Street B2
Castle Street A2
Clarence Street A2
Corporation Street A1
Cranmer Road C2
Duke Street C2
East Reach C2
East Street B1
Eastbourne Road C2
Elm Grove A3
Elms Close A3

Gwynne Lane C1
Haydon Road C2
High Street B1
Holway Avenue C1
Kingston Road B3
Linden Grove A3
Magdalene Street B2
Manor Drive A1
Middle Street B2
Mount Street B1
Mountway B1
North Street B2
Northfield Road A2
Park Street A1
Paul Street B1
Priory Avenue C2
Priory Bridge Road B3–C2
Queen Street C1
Railway Street A3

Riverside A2
Silver Street C1
South Street C1
St Augustine Street C2
St James Street B2
St John's Road A1
Staplegrove Road A2
Station Road B3
Stephen Way B2
The Avenue A3
The Bridge B2
The Crescent A1
Tower Street A1
Trinity Street C1
Upper High Street A1
Victoria Gardens C2
Winchester Street C2
Wood Street A2
Yarde Place A2

TOWN PLANS

TELFORD

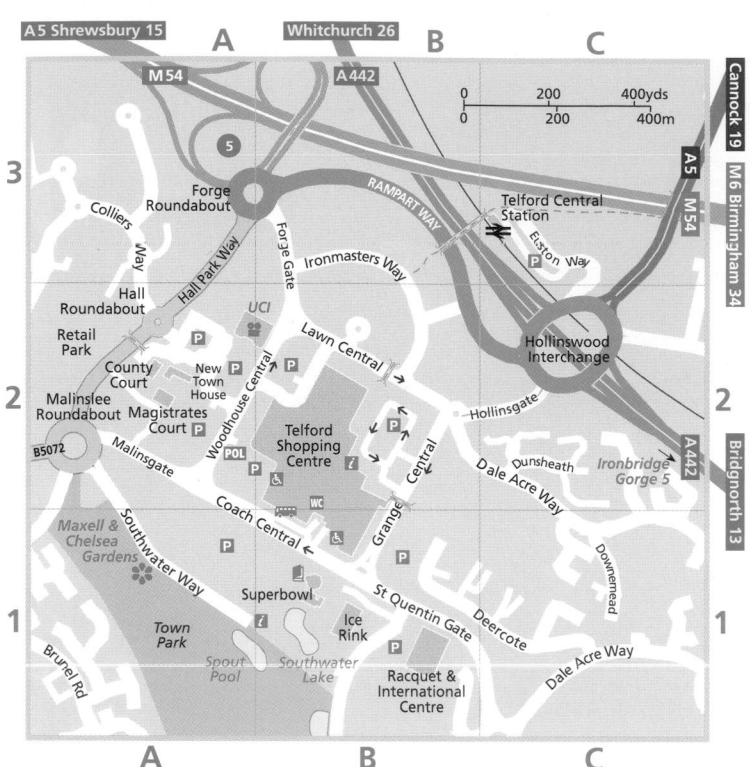

TENBY

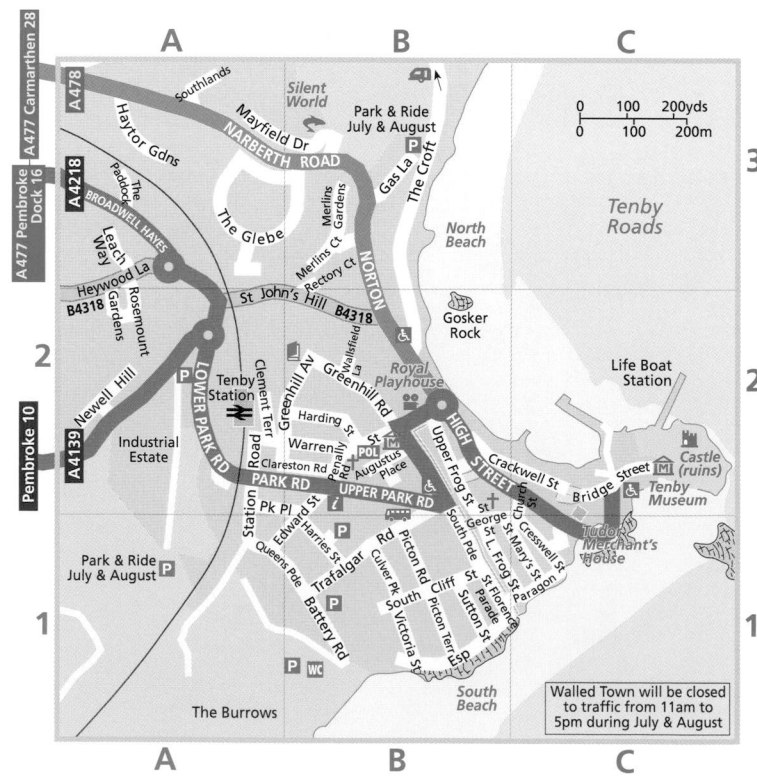

THETFORD

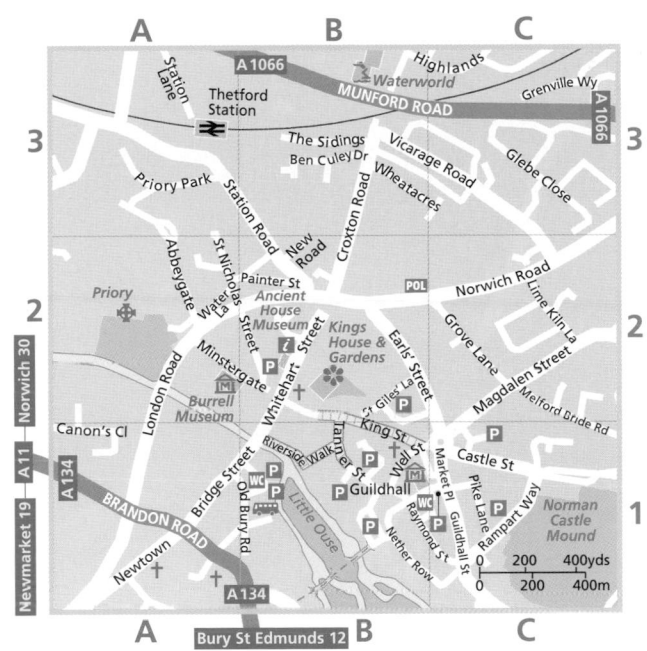

THIRSK

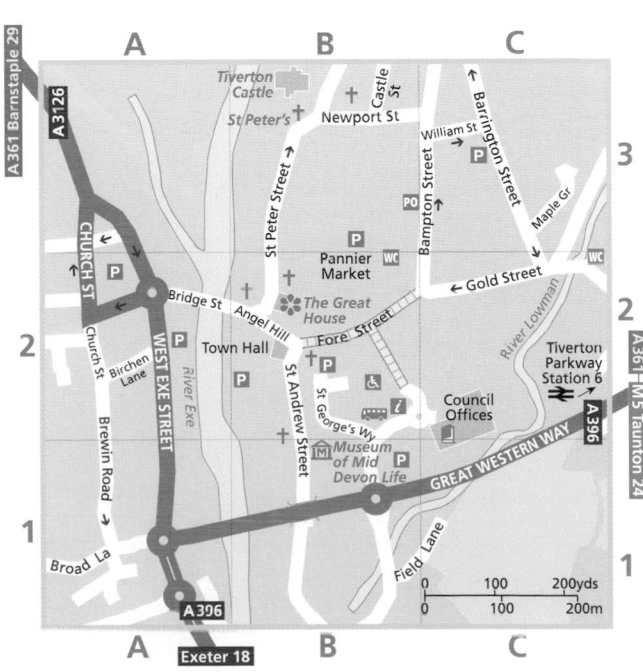

TIVERTON

TOWN PLANS

TORQUAY

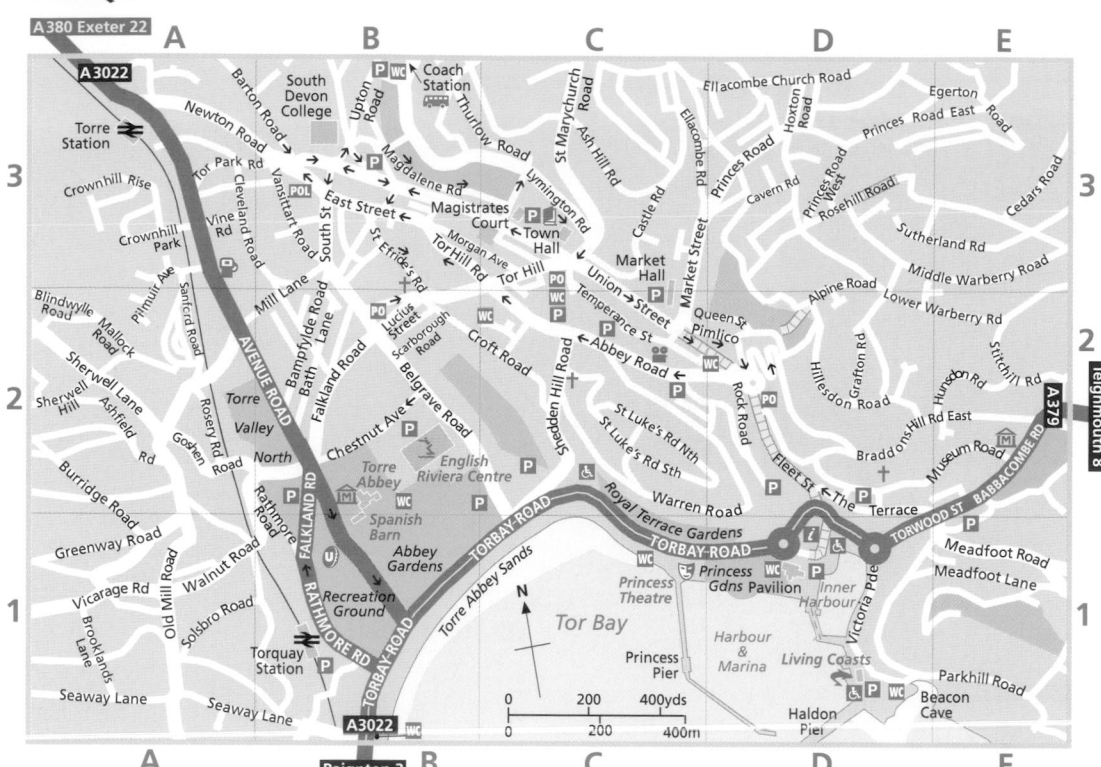

TUNBRIDGE WELLS, ROYAL

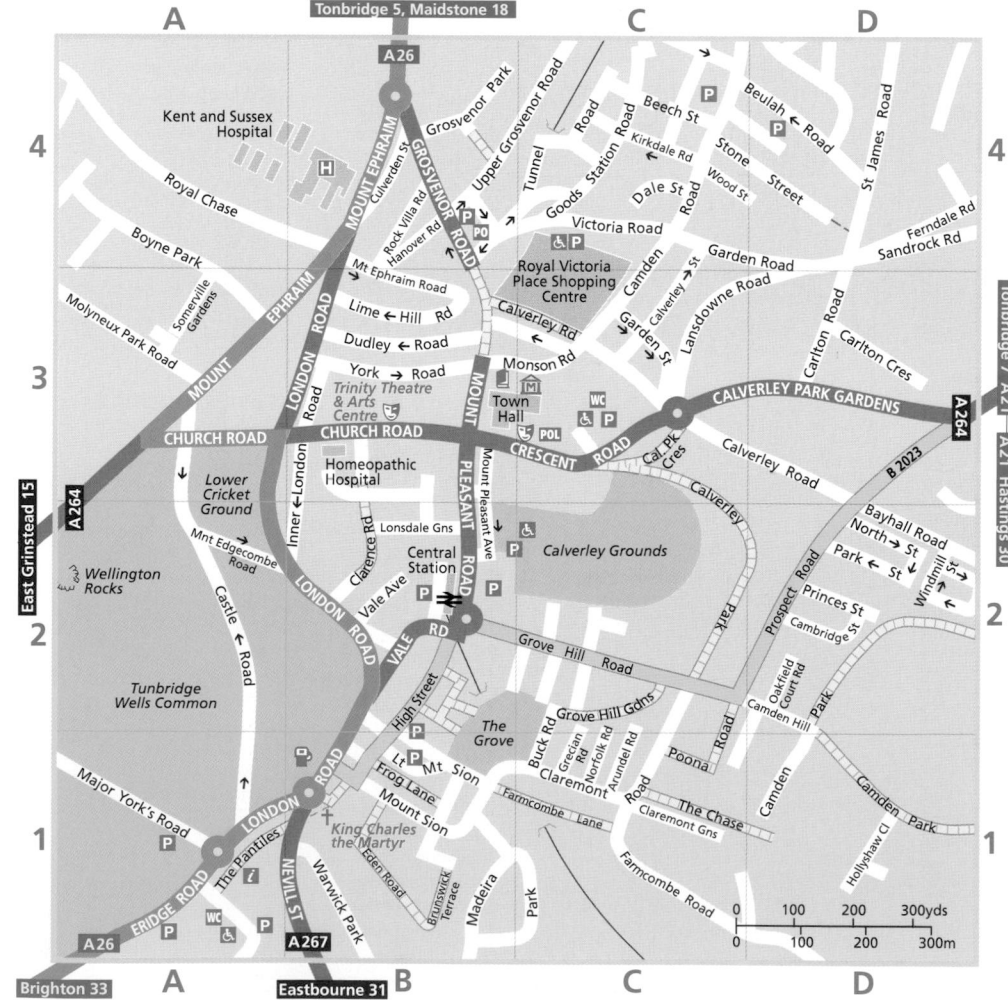

WALSALL

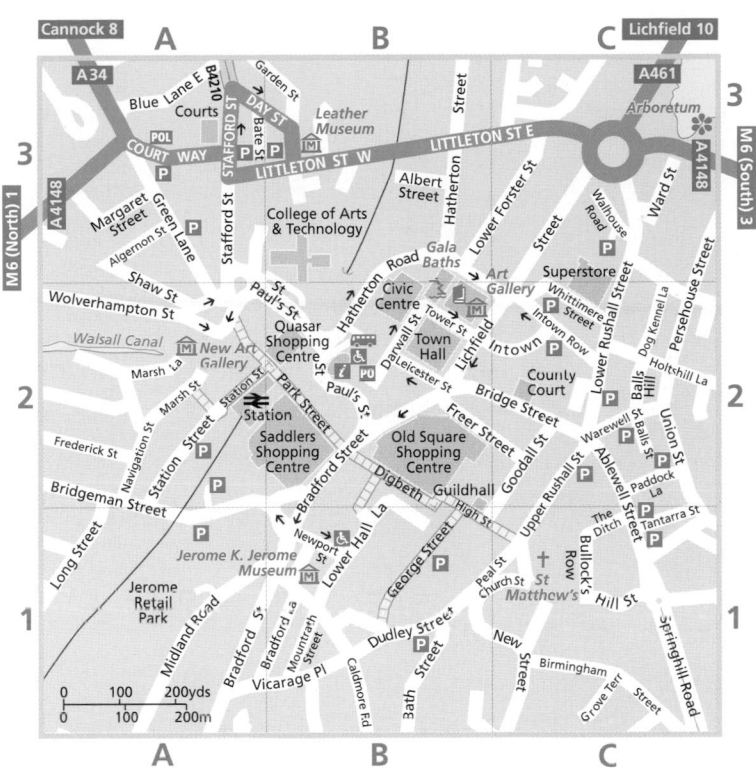

WARRINGTON

WARWICK

WATFORD

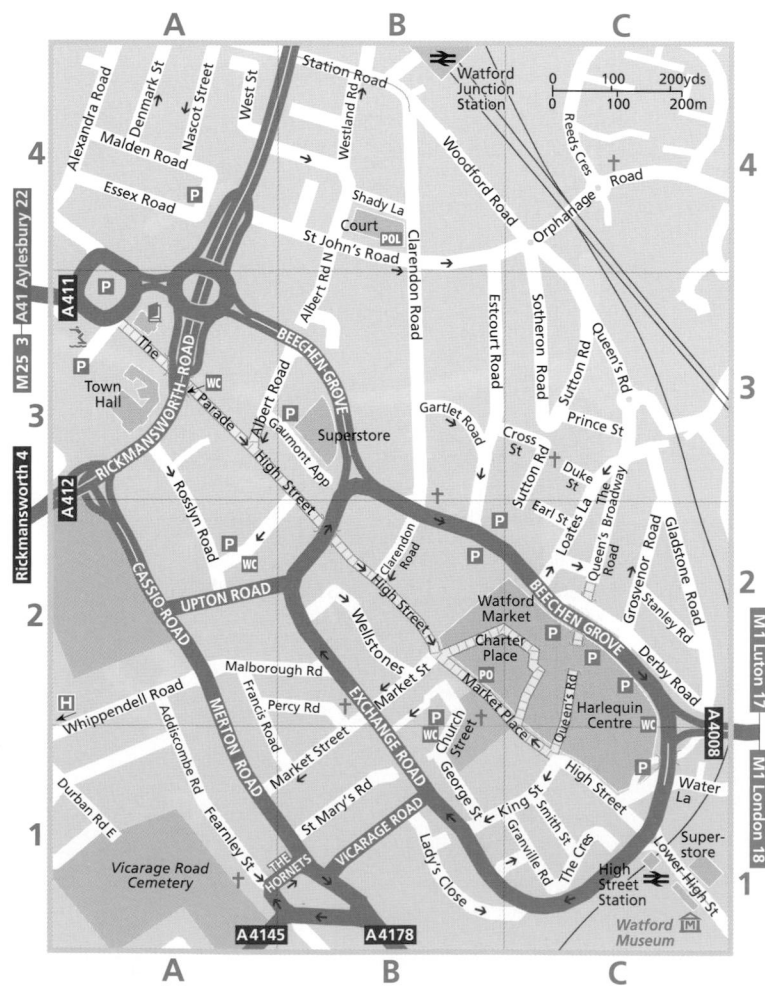

ULLAPOOL

STREET INDEX

Argyle Street **C2**
Castle Terrace **A3**
Custom House Street **C3**
Fraser Place **B3–C3**
Ladysmith Street **B3**
Latheron Lane **B2**
Market Street **C2**
Mill Street **C2**
Moss Road **C3**
Pulteney Street **B2–C2**

Quay Street **B2**
Riverside Terrace **B3**
Royal Park **C2**
St Valery Place **A3**
Seaforth Road **A2–B2**
Shore Street **B2–C2**
West Argyle Street **A2–B2**
West Lane **B2–B1**
West Shore Street **A1–B1**
West Terrace **A2**

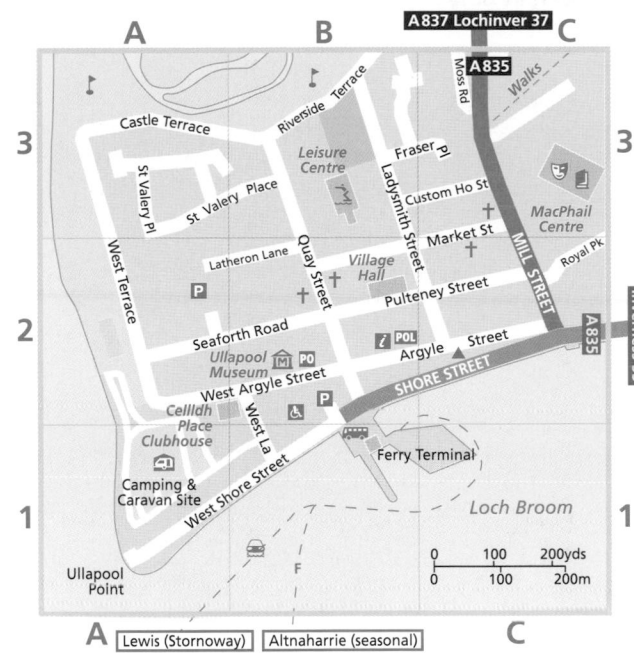

WELSHPOOL

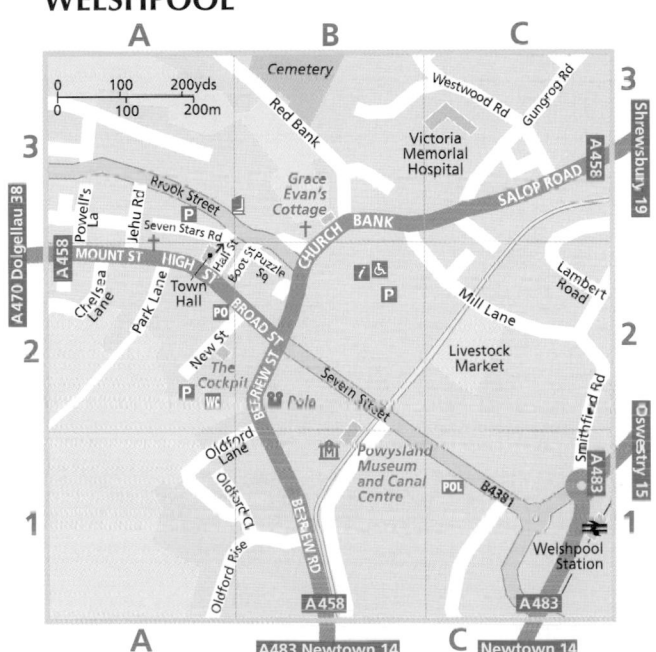

STREET INDEX

Berriew Road **B1**
Berriew Street **B2**
Boot Street **B2**
Broad Street **A2**
Brook Street **A3**
Chelsea Lane **A2**
Church Bank **B2**
Gungrog Road **C3**
Hall Street **A2**
High Street **A2**
Jehu Road **A3**
Lambert Road **C2**
Mill Lane **C2**

Mount Street **A2**
New Street **A2**
Oldford Close **A1**
Oldford Lane **A1**
Oldford Rise **A1**
Park Lane **A2**
Powell's Lane **A3**
Puzzle Square **B2**
Red Bank **B3**
Salop Road **C3**
Seven Stars Road **A3**
Severn Street **B2**
Smithfield Road **C1**
Westwood Road **C3**

WEYMOUTH

STREET INDEX

Abbotsbury Road **A2**
Alma Road **A2**
Barrack Road **B1**
Bath Street **B3**
Commercial Road **A2**
Custom House Quay **B1**
East Street **B1**
Franchise Street **A1**
Granville Road **A2**
Great George Street **B2**
Holland Road **A2**
King Street **B3**
Marsh Road **A1**
New Street **B2**
Newberry Road **B1**
Newstead Road **A2**
Newton's Road **B1**
North Quay **A1**
Nothe Parade **B1**
Orion Road **A1**

Park Street **B2**
Rodwell Avenue **A1**
St Leonard's Road **A1**
St Mary Street **B2**
St Nicholas Street **B1**
Stavordale Road **A2**
The Esplanade **B2**
Thomas Street **B2**
Trinity Road **B1**
Westham Road **A2**
Weston Road **A1**
Westwey Road **A2**
Wyke Road **A1**

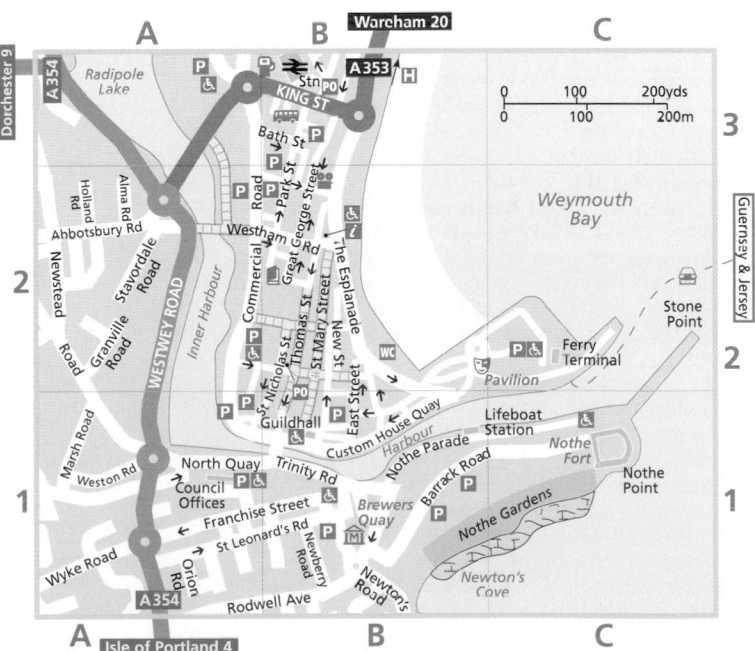

TOWN PLANS

WESTON-SUPER-MARE

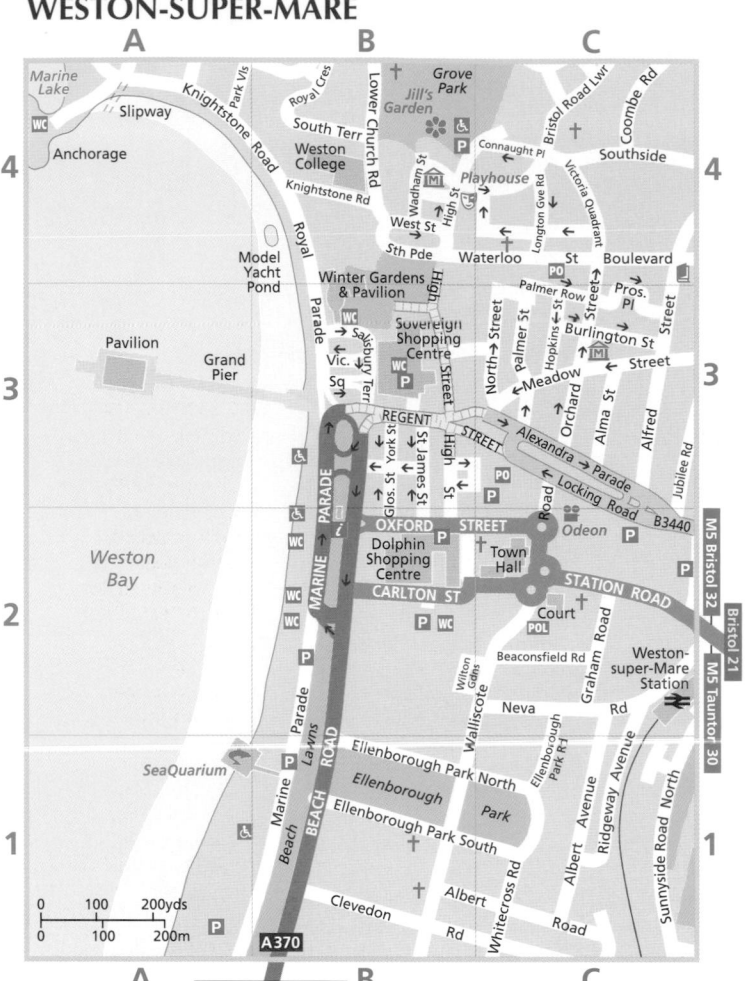

WIGAN

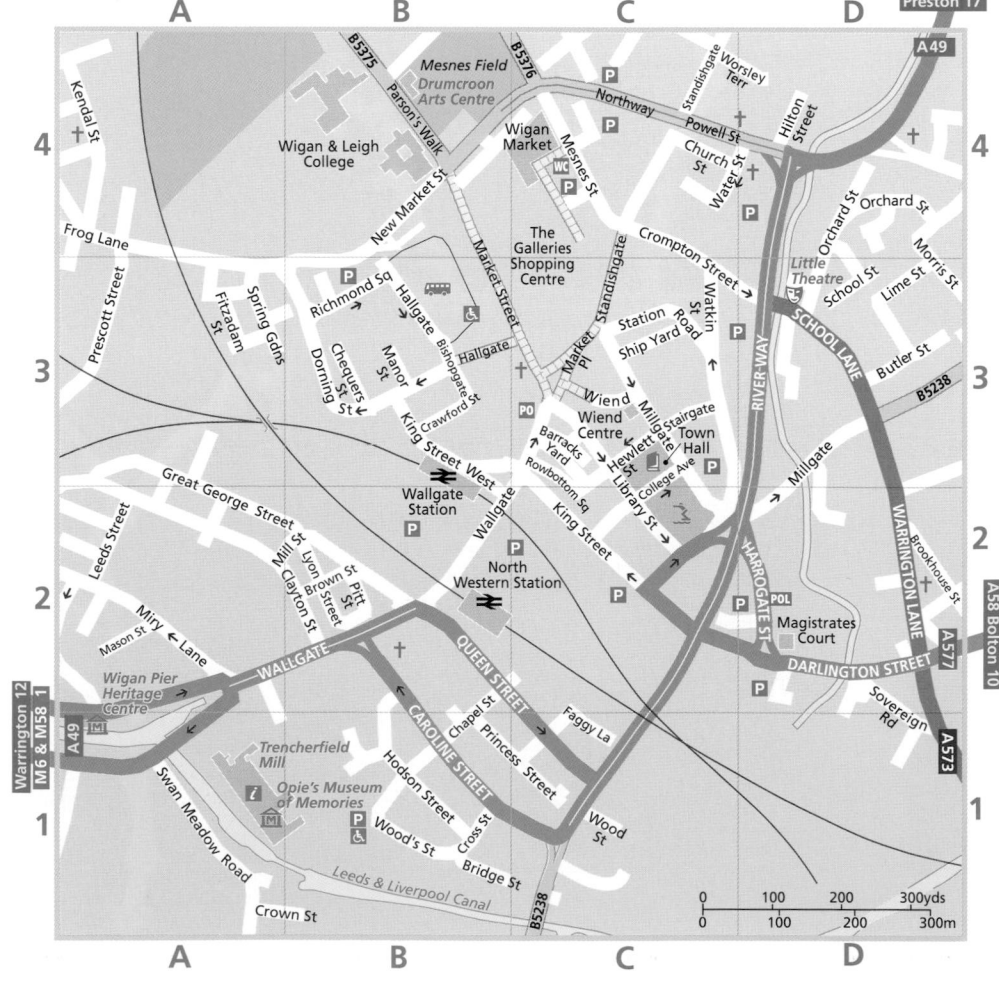

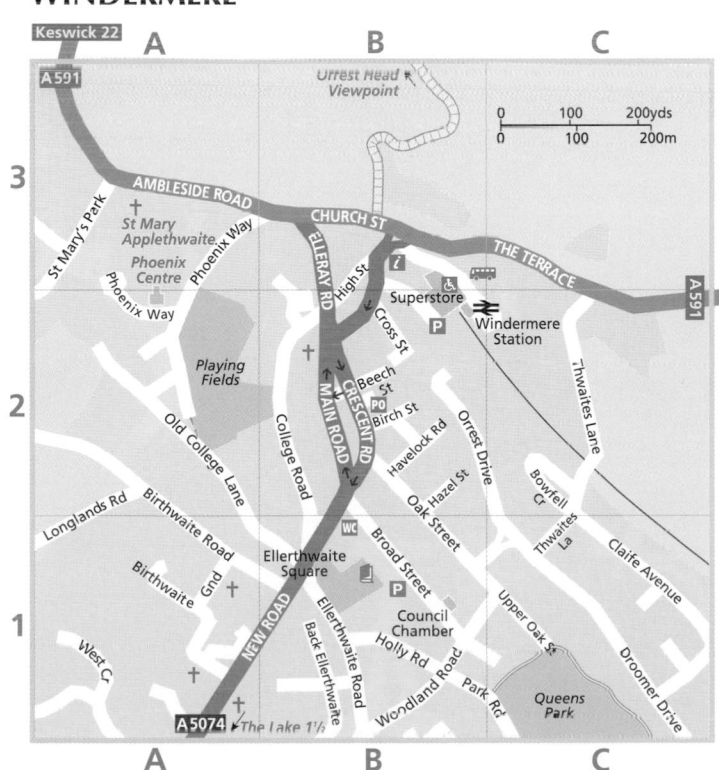

WINCHESTER

A34 Newbury 26 · A
B · A33 Basingstoke 19
C
D
E

A34 Newbury 26
A33 Basingstoke 19

B3045
B3047

WC
P

Cattle Market
King Alfred Pl

North Walls Recreation Ground

Ebden Rd

Moss Rd

4

Brassey Rd
Owens Rd

Andover Road

Worthy Lane
Hyde Street
King Alfred Terr

P
WC
Recreation Centre

Park Avenue

River Itchen

Street

Beggars Lane

St Martins Close

Historic Resources Centre

Hyde Close

Victoria Road

Hyde Abbey Rd

Gordon Road

Hatherley Rd
Cranworth Road

B3044

Swan Lane

P

POL
P

Durngate

Wales Street

St John's Street

Magdalen Hill

St Giles Hill

B3404

Fairfield Road

Stockbridge Road

Winchester Station

City Road
North Walls
B3330
North Walls

Upper Brook St

Middle Brook St

Lower Brook St

Union St

Eastgate Street

Water Lane

Ball Hill

A31 Alton 18

A272 Petersfield 20

B3049
A30 Salisbury 23

St Pauls Hill

Sussex Street

Theatre Royal
Tower Rd

St Peter Street
Parchment Street

P
Friarsgate

P

Blue

St John's Hosp & Chapel

City Mill

STREET INDEX

Andover Road B4
Broadway D2
Chesil Street E2
City Road B3
College Walk E1
Culver Road C1
Eastgate Street E3
Ebden Road E4
Elm Road A2
Friarsgate D3
Gladstone Road B3
Gordon Road C4
High Street B2
Hyde Close B4
Hyde Street B4
Jewry Street C3
Magdalen Hill E3
Moss Road E4
North Walls C3
Owens Road A4
Parchment Street C3
Romsey Road A1
St Cross Road C1
St George's Street C2
St Pauls Hill A3
Southgate Street C2
Stockbridge Road A3
Sussex Street B3
Swan Lane D3
Tanner Street D2
Tower Road B3
Union Street D3
Upper High Street B2
Wales Street E4
Water Lane E3
Wharf Hill E1
Worthy Lane B4

St Paul's Hospital
Elm Road

Clifton Road
Gladstone Rd
Cross St
Upper High St

County Offices
Staple Gardens
Jewry Street
Southgate St
St Clement St

Brooks Shopping Centre
Tanner St

PO

Broadway

Colebrook Street

Chesil Street

Chesil

2

Oram's Arbour
Middle Road

West End Terrace
Step Terr
Clifton Terrace
Clifton Hill

Plague Mon
PO
Westgate
St

High Street
Old Guildhall
City Cross
The Square
Market Lane
City Museum

City Offices

Abbey Gdns
Guildhall & Art Gallery

King Alfred's Statue
River Itchen

P

2

Hussars & Gurkha Museums
Green Jackets Museum
POL

Great Hall
Law Courts
Peninsula Barracks

Royal Hants Regimental Museum

Cathedral

Wolvesey Castle

HM Prison
Romsey Road

Square
Peninsula
Light Infantry Museum

Archery Lane

St Thomas St
Symonds St

B3355

Deanery
Cheyney Court

M3 London 64

M3 Southampton 13

B3040
A3090 Romsey 11

Royal Hampshire County Hospital

St James Lane
Christchurch Rd

Constables Gate

St James Lane

Edgar Rd
St Cross Road

St Swithun Street
Canon Street
Culver Rd

College Street
Kingsgate St

Jane Austen's House

Winchester College

College

Walk

Wharf Hill

A
B
M3 Southampton 13 · C
D
E

Park & Ride

A272 · A34
A33 · M3

P 9 BARFIELD

A3090
10
A31
A272

11
ST CATHERINE'S
11
M3

WINDERMERE

Keswick 22 · A
B
C

A591

Orrest Head Viewpoint

0 100 200yds
0 100 200m

3

St Mary's Park
AMBLESIDE ROAD
CHURCH ST
THE TERRACE

3

St Mary Applethwaite
Phoenix Centre
Phoenix Way

ELLERAY RD
High St

i

Kendal 19
A591

Superstore
P
Windermere Station

Phoenix Way

Cross St

Thwaites Lane

2

Playing Fields

Old College Lane
College Road

MAIN ROAD
CRESCENT RD

Beech St
Birch St

Havelock Rd
Oak Hazel St

Bowfell Cr

2

Longlands Rd
Birthwaite Road

Birthwaite Gnd

Ellerthwaite Square

NEW ROAD

Broad Street
Back Ellerthwaite Road
Ellerthwaite Road

WC

P
Council Chamber

Holly Rd

Oak Street

Upper Oak St

Thwaites La
Claife Avenue

1

West C
A5074
The Lake 1½

Woodland Road

Park Rd

Queens Park

Droomer Drive

1

A
B
C

STREET INDEX

Ambleside Road A3
Back Ellerthwaite Road B1
Beech Street B2
Birch Street B2
Birthwaite Ground A1
Birthwaite Road A2
Bowfell Crescent C2
Broad Street B1
Church Street B3
Claife Avenue C1

College Road B2
Crescent Road B2
Cross Street B2
Droomer Drive C1
Elleray Road B3
Ellerthwaite Road B1
Havelock Road B2
Hazel Street B2
High Street B3
Holly Road B1
Longlands Road A1
Main Road B2

New Road A1
Oak Street B2
Old College Lane A2
Orrest Drive B2
Park Road B1
Phoenix Way A3
St Mary's Park A3
The Terrace B3
Thwaites Lane C1–C2
Upper Oak Street C1
West Crescent A1
Woodland Road B1

TOWN PLANS

WINDSOR

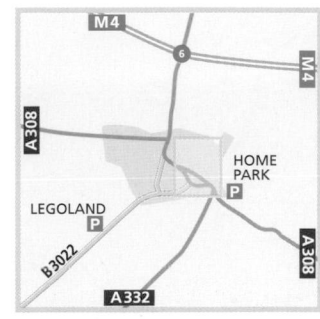

Park & Ride

WOLVERHAMPTON

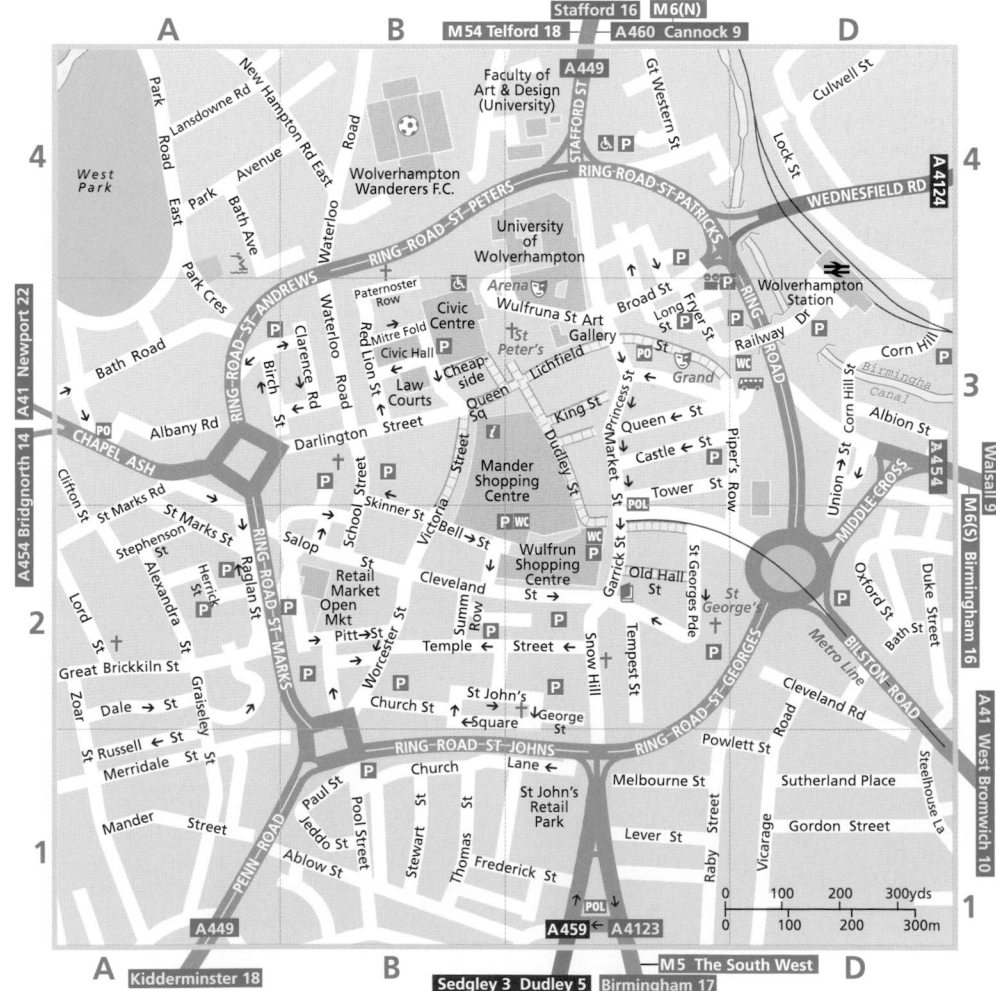

WORCESTER

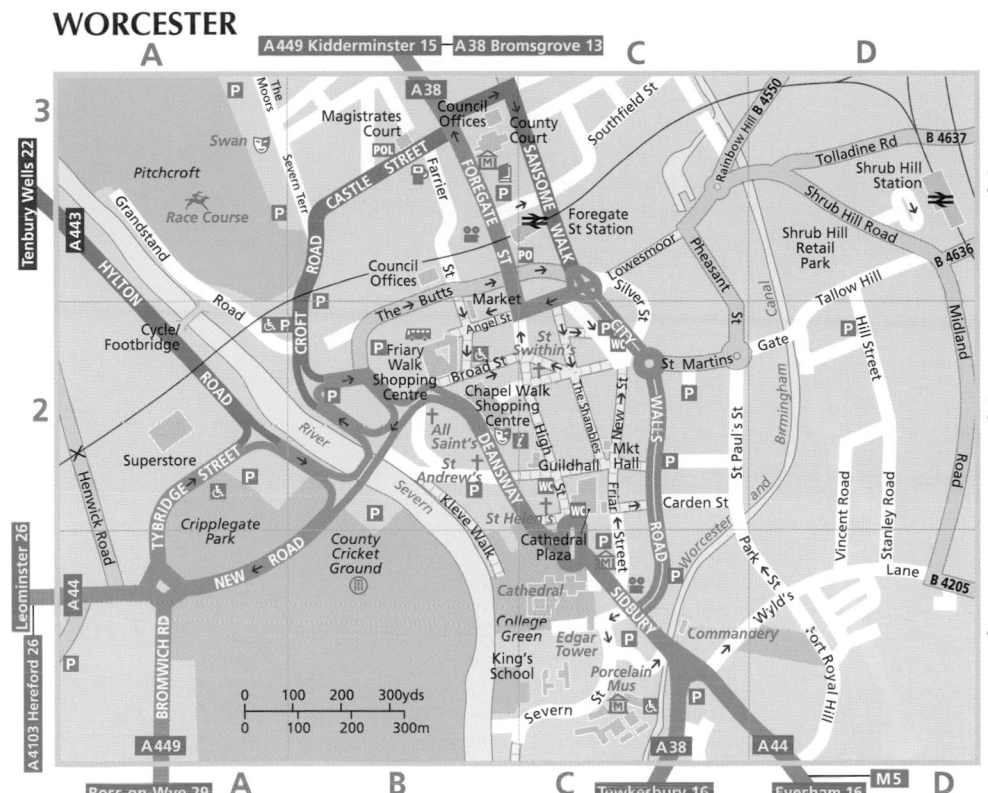

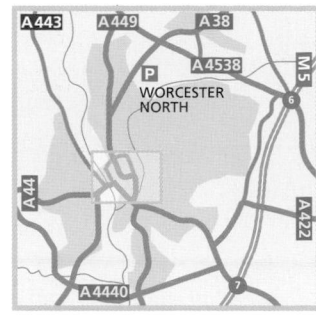

Park & Ride

WORTHING

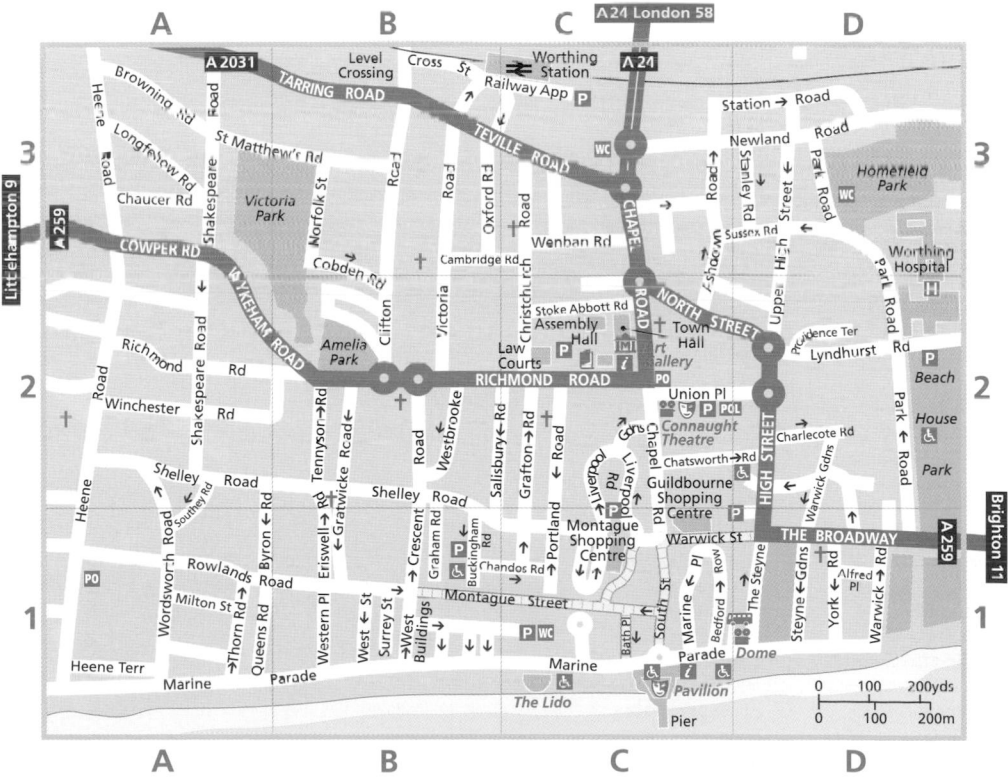

WREXHAM

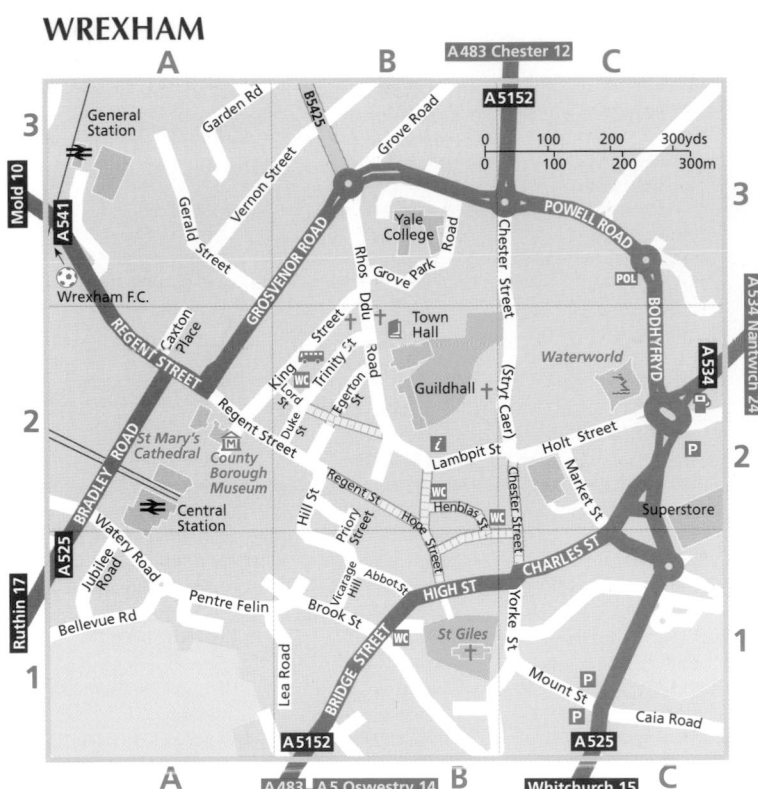

YEOVIL

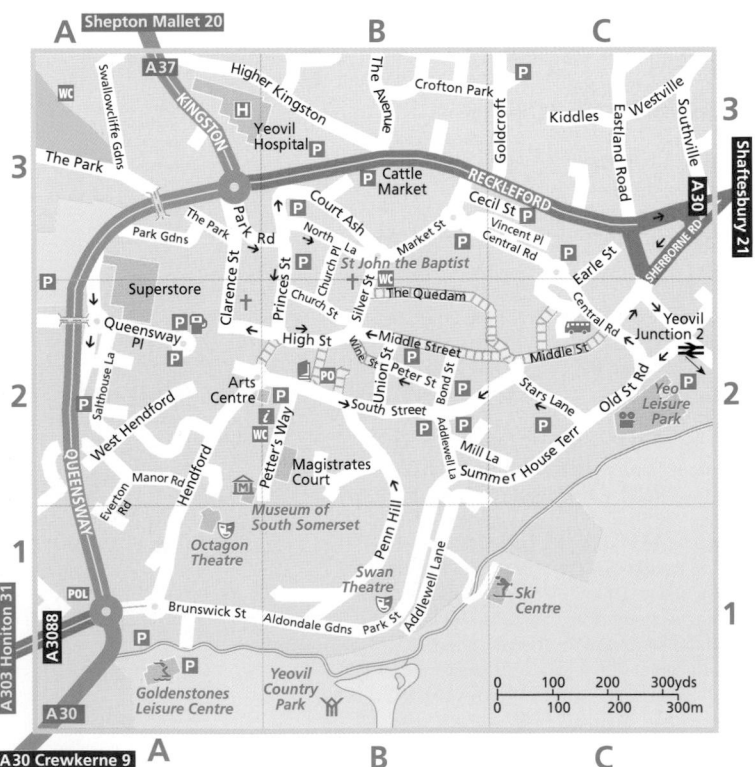

YORK

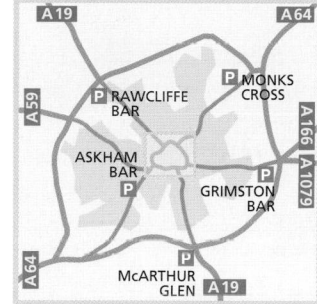

Park & Ride

TOWN PLANS

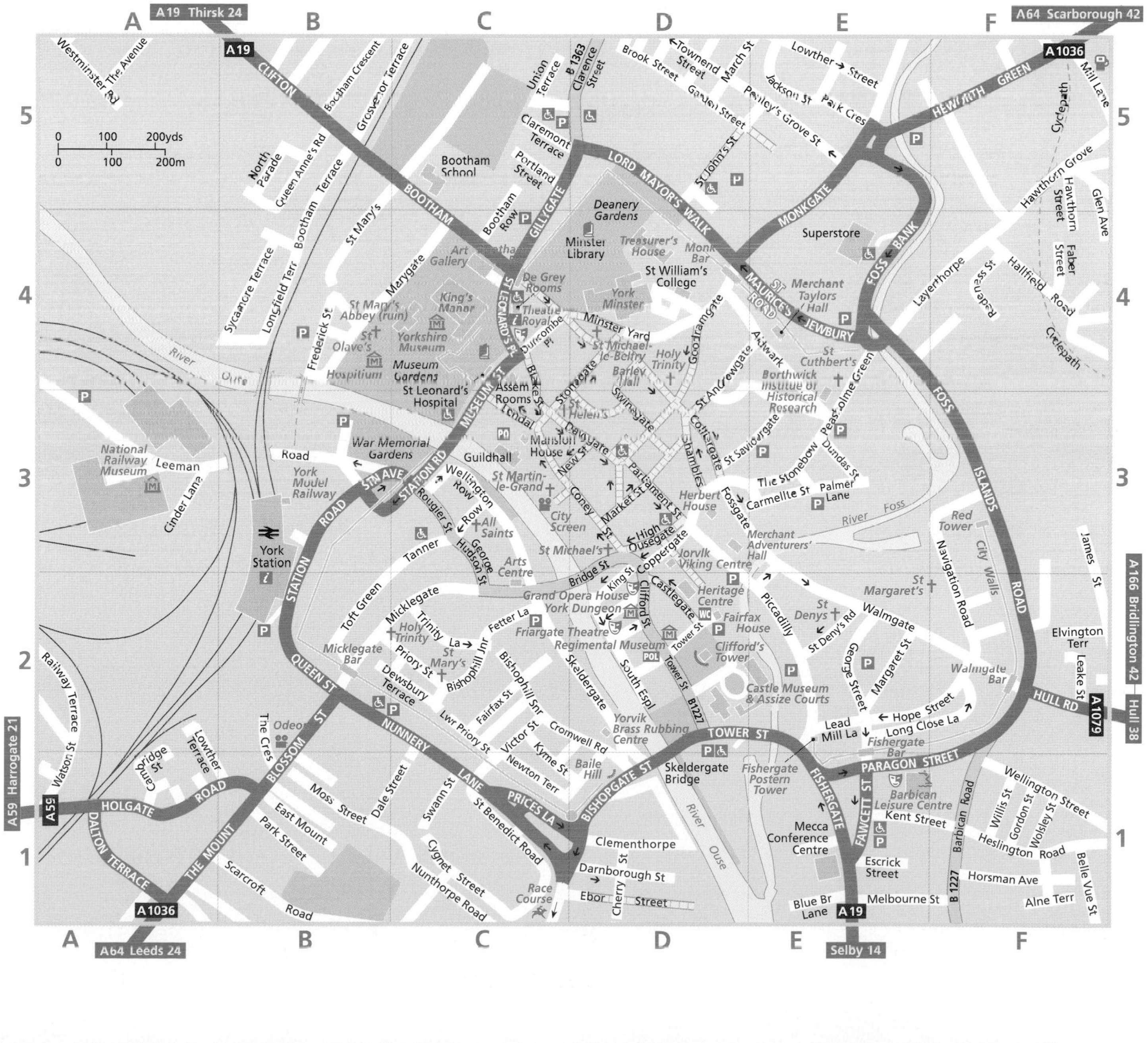

Touring guide

There are a wealth of places to visit throughout Britain and Ireland. Vibrant, bustling cities contrast with quaint rural villages, rugged moors with breathtaking coastlines, and medieval churches with dazzling modern architecture. The following pages are packed with suggestions for places to visit, attractions and diversions arranged by area to help you plan holidays and excursions.

Finding your way back to the map

Each page of the touring guide corresponds to one (and sometimes two) of the main map pages. Cross-references to the map pages are given at the top of each touring page. The attractions are listed under the name of the nearest village or town or, as in the case of famous houses or castles, are described separately. Where an entry covers more than one attraction, individual places of interest are picked out in bold type. Each entry has a two-figure grid reference to its map page for easy location. Where more than one map area is covered on a page, the relevant map page number is included in the reference. Information on attractions in major cities is given in the City Routes section, pages 270–301.

For further details about the places listed, including addresses, opening times, prices and telephone numbers, contact the local tourist information centres, whose telephone numbers are listed for each area.

Where to eat

For each touring area, we give a selection of good pubs to stop off for meals and refreshments. All pubs in Britain have been specially selected from The Good Pub Guide 2002 for their high quality of food, atmosphere and suitability for families with children. Managements and policies do change, however, so it is always advisable to check ahead. Many of the pubs we list are very popular and so it is also worth booking a table to avoid disappointment.

Symbols

When an attraction is followed by ❧, it means the property is owned by the National Trust and entry is free for members of the scheme. Likewise, the symbol ⌗ denotes properties which belong to the English Heritage and to which admission is also free for members.

Useful numbers

English Heritage (020) 7373 7737
National Trust (020) 8315 1111
National Trust Scotland (0131) 243 9300
Historic Houses Association (01462) 896688
Civic Trust (020) 7170 4299
National Parks (029) 2049 9966
Royal Horticultural Society (020) 7821 3000
Forestry Commission (0845) 3673787

Maritime memories *Towering over Liverpool's pier is the grand Port of Liverpool Building, a vestige from the city's past as a major port for passenger liners.*

Rural retreats *As well as busy towns and cities, the touring guide includes many secluded coastal and country villages, for those seeking a more peaceful trip.*

SHETLAND
488
Lerwick

Kirkwall
ORKNEY
488

487
Thurso
Stornoway
Wick
OUTER HEBRIDES
486
Ullapool

483
Portree
Inverness
484
485
SCOTLAND
Aberdeen

481
Fort William
481
482
Tobermory
Pitlochry
Forfar

479
479
Dundee
480
Oban
Perth
St Andrews
487
476
Stirling
477
478
Glasgow
EDINBURGH

473
474
475
Berwick-upon-Tweed
Ayr
Selkirk
Alnwick
471
471
472
Dumfries
495
Londonderry
495
Larne
Stranraer
Carlisle
Newcastle upon Tyne
Donegal
NORTHERN IRELAND
468
468
469
470
Sligo
BELFAST
465
Darlington
Middlesbrough
454
Kendal
466
467
Newry
Douglas
Scarborough
493
494
ISLE OF MAN
462
463
464
Westport
York
REPUBLIC
Blackpool
Bradford
Kingston upon Hull
Galway
Drogheda
459
Preston
LEEDS
461
OF
460
IRELAND
DUBLIN
454
455
MANCHESTER
456
Huddersfield
Doncaster
491
492
Holyhead
LIVERPOOL
457
458
458
Limerick
Chester
SHEFFIELD
Lincoln
448
449
450
Boston
453
Killarney
Waterford
Dolgellau
STOKE ON TRENT
451
452
King's Lynn
Norwich
Cork
Shrewsbury
Derby
Nottingham
489
490
WALES
Wolverhampton
Leicester
Peterborough
446
Great Yarmouth
442
443
444
445
Lowestoft
Fishguard
Newtown
Coventry
440
441
Aberystwyth
BIRMINGHAM
Northampton
Cambridge
436
437
438
Worcester
439
Ipswich
Hereford
ENGLAND
Colchester
430
Carmarthen
Brecon
432
Oxford
Luton
434
Harwich
430
431
Gloucester
433
435
Swansea
Newport
LONDON
Southend-on-Sea
CARDIFF
Bristol
Reading
428
429
Margate
424
425
426
427
Guildford
Maidstone
Canterbury
Bath
Winchester
422
Royal Tunbridge Wells
Dover
Barnstaple
Taunton
Salisbury
421
Brighton
423
418
419
420
Eastbourne
Southampton
417
Okehampton
413
Exeter
Bournemouth
Portsmouth
414
415
Weymouth
416
411
Newquay
Torquay
Truro
Plymouth
412
410
Penzance
410

CELTIC SEA

ATLANTIC OCEAN

NORTH SEA

ENGLISH CHANNEL

BELGIUM

FRANCE

415

Key to the touring guide pages 410–495

Western Cornwall and the Isles of Scilly

CHYSAUSTER [B3] Ruined houses in England's oldest street are part of what was probably a Celtic mining village 2000 years ago. They had central courtyards and paved floors fitted with drainage channels.

EDEN PROJECT [H5] See picture.

FALMOUTH [F3] A busy port since Tudor times, Falmouth had the first mail packet station in 1688. Ships took mail overseas from here for 150 years. At the entrance to the **Roads** is **Pendennis Castle ▣** of 1539–43. The **National Maritime Museum Cornwall** on the harbourside houses the National Small Boat Collection.

GWENNAP PIT [E4] John Wesley, founder of Methodism, preached to mining folk here in 1762, and the pit is still a Methodist centre today. Nearby **St Day** was once the mining capital of Cornwall.

HELFORD RIVER [E2] Wading birds probe the mud of the Helford estuary at low tide. The river runs through leafy creeks to **Gweek**, with its **Seal Sanctuary**, before turning inland.

HELSTON [D2] A boulder in the wall of the **Angel Hotel** is said to have given the town its name – after the 'Hell's stone' dropped by the Devil when challenged by St Michael. The Furry Dance in May is said to mark the saint's victory. The enchanting gardens of the **Trevarno Estate**, now open to the public, are close by.

ISLES OF SCILLY [A4/A5] Of the 100 or so islands 28 miles off Cornwall's south-west tip, only five

are inhabited. Tresco is famed for its subtropical **Abbey Gardens**, and is reached either by helicopter from Penzance or by boat from St Mary's, the largest island. Huge colonies of sea birds roost on the cliffs, porpoises leap clear of the crystal-clear water, and daffodils bloom in winter.

LANDS END [A2] Bare granite cliffs often buffeted by stormy seas give England's most westerly point an awesome grandeur. **Longships lighthouse** is offshore.

LIZARD PENINSULA [D1] One of the most scenic stretches of the Coast Path winds along the clifftop from the cliffs above **Mullion Cove** to the lighthouse on **Lizard Point**. During summer, clamouring colonies of kittiwakes and guillemots inhabit the cliffs, and the turf is carpeted with fragrant flowers. At **Kynance Cove 🌿**, serpentine rock is coloured red, white, yellow, black and grey-green.

MOUSEHOLE [B2] Narrow streets with stone-built cottages cluster round the quay of this fishing village. In nearby **Paul** is the grave of Dolly Pentreath, who died in 1777, and is believed to have been the last person to speak only Cornish. Nearby is a boulder honouring eight lifeboatmen who died on a mission in 1981.

NEWLYN [B2] The screaming of scavenging gulls is a reminder that the town's chief activity is landing and selling fish. Newlyn is popular with artists and the local **art gallery** has some excellent avant-garde art. There are also tours of the last working **Salt Pilchard Works** here.

PENZANCE [B2] Subtropical plants flourish in the sheltered **Morrab Gardens** close to the seafront of this popular resort. Sir Humphry Davy, who invented the miner's safety lamp, was born in the town. There are stunning views across to **St Michael's Mount** and the sandy beaches fringing **Mount's Bay**.

PRUSSIA COVE [C2] In the 18th century, the beach was the scene of John Carter's smuggling exploits. Known as the King of Prussia, he built the *King of Prussia Inn* at the head of the cove and fortified it with guns.

ST IVES [C4] The town was a pilchard-fishing port for centuries and the 12th-century **pier church** has relics from a time when fishermen paid a friar to bless their boats. St Ives has long attracted artists, including the sculptor Barbara Hepworth, who died in 1975. There is a **Tate Gallery** and a **Barbara Hepworth Museum**.

ST JUST [A3] Once a busy centre for the miners who worked at the tin mine at **Cape Cornwall**, the village is today a good place to explore the area's past, such as the Iron Age village of **Carn Euny** and the old mines at **Botallack** and **Pendeen**.

ST JUST-IN-ROSELAND [F3] Shrubs such as bamboo, rhododendron and camellia frame this 13th-century church, which overlooks tranquil **St Just Pool**, an inlet of the **Carrick Roads**. South of the King Harry Ferry is **Trelissick Garden 🌿**, a wooded estate famed for its rare shrubs.

ST MAWES [F3] This sheltered town provides ideal moorings for exploring the inlets of the Carrick Roads by boat. The sturdy **castle ▣** in the shape of a clover leaf was built for Henry VIII in the 1540s to guard the eastern approaches to the Carrick Roads. Across the water is **Pendennis Castle**.

TOURIST INFORMATION

Falmouth (01326) 312300
Helston (01326) 565431
St Mary's, Isles of Scilly
    (01720) 422536
Penzance (01736) 362207
St Ives (01736) 796297
Truro (01872) 274555

THE GOOD PUB GUIDE

Ludgvan [C3] *White Hart*
    (01736) 740574
Mousehole [B2] *Ship Inn*
    (01736) 731234
Mylor Bridge [E3] *Pandora*
    (01326) 372678
Penzance [B2] *Turks Head*
    (01736) 363093
Philleigh [F3] *Roseland*
    (01872) 580254
Ruan Lanihorne [F4] *Kings Head* (01872) 501263
St Ives [C3-4] *Sloop Inn*
    (01736) 796584
St Mawes [F3] *Rising Sun*
    (01326) 270233

ST MICHAEL'S MOUNT [C2] Near **Marazion** lies a small island where the Archangel Michael is said to have appeared to fishermen in AD 495. The mount is topped by a 14th-century **castle 🌿**. A causeway is uncovered briefly at low tide.

WENDRON [D3] Outside the village is the 18th-century Poldark tin mine which features an underground post box. A heritage centre relates the history of Cornish mining.

ZENNOR [B3] This remote coastal village is clustered round the 12th-century church of **St Senara**. A carved pew-end tells of a mermaid captivated by the singing of a local chorister who followed her into the sea at **Pendour Cove**. Nearby is **Zennor Quoit**, Britain's largest Stone Age burial chamber.

Paradise in a clay pit *Huge biomes (conservatories) nurture plants from rainforests to temperate habitats at the **Eden Project**. The Humid Tropics Biome is the largest greenhouse in the world at 240m (787ft) long, 110m (361ft) wide and 50m (164ft) high.*

Central and northern Cornwall

TOURIST INFORMATION

Bodmin (01208) 76616
Fowey (01726) 833616
Looe (01503) 262072
Lostwithiel (01208) 872207
Mevagissey (01726) 844857
Newquay (01637) 854020
Padstow (01841) 533449
Truro (01872) 274555

THE GOOD PUB GUIDE

Egloshayle [F5] *Earl of
   St Vincent* (01208) 814807
Fowey [G3] *Ship Inn*
   (01726) 834931
Lanlivery [F3] *Crown*
   (01208) 872707
Lostwithiel [F4] *Royal Oak*
   (01208) 872552
Mitchell [D3] *Plume of Feathers*
   (01872) 510387
Mithian [C3] *Miners Arms*
   (01872) 552375
Polperro [H3] *Old Mill House*
   (01503) 272362
St Kew [F5] *St Kew Inn*
   (01208) 841259
St Mawgan [D4] *Falcon*
   (01637) 860225

TOURING GUIDE

PADSTOW [E5] The **Court House**
was used by Sir Walter Raleigh as
Lord Warden of the Cornish
stannaries in 1585. Near **Rock** is the
15th-century church of **St Enodoc**,
recovered from the sands in 1863.

PERRANPORTH [C3] The ruins of
St Piran's Oratory, a 6th–7th century
chapel dedicated to the patron saint
of tin miners, are buried under the
sands. At **St Piran's Round** is an
earthwork amphitheatre, where
medieval mystery plays were held.

POLPERRO [H3] See picture.

RESTORMEL CASTLE [G4] On a hill
north of Lostwithiel stand the ruins of
the circular **castle**, which once
sheltered the Black Prince. The hill
was artificially steepened in about
1300, and the Norman shell given
further protection by a moat.

ST AGNES BEACON [C3] In the
16th century, fires blazed on the
191m (628ft) summit of this natural
lookout point to warn of the approach
of the Spanish Armada.

ST CLEER [H4] Close by the village
is spectacular **Trethevy Quoit ⚏**,
a prehistoric burial chamber with a
huge capstone supported on stone
slabs almost 5m (15ft) high. To the
west of the village are **Golitha Falls**.

TRURO [D2] Although 10 miles
inland, Truro was a thriving port until
the river silted up during the 17th
century. The three-spired **cathedral**
dates from 1910; Lemon Street has
well preserved Georgian buildings.

*Valley village The tiny streets which climb the steep slopes from **Polperro's**
quaint harbour are so narrow that traffic is banned in the village. Smuggling
was rife in the area in the 18th century, and the country's earliest Preventive
Station was set up here in 1801 to patrol the coastline.*

BEDRUTHAN STEPS [D4] According
to legend these massive stacks of
granite near **Trenance** were stepping
stones for the giant Bedruthan ⚘.

BLISLAND [G5] Set on Bodmin Moor
above the River Camel, in medieval
times it was called Blisland-juxta-
Montern, or Blisland near the
Mountain – probably a reference to
Brown Willy, north-east of the village.

BODMIN [F4] The large 15th-century
church is dedicated to the Cornish
saint, Petroc. **St Guron's Well** in the
churchyard is 1400 years old. An
18th-century jail now houses an
exhibition on crime and punishment.
Restored steam locomotives on the
Bodmin and Wenford Railway travel
through picturesque scenery. North of
Bodmin, 18th-century **Pencarrow
House** is set in lovely grounds and
holds fine paintings and furniture.

BODMIN MOOR [G5] Bleak and
windswept, and at times clothed in
mist, the 80 sq mile moor lends itself
to myth and mystery, not least at
Dozmary Pool, linked with Arthurian

legend. **Brown Willy** and **Rough Tor**,
Cornwall's highest points, both rise to
more than 396m (1300ft).

CARDINHAM WOODS [G4] Red
and roe deer may be seen here; trails
include a riverside walk.

DULOE STONE CIRCLE [H3] The
small eight-stone circle has quartz-
hewn stones up to 3m (9ft) tall and
some 3000 years old.

FOWEY [G3] At the quay, ships with
china clay from **St Austell** mingle with
pleasure craft. Fowey grew as a resort
after Sir Arthur Quiller-Couch made it
his 'Troy Town' in 1888. Daphne du
Maurier lived at **Menabilly**.

LANHYDROCK [F4] An 1881 fire
destroyed all but the gatehouse and
north wing of this 17th-century house
⚘. It was rebuilt later in the 19th
century. Lanhydrock has fine gardens
and views of the Fowey valley.

LOOE [H3] The old pilchard-fishing
port is now a seaside resort and shark-
fishing centre. East Looe's 16th-
century **guildhall** is a museum. West
Looe has the 16th-century **Jolly Sailor
Inn** and the **Church of St Nicholas**.

MEVAGISSEY [F2] Traditional slate
and cob cottages line the harbour. To
the north-west are the Victorian **Lost
Gardens of Heligan**, nurtured back to
their former glory after falling into
neglect after the First World War.

MINIONS [H5] The **Hurlers ⚏**, three
Bronze Age stone circles, lie just west
of the village. **The Cheesewring** on
Stow's Hill, a pile of granite slabs,
resembles tools for pressing curds.

NEWQUAY [D4] The 'new' quay
dates from the 16th century. Pilchard
fishermen kept watch for shoals from
clifftop lookouts called huers' huts –
one can be seen on the cliffs. This
lively resort has fine surfing beaches.

South-western Devon and the English Riviera

ANTONY HOUSE [B3] Built for Sir William Carew in the early 18th century, it is still the home of the Carew-Pole family, and retains much of the original furniture.

BUCKFASTLEIGH [E4] The great **abbey** of Buckfast, founded in 1018 and abandoned in 1539 lies north of the town. Its ruins were discovered in 1882, and the abbey rebuilt from 1906–38 by six Benedictine monks.

BUCKLAND ABBEY [C4] Sir Francis Drake, the Elizabethan sea captain, bought the 13th-century **abbey** ✤ in 1580–82, after his return from sailing round the world. It was his home until his death in 1596.

BURGH ISLAND [D/E2] At high tide, a tractor carries visitors to the island, with its dramatic cliffs, chic Art Deco hotel and 14th-century *Pilchard Inn*.

COLETON FISHACRE [G3] Colourful gardens surround the Arts and Crafts style house of the D'Oyly Cartes and extend into woodland gardens. A clifftop walk gives breathtaking views.

DARTINGTON [F4] Set in 16th and 17th-century buildings, shops in the **Dartington Cider Press Centre** sell pottery, crystal and farm foods. The 14th-century Dartington Hall is now a rural crafts and study centre.

DARTMOOR [D4/5] A bleak, lonely moor with granite tors (see picture), Dartmoor also has some of Devon's loveliest villages. Its prehistoric relics include **Hembury Castle**, an Iron Age hill fort, and **Grimspound**, a Bronze Age village featured in Sir Arthur Conan Doyle's *The Hound of the Baskervilles*. Dartmoor is now a national park covering 365 sq miles.

DARTMOUTH [G3] Once a port trading in cloth and Bordeaux wines, the town is now home to the **Britannia Royal Naval College**. It overlooks the River Dart estuary, guarded by a 15th-century **castle** ⌗ on a rocky headland.

DITTISHAM [G3] Famed for plums and cider, the village, set on the Dart, has a church with a Norman font and an unusual carved stone 15th-century pulpit. There is a river ferry to the gardens at **Greenway** ✤, once home of the detective writer Agatha Christie.

KENT'S CAVERN [G4] Flint weapons and the bones of hunted animals, such as mammoths and cave bears, have been found at the limestone caves, which were inhabited more than 450 000 years ago.

KINGSBRIDGE [E2] At the head of a broad estuary, the town's steep streets include the 16th-century **Shambles** and **Squeezebelly Lane**. **Fore Street** has some fine Georgian houses.

KITLEY CAVES [D3] First uncovered in the early 19th century, evidence remains of Stone Age cave bears, mammoths and hyenas. (Visits by appointment, call 01752 880885.)

MOUNT EDGCUMBE [C3] Laid out in 1761–1800, it was the earliest landscaped park in Cornwall, with grounds including a deer park and two fishing villages, offering fine views over Plymouth Sound. The 1547 mansion was burnt down in an air raid in 1941 and later rebuilt.

NEWTON FERRERS [C2] Set amid woodlands beside a creek off the River Yealm, the village is a popular yachting haven.

PAIGNTON [G4] Once a small fishing village, today Paignton is a popular seaside resort, its small harbour sheltering mainly holiday craft. The **Torbay and Dartmouth line** steam trains terminate here.

PLYMOUTH [C3] The estuaries of the Tamar and Plym join to form **Plymouth Sound**, which is crowded with naval and merchant ships, fishing boats and pleasure craft. A statue of Sir Francis Drake stands on **Plymouth Hoe**, but the **Royal Citadel** now occupies the green where he may have played bowls. **Smeaton's Tower**, a former Eddystone lighthouse, was moved to the Hoe in 1882. Drake, Raleigh, Frobisher, Captain Cook and the Pilgrim Fathers – in the *Mayflower* – all sailed from Barbican quay on **Sutton Harbour**. The **National Marine Aquarium** has hundreds of fish in habitats including a deep sea reef and a river estuary, along with Europe's largest collection of seahorses.

ST GERMANS [B3] The village has an outstanding **church** with two west towers and a Norman doorway. Balconied **almshouses** dating from 1538 overlook the small harbour.

SALCOMBE [E1] Devon's most southerly resort has a climate so mild that palm, orange and lemon trees grow on the harbour shores. A yachting centre, Salcombe's annual regatta was established in 1857.

SALTASH [B3] Tin was once exported from this fishing port which lies on a steep hill on the Cornish side of the Tamar. Brunel's **Prince Albert Bridge** carries the railway over the river.

SALTRAM HOUSE [C3] Devon's largest country house is an 18th-century mansion with some remains of the original Tudor house. The saloon and dining room are by Robert Adam, and there are ten paintings by Sir Joshua Reynolds.

SLAPTON LEY [F2] South-west England's largest natural lake and its marshes are part of a nature reserve with rare plants such as strapwort and birds such as Cetti's warbler.

THURLESTONE [E2] Black timbers at the *Village Inn* come from a galleon wrecked in 1588 in Hope Cove. Offshore is the **Thurlestone Rock**, a rock with a hole mentioned in the *Domesday Book* of 1086.

TORQUAY [G4] The town's central area overlooking Torbay retains its early 19th-century architecture. A broad green meadow between beach and town is a relic of the days when the land was owned by **Torre Abbey**, part of which survives as a museum (in Kings Drive). The novelist Agatha Christie was born here in 1890.

TOTNES [F4] Once a wealthy medieval town exporting wool and tin; on summer Tuesdays a small Elizabethan market is held in the town centre. Charles Babbage, who invented the first automatic digital computer, was educated in the town.

Rocky features *Bowerman's Nose is one of Dartmoor's stranger granite tors – rugged piles of deeply jointed rock that often form odd shapes. The tors are the remains of mountains that have been worn away by aeons of weathering.*

Northern Cornwall and Western Devon

*Surfer's paradise The deep, foamy waves which roll into north Cornish resorts such as Bude – seen here from **Wrangle Point**, to the north – have become a major draw for surfers.*

TOURIST INFORMATION

Boscastle (01840) 250010
Bude (01288) 354240
Camelford (01840) 212954
High Moorland Visitor Centre,
    Princetown (01822) 890414
Holsworthy (01409) 254185
Launceston (01566) 772321
Okehampton (01837) 53020
Tavistock (01822) 612938
Wadebridge (01208) 813725

THE GOOD PUB GUIDE

Boscastle [B3] *Wellington Hotel* (01840) 250202
Hatherleigh [F5] *Tally Ho Inn* (01837) 810306
Horndon [F2] *Elephant's Nest* (01822) 810273
Iddesleigh [G5] *Duke of York* (01837) 810253
Lydford [F3] *Castle Inn* (01822) 820241
Peter Tavy [F2] *Peter Tavy Inn* (01822) 810348
Port Isaac [A2] *Golden Lion* (01208) 880336
St Kew [A2] *St Kew Inn* (01208) 841259
Sheepwash [F5] *Half Moon* (01409) 231376
Tregadillett [D2] *Eliot Arms* (01566) 772051

TOURING GUIDE

ALTARNUN [C2] Set on the edge of Bodmin Moor, the village has granite-built cottages, an ancient packhorse bridge and 'the Cathedral of the Moor' – the **church** of **St Nonna**, noted for its 16th-century carved bench-ends. The vicar of Altarnun plays a key role in the novel *Jamaica Inn* by Daphne du Maurier.

BOSCASTLE [B3] Slate was once exported from the ancient **harbour**, which runs between narrow cliffs to the lime-washed village. While he was helping to restore nearby **St Juliot** church, the novelist Thomas Hardy met the rector's sister-in-law, Emma Gifford; they were married in 1874. At **Pentargon Bay**, to the north, an impressive waterfall plunges to the sea down a chasm, and there are fine views from **Beeny Cliff** – the subject of a poem by Thomas Hardy.

BRENT TOR AND LYDFORD GORGE [F2/3] The small 12th-century church of **St Michael de Rupe** stands atop windswept **Brent Tor** at some 335m (1100ft). **Whitelady Waterfall** at Lydford Gorge, to the north-east, drops 27m (90ft).

BUDE [C5] Surfers flock to this Atlantic seaside resort with wide, sandy beaches below the cliffs. The poet Alfred, Lord Tennyson, wrote of its 'long wave' and 'thundering shore'. In the 1800s the town was infamous for its wreckers – people who plundered shipwrecks. Nearby **Stratton** was the birthplace of the

Cornish giant, Anthony Payne, who fought for the Royalists in 1643 at their victorious Battle of Stamford Hill, near Stratton.

CRACKINGTON HAVEN [B4] Much of this coast belongs to the National Trust, and there are breathtaking views from the cliffs. At **St Gennys churchyard** on nearby **Pencannow Point**, the graves of sailors are evidence of the many ships that this wild coast has claimed.

HATHERLEIGH [F5] Once, the 15th century **George Hotel** in this small market town was the main coaching stage between Devon's two coasts. On **Hatherleigh Moor** is a monument to Lt Col William Morris CB, a hero of the Charge of the Light Brigade in 1854; it offers outstanding views of Dartmoor. At **Sheepwash** village to the west, the **Church of St Lawrence** has an unusual painted porch roof.

HOLSWORTHY [D4] Every three hours during the day, the town resounds to hymn tunes from the carillon of the 13th-century church. Holsworthy is said to be the last place in England where a man was put in the stocks – in 1861.

LAUNCESTON [D3] The ruined Norman **castle** its keep now 1m (3ft) out of true, overlooks the narrow, hilly streets of the town. The **South Gate** was part of the medieval town walls. The granite church of **St Mary Magdalene**, built in 1511–24, has

many carvings on its outside walls – among them minstrels said to depict a noted local group of 1440.

LISKEARD [C1] This hilltop market town was once one of Cornwall's stannary towns, where tin was tested for purity. It has Cornwall's second largest church, partly Norman.

MORWELLHAM QUAY [E1] Visitors can join the guides in Victorian dress, journey into a copper mine, be educated in an 1800s schoolroom or visit the nature reserve at this open-air **museum**, set in the once busy quay.

OKEHAMPTON [G4] The ruined Norman keep of the castle looks over the town from a hill by the West Okement river. To the south there are waymarked trails onto Dartmoor; to the north trails lead through **Abbeyford Woods**, where part of the **Tarka Trail** follows a riverside route described in *Tarka the Otter* (1927) by Henry Williamson. The **Museum of Dartmoor Life**, in a converted Victorian mill, recalls the lives, homes and occupations of local people.

PORT ISAAC [A2] The slate cottages of this fishing village huddle below high cliffs. Park at the hilltop and walk round the narrow streets. Nearby **Port Gaverne** was once the port for **Delabole Slate Quarry** to the north-east. The quarry is over 600 years old; visitors can gaze into its 130m (425ft) depths from a viewing platform. At the **Delabole Wind Farm and Gaia**

Energy Centre, visitors can get a close-up view of the wind turbines. It was Britain's first wind farm and the Energy Centre has exhibitions about alternative power sources, including wave and solar energy.

STICKLEPATH [G4] The village became part of the Industrial Revolution in the 19th century, when the fast-flowing River Taw was harnessed to drive mills. One of these mills was used for the **Finch Brothers' foundry**, which made many types of hand tool between 1814 and 1960. Today the foundry is a museum.

TAVISTOCK [F2] In the 19th century, this market town on the fringe of Dartmoor was one of the world's foremost copper mining centres. Sir Francis Drake is believed to have been born at **Crowndale Farm**, around 1542. The canal-side **Drake's Walk**, which starts near his statue in Plymouth Road, passes the site.

TINTAGEL CASTLE [B3] Legend has it that King Arthur, who was probably a 6th-century British leader, was born here. The atmospheric ruins of the cliff-top **castle** on Tintagel Head actually date from the 12th–13th centuries, but local landmarks, including **Merlin's Cave**, play on the enduring legend of Arthur, the wizard Merlin, and the Knights of the Round Table. On Tintagel's main street, **King Arthur's Great Halls** has 73 stained glass windows with stories of Arthur and his knights. Good visitor centre.

TOURING GUIDE

FROM MAP ON PAGES 72–73

Exeter and the south Devon coast

Gothic splendour *Exeter's ornate cathedral towers over the quaint cobbled lanes of the city's old quarter. The cathedral's west face has fine 14th-century sculpture.*

TOURIST INFORMATION

Axminster (01297) 34386
Budleigh Salterton
 (01395) 445275
Chard (01460) 67463
Crediton (01363) 772006
Dawlish (01626) 215665
Exeter (01392) 265700
Exmouth (01395) 222299
Honiton (01404) 43716
Lyme Regis (01297) 442138
Ottery St Mary (01404) 813964
Seaton (01297) 21660
Sidmouth (01395) 516441
Teignmouth (01626) 215666
Tiverton (01884) 255827

THE GOOD PUB GUIDE

Axmouth [F3] *Ship Inn*
 (01297) 21838
Beer [F3] *Dolphin*
 (01297) 20068
Cheriton Bishop [A3] *Old Thatch Inn* (01647) 24204
Cockwood [C2] *Anchor* (01626) 890203
Exeter [C4] *Double Locks Hotel* (01392) 256947
Haytor Vale [A2] *Rock Inn* (01364) 661305
Lyme Regis [G3] *Pilot Boat* (01297) 443157
Sidford [E3] *Blue Ball* (01395) 514062
Stockland [F5] *Kings Arms* (01404) 881361
Tipton St John [D3] *Golden Lion* (01404) 812881

A LA RONDE [D2] An unusual 16-sided **cottage** 🌺 on the fringe of Exmouth, it was designed by two cousins, Jane and Mary Parminter, after their 18th-century Grand Tour. The design is based on the Byzantine church of San Vitale in Ravenna, Italy, and the shell decoration echoes San Vitale's mosaics.

AXMINSTER [G4] Famous for its carpet-making industry, the town still holds a **Thursday market**, including free concerts in **St Mary's Church**.

AXMOUTH AND SEATON [F3] In its time the River Axe estuary has hosted Phoenician traders, Roman war galleys and Viking longships. Both Axmouth and Seaton were busy medieval havens that declined with the silting up of the river. Today Axmouth is a fine village, and Seaton a seaside resort. **Open-top trams** run between Seaton and Colyton.

BEER HEAD [F3] The most westerly of the English Channel's **chalk cliffs**, Beer Head rises above the fishing village of Beer. Jack Rattenbury, a local smuggler, published his *Memoirs of a Smuggler* in 1837.

BUDLEIGH SALTERTON [D2] The town grew up round salt pans at the mouth of the Otter. **Hayes Barton**, a 13th-century farmhouse on the northern outskirts, was the birthplace of Sir Walter Raleigh in 1552.

CASTLE DROGO [A3] Towering over the Teign's wooded gorge, Drogo 🌺 resembles a medieval fortress. In fact it was designed by Edward Lutyens early in the 20th century.

CHARD [G5] Somerset's highest town, Chard has steep and narrow streets. The 16th-century **courthouse** was the scene of one of Judge Jeffreys' 'Bloody Assizes'. A 200-year-old working corn mill, **Hornsbury Mill** is set in landscaped water gardens.

COMPTON CASTLE [B1] More a fortified manor house 🌺 than a castle, nevertheless it has a portcullis and arrow slits in the walls.

CREDITON [B4] Fire destroyed much of the town centre in the 18th century, but among the surviving ancient buildings is the 13th-century **Chapter House**, now a museum. St Boniface was born here in about AD 680.

DARTMOOR [A1/2] See p412.

DAWLISH [C2] Brilliant red cliffs flank the small seaside town. Dawlish Water flows through **The Lawn**, a delightful landscape garden.

EXETER [C3] Much of the area round the cathedral survived Second World War bombing; the **Guildhall** dates from 1330. William of Orange stayed at the **Deanery** during the Glorious Revolution of 1688, and the nearby

Ship Inn was a favourite haunt of Sir Francis Drake who also frequented **Mol's Coffee House** (now a map shop) in the Cathedral Close. **Underground passages** once carried water into the city and can be toured.

EXMOUTH [D2] The world's largest 00 gauge railway, the **Exmouth Model Railway**, is housed near the sea-front. **The World of Country Life**, to the east, displays collections of steam engines and farm machinery.

FORDE ABBEY [G5] Much of the original abbey, founded more than 800 years ago, remains. Later converted into a country house, it has attractive 18th-century gardens. To the south-east, a **hill fort** at Pilsdon Pen crowns the highest point in Dorset.

GOLDEN CAP [H3] A bright band of sandstone tops this cliff 🌺 above Lyme Bay – at 618ft (188m) the highest cliff on the south coast. It has views extending from Portland Bill to Start Point, and inland to Dartmoor.

HALDON FOREST [B/C2] Way-marked walks offer superb views of Dartmoor and Exeter. Buzzards and sparrow-hawks may be spotted here. To the south is **Ugbrooke House**, designed by Robert Adam and set in parkland by 'Capability' Brown.

LAPFORD [A5] The hilltop village is worth visiting for the wood carvings

in the mainly 15th-century church of **St Thomas of Canterbury**. It may have been built by William de Tracy, one of the murderers of Archbishop Thomas Becket, as a reparation for his crime.

LYME REGIS [G3] This Dorset town and its dramatic 13th-century breakwater, or **Cobb**, were made famous by John Fowles's novel and the later film *The French Lieutenant's Woman*. **Fossils** 150 million years old, discovered in the cliffs in 1811, are shown in the town's **Philpot Museum**.

TEIGNMOUTH [C1] Slabs of local granite used to build old London Bridge (1825–32) were shipped from the **quay**. Now the town is a holiday resort and a working port for small ships. The poet John Keats lived in **Northumberland Place**.

WHITCHURCH CANONICORUM [H4] The **Norman church** has a shrine dedicated to St Wite, and it still contains her relics. Medieval pilgrims thrust their diseased limbs into holes in the shrine in hope of a cure.

YARNER WOOD [A2] This national nature reserve has fine ancient oakwoods. **Becka (or Becky) Falls** are north-west off B3344 on a private estate, but are open to the public.

Southern Dorset and the Channel Islands

ABBOTSBURY [B3] The village has a huge **tithe barn** from a former 11th-century abbey, and fine **subtropical gardens**. Overlooking Abbotsbury is ruined **St Catherine's Chapel** ⌗.

ATHELHAMPTON [D4] The Great Hall of this early Tudor house has a minstrels' gallery and carved linenfold wall panelling.

BLACK DOWN [B3] An **obelisk** to Sir Thomas Masterman Hardy, Lord Nelson's flag captain at the Battle of Trafalgar, stands on the hill.

BLANDFORD FORUM [E5] A handsome Georgian town, it was almost totally rebuilt after a 1731 fire. The **Corn Exchange** and **Church of St Peter and St Paul** are especially fine.

BOURNEMOUTH [G3] A popular resort, Bournemouth has parks, gardens, two piers and long sandy beaches. Robert Louis Stevenson wrote *Kidnapped* and *The Strange Case of Dr Jekyll and Mr Hyde* while living here. **St Peter's churchyard** has the tomb of Mary Shelley, author of *Frankenstein*. A Victorian mansion houses the **Russell-Cotes Art Gallery and Museum**.

BROWNSEA ISLAND [F3] Lord Baden-Powell held the first Scout camp on the island in 1907. Now its heath and woods 🦌 include a nature reserve and one of Britain's few remaining red squirrel colonies.

CERNE ABBAS [C4] Cut into the chalk hillside above the village is the **Cerne Giant**, thought to be a fertility symbol more than 1500 years old. The village has **medieval stocks**, half-timbered flint houses, and a bridged rivulet running along Abbey Street to the site of a 10th-century **abbey**.

CHANNEL ISLANDS [INSET] The islands are popular for their mild climate and extensive beaches. **La Hougue Bie** in St Helier on Jersey is a fine prehistoric tomb. The **German Underground Hospital** was hewn out of rock by forced labour during the Second World War. Guernsey's capital, St Peter Port, was the home of the French poet and novelist Victor Hugo; his house is now a **museum**. Alderney is a wildlife haven with rare black rabbits and blonde hedgehogs.

CHESIL BEACH [B2] See picture.

CHRISTCHURCH [H3] A stronghold against the Danes in the 9th century, Christchurch's 1094 **Priory** is Britain's longest parish church, at just over 91m (300ft). It also has the country's two oldest bells, dating from 1370. South of the harbour is **Hengistbury Head**, rich in archaeological remains and wildlife, and a fine viewpoint.

CLOUDS HILL [D3] Soldier and writer T E Lawrence (Lawrence of Arabia) lived in this cottage 🦌. **St Nicholas's Church** in Moreton has windows by Lawrence Whistler and Bovington camp has a **tank museum**.

CORFE CASTLE [F2] The castle's gaunt ruins 🦌 stand on a mound above the village. The Saxon king Edward the Martyr was murdered here in 978 while visiting his half-brother Ethelred.

DORCHESTER [C3] The town dates back to Roman times and its tree-lined **Walks** follow the Roman walls. The **Antelope Hotel** was the scene of a 'Bloody Assize' in 1685, when dreaded Judge Jeffreys sentenced 292 men after the Monmouth rebellion. A **dinosaur museum** contains fossils and life-size reconstructions. **Max Gate** 🦌 was the home of the writer Thomas Hardy. He was born at Higher Bockhampton, nearby.

ISLE OF PORTLAND [C1] The famed pale limestone from this peninsula has been used to face buildings such as Buckingham Palace and St Paul's Cathedral. **Portland Castle** ⌗ was a coastal fort and Portland Bill's **lighthouse** dates from 1906.

LULWORTH COVE [D2] This neat, horseshoe-shaped cove has been perfectly chiselled by the sea. The cliffs rise higher than 122m (400ft) at Hambury Tout. To the west of the cove is **Durdle Door**, a rock arch.

MAIDEN CASTLE [C3] A Celtic tribe made this immense **earthwork** ⌗ in the 1st century BC and excavations have shown that the site was also used in the Stone Ages.

POOLE [F3] Built on an almost landlocked bay, the port has one of Britain's largest shallow anchorages. Its ancient heart by the harbour is crowded with old inns and 18th-century warehouses.

SWANAGE [F2] Purbeck marble was quarried locally and rare lowland heath still survives at Arne and at Studland 🦌, where a nature reserve shelters native British reptiles. A coast path from Shell Bay to Durlston Head gives superb views of **Tilly Whim Caves** and **Dancing Ledge**.

WAREHAM [F3] The stone coffin of Edward the Martyr lies in **St Mary's Church**. The Quay and Abbot's Quay are packed with small boats. The **Blue Pool**, a disused claypit in nearby Furzebrook, changes colour as the clay particles reflect changing light.

WEYMOUTH [C2] George III turned this into a popular resort after he holidayed here in 1789. Grand Georgian buildings remain from that time. Attractions include a **sea life centre** and displays on the town's history at the **Timewalk museum**.

WIMBORNE MINSTER [F4] A figure of a grenadier on the clock of the local church strikes the quarter-hours

TOURIST INFORMATION

Alderney (01481) 823737
Blandford Forum
 (01258) 454770
Bournemouth (01202) 451700
Bridport (01308) 424901
Christchurch (01202) 471780
Dorchester (01305) 267992
Guernsey (01481) 723552
Jersey (01534) 500777
Poole (01202) 253253
Ringwood (01425) 470896
Sark (01481) 832345
Swanage (01929) 422885
Wareham (01929) 552740
Weymouth (01305) 785747
Wimbourne Minster
 (01202) 886116

THE GOOD PUB GUIDE

Burton Bradstock [A3] *Anchor* (01308) 897228
Cerne Abbas [C4] *Royal Oak* (01300) 341797
East Chaldon [D2] *Sailors Return* (01305) 853847
Colehill [F4] *Barley Mow* (01202) 882140
Corfe Castle [F2] *Greyhound* (01929) 480205
Corscombe [A5] *Fox* (01935) 891330
King's Mills [Guernsey] *Fleur du Jardin* (01481) 257996
Plush [C4] *Brace of Pheasants* (01300) 348357
St Brelade [Jersey] *Old Portelet Inn* (01534) 741899
Upwey [C3] *Old Ship* (01305) 812522

TOURING GUIDE

Shingle landmark *Chesil Beach* extends for 17 miles and is formed from stones deposited by the sea. The pebbles are the size of potatoes at the east end of the beach but decrease to the size of chick peas by the west end.

Southern Hampshire and the Isle of Wight

BEAULIEU ABBEY [B4] The remains of a Cistercian abbey stand near the Beaulieu River. Its gatehouse is now part of **Palace House**. In the grounds is the **National Motor Museum**.

BLACKGANG CHINE [C2] There are spectacular views from the clifftop gardens and theme park here, and from the coast road to Alum Bay, where **The Needles** jut into the sea.

BOGNOR REGIS [H4] Sir Richard Hotham, a London hatter, arrived in Bognor in 1787, and transformed it from a fishing hamlet into a genteel health resort. It gained the title Regis after a visit by George V in 1929.

BOSHAM [G4] In 1064, Harold Godwin, who later became King Harold, prayed at the Saxon church in Bosham (pronounced Bozzam) before going to Normandy to swear fealty to Duke William. This visit led in 1066 to the Battle of Hastings.

BOW HILL [G5] Amid fine South Downs scenery, the hill is noted for its yew trees, in medieval times used to make English longbows. Some of Europe's finest yew woods are in **Kingley Vale Nature Reserve**.

BROCKENHURST [A4] A renowned New Forest snake catcher, Harry 'Brusher' Mills, has a distinctive headstone in the town's churchyard. A churchyard yew 6m (20ft) round is said to be the New Forest's oldest tree.

BUCKLERS HARD [C4] In the late 18th century this village at the mouth of Beaulieu River was a shipbuilding centre. Among the vessels launched here was HMS *Agamemnon,* Lord Nelson's command when he left for the Mediterranean in 1793.

CHICHESTER [G5] Laid out by the Romans in about AD 70, the city is quartered by four main streets centred on the **Market Cross** of 1501 and the nearby 900-year-old **cathedral**, its 84m (277ft) spire a local landmark. The **Festival Theatre** of 1962 is just outside the city's medieval walls.

COWES [C4] The town flanks the Medina, its two parts linked by a 'floating bridge' ferry. The **Royal Yacht Squadron headquarters** is the starting point for yachting races. Cowes Week began in 1776 and is now an annual

yachting highlight in August. Nearby **Ryde** has broad sands and a pier ½ mile (800m) long built in 1813.

FAREHAM [D5] In the 18th century Portsmouth naval officers lived in the Georgian houses on the High Street. Nearby **Titchfield Abbey ⌘**, with a fine four-storey gatehouse, dates from the 13th century. In 1647, Charles I was arrested there.

FISHBOURNE ROMAN PALACE [G5] No Roman palace in northern Europe was more splendid than Fishbourne in the 1st century AD. Covering 4ha (10 acres), it had four wings round formal gardens, and walls inlaid with marble. **The Trundle**, on a 206m (676ft) hill north of Chichester, has fine views. It was a stronghold of the Atrebates, a powerful tribe of British Celts.

GOSPORT [E4] *Holland I*, the Royal Navy's first submarine, launched in 1901, is on view at the **Submarine Museum**. Old naval stores in the harbour now house **Explosion!**, a museum of naval firepower. From the **Falklands Gardens** there are good views across Portsmouth Harbour.

HAVANT [F5] Until early last century, parchment was made in the town – the 1919 Treaty of Versailles was printed on Havant parchment. **Hayling Island** has fine, 'blue flag' beaches, yachting and windsurfing.

LYMINGTON [B4] Today a sailing resort, this river-mouth port and old market town was a salt refining centre until the 18th century. Old salterns can be still seen on the marshes.

LYNDHURST [A5] Set at the heart of the New Forest, the town has the forest's Visitor Centre and museum. In the churchyard is the grave of Alice

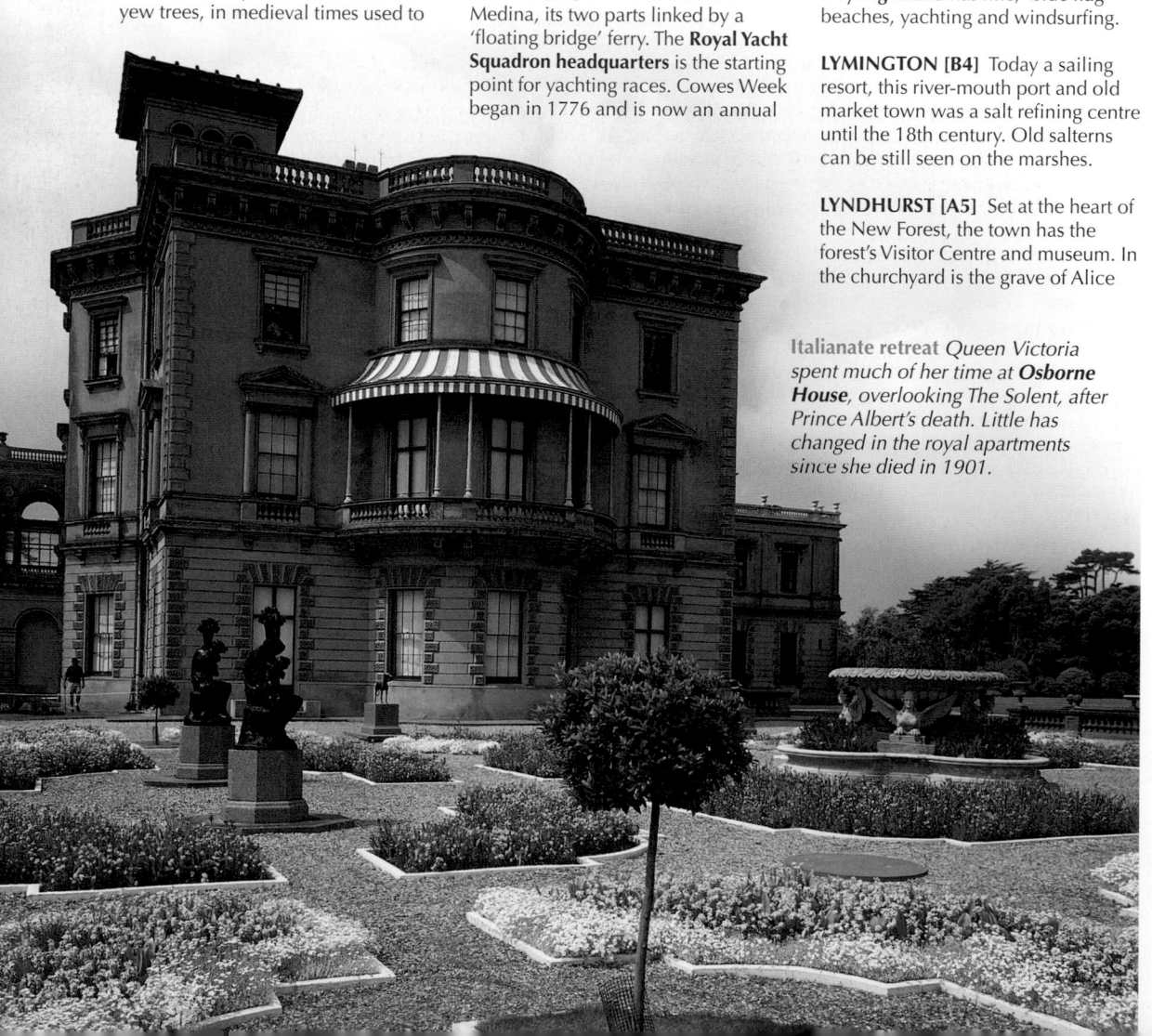

*Italianate retreat Queen Victoria spent much of her time at **Osborne House**, overlooking The Solent, after Prince Albert's death. Little has changed in the royal apartments since she died in 1901.*

Hargreaves (née Liddell), the inspiration for Lewis Carroll's book, *Alice's Adventures in Wonderland*.

MINSTEAD [A5] Sir Arthur Conan Doyle, creator of Sherlock Holmes, is buried in the village churchyard.

NEWPORT [C3] Roman hot and cold plunge baths are on show at the Cypress Road **Roman Villa**, evidence that the island's capital dates back some 2000 years. In times of trouble, people fled to nearby **Carisbrooke Castle ⌘** where, in 1647–8, Charles I was imprisoned for 10 months.

OSBORNE HOUSE [D4] See picture.

PORTSMOUTH [E4] See City Routes pp296–297.

SANDOWN [D3] Golden sands stretch for 6 miles along the large bay at Sandown. **Shanklin**, nearby, is on the cliffs, with a lift to the esplanade and beach. **Shanklin Chine**, a deep, winding, wooded ravine, has waterfalls that are floodlit in summer.

SOUTHAMPTON [B5] See City Routes pp296–297.

FROM MAP ON PAGES 78–79

The South Downs and the Sussex coast

Beside the sea *Construction of the 525m (1722ft) long Victorian pier at Brighton began in 1891 and was completed in 1899. By 1901, one building housed dining, reading and smoking rooms and a concert hall.*

TOURING GUIDE

ALFRISTON [F4] The thatched 14th-century **Clergy House** ✄, once used as a lodging for visiting priests, was the National Trust's first property, acquired in 1896 for £10. Other buildings of note are the **Star Inn** and a magnificent parish **church** known as the 'Cathedral of the Downs'.

ARUNDEL [A5] For over 900 years the mighty **castle** of the Dukes of Norfolk has dominated this small town. The castle was restored in the 19th century, but the keep has changed little since it was built after the Norman conquest. The Roman Catholic **cathedral** dates from 1869.

BEACHY HEAD [G4] 'Beau chef', or 'beautiful head', was the apt name the Normans gave to this spectacular headland. There are good views from the cliffs to the west. High above the beach and lighthouse, brilliant white cliffs rise 163m (534ft), with views to the Isle of Wight and Dungeness.

BEXHILL [H5] The modernist **De La Warr Pavilion**, built in 1935, is found in this peaceful seaside resort.

BRIGHTON AND HOVE [D4/5] Once the Prince Regent had set his seal of approval on Brighton in the 1780s, its popularity as a seaside resort earned it the name of 'London by the sea'. The **Royal Pavilion**, with its lavish interiors, is one of Britain's most extraordinary buildings – Queen Victoria disapproved and sold it to the town. Hove, with stuccoed Regency terraces, is a quieter resort.

CHARLESTON FARMHOUSE [F5] The artist Vanessa Bell lived here from 1916 until her death in 1961. With contributions from other artists, she decorated it in a colourful, distinctive style. Today the house is a shrine to the Bloomsbury Group of writers, artists and intellectuals.

DITCHLING BEACON [D5] There are fine views from this downland high point, 248m (813ft), located on the South Downs Way that runs from Eastbourne to Winchester.

EASTBOURNE [G4] The majestic Grand Hotel on the esplanade sums up Eastbourne. It was built in 1875, and the visitors' book is full of famous names. The town prides itself on its aristocratic origins – it was laid out by the Duke of Devonshire in 1834. There are fine parks and gardens, and a 3 mile long esplanade.

FIRLE PLACE AND BEACON [F5] The Tudor mansion – much altered around 1730 – was built by the Gage family, who still own it. Nearby is the viewpoint of **Firle Beacon**, 217m (713ft) high, with views that extend to the Channel and the Weald.

FRISTON FOREST [F4] First planted in 1926, the forest – mainly of beeches – has waymarked trails. At **Crowlink** ✄ to the south you can walk on National Trust downs above the Seven Sisters cliffs.

HERSTMONCEUX CASTLE [G5] The Royal Greenwich Observatory, driven out of London in 1957 by severe air pollution, was housed in this moated castle until 1990. The observatory is now in Cambridge, but you can visit the grounds and Science Centre.

LEWES [E5] Looming above the town from the top of a great mound, the Norman **castle** has two distinctive octagonal towers and a superb barbican gateway. Its grounds were turned into gardens in the 18th and 19th centuries. Among a number of historic buildings is the 15th-century **Anne of Cleves house** given by Henry VIII to his fourth wife in 1538. The diarist John Evelyn (1620–1706) spent his boyhood at **Southover Grange**.

LITTLEHAMPTON [A4] Caen stone, used for building Sussex churches and castles, was once imported through this town at the mouth of the fast-flowing River Arun. In the 18th century a shipbuilding centre, it now caters mainly for amateur yachtsmen.

LONG MAN OF WILMINGTON [F4] Driving between Wilmington and Alciston, you cannot miss the 69m (226ft) tall figure, cut into the chalk on Windover Hill. Whether the Long Man is prehistoric or Saxon, or if he represents man or god, is unknown.

MICHELHAM PRIORY [G5] Part of the ruined 13th-century priory ✄, mirrored in a tranquil moat, has been restored to give an idea of medieval monastic life. Even the physic garden is laid out in its original form.

NEWHAVEN [E4] When, in 1579, a tremendous storm altered the course of the Ouse, it created a 'new haven' – today's port. **Newhaven Fort**, a coastal defence, is now a museum.

PEVENSEY CASTLE [G5] The castle began its 1700 years of military history about AD 340 as Anderida, a Roman fort. In 1066, William the Conqueror camped inside its walls. The medieval castle built on the site had gun emplacements added in the Second World War.

SEAFORD [F4] Made a 'limb', or auxiliary, of the Cinque Port of Hastings in 1229, Seaford had the duty of providing ships and men for coastal defences. The storm that created Newhaven ended Seaford's importance as a port. A Martello tower now houses the town **museum**.

SEVEN SISTERS [F4] From Beachy Head or the viewpoint at **Birling Gap** ✄, you can see this entire stretch of undulating chalk cliffs, like frozen waves of green turf rolling westwards to **Cuckmere Haven**. The **Seven Sisters Country Park** is located in the picturesque Cuckmere valley.

SHOREHAM-BY-SEA [C5] Just before it reaches the sea, the River Adur turns sharply to create the town's sheltered inner harbour. The river footbridge gives a good view of Shoreham and its Norman church. **Marlipins**, a 12th-century chequered flint building, houses a museum of local history. Shoreham's **art deco airport** buildings recall a more leisurely age of travel.

WORTHING [B4] Although the town dates back to Roman times, it was still a hamlet when George III sent his sickly daughter Amelia to convalesce here. Fashionable England then flocked here too and it became a popular resort. Today Worthing is the largest town in West Sussex.

North Devon and western Exmoor

TOURIST INFORMATION

Barnstaple (01271) 375000
Bideford (01237) 477676
Braunton (01271) 816400
Combe Martin (01271) 883319
Exmoor National Park, County
    Gate (01598) 741321
Holsworthy (01409) 254185
Ilfracombe (01271) 863001
Lynmouth, National Park Visitor
    Centre (0845) 6603232
Lynton (0845) 6603232
South Molten (01769) 574122
Tarka Trail (01237) 423655
Woolacombe (01271) 870553

THE GOOD PUB GUIDE

Berrynarbor [F5] *Olde Globe*
(01271) 882465
Buckland Brewer [E2] *Coach &
    Horses* (01237) 451395
Chittlehamholt [G2] *Exeter Inn*
(01769) 540281
Horns Cross [D2] *Hoops*
(01237) 451222
Umberleigh [G2] *Rising Sun*
(01769) 560447

APPLEDORE [E3] A historic boating centre, Appledore is defined by fishing boats, lobster pots and cobbled streets. It has a fine **Maritime Museum**, and a ferry crosses the river estuary to sandy beaches at Instow.

ARLINGTON COURT [G4] A fine Regency mansion 🦋 set in a thickly wooded park, it was home to the Chichester family. Its many treasures include a William Blake painting found on top of a pantry cupboard.

BADGWORTHY WATER [H4/5] At the heart of Doone Country, the scenic river valley was the setting for R.D. Blackmore's novel *Lorna Doone*.

BARNSTAPLE [F3] Once a busy port, the town claims to be England's oldest borough, and is still a thriving farming centre. Fine 18th-century architecture can be seen in the colonnaded **Queen Anne's Walk**, once the Merchants' Exchange where traders gathered to seal deals on the **Tome Stone**.

BIDEFORD [E3] A **medieval bridge** spans the river at the busy port of Bideford. Westward Ho!, a nearby resort, was named after Charles Kingsley's book of the same name. Sheep racing, shearing, sheepdog training and duck-herding trials are seen at **The Big Sheep**, near Abbotsham.

BRAUNTON BURROWS [E3] These magnificent sand dunes are rich in wildlife. They are mainly a national **nature reserve** but parts are army ranges. There are fine views from the cliffs around **Baggy Point** 🦋.

CHULMLEIGH [G1] In this hilly town by the Little Dart River, the 15th-century church of **St Mary Magdalene** is noted for its fine carvings. The *Barnstaple Inn* dates from 1633.

CLOVELLY [D3] See picture.

COMBE MARTIN [F5] The resort is a good base for exploring the Exmoor coast. **Little and Great Hangman** are striking headlands nearby. The *Pack O'Cards Inn* was built in 1690 by George Ley after a win at cards.

EGGESFORD FOREST [G1] In 1956 the Queen unveiled a stone here marking the planting of 405,000ha (1 million acres) of trees throughout Britain. There are waymarked trails through the woods first planted by the Forestry Commission in 1919.

GREAT TORRINGTON [F2] During the Civil War, the local church was accidentally blown up. A **visitor centre** tells the story. The town is now

Village scene *Lined by 16th-century cottages, the cobbled, car-free high street of* **Clovelly** *drops 122m (400ft) towards the Tudor walls of the harbour.*

home to Dartington Crystal. Nearby **Rosemoor (RHS)** has fine roses, tropical plants and a winter garden.

HARTLAND QUAY [C2] A former port, financed by Sir Francis Drake, Sir Walter Raleigh and Sir John Hawkins, its quay was later destroyed by storms. Nearby is **Hartland Abbey**, a mansion with a 12th-century abbey.

HEANTON PUNCHARDON [F4] There are panoramic views from the village, set on a high ridge above the Taw estuary. Nearby is **Marwood Hill garden**, noted for its camellias and rare flowering shrubs.

HEDDON'S MOUTH [G5] This secluded cove at the mouth of the River Heddon valley is a 1 mile walk from *Hunter's Inn*. To the east, a cliff path leads to **Woody Bay**, with its oak woods and waterfall.

HELE CORN MILL [F5] The 16th-century **water mill** has a working overshot (top-fed) 5.5m (18ft) wheel.

ILFRACOMBE [F5] A popular holiday resort since the arrival of the railway in 1874, Ilfracombe has a number of sheltered **beaches** and coves.

LUNDY [B5] Once a pirate haunt, this tiny island 🦋 whose cliffs reach 122m (400ft) is rich in wildlife. There are more than 400 bird species as well as grey seals, sika deer and soay sheep. It has three **lighthouses** and a **castle**, but no roads. Access is by boat from Bideford or Ilfracombe.

LYNTON AND LYNMOUTH [H5] A clifftop resort on the edge of Exmoor, Lynton is reached by a steep, water-powered **cliff railway**. In 1952 Lynmouth, its twin resort, was partly destroyed by a flood, but the 18th-century **quay** survived.

MORWENSTOW [C2] The former vicar, Robert S. Hawker, revived the medieval custom of the Harvest Festival. On a notoriously perilous coast, he aided shipwreck survivors and buried victims in the **churchyard**.

PARRACOMBE [G5] Set in the steep Heddon valley, the village has a fine but disused 11th-century church – **St Petrock's**. It was saved in 1878 after a protest led by John Ruskin.

SIMONSBATH [H4] Exmoor's highest village, at 335m (1100ft) is a good centre for exploring the moor. The

wilderness of **The Chains**, 487m (1599ft), rises to the west, with **Pinkworthy Pond** below. To the south-west are **Five Barrows**, 493m (1617ft), and **Hangley Cleave**, 483m (1585ft).

SOUTH MOLTON [H3] This former wool-trading centre on the edge of Exmoor has fine Georgian buildings including the **Guildhall**. Henry Williamson, the author of *Tarka the Otter*, lived at **Shallowford House**.

SWIMBRIDGE [G3] The Rev. Jack Russell, the vicar here, was a founder member of the Kennel Club and the breeder of the Jack Russell terrier. The *Jack Russell Inn* is named after him.

TAPELEY PARK [E3] A fine 17th-century house, it has terraced Italian gardens and a considerable collection of William Morris furniture. John Christie, who grew up here, founded the Glyndebourne Opera Festival.

THE VALLEY OF THE ROCKS [H5] **Castle Rock**, with its piled slabs of limestone, dominates the dry, grassy valley. Other strangely weathered rocks in the valley include **Ragged Jack** and the **Devil's Cheesewring**.

WATERSMEET [H5] Hoar Oak Water and the East Lyn river meet at the steep, wooded **gorge** 🦋 and cascade in a rush to the sea. A former fishing lodge now provides refreshments.

WOOLACOMBE [E4] A superb beach backed by sand dunes stretches for 2 miles and is a highlight of this popular swimming and surfing resort. A cliff path runs from Mortehoe to **Morte Point**, a treacherous reef that has wrecked many a ship.

Exmoor, the Quantocks and the Somerset Levels

Subterranean dwellings Stone Age people inhabited the eerie limestone caverns at **Wookey Hole** *some 50,000 years ago. Tours use special light effects to illuminate geological features and bring to life the stories of those who existed here.*

BRENT KNOLL [F5] The hill above the village is topped by an **Iron Age fort** 🐾. Medieval carved bench-ends in the **church** insult an abbot who tried to seize parish revenues.

BRIDGWATER [F4] This market town on the Parrett was once a busy port. The Duke of Monmouth viewed the king's army from **St Mary's Tower** before the Battle of Sedgemoor.

BURNHAM-ON-SEA [F5] The **'Whitehall Carvings'** in the church are by Grinling Gibbons and Arnold Quellin. They were originally ordered by James II for Whitehall Palace.

CULBONE CHURCH [A5] Said to be England's smallest church still in use, the medieval **St Bueno's** seats just 36 people. It is a 2 mile (3km) walk from Porlock Weir or the A39.

DULVERTON [B3] An unspoiled town amid thick woods, Dulverton was the birthplace of Sir George Williams, who founded the YMCA.

DUNSTER [C4] This scenic village has a 13th-century **castle** 🐾, and a **priory church**. It also has a medieval **packhorse bridge**, a **Yarn Market** ⬡ and an 18th-century **watermill** 🐾.

EBBOR GORGE [H5] A wooded chasm in the Mendip Hills, the gorge is part of a **nature reserve**, with waymarked walks and superb views.

GLASTONBURY [H4] **King Arthur and Queen Guinevere's tomb** is in the ruined 13th-century **abbey**. The **'Holy Thorn'** is said to have descended from

one struck from the staff of St Joseph of Arimathea. Legend has it that the Holy Grail was hidden at the **Chalice Well**. **St Michael's Tower** sits at the peak of **Glastonbury Tor** 🐾. The village has a **museum of rural life**.

ILMINSTER [G1] The market town has a colonnaded **market house** and a handsome 15th-century **church.**

MEARE [G4] Originally Meare was a lake village of the Somerset swamps. Fish was stored in 14th-century **Fish House** for the abbots of Glastonbury.

MINEHEAD [C5] A holiday resort on a wide bay, it has vast sands at low tide and a characterful old town.

MONTACUTE HOUSE [H2] See picture.

MUCHELNEY ABBEY [G2] Remains of a 12th-century **abbey** ⬡ rise out of the Somerset Levels.

PORLOCK [B5] This village lies below a steep hill with hairpin bends – Victorian tourists had to get out of their carriages and walk up the hill.

QUANTOCK HILLS [D/E4] Crowned by moors, the hills stretch for miles through scattered farms, sunken lanes and hamlets. Samuel Taylor Coleridge had a **cottage** 🐾 in Nether Stowey and he and William Wordsworth wrote the *Lyrical Ballads* of 1798 while staying in the area.

SEDGEMOOR [G4] In 1685, James II's army defeated the Duke of Monmouth on this marshy site. Prisoners were hanged from the belfry in the **church** at Westonzoyland.

STOKE PERO COMMON [B4] A steep, twisting road climbs to this lonely Exmoor common. Gorse-topped **Selworthy Beacon** is visible to the north-east. South-east is **Dunkery Beacon**, Somerset's highest point.

STREET [H4] James Clark built a factory here in the 1820s to line slippers with sheepskin. There is a **shoe museum** at Clark's Village.

TAUNTON [E2] Somerset's county town is famous for its cider. Its historic buildings include the **Norman castle** and **St Mary Magdalene's Church**.

TIVERTON [B1] This former lace-making town has a 12th–14th-century pink sandstone **castle**. **Old Blundell's School** was featured in the novel *Lorna Doone* by R.D. Blackmore.

WASHFORD [C4] Ruined **Cleeve Abbey** ⬡ has a 14th-century dormitory and 15th-century refectory. An old **radio station** houses a jungle with exotic animals. In Willeton, close by, is the **Bakelite Museum** of vintage plastics.

WELLINGTON MONUMENT [D2] On the Blackdown Hills is an obelisk honouring the Duke of Wellington.

WINSFORD [B3] At Spire Cross outside the village is the **Caratacus Stone** with a Latin inscription. Nearby Tarr Steps has an old **clapper bridge**.

WOOKEY HOLE [H5] See picture, above.

Elizabethan splendour Montacute House 🐾 *was built in the 1590s for Sir Edward Phelips, a successful lawyer and politician. Paintings from the National Portrait Gallery are displayed in its spectacular Long Gallery.*

East Somerset, Salisbury Plain, Cranborne Chase

Fabulous backyard *Cottages on Gold Hill in* **Shaftesbury** *stand by the walls of King Alfred's Abbey and overlook the verdant Blackmore Vale.*

AMESBURY [G4] The town's Norman **abbey church** stands on the site of a priory to which Queen Guinevere is said to have retreated after the death of King Arthur.

ASHMORE [E2] On a clear day, the view from the village extends to the Isle of Wight. The village pond is, at midsummer, the setting for the Morris dance 'Filly Loo' ceremony.

CADBURY CASTLE [B3] Some locals believe the hilltop earthwork was the site of Camelot. At North Cadbury, **St Michael's Church** has unusual 16th-century carved bench-ends, including one that depicts a Tudor mousetrap.

CRANBORNE [F1] Amid the colour-washed cottages and elegant houses stands a Jacobean manor house, built around King John's **hunting lodge** of 1208. John Tradescant laid out the gardens in the 17th century.

DOWNSIDE ABBEY [B5] French monks fleeing the Revolution founded a Benedictine abbey here in 1814.

The vast **abbey church** was built in 1880–1925 with soaring Gothic arches in the nave.

EAST COKER [A1] William Dampier, a pirate turned explorer, was born here in 1652. His rescue of the marooned Alexander Selkirk in 1709 inspired Daniel Defoe's *Robinson Crusoe*. The ashes of the poet T.S. Eliot are buried in the local **church**.

FROME [C5] In the old market town, medieval **Cheap Street** still has a water channel running down its centre. The bridge over the River Frome has an 18th-century **lockup**.

GREAT WISHFORD [F3] On May 29, Oak Apple Day, the people of the village gather firewood from nearby Grovely Wood and deck the church and houses with branches of oak.

HAMBLEDON HILL [D1] There are good views of the Stour valley from the hill's summit, crowned by an Iron Age **hill-fort**. To the south-east is a causewayed **camp** where Stone Age

farmers herded livestock some 4500 years ago. The neighbouring Hod Hill's **hill-fort** was taken over by a Roman legion in AD 43.

HORNINGSHAM [D4] The 1566 **Meeting House** in this village of thatched cottages may be the oldest Nonconformist church in England.

LONGLEAT HOUSE [D4] Longleat was the first stately home to be opened to the public, and its well-known safari park, where lions roam free, was established in 1966. The Elizabethan mansion was designed by Robert Smythson and 'Capability' Brown landscaped the park.

LYTES CARY MANOR [A3] For 500 years this medieval house ✿ was the home of the Lyte family and their horse and swan emblems appear in the plasterwork in the 15th-century great hall, with its minstrels' gallery.

NADDER VALLEY [F3] Cattle graze in the rich farmlands of the valley, which has many attractive villages such as Tisbury – with its thatched **tithe barn**.

NEWTON TONY [H4] Celia Fiennes, one of Britain's earliest travel writers, lived at the **manor house** here.

SALISBURY [G3] A 123m (404ft) high spire crowns Salisbury's splendid Early English **cathedral**. A clock dating from 1386 in the nave is said to be the world's oldest working clock. In the Close are the medieval **Bishop's Palace** and fine houses including **Mompesson House** ✿ and **King's House**. The city has a large market and old timbered buildings, such as the 16th-century **Joiners' Hall**.

SHAFTESBURY [D2] See picture (above).

SHEPTON MALLET [B4] Weavers' cottages and mill owners' houses recall the town's past as a wool centre. There is a fine **cross** in the marketplace and a restored 1450 **Shambles**, or meat market. At nearby Cranmore, steam trains run along a track known as the **Strawberry Line**.

SHERBORNE [B2] The town is dominated by its fan-vaulted 15th-century **abbey**, whose golden stone blends with the monastic buildings of **Sherborne School**. The 12th-century **castle** ✚ is in ruins. In 1594, a **new castle** was built for Sir Walter Raleigh.

STONEHENGE [G4] See picture (below).

STOURHEAD [C3] The Palladian **mansion** ✿ has gardens with rare trees and lovely foliage colours.

STURMINSTER NEWTON [C1] The bustling town has a working 17th-century **water mill**. An old sign on the 15th-century **bridge** threatens vandals with 'transportation for life'. Nearby **Fiddleford Manor** ✚ has a 14th-century hall and living room.

WELLS [A5] England's smallest city is famed for its fine three-towered **cathedral**. The moat round the **Bishop's Palace** is fed from the springs that gave Wells its name. **Vicars' Close**, built in 1348, is the oldest complete medieval street in Europe.

WILTON [F3] Fine quality carpets have been woven at the Royal Wilton Factory for 300 years. **Wilton House**, built in the 1540s, has a 'Double Cube' room designed by Inigo Jones. In the 1940s, the D-Day invasion was planned here.

WYLYE VALLEY [E/F4] Izaak Walton, the author of *The Compleat Angler*, loved to fish in this scenic river valley and John Constable painted here.

YEOVIL [A2] Aircraft have replaced gloves and sailcloth as the main industry here. The Perpendicular 14th-century **St John's Church** has fine architecture.

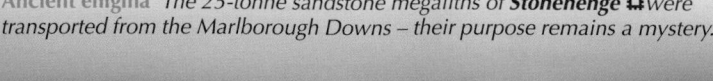

Ancient enigma *The 25-tonne sandstone megaliths of* **Stonehenge** ✚ *were transported from the Marlborough Downs – their purpose remains a mystery.*

Winchester and the North Downs

TOURIST INFORMATION

Aldershot (01252) 320968
Alton (01420) 88448
Andover (01264) 324320
Basingstoke (01256) 817618
Farnham (01252) 715109
Guildford (01483) 444333
Midhurst (01730) 817322
Petersfield (01730) 268829
Petworth (01798) 343523
Romsey (01794) 512987
Winchester (01962) 840500

THE GOOD PUB GUIDE

Arford [F4] *Crown*
(01428) 712150
Beauworth [D3] *Milburys*
(01962) 771248
Charleshill [G4] *Donkey*
(01252) 702124
Chilgrove [F1] *White Horse*
(01243) 535219
Crawley [B3] *Fox & Hounds*
(01962) 776006
Droxford [D2] *White Horse*
(01489) 877490
Elsted [F2] *Three Horseshoes*
(01730) 825746
Longstock [B4] *Peat Spade*
(01264) 810612
Owslebury [C2] *Ship*
(01962) 777358
Sparsholt [B3] *Plough*
(01962) 776353
Tillington [H2] *Horse Guards*
(01798) 342332
Trotton [F2] *Keepers Arms*
(01730) 813724

ANDOVER [B5] A **market** is still held on Thursdays and Saturdays in this ancient town beside the Anton river. It has a 19th century grand **guildhall**, and the **Museum of the Iron Age** contains finds from Danebury Ring hill-fort. Whitchurch, to the east, has a working **silk mill** and uses Victorian machinery to produce fine silks.

BIGNOR ROMAN VILLA [H1] One of Britain's largest Roman villas, with 65 rooms, Bignor has outstanding 4th-century mosaics, including a 25m (82ft) design and *Venus with Gladiators,* one of Europe's finest.

BLACK DOWN [G3] In 1796, a hand-operated shutter telegraph was sited on the hill for sending Admiralty messages between London and Portsmouth. The poet Lord Tennyson loved the view and built **Aldworth House** on its eastern slope in 1868–9.

BROADLANDS [B2] 'Capability' Brown landscaped the grounds of this Palladian mansion in the 1700s. It was for a time the home of Lord Palmerston, and later the home of Lord Mountbatten – the Mountbatten Exhibition celebrates his life.

BURY [H1] John Galsworthy, Nobel prize winner and author of *The Forsyte Saga,* bought **Bury House** in 1920. On his death in 1933 his ashes were scattered in the grounds.

CHAWTON [E4] Jane Austen lived in the village from 1809 to 1817. She was born at **Steventon**, where her father was the rector. Steam locomotives run on a picturesque route between nearby Alton and Alresford on the **Watercress Line**.

COLDEN COMMON [C2] At the **Marwell Zoological Park**, over 200 rare or endangered species roam in 100 acres of grounds.

DEVIL'S PUNCH BOWL [G4] A vast hollow on **Hindhead Common** ❧, the Punchbowl is some 2 miles long, and

Grand designs In 1688–93, the Duke of Somerset rebuilt 12th-century **Petworth House** ❧*. It has many paintings by J.M.W. Turner, a frequent guest.*

is one of the biggest craters in Europe to have been eroded by springs above. It is overlooked by **Gibbet Hill**; a stone cross marks the spot where the gibbet once stood.

FARNHAM [F5] The ruined keep ⌗ of a 12th-century **castle**, until 1927 used as the palace of the bishops of Winchester, overlooks the town. Castle Street has fine Georgian houses and the gabled **Windsor Almshouses** of 1619. William Cobbett, the farmer and politician who wrote *Rural Rides*, was born in Bridge Square at what is now the *William Cobbett* pub.

GODALMING [H4] In 1881, the narrow streets of the town were the first in Britain to have electric lighting. The town was once a stagecoach stop between Portsmouth and London, and in 1698 Peter the Great, Tsar of Russia, stayed at the *King's Arms* and *Royal Hotel.* At Hambledon to the south is **Oakhurst Cottage** ❧.

GUILDFORD [H5] On Stag Hill to the north-west of the town stands the red brick **cathedral** – a 20th-century landmark. On Castle Hill, the ruined keep of the 12th-century **castle** overlooks the town from fine gardens. In the steep High Street are the Jacobean **Abbot's Hospital**, with its huge gatehouse, and the 16th-century **guildhall** with a gilded clock of the 1680s. At **Dapdune Wharf**, there is a restored Wey barge, models and interactive displays.

HASLEMERE [G3] The town's annual early music festival honours local musician Arnold Dolmetsch. His family still make early instruments, including harpsichords, lutes, viols and recorders here. A stained-glass window by Sir Edward Burne-Jones in **St Bartholomew's Church**, is in memory of Lord Tennyson, who died at nearby **Aldworth House** in 1892.

MIDHURST [G2] Knockhundred **Row** may take its name from medieval times, when the local lord could knock on 100 doors and call upon 100 men to defend his castle. The *Spread Eagle Hotel* dates from 1430, and the ruins of **Cowdray House**, where Queen Elizabeth I stayed, from 1530. The writer H.G. Wells was a pupil at the **Grammar School**.

MOTTISFONT ABBEY [A3] The converted 12th-century **Augustinian priory** ❧ is now home to the national collection of old roses.

OLD WINCHESTER HILL [D2] Crowned by the earthen ramparts of a **hill-fort** 5000 years old, the hill is now a national **nature reserve**. Its chalk downland is home to beeches, yews, juniper and rare wildflowers. The butterflies include dark green and Duke of Burgundy fritillaries, and the rare chalk-hill blue.

PETWORTH [H2] See picture, above.

ROMSEY [B2] The splendid Norman **Abbey Church** of this ancient wool and brewing town was built round the church of a nunnery in AD 907. Lord Mountbatten is buried in the south transept. Among other old buildings is the 13th-century **King John's House**.

SELBORNE [E3] The village is little changed since the days of the Rev Gilbert White, who wrote *The Natural History and Antiquities of Selborne.* Even the lime trees he planted to hide a butcher's shop still flourish. His home, **The Wakes**, is now a museum.

UPPARK HOUSE [F2] This late 17th-century house ❧ was restored after a disastrous fire in 1989. As well as beautiful furniture, ceramics, and textiles, it also houses a collection of Grand Tour paintings. The writer H.G. Wells's mother was housekeeper here.

WAGGONERS WELLS [G3] Lord Tennyson was one of the many 19th-century visitors to this beauty spot near the village of Bramshott. The three **ponds** and **waterfalls** ❧ were once part of a 17th-century hydraulic system that operated hammers for the Wealden iron industry.

WINCHESTER [C3] This old Roman city became King Alfred's capital in the 9th century. William the Conqueror made it a joint capital with London, and was crowned in the **Old Minster**. The 1079 **cathedral** is the longest Gothic cathedral in Europe, at 170m (556ft); the choir houses the remains of King Canute and William Rufus. At the **Hospital of St Cross**, founded in 1133–6, wayfarers may still ask for a 'dole' of bread and ale. Jane Austen, the novelist, died at **No. 8 College Street**. **Winchester College**, founded in 1382 for poor scholars by William of Wykeham, is nearby.

WINKWORTH ARBORETUM [H4] Dr Wilfrid Fox presented the gardens ❧, with two lakes and landscaped wooded hillsides, to the National Trust in 1952. There are more than 1000 species of rare trees and shrubs, including magnolias and maples, as well as magnificent displays of bluebells and azaleas in spring.

TOURING GUIDE

Sussex and the Weald of Kent

Fairy-tale home *Anne Boleyn spent her childhood in the double-moated* **Hever Castle**, *built in 1270. The American millionaire William Waldorf Astor restored it in 1903, adding a 14ha (35 acre) lake and a Tudor 'village'.*

TOURIST INFORMATION

Ashdown Forest Information
Centre (01342) 823583
Battle (01424) 773721
Burgess Hill (01444) 238202
Horsham (01403) 211661
Royal Tunbridge Wells
(01892) 515675
Tonbridge (01732) 770929

THE GOOD PUB GUIDE

Chiddingly [F1] *Six Bells*
(01825) 872227
Danehill [E3] *Coach & Horses*
(01825) 740369
East Chiltington [D1] *Jolly
Sportsman* (01273) 890400
Fletching [E2] *Griffin Inn*
(01825) 722890
Hartfield [E4] *Anchor Inn*
(01892) 770424
Langton Green [F4] *Hare*
(01892) 862419
Leigh [C5] *Plough*
(01306) 611348
Penshurst [F4] *Bottle House*
(01892) 870306
Tunbridge Wells [G4] *Royal
Wells Inn* (01892) 511188

ASHDOWN FOREST [E3] Once the forest was a king's hunting ground; near Crowborough is **King's Standing**, a vantage point where the monarch viewed the chase. **Wych Cross visitor centre** is at the heart of the forest's 22 sq miles of heathland.

BATTLE [H2] William the Conqueror built the **abbey ⚒**, now a ruin, on the site of the Battle of Hastings. The high altar stands at the point where Harold, the Saxon king, fell.

BODIAM CASTLE [H3] Built in 1385–9 against a French invasion that never took place, this moated fortress ❧ is a fine example of medieval military architecture.

BOX HILL [B5] Once covered with box trees, the 172m (564ft) hill ❧ is part of a country park of woods and chalk downs. Near the foot of the hill is an ancient trackway, now on the North Downs Way, which may once have linked Stonehenge to the coast.

BURWASH [G2] In the 16th–17th centuries the village was a prosperous centre of the Wealden iron industry. **Bateman's ❧** was the writer Rudyard Kipling's home; his letters, papers and 1928 Rolls-Royce can be seen.

CHARTWELL [E5] Sir Winston Churchill's country home from 1922, the house ❧ has sweeping views across the Kentish Weald. Churchill

built the kitchen garden wall himself and deep yellow roses in the garden mark the Churchills' golden wedding.

CHIDDINGSTONE [E5] The Chiding Stone that this village ❧ may take its name from was where chattering women were once scolded. The stone stands near the 17th-century **castle**, a house refurbished in the 19th century in neo-Gothic style.

DITCHLING [D1] **Wings Place** was allegedly given to Anne of Cleves, Henry VIII's fourth wife, in 1540, as part of their divorce settlement. In the 17th century, dissenters from the Church of England gathered in the **Old Meeting House**, and the weather-boarded house called **Candles** was once a candlemaker's workshop.

DORKING [B5] Once a posting station on Stane Street, the Roman route from Chichester to London, the High Street follows the line of the old road. Charles Dickens once stayed at the *White Horse*, a 15th-century inn.

EAST GRINSTEAD [D4] A terrace of half-timbered Sussex hall houses from the 15th and 16th centuries lines the High Street of this lively market town. **Sackville College** was built to provide homes for poor townspeople in 1619.

FRIDAY STREET [B5] In the 17th century, this red-brick hamlet with a pine-shaded lake was a centre of the Wealden iron industry. The local inn is named after Archbishop Stephen Langton, who was born here in 1150.

HEVER CASTLE [E4] See picture.

HORSHAM [B3] The **Carfax**, an area ringed by 19th-century buildings, is one of the most attractive parts of this town. Also notable is the **Causeway**, with the 13th-century **church**, the gabled **town hall** and a **museum**.

IGHTHAM MOTE [F5] The manor house ❧ of half-timbering and mellow brick probably takes its name from 'moot', a Saxon meeting place, rather than its surrounding moat.

LEITH HILL [B4] The highest point in Surrey, at 294m (965ft), the hill is crowned by a tower folly ❧. On a clear day you can see north to St Paul's Cathedral in London and south as far as the English Channel.

PENSHURST PLACE [F4] Sir Philip Sidney, the Elizabethan poet and courtier, was born in 1558 at this stately home, with a Baron's Hall – its roof is 18m (60ft) high. His portrait is in the state dining room.

POLESDEN LACEY [B5] Built on the gentle slopes of the Surrey Downs in the 1820s, the gold stone house ❧ was remodelled in the 1900s. Its furnishings, walled rose gardens and elegant terraces recall Edwardian times. Entertainments are staged in the open-air theatre.

ROYAL TUNBRIDGE WELLS [F4] In 1606 a chalybeate, or iron salts, spring was discovered, and the town became popular as a spa – especially after the dandy Richard 'Beau' Nash came to visit in 1735. **Nash House** in Mount Sion was his gaming house. It was made a royal borough in 1909.

SHERE [A5] A sunny day by the Tilling Bourne brings crowds to this attractive village below the North Downs and its ancient *White Horse* inn. The 12th-century church has the remains of an anchorite cell of 1329.

TONBRIDGE [F5] At the heart of the town is a ruined Norman **castle** with a huge 13th-century gatehouse. The novelist E.M. Forster went to Tonbridge School. The **Hop Farm Country Park**, to the east, is a working museum of hop growing, set in oast-houses.

WILDERNESS WOOD [F2] At this scenic wood near Hadlow Down in the High Weald, age-old forestry skills are demonstrated and there is an exhibition of trees and wood.

YALDING [H5] The Medway, Teise and Beult rivers meet at the village. At **Yalding Organic Gardens**, a tour through gardening history has been created in 14 separate areas.

Romney Marsh and the White Cliffs of Dover

ASHFORD [C4] When steam engines were built here in the 19th century, the ancient market town, which still retains some Georgian houses, became an industrial centre.

BARFRESTONE [F5] The 11th-century church is one of Britain's most richly decorated Norman churches. It has superb stone carvings, especially round the south door.

BIDDENDEN [B4] Siamese twins, born here in about 1135, and known as The Biddenden Maids, can be seen on the village sign. Many of the 15th–17th century half-timbered buildings once had wool weavers in their large-windowed attics.

CRABBLE CORN MILL [F4] This Georgian water mill once ground grain into flour for the garrison at Dover Castle. It is still operating.

DEAL [G5] A **castle** laid out in the shape of a Tudor rose, built in case of an invasion by French and Spanish forces, dominates the quiet fishing port's seafront. The ball of the 1854 **Time Ball Tower**, which gave time signals to ships, can still be seen.

DOVER [F4] For more than 800 years, the great **castle** on the White Cliffs has watched over the English Channel. The castle is one of Britain's biggest and most complete, and has a network of tunnels in the cliffs. The tunnels provided a safe operations centre for the Dunkirk evacuation and the Battle of Britain. A Roman lighthouse stands on cliffs nearby and the **Roman Painted House** (New Street) has stunning frescoes.

DUNGENESS [D2] This vast, misty shingle headland, the scene of many shipwrecks, had a lighthouse in 1615. Near today's lighthouse, an old one of 1904 gives all-round views. There is a visitor centre for the two nuclear power stations, and an **RSPB** reserve.

DYMCHURCH [D3] At high tide this seaside resort on Romney Marsh is some 2m (7ft) below sea level, and is protected by a huge sea wall. Visitors can see the Court Room of the 'Lords of the Level', who maintained the drainage systems of the Marsh from 1252. A Martello tower with walls 4m (13ft) thick is now a museum.

FOLKESTONE [E4] The beach, reached by lift, lies below the 60m (200ft) cliffs topped by **The Leas** gardens. **East Cliff Sands**, the main bathing beach, is east of the harbour.

FOLKESTONE WARREN [E4] Grassy chalk terraces and woods along the cliffs of **East Wear Bay** are now a country park. There are superb sea views from **Abbot's Cliff**. (Red flags fly when the army rifle range is in use.)

GODMERSHAM [D5] Jane Austen often visited the Georgian house of **Godmersham Park**, the home of her brother, Edward Knight. She modelled the mansion in her book *Mansfield Park* (1814) on it.

HASTINGS [A1] On West Hill, the ruins of a Norman castle overlook Hastings Old Town. The 1066 Story at the **castle** tells of the town's historic past. The harbour **Fishmarket** and the net sheds by the **Fishermen's Museum** contrast with the modern pier and the wide promenade that runs west to St Leonards and its Regency buildings.

HAWKINGE [E4] An RAF fighter station in 1940, the airfield is now the **Kent Battle of Britain Museum**, with Britain's biggest collection of British and German 1940s flying equipment.

HYTHE [E3] The town is separated from the old Cinque Port by the tree-lined **Royal Military Canal** of 1804–9. The knights who killed Archbishop Thomas Becket met at **Saltwood Castle** on the night before the murder.

LANGDON CLIFFS [F4] See picture.

LYDD [C2] The 40m (132ft) tower of the 14th-century church of All Saints, 'the Cathedral of Romney Marsh', dwarfs the town's buildings. At nearby **Lydd-on-Sea**, the Romney, Hythe and Dymchurch railway separates a row of seaside houses from the beach.

NEW ROMNEY [D3] Violent storms in the 13th century diverted the course of the River Rother, cutting this Cinque Port off from the sea. The station has a **Toy and Model Museum**.

ROLVENDEN [A3] The garden at **Great Maytham Hall** is said to have inspired Frances Hodgson Burnett's book *The Secret Garden* (1907).

ROMNEY MARSH [D3] Hardy, hornless Romney sheep graze in fields edged by reed-lined dykes. Notable Marsh village churches include **Brookland** with its conical belfry and **Ivychurch** with a beacon turret.

ROYAL MILITARY CANAL [B2–C3] Built in 1804–9, the canal runs for 23 miles and was intended as a second line of defence against Napoleon if troops posted in Martello towers failed to stop invaders.

RYE [B2] A hilltop church looks across the town's timbered houses, cobbled streets and a medieval gate. The *Mermaid Inn* was a smugglers' haunt, and the American writer Henry James lived at **Lamb House**.

Dazzling landmark The view from Langdon Cliffs extends to France on a clear day. South Foreland Lighthouse, the first to have a permanent electric light, was used by Guglielmo Marconi in a radio trial in 1898.

TOURIST INFORMATION

Ashford (01233) 629165
Deal (01304) 369576
Dover (01304) 205108
Folkestone (01303) 258594
Hastings (01424) 781111
Hythe (01303) 267799
New Romney (01797) 364044
Rye (01797) 226696
Tenterden (01580) 763572

THE GOOD PUB GUIDE

Brookland [C3] *Woolpack*
(01797) 344321
Deal [G5] *Kings Head*
(01304) 368194
Hawkhurst [A3] *Queens*
(01580) 753577
Icklesham [B2] *Queens Head*
(01424) 814552
Pett [B1] *Two Sawyers*
(01424) 812255
Pluckley [B5] *Dering Arms*
(01233) 840371
Rye [B2] *Mermaid Inn*
(01797) 223065
Sandgate [E4] *Clarendon*
(01303) 248684

SISSINGHURST GARDEN [A4] The writer Vita Sackville-West and her husband, the diplomat Sir Harold Nicolson, created a series of small gardens here in the 1930s. Only the turreted gate tower and a few restored parts remain of **Sissinghurst Castle**, an Elizabethan mansion demolished 200 years ago.

STONE IN OXNEY [B3] In this marshland village, the restored 15th-century **church** has two unusual relics: a Roman altar stone to Mithras, the god of light, and dinosaur bones dug up in a local quarry in 1935.

TENTERDEN [B3] The town was a port until the 17th century, when the channel from the River Rother silted up. **Smallhythe Place** is a 16th-century, half-timbered house; it was the home of actress Ellen Terry and is now a theatrical museum.

WALMER [G5] William Pitt the Younger, used the Tudor-rose shaped, 16th-century **castle** as his official residence in 1792–1806. The gardens were laid out by Pitt's eccentric niece.

WINCHELSEA [B2] Set amid marshland, the hilltop town is part of an old walled town built in 1283 by Edward I after the sea had engulfed an earlier settlement. The streets are laid out in a gridiron pattern.

WYE AND CRUNDALE DOWNS [D5] One of the best stretches of chalk grassland and woods in the North Downs forms a national nature reserve. There are panoramic views.

TOURING GUIDE

Swansea and the Gower Peninsula

CULVER HOLE [C4] A narrow cleft in the cliffs near Port-Eynon Point was sealed off long ago by an 18m (60ft) wall of unknown origin which is pierced with window-like openings, resembling a dovecot. At low tide it can be reached from Port-Eynon.

LLANTWIT MAJOR [H2] Britain's first school was founded here by St Illtyd some 1500 years ago. The patron saint of Wales, St David, is said to have been a pupil. There are views of the Bristol Channel from the nearby **Seawatch Centre**, housed in a former coastguard station. To the west is **St Donat's Castle,** now a school. Nearby are **Tressilian Bay**, with smugglers' caves, and **Nash Point**, from where there are fine views.

MARGAM COUNTRY PARK [G4] An 1840s **mansion** set in extensive grounds on the site of a ruined 12th-century abbey, Margam has a magnificent orangery, now housing exhibitions. Attractions include a vast maze, gardens, woods and parkland. **Margam Sands** beach is nearby.

MERTHYR MAWR [G3] Thatched stone dwellings surround the green, and there is a medieval **Dipping Bridge** over the Ogmore – it has large holes in the parapet through which unwilling sheep were pushed into the river to be washed. The ruins of **Candleston** and **Ogmore castles** are close by, and upriver are the remains of the fortified **Ewenny Priory**. The warren or burrows, an area of grassy dunes, stretches west along the Ogmore estuary.

THE MUMBLES [E4] Until the 1950s, a train ride round the bay to **Mumbles Head** was a day out for Swansea folk. Now part of the old rail line is a promenade to the pier at The Mumbles resort, the gateway to the Gower peninsula.

NEATH [F5] Sited at the gateway to the Vale of Neath, the industrial town became a centre of copper smelting in 1584. By the 18th century furnaces were even set up in the 12th-century abbey ruins. The Welsh Rugby Union first met at the **Castle Hotel** in 1881.

OYSTERMOUTH [E4] In **All Saints'** churchyard is the grave of Dr Thomas Bowdler; his expurgated editions of Shakespearean plays gave rise to the word 'bowdlerise'. A window in the **church** depicts one of the earliest railways – a horse-drawn tram of 1800 on the line to The Mumbles. The ruins of **Oystermouth Castle** overlook the bay.

PORTHCAWL [G3] The former coal port is now one of South Wales's largest seaside resorts, with three sandy bays, a vast pleasure park and a fine golf course. **Kenfig Pool** and **Dunes Nature Reserve**, to the north-west, lie above a town buried by sand in medieval times.

PORT TALBOT [F4] Aberavon was the town's name until 1836, when it was renamed after the Talbot family, local landowners. There is good surfing on Aberavon beach, and **Afon Lido** is one of Wales's largest leisure centres. Port Talbot also has the biggest tidal harbour in Britain, and one of the largest steelworks in Europe. The actor Richard Burton was born at nearby Pontrhydyfen, which is on the way to the scenic **Afan Argoed Country Park**, where there is a **Welsh Miners' Museum**.

SWANSEA [E5] See City Routes pp298–299.

TOURIST INFORMATION

Bridgend (01656) 654906
Llandeilo (01558) 824226
Mumbles (01792) 361302
Porthcawl (01656) 786639
Sarn (01656) 654906
Swansea (01792) 468321

THE GOOD PUB GUIDE

Monknash [H3] *Plough & Harrow* (01656) 890209
Reynoldston [C5] *King Arthur Hotel* (01792) 390775

TREORCHY [H5] The former mining village is famous for its male voice choir. Visitors can attend their twice-weekly rehearsals. Miners' choirs still flourish in Wales, despite the closure of the mines.

WHITEFORD BURROWS [C5] An area of sand dunes is an extensive nature reserve with golden plovers, redshanks and oystercatchers.

WORMS HEAD [B4] Reached by a promontory battered by waves, the headland has a nature reserve and a cliff arch where the sea spouts through a blowhole. Further up the coast is Burry Holmes, an islet with a ruined **chapel** and Iron Age **fort**, accessible by foot at low tide. Inland is 13th-century **Weobley Castle**.

Remote splendour *The rugged headland around Rhossili Bay on the Gower peninsula is inhabited by wild ponies and seabirds. Seals bask on the rocks in secluded coves.*

Bristol, Cardiff and the Severn estuary

Atmospheric ruins Founded in 1131 by Walter de la Clare, a lord of Chepstow, Tintern Abbey's ruined arches attracted many 18th-century artists and have been immortalised in a poem by William Wordsworth .

TOURIST INFORMATION

Barry (01446) 747171
Bristol (0906) 711 2191
Caerleon (01633) 422656
Caerphilly (029) 2088 0011
Cardiff (029) 2022 7281
Cheddar (01934) 744071
Chepstow (01291) 623772
Newport (01633) 842962
Weston-super-Mare
 (01934) 888800

THE GOOD PUB GUIDE

Almondsbury [H4] *Bowl*
 (01454) 612757
Blagdon [G1] *New Inn*
 (01761) 462475
Chepstow [G5] *Boat Inn*
 (01291) 628192
Creigiau [B4] *Caesar's Arms*
 (029) 2089 0486
East Aberthaw [B2]
 Blue Anchor (01446) 750329
Littleton-upon-Severn [G4]
 White Hart (01454) 412275
St Hilary [B3] *Bush*
 (01446) 772745
Stanton Wick [H2] *Carpenters
 Arms* (01761) 490202

AVON GORGE [G3] Ancient Leigh Woods crown a nature reserve on the west bank of the Avon, near **Clifton Suspension Bridge**

AXBRIDGE [F1] The ancient market town shelters below the Mendip Hills. **King John's hunting lodge**, a half-timbered building in the High Street, dates from the 16th century. Now a local **museum**, it contains a bull anchor, once used in bull-baiting, and the old stocks.

BANWELL [E1] The village's 14th-century **church** is one of the finest in the area, and has some outstanding 15th-century Flemish stained glass, installed in 1855. Nearby **Banwell Caves** were discovered in 1824; the finds, which included the ancient skull of a great cave lion, are now displayed in Taunton Museum. The caves are closed to the public to protect the fossilised remains.

BARRY AND PENARTH [C2/3] Sandy beaches and pleasure parks offer traditional seaside holidays at **Barry Island**, actually a peninsula. Nearby, Penarth's Victorian **esplanade** and 100-year-old **pier** give it a 19th-century atmosphere. Beside the old coal docks is a busy **waterfront**, and there are wide views across the Bristol Channel from the cliffs at Penarth

Head. At **Cosmeston Lakes Country Park** to the south is a reconstructed medieval village, open to visitors.

BERKELEY [H5] Edward Jenner, who discovered the means of vaccination against smallpox, was born here in 1749. **Berkeley Castle** was in 1327 the scene of the brutal murder of King Edward II – the dungeon where he was imprisoned can still be seen.

BRISTOL [G3] See City Routes pp272–273.

CAERPHILLY [C4] One of Britain's largest and finest medieval **castles** covers 12ha (30 acres) of the town, its moats and battlements are largely intact with a ruined tower leaning at a greater angle than the Tower of Pisa. Gilbert the Red built it in 1268–71. The town is famous for Caerphilly cheese, now mostly made over the border in Somerset.

CARDIFF [C3] See City Routes pp274–275.

CASTELL COCH [C4] The rounded towers and conical spires of **Red Castle** rise above a wooded gorge. It was built in the late 19th century by the 3rd Marquess of Bute. The interior is covered with paintings based on the Bible and classical mythology.

CHEDDAR GORGE [F1] A narrow cleft in the Mendips is flanked by cliffs around 213m (700ft) high. Of the many caves with stalactites and stalagmites, **Gough's Cave** is the most spectacular. **Black Rock Nature Reserve**, part of Mendip Forest, is farther along the gorge.

CHEPSTOW [G5] The port grew round the 11th-century **castle** on a spur above the Wye, near its confluence with the Severn. Old warehouses by the quay date back to Chepstow's heyday in the 18th and 19th centuries. Spanning the scenic Wye gorge upriver are John Rennie's graceful cast-iron **road bridge** of 1816, and Isambard Kingdom Brunel's 1852 **rail bridge**.

CLEVEDON COURT [F3] The home of the Elton family since 1709, the 14th-century house has a hall dating from 1300 and collections of Eltonware pottery and Nailsea glass – in the style of the nearby Nailsea works during 1788–1883. The sedate resort of Clevedon has a recently restored Victorian **pier**.

COWBRIDGE [A3] An occasional livestock market is held in this market town sited in the Vale of Glamorgan. Nearby are 16th-century **Beaupre (or 'Bewper') Castle**, and **Llanerch Vineyard**, the largest in Wales.

CWMCARN FOREST DRIVE [D5] Scattered along some 20 miles beside the Ebbw river, the forest is a 1920s re-creation of the ancient Forest of Machen, which was destroyed by sheep grazing and industrial needs such as pit props. From Cwmcarn, a scenic drive climbs for some 7 miles through tree-clad hills. At 419m (1374ft), the **hill-fort** of Twmbarlwm has fine views.

LLANTRISANT [B4] In the **parish church** there is a 7th-century stone depicting the Resurrection. Since the 1970s, the town has been the home of the Royal Mint. There is a statue of Dr William Price, who campaigned in the 19th century to legalise the cremation of dead bodies.

NEWPORT [E4] See City Routes pp274–275.

PONTYPRIDD [B4] The single-arched stone **bridge**, now disused, across the Taff was built in 1756. Its span of 43m (140ft) was the longest in Britain until the building of London Bridge in 1831. In **Ynysangharad Park**

is a memorial to Evan James and his son James, who wrote 'Land of My Fathers', the Welsh National Anthem since 1856.

RHOOSE [B2] There are superb views across the Bristol Channel to Somerset from the nearby clifftops. **Porthkerry Country Park**, which has a 19th-century 18 arch **viaduct** amid woodland scenery, is close by.

ST FAGANS CASTLE [C3] The **Museum of Welsh Life** is housed in this E-shaped 16th-century mansion and grounds. The magnificent range of re-erected rural buildings include an 18th-century chapel, a circular thatched cockfighting pit and a beehive pigsty of 1800. Indoor galleries have displays on costume, agriculture and social life.

THORNBURY [H4] The cricketer Dr W.G. Grace spent his boyhood in the town. The **church** is mainly Perpendicular and dates from the early 16th century. There are tours of **Oldbury nuclear power station** which has hands-on displays.

TINTERN ABBEY [G5] See picture.

WESTON-SUPER-MARE [E2] Wide sands, a long promenade and two piers make this resort popular. A museum holds a collection of over 50 helicopters and autogyros and the Seaquarium has over 30 displays ranging from starfish to sharks. A ferry ride across the Axe leads to a viewpoint at **Brean Down**, a bird sanctuary. North of the town there are walks in **Weston Woods**.

FROM MAP ON PAGES 96–97

The Wiltshire Downs and the Vale of Pewsey

Dutch elegance *Set in an ancient deer park, Dyrham Park* ❧ *was built in the Dutch baroque style in 1692 for William Blathwayt, William III's Secretary of War.*

TOURIST INFORMATION

Avebury (01672) 539425
Bath (0906) 711 2000
Bradford-on-Avon
  (01225) 865797
Chippenham (01249) 706333
Devizes (01380) 729408
Malmsbury (01666) 823748
Marlborough (01672) 513989
Melksham (01225) 707424
Swindon (01793) 530328
Tetbury (01666) 503552
Trowbridge (01225) 777054
Westbury (01373) 827158

THE GOOD PUB GUIDE

Axford [G2] *Red Lion*
  (01672) 520271
Brinkworth [E4] *Three Crowns*
  (01666) 510366
Combe Hay [B1] *Wheatsheaf*
  (01225) 833504
Ford [C3] *White Hart*
  (01249) 782213
Lacock [D2] *George Inn*
  (01249) 730263
Norton St Philip [B1] *George*
  (01373) 834224
Seend [D2] *Barge Inn*
  (01380) 828230
Sherston [C4] *Rattlebone Inn*
  (01666) 840871
Whitley [C2] *Pear Tree Inn*
  (01225) 709131
Woodborough [E1] *Seven Stars*
  (01672) 851325
Wootton Rivers [F2] *Royal Oak*
  (01672) 810322

ASHDOWN HOUSE [G4] The white four-storey house ❧ has a grand oak staircase and a cupola topped by a golden ball. It was built by Lord Craven for Elizabeth of Bohemia, James I's daughter, but she died of the plague before the house was finished.

AVEBURY [F2] A large prehistoric **stone circle** ⌗ dominates the village. Other prehistoric monuments nearby are **Windmill Hill**, **Silbury Hill** and **The Sanctuary**, linked to Avebury by stone-lined West Kennet Avenue.

BATH [B2] See City Routes pp272–273.

BOWOOD HOUSE [D2] The fine park surrounding this 18th-century house is landscaped by 'Capability' Brown. Next to the **art gallery** is the **laboratory** where in 1774 Dr Joseph Priestley identified oxygen gas.

BRADFORD-ON-AVON [C2] Once a busy wool centre, the town's fine buildings include weavers' cottages and merchants' houses. A tiny **chapel** on the nine-arched bridge became a lock-up in the 17th century. There is a 14th-century **tithe barn** nearby.

CASTLE COMBE [C3] Lying in a shaded valley are weavers' cottages with lattice windows and a three-arched bridge over the Bybrook river.

CHIPPENHAM [D3] A busy farmers' market is held every second Tuesday in this town of Cotswold-stone houses. The town hall is from the 15th century.

CLAVERTON MANOR [B2] In 1897, 23-year-old Winston Churchill made his first political speech at a fête here. Since 1961 the neoclassical house has housed the **American Museum**, showing 17th–19th century domestic life, including native art.

CROFTON BEAM ENGINES [G2] Two steam-driven beam engines of 1812 and 1845, the oldest still in working order, were built to pump water to the upper level of the Kennet and Avon Canal.

DEVIZES [E2] Wiltshire's central market town has fine Georgian houses and two Norman **churches**. *The Bear Hotel*, a coaching inn of 1599, was the boyhood home of the painter Sir Thomas Lawrence. At **Caen Hill Locks**, the Kennet and Avon canal drops 72m (237ft) in 29 locks.

DYRHAM PARK [B3] See picture.

GREAT COXWELL BARN [G5] Built by Cistercian monks in the 13th century, the 46m (152ft) long barn ❧ has a massive stone-tile roof. Artist and designer William Morris lived at nearby **Kelmscott Manor**.

INKPEN HILL AND WALBURY HILL [H2] These twin summits linked by a ridge walk are England's highest chalk hills and offer fine views. Walbury has an Iron Age **hill-fort**.

LACOCK ABBEY [D2] The 1232 **abbey** ❧ is the home of the Talbot family, of whom William Henry Fox Talbot was the pioneer of photography. In Lacock village ❧ there are many attractive buildings.

MALMESBURY [D4] In the centre of the ancient town is an octagonal 15th-century **market cross**. The **parish church** is all that remains of a huge 7th-century abbey. Its Norman porch has fine sculpture, and a stained-glass window depicts the exploits of a monk, Elmer, who launched himself from the top of the tower in an attempt to fly. He broke both legs.

MARLBOROUGH [F2] The colonnaded High Street is one of the widest in England. On the site of the Norman castle is **Marlborough College**, a public school. Among its pupils were William Morris and Sir John Betjeman. In the grounds, **Castle Mound** is said to be Merlin's tomb.

SAVERNAKE FOREST [G2] A royal hunting ground since Saxon times, the forest has been privately owned since 1540. In the 18th century it was replanted with oaks and beeches, when 'Capability' Brown planned the Grand Avenue of beeches.

SWINDON [F4] Set in the former Great Western Railway buildings in Swindon, the **Steam Museum** tells the history of this railway line.

TETBURY [C5] The 17th-century **town hall** of this small Cotswold market town is built above rows of pillars. Neo-Gothic **St Mary's Church** of 1777–81 has a passage round most of the building. At **Westonbirt Aboretum** to the south, there are walks in woods which include giant maples dating from 1810.

TROWBRIDGE [C1] Wiltshire's old county town, a medieval weaving centre, still makes suit cloth. Sir Isaac Pitman, who invented the best-known shorthand system, was born here in 1813. To the east, **Ilford Manor** has a romantic Italianate garden, created by the architect and landscape gardener Harold Peto in 1898.

WESTBURY WHITE HORSE [D1] Cut in the chalk of Bratton Down on Salisbury Plain in 1778, the White Horse ⌗ is said to have replaced an earlier one marking Alfred's defeat of the Danes at Ethandun in AD 878.

The Berkshire Downs and the Thames Valley

ABINGDON [C5] The town grew up round a Benedictine **abbey** whose remains include a 15th-century gatehouse. In the market place is the open-colonnaded **County Hall**.

ASCOT [G2] The Berkshire town is famous for its **racecourse**, founded by Queen Anne in 1711. The Royal Ascot meeting is in June, the main race being the Ascot Gold Cup.

ASTON ROWANT [E5] There are superb views across the Vale of Aylesbury from Beacon Hill in the Chilterns nature reserve.

BURNHAM BEECHES [G4] Stately beech woods, with some trees gnarled and centuries old, grow here.

CHALFONT ST GILES [G5] The poet John Milton lived here in 1665, where he completed *Paradise Lost* and wrote *Paradise Regained*. Personal relics of the poet are on view in his **cottage**.

CLIVEDEN [G4] A grandiose Italianate 19th-century mansion 🏛, it was built by Sir Charles Barry and once belonged to the Astor family.

COOKHAM [F4] Artist Sir Stanley Spencer was born and lived in this village. There is a **Stanley Spencer Gallery**, and his *Last Supper* is in the **church**. The Keeper of the Royal Swans is based near Cookham Bridge.

DONNINGTON CASTLE [B2] Royalist forces held out against a Parliamentarian force for 20 months in 1644–6. Only the gatehouse ⌗ survived, but a star-shaped Royalist earthwork can still be traced.

DORCHESTER [C5] Brick and timber-framed houses adorn the village. A Roman military centre,

Dorchester was the cathedral city of the Saxon kingdom of Wessex. In the 12th-century **abbey** is a fine window showing Christ's descent from Jesse.

ETON [G3] **Eton College**, a public school, was founded by Henry VI in 1440. The boys wear wing collars and tailcoats, and old Etonians include 20 British prime ministers.

EWELME [D5] In the 15th-century village **church** is the superb alabaster tomb of Alice, Duchess of Suffolk, who was the granddaughter of poet Geoffrey Chaucer. The author Jerome K. Jerome is buried in the churchyard.

GREYS COURT [E4] Until 1914, the water for this gabled house 🏛 was raised from a well by a donkey treading a vertical wheel. In the 16th century, the house was rebuilt within a 14th-century fortified manor.

HAMPSTEAD NORREYS [C3] Exotic plants and animals, including a collection of orchids, are found in 20,000 sq ft (1840m²) of rainforest.

HENLEY-ON-THAMES [E4] An elegant riverside town, it is famed for its annual regattas. The 18th-century five-arched **bridge** spans the Thames.

MAIDENHEAD [F4] North of the town, the Thames is spanned near Boulter's Lock by an 18th-century **road bridge** and Isambard Kingdom Brunel's 1838 **rail bridge**.

MAPLEDURHAM HOUSE [D3] This Elizabethan mansion has a decorated oak staircase and a working water mill. The house was the inspiration for Soames Forsyte's home in John Galsworthy's *The Forsyte Saga*.

MARLOW [F4] The town has an elegant **suspension bridge** spanning the Thames. In 1817–18, the poet

Percy Bysshe Shelley and Mary Godwin lived at **Albion House** in West Street, where he wrote *The Revolt of Islam* and she *Frankenstein*.

NEWBURY [B2] The former cloth-making town today thrives on horse racing and high-tech industry. Two Civil War battles were fought nearby.

PANGBOURNE [D3] Hilly, wooded country around the village inspired Kenneth Grahame's *The Wind in the Willows*. He lived at **Church Cottage**. Nearby is the 1917 **Nautical College**.

READING [E3] The medieval town prospered from the wool trade. Henry I is buried in the now ruined **abbey**. The dramatist Oscar Wilde was imprisoned in the **jail** in 1895–7. The **Museum of Reading** houses a Victorian copy of the Bayeux Tapestry.

STONOR PARK [E4] An ancient interior lies behind the 18th-century facade of this red-brick house, the home of the Stonor family for 800 years. The Jesuit Edmund Campion set up a secret printing press in the attic.

STRATFIELD SAYE HOUSE [D2] Arthur Wellesley, the 1st Duke of Wellington, adapted the 17th-century mansion built by Sir William Pitt. Relics of the Iron Duke are on display, and Copenhagen, his horse, is buried in the grounds.

THE VYNE [D1] This splendid red-brick Tudor house 🏛 was built by Lord Sandys, who served Henry VIII. Its classical portico was the first to be added to an English country mansion.

WALLINGFORD [D4] The ancient town has a handsome 17-arched **bridge**. The Norman **castle**, now ruined, was a Royalist stronghold in the Civil War. Agatha Christie is buried in nearby **Cholsey churchyard**.

WANTAGE [B4] Alfred the Great was born in the town and his **statue** stands in the market place. Cobbles in an alley off Newmarket Street are in fact the knucklebones of sheep.

WEST WYCOMBE [F5] **West Wycombe Park** 🏛 was built by Sir Francis Dashwood, founder of the

dissolute Hellfire Club in the mid 18th century. Nearby is his **mausoleum**, a **church** topped by a golden ball and the **Hellfire Caves**, in which orgies were held.

WINDSOR [G3] The 900-year-old **castle** is the Queen's official residence. The State Apartments, Queen Mary's Dolls' House and the medieval St George's Chapel, with Gothic architecture, can be visited.

TOURIST INFORMATION

Abingdon (01235) 522711
Aldershot (01252) 320968
Basingstoke (01256) 817618
Bracknell (01344) 868196
Dorchester (01305) 267992
Fleet (01252) 811151
Henley-on-Thames
 (01491) 578034
High Wycombe
 (01494) 421892
Maidenhead (01628) 796502
Marlow (01628) 483597
Newbury (01635) 30267
Reading (0118) 956 6226
Wallingford (01491) 826972
Wantage (01235) 760176
Wokingham (0118) 978 3185

THE GOOD PUB GUIDE

Blewbury [C4] *Blewbury Inn*
 (01235) 850496
Bray [G3] *Crown*
 (01628) 621936
Cookham [G4] *Bel & the Dragon* (01628) 521263
Eversley [E2] *Golden Pot*
 (0118) 973 2104
Hambledon [E4] *Stag & Huntsman* (01491) 571227
Henley [E4] *White Hart Hotel*
 (01491) 649018
Highmoor [D4] *Rising Sun*
 (01491) 641455
Sonning [E3] *Bull Inn*
 (0118) 969 3901
South Stoke [D4] *Perch & Pike*
 (01491) 872415
West Ilsley [B4] *Harrow Inn*
 (01635) 281260
Winterbourne [B3]
 Winterbourne Arms
 (01635) 248200
Wooburn [G4] *Chequers*
 (01628) 529575

TOURING GUIDE

Tranquil scene *The Romans had to build a causeway to ford turbulent waters at Goring Gap in the Chilterns but today weirs and locks allow a smooth passage for boats.*

The villages and suburbs of London

BROMLEY [E2] A busy suburban centre, Bromley was once a market town. The writer H.G. Wells was born there in 1866. The old **palace** of the bishops of Rochester, now the civic centre, dates from 1775.

BROOKLANDS MUSEUM [A2] Set at the world's first concrete racetrack, the museum displays vintage racing cars and motorbikes as well as a collection of historic aircraft.

CROYDON [D2] Once the summer residence of the archbishops of Canterbury, Croydon is now a commercial centre. Old and new buildings mingle, such as the Whitgift Almshouses of 1596 and the 1962 Fairfield Halls – a venue for concerts and art exhibitions.

DARTFORD [F3] A traffic junction for 2000 years, Dartford was first a ford on the Darent. The Dartford Road Tunnel and the Queen Elizabeth II bridge – Europe's longest cable-stayed bridge when it opened in 1991 – now take traffic between Kent and Essex.

DULWICH [D3] The first English purpose-built art gallery, **Dulwich Picture Gallery**, designed by Sir John Soane, was opened in 1817. **Dulwich College** was founded in 1619 for the poor. Now it is a public school.

HAMMERSMITH [C3] Charles II, it is said, used to meet Nell Gwyn, his mistress, at the 17th-century riverside *Dove Inn*. **Fulham Palace**, nearby, was the Bishops of London's residence from AD 691 until 1973.

Chinese folly *The 50m (164ft) tall pagoda in* **Kew**'s *Royal Botanic Gardens was built in 1761 for George III's mother, Princess Augusta, who founded the garden.*

HARROW [B4] St Mary's Church spire at Harrow on the Hill is a landmark for Harrow School, founded in 1571; pupils still wear straw boaters in summer. Among old Harrovians are Sir Winston Churchill and Lord Byron and the writer Anthony Trollope.

HIGHGATE AND HAMPSTEAD [C4] Elegant 17th and 18th-century houses mark old Highgate village, once a fashionable London retreat. There are fine views from **Parliament Hill** on Hampstead Heath. **Fenton House** ❦ dates from 1693. It has an outstanding

collection of porcelain and early keyboard instruments – many of which are in working order.

KEW [B3] The houses round Kew Green were built for courtiers of George III (1760–1820). The **Royal Botanic Gardens**, established in 1759, are world renowned and now have more than 40,000 plant species.

KINGSTON UPON THAMES [B2] The medieval bridge was the first crossing above London Bridge until 1729; it was replaced in 1828. The restored **Market House** of 1838 presides over a market that was first recorded in the 13th century. In front of the guildhall is the **Coronation Stone**; seven 10th-century Saxon kings may have been crowned on it.

KNOLE HOUSE [F1] The 15th-century house, set in a deer park, was enlarged in 1603 and has changed little. The house has magnificent state apartments, intricate plasterwork ceilings and 17th-century furniture.

RICHMOND UPON THAMES [B3] London's oldest river bridge, built in 1774–7, spans the Thames here. All that is left of **Richmond Palace**, is the Gate House and Old Palace Yard.

ROMFORD [F4] A market town since 1247, Romford's chief industry was brewing. Nearby **Havering-atte-Bower** is named for its former medieval royal palace, The Bower. **Barking**, to the south, still has the gate tower of its medieval abbey.

TILBURY FORT [G3] This low, squat building ⌖ with a triple moat was built in the 1670s to guard the river. Here in 1588, at an earlier Tudor fort

on the site, Elizabeth I made her famous speech to her forces as the Spanish Armada approached.

WOODFORD [D5] On the green of this leafy suburb is a statue of its most famous MP, Sir Winston Churchill, who represented the town from 1945–1959. At nearby **Walthamstow** is the childhood home of William Morris, the artist and designer.

THE GOOD PUB GUIDE

Cobham [B2] *Cricketers* (01932) 862105
Horndon on the Hill [G4] *Bell Inn* (01375) 642463
Ightham [F1] *George & Dragon* (01732) 882440
Ightham Common [F1] *Harrow* (01732) 885912
Laleham [A2] *Anglers Retreat* (01784) 440990
Richmond [B3] *White Cross* (020) 8940 6844

Protected view *The outlook from* **Richmond Hill**, *with its sweeping vista down to the meadows which border the Thames, is preserved by an Act of Parliament passed in 1902.*

The Thames estuary, east Essex, the Medway towns

Leeds Castle *The medieval castle stands on two islands in the middle of a lake. Built around 1119, it was bought by Edward I in 1278 for his queen, Eleanor of Castile.*

TOURIST INFORMATION

Broadstairs (01843) 865650
Canterbury (01227) 378100
Faversham (01795) 534542
Herne Bay (01227) 361911
Maidstone (01622) 602169
Margate (01843) 583334
Ramsgate (01843) 583333
Rochester (01634) 843666
Sandwich (01304) 613565
Southend-on-Sea
    (01702) 215120
Whitstable (01227) 275482

THE GOOD PUB GUIDE

Boyden Gate [F2] *Gate Inn*
(01227) 860498
Burnham-on-Crouch [C5]
White Harte (01621) 782106
Dargate [D2] *Dove*
(01227) 751360
Faversham [D2] *Albion Tavern*
(01795) 591411
Hollingbourne [B1] *Dirty Habit*
(01622) 880880
Newnham [C1] *George Inn*
(01795) 890237
Oare [D2] *Shipwrights Arms*
(01795) 590088
Paglesham East End [C5] *Plough & Sail* (01702) 258242

TOURING GUIDE

AYLESFORD [A1] The Carmelite Friary founded here in 1242 was one of Europe's earliest. It was converted into a house, **The Friars**, after the Dissolution of the Monasteries. The remains of an ancient burial chamber, **Kit's Coty House ⌗**, are nearby.

BIRCHINGTON [F2] The poet and painter Dante Gabriel Rossetti is buried in All Saints' churchyard. **The Powell-Cotton Museum** of African and Asian animals is at Quex House.

BROADSTAIRS [G2] A seaside resort that was popular in the 19th century, Broadstairs – its seafront a series of small bays – still has quite a Victorian air. Viking Bay is sheltered by a pier that dates from the 16th century. At the battlemented **Bleak House**, overlooking the harbour, Charles Dickens wrote *David Copperfield*.

CANEWDON [B5] The name means 'Canute's town'. In the 11th century, the Danish leader Canute is said to have had his headquarters on **Beacon Hill** before defeating Edmund Ironside at the Battle of Ashingdon in 1016.

CANTERBURY [E1] The ruins of the **abbey** founded by St Augustine in AD 598 lie outside the medieval walls that still partly enclose the city. The **cathedral** was begun in 1070, and pilgrims have flocked there since Archbishop Thomas Becket was murdered on the altar steps in 1170. The Miracle Windows depict his life.

CANVEY ISLAND [B4] Much of the island is occupied by holiday homes, and most of it is below the high-tide level. A huge concrete wall, built after floods in 1953, keeps out the sea.

CHATHAM [A2] Visitors to the Ropery in Chatham Dockyard can still see rope being made as it was in Nelson's day. From 1547 until 1984 the dockyard built ships for the Royal Navy. It is now a working museum.

ELMLEY MARSHES [C2] Mud flats, salt marshes, creeks and lagoons by the north banks of the Swale attract thousands of wetland birds. Many of them can be seen from the **RSPB centre** at Kingshill Farm.

FAVERSHAM [D2] This old town was a centre of the explosives industry until 1934. **Chart Gunpowder Mills** of 1760 are the oldest of their kind in the world. Today the town has one of the major breweries in Kent. The **Church of St Mary of Charity** is Early English and the **guildhall** is raised on a 16th-century arcade. The **Fleur de Lis Heritage Centre** recalls 1000 years of Faversham's history.

GILLINGHAM [A2] Much of Chatham Dockyard extended into this Medway town. There is a memorial to a local sailor, Will Adams, born in 1564, who landed in Japan in the early 17th century and became a samurai warrior and a diplomat. James Clavell's novel *Shogun* is based on his exploits.

HERNE BAY [E2] The Victorians turned this former fishing village into a resort in the 19th century. The high clock tower on the seafront dates from 1837. At Reculver to the east, only twin towers remain of a 12th-century Norman church ⌗ built on the site of a Saxon church of AD 669.

LEEDS CASTLE [B1] See picture.

LEIGH-ON-SEA [B4] Seaside walks, jellied eels and freshly caught cockles from Maplin Sands are the main attractions of this old fishing village.

MAIDSTONE [A1] The Medway flows through Kent's county town, which has fine medieval buildings. They include **All Saints' Church** and the country house of the archbishops of Canterbury. Nearby Sandling has the **Museum of Kent Life**.

MARGATE [G3] A local glovemaker invented the covered bathing machine here in 1753. Now Margate is a popular resort with 9 miles of sandy beach and attractions such as the **Dreamland** theme park and **Margate Caves** – once medieval dungeons. Seashells decorate the 2000-year-old **Shell Grotto**.

MINSTER [C3] This Isle of Sheppey village has one of England's oldest existing places of worship, a church founded in about AD 670.

RAMSGATE [G2] A seaside resort, cross-Channel port and yachting centre, Ramsgate has a busy harbour and sandy, south-facing beaches below chalk cliffs. **St Augustine's Church** was designed and funded by Augustus Pugin in the 1840s. He is also buried there. A stained-glass window in the **Church of St George** commemorates the British Army's evacuation from Dunkirk in 1940.

RICHBOROUGH CASTLE [G2] This ruined Roman fortress ⌗ of the 1st century AD once guarded the southern end of the **Wantsum** from Saxon raiders. The Wantsum was a channel that cut off Thanet from the mainland.

ROCHESTER [A2] The **castle keep ⌗** of 1126 was built to guard Watling Street as it crossed the Medway. The small but grand **cathedral** is noted for its Norman west door. Charles Dickens lived at Gad's Hill for 12 years and spent much of his time in Rochester. Scenes in *The Pickwick Papers* and *Great Expectations* are set there. Miss Haversham's house was inspired by **Restoration House**.

SANDWICH [G1] Since the Stour silted up in the 16th century, this old town, with winding medieval streets and fine Tudor buildings, has been a market town 2 miles inland. In the 11th century it was a leading port.

SOUTHEND-ON-SEA [B4] This large shopping centre and seaside resort began as the 'south end' of Prittlewell, now a suburb. At Prittlewell, a local history museum and vintage radio, TV and gramophone collection is housed in the remains of a 12th-century **priory**. In the 19th century, Southend became popular for day-trips from London. Its pier, at 1 mile 587 yd, is the world's longest.

TWO TREE ISLAND [B4] Windswept mud flats and saltings – reached by a boat that puts out from a road by Leigh-on-Sea station – are a national nature **reserve** where large numbers of wildfowl spend the winter.

WHITSTABLE [E2] Colourful fishermen's cottages fringe the busy harbour, which has one of Europe's largest oyster hatcheries.

The Pembrokeshire coast and south-west Wales

Map on pages 104–105

CAREW CASTLE [G2] The Norman castle's walls and round towers rise above a tidal creek, and the restored tidal mill on the causeway is the only one in Wales still working.

DALE PENINSULA [E2] St Ann's Head, at the windswept tip of the peninsula affords fine views. In August 1485, Henry Tudor landed at **Mill Bay** on his way to win the crown from Richard III at Bosworth Field.

DINAS HEAD [G5] Seals, guillemots, shags, razorbills and fulmars can be seen on a walk round the headland.

EFAILWEN [H4] In 1839, a tollgate here was attacked, the first of the Rebecca Riots against tolls and taxes, where the leaders dressed as women and took the name of Isaac's wife in the Old Testament.

FISHGUARD [F5] The last invasion of Britain took place here in February 1797: French mercenaries landed at **Carregwastad Point** to stir up a rebellion against George III but were defeated.

HAVERFORDWEST [F3] From the 15th–19th centuries the county town of Pembrokeshire was a busy port. The 12th-century **castle** has fine views over the Cleddau valley.

LLANDISSILIO [H3] Ancient relics, include the 5th–6th-century stones in the church wall. **Penrhos Cottage** was built overnight by poor people in the 19th century to gain squatter's rights.

MANORBIER CASTLE [G1] Once the centre of a prosperous Norman farming estate, the 12th–13th-century castle was the home of Gerald of Wales, a famous medieval scholar; his effigy is in the cathedral at St David's.

MARLOES [D2] The extensive sands, a good surfing area, are backed by rock pools and cliffs. Leeches at **Marloes Mere** were highly prized by 18th-century Harley Street doctors.

MILFORD HAVEN [E2] American Quakers built a whaling port here in 1790. Lord Nelson described Milford Haven Waterway as one of the finest harbours in the world. Until 1814 it was a naval dockyard; today it is a large oil port.

NEWPORT [G5] A former port and shipbuilding centre, Newport is today visited for its rocky shores and the sandy beach at Parrog. To the east near Nevern are **Pentre Ifan Stone Age burial chamber**, and **Castell Henllys**, with re-created roundhouses of an Iron Age hill-fort.

PEMBROKE [F1] On a wooded bluff jutting out to sea is a massive **castle** with a circular **Great Keep** 23m (75ft) high. Henry VII was born here in 1457. During the Second World War, Pembroke Dock was a base for Sunderland flying boats.

PICTON CASTLE [G3] Paintings by artist Graham Sutherland (1903–80) are housed in the castle of 1302.

*Medieval resort Town walls built some 600 years ago ring **Tenby**'s streets and castle and include an arched barbican gateway. St Florence Parade was once a moat that surrounded the fortification.*

ST DAVID'S [D4] Britain's smallest city has Wales's largest and finest cathedral, begun in 1181. There are ruins of a huge 13th-century **Bishop's Palace** with fine arcaded parapet.

SEALYHAM [F4] Captain Jack Edwardes bred the Sealyham terrier around 1900 to chase out foxes and badgers from their holes.

SKOMER AND SKOKHOLM [D2] Known as the 'Dream Islands', the islands are nature reserves, and home to Manx shearwaters and puffins.

SOLVA [D4] A thousand years ago the boating centre was a Viking haunt. **Tobacco Cove** was a hiding place for 18th-century smugglers' contraband. In the 19th century, emigrants sailed for America from Solva.

TENBY [H1] See picture.

Map on pages 106–107

ABERDULAIS FALLS [G1] For more than 300 years, these **waterfalls** powered a copper-smelting works. Now they provide energy for a large electricity-generating water wheel.

CARMARTHEN [C3] The former Roman city has the remains of a 500-seat amphitheatre. In 1451, an early **eisteddfod** of Welsh bards was held here. Merlin the wizard is said to have been born nearby in AD 480.

CARN GOCH [F4] In 150 BC some 2000 Celtic people and their livestock lived in this Iron Age camp, 213m (700ft) up the Black Mountain.

CARREG CENNEN CASTLE [F3] High on a grassy crag 91m (300ft) above the Cennen, the 13th–14th-century castle (**Cadw**) has one of Wales's most dramatic defensive positions.

CRAIG-Y-NOS [G3] This town is a good starting point for nearby **Dan-yr-Ogof Caves**, now part of the National Showcaves Centre, with the 21m (70ft) Cathedral Cave.

DINEFWR CASTLE [E4] Built by Lord Rhys, who led the Welsh against the Normans, the castle was the 10th-century seat of Hywel Dda who gave Wales a legal system. **Newton House** has White Park cattle, an ancient breed, possibly used for sacrifice by Druids.

KIDWELLY [C2] Until the 1940s the town made tin plate. Today, the chimney of a tin-plate works marks the **Industrial Museum**, with steam engines and rolling mills on show.

LAUGHARNE [B2] The town inspired the setting of Llareggub in Dylan Thomas's *Under Milk Wood*. The **Boat House** was his home until 1949.

LLANDOVERY [G5] Set beside the River Tywi, Llandovery has a ruined medieval **castle**, a cobbled square and a regular livestock market.

LLANELLI [D1] A stretch of 14 miles of coastline has been designated as a coastal park with a wetland nature reserve, landscaped woodland and a restored promenade.

PAXTON'S TOWER [D3] Sir William Paxton built the hilltop **folly** in 1811, in memory of Lord Nelson.

PEMBREY COUNTRY PARK [C1] Sands stretch for 8 miles beside Carmarthen Bay backed by dunes, pine woods and grassland.

PENDINE SANDS [B2] Several land speed record attempts have been made here. The sands can be visited when the military range is not in use.

PUMSAINT [F5] The village name means 'five saints'. Near **Dolaucothi mine** is the spot where the five are said to have sheltered in a storm.

YSTRADGYNLAIS [G2] Two rows of yellow-brick arches are all that is left of the 1612 **Ynyscedwyn Ironworks**.

The Brecon Beacons and the Forest of Dean

ABERGAVENNY [D3] Mountains ring this market town on the eastern fringe of the Brecon Beacons. The ruined **castle** dates from 1090; a grim betrayal by the Norman lord William de Braose occurred here on Christmas Day in 1176 – the Welsh lord Sitsyllt and his men were killed at a feast to mark a truce.

BLAENAVON [D2] Now a free museum, **Big Pit** was in use for 100 years until 1980. Visitors go down the pit shaft in a cage to the coal face, pit ponies' stables and workshops.

BRECON [B4] The 16th-century sandstone tower of **St Mary's Church** marks the centre of the old town with alleys lined with antique shops. In 1755 the actress Mrs Siddons was born here. The medieval **Cathedral Church** was restored in 1874–5. The Brecon Jazz Festival is in August.

CLYDACH GORGE [D3] Beechwoods line the steep river gorge and its waterfalls. The river once powered the 19th-century **Clydach Ironworks**, which has been restored.

FOREST OF DEAN [H2/3] Covering 35sq miles, in 1938 the forest became England's first National Forest Park. It has one of the largest areas in Britain of oaks over 150 years old.

GOODRICH CASTLE [G3] In the 12th century the red sandstone **castle** was built to guard the river crossing. It was ruined by Cromwell's forces in 1646 when they defeated the defending Royalist garrison.

HEREFORD [G5] Inside the cathedral is the *Mappa Mundi*, a map of the world drawn on vellum in the late

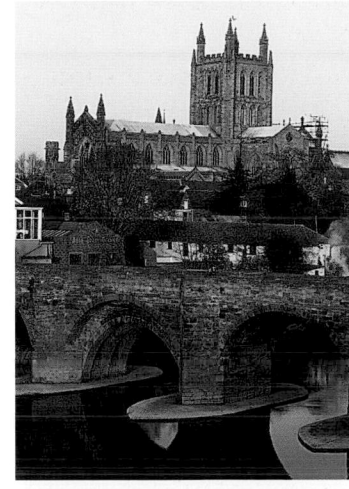

Library treasures *Hereford's 11th-century cathedral has the world's largest chained library, with more than 1500 books and manuscripts, some more than 1000 years old.*

13th century showing Jerusalem at its centre. The **Hereford Cider Museum** celebrates the fine produce of local orchards. Nell Gwynne, the mistress of Charles II, is believed to have been born in Gwynne Street.

KILPECK CHURCH [F4] Remarkable Norman carving can be seen at this small 12th-century church built of red sandstone. On the south doorway is a tree of life with warriors, dragons and flowers, while outside the building is a frieze of some 80 human, animal and monster heads.

LLANTHONY PRIORY [D4] The beauty and isolation of the **Vale of Ewyas** attracted Augustinian monks to build a large priory there in 1108, but

30 years later civil strife drove them to Gloucester. A small establishment continued until 1538.

LLANGORSE LAKE [C4] A yachting centre and wildfowl haunt with a shoreline 5 miles long, Llangorse is the largest natural lake in South Wales. Legend tells of a sunken palace and of church bells pealing under the water.

MERTHYR TYDFIL [B2] In the 19th century, the town was the iron-making capital of the world. By 1831 it was the largest town in Wales. **Cyfarthfa Castle**, built in mock-Gothic style in 1825, is now a free art gallery and museum. Keir Hardie, a founder of the Labour Party, was MP for Merthyr from 1900 until 1915.

MONMOUTH [G3] The fortified 13th-century gateway above the bridge is the only one of its kind in Britain. Henry V was born in 1387 in the **castle**. He figures on the façade of the 1724 **Shire Hall** in Agincourt Square, where there is a statue of Charles S. Rolls, one of the co-founders of Rolls-Royce motors.

PARTRISHOW [D4] The tiny church of **Merthyr Issui** was named after a murdered hermit. It has a decorated 11th-century font and a 15th-century screen with open-work tracery that includes a Welsh dragon.

RAGLAN CASTLE [F2] A grand moated **fortress-palace (Cadw)**, it was started in the 1430s. Lord Raglan gave the order that led to the ill-fated charge of the Light Brigade in 1845 during the Crimean War.

ROSS-ON-WYE [G4] Set high above the Wye on a sandstone bluff, the town is dominated by the spire of the medieval **St Mary's Church**. The 17th-century **Market House** has weathered open-plan pillars and arches. **Prospect Gardens** were laid out by John Kyrle.

SUGAR LOAF [D3] Pen-y-fân, has fine views from its conical 596m (1955ft) summit. It can be reached off the A40 at Pentre Road, Abergavenny.

TOURIST INFORMATION

Abergavenny (01873) 857588
Brecon (01874) 622485
Chepstow (01291) 623772
Coleford (01594) 812388
Hereford (01432) 268430
Merthyr Tydfil (01685) 379884
Monmouth (01600) 713899
Ross-on-Wye (01989) 562768

THE GOOD PUB GUIDE

Crickhowell [D3] *Bear* (01873) 810408
Llangynidr [C3] *Coach & Horses* (01874) 730245
Pontypool [D1] *Open Hearth* (01495) 763752
Raglan [F2] *Clytha Arms* (01873) 840206
Talybont-on-Usk [C4] *Star* (01874) 676635
Walterstone [F4] *Carpenters Arms* (01873) 890353
Usk [E1] *Nags Head* (01291) 672820

SYMONDS YAT [G3] From the **Yat Rock** there are stunning vistas of the Wye as it makes a horseshoe loop. The village has a dramatic gorge.

TALGARTH [C5] Early Medieval towers are reminders that the town was in the path of the 11th-century Norman advance into Wales. To the south is 12th-century **Castell Dinas**, which guarded a mountain pass.

TRETOWER COURT [C3] The fine medieval **manor house (Cadw)** was mostly the work of Sir Roger Vaughan, said to have been the wealthiest commoner in Wales during the 15th century. Near the Court are the remains of **Tretower Castle**, dating from the 12th century.

Y GAER [B4] One of a network of Roman camps in the area, the fort could house up to 1000 men and was used on and off from AD 75 to about AD 400. Some 10 miles west, are the ramparts of **Y Pigwyn**, a Roman marching camp which was a base used during campaigns against the Celtic inhabitants in AD 47–78.

TOURING GUIDE

High peak *The highest spot in western Wales, **Pen-y-Fân** lies at the heart of the Brecon Beacons. Excavations on a Bronze Age cairn on the mountain unearthed flint arrowheads and a bronze spearhead.*

FROM MAP ON PAGES 110–111

The Severn Valley and the Cotswolds

Exemplary style *Built in the early 1600s,* **Chastleton House** *is one of England's finest Jacobean houses and has much original furniture.*

TOURIST INFORMATION

Burford (01993) 823558
Cheltenham (01242) 522878
Chipping Norton
 (01608) 644379
Cirencester (01285) 654180
Gloucester (01452) 396572
Ledbury (01531) 636147
Moreton-in-Marsh
 (01608) 650881
Newent (01531) 822468
Stow-on-the-Wold
 (01451) 831082
Stroud (01453) 760960
Tewkesbury (01684) 295027
Upton upon Severn
 (01684) 594200
Winchcombe (01242) 602925
Witney (01993) 775802
Woodstock (01993) 813276

THE GOOD PUB GUIDE

Ashleworth [B4] *Queens Arms* (01452) 700395
Bledington [F4] *Kings Head* (01608) 658365
Bourton-on-the-Water [F3] *Kingsbridge Inn* (01451) 820371
Little Barrington [F3] *Inn for All Seasons* (01451) 844324
Lower Oddington [F4] *Fox* (01451) 870555
Nailsworth [B1] *Egypt Mill* (01453) 833449
Paxford [F5] *Churchill Arms* (01386) 594000
Sapperton [C2] *Bell* (01285) 760298
Tetbury [C1] *Gumstool* (01666) 890391

BIBURY [E2] William Morris, the artist-designer, called Bibury the most beautiful village in England. **Arlington Row** (not open to the public) is a terrace of 16th–17th-century cottages.

BLENHEIM PALACE [H3] When the 1st Duke of Marlborough defeated the French at Blenheim, he was rewarded with this costly mansion by Sir John Vanbrugh. Sir Winston Churchill was born here and is buried at Bladon.

BOURTON-ON-THE-WATER [F3] Five stone bridges span the Windrush as it flows through this scenic village. Attractions include an exhibition of village life, a model railway, a motor museum and a model of the town .

BURFORD [F2] The grandeur of the medieval **Church of St John the Baptist** reflects Burford's past as a rich wool town. Traders still set up stalls at the 16th-century **Tolsey**, or toll house.

CASTLEMORTON COMMON [B5] Ancient rough-grazing land that was never enclosed, the common lies below Herefordshire Beacon, 340m (1114ft) high, in the Malverns.

CHASTLETON HOUSE [F4] See picture.

CHEDWORTH ROMAN VILLA [E3] The wealthy Romano–British family that lived here in the 2nd century AD enjoyed steam baths and a sauna. The villa has striking mosaic floors, two bath houses and a water shrine.

CHELTENHAM [D4] This spa town gained popularity after George III visited in 1788 and most of the Regency buildings date from that time. The **Pittville Pump Room** still dispenses spa waters.

CHIPPING NORTON [G4] St Mary's is one of Gloucestershire's biggest churches. **Cornwell**, nearby, was rebuilt as an 'ideal' village in the 1930s. To the north are the **Rollright Stones**, a Stone Age burial site.

CIRENCESTER [D2] The outline of a Roman amphitheatre can be seen here and the **Corinium Museum** has Roman relics. The large Norman **Church of St John the Baptist** was rebuilt using money from the 15th–16th-century wool trade.

COOPER'S HILL [C3] People have rolled cheeses down this steep hill at Whitsuntide for centuries – maybe as part of ancient Sun worship. The hill is a nature reserve, and looks out across the Severn Vale into Wales.

DEERHURST [C4] St Mary's Church, which dates from AD 804, was once part of a Saxon monastery and has the finest Saxon font in Britain. Nearby is **Odda's Chapel**, built in 1056.

EASTNOR CASTLE [A5] The castle's turreted Gothic towers and keep were built around 1812. The Victorian Gothic revivalist Sir George Gilbert Scott designed the Great Hall, and Augustus Pugin the Drawing Room.

FRAMPTON ON SEVERN [A2] The village green, overlooked by Georgian houses, is one of the largest in England. Ships pass close to **St Mary's Church**, which is by the **Gloucester and Sharpness Canal**.

GLOUCESTER [B3] The cathedral, founded in 1089, houses Edward II's tomb. New docks and a ship canal linked the city to the Severn mouth in 1827. The **Soldiers of Gloucester** and **National Waterways Museums** are found in the rejuvenated dock area.

HAILES ABBEY [E4] Medieval pilgrims were drawn to the 13th-century **abbey**, now a ruin , , by a relic believed to be Christ's blood.

MINSTER LOVELL [G2] The village and the ruins of the 15th-century **Minster Lovell Hall** stand beside the Windrush. Francis, 9th Baron Lovell, joined the abortive rebellion of Lambert Simnel. He later vanished and legend says he hid in a secret chamber at the hall; workmen found a man's skeleton in 1708.

MORETON-IN-MARSH [F4] Old houses and coaching inns line the main street and the 16th-century curfew tower has its original bell. **Sezincote**, built in Indian style with onion-shaped domes, and **Chastleton House** (see picture), are nearby.

PAINSWICK [C2] The churchyard's 99 trimmed yews were planted about 1792. The rare 18th-century **Rococo Garden** has a flamboyant design.

SLIMBRIDGE [A2] Amid the Severn estuary wetlands, the Wildfowl Trust has one of the world's largest collections of wildfowl.

SNOWSHILL MANOR [E5] The Tudor manor has a vast display of objects, from cuckoo clocks and bicycles to Japanese armour.

STOW-ON-THE-WOLD [F4] The highest town in the Cotswolds is on the route of the ancient salt way, along which salt was carried for export. The market place still has a medieval cross and stocks.

SUDELEY CASTLE [D4] Henry VIII's sixth wife, Catherine Parr, who died in 1548, is buried in the castle chapel. A ruined 15th-century banqueting hall remains, but most of the castle dates from the 19th century. Nearby **Winchcombe** has a 15th-century church and a railway museum.

TEWKESBURY [C5] The large and splendid 12th-century abbey church of **St Mary the Virgin** has a 45m (148ft) high Norman tower. Local people bought it from Henry VIII in 1540 for £453 to save it from ruin at the dissolution of the monasteries.

WITNEY [G2] Blankets have been made at Witney for 600 years, and merchants once met in the **Blanket Hall** of 1721. The 17th-century Buttercross stands on pillars – it once served as a covered market. At nearby **Cogges Manor Farm Museum**, guides in costume reveal what rural life was like in late 19th-century Oxfordshire.

Oxford and the Vale of Aylesbury

AMPTHILL [G5] In Ampthill Park, west of the 18th–19th-century town centre, the site of Ampthill Castle is marked by **Catherine's Cross**. Henry VIII's first wife, Catherine of Aragon, lived there at the time of their divorce.

AYLESBURY [E3] Fragments of historic Aylesbury, the county town of Buckinghamshire, are found in the Market Square, where the 15th-century *King's Head Inn* ⅍ has a medieval gateway and a window containing 15th-century glass.

BANBURY [A5] The medieval market cross of nursery-rhyme fame was destroyed by Puritans in 1600, but replaced in 1859. The town still has some fine coaching inns, and there are Thursday and Saturday markets.

BERKHAMSTED [F2] William the Conqueror is said to have accepted the throne from the Saxons here after 1066. His double-moated **castle** is now a ruin ⌗.

BRILL [C3] An old post-mill of 1689 stands near this hilltop village, which has an Elizabethan manor house and a village green. Grassy mounds below the mill are relics of clay quarrying.

BUCKINGHAM [D5] Most of the ancient market town was rebuilt after a fire in 1724. A 15th-century **chantry chapel** ⅍ with a Norman doorway survives. The Georgian **Old Gaol** houses a **museum**.

CLAYDON HOUSE [D4] Much of the mansion ⅍ was demolished in 1792, before it was 50 years old. The surviving west wing has 18th-century rococo and Chinese interiors.

COOMBE HILL [E2] The 260m (853ft) Chiltern summit ⅍ is topped by a monument to the Boer War. To the south-west, **Chequers**, the country residence of the prime minister, can be glimpsed through the trees. To the east are **Wendover Woods**, with waymarked walks.

DUNSTABLE [G3] Watling Street passes through this former Roman posting station. The Norman nave of **St Peter's Church** is all that remains of a 12th-century priory.

*City of spires **Oxford's** university buildings set the tone of the elegant city. The domed Radcliffe Camera is part of the Bodleian Library, which holds more than 7 million books.*

*Sacred memorial The shrine in **St Albans** cathedral marks the site where Alban, a Roman soldier and England's first Christian martyr, was killed in about AD 209.*

DUNSTABLE DOWNS [F3] Gliders cruise over the Downs (partly ⅍), which give views over the Vale of Aylesbury. At the eastern end of the Chilterns is **Sharpenhoe Clappers** ⅍, once the site of an Iron Age hill-fort.

LUTON [H4] Until about 100 years ago Luton was famed for straw hats. Now it is better known for its airport and for motor vehicle production. The **Luton Museum** in Wardown Park tells of the town's straw-plaiting industry.

OXFORD [B2] Fine buildings in this academic city include the **Ashmolean Museum** of 1683, Britain's oldest public museum, and Sir Christopher Wren's **Sheldonian Theatre**. **University College**, one of the oldest, was founded in 1280, and Henry VIII established the largest, **Christ Church**. The 15th-century tower of **Magdalen** (pronounced Maudlin) **College** is one of the city's famous landmarks.

ROUSHAM HOUSE [A4] The oak front door of this house of 1635 has holes through which Civil War Royalist defenders could train their muskets. The gardens beside the Cherwell are much as William Kent created them in the 1730s.

ST ALBANS [H2] See picture (left). As Verulamium, the town was a main centre of Roman Britain – remains include the theatre at Bluehouse Hill.

SHAW'S CORNER [H3] George Bernard Shaw lived in this house ⅍ in the village of Ayot St Lawrence and wrote *Pygmalion* (1913) here. The house is now the Shaw museum.

SHOTOVER COUNTRY PARK [B2] Nature trails lead through this heath, wood and marshland, once a royal hunting ground. **Brasenose Wood** provided some of the oak used in Oxford's historic buildings.

STANTON HARCOURT MANOR [A2] The house has a huge medieval kitchen and a tower where the poet Alexander Pope is said to have translated part of the *Iliad*.

STOWE [C5] Pavilions, monuments, follies and bridges adorn these extensive 18th-century gardens ⅍. The house, one of England's largest, became a public school in 1923.

WADDESDON MANOR [D3] Built in the 1870s, the manor ⅍ is in the style of a French Renaissance château. It has a fine collection of French 18th-century decorative arts, and classic vintage wines. An ornate rococo aviary has many exotic birds.

TOURIST INFORMATION

Abingdon (01235) 522711
Aylesbury (01296) 330559
Banbury (01295) 259855
Bicester (01869) 369055
Buckingham (01280) 823020
Dunstable (01582) 471012
Hemel Hempstead
  (01442) 234222
High Wycombe
  (01494) 421892
Luton (01582) 401579
Milton Keynes (0870) 120 1269
Oxford (01865) 726871
St Albans (01727) 864511
Thame (01844) 212834
Wendover (01296) 696759

THE GOOD PUB GUIDE

Caulcott [B4] *Horse & Groom*
  (01869) 343257
Chinnor [D1] *Sir Charles Napier*
  (01494) 483011
Easington [C2] *Mole & Chicken*
  (01844) 208387
Great Hampden [E1] *Hampden Arms* (01494) 488255
Long Crendon [C2] *Angel*
  (01844) 208268
Murcott [B3] *Nut Tree*
  (01865) 331253
Oxford [A2] *Isis Tavern*
  (01865) 247006
Thame [D2] *Swan*
  (01844) 361211

WHIPSNADE TREE CATHEDRAL

[G3] On part of **Whipsnade Downs** ⅍, trees have been planted to form a cathedral. The structure was created in the 1930s by the landowner at the time, Edmund Kell Blyth, in memory of friends lost during World War I.

WOBURN ABBEY [F5] This palatial mansion was converted from a medieval abbey; the park was landscaped by Humphry Repton. **Woburn Safari Park** is one of Britain's largest.

TOURING GUIDE

The northern Home Counties

AUDLEY END [D5] Thomas Howard, 1st Earl of Suffolk and treasurer to James I, built the palatial house ✠ in the early 1600s. To reduce the upkeep, half of it was pulled down in the 18th century, leaving the Great Hall and two wings. 'Capability' Brown laid out the park in 1762.

BALDOCK [B5] The Knights Templar founded the town in the 12th century, and called it 'Baghdad'. The 14th-century tower on **St Mary's Church** has a very thin spire, or 'Hertfordshire spike'. The finest Hertfordshire spike is on the church at nearby **Ashwell**.

BISHOP'S STORTFORD [D3] Cecil Rhodes, the founder of Rhodesia (now Zimbabwe and Zambia), was born here in 1853. **Nettleswell House**, his birthplace, is now a museum.

diesel-powered trains run on the **Colne Valley Railway** and a **museum** has vintage engines and carriages.

CHELMSFORD [F2] The Romans founded Chelmsford in the 1st century AD. **St Mary's Cathedral** has some fine 15th-century chequered flintwork on its porch.

COGGESHALL [H4] The town was a prosperous medieval cloth-weaving centre. **Paycocke's** 🌿 is a fine 16th-century merchant's house. The timber framed **Coggeshall Grange Barn** 🌿, dates from 1140 and is a remnant of a 12th-century Cistercian monastery.

CRESSING [G3] Watercress was once farmed in this village. It has two **medieval barns** built by the Knights Hospitallers, a religious order.

danced here in 1561. The exiled Louis XVIII stayed in the hall and descendants of his retainers still live in the village.

GREAT BARDFIELD [F4] The pretty village has medieval **pargeted houses**, a 14th-century **church** with a rare stone screen and a windmill.

GREAT DUNMOW [E3] Every leap year, the **Dunmow Flitch Trials** take place here. A side, or flitch, of bacon is given to the married couple who have lived most harmoniously for a year and a day.

HATFIELD FOREST [D3] Huge oaks and hornbeams can be seen in this former Royal hunting forest 🌿 with wide, grassy rides and a nature trail.

HATFIELD HOUSE [A2] Robert Cecil, Earl of Salisbury, built the fine Jacobean house in 1607–11. Set in a large park, it has formal gardens next to a wing of the Old Palace where Elizabeth I spent much of her youth.

HODDESDON [C2] The **Rye House Gatehouse** is the only remnant of a former 15th-century manor. It holds an exhibition on the Rye House plot, the attempt to assassinate Charles II.

KNEBWORTH HOUSE [A3] Built in 1490 by Robert Lytton, the Tudor courtyard house was later restyled in High Gothic.

MALDON [H2] A port since Roman times, the hilltop town has a 13th-century **church** and the 15th-century brick-built **Moat Hall** was the site of a battle in AD 991, when Viking invaders defeated the local Saxons. In the **Maeldon Centre** is a 6m (42ft) embroidered appliqué hanging that commemorates its 1000-year history.

MOLE HALL [E4] Animals, including otters, deer and wildfowl, can be seen in the **wildlife park** set around a moated 13th-century manor house.

MUCH HADHAM [C3] The village has a Jacobean **Bishop's Palace**. Henry Moore, who lived at nearby **Perry Green**, carved the faces on the tower door of the **church**. The **Henry Moore Foundation** is nearby.

THE RODINGS [E3] Eight charming Roding villages are set amid fertile farmland, with old churches, moated halls and half-timbered cottages. They derive the name Roding from a Saxon tribe, the Hrodingas.

ROYSTON [C5] The town grew up round the crossing point of the prehistoric Icknield Way and the Roman Ermine Street. A **cave** with wall carvings, thought to have been cut by the Knights Templar in the 13th century, lies beneath Melbourn Street.

TOURIST INFORMATION

Bishop's Stortford
 (01279) 655831
Chelmsford (01245) 283400
Hertford (01992) 584322
Letchworth (01462) 487868
Maldon (01621) 856503
Saffron Walden (01799) 510444
Waltham Abbey
 (01992) 652295
Witham (01376) 502674

THE GOOD PUB GUIDE

Ayot St Lawrence [A3] *Brocket Arms* (01438) 820250
Coggeshall [H4] *Compasses* (01376) 561322
Fuller Street [F3] *Square & Compasses* (01245) 361477
Great Yeldham [G5] *White Hart* (01787) 237250
Harlow [D2] *Rainbow and Dove* (01279) 415419
Little Braxted [G5] *Green Man* (01621) 891659
Little Hadham [C4] *Nags Head* (01279) 771555
Maldon [H2] *Blue Boar* (01621) 855888
Watton at Stone [B3] *George & Dragon* (01920) 830285
Young's End [F3] *Green Dragon* (01245) 361030

SAFFRON WALDEN [D5] Until the 18th century, the market town was a major producer of saffron. Only the 12th-century keep of **Walden Castle** remains. Medieval buildings include the ornately pargeted **Sun Inn** 🌿 and **St Mary's Church**. The large turf maze on the common may be 800 years old.

STANSTED MOUNTFITCHET [D4] A replica timber-built Norman castle, **Mountfitchet Castle** is on the site of a similar castle, destroyed by King John in 1215. A nearby **toy museum** contains over 30,000 playthings.

STEVENAGE [A4] Built in the 1950s, the new town grew out of an old market town. Nearby Hitchin retains a medieval air, and the 15th-century **Church of St Mary** is Hertfordshire's largest parish church. To the north is Letchworth, Britain's first garden city.

THAXTED [E4] The tall spire of a huge **church** of 1500 soars over the town – its medieval wealth came from cutlery. The highwayman Dick Turpin was born at nearby Hempstead.

WARE [C3] An old malting and coaching town, it is famous for the **'Great Bed of Ware'** that slept 12, which is mentioned in Shakespeare's *Twelfth Night*.

WITHAM [G3] A plaque marks the former home of the writer Dorothy L. Sayers, best known for her detective novels featuring Lord Peter Wimsey.

Working windmill *The largest of its kind left in Essex, the restored 1790 post mill in **Aythrorpe Roding** was originally used to grind corn into flour.*

BRAINTREE [G4] Once a medieval wool-weaving centre, the town turned to silk weaving in the 19th century when the Courtauld family opened a factory there. **Warner's silk archive** will open in 2005.

CASTLE HEDINGHAM [G5] One of the country's finest Norman keeps, Hedingham Castle dominates the village. Built in about 1140, it has an early Tudor moat bridge that may have been added in1496 for a visit by Henry VIII. There is a banqueting hall with a minstrels' gallery. Steam and

DANBURY [G2] Nine **woods** grouped round the hilltop village provide a circular walk and are home to diverse plants, birds and butterflies.

FURNEUX PELHAM [C4] A 15th-century **church** here has a timber roof with painted angels, a clock inscribed with 'Time flies' and 'Mind your business', and windows by William Morris and Edward Burne-Jones.

GOSFIELD HALL [G4] The panelled Queen's Gallery in the 16th-century hall was named after Elizabeth I who

East Essex and Constable country

TOURIST INFORMATION

Clacton-on-Sea (01255) 423400
Colchester (01206) 282920
Felixtowe (01394) 276770
Harwich (01255) 506139

THE GOOD PUB GUIDE

Burnham-on-Crouch [A1]
  White Harte (01621) 782106
Chelmondiston [D5] *Butt &*
  Oyster (01473) 780764
Erwarton [D5] *Queens Head*
  (01473) 787550
Fingringhoe [B3] *Whalebone*
  (01206) 729307
Langham [B4] *Shepherd & Dog*
  (01206) 272711
Stoke-by-Nayland [A5] *Angel*
  (01206) 263245

BOURNE MILL [B4] Sir Thomas Lucas's fishing lodge of 1591 became a **mill** ❧ in the 19th century, and was in use until 1914. The waterwheel is still in working order.

BRIGHTLINGSEA [B3] A boating centre on the Colne estuary, the old fishing port is surrounded by water on three sides. The Perpendicular **church** has one of East Anglia's finest towers, 29m (94ft) high.

BRADWELL-ON-SEA [B2] Set amid marshland, the isolated town has a restored Saxon **chapel**, the site of an annual pilgrimage. There are free tours of the nuclear power station.

BURNHAM-ON-CROUCH [A1] The old-fashioned yachting resort holds lively regattas in the summer.

CLACTON-ON-SEA [C3] A popular seaside resort geared for family holidays, Clacton has a pier, a long sandy beach, a promenade, public gardens and amusement centres.

COLCHESTER [A4] Britain's oldest recorded town was a Celtic capital captured by the Romans in AD 44, and sacked by Celtic Queen Boudicca 11 years later. The town's **Norman castle** has the largest castle keep in Europe, now a **museum**. Ruined **St Botolph's Priory** ✠, built around 1100, is one of the city's many medieval buildings. To the south-west, **Colchester Zoo** has a good collection of animals including over 2000 rare and endangered species.

DEDHAM [B5] Artist John Constable went to school in Dedham village and, across the river, the thatched **Flatford Bridge Cottage** ❧ has displays on his art and life.

Pretty as a picture John Constable's father was miller at the picturesque **Flatford Mill** *which featured in some of the artist's best-known works.*

EAST BERGHOLT [B5] The house where the painter John Constable was born in 1776 has gone, but much of the 16th–17th century village remains as it was in his boyhood. A timber bell-cage in the **churchyard** was built in 1531 to house the five church bells, said to be the heaviest in the country; together they weigh some 4 tons.

FELIXSTOWE [E5] A quiet seaside resort, the town is also Britain's largest container port. It owes its dual nature to a 19th-century snub. In the 1870s, nearby Harwich rejected Colonel George Tomline as its potential Member of Parliament. Tomline, in retaliation, developed the village of Felixstowe into a rival port and resort. **Landguard Fort**, from the 18th century, is the only English fort to have repelled a full-scale invasion attempt; Admiral De Ruyter's Dutch forces were defeated here in 1667.

FINGRINGHOE WICK [B3] These mud flats, salt marshes and gravel pits on the Colne estuary, noted for wintering Brent geese, are a nature reserve with wildlife typical of the Essex marshes; the Essex Naturalists' Trust is based here.

FLATFORD MILL [B5] See picture (above).

FRINTON-ON-SEA [D3] See picture (below).

HARWICH [D4] The town has been a port and naval base since the reign of Edward III, and seafarers such as Sir Francis Drake fitted out their ships here in the 16th century. The old part of the town retains its 13th-century grid layout. A **treadmill crane** used in the shipyard from 1667 until 1927 can be seen near the Green, and the circular Redoubt **fort** of 1808 was built as a defence against Napoleon.

LAYER MARNEY TOWER [A3] The first Lord Marney died in 1523 before the building of his mansion could begin. Dating from about 1520, a red-brick gate tower decorated with shells and dolphins, was the only part completed; it is the tallest Tudor gate tower in Britain. In Layer-de-la-Haye nearby is a wetlands nature reserve.

MANNINGTREE [C4] The small market and sailing centre was the headquarters of Matthew Hopkins' witch hunt in the 1640s; he hanged more than 100 people until he himself was hanged in 1647. The nearby port of Mistley has a **churchyard** with two towers that are the sole remains of a neo-classical **church** ✠ of 1776 built by architect Robert Adam.

MERSEA ISLAND [B3] Linked to the mainland by a causeway which can disappear at full tide, the island's coast is a nature reserve.

PIN MILL [D5] Barge building was once the lifeblood of this Orwell estuary beauty spot, today a popular amateur sailing centre. The **Cliff Plantation** ❧ provides an attractive riverside walk.

TATTINGSTONE WONDER [C5] What appears to be a medieval church is actually a famous folly – a trio of cottages transformed in 1790 by the local squire, Edward White, to enhance the view from his house.

WALTON ON THE NAZE [D3] The Naze is a headland to the north of this seaside resort with a 244m (800ft) long pier. The extensive salt marshes are a nature reserve.

WIVENHOE [B4] Ships have been built in the small riverside town for at least 400 years. **Garrison House**, said to have been a billet for Cromwell's troops in the Civil War, has fine pargeting.

Fashionable Frinton Fine sands and a lively atmosphere attracted film stars and royalty to the Essex coastal resort of **Frinton-on-Sea** *in its 1920s heyday.*

TOURING GUIDE

Cardigan Bay and the central Cambrians

ABERAERON [E4] In the early 19th century a landowner developed this small port into an elegant Regency town and shipbuilding centre. Today it is a popular holiday resort.

CARDIGAN [B2] Once a major port, Cardigan is now a market town on the Teifi. A medieval seven-arched **bridge** spans the river, and the **guildhall** has fine arches and clock tower. The **castle**, now a ruin, was in 1176 the venue for the first recorded assembly of bards, the start of the **Eisteddfod**.

CEMAES HEAD [B3] The marbled look of the cliff face results from the compression of sand and mud layers over thousands of years. There are fine views across the Teifi estuary and to the nature reserve of Cardigan Island.

CORS CARON [G4] Some of Europe's richest raised peat bog, with three distinct domes, forms this nature reserve. Red kites, sedge warblers and otters thrive here.

CWMTYDU [D3] Narrow lanes lead to secluded Cwmtydu beach, with its caves and rockpools. **Caerllan** 🦡,

nearby, offers a 3½ mile walk along the cliff to New Quay with breath-taking views.

DEVIL'S BRIDGE [H5] Plunging in spectacular cascades to join the Rheidol, the Mynach has carved a 91m (300ft) deep ravine spanned by a trio of bridges one above the other. The oldest is a medieval stone bridge, built, legend says, by the Devil to help a woman to cross the river with her cow, with the proviso that he kept the first creature across; she outwitted him by sending her dog first. The second bridge was built in 1753 and the iron road bridge in 1901. There is a steep path to the ravine floor.

DOLAUCOTHI [G2] Gold was mined here for some 2000 years until 1938. The mine 🦡 is east of Pumsaint village in wooded cliffs. Jagged seams worked by Roman slaves, remains of the Roman water channels, and 1930s mining gear can still be seen.

LAMPETER [F2] The town has been a cattle-trading centre since the 13th century. It is the home of the oldest Welsh university, St David's

University College, founded by the Bishop of St David's in 1822.

LLANDDEWI-BREFI [G3] St David's Church stands on a mound beside the village square. The ground is said to have risen at this spot in AD 519 so that St David could be seen when he addressed the Synod of Brefi. In the church are early Christian stones with Latin inscriptions.

LLYN BRIANNE [H2] The long reservoir stretches into the Cambrians and the Tywi Forest. When it is full, water cascades down 400m (1312ft). At nearby **Dinas** is an RSPB reserve with a trail to the cave of Twm Shon Catti, a 16th-century outlaw.

MWNT [B3] A steep path near the 13th-century **Holy Cross Church** (the smallest church in Wales) leads down from the headland to the beach 🦡.

NEW QUAY [D4] Terraced houses rise behind a scenic harbour at this old fishing port, where in October 1745 some half a million herring were caught in one night. There are fewer boats today, but tourists come to savour the seafaring atmosphere. Near Cei Bach, the 17th-century **Llanina church** is one of the smallest in Wales (see Mwnt, above).

PONTRHYDFENDIGAID [H4] Since 1963, a week-long Eisteddfod has been held each May in this village

TOURIST INFORMATION

Aberaeron (01545) 570602
Nant-yr-Arian Visitor Centre,
Rheidol Forest (01970) 890694
New Quay (01545) 560865

THE GOOD PUB GUIDE

Abercych [C2] *Nags Head*
(01239) 841200
Cilgerran [B2] *Pendre*
(01239) 614233
Llwyndafydd [D3] *Crown*
(01545) 560396

straddling a stream at the start of the Teifi. A pavilion seating 3000, endowed by Sir David John James (1888–1967), houses the event.

ST DOGMAELS [B2] The small town of St Dogmaels grew up around an abbey believed to have been founded in the 7th century. It was rebuilt by the Normans in 1115. The ruins lie beside the parish church, where a stone inscribed with Celtic and Latin script was used to decipher the Celtic languages of Irish and Scots Gaelic, and Manx. Nearby is **Y Felin**, a restored 17th-century water mill still producing stoneground flour.

SARN HELEN [G3] A section of the Roman road can be seen at the A485–B4578 junction between Lampeter and Tregaron. The road may have been named after Helen, the wife of a 4th-century Roman ruler, Magnus Maximus, but 'sarn heolen' is also Welsh for a paved causeway.

STRATA FLORIDA [H4] One of the great cultural centres of medieval Wales, this remote abbey in the Teifi valley was founded in 1164 by Cistercian monks and nurtured by Prince Rhys of Deheubarth. A number of Welsh princes are buried there. The name is from the Welsh Ystrad-fflur, or Vale of Flowers. The imposing ruins **(Cadw)** are entered through a Norman arch.

TREGARON [G4] Twm Shon Catti, an outlaw known as the Welsh Robin Hood, was born in this small country town in 1530. Until this century, Tregaron's position in the Cambrian foothills made it one of the main staging posts for drovers taking herds of Welsh Black cattle to English markets via the remote Abergwesyn Pass. Today, farmers gather here to trade sheep.

VALE OF RHEIDOL [G5] See picture.

YSBYTY CYNFYN [H5] The lonely church here once stood within a prehistoric stone circle, of which only five huge stones remain. Now the ancient stones, the tallest of them 3.3m (11ft) high, are embedded in the churchyard walls.

Valley line The **Vale of Rheidol** steam railway line runs from Aberystwyth to Devil's Bridge and was built in 1902 to transport lead from local mines. There are superb views of the wooded Rheidol valley on the hour-long journey.

Mid Wales and the Welsh borders

Freshwater supply *Craig Goch reservoir is one of a chain of reservoirs and dams in the* **Elan Valley.** *They were built between 1892 and 1904 to supply water to the people of Birmingham.*

TOURIST INFORMATION

Builth Wells (01982) 553307
Elan Valley Visitors Centre (01597) 810898
Hay-on-Wye (01497) 820144
Kington (01544) 230778
Knighton (Offa's Dyke) (01547) 528753, 529424
Leominster (01568) 616460
Llandrindod Wells (01597) 822600
Llanwrtyd Wells (01591) 610666
Ludlow (01584) 875053
Presteigne (01544) 260650
Rhayader (01597) 810591

THE GOOD PUB GUIDE

Brimfield [H4] *Roebuck* (01584) 711230
Dorstone [F2] *Pandy* (01981) 550273
Hay-on-Wye [F2] *Kilverts* (01497) 821042
Llandrindod Wells [D4] *Bell Country Inn* (01597) 823959
Old Radnor [E3] *Harp* (01544) 350655
Pembridge [G3] *New Inn* (01544) 388427
Presteigne [F4] *Radnorshire Arms* (01544) 267406
Titley [F3] *Stagg* (01544) 230221
Wellington [H2] *Wellington* (01432) 830367
Weobley [G3] *Salutation* (01544) 318443
Winforton [F2] *Sun Inn* (01544) 327677

BERRINGTON HALL [H4] The red sandstone mansion ❧ was designed by Henry Holland. 'Capability' Brown landscaped the park.

BUILTH WELLS [C3] Once the town was a collecting place on the old cattle drovers' route to England. It became a fashionable spa in the early 19th century. At nearby **Cilmeri**, a memorial stone stands where Llywelyn ap Gruffydd, the last of the Welsh princes, died in 1282.

CLYRO [E2] Francis Kilvert, a curate in this border village in 1865–72, wrote diaries that recorded life in the countryside. There are fine views of the Wye valley and Black Mountains.

CROFT CASTLE [G4] The 14th–15th-century walls and turrets of this fortified house ❧ conceal an 18th-century interior. The park has huge oaks and an avenue of Spanish chestnuts, some over 350 years old.

EARDISLAND [G3] Set beside the River Arrow, the village is noted for its black-and-white houses, such as **Staick House**, a yeoman's hall of about 1300. Nearby **Burton Court** is an 18th-century house built round a 14th-century **Great Hall**.

ELAN VALLEY [B4] See picture (above). A trail through the valley follows a 5½ mile route along the man-made reservoirs. The many birds to be seen include the rare red kite.

HAY-ON-WYE [E2] The market town is noted for its secondhand bookshops. To the south, steep **Hay Bluff** has views of the Malvern Hills and Snowdonia. Nearby **Gospel Pass** is the highest point on one of the few roads through the Black Mountains.

KINGTON [F3] The *Red Book of Hergest*, a source for the *Mabinogion*, a medieval collection of Welsh tales, takes its name from **Hergest Court**, a local, 15th-century manor. **Bradnor Hill** ❧ has England's highest golf course. At **Hergest Croft Gardens**, nearby, is a fine collection of exotic trees and a valley with 9m (30ft) tall rhododendrons.

KNIGHTON [F5] Quaint, narrow streets define the riverside market town. The **Offa's Dyke Centre** recalls the boundary's history.

LEOMINSTER [H3] The town was once noted for fine wool, known as Lemster Ore. **St Peter and St Paul Church** has a Norman doorway, ornate carvings and a ducking stool. **Grange Court**, an outstanding timber-framed house of 1633, was built by John Abel, carpenter to Charles I.

LLANDRINDOD WELLS [D4] The Victorian passion for spas and the railway's arrival in 1867 created a prosperous resort, with elegant buildings and wide streets. The waters are today available at **Rock Park Spa**, close to the **Pump Room**. Nearby is the Roman fort of **Castell Collen**.

LLANWRTYD WELLS [B2] On August Bank Holiday Monday, the small mountain town hosts the eccentric Bog Snorkelling World Championships. Nearby, a scenic road in the Irfon valley climbs the **Abergwesyn Pass**.

LUDLOW [H5] A well-preserved medieval town, Ludlow has splendid half-timbered buildings, such as the early 17th-century *Feathers Hotel*. The **castle** was built in about 1086 and later became a royal palace. Ludlow's past wool-trade wealth is reflected in the fine **Church of St Laurence**.

Home front *Weobley is dominated by colourful timber-framed houses. It is part of the Black and White Village Trail, a 40-mile route taking in some of Britain's most picturesque villages.*

OFFA'S DYKE [F1–5] The earthwork, 8m (26ft) high in places, was built in the 8th century by Offa, the king of the Anglo-Saxon kingdom of Mercia, to mark his boundary with the Welsh. The **Offa's Dyke Path**, runs for 177 miles from Sedbury cliffs to Prestatyn.

PEMBRIDGE [G3] The 14th-century *New Inn* is just one of the many well-preserved black-and-white buildings in the village. **St Mary's Church** has a detached pyramidal timber belfry.

PRESTEIGNE [F4] North of this town a 17th-century bridge spans the River Lugg, which marks the border with England. A 19th-century shire hall houses the **Judges' Lodging Museum**, and there are secret passages and a priest's hole in the *Radnorshire Arms*.

RADNOR FOREST [E4] A grassy plateau rising to 660m (2165ft), with rolling hills and deep valleys, the 'forest' is open sheep-grazing country with stretches of forestry plantation. There are footpaths and tracks but no roads. The aptly named 'Water-break-its-neck' waterfall drops into a gorge.

WEOBLEY [G3] See picture (left).

Worcester, Warwick and Shakespeare country

ALCESTER [F3] The town sits at the meeting of two Roman roads and the Alne and Arrow rivers. Medieval and Tudor half-timbered buildings mingle with red-brick Georgian façades. Nearby is **Ragley Hall** of 1680, with ornate plasterwork by James Gibbs.

BADDESLEY CLINTON [H5] The hall is one of England's finest medieval moated houses ❦. Nearby is **Packwood House** ❦, originally Elizabethan but re-created as Jacobean; it has a 17th-century garden of topiary yews thought to depict the *Sermon on the Mount*.

BEWDLEY [C5] A stone bridge built in 1798 by Thomas Telford spans the Severn here. There are fine Georgian houses, including the birthplace of Stanley Baldwin, three times prime minister, and a **museum** in the cobbled **Shambles**. The Severn Valley Railway, a standard-gauge steam railway, runs through Bewdley.

BIDFORD-ON-AVON [G3] A Roman road crossed the river here, and an eight-arched 15th-century **bridge** was a medieval crossing point. Shakespeare is said to have drunk with fellow playwright Ben Jonson at the former *Falcon Inn*.

BROMYARD [B3] Hopfields and orchards surround the town, which still has its medieval street pattern. From **Bromyard Downs** there are views of Wales and the Malverns. **Lower Brockhampton** ❦ nearby is a moated manor with a rare half-timbered gatehouse.

BURFORD HOUSE GARDENS [A4] Set on the River Teme, these gardens are home to a national collection of clematis, among other plants.

CHARLECOTE PARK [H3] In 1572 Elizabeth I stayed here on her way to Kenilworth. The house ❦, built in the 1550s, was restored in Elizabethan style in the 1830s. It is said that in the 1580s, Sir Thomas Lucy, the estate owner, fined William Shakespeare for poaching deer, and that after writing lewd verses on the gatehouse wall, the playwright left for London.

COUGHTON COURT [F4] Since 1409 the house has been the home of the Roman Catholic Throckmorton family. There are priests' holes under the Tower Room. The building was damaged in the Civil War and in 1688 by a Protestant mob. On November 5, 1605, the wives of the conspirators in the Gunpowder Plot waited for news in the Court's gatehouse.

EVESHAM [F2] In the centre of the market town is an ornate gate and **bell tower**. It dates from 1539, and is all that is left of a Benedictine monastery. An obelisk on **Green Hill** marks the battlefield of 1265, where the future Edward I defeated Simon de Montfort.

HANBURY HALL [E4] The elegant 18th-century country house ❦ boasts beautifully painted ceilings and a fine staircase. Other features include an orangery and an icehouse.

HARTLEBURY CASTLE [D5] The castle has been the official residence of the Bishops of Worcester since 850. Some of the elegant state rooms are open to the public.

HENLEY-IN-ARDEN [G4] The quaint town grew up beside the Forest of Arden. The forest court still meets yearly in the 15th-century **guildhall**.

KENILWORTH CASTLE [H5] Queen Elizabeth I gave the **castle** ⌗ to Robert Dudley, Earl of Leicester, in 1563. Her entertainment here in grand style inspired Sir Walter Scott's novel *Kenilworth*. The castle's 13th-century outer walls still stand, and the ruins include a 12th-century Norman **keep** and 14th-century **Great Hall**.

LEIGH BROOK [C3] Kingfishers and dippers may be seen at the Knapp reserve in a valley of the brook. Above is **Old Storridge Common**, at 204m (670ft), a fine viewpoint.

LOWER BROADHEATH [D3] The composer Sir Edward Elgar was born here in 1857. His birthplace is now a museum.

MALVERN HILLS [C2] See picture.

STOURPORT-ON-SEVERN [D5] The town grew up in the 1760s after James Brindley built the **Staffordshire and Worcestershire Canal** to join the rivers Severn and Stour. An iron bridge of 1870 spans the Severn.

STRATFORD-UPON-AVON [H3] The house where William Shakespeare was born in 1564 is now a national memorial; he is buried in **Holy Trinity Church**. The Royal Shakespeare Company performs at the **Royal Shakespeare Theatre**, the **Swan Theatre** and **The Other Place**.

TENBURY WELLS [A4] Queen Victoria called this market town on the Teme: 'My lovely town in the orchard'. A coaching stop on the road to Wales, this was also briefly a spa in the 19th century. The **Round Market** of 1811 is, in fact, oval.

WITLEY COURT [C4] Once a huge 19th-century Italianate style stately home, it is now a spectacular ruin ⌗.

In the grounds is the Jerwood Foundation's collection of modern British sculptures.

WORCESTER [D3] Soaring above the town is the 14th-century tower of the **cathedral**, in whose nave is the tomb of King John. The city's buildings include the 15th-century **Greyfriars** ❦ and 18th-century **guildhall**. The **Museum of Worcester Porcelain** has a large collection of Royal Worcester porcelain, made here since 1751.

WYRE FOREST [C5] Fast-flowing Dowles Brook is at the heart of the forest beside the River Severn.

Golden hills *The **Malvern Hills** rise steeply from the Severn plain. The restorative spring waters which gush out from the rocks in these hills are still bottled and exported today.*

The shires of central England

ALTHORP [E4] John Spencer bought the original house in 1508. The grand entrance hall dates from the 1730s, and the elegant exterior from the 1780s. The fine art collection includes paintings by Gainsborough, Reynolds and Van Dyck. Diana, Princess of Wales is buried in the grounds and the stable block houses a museum containing memorabilia and books of condolences collected on her death.

CANONS ASHBY HOUSE [D3] See picture (right).

DAVENTRY [D4] Charles I stayed six nights at the *Wheatsheaf Inn* in 1645, before the Battle of Naseby. His army camped nearby on **Borough Hill**, the site of a huge Iron Age hill-fort.

HARROLD-ODELL COUNTRY PARK [H3] Water meadows and lakes have been made into a country park by the Great Ouse. Wildlife includes feral mink, kingfishers, and muntjac deer.

NORTHAMPTON [E4] Boots and shoes have been made here since medieval times. In the 17th century the town shod Cromwell's army; the walls and Norman castle were destroyed as punishment in the Restoration. Queen Victoria's wedding shoes can be seen at the **Central Museum and Art Gallery**. **St Sepulchre's** is one of four round churches left in England.

OLNEY [G3] William Cowper, poet of the 'Olney Hymns', lived in this small town by the Great Ouse in 1768–86. His home is now a museum. Every Shrove Tuesday there is a pancake race in the town.

ROYAL LEAMINGTON SPA [A4] Iron and salt springs made the town fashionable in the late 18th century. **The Royal Pump Room**, built in 1814 and recently restored, houses an art gallery and museum. The gardens, overlooked by Regency and Victorian terraces, are beautifully laid out.

RUGBY [C5] Engineering and the railways spurred Rugby's industrial growth. The public school was founded in 1567 and a small museum relates its history; *Tom Brown's Schooldays* by Thomas Hughes was set at Rugby. Rugby Art Gallery and Museum holds a fine collection of modern art and Roman artefacts.

STANFORD ON AVON [D5] The village straddles the River Avon and the county border; its 14th-century church is in Northamptonshire, and nearby **Stanford Hall**, a 1690 William and Mary house, is in Leicestershire.

STOKE BRUERNE [E2] See picture (below right).

STONELEIGH [A5] Half-timbered houses line the village's main street. At **Stoneleigh Abbey** only the gatehouse and doorways of the 1154 Cistercian monastery survive but the grand interiors and facade added by the Leigh Family in the 18th century are undergoing restoration.

SULGRAVE MANOR [D2] The manor was the home of Colonel John Washington, the great grandfather of George Washington, first President of the USA. The family coat of arms is said to have inspired the US flag.

*Historic canal The Grand Union Canal winds through the charming village of **Stoke Bruerne**, where a 19th-century corn mill contains a canal museum. On display in the museum is a reconstructed, fully furnished, traditional narrowboat.*

*Courtyard manor Dating from the 1550s, **Canons Ashby House** ❧ belonged to relatives of the poet John Dryden, who visited the manor in the 1650s.*

TOWCESTER [E2] Known for its racecourse, this small town is on the Roman **Watling Street**. The *Saracen's Head* inn was the setting for Charles Dickens's *The Pickwick Papers*. The poet Edith Sitwell is buried in **St Mary's** churchyard at Weedon Lois.

WARWICK [A4] The 14th-century **castle** was the home of the earls of Warwick until 1978, including Warwick the Kingmaker – who in the Wars of the Roses made kings of both the Yorkist Edward IV and Lancastrian Henry VI. The **Lord Leycester Hospital** of 1571 and the 15th-century Beauchamp Chapel in **St Mary's Church** survived the 1694 fire.

WELLINGBOROUGH [G4] In the 19th century the town grew into a centre of shoe-making and ironworking. Oliver Cromwell stayed in the 17th-century inn, now the *Hind Hotel*, on the way to the Battle of Naseby in June 1645.

TOURIST INFORMATION

Daventry (01327) 300277
Kettering (01536) 410266
Northampton (01604) 838800
Royal Leamington Spa (01926) 742762
Rugby (01788) 534970
Warwick (01926) 492212
Wellingborough (01933) 276412

THE GOOD PUB GUIDE

Badby [D3] *Windmill* (01327) 702363
Biddenham [H3] *Three Tuns* (01234) 354847
Chacombe [C2] *George & Dragon* (01295) 711500
Dunchurch [C5] *Dun Cow* (01788) 810305
Farthingstone [D3] *Kings Arms* (01327) 361604
Odell [H3] *Bell* (01234) 720254
Shenington [B2] *Bell* (01295) 670274
Sulgrave [D2] *Star* (01295) 760389
Turvey [G3] *Three Cranes* (01234) 881305; *Three Fyshes* (01234) 881264

TOURING GUIDE

Cambridge and the southern Fens

TOURIST INFORMATION

Bedford (01234) 215226
Cambridge (0906) 586 2526
Huntingdon (01480) 388588
Newmarket (01638) 667200
St Neots (01480) 388788

THE GOOD PUB GUIDE

Broom [B2] *Cock*
(01767) 314411
Cambridge [E3] *Cambridge Blue* (01223) 361382
Fordham [G5] *White Pheasant*
(01638) 720414
Fowlmere [E2] *Chequers*
(01763) 208369
Grantchester [E3] *Green Man*
(01223) 841178
Horningsea [E4] *Crown & Punchbowl* (01223) 860643
Houghton Conquest [A2]
Knife & Cleaver
(01234) 740387
Lidgate [H3] *Star*
(01638) 500275
Madingley [D4] *Three Horseshoes* (01954) 210221

*Seat of learning The chapel of King's College in **Cambridge** dates from 1547 and is renowned for its annual carol service, the Festival of Nine Lessons and Carols. It boasts a fan-vaulted roof and fine stained glass.*

ANGLESEY ABBEY [F4] Built in 1600 on the site of an Augustinian priory, this Jacobean house ❧, is full of treasures collected by the first Lord Fairhaven. He also created a fine garden with an **arboretum**.

BEDFORD [A3] A five-arched bridge dating from 1813 crosses the Great Ouse as it flows through the town. Of the Norman castle that guarded the river until 1224, only the mound remains. The **John Bunyan Museum** is housed in the Bunyan Meeting House, on the site of the barn where Bunyan once preached.

BURWELL [F4] The wide main street of this sprawling Fenland village has pink, white and yellow houses. The tower of **St Mary's Church**, octagonal at the top, is a local landmark.

CAMBRIDGE [E3] Peterhouse, the first college of this university city, was founded in 1284. Many of the city's finest buildings are on **King's Parade** and **Trinity Street**. A large collection of English and European art is found at the **Fitzwilliam Museum**. **Kettle's Yard** has a fine display of 20th-century art.

CLARE [H2] In the village are the remains of a 13th-century friary, founded by the Clare family. The 15th-century **Ancient House**, now a museum, and other village buildings display richly patterned plasterwork.

DUXFORD [E2] This branch of the Imperial War Museum, housed in a glass-walled aircraft hangar, displays 180 civil and military aircraft.

ELSTOW [A2] John Bunyan was born at nearby Harrowden and spent his childhood here. The 16th-century **Moot Hall** houses a small museum.

GODMANCHESTER [C4] The town's bridge of 1332 was built out from both banks of the Ouse at the same time, and is misaligned. Fine buildings include **Island Hall**, a restored 18th-century mansion.

GRAFHAM WATER [B4] The huge reservoir provides a sanctuary for waterfowl such as wigeons and wintering goldeneyes. A walk leads round the 10 mile shore.

GRANTCHESTER [E3] Rupert Brooke's poem 'The Old Vicarage, Grantchester' immortalised the village. Brooke was one of many poets – including Chaucer, Spenser, Milton and Byron – to be attracted by its idyllic setting on the Cam.

HEMINGFORD GREY [C5] The 12th-century moated **manor** in this riverside village was the model for the children's story *Green Knowe*, by Lucy Boston. Medieval **St James's Church** has a truncated spire; the top was blown off during a gale in 1741.

HUNTINGDON [C5] Oliver Cromwell was born in Huntingdon and was the town's MP in 1628–9. The grammar school he attended – the diarist Samuel Pepys went there 30 years later – is now a **Cromwell museum**. Nearby **Houghton Mill** ❧ is on an island in the Ouse.

KIMBOLTON [A4] The **castle** where Catherine of Aragon lived after her divorce from Henry VIII, is now a school. It was reshaped by John Vanbrugh, and the Robert Adam gatehouse was added in around 1766.

NEWMARKET [G4] The headquarters of horse racing and breeding in Britain since the 17th century, Newmarket has two racecourses and is the home of the **National Stud**, which can be toured. **The Jockey Club** was founded in the town in the 1750s, and its headquarters are next to the **National Horseracing Museum**.

ST IVES [D5] The market town on the Great Ouse was a village called Slepe until a priory, dedicated to the Persian bishop St Ivo, was built here around 1050. A six-arched stone bridge of 1425 spanning the river has a tiny two-storey **chapel** – one of very few medieval bridge chapels in England.

ST NEOTS [B4] Named after a 10th-century priory founded in honour of St Neot, the small riverside town has

Georgian buildings, river terraces and a 15th-century church featuring fine roof carvings.

SANDY [B2] The Royal Society for the Protection of Birds has its headquarters in the Victorian Lodge. Birds in the nature reserve include all three species of British woodpecker.

SHUTTLEWORTH COLLECTION [B2] A Spitfire, a De Havilland Moth and a Sopwith Pup are among historic aircraft on show at Old Warden Aerodrome. At nearby **Old Warden Park** is a 19th-century Swiss Garden with a fernery and grotto.

WICKEN FEN [F5] One of the few fens that remains undrained, Wicken Fen is now a nature reserve ❧. Today, water is pumped in to keep the fen waterlogged so that marshland plants, such as hemp agrimony, marsh fern and great fen sedge can survive.

WILLINGTON [B2] A distinctive 16th-century **dovecote** and **stables** ❧ are all that remain of a mansion built by Cardinal Wolsey's Master of the Horse, Sir John Gostwick.

WIMPOLE HALL [D3] This imposing 17th-century mansion ❧ is set in a park landscaped by Humphry Repton and 'Capability' Brown. Rare breeds of cattle, pigs and sheep are housed in a 1790s model farm.

The Dove and Waveney valleys and the Suffolk coast

ALDEBURGH [H3] Among devotees of this fishing village and resort with a half-timbered Tudor moot hall were the writers Wilkie Collins and George Meredith. The village's music festival was founded in 1948 by Peter Pears and Benjamin Britten, who are buried in the churchyard of the 15th-century **Church of St Peter and St Paul**.

BLYTHBURGH [H5] Holy Trinity Church, one of the finest in Suffolk, dates from the 15th century when the village was a busy port. Its tie-beam roof is jointed without a single nail.

BURY ST EDMUNDS [B4] Norman Britain's first planned town was laid out round a Benedictine **abbey**. The abbey once housed the shrine of St Edmund, the last East Anglian king. A park surrounds the abbey ruins ✠. The **Theatre Royal** ✹ is one of only three Georgian playhouses in England and 12th-century **Moyse's Hall** is East Anglia's oldest secular building. *The Nutshell* is Britain's smallest pub.

DUNWICH [H5] Most of this former Roman and medieval port, which once had a bishop's palace and nine churches, lies under the sea. In 1326 waves engulfed 400 houses, by 1677 the sea had risen to the marketplace and in the 1920s **All Saints' Church** crumbled with the cliffs.

EYE [D5] Settled round its castle hill, the town once lay amid marshes – Eye comes from the Saxon for island. The tower of the **Church of St Peter and St Paul** has good 15th-century stone and flint decoration.

FRAMLINGHAM [F4] The high walls and 13 towers of the **castle** ✠ rise above the town. **St Michael's Church** has the tombs of Henry Fitzroy, the bastard son of Henry VIII, and the 3rd and 4th dukes of Norfolk.

HADLEIGH [C2] The medieval and Georgian buildings of this former wool-trading town have walls with traditional Suffolk colour-washes and decorative plasterwork, or pargeting. Notable buildings include the 15th-century **Guildhall** and **St Mary's Church**, which contains a handsome organ case, brasses and memorials.

HALESWORTH [G5] The small market town grew up after the Blyth was made navigable to barges in 1756. The botanist Sir Joseph Dalton Hooker, who succeeded his father as director of Kew Gardens, was born in Halesworth in 1817.

HOXNE [E5] Goldbrook Bridge, off the B1118, is said to bear the curse of St Edmund – he hid below it to elude the Danes, but was betrayed by his glinting spurs. A stone cross marks the supposed place of his execution.

ICKWORTH HOUSE [A4] Frederick Hervey, 4th Earl of Bristol, never lived to see his house-cum-gallery ✹ finished. The 30m (100ft) high rotunda holds the art collection.

IPSWICH [E2] A busy port at the head of the Orwell estuary, Ipswich is a thriving commercial and shopping centre. It has 12 medieval churches, the Tudor **Ancient House** with ornate 17th-century plasterwork and the **Christchurch Mansion,** dating from 1548, which is now a museum.

LAXFIELD [F5] The village's many thatched and timbered buildings include the **guildhall** of 1461. In the **church** is a memorial to the 17th-century Puritan William Dowsing, born here. He smashed ornaments in some 150 Suffolk churches, but dealt leniently with his birthplace.

LAVENHAM [B2] The town's blue cloth stamped with a fleur-de-lys was famous in medieval times, but the trade was declining when the half-timbered Tudor **guildhall** ✹ was built in 1528–9. Its display of 700 years of the medieval woollen cloth trade is unique. The splendid **church** has a stone and flintwork tower.

LONG MELFORD [B2] Wool merchants built the affluent village in the 1490s. Flanking the high street are the lawns of **Melford Hall** ✹, a turreted Tudor mansion, where Beatrix Potter, the children's author, often stayed. Another Tudor mansion, **Kentwell Hall**, is approached by a 1 mile long avenue of limes.

MINSMERE [H4] In the freshwater marsh and heathland adjoining **Dunwich Heath** ✹ is an **RSPB** reserve. Birds such as avocets, bitterns and nightjars breed here.

NEEDHAM MARKET [D3] Houses dating from the 13th century line the high street. **St John the Baptist Church** has a magnificent double hammerbeam roof – lacking cross beams, it resembles the interior of a ship's hull.

ORFORD [G2] The well-preserved keep of the 12th-century **castle** ✠ has 18 irregular sides. From the top there are good views of the quay and the marshes at Orford Ness. Oysters are farmed around Butley, nearby.

ORFORD NESS [G2] The Ore estuary and the Alde flow beside the sea for about 10 miles, behind a shingle spit. A ferry runs to the headland (partly ✹) at limited times. Wildfowl and waders such as avocets breed in the Havergate Island reserve (**RSPB**, permits only).

SNAPE [G3] Newton Garrett, who had a malt business at this River Alde port from 1841, was the father of Elizabeth Garrett Anderson, Britain's first woman doctor. The annual Aldeburgh Festival is held at **The Maltings**, once a barley store.

SOUTHWOLD [H5] The resort has its own brewery, as well as pastel pink and blue cottages, jaunty beach huts and a lighthouse of 1890. The 15th-century Perpendicular **Church of St Edmund**, has Southwold Jack, a wooden soldier who strikes a bell at the start of each service.

STOWMARKET [C3] The Gipping navigation link to Ipswich in 1973 brought industry to the town which had long been a trading centre. There is an open-air **Museum of East Anglian Life**.

SUDBURY [B2] Half-timbered 19th-century houses are reminders of the town's prosperous days of silk weaving. Thomas Gainsborough, the artist, was born here – his house is now a **museum**.

SUTTON HOO [F2] A visitor centre tells the story of the Anglo Saxon ship burial ✹, displaying a replica of the burial ship and some of the treasures found on site.

THORPENESS [H3] See picture.

TOURIST INFORMATION

Aldeburgh (01728) 453637
Bury St Edmunds
(01284) 764667
Ipswich (01473) 258070
Lavenham (01787) 248207
Southwold (01502) 724729
Stowmarket (01449) 676800
Sudbury (01787) 881320
Woodbridge (01394) 382240

THE GOOD PUB GUIDE

Cavendish [A2] *Bull*
(01787) 280245
Cotton [D4] *Trowel & Hammer*
(01449) 781234
Dennington [F4] *Queens Head*
(01728) 638241
Great Glemham [F4] *Crown*
(01728) 663693
Lavenham [B2] *Angel*
(01787) 247388
Rattlesden [C3] *Brewers Arms*
(01449) 736377

WALBERSWICK [H5] Across the water from Southwold, this pleasant seaside village with fine houses was a thriving 15th to 16th-century port. The ruined 15th-century **church** encloses a later building.

WOODBRIDGE [F2] The town has Georgian houses and the **Shire Hall** of 1575. The **Suffolk Horse Museum** tells the story of the Suffolk Punch.

TOURING GUIDE

Lofty dwelling
The House in the Clouds rises above **Thorpeness***, a holiday resort. The 'cottage' at the top once housed a huge tank that supplied water to the resort.*

Southern Snowdonia and the Cambrian Mountains

*Abode of eagles **Cadair Idris**, at 893m (2930ft), is the highest peak in southern Snowdonia. A path ascends its southern flank from the car park east of Tal-y-llyn lake on the A487, giving superb views of the area's rugged beauty.*

TOURIST INFORMATION

Aberdovey (01654) 767321
Aberystwyth (01970) 612125
Barmouth (01341) 280787
Dolgellau (01341) 422888
Llanidloes (01686) 412605
Llywernog Mine
  (01970) 890620
Machynlleth (01654) 702401
Tywyn (01654) 710070

THE GOOD PUB GUIDE

Aberdovey [D3] *Penhelig Arms*
(01654) 767215
Dolgellau [E5] *George III*
(01341) 422525
Tal-y-llyn [E4] *Tynycornel*
(01654) 782282

ABERDOVEY [D3] The resort (also known as Aberdyfi) lies on the mountain-backed Dyfi estuary. 'The Bells of Aberdovey', a song from the opera *Liberty Hall* by Charles Dibdin, recalls a legend of a lost town offshore, with bells ringing under the sea. To the south, is Ynslas **nature reserve** where red kites can be seen.

ABERYSTWYTH [C2] Fronted by a grand Victorian promenade, the town's harbour shelters fleets of pleasure craft. A ruined **castle** of 1277 crowns a rocky headland. On the seafront is the neo-Gothic **University College of Wales** of 1872. The **National Library of Wales** holds many Celtic manuscripts, including the 'Black Book of Carmarthen'. A cliff railway climbs to Constitution Hill.

BARMOUTH [D5] Set against the dramatic backdrop of **Cadair Idris**, Barmouth overlooks the Mawddach Estuary. At **Ty Gwyn**, a medieval **tower house**, Jasper Tudor, uncle to Henry VII, reputedly planned the overthrow of Richard III in 1485.

Ty Crwn has displays of treasures from wrecks. A steep walk leads to **Dinas Oleu**, 'fortress of light'.

CADAIR IDRIS [E5] See picture.

CORRIS [E4] In an attractive setting beneath the crags of **Cadair Idris**, the town has a **craft centre** and there are boat trips into nearby underground **caves** with reconstructed scenes from Arthurian legend.

DINAS-MAWDDWY [F5] Until 1668 this remote village at the foot of the wooded Aran peaks had its own mayor and council. The Red Robbers of Mawddwy terrorised the area, until the last was executed in 1554.

DOLGELLAU [E5] In the 19th century a minor gold rush gripped the town, and a nugget found in 1920 made wedding rings for Queen Elizabeth in 1947 and the Princess of Wales in 1981. To the north are **Precipice Walk**, with splendid views, and the ruins of the 12th-century **Cymer Abbey**.

FAIRBOURNE [D5] In 1890, flour manufacturer Sir Arthur McDougall built a horse-drawn tramway to bring in building materials. The narrow-gauge railway now takes passengers across the dunes to Porth Penrhyn.

LLANBADARN FAWR [D2] St Padarn founded a monastery here in the 6th century and the village that grew around it became Aberystwyth. The village now lies on its outskirts.

LLANIDLOES [G2] The Severn and Clywedog rivers meet at this former centre of flannel making and lead mining. John Wesley preached outside the Elizabethan timbered **market hall** in the 18th century.

LLYWERNOG MINE [E2] A former silver-lead mine is now an open-air museum where visitors can follow a **Miners' Trail** above ground and go on an underground 'cap-lamp' tour.

MACHYNLLETH [E4] At the centre of the town is an ornate **clock tower**, built in 1874 to mark the 21st

birthday of the 5th Marquess of Londonderry. Owain Glyndwr, who in 1404 led a rebellion against Henry IV, is said to have held his first parliament here; a **museum** recalls the story. The impressive **Museum of Modern Art** includes fine collections by Welsh contemporary artists and an 18th-century **mansion** holds displays on the history and legends of the Celts. To the north of the town, the **Centre for Alternative Technology** has solar and wind power demonstrations.

NANT-YR-ARIAN [E2] Red kite feeding takes place daily at the Visitor Centre in the horseshoe-shaped valley. Waymarked walks through the Rheidol Forest give superb views of Rheidol Vale, and beyond to Aberystwyth and Cardigan Bay.

PENMAENPOOL [D5] A signal box of the old Aberystwyth and Welsh Coast Railway is now an **RSPB** observatory. Curlews, redshanks, oystercatchers and shelducks may be seen on the shore.

PLYNLIMON [E2] From a distance, the chain of rolling hills rising to 752m (2467ft) appears to be one whale-backed mountain. The rivers Severn and Wye rise here. A 2 mile track leads to the summit from Eisteddfa Gurig, off the A4.

TAL-Y-BONT [D2] Lying beside the Leri, the village was a wool centre in the 18th and 19th centuries. A scenic road leads east to **Nant-y-moch Reservoir** below **Plynlimon**, with superb views of the mountain.

TYWYN [C4] A seaside resort set among sand dunes, Tywyn is also the terminus of the narrow-gauge **Talyllyn Railway**, built in 1865 and saved in the 1950s by volunteers. The steam trains climb the scenic Fathew valley to **Abergynolwyn**, a walks centre. A 7th-century tombstone in Tywyn's 11th-century church of **St Cadfan** bears an inscription believed to be the earliest example of written Welsh.

Offa's Dyke and the upper Severn Valley

ATTINGHAM PARK [F5] A modest Queen Anne house of 1701 was transformed into a neoclassical mansion ❀ with a magnificent 122m (400ft) long façade in the 1780s by the 1st Lord Berwick.

BISHOP'S CASTLE [C2] The town is named for the Norman Bishop of Hereford who built a castle here in 1085–1100; only a few stones remain. The medieval half-timbered 'House on Crutches' is now a **museum**. To the south east is Walcot Hall, a Georgian house built for Clive of India and set in an arboretum with a mile-long lake.

BOSCOBEL HOUSE [H4] In 1651, Charles II hid here after the Battle of Worcester. The 'Royal Oak' is said to be descended from an oak in which the king hid from Cromwellian troops. Nearby **White Ladies Priory ⌗** was another of his hiding places.

BRIDGNORTH [G3] Split between clifftop High Town and Low Town, on the Severn's banks, Bridgnorth is linked by the old **Cartway**, lined with cave houses until the 19th century, and a **cliff railway**. To the south is **Dudmaston**, a 17th-century house ❀ with a an important art collection, including Dutch flower paintings.

BROWN CLEE HILL [F2] The highest hill in Shropshire rises to just under 550m (1800ft) and has superb views. **Nordy Bank** is the best preserved of three Iron Age hill-forts.

BUILDWAS ABBEY [F4] The abbey ⌗ was founded in 1135 for Savignac monks, who later merged with the Cistercians.

CHURCH STRETTON [E3] Lying between **Long Mynd** and the **Stretton Hills**, the village was a spa in the 19th century. On the summit of nearby **Caer Caradoc** is an Iron Age hill-fort.

CLUN [C2] The ruined Norman **castle ⌗** bears the scars of numerous medieval conflicts. During the Civil War the townsfolk, sick of harassment by both Royalists and Roundheads, fought against both sides.

COSFORD [H4] The Royal Air Force Museum holds an impressive collection of aircraft ranging from Vulcan bombers to airliners.

GREGYNOG [A3] The Davies sisters, Gwendoline and Margaret, made their black and white Victorian mansion into an arts centre in 1919. Their art collection is now housed in the National Museum of Wales.

IRONBRIDGE & COALBROOKDALE [G4] The **Coalbrookdale Museum of Iron** is based round the blast furnace of 1709. Industrial life in the 19th century is recreated in the **Blists Hill Victorian Town**, which includes the **Jackfield Tile** and **Coalport China** museums, and shops and cottages.

KINVER EDGE [H2] Five ranges of hills, including the Cotswolds and the Malverns, can be seen from this sandstone ridge ❀. Caves carved from the rock were once dwellings.

LILLESHALL [G5] The 12th-century **abbey ⌗** was ruined during a Parliamentarian siege in the 1640s. A hill above the village has good views of the Wrekin.

LLANFYLLIN [A5] An old market town close to the meeting of the Cain and Abel rivers, its name comes from St Myllin, said to have been the first Briton to baptise by full immersion.

LONG MYND [D3] Much of the high rounded ridge (part ❀), is heather moor. A track from Church Stretton joins the 7 mile long **Port Way**, used 3500 years ago by prehistoric traders.

MONTGOMERY [B3] Perched on a craggy ridge above the town, with its timber-framed and Georgian inns and houses, are the ruins of Henry III's **castle** of 1223.

MUCH WENLOCK [F3] The market town with half-timbered buildings grew round **Wenlock Priory ⌗** – refounded in about 1080 from a 7th-century nunnery by the Mercian king Leofric, husband to Lady Godiva. The old market hall is now a museum.

NESSCLIFFE HILL COUNTRY PARK [D5] Woodland paths lead to the hill top and an Iron Age hill-fort. A 16th-century highwayman, Humphrey Kynaston, used a cave as a hideout.

NEWTOWN [A3] The 19th century Welsh flannel industry centred on Newtown. Robert Owen, pioneer of the cooperative movement, was born here; a **museum** relates his history.

POWIS CASTLE [B4] Since 1587, the **castle ❀** has been the Herbert family home. They created the splendid formal gardens in the 17th century. Lord Clive, Clive of India's son, married into the family in 1784; his family treasures are on show.

SHREWSBURY [E5] The centre of the town is in a great loop of the Severn, guarded by the medieval walls and the Norman **castle**. There are fine half-timbered Tudor houses such as the **Abbot's House** of around 1457.

STIPERSTONES [D3] The ridge's jagged 536m (1759ft) summit is the result of shattering by frost at the last

TOURIST INFORMATION

Bishop's Castle (01588) 638467
Church Stretton (01694) 723133
Ironbridge (01952) 884391
Shrewsbury (01743) 281200
Telford (01952) 238008
Welshpool (01938) 552043

THE GOOD PUB GUIDE

Bishop's Castle [C2] *Three Tuns* (01588) 638797
Bridges [D3] *Horseshoe* (01588) 650260
Bridgnorth [G3] *Lion O'Morfe* (01746) 710678
Bromfield [E1] *Cookhouse* (01584) 856565
Cressage [F4] *Cholmondeley Riverside* (01952) 510900
Hopton Wafers [F1] *Crown* (01299) 270372
Ironbridge [G4] *Malthouse* (01952) 433712
Shrewsbury [E5] *Armoury* (01743) 340525
Wentnor [D3] *Crown Inn* (01588) 650613
Wistanstow [D2] *Plough* (01588) 673251

Ice Age. Witches are said to gather here, and one rocky outcrop is called **The Devil's Chair**.

STOKESAY CASTLE [D2] An almost intact fortified manor house ⌗, Stokesay was built around 1290 by Lawrence of Ludlow, a wool trader. Just north, the grass-roofed Secret Hills Discovery Centre has displays on local nature and culture.

TELFORD [G4] The town is named after the engineer Thomas Telford, who was Shropshire's County Surveyor. The ironmaster Abraham Darby the first lived at 16th-century **Madeley Court**, now a hotel.

TITTERSTONE CLEE HILL [F1] The pitted hilltop is the result of medieval coal digging and modern quarrying for black basalt. The view includes the Malvern Hills and the Welsh uplands.

TONG [H4] Charles Dickens used the churchyard as the model for Little Nell's resting place in *The Old Curiosity Shop*. The **Great Bell of Tong**, first cast in 1518, weighs 2 tons.

WELSHPOOL [B4] For more than 700 years, a market has been held here. The town's cockpit dates from the 1700s and was in use until 1849.

WENLOCK EDGE [E2/3] The limestone ridge was a coral reef in a tropical sea 420 million years ago.

THE WREKIN [F4] A hump of volcanic lava 900 million years old has earthworks on its summit made by the last tribe to resist the Romans.

An iron legacy Spanning the Severn gorge at **Ironbridge** *is the world's first large cast-iron bridge* ⌗, *built by Abraham Darby III in 1779. It is a symbol of the town's key role in pioneering the mass production of iron.*

TOURING GUIDE

Birmingham and the West Midlands

Ancient woodland *Mature oak, ash and lime trees surround long-disused slate quarries in Swithland Wood, part of Charnwood Forest. The elusive lesser spotted woodpecker may be found here.*

TOURIST INFORMATION

Ashby-de-la-Zouch
 (01530) 411767
Birmingham (0121) 2022 5099
Bosworth Battlefield
 (01455) 290429
Coventry (024) 7622 7264
Dudley (01384) 812830
Hinckley (01455) 635106
Lichfield (01543) 308209
Tamworth (01827) 709581
Wolverhampton
 (01902) 556110

THE GOOD PUB GUIDE

Alrewas [D5] *The Old Boat*
 (01283) 791468
Berkswell [E1] *Bear*
 (01676) 533202
Birmingham [C1] *Peacock*
 (01564) 823232
Brierley Hill [B2] *Vine*
 (01384) 78293
Coventry [F2] *Rose & Castle*
 (024) 7661 2822
Dunchurch [G1] *Dun Cow*
 (01788) 810305
Himley [A3] *Crooked House*
 (01384) 238583
Monks Kirby [G2] *Bell Inn*
 (01788) 832352
Newton Burgoland [F4]
 Belper Arms (01530) 270530
Rugby [G1] *Golden Lion*
 (01788) 832265
Sedgley [A3] *Beacon*
 (01902) 883380

ARBURY HALL [F2] George Eliot, the novelist, was born on the estate in 1819. She used the house as a model for Cheveral Manor in her *Scenes of Clerical Life*. The ornate plaster ceilings are part of an 18th-century Gothic restyling by Sir Roger Newdigate, also the founder of the Oxford poetry prize.

ASHBY-DE-LA-ZOUCH [F5] Alan la Zouch, in 1160 the Breton lord of the manor, gave his name to the town. The **Hastings Tower** of the 1470s, 24m (80ft) high, dominates the 12th-century castle ⌗. A finger pillory in **St Helen's Church** was once used on sleepy or disorderly churchgoers.

BIRMINGHAM [C2] See City Routes pp298–299.

BOSWORTH FIELD [G3] On this site in 1485 Richard III lost his throne and his life to Henry VII, the first Tudor monarch. A visitor centre has displays on the battle, and there is a trail featuring the spring where Richard took a drink before the battle.

BRADGATE PARK [H5] Enclosed long ago from **Charnwood Forest**, the park holds the ruins of **Bradgate House**, the birthplace in 1537 of Lady Jane Grey, great-niece of Henry VIII,

who in 1553 was queen for nine days after the death of Edward VI, but was then executed. **Old John**, a hilltop folly in the shape of a tankard, was built in memory of a local miller who is said to have been killed in the 1700s by a pole falling from a bonfire.

CANNOCK CHASE [C5] A remnant of a former royal hunting ground, attractive places include **Sherbrook Valley** and **Seven Springs**. There are some 28sq miles of woods and heath where fallow deer roam.

CHARNWOOD FOREST [H5] See picture. Four counties can be seen from **Beacon Hill**, 248m (814ft) high, in the 24sq mile ancient forest of heaths, woods and crags.

COALVILLE [G5] The town's former **Snibston Colliery** is now the centre of a **Discovery Park** that includes a museum of science and industry and a nature reserve.

COVENTRY [F1] Most of the city centre was reduced to rubble during the Second World War. **St Mary's Guildhall,** founded in 1342, and **Ford's Hospital** of 1509 survived, but not the medieval cathedral – its shell is now joined to the striking modern **St Michael's Cathedral**, built in

1954–62 by Sir Basil Spence. Coventry was the birthplace of the British car industry and the **Coventry Transport Museum** boasts an unrivalled collection of British cars, vehicles and bicycles. The **Herbert Art Gallery and Museum** has lively displays on the city's history.

LICHFIELD [D4] More than 100 statues embellish the west front of the 12th-century three-spired **cathedral**. The 18th-century city was noted for its literary figures, including Dr Samuel Johnson, who lived here until 1737; his birthplace in **Market Street** is now a museum. His contemporaries in the city included the actor David Garrick and the poet Anna Seward.

MERIDEN [E2] The 15th-century **cross** in the middle of the village green is said to mark the centre of England. The 18th-century **Forest Hall** is the headquarters of the Woodmen of Arden archery society, which was founded in 1785.

MOSELEY OLD HALL [B4] Behind the rich panelling of the Elizabethan house ❧ are hiding places used by Charles II after the Battle of Worcester in 1651. The garden is planted in 17th-century style, with many herbs.

SUTTON COLDFIELD [D3] The market town has medieval origins. Some 16th-century stone houses built by the town's benefactor, Bishop Vesey of Exeter, still stand. **Sutton Park** covers 4sq miles of woods, moors and lakes.

TAMWORTH [E4] King Offa of Mercia had a palace and a mint here in the 8th century. Tamworth was first fortified by Ethelfleda, Alfred the Great's daughter, in the 10th century. The **castle** has a fine **keep**, a **Great Hall** of the mid 15th century and parts of a Norman herringbone wall. Sir Robert Peel (1788–1850), MP for Tamworth and twice prime minister, lived at nearby **Drayton Manor Park**, now a theme park.

WALL [D4] Once a Roman posting station on **Watling Street**, excavations carried out in the village in the 19th century revealed one of Britain's most complete **Roman bathhouses** ⌗.

WESTON PARK [A5] English, Flemish and Italian paintings can be seen in this house of 1671, the home of the earls of Bradford. The park was laid out by Capability Brown.

WOLVERHAMPTON [B3] See City Routes pp298–299.

Leicestershire and the western fens

BOURNE [F5] Earthworks here are thought to be the remains of the 11th-century manor of Hereward the Wake, the last Saxon to resist William the Conqueror. **Grimsthorpe Castle**, of the 13th century, was remodelled by Sir John Vanbrugh in the 1720s.

BURGHLEY HOUSE [E4] Domes, pinnacles and tall chimneys crown the late-Elizabethan palace, built in 1565–87 for William Cecil, the 1st Lord Burghley. The interior includes 18 state rooms, oriental porcelain and a large private collection of Italian art.

BURTON LAZARS [C5] The Order of St Lazarus of Jerusalem built a leper hospital on a hilltop around 1160. Local spring waters were thought to be a cure for leprosy.

CROWLAND [G4] The town grew up round **Croyland Abbey**, founded in AD 716. Parts of the abbey survive in the parish **church**. In the town centre is a 14th-century triangular **bridge**.

DEENE PARK [D3] See picture.

GEDDINGTON [D2] This village has one of the three remaining **Eleanor Crosses** – put up by Edward I, one on each of the 12 places where his wife Eleanor's coffin rested on its journey from Nottinghamshire to Westminster Abbey in 1290. There is another cross at Hardingstone near Northampton.

HALLATON [C3] On Easter Monday, a market cross in the square is the centre of a robust 'ball' game which uses a small barrel rather than a ball.

KIRBY HALL [D3] Ruined and in parts roofless, the stone mansion ⌗ of the 16th and 17th centuries is noted for its rich and varied architecture, which includes Elizabethan gables and Renaissance balustrades.

LEICESTER [A4] Hosiery was the town's main industry in the 18th century. The 7th-century **St Nicholas's Church** has Roman stones in its tower, and the **Jewry Wall** ⌗ stands beside the Roman baths site; a museum in the wall relates its history. Leicester's fine old buildings include the **guildhall** of 1390 and two historic 16th-century houses, **Wygston's Chantry House** and **Skeffington House**, now part of the **Newarke Houses Museum**. An outstanding planetarium is the highlight of the **National Space Science Centre** which has high-tech displays. To the west of the town is **Kirby Muxloe Castle** ⌗, a 15th-century brick manor house.

LITTLE DALBY [C5] A housekeeper at **Little Dalby Hall** is said to have invented Stilton cheese in 1720. A farmer's wife sent some to her brother-in-law, the landlord of the *Bell* at Stilton in Huntingdonshire; after that, its fame spread far and wide.

LYDDINGTON [D3] **Bede House** ⌗, with mullioned windows and a fine oak ceiling, was built in the 15th century for the bishops of Lincoln.

MARKET DEEPING [F5] The early 14th-century rectory in this old coaching town is England's oldest inhabited parsonage. There are some fine 18th-century ironstone houses in the town centre.

MARKET HARBOROUGH [B2] There has been a market here since 1202. From the market place, the 14th-century spire of the **Church of St Dionysius** soars to 49m (161ft). The half-timbered **Old Grammar School**, built in 1614, is set on wooden pillars that once sheltered a butter market.

MELTON MOWBRAY [C5] The town is renowned for Stilton cheese and pork pies. In 1837, the Marquis of Waterford and friends literally 'painted the town red', including the swan over the former *Swan Inn.* **Tumbledown Farm** is a traditional working farm with rare breeds.

OAKHAM [D4] An old Rutland town, it has an octagonal butter cross and the great hall of the 12th-century **castle** is hung with decorative horseshoes. The **Rutland County Museum** is in the former riding school of the town militia.

OUNDLE [E2] Lying in a loop of the River Nene, Oundle has narrow alleys between its 17th and 18th-century houses and inns. **Lyveden New Bield** is an abandoned Elizabethan garden lodge in the shape of a Greek cross.

PETERBOROUGH [G3] The city was built on the site of a monastery of AD 650. The 12th-century **cathedral** has a Norman nave with a painted ceiling of about 1220.

RAMSEY [H2] A richly carved 15th-century gatehouse ⌗ and an ornate oriel window are all that remain today of a Benedictine abbey, which was founded in AD 969 on island in the fens, south-east of the town.

RUSHTON [C2] The **Triangular Lodge** ⌗, in the grounds of 16th-century **Rushton Hall**, now a school, is a folly of the 1590s. All its features are divisible by three, symbolising the Holy Trinity. Britain's biggest dovecote is at nearby **Newton**.

RUTLAND WATER [D4] The lake attracts many wildfowl. Nearby is a 12th-century **church** at **Edith Weston**, named after Edward the Confessor's widow. **Normanton Church** of 1764 is now a water museum.

STAMFORD [E4] Ringed by medieval walls, the town was once a busy coaching stop and the 16th-century

George Hotel has rooms marked 'York' and 'London' for resting passengers. Well preserved buildings include the **Assembly Rooms** of 1727 and the former **theatre** of 1768. In St Martin's cemetery is the grave of Daniel Lambert, who weighed 330kg (52 stone) when he died in 1809. **Tolethorpe Hall** has Europe's finest open-air theatre in its grounds.

THORNEY [H4] Settled by monks in the 7th century, 400 years later it was a hideout of Hereward the Wake, the last Saxon to resist the Normans. The **abbey** is part of the church, and gravestones recall how the Duke of Bedford gave shelter to religious refugees in the 1600s.

TOURING GUIDE

Military mansion Deene Park was home to the 7th Earl of Cardigan who led the 1854 Charge of the Light Brigade at Balaclava in the Crimean War. Many of the Earl's military mementos can be seen at the house which is medieval in origin but with a mixture of Tudor and Regency styles.

The Bedford Levels and western Norfolk

TOURIST INFORMATION

Ely (01353) 662062
King's Lynn (01553) 763044

THE GOOD PUB GUIDE

Gorefield [B5] *Woodmans Cottage* (01945) 870669
King's Lynn [D2] *Tudor Rose* (01553) 762824
Larling [G2] *Angel* (01953) 717963
Mundford [E3] *Crown* (01842) 878233
Sutton Gault [B2] *Anchor* (01353) 778537
Stow Bardolph [D4] *Hare Arms* (01366) 382229

Medieval port *By the 14th century, King's Lynn had become a major port on the river Ouse and its former wealth is reflected in buildings such the Custom House, built in 1683, and St George's Guildhall of 1407.*

as Bewick's swans, and a breeding ground for black-tailed godwits and ruffs.

SWAFFHAM [F4] John Chapman, known as the 'Pedlar of Swaffham', is said to have dug up two pots of gold and used them to pay for the north aisle of the 14th-century **church**. In the marketplace, the domed **butter cross** of 1783 is topped by a statue of Ceres, the Roman goddess of agriculture. Elegant buildings in the town include the 19th-century **Corn Hall** and **Assembly Rooms**.

THETFORD [F2] The capital of East Anglia under the Danes in the 9th century, Thetford was in 1075–94 the seat of East Anglian kings and bishops. **Castle Hill's** Iron Age earthworks, and the mound of the Norman **castle**, are now part of a public park, and there are ruins of a **Cluniac priory** ✠ and the **Church of the Holy Sepulchre** ✠, both dating from the 12th century. Near **King's House** is a statue of Thomas Paine, the author of *The Rights of Man*, who was born in White Hart Street in 1737.

WELNEY WILDFOWL REFUGE [C3] Birds such as ruffs, black-tailed godwits, tufted ducks and sedge warblers breed in these wetland meadows. Frequent winter visitors include Bewick's swans and wigeons.

WISBECH [B5] At the centre of a flower and fruit-growing area, this old port on the River Nene is 11 miles inland. It has Georgian houses built during its trading heyday. **Peckover House** ✿, built in about 1722, has a fine Victorian garden. Octavia Hill, one of the founders of the National Trust, was born in the town in 1838; a museum has displays on her life.

CASTLE ACRE [F5] Set in a wooded valley, the village has the ruins of a **priory** founded in 1090. On a green mound are the flint remains of an 11th-century **castle** ✠ built by William de Warenne, William the Conqueror's son-in-law.

COCKLEY CLEY [E4] A camp of the Celtic Iceni tribe during the 1st century AD, the village now has a replica of an Iceni stockaded village of AD 60 – the year that Queen Boudicca led the tribe in a revolt against the Romans.

DOWNHAM MARKET [D4] During the 1760s, Lord Nelson went to school in this old market town by the Great Ouse. Nearby **Denver Sluice**, with its tower windmill, teems with sailing boats in summer.

EAST DEREHAM [G5] On the town's main street, formerly the marketplace, the **Cowper Memorial Chapel** stands on the site of the poet William Cowper's home. He died in 1800, and his tomb is in **St Nicholas's Church**. Nearby are the **Roots of Norfolk Museum** in a former workhouse at **Gressenhall**, and the ruins of an 11th-century **cathedral** and **bishop's palace** ✠ at **North Elmham**.

EAST WRETHAM HEATH [G2] The sandy heaths and reed-fringed meres of true Breckland landscape can still

be seen here. Roe deer, badgers, adders, common lizards, wildfowl and birds of prey are among the wildlife sheltered by a ½ sq mile nature reserve.

ELY [C1] When St Etheldreda founded a monastery at Ely in AD 673, it was an island – Eel Island – set amid marshy wilderness. After 1066 the Anglo-Saxon folk hero Hereward the Wake retreated here. The **cathedral** was built on the highest point of the island in 1083, but its lantern tower

Chequered guildhall *On show in the vaulted undercroft beneath the Trinity Guildhall in King's Lynn is the 14th-century King John Cup.*

was added later. Supported by eight massive oak beams, the tower lets a stream of light into its 76m (248ft) long nave. Inside the cathedral is a stained-glass museum. Many of Ely's finest buildings are near the cathedral close; the 14th-century **Ely Porta** (gatehouse) was once the main entrance to the abbey.

KING'S LYNN [D5] See pictures.

OXBURGH HALL [E4] Henry VII is said to have stayed at this moated Tudor manor house ✿ – in the King's Chamber of the 25m (80ft) high gatehouse of 1482. In a former bedroom is embroidery work by Mary, Queen of Scots.

OUSE WASHES [B2] A strip of water meadows and ditches ½ mile wide and stretching 20 miles forms the Washes, which were created by fen drainage in the 17th century. Cornelius Vermuyden, a Dutch land reclamation engineer employed by the Earl of Bedford, straightened and embanked the Bedford rivers to contain winter flooding on the land between. The area is now a nature reserve for wintering wildfowl, such

Norwich and the Norfolk Broads

ACLE [D5] Central Norfolk's rolling country meets the flatlands of the coast here. Nearby is **Stacey Arms Windpump**, built in 1883 to pump water off the low-lying land.

BAWBURGH [B4] Pilgrims came to the village, until the 16th-century Reformation, to benefit from the healing properties claimed for **St Walstan's Well**. This was said to have sprung up where Walstan, a farm labourer, was buried in 1016. The church of **St Walstan and St Mary** now stands by the well.

BECCLES [D3] Much of the quaint riverside town was rebuilt in red brick in the 1700s after a fire. Surviving buildings include the 14th-century **church** and **Roos Hall**, home of Sir John Suckling, Lord Nelson's ancestor.

BREYDON WATER [E4] Widgeons and lapwings winter at the estuary. On the southern shore, the Roman keep of **Burgh Castle** ⌗ dates from AD 300. The seven-storey **Berney Arms** ⌗ nearby is one of the tallest windmills that once drained the marshes.

THE BROADS [D5] See picture.

Messing about in boats
A network of 200 miles of linked waterways, the **Broads** *were produced by medieval peat digging. In summer the winding rivers are packed with boats.*

BUNGAY [C2] Only a twin-towered gatehouse of 1294 remains from **Bungay Castle**, a stronghold of the Bigod family, who were once the earls of Norfolk. Near the **Butter Cross** of 1689 in the marketplace is a weather vane in the shape of Old Shuck, a monstrous dog that was once said to haunt the area.

CAISTER-ON-SEA [E5] Roman walls and the **town gate** of about AD 125 have been excavated ⌗. The moated ruins of 15th-century **Caister Castle** have a 30m (98ft) tower; a museum in the grounds displays vintage cars.

CAISTOR ST EDMUND [B4] After crushing Queen Boudicca's revolt, the Romans built Venta Icenorum, today Caistor St Edmund, in AD 70 as the capital for her Iceni tribe. **St Edmund's Church** has some Roman bricks in its walls and porch, and a 15th-century carved font.

COVEHITHE [E2] Its tower a sailors' landmark, the ruined **St Andrew's Church** stands on the cliffs. In 1672, a thatched church was built inside the medieval shell. For centuries the cliffs have been slowly crumbling into the sea; a house on the cliffs to the south had to be abandoned in 1990.

DISS [A2] Clustered round a large mere, or lake, the town is a mix of 16th–19th-century buildings dominated by the Norman tower of **St Mary's Church**. At Bressingham nearby the steam museum has the locomotive *Royal Scot*.

EARSHAM [C2] One of the world's largest collections of otters can be seen at the **Otter Trust**, in natural riverside enclosures in the wooded Waveney valley. Otters are bred here for reintroduction to the wild.

GREAT YARMOUTH [E4] The port flourished for 1000 years before Victorian fervour for the seaside made it a busy resort. **South Quay** has two fine 17th-century merchants' houses ⌗, and an **Elizabethan house** ❀ is a museum of 16th to 19th-century domestic life. Anna Sewell, author of *Black Beauty*, was born here in 1820.

LOWESTOFT [E3] The UK's most easterly port has an award-winning beach. The inner harbour divides the town and brings ships into its heart. Narrow lanes, called 'Scores', radiate from the old town's historic High Street. A transport museum displays restored vehicles and features a reconstructed 1930s street scene. Nearby **Oulton Broad** is a yachting and powerboat centre.

NORWICH [B4] By AD 850 Norwich was trading with the Rhineland and in 1066 it was one of England's largest cities. At **Tombland**, its Saxon heart, is the **cathedral**, begun in 1096 by the Normans. Its 15th-century spire is, at 96m (315ft), England's second highest after Salisbury. Near the south door is the tomb of Nurse Edith Cavell, who was executed by the Germans in 1915. Nearby **Elm Hill** is a preserved medieval street. The **castle keep**, originally Norman, houses the regional museum and includes paintings by the Norwich School. On the **University of East Anglia campus** stands the 1978 **Sainsbury Centre**, designed by Sir Norman Foster, with displays of ethnic and modern art, and **Earlham Hall**, home of Elizabeth Fry, the 19th-century prison reformer.

RANWORTH [D5] St Helen's Church has an exquisite 500-year-old painted screen and wide views from its tower.

TOURIST INFORMATION

Beccles (01502) 713196
Diss (01379) 650523
Great Yarmouth
   (01493) 842195
Lowestoft (01502) 533600
Norwich (01603) 727927

THE GOOD PUB GUIDE

Bawburgh [B4] *Kings Head*
   (01603) 744977
Norwich [B4] *Adam & Eve*
   (01603) 667423
Reedham [D4] *Railway Tavern*
   (01493) 700340
Tivetshall St Mary [B2]
   Old Ram (01379) 676794
Woodbastwick [C5] *Fur & Feather* (01603) 720003

ST BENET'S ABBEY [D5] Little of this 9th-century Benedictine abbey is left except its gatehouse, which has a derelict 18th-century windpump built into it. The Bishop of Norwich arrives by wherry (boat) once a year to conduct a service at the abbey.

WESTON LONGVILLE [A5] In the village **church** is a portrait of James Woodforde, rector in 1776–1803. He kept a journal full of domestic detail in 1758–1802, published in 1924–31 as *The Diary of a Country Parson*. It records dinners that began with such delicacies as calf's head and roast swan. The pond where the rector hid smuggled gin still survives.

WYMONDHAM [A4] At the centre of the town is a 17th-century market cross with a raised octagonal chamber which was once the courthouse. The **abbey church** is unusual in having a tower at each end – in 1349 the Pope had it split in two because it was so bitterly claimed by both townsfolk and monks. The choir and octagonal tower went to the monks and the nave and north aisle to the townsfolk, who built the square tower about 1450. A former prison houses the **Heritage Museum**, with displays on prison life in past times.

TOURING GUIDE

Snowdonia and the Lleyn Peninsula

BARDSEY ISLAND [A1] Separated from the Lleyn Peninsula by a treacherous strait, Bardsey has been a place of pilgrimage and religious retreat since the 4th century AD.

BEDDGELERT [F4] The name of the village was long believed to mean 'grave of Gelert', referring to a dog killed by Llywelyn the Great – but the tale was made up, to win trade, by an 18th-century innkeeper. The 18th–19th-century **Sygun Copper Mine** is to the north-east.

BETWS-Y-COED [H5] The village lies in a glen where the rivers Llugwy, Lledr and Conwy meet. To the west, the **Swallow Falls** cascade down the Llugwy. South of the village is Thomas Telford's iron bridge of 1815.

BLAENAU FFESTINIOG [G4] Jagged slate quarries scar the mountains ringing the town. At the 19th-century **Llechwedd Slate Caverns** visitors can take a tram through the chambers or travel down to a deep mine.

CAERNARFON [E5] The old town clusters below the **castle (Cadw)**, begun in 1283 as a fortress and palace for Edward I. At the **Roman Segontium fort (Cadw)**, 1000 troops were stationed from the 1st to 4th centuries AD. **Air World** has a collection of aeroplanes and helicopters and the **Inigo Jones Slateworks**, established in 1861, is now a museum.

CAPEL CURIG [G5] Ringed by mountains, the village is at the meeting place of the rivers Ogwen and Nantgwryd. It is an angling centre and a base for Snowdonia.

CLYNNOG-FAWR [D4] A village of whitewashed houses, it was once on the pilgrimage route to Bardsey Island. The beautiful church was founded by St Beuno in the 7th century. **St Beuno's Well** is said to have curative powers.

COED-Y-BRENIN [G2] The name means 'The King's Forest', in honour of the Silver Jubilee of George V in 1935. It shelters otters, polecats and fallow deer. Forest trails lead to waterfalls, rapids and viewpoints.

CRICCIETH [E3] A ruined **castle** sits on the headland giving fine views over Cardigan Bay; it was built by Llywelyn the Great about 1230, taken by the English in 1283 and sacked by Owain Glyndwr in 1404.

DOLBADARN CASTLE [F5] Set high above the Llanberis Pass, the **castle (Cadw)** has a 13th-century keep built by Llywelyn the Great. From 1255 until around 1275 it was the prison of Owain Goch, the brother and rival of Llywelyn ap Gruffydd.

DOLWYDDELAN CASTLE [G4] Astride a crag above the Lledr valley is the tower of the 12th-century **castle (Cadw)**. Llywelyn the Great may have been born there in 1173.

HARLECH [F2] Set on a vast rock, **Harlech Castle** was built in 1283–9 for Edward I. In 1404 Harlech was taken by Owain Glyndwr, who made the town his capital until the English took it back in 1409. The longest siege lasted from 1461–68 with the Yorkists victorious over the Lancastrians – an event said to have inspired the song 'Men of Harlech'.

LLANBEDR [F2] Grey stone, slate-roofed houses lie below the craggy slopes of **Rhinog Fawr**. The remote **Roman Steps** were probably a medieval packhorse route.

LLANBERIS [F5] The village is a base for the ascent of **Snowdon**, on the **Mountain Railway** or on foot. For 160 years slate was mined at Dinorwic quarry, now the **Welsh Slate Museum**. There are tours of **Dinorwic Pumped Storage Station**, set deep in the mountains. The **Llanberis Lake Railway** has steam trips by the shore of Llyn Padarn.

LLANRWST [H5] A 17th-century stone bridge, attributed to Inigo Jones, spans the River Conwy. Llywelyn the Great, who died in 1240, may lie in a stone coffin in the church. **Gwydir Uchaf Chapel (Cadw)** is noted for its 17th-century painted ceiling. Nearby, at **Trefriw**, is a working woollen mill.

LLANYSTUMDWY [E3] David Lloyd George grew up at Highgate Cottage. In the **Lloyd George Museum** there is a 'talking head' of the MP reciting his most rousing speeches. To the north-west at Llangybi is **St Cybi's Well** (also known as Fynnon Gybi), which is thought to have healing properties.

MYNYDD MAWR [A2] There are spectacular views from this headland between the cliffs of **Braich y Pwll** and **Pen y Cil**. **Porth Oer** bay is also known as Whistling Sands.

PLAS-YN-RHIW [B2] A small medieval manor house with Tudor and Georgian additions, it was owned by the Misses Keating, who from 1938–66 rescued much of the old estate. The gardens overlook **Porth Neigwl**, or Hell's Mouth, where ships were often driven ashore during gales.

PORTHMADOG [F3] The resort was once a port exporting slate from the quarries at Blaenau Ffestiniog. The narrow-gauge **Ffestiniog Railway**, built in 1811 by local MP William Madocks, now carries tourists on a scenic run high above the estuary. Trains also run on the restored West Highland Railway.

TOURIST INFORMATION

Betws-y-coed (01690) 710426
Blaenau Ffestiniog
  (01766) 830360
Caernarfon (01286) 672232
Harlech (01766) 780658
Llanberis (01286) 870765
Porthmadog (01766) 512981
Portmeirion (01766) 770000
Pwllheli (01758) 613000

THE GOOD PUB GUIDE

Abersoch [C2] *St Tudwal's Inn*
(01758) 712539
Betwys-y-coed [H5] *Ty Gwyn*
(01690) 710383
Porthmadog [F3] *Ship*
(01766) 512990

PORTMEIRION [F3] See picture.

PWLLHELI [D2] Sandy beaches stretch on each side of the almost landlocked harbour. The oldest part of the town, with canopied Victorian shops, is set back from the seafront. **Plas Glyn-Y-Weddw**, a Victorian Gothic mansion, houses a fine gallery.

SNOWDON [F4] Six walkers' tracks and the **Snowdon Mountain Railway**, opened in 1896, lead to the summit, with fine views. Arctic alpine plants, including the rare Snowdon lily, thrive on the slopes.

TOMEN-Y-MUR [G3] Close by Sarn Helen – the main Roman north-south road in west Wales – is the site of a **Roman fort** of the 1st–2nd centuries AD. The fort had a bathhouse, parade ground and an amphitheatre.

TREMADOG [F3] The birthplace in 1888 of T.E. Lawrence, or Lawrence of Arabia, the town was built in the early 19th century by the local MP, William Madocks. He intended it as a stop on a London-Dublin route that never materialised.

TRE'R CEIRI [D3] An Iron Age hill fort perched at almost 488m (1600ft) offers views of Snowdonia, Anglesey and Ireland. Occupied in the 2nd–4th centuries AD, the fort has 150 stone huts ringed by a wall 4m (13ft) high and 4.5m (15ft) thick in places.

TY MAWR [H4] Bishop William Morgan, who first translated the Bible into Welsh, was born in this picturesque stone house in the secluded Wybrnant valley in about 1541. **Penmachno Church** nearby has a collection of early Christian inscribed stones.

*Fantasy world An eccentric village in a riot of contrasting styles, **Portmeirion** was designed in the 1920s by Clough Williams-Ellis as a living exhibition of architecture.*

North-east Wales and western Cheshire

Victorian waterway *The* **Llangollen Canal** *runs for 41 miles from Nantwich to Llangollen, flowing along aqueducts built by Thomas Telford and William Jessup.*

PISTYLL RHAEADR [C2] The highest waterfall in England and Wales drops 73m (240ft) to a deep pool.

PONT-CYSYLLTE [E3] The 19-arched aqueduct – Britain's longest – was built by Thomas Telford in 1805.

RUTHIN [D5] The town grew up round the Norman castle. **St Peter's Square** contains the **Old Court House** of 1401 and **Exmewe Hall** of 1500. Beside the hall is the **Maen Huail stone**, where King Arthur is said to have beheaded Huail, a rival in love. **St Peter's Church** has 400 carved oak panels, given by Henry VII.

WEM [H2] Judge Jeffreys of the 17th-century Bloody Assizes bought the town in 1604 for £9000. **Hazlitt House** was the boyhood home of the essayist and critic William Hazlitt.

WHITCHURCH [H3] Sir Edward German, composer of the operetta *Merrie England*, was born in this border town in 1862. **St Alkmund's Church**, built in 1713, replaced a church that collapsed in 1711. Not very far away, at Hodnet, is a traditional rocking-horse workshop.

WHITTINGTON [F2] A moat, two towers and a gatehouse remain of the 13th-century **castle**. In 1371, Dick Whittington, who was Lord Mayor of London three times, is said to have left the village to seek his fortune.

WREXHAM [F4] In this industrial and market town just within the Welsh border is the 15th-century **St Giles's Church**, with a 41m (136ft) pinnacled tower. The churchyard gates are the work of the local ironmasters John and Robert Davies in 1720. **Bersham Ironworks Museum**, once their home, is west of the town.

BALA [B3] A major religious centre in the 18th century, Bala's leading figure was the Rev Thomas Charles, a champion of Welsh Methodism and the Sunday School movement. The **Bala Lake Railway** affords spectacular vistas of the lake and surrounding mountains from open-top carriages.

BEESTON CASTLE [H5] Built about 1220 by Ranulf, Earl of Chester, the ruined **castle** ⚑ stands on a 152m (500ft) high crag.

CHIRK [E3] The village grew up round an 11th-century castle, of which only a small mound is left. **Chirk Castle** ⚘ to the west dates from 1310. Previous owners include Robert Dudley, a favourite of Elizabeth I. Since 1525 it has been home to the Myddletons; its interiors reflect 400 years of decorative styles.

CORWEN [C3] Owain Glyndwr gathered his forces here before the Battle of Shrewsbury in 1403. Nearby **Rug Chapel (Cadw)** of 1637 has a fine painted roof and friezes. In **Llangar**

Church (Cadw), to the south, there are elaborate 14th–18th century wall paintings.

ERDDIG [F4] The 17th-century **mansion** ⚘ still has its domestic and estate buildings and many furnishings. In the gardens are 18th-century fruit trees, such as Orange Apricock.

GRESFORD [F4] The pure peal of the bells from the village **church** is often described as being one of the Seven Wonders of Wales. A yew tree in the churchyard is believed to be about 1,400 years old.

LAKE VYRNWY [B1] Overlooked by a Gothic tower, the dark lake was created in the 1880s from the river Vyrnwy and eight tributaries to provide water for Liverpool. When the water level is low, you can see the remains of the original village.

LLANARMON DYFFRYN CEIRIOG [D2] John Hughes, who wrote the song 'Men of Harlech', was born in the village in 1832. At nearby **Glyn**

Ceiriog there is a Memorial Institute to him. The **Chwarel Wynne** slate mine and quarries can be visited.

LLANGOLLEN [E3] The spectacular **Horseshoe Weir** was built in 1801 by Thomas Telford to supply water to the **Llangollen Canal**. The hilltop ruins of **Castell Dinas Bran**, built in the mid 13th century, look across to **Plas Newydd**. From 1780–1829 it was home to the 'Ladies of Llangollen' – Lady Eleanor Butler and the Hon Sarah Ponsonby, who entertained guests such as Sir Walter Scott and the Duke of Wellington. Steam and diesel trains on the **Llangollen Railway** run to the village of Carrog on the Dee. To the north are the ruins of **Valle Crucis Abbey (Cadw)**, founded in 1201.

OSWESTRY [E2] The town is named after Oswald, King of Northumbria, who was defeated here by King Penda of Mercia in AD 642 and crucified on 'Oswald's Tree'. **Old Oswestry** ⚑ is an Iron Age hill fort of 300 BC. The Cambrian Railway Museum is a delight for steam engines enthusiasts.

Stoke-on-Trent and the Potteries

Valley spa town *Matlock Bath became popular during the 17th century for its warm springs. The 1910 Pavilion housed the Pump Room when the town was a spa – it is now the Peak District Mining Museum.*

ARBOR LOW [G5] Nearly 50 stones lying flat and each weighing around 8 tonnes, form a circle ✿ more than 4000 years old. The site may have been used for religious rites.

ASHBOURNE [G4] This market town at the edge of the Peak District was the model for 'Oakbourne' in George Eliot's 1859 novel *Adam Bede*. Every Shrovetide, a football game with the goals set 3 miles apart is played here.

BURTON UPON TRENT [G1] Known for brewing since medieval times, the town benefited from the high gypsum content of the local water. The **Museum of Brewing** tells its history; Bass began brewing here in 1777.

CREWE [B5] For about 100 years from 1837, Crewe was one of the world's biggest railway junctions. **The Railway Age** collection, with diesel and steam engines, tells the story.

DOVEDALE [F4] A tree-clad gorge of the Dove with fantastic limestone rock shapes whose imaginative names

include **Dovedale Castle**, the **Twelve Apostles** and **Lion's Head Rock**.

KEDLESTON HALL [H3] A grand neoclassical mansion ❧ built in 1759–65, the hall was the first great work of Robert Adam. It has England's most complete Adam interiors, and an Indian collection by Lord Curzon, Viceroy of India in 1898–1905.

LEEK [E5] A silk-weaving centre in the 17th–19th centuries, the town is on the edge of the Dark Peaks. Nearby at Upper Hulme rise **The Roaches** and **Hen Cloud**. **Brindley Mill** of 1752 was built by Leek millwright James Brindley, who in the 1760s built the Bridgewater Canal, the first canal in Britain.

LITTLE MORETON HALL [C5] A medieval moated manor house, the delightful half-timbered **hall** ❧ has leaded windows, a 21m (68ft) long gallery and the **Tudor Knot Garden**. Nearby is **Mow Cop** ❧, a 333m (1091ft) high hill topped by a 1750s castle folly, built as a summerhouse.

MATLOCK [H5] Split into two parts – **Matlock Bridge**, by the stone river bridge, has emerged from the original village, and **Matlock Bank**, on the hill above, the town developed round tepid springs in the 19th century. Their popularity peaked after 1853, when John Smedley opened a hydropathic treatment centre.

MATLOCK BATH [H5] See picture (left).

NANTWICH [A4] This old salt town is rich in timber-framed buildings. The 14th-century **St Mary's Church** is a rare survivor of a great fire of 1583. The herbalist John Gerard was born in the town in 1545.

REPTON [H2] In the 7th century the town was the capital of South Mercia, and there are 9th-century carvings in the crypt of **St Wystan's Church**. Repton public school was founded in 1557; its gateway once belonged to a 12th-century priory.

SHUGBOROUGH [E1] The seat of the earls of Lichfield since 1624, the estate ❧ includes a mansion of 1693 with an Ionic portico of the 18th century, and a stable block housing the **County Museum.** In the grounds, neoclassical monuments include the **Triumphal Arch** and **Tower of the Winds**; the 1805 farm is a working farm museum.

STAFFORD [D1] In the 18th century this county town thrived as a shoe-making centre. The **High House** of 1595 is one of England's largest timber-framed town houses. The author Izaak Walton, who wrote *The Compleat Angler*, was born in Stafford in 1593. The playwright Richard Brinsley Sheridan, MP from 1780–1806, lived at **Chetwynd House**, now the main post office.

STOKE-ON-TRENT [D4] The six Potteries towns merged to form this city in 1910. The Wedgwood, Davenport, Spode, Copeland and Minton firms began in the 18th century. Visitor centres include **Spode** and **Wedgwood,** and the **Gladstone Pottery** which has 19th-century bottle kilns. Arnold Bennett, born in Hanley in 1867, based many of his novels, such as *Clayhanger*, in The Potteries.

SUDBURY HALL [G2] Carving by Grinling Gibbons and a staircase with rich plasterwork can be seen in this 17th-century house ❧. It also has a **Museum of Childhood** with chimney climbs for adventurous children.

TUTBURY [G2] Glass-making has been the village livelihood for more than 200 years. Mary, Queen of Scots, was a prisoner in the ruined castle in 1569 and 1585. The tower on top of the motte is an 18th-century folly.

TOURIST INFORMATION

Ashbourne (01335) 343666
Burton upon Trent
   (01283) 508111
Congleton (01260) 271095
Crewe/Nantwich
   (01270) 610983
Leek (01538) 483741
Market Drayton
   (01630) 652139
Matlock Bath (01629) 55082
Stafford (01785) 619619
Stoke-on-Trent (01782) 236000

THE GOOD PUB GUIDE

Ashbourne [G4] *Green Man*
   (01335) 345783
Barthomley [C4] *White Lion*
   (01270) 882242
Butterton [F5] *Black Lion*
   (01538) 304232
Eccleshall [C2] *George*
   (01785) 850300
Onecote [F4] *Jervis Arms*
   (01538) 304206
Salt [E2] *Holly Bush*
   (01889) 508234
Stafford [D1] *Moat House*
   (01785) 712217
Warslow [F5] *Greyhound*
   (01298) 84249
Weston [B4] *White Lion*
   (01270) 500303
Wrenbury [A4] *Dusty Miller*
   (01270) 780537

UTTOXETER [F2] The town has flat racing, steeplechasing, and a livestock market. Old coaching inns such as the *Old Talbot* were once stops on the London–Liverpool run.

WIRKSWORTH [H4] The town's lead merchants' houses reflect mining wealth up to the 19th century. There is a coffin lid of AD 800 in 13th-century **St Mary's Church**.

Blessing the wells *Tissington, in Derbyshire, was in 1349 the first place to record a 'well dressing'. The well is dressed with a mosaic of petals, leaves and other natural materials, pressed into shallow clay.*

Derby, Nottingham and western Lincolnshire

ATTENBOROUGH NATURE RESERVE [C2] Reedbeds and scrub round flooded gravel pits are the haunt of warblers and kestrels; common terns nest on the islands.

BELTON HOUSE [G3] Built in 1685–8, the late Restoration house ✤ has Grinling Gibbons carvings and plasterwork ceilings by Edward Goudge. The landscaped park has formal gardens and an orangery.

BELVOIR CASTLE [F2] The Gothic castle dates from 1816, when a fortress on a Norman site was remodelled by James Wyatt for the Duke of Rutland.

BESTWOOD COUNTRY PARK [C4] Once a part of **Sherwood Forest**, the park was leased to Sir John Byron in the 16th century, and in the 1680s Charles II gave it to Nell Gwyn, his mistress. Woodland glades are home to birds such as green woodpeckers and spotted flycatchers.

BOOTHBY PAGNELL [G2] This small 12th-century **manor house** (open by appointment only), in the grounds of Boothby Pagnell Hall, was built as a dwelling house for a Norman knight.

BOTTESFORD [F3] The **church** has Leicestershire's tallest spire, 64m (210ft) and a monument to the 6th earl of Rutland whose two sons, it was said, died from sorcery. This led to the 1618 'Witches of Belvoir' trial.

BOURNE WOOD [H1] A remnant of an ancient forest 7000 years old with woodland plants such as bellflowers.

BREEDON ON THE HILL [A1] The 12th-century church has a Saxon stone frieze of fantastical beasts, which may be a relic from a 7th-century monastery on the site.

CALKE ABBEY [A1] Since the death in 1924 of the last baronet, Sir Vauncey Harpur Crewe, the baroque **mansion** ✤ has been kept unchanged. The 1650s church at **Staunton Harold** ✤ is one of the few built as an act of defiance during the Commonwealth.

COLSTERWORTH [G1] Woolsthorpe Manor ✤ was the birthplace of Sir Isaac Newton (1642–1727). In **St John Baptist Church**, a sundial bears a carving by the nine-year-old Newton.

CRANWELL [H4] The **Cranwell RAF college**, finished in 1933, was the world's first military air academy. At North Rauceby, the **Aviation Heritage Centre** tells the story of the college and the history of this working base.

CRICH [A4] Beside the village is the **National Tramway Museum**. High above it is **Crich Stand**, a 291m (955ft) cliff, with a tower built in 1923 as a memorial to Sherwood Foresters killed in the First World War.

DERBY [A3] See City Routes pp292–293.

EAST STOKE [E4] In 1487, two years after the Battle of Bosworth, Lambert Simnel, who wanted to restore the House of York, engaged Henry VII outside East Stoke, and lost. A tablet in **East Stoke churchyard** remembers the four Yorkist leaders and the 7000 unnamed men killed in battle.

EASTWOOD [B4] D. H. Lawrence (1885–1930), author of *Lady Chatterley's Lover*, was born here. His book *Sons and Lovers* (1913) was based on his early years when the family lived at 28 Garden Road.

GRANTHAM [G3] The 13th-century **St Wulfram's Church** spire soars 86m (282ft) above **Grantham House** ✤. The **Royal Hotel** is one of Britain's oldest coaching inns. Former Prime Minister Baroness Thatcher was born here in 1925. Sir Isaac Newton went to the **King's School** in the 1650s.

HARDWICK HALL [B5] The mansion ✤ was built by Bess of Hardwick in the 1590s. **Stainsby Mill** ✤, 18th-century, is in the estate. Thomas Hobbes, author of *Leviathan*, is buried at **Ault Hucknall church**.

HUCKNALL [C4] Lord Byron lies in his family vault in **St Mary Magdalen's Church**. His body was brought from Greece, where he died in 1824, fighting for Greek independence.

LOUGHBOROUGH [C1] Bells have been made in the town since 1839. There is a **Bell Foundry Museum**. The **War Memorial Tower** in Queen's Park has a carillon of 47 bells.

MELBOURNE HALL [A2] An 18th-century, greystone mansion rebuilt from an earlier house, the hall has fine formal gardens. It was the home of two 19th-century prime ministers, Lord Melbourne and Lord Palmerston. Thomas Cook, the travel agent, was born in Melbourne in 1808.

NEWARK-ON-TRENT [E4] Beside the river is the Norman castle, a ruined 52m (170ft) high shell not open to the public. King John died there in 1216. In the marketplace are the 15th-century *Old White Hart* inn and the **town hall** dating from 1774–6. The actor Donald Wolfit was born in 1902 at neighbouring Balderton.

TOURIST INFORMATION

Derby (01332) 255802
Grantham (01476) 406166
Loughborough (01509) 218113
Newark-on-Trent
  (01636) 655765
Nottingham (0115) 915 5330
Nottingham-West Bridgford
  (0115) 977 3558

THE GOOD PUB GUIDE

Beeston [C3] *Victoria* (0115) 925 4049
Caunton [E5] *Caunton Beck* (01636) 636793
Derby [A3] *Olde Dolphin* (01332) 267711
Grimsthorpe [H1] *Black Horse* (01778) 591247
Hose [E2] *Rose & Crown* (01949) 860424
Kegworth [B2] *Cap & Stocking* (01509) 674814
Kimberley [B4] *Nelson & Railway* (0115) 938 2177
Loughborough [C1] *Swan in the Rushes* (01509) 217014
Melbourne [A2] *John Thompson* (01332) 862469
Upton [E4] *French Horn* (01636) 812394

NEWSTEAD ABBEY [C4] Built by Henry II in 1170 to atone for the murder of Thomas Becket, and converted into a house by Sir John Byron in 1540. Lord Byron inherited the decaying abbey in 1798. Many of his relics are still on display.

NOTTINGHAM [C3] See City Routes pp292–293.

PAPPLEWICK [C4] Six boilers and two beam engines operate at **Papplewick Pumping Station** of 1884. The village **church** has graves of 42 pauper children apprenticed at the local mill.

ROLLESTON [E4] Illustrator Kate Greenaway (1846–1901) spent part of her childhood in the village.

SHERWOOD FOREST [D5] The ancient oak wood is now a country park, with a trail to the 500-year-old **Major Oak**. Robin Hood and Maid Marian were said to have married at **St Mary's Church**, Edwinstowe.

SOUTHWELL [E4] The **Minster** dates from 1108. Its **Chapter House** has delicate stone carvings of foliage, called 'the leaves of Southwell'. Charles I gave himself up to the Scots in the *Saracen's Head* inn at the end of the Civil War in 1646.

Historic tavern Ye Olde Trip to Jerusalem, *in* **Nottingham**, *is built into the sandstone rock below the castle and dates from 1189.*

TOURING GUIDE

The Wash and west Norfolk farmlands

BOSTON [C3] **Boston Stump**, the 83m (272ft) high lantern tower of the 14th-century **St Botolph's Church**, was once a beacon for travellers in the fens and ships in The Wash. In the Middle Ages Boston became wealthy from its wool trade with Flanders. In 1630, a band of Puritans sailed from here to found Boston, Massachusetts; a museum relates the story.

BRANCASTER STAITHE [H3] A wide beach with salt marsh and sand dunes, the **staithe** ⚓ stretches for some 4 miles along the tidal foreshore. It includes the site of a Roman fort, **Branodunum**. At nearby Titchwell Marsh is a **bird sanctuary**.

CASTLE RISING [G1] 'Rising was a seaport when Lynn, it was a Marsh', goes a local rhyme – but the Babingley river silted up long ago and now the town is inland. The massive Norman **castle** ⌗ stands almost intact on high earth banks. In the 14th century, Edward III imprisoned his mother Isabella here for 30 years, after her part in the murder of his father, Edward II.

EAST KIRBY [C5] On a wartime airfield is a fine collection of Second World War aircraft including the Avro Lancaster NX611, *Just Jane*.

FISHTOFT [D3] In 1607, a group of persecuted Puritans attempted to emigrate to the Netherlands. At **The Haven**, formerly known as Scotia Creek, a memorial marks the point where they tried to set sail and were arrested after their ship's captain had betrayed them.

FREISTON SHORE [D3] Redshanks, brent geese, snow buntings and Lapland buntings are among the thousands of birds that flock to the creeks and marshes of this Wash-side hamlet, sheltered behind a sea wall.

FRISKNEY FLATS AND DECOY WOOD [E4/5] The land along Friskney Sea Lane has been reclaimed from the sea in stages. The **Decoy Wood**, with a pond where wild ducks were once netted, is a breeding site for some 40 species of birds, including goldcrests and redpolls.

GIBRALTAR POINT [F5] Some of the most extensive salt marshes in Europe border the sand-spit nature reserve at the mouth of The Wash. Birds such as ringed plovers and little terns nest on the shingle in summer. It is also home to a large population of skylarks.

HEACHAM [G3] A tablet in the church of the seaside village recalls the American Indian princess Pocahontas, who married John Rolfe of **Heacham Hall** in 1614.

HECKINGTON [A3] One of the most famous churches in Lincolnshire, **St Andrew's** was built in 1308–40 in Decorated style by the monks of **Bardney Abbey** to the north. The east window has superb flowing tracery, and among the finely carved figures on the Easter Sepulchre are those of a mermaid and a bagpiper.

HOLBEACH [D1] Reclaimed from the Wash over a period of 1300 years, the town is now one of the country's largest parishes. **All Saints' Church**

was built in the 14th century with wealth accrued from exporting wool and salt. Salterns, or salt-waste tips, are still visible.

HOUGHTON HALL [H2] The Palladian house was built by Colen Campbell in 1722–31 for Sir Robert Walpole, England's first prime minister. Furniture, china, paintings and over 20,000 model soldiers are on display to the public.

HUNSTANTON [G3] A lively resort with long sands and a promenade, it has striped cliffs – with thin layers of red chalk between layers of white chalk and brown sandstone. The **Sea Life Aquarium** here has an underwater viewing tunnel. On the cliffs are the ruins of the chapel of **St Edmund**, who is said to have landed here in AD 850.

REVESBY [C5] The village was built mainly in the late 19th century in the grounds of **Revesby Abbey**. An earlier house on the site was the home of the naturalist Sir Joseph Banks, who sailed with Captain Cook in 1768–71.

SANDRINGHAM HOUSE [G2] Bought in 1862 as part of a farming and shooting estate for Edward VII while he was Prince of Wales, the red-brick house was converted in Jacobean style in 1870, and has remained a royal residence. The house and grounds may be visited.

SLEAFORD [A4] In the square of this market town, fine buildings include the Georgian former *Bristol Arms*, the **Sessions House** of 1831 and the 12th-century **Church of St Denys**, with a spire 44m (144ft) high. The massive **Bass Maltings** of 1892–1905 is more than 305m (1000ft) long.

SPALDING [B1] Once a bulb-growing centre, Spalding lies by the South Holland fens and hosts the

TOURIST INFORMATION

Boston (01205) 356656
Hunstanton (01485) 532610
Sleaford (01529) 414294
Spalding (01775) 725468
Wisbech (01945) 583263

THE GOOD PUB GUIDE

Aswarby [A3] *Tally Ho* (01529) 455205
Brancaster Staithe [H3] *Jolly Sailors* (01485) 210314 *White Horse* (01485) 210262
Burnham Market [H3] *Hoste Arms* (01328) 738777
Coningsby [B5] *Old Lea Gate Inn* (01526) 342370
Dyke [A1] *Wishing Well* (01778) 422970
Gedney Dyke [D2] *Chequers* (01406) 362666
Snettisham [G2] *Rose & Crown* (01485) 541382
Surfleet [B2] *Mermaid* (01775) 680275
Thornham [G3] *Lifeboat* (01485) 512236
Titchwell [H3] *Manor Hotel* (01485) 210221
Woodhall Spa [B5] *Abbey Lodge* (01526) 352538

Flower parade every year on Spring Bank Holiday Saturday. It has fine Georgian houses beside the Welland. Sir Isaac Newton was a member of the Gentlemen's Society, founded in **Ayscoughfee Hall** in 1710. The hall now houses a local history museum.

TATTERSHALL [B5] The tower of the moated castle ⚓ was begun in the 1430s by Ralph Cromwell, Lord High Treasurer to Henry VI, and restored by Lord Curzon, Viceroy of India, in 1911–14. Cromwell also built Holy Trinity Church and founded **Tattershall College** ⌗.

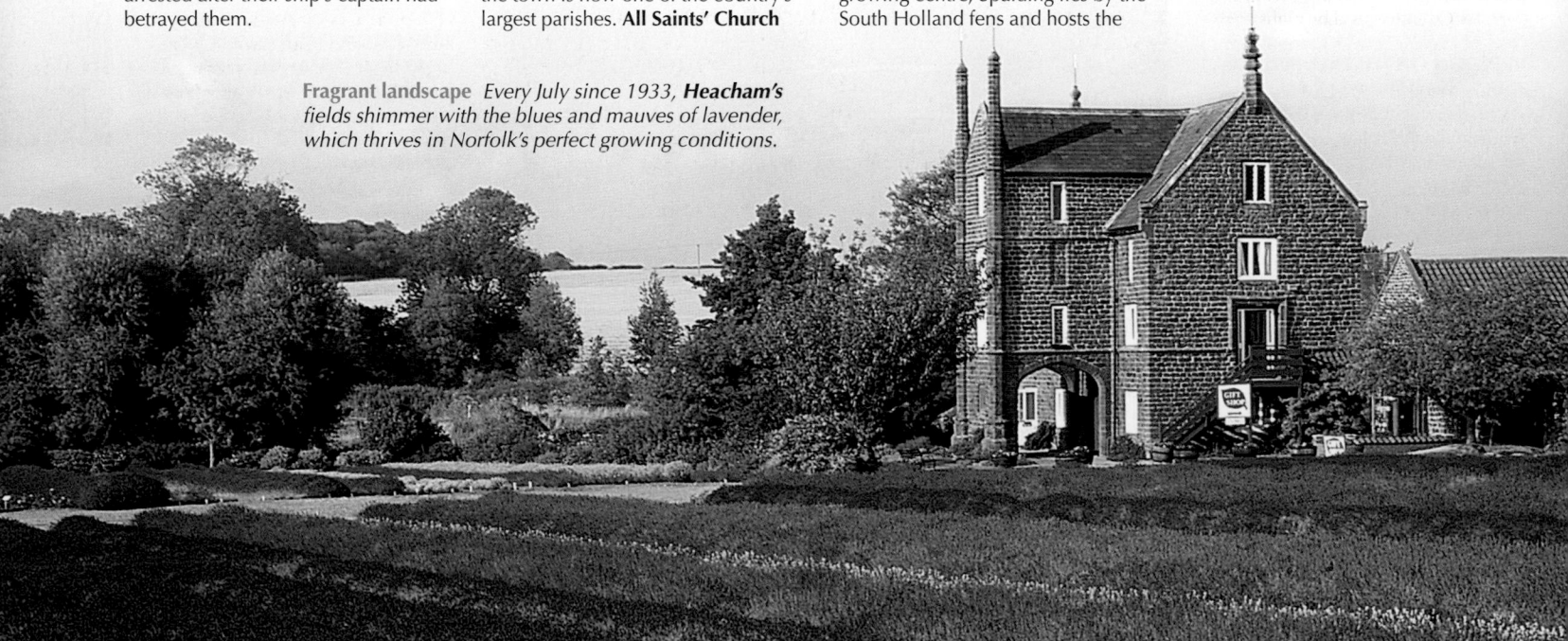

Fragrant landscape *Every July since 1933, **Heacham's** fields shimmer with the blues and mauves of lavender, which thrives in Norfolk's perfect growing conditions.*

North Norfolk and the North Sea coast

AYLSHAM [D2] Handsome red-brick and flint merchants' houses dating from the 18th century are a legacy of 500 prosperous years of making linen and worsted cloth. Steam trains run to Wroxham along narrow-gauge tracks on the **Bure Valley Railway**.

BLAKENEY AND BLAKENEY POINT [C3/4] See pictures.

BLICKLING HALL [D2] Anne Boleyn, Henry VIII's second wife, spent her childhood on this estate, but in an earlier house. It was replaced in 1619–29 by the present mansion 🐾, designed by Robert Lyminge. In the grounds are formal beds, lakes and an orangery of the late 18th century.

THE BURNHAMS [A3] The villages of Burnham Thorpe, Burnham Deepdale, Burnham Overy and Burnham Market cluster near a much-silted sea inlet. Lord Nelson was born in Burnham Thorpe in 1758 – timbers from *HMS Victory* were used for the parish church cross and lectern.

CLEY NEXT THE SEA [C3] In the middle ages, Cley, now 1 mile inland, was a busy port. Ships bore wool to the Low Countries and brought back Dutch tiles. The town's former wealth is reflected in the huge 13th–15th-century **St Margaret's Church**. The remains of the old quay include the 18th-century **Custom House**.

CROMER [E3] A popular resort early in the 20th century, fishing flourishes here and Cromer crabs are especially famed. The **RNLI Lifeboat Museum** honours men such as Cox'n Henry Blogg, awarded the George Medal for helping to save hundreds of lives between 1909 and 1947.

FAKENHAM [B2] The town has a racecourse and holds a lively Thursday market. Nearby **Thursford** has a collection of mechanical organs and a Wurlitzer cinema organ.

FELBRIGG HALL [D3] A Tudor house was rebuilt in the 1620s to create the mansion 🐾, extended in 1674–86.

*Wildlife haven Sea lavender and edible samphire grow at **Blakeney Point** 🐾 and common seals breed on offshore sandbanks in June and July. In summer, the spit is home to common and Sandwich terns, oystercatchers and ringed plovers; brent geese visit in winter.*

The neo-Gothic library, added about 1750, displays books that belonged to Dr Johnson, the 18th-century writer.

GREAT WITCHINGHAM [D1] Covering 40 acres of parkland, the **Norfolk Wildlife Park** is home to a wide range of British and European wildlife, and also has wallabies, lynxes, iguanas and snakes.

HICKLING BROAD [G1] The biggest of the Broads, this area of open water, reed beds, marsh and woods is designated as a nature reserve (permit needed). Rare marsh harriers may be seen, as well as swallowtail butterflies during the months of June and July.

HOLKHAM HALL [A3] The Palladian house stands amid rolling parkland laid out by 'Capability' Brown. It was built in the 18th century for Thomas Coke by William Kent.

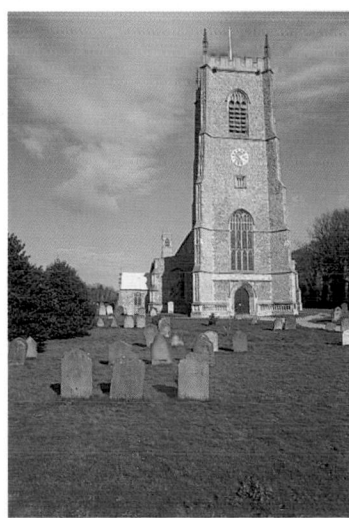

*Wool churches Many large and splendid Norfolk churches, such as here at **Blakeney**, were built with wealth generated by the area's flourishing medieval wool trade.*

HOLT [C3] A small town of Georgian buildings and antique shops, it was the birthplace in 1519 of Sir Thomas Gresham, who built London's original stock exchange, the Royal Exchange.

LETHERINGSETT [C3] The village was planned by the 18th-century landowners, the Barons Cozens-Hardy. The restored Norman **church** has a round tower with an 18th-century barrel organ that needs two people to work it.

LITTLE WALSINGHAM [B3] Pilgrims have flocked to the **Shrine of Our Lady** for more than 900 years. In 1061 the Virgin Mary came in a vision to Richeldis de Faverches, the lady of the manor, and told her to build a chapel as a replica of Christ's childhood home in Nazareth. At **Binham** the 11th-century priory ruins ⌘ hold the Tobruk Cross, a Second World War memorial made of shell cases.

NORTH WALSHAM [E2] In the marketplace is a 16th-century three-tiered market cross. The **Church of St Nicholas**, has a monument to Sir William Paston, who died in 1610. He founded Paston School, which Horatio Nelson attended in 1768–71.

PASTON [F3] Only a barn remains of the medieval **Paston Hall**. The Paston Letters – correspondence by family members in 1422–1509 – are prized for their detail on political events.

SALLE [D1] Outside the tiny village is one of Norfolk's largest Perpendicular churches, the 15th-century **St Peter and St Paul**, funded by local wool merchants including the Boleyns.

SCOLT HEAD [A4] An island sand spit separated from the mainland by a narrow tidal creek, both common and sandwich terns nest here. Dune plants include sea holly and saltwort.

SHERINGHAM [D3] The **North Norfolk Steam Railway** runs trains to Holt; the station has steam engines and memorabilia on display. Inland at Upper Sheringham is **Sheringham Park** 🐾. Viewing towers offer fine views over countryside and coast.

STIFFKEY MARSHES [B3] In summer the **marshes** 🐾 are alive with purple sea lavender. Common seals may be seen resting on sandbanks by the sea.

WELLS-NEXT-THE-SEA [B3] Boats fishing for lobster and crab come to the quay along a winding creek. The **Buttlands** green was used in the 16th century for longbow practice. A narrow-gauge light **railway** runs trains to Walsingham.

WORSTEAD [E2] The village gives its name to worsted cloth. **Weavers' houses**, built to hold looms, remain. The **church** has fine flushwork – flint decoration – and a 15th-century painted screen.

TOURING GUIDE

The Isle of Man and western Anglesey

Map on page 154

ANDREAS [C4] Viking stones about 1000 years old, some carved with scenes from Norse legends, can be seen in the village parish **church**.

BALLASALLA [B1] On the village outskirts is ruined **Rushen Abbey**, founded by Viking Olaf I in 1134.

CALF OF MAN [A1] Colonies of puffins, kittiwakes, guillemots and razorbills share the cliffs of the island reserve **(MNH, MNT)**.

CASTLETOWN [B1] Magnus, the island's last Viking king, died here in 1265, and the town was the seat of the Manx parliament until 1874. **Castle Rushen (MNH)**, with parts dating from 1153, was originally the castle of the Viking kings. The **Manx Nautical Museum (MNH)** houses *Peggy*, a 1791 armed yacht, and a re-created sailmaker's loft.

CREGNEASH [A1] **Meayll Stone Circle** nearby is thought to be 4000 years old, and includes six pairs of stone burial chambers. On the cliffs to the south, **The Chasms** are narrow rifts caused by earth movements.

CROSBY [B2] The **Church of St Runius Marown** is typical of many medieval churches on the Isle of Man. The chapel of **St Trinian** has been kept roofless, it is said, by a local buggane, or goblin.

CURRAGHS WILDLIFE PARK [C4] Manx cats and Loghtan sheep can be seen in the park, along with more than 100 kinds of animals and water birds from all over the world.

*Relics of an earlier life Former crofters' and fishermen's homes at **Cregneash** now house a folk museum (MNH) showing Manx life as it was at the turn of the century.*

Record breaker *The **Laxey Wheel** (MNH) is the world's largest water wheel, with a diameter of 22m (72ft 6in) and 168 buckets. It was built in 1854 to pump water from the mines.*

DHOON GLEN [D3] Between the glen's steeply wooded slopes, a stream drops over two waterfalls to reach the coast at **Dhoon Bay**.

DOUGLAS [C2] Horse-drawn trams plying the Victorian promenade lend an old-world look to Man's capital. In the **Manx Museum (MNH)**, exhibits vary from Stone Age tools to Viking warships. Tram cars of 1893 are still in use on the **Manx Electric Railway**. The **Isle of Man Steam Railway** runs trips from the harbour to Port Erin.

GLEN HELEN [B3] Firs and spruces hug the slopes, and the rivers Neb and Blaber rush below them. Paths lead down to the Rhenass waterfall.

GLEN MAYE [A3] A path snakes down a wooded ravine to a pebbly shore below the rugged cliffs.

LAXEY [C3] See picture (left).

MAUGHOLD [D4] Saint Maughold landed on the headland in the 5th century, and founded a monastery. There are Celtic and Norse monuments in the churchyard.

PEEL [B3] **Peel Castle (MNH)** stands on **St Patrick's Isle**, reached by a causeway. In the 11th century the castle was the ruling seat of the Norse Kingdom of Mann and the Isles; its curtain walls enclose a ruined 9th-century **chapel** and **Round Tower**, a **Viking palace** and a ruined 13th-century **cathedral**. A **museum** holds the 'Story of Man' exhibition with displays on the history and folklore of the island.

PORT ERIN [A1] Sheltered between two headlands, the resort is the terminus of the steam railway from Douglas, opened in 1874: it has a splendid **museum of steam engines and coaches** where Manx engines of more than 120 years old can be seen. **Milner's Tower** is a key-shaped monument built in 1884.

POINT OF AYRE [D5] From the low-lying northern tip of Man, views extend as far as the hills of Galloway. The coastal strip to the west is known as **The Ayres (MNT)**. Birds that breed in the area include terns and waders.

RAMSEY [D4] Palm trees flourish in Man's second largest town, sheltered by the slopes of **North Barrule**. The **Albert Tower** commemorates a royal visit in 1847. The **Grove Rural Life Museum (MNH)** is housed in the Victorian summer retreat of a Liverpool merchant.

SNAEFELL [C3] The highest point on the Isle of Man at 621m (2036ft), the peak is snow-capped for much of the year. An electric railway ascends the mountain from Laxey to give visitors breathtaking views of the island.

TYNWALD HILL [B3] The name comes from the Old Norse *thing vollr*, or 'assembly field'. Each year on July 5, acts passed by the Manx parliament in Douglas are proclaimed on the tiered hillside by two judges or 'deemsters'. The ceremony, carried out in Manx and English, dates from at least AD 979.

Map on page 155

ABERFFRAW [G1] More than 700 years ago the town was Gwynedd's capital. Nothing is left of the palace of the last prince, Llywelyn ap Gruffydd, who died in 1282. A cliff path leads to the 7th-century **St Cythan's Church**.

TOURIST INFORMATION

Castletown (01624) 825005
Douglas (01624) 686766
Holyhead (01407) 762622
Laxey (01624) 862007
Manx Wildlife Trust
  (01624) 801985
Onchan (01624) 621228
Peel (01624) 842341
Port Erin (01624) 832298
Port St Mary (01624) 832101
Ramsey (01624) 810146

THE GOOD PUB GUIDE

Peel [B3] *Creek Inn*
  (01624) 842216
Port Erin [A1] *Falcon's Nest*
  (01624) 834077

AMLWCH [H4] In the late 18th century, copper deposits in the nearby **Parys Mountain** turned a fishing port into a mining boom town. **Amlwch Port**, built in 1793, was in the early years of the 19th century the biggest copper port in the world.

BRYNSIENCYN [H1] The **Anglesey Sea Zoo** displays local marine life in transparent tanks. North-west of the town near Llangaffo is a prehistoric burial chamber.

CEMLYN BAY [G4] A long shingle arm separates the **bay** from a lagoon that attracts birds such as red-breasted mergansers and Arctic terns.

HOLYHEAD [F3] Anglesey's largest town has been a port for Ireland since Thomas Telford completed the road from London to Holyhead; the 1821 **Admiralty Arch** marks its end. The harbour breakwater took nearly 30 years to build and at 567m (1860ft) is Britain's longest. The walls of the Roman fort of **Caer Gybi** ring the medieval **St Cybi's Church**.

HOLYHEAD MOUNTAIN [F3] Anglesey's highest point rises a craggy 220m (722ft). Ramparts of the Iron Age hill-fort of **Caer y Twr** ring the summit, and on the slopes are the **Cytiau'r Gwyddelod** ('huts of the Irish') – stone circles of huts 1700 years old. Nearby **South Stack** rock has an **RSPB** reserve.

LLANDDWYN ISLAND [G1] A rocky ridge reached at low tide, the island lies at the western end of the beach of **Llanddwyn Bay**. Near the lighthouse are the ruins of the **Church of St Dwynwen**, the 5th-century Welsh patron saint of lovers. Shags and cormorants nest on the island.

LLANGEFNI [H2] The town is the main market centre of Anglesey. The **Oriel Ynys Môn** museum has work by the wildlife artist Charles F. Tunnicliffe (1901–79), who lived on the island from 1947.

Eastern Anglesey and the Conwy and Clwyd valleys

ABER FALLS [C1] Lovely **Coedydd Aber** glen is the start of a 3-mile nature trail that climbs to the breathtaking Aber Falls.

BANGOR [B2] A small university and cathedral city, Bangor dates back to St Deiniol, a 6th-century noble who founded a monastery here. The **cathedral**, with 12th-century origins, has a **Bible Garden**, where biblical plants are grown. The 1896 pier juts into the Menai Strait.

BEAUMARIS [B2] The **castle (Cadw)** is the last of Edward I's 'iron ring' of fortresses; it was started in 1295 but was never completed. The **Courthouse** dates from 1614, and the **jail** was built in 1829 by Joseph Hansom, designer of the hansom cab.

BODNANT GARDEN [D2] Situated in 80 acres of woodland in a sheltered valley, the garden was started in 1875 and is renowned for the rhododendrons and azaleas.

CONWY [D2] On a rocky site above the Conwy estuary, the **castle (Cadw)** has eight towers and a Great Hall 38m (125ft) long. Some of the town's original walls remain, with 22 towers and three gateways. Thomas Telford's 1826 **suspension bridge** 🏛, now a footbridge, spans the Conwy. **Ty Bach**, a tiny fisherman's cottage is on the quayside; 14th-century **Aberconwy House** 🏛 and **Plas Mawr (Cadw)**, a 16th-century Elizabethan town house, are in the town. Nearby is **Felin Isaf**, a restored 17th-century river mill.

DENBIGH [G1] The **castle (Cadw)** ruins adjoin the remains of the medieval town walls. The castle dates back to the 11th century, but is mostly the work of 1282, when it was built for Edward I by the Earl of Lincoln. The explorer Henry Morton Stanley was born in the town in 1841.

GREAT ORMES HEAD [D3] The clifftop summit can be reached by cable car, funicular tramway, road, or on foot through the Happy Valley. Birds such as choughs, guillemots and razorbills may be seen.

HOLYWELL [H2] A farm museum has reconstructed buildings including a 17th-century cottage and a Victorian farmhouse. Nearby, **St Winefride's Well** is the source of a holy spring and a centre of pilgrimmage.

LLANDUDNO [D3] Flanked by the headlands of the Great Orme and Little Orme, the resort promenades on Llandudno Bay and Conwy Bay. A White Rabbit statue commemorates Charles Dodgson (Lewis Carroll); the author of *Alice's Adventures in Wonderland* often visited the town as a guest of Dean Liddell, whose daughter Alice was the inspiration for the fictional Alice. To the south is the **Welsh Mountain Zoo**.

LLANFAIR PG [A2] The longest village name in the UK, with 58 letters, is usually abbreviated to this. A column in the village dating from 1816 commemorates the Marquess of Anglesey's achievements in the Battle of Waterloo.

MENAI BRIDGE [B2] See picture.

MOELFRE [A3] Many ships wrecked on the headland have been helped by the village lifeboat. In 1859 the *Royal Charter* sank in a storm, taking with it some 1450 lives and a fortune in gold. A memorial stands on the clifftop; inland are the ruins of **Din Lligwy**, a 4th-century village.

PENMAENMAWR [C2] The resort, whose name means 'large stone head', was one of Gladstone's favourites. A 400m (1300ft) climb leads to **Cefn Coch** stone circle.

PENMON [B3] Priory ruins (Cadw) dating from the 13th century mark the site of a monastery founded in the 6th century by St Seiriol. Beyond **Trwyndu**, or Black Point, is **Puffin Island**, or Ynys Seiriol, home to seals, shags and cormorants, but few puffins.

TOURIST INFORMATION

Bangor (01248) 352786
Colwyn Bay (01492) 530478
Conwy (01492) 592248
Llandudno (01492) 876413
Llanfair PG (01248) 713177
Prestatyn (01745) 889092
Rhyl (01745) 355068

THE GOOD PUB GUIDE

Beaumaris [B2] *Ye Olde Bull's Head* (01248) 810329
Bodfari [G1] *Dinorben Arms* (01745) 710309
Halkyn [H2] *Britannia* (01352) 780272
Llanbedr-y-cennin [D1] *Olde Bull* (01492) 660508
Llannefydd [F2] *Hawk & Buckle* (01745) 540249
Llanynys [G1] *Cerrigllwydion Arms* (01745) 890247
Red Wharf Bay [B3] *Ship* (01248) 852568
Ty-n-y-groes [D2] *Groes* (01492) 650545

PENRHYN CASTLE [B2] The fantasy neo-Norman **castle** 🏛 was built in 1820–40 by Thomas Hopper for G.H. Dawkins-Pennant, using slate quarried from the Penrhyn mines.

PLAS NEWYDD [A1] Home of the Marquess of Anglesey, the ivy-clad house 🏛, was altered extensively in the 18th century. The 1st Marquess lost a leg in 1815 at the Battle of Waterloo and many Napoleonic War relics are on show. The former dining room contains Rex Whistler's largest mural, painted in 1936–40. Nearby, at **Bryn Celli Ddu**, is a well-preserved stone age passage burial chamber.

RHYL AND PRESTATYN [F3] Six miles of beach and promenade link the two resorts. Near Prestatyn are the north end of the **Offa's Dyke Path** and **Graig Fawr** 🏛, a limestone hill. **Rhuddlan Castle**, south of Rhyl, was begun in 1277 by Edward I.

ST ASAPH [F2] Britain's smallest medieval **cathedral,** founded by St Kentigern in the 6th century, was destroyed in 1282 and rebuilt in the 14th century. Explorer Henry Morton Stanley entered St Asaph workhouse in 1847, aged six, and ran away to sea at 15. To the east is **Bodelwyddan Castle**, built in white limestone and furnished with pieces from London's Victoria and Albert Museum.

Fording the strait *Thomas Telford's iron and limestone suspension bridge across the Menai Strait was the world's longest bridge, at 386m (1265ft), when it was built in 1826. With a height of 30m (100ft), the* **Menai Bridge** *enables tall ships to pass beneath it.*

TOURING GUIDE

Manchester, Merseyside and the Cheshire Plain

The new rising from the old Salford's striking **Lowry centre** of 2000 overlooks the Manchester Ship Canal, which opened in 1894.

ALDERLEY EDGE [G2] A ridge of red sandstone, 198m (650ft) high, offers rugged walks and views across the Pennines. At the Wizard of the Edge cave, legend says, knights still wait until summoned to save their country. At **Nether Alderley** ❧ a 15th-century water mill is still in working order.

CHESTER [C1] Set within a loop of the River Dee, the city is ringed by about 2 miles of Roman and medieval walls. Between the western wall and the river is **The Roodee**, the site of Chester races since 1540. Among the ancient streets are **the Rows** – two tiers of half-timbered, galleried medieval shops. The **cathedral** dates mainly from the 14th century and the Chester Imp lurks above the nave. From **King Charles's Tower**, Charles I watched the defeat of his troops on Rowton Heath in 1645.

DEE ESTUARY [A3] From **Burton Mill Wood** ❧ on the Cheshire shore, there are views across vast stretches of mud flats, sand and salt marsh from **Point of Ayr** to **Connah's Quay**. More than 110,000 waders winter at the estuary, which is home to two-thirds of Britain's winter wildfowl.

ELLESMERE PORT [C2] In the early 19th century, Thomas Telford built a tidal basin where the **Shropshire Union Canal** joins the Mersey and the town grew up around it. In the old docks, which linked the canal with the **Manchester Ship Canal**, is the **Boat Museum**, with around 50 different canal craft.

JODRELL BANK [G2] The huge dish, 76m (250ft) across, of a radio telescope, dominates the **Jodrell Bank Science Centre**. Built in 1957 by Sir Bernard Lovell, it receives radio waves from space. An observation pathway allows visitors a good view.

LIVERPOOL [C4] See City Routes pp282–283.

MACCLESFIELD [H2] The restored **Paradise Mill** and **Silk Museum**, housed in an 1813 Sunday School, recall the town's past as a centre of the silk industry. To the south, 15th-century **Gawsworth Hall** was once the home of Mary Fitton, possibly the 'dark lady' in Shakespeare's sonnets.

MANCHESTER [H4] See City Routes pp288–289.

NORTHWICH [F2] The **Salt Museum** tells the story of salt mining in the area. The **Lion Salt Works** at Marston opened in 1842 and pumped brine up to 1986. Boats were carried between the River Weaver and the Trent and Mersey Canal by the **Anderton Boat Lift**, completed in 1875.

PORT SUNLIGHT [C3] This garden village was built in 1888–1914 by the soap-maker William Hesketh Lever

for his factory workers – he believed they should benefit from the wealth they helped to create. Impressive Pre-Raphaelite and 18th-century art can be seen in the **Lady Lever Art Gallery**.

ST HELENS [D4] Since the early 18th century the town has been a glass-making centre. The **World of Glass** museum explores the history and future of the ancient craft. Sir Thomas Beecham, the conductor, was born here in 1879.

SALFORD [G4] Salford factories are frequently featured in the paintings of Manchester-born artist L.S. Lowry. **The Lowry**, a new gallery on the Salford Quays, has more than 300 of his paintings and drawings.

SPEKE HALL [C3] When the Norris family began the building of their black-and-white half-timbered mansion in the early 16th century, Liverpool was a small fishing port 8 miles away. Completed in 1612, the house is built around a cobbled court-yard; it includes a Great Hall, fine plasterwork and tapestries, priest holes and a Victorian kitchen.

STOCKPORT [H3] The former cotton mill town is dominated by a huge railway viaduct, opened in June 1840. The economist Richard Cobden was its MP from 1841 to 1847. Stockport's hat-making days are recalled at the **Museum of Hatting**. Visitors can go

underground in the **Stockport Air Raid Shelters** to explore the network of tunnels where more than 7000 people took cover each night during the Blitz. Nearby are 14th-century **Bramall Hall** and **Lyme Park**, a Tudor mansion with an Italianate exterior.

WIGAN [E5] A jetty on the canal basin, Wigan Pier became a music-hall joke during the 19th century. The **Wigan Pier Experience** recreates work in a Victorian mill and houses the Trencherfield Mill Engine, the world's largest original working steam engine. **Opie's Museum of Memories**, on the same site, looks back at domestic life in industrial Britain.

Time to celebrate *The ornate clock adorning **Chester**'s Eastgate was built in 1897 to honour Queen Victoria on her Diamond Jubilee.*

The Peak District and Nottingham's coal towns

ASHFORD IN THE WATER [D1]
Black limestone was quarried here from 1748 to 1905. Nearby are the **Monsal Dale viaduct** of 1863, and the 'Cathedral of the Peak', **Tideswell's** 14th-century church.

BAKEWELL [D1] Famous for its jam puddings topped with an egg mixture, this town on the Wye also has a noted market. **Bath House**, built in 1697, adjoins **Bath Gardens**, laid out in 1814 as part of the Duke of Rutland's plans for a spa. Nearby is **Haddon Hall**, a medieval manor house.

BARNSLEY [E5] The pits that for 500 years made Barnsley a rich coal-mining centre are now closed. The **Cooper Gallery** has fine French and Dutch paintings. Much of the land around the manufacturing town was once owned by the ruined **Monk Bretton Priory**, founded in 1154.

BOLSOVER [G2] Situated on a lime-stone ridge with views to the peaks, Bolsover was once a mining town. The 17th-century **castle ⚑**, a hilltop mansion, was built by the Cavendish family, who also built **Chatsworth** and **Hardwick Hall ✿**. It includes the **Little Castle** Jacobean folly and the early riding school of 1620–1630.

BUXTON [C2] Warm springs and an impressive setting made Buxton a popular spa. The **Devonshire Royal Hospital** building has a 19th-century domed roof 48m (156ft) across and the elegant **Crescent** was built by the 5th Duke of Devonshire in the 1780s.

CASTLETON CAVERNS [D3] Below the keep of **Peveril Castle ⚑** is the entrance to **Peak Cavern**, extending 610m (2000ft) underground. The caverns are rich with coloured minerals, stalactites and stalagmites. There is a canal trip through **Speedwell Cavern**, first used by 18th-century miners. A hill-fort of 1200 BC tops nearby **Mam Tor**, or 'mother hill'

CHATSWORTH HOUSE [E2] See picture.

CHESTERFIELD [F2] The twisted spire of the 14th-century church is a local landmark. A **Museum and Art Gallery** tells the town's story. The railway pioneer George Stephenson (1781–1848) is buried in **Holy Trinity Church**.

CONISBROUGH CASTLE [G4] A ruined circular keep ⚑ is all that survives of the castle of 1180. A carved 12th-century tomb chest is found in **Conisbrough church**. The **Earth Centre**, east of Conisbrough, has gardens, wetlands and exhibiton areas with the theme of sustainable development. It was created on land once used by the coal industry.

CRESWELL CRAGS [G2] A limestone ravine, the crags have caves where traces of occupation go back some 70,000 years. Bones of cave lions and mammoths have been found, along with arrowheads and tools left by Stone Age hunters.

DENBY DALE [D5] A large pie plate recalls the village tradition of baking a giant pie on special occasions; the first pie, in 1788, marked George III's recovery from illness. Nearby is **Cannon Hall**, a 17th-century country house that is now a museum.

DONCASTER [H5] Roman in origin, the town is best known for its butterscotch and its racecourse, where the St Leger has been run since 1776. The 1748 **Mansion House** is a relic of Doncaster's 18th-century wealth. **St George's Church**, with its pinnacled tower, is by George Gilbert Scott. The **Museum of South Yorkshire Life** is in 18th-century **Cusworth Hall**.

EYAM [D2] London cloth sent to a local tailor brought the plague to the village in 1665–6. The 350 villagers put themselves in quarantine for 13 months to stop its spread; more than a third died. The **Plague Cottages**, the seat of the outbreak, can still be seen and stones outside the village mark where money was disinfected. **Eyam Hall** is a 17th-century manor house with a fine Jacobean staircase and flagstoned hall.

GLOSSOP [B4] The **Snake Pass** leads from the Pennines into the small town. It expanded in the 19th-century cotton boom, and has some fine mill buildings. **Old Glossop**, round the mainly 17th-century church, is distinct from the 19th-century development. Nearby, the remains of a **Roman fort**, Melandra, include ramparts and a bathhouse.

HATHERSAGE [D3] Little John, giant henchman of Robin Hood, is said to be buried in the churchyard. Brasses of the Eyre family, a name used by Charlotte Brontë in her novel *Jane Eyre*, are in 14th-century **St Michael's Church**. The **Round Building** was converted from a disused gasometer to house a modern cutlery factory.

ROTHERHAM [F4] See City Routes pp294–295.

SHEFFIELD [E3] See City Routes pp294–295.

WORKSOP [H3] The industrial town on the edge of the Nottinghamshire coalfield has a church belonging to an Augustinian priory founded in 1103. It has a Norman nave, a 14th-century gatehouse and 20th-century east end. The 12th-century yew door has fine scrollwork. **Mr Straw's House ✿**, a suburban semi-detached house with mainly 1920s furnishings, is a fascinating time capsule. A replica of the *Mayflower* can be seen in nearby Babworth church.

ROTHERHAM [F4] See City Routes pp294–295.

SHEFFIELD [E3] See City Routes pp294–295.

TOURIST INFORMATION

Bakewell (01629) 813227
Barnsley (01226) 206757
Buxton (01298) 25106
Chesterfield (01246) 345777
Doncaster (01302) 734309
Rotherham (01709) 835904
Sheffield (0114) 221 1900
Sherwood Forest Visitor Centre
   (01623) 824490
Worksop (01909) 501148

THE GOOD PUB GUIDE

Bamford [D3] *Yorkshire Bridge Inn* (01433) 651361
Buxton [C2] *Bull i' th' Thorn* (01298) 83348
Castleton [D3] *Castle Hotel* (01433) 620578
Froggatt Edge [D2] *Chequers* (01433) 630231
Grindleford [D2] *Maynard Arms* (01433) 630321
Hathersage [D3] *Plough* (01433) 650319

TOURING GUIDE

Palace in the Peaks *Set in a vast estate, **Chatsworth House** is the palatial seat of the dukes of Devonshire. The ornate interior, with its 20m (64ft) long Painted Hall, has a superb art collection. Joseph Paxton, who designed the Crystal Palace, relaid the gardens in the 1830s and moved Edensor village from the east to the west of the estate to improve the view.*

The Lincolnshire wolds, fens and marshlands

Pages 162–3

CLUMBER PARK [A2] One of the 'Dukeries' – estates granted to five noble dukes by monarchs in the 18th century – Clumber 🌿 was enclosed as a hunting park for Queen Anne by the 3rd Duke of Newcastle in 1707. Within the park are a lake, and a 3 mile double lime avenue. The mansion was demolished in 1938, but the fine Gothic chapel of 1886–9 remains. The Clumber spaniel, a gun dog, was bred on the estate.

DODDINGTON HALL [D2] Built for the Bishop of Lincoln's Recorder in the 1590s, the mansion stands amid formal gardens. The **Church of St Peter** was rebuilt in 1770 by Sir John Delaval, the hall's owner, as a burial place for his daughter.

HORNCASTLE [H1] A market centre since the 13th century, the town has traces of a Roman garrison. Until the mid 20th century, Europe's largest annual horse fair was held here for ten days every August.

LAXTON [B1] The 18th-century land enclosures passed Laxton by; it is the only place in England that carries on medieval open-field strip farming. Three large fields are farmed on a three-year cycle, with one field left fallow each year.

LINCOLN [E2] Steep cobbled streets descend from the **cathedral**, with its Norman west front and triple towers. **Bailgate**, north of the 11th-century **castle**, was at the heart of the Roman town; at the north end, **Newport Arch** is the only Roman gateway still used by traffic. On Steep Hill is the early 12th-century **Jew's House**. The quay at **Brayford Pool** on the Witham was an 18th and 19th-century port, linked by canal to the sea.

LUDFORD [G3] Salt was brought from coastal salt pans to Lincoln along the old Salter's Way. Horned helmets mark the route of the nearby **Viking Way**, that runs 116 miles from Oakham to the Humber Bridge. East of Ludford, is the site of the lost village of **Calcethorpe**.

MARKET RASEN [F3] In this Wolds town, **St Thomas's Church** dates from Norman times. The National Hunt racecourse has 17 annual fixtures.

SHERWOOD FOREST [A1/2] Some of the oldest forest remnants are near Edwinstowe, where Robin Hood and Maid Marian were said to have been married at St Mary's. The last strip of ancient oak wood is now a country park, with a trail to the 500-year-old Major Oak.

THORESBY [A2] The original **Thoresby Hall** was burnt down in 1745 but its Victorian re-creation of 1865–75 has an exhibition gallery.

WALESBY [F4] On a remote hilltop above the village is the restored 12th-century **'Ramblers' Church'**. It has a fine rood screen, a 17th-century marble altar and Jacobean pulpit.

BURGH LE MARSH [C1] The village stands on raised ground amid the marshes. Its **tower mill**, with five sails and five storeys, is 'left-handed' – its sails of about 1870 rotate clockwise.

CALCEBY [B2] Founded by Danish settlers, medieval Calceby made a living from coastal salt pans. Though it survived for 200 years after the Black Death, it is today one of the 'lost villages' of Lincolnshire with its hillside **church** an ivy-covered ruin.

DONNA NOOK [B4] Ringed plovers and little grebes, or dabchicks, live on the mud flats and saltings of this coastal reserve, and common and grey seals may be spotted offshore.

GUNBY HALL [C1] Built of red brick and stone in 1700, but greatly changed in the 1800s, the hall has a

Poet at the cathedral *A statue of Alfred Lord Tennyson stands in the shadows of **Lincoln Cathedral**; the Victorian Poet Laureate was born in 1809 in Somersby near Horncastle. Only the west front remains from the 11th-century Norman cathedral; the rest of the structure is a later Gothic addition.*

Pages 164–5

ALFORD [C2] The timbered **manor house** of 1540, now a folk museum, was later encased in brick to become a 'house within a house'. The five-sailed **mill** of 1813 is 29m (95ft) high.

ALVINGHAM [B4] The **Louth Navigation Canal** allowed small ships to get to Louth warehouses until 1924.

fine oak staircase and wainscoted rooms. On the estate stands Monksthorpe Chapel 🌿, one of the finest examples of a Baptist chapel

HALTON HOLEGATE [B1] The 15th-century hilltop **St Andrew's Church** has a pinnacled tower and carved pews adorned with angels, owls and foxes carrying geese. The red-brick **Old Hall** dates from the 18th century.

HARRINGTON HALL [B2] After a fire in 1991, the 17th-century mansion was rebuilt. The gardens are said to have inspired Tennyson's poem 'Maud', with the much-quoted line: 'Come into the garden, Maud'. Rosa Baring, the real Maud, lived at Harrington Hall with her guardian.

LOUTH [A3] Soaring above the narrow streets, Georgian houses and old inns is the 90m (295ft) high spire of the fine 15th-century Perpendicular church of **St James**. Sir John Franklin, explorer of the North-west Passage, and Lord Tennyson both attended **Louth Grammar School**.

MABLETHORPE [C3] The terraced promenade overlooks 6 miles of sandy beach. **The Seal Sanctuary** at North End nurses injured seals and sea birds back to health. At low tides, the stumps of a forest engulfed by the sea 7500 years ago are exposed.

OLD BOLINGBROKE [A1] A few grassy mounds mark the site of the 13th-century castle ⚔ where Henry IV, son of John of Gaunt, Duke of Lancaster, was born in 1367. Taken by Cromwell after the Battle of Winceby in 1643, the castle fell into decay.

SKEGNESS [D1] Planned as a resort from 1877 by Lord Scarborough, it has tree-lined avenues, swimming pools and extensive seafront gardens. The 562m (1843ft) long **pier** was lost in gales in 1978.

SNIPE DALES COUNTRY PARK [A1] Long-billed snipe and woodcocks probe the muddy streams of the park at dusk, and there are also short-eared owls, sand martins and six kinds of warbler. Oak, ash, willow and alder trees have been planted to re-create woods that were once commonly found in the southern Wolds.

The Lancashire coast and the cotton towns

ACCRINGTON [G3] The town was known in the 19th century for its smooth red bricks, called 'Accrington Bloods'. In **St John's Church**, the Pals Chapel is a memorial to those killed on the Somme in the First World War.

AINSDALE DUNES [B2] Natterjack toads and sand lizards thrive in the nature reserve behind the beach.

BLACKBURN [F3] **The Lewis Textile Museum** tells the story of the town's heyday as a cotton centre during the 18th–19th centuries; working models include the spinning jenny invented by James Hargreaves in 1764.

BLACKPOOL [B4] Britain's biggest seaside resort is dominated by the 158m (518ft) high **Blackpool Tower**, inspired by the Eiffel Tower and built in 1894. Blackpool had the UK's first tram system in 1885, and overhead-wire trams still run regularly along the front to Fleetwood. In the **Winter Gardens** is the Opera House, with Britain's largest stage. **Stanley Park** has gardens and a boating lake, and nearby is **Blackpool Zoo**.

BOLTON [F1] In **Churchgate**, the 13th-century *Man and Scythe* inn is said to be where the 7th Earl of Derby spent his last hours before execution by Cromwell in 1651. At that time Bolton had long been a cloth-making town, and Richard Arkwright patented a water powered spinning frame here in 1769. Samuel Crompton, inventor of the spinning mule – a speedier version of the jenny – lived at **Hall i' th' Wood**. **Smithills Hall**, a restored manor, has a 14th-century Great Hall and panelled drawing room.

BURNLEY [H4] By the end of the 19th century, Burnley was the world's largest producer of cotton cloth. In the centre is the **Victorian Weavers' Triangle**, where mills and workers' houses line the **Leeds and Liverpool Canal**, along which raw cotton and finished cloth used to be transported. Nearby are 17th-century **Gawthorpe Hall**, rebuilt in the 1850s, and **Towneley Hall**, a 14th-century house with a fine entrance hall.

BURY [G2] Sir Robert Peel, twice prime minister and founder of the Metropolitan Police – originally known as 'Peelers' – was born in Bury in 1788. John Kay, inventor of the flying shuttle, was born in 1704 at **Walmersley** to the north of the town.

CHORLEY [E2] Henry Tate, the sugar magnate and benefactor of London's Tate Gallery, was born here in 1819. Nearby is 17th-century **Astley Hall**, where the Long Gallery has a long shovelboard table.

CLITHEROE [F5] On a hill above the former cotton town are the ruins of a Norman **castle** with probably England's smallest keep, 11m (35ft) square. In 1612 ten homeless women sheltering on **Pendle Hill** nearby were hanged as witches.

HEALEY DELL [H2] Set in a narrow, wooded gorge, the nature reserve has marsh violets, marsh marigolds and cuckooflowers. Bird life includes woodcocks, redpolls and waxwings.

HOGHTON TOWER [E3] The 16th-century mansion, visited by James I, is set on a wooded hill and has a Tudor well house with a horse-drawn pump.

HYNDBURN DEER WALKS [F4] Fallow, roe and sika deer may be spotted on waymarked trails in the area around **Great Harwood**.

LYTHAM ST ANNE'S [B3] A resort with sandy beaches at the mouth of the Ribble, it is also a venue for major golf tournaments. There is a restored **windmill** on the seafront.

MARTIN MERE [C2] Run by the Wildfowl Trust, the mere is a haven for wetland birds, and whoopers and Bewick's swans winter here.

PRESTON [E3] In 1648, Cromwell routed Charles I's Scottish allies at Preston. Richard Arkwright, pioneer of the factory system in 1771 was born here. The **National Football Museum** has an impressive collection of memorabilia, with displays on the game's history, rules, tactics and equipment. The **Ribble Steam Railway** will reopen in mid-2005. Meanwhile, a **museum** displays steam, electric and diesel locomotives.

RIBBLE MARSHES [B3] Wildfowl such as wigeon, teal and a large number of pink-footed geese, live or winter on this estuary, a national nature reserve.

Textile town *An old Lancashire cotton mill towers over* **Rochdale**, *high in the foothills of the Pennines. The Cooperative Movement began in the town in 1844, in a shop in Toad Lane that is now the Rochdale Pioneers Museum.*

TOURIST INFORMATION

Accrington (01254) 872595
Blackburn (01254) 681120
Blackpool (01253) 478222
Blackpool Pleasure Beach
  (0870) 4445566
Bolton (01204) 334321
Burnley (01282) 664421
Bury (0161) 253 5111
Cleveleys (01253) 853378
Clitheroe (01200) 425566
Fleetwood (01253) 773953
Lytham St Anne's
  (01253) 725610
Preston (01772) 253731
Rochdale (01706) 864928
Southport (01704) 533333

THE GOOD PUB GUIDE

Belmont [F2] *Black Dog*
  (01204) 811218
Chipping [E5] *Dog & Partridge*
  (01995) 61201
Croston [D2] *Black Horse*
  (01772) 600338
Downham [G5] *Assheton Arms*
  (01200) 441227
Goosnargh [E4] *Ye Horns*
  (01772) 865230
Little Eccleston [C5] *Cartford*
  (01995) 670166
Longridge [E4] *Derby Arms*
  (01772) 782623
lytham [C3] *Taps*
  (01253) 736226
Mawdesley [D2] *Red Lion*
  (01704) 822208/822999
Ribchester [E4] *White Bull*
  (01254) 878303

RIBCHESTER [E4] Exhibits in a **museum** in this former Roman town include the famous Ribchester helmet among other Roman finds.

ROCHDALE [H2] See picture (left).

RUFFORD OLD HALL [D2] One of Lancashire's finest half-timbered houses, the hall, built about 1480, has a richly carved roof. Nearby is the **Camelot Adventure Theme Park**.

SOUTHPORT [B2] A seaside and golfing resort with extensive sands, it has fine **Botanic Gardens** and a ¾ mile long **pier**. A **museum** has displays on the history of British lawnmowers.

TOURING GUIDE

Pleasure beach **Blackpool's 7 mile long beach is backed by a boisterous promenade with its Golden Mile of slot machines, candy floss, cabaret and amusement rides, and three 19th-century piers.**

West Yorkshire and the central Pennines

TOURIST INFORMATION

Bradford (01274) 433678
Halifax (01422) 368725
Hebden Bridge (01422) 843831
Holmfirth (01484) 222444
Huddersfield (01484) 223200
Leeds (0113) 242 5242
Oldham (0161) 627 1024
Selby (01757) 212181
Wakefield (0845) 601 8353

ALMONDBURY [C2] Castle Hill, rising above the village, has an Iron Age hill-fort and there are views of the Peak District from the 305m (1000ft) high **Jubilee Tower**.

BATLEY [D3] The manufacture of shoddy began here in 1813. The **Bagshaw Museum**, in a neo-Gothic mansion in Wilton Park, displays many curious objects collected by the Bagshaw family on their world travels.

BOSTON SPA [F5] Mineral springs found in 1744 made Boston Spa a resort. Cottages at **Clifford** are built from the honey-coloured magnesian limestone also used for York Minster.

GOLCAR [B2] Three 19th-century weavers' cottages house the **Colne Valley Museum**, which re-creates local clog-making and weaving in the days before mass production.

HALIFAX [B3] The town profited from wool weaving, which paid for **Piece Hall** of 1779, where merchants sold homespun cloth in 315 galleried rooms round its colonnaded piazza.

HAWORTH [B4] See picture.

HEBDEN BRIDGE [A3] The tall houses of this former mill town stand flush against the hillside. Traditional clogs can be bought at the **Walkley**

a local history museum in the 17th-century grammar school. The poet Sylvia Plath (1932–63) is buried in the new churchyard.

HOLMFIRTH [C1] The TV comedy *Last of the Summer Wine* brought fame to this former weaving town. Bamforths, famed for saucy seaside postcards, also made silent films here in the early 20th century.

HUDDERSFIELD [C2] St George's Square, with Italianate warehouses and offices, is the hub of this 19th-century cloth town. The railway station has a fine neo-classical façade. The entrance to the **Cloth Hall** of 1776 has been re-erected in **Ravensknowle Park**, which also has the **Tolson Museum**. Works by L. S. Lowry, Henry Moore and David Hockney hang in the art gallery.

LEEDS [E4] See City Routes pp280–281.

THE GOOD PUB GUIDE

Goose Eye [B5] *Turkey*
(01535) 681339
Heckmondwike [C3] *Old Hall*
(01924) 404774
Ledsham [F4] *Chequers*
(01977) 683135
Leeds [E4] *Whitelocks*
(0113) 245 3950
Linton [E5] *Windmill*
(01937) 582209
Penistone [D1] *Cubley Hall*
(01226) 766086
Pool [D5] *White Hart*
(0113) 202 7901
Ripponden [B2] *Old Bridge*
(01422) 822595
Shelley [C2] *Three Acres*
(01484) 602606
Uppermill [B1] *Church Inn*
(01457) 820902
Widdop [A4] *Pack Horse*
(01422) 842803

*Author siblings The Parsonage at **Haworth** on the edge of the moors was home to the Brontë family from 1820–61. The sisters Emily, Charlotte and Anne wrote their novels here, including* Wuthering Heights *(by Emily),* Jane Eyre *(by Charlotte) and* Agnes Grey *(by Anne). It is now a museum.*

BRADFORD [C4] See City Routes pp280–281.

CASTLEFORD [F3] This former coal-mining centre began as the Roman town of Lagentium. Henry Moore, the sculptor, was born here in 1898.

DEWSBURY [D3] This Calder valley town was the centre of the local wool industry by 1900. The parish church has fragments of a Saxon cross. The father of the Brontë sisters was the curate here from 1809–11.

Clog shop. North-west of the town, **Hardcastle Crags** ❧ overhang **Hebden Water**.

HEMINGBROUGH [H4] Soaring 58m (189ft) over the village is the 15th-century spire of **St Mary's**; it is claimed that a misericord inside dates from 1200 and is Britain's oldest.

HEPTONSTALL [A3] Millstone grit buildings cling to the steep village hillside. An octagonal **Wesleyan chapel** dates from 1764, and there is

MARSDEN [B2] This mill town grew as a staging post on the route across Standedge Fell. Nearby, Huddersfield Narrow Canal and the railway enter the 3 mile **Standedge Tunnel**, the longest canal tunnel in England. The **Standedge Visitor Centre** is housed in a former canal warehouse.

NOSTELL PRIORY [F2] Most of the furniture in this 1735 mansion was made for it by Thomas Chippendale. The state rooms and a 1766 wing are by Robert Adam.

OAKWELL HALL [D3] A moated Elizabethan manor house, Oakwell is furnished in 17th–18th-century style. At Gomersal the **Red House Museum** is housed in a 17th-century mansion.

OLDHAM [A1] Cloth was made here in the 1600s, but from the 1790s it was cotton rather than wool that brought wealth. In 1832, the radical campaigner William Cobbett became its first MP; Winston Churchill took his first parliamentary seat from here in 1900 – Epstein's bust of him is in the art gallery.

PONTEFRACT [F3] Famous for its racecourse, the town is also known for Pontefract cake, a sweet made from liquorice. Little remains of the Norman castle, where Richard II died, or was perhaps murdered, in 1400. It was destroyed by Cromwell in 1649.

SALTAIRE [C4] Sir Titus Salt, a textile millionaire, built Saltaire as a model village for his mill workers from 1852 to 1872. Works by the Yorkshire-born artist David Hockney are displayed at the **1853 Gallery** in Salt's mill.

SELBY [H4] The fine three-towered 12th-century abbey church avoided destruction during the Dissolution of the Monasteries after 1536 by becoming the parish church.

WAKEFIELD [E3] The cathedral church of **All Saints** has Yorkshire's tallest spire at 83m (274ft). The chief Yorkshire cloth town for 700 years, in the 17th century trade migrated to Bradford and Leeds. The city art gallery has early sculptures by Henry Moore and Barbara Hepworth.

Humberside and the wolds of East Yorkshire

BARTON-UPON-HUMBER [D3] This Georgian market town has two fine churches – **St Peter's** ⌗, with a 7th-century Saxon tower 21m (70ft) high, and the 13th-century **St Mary's**, with an eight-pinnacled tower.

BEVERLEY [D5] One of England's finest Gothic churches, the **Minster** dates from the 13th–15th centuries. Treasures include the ornate Percy Tomb, a Saxon sanctuary chair and 68 misericords carved with cameos such as a pig playing a harp. Charles I stayed at **Bar House** in 1642 during the Royalist siege of Hull.

BLACKTOFT SANDS [B3] Bearded tits, reed warblers, reed buntings and rare water rails breed in this ¾sq mile tidal reed swamp fringed by salt marsh – an RSPB reserve.

BRIGG [D1] A fair held in the market town since 1235 has been immortalised in the tone poem *Brigg Fair*, by composer Frederick Delius. Brigg is a good base for exploring the villages of the Lincolnshire Wolds.

BURTON CONSTABLE HALL [F4] The mansion, built about 1570 and later remodelled, has furniture by Chippendale, rooms by Robert Adam and a park by Capability Brown.

CAISTOR [E1] The massive tower of the 13th-century golden-stone **Church of St Peter and St Paul** dominates the surrounding Wolds. There are wide views from the top.

CLEETHORPES [G1] Flower-filled parks and gardens, a 90m (300ft) long pier and more than 3 miles of sandy beaches have drawn holiday-makers since the 19th century. Today it also has the **Pleasure Island** theme park and a coastal light railway.

ELSHAM HALL COUNTRY PARK [D2] Nature trails, including a wild butterfly walk, lead through the wooded grounds of Elsham Hall.

EPWORTH [B1] John Wesley, the founder of Methodism, was born in 1703 in the **Old Rectory**. It was burned down in 1709 by a mob opposed to Wesley's father's views, and later rebuilt.

GOODMANHAM [C5] In AD 627, Paulinus converted Edwin, King of Northumbria, and his high priest Coifi to Christianity. The Norman **Church of All Hallows** stands on the site of Coifi's pagan temple.

GOOLE [A3] Goole became a busy port after the **Aire and Calder Canal** of 1826 linked it to the Yorkshire coalfields. The **Museum and Art Gallery** has paintings by the Goole artist Reuben Chappell (1870–1940).

GRIMSBY [G2] Reputedly founded by Grim, an 11th-century Danish fisherman, this is still a busy fishing port. **The Dock Tower** is a 100m (330ft) copy of the Siena Town Hall tower in Italy. In the **National Fishing Heritage Centre**, exhibits include a restored 1950s trawler.

HEDON [F3] The Perpendicular tower of **St Augustine's Church** rises 39m (128ft) above this former port. The main street has fine 18th-century buildings, and the town's silver collection includes a 15th-century civic mace, the oldest in Britain.

HOWDEN [B3] Georgian buildings, cobbled streets and a 13th-century minster define the market town of Howden. In the early 20th century it was a base for airship design; Neville Barnes Wallis and the novelist Nevil Shute worked here on the R100, Britain's last working airship.

KILNSEA [H2] At the mainland end of Spurn Head, this hamlet is part of an earlier village lost under the sea. A plaque on a house of 1847 records its distance from the sea as 488m (534yd); today the high tide is only 183m (200yd) away.

KINGSTON UPON HULL [E3] Developed by Edward I from a Cistercian monastic settlement at the mouth of the River Hull, one of the few medieval remains is the 13th-century **Holy Trinity Church**. **Queen's Gardens** cover the first docks of 1778; the docks now service fishing fleets, cargo ships, oil tankers and ferries. **Wilberforce House**, was the home of William Wilberforce, the antislavery activist, and the **Maritime Museum** brings Hull's whaling and fishing industries to life. Europe's deepest fish tank is contained in an angular building above the Humber Estuary. Visitors to **The Deep** can ascend through the 9m (30ft) tank in a glass lift and see 500 species of fish.

MELTON GALLOWS [D2] James I is said to have had these gallows built in the 17th century as a warning to the feuding families of Ross and Tyrwhitt. Nearby **Wrawby windmill**, built over 200 years ago, is one of the few post-mills left in Britain. It still grinds corn.

NORMANBY HALL [C2] Deer and peacocks roam the parkland round a country house of 1830 by Robert Smirke, who was the architect of the British Museum. Its Farming Museum has displays on various crafts.

PATRINGTON [G3] The 14th-century **Church of St Patrick**, in Decorated style, has a tall spire, an outstanding Easter Sepulchre, ornate window tracery and stone carvings.

SANDTOFT [A1] The **Transport Centre** has one of the largest trolley and motor bus collections in Britain.

SCUNTHORPE [C2] An industrial centre beside the Trent, the town grew in the 19th century when ironstone was extracted for making steel. At Frodingham, one of the five villages that formed the city, the **Church of St Lawrence** has a 12th-century tower and nave, and a fine oak roof. In the **North Lincolnshire Museum** is a rebuilt ironworker's cottage.

SKIDBY MILL [D4] There are wide views from the old East Riding's last windmill, restored in 1974. Built in 1821, it has been powered by electricity since 1954.

SPURN HEAD [H2] See picture.

TOURIST INFORMATION

Beverley (01482) 867430
Brigg (01652) 657053
Cleethorpes (01472) 323111
Humber Bridge (01482) 640852
Kingston-upon-Hull
(01482) 223559
Withernsea (01964) 615683

THE GOOD PUB GUIDE

Barnoldy le Beck [F1] *Ship* (01472) 822308
Beverley [D5] *White Horse* (01482) 861973
Coniston [F4] *Gardeners' Country Inn* (01964) 562625
Hull [E3] *Minerva* (01482) 326909
Sutton upon Derwent [A5] *St Vincent Arms* (01904) 608349
Thorganby [A5] *Jefferson Arms* (01904) 448316

THORNTON ABBEY [E2] Standing amid farmland is the 15m (50ft) high abbey gatehouse ⌗ of 1382, still virtually intact. The façade is finely carved with statues, and the three-storey building has a large hall and various chambers. Two chapter house walls also remain from the vast Augustinian abbey.

Shifting sands *Spurn Head is a narrow spit of sand and shingle. It is constantly reshaped by the sea, but its dense vegetation supports many butterflies and moths, and migrating birds such as wheatears and whinchats. In winter, curlews and Brent geese visit the mud flats on its west side.*

TOURING GUIDE

Morecambe Bay and the Forest of Bowland

ARNSIDE [F4] A shipbuilding centre in the 18th century, the village is now a yacht haven. From **Beetham**, a riverside walk leads to 18th-century **Heron Corn Mill**. **Arnside Knott** 🦋, offers good walks and fine views.

BARROW-IN-FURNESS [C4] The arrival of the Furness Railway in 1846 sparked the town's growth as an iron

DUNSOP BRIDGE [H2] The gateway to the **Trough of Bowland** from the Ribble Valley, the hamlet is near the exact centre of Britain.

FLOOKBURGH [E4] The village takes its name from flukes, the local word for flounders. The weather vane on the west tower of the church is in the shape of a fluke.

A topiary extravaganza **Levens Hall** was built between 1570–90 around a 13th-century pele tower. It has fine plasterwork and woodwork and a superb mature topiary garden first laid out in 1692.

and steel making centre. By 1870 the steelworks were the world's largest. Since 1896, the Vickers shipyard has built warships, especially submarines, for the Royal Navy. To the north-east are the red sandstone ruins of **Furness Abbey** ⚜, founded in 1123.

CARTMEL [E4] The splendid priory church escaped Dissolution in 1536. The 14th-century **priory gatehouse** 🦋 also remains. Nearby is **Holker Hall**, with fine gardens, a deer park and the **Lakeland Motor Museum**.

DALTON-IN-FURNESS [C4] The monks of Furness Abbey built **Dalton Castle** 🦋, as a manorial courthouse held by lords of the manor of Furness.

GRANGE-OVER-SANDS [E4] The town is named after the grange, or granary, built by the Augustinian monks of nearby **Cartmel Priory**, founded in 1188. Lovely ornamental gardens adorn the seafront.

HALTON [F3] A little upstream from this popular salmon-fishing centre is the **Crook o' Lune**, a beautiful stretch of the river painted by J.M.W. Turner in the 19th century.

KIRKBY LONSDALE [G4] 'I do not know…a place more naturally divine,' wrote the 19th-century art critic John Ruskin of this Lune Valley market town with quaint cottages and Georgian houses.

LANCASTER [F3] An 11th-century castle towers over the **Lune**: parts are still used as a court and prison. Below are the 15th-century **Priory Church of St Mary**, fine Georgian houses and medieval alleys round the Market Square, where in 1651 Charles II was proclaimed king – prematurely. **The Custom House** of 1764 houses the **Maritime Museum**. In **Williamson Park** is the Ashton Memorial – the 'Taj Mahal of the North'.

LEIGHTON MOSS [F4] The booming of bitterns may be heard on this **RSPB** reserve, one of the bird's few British breeding grounds.

LEVENS HALL [F5] See picture (left).

MORECAMBE [E3] See picture (below).

NEWTON [C4] The radical politician John Bright, a leader of the campaign to repeal the Corn Laws, which kept the price of bread high, went to the Quaker school here. His initials are carved into the back of a bench in the 1767 Quaker meeting house.

PIEL ISLAND [C3] In 1487 the island was the landing place of Lambert Simnel, who tried to pass himself off as the Earl of Warwick and take the throne from Henry VII. There is a ruined 14th-century castle ⚜ – to reach it catch the ferry from Roa Island, half a mile away.

SLAIDBURN [H2] The **Hark to Bounty** inn takes its name from a local story. Bounty, a foxhound, was left outside while his master drank. When the dog barked he would exclaim 'Hark to Bounty!' The Forest of Bowland Court once sat at the inn and the jury box survives.

SWARTHMOOR HALL [D4] In 1652 Judge Thomas Fell, the hall's owner, gave shelter to George Fox, founder of the Quakers. The hall became the sect's first settled centre.

TROUGH OF BOWLAND [G2] At the top of this high pass are superb

TOURIST INFORMATION

Barrow-in-Furness
  (01229) 894784
Cleveleys (01253) 853378
Fleetwood (01253) 773953
Grange-over-Sands
  (015395) 34026
Lancaster (01524) 32878
Morecambe (01524) 582808
Ulverston (01229) 587120

THE GOOD PUB GUIDE

Beetham [F4] *Wheatsheaf* (015395) 62123
Casterton [G4] *Pheasant* (015242) 71230
Conder Green [F2] *Stork* (01524) 751234
Dalton-in-Furness [C4] *Black Dog* (01229) 462561
Kirkby Lonsdale [G4] *Pheasant Inn* (01524) 271230
Newton [C4] *Parker's Arms* (01200) 446236
Ulverston [D4] *Bay Horse*, (01229) 583972; *Farmer's Arms* (01229) 584469
Whitewell [G1] *Inn at Whitewell* (01200) 448222
Yealand Conyers [F4] *New Inn* (01524) 732938

views over the Hodder and Wyre valleys. Red grouse, snipe and meadow pipits flourish on the moors.

ULVERSTON [D4] The film comedian Stan Laurel was born in the town in 1890; the **Laurel and Hardy Museum** is devoted to his famous partnership with Oliver Hardy.

WALNEY ISLAND [C3] South Walney reserve has Europe's largest ground-nesting site of herring gulls and lesser black-backed gulls. North Walney reserve has the rare natterjack toad and the Walney geranium – a plant found nowhere else in Britain.

WARTON [F4] The village has a ruined 14th-century rectory ⚜. The church tower was built by an ancestor of George Washington, first president of the United States of America.

Seas of sand *With miles of wide sandy beaches, **Morecambe** burgeoned in the 19th century as a resort for mill workers. There are fine views over the expanse of Morecambe Bay from the promenade.*

The Yorkshire Dales and the central Pennines

TOURIST INFORMATION

Boroughbridge (01423) 323373
Harrogate (01423) 537300
Ilkley (01943) 602319
Knaresborough (01423) 866886
Otley (0113) 247 7707
Pateley Bridge (01423) 711147
Ripon (01765) 604625
Settle (01729) 825192
Skipton (01756) 792809
Thirsk (01845) 522755
Wetherby (01937) 582151

THE GOOD PUB GUIDE

Appletreewick [D2] *Craven Arms* (01756) 720270
Asenby [H4] *Crab & Lobster* (01845) 577286
Boroughbridge [H3] *Black Bull* (01423) 322413
Buckden [C4] *Buck Inn* (01756) 760228
Burnsall [D3] *Red Lion* (01756) 720204
Cray [C4] *White Lion* (01756) 760262
Ferrensby [G3] *General Tarleton* (01423) 340284
Hetton [C2] *Angel* (01756) 730263
Hubberholme [C4] *George* (01756) 760223
Litton [B4] *Queens Arms* (01756) 770208
Ramsgill [E4] *Yorke Arms* (01423) 755243)
Ripley [F3] *Boar's Head* (01423) 771888
Settle [B3] *Golden Lion* (01729) 822203
Starbotton [C4] *Fox & Hounds* (01756) 760269

Eroded pavements *Bald outcrops of porous limestone are easily sculpted into dramatic fissures, caves and underground potholes by wind and rain. These flat-topped 'pavements' of clefted rock lie near Malham Cove.*

ALDBOROUGH [H3] The chief town of the Celtic Brigantes tribe became a Roman centre in AD 71, and two mosaic pavements from a house of the 2nd or 3rd century can be viewed in the Roman Town ✿. In 14th-century **St Andrew's Church** is a statue of the god Mercury, whose temple reputedly stood on this site.

BOLTON ABBEY [D2] Nearby, the ruined 12th-century Augustinian priory stands amid meadows and woods beside the **Wharfe**, a setting used by Sir Edwin Landseer in his 1834 painting *Bolton Abbey in Olden Time*. The priory's nave is now incorporated in the village church.

BOROUGHBRIDGE [G3] West of the village are the **Devil's Arrows**, three standing stones – possibly fertility symbols – some 3000 years old and about 6m (20ft) high. Hewn from millstone grit, they were hauled about 7 miles from Abbey Plain near Knaresborough.

BRIMHAM ROCKS [F3] On moors high above the Nidd, these huge gritstone outcrops ❧ have been weathered into strange shapes.

FOUNTAINS ABBEY [F3] Founded in 1132 beside the Skell, Fountains ❧ became the richest Cistercian abbey in England. Its remains are beautifully preserved. **Studley Royal Water**

Gardens, in which the ruins stand, were laid out in the 18th century. Displays at **Fountains Hall** recount the history of the abbey.

GRASSINGTON [D3] This Dales village has a cobbled square and a stone bridge of 1603 spanning the Wharfe. Two 18th-century lead miners' cottages house the **Upper Wharfedale Folk Museum**.

HARROGATE [F2] Visitors have crowded this spa town since 1571, when William Slingsby found the Tewit Well. The 1897 **Victorian Royal Baths Assembly Rooms** today house Turkish baths. **The Royal Pump Room**, built in 1842 over a sulphur well, has a local history museum. The town is an exhibition and conference centre.

ILKLEY [E1] When Squire Middleton built baths at White Wells in 1756, fed by a spring on Ilkley Moor, Ilkley became a spa. The 16th-century **Manor House**, now a museum, is on the site of a Roman fort of AD 79, and **All Saints' Church**, partly 13th century, has Roman altars and three Saxon crosses. The moor, made famous in the song 'On Ilkla Moor baht 'at', has many rocks with 3000-year-old cup-and-ring carvings.

KETTLEWELL [C4] This Wharfedale village is close to 702m (2302ft) **Buckden Pike**. To the south, rugged **Kilnsey Crag** rises above Kilnsey village, named for the limekilns once scattered over the hillsides.

KNARESBOROUGH [G2] A chemist's shop in the marketplace, in use since 1720, claims to be England's oldest. Above the town, a ruined 14th-century castle looks down on a gorge of the Nidd spanned by a 19th-century railway viaduct. At **Dropping Well** nearby, water mixes with lime and turns objects hung above the rock face to stone.

MALHAM COVE [B3] Scree reaches down on each side of the cliff to a stream at its base. At the top are limestone pavements – flat rocks with deep clefts in which plants grow. Paths lead to magnificent **Gordale Scar**, where waterfalls plunge 76m (250ft) into a ravine.

RIPLEY [F3] Home to the Ingilbys since the 14th century, the castle was rebuilt in the 18th century with gardens designed by 'Capability' Brown. In 1827 Sir William Amcotts Ingilby remodelled Ripley to resemble a French village in Alsace Lorraine.

RIPON [G4] In the market square, a 28m (90ft) obelisk supports a gilded horn – a symbol of the horn presented by Alfred the Great in AD 886. The cathedral has a 13th-century west front; its 7th-century crypt is the remains of a Saxon church.

SETTLE [B3] Set below **Castleberg Crag**, the town has narrow lanes with 17–18th-century houses. **The Shambles**, or market, of 1680 has three storeys – living quarters are above the shops. George Birkbeck, born here in 1776, founded Birkbeck College. The **Carlisle to Settle** railway was a feat of Victorian engineering.

SKIPTON [C2] In this market town the 11th-century castle has a yew tree planted by Lady Anne Clifford, who restored the castle in the 1650s. The region's geology, natural history and archaeology are explained in the **Craven Museum** in the Town Hall.

STUMP CROSS CAVERNS [D3] Weirdly shaped stalagmites and stalactites, which began to form some 500,000 years ago, can be seen in these limestone caverns.

The Yorkshire Wolds and the Derwent Valley

BEMPTON CLIFFS [H4] The **RSPB** reserve is the only mainland site in Britain with a colony of gannets; they nest between May and July. During summer, chalk cliffs pulsate with puffins, razorbills, guillemots, kittiwakes and other sea birds.

BISHOP WILTON [D2] A clear beck runs through this village set in a green hollow. **St Edith's Church** has an unusual black-and-white mosaic floor depicting birds such as lapwings, magpies and ducks.

BOYNTON [G3] **St Andrew's Church** has a reminder that the Strickland family of **Boynton Hall** introduced the turkey from the USA in the 18th century. At nearby Rudston, in **All Saints' churchyard**, is a 8m (25ft) high, 46 ton standing stone that was erected some 2000 years ago.

BRIDLINGTON [H3] The resort town is perched above the busy fishing harbour. **St Mary's Church** was once the nave of a 12th-century priory church, and **Bayle Museum** is in the 14th-century gatehouse of the priory. Nearby **Sewerby Hall**, an 18th-century mansion opened to the public in 1936 by Amy Johnson, the pioneer aviator, has an Amy Johnson museum.

BURTON AGNES [G3] **Burton Agnes Hall**, built in 1598–1610, has a turreted gatehouse, a Great Hall, and a collection of Impressionist art. Close to the hall is a Norman **manor ⌗** dating from 1173.

BYLAND ABBEY [A4] Sheltered by the Hambleton Hills, the medieval **abbey** ruins ⌗ include a 13th-century tiled floor and a wide rose window.

CASTLE HOWARD [C3] See picture.

COXWOLD [A4] Laurence Sterne, the 18th-century novelist, was vicar at **St Michael's Church**. His house was named Shandy Hall after his novel *The Life and Opinions of Tristram Shandy*. At nearby **Newburgh Priory**, a brick vault unopened since 1660 is said to be Oliver Cromwell's tomb.

DRIFFIELD [F2] Known as the capital of the Wolds, this market town has **All Saints' Church** with a 34m (110ft) 15th-century tower.

FILEY [G5] Sandy beaches stretch for 6 miles along **Filey Bay**, sheltered by Filey Brigg, a breakwater of jagged rock. The **Wolds Way** and the **Cleveland Way**, meet at Filey.

HELMSLEY [B5] On the edge of the moors in Ryedale, this handsome limestone town is dominated by its ruined 12–13th century **castle ⌗** and defended by two rings of ditches. A fortified gate and a fine Tudor hall remain intact. **Duncombe Park**, built in 1713 and home to the Feversham family for nearly 300 years, has fine landscaped gardens.

Baroque splendour **Castle Howard** was built in 1699–1726 by John Vanbrugh and Nicholas Hawksmoor for Charles Howard, 3rd Earl of Carlisle. The house has a collection of post-1700 costume, and paintings by artists including Van Dyck, Holbein, Gainsborough and Reynolds.

HORNSEA [H1] Renowned for its pottery, this seaside resort began as a spa in 1730, when visitors were drawn by its chalybeate spring. A 16th-century farmhouse has a **Museum of Village Life**. A local man built **Bettison's Folly**, a 15m (50ft) tower, in 1844 so his servants could watch for him and have a meal prepared. At **Hornsea Mere** birds, including herons, grebes, reed warblers and teal, find sanctuary to the east of the lake.

KILBURN [A4] Thomas Taylor, a grocer, impressed by the White Horse of Uffington in Oxfordshire, carved the 96m (314ft) figure of a horse in the hillside above Kilburn in 1857. Craftsman Robert Thompson became world-renowned as the Mouseman of Kilburn; his mouse trademark carved on furniture and other oak woodwork.

MALTON [D4] One of the north's largest livestock markets is held here. Horses are bred in the area and thoroughbreds are trained on nearby Langton Wold. Relics from a Roman fort of about AD 70 are on display in the **Roman Museum** in the 18th-century former town hall.

NUNNINGTON HALL [C4] As well as tapestries and a panelled hall, this manor house ✤ has a series of rooms that are one-eighth normal size and in styles of different periods.

PICKERING [D5] One of Britain's oldest market towns, founded as a Celtic settlement in 270 BC. The castle ⌗ was a hunting lodge of medieval kings. Wallpaintings in the church of **St Peter and St Paul** include subjects such as Salome dancing for Herod.

POCKLINGTON [D1] Twisting alleys in this market town lead to **All Saints' Church**, with its fine 15th-century tower. An exhibition of amusement machines is housed in a former cinema. At **Burnby Hall**, the lakes have more than 50 kinds of water lily.

RIEVAULX ABBEY [B5] The Gothic ruins of the **abbey ⌗** soar upwards in three-tiered walls and arcades of pointed arches. It was founded by French Cistercian monks in 1132, but the ruins date mainly from the 13th century. **Rievaulx Terrace ✤**, laid out on the hillside above in 1758, gives views over the ruins and across to Ryedale and the Hambleton Hills.

SLEDMERE HOUSE [E3] Completed in 1751, the house is filled with Chippendale, Sheraton and French furniture. At **Duggleby Howe**, 4000-year-old tools made of antlers were found in a Stone Age burial mound.

YORK [B2] Chief among the city's many glories is the huge **Minster**, built 1220–1470, and its treasury of medieval stained glass. Founded by the Romans in AD 71 as Eboracum, York has remnants of its Roman walls. Viking invaders in the 9th century knew the city as Jorvik, and the **Jorvik Viking Centre** tells of Viking days. In the **Castle Museum**, there are period rooms dating from 1870 and three Victorian streets. The castle was once a prison, where in 1739 Dick Turpin the highwayman spent the night before he was hanged. The **National Railway Museum** traces the history of the railways, including *Mallard* of 1938, the fastest steam locomotive.

The Lake District and the Cumbrian Fells

AMBLESIDE [F2] Lying at the foot of **Wansfell Pike**, the oldest part of this resort is on the hillside above 17th-century **Bridge House**, which spans Stock Ghyll stream. North of the town, the brook gushes over rocky ledges as Stockghyll Force waterfall.

BOWNESS-ON-WINDERMERE [F2] Steamer trips run from Bowness and Ambleside, and the **Lakeside and Haverthwaite Railway** offers steam-train rides. **Windermere Steam Boat Museum** and the **National Park Visitor Centre**, Brockhole are nearby.

COCKERMOUTH [C5] Pastel-toned Georgian and Victorian houses line the streets. William Wordsworth was born in **Wordsworth House** in 1770. **Jennings's Brewery** is open for tours, and there are toy, mineral and printing museums, and an art gallery.

CONISTON [E2] The **Old Man of Coniston** towers over this former copper-mining village. **Brantwood**, across the lake, was home to the writer and social reformer John Ruskin and is filled with his furniture, paintings and books; he is buried in Coniston churchyard. The restored Victorian steam yacht *Gondola* plies the lake. **Grizedale Forest** has sculpture trails and nature trails.

DALEMAIN [G5] An 18th-century pink sandstone façade hides the mainly medieval and Elizabethan

core of this house, which includes a pele tower – a refuge from Scots raiders. Nearby **Dacre** has four stone bears in the churchyard.

DERWENT WATER [E4] Wooded islets stud the mountain-ringed lake. There are boat trips from six piers, and superb views from the east shore.

GOSFORTH [C2] By the church is a stone cross of about AD 1000. Its carvings of beasts and men blend old Norse legend and Christianity, and may represent good overcoming evil.

GRASMERE [E3] **Dove Cottage** was home to William Wordsworth from 1799–1808. There is a **Wordsworth Museum** by the cottage. For the 37 years before his death in 1850, the poet lived at nearby **Rydal Mount**. His grave is in Grasmere churchyard.

HAWKSHEAD [E2] The town is little changed from the early 20th century, when Beatrix Potter knew it and married solicitor William Heelis. His offices now form the **Beatrix Potter Gallery**. Wordsworth's desk can be seen at the old grammar school.

HILL TOP [F1] Beatrix Potter bought this farmhouse in **Near Sawrey** in 1905 and it has been kept just as she left it. The farmer stayed as a tenant, and here she wrote stories such as *The Tale of Mr Jeremy Fisher* and *The Tale of Jemima Puddle-Duck*.

KENDAL [G1] Among many historic parts of the town are the 18th-century yards, built to house weavers. **Abbot Hall** has an art gallery with several portraits by George Romney, and has the **Museum of Lakeland Life and Industry** in the stable block.

KESWICK [E4] The town grew from the 1850s, when the railway brought in tourists. **The Moot Hall** dates from 1813. **Cumberland Pencil Museum** gives details of a local industry. Above Derwent Water, is the early Bronze Age **Castlerigg Stone Circle**.

RAVENGLASS [C2] Once a Roman naval base, the village has a ruined **Roman bath house**. Today it is the terminus of the **Ravenglass and Eskdale Railway**, built in the 1870s for the local iron industry. Nearby **Muncaster Castle** has the **World Owl Centre** in its grounds.

SIZERGH CASTLE [G1] The castle, home of the Strickland family for 750 years, is decorated with fine Elizabethan wood carving.

STOTT PARK BOBBIN MILL [F1] Reels and bobbins for Lancashire's 19th-century cotton mills were made at the mill from 1835 to 1971.

TOWNEND [F2] This yeoman's, or freeholder's, farmhouse of about 1626 was, until 1943, the home of the Browne family. It retains many pieces of fine, hand-carved furniture.

ULLSWATER [F4] Steamers plying Ullswater afford splendid views of **Helvellyn**, at 950m (3117ft), the third highest peak in the Lake District. **Aira Beck** drops 21m (70ft) over the Aira Force waterfall before it flows into Ullswater.

WAST WATER [D3] A scree-strewn slope drops 610m (2000ft) to the deepest lake in England, next to **Scafell Pike**, England's highest

mountain. North-east is **Great Gable's** pyramidal peak – the Lake District National Park's emblem.

WHITEHAVEN [B4] Built as a coal port, the town was second only to London until the early 1800s, when Liverpool eclipsed it. There are many fine 18th-century buildings. The **Beacon Heritage Centre** tells the Whitehaven story.

TOURIST INFORMATION

Ambleside (015394) 32582
Borrowdale (017687) 77294
Bowness-on-Windermere
(015394) 42895
Cockermouth (01900) 822634
Coniston NP (015394) 41533
Grasmere NP (015394) 35245
Hawkshead NP
(015394) 36525
Kendal (01539) 725758
Keswick (017687) 72645
Lake District Visitor Centre
(015394) 46601
Penrith (01768) 867466
Whitehaven (01946) 852939
Windermere (015394) 46499

THE GOOD PUB GUIDE

Crosthwaite [F1] *Punch Bowl*
(015395) 68237
Askham [G4] *Punch Bowl*
(01931) 712443
Buttermere [D4] *Bridge Hotel*
(017687) 70252
Coniston [E2] *Black Bull*
(015394) 41335
Crosthwaite [F1] *Punch Bowl*
(015395) 68237
Grasmere [E3] *Travellers Rest*
(015394) 35604
Hawkshead [E2] *Drunken Duck*
(015394) 36347
Loweswater [C4] *Kirkstile Inn*
(01900) 85219
Seathwaite [D2] *Newfield Inn*
(01229) 716208
Troutbeck [F2] *Queens Head*
(015394) 32174

TOURING GUIDE

*Poet's paradise The wonderful landscape around **Grasmere** inspired the poet William Wordsworth to write some of his finest poetry praising the beauty of the natural world. In The Recluse he wrote of Grasmere's 'crags and woody slopes…its one green island and its winding shores'.*

FROM MAP ON PAGES 180–181

The high dales of Durham and North Yorkshire

APPLEBY-IN-WESTMORLAND [A4] Boroughgate leads past this attractive market town's 16th-century **Moot Hall** to the Norman **castle**, which was restored in the 17th century.

AYSGARTH FALLS [E1] See picture (below left).

BARNARD CASTLE [E4] High above the Tees is the **castle ⌗** that gives the

*Sheltered cascades In a wooded gorge the Ure tumbles over three ledges, extending for ½ mile, called the **Aysgarth Falls**. The cloth for the red shirts of the 19th-century Italian patriot Garibaldi and his followers was woven at nearby Yore Mill; today it houses the **Yorkshire Carriage Museum**.*

town its name. In the **Bowes Museum** is the art collection of the coal magnate who built the château-style house in 1869. The ruins of **Egglestone Abbey ⌗** are nearby.

BEDALE [G1] Georgian houses line the cobbled square of this market town. **Bedale Hall**, now a museum, has an ornate ballroom. **Thorp Perrow Arboretum** is nearby.

BINCHESTER ROMAN FORT [G5] This 1st-century AD cavalry fort has tall earth ramparts and a hypocaust, which probably heated the bath house of the commanding officer.

BISHOP AUCKLAND [G5] In the town marketplace is a neo-Gothic gateway of 1760. It is the entrance to **Auckland Castle**, the residence of the prince bishops of Durham for some 800 years. Older areas like **St Peter's**

Chapel, originally built in the 12th-century as a banqueting hall, lie beneath its 18th-century façade.

BOWES [D3] Charles Dickens based 'Dotheboys Hall' in *Nicholas Nickleby* on a school in the village and William Shaw, inspiration for the character of Wackford Squeers, is buried in St Giles' churchyard. **Bowes Castle ⌗** has a 12th-century keep.

BROUGH [B3] On the edge of this village the ruins of **Brough Castle ⌗** occupy a site fortified since Roman times. The Norman castle was extensively altered in the 1650s.

BUTTER TUBS PASS [C2] Swaledale and Wensleydale are linked by the pass which rises to a height of 526m (1726ft). Farmers going to market used to cool butter by lowering it into the 18–24m (60–80ft) deep potholes, or 'Butter Tubs', at the top of the pass.

CASTLE BOLTON [E1] Mary, Queen of Scots was imprisoned in **Bolton Castle**, a fortified manor house, from 1568–9. The castle is partly in ruins, but still 30m (100ft) high in some places.

DARLINGTON [G3] A Victorian covered market marks the town's role as a commercial centre that

developed as a railway engineering town in the 19th century. *Locomotion* (see picture), George Stephenson's steam engine, can be seen in the **Railway Centre and Museum**. In Morton Park Way, the sculptor David Mach used 185,000 bricks to create *Train*, a 46m (150ft) long locomotive.

DENT [B1] High hills rise all around Dent's cobbled streets, an isolated village set in lovely Dentdale. The **Dent Fault**, which cuts through the valley, has limestone fells on its east side and weathered slate to its west.

ESCOMB [F5] St John's Church dates from the 7th or early 8th century and is one of the best-preserved Saxon buildings in Britain. It was built from dark gritstone, much of which came from the Roman fort at **Binchester**.

GRINTON [E2] The village church was founded in Norman times but extended in the 15th century. Bodies for burial were carried there along a path known as the Corpse Way.

GUNNERSIDE [D2] Once the Dales lead-mining centre, the village is beside Gunnerside Gill, where the waters rush through a steep-sided valley. The ruins of the **Old Gang lead mine** dominate the area.

HAMSTERLEY FOREST [E5] Nature trails lead through the forest's varied terrain where red squirrels and roe deer can be seen among the trees.

HAWES [C1] Wensleydale's main town has large livestock markets. In the **Dales Countryside Museum**, displays on local life include lead-mining and sheepfarming. At **The Ropeworks**, across the street, visitors can watch ropes being made, and at the Wensleydale cheese factory, slightly out of town, the process of making the famous cheese can be seen – and the results tasted.

JERVAULX ABBEY [F1] In spring, purple aubrietia drapes the ruins of this Cistercian abbey, pronounced 'Jervo'. The first Wensleydale cheese was made here by abbey monks.

KIRKBY STEPHEN [B3] A house near the church in this wool town has an open gallery where women used to spin and weave. In the church is a 10th-century cross shaft with an odd Anglo-Danish carving of a devil.

KISDON GORGE [C2] The swift-flowing Swale cascades through this steep, wooded gorge, a short walk from Keld. **Cartrake Force** and **Wain Wath Force** waterfalls are nearby.

MIDDLEHAM [F1] While he was Protector of the North, the future Richard III used the castle's keep **⌗** as his headquarters from 1472.

TOURIST INFORMATION

Appleby (017683) 51177
Aysgarth Falls (01969) 663424
Barnard Castle (01833) 690909
Bedale (01677) 424604
Bishop Auckland
(01388) 604922
Darlington (01325) 388666
Hawes NP (01969) 667450
Kirkby Stephen (017683) 71199
Leyburn (01969) 623069
Northallerton (01609) 776864
Reeth (01748) 884059
Richmond (01748) 850252

THE GOOD PUB GUIDE

Constable Burton [F1] *Wyvill Arms* (01677) 450581
East Witton [F1] *Blue Lion* (01969) 624273
Langthwaite [E2] *Charles Bathurst Inn* (01748) 884567
Leyburn [F1] *Sandpiper* (01969) 622206
Romaldkirk [D4] *Rose & Crown* (01833) 650213

RABY CASTLE [F4] This large, battlemented castle was built in the mid 14th century on the site of an earlier fortified manor house. Its vaulted kitchen is medieval, but much of the interior was remodelled in the 18th and 19th centuries.

*Pulling power In 1825, Locomotion, on show in **Darlington**, hauled the world's first passenger train from Shildon to Stockton via Darlington.*

RICHMOND [F2] Narrow 'wynds', or lanes, descend from the cobbled marketplace of this hilltop town. The 12th-century keep of **Richmond Castle ⌗** stands 30m (100ft) high and overlooks the Swale gorge. In the marketplace is the **regimental museum** of the Green Howards.

The North York moors and the Cleveland Hills

DALBY FOREST [F1] A remnant of the medieval Forest of Pickering that once stretched to Whitby, Dalby now has conifer plantations.

DANBY RIGG [D3] Cairns and dykes some 2000 years old still stand on this moor and one stone, 1.8m (6ft) high, survives from a Bronze Age circle.

FALLING FOSS [F2] From the forest trail car park, a track leads to this 12m (40ft) waterfall on May Beck.

FYLINGDALES MOOR [F2] A missile early-warning system in the shape of a truncated pyramid towers above the Ministry of Defence site here.

GOATHLAND [E2] High amid the moors, the stone-built village is the setting for the TV series *Heartbeat*. It has a station on the North Yorkshire Moors Railway and an old livestock pound. Close by is **Mallyan Spout**, a 21m (70ft) waterfall on the West Beck.

GREAT AYTON [C3] Captain James Cook lived here as a child; his school is now the **Captain Cook Museum** and a monument to him stands 15m (50ft) high on Easby Moor. **Roseberry Topping** 🞔, nearby, is a 320m (1050ft) hill with superb views.

GUISBOROUGH [C4] Robert de Brus – an ancestor of the Scottish king Robert Bruce – founded a priory here

in 1119. Its remains include the **gatehouse** and the 14th-century east end of the **abbey church** 🞔.

HOLE OF HORCUM [E1] This huge natural amphitheatre has been worn away over the centuries by spring water. From the southern slope there are views over the **Vale of Pickering**.

HUTTON LE HOLE [D1] A medieval cruck house and an Edwardian photographic studio can be seen at the **Ryedale Folk Museum**. Remains of animals such as spotted hyenas, which lived in Britain about 150,000 years ago, were found in a cave at nearby **Kirk Dale**.

KIRKLEATHAM [C4] The Old Hall, now a **Museum of Local Life**, was one of Britain's first lending libraries. Other fine buildings are the **Turner Mausoleum**, built onto 10th-century **St Cuthbert's Church**, and the 1742 **chapel** attached to the hospital.

LEALHOLM [E3] An 18th-century stone bridge and stepping stones cross the Esk at this riverside village.

MIDDLESBROUGH [B4] See City Routes pp300–301.

MOUNT GRACE PRIORY [B2] Monks at this Carthusian priory 🞔, founded in 1398, swore a vow of silence and lived in separate cells.

ROBIN HOOD'S BAY [G3] Visitors must park at the top and walk down the steep, narrow streets, lined with stone cottages, to the quay and fossil-rich bay. The **Fisherhead museum** recalls the village's history as a major 19th-century fishing centre.

SALTBURN-BY-THE-SEA [D4] The hydraulic lift, built in 1884, that links the town with the pier 37m (120ft) below is the oldest in Britain.

SANDSEND [F3] In 1607 one of Cleveland's first alum works began quarrying here. Two streams lead to Mulgrave Woods and the ruins of Mulgrave Castle.

SCARBOROUGH [G1] Sea bathing in Britain is said to have begun at Scarborough in the 1660s, a spa since 1620. Bathing machines were used in 1733, the first recorded use in Europe. Today the town is a large resort and conference centre. A 12th-century **castle** 🞔 stands on the 90m (300ft) high cliffs on the site of a Roman signal station. The novelist Anne Brontë is buried at **St Mary's Church**.

SKINNINGROVE [D4] The discovery of ironstone at this fishing village in 1848 changed it into an iron and steel centre. Mines in the area were active until the 1950s – the **Tom Leonard Mining Museum** tells their story.

STAITHES [E4] When Captain Cook was an apprentice here in 1745, up to 50 fishing cobles sailed out daily.

TOURIST INFORMATION

Danby NP (01439) 772737
Great Ayton (01642) 722835
Guisborough (01287) 633801
Low Dalby (01751) 460295
Middlesbrough (01642) 729700
Ravenscar (National Trust
    Coastal Information Centre)
    (01723) 870138/870423
Saltburn-by-the-Sea
    (01287) 622422
Scarborough (01723) 383636
Stockton-on-Tees
    (01642) 393936
Whitby (01723) 383637

THE GOOD PUB GUIDE

Danby [D3] *Duke of Wellington*
    (01287) 660351
Fadmoor [D1] *Plough*
    (01751) 431515
Levisham [E1] *Horseshoe*
    (01751) 460240
Osmotherley [B2] *Golden Lion*
    (01609) 883526
Rosedale Abbey [D2] *Milburn
    Arms* (01751) 417312

Now, tourism is the village's mainstay and there is a **Captain Cook Heritage Centre**. **Dog Loup**, an alley to the harbour, is 18in (457mm) wide.

WADE'S CAUSEWAY [E2] A well-preserved stretch of Roman road, open only to walkers, extends for 1¼ miles across Wheeldale Moor.

WHITBY [F3] See picture.

TOURING GUIDE

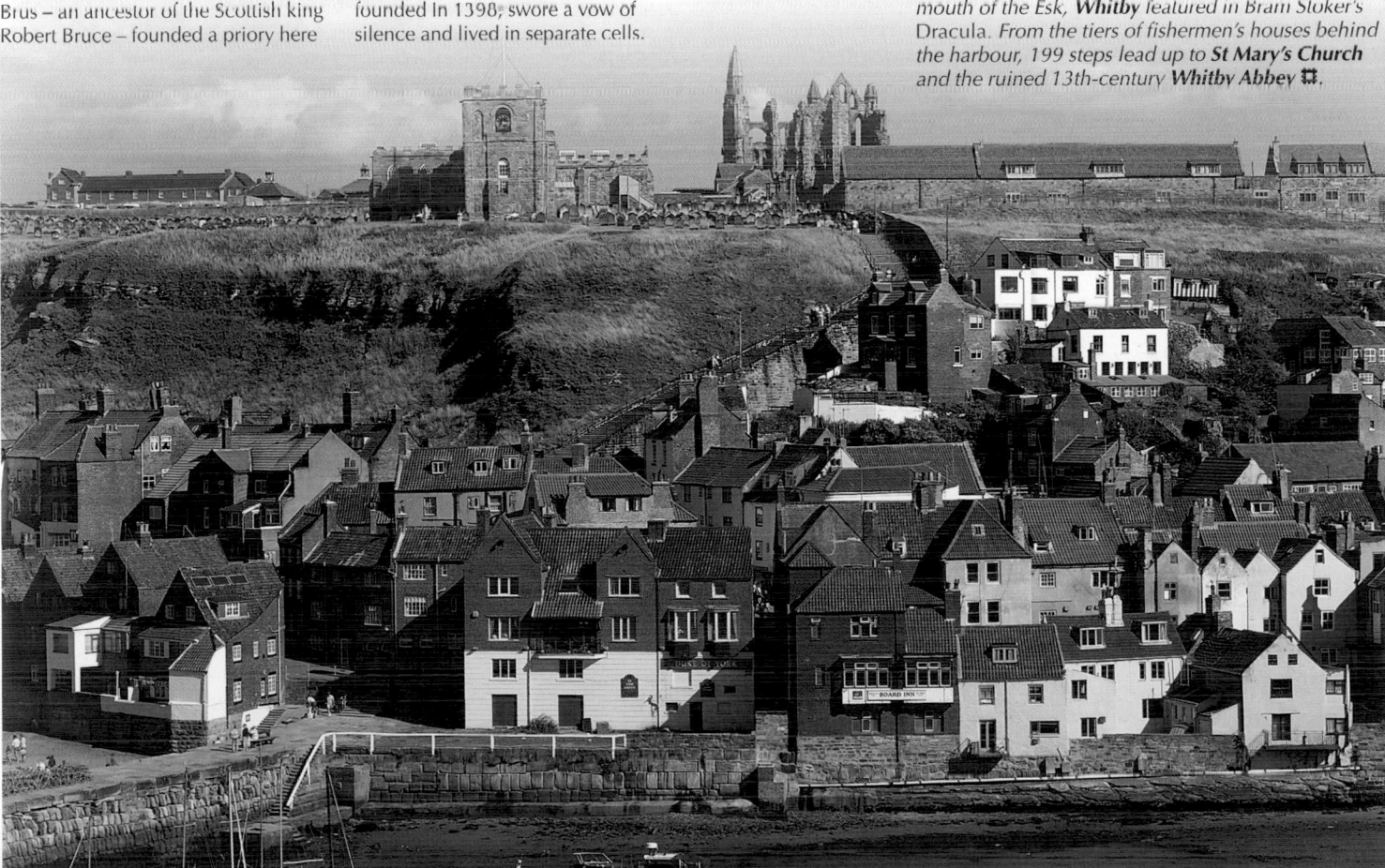

Inspirational setting *A former whaling port on the mouth of the Esk,* **Whitby** *featured in Bram Stoker's* Dracula. *From the tiers of fishermen's houses behind the harbour, 199 steps lead up to* **St Mary's Church** *and the ruined 13th-century* **Whitby Abbey** 🞔.

The Rhins of Galloway and southern Dumfries

Map on page184–5

CASTLE KENNEDY GARDENS [D4]
Soldiers shaped these gardens in the 18th century. Terraces are adorned with vivid trees and shrubs.

CORSEWALL POINT [B5] The beam of **Corsewall lighthouse** marks the windswept north-west tip of the Rhins peninsula for shipping. It was built by Robert Stevenson, the father of the writer Robert Louis Stevenson.

CREETOWN [G4] Rocks, crystals and gemstones can be seen in the **Gem Rock Museum**, including an agate that holds a water drop 200 million years old. A granite tower marks Queen Victoria's Diamond Jubilee.

DRUMMORE [D2] Scotland's most southerly village, the port once traded in coal, lime and smuggled goods. It is now a centre for sea-angling. Some 4 miles to the north-west are the **Logan Botanic Gardens**.

GARLIESTON [G3] This bright village of colourful cottages was once a shipbuilding centre. **Galloway House** has fine azaleas and rhododendrons.

GLENLUCE [D4] A derelict viaduct, on the former Carlisle–Stranraer railway, dominates the village. **Glenluce Abbey (NTS, HS)** still has much of its 15th-century chapter house, with a fine vaulted ceiling.

KIRKMADRINE [C3] This small church **(HS)** has three carved 5th–6th-century stones, some of Britain's earliest Christian memorials.

LUCE SANDS [D3] A long arc of sand sweeps round the head of **Luce Bay**. Much of the beach is a firing range, but there are forest walks and picnic sites to the east.

MULL OF GALLOWAY [D1] Seven tides meet at the southernmost point of Scotland. In summer, many sea birds can be seen on the 76m (250ft) high cliffs (an **RSPB** reserve).

NEWTON STEWART [G5] This market town was founded in 1677 and is a good base for exploring Galloway Forest Park. At **Creebridge** there is a mohair and knitwear outlet.

PORTPATRICK [B3] Until storms ruined the harbour walls in the 1840s, Portpatrick was the port for a packet boat to Northern Ireland. The resort offers golf, watersports and cliff walks.

PORT WILLIAM [F2] A sailing and shark-fishing centre in Luce Bay, the village was notorious for smuggling in the 18th century. **Monreith House** to the south was the home of Sir William Maxwell, the village's founder. On the coast near Monreith village there is an otter sculpture commemorating the author Gavin Maxwell.

STRANRAER [C4] Ferries ply daily to Belfast from this port on Loch Ryan. The **Castle of St John** was the headquarters of Viscount Dundee, or John Graham of Claverhouse, known as 'Bluidy Clavers' for his repression of Protestant Covenanters.

WHITHORN [G2] St Ninian built Scotland's first church here in about AD 397. A barrel-vaulted crypt and roofless nave remain from the **12th-century priory**. Early Christian crosses are displayed in the **Priory Museum**.

WIGTOWN [G4] Until its harbour silted up in 1914, Wigtown was a busy port. Now it is a base for touring the Machars peninsula. A monument to martyred Covenanters stands on Windyhill. Nearby is the ruined 17th-century **Baldoon Castle**, the setting for *The Bride of Lammermoor*, a novel by Sir Walter Scott.

Map on page186–7

ABBEY TOWN [G3] This farming village grew around the 12th-century Cistercian abbey of **Holm Cultram**. Robert Bruce sacked the abbey in

1322, but **St Mary's Church** was restored in 1883. **Silloth**, to the north-west, takes its name from the laths, or granaries, where monks stored grain.

BALCARY POINT [C3] Wading birds such as dunlins and redshanks forage offshore. Smugglers built **Balcary House** in the 18th century to store contraband from the Isle of Man.

BOWNESS-ON-SOLWAY [G4] Once the Roman fortress of Maia, the main road follows the line of Maia's central thoroughfare. **Glasson Moss**, nearby, is a national nature reserve of moss and peat bog. (Visits by permit only.)

CAERLAVEROCK CASTLE [E5] See picture.

CASTLE DOUGLAS [C4] Today's market town was once a busy cotton-spinning centre. At **Carlingwark Loch** are two crannogs or Bronze Age islets made of brushwood and logs. To the north-west is the **Mote of Urr**, a large, man-made castle mound.

ECCLEFECHAN [G5] Arched House (NTS), now a museum, was the birthplace of the historian Thomas Carlyle in 1795.

GATEHOUSE OF FLEET [A4] The history of this town, which prospered from cotton manufacturing, is told at the **Mill on the Fleet Heritage Centre**. In the 15th-century **Cardoness Castle (HS)** nearby is a 'murder hole' for pouring hot pitch on beseigers.

GRETNA GREEN [H5] Couples from England eloped to get married here after 1754, when English law forbade unlicensed marriages. Runaways were married at the blacksmith's, **Gretna Hall** and the **tollhouse** at Sark Bridge; all three are now museums.

Triangular castle *The splendid 13th-century Caerlaverock Castle is three-cornered, with a 15th-century gatehouse. The nearby nature reserve is a winter haven for birds, including barnacle geese from Spitzbergen.*

KEN-DEE MARSHES [B5] The valley of Loch Ken and the Dee is a haven for birdlife. A flock of white-fronted geese from Greenland winter here.

KIPPFORD [C3] At low tide a shingle spit leads to **Rough Island (NTS)**, a bird sanctuary where terns nest. Views from the cliff-top **Jubilee Path (NTS)**, which leads to Rockliffe, extend to the Lake District. Nearby is the **Mote of Mark (NTS)** a 6th-century Celtic fort.

KIRKCUDBRIGHT [B3] By the harbour at Kircudbright (pronounced 'Kirkoobree') is **MacLellan's Castle (HS)** of 1582, a turreted mansion with a spyhole – or 'laird's lug' – in the fireplace of the Great Hall.

MABIE FOREST [D5] This hillside forest has fine views of the granite heights of Criffel, Caerlaverock and the Solway Firth.

NEW ABBEY [E5] Sweetheart Abbey **(HS)** dominates this greystone village. It was founded by Devorgilla Balliol in memory of her husband. It is said that she carried his heart in a casket and when she died it was buried with her at the abbey, hence its name.

RUTHWELL [F5] The 7th-century **Ruthwell Cross** is found in the church of this secluded village. Its 5m (18ft) high shaft has figures and runic verses from the Anglo-Saxon poem *The Dream of the Rood*, the earliest known poem in the English language.

THREAVE CASTLE [B4] South of the ruined 14th-century castle are the islands of the Threave Wildfowl Refuge, where wild geese and ducks such as teal spend winter. Nearby is **Threave Garden**, with more than 200 types of daffodil in spring.

The Cumbrian Fells and Hadrian's Wall

Roman frontier *Hadrian's Wall took just over seven years to build and extended for 73 miles. Stone-built up to 4m (14ft) high, the wall was manned by 18,000 troops.*

TOURIST INFORMATION

Alston (01434) 382244
Brampton (016977) 3433
Carlisle (01228) 625600
Corbridge (01434) 632815
Haltwhistle (01434) 322002
Hexham (01434) 652220
Once Brewed NP
   (01434) 344396
Penrith (01768) 867466
Southwaite (016974) 73445/6
Stanhope (01388) 527650

THE GOOD PUB GUIDE

Allenheads [F3] *Allenheads Inn*
   (01434) 685200
Armathwaite [C3] *Dukes Head*
   (016974) 72226
Caldbeck [A2] *Oddfellows Arms*
   (016974) 78227
Garrigill [E2] *George & Dragon*
   (01434) 381293
Melmerby [D2] *Shepherds*
   (01768) 881217

ALLEN BANKS [F4] Roe deer and red squirrels can be seen among the trees that cling to the steep banks of the Allen. The east bank gives good views of Hadrian's Wall. At **Allen Gorge**, the banks plunge 76m (250ft) to riverside paths through woodland.

ALLENDALE TOWN [F4] On New Year's Eve the town is the scene of an ancient pagan ceremony in which men parade to the market square with barrels of blazing tar on their heads.

ALSTON [E3] Standing 290m (950ft) above sea level, there are splendid views of the Pennines from Alston, including Cross Fell – the highest peak in the chain at 893m (2930ft). To the south-west, an old lead mine and miners' living quarters have been restored at the **Killhope North of England Lead Mining Museum.**

ARMATHWAITE [C3] Houses cluster round the village bridge over the Eden, and nearby are the ruins of a medieval castle, which is now part of a Georgian mansion. The 12th-century **Chapel of Christ and St Mary** was rebuilt in the 17th century. A riverside walk leads to the village of Wetheral. Nearby stands a 15th-century gatehouse ✠ that was once part of a Benedictine priory of 1106.

BIRDOSWALD ROMAN FORT [D5] The gateway, tower and walls of this massive Roman fort ✠, built around AD 125, stand sentinel by Hadrian's

Wall. The fort, known to the Romans as Camboglanna, was built to defend the bridge over the **Irthing gorge**. An exhibition tells its history and of the life of the Roman garrison.

BLANCHLAND [G3] This 18th-century village in the River Derwent valley was created round an abandoned monastery. Remains of cloisters can be seen by the village inn, which is on the site of the abbot's guesthouse. The post office is built into the abbey gatehouse.

BRAMPTON [C4] Wooded hills shelter this small market town. Its cobble-lined main street leads to an octagonal **Moot Hall** of 1817, now an information centre. The parish **church** of 1874 has stained-glass windows by William Morris and Edward Burne-Jones, as does **Lanercost Priory** ✠, to the north-east. The priory's north aisle served as the parish church until 1740, when the nave was restored. Close by, a splendid 15th-century bridge spans the River Irthing.

CALDBECK [A2] John Peel, hero of the song 'D'ye ken John Peel?', hunted from this village, and his hunting coats were made at the village's former wool mills. Peel died aged 78, after a fall from his horse; his grave is in **St Kentigern's churchyard.**

CARLISLE [B4] On a bluff above the rivers Eden and Caldew, the **castle** ✠ of 1092 overlooks the busy city

founded by the Romans in about AD 78. In medieval times, Carlisle was repeatedly invaded by the Scots, and the castle was repaired after each assault. Parts of the city's 12th-century **walls** remain. The **cathedral** was created from an earlier church in 1133; twice damaged by fire, it is noted for its 14th-century stained glass and carved choir stalls. The **guildhall** of 1391 has a local history museum. **Tullie House**, built in 1689, houses the city museum.

CHESTERS FORT [G5] Built to house 500 men, Britain's best-preserved Roman cavalry fort ✠ is by the North Tyne near Hadrian's Wall.

CORBRIDGE [G4] A 14th-century pele tower beside **St Andrew's Church** was built when the town was troubled by Scottish raiders. A storehouse among the ruins at the **Roman Corstopitum** ✠ nearby is Britain's largest Roman building.

HALTWHISTLE [E4] This neat village by the River South Tyne is a good base for visiting Hadrian's Wall. It has a fine 13th-century **church** with a 16th-century tombstone to John Ridley, whose brother-in-law Nicholas Ridley, Bishop of London, was burnt at the stake in 1555.

HEXHAM [G4] The graceful Early English architecture of the **priory church** soars above the town's marketplace. Built in 1180–1250 and

restored in the 19th century, it stands on the site of an abbey founded in AD 674 by St Wilfred, of which the crypt and a Saxon throne survive. A fine carved choir screen fronts the Chantry. In the 14th-century jail is the **Border History Museum** with artefacts and reconstructions that tell the story of the reivers.

HOUSESTEADS ROMAN FORT [E5] Named Vercovicium, or hilly place, by the Romans, this is one of the best-preserved Roman forts 🏛, ✠ in Britain. In the 3rd century it housed a garrison of some 1000 men. The ruins include the commandant's house, barracks, granaries, a hospital and sections of the fort walls 2m (8ft) high.

KIRKOSWALD [C2] Converted from a pele tower, the two-storey college of 1450 housed priests from 15th-century St Oswald's Church. The church stands about 183m (200yd) from its Victorian bell tower, which is set on a hill to call people to prayer.

LITTLE SALKELD [C2] Cottages cluster near the village's restored 18th-century **water mill** on the Eden. To the north is a Bronze Age stone circle – **Long Meg and her Daughters.** Long Meg aligns with the midwinter Sun; her daughters form a circle 171m (560ft) across.

PENRITH [C1] A 14th-century **castle** marks the busy market town as a former stronghold against Scottish raiders. **Penrith Museum** is housed in a 17th-century girls' school.

TALKIN TARN COUNTRY PARK [C4] A watersports centre, this large lake is ringed by rich woodlands. Starting at the Victorian boathouse, waymarked trails lead among trees such as western hemlock and mountain ash.

TOURING GUIDE

North County Durham and Tyne and Wear

*Parkland splendour An avenue of ancient oaks crosses a landscaped 18th-century estate ❧ and leads to **Gibside Chapel**. The Palladian chapel by James Paine has box pews and a three-tiered mahogany pulpit.*

TOURIST INFORMATION

Durham (0191) 384 3720
Gateshead (0191) 478 4222
Hartlepool (01429) 869706
Newcastle upon Tyne
  (0191) 277 8000
North Shields (0191) 200 5895
Peterlee (0191) 586 4450
South Shields (0191) 454 6612
Sunderland
  (0191) 553 2000/1/2
Whitley Bay (0191) 200 8535

THE GOOD PUB GUIDE

Hedley on the Hill [A4] *Feathers*
  (01661) 843607
New York [C5] *Shiremoor Farm*
  (0191) 257 6302
Shincliffe [C2] *Seven Stars*
  (0191) 384 8454

JESMOND DENE [C5]
A woodland valley along the Ouseburn shelters **St Mary's Chapel**, the oldest church in Newcastle, and the ruins of a 19th-century banqueting hall.

MARSDEN BAY [D5]
High limestone cliffs fringe the bay, and isolated rock stacks rise from the beach. A lift takes visitors to caves at the base of the cliffs, where there is a pub dating from 1782.

NEWCASTLE UPON TYNE [B5]
See City Routes pp290–291.

PRUDHOE CASTLE [A4]
Part of the walls of this ruined 12th-century castle ⌗ are incorporated in the Percy family's 19th-century manor house, by the gatehouse. Thomas Bewick, the wood engraver and naturalist was born at nearby **Cherryburn** ❧.

SOUTH SHIELDS [D5] At this busy port, industrial Tyneside gives way to seaside, with a sandy beach and promenades. A trail following the footsteps of the writer Catherine Cookson, born locally in 1906, ends at the Museum. Beside the site of the **Roman Arbeia** of about AD 80, whose granaries fed the troops on Hadrian's Wall, there is a replica gateway. The actress Flora Robson (1902–84) was born in the town.

SUNDERLAND [D4] Centuries of coal mining, shipbuilding, pottery and glass-making made this port a flourishing town. The **River Wear Trail** explores the city's industrial heritage, and the **Museum and Art Gallery** has fine 19th-century lustreware pottery. **The National Glass Centre** is housed in a breathtaking modern structure with a glass roof. Nearby are **Monkwearmouth Station Museum** and 19th-century **Fulwell windmill**.

TYNEMOUTH [D5] On a headland beside the Tyne estuary, the ruins of **Tynemouth Castle** ⌗ enclose the remains of a priory of 1090. Relics of the Volunteer Life Brigade of 1864, Britain's first, are displayed in the **Watch House**.

WALLSEND [C5] At the eastern end of Hadrian's Wall, the town has finds from the Roman fort of Segedunum. The liner *Mauretania*, which for 22 years held the record for the fastest Atlantic crossing, was launched from here in 1907.

WASHINGTON [C4] Washington Old Hall ❧, restored in the 17th century, was for 430 years until 1613 the home of the ancestors of George Washington, the first president of the United States.

WHITLEY BAY [D5] A causeway leads to the **St Mary's Island** lighthouse at low tide – climb its 137 steps for fine views from the top.

WYLAM [A5] George Stephenson, co-inventor in 1829 of the steam locomotive *Rocket*, and father of the railways, was born in 1781 in a small cottage ❧ near the village.

BEAMISH [B3] Life in the early 1800s and 1900s has been vividly recreated at the **North of England Open Air Museum**. The 300-acre museum has a manor house, town, colliery village, working farm and railway station. Trams and buses carry visitors around the site and children will enjoy the Hall of Mirrors and rides at a Victorian fairground.

CAUSEY ARCH [B4] The single-span stone bridge of 1725–6 across the wooded gorge of **Beamish Burn** is one of the world's oldest railway bridges. It carried horse-drawn wagons on wooden rails from Tanfield Colliery to Gateshead. At nearby **Marley Hill** during the summer, steam engines of the **Tanfield Railway** still take passengers along part of the track.

DERWENT WALK COUNTRY PARK [B4] Woods, meadows, ponds and wetlands flank the Derwent Walk, an 11 mile disused railway track from Swalwell to Consett.

DURHAM [C2] In medieval times one of England's foremost cities, Durham stands in a tight loop of the Wear on a lofty sandstone outcrop crowned by its Norman **cathedral**. The **castle**, the palace of the prince bishops of Durham for nearly 800 years until 1837, is today the foundation college of Durham University. Riverside paths give fine views of the city. On Elvet Hill, the **Oriental Museum** has a 'Marvels of China' gallery and is devoted to art and antiquities from the Orient, with displays of ceramics, carvings, paintings and costumes. Durham County Cricket Club's stunning new ground, set in beautiful countryside, is just north at **Chester-le-Street**.

FINCHALE PRIORY [C3] A cross on the floor of this priory ⌗ marks the tomb of St Godric, a reformed pirate. The ruins, set beside the Wear, date from the 13th century.

GIBSIDE CHAPEL [B4] See picture (above).

HARTLEPOOL [E1] See City Routes pp300–301.

HYLTON CASTLE [D4] This keep gatehouse ⌗ was built in the 15th century to defend a ford of the Wear. It is said to be haunted by the ghost of a stablelad, known as The Cauld Lad.

JARROW [C5] The Saxon church of **St Paul**, now in the shadow of oil storage tanks, is a reminder that this industrial town began as a monastic settlement where the Venerable Bede (AD 673–735) lived. Nearby **Bede's World** tells his story. A plaque on the town hall recalls the 1936 march after the steelworks and shipyard closed.

*Learned seat Bede's Chair can be seen at **Jarrow Monastery**. Bede was nine when he went to the monastery in AD 682. His book, The Ecclesiastical History of the English People, is a major source of Britain's early history.*

South Ayrshire, Dumfries and Galloway

Map on page 192–3

BALLANTRAE [A2] The village fronts a sand and shingle beach. The ruins of **Ardstinchar Castle** guard the mouth of the Stinchar, a haven for little terns and oystercatchers.

CULZEAN CASTLE [B5] Robert Adam built the battlemented and turreted clifftop castle (**NTS**). It has a splendid round drawing room and oval staircase. Dwight D. Eisenhower, US president, was given a flat in the castle, and a room is devoted to him.

DALMELLINGTON [E4] The village's 18th-century weaving days are relived in the **Cathcartson Visitor Centre**. At nearby Minnivey is the **Scottish Industrial Railway Centre**.

DUNURE [C5] In the 18th century, Dunure was a whisky smuggling and fishing village. At ruined **Dunure Castle**, the 4th Earl of Cassillis, it is said, roasted the Abbot of Crossraguel to force him to hand over land. An optical illusion at nearby **Croy Brae** (Electric Brae) makes a car travelling uphill seem to be going downhill.

GALLOWAY FOREST PARK [D2] See picture.

GIRVAN [B3] Fishing boats still sail from the harbour of this holiday resort with a long beach. In 1328, Robert Bruce held his court in the gardens on **Knockcushan Hill** above the harbour. In the Firth of Clyde, 10 miles to the west of Girvan, is **Ailsa Craig**. It is part of an extinct volcano and rises to 338m (1109ft). Razorbills, guillemots and puffins breed here.

KIRKOSWALD [B4] Robert Burns came here to study surveying. Souter Johnnie, the cobbler or 'souter' of Burns's 'Tam o'Shanter', lived in a thatched cottage (**NTS**) built in 1785.

LOCH DOON [E3] Framed by hills all round, this small lake became a giant loch in the 1930s, when the Galloway Hydro-Electric Scheme made it into a reservoir. To avoid

submersion, the ruined 14th-century **Loch Doon Castle** was moved to a site by the west shore.

MAIDENS [B4] Offshore rocks give this fishing village and resort its name. To the south, **Turnberry Lighthouse** is on the site of a castle thought to be the birthplace of Robert Bruce.

MAYBOLE [C5] The baronial-style 16th–17th-century **castle** of the earls of Cassillis is now a private house. The earls are buried in the ruined 15th-century **Collegiate Church**. The ruins of 13th-century **Crossraguel Abbey**, nearby, include a turreted gatehouse and the abbot's tower.

MONIAIVE [H3] James Renwick, the Covenanter martyr, was born in this village. A monument to him is on a hill nearby. Annie Laurie, named in the Scottish ballad, was born at **Maxwelton House**, to the East.

SANQUHAR [H5] The town post office, the world's oldest, was in existence by 1763. Postal artefacts and interactive displays can be seen at the **Post Office Museum**. A monument marks the spot where a group of Covenanters issued the Declaration of Sanquhar, renouncing allegiance to Charles II.

Map on page 194–5

BEATTOCK HILL [C4] An Iron Age fort crowns the hill, which affords extensive views over Annandale.

BEWCASTLE [H1] A magnificent carved 7th-century cross shaft is in the village churchyard. There are four pele towers nearby – **High** and **Low Grains**, **Crew Castle** and **Woodhead**.

CASTLE O'ER FOREST [E3] A picnic site by the B723 is the base for forest walks. Nearby is **Castle O'er** Iron Age

hill fort. To the north there are groups of standing stones, the **Girdle Stanes** and **Loupin Stanes**.

CRAIGCLEUCH HOUSE [F2] Items brought back by Scottish explorers from all over the world are displayed in this 19th-century mansion. Chinese silk paintings and African sculptures are among its treasures.

DEVIL'S BEEF TUB [C5] Raiders once hid stolen cattle in this natural amphitheatre. The River Annan begins in the 200m (656ft) hollow.

DRUMLANRIG CASTLE [A3] This huge Renaissance mansion, has paintings by Rembrandt and Holbein, and relics of Bonnie Prince Charlie.

DUMFRIES [B1] Robert Burns lived in this former seaport. At his **house** and the **Burns Centre** are poems and period furniture, and his verses are engraved on windows at the Globe Inn, Burns's local howff, or tavern.

FOREST OF AE [C3] Trees meet overhead on the minor road through the Forest of Ae. A picnic site by a stream is fringed by spruce and alder, and there are marked walks.

GREY MARE'S TAIL [D5] These graceful falls (**NTS**) tumble 60m (200ft) to enter **Moffat Water**. Wild goats graze the high slopes.

HAWICK [H5] The chief town of the region, Hawick was ruined by English raiders in 1570. Hawick's history is recounted at **Drumlanrig's Tower**.

HERMITAGE CASTLE [G3] In 1566 Mary, Queen of Scots, rode 40 miles from Jedburgh to the 14th-century castle (**HS**) and back in a day to visit her wounded lover Bothwell.

LANGHOLM [F2] Twisting streets meet in a small square dominated by the **Town House**. Langholm Castle was owned by ancestors of Neil Armstrong, the first man on the Moon.

LEADHILLS [A5] One of the earliest subscription libraries was founded here in 1741 by lead miners. It was

named after the poet Allan Ramsay, who was born in the village in 1686. Ramsay encouraged the miners to start a library and contributed books from his Edinburgh bookshop.

LOCHMABEN [C2] On a peninsula in Castle Loch are the ruins of a 14th-century **castle**. By the town hall is a statue of William Paterson who was born in 1658 at nearby Tinwald and founded the Bank of England in 1694.

LOCKERBIE [D2] This small market town centres on the **Old Tower**, once its jail. In a battle between feuding Johnstones and Maxwells, many of the 700 defeated Maxwells were slashed about the head with swords – a stroke known as the 'Lockerbie lick'.

MOFFAT [C4] The ram statue on the Colvin Fountain symbolises Moffat's importance as a wool centre. It became a spa and resort after the discovery of a mineral spring in 1633; the **Baths Hall** is now the town hall.

WANLOCKHEAD [A5] Gold was panned here from the 1400s, but was supplanted by lead mining. Loch Nell Mine, with 183m (600ft) deep galleries, is part of the **Museum of Lead Mining** which also has a restored beam engine.

TOURIST INFORMATION

Girvan (0845) 2255 121
Hawick (0870) 608 0404
Moffat (01683) 220620
Sanquhar (0845) 2255 121

THE GOOD PUB GUIDE

Kingholm Quay [page 194 B1]
  Swan (01387) 253756
Moffat [page 194 C4]
  Black Bull
  (01683) 220206
Tushielaw [page 195 F5]
  Tushielaw Inn
  (01750) 62205

TOURING GUIDE

Spectacular outlook The **Galloway Forest Park**, a Forestry Commission reserve, covers mountains, lochs and forests, and has camping sites and nature trails. To the west, forest walks lead by Loch Trool.

The Cheviot Hills and northern Northumberland

ALNMOUTH [G5] Before the Aln changed its course in 1806, this village of colour-washed houses was a thriving port. Now a popular sailing and golfing resort, it has a **golf course** laid out in 1869.

ALNWICK [G5] The 1816 **Tenantry Column** was put up by tenants after rents had been reduced. The **Hotspur Tower** of 1450 is all that survives of the town fortifications. Just outside town are **Hulne Park**, with a Gothic folly of 1781, the **Brizlee Tower** and a ruined 13th-century **Carmelite priory**.

AMBLE [H4] Until the Second World War, the Amble area had as many as 80 coal mines. Today, fishing boats and pleasure craft fill the harbour, which also has a boatbuilder's yard. There is a **nature reserve** on Amble Dunes and there are boat trips to nearby **Coquet Island**.

BELLINGHAM [C2] Former ironworks in this small market town provided the metalwork for the Tyne Bridge. **St Cuthbert's Church** has a stone roof to protect it from 16th-century Border raiders. To the north west, **Black Middens Bastle House** is a fortified 16th-century farmhouse.

BELSAY HALL [F1] A 19th-century hall ✿ is set in landscaped grounds including the Quarry Garden, ablaze with exotic flowering trees. Nearby are a 14th-century **tower house** and ruined 17th-century **mansion**.

BRINKBURN PRIORY [F3] In a peaceful setting by the Coquet, the 12th-century **priory** ✿ is mostly a ruin, but the Norman and Early English church was restored in the 19th century. A fine William Hill organ and a bell were donated by the industrialist Sir William Armstrong in 1866. As there was nowhere to hang the bell, a turret was removed and a timber bellcote built in its place.

CARTER BAR [B4] An upright stone at the top of this pass marks the England-Scotland border. The Wardens of the Middle Marches used to meet here to resolve disputes.

CHEW GREEN [C4] Three Roman earthwork camps dating from AD 80 are reached by a stiff walk through the Redesdale Forest on the Pennine Way.

COQUET ISLAND [H4] Boats from Amble make trips round this **RSPB** reserve, the southernmost eider duck breeding ground (no landing).

DRURIDGE BAY [H3] Sands 6 miles long curve round the bay. In **Druridge Bay Country Park** is Ladyburn Lake, an open-cast mine until 1989, now used for water sports.

ELSDON [D3] In medieval times, the **vicarage** was fortified as a refuge from border raiders. Horse skulls found in the 14th-century **church** in 1877 may have been put there as a supposed protection from lightning.

HOLYSTONE FOREST [D4] This scenic area of the Northumberland Forest Park has many waymarked walks, including one to The Lady's Well ❧. The longest leads to the 429m (1407ft) summit of Dove Crag in the Simonside Hills, where many rocks on the heather-clad slopes bear 'cup-and-ring' Bronze Age carvings.

HOWICK [H5] **Rumbling Kern**, a gully south of this hamlet, takes its name from the organ-like noise made when the sea runs in. It is reached by a coastal path. Inland are the terraced gardens of 18th-century **Howick Hall**.

KIELDER FOREST [B3] Europe's largest planted forest covers 200 sq miles. Waymarked trails lead through conifers, and **Kielder Water** offers boating, fishing and water sports. The 18th-century **Kielder Castle** has a visitor centre, and is the start of a 12 mile drive.

MORPETH [G2] Riverside walks lead beside the Wansbeck, which flows through this bustling market town.

The **parish church** dates from the 14th century, and the **town hall** was designed by John Vanbrugh in 1714. A clock on the 15th-century tower of the former jail sounds the curfew. The **Chantry Bagpipe Museum** includes pipes from Northumberland, the Borders, Ireland, Greece and Italy.

NEWBIGGIN-BY-THE-SEA [H2] Only fishing boats and pleasure craft now use this former coal port. At the former **Woodhorn Colliery**, where old workings have been landscaped to form woods and a lake, the mining museum will reopen in 2006. Nearby **Bedlington** gives its name to a terrier, noted for speed and endurance, that was bred from the Rothbury terrier, used to rid mines of rats.

OTTERBURN [D3] Ballads on both sides of the border – such as the 'Ballad of Chevy Chase' – recall the battle that took place north of the village in 1388. The Scots won the day but lost their leader, Earl Douglas; Sir Henry Percy (Hotspur), the English leader, was captured. **Otterburn Mill**, first recorded in 1245, sells tweed.

ROTHBURY [F4] This market town is a popular base for walks in the **Cheviot Hills**. **Cragside** ❧ nearby was the 19th-century home of Sir William Armstrong, who invented the Armstrong gun during the Crimean War. The house was designed by the Victorian architect Norman Shaw in a blend of Elizabethan and Gothic styles, and it was the first house in the world to be lit by hydroelectricity. It is set in the landscaped grounds of Cragside Country Park.

SEATON DELAVAL HALL [H1] Built by John Vanbrugh, this mansion of the early 18th century, magnificent in spite of its modest size, is often regarded as his masterpiece.

TOURIST INFORMATION

Alnwick (01665) 510665
Amble (01665) 712313
Bellingham (01434) 220616
Craster (01665) 576007
Kielder Castle Visitor Centre (01434) 250209
Kielder Water, Tower Knowe Visitor Centre (0870) 2403549
Morpeth (01670) 500700
Rothbury NP (01669) 620887

THE GOOD PUB GUIDE

Great Whittington [E1] *Queens Head* (01434) 672267
Matfen [E1] *Black Bull* (01661) 886330
Newton-on-the-Moor [G4] *Cook & Barker Arms* (01665) 575234
Stannersburn [B2] *Pheasant,* (01434) 240382
Throptton [E4] *Three Wheat Heads* (01669) 620262

WALLINGTON HOUSE [E2] William Blackett, a coal and lead-mining magnate, built this mansion ❧ in 1688. Its treasures include murals by William Bell Scott, commissioned in the 1850s by Sir Walter and Lady Trevelyan, and outstanding porcelain.

WARKWORTH [H4] Stone houses climb from the fortified medieval bridge over the Coquet to the shell of **Warkworth Castle** ✿, from the 1330s a Percy stronghold and the birthplace in 1364 of Sir Henry Percy, Shakespeare's Hotspur. Upriver from the village, reached by boat, is a **hermitage** ✿ of the 14th century carved into the river cliff.

The Windsor of the North *Set in beautifully landscaped grounds, the Norman castle at **Alnwick** has been the home of the Percy family since 1309. The gardens have recently been redeveloped with a spectacular Grand Cascade, using fountains and canals, as the centrepiece.*

The Firth of Clyde, Ayr and Kilmarnock

*Poet's birthplace Thatched Burns cottage in **Alloway**, where Robert Burns was born in 1759, contains original furniture. It is joined to the Burns Museum.*

AIRDS MOSS [E1] In this high and barren moorland, the **Cameron Stone** marks the spot where, in 1680, Government troops defeated the Covenanters, whose leader, Richard Cameron, was killed.

ARDROSSAN [B3] Boats sail to Arran from this port and resort, laid out round sandy South Bay. The ruined 12th-century **castle** stands above the town. Offshore is little Horse Isle, a **bird sanctuary**. Nearby Saltcoats, given its charter by James V in 1528, is named after the saltworks close by.

AUCHINLECK [E1] Coal was mined near this village until the Barony Colliery closed in 1989. James Boswell, the friend and biographer of Dr Johnson, was the son of Lord Auchinleck. Boswell and Dr Johnson began their tour of the Hebrides from the village in 1773. Boswell is buried beside the church of 1683, which is now a **Boswell museum**.

AYR [C1] Once a major port, Ayr is now a popular seaside resort. The **world's last sea-going paddle steamer**, the *PS Waverley*, makes summer trips to Arran. The poet Robert Burns was baptised in the 17th-century **Auld Kirk**. Burns was born in nearby Alloway (see picture, above), which has the **Burns Museum** and the **Land o' Burns Centre**. Close by stand the **Auld Brig o' Doon** and **Alloway Kirk**, which feature in Burns's poem 'Tam o' Shanter', the Grecian-style **Burns Monument** of 1823 and **Rozelle House**, a 1750s mansion.

BOTHWELL [G5] The 13th-century red sandstone **Bothwell Castle** rises above the River Clyde just outside the market town. **St Bride's Church** has

windows by Edward Burne-Jones. Blantyre close by was the birthplace in 1813 of the missionary and explorer David Livingstone; the mill tenement where he grew up is now a **museum** where his famous explorations can be learnt about.

CRAIGNETHAN CASTLE [H4] Set on a precipice above Clydesdale, this well-preserved 16th-century castle has a caponier – a vaulted gun chamber built across a dry moat. The castle appears in Sir Walter Scott's novel *Old Mortality*.

CUMNOCK [E1] The town became a shoemaking, coal mining and weaving centre in the 18th century. The Labour MP James Keir Hardie lived here from 1880. William Murdoch, the pioneer of coal-gas lighting, was born in nearby **Lugar**.

EAGLESHAM [E4] This town was built by the 12th Earl of Eglinton in the 1790s. Streets of weavers' cottages enclose the Orry, a park. To the east, in East Kilbride is the **Museum of Scottish Country Life**.

FAIRLIE [B4] The ruined tower of a 15th-century **castle** stands in stark contrast to **Hunterston nuclear power station**, which can be visited.

GREAT CUMBRAE ISLAND [A5] Millport's sandy beaches draw crowds of tourists in summer. The **Cathedral of the Isles** is Scotland's smallest.

IRVINE [C3] Ruined 14th-century **Seagate Castle** was visited by Mary, Queen of Scots in 1563 and Robert Burns lived in the town in 1781–2; the **Burns Club** is a museum. In a huge building shaped like a sand

dune is a **museum** exhibiting a wide range of inventions and the work of the Nobel Laureates.

KELBURN COUNTRY CENTRE [B5] This romantic glen is threaded by Kel Burn, which cascades in waterfalls. Walks give fine views over the Firth of Clyde. **Kelburn Castle** has a 13th-century keep and splendid gardens.

KILMARNOCK [D3] The first edition of Robert Burns's poems was printed here; a copy is in the museum in **Dean castle**. In Kay Park is the **Burns Monument**. The Johnnie Walker whisky-bottling plant can be toured.

LARGS [B5] A festival in September recalls Alexander III's victory in 1263 over the Vikings. Today Largs is a water sports and yachting centre. The **Vikingar! museum** has interactive displays on the Vikings. **Skelmorlie Aisle** in a churchyard off Main Street is a Renaissance mausoleum.

LOCHWINNOCH RESERVE [C5] From a nature centre tower, and hides at **Aird Meadow**, many wintering and breeding birds can be seen. Diverse wetland plants grow here.

MAUCHLINE [E2] Robert Burns and his wife Jean Armour lived here and their cottage is now a **museum**. **Poosie Nansie's Tavern** features in Burns's 'The Jolly Beggars' and is still a pub. A red sandstone tower is the **National Burns Monument**. The round granite stones used in the game of curling are made in Mauchline.

MOTHERWELL AND WISHAW [G5/H4] Between the two merged towns are the **Ravenscraig Steel Works**, until the 1980s one of Britain's largest steel makers, and currently under regeneration. Metal for the hulls of the ocean liners *Queen Mary* and *Queen Elizabeth* was forged here. Motherwell has Scotland's biggest **theme park**. To the south, an

TOURIST INFORMATION

Ayr (0845) 2255 121
Hamilton (01698) 285590

THE GOOD PUB GUIDE

Coylton [D1] *Finlayson Arms* (01292) 570298
Symington [C2] *Wheatsheaf Inn* (01563) 830307

18th-century **lodge** built for the Dukes of Hamilton is in the grounds of **Chatelherault Country Park**.

PRESTWICK [C2] This seaside and golfing resort is one of Scotland's oldest burghs. The ruins of **St Nicholas's Church** date from the 12th century. Robert Bruce reputedly cured a skin disease by drinking from a well near the shore, now known as **Bruce's Well**. The first British Open Golf Championship was held at the **Old Prestwick Golf Course** in 1860.

SORN CASTLE [E2] On a cliff above the Ayr, the 15th-century castle has a fine setting. It is only open to the public in summer but the gardens can be visited throughout the year.

STAIR [D1] Robert Burns and his friends drank at the **Stair Inn** in this River Ayr hamlet. Whetstone, used for sharpening knives, has been mined locally since the 18th century.

STEWARTON [D4] Knitwear is the mainstay of the town, still famed for its tam-o'-shanter caps – hence its nickname of 'Bonnet Toun'.

TARBOLTON [D2] See picture, below.

TROON [C2] The Royal Troon golf course was founded here in 1878. A spit of land extends from the resort into the Clyde. To the north-east is **Dundonald Castle ⌗**, where the first Stuart king, Robert II, died in 1390.

*The Bachelors' Club A 17th-century thatched house in **Tarbolton** was the home of a debating society formed by Robert Burns and his friends.*

The Pentland Hills and the Clyde Valley

ABBOTSFORD [G2] The world of Walter Scott's romantic historical novels is embodied in this mansion overlooking the Tweed. It has weapons and relics such as Burns's drinking glass and a clasp from Napoleon's cloak.

BIGGAR [B3] Set round a broad main street, this market town has Scotland's oldest gasworks, dating from 1839. **Gladstone Court** has a re-created 19th-century street and the **Greenhill Covenanters' House** is a rebuilt 17th-century farm. **St Mary's Kirk** of 1545 was the last church built in Scotland before the Reformation separated Protestants from the Roman Catholic Church.

BORTHWICK [F5] Twin keeps and massive wings make 15th-century **Borthwick Castle**, now a hotel, one of Scotland's largest pele towers – more than 30m (100ft) tall, with walls 4.3m (14ft) thick. Mary, Queen of Scots, and the 4th Earl of Bothwell stayed here after marrying in 1567.

in Italian style with an arcaded courtyard and four kitchens; here the Earl entertained James VI.

INNERLEITHEN [E3] This mill town beside the Tweed was a spa in the 19th century, and its spring was the basis for Walter Scott's novel *St Ronan's Well*. **Robert Smail's Printing Works (NTS)** is a museum of 19th-century printing. Nearby at Walkerburn, the **Scottish Museum of Woollen Textiles** traces the history and development of this craft.

LANARK [A3] A busy agricultural centre, this market town perches on a plateau high above the Clyde. The bell of **St Nicholas's Church** is from 1110. In the High Street is a statue of William Wallace, who began his fight for Scottish independence here by overthrowing the English garrison.

LAUDER [G4] The 17th-century town hall and tollbooth dominate the marketplace. The parish church of about 1670 is in the shape of a cross

MELROSE [G2] The abbey **(HS)**, founded in 1136 and rebuilt in the late 14th century, is an imposing ruin with flying buttresses and sculpted figures; Robert Bruce's heart is buried here. Nearby is **Dryburgh Abbey** built in 1150. Walks take in the three peaks of the Eildon Hills.

NEIDPATH CASTLE [D3] The 14th-century stronghold stands in a wooded gorge on the River Tweed. Neidpath Castle, later converted to a tower house, has walls that are 3m (11ft) thick. The bedroom where Mary, Queen of Scots, once stayed can still be seen although its ceiling collapsed to reveal a medieval vault. There is also a pit prison, a period kitchen and a small museum.

NEW LANARK [A3] Robert Owen (1771–1858) converted this village of cotton mills into a model village for his workers. Today, restored mills, houses and such ventures as the **Institute for the Formation of Character** of 1816, can still be visited. The **Falls of Clyde**, which powered the cotton mills, are now part of a nature reserve.

NEWTONGRANGE [E5] The Lady Victoria Colliery, which opened in the 1890s, is now the **Scottish Mining Museum**. The 'magic helmet' tour guides you around the colliery, which produced 40 million tons of coal in its lifetime, and ex-miner guides offer anecdotes about life in the mine.

PEEBLES [E3] Tweeds and knitwear are made in the quiet town by the Tweed, and there is salmon fishing on the river. The brothers William and Robert Chambers, publishers of *Chambers Encyclopaedia* in 1859–68, were born in Peebles; the **Chambers Institute** has a library and museum.

ST MARY'S LOCH [D1] See picture (left).

SELKIRK [G2] More than four centuries ago this attractive town made leatherware; since then the townspeople have been known as 'souters', or shoemakers. In the old town hall, the courtroom is still as it was when the novelist Walter Scott was sheriff from 1799 until his death in 1832. Ironmongery thrived in the 18th–19th centuries, and **Halliwell's House Museum** is set out as a typical ironmonger's shop.

TIBBIE SHIELS INN [D1] Originally a fishing inn, the Tibbie Shiels stands on an isthmus between **St Mary's Loch** and the **Loch of the Lowes**. Tibbie Shiels was the name of the first hostess, from 1823 until her death in 1878. The inn was popular with the poet James Hogg and the writer and publisher Robert Chambers. The **Grey Mare's Tail** waterfall is nearby.

THE GOOD PUB GUIDE

Innerleithen [E3] *Traquair Arms* (01896) 830229
Melrose [G2] *Burts Hotel* (01896) 822285
Penicuik [D5] *Howgate Restaurant* (01968) 670000

Reflective pursuit *Monks grew fruit at **Priorwood Garden (NTS)** in Melrose. Ironwork, thought to be by Lutyens, adorns the garden walls.*

TRAQUAIR HOUSE [E3] Said to be Scotland's oldest continuously inhabited house, the fortified mansion was once the home of William the Lion, King of the Scots in 1165–1214. The present house dates mainly from the 1680s and is said to have been visited by 27 English and Scottish monarchs. The Bear Gates have been closed since Bonnie Prince Charlie rode out through them in 1745; the 5th Earl vowed that they would not reopen until a Stuart sat on the throne. Traquair Ale is produced in the 18th-century brewhouse and a museum has displays on the beer.

TWEEDSMUIR [C1] The local church was built in 1874, but a stone in the churchyard is dated 1685 and pays tribute to a martyred Covenanter. The statesman and novelist John Buchan, Lord Tweedsmuir (1875–1940), took his title from the area, which is today popular with walkers.

Still waters *Enfolded within the Ettrick hills, tranquil **St Mary's Loch** is one of southern Scotland's loveliest stretches of water. A pleasant walk along the eastern shore is part of the 212-mile Southern Upland Way.*

CRAWFORD [B1] The remains of the 16th-century **Tower Lindsay**, once the seat of the earls of Crawford, stand on a bend on the Clyde.

CRICHTON CASTLE [F5] Crowning a hill beside **Tyne Water**, the castle began as a 14th-century tower house. Its striking appearance, even in ruins, is due to Francis Stuart, 5th Earl of Bothwell, who rebuilt it in 1585,

with four equal arms. On the outskirts of Lauder, **Thirlestane Castle** has splendid Restoration plasterwork ceilings, and there are some 7000 historic toys on display.

MEGGET RESERVOIR [D1] The picturesque valley reservoir has good trout fishing. Up the hill is the ancient **Megget Stone**, once marking the border of Selkirk and Peebleshire.

The Borders, Berwick-on-Tweed and Holy Island

BAMBURGH [F2] The pink castle high above the shore dates from the 12th century and was restored in about 1894. A 7th-century gold plaque dates from the time when Bamburgh was an Anglo-Saxon stronghold. In the churchyard is a memorial to Grace Darling, who in 1838 at the age of 22, rowed out with her father, a lighthouse keeper, to the wrecked *Forfarshire* off the Farne Islands, and saved nine men.

BEADNELL [G2] Flat-bottomed fishing boats, called cobles, are moored in the harbour, which has large 18th-century limekilns. Sands stretch round Beadnell Bay for 2 miles to **Snook Point**.

BERWICK-UPON-TWEED [F4] The Elizabethan town walls provide a 2 mile walk. This most northerly English town changed hands 13 times between the Scots and English. In The Parade are a fine 17th-century church and the old barracks, housing part of the **Burrell Collection**.

CHILLINGHAM CASTLE [F2] A herd of Wild White cattle, perhaps bred from oxen kept by ancient Britons, has lived wild for more than 700 years in the park of the 14th-century castle. Wild White cattle may have been used for sacrifices by the Druids.

COLDSTREAM [C3] Soldiers and raiders headed here, where the Tweed could be forded, when bridges over the river were few. In 1659 General Monck, commander of Cromwell's Scottish army, took a regiment – later the Coldstream Guards – from here to reinstate Charles II.

CRASTER [G1] Kippers are smoked in sheds near the harbour of 1906, where fishing cobles and pleasure craft berth. Many of the village cottages are of dark whinstone, quarried nearby until the 1930s.

DUNS [B4] A statue of Duns Scotus, the philosopher, who was probably born in this market town in about 1265, stands in the park. A museum honours Jim Clark, world motor-racing champion of 1963 and 1965, who lived in the town. Nearby is **Duns Law**, 218m (715ft) high.

DUNSTANBURGH CASTLE [G1] A huge curtain wall encloses the ruined clifftop castle, of 1313, one of the largest Border castles. It can be reached only by a short coastal walk from Craster. In 1380 John of Gaunt rebuilt the gatehouse as a keep.

FARNE ISLANDS [G3] Half of these 28 rocky islands are covered at high tide, but some have high cliffs that are alive with sea birds during summer; grey seals can be seen all year. **Inner Farne** has a tower of 1500 on the site of a cell built in AD 676 by St Cuthbert. He died here in 687 and the chapel built in his memory can be visited.

FLODDEN FIELD [C3] A cross in a field marks the site of the battle of 1513, in which 10,000 Scots and 4000 English died, among them James IV of Scotland. The Earl of Surrey marched from Newcastle with 20,000 men, who routed the Scottish invaders. **Etal Castle**, a 14th-century ruin, is to the east.

HOLY ISLAND [F3] (See picture.) A monastery founded by St Aidan in AD 635 was destroyed by Viking raiders. The monks penned the fine illuminated Lindisfarne Gospels, now in the British Museum. There are also ruins of a 12th-century **priory**.

JEDBURGH [A1] Sited on a major north–south route, this market town on the banks of **Jed Water** was often attacked by the English in medieval times, and its ruined red sandstone abbey, founded in 1138, was often ransacked. The roofless **abbey church** has superb walls. Mary, Queen of Scots, stayed at the tower house in 1566; now it tells her life story. Mint-flavoured sweets known as Jeddart snails are a local speciality.

KELSO [B2] Elegant Georgian buildings face the market square. Now in ruins, the **abbey (HS)** founded in 1128 has Norman and early Gothic features. **Floors Castle**, a house of 1721, has superb tapestries.

MANDERSTON [C4] This opulent mansion, remodelled in 1901, has a marble stairway with a silver handrail and ballroom curtains embroidered in gold and silver.

NEWTON POOL NATURE RESERVE [G1] More than 30 bird species, including teals and sedge warblers, breed at this freshwater lake.

TOURIST INFORMATION

Adderstone (01668) 213678
Berwick-upon-Tweed (01289) 330733
Craster (01665) 576007
Eyemouth (0870) 608 0404
Jedburgh (0870) 608 0404
Kelso (0870) 608 0404
Seahouses (01665) 720884
Wooler (01668) 282123

THE GOOD PUB GUIDE

Bamburgh [F2] *Victoria Hotel* (01668) 214431
Belford [E2] *Blue Bell* (01668) 213543
Chatton [E2] *Percy Arms* (01668) 215244
Craster [G1] *Jolly Fisherman* (01665) 576461
Dunstan [G1] *Cottage* (01665) 576658
Seahouses [G2] *Olde Ship* (01665) 720200

NORHAM CASTLE [D4] This keep by the Tweed dates from about 1160 and is 27m (90ft) high. It fell to James IV in 1513, in the invasion that ended at the Battle of Flodden.

PRESTON TOWER [F2] This 14th-century pele tower gives a good idea of how these defensive towers looked. Inside is a room furnished in medieval style, and also a dimly lit prison cell.

SEAHOUSES [G2] The harbour comes to life when the fishing boats land their catches. Boat trips reach the Farne Islands in about an hour. To the north are **St Aidan's Dunes**.

SMAILHOLM TOWER [A2] This fine 16th-century fortified farmhouse **(HS)** has a ledge round the top of its five storeys from which to watch for raids. As a child at nearby **Sandyknowe farmhouse**, Walter Scott was inspired by his grandmother's songs and stories, and also by the tower, with images for his Border ballads. Today the tower displays tapestries and costume figures based on the ballads.

WOOLER [D2] This market town is a good hill-walking base. **The Cheviot**, 815m (2674ft), from where there are fine views, can be reached from **Langleeford** village to the south-west.

TOURING GUIDE

Religious retreat *Low tides reveal a causeway from Beal to **Holy Island**, also known as Lindisfarne. Lindisfarne Castle, a Tudor fortress, was restored by Sir Edwin Lutyens in 1903.*

Argyll and Bute and western Strathclyde

Sailing by *The **Crinan Canal** is popular with fans of small-boats – many yachts, dinghies and fishing boats stream through its 15 locks. The waterside hamlets of Ardrishaig and Crinan are good points from which to view this parade of small boats.*

TOURIST INFORMATION

Balloch (08707) 200607
Drymen (08707) 200611
Dumbarton (08707) 200612
Dunoon (08707) 200629
Helensburgh (08707) 200615
Paisley (0141) 889 0711
Rothesay 08707 200619

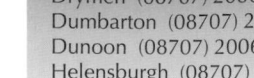

THE GOOD PUB GUIDE

Drymen [G4] *Clachan Inn*
(01360) 660824
Dunoon [D3] *Coylet Inn*
(01369) 840426
Glasgow [H2] *Babbity Bowster*
(0141) 552 5055
Houston [G2] *Fox & Hounds*
(01505) 612448
Lochwinnoch [F1] *Brown Bull*
(01505) 843250
Tarbert [A2] *Victoria Hotel*
(01880) 820236

AUCHINDRAIN [C5] Although most joint-tenancy farms were swept away in the 18th–19th centuries, a dozen families shared the rent and labour here until the early 20th century, when it was taken over by a single tenant. Now the farm is a museum, with restored cottages and 18th-century farming and domestic items.

CRARAE GLEN GARDEN [B5] A burn tumbles through the glen to Loch Fyne, with footbridges that link paths on each side of this woodland garden. Three generations of Campbell lairds created the garden.

CRINAN CANAL [A4] (See picture right). A short cut for boats from Loch Fyne to the sea, the 9 mile long canal was begun in 1793 by John Rennie. Although it saved vessels a haul of some 120 miles round the Mull of Kintyre, the canal was never a great commercial success.

DUMBARTON [G3] Castles built on airy Dumbarton Rock, high above the Clyde, have played their part in Scottish history. The first fort in the 5th century was for 400 years the capital of the Kingdom of Strathclyde. *Cutty Sark* was launched here in 1869.

DUNADD FORT [A4] Four tiers of walls defend this bleak hilltop fort **(HS)**, reached by a footpath and looking over the flatness of Moine Mhor. This site was the capital of the ancient kingdom of Dalriada.

DUNOON [D3] This holiday resort has two lovely bays and a ruined medieval castle. Mary Campbell,

Robert Burns's sweetheart, was born in the town. Her statue gazes over the Firth of Clyde. The beautiful **Cowal peninsula** lies behind the town.

GREENOCK [E3] James Watt, the pioneer of steam power, was born in the town in 1736. A statue, a dock, a college and a scientific library all commemorate him. The Clyde roadstead off Greenock was an Atlantic convoy assembly point in the Second World War; on **Lyle Hill** is a Cross of Lorraine memorial to Free French sailors who died in the Battle of the Atlantic in 1940–5.

HELENSBURGH [F3] (See picture below). John Logie Baird, pioneer of television, was born in the town in 1888. Henry Bell, who invented the first seagoing steamship, the *Comet* of 1812, lived in Helensburgh.

KILMARTIN [A5] The grey-stone village dates from the 19th century, but the site was inhabited much

earlier. In the church are two finely carved early Christian crosses and outside are medieval sculpted stones. A track leads from the village past **Nether Largie Linear Cemetery (HS)**, which has Bronze and Stone Age burial chambers, and **Temple Wood Stone Circles (HS)**, dating from before 3000 BC. **Carnasserie Castle (HS)**, blown up by the army of James II, is north of Kilmartin.

KILMUN ARBORETUM [D3] Behind the village of Kilmun, paths climb through larch, spruce, cedar, hemlock and pine to glorious views. There are also dawn redwoods, known only from fossils until living specimens were found in China in 1945.

OLD KILPATRICK [G2] The village is thought to have been the birthplace of St Patrick. Still to be seen is part of the western end of the **Antonine Wall**, built in about AD 141, that extended for 37 miles from Bridgeness on the Firth of Forth.

POLLOK HOUSE AND PARK [H1] The collection of Spanish paintings at the Georgian Pollok House **(NTS)** includes pieces by El Greco and Goya. The **Burrell Collection** has some 8000 works given by William Burrell, a ship owner. The estate's Country Park is centred on the Old Stables Courtyard, by a weir on the White Cart Water.

ROTHESAY [C1] Largest of the Firth of Clyde resorts, Rothesay is the main town of the 15 mile long Island of Bute; 19th-century houses back the sandy beach, and the ruins of the **castle**, begun in the 13th century, are nearby. **Mount Stuart**, the seat of the Marquess of Bute, is set in 300 acres (122 ha) of woodlands near Kerrycroy to the south.

SKELMORLIE [D2] This bright resort has a beach of flat red rocks. A turreted 'hydropathic' on the clifftop was an austere 19th-century health farm popular until the 1930s.

SKIPNESS [A1] A huge red 13th-century castle dwarfs the village and its sandy beach. The castle was a major Campbell stronghold until it was abandoned around 1700.

TIGHNABRUAICH [B2] Pronounced Tie-na-broo-ach, the name means 'House on the Hill' in Gaelic. The mainly Victorian hilltop village has fine views to the north.

WEMYSS BAY [D2] Pronounced 'Weems', this Firth of Clyde port was for generations the gateway by paddle steamer to Clydeside resorts. Ferries still ply to Bute.

YOUNGER BOTANIC GARDEN BENMORE [D4] The garden has an extensive and spectacular collection of trees and shrubs, including more than 350 species of rhododendron.

Stylish living *In Helensburgh, overlooking the Clyde estuary, is Charles Rennie Mackintosh's **Hill House**. Built for the publisher, Walter Blackie, in 1902–4 in Art Nouveau style, it is thought to be his finest domestic work. Mackintosh's wife, Margaret, also contributed many decorative features.*

Glasgow and the Clyde valley

ABERFOYLE [A5] This busy resort is a centre for visiting the Trossachs and the Queen Elizabeth Forest Park. To the north is **Duke's Road**, the A821, built by the Duke of Montrose in 1820; beside it a hilltop viewpoint looks across Ben Venue, Loch Katrine and Ben Ledi. Trails and a forest drive wind through **Achray Forest**.

*Imposing fortress **Stirling Castle** (HS) dates from the 15th and 16th centuries. The castle esplanade looks across the old marshes, towards the southern highlands.*

ALMONDELL [F2] This beautiful wooded country park has picnic areas and riverside paths.

ALVA GLEN [D5] This sheer-sided ravine in the Ochil Hills has ferns, mosses and waterfalls. A path to Alva village gives good views of the lowlands below the Forth.

BANNOCKBURN [D4] Robert Bruce's army defeated Edward II's English forces here in 1314, and won Stirling Castle. Bruce's command post is marked by an equestrian statue of 1964. The **Bannockburn Heritage Centre (NTS)** recounts the battle.

BEECRAIGS [E2] Woodlands with marked walks surround a loch. A path ascends to an Iron Age fort on **Cockleroy**, 278m (912ft) high.

BLAIR DRUMMOND [C5] Scotland's safari and leisure park has llamas, tigers, giraffes and camels – as well as yakmacs (a cross between yaks and Highland cattle). A boat safari takes in Chimpanzee Island.

BO'NESS [E3] Once this hillside town was Scotland's third largest port; its industrial past is recalled in the museum at 16th-century **Kinneil House**. In the grounds is a Roman fort, and the cottage in which James Watt experimented with the steam engine in the late 1760s. The **Bo'ness and Kinneil Railway** runs to Birkhill.

CAMBUSKENNETH ABBEY [D4] A detached belfry survives from this Augustinian abbey **(HS)** beside the Forth. It was probably founded by David I in 1147. Robert Bruce held his parliament here in 1326, and James III is buried in the abbey.

CLACKMANNAN [E4] By the town's 16th-century tollbooth is the **Clach of Mannan** – a stone believed to be sacred to the pagan god Mannan. A medieval tower nearby is said to have been a residence of Malcolm IV.

CULROSS [E4] The Old Burgh of Culross is a well-preserved small harbour town of the 16th–17th centuries. A **Town House (NTS)** of 1626 houses the Visitor Centre. The ruined Cistercian **abbey** of 1215 has a restored church.

DALMENY [G3] The fine south door of St Cuthbert's, the 12th-century Norman church, has intricate carvings, surmounted by an arcade of interlaced arches. To the east is Gothic style **Dalmeny House** of 1817. The 5th Earl of Rosebery crammed the house with tapestries, paintings and Napoleonic mementos.

DOLLAR [E5] The **Dollar Academy** of 1818–20, endowed by John McNabb, a poor boy of the town who became a sea captain and rich merchant, is now a private school. **Tillicoultry**, a 19th-century weaving village, is reached via the Mill Heritage Trail. **Castle Campbell (HS)** rises above the woods of Dollar Glen **(NTS)** north of Dollar.

DUNFERMLINE [G4] Scotland's royal capital in the 11th–17th centuries, the town was once famous for its damask linen and still makes silk. Steep streets lead to the abbey where Robert Bruce is buried. Charles I was born in the palace, now a ruin. The US steel magnate, Andrew Carnegie, was also born in the town; his cottage is a museum. He gave **Pittencrieff House** and the **Carnegie Library** to the town.

FALKIRK [D3] Iron produced at nearby Carron was worked here from 1760, but now the town is a shopping and leisure centre. Here the Scottish patriot William Wallace was defeated in battle by Edward I, and in 1746 Bonnie Prince Charlie routed an English army. At **Rough Castle**, to the west, the ditch and rampart of a fort on the Antonine Wall can be seen. The **Falkirk Wheel**, nearby, is the only rotating boat lift in the world and connects the Forth and Clyde canal with the Union canal.

FINTRY [B4] Sheep farming has been a way of life in this village since the 13th century, apart from some 50 years from the 1790s when a cotton mill operated. The mill ruins stand by 15th-century **Culcreuch Castle**. The **Loup of Fintry**, east of the village, is a 27m (90ft) waterfall.

GARTMORN DAM [E4] Scotland's oldest man-made reservoir of 1713 is now at the centre of a country park. There are many birds to be seen, especially wildfowl.

GLASGOW [A2] See City Routes pp278–279.

HOPETOUN HOUSE [F3] William Adam and his sons Robert and John enlarged and decorated this classical mansion in the mid-18th century. It was built in 1699 on the shores of the Firth of Forth. To the west is the **House of the Binns (NTS)**; a secret passage is said to lead to 15th-century **Blackness Castle**, which was the setting for Zeffirelli's film of *Hamlet*.

LAKE OF MENTEITH [A5] Because of a map-maker's error, this is Scotland's only 'lake'. A ferry runs from Menteith to the island of Inchmahome; it has ruins of a priory **(HS)** where 5-year old Mary, Queen of Scots, was sent in 1547, before going to France.

LINLITHGOW [F3] The ruined palace **(HS)** of 1425, birthplace of Mary, Queen of Scots, is by the loch. The county town, one of Scotland's oldest, was founded in the 12th century. **St Michael's Church**, 15th century, has superb window tracery.

MENSTRIE CASTLE [D5] William Alexander, 1st Earl of Stirling, was born here in 1567. He was granted land in Canada by James VI in 1621, and named it Nova Scotia, Latin for 'New Scotland'. Money for settling the land was raised by selling baronetcies, and baronets' coats of arms are on display.

RUMBLING BRIDGE [F5] Spanning a steep gorge of the Devon, this bridge has a lower part of 1713 and an upper part of 1816. There is a riverside walk with picnic areas, and a double cascade downstream at **Cauldron Linn**. Beyond the bridge the road winds through purple moorland skirting the Ochil Hills.

STIRLING [C4] The Old Town, which slopes down from the **Castle (HS)**, retains fine mansions, including **Argyll Lodging (HS)** and **Mar's Wark (HS)**. The Castle **(HS)** is perched above on a huge sheer-sided crag. The Chapel Royal, where Mary, Queen of Scots, was crowned in 1543, at the age of nine months, was later rebuilt. In 1567 James VI of Scotland – later to be James I of England – was crowned in the **Church of the Holy Rude**.

WALLACE MONUMENT [D5] This 67m (220ft) tall monument was erected where William Wallace (c1270–1305) camped before the Battle of Stirling Bridge. There are 246 steps to a platform that affords extensive views of the Pentlands, Fife and Ben Lomond.

TOURIST INFORMATION

Aberfoyle (08707) 200604
Bo'ness (08707) 200608
Dunfermline (01383) 720999
Edinburgh (0845) 2255 121
Falkirk (08707) 200614
Glasgow (0141) 204 4400
Kirkcaldy (01592) 267775
Linlithgow (0845) 2255 121
Stirling (08707) 200620

THE GOOD PUB GUIDE

Kippen [B4] *Cross Keys* (01786) 870293
Linlithgow [F3] *Champany Inn* (01506) 834532
Thornhill [B5] *Lion & Unicorn* (01786) 850204

Edinburgh, the Firth of Forth and East Lothian

*Smuggler's haven Cobbled streets climb from the harbour in the fishing port of **Eyemouth**. In the 18th century several houses had secret passages to the shore for smuggling.*

TOURIST INFORMATION

Dunbar (01368) 863353
Edinburgh (0131) 473 3800
Kirkcaldy (01592) 267775
North Berwick (01620) 892197
Old Craighall (0131) 653 6172
Penicuik (01968) 673846
Visit Scotland (0845) 2255 121

THE GOOD PUB GUIDE

East Linton [D3] *Drovers Inn*
(01620) 860298
Edinburgh [A3] *Starbank*
(0131) 5524141
Elie [C5] *Ship Inn*
(01333) 330246
Gifford [D2] *Tweeddale Arms*
(01620) 810240

tolbooth and **Esk Bridge** date from the 16th century. James IV is said to have played on its original golf links in 1504; they are now a **racecourse**.

NORTH BERWICK [D4] An airy seaside and golfing resort, North Berwick grew in late Victorian and Edwardian days. Sandy beaches stretch on each side of the harbour, which is a yachting and diving centre. Boat trips round the 107m (350ft) **Bass Rock** offer a chance to see gannets, shags and other sea birds. **North Berwick Law**'s conical summit gives views inland and over the Forth.

PRESTONPANS [B2] Monks used local coal to heat sea water and extract salt – it was salt-panning that gave this town its name. A former colliery houses a **mining museum**. It tells the story of local industry and guided tours are offered. Visitors can see a historic Cornish beam engine – the only one in Scotland – and a brick kiln. Bonnie Prince Charlie routed the English army at the Battle of Prestonpans in 1745.

ST ABB'S HEAD [H2] These dark dramatic cliffs **(NTS)**, capped by a lighthouse, are the highest on Scotland's east coast, towering to 94m (308ft). In summer they swarm with nesting sea birds, including shags, guillemots and puffins. A remote camera link allows visitors to observe sea birds in the nesting season.

TANTALLON CASTLE [D4] Once a fortress of the 'Red' Douglas clan, the ruined 14th-century **castle (HS)** stands on a rocky promontory jutting into the Firth of Forth; the battlements offer wide views. In 1651 it fell to General Monck after a 12-day siege.

TRAPRAIN LAW [D2] The long, whale-backed hill rising to 221m (725ft) gives wide views. There are earthworks of an Iron Age **hill-fort** which was once the capital of the Celtic Votadini tribe.

DALKEITH [B2] The 1708 **palace** is built round a 12th-century castle in Dalkeith Park, at the end of the wide cobbled High Street. The palace is not open, but there are walks by the Esk.

DIRLETON [D3] Although badly battered by Cromwell in 1650, the 13th-century **castle (HS, NTS)** still has its drum towers, kitchen, chapel, great hall and prison. Pink stone buildings of the 17th and 18th centuries flank the green. The **Yellowcraig Nature Trail** leads through woods and dunes.

DUNBAR [E3] A sandstone tower is all that remains of the **castle** where in 1339 'Black Agnes', the Countess of March and Dunbar, jeered at English besiegers from the battlements. Mary, Queen of Scots, came here in 1566 with her husband, Lord Darnley, and a year later with Bothwell, suspected of murdering Darnley. Cromwell took the fortress in 1650.

DUNGLASS BURN [F2] Trees and ferns cling to the sheer sides of a gorge cut by a burn which flows near Cockburnspath. Three bridges span it, one of 1768 giving dizzying views of the gorge.

EAST FORTUNE [D3] On an airfield is Scotland's **Museum of Flight** with over 40 aircraft on display, including Britain's oldest aeroplane, dating from 1896.

EAST WEMYSS [B5] In the village is ruined **Macduff's Castle**, the reputed home of the Macduff of Shakespeare's *Macbeth*. On the rocky shore are **caves** with wall inscriptions dating from Bronze Age to medieval times.

EDINBURGH [A3] See City Routes, pp276–277.

ELIE AND EARLSFERRY [C5] United as one burgh, the two towns share a sheltered bay and beach. Elie has a **golf course** of 1589. To the south, Chapel Ness has **chapel ruins** and offers fine views of the bay.

EYEMOUTH [H1] See picture.

GIFFORD [D2] This estate village, with its tree-lined green, replaced one pulled down to make way for the park of **Yester House**, built in 1699 for the 2nd Marquis of Tweeddale. The Adam brothers added to it later. A plaque in the **church** notes the birth in 1723 of

US congressman John Witherspoon, who signed the Declaration of Independence in 1776.

KIRKCALDY [A4] The main street of this industrial town stretches for more than 1 mile, and has earned it the nickname of 'Lang Toun'. The economist Adam Smith, who wrote *The Wealth of Nations*, was born in Kirkcaldy in 1723. Also born here were architect Robert Adam in 1728, and in 1827 Sir Sandford Fleming – who pioneered the adoption of standard time. **Sailors' Walk** has fine 17th-century houses **(NTS)**. The ruins of **Ravenscraig Castle** of 1459 are in a coastal park.

LENNOXLOVE [D2] The house takes its name from Frances Stewart, Duchess of Lennox, who was the model for Britannia on British coins. On display are the map and compass belonging to Rudolf Hess, Hitler's deputy, who in May 1941 flew alone to Lanarkshire, it is said, to start peace talks with the British Government.

MUSSELBURGH [B2] Founded by the Romans, Musselburgh is today a busy town with a small harbour. Its

The Argyll coast, Loch Awe & central Perthshire

Map on pages 210–11

ARDUAINE GARDENS [A2] With fine rhododendron collections, the gardens (**NTS**) give views of the 'slate islands' of Seil, Luing and Shuna.

CRIANLARICH [G3] Three glens meet at this village between the peaks of Ben Lui, Ben More and Ben Challum. A gentle walk along Glen Falloch leads to the **Falls of Falloch**.

DALMALLY [E3] Walkers and anglers frequent the village. To the south-west, **Monument Hill** has a memorial to the poet Duncan Bàn Macintyre. The summit affords views of ruined **Kilchurn Castle (HS)** by Loch Awe.

EASDALE [A2] Above the village, **Dun Mor** gives views across the old slate quarries. In nearby **An Cala Garden** are flowering shrubs, roses and rock gardens. Clachan bridge 'the bridge over the Atlantic' links the island of Seil to the mainland.

FORD [B1] The hamlet is sited at the southern tip of Loch Awe. On the east side is **Fincharn Castle**, a Macdonald stronghold. The **Falls of Blarghour** near Ballimeanoch drop 28m (90ft).

GLEN NANT [D3] Nature trails wind through woods of oak, ash, birch and hazel in the Forest Nature Reserve.

INVERARAY [D1] Outside the Georgian town, a neo-Gothic **castle** of 1745 has a balcony for the Duke's piper. The castle can be visited.

INVERLIEVER FOREST [C1] Deer, badgers and wildcats inhabit the forests and glens on Loch Awe's west shore. Paths from Dalavich lead to waterfalls and hilltop views.

LISMORE [B5] The tiny **church** on this island was a medieval cathedral, the seat of the Bishop of Argyll from 1200–1507. On the west coast are the ruins of two 13th-century **castles**.

LOCHGOILHEAD [F1] Set beside Loch Goil, the village is largely Victorian and its **church** has a 16th-century altar. To the south are ruins of 15th-century **Carrick Castle**.

LOCH KATRINE [H1] Eilean Molach features in Walter Scott's *The Lady of the Lake*. The 1900 **steamer** *Sir Walter Scott* departs from a visitor centre.

LOCH LOMOND [G1] See picture.

OBAN [B3] Steep climbs from the busy port offer views across to Kerrera Island. **McCaig's Tower** dates from 1897. Ruined 12th-century **Dunollie Castle** was a MacDougall stronghold.

REST AND BE THANKFUL [F1] A stone seat, now gone, gave this pass its name. To the west, in **Ardkinglas Woodland Garden**, a 63m (206ft) fir is one of the tallest trees in Britain.

Map on pages 212–13

BALQUHIDDER [A3] The heather-covered slopes of the **Braes of Balquhidder** surround the village. The outlaw Rob Roy MacGregor is buried in the churchyard.

BEN LAWERS [B5] Rising to 1214m (3984ft), the mountain is a National Nature Reserve. Birdlife includes ring ouzels and ptarmigans. A visitor centre is the start of a nature trail.

BIRNAM [F5] Beatrix Potter spent childhood holidays here and the **Beatrix Potter Garden** has characters

from her stories. **Birnam Oak** may be the last relic of the Birnam Wood in Shakespeare's *Macbeth*. From Inver, the **Hermitage Woodland Walk (NTS)** leads past the Falls of the Braan.

BLAIRGOWRIE [H5] Set at the heart of raspberry-growing country, this is a former flax-milling town. Now it is a centre for outdoor activities: fishing, walking and golf – there are 5 golf courses near the town.

CALLANDER [B1] A **visitor centre** tells the story of Rob Roy MacGregor, outlaw and folk hero. A path ascends Callander Craig giving fine views. To the east are the dramatic **Bracklinn Falls**; the **Falls of Leny** are near the road over the narrow Pass of Leny.

COMRIE [D3] This village lies on the Highland Boundary Fault; tremors are recorded at **Earthquake House**. Close by is **Deil's Caldron**, where the River Lednock runs into a hole in the rock.

CRIEFF [E3] Formerly a cattle-trading centre, the town was also a Victorian spa. North is the **Glenturret whisky distillery**. South are **Drummond Castle Gardens** and Scotland's oldest **library**, of 1691, at Innerpeffray.

DOUNE [C1] The Duke of Albany built **Doune Castle (HS)** in the late 14th century. The gatehouse includes the Lord's Hall with a musicians' gallery and double fireplace.

DUNBLANE [D1] The **cathedral (HS)** is mainly 13th century with a Norman tower. The **Dean's House** is a local history museum. A 16th-century **bridge** spans nearby Allan Water.

DUNKELD [F5] Above the River Tay are ruins of a 14th-century **cathedral**. Restored **whitewashed cottages (NTS)** date from 1689 when much of the town was rebuilt.

KENMORE [D5] In a spectacular setting at the eastern end of Loch Tay, Kenmore was developed as a model village for estate workers and has a

reconstructed **crannog**, or prehistoric loch dwelling. The area is noted for excellent salmon fishing.

LOCH LEVEN [G1] Pink-footed and greylag geese breed here. **St Serf's Island** has priory ruins, and on Castle Island is **Loch Leven Castle**, once the prison of Mary, Queen of Scots.

LOCH OF LOWES [G5] An observation hide on the southern shore of the loch allows views of ospreys, tufted duck, redstarts and woodpeckers in the **nature reserve**.

PERTH [G3] John Knox's sermon at **St John's Kirk** in 1559 started the Scottish Reformation. **The Fair Maid's House** was the home of Walter Scott's heroine Catherine Glover. Balhousie Castle has the **Black Watch Museum**.

SCONE PALACE [G3] Scottish kings were crowned on Moot Hill from 1153 until 1488. The famous coronation stone, the Stone of Scone, was seized by Edward I in 1296 but was returned to Scotland in 1996.

TOURIST INFORMATION

Blairgowrie (01250) 872960
Callander (08707) 200628
Crieff (01764) 652578
Dunblane (08707) 200613
Dunkeld (01350) 727688
Inveraray (08707) 200616
Killin (08707) 200627
Kinross (01577) 863680
Lochgilphead (08707) 200618
Oban (08707) 200630
Perth (01738) 450600

THE GOOD PUB GUIDE

Arduaine [p210 B2] *Loch Melfort Hotel* (01852) 200233
Crianlarich [p211 G3] *Ben More Lodge* (01838) 300210
Inveraray [p210 D1] *George* (01499) 302111
Kilmahog [p212 B1] *Lade* (01877) 330152
Oban [p210 B3] *Oban Inn* (01631) 562484

TOURING GUIDE

Bonnie bonnie banks **Loch Lomond**, *Scotland's largest loch and the setting for a famous ballad, lies at the foot of Ben Lomond (**NTS**). Rob Roy's Cave, a MacGregor meeting place, is on the loch's eastern shore.*

Eastern Fife and the Firth of Tay

ANSTRUTHER [D1] This picturesque East Neuk fishing village has a fishing museum. There are boat trips in summer to the **Isle of May** where puffins and seals can be seen.

ARBROATH [E5] Pervading this fishing port and holiday resort is the scent of 'smokies' – or cured haddock. William the Lion is buried in the ruined red sandstone **abbey (HS)**, which he founded in 1178. The **Signal Tower**, now a museum, originally relayed messages to the 19th-century **Bell Rock lighthouse** offshore. The Bell Rock was also the Inchcape Rock made famous in a poem by Robert Southey.

BALMERINO ABBEY [B3] The ruined hilltop Cistercian **abbey (NTS)** was founded by Alexander II and his mother, Queen Ermengarde, who is buried here. Nearby is a Spanish chestnut tree about 450 years old.

CRAIL [E1] Hidden beneath this pretty fishing village is a network of underground **caves** built for the relocation of the Scottish government in the event of a nuclear attack.

DUNDEE [B4] From **Dundee Law**, a 174m (571ft) hill of volcanic rock at the city centre, there are views of the 18th-century docks. The wooden frigate **HMS Unicorn**, now a museum, and Captain Scott's ship **Discovery**, can be seen. Dundee is renowned for its fruit cakes and jam, and is home to *The Beano* comic. Nearby is 15th-century **Broughty Castle**, with a whaling museum.

FALKLAND [A1] The burgh of 1458 at the foot of the Lomond Hills has fine 17th–19th-century houses. **Falkland Palace (NTS)** of the 16th century was a favourite residence of James V and Mary, Queen of Scots. The grounds have a 16th-century tennis court. Walks in the surrounding **Lomond Hills** offer lovely views.

KIRKTON OF LARGO [C1] A fine 17th-century spire tops the **church** of 1243 in this hamlet; Andrew Wood (1460–1550), the admiral who fought for James III against the English in 1498, is buried there. At the foot of the volcanic mound of **Largo Law** nearby is ruined **Largo House** of 1750, designed by John Adam.

Norman remains The ruins of twin-towered St Andrew's Cathedral, once the largest cathedral in Scotland, date from 1161. St Rule's Tower nearby was built to guide pilgrims to a small shrine which housed relics of St Andrew.

LOWER LARGO [C1] Alexander Selkirk, the castaway who inspired Daniel Defoe's *Robinson Crusoe*, was born in the former fishing hamlet in 1676. A **statue** erected in 1885 marks the site of his cottage.

MEIGLE [A5] Superb carved Pictish stones from the 7th–10th centuries are displayed in a **museum (HS)** in the village. All the stones were found in or near the churchyard.

PITTENWEEM [D1] The fishing port's name is Pictish for 'Place of the Cave', and refers to the **cave** where the 7th-century missionary St Fillan is said to have lived. His stone bed and the spring where he drank can be seen. By the harbour are 16th-century Dutch-gabled houses – **The Gyles**. The nearby 14th-century **Kellie Castle (NTS)** has fine 16th-century towers.

ST ANDREWS [D2] Golf has made the town famous. The Royal and Ancient Golf Club of 1754 is golf's ruling body, and the 15th-century Old Course is the world's oldest. Opposite the club is the **British Golf Museum**. At the university of 1411, Scotland's oldest, the students wear scarlet gowns. **St Andrew's Castle**, today in ruins, was the scene of Cardinal Beaton's murder in 1546. An **aquarium** has displays of tropical fish and the town's **Botanic Garden** is set in landscaped grounds with several greenhouses.

ST MONANS [D1] Steep streets lead down to the harbour and boat-builders' yards. By the shore is the

TOURIST INFORMATION

Arbroath (01241) 872609
Carnoustie (01241) 852258
Dundee (01382) 527527
St Andrews (01334) 472021

THE GOOD PUB GUIDE

Anstruther [D1] *Dreel Tavern* (01333) 310727
Broughty Ferry [C4] *Fishermans Tavern* (01382) 775941
St Monans [D1] *Seafood Restaurant and Bar* (01333) 730327

18th-century **St Monan's Windmill**, with displays on the old salt-panning industry. **St Monan's Church** dates from about 1360.

SCOTSTARVIT TOWER [B2] Sir John Scot (1585–1670), the author of the libellous political memoirs *Scot of Scotstarvit's Staggering State of Scots Statesmen*, lived in the tower of 1579. To the north is **Hill of Tarvit (NTS)**, a 17th-century mansion remodelled in 1906, and a **deer park**.

TEALING [C4] In the village is an Iron Age **earth-house (HS)**, now roofless and exposing a 25m (80ft) stone-lined underground passage. Close by is a fine **dovecote (HS)**.

TENTSMUIR POINT [C3] Wildfowl and winter waders, such as little stint and grey plovers, frequent the marsh and woodland at the nature reserve. Flowering plants, including Grass-of-Parnassus, grow on the dunes.

The Inner Hebrides and the Western Highlands

TOURIST INFORMATION

Aberfeldy (01887) 820276
Pitlochry (01796) 472215
Tobermory (08707) 200 625
Visit Scotland 0845 2255 121
   for Ballachulish
        Fort William
        Kilchoan
        Mallaig
        Ralia, near Newtonmore
        Spean Bridge
        Strontian

THE GOOD PUB GUIDE

Pitlochry [p219 G2] *Moulin*
   (01796) 472196
Weem [p219 G1] *Ailean*
   Chraggan (01887) 820346

FALLS OF BRUAR [F2] On visiting
the three-tiered waterfall, Robert
Burns observed that it should be
veiled by trees and as a result the falls
now cascade through pine woods.

FORT WILLIAM [A3] Set at the foot
of Ben Nevis, the town is a tourist
hub. Nothing survives of the fort that
gave the town its name. A **museum**
details local and natural history.

GLENCOE [A1] See picture.

GLEN NEVIS [A/B2] A beautiful glen
sweeps up from open meadows to
Ben Nevis's steep western slopes.
At the eastern end a waterfall drops
more than 305m (1000ft).

GLEN ROY [C4] Three terraces on
the slopes of this vast glen mark the
successive shorelines of a lake formed
during the Ice Age.

KILLIECRANKIE [G2] The tree-lined
pass (NTS) was the site of a fierce
battle in 1689 between the Jacobites
and the troops of William III. A **visitor
centre** has displays on the battle.

KINGUSSIE [F5] An open-air **folk
museum** includes a Hebridean black
house. At Newtonmore is the **Clan
Macpherson Museum**. To the north
at Kincraig is a **wildlife park** with
reindeer, bison and rare breeds.

PITLOCHRY [G1] The town thrives
on tourism, whisky and tweeds. From
a viewing platform on man-made
Loch Faskally, salmon can be seen
swimming upstream to spawn.

QUEEN'S VIEW [G2] Queen Victoria
was very fond of this view from above
Loch Tummel looking west towards
the pyramidal cone of **Schiehallion**,
which soars to 1083m (3554ft).

SPEAN BRIDGE [B3] The hamlet
grew up round the bridge built by
Thomas Telford in 1819. At nearby
Gairlochy, two locks raise the
Caledonian Canal to Loch Lochy.

Savage grandeur *The heather-clad steep slopes and dramatic jagged peaks of*
Glencoe *witnessed an infamous massacre of the Macdonald clan, which is
related at a visitor centre. At the heart of the glen, a rock platform known as
The Study looks across to the Three Sisters peaks on the south side.*

Map on pages 216–17

ARDTORNISH [F1] From the garden
visitors can view Victorian Gothic
Ardtornish House and the restored
14th-century **Kinlochaline Castle**.

ARISAIG [F4] Once a busy port, the
harbour is packed with pleasure craft.
Sandy beaches lie to the north. By
St Mary's Church is a ruined **chapel**
with carved medieval gravestones.

ARMADALE CASTLE [E5] A romantic
neo-Gothic ruin, the castle dates from
1815 and houses the **Clan Donald
Centre**. In the grounds are nature
trails and an arboretum.

CANNA [C5] Crofting and lobster
fishing are the main occupations on
Canna **(NTS)**. Only a Celtic cross and
a column remain in **A'Chill town**,
deserted in the 1840s Clearances.

CASTLE TIORAM [F2] Perched on
an islet in Loch Moidart, this 14th-
century stronghold was once the seat
of the Macdonalds. In 1715, fearing
the Campbells were about to take the
castle, the chief burnt it down.

COLL [B1] Arinagour is the island's
main village. Small lochs dot the
inland moors, and corncrakes nest in
the **RSPB** reserve in the south-west.

DERVAIG [D1] In a converted barn,
Mull Little Theatre claims to be the
smallest professional theatre in
Britain. To the south, **The Old Byre
Heritage Centre** tells Mull's history.

EIGG [D3] **An Sgurr**, a volcanic
ridge, soars to 394m (1292ft). At
Camas Sgiotaig are the **Singing Sands**,
which creak when walked upon.

GLENFINNAN [G3] A **monument
(NTS)** honours the Highlanders who
rallied here to Bonnie Prince Charlie
in 1745; a **visitor centre** tells the
story. The West Highland Railway
runs over a spectacular **viaduct** and
the station has a **railway museum**.

LOCH MORAR [F4] Morar is, at
310m (1017ft), Great Britain's deepest
lake. In its depths, according to
legend, lurks a monster called Mhorag.

MALLAIG [F4] In this busy ferry port
the **Mallaig Marine World** exhibits sea
creatures and a **heritage centre** has
displays on the town's past.

POINT OF ARDNAMURCHAN [D2]
A **lighthouse** stands at the most
westerly point on mainland Britain. At
Glenmore is a **natural history centre**.

RUM [C4] Sea eagles, extinct in
Scotland since 1916, were
reintroduced to this island reserve
(SNH) in 1974. There are also red
deer, otters and wild goats.

TOBERMORY [E1] The crescent of
brightly painted houses around the
fine harbour lend Mull's capital a
Mediterranean air. To the south,
Aros Park offers cliff and forest walks.

Map on pages 218–19

ABERFELDY [G1] The woods of silver
birches inspired Robert Burns's poem
'The Birks o' Aberfeldy'. Outside the
town stands a five-arched stone **Tay
bridge**, designed by William Adam.

BEN NEVIS [B2] A path leads to
the mountain's summit from the
west. The north face, however, is a
challenge for experienced climbers.
On a clear day, the Hebrides and
Irish hills are visible from the top.

BLACK WOOD OF RANNOCH [E1]
This pine and birch wood is one of
the last surviving parts of a primeval
forest. Walks from Carie include a
long trail towards **Glen Lyon**, with
good views over **Loch Rannoch**.

BLAIR ATHOLL [G2] A working
water mill dates from 1613 and
the **Atholl Country Life Museum** has
displays of rural life. **Blair Castle** is
the base of Britain's only private army,
the Atholl Highlanders.

CAIRNGORM NATIONAL PARK [G5]
Britain's largest national park covers
1400sq miles. Roe deer, red squirrels,
wildcats and many other species
abound. A 15th-century **castle** ruin
stands on an island in **Loch an Eilein**,
and a chair lift climbs 1245m (4084ft)
to the top of Cairn Gorm.

CASTLE MENZIES [F1] The restored
16th-century fortified house was the
seat of the chiefs of Clan Menzies. In
1746 Bonnie Prince Charlie stopped
here on his way to fight at Culloden.

DALWHINNIE [E3] Set at the head of
lonely Loch Ericht, this is one of the
highest villages in the Highlands, at
362m (1188ft). **Cluny's Cave**, where
Bonnie Prince Charlie is said to have
hidden, is on the loch's western shore.

The Dee Valley and the Braes of Angus and Strathmore

TOURIST INFORMATION

Aberdeen (01224) 288828
Ballater (013397) 55306
Banchory (01330) 822000
Braemar (013397) 41600
Brechin (01356) 623050
Carnoustie (01241) 852258
Forfar (01307) 467876
Kirriemuir (01575) 574097
Montrose (01674) 672000
Stonehaven (01569) 762806

THE GOOD PUB GUIDE

Aberdeen [G5] *Prince of Wales* (01224) 640597
Kirkton of Glenisla [B2] *Glenisla Hotel* (01575) 582223
Stonehaven [G3] *Lairhillock* (01569) 730001

ABERDEEN [G5] Built largely of local granite, the most northerly city in Britain displays the stone to good effect in Union Street, which runs from the **Mercat Cross** of 1686. A museum of civic life is in **Provost Skene's House** of 1545, and a maritime museum in **Provost Ross's House** of 1593 **(NTS)**. The **Union Terrace Gardens** are an oasis in the city's heart, and the harbour fish market is Scotland's largest. Marischal College and King's College joined in 1860 as Aberdeen University.

ABERLEMNO [D1] See picture (right).

BALLATER [C4] Granite houses and hotels date from the late 18th century when the town was a popular spa. The old Victorian **railway station** has been restored with displays on its royal connections. Paths climb nearby **Craigendarroch's** slopes, and red deer live in **Glen Muick**.

BALMORAL CASTLE [B4] Prince Albert built turreted Balmoral in 1852–5 on the site of an earlier castle, Bouchmorale – Gaelic for 'majestic dwelling'. In the ballroom there are exhibits from the royal collection, and the grounds have formal gardens and rare conifers. The Royal Family have spent holidays here since the 1850s, and attend nearby **Crathie Church**.

BANCHORY [E4] Hill and woodland walks, fishing and golf attract visitors to the village resort. A plaque marks the birthplace in 1843 of James Scott Skinner, composer of Scottish fiddle tunes. Leaping salmon can be seen from the **Bridge of Feugh** in spring.

BRAEMAR [A4] Towered and turreted **Braemar Castle** was built by the Earl of Mar in 1628 as a hunting seat, and fortified after the Jacobite uprising of 1745. Highland games feature at the annual Braemar Royal Highland Gathering. Robert Louis Stevenson wrote *Treasure Island* here in 1881.

BRECHIN [E2] Red sandstone buildings line the streets of the old town, on the banks of the River South Esk. Next to the parish **church**, which began as a 13th-century cathedral, stands the **Round Tower (HS)**, built by Irish masons in AD 990–1012.

CAIRN O'MOUNT [E3] For more than 2000 years, a cairn has marked the top of this exposed pass. Macbeth was among those who led armies this way during Scotland's war-torn past.

Pictish picture *Depicting beasts, a Celtic cross and a battle, the 8th-century slab stands in* **Aberlemno** *churchyard. Stones by the B9134 may have been boundary markers.*

CATERTHUN FORTS [D2] Two Iron Age forts **(HS)** facing each other across a Grampian pass date from 200 BC–AD 100. **White Caterthun** has stone walls and earthworks. The earlier fort, **Brown Caterthun**, is ringed by six lines of earthworks.

CRATHES CASTLE [E4] See picture (right).

DRUM CASTLE [F4] The Irvine family held Drum Castle **(NTS)** for 653 years from 1323. Its 13th-century keep is adjoined by a Jacobean mansion of 1619. The **Old Wood of Drum** lies north-west of the castle. To the north is **Cullerlie Stone Circle (HS)**, which may be 4000 years old.

DUNNOTTAR CASTLE [G3] An exposed crag jutting into the sea is crowned by the ruins of the 14th-century fortress. The Scottish crown and sceptre were kept here during the period of the Commonwealth. Cromwell took the castle in 1652 but the regalia was smuggled out.

EDZELL [E2] An arch at the entrance to the village commemorates the 13th Earl of Dalhousie. Ruined 16th-century **Edzell Castle (HS)** is best known for its 17th-century pleasance, or walled garden, which has heraldic and symbolic sculptures and a box hedge trimmed to spell out the Lindsay family motto *Dum Spiro Spero* – 'While I Breathe I Hope'.

FASQUE [E3] The **Fettercairn distillery** nearby offers a video presentation, tours and tastings.

FORFAR [D1] An octagonal turret marks the site of the **castle** where Malcolm III is said to have held a parliament in 1057 – the same year that he killed Macbeth. During the 1650s, this town was the scene of many witch hunts; the Forfar Bridle, an iron collar used to gag those about to be burnt at the stake, is a grim relic in the **Meffan museum** in the town.

FOWLSHEUGH [G3] A cliffside **RSPB** reserve, it is one of the largest of eastern Scotland's mainland sea-bird colonies. In May and June, kittiwakes, razorbills and guillemots nest in thousands on the ledges. Fulmars, shags and puffins may also be seen.

GLAMIS [C1] The castle has been the Lyon (later Bowes-Lyon) family home since 1372. Queen Elizabeth, the late Queen Mother, spent her childhood here. Duncan's Hall was the setting for the murder of King Duncan in Shakespeare's *Macbeth*. In the village, the **Angus Folk Museum (NTS)** is in a row of six 18th-century cottages.

HOUSE OF DUN [E2] William Adam designed the mansion **(NTS)** for David Erskine, Lord Dun, whose armorial bearings are part of the plasterwork ceiling in the saloon. In the grounds are woodland trails.

KIRRIEMUIR [C1] James Barrie, the creator of *Peter Pan*, was born here. Barrie is buried in the churchyard and his two storey home is now a **museum (NTS)** with rooms as they may have been in his day. The outside wash-house is said to have been his first theatre. A 16th-century townhouse houses a museum with displays on the glens.

LUNAN BAY [E1] Semiprecious stones such as amethysts and agates are found in the dune-backed sands. Ruined 15th-century **Red Castle** on the clifftop was built of sandstone from nearby Red Head.

MONTROSE [E1] This resort and North Sea oil supply base has narrow, winding closes leading from gable-ended town houses. The parish **church** steeple has a curfew bell, 'Big Peter', that rings each night at ten o'clock. The **Montrose Basin**, a tidal lagoon and nature reserve, shelters greylag and pink-footed geese.

REEKIE LINN [B1] The Isla plunges down this waterfall and through a deep gorge. The **Loch of Kinnordy** nearby is an **RSPB** reserve, where water birds include tufted ducks.

STONEHAVEN [G3] Cottages huddle beside the harbour, the oldest part of the fishing port and resort. A 16th-century **tolbooth** is a local history and fishing museum; clergy imprisoned here in 1748 baptised fishermen's children through a cell window.

Pepper-pot castle *Painted ceilings and turreted roofs are features of 16th-century* **Crathes Castle** *(NTS). Eight separate gardens are bordered by yew hedges dating from 1702.*

Glen Shiel and the Isle of Skye

Bridging the gap Set against a stunning backdrop of the dramatic Cuillins mountain range, the Kyle of Lochalsh bridge connects the island of Skye to the Scottish mainland. Nearby Lochalsh Woodland Garden (NTS) has lochside walks and many exotic plants.

TOURING GUIDE

BEINN EIGHE [G5] Rising from Loch Maree, the jagged mountain is part of Britain's oldest national nature reserve (**SNH**). Waymarked trails lead amid moors and pinewoods, which are home to wildcats and pine martens.

BROADFORD [D2] The crofting village lines Broadford Bay, with the red granite mountain, Beinn na Caillich, to the south. It is said Bonnie Prince Charlie blended the whisky liqueur Drambuie here in about 1745. An **environmental centre** displays lizards and snakes in a serpentarium.

COLBOST FOLK MUSEUM [A4] An illicit whisky still can be seen at this restored crofter's cottage. Part of the museum is a **water mill** at Glendale. Farm tools are displayed at **Borreraig Park Exhibition Croft** to the north.

DUN BEAG BROCH [B3] Perched on a hilltop, the 2000-year-old broch (**HS**) is one of the finest on Skye. Its walls, once 12m (40ft) high, still reach above head height.

DUNTULM CASTLE [C5] On top of a sheer cliff are the ruins of an early 16th-century stronghold of the Macdonalds of Sleat. Duntulm was abandoned in 1730 after a nurse accidentally dropped the laird's young son into the sea – his ghost is said to haunt the castle.

DUNVEGAN [B4] Among the castle's relics is the Fairy Flag, said to have the power to protect the clan. It also has a trapdoor dungeon. A village **museum** tells the story of the 2.36m (7ft 9in) giant, Angus Macaskill, born in 1823 on Berneray in the Outer Hebrides.

EILEAN DONAN CASTLE [F2] The forbidding stronghold was destroyed by the English navy during the 1719 Jacobite uprising. Restored in 1932 as a clan war memorial and museum, it has Macrae portraits and furniture.

ELGOL [C1] From the bay there are views of Rum, Soay, Canna and Eigg; boat trips to these islands depart from Kirkibost. **Loch Coruisk**, hemmed in by the rugged Cuillins, can be visited by boat from Elgol.

GLEN AFFRIC [H2] The paintings of Edwin Landseer (1802–73) made the glen's crags, hanging woods and roaring waters familiar to many. Waymarked walks start from the car park between Loch Affric and Loch Beinn a' Mheadhoin.

GLENELG [F2] Bernera Barracks stand in ruins to the north of the seasonal ferry port to Skye. At nearby Gleann Beag are Dun Telve and Dun Troddan, two Iron Age **brochs** (HS).

KILMUIR [C5] A white Celtic cross in the churchyard marks the burial place of Flora Macdonald in 1790. Nearby, the **Skye Museum of Island Life** recalls 19th-century crofting life.

KINTAIL FOREST [G1] The chain of peaks known as the **Five Sisters of Kintail** dominate the wilds of Kintail Forest (NTS), which is populated by red deer and feral goats. Walks start from the Morvich visitor centre (NTS). A 5 mile walk from Dorusduain leads to the dramatic **Falls of Glomach**.

KYLEAKIN [E2] Seal-spotting cruises operate from here in summer. Under the bridge is **Eilean Ban**, the island where the author and naturalist Gavin Maxwell lived for a year. Ruined 13th-century **Castle Moil** was built as a defence against Norsemen.

KYLE OF LOCHALSH [E2] See picture.

MACLEOD'S TABLES [A3] The name given to this pair of flat-topped hills dates from the 16th century, when a Macleod held an open-air banquet for James V on one of them.

PLOCKTON [F3] Palm trees line the sheltered waterfront of the town where the TV series *Hamish Macbeth* was filmed. There are boat trips to seal colonies on islands in Loch Carron. Nearby **Craig Highland Farm** has rare breeds, and there is a woodland garden at **Duirinish Lodge**. **Strome Castle (NTS)**, once a Macdonald stronghold, was destroyed in 1602.

PORTREE [C3] Brightly painted houses border the harbour of Skye's only town. *McNab's Inn*, where the Royal Hotel now stands, is where the fugitive Bonnie Prince Charlie parted company with Flora Macdonald in 1746. Both his story and Skye's history are told at the nearby **Aros Experience and Visitor Centre**.

QUIRAING [C5] Pinnacles and pillars such as the 36m (120ft) high **Needle** are features of the dramatic basalt ridge. To the south-east, **Loch Mealt** cascades over a cliff into the sea.

RAASAY [D3] Flat-topped **Dun Caan** rises to 443m (1455ft) amid ravines and woods on this 13 mile long island. **Raasay House**, now an outdoor centre, and **Brochel Castle** were once owned by the Macleods, whose support for the Jacobite cause in 1745 led to the island's virtual destruction by government troops.

SANDAIG [E1] Wild otters may be seen along the remote shore, once the home of the writer Gavin Maxwell. Visitors walk along a forest track from Upper Sandaig to leave shells and pebbles on the memorial to the author and Edal, his beloved pet otter.

SKYE FOLK MUSEUM [D2] The crofter's house at Luib has its thatched roof held fast by ropes and rocks and is furnished in period style. Displays tell of Bonnie Prince Charlie in Skye.

THE STORR [C4] Pointed pinnacles and blunt towers top the basalt ridge. The tallest stack is the **Old Man of Storr** at 49m (160ft); it can be reached by woodland paths.

TORRIDON [F4] Crags, corries and quartz-capped peaks characterise this huge nature reserve (**NTS**). There are tame red deer at the **Deer Museum (NTS)** in the village. The **Countryside Centre (NTS)** explains the area's natural history. Walks start from a car park beside Upper Loch Torridon.

UIG [C5] Backed by an arc of green hills, this small fishing port has ferries to Harris and North Uist in the Outer Hebrides, and is a windsurfing, canoeing and riding centre. Above the bay is a 19th-century **folly** tower.

Loch Ness, the Moray Firth and Strathspey

TOURIST INFORMATION

Elgin (01343) 542666
Forres (01309) 672938
Tomintoul (01807) 580285
Visit Scotland 0845 2255 121
  for Aviemore
          Daviot Wood
          Fort Augustus
          Grantown-on-Spey
          Inverness
          Nairn
          North Kessock
          Strathpeffer

THE GOOD PUB GUIDE

Cawdor [E4] *Cawdor Tavern*
(01667) 404777
Cromarty [E5] *Royal*
(01381) 600217
Fort Augustus [B1] *Lock Inn*
(01320) 366302

Flanked by hills and overlooked by the ruins of Urquhart Castle, the waters of the legendary Loch Ness, home to the elusive monster, are 24 miles long and over 230m (750ft) deep in places.

AVIEMORE [F1] Below the **Rock of Craigellachie** – the Clan Grant rallying point – is a huge complex in Britain's main **winter-sports** area, which offers go-karting and concerts.

BOAT OF GARTEN [F1] Named after a former ferry, the village is a terminus of the **Strathspey Railway**, whose steam trains follow a scenic route to Aviemore. To the east on **Loch Garten** is an **RSPB** hide for viewing ospreys.

BRODIE CASTLE [F4] Set amid landscaped grounds, the medieval tower of the 16th-century castle has been the home of the Brodie family since 1249. A Pictish monument, **Rodney's Stone**, is in the grounds.

BURGHEAD [G5] Stone granaries by the harbour recall Burghead's days as a grain-shipping port. **Burghead Well**, a spring-fed rock pool, may have been an early Christian baptistry. The nearby **Clavie Stone** is the scene each January 11, the old New Year, of an old Norse ritual – a blazing tar barrel is broken up after being carried through the town.

CAWDOR CASTLE [F4] Shakespeare set Macbeth's murder of Duncan in an earlier castle on this site. The castle keep dates from 1372 with some 16th–17th-century additions. The grounds have three landscaped gardens and woodland trails.

CRAIG PHADRIG [D3] Rising to 171m (561ft) the hill gives wide views towards Inverness and the Beauly Firth. The Iron Age **fort** on its crest is believed to have been the work of Brude, a Pictish king.

CROMARTY [E5] This Black Isle burgh has some fine 18th-century buildings. Its history is given at the museum in the **Cromarty Courthouse**. The thatched cottage **(NTS)** of amateur folklorist, naturalist and writer Hugh Miller is now a **museum**. Boat trips offer sightings of blue-nose dolphins and whales.

CULBIN FOREST [G5] Storms in the 17th century submerged Culbin village beneath the sands. A forest now covers the reclaimed land, stretching from Nairn to Findhorn Bay. Wildlife includes the capercaillie, a bird that became extinct in Britain in 1783; it was reintroduced in 1837.

CULLODEN [E3] Stone cairns mark the place on Culloden Moor where 1000 of Bonnie Prince Charlie's Highlanders met their deaths on a rainy day in April 1746, routed by the Duke of Cumberland's army. The **battlefield (NTS)** has a visitor centre that tells the story.

DINGWALL [C4] Settled by the Vikings, the market town is now overlooked by a tower on **Mitchell Hill** to the Victorian general Sir Hector MacDonald. Dingwall was the birthplace of Macbeth, ruler of Scotland in 1040–57. The **Town House Museum** sets out local history.

DRUMNADROCHIT [C2] Tucked into Glen Urquhart where it meets Loch Ness, the village is a tourist centre. An exhibition recounts the search for the **Loch Ness monster**.

ELGIN [H5] Known as the 'Lanthorn of the North', the 13th-century **cathedral** still stands although it was partly destroyed in 1390 by the 'Wolf of Badenoch', Robert II's outlawed son. Elgin, a market town and tourist centre, has an Italianate **museum** with fossils and Pictish stones.

FINDHORN [G5] The village is the third to be built here – the first was buried by sand in storms, the second overwhelmed by floods in 1701. Once a trading port, Findhorn is now a sailing and water-sports centre.

FORRES [G4] Soaring above the busy town is **Nelson Tower**. **Sueno's Stone (HS)** is a slender sandstone pillar etched with warrior carvings, thought to be about 1000 years old. A local Victorian **distillery** is open to visitors.

FORT AUGUSTUS [B1] An **abbey** now occupies the site of the fort, named after William Augustus, Duke of Cumberland. The town is a boating, walking and fishing centre. Six locks built by Thomas Telford connect Loch Ness with the Caledonian Canal.

FORT GEORGE [E4] This artillery fort protected by 1 mile of ramparts has stayed virtually unaltered since its completion in 1769. It has the regimental **Museum of the Queen's Own Highlanders**.

FORTROSE [E4] The ruined **cathedral (HS)** dates from about 1400. Standing beside a lighthouse on the headland is the **Brahan Seer Stone**, which commemorates a 16th-century seer, Coinneach Odhar.

FOYERS [C2] Thundering through a wooded ravine, the River Foyers plunges down the two-tiered **Falls of Foyers**, dropping 27m (90ft).

GLENMORE FOREST PARK [G1] Sweeping up from the shores of Loch Morlich to the Cairngorm summits, the park is the home of the only herd of reindeer in Britain.

GRANTOWN-ON-SPEY [G2] Laid out in 1776 as part of the expansion of the Highland linen industry, the town is now an angling and ski resort. At Dulnain Bridge, more than 300 varieties of heather and shrubs can be seen at the **Speyside Heather Centre**.

INVERNESS [D3] Known as the 'capital of the Highlands', the town straddles the broad River Ness, and bridges lead to the Ness Islands. **Abertarff House (NTS)** of 1593 is the town's oldest building. The 19th-century **castle**, on the site of earlier fortifications, is now a courthouse and council offices. A museum in **Castle Wynd** has Jacobite relics. To the west, Beauly has **priory** ruins **(HS)** dating from the 13th century.

LOCH NESS [C2] See picture.

NAIRN [F4] Founded by royal charter in the 12th century, this ancient town became a fashionable Victorian watering place. The old district of **Fishertown** has narrow alleys and fishermen's cottages. A museum in **Viewfield House** explains local history. There are two sweeping sandy beaches and two golf courses.

PLUSCARDEN ABBEY [H4] Looming above a quiet valley is the lofty central tower of this 13th-century priory. Restored by Benedictines in 1948, it became an abbey in 1974.

RANDOLPH'S LEAP [G4] As the Findhorn races through a gorge, it forms a series of waterfalls and whirlpools below woodland paths.

Aberdeenshire and the Moray Coast

ADEN COUNTRY PARK [F4] Spread around an 18th-century farmstead, the park has a wildfowl lake.

ALFORD [C1] A base for visits to the castles of **Kildrummy (HS)** and **Craigievar (NTS)**, it has a **transport museum** and a narrowgauge railway to **Haughton Country Park**.

BALMEDIE [F1] Sandy beaches and huge dunes stretch for miles between the rivers Ythan and Don. Wading birds to be seen include redshanks, ringed plovers and sanderlings.

BANFF [D5] This resort has fine 17th–18th-century town houses. **Duff House (HS)** is home to the Scottish Collection of Country House Art.

BENNACHIE [D2] Rugged granite **Mither Tap** is one of several peaks on this wooded ridge at the centre of a forest reserve. The heather-clad summit affords spectacular views.

BULLERS OF BUCHAN [G3] The sea roars into this immense cliff chasm. A dizzying clifftop path leads round the rim, 30m (100ft) above the waves.

FOCHABERS [B4] George Baxter founded a food business here in 1868; a visitor centre tells the story of its worldwide success.

FRASERBURGH [F5] The fishing port has more than 2 miles of dunes and sands. **Fraserburgh Castle** was converted in 1787 into Kinnaird Head lighthouse **(HS)** and is now a museum. Nearby, 16th-century **Wine Tower** has three floors, but no stairs.

FYVIE CASTLE [E3] The towers of the 13th-century castle **(NTS)** are named after family owners. The Gordons, the

owners from 1733-1847, are said to have ridden their horses up the 3m (10ft) wide spiral staircase.

HADDO HOUSE [E3] Set in a large country park, the mansion **(NTS)** was owned by the Gordons, earls of Aberdeen. The 4th earl was prime minister in 1852–5.

HUNTLY [C3] The rivers Bogie and Deveron meet at the market town. **Huntly Castle (HS)** has a doorway with fine heraldic ornament and a prison with 15th-century graffiti.

INVERUGIE [G4] Beside the River Ugie is a ruined 16th-century **castle**, the birthplace of James Keith, a Jacobite in the 1715 uprising.

INVERURIE [E2] The Bass, a high mound, was the site of a Norman castle. **Brandsbutt Stone (HS)** has ogham inscriptions and Pictish symbols. Nearby are prehistoric **Loanhead Stone Circle (HS)** and the 9th-century **Maiden Stone (HS)**.

KEITH [B4] The bridge of 1609 over the River Isla links the old and new parts of the town. The 1786 **Milton whisky distillery**, now called Strath Isla, is on the Malt Whisky Trail.

LEITH HALL [C2] This turreted mansion of 1649 **(NTS)** was home to the Leith-Hay family until 1945.

LOSSIEMOUTH [A5] Fine, sandy beaches flank the resort and fishing town. James Ramsay Macdonald, Britain's first Labour prime minister, was born here in 1866.

MACDUFF [D5] An **aquarium** with a huge open-roofed tank contains local marine life and touch pools.

MONYMUSK [D1] St Mary's Church of 1140, built of red stone, was restored in 1929. South-east is **Castle Fraser (NTS)**, said to be haunted by the ghost of a murdered princess.

OLD DEER [F4] The only relic from the 6th-century Celtic **abbey** is the 9th-century Book of Deer, now in Cambridge University library. Nearby are stone ruins of **Deer Abbey (HS)**.

OLD SLAINS CASTLE [G2] Gaunt and ruined, the medieval tower was destroyed by James VI in 1594 after he uncovered a plot against him. Later pardoned, the owner, the Earl of Erroll, built **New Slains Castle** farther up the coast above Cruden Bay.

OYNE [D2] An earth mound houses **Archeolink**, a history centre with displays on ancient crafts and rituals. Outside are the remains of an Iron Age **hill fort**.

PENNAN [E5] A single row of whitewashed cottages is built into the cliff face at this charming fishing village. It was the setting for the 1982 film *Local Hero*.

PETERHEAD [G4] The pink granite harbour of this seaport was built by convicts from Peterhead Prison. The **Arbuthnot Museum** covers local fishing and whaling history.

PITMEDDEN GARDEN [E2] See picture.

PORTSOY [C5] Harbourside warehouses once stored local serpentine marble for export. There are coastal walks to Sandend Bay and to ruined 16th-century **Boyne Castle**.

ROSEHEARTY [F5] The quiet resort has been a port since the 14th century. Nearby **Pitsligo Castle** of 1424 was abandoned by its Jacobite laird in 1746 after the Battle of Culloden.

TOURIST INFORMATION

Aberdeen (01224) 288828
Alford (019755) 62052
Banff (01261) 812419
Dufftown (01340) 820501
Fraserburgh (01346) 518315
Huntly (01466) 792255
Inverurie (01467) 625800

THE GOOD PUB GUIDE

Bridge of Alford [C1] *Forbes Arms Hotel* (019755) 62108
Fochabers [B4] *Gordon Arms Hotel* (01343) 820508

SANDS OF FORVIE [F2] Pink-footed and greylag geese winter in this dunes nature reserve,which stretches for 4 miles. In summer a colony of eider ducks breed in the sands.

TAP O' NOTH [C2] The summit of the hill is a hollow, ringed by the remains of a vitrified Iron Age **fort**, its stones fused together by fire.

TOLQUHON CASTLE [E2] A secluded pink sandstone ruin, the 15th-century **castle (HS)** stands in a wooded glen. **Tolquhon Gallery** has a changing exhibition of works by Scottish artists.

TURRIFF [D4] This town may have been the capital of a 6th-century Pictish prince. A double belfry and a bell survive in the ruined **church**.

UDNY GREEN [E2] Udny Castle, a 15th–17th-century turreted tower house, rises high above the village. A **mort-house** of 1832 in the churchyard was built to foil bodysnatchers.

WHITE COW AND LOUDON WOODS [F4] In a clearing in Loudon Wood is the prehistoric **Buchan stone circle**. The road to Strichen gives views of a white horse and stag etched on Mormond Hill.

Box symmetry *The* **Pitmedden Garden** *(NTS) was laid out in 1675 along French classical lines with 3 miles of box hedges cut to form designs and Latin mottoes.*

TOURING GUIDE

FROM MAP ON PAGES 228–229

The Flow Country to John o'Groats

Off to market! The small rural village of **Lairg** by Loch Shin is filled with jostling sheep in August when it hosts Britain's biggest sheep fair. Nearby is a salmon leap at Shin Falls and the dramatic Cassley Waterfall.

ACHILTIBUIE [B2] A hydroponicum, an extraordinary soil-free complex of glasshouses, contains plants as diverse as figs, lilies and bananas.

AUCKENGILL [H5] A former school house is now the **Northlands Viking Centre**, explaining the area's cairns and brochs, and the archaeology of pre-Viking and Norse Caithness.

BETTYHILL [E5] The village grew as a crofting settlement for tenants evicted during the Clearances. The **Strathnaver Museum**, housed in an 18th-century church, gives details.

CAPE WRATH [C5] Atlantic breakers pound the towering cliffs of the headland, which can be reached in summer by a passenger ferry across the Kyle of Durness. **Clo Mor**, to the south-east, is Britain's highest mainland cliff at 281m (921ft) tall.

CORRIESHALLOCH GORGE [C1] Birch, rowan and hazel cloak this deep, 1 mile long chasm (**NTS**), which plunges to 60m (200ft) and is 30m (100ft) wide. Lush ferns cling to its walls. The **Falls of Measach** drop into the Droma far below.

DORNOCH [F1] Extensive sands and a golf course flank this town. The 13th-century **cathedral** was burnt down in 1570 and rebuilt in the 19th century. Janet Horne, one of the last women in Scotland to be tried as a witch, was burnt here in 1722.

DOUNREAY [F5] Gleaming against the sky above the coastline is the steel sphere of the Dounreay **nuclear reactor**, now decommissioned. There is a permanent summer exhibition about it at the site.

DUNBEATH [G3] From this former fishing village, the Beatrice Oil Field platforms in the North Sea are visible. Nearby, the **Laidhay Croft Museum**, in a thatched longhouse, evokes crofting life during the 1930s.

DUNROBIN CASTLE [F2] This medieval seat of the earls and dukes of Sutherland was redesigned in 1844 in French chateau style. At Brora, the **Clynelish Distillery** is open to visitors. On Beinn a Bhragaidh is a huge **statue** of the 1st Duke of Sutherland.

EAS A' CHUAL ALUINN [C3] Britain's highest waterfall drops 201m (658ft) from the heights of Glas Bheinn. It can be viewed by boat from Loch Glencoul, or on a 3 mile walk.

FEARN ABBEY [F1] In the 16th century, a local prophet, Brahan Seer, predicted that disaster would strike at this 13th-century church. During a service in 1742 the roof collapsed, killing 44 people.

GREY CAIRNS OF CAMSTER [H4] Two Stone Age cairns some 5000 years old make up this restored burial site (**HS**). Human and animal bones were found in one of the two chambers in the long cairn.

HANDA ISLAND [C4] Puffins and shags nest on the reserve (**SWT**), which is reached by boat from Tarbet in summer. Grey seals, whales and dolphins can be seen offshore.

HELMSDALE [G3] Crofts surround the former fishing village, where Highland history is explained at the **Timespan Visitor Centre**. To the north the road climbs the **Ord of Caithness** pass giving fine views.

INVEREWE GARDENS [A1] Osgood Mackenzie prepared the garden (**NTS**) in 1862. Exotic plants such as Himalayan lilies flourish in the mild climate brought by the North Atlantic Drift, an extension of the Gulf Stream.

INVERPOLLY [B2] Red deer, otters, pine martens, golden eagles and wild cats are among the wildlife found in the mountainous nature reserve. A path ascends the pinnacled peak of **Stac Pollaidh**, 612m (2009ft), which is often likened to a porcupine.

JOHN O' GROATS [H5] The hamlet owes its name to a Dutchman, Jan de Groot, who once ran a ferry to Orkney. Nearby is Duncansby Head, the mainland's north-east tip, and the 64m (210ft) high **Duncansby Stacks**.

KNOCKAN CLIFF [C2] In 1859, a geologist studying the cliff noticed that its topmost rock layer was older than its bottom one: an upheaval in the earth's crust 400 million years ago in effect turned the cliff upside down. This discovery helped towards the understanding of mountain formation.

LAIRG [E2] See picture.

LOCHINVER [B3] The cone-shaped mountain, Suilven, looms over the water-skiing and fishing resort. Near Stoer, there are fine views of the 60m (200ft) **Old Man of Stoer**, a rock stack.

TOURIST INFORMATION

Visit Scotland 0845 2255 121
for Bettyhill
Dornoch
Durness
Lairg
Lochinver
Thurso
Ullapool
Wick

THE GOOD PUB GUIDE

Lybster [H4] *Portland Arms* (01593) 721721
Ullapool [C2] *Ferry Boat* (01854) 612366

LYBSTER [H4] An octagonal lighthouse guards the harbour of this 19th-century fishing village. To the east, the **Hill o' Many Stanes (HS)** has some 200 stones in a fan shape dating from Stone Age to Bronze Age times.

SMOO CAVE [D5] A huge cave in the cliff near Durness, it is entered by a chamber where Allt Smoo burn tumbles some 24m (80ft) from a hole in the roof. Boat trips venture into an inner chamber in summer.

STRATH OF KILDONAN [F3] In the 1860s the area was renamed Baile an Or – 'the town of the gold' – after a brief goldrush. Gold panning equipment can be hired from Strath Ullie craft shop in Helmsdale.

TAIN [E1] Most houses in the burgh are of local honey-coloured sandstone. Dominating the High Street is the turreted 18th-century **Tolbooth**. A **distillery** and a **cheese factory** have guided tours.

THURSO [G5] Caithness's chief town was the centre of Scottish trade with Scandinavia in medieval times. Ruined **St Peter's Church** is 13th century. **Dunnet Bay** nearby attracts windsurfers.

TONGUE [E4] The town flanks the east side of the Kyle of Tongue, a shallow sea inlet. In the **church** of 1680 is a Laird's Loft, or gallery. Nearby is the fortress of **Castle Varrich**, built by the Mackays in the 15th–16th centuries.

ULLAPOOL [C2] Yachts and trawlers add to the waterside bustle of the former herring port beside Loch Broom. There are Summer Isles cruises and ferries to Stornoway.

WICK [H4] Until the mid 20th century, Wick was one of Britain's busiest herring-fishing ports. A Heritage Centre relates its history. At **Caithness Glass**, visitors can see hand-blown glass being made. To the south is the **Castle of Old Wick (HS)**, a medieval tower house.

The Hebrides and the Western Isles

ARNOL [G5] A typical 19th-century thatched croft is today the **Black House Museum (HS)**. Another **crofting museum** can be seen at Siabost.

BARRA [E1] High above Castlebay is **Kisimul Castle**, the home of the piratical Macneils in medieval times. The novelist Compton Mackenzie is buried in **St Barr's Church**.

BENBECULA [E2] On Rueval is a **cave** where in 1746 Bonnie Prince Charlie waited for Flora Macdonald.

BOWMORE [B2] See picture (right).

BRODICK CASTLE [C1] Paintings, fine furniture and porcelain adorn the 13th-century castle **(NTS)** on Arran.

BRODICK COUNTRY PARK [C1] Woods of oaks and beeches can be explored on nature trails. A visitor centre gives details on local birds.

Our Lady of the Isles *Erected in 1957, this impressive 9m (30ft) high granite statue gazes over farmland near West Gerinish on **South Uist**. A ruin in the nearby village of Milton was the birthplace of Flora Macdonald.*

BURG [B4] The rugged area **(NTS)** is best known for **MacCulloch's Fossil Tree** – an ancient trunk fossilised in basalt cliffs. It can be reached by an arduous 7 mile walk from Tiroran.

BUTT OF LEWIS [G5] Gales buffet the most northerly tip of the Hebrides and its lighthouse. Nearby Eoropaidh has 12th-century **St Moluag's Church**.

CALLANISH [F4] Prehistoric stones **(HS)** surround a chambered tomb which is cast in shadow at sunset on the spring and autumn equinoxes.

CAMPBELTOWN [C1] A former herring port, it has a **distillery**, open to visitors in summer, and a **heritage centre**. In a cave on **Davarr Island** is a painting by Archibald Mackinnon.

CARSAIG ARCHES [B4] The basalt arches can be reached at low tide. Polecats, otters and golden eagles may be seen from Mull's south coast.

COLONSAY [B3] At **Dun Ghallain** is a cave where the MacFie clan hid. On the East coast, **MacFie's Stone** marks where their chief was murdered.

CORRYVRECKAN WHIRLPOOL [B3] The roaring maelstrom of white water is in the strait between Scarba and Jura and can only be reached by foot. It is best seen an hour after low tide.

DUART CASTLE [C4] The 13th century castle contains displays of family relics and clan history.

DUN CARLOWAY [F5] The walls of this well-preserved Iron Age tower **(HS)**, dating from the 1st century BC, are still 6m (20ft) high.

DUNSTAFFNAGE CASTLE [C4] Flora Macdonald was briefly imprisoned in the 13th-century castle **(HS)**. The chapel has ornate Gothic windows.

ERISKAY [E1] Known for the haunting 'Eriskay Love Lilt', it was on this island that Bonnie Prince Charlie first set foot on Scottish soil in 1745.

FINLAGGAN CASTLE [B2] From the 12th–16th century, Macdonald clan chiefs held parliaments here. A nearby cottage tells the ruined castle's story.

*Island spirit Flavoured with peat and seaspray, Islay's whisky has a unique taste; there are tours of a distillery in **Bowmore**. The design of the round church here was meant to prevent the Devil hiding in corners.*

GIGHA ISLAND [B2] Forts and standing stones are scattered across Gigha. Palms and rhododendrons flourish at **Achamore House**.

IONA [A4] St Columba landed here in AD 563 and founded a **monastery**. Three Celtic crosses stand near the restored late 15th-century **abbey**.

JURA [B2–B3] Red deer and sheep are numerous on the island. A walled garden at **Jura House** has plants from Australia and New Zealand.

KILDALTON CROSS [B2] The Celtic cross **(HS)** may date from the 9th–10th century. The **Mull of Oa** has a monument to 650 US troops who drowned offshore in 1918.

KILMORY [C2] The 13th-century **chapel (HS)** has carved medieval grave slabs. **Macmillan's Cross** of the 15th century depicts a hunting scene.

LOCHBUIE [B4] Prehistoric standing stones and stone circles can be seen in the area. Closed to the public, 15th-century **Moy Castle** was the bastion of the MacLaines of Lochbuie.

LOCH DRUIDIBEG [E2] The nature reserve **(SNH)** has greylag geese, hen harriers and golden eagles. Wild orchids grow on the machair.

LOCHGILPHEAD [C3] A crescent of painted stone houses overlook Loch Gilp. In nearby **Kilmory Castle Gardens**, ferns, rare alpines and rhododendrons line woodland paths.

TOURIST INFORMATION

Bowmore (Islay)
  (08707) 200617
Brodick 0845 2255 121
Campbeltown (08707) 200609
Castlebay (Barra)
  (01871) 810336
Craignure (08707) 200 610
Lochboisdale (South Uist)
  (01878) 700286
Lochgilphead (08707) 200 618
Lochmaddy (North Uist)
  (01876) 500321
Stornoway (Lewis)
  (01851) 703088
Tarbert (L. Fyne) (08707) 200624
Tarbert (Harris) (01859) 502011

THE GOOD PUB GUIDE

Ardfern [C3] *Galley of Lorne*
  (01852) 500284
Crinan [C3] *Crinan Hotel*
  (01546) 830261
Kilberry [C2] *Kilberry Inn*
  (01880) 770223

LOCH GRUINART [A2–B2] Barnacle and white-fronted geese winter on the **RSPB** reserve; breeding birds include buzzards and hen harriers.

LOCHRANZA [C2] The Claonaig to Arran ferry port has a ruined 16th-century **castle** on the site of a building where Robert Bruce may have stayed.

NORTH UIST [E3] Ancient forts and standing stones dot the island. In the south-west are ruins of 13th-century **Trinity Temple**.

RODEL [F3] **St Clement's Church (HS)** has fine tombs and an effigy of a 16th-century chief in armour.

SADDELL ABBEY [C1] The 12th-century ruin has tombstones depicting priests, warriors and war galleys.

SHIANT ISLANDS [G3] Hexagonal columns rise on the north of **Garbh Eilean**. Puffins and seals abound.

SOUTHEND [C1] St Columba is said to have landed near **Keil chapel** in AD 563; carved in a rock nearby are **St Columba's Footprints**.

SOUTH UIST [E2] See picture (left).

STAFFA [B4] Columns of basalt ring the uninhabited island **(NTS)**. **Fingal's Cave**, made famous by Mendelssohn's music, can be visited by boat.

TIREE [A4] **Dun Mor** is a 1st-century BC broch; nearby the **Ringing Stone** sounds a musical note when struck. At Hynish a **museum** tells the history of Skerryvore Lighthouse.

TOROSAY CASTLE [C4] Built in the Scots Baronial style, the castle has fine portraits and period furniture.

TOURING GUIDE

FROM MAP ON PAGES 232–233

The islands of Orkney and Shetland

BIRSAY [A4] Ruins of the Earl's Palace overlook Birsay Bay. Offshore is the **Brough of Birsay**, where Picts and Vikings settled. Remains of the **hall** and 12th-century **church (HS)** of Thorfinn the Mighty still stand.

BLACKHAMMAR CAIRN [B4] Beside the road on Rousay is a Stone Age **burial chamber** 14m (47ft) long and lined with stalls. Entry is by a trap door. **Taversoe Tuick,** a two-tiered burial chamber, is nearby.

BROCH OF GURNESS [B4] Three lines of earthworks circle the drystone walls of the splendid 2000-year-old broch **(HS)**, or fortified tower.

CROFT HOUSE MUSEUM [F1] The croft house, roofed with turf and straw, gives an idea of what crofting life was like in the 19th century.

ESHA NESS [E4] The promontory has sea-sculpted rocks such as **Calder's Geo**, a collapsed cave. From Loch of Houlland, a stream feeds the sheer-sided **Holes of Scraada** and drains through a rock tunnel.

HERMA NESS [G5] At Britain's most northerly point, cliffs rise to 180m (600ft), and gannets and puffins can be seen in the national nature reserve.

HOY [A3] Much of the island is mountainous and rare alpine plants thrive here. The **Old Man of Hoy** is a rock stack at the edge of the sea, and on moorland the **Dwarfie Stane (HS)** is a two-chambered grave hewn out of rock some 5000 years ago.

ITALIAN CHAPEL [B3] Italian prisoners of war created the chapel in 1943 from two corrugated Nissen huts and scrap materials. The interior has medieval style wall paintings, a concrete altar and altarpiece, and an ornate screen.

JARLSHOF [F1] A settlement for some 3000 years from the Stone Age, Jarlshof is a remarkable site **(HS)** with Bronze Age houses, or 'wheel-houses', of the 2nd–3rd century AD, and 9th-century Norse farmsteads.

KIRKWALL [B3] Orkney's capital faces a harbour busy with ferries and lobster boats. The **cathedral** of red and yellow sandstone was founded in 1137 by the Norse earl Rognvald. The **Bishop's Palace** is also 12th century, but the Renaissance style **Earl's Palace** was built in about 1600. The **Orkney Wireless Museum** takes a nostalgic look back as far as crystal sets. The **Orkney museum** in Tankerness House covers local history of the last 5000 years. A chambered tomb, dating from 3500 to 2500 BC, on **Wideford Hill** has views of the **Pentland Firth**.

LERWICK [F2] North Sea oil has brought fortune to the most northerly town in the British Isles, but its harbour is still busy with fishing boats. Many buildings have loading piers, or 'lodberries'. On a loch islet is the Iron Age **Clickhimin Broch (HS)**.

MAES HOWE [B3] The workmanship in the 4500-year-old tomb **(HS)** suggests that it was a chieftain's burial place. An 11m (36ft) long stone-lined passage leads to a beehive-shaped burial chamber 35m (115ft) across. Runic graffiti left by Viking raiders moan that others had snatched the finest treasure. To the north, near the Loch of Harray, are **Click Mill** and **Corrigall Farm Museum**.

MARWICK HEAD [A4] On top of the cliffs is a **memorial** to Lord Kitchener, the First World War general who died when HMS *Hampshire* struck a German mine offshore in 1916.

MID HOWE [B4] Settlers built this Stone Age cairn **(HS)** some 5000 years ago; 23 people have been found buried there. Nearby is **Mid Howe Broch (HS)**, built 1000 years later.

MOUSA [F1] One of Scotland's most complete Iron Age **brochs (HS)** stands on this uninhabited island. Its circular drystone walls, 13m (43ft) high, are built around a courtyard. Stairs in the 6m (20ft) wide walls lead to a parapet with fine views.

NORTH RONALDSAY [D5] Sheep eat seaweed on the shores of the most northerly Orkney isle. A 2m (6ft) wall rings the island to stop them from grazing the crops. The **lighthouse** is one of Britain's tallest land lights.

NOSS [G2] One of the largest bird breeding sites in Europe, the island is a nature reserve, with superb views from a clifftop path. Black guillemots and gannets can be seen here.

PAPA WESTRAY [B5] Two houses at **Knap of Howar (HS)** date back 5500 years, and may be the oldest existing dwellings in north-west Europe. **Holm of Papa** nearby has a chambered tomb **(HS)** with 14 beehive cells. Arctic terns nest on **North Hill RSPB reserve** in summer.

RING OF BRODGAR [A3] Of some 60 stones set in a circle 104m (340ft) wide, 27 still stand. Set between the lochs of Stenness and Harray in an area studded with ancient cairns, the ring **(HS)** was built in about 2000 BC. Like the nearby **Standing Stones of Stenness (HS)**, it may have had astronomical purposes.

ST MARGARET'S HOPE [B2] To the south is the Stone Age **Tomb of the Eagles**, once used for ritual animal sacrifice.

ST NINIAN'S ISLE [F1] A treasure of 28 pieces of Pictish silver was unearthed in 1958 in the ruined 12th-century **chapel** on the isle. It may have been buried by monks to evade raiding Vikings around AD 800.

SCALLOWAY [F2] Dominating the harbour are the ruins of a **castle** built in about 1600. The **museum** explains a Second World War operation called the 'Shetland Bus': Norwegian patriots smuggled saboteurs into German-occupied Norway from Scalloway, and then brought back the refugees they had smuggled out.

SKARA BRAE [A4] See picture.

STROMNESS [A3] Crab and lobster fishing is the mainstay of the town; many gable-ended houses have their own jetties. Stromness grew in the 18th century as a trading centre, and the Hudson's Bay Company's ships called here on the fur-trading run to Canada; later, whaling and herring fishing predominated. **The Pier Arts Centre** has a 20th-century collection.

SYMBISTER [G3] Until a salt tax ruined trade in 1712, **Pier House**, a 17th-century Hanseatic booth on the quay, was used by Baltic traders to display goods exchanged for fish, wool and butter.

WESTRAY [B5] Pierowall's ruined medieval **church (HS)** has lettered tombstones. **Noltland Castle (HS)**, begun in the 1560s but never completed, has gun loops in a Z-plan. **Noup Head**, an RSPB reserve on top of the cliffs, has one of Britain's largest sea bird colonies.

YELL [F4] Otters and seals swim around the island with its small lochs, peat hills and scattered crofts. There are two **RSPB** reserves, **Lumbister and Black Park**. On the Otterswick shore is the **'White Wife'** figurehead from a German ship wrecked in 1924.

TOURIST INFORMATION

Kirkwall (01856) 872856
Lerwick (01595) 693434
Stromness (01856) 850716

THE GOOD PUB GUIDE
Kirkwall [B3] *The Albert Hotel*
(01856) 876000

Beach residence In 1850 a storm blew away sand, burying the 4500-year-old village (HS) of Skara Brae. Seven or eight stone houses are linked by narrow, roofed lanes, and there is an open square, or marketplace.

Killarney and the south-west of Ireland

On the waterfront *The colourful port of **Dingle** is a lively base for touring the Dingle peninsula. There are boat trips from the harbour to visit Fungi, a bottle-nose dolphin.*

TOURIST INFORMATION

Bantry 353 (0) 27 50229
Cahirciveen 353 (0) 66 9472589
Clonakilty 353 (0) 23 33226
Dingle 353 (0) 66 9151188
Glengariff 353 (0) 27 63084
Kenmare 353 (0) 64 41233
Killarney 353 (0) 64 31633
Listowel 353 (0) 68 22590
Skibbereen 353 (0) 28 21766
Tralee 353 (0) 66 7121288

GOOD PLACES TO STOP

Baltimore [E1]
  Bushe's Bar 353 (0) 28 20125
  Casey's 353 (0) 28 20197
Bantry [E2]
  Blairs 353 (0) 21 438 1470
  Snug Bar 353 (0) 27 50057
Cloghroe [G3] *Blairs*
  353 (0) 21 438 1470
Clonakilty [F1] *Malthouse*
  Granary 353 (0) 23 34335
Dingle [B4] *Lord Bakers*
  353 (0) 66 915 1277
Kenmare [D3] *Mickey Ned's*
  353 (0)64 40200
Kinsale [G2]
  Crackpots 353 (0) 21 477 2847
  Man Friday
  353 (0) 21 477 2260
Skibbereen [E1] *Ty Ar Mor*
  Seafood 353 (0) 28 22100

ABBEYFEALE [E5] The town, nestled in the foothills of the Mullagharierk Mountains, takes its name from a Cistercian abbey. At nearby **Listowel** two ivy-clad towers are all that is left of the 15th-century **castle**. The **Lartigue Railway** – the world's first monorail – ran between Ballybunnion and Listowel from 1888 to 1924.

ARDFERT [D5] St Brendan founded a monastery in the village in the 6th century. Today the 13th-century **St Brendan's Cathedral (NM)** is a majestic ruin. At **Banna Beach** to the west is **Casement's Fort**, a prehistoric circular rampart.

BALLINASCARTY [F2] The Ford family left by cart from here in 1847 to flee the potato famine, and sailed to the USA. William Ford, whose son Henry founded the Ford motor company, was among them.

BANTRY [E2] A fishing port and market town set at the head of a scenic bay, it survived two attacks by French troops allied with Irish nationalist leader Wolfe Tone in 1689 and in 1796. **Bantry House** contains treasured objects such as Marie Antoinette's bookcases.

BEARA PENINSULA [C2–D2] There are dramatic views from the Healy Pass, which crosses the central Caha Mountains. **Hungry Hill**, the highest peak at 686m (2251ft), has a 235m (770ft) waterfall. Daphne du Maurier's novel *Hungry Hill* is set round the copper mines at Allihies. **Dursey Island**, off the tip of the peninsula, is reached by Ireland's only cable car.

CAHERDANIEL [C2] Derrynane House, in the Derrynane National Park, was Daniel O'Connell's home. Known as 'The Liberator', O'Connell campaigned for full citizens' rights for Irish Catholics, achieved in 1829.

CLONAKILTY [F1] A thriving linen-making centre in the 19th century, it is now a lively market town. Nearby **Timoleague** has the ruins of a 14th-century Franciscan friary. A memorial to Michael Collins, the nationalist leader who was born in nearby Woodford in 1890 and who died in 1922, stands at Sam's Cross Road.

DINGLE [B4] See picture.

DINGLE PENINSULA [B4–5] Behind the Dingle's long, sandy beaches and rugged cliffs are lakes, mountains and soft green fields. There are many prehistoric sites, ancient forts and early Christian monuments. The 95 mile **Dingle Way** round the peninsula crosses the mountains at Ireland's highest pass, the **Connor**.

GALLARUS ORATORY [B4] The early Christian chapel, shaped like an upturned boat, has stood solid and watertight since the 8th–12th centuries. Its walls, more than 1m (3ft) thick, are corbelled – laid with stones that successively jut farther inwards.

GAP OF DUNLOE [D3] Rapids cut through this pass between the Purple Mountain and MacGillycuddy's Reeks. Jaunting cars (ponies and traps) can be hired at **Kate Kearney's Cottage** for the winding 4 mile ride through to **Lord Brandon's Cottage**.

GLANDORE [E1] East of the village is **Dromberg Stone Circle**, more than 2000 years old. Cremated bones were placed in a pit, 9m (17ft) wide, which was enclosed by 17 standing stones.

GLENGARRIFF [D2] In a wooded inlet at the head of Bantry Bay, the village has a mild climate that allows plants such as arbutus and fuchsia to thrive. On **Garinish Island**, exotics such as camellias flourish in a 1920s Italianate garden.

KANTURK CASTLE [F4] The lofty ruins of this unfinished castle are south of the market town of Kanturk. In 1615 the English government forbade completion of the castle, by then four storeys high.

KENMARE [D3] Set on the Roughty river, the town takes its name from the Irish *Ceann Mara* – 'Head of the Sea'. Its lace-making industry began during the potato famine of 1845–51, when local nuns employed starving women and girls to make needlepoint lace.

KILLARNEY [D4] Beautifully situated beside three lakes at the foot of MacGillycuddy's Reeks, the town has been a tourist centre since the 1750s. **St Mary's Cathedral** was designed by Augustus Pugin in 1855. Near the Franciscan **friary**, with fine stained glass, is a **monument** to four of Kerry's 17th–18th-century Gaelic poets.

KILLARNEY NATIONAL PARK [D3] Two of Killarney's lakes – Leane and Muckross – lie within the park, which borders the third, Upper Lake. Ireland's only herd of native red deer roam here. By Lough Leane stand the remains of the 15th-century **Muckross Abbey**. Muckross House of 1843 houses the **Kerry Folklife Centre**.

LOUGH HYNE [E1] Forested hills ring this almost landlocked sea inlet. Rare fish such as the triggerfish and the red-mouth goby are carried into the lough's deep salt waters.

MALLOW [G4] The market town on the Blackwater was, in the 18th and 19th centuries, Ireland's chief spa – the 'Irish Bath'. **Mallow Castle** is a ruined fortified house of the 1590s; in its park are white fallow deer.

THE SKELLIGS [A2] Three dark rock pinnacles rise up out of the Atlantic. Monks lived in a clifftop settlement on **Skellig Michael** in the 6th–12th centuries. Several stone beehive huts, a cemetery and the remains of a church and two chapels survive.

SKIBBEREEN [E1] The small fishing port on the River Ilen was founded in 1631 after Algerian pirates sacked the neighbouring port of Baltimore, massacring its inhabitants. The fine Protestant **cathedral** of 1826 is in classical Greek style.

TRALEE [D4] The town owes its fame to the 1800s song 'The Rose of Tralee' and there is an annual Rose of Tralee festival. The town has fine 18th century houses, an 1861 Dominican church and a Victorian courthouse.

Waterford, southern Wexford & eastern Cork

Emerald realm *Locals erected the statue of Christ the King in 1950. It looks over the* **Glen of Aherlow** *towards the distant Galty Mountains.*

TOURIST INFORMATION

Blarney 353 (0) 21 4381624
Caher 353 (0) 52 41453
Clonmel 353 (0) 52 22960
Cork 353 (0) 21 4255100
Cork Airpt: freephone at t'minal
Dungarvan 353 (0) 58 41741
Kinsale 353 (0) 21 477 2234
Midleton 353 (0) 21 46 13702
New Ross 353 (0) 51 421857
Rosslare (Kilrane)
    353 (0) 53 33232
Tramore 353 (0) 51 381572
Waterford 353 (0) 51 875823
Wexford 353 (0) 53 23111
Youghal 353 (0) 24 92447

GOOD PLACES TO STOP

Cobh [B3] *Water's Edge*
    353 (0) 21 4815566
Dungarvon [C4] *Tannery Rest*
    353 (0) 58 45420
New Ross [F5] *Kennedy's Pub*
    353 (0) 51 425188
Waterford [E4] *Bodega!*
    353 (0) 51 844177
    Gatchell's 353 (0) 51 332575

inland port. The **J F Kennedy Arboretum**, to the south, was planted in memory of the US president. His great-grandfather was born nearby.

ANNE'S GROVE [A4] The beautiful 18th-century gardens stand beside the River Awbeg. **Doneraile Court Park** nearby has a herd of Irish red deer in its wildlife sanctuary.

ARDMORE [C3] A fine 30m (100ft) high round **tower** some 800 years old overlooks the village. Inside the **cathedral** are two pillars carved with ancient Irish ogham script.

BLARNEY CASTLE [A3] The **keep** is all that is left of the 15th-century castle built by Cormac MacCarthy. In the battlements is the limestone block known as the **Blarney Stone**.

CAHER [C5] Perched on an island in the Suir, the 15th-century battlements and barbican gateway of **Castle Caher** dominate the market town. John Nash designed the Protestant **church** and the nearby **Swiss Cottage**.

CAPPOQUIN [C4] The 18th-century mansion, **Cappoquin House**, was burned down in 1923 and rebuilt to make the most of the views of the Blackwater. In the Knockmealdown Mountains to the north is **Mount Melleray Monastery**.

CARRICK-ON-SUIR [D5] **Ormonde Castle**, a manor house of 1584, was added to the 1309 castle by 'Black Tom', the 10th Earl of Ormonde.

CLONMEL [C5] Edward I fortified the town and some ramparts are visible near **St Mary's Church**. A plaque on

the **West Gate** honours the author Laurence Sterne, who was born here. The other gate, the **Main Guard**, was built as a courthouse in 1674.

CLOYNE [B3] The village grew round a 6th-century monastery founded by St Colman. The **Round Tower** and a remnant of the **Fire House**, an early oratory, survive. **St Colman's Cathedral**, dating from 1250, has an alabaster effigy of the philosopher George Berkeley, Bishop of Cloyne in 1734–52. The **Jameson whiskey distillery** is at nearby Midleton.

COBH [B3] The *Sirius*, the first transatlantic steamer, sailed from the harbour in 1838. The towering blue granite **cathedral** dates from 1868. On the quay, a memorial recalls the loss of the liner *Lusitania*, which was torpedoed offshore in May 1915. Mud flats at nearby **Foaty Island** attract wildfowl. Rare trees and shrubs can be seen in the **Fota House arboretum**.

CORK [A3] Ireland's third largest city, at the mouth of the River Lee, was founded by St Fin Barre in the 7th century as a monastic settlement. The three Gothic spires of **St Fin Barre's Cathedral** soar over 18th-century houses, warehouses and quays.

DUNGARVAN [C4] King John built the **castle**, now a ruin, in 1185. On a spit of land to the harbour's east is a **friary** founded in 1290, now part of a 19th-century church. It has fine views of **Helvick Head**.

FERMOY [B4] John Anderson, a Scottish businessman, built the **Grand Hotel** and the **barracks** to serve his mail coach service between Dublin and Cork. **Castle Hyde** was the home of Ireland's first president, Dr Douglas Hyde. At **Glanworth**, to the north, a ruined **castle** overlooks a 12-arched stone **bridge** of 1446, Ireland's oldest.

GLEN OF AHERLOW [B5] See picture.

KILMALLOCK [A5] The town's defences were razed by Cromwell, but part of the town walls, one of the gateways and a pele tower survive.

KINSALE [A2] A Spanish invasion force and their Irish allies were defeated here by the English after a siege in 1601. The courthouse, now a **museum**, has siege relics. **Charles's Fort (NM)** is a splendid example of 17th-century military architecture.

LISMORE [C4] King John established a **castle** here in 1185, and it was remodelled in the 19th century; the grounds are open in summer. **St Carthage's Cathedral**, with a shapely spire, was built in the 17th century.

MITCHELSTOWN CAVES [B5] Fine rock formations can be seen in this cave system. The roof of the Middle Cave glistens with calcite crystals.

NEW ROSS [F5] Brightly painted shop fronts crowd the narrow streets that climb the hillside around this

SALTEE ISLANDS [F/G4] Puffins, Manx shearwaters and gannets nest amid the grasses and sea pinks at Ireland's largest bird sanctuary. Boats take visitors from **Kilmore Quay**.

TACUMSHIN LAKE [G4] This salt lake is popular with windsurfers. Druid priestesses may have lived on the island in nearby **Lady's Island Lake**; it has ruins of a **castle** and a **priory**.

WATERFORD [E4] **Reginald's Tower** of about AD 1000 – now a **museum** – and the remains of 9th-century **walls**, recall the city's Viking origins. Narrow streets and the ruins of **Blackfriars Abbey** survive from medieval days. Crystal glass manufacture began here in the late 18th century. John Roberts, a local architect, designed the **City Hall**, the **Chamber of Commerce** and two **cathedrals** in the 18th century.

WEXFORD [G5] When the harbour silted up in the 19th century, it ended Wexford's 1000 years as a port. Henry II spent six weeks in the tower of **Selskar Abbey** as a self-imposed penance for his part in the murder of Thomas Becket. Outside the town are wetlands known as the **Slobs**, a wildfowl reserve. In winter, white-fronted geese from Greenland gather on the South Slobs in huge flocks.

YOUGHAL [C3] A four-storey **clock tower** spans the main street of Youghal (pronounced Yawl). Sir Walter Raleigh was mayor in 1588–9.

Southern Galway, Clare & northern Limerick

ADARE [F1] This pretty village of thatched cottages has three medieval abbeys, two in use as parish churches. The **priory** of 1315 has carved shields of the Fitzgeralds, earls of Kildare.

ARAN ISLANDS [C4] Fishing, farming and tourism are the main occupations on the three islands of Inishmore, Inishmaan and Inisheer. Inishmore has four prehistoric forts, among them the vast **Dun Aengus** on a 90m (300ft) cliff. On Inisheer is **O'Brien's Castle**, a ruined 15th-century tower house.

ASKEATON [E1] **Desmond Castle**, a 16th-century tower house, has a grand hall 27m (90ft) by 9m (30ft). At the 15th-century Franciscan **friary**, black marble pillars form the cloister, and a statue of St Francis has its face worn by kisses from people seeking a cure for toothache. In the 1930s, flying boats first made commercial transatlantic flights from **Foynes**, to the west; a **museum** tells the story.

BALLINASLOE [G5] Horse selling and buggy racing thrive in this town, whose annual livestock fair (the first week in October) is Ireland's biggest.

BUNRATTY CASTLE [F2] Built in the 15th century, the castle has been restored complete with drawbridge, corner turrets and rectangular keep.

THE BURREN [F3] Water seeping through limestone rock (see picture) into underground streams has gouged out caves below, among them **Ailwee Cave**, which is drained and lit. On the surface there are earthworks and tombs such as **Poulnabrone Dolmen**. There is a display centre at **Kilfenora**.

CARRIGAHOLT [C1] The Irish village name means 'rock of the fleet', and refers to ships of the Spanish Armada that sheltered in the Shannon estuary. There are splendid views from **MacMahon Castle**, a medieval ruin.

CASTLE MATRIX [E1] Sir Walter Raleigh restored this 15th-century tower house, which is now the **Irish International Arts Centre**.

CLARINBRIDGE [E4] Oyster-lovers meet at the village each September for the **Oyster Festival**. Local oysters are renowned for their full flavour.

CLIFFS OF MOHER [D3] Sheer, dark, limestone cliffs rise to 204m (668ft) and extend for 5 miles. Guillemots, kittiwakes and other sea birds share the cliff ledges.

CLONMACNOISE [H5] In a meadow by the Shannon are the ruins of the **monastery** founded in AD 545 but destroyed by English troops in 1552. The extensive ruins include a 10th-century cathedral, two round towers, eight churches and some 200 graves inscribed in Irish.

COOLE PARK [E4] Once a literary centre, the house was demolished in 1941, but the grounds can still be visited. The poet W. B. Yeats, who wrote a poem 'The Wild Swans at Coole', was a frequent visitor; there are still swans on **Coole Lough**.

CORROFIN [E3] Among the items in the **Clare Heritage Centre** is a T-shaped early Christian cross used for marking parish boundaries.

CURRAGHCHASE [E1] Forest walks beneath hornbeam, ash and elm trees ring the ruined house of Aubrey de Vere, the 19th-century poet.

DUNDRUM [H1] **Marl Bog Forest Walk** by the village is a good place for observing bogland wildlife.

ENNIS [E3] Clare's county town grew round its 13th-century **friary (NM)** and still has a medieval air. Gazing over the High Street is a statue of Daniel O'Connell, the county's MP in 1828–31. In the **Clare museum** are artefacts relating to Éamon De Valéra, who became the Republic's president in 1959. The town also has a fine classical **courthouse** of 1850.

GALWAY [E5] The city has been a focus of trading on Galway Bay for some 1000 years. The **Spanish Arch** of 1584 is a monument to a past trading partner, and the 16th-century

mansion, **Lynch's Castle**, now a bank, was built by a wealthy merchant. Dominating the city's skyline is the copper-domed limestone **cathedral**.

KILLALOE [G2] This market town sheltered beneath hills is said to be the site of Kincora, the palace of Brian Boru, who became High King of Ireland in 1002. There are inscriptions in ancient Irish ogham and runic text on the **Thorgrim Stone** in the 13th-century **St Flannan's Cathedral**.

KILRUSH [D2] Sailing and fishing boats throng the marina, and trips run to **Scattery Island**, the site of a monastic settlement, where there are several 9th–15th-century churches and a round tower 26m (85ft) high.

KNAPPOGUE CASTLE [E2] In the 15th century, it was a stronghold of the MacNamaras, and there are many of their tombs at the Franciscan friary in nearby **Quin**. The **Craggaunowen Project** to the east re-creates early Irish history. It includes a crannog (a man-made island), a ring fort and the leather-hulled *Brendan*, based on St Brendan's 6th-century boat, in which explorer Tim Severin crossed the Atlantic in 1976–7.

LIMERICK [F2] Founded by Vikings in the 9th century, Limerick is a port and manufacturing centre. The ruins of **King John's Castle** of 1210 bear the scars of the city's past battles. The **Treaty Stone** on Thomond Bridge is said to be where a treaty was signed in 1691. **St John's Cathedral** has Ireland's highest tower, 280ft (85m), and 12th-century **St Mary's Cathedral** has the only carved misericords (tip-up seats) left in Ireland.

LISDOONVARNA [D3] Ireland's only spa grew in the 1800s, thriving as a Victorian health resort. People still come to bathe in its waters.

LOUGHREA [F4] St Brendan's **Cathedral**, built in the idiom of the Arts and Crafts Movement, is the glory of this pretty market town. There is also a ruined Carmelite **friary** and the de Burgo family's 13th-century **castle**.

NENAGH [G3] The massive Norman keep of the 13th-century **Butler Castle (NM)** looms over the market

town, its five storeys of 6m (20ft) thick walls soaring to 30m (100ft). There is also a Franciscan **friary** of 1250, a classical **courthouse** of 1843 and a Victorian **town hall**. The scaffold and condemned cells at the **Governor's House** and jail can be visited.

PORTUMNA [G4] Three bridges cross the Shannon in this market town. The **castle (NM)**, built by the Earl of Clanrickarde before 1618, is a magnificent fortified house. Within its grounds on the edge of the **Portumna Forest Park** are a ruined 15th-century Dominican **priory** and a formally laid out garden.

THOOR BALLYLEE [F4] Home of the poet W. B. Yeats from 1917 to 1929, the restored 16th-century tower and cottage is still furnished as it was when he lived there.

TIPPERARY [G1] A dairying centre of the Golden Vale pasturelands, the town has been made famous by the song 'It's a long way to Tipperary'; during the First World War it became a marching song. Red Kelly, born here in about 1820, was deported to Australia and became the father of the notorious outlaw Ned Kelly.

TOURING GUIDE

Pavement of rock Fissured rock, known as **The Burren**, defines more than 100 sq miles of landscape. Its bleakness is only broken by plants such as maidenhair ferns and arctic-alpine mountain avens which thrive in the gaps.

Dublin & Ireland's central lowlands

Watchful eye *A statue of George Salmon, provost of Trinity College, Dublin from 1888, guards the college entrance. He died in 1904, the year that Trinity admitted women – a change he was fervently against.*

TOURIST INFORMATION

Arklow 353 (0) 402 32484
Athlone 353 (0) 90 6494630
Athy 353 (0) 59 8633075
Birr 353 (0) 509 20110
Carlow 353 (0) 59 9131554
Cashel 353 (0) 62 61333
Dublin 353 (0) 187 88053
Enniscorthy 353 (0) 54 34699
Gorey 353 (0) 55 21248
Kildare 353 (0) 45 521240
Kilkenny 353 (0) 56 7751500
Portlaoise 353 (0) 502 21178
Wicklow 353 (0) 404 69117

GOOD PLACES TO STOP

Cashel [A1] *Cashel Palace Hotel*
353 (0) 62 62707
Dublin [F5] *Bad Ass Cafe*
353 (0) 1 671 2596
Doheny & Nesbitt
353 (0) 1 676 2945
Morrison Hotel
353 (0) 1 887 2400
O'Neills 353 (0) 1 677 5213
The Vaults 353 (0) 1 605 4700
Dun Laoghaire [F5] *Caviston's
Seafood Restaurant*
353 (0) 1 284 9120

ARKLOW [F2] A major port in the 19th century, it is still a shipbuilding centre. *Gypsy Moth IV,* in which Sir Francis Chichester sailed round the world in 1966–7, was built here.

ATHY [D3] **White's Castle** of 1507 guards the **Crom-a-boo Bridge** across the Barrow. By the nearby ruins of the 13th-century **Moone Abbey** is a 9th-century 5m (17ft) high cross.

AVOCA [F3] The rivers Avonmore and Avonbeg are immortalised in Thomas Moore's poem, 'The Meeting of the Waters'. The 1723 hand-weaving mill is one of the oldest in Ireland. More recently Avoca was the setting for TV's *Ballykissangel.*

AVONDALE FOREST PARK [F3] **Avondale House** within the park was the home of Irish patriot and MP Charles Stewart Parnell (1846–91).

BIRR [A4] The ancient Seefin stone, which marked 'The Navel of Ireland', is at the **Heritage Centre. Birr Castle** has a giant telescope, built in 1845 by the 3rd Earl of Rosse.

BRAY [F4] Dubliners flock to this Victorian resort, where the novelist James Joyce lived in 1888–91. The mock-Tudor **Kilruddery House** lies south of the town.

CARLOW [D3] The town grew round a **keep**, built in 1207–13 to guard a river crossing. A **Celtic cross** marks the burial site of 600 killed in the 1798 Rebellion against the British. The 4000-year-old **Browneshill Dolmen** has a 100 ton capstone.

CASHEL [A1] The **Rock of Cashel (NM)** is topped by ruined **St Patrick's Cathedral**, and **Cormac's Chapel** of 1127–34, with carvings of beasts and human figures. The **Vicars' Choral Hall** has the **St Patrick's Cross** and a 4th-century **Coronation Stone.** The folk village in Cashel has **Bothàn Scóir,** a 17th century peasant house.

CELBRIDGE [E5] Esther Vanhomrigh, daughter of a Dutch merchant and the 'Vanessa' of Jonathan Swift's writings, lived in **Celbridge Abbey. Castletown House** is a classical mansion of 1722.

DUBLIN [F5] Ireland's capital sits on Dublin Bay, with the Liffey flowing through its centre. Fine Georgian buildings include the **Four Courts, Custom House,** and the **Rotunda Hospital** – Europe's first permanent maternity hospital. South of the river are **Trinity College,** the **National Museum** and the **National Gallery. St Patrick's Cathedral** dates from 1225; Jonathan Swift, author of *Gulliver's Travels,* was Dean from 1713–45.

ENNISCORTHY [E1] Blue stone **St Aidan's Cathedral** is by Augustus Pugin. In 1828, a 27 day rising against the British took place on **Vinegar Hill**; a shell of the rebels' fort remains. The poet Edmund Spenser (1552–99) once leased the 13th-century **castle.**

ENNISKERRY [F4] South of the village is **Powerscourt House,** a ruined 1740 mansion with terraced gardens giving views across the Dargle valley. In a wooded grove of the **deer park,** Ireland's highest waterfall tumbles 121m (398ft).

FERNS [E1] The seat of the Leinster kings, Ferns was plundered for ten centuries by the Danes, Irish and English. The 13th-century **castle** has a tower with a circular chapel.

GLENDALOUGH [E3] St Kevin set up a monastery here in the 6th century. A rock ledge with a stone oratory is known as **St Kevin's Bed**.

HOWTH [F5] The town is a fishing and sailing centre, with the ruins of **Howth Abbey** of 1042, and a 12th-century **castle** with fine gardens.

KILDARE [D4] Horse racing still dominates the town. The Curragh racing country can be viewed from the tower in the grounds of **St Brigid's Cathedral.** Nearby are the **National Stud and Horse Museum,** and the **Japanese Gardens** of 1910.

KILKENNY [C2] The **castle** was the seat of the earls of Ormonde from 1391 to 1935. **St Canice's Anglican cathedral** was built in 1280 on the site of a 6th-century monastery. The **Black Abbey** was founded in 1225.

MAYNOOTH [E5] The Catholic seminary of **St Patrick's College** was founded in 1521, closed in the Reformation and reopened in 1795. The **castle** ruins are by the college.

NAAS [D4] Before the 14th century, Naas was a stronghold of the kings of Leinster; the Irish name, 'An Nás', means 'Castle of the Kings'.

PORTLAOISE [C3] The O'Moores had a fort here until the 16th century,

when the English ousted them, built a town behind the fort and named it Maryborough. On the **Rock of Dunamase** – shown by Ptolemy on maps of AD 140 – are the ruins of 12th-century **Masg Castle.**

ROSCREA [A3] Ruins of 12th-century **St Cronan's Abbey** are found in the town. The 18th-century **Damer House** stands within the walls of the **castle's** 13th-century gate tower.

THOMASTOWN [C1] The town has fragments of medieval walls, a **castle** and a scenic water garden. The 15th-century cloisters at **Jerpoint Abbey** have carved figures, including a man with stomach ache.

THURLES [A2] A market town beside the Suir, Thurles has a fine 19th-century **cathedral.** A statue in **Liberty Square** celebrates Archbishop Croke, founder in 1884 of the Gaelic Athletic Association (GAA).

TULLAMORE [B5] A hot-air balloon fell and exploded in Tullamore in 1785, destroying 100 houses. The town's liqueur distilling industry was established in 1798, when the Dublin-River Shannon Grand Canal reached it. Neo-Gothic **Charleville Castle** nearby dates from 1800–12.

WICKLOW [F3] Settled by the Danes during the 9th century, this seafaring town derives its name from Wykinglo – 'Viking's meadow'. On a knoll by the harbour are the ruins of **Black Castle,** dating from 1176. **Wicklow Head** offers excellent views of the sea and mountains.

Mayo, Sligo, Roscommon and northern Galway

ACHILL ISLAND [B3] On Ireland's largest offshore island, the peaks of **Croaghaun** and **Slievemore** rise above a rugged wilderness of heath and bog. Dolphins, seals and basking sharks may be seen below sheer cliffs to the north and west.

BALLINA [E4] On the east bank of the River Moy stand the ruins of a 15th-century **friary**. On the west bank is the **Dolmen of the Four Maols**, dating from the Bronze Age, named after four foster-brothers hanged in the 6th century for murdering their master. Mary Robinson, Ireland's president from 1990–7, spent her childhood in Ballina.

BALLINTOBER ABBEY [D2] Mass has been celebrated at the **abbey** since its foundation in 1216 – except for five weeks in the 1840s famine. Tioboid na Long ('Theobald of the Ships'), son of 'Pirate Queen' Grace O'Malley, was murdered nearby in 1629 and is buried in the **de Burgo Chapel**.

BALLINTOBER CASTLE [G2] From this early 13th-century **castle's** mighty walls the powerful O'Conor clan ruled Connaught until the 17th century. It is thought to be Ireland's earliest stone castle.

BALLYMOTE CASTLE [F4] Richard de Burgo, the 'Red Earl' of Ulster, built this **fortress (NM)** around 1300. It changed hands between English and Irish before falling in the 17th century to General Ireton, Oliver Cromwell's chief officer in Ireland.

BENWEE HEAD [C5] See picture.

BOYLE [G3] Cistercian monks founded **Boyle Abbey (NM)** in the 12th century. Its church has rounded Romanesque arches on one side of the nave and pointed Gothic arches on the other.

CARRICK-ON-SHANNON [H3] Boating enthusiasts and anglers enjoy the tranquil waterways of Leitrim's small but bustling county

town. **Costello Chapel**, only 5m (16ft) long, is the smallest chapel in Ireland, built in 1877 by Edward Costello, in memory of his wife Josephine.

CASTLEBAR [D3] In 1798, the town was seized by a Franco-Irish army led by General Humbert; the routed British garrison took flight so fast the event was called the 'Races of Castlebar'. At **Straide** is a **museum** to Michael Davitt (1846–1906), founder of the National Land League to protect tenant farmers from eviction.

CÉIDE FIELDS [D5] Preserved beneath 2m (6ft) of blanket bog for centuries, **Céide Fields (NM)** are one of the world's most extensive Stone Age monuments. Excavations have uncovered houses, pottery, flint tools, tombs, fields enclosed by drystone walls, and stumps of pine forest cleared by early settlers.

CLIFDEN [B1] Connemara's chief town is a lively fishing port and angling centre. To the west stand the ruins of **Clifden Castle** built by John d'Arcy, founder of the town, in 1815. On the moors behind Mannin Bay is a monument to John Alcock and Arthur W. Brown, who made the first nonstop flight across the Atlantic, landing near the spot where Marconi set up the first transatlantic wireless telegraphy station in 1907.

CLONALIS HOUSE [F2] Family belongings and archives of the O'Conors, who can trace back their lineage 60 generations to the High Kings of Ireland, fill this Victorian mansion near the market town of **Castlerea**. Treasures include a harp played by the blind harpist Turlough O'Carolan (1670–1738).

CONG [D1] Turlough O'Conor, High King of Ireland, founded **Cong Abbey** in 1128 where monks guarded the Cross of Cong, reputed to contain a fragment of the true Cross; it is now in the National Museum in Dublin. The town was used for scenes in the 1952 film *The Quiet Man*, with John Wayne and Maureen O'Hara.

CONNEMARA NATIONAL PARK [C1] Four of the **Twelve Pins**, a cluster of conical mountains at the heart of Connemara, are within the park, as is the Polldark gorge.

CROAGH PATRICK [C2] Thousands of pilgrims continue a centuries-old tradition as they climb to the summit in remembrance of St Patrick, who is said to have spent the 40 days of Lent here in AD 441.

DOWNPATRICK HEAD [D5] See picture.

KILLARY HARBOUR [C1/2] Lofty heights line a beautiful inlet, running 8 miles inland. To the north it is framed by the Mweelrea Mountains and to the south by the Maumturks.

KNOCK [F2] A million pilgrims flock annually to the shrine and basilica of Ireland's most revered Christian site. On a stormy night in August 1879, a group of villagers saw an apparition of the Virgin Mary, St Joseph and St John the Evangelist here.

KYLEMORE ABBEY [C1] A castellated neo-Gothic mansion built in the 1860s by English shipping magnate, Mitchell Henry, it is now run as a school. The grounds and part of the building are open – the chapel is Norwich Cathedral in miniature.

ROSCOMMON [G2] An effigy of Felim O'Conor, King of Connaught, can be seen in the ruined church of the

TOURIST INFORMATION

Achill 353 (0) 98 45384
Ballina 353 (0) 96 70848
Boyle 353 (0) 71 9662145
Carrick 353 (0) 78 20170
Castlebar 353 (0) 94 9021207
Clifden 353 (0) 95 21163
Knock 353 (0) 94 9388193
Oughterard 353 (0) 91 552808
Roscommon 353 (0) 90 6623342
Sligo 353 (0) 71 9161201
Tuam 353 (0) 93 25486/24463
Westport 353 (0) 98 25711

GOOD PLACES TO STOP

Sligo [G5] *Atrium Restaurant* 353 (0) 71 914418

Dominican friary he founded in 1253. In the 18th century the county jail had a female executioner, 'Lady Betty'; condemned to death for murder, she escaped execution by offering to take over as hangman. The **castle** was partly destroyed by Cromwell in 1652.

SLIGO [G5] The Dominican **abbey (NM)**, of 1252, has Ireland's only surviving sculpted high altar. In nearby Lough Gill is **Innisfree** – made famous by W.B. Yeats in his poem, 'The Lake Isle of Innisfree'. Ireland's largest Bronze Age burial ground is **Carrowmore Megalithic Cemetery**.

STROKESTOWN [G2] The village was laid out round Palladian **Strokestown Park House** in the 1730s and the wide main streets are modelled on Vienna's *Ringstrasse*.

TUAM [E1] The 12th century **High Cross** now in the cathedral once stood in the middle of the town. In the 6th century AD, St Jarlath founded a monastery here. The Protestant cathedral of 1878 incorporates a superb Romanesque chancel arch. There is a **Museum of Milling** housed inside a 17th-century corn mill.

WESTPORT [D2] Lime trees shade **The Mall**, which flanks both sides of the River Carrowbeg as it flows through this former port, now a fishing centre, on an inlet of Clew Bay. The town was laid out in 1780 by James Wyatt for the 2nd Earl of Altamount, who lived in **Westport House** where, as well as family treasures, there are dungeons, fountains and a children's zoo.

TOURING GUIDE

Sculpted by Nature – Downpatrick Head is a great stack which was part of the mainland until 1393 when heavy seas caused it to break away. The windswept cliffs at Benwee Head to the west afford breathtaking views of the coasts of Mayo and Donegal, including the Mullet peninsula and the Stags of Broad Haven.

Meath, Louth, Cavan, Armagh and Fermanagh

ARMAGH [D5] The city is named for the legendary warrior queen, Macha, Ard Mhacha, or 'Macha's Height'. Her palace was at **Navan Fort**, seat of Ulster kings for 600 years. St Patrick founded a church and monastic school in the city around AD 445, and it became the ecclesiastical capital of Ireland, with two hilltop **cathedrals**. Local architect Francis Johnston built the **County Courthouse** of 1809, laid out the **Mall**, and designed the **Observatory**. A heritage centre tells the history of the city in Georgian times and the **County Museum** has a gallery of local artists including George Russell (1867–1935), poet, painter and writer, known as 'A.E.'.

ATHLONE [A1] For centuries the town guarded the main Shannon crossing. The 13th-century **castle** was besieged by William of Orange's army for a week in the 1690s.

BECTIVE ABBEY [D1] The **abbey** ruins are mostly 15th century, but the **monastery** was founded in 1147. The headless body of Hugh de Lacy, a governor of Ireland, was interred here after his murder in 1186; his head is in St Thomas's Abbey, Dublin.

BOYNE ESTUARY [F2] See picture.

CARLINGFORD [F3] The peak of Slieve Foye towers over the village. **King John's Castle**, a 13th-century fortress, is by the harbour. The **Mint** and **Taafe's Castle** are fortified 15th–16th-century houses. Terns nest on **Green Island** and **Blockhouse Island** ❧ at the mouth of Carlingford Lough.

CARRICKMACROSS [D3] Lace has been hand-stitched in the town since the early 19th century. **St Joseph's Church** has some splendid 1920s stained-glass windows.

CASTLE WARD [G5] An unusual mix of Classical and Gothic styles, the grounds of the 1760 mansion ❧ extend to the shores of **Strangford Lough** with its wild life centre

CASTLEWELLAN FOREST PARK [F5] A fine **arboretum**, planted in the 18th century, lies at the heart of the park. Farther south, **Tollymore Forest Park** has river and hill walks.

CLONES [C4] The town's tradition of crochet lace-making dates from the early 19th century. A 10th-century **High Cross** depicts various Biblical scenes. Vikings destroyed the 6th-century **monastery** in AD 836.

DOWNPATRICK [G5] St Patrick landed at nearby Saul around AD 432. When he converted Dichu, a local prince, and founded a monastery here, the town was already a large settlement. Ruined **Inch Abbey** nearby was a Benedictine abbey refounded by Cistercian monks in 1187.

DROGHEDA [E2] In 1412 two towns were joined to make Ireland's largest English-held town. It stood against Cromwell in 1649, and was put to the sword. **St Lawrence's Gate** is the only surviving town gate, and **Magdalene Tower** was the belfry of a Dominican friary of 1224. **St Peter's Church** has the embalmed head of St Oliver Plunkett, Archbishop of Armagh, executed for treason in 1681.

DUNDALK [E3] In this border port, the **courthouse** of 1818 is a copy of the Temple of Theseus in Athens, while the **cathedral** was modelled on King's College Chapel, Cambridge. In a restored 18th-century warehouse is the **County Museum**.

DUNSANY CASTLE [E1] Built on the **Hill of Tara** in 1180, the **castle** has been the home of the Plunkett family since the 15th century.

ENNISKILLEN [B5] The town was once a stronghold of the Maguires whose 15th-century **castle** became a barracks in the 18th century. The **Watergate** houses county and regimental museums and the **Portora Royal School** was founded in 1608 by James I; past pupils include Oscar Wilde and Samuel Beckett. To the south is 18th-century **Florence Court** ❧; to the east is **Castle Coole** ❧, a mansion of 1789–95.

FORE [C2] The former walled town has a 13th-century **priory**. The tiny 7th-century's **St Fechin's Church** is one of the 'seven wonders' of Fore that include water that never boils and wood that will not burn.

KELLS [D2] A round tower, crosses and the 9th-century stone-roofed **St Columcille's House** remain from the monastery founded here by St Columba in the 6th century. In the youth hostel, church and town hall are copies of the *Book of Kells* of around AD 800, an illuminated Latin manuscript of the Gospels, now kept at Trinity College, Dublin.

KILLYKEEN FOREST PARK [B3] Herons, great crested grebes and kingfishers can be seen here. Some islands in Lough Oughter may have been artificial islands, or crannogs.

LONGFORD [A2] The 61m (200ft) 'pepperpot' tower of **St Mel's Cathedral** of 1840–93 dominates the town. Nearby **Carrigglass Manor** was rebuilt in 1837 in Tudor style. A timber causeway of 48 BC was unearthed in nearby **Corlea Bog**.

MELLIFONT ABBEY [E2] Ireland's first Cistercian abbey **(NM)**, now a ruin, was founded in 1142. It later became a fortified mansion and in 1690 was used as William of Orange's base during the Battle of the Boyne.

MONAGHAN [C5] In the 17th century the town was seized by the English who developed its three wide squares. The **Cross of Clogher**, dating from 1400, is in the **County Museum**.

MONASTERBOICE [E2] St Buite founded a monastery here in the 6th century. Two **churches**, a round **tower** and three **crosses**, including the 10th-century **Cross of Muiredach**, remain.

MOURNE MOUNTAINS [F4] **Slieve Donard** ❧, the highest peak at 852m (2796ft), offers fine views. Primroses, bell heather and pyramidal orchids

Watch towers
*Two beacons, Lady's Finger and Maiden's Tower, overlook the **Boyne estuary**. Local legend has it that a maiden threw herself off Maiden's Tower thinking her lover was lost at sea.*

TOURIST INFORMATION

Armagh 028 3752 1800
Athlone 353 (0) 90 649 4630
Banbridge (028) 4062 3322
Cavan 353 (0) 49 4331942
Downpatrick (028) 4461 2233
Drogheda 353 (0) 41 9837070
Dundalk 353 (0) 42 9335484
Enniskillen (028) 6632 3110
Kilkeel (028) 417 62525
Longford 353 (0) 43 46566
Monaghan 353 (0) 47 81122
Mullingar 353 (0) 44 48650
Newcastle (028) 4372 2222
Newgrange 353 (0) 41 9880305
Newry (028) 3026 8877
Trim 353 (0) 46 9437111

GOOD PLACES TO STOP

Ballyconnell [B4] *Anglers' Rest* 353 (0) 49 952639
Downpatrick [G5] *Denvirs* (028) 4461 2012
Kells [D2] *Ground Floor Restaurant* 353 (0) 46 9249688

thrive on 5000-year-old dunes at the **Murlough National Nature Reserve** ❧ to the north-east.

NEWGRANGE [E2] A Stone Age passage grave at **Newgrange (NM)** is 5000 years old. **Newgrange Farm** has displays on past rural life and vintage farm machinery.

NEWRY [E4] The **town hall** is built over the River Newry and straddles the border of Down and Armagh. The first Irish Protestant **church** was built here in 1578, and the 1829 **Catholic cathedral** was Ireland's first since the Reformation. The **Newry Canal** of 1741 was the first in the British Isles.

QUOILE PONDAGE [G5] A nature reserve was created when two flood-control barrages were built on the River Quoile estuary. Many wildfowl breed here, and marsh plants and scrub grow in the former estuary.

SWORDS [F1] An 11th-century **tower** and a ruined 15th-century **church** are relics of the abbey St Columba founded here in AD 550. **Swords Castle** is a fortified manor built by the Archbishop of Dublin in about 1200. At the nearby resort of **Malahide**, the castle was the home of the Talbots from 1185 to 1973. It houses paintings from the National Portrait Gallery of Ireland.

WINDY GAP [E/F5] Cliffs hem in the pass on the Cooley peninsula. Nearby is the **grave of the Long Woman** – she is said to have been a Spanish princess, rescued from pirates by a local man, who then married her. He told her he owned all the lands that could be viewed from this hill; when she saw how little was visible she died of shock!

The north of Ireland from Donegal to Antrim

Natural geometry *Tradition holds that the black basalt columns of* **Giant's Causeway** 🌿 *were built by folk hero Finn MacCool to make a path to the island of Staffa. In fact, they result from volcanic eruptions 60 million years ago.*

TOURIST INFORMATION

Antrim (028) 9442 8331
Ballycastle (028) 2076 2024
Ballymena (028) 2563 8494
Ballymoney 028 2766 2280
Ballynahinch (028) 9756 1950
Bangor (028) 9127 0069
Belfast (028) 9024 6609
Buncrana 353 (0) 74 9362600
Bundoran 353 (0) 71 9841350
Carnlough 028 2888 5236
Carrickfergus 028 9336 6455
Coleraine 028 7034 4723
Cookstown 028 8676 6727
Donegal 353 (0) 74 9721148
Dungannon (028) 8776 7259
Dunglow 353 (0) 74 9521297
Giant's Cswy (028) 2073 1855
Larne (028) 2826 0088
Letterkenny 353 (0) 74 9121160
Limavady (028) 7776 0307
Lisburn (028) 9266 0038
Londonderry (028) 7126 7284
Magherafelt (028) 7963 1510
Omagh (028) 8224 7831
Portrush (028) 7082 3333
Strabane (028) 7188 3735

TOURING GUIDE

Map on pages 246–47

ARDARA [C2] A pretty town, set on a sea inlet by steep hills, its **Holy Family Church** of 1904 has a fine stained-glass window of 1954 by Evie Hone.

BALLYSHANNON [C1] Georgian shops and barracks of 1700 can be seen in the former British garrison town. **Bundoran** close by has fine sandy beaches, while **Belleek** pottery can be seen at its visitor centre.

BUNBEG [C4] The village lies at the heart of the Irish-speaking Gweedore region. **Dunglow** nearby is capital of the scenic area of **The Rosses**.

COLERAINE [G4] Linen exports led to the town's expansion in the 18th and 19th centuries. There are scenic locks at **The Cuts**, and 9000-year-old **Mountsandel** is Ireland's oldest settlement. Fine buildings include **St Patrick's Church** and the **town hall**.

DONEGAL [C2] Magee's 1866 shop still sells handwoven tweed. The 17th-century **Diamond** was planned by Sir Basil Brooke, who rebuilt the **castle** in 1610, adding a Jacobean manor. At **Donegal Abbey**, the monks began the *Annals of Four Masters*, a history of Ireland from pre-history to 1616.

GIANT'S CAUSEWAY [H5] See picture.

GLENVEAGH NATIONAL PARK [D4] Lough Beagh and its surrounding mountains, where red deer shelter in woods and peregrines patrol the slopes, lie in this park **(NM)**.

LETTERKENNY [D3] The 66m (215ft) spire of **St Eunan's** neo-Gothic cathedral towers above one of Ireland's longest main streets. St Columba was born near **Church Hill** to the north in AD 521.

LIMAVADY [G4] An 18th-century linen centre, it has a six-arched bridge across the Roe. Jane Ross heard a fiddler playing 'Londonderry Air', the melody to 'Danny Boy', here in 1851 and wrote down the tune.

LONDONDERRY [F3] The 17th century walls still encircle the old city. **St Columb's** Church of Ireland cathedral dates from 1633, and **St Eugene's** Catholic cathedral from 1851. At **Dungiven** is a 12th-century Augustinian **priory**. At **Ballyarnet**, an exhibition marks where Amelia Earhart, the first woman to fly the Atlantic solo, landed in 1932.

MAGHERA [G3] Animal and floral carvings adorn the west door of the 10th-century **church**. Nearby is 6000-year-old **Tirnony Dolmen.**

OMAGH [F1] The 1899 neo-Gothic **Sacred Heart Cathedral** has twin spires of different heights. 'Jimmy' Kennedy, who wrote 'The Teddy Bears' Picnic', and playwright Brian Friel were born here. The **Ulster-American Folk Park** re-creates old American and Irish villages.

RATHMELTON [E4] The town was a major port in the 18th century; it was from **Rathmullan** that the Celtic earls of Tyrone and Tyrconnell fled in 1607 ending the rule of the Irish chieftains; the story is told at the **battery fort.**

STRABANE [E3] Gray's Printing Press 🌿 celebrates the town's past as a printing centre. John Dunlap, who published the first US daily paper in 1784, and printed the Declaration of Independence, is said to have learned his trade at Gray's. Novelist Flann O'Brien was born here in 1911.

Map on page 248

ANTRIM [A2] The town grew up round a 5th-century monastery, of which only the 10th-century round tower remains. **Antrim Castle** of 1662 has splendid public gardens opposite the 1726 **courthouse**.

BALLYCASTLE [A4] The largest town in the Antrim glens, its **Holy Trinity Church** has a striking blue ceiling. By the beach is a memorial to Guglielmo Marconi, who in 1898 made radio contact with **Rathlin Island**.

BALLYMENA [A3] Grey basalt is the main constituent of many buildings including the neo-Gothic **St Patrick's Church** and the 1721 parish **church**.

BANGOR [C2] A resort since Victorian times, Bangor now has the largest marina in Ireland. **Bangor Castle** of 1859, set on a wooded hill, is now the town hall.

BELFAST [B2] From the 17th century, linen weaving brought prosperity to Belfast, with engineering and shipbuilding in the 19th century. The *Titanic* was built in Belfast's docks. Much of the city is of red brick, but the **Royal Courts of Justice** and the copper-domed **City Hall** are of white Portland stone. **Queen's University** is in Tudor Gothic style. The lavish **Opera House**, and the **Crown Liquor Saloon** 🌿, are among the finest Victorian buildings. In **St Anne's Cathedral** is the tomb of the Unionist Edward Carson. The **Ulster Museum** in the **Victorian Botanic Gardens** has a fine collection of Irish paintings.

GOOD PLACES TO STOP

Belfast [p248 B2] *Crown Liquor Saloon* (028) 9027 9901
Morning Star (028) 9023 5986
Letterkenny [p246 D3] *Castle Grove* 353 (0) 74 9151118
Limavady[p247 G4] *Lime Tree* (028) 7776 4300

CARRICKFERGUS [B2] A five-storey **castle keep** of 1180 stands above the harbour. William of Orange landed here in 1690, and a **Williamite Trail** leads to the town walls of 1608. Louis MacNeice (1907–63) lived in the town, and at **Kilroot**, Jonathan Swift wrote *A Tale of a Tub* in 1694–6.

GLENS OF ANTRIM [A4–B3] Nine steep glens carved by rivers through a high moorland plateau are among Ireland's famous beauty spots.

LISBURN [B1] Linen was bleached on the banks of the Lagan by Huguenot weavers in the 17th century. The **Lisburn Museum and Irish Linen Centre** are in the 17th-century Market House

LURGAN [A1] Master McGrath, the greyhound that won the Waterloo Cup three times between 1868–71, is in the town's coat of arms and is buried in the park. Poet George 'A.E.' Russell, was born here in 1867. Nearby **Portadown** is famous for roses and for roach fishing on the Bann.

RATHLIN ISLAND [A5] Scottish leader Robert Bruce took refuge in a cave on the rocky island in 1306. He learned patience, it is said, while watching a spider spin its web. Puffins are among the birds that can be seen at **Kebble Nature Reserve**.

Making the most of your journey

The following pages offer practical information on a number of situations which drivers may encounter on the road, from critical problems such as giving first aid following a collision, to essential advice on driving on the Continent.

498–503
What to do when an accident happens

If you have a serious accident, it is important to know the basics of first aid. Here are clear instructions on how to give cardio-pulmonary resuscitation (CPR) to someone whose breathing has stopped, along with advice on strapping fractures and controlling bleeding. We also give details on how to gather information for an insurance claim.

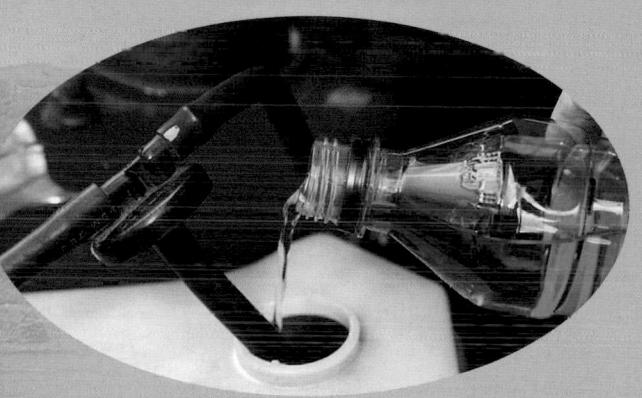

504–505
Dealing with breakdowns

Most of the time, breakdowns are completely avoidable. Follow our maintenance and pre-journey checklists to minimise the risk that it will happen to you. And if it does, follow the advice on the best way to get help.

510–511
Driving abroad

Getting to Europe by car is easier than ever. Make sure you have the right documentation, insurance and equipment with our guide to driving on the Continent.

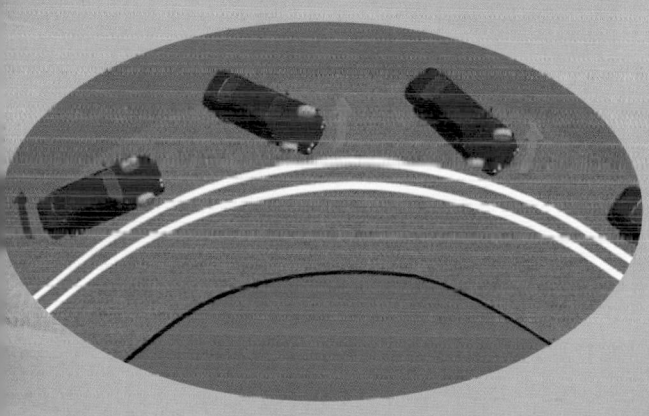

506–507
Driving in difficult situations

Find advice on how to cope with a skid and how to deal with a burst tyre. Plus important information on stopping distances and lots of tips on how to avoid one of the driver's main challenges – tiredness.

508–509
Travelling with children

Cut the stress of driving with children with tips on choosing the best car seat, avoiding travel sickness, how to pack the car and lots of tried and tested games for children of all ages.

512–515
Reading road signs

All the most common road signs and markings are covered in an informative guide.

What to do when an accident happens

If you are the first at the scene of an accident there are three main actions you must take in the following order. First, ensure safety and call for help, second make the vehicles involved safe and finally, attend to the people who are injured.

Ensure safety

TURN ON HAZARD LIGHTS and park well clear of the vehicles involved. If necessary, position your car so that it protects a casualty in the road. Keep it at least 14m (46ft) away; turn it so that it cannot move forwards if pushed by another vehicle and put the front wheels on full steering lock. At night, position it so that the headlights light up the scene.

Assess the situation Before you act, take a moment to assess the situation and get out of your car on the side away from the traffic. Do not rush straight from the car to the injured, or you, too, may be hit by a vehicle – especially on a motorway.

Call for help If on a motorway, use an emergency telephone as they are connected directly to the police. If you use a mobile telephone you will have to tell the emergency services details of your location. You can check the location from the marker post at the side of the carriageway. Give the exact location if you can, the type of accident and the number of vehicles and casualties involved. If possible, put on something bright – a high-visibility tabard or jacket is good for this purpose.

Warn other drivers by placing a warning triangle, if you have one, at least 50m (166ft) behind the crashed vehicles. On a motorway or dual carriageway put the triangle on the hard shoulder about 150m (492ft) behind the crashed vehicles. If using a warning triangle, be very careful when putting it out and retrieving it.

Make the vehicles involved safe

DO NOT MOVE ANY VEHICLES unless it is absolutely necessary to avoid another accident. Where damage is minor, it is best to move vehicles only if they are causing an obstruction.

To cut down the risk of fire, switch off the ignition in the vehicles. Leave ignition keys in place in case cars have to be moved and put the handbrake on.

Do not smoke, and warn others not to do so. Keep well away from a vehicle which is smouldering or on fire, as the petrol tank may explode.

Do not approach a crashed vehicle which has spilled chemicals or flammable material – warn the emergency services and keep bystanders well away.

Attend to the injured

DO NOT MOVE INJURED PEOPLE – whether they are inside or outside a vehicle – unless they are in immediate danger from fire, spillage or oncoming traffic, or they require resuscitation. There is a risk of spinal injury in road accidents, and permanent paralysis can be caused by movement.

If you have to move someone to get them out of danger, hold them under the arms and drag them away, making sure that the neck is supported in line with the body as much as possible.

> Always give first aid in the following order:
>
> **First** TO THOSE WHO ARE UNCONSCIOUS AND NOT BREATHING
>
> **Second** TO THOSE BLEEDING SEVERELY
>
> **Third** TO THOSE UNCONSCIOUS BUT BREATHING
>
> **Fourth** TO THOSE INJURED AND CONSCIOUS

Dealing with an unconscious casualty

Remember the ABC rule: A for AIRWAY – clear the airway; B for BREATHING – check the breathing; C for CIRCULATION – check the circulation.

Clear the airway

1 **Tilt head back** by lifting the chin with two fingers. This lifts the tongue, which may be pressing on the back of the throat. An unconscious casualty may die unless the airway is kept open. However, if there is a possibility of spinal injury, ask another person to support the head in a straight line with the neck while you tilt the chin back, or steady the head yourself with a hand on the forehead. Use the minimum chin tilt necessary to keep the airway open.

2 **Clear an obstruction** such as blood from the mouth by turning the head to one side and sweeping inside the mouth with two fingers.

Check the breathing

1 **Place your ear** next to the person's mouth and nose and look along the chest. If it is rising and falling, there is breathing.

2 **If you have a small hand mirror**, hold it next to the mouth and nose. If it clouds over and clears, this indicates that breathing is occurring.

3 **If the person is breathing**, support the airway to prevent the tongue, blood or vomit from obstructing it. Continue to hold the airway open until help arrives.

Check the circulation

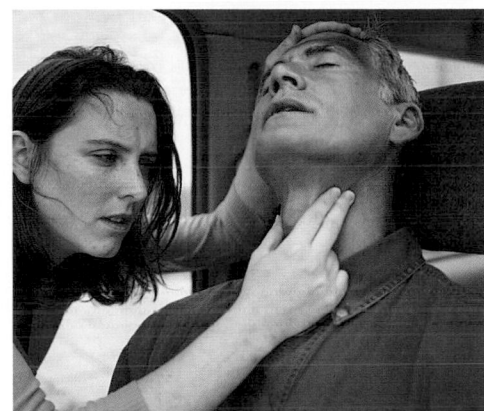

1 **If the person is not breathing,** check the circulation by feeling for a pulse at the neck. If there is a pulse, start the **kiss of life** (see p500).

2 **If there is no pulse** and the heart has stopped, you will need to use chest compressions as well to provide an artificial circulation. The combined process is known as cardio-pulmonary resuscitation or **CPR** (see p500).

3 **When the pulse** is restored, continue with the **kiss of life** (see p500) until the person's breathing is restored; then place in the recovery position (see p501).

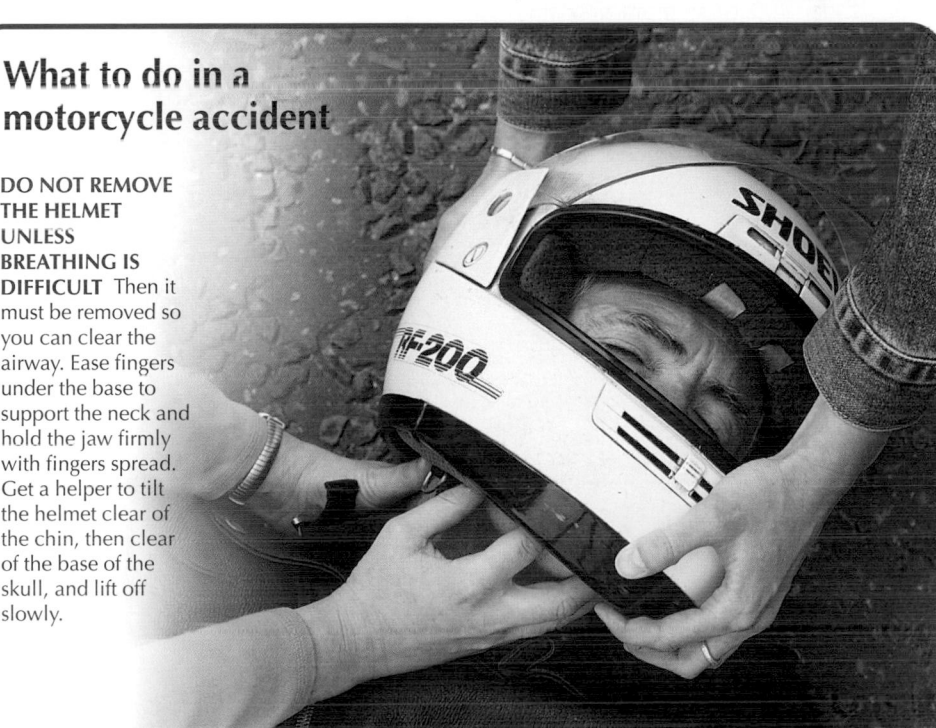

What to do in a motorcycle accident

DO NOT REMOVE THE HELMET UNLESS BREATHING IS DIFFICULT Then it must be removed so you can clear the airway. Ease fingers under the base to support the neck and hold the jaw firmly with fingers spread. Get a helper to tilt the helmet clear of the chin, then clear of the base of the skull, and lift off slowly.

ACCIDENTS **FIRST AID**

Giving the KISS OF LIFE

When starting CPR the rescuer should give two inflations (breaths) as described here, before starting chest compressions.

1 Using the finger and thumb of one hand, close the person's nostrils and support the jaw with your other hand.

2 Take a deep breath, seal your lips round the person's open mouth and then breathe out. Continue this procedure every six seconds until breathing is restored.

3 Once breathing has started, keep the airway open. If you have to leave the person, put them outside the car in the recovery position (see p501).

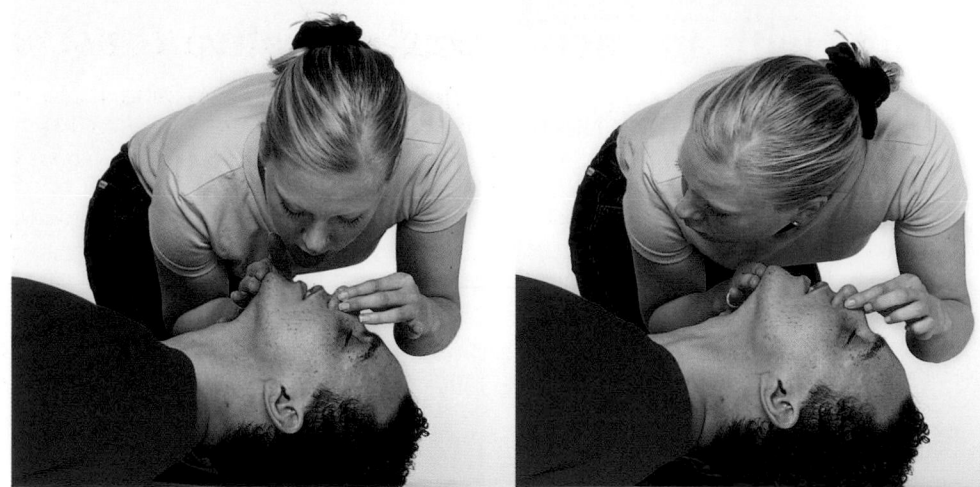

Giving CHEST COMPRESSIONS

1 Kneel down next to the person. Locate one of the lowest ribs with the index and middle fingers of your hand. Move your fingers along the rib until the lower rib meets the breastbone. Keep the middle finger at this point, placing the index finger above it on the breastbone.

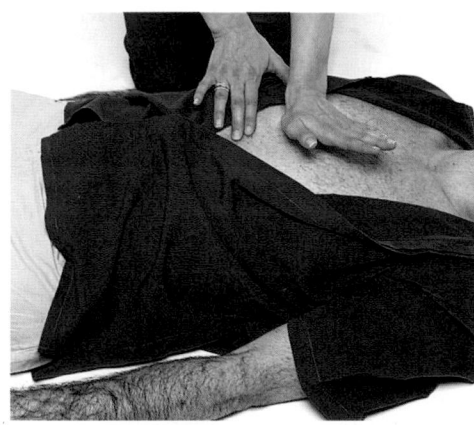

2 Put the heel of the other hand on the breastbone and move it down to the index finger. You should apply pressure at this point.

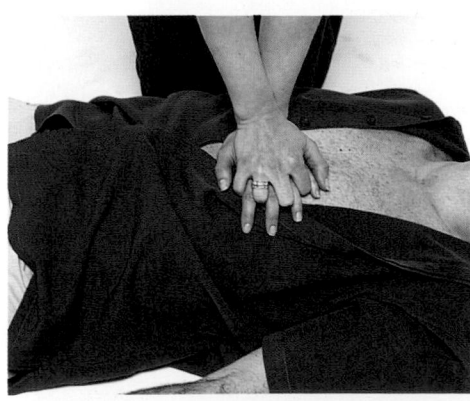

3 Place the heel of your first hand on top of this hand and then interlock your fingers.

4 Lean over the casualty Then press vertically down, keeping your arms straight, and depress the breastbone by 4–5cm (1½–2in). Remove the pressure but do not move your hands.

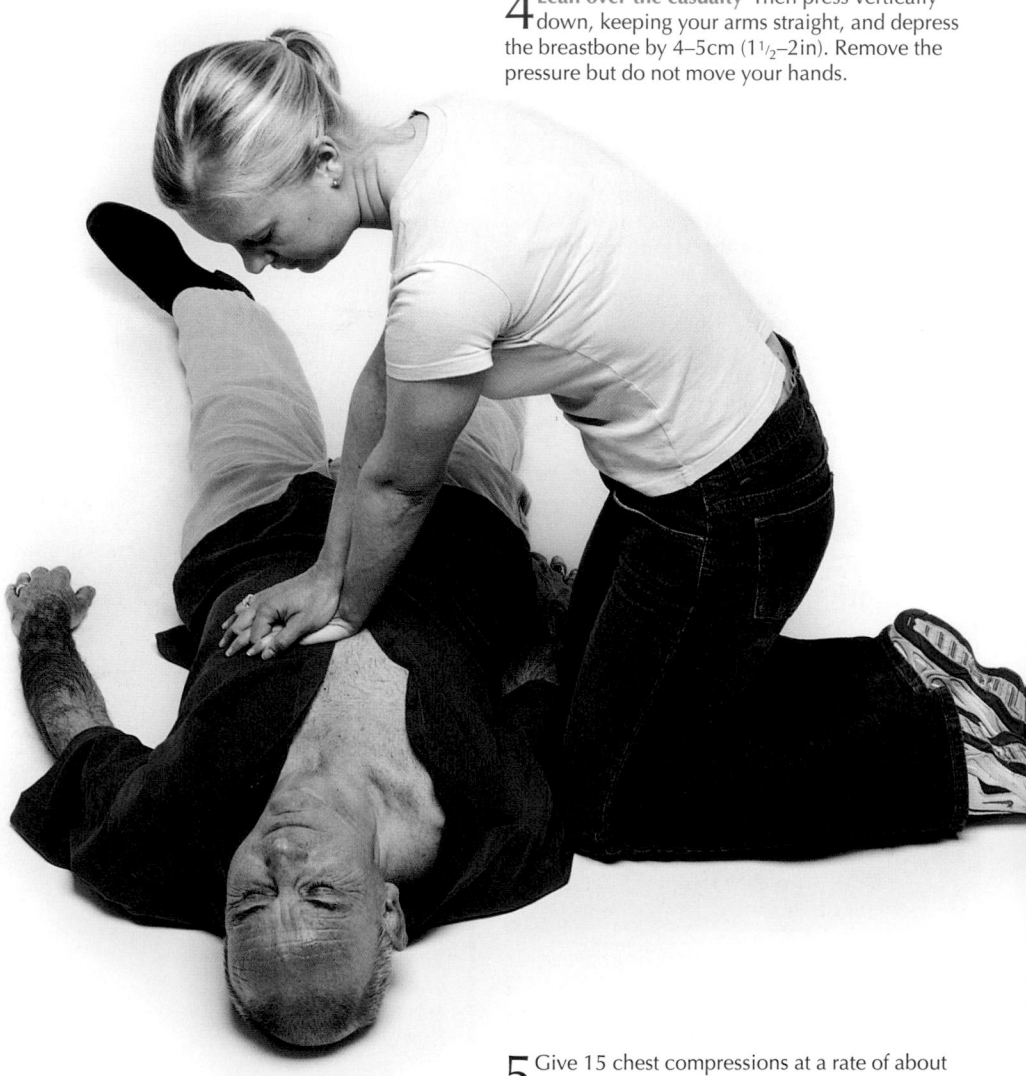

5 Give 15 chest compressions at a rate of about 100 compressions per minute. Then give two breaths of artificial ventilation (see above). Carry on alternating 15 compressions with two breaths until help arrives.

Using the RECOVERY POSITION

If an unconscious casualty has a pulse and is breathing, support the airway until help arrives. If you must leave the person, the recovery position helps keep the airway open.

1 **Kneel beside the person** and raise the far leg to bend at the knee. Place the arm nearest to you at right angles to the body, with elbow bent and palm uppermost. Fold the other arm across the chest and rest the back of hand under the cheek.

2 **Put your hand on the far knee** and pull it towards you, supporting the person's head as you do so. Use your knees as a support and control during the manoeuvre.

3 **With the person now turned** onto one side, align the bent knee so that it rests at right angles to the body, propping it in a secure and comfortable position.

4 **Tilt the chin up** to straighten the throat and clear the airway, then rest the cheek on the back of the hand, as in 3 above. Cover with a coat or rug to maintain body heat.

Dealing with a conscious casualty

• Speak reassuringly to an injured person, who may be suffering from shock. Do not give food, liquid, cigarettes or alcohol – this may cause further harm to unseen injuries and could interfere with an anaesthetic and delay hospital treatment.

• Do not move the person unless it is absolutely essential. Ask where the pain or numbness is, to help you to identify the injuries. Examine an injured area gently; ask the casualty to help to support it, if possible.

• Apply a bandage or sling only if it is necessary to stem excessive bleeding or to move someone. It will be removed at the hospital, and meanwhile ambulance personnel may have to put splints on a fractured limb.

Treating external bleeding

1 If the person is mobile, get them to lie down. Bleeding is slowest when lying down. Unconscious casualties should not be moved.

2 Carefully and gently remove or cut away clothing to expose the wound. Look for possible fractures – likely if there is swelling, pain or loss of use, or if the limb is in an unnatural position.

A FOREIGN OBJECT IN THE WOUND

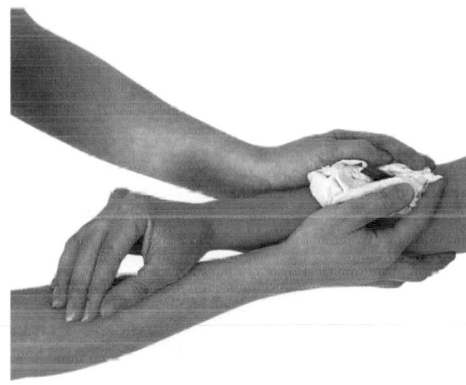

1 If there is glass, metal or another object in the wound, don't remove it but do not bandage directly over a foreign object in a wound. Put raised pads, made from rolled cotton wool or another absorbent material, round the object to prevent pressure bearing down on it.

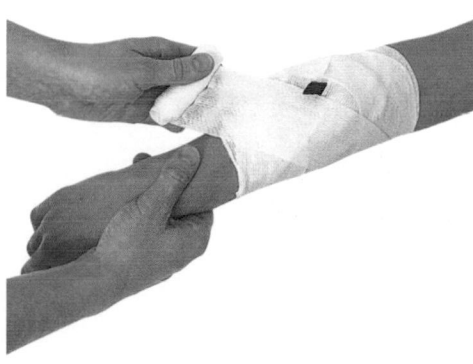

2 Bandage carefully around the raised pad leaving the object uncovered so that it does not become embedded further into the body.

NO FOREIGN OBJECT IN THE WOUND

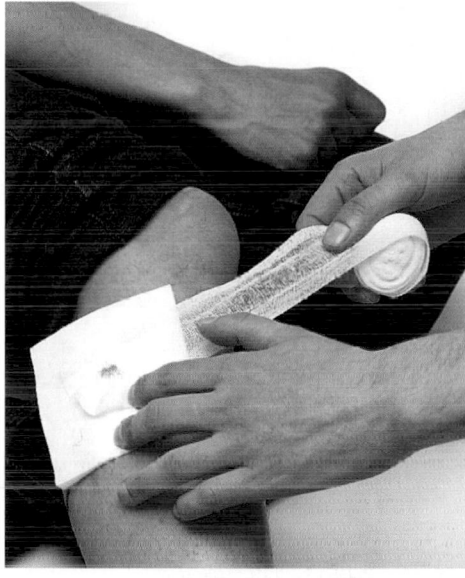

1 If there is no foreign body in the wound, and the limb is not fractured, make a pad of clean, absorbent material and press it down firmly over the wound to stem the bleeding. If nothing else is available, press paper tissues over the wound.

2 Bandage the wound firmly using a scarf or a strip of clean linen. If blood seeps through, put another bandage on top. Do not apply a tourniquet to ease the bleeding – if applied incorrectly it can cut off circulation and result in the loss of a limb.

3 Provided there is no fracture to an injured limb, raise it so that the wound is above the level of the heart to slow the bleeding.

4 Get medical attention as soon as you can, but do not leave the person alone for any longer than is necessary.

5 Keep an injured person warmly covered, reassured and as still as possible. Don't give anything to eat or drink – or to smoke.

Treating internal bleeding

1 If an injured person is bleeding from the nose, mouth or ear, place in a half-sitting position with the head tilted towards the side from which the blood is coming.

2 Cover the bleeding point with a pad of clean material or cotton wool, but do not apply pressure. Call for an ambulance.

3 If the person loses consciousness before the ambulance arrives, put in the recovery position, injured side lowest (see page 500).

Dealing with broken bones

Do not move someone with a possible fracture unless they are in immediate danger. Help the injured person into the position in which they are most comfortable, and support the limb with a rolled-up blanket or coat while waiting for an ambulance.

If you have to move the person:
First protect any wound by covering it with a clean, non-fluffy cloth such as a handkerchief. If a bone is protruding, put a sterile pad made from a clean handkerchief or similar material round it as a protection.

IMMOBILISING A BROKEN LEG

1 **First, bandage over a protective pad**. Don't tie too tightly, as this can affect blood circulation.

2 Immobilise the injured leg by putting padding between the ankles and knees (above).

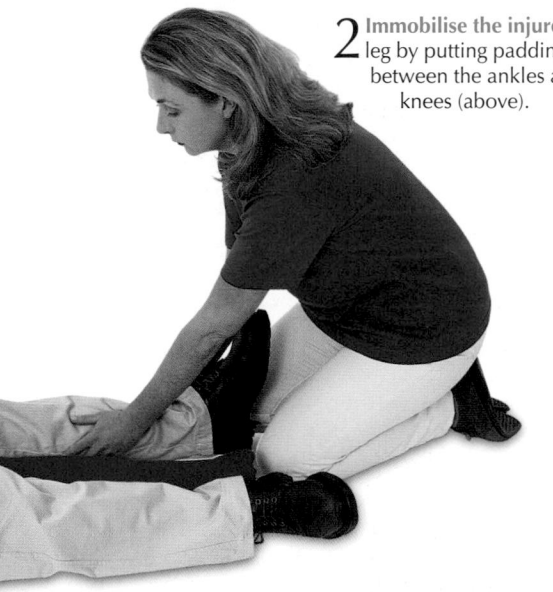

3 **Tie the legs together** with bandages or other strips of firm material. Tie above and below the fracture, but not on top of it.

SUPPORTING A BROKEN ARM
Don't use force to move the arm. Position it gently and strap it to the body, avoiding the injured part.

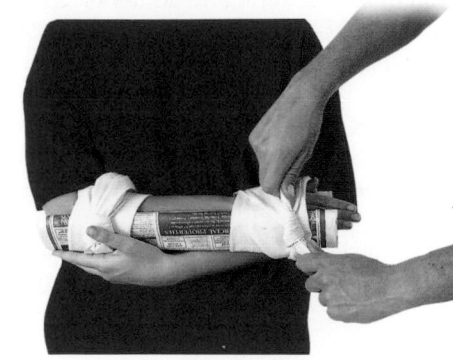

1 **If the arm will bend easily,** place it across the chest, putting some padding such as a rolled newspaper between it and the body (above).

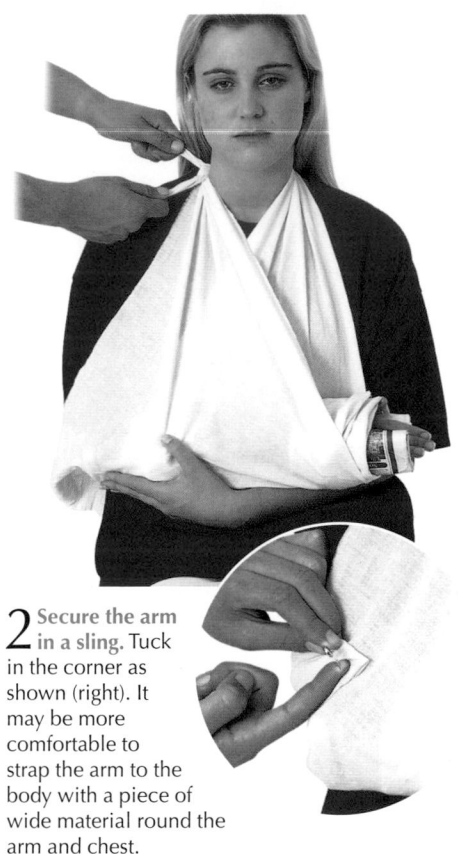

2 **Secure the arm in a sling.** Tuck in the corner as shown (right). It may be more comfortable to strap the arm to the body with a piece of wide material round the arm and chest.

3 Move the person very carefully to a more sheltered place. If necessary, get other people to help you to do this.

Eye injuries

1 If a person has an object embedded in the eye, do not attempt to remove it, as you may cause further damage.

2 Cut a hole in a piece of clean cloth and put it over the eye. Place a paper or plastic cup over the cloth to protect the eye.

3 Hold the cup in place with a bandage. Tell the person not to move the eyes to prevent worsening the injury.

Burns & scalds

• For a chemical burn, wash thoroughly with cold water and remove any contaminated clothing, taking care to protect yourself.
• If the burned person is unconscious but breathing, treat the burns and place in the recovery position (see page 500).
• If the mouth and throat are scalded or burned, speak reassuringly and give the person cold water, ice cubes or ice cream to suck in order to reduce the swelling.

1 Remove any tight clothing, rings or a wristwatch before the area begins to swell. Cool a superficial burn by applying clean, cold water or similar cold fluid (milk or soft drink) for ten minutes or longer, until the pain has eased.

2 Cover the burn with clean, dry, non-fluffy material – a handkerchief, for example. Hold it in place with a soft towel or other material. If the burn is widespread, lay the person down gently, speak reassuringly and cool with clean water. Call for an ambulance.

IF SOMEONE HAS CLOTHING ON FIRE
1 Hold a blanket or coat in front of you as you approach, then wrap it round the person to smother the flames. Lay the victim on the ground with the burnt side uppermost. Remove hot clothing that can be taken off easily, but don't take off any fragments that have stuck to the skin. Cool the burn by applying clean, cold water.

2 Don't apply lotions or ointments, as they may cause infection. Don't apply any plasters and don't prick any blisters.

Insect & animal bites

Bites Wash a dog or cat bite thoroughly with soap and warm water or a mild antiseptic and cover with a clean dressing. If the skin is broken, get the

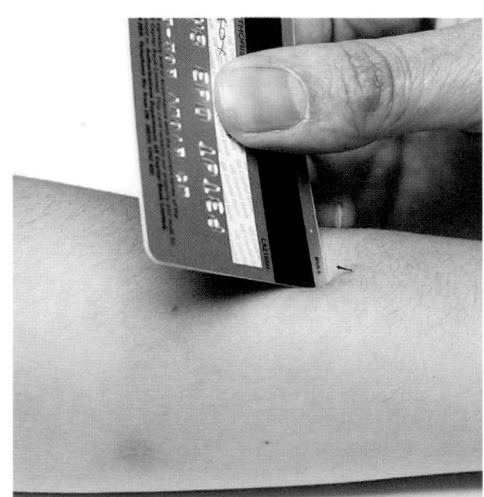

wound looked at by a doctor as soon as possible.

Stings If a sting is left in the skin, remove it by a scraping action (for instance with a fingernail or credit card edge) to avoid squeezing more poison into the skin. Don't use tweezers to pluck it out. If available, apply an ice cube to dull the pain.

What you need in a basic FIRST-AID KIT

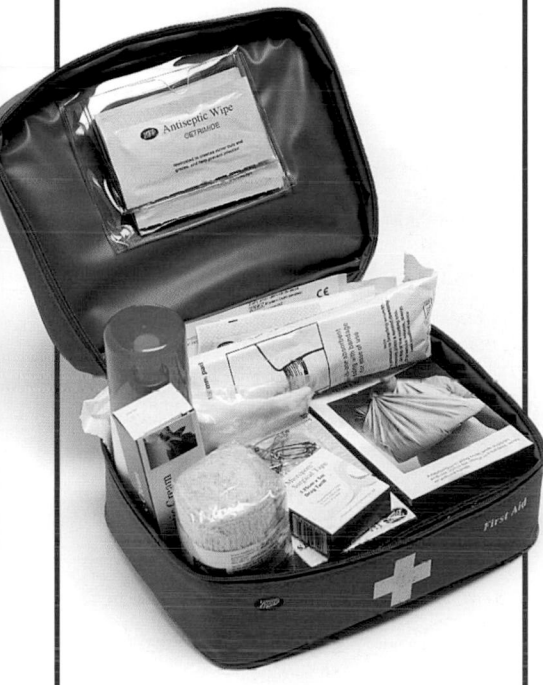

- First-aid manual, including CPR instructions (it may be worth bookmarking the relevant pages)
- Assorted adhesive plasters
- Aspirin (for adults) and paracetamol (for children) Do not give aspirin to children under 16
- Latex gloves
- Antihistamine cream
- Antiseptic lotion and antiseptic wipes
- Safety pins
- Sterile dressings of various sizes; sterile eye dressing with bandage attached
- Tubular gauze bandages for finger injuries
- Roll of micropore tape
- Spray-on dressing
- Burn dressings
- Sterile gauze
- Cotton wool
- Triangular bandages
- Stretch bandages
- Survival blanket for covering injured people, especially in cold or wet conditions

Insurance requirements

You must stop after an accident that involves damage or injury to another person or vehicle. The same applies to a collision with an animal such as a dog, horse, cow, goat or sheep, or roadside property such as a fence.

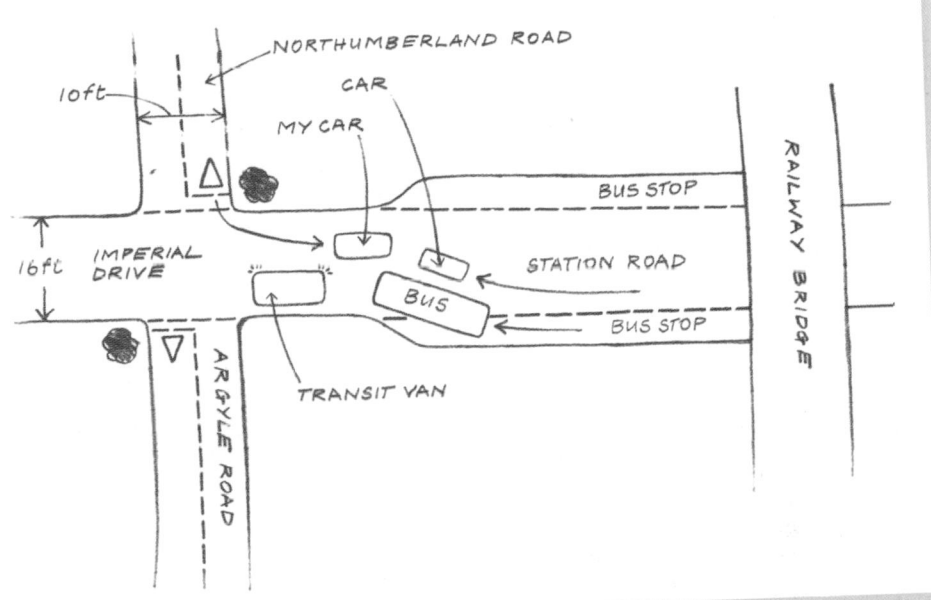

Make a sketch-map *showing the final positions of all the vehicles involved, the length of any skid marks and where there is broken glass on the road. Record weather, road conditions at the time and the estimated speeds of the vehicles. Note down the road names and any landmarks. If you have a camera with you, take photos of the scene from different angles.*

1 Record the registration numbers of vehicles involved and exchange names and addresses, and insurance company names and addresses, with the other driver or drivers. You must also give your own name and address, and the vehicle owner's if different, and your vehicle's registration number to anyone who has reason to require them. If you are unable to give all the information required at the time report additional details to the police within 24 hours.

2 Do not admit liability for the accident, or get involved in discussions about the cause, especially if you think the fault is yours. If you admit blame, your insurers may refuse you cover. Do not apologise, even as an act of courtesy; an apology may be used as evidence against you in both civil and criminal proceedings.

3 Quickly sketch the scene of the accident noting down all relevant details (see above). Be careful that you don't stand in the way of oncoming traffic while sketching or photographing the scene.

4 If details have been exchanged, there is no need to report a damage-only collision to the police unless another driver cannot be traced or refuses details. Call the police if anyone is hurt, including you, or if you think another driver has committed an offence. You have no right to detain anyone until the police arrive. An officer may ask to see your driving licence, insurance certificate and MOT certificate; if you don't have them, you may have to produce them within seven days.

5 Making a statement You are not obliged to make a statement to the police. Be aware that you may regret making one in haste, and that your own words may be given in evidence against you. On the other hand, if you have a valid excuse you would be wise to make a statement carefully and in detail. If, when the police question you, you fail to say something in your favour and try to bring it up at a later hearing, the court may infer that you concocted that evidence. If you do make a statement, you can write it out yourself or have an officer write it for you; read it carefully and make any necessary corrections before signing. Otherwise just give your name, address and insurance particulars, and get the help of a solicitor as soon as possible.

6 Collisions with parked vehicles If a parked vehicle is involved in an accident, you are not obliged to search for the owner. But it may be easier in the long run if you enquire at nearby buildings, and if necessary wait a short time for the owner to return. You should record the vehicle's make, model, colour and registration number, the damage caused, and if there is any other damage to the vehicle not caused by the accident. Report the matter to the police and your insurers. If you decide to leave a note on the parked vehicle, beware of admitting liability.

Dealing with a breakdown

Motoring organisations such as the AA and RAC estimate that four out of five breakdowns are avoidable. Regular servicing and a few basic checks before you set off will greatly reduce the risk of problems. If a breakdown does occur, follow our advice to get out of danger and call for help as swiftly as possible.

Checks to make before your journey

Have your car serviced at the recommended intervals and check the following parts and systems regularly. You will greatly reduce the risk of breaking down and the cost and aggravation that results.

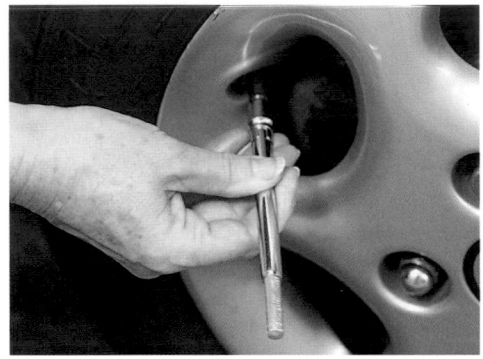

Tyres Look up the correct tyre pressures for your car and check them once a fortnight with a gauge (above) or garage air line.
• Check for cuts in the sidewalls.
• If you are constantly topping up the air in a tyre it may have a slow puncture caused by an embedded nail or other sharp object or a faulty tyre valve.
• Always ensure that your spare tyre is in good condition and easily accessible.

Water Check the coolant level regularly and top up as necessary when the engine is cold.
• Have the antifreeze concentration checked before the winter. When buying antifreeze check that it contains ethylene glycol as cheaper substances such as methanol offer less protection for the engine. The correct mix for year-round protection is 1 part antifreeze to 2 parts water. This gives an antifreeze mix of approximately 30 per cent.

Engine oil Have the oil and filter changed at the recommended service intervals.
• Check the dipstick once a fortnight and always before a long journey.

1 Remove the dipstick and clean it by wiping downward along the length with a clean rag or absorbent paper, replace and then remove after a few seconds to check the level again.

2 The level should fall between the minimum and maximum levels marked on the tip of the dipstick.

3 If the oil level is near or below the minimum marked, remove the oil-filler cap and top up. Keep a supply of the engine oil recommended by the manufacturer.

Toolkit Every car should have a basic toolkit containing a jack and wheel removal tools – and the key or removal tool if locking wheel nuts are fitted. Make sure the toolkit is easy to get at and that you know where the jacking points are.

Windscreen Look out for minor chips and cracks. Small chips can be repaired by a windscreen specialist but the screen must be replaced if cracks are larger.

Power steering Check the fluid reservoir once a month and ensure it is checked at every service.
• Top up using the correct hydraulic fluid. Details will be given in the car handbook.

Screenwash Check regularly and top up if necessary – especially if you are going on a long journey. It is worth using a good screenwash additive to clean oily grime effectively. It will also freeze more slowly in winter.
• Screenwashes are concentrates which are mixed up with water according to requirements.
• The bottle holding the screenwash has a wiper symbol on the cap. Flip up the cap to pour diluted screenwash into the bottle.

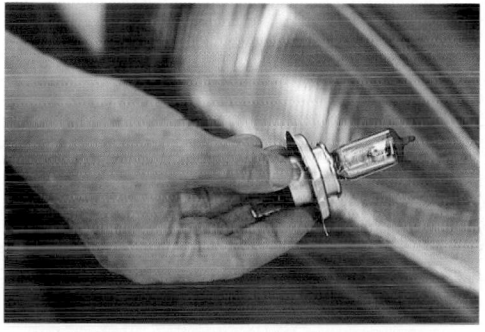

Lights Check your lights including indicators, brake and fog lights, every week and replace it faulty.
• When replacing a halogen bulb, hold it by the shroud at the back as grease from your fingers can shorten the life of the bulb.

Windscreen Look out for minor chips and cracks in the windscreen: small chips can be repaired but you should replace the screen if cracks are larger.
• Fit new wiper blades if the rubber is torn – most wipers are attached using a simple clip.

Common causes of mechanical breakdown

Most problems can be easily fixed at the roadside – but the great majority can be avoided altogether.

Flat battery Most battery problems arise from faulty terminals and clamp connections and loss of voltage.
• When the car is serviced, terminals should be cleaned and protected from corrosion by a layer of petroleum jelly. Connections should be checked and secured if necessary.
• If you rarely drive for long distances, it is worth charging your battery once a fortnight to prolong its life; however modern maintenance-free batteries need no top-up.

Lost keys If you lose the keys to your car, only an authorised dealer is likely to be able to help, and even then it may take a few days to get a replacement. **Always** carry a spare set.

Flat or damaged tyres and wheels Make sure tyres are at the correct pressure for the load and average speed and adjust accordingly.
• If you hit a kerb, the sidewalls and wheel rims may be damaged, resulting in a slow loss of air. Get the tyre checked by a specialist and replace or repair if necessary.
• Make sure the wheels are correctly aligned – misalignment is indicated by uneven wear on the tyres.

Faults in the alternator and generator Battery problems and dim headlights when the engine is idling may be an indication of problems.
• The alternator belt may also operate the radiator fan and water pump. A red ignition light and swift rise in engine temperature may mean the belt is broken. Stop at once.

Starter motor Problems with starting can be avoided with regular maintenance.

Distributor cap Keep the cap clean and dry.
• Cracked insulation may allow ignition voltage to leak away – a particular problem in damp weather when there is no ignition spark.
• Always replace the cap at the intervals recommended by the manufacturer or if the weather protection surrounding the cap splits.

Problems with fuel Always make sure you fill up the tank at the beginning of your journey.
• Use the right fuel for your car. Cleaning an engine which has been contaminated by the wrong kind of fuel (for example diesel in a petrol engine) is both expensive and time-consuming.

Clutch cables The clutch is subject to considerable stress so replace the clutch cable at the very first signs of wear.

Spark plugs Always replace plugs at the intervals recommended by the manufacturer.

High-tension leads Damp and dirt are the enemies of HT leads and their connections, entering cracks in the insulation and reducing ignition voltage. When the car is serviced, check the leads and replace if damaged.

If your car does break down

Wherever you break down, think of other road users first and get your vehicle off the road if you can. In addition:

• Warn other traffic by using hazard warning lights if you are causing an obstruction.
• If you have a warning triangle, place it at least 45m (147ft) behind your vehicle on the same side of the road. On a motorway, be careful when putting the warning triangle on the hard shoulder.
• Keep sidelights on if it is dark or visibility is poor.
• Do not stand between your vehicle and oncoming traffic.
• At night or when visibility is poor, do not stand where you may prevent other road users seeing your lights.

On a motorway
If you can, try to leave the motorway at the next exit or pull into a service area. If this is not possible:
• Pull onto the hard shoulder, stopping as far to the left as possible, with the wheels turned to the left.
• Stop near an emergency telephone (these are situated at approximately one mile intervals along the hard shoulder.
• Leave the vehicle using the left-hand door and make sure your passengers do the same.
• You must leave animals in the vehicle, or in an extreme emergency, keep them under proper control on the verge.
• Ensure passengers stay away from the carriageway and the hard shoulder and that children do the same and are kept under control.
• Do not attempt to undertake any repairs.
• Walk to an emergency telephone on your side of the carriageway. Follow the arrows on the posts at the back of the hard shoulder. The telephone is free of charge and connects directly to the police who will call the AA, RAC (if you are a member), or a local breakdown service and tell you how long you have to wait. Use these in preference to a mobile telephone.
• Give full details about your breakdown and the make and colour of your car to the police. Inform them if you are a vulnerable motorist such as a woman on her own or have children or other vulnerable people with you.
• Return and wait close to your vehicle, well away from the carriageway and hard shoulder.
• If you feel at risk from another person, return to the vehicle by the left-hand door and lock all the doors. Leave the vehicle again as soon as the danger has passed.

If you have to stop in a driving lane
• Do not attempt to place any warning device on the carriageway.
• Switch on the hazard warning lights.
• Leave the vehicle only when you can safely get clear of the carriageway.
• If possible put on a high-visibility jacket or a brightly coloured garment before getting out.

If you are disabled
• Stay in the vehicle.
• Switch on the hazard warning lights.
• Display a 'Help' pennant from the window or if you have a car or mobile telephone, contact the emergency services and be prepared to advise them of your location.

Driving in difficult situations

A good driver should 'read the road' and be ready to react to any situation. Skilful driving requires alertness, patience, courtesy to other road users and, above all, knowledge of the best way to deal with problems or hazards – from difficult weather conditions such as snow or heavy rain, to sudden emergencies such as a burst tyre.

In adverse weather

Try to avoid driving in bad weather. If your journey is essential, make sure you drive more slowly and carefully than usual.

Strong winds & crosswinds
• Keep a firm grip on the steering wheel to avoid being pulled out of lane, especially on exposed stretches of motorway, bridges or viaducts.
• When moving from a sheltered area to an exposed section of road, be prepared for sudden crosswinds.

• Watch out for cyclists or motorcyclists who may be blown into your path and allow them extra room when overtaking.
• When overtaking a high-sided vehicle, adjust your steering to allow for being pulled towards it as you pass, and then pushed away beyond it.
• When towing a caravan or trailer, listen for radio forecasts of strong winds. Avoid high bridges and high, exposed routes.

Heavy rain and spray
• Slow down and turn on dipped headlights so that you can be seen clearly.
• Turn on demisters and the rear-window heater.

• If your car aquaplanes – slides on water not channelled away by the tyres – don't brake or steer sharply; ease pressure on the accelerator until the tyres regain grip.
• Avoid overtaking heavy goods vehicles, as their spray can completely obscure your vision.
• Keep the windscreen clean and the washer bottle filled with water.

Mist and fog
• Drive with dipped headlights.
• Keep the screen clear inside and out by using windscreen wipers and the demister.
• You must use fog lamps when visibility is seriously reduced; when you cannot see for more than 100m (328ft) ahead. You can also use front or rear fog lamps but switch them off when visibility improves as they dazzle other road users and may obscure your brake lights.
• Use the nearside kerb or verge as a guide. Don't drive too near to the centre line: you risk colliding with cars coming from the opposite direction.
• To hear other vehicles, turn off the radio, cassette or CD player and wind down your window.
• Drive slowly enough to stop within the distance clear ahead, taking into account that roads are more slippery in fog than in rain.
• Keep well behind the vehicle in front, and don't blindly follow its rear lights as a guide.
• Avoid overtaking.
• If you must stop, pull off the road. If forced to stop on the hard shoulder or carriageway, switch on hazard warning lights.

Ice and snow
• Make sure tyres are at the recommended pressures, so that they give the best grip possible.
• Keep your speed down and leave plenty of space between your car and other vehicles.
• A high gear – no lower than third, or Drive on an automatic – reduces the chances of wheelspin.
• Brake and accelerate gently. Don't brake and steer at the same time. Brake with a pumping action to avoid the wheels locking.
• To maintain traction, avoid changing down through the gears any more than you have to.
• Approach corners and bends at a gentle, steady speed in high gear and steer smoothly.
• On an icy hill, don't stop or change gear as you ascend, because you may lose tyre grip and slide. Try to keep going in third gear.
• In falling snow, use dipped headlights and stop regularly to clear windows and lights.
• If the car gets stuck, don't accelerate hard,

Stopping distances

Always keep to a speed that allows you to stop well within the distance you can see to be clear ahead of you.
• Leave sufficient space between you and the vehicle in front so that you can pull up safely if it suddenly slows down or stops. Never drive closer than the stopping distances that are shown in the diagram below.
• Allow at least a two-second gap between you and the vehicle in front on roads with heavy traffic.
• In ice, snow and rain, double the safety gap.

20 20ft 20ft — At 20mph it takes 40ft (12m) or 3 car lengths to stop

30 30ft 45ft — At 30mph it takes 75ft (23m) or 6 car lengths to stop

40 40ft 80ft — At 40mph it takes 120ft (36m) or 9 car lengths to stop

50 50ft 125ft — At 50mph it takes 175ft (53m) or 13 car lengths to stop

60 60ft 180ft — At 60 mph it takes 240ft (73m) or 18 car lengths to stop

70 70ft 245ft

THINKING DISTANCE

BRAKING DISTANCE

What it takes to stop *The shortest distance in which a car can come to a halt increases dramatically with speed. Even with good brakes and tyres and perfect road conditions, a car about 13ft (4m) long doing 70mph (112.5km/h) will travel 24 times its own length. Stopping distances in snow or ice can be ten times those in normal conditions.*

70mph it takes 315ft (96m) or 24 car lengths

because the wheels will spin, packing snow into the tyre treads. This reduces grip.
• To get out of snow, put sacking, twigs, sand or grit immediately in front of the driving wheels. With the front wheels straight, select second gear, and accelerate gently, letting the clutch out slowly to avoid wheel spin.
• Ask passengers or passers-by to help to push the car. Make sure they stand at the side, away from the driving wheels, so that the car doesn't roll or slide into them.
• Once the car is moving, drive until you are on a firmer, more level surface.

If you are stranded in a blizzard:
• Stay in the car.
• Keep awake. Play the radio or a tape, but not for too long at a time or you will drain the car battery.
• Wrap up warm in rugs, clothing or newspapers.
• Don't drink alcohol.
• Don't switch on the engine to use the heater unless the exhaust is clear of snow, otherwise poisonous fumes could enter the car.
• Run the engine and heater for about 10 minutes every hour – not longer or you will use up fuel, and may become drowsy.
• Open a window occasionally – on the side away from drifting snow – to let in air.

Dealing with an emergency

Burst tyre
• Don't change gear to slow down.
• If a front tyre has burst, the car will pull towards the side with the damage. Don't brake. Turn the steering wheel smoothly in the opposite direction to the sideways pull, and hold a straight course.
• If a rear tyre has burst, the back end of the car may slide to one side. Brake very gently and grip the steering wheel firmly to keep the car steady.
• Signal left, and if possible steer the car to the side of the road and roll to a stop.
• If a tyre bursts in the outside lane of a motorway and you can't safely move across to the hard shoulder, pull into the central reservation, if you can. Turn on hazard lights and wait for assistance.
• Never change a wheel on a motorway or hard shoulder – call for assistance.

Shattered windscreen
Most cars have laminated windscreens – with a layer of plastic sandwiched between glass. This may crack or chip but should not shatter.

• If your windscreen shatters, don't punch out an area of glass – you could cut your arms and eyes.
• Lean forward to get a better view and quickly signal and move left to stop.
• Cover the demister slots on top of the dashboard and spread newspaper or a blanket over the bonnet. Pad your hand with a glove or cloth, get back inside the car and push out as much glass as you can onto the paper.
• Dust fragments off the dashboard and wrap the glass in the newspaper or blanket. Don't leave glass by the roadside – dispose of it safely.
• If glass has fallen into the heater vents, don't use the demister until the system has been cleaned, or the fan will blow fragments of glass into the car.
• Fit a temporary windscreen if you have one – it is normally wrapped around the front door jambs and held in place by the closed doors.
• Otherwise, either cover the rubber flange that held the screen with adhesive or masking tape to

Controlling a rear-wheel skid *The car is skidding with the rear tyres losing grip on the road, and as the rear end swerves violently left, the driver steers to the left to bring the wheels into line. As the car swings back into line, the driver continues steering left, straightening the wheels only when the skid is completely under control.*

stop glass fragments flying out, or remove it completely, or protect your eyes with sunglasses.
• Drive carefully to the nearest service station or telephone to arrange for an emergency windscreen to be fitted.

Controlling a skid
• Skids occur when tyres lose their grip on the road surface. They are most likely to happen when slowing or speeding up, or on corners or hills.
• Be particularly careful on slippery roads, wet with rain, snow or ice, or where there are patches of loose shale, oil or wet leaves.
• Even on a dry road, never brake violently. The car may skid because its weight is pitched to the front, and with a loss of weight to the rear, the rear wheels tend to lock and the body swings.
• Avoid driving in shoes or boots with very thick soles, which make control of the brake, clutch and accelerator difficult.
• To control a skid, don't press the brake pedal or the accelerator.
• For a slight slide, turn the steering in the direction of the skid and ease off the accelerator until tyre grip is regained.
• If the skid is more violent, take your feet right off the brake and accelerator, and steer sharply in the direction of the skid. If the rear of the car swings left, turn the steering left to bring front and rear wheels into line. If the car rear swings right, turn the steering to the right.
• Once the skid is controlled, straighten the steering, and don't accelerate or brake until all four wheels are in line.

Personal safety

Security while driving
• Don't keep valuables where they can be seen when you are driving or parked.
• In built-up areas, keep windows and the sun-roof closed and doors locked, especially where you have to stop – at traffic lights, for example – in case someone tries to enter your vehicle.
• Beware of giving lifts to strangers. If a hitchhiker threatens you with a weapon, do as you are told. Hand over the items demanded, and don't struggle. If you can get to a place full of people, make as much noise as you can to attract their attention – this may scare off the attacker. If you think you may be in serious danger, stop the car and get out as fast as you can.

• Beware of someone flagging you down for help – this could be a trap. Slow down and change to a low gear so that you can accelerate away if necessary. If you stop, make sure your doors are locked, keep the engine running and be ready to drive off quickly. If you are uncertain whether the situation is genuine, drive on until it is safe to contact the police.
• If another driver is trying to ram your car or force you off the road, don't retaliate. Keep calm and drive to a well-lit, busy place, or directly to a police station.

Avoiding fatigue at the wheel

Driver fatigue is one of the most common causes of serious accidents – drowsy drivers are thought to cause over 20 per cent of motorway crashes. To minimise the risk of falling asleep:

• Make sure you are fit to drive. Do not go on a journey of more than an hour if you feel at all tired.
• Do not go on long journeys between midnight and 6am, when your natural alertness will be at its lowest level.
• Plan plenty of breaks into your journey. You should try to stop for at least 15 minutes once every two hours.
• If you start to feel at all sleepy, stop in a safe place – pull into a service station and park for example. Do not under any circumstances stop on the hard shoulder.
• The most effective way to counteract drowsiness is to take a short nap (of about 15 minutes) or drink two cups of strong coffee. Though fresh air, exercise or turning up the radio may help you to wake up briefly, they are not as effective.
• Bright sunlight puts strain on the eyes and increases fatigue. Try sunglasses with polarised lenses to cut out dazzling light. If you wear glasses, make sure your sunglasses have prescription lenses. Remember that your visibility will reduce if you enter a tunnel or a dark car park.

Travelling with children

Whether it's a short hop to the supermarket or a longer journey to a holiday destination, travelling with children can be a daunting experience. Safety is the primary concern – make sure you choose the correct restraint for the size and age of your child. And follow our tips for avoiding travel sickness and keeping children entertained on a long journey.

Child safety

Every year in the UK an average of 200 children under five are badly injured and a further 20 are killed while passengers in cars. It is essential that children of all ages are suitably restrained within the car, both for their own safety and that of the driver and other passengers. The Highway Code, rule 76 states that 'the driver must ensure that all children under 14 years of age wear seat belts or sit in an approved child restraint. This should be a baby seat, child seat, booster seat or booster cushion appropriate to the child's weight and size, fitted to the manufacturer's instructions.'

Carrying your child in the car
• It is almost always safer to carry children appropriately restrained in the back of the car.
• If it is just you and one child, it may be better to use the front to avoid distraction and give the child reassurance, but only if the child is very restless.
• If no restraints are available for a child under three, it is better for the child to wear an adult belt in the back than no restraint at all, but this is far from ideal and not recommended for long journeys. It is illegal for a child of this age to travel in the front without a proper child restraint.

Choosing the right car seat

Child seats broadly cover the following categories, according to the child's age and weight.

• **Infant carriers** Birth to 10kg (6–9 months), though some are suitable for children up to 13kg or approximately 15 months.
• **Child seats** 9–18kg (9 months–4 years)
• **Booster seats** 15–25kg (4–6 years)
• **Booster cushions** 22–36kg (6–11 years)
• Before you choose a seat, check your child's weight in kilograms.
• Check that the model you choose is suitable for your make of car.
• All restraints should confine and support both the head and body in the event of a head-on or sideways collision.
• Don't rely on the age limit given with the seat – base your decision on the weight and size of your child and how they fit in the seat, but don't move your child onto a larger restraint too soon.

Infant carriers
Rear-facing seats, which give even support to the head, neck and back are the safest for newborn babies. Some can be used for children up to 15kg. They are fitted using an adult lap and diagonal belt and the child is restrained by a harness within the seat. As no additional fixtures are needed, they can be easily moved from one car to another.
• **IMPORTANT** Under no circumstances must a rear-facing baby carrier be used in the front of a car fitted with a passenger airbag. If the airbag inflates

Sitting comfortably
When choosing a seat for your child, bear the following points in mind.

1 Check adult seat belts are long enough. Some seats have an 'alternative belt route' that can be used when belts are too short.

2 Ensure the seat can be installed in your model of car and that it sits securely at an angle comfortable for the child.

3 Choose one with an adjustment system that is quick and simple to alter. Make sure your supplier will accept the seat back if it won't fit your car.

UK legal requirements

AGE/HEIGHT	FRONT SEAT	BACK SEAT
Child under 3 years	Appropriate child restraint must be worn	Appropriate child restraint must be worn if available
Child 3–11 years and under 5ft (1.5m)	Appropriate child restraint must be worn if available; if not an adult belt must be worn	Appropriate child restraint must be worn if available; if not an adult belt must be worn
Child 12 or 13 years or more than 5ft (1.5m)	Adult seat belt must be worn if available	Adult seat belt must be worn if available

suddenly it could cause severe injury or death to the child in the seat.

• The seat covers should be simple to remove, clean and replace.

• With tiny babies, a wrap-around body support may provide extra protection within the carrier.

Child seats

Once a child is able to sit up unaided, a child seat may be used. The child is held in the seat by a five-point harness, with the frame attached to the car using adult seatbelts. It is very important to choose a seat that is compatible for your car – check application lists on the box or seek advice from the manufacturer's customer service department.

• Ask the retailer to show you how to install the seat correctly and keep instructions close at hand.

• Always make sure that the adult seat belt passes through all of the correct belt-guides and that the buckle isn't bent or lying on the seat frame.

• For maximum protection, the seat must be fitted very securely. Place the seat in the car, kneeling into it to compress the car seat cushion while pulling the adult seatbelt as tight as possible. It should be so tight that if you rock the child seat the car will rock as well.

• Look for a seat with a harness that is simple to adjust and consider one which can be reclined when the child is sleeping.

• Check the seat before each journey and tighten again if necessary.

• The harness should have no twists and should be comfortably tight. Place your hand flat on the child's chest and pull the harness up tight against it.

Booster seats

Lighter and less rigid than a child seat, booster seats will still give a child's head and neck greater protection in an accident.

• The seat and child are held in by the adult lap and diagonal seat belt. Frequently the seat back can be removed and the remaining base used as a booster cushion for older children.

• Ensure the diagonal belt lies across the child's shoulder, not the neck.

• The belt should lie flat, not twisted. The lap belt should lie across the thighs, not the abdomen.

• Do not pass the diagonal belt under child's arm.

• For children under 3, static belts should be used; most automatic belts can be converted to static operation using the so-called ALR/ELR facility.

Booster cushions

The booster lets the child sit higher and more comfortably in the car. Many can be converted into cushions with the removal of the back part.

• Don't be tempted to use an ordinary cushion as it may fly out in the event of an accident.

• Adult seat belts hold the child and cushion in place. They are passed through 'ears' at the rear of the cushion.

• The diagonal belt should pass over the shoulder, not the neck and the lap belt should go across the top of the thighs, not the abdomen.

• Some are fitted with an additional strap and clip that lowers the over-shoulder height of the diagonal part of the seat belt. This may improve the fit and comfort by pulling the belt away from the neck.

Make sure the seatbelt stays buckled

It doesn't take long for most children to learn how to undo their seatbelt buckles. Try these techniques to persuade them to keep them done up – or that there is no advantage in undoing the belt.

• Show them that the car won't go (or soon stops) with the belt undone.

Games to play

Keeping children entertained on a journey of any length can try the most patient of parents. The following games should help to alleviate boredom and are an excellent distraction even for children prone to travel sickness.

20 Questions The first player thinks of an object which can be classified as 'animal', 'vegetable' or 'mineral'. The other players guess the category and then ask questions which must be able to be answered with a yes or a no, for example: 'Does it have a long nose.' If the answer isn't reached after 20 questions, each players is allowed to make a guess. The game then moves on to the next player.

Name Game One player thinks of a name and tells the group whether it is a boy or girl's name and the first letter. The group then tries to guess the name by calling out all the names they know which start with that letter.

Alphabet Memory Game The first person starts with the letter A, saying 'A is for . . .' (any word beginning with A, eg Apple, Aardvark). The next person does the letter B, but must remember what A was. So they would say, A is for Apple, B is for Bumblebee and so on. By the time you reach Z, the children will have to recite every name from A to Z.

Geography A terrific game for children aged about 8 and up. The first player names a country such as Scotland. The next player must name a country beginning with the last letter of the previous name, for example Denmark. This continues until one player can't continue – names shouldn't be repeated. You can also use city names, rivers, oceans, counties – or whatever you fancy.

Categories One player thinks of a category and the others take turns listing items that fit the category. When one player can't think of any more items in that category he or she is out. The game continues until one of the last two players can't continue any longer. The other player can't win unless he or she can name at least one more thing in the category. The possibilities for categories are endless – the wider the better.

I-Spy Straightforward version. first player spies something out of the window and the others have to ask a series of questions to guess what the object in question is.

Reverse I-Spy The 'spy-er' is told by the others something about what they have to spy; something that is yellow, or bendy, or edible (a banana for example).

Car Scrabble The players are each given a word which they have to fill out from letters which they see along the roadside. If someone is prepared to keep score, you can play with the letter point values in Scrabble.

• Try telling the child that if the belt isn't done up they won't get to their destination (something appealing like a friend's house or a party).

• A raised seat increases the child's field of view and may help to hold their interest in the journey.

• A 'play tray' attachment may give some distraction and make the buckle less tempting.

Trouble-free travel

Before you start

• Fit a child view mirror to the windscreen so that you can easily see your child in the back.

• Sun shades protect children from UV rays and help to prevent motion sickness.

• Pack the car before the children get in, allowing plenty of space to stretch their legs and relax.

• Make sure any items not in the trunk are secured and cannot slip forward and injure the child.

• Let your child keep a couple of favourite toys close to hand for comfort.

On the journey

• Stop every couple of hours on a long journey to let children crawl or run around and let off steam.

• Encourage children to use the toilet every time you stop.

• A selection of tapes or CDs of favourite stories or songs is a good distraction – particularly for children who suffer from travel sickness.

Food and drink

• Pre-pack a snack for each child to avoid passing food backwards and forwards from front to back.

• Carry drinks – even for older children – in spill proof containers.

• Keep food simple – avoid drippy fillings and lots of bits – to minimise mess.

• Don't give young children boiled sweets or anything else they might choke on.

Motion sickness

A number of children suffer from motion sickness when travelling in a car. Symptoms range from dizziness and mild nausea to sweating and actual vomiting. Those affected tend to be aged between 3 and 12, and girls are more susceptible than boys. It is caused by a mismatch between the signals received by the brain from the ear – which controls balance – and the eye. You can minimise the effects of motion sickness by following some of these tips.

• Put sun shades over the side windows to stop the child from looking sideways.

• Seat the child high up so that he or she can see out of the front window.

• Discourage reading or looking down at toys.

• Avoid heavy meals before setting out.

• Encourage the child to sip a drink but not to gulp large quantities of fluid in one go. Avoid very sweet or carbonated drinks.

• If you are caught in a traffic jam, close the windows to minimise the effects of traffic fumes.

• Motion-sickness tablets, taken two to three hours before travel, may help. Ask a pharmacist for the most suitable varieties for your child.

DRIVING INFORMATION

Driving abroad

High speed ferries and the Channel Tunnel have brought continental Europe ever closer. More drivers take their cars for a seamless journey and unlimited freedom of movement. You must, however, be aware of differences in the law and in driving practice abroad, particularly with regard to speed limits and the level of alcohol allowed.

Driving on the right-hand side

When driving on the right in a car with right-hand drive, the trickiest manoeuvres are turning left and overtaking. Make sure you use the left-hand wing mirror to check for following traffic.

• You will need to adjust your headlight beam to the right. You can buy a kit for the purpose.
• Don't overtake when first driving abroad unless you really have to. When overtaking, allow more space between your car and the one in front so you can see farther down the road. Then ease out gradually until you have a clear view. A front-seat passenger can help by letting you know about oncoming traffic.
• Beware of looking the wrong way at junctions – this causes more accidents than driving on the wrong side of the road.
• When turning left, you have to cross the path of oncoming traffic. As you turn into the new road, remember to go into the right-hand lane.
• Be particularly careful when setting off from a service station on the left hand side of the road.
• Not all main roads have priority over side roads – watch for traffic coming from the right.
• Give way to trams and to people getting on or off.
• Be careful at roundabouts. Traffic flows counter-clockwise – make sure you go the right way.
• If hiring a left-hand drive vehicle, take time to familiarise yourself with the different control layout and get used to changing gear with your right hand.

Driving in Europe

In all countries a full UK driving licence is required and most European countries require drivers to be 18, rather than 17 as in the UK. Some countries now require drivers to have EC model licences which have a photograph included or some form of additional photographic ID such as a passport if they have the old-style UK licence. Both driver and passengers require a full 10-year passport.

International Driving Permit

Some countries require an International Driving Permit as well as a full UK driving licence.

Insurance

Check with your insurance company that you are covered for driving abroad. Motoring organisations strongly recommend that you obtain an International Motor Insurance Certificate (Green Card) from your insurer, though this is not generally needed in the EC. It may also be worth taking out a policy designed for driving abroad.

Vehicle documentation

When driving in Europe you need the original Vehicle Registration Document or, in its absence, a letter or authority from the owner and a Vehicle on Hire Certificate (VE103B) instead.

Speed limits

Although road speeds are in many cases higher than those in the UK, they are strictly adhered to. Radar sensors and police patrols are frequent and effective at trapping the speeding motorist. In France, any driver caught at more than 25km/h (15mph) above the speed limit may have their licence immediately confiscated. In most countries, speeding and other traffic violations may incur an on the spot fine.

Seat belts

Most cars in continental Europe must now have seat belts fitted in the front and rear of the car by law. Always wear seat belts and ensure that your backseat passengers, especially children, are wearing them as well. A number of countries also have particular restrictions and requirements for young children travelling in the front seat of the car.

Drinking and driving

Many European countries have very strict drink driving laws, rigorously implemented. The limit in the UK is 80mg of alcohol per 100ml of blood; in Belgium, France, Germany and the Netherlands it is 50mg. The limit in many countries limits drivers to a single drink – if in any doubt don't drink and drive at all.

Road tolls and charges

Toll charges are increasingly common across Europe. You can pay by credit card at most tolls, but you will need plenty of change in order to use the automatic cash booths; if not, you will have to use manual booths instead. In some countries you can buy longer term passes at the border or at service stations nearby.

Health matters

Make sure you have a copy of the form E111 from the leaflet Health Advice for Travellers (ref T6) obtainable from UK post offices or from FREEFONE 0800 555777. You will need this form if you need medical treatment in any country within the European Union. If you wear spectacles to drive, make sure you have a spare pair with you – they are required by law in Spain and Switzerland.

Essential kit

Always take the following items: a GB sticker, a first-aid kit, fire extinguisher, warning triangle, headlamp beam reflectors and spare lamp bulbs, most of which are required by law in many European countries.

Toll roads *Pay-as-you-go tolls are charged on most motorways in France, Spain and Italy; and in Austria and Switzerland, tolls are charged for driving on the autobahns. Some of them can be very expensive and it is worth factoring toll charges into the cost of your holiday.*

Legal checklist for driving in Europe

COUNTRY	Town	Open	Motorway	DRIVING LICENCE Legal age and licence requirements	SEAT BELTS Type and legal requirements
Austria	50	100	130	18, UK licence (pink or pink/green) accepted. Old style licences accepted only if accompanied by an identity document with a photograph e.g. passport.	Compulsory. Children under 12 are forbidden to travel in the front seat without a child restraint.
Belgium	50	90	120	18, UK licence	Compulsory
Bulgaria	50	90	120	18, UK licence and IDP required	Compulsory. No children under 12 in front.
Croatia	50	80	130	18, UK licence	Compulsory. Children under 12 are forbidden to travel in the front seat.
Czech Republic	50	90	130	18, UK licence and IDP required where licence does not incorporate photograph	Compulsory. Children under 12 or under 5ft (1.5m) are forbidden to travel in the front seat.
Denmark	50	80	110	17, UK licence	Compulsory. Children under 3 need child restraint.
Finland	50	80	120	18, UK licence	Compulsory. Children must use seat belt or restraint.
France & Monaco	50	90	130	18, UK licence (speed restrictions for those who have held a licence for less than 2 years)	Compulsory.
Germany	50	100	130	17, UK licence	Compulsory. Children under 12 and under 5ft (1.5m) are forbidden to travel in the front seat without a child restraint.
Greece	50	110	120	17, UK licence	Compulsory. Children under 10 are forbidden to travel in the front seat without a child restraint.
Hungary	50	90	130	18, UK licence and IDP required where licence does not incorporate photograph	Compulsory. Children must use seat belt or child restraint in front.
Ireland	30	60	70	17, UK licence	Compulsory. Children under 12 forbidden to ride in the front without a child restraint.
Italy & San Marino	50	90	130	18, UK licence – IDP with old-style licence	Compulsory. Children under 4 forbidden to travel without child restraint. Children between 4 and 12 require suitable restraint in front seat
Luxembourg	50	90	120	17, UK licence	Compulsory. Children under 12 and under 5ft (1.5m) are forbidden to travel in the front seat without a child restraint. Children under 3 require safety seat in back.
Netherlands	50	80	120	18, UK licence	Compulsory. Children under 3 must travel in the rear with a suitable safety system. Children over 12 may travel in front with suitable restraint.
Norway	50	80	90	17, UK licence	Compulsory. Children under 4 need child restraint.
Poland	60	90	130	18, UK licence and IDP required	Compulsory. Children under 10 need child restraint.
Portugal	50	90	120	18, UK licence but with special requirements for those who have held a licence for under a year. IDP required with old-style licence.	Compulsory. Children under 12 need child restraint.
Slovakia	60	90	130	18, UK licence	Compulsory. Children under 12 and under 5ft (1.5m) are forbidden to travel in the front seat.
Slovenia	50	100	130	18, UK licence and IDP	Compulsory. Children under 12 forbidden to ride in the front.
Spain	50	90	120	18, UK licence – IDP with old-style licence	Compulsory. Children under 12 need child restraint.
Sweden	50	70	110	18, UK licence	Compulsory. Children under 7 need child restraint.
Switzerland & Liechtenstein	50	80	120	18, UK licence	Compulsory use front and back. Under 7's are forbidden to travel in the front seat without a child restraint.

DRIVING INFORMATION

Reading road signs

The shapes and colours of British road signs are related to their function. In general, circular signs give orders, triangular signs give warnings and rectangular signs give information. Direction signs on motorways are blue and on primary routes they are green.

Signs giving warning

The symbol inside a red triangle (or in the Republic of Ireland on a yellow diamond) denotes the kind of danger ahead. There may be a plate attached giving more details.

A thickened line indicates the priority through the junction

School crossing ahead

Risk of falling or fallen rocks

Side winds

Road works

Hump bridge

Crossroads

Side road

Staggered junction

T-junction

Bend to right (left if reversed)

Junction on bend (may be reversed)

Road narrows on right (left if reversed)

Road narrows on both sides

Dual carriageway ends

Loose chippings

Quayside or river bank

Opening or swing bridge

Low-flying aircraft or sudden aircraft noise

Available width of headroom indicated in feet and metres

Slippery road

Pedestrian crossing

Other warning signs

At level crossings

Level crossing with gate or barrier

Level crossing without gate or barrier

Light signals ahead – used with triangular warning sign

St Andrew's Cross used at crossings without gates or barriers

Roundabout

Soft verges

Deviations in the road

Sharp deviation off route to left (or to right if the chevrons are reversed)

Temporary sharp deviation of route to left (or the right if the chevrons are reversed)

Barrier indicating the boundary of an area of highway closed to vehicular and pedestrian traffic

Two-way traffic crosses one-way road

Double bend (may be reversed)

Two-way traffic straight ahead

Uneven road

Traffic signals (may warn of a pelican crossing)

Migratory toad crossing

Horse riders likely to be in road

Cattle likely to be crossing road

Farm traffic on road

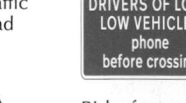

DRIVERS OF LONG LOW VEHICLES phone before crossing

Irish road signs Some Irish signs differ; those giving warnings are yellow and diamond-shaped.

Steep hill upwards with 1 in 5 gradient

Slow-moving vehicles on hill

STOP 100 yds

Distance to STOP line ahead

Road tunnel

Risk of grounding (Long low vehicles must obtain permission to drive over crossing)

Level crossing without gate or barrier

Road bends

Major road ahead

Junction with lesser road

Signs that give orders

Blue discs mostly give positive instructions. Red discs and white discs with red borders are mostly prohibitive. Give Way and Stop signs stand out by their distinctive shapes.

 Turn left ahead

 Trams only

 One-way traffic

 Minimum speed

 End of minimum speed

 Keep left (or right if reversed)

 Pass either side

 Pedal cycles only

 Mini roundabout

 Waiting restrictions apply

 No stopping (clearway)

 National speed limit applies

 Maximum speed

 No entry for vehicular traffic

 No vehicles except motorcycles without sidecars

 No U turns

 Overtaking prohibited

 No cycling

 No pedestrians

 All motor vehicles prohibited

 No vehicles except bicycles being pushed by hand

 Give priority to vehicles coming from the opposite direction

 No goods vehicles over maximum gross weight shown in tonnes

 No right turn (no left turn if reversed)

 Give way (Ireland)

 Give way to traffic on major road

 School crossing patrol

Signs giving information

In Britain, information signs are rectangular. Primary route signs are green and those on lesser routes are white with black borders. Motorway signs are blue. For tourist attractions and facilities, brown rectangular signs are used.

 Priority over oncoming vehicles

 No through road

 Use the appropriate traffic lane for the junction ahead

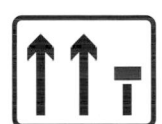 Number of traffic lanes reduced ahead

Road works and diversions

Where the flow of traffic has to be restricted to allow road maintenance or improvements, one or more lanes of the carriageway may be closed. Yellow signs indicate lane diversions, sometimes onto the opposite carriageway in a contraflow arrangement.

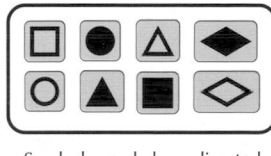 Symbols used along diverted routes to help drivers follow the required route.

 Restrictions ahead on motorway because of road works.

 Parking available (Ireland)

 Distance to parking place ahead

 Parking place for towed caravans

 Vehicles may park partially on the verge or footway

 Escape lane ahead for vehicles unable to stop on steep hill.

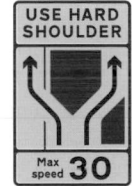 Diversion of the two lanes open to traffic; the left-hand lane uses the hard shoulder, the right-hand lane uses the other carriageway.

 Diversion from a motorway or other main road

 **Hospital** A blue sign means Accident and Emergency facilities are not available, a red sign that they are; restrictions are indicated.

Route direction signs

Primary routes For primary routes (which usually allow faster travel than ordinary roads), the direction signs have green backgrounds. Ring roads that bypass town centres are shown by an R sign. Where a ring road is not a primary route, the R sign appears in black on a white background.

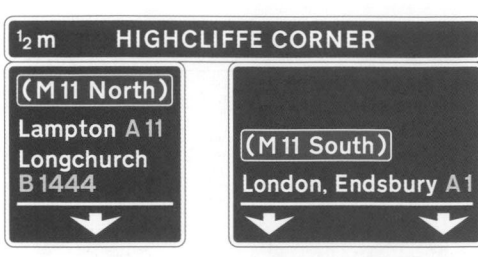

A gantry sign over the road before a junction directs traffic into the correct lane for the destination required.

Ring road

Primary road
and lesser route in white

Other (non-primary) routes The sign below shows a roundabout with a primary route to the left and other routes ahead and to the right.

The primary route leads to a motorway, and for traffic turning onto the primary route there is a dedicated lane (slip road) to help avoid the roundabout.

A confirmation sign giving the number of the road being followed; a road number in brackets is a road that can be joined farther on.

Tourist signs Signs with a brown background give directions to various named tourist attractions, and may also show a symbol indicating the type of attraction.

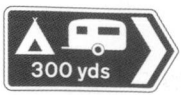

At junctions, repeat signs may show the symbol alone

The examples shown are:

1 English Heritage
2 National Trust
3 Picnic area
4 Zoo
5 Castle
6 House of architectural or historical interest
7 Country park
8 Museum or art gallery
9 Air museum
10 Flower garden
11 English Tourist Board recognised attraction
12 Scottish Tourist Board recognised attraction

Motorway signs

On motorways, the blue and white signs are designed to be clearly seen and easily understood while driving at speed. Most exits are clearly numbered; this simplifies route-planning.

Start of motorway

Countdown markers These indicate the distance to the start of a junction deceleration lane. Each bar represents about 90m (300ft).

Motorway slip road On a motorway slip road, a sign may show the destinations reached along a primary route on a green panel, or along a non-primary route on a white panel.

End of motorway The sign is at the motorway end or on its slip road. Here motorway regulations cease.

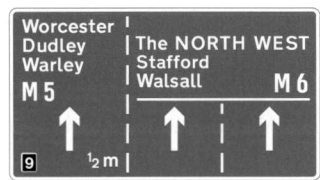

Increase or decrease in lanes Traffic in the left lane is leaving the main carriageway.

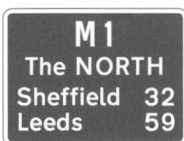

Route confirmation sign Beyond a junction, a route sign gives main destinations ahead, with distances to those destinations shown in miles.

Junction sign Warning of a junction is usually 1 mile (1.6 km) before the exit slip road, then again ¹/₂ mile later. The sign gives the number of the road being joined, the main destinations and the number of the junction.

Hazard signals and emergency phones

Gantry signals Signals are sited on gantries over the road or on posts beside the carriageway. At most times they are blank, and are switched on by the police only if road, traffic or weather conditions are abnormal. Hazard signals tell drivers what action to take – reduce speed to 50mph (80km/h) or change lanes, for example. Amber lights flashing alternately above and below a signal are warnings to draw attention to the signal itself.

Do not proceed in this lane

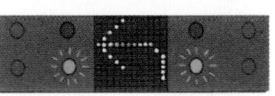

Leave motorway at next exit

End of restriction

Carriageway signals Signals on the far edge of the hard shoulder and on the central reservation concern drivers in all lanes. The reason for the restriction signalled, such as a speed limit or a lane closure, may not be apparent at first, but there may be an accident ahead, for instance, or a belt of fog, and traffic approaching must be warned and controlled.

Emergency telephones SOS telephones about 1 mile (1.6km) apart on the hard shoulder are linked to a police switchboard

Marker post Pointer at every 90m (300ft) to nearest phone

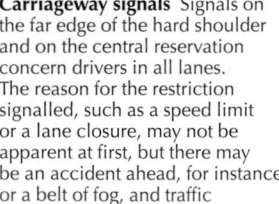

Temporary maximum speed limit advised

Lane closed ahead (right-hand lane)

Markings on the road and kerb

White lines marked on the carriageway are used to separate traffic lanes or to indicate restrictions or hazards. Yellow or red lines along the edge of the road and on the kerb indicate that there are waiting, parking or loading restrictions.

Markings on the carriageway

Double white in the centre of the carriageway If the line **nearest to you is unbroken**, it must not be crossed or straddled, except to get out of a property or side road, avoid a stationary vehicle or overtake a cyclist, horse or road work vehicle moving at less than 10mph (16kph). Where **both lines are unbroken**, drivers in both directions are similarly restricted. A **white arrow** indicates the direction traffic must pass double white lines.

Short broken white lines mark the edges of a traffic lane. Keep within them.

Long broken white lines warn of a hazard. Do not cross the lane unless the road is clear for a long way ahead. Longer broken lines (right) warn of a greater hazard when overtaking.

White diagonals or hatched markings separate traffic lanes, protect traffic turning right, or keep traffic away from the road edge. If the border is solid, do not enter except in an emergency. If it is broken, only enter if it is safe to do so.

Red road markings Roads edged with double or single red lines are designated as Red Routes, and are also marked by signs. Traffic must not stop on red routes during specified times.

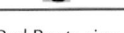

Red Route sign

Lines indicate Red Route

Waiting restrictions Yellow lines are a guide to the waiting restrictions in force. Generally, two yellow lines are an indication of more stringent restrictions than a single line. For full information, read plates posted nearby, or entry signs to controlled parking zones.

No waiting, except for loading and unloading, during the times on the nearby plates. If no days or dates are given, waiting is not allowed at any time.

At any time — No waiting

No waiting, except for loading and unloading, during the times indicated.

8 am - 6 pm

No waiting between times shown. Arrow gives direction of restricted area

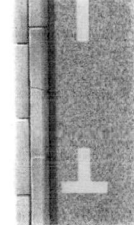

P Mon - Sat 8 am - 7 pm 20 mins No return within 40 mins

Limited waiting in bay

Waiting limited to, or prohibited at times, on blue or yellow plates. These are being phased out. Bays with broken white lines and white information plates will replace some.

Loading restrictions Yellow marks on the kerb or carriageway edge are a guide to the loading restrictions in force, as indicated on nearby black and white plates. In general, the more lines, the greater the restriction. If plates give no dates, the restrictions are in force every day including Sundays and Bank Holidays.

No stopping 7 am - 7 pm except buses

Bus stop clearway The sign is accompanied by a thick yellow line and BUS STOP marked on the carriageway. Vehicles other than buses may stop between the times shown on the sign.

URBAN CLEARWAY Monday to Friday am 8.00 - 9.30 pm 4.30 - 6.30

Urban clearway No stopping is allowed except to set down or pick up passengers, during the times shown. Waiting restrictions may apply at other times.

No loading at any time

Double lines: no loading at all

No loading Mon - Fri 11 am - 3 pm

Single line: no loading or unloading at certain times

LOADING ONLY

Loading only

Reserved for loading

Bus and cycle lanes

Special lanes for buses or bicycles These are shown by both signs and road markings. They may be in operation for 24 hours a day, or for periods indicated on roadside plates. The signs give details of the vehicles that may use the lane. Outside the period of operation, all vehicles may use a bus lane and generally may enter to stop for loading or unloading.

Lane reserved for buses

Lane reserved for cyclists

Lane reserved for buses, cyclists and taxis ahead

Lane for cycling in traffic direction

Hatched and zigzag lines

Box junction You must not enter the box until your exit is clear, unless you intend to turn right and are waiting for oncoming traffic to stop, or cars in the box are stationary and waiting to turn right.

Zigzag lines On a zebra or pelican crossing, you must not park or wait within the area bounded by zigzag lines, except to give way to pedestrians on the crossing or in circumstances beyond your control.

Yellow zigzag lines mark school areas. Do not stop or wait on these lines, even to pick up or set down children or other passengers.

A gazetteer of nearly 30,000 entries

Index of places

This gazetteer of cities, towns, suburbs and villages in the United Kingdom and the Republic of Ireland is an index to the maps on pages 64–248. The reference after each name gives the map page number and the letter code of the grid square in which the place appears. If two or more placenames are spelt the same way they are distinguished by their county or administrative area. A list of counties, unitary authorities and administrative areas is given below, together with the abbreviated forms used in the gazetteer.

ENGLAND

Barking & Dagenham	*Bar & Dag*
Barnet	*Barn*
Barnsley	*Barns*
Bath & North East Somerset	*B & NE Som*
Bedfordshire	*Beds*
Bexley	*Bex*
Birmingham	*Bham*
Blackburn	*Bburn*
Blackpool	*Bpool*
Bolton	*Bolt*
Bournemouth	*Bmth*
Bracknell Forest	*Brack*
Bradford	*Brad*
Brent	*Brent*
Brighton & Hove	*B & H*

Bristol, City of	*C of Bris*
Bromley	*Brom*
Buckinghamshire	*Bucks*
Bury	*Bury*
Calderdale	*Cald*
Cambridgeshire	*Cambs*
Camden	*Camd*
Cheshire	*Ches*
Cornwall	*Corn*
Coventry	*Cov*
Croydon	*Croy*
Cumbria	*Cumb*
Darlington	*Darl*
Derby, City of	*C of Derby*
Derbyshire	*Derbs*
Devon	*Devon*
Doncaster	*Donc*

Dorset	*Dors*
Dudley	*Dud*
Durham	*Dur*
Ealing	*Ealing*
East Riding of Yorkshire	*E R of Yorks*
Enfield	*Enf*
Essex	*Esx*
Gateshead	*Gate*
Gloucestershire	*Glos*
Greenwich	*Green*
Hackney	*Hack*
Halton	*Halton*
Hammersmith & Fulham	*Ham & Ful*
Hampshire	*Hants*
Haringey	*Harg*
Harrow	*Harw*

Hartlepool	*Hpool*
Havering	*Haver*
Herefordshire	*Herefs*
Hertfordshire	*Herts*
Hillingdon	*Hilln*
Hounslow	*Houns*
Isle of Wight	*IOW*
Islington	*Isling*
Kensington & Chelsea	*Ken & Chel*
Kent	*Kent*
Kingston upon Hull, City of	*C of Hull*
Kingston upon Thames	*Kings*
Kirklees	*Kirk*
Knowsley	*Knows*
Lambeth	*Lamb*

Lancashire	*Lancs*
Leeds	*Leeds*
Leicester, City of	*C of Leics*
Leicestershire	*Leics*
Lewisham	*Lew*
Lincolnshire	*Lincs*
Liverpool	*Lpool*
London, City of	*C of L*
Luton	*Ltn*
Manchester	*Man*
Medway Towns	*MT*
Merton	*Mert*
Middlesbrough	*Midbro*
Milton Keynes	*MK*
Newcastle upon Tyne	*N on Tyne*
Newham	*Newm*
Norfolk	*Nflk*

Northamptonshire — Northants
North East Lincolnshire — NE Lincs
North Lincolnshire — N Lincs
North Somerset — N Som
North Tyneside — N Tyne
Northumberland — Northld
North Yorkshire — N Yorks
Nottingham, City of — C of Nott
Nottinghamshire — Notts
Oldham — Oldm
Oxfordshire — Oxon
Peterborough — Pbro
Plymouth, City of — C of Plym
Poole — Poole
Portsmouth — Ptsmth
Reading — Read
Redbridge — Redb
Redcar & Cleveland — Red & Clev
Richmond upon Thames — Rich
Rochdale — Roch
Rotherham — Roth
Rutland — Rut
St Helens — St Hel
Salford — Salf
Sandwell — Swell
Setton — Seft
Sheffield — Sheff
Shropshire — Shrops
Slough — Slough
Solihull — Soli
Somerset — Som
Southampton — Sotton
Southend-on-Sea — S on Sea
South Gloucestershire — S Glos
South Tyneside — S Tyne
Southwark — Swark
Staffordshire — Staffs
Stockport — Stock
Stockton-on-Tees — S on Tees
Stoke-on-Trent, City of — C of Stoke
Suffolk — Sflk
Sunderland — Sund
Surrey — Sry
Sutton — Sutt
Sussex, East — E Ssx
Sussex, West — W Ssx
Swindon — Swin
Tameside — Tside
Telford & Wrekin — T & W
Thurrock — Thurr
Torbay — Tby
Tower Hamlets — T Ham
Trafford — Traff
Walsall — Wals
Wandsworth — Wand
Wakefield — Wfield
Warrington — Warr
Warwickshire — Warks
Waltham Forest — Wal F
West Berkshire — W Berks
Westminster, City of — C of W
Wigan — Wig
Wiltshire — Wilts
Windsor & Maidenhead — W & M
Wirral — Wir
Wokingham — Wokm
Wolverhampton — Wolv
Worcestershire — Worcs
York — York
Yorkshire, North — N Yorks

Wales
Conwy — Cnwy
Anglesey — Anglsy
Blaenau Gwent — BG
Bridgend — Brid
Caerphilly — Caer
Cardiff — Crdff
Ceredigion — Cere
Carmarthenshire — Carm
Denbighshire — Denb
Flintshire — Flint
Gwynedd — Gwyn
Merthyr Tydfil — MT
Monmouthshire — Mon
Neath & Port Talbot — N & PT
Newport — Nwprt
Pembrokeshire — Pemb

Powys — Pwys
Rhondda Cyon Taff — RCT
Swansea — Swan
Torfaen — Trfn
Vale of Glamorgan — V of G
Wrexham — Wrex

Scotland
Aberdeen, City of — C of Aber
Aberdeenshire — Aber
Angus — Angus
Argyll & Bute — A & B
Ayrshire, East — E Ayr
Ayrshire, North — N Ayr
Ayrshire, South — S Ayr
Borders — Bdrs
Clackmannan — Clmnn
Dumfries & Galloway — D & G
Dundee, City of — C of Dun
East Dunbartonshire — E Dun
Edinburgh, City of — C of Edin
Falkirk — Falk
Fife — Fife
Glasgow, City of — C of Glas
Highland — Hghld
Inverclyde — Invclyd
Lanarkshire, North — N Lan
Lanarkshire, South — S Lan
Lothian, East — E Loth
Lothian, West — W Loth
Midlothian — Midln
Moray — Moray
Orkney Islands — Ork
Perth & Kinross — P & K
Renfrewshire — Ren
Renfrewshire, East — E Ren
Shetland Islands — Shet
Stirling — Stir
West Dunbartonshire — W Dun
Western Isles — W Is

Self-governing islands
Channel Islands — Ch Is
Isle of Man — IOM
Isles of Scilly — Is OS

Northern Ireland
Antrim — Ant
Armagh — Arm
Down — Down
Fermanagh — Ferm
Londonderry — Londy
Tyrone — Tyr

Republic of Ireland
Carlow — Carl
Cavan — Cav
Clare — Clare
Cork — Cork
Donegal — Dngl
Dublin — Dub
Galway — Gal
Kerry — Kerry
Kildare — Kild
Kilkenny — Kilk
Laois — Laois
Leitrim — Leit
Limerick — Lim
Longford — Long
Louth — Louth
Mayo — Mayo
Meath — Meath
Monaghan — Mongh
Offaly — Ofly
Roscommon — Rosc
Sligo — Sligo
Tipperary — Tipp
Waterford — Wat
Westmeath — Wmth
Wexford — Wex
Wicklow — Wklw

A

Abbas Combe 84 C2
Abberley 122 C4
Abberton *Esx* 116 B3
Abberton *Worcs* 123 E3
Abberwick 197 F5
Abbess Roding 115 E2
Abbey *Devon* 82 D1
Abbey *Gal* 239 G4
Abbey-cwm-hir 120 D5
Abbey Dore 109 E4
Abbeydorney 234 D5
Abbeyfeale 235 E5
Abbey Hulton 146 D4
Abbeylands 154 C2
Abbeylara 244 B2
Abbeyleix 240 C3
Abbey St Bathans 209 F1
Abbeyshrule 244 B1
Abbeystead 173 G2
Abbey Town 187 G3
Abbey Village 167 E4
Abbotrule 196 A5
Abbots Bickington 80 D1
Abbots Bromley 147 F1
Abbotsbury 74 B3
Abbotsham 81 E3
Abbotskerswell 69 G4
Abbots Langley 113 G1
Abbots Leigh 95 G3
Abbotsley 126 C3
Abbots Morton 123 F3
Abbots Ripton 126 C5
Abbot's Salford 123 F3
Abbotswood 86 B2
Abbotts Ann 86 A4
Abdon 133 F2
Aber 119 E2
Aberaeron 119 E4
Aberaman 108 B1
Aberangell 131 F4
Aberargie 213 H2
Aberarth 119 E4
Aber-banc 118 D2
Aberbargoed 108 C1
Aberbeeg 108 D1
Abercanaid 108 B2
Abercarn 94 D5
Abercastle 105 F5
Aberceglr 131 F4
Aberchalder 218 C5
Aberchirder 226 D4
Abercraf 107 G3
Abercromble 214 D1
Abercwmboi 108 B1
Abercych 118 C2
Abercrynafon 108 B3
Abercrynon 94 B5
Aber-Cywarch 131 F5
Aberdalgie 213 G3
Aberdare 108 B2
Aberdaron 142 B2
Aberdeen 221 G5
Aberdour 207 G4
Aberdulais 107 G1
Aberdyfi 130 D3
Aberedw 120 D2
Abereiddy 104 D4
Abererch 142 D3
Aberfan 108 B1
Aberfeldy 219 G1
Aberffraw 155 G1
Aberffrwd 130 D1
Aberford 169 F4
Aberfoyle 205 H5
Abergavenny 100 D3
Abergele 157 F2
Aber-Giar 119 F2
Abergorlech 107 E5
Abergwesyn 120 B3
Abergwili 106 C3
Abergwydol 131 E4
Abergwynant 130 D5
Abergwynfi 93 G3
Abergwyngregyn 156 C2
Abergynolwyn 130 D4
Aberhafesp 131 H3
Aberhosan 131 F3
Aberkenfig 93 G4
Aberlady 208 C3
Aberlemno 220 D1
Aberllefenni 131 E4
Abermeurig 119 F3
Abermule 132 B3

Abernaint 144 D1
Abernant 106 B4
Aber-nant 108 B2
Abernethy 213 H2
Abernyte 214 A4
Aberporth 118 C3
Abersky 224 D2
Abersoch 142 C2
Abersychan 108 D2
Aberthin 94 B3
Abertillery 108 D2
Abertridwr *Caer* 94 C4
Abertridwr *Pwys* 144 C1
Abertysswg 108 C2
Aberuthven 213 F2
Aber Village 108 C3
Aberyscir 108 A4
Aberystwyth 130 C2
Abhainn Suidhe 231 F4
Abingdon 98 B5
Abinger Common 88 B5
Abinger Hammer 88 A5
Abington *Lim* 239 G2
Abington *S Lan* 200 A1
Abington Pigotts 126 D2
Abingworth 88 B2
Ab Kettleby 149 E1
Ablington 111 E2
Abney 160 D2
Aboyne 220 D4
Abram 159 E5
Abriachan 224 C3
Abridge 114 D1
Abronhill 206 C3
Abson 96 B3
Abthorpe 125 E2
Aby 164 B2
Acaster Malbis 176 B1
Acaster Selby 169 G5
Accrington 167 G3
Acha 216 B1
Achabraid 204 A3
Achachork 222 C3
Achahoish 230 C2
Achalader 211 G5
Acha Mòr 231 G4
Achanalt 224 A5
Achandunie 224 D5
Ach' an Todhair 218 A2
Achany 228 D2
Achaphubuil 218 A3
Acharacle 217 F2
Achargary 229 F4
Acharn *Angus* 220 B3
Acharn *Hghld* 217 F1
Acharn *P & K* 212 D5
Achath 226 D1
Achavanich 229 G4
Achduart 228 B2
Achentoul 229 F3
Achfary 228 C4
Achgarve 228 A2
Achiemore *Hghld* 228 D5
Achiemore *Hghld* 229 F5
A' Chill 216 C5
Achill Sound 242 B3
Achiltibuie 228 B2
Achina 229 E5
Achindown 225 E4
Achinduich 229 E2
Achinduin 210 B4
Achingills 229 G5
Achintee 223 G3
Achintraid 223 F3
Achleck 216 D1
Achleek 217 G2
Achluachrach 218 C3
Achlyness 228 C4
Achmelvich 228 B3
Achmore *Hghld* 223 F3
Achnaba 210 C4
Achnabat 224 D2
Achnacarnin 228 B3
Achnacarry 218 B4
Achnacloich *A & B* 210 C4
Achnacloich *Hghld* 222 D1
Achnaconeran 224 B1
Achnacreebeag 210 C4
Achnacrolsh 210 B5
Achnadrish 216 D1
Achnafalnich 211 F3
Achnagarron 224 D5
Achnaha 216 D2
Achnahanat 228 D2

Achnahannet 225 F2
Achnairn 228 D2
Achnaluachrach 229 E2
Achnamara 230 C3
Achnasaul 218 B4
Achnasheen 223 H4
Achnashelloch 204 A4
Achosnich 216 D2
Achreamie 229 G5
Achriabhach 218 B2
Achriesgill 228 C4
Achrimsdale 229 F2
Achterneed 224 C4
Achurch 137 E2
Achuvoldrach 228 D5
Achvaich 229 E2
Achvarasdal 229 F5
Ackergill 229 H4
Acklam *Midbro* 182 B4
Acklam *N Yorks* 176 D3
Ackleton 133 H3
Acklington 197 G4
Ackton 169 F3
Ackworth Moor Top 169 F2
Acle 140 D5
Acock's Green 134 D2
Acol 103 G2
Acomb 189 G5
Aconbury 109 G5
Acre 167 G3
Acrefair 145 E3
Acton *Arm* 245 E5
Acton *Ches* 146 A4
Acton *Ealing* 100 C4
Acton *Sflk* 128 B2
Acton *Shrops* 132 C2
Acton Beauchamp 122 B3
Acton Bridge 159 E2
Acton Burnell 133 E4
Acton Green 122 B3
Acton Pigott 133 E4
Acton Round 133 F3
Acton Scott 133 E2
Acton Trussell 146 D1
Acton Turville 96 C4
Adamhill 198 D2
Adamstown 237 F5
Adamthwaite 180 B2
Adare 239 F1
Adbaston 146 C2
Adber 84 B2
Adderbury 124 C1
Adderley 146 B3
Adderstone 203 F2
Addiewell 207 E1
Addingham 174 D1
Addington *Bucks* 112 D4
Addington *Croy* 100 D2
Addington *Kent* 101 G1
Addlestone 100 A2
Addlethorpe 164 C1
Adeney 146 B1
Adfa 131 H4
Adforton 121 G5
Adlsham 103 F1
Adlestrop 111 F4
Adlingfleet 170 B3
Adlington *Ches* 160 A3
Adlington *Lancs* 167 E2
Admaston *Staffs* 147 F1
Admaston *T & W* 133 F5
Admington 123 H2
Adrigole 234 D2
Adsborough 83 F3
Adstock 112 D4
Adstone 124 D3
Adversane 88 A2
Advie 225 H3
Adwell 112 C1
Adwick le Street 169 G1
Adwick upon Dearne 161 G5
Adziel 227 F4
Ae 194 B2
Affleck 227 E2
Affpuddle 74 D3
Afon-wen 157 G2
Agglethorpe 174 D5
Aghaboe 240 B3
Aghabullogue 235 F3
Aghada 236 B2
Aghadowey 247 G4
Aghagallon 248 A1
Aghagower 242 D2

Aghalee 248 A1
Aghamore *Leit* 243 F3
Aghamore *Mayo* 243 H3
Aghavas 244 A3
Aghern 236 B4
Aghleam 242 B4
Aghnacliff 244 B3
Aghnamullen 244 D4
Aglionby 188 B4
Aglish 236 C4
Ahakista 234 D1
Ahascragh 239 G5
Aherla 235 G3
Ahoghill 248 A3
Aignis 231 G4
Aike 171 E5
Aikers 232 B2
Aiketgate 188 B3
Aikton 187 H3
Ailey 121 F2
Ailsworth 137 F3
Ainderby Quernhow 175 G5
Ainderby Steeple 181 H1
Aingers Green 116 C3
Ainsdale 166 B2
Ainstable 188 C3
Ainsworth 167 G2
Ainthorpe 182 D3
Aintree 158 C4
Aird *A & B* 210 A1
Aird *D & G* 184 C4
Aird *W Is* 231 G5
Aird a' Mhachair 231 E2
Aird a' Mhulaidh 231 F4
Aird Asaig 231 F4
Aird Dhail 231 G5
Aird Mhidhinis 231 E1
Aird of Sleat 217 E5
Aird Ruairidh 231 E2
Aird Thunga 231 G5
Aird Uig 231 F5
Airdre Mill 225 G3
Airdrie 206 C2
Airdriehill 206 C2
Aireland 186 C4
Airidh a Bhruaich 231 F4
Airmyn 170 A3
Airntully 213 G4
Airor 217 F5
Airth 206 D4
Airton 174 C2
Airyhassen 185 F3
Aisby *Lincs* 149 H3
Aisby *Lincs* 162 D4
Aiskew 181 G1
Aislaby *N Yorks* 176 D5
Aislaby *N Yorks* 183 F3
Aislaby *S on Tees* 182 A3
Aisthorpe 162 D2
Aith *Ork* 232 A4
Aith *Ork* 232 C4
Aith *Shet* 233 F3
Aith *Shet* 233 G4
Aithsetter 233 F1
Altnoch 225 G3
Akeld 202 D2
Akeley 125 E1
Akenham 128 D2
Albaston 71 E1
Alberbury 132 D5
Albourne 88 C2
Albrighton *Shrops* 133 H4
Albrighton *Shrops* 145 G1
Alburgh 140 C2
Albury *Herts* 114 C4
Albury *Sry* 88 A5
Albury End 114 C4
Alby Hill 152 D2
Alcaig 224 D4
Alcaston 133 E2
Alcester 123 F3
Alciston 79 F5
Alcombe 82 C5
Alconbury 126 B5
Alconbury Weston 126 B5
Aldborough *Nflk* 152 D2
Aldborough *N Yorks* 175 H3
Aldbourne 97 G3
Aldbrough 171 F4
Aldbrough St John 181 G3
Aldbury 113 F3
Alclune 219 G2
Aldeburgh 129 H3
Aldeby 140 D3

ALDENHAM–ASH

521
BARROW–BIGTON

Barrow *Shrops* 133 G4
Barroway Drove 138 C4
Barrowburn 196 D5
Barrowby 149 F3
Barrowden 136 D4
Barrowford 167 H4
Barrow Gurney 95 G2
Barrow-in-Furness 172 C4
Barrow Nook 166 C1
Barrow Street 84 D3
Barrow upon Humber 171 E3
Barrow upon Soar 148 C1
Barrow upon Trent 148 A2
Barry *Angus* 214 D4
Barry *V of G* 94 C2
Barry *Long* 244 A1
Barry Island 94 C2
Barryroe 235 G1
Barsby 136 B5
Barsham 140 D2
Barston 135 E1
Bartestree 122 A2
Barthol Chapel 227 E3
Barthomley 146 C4
Bartley 86 A1
Bartlow 127 F2
Barton *Cambs* 127 E3
Barton *Ches* 145 G4
Barton *Glos* 111 E4
Barton *Lancs* 166 C1
Barton *Lancs* 166 D4
Barton *N Yorks* 181 G3
Barton *Tby* 72 C1
Barton *Warks* 123 G3
Barton Bendish 139 E4
Barton End 96 C5
Barton Hartshorn 112 C4
Barton in Fabis 148 C2
Barton in the Beans 135 F4
Barton-le-Clay 113 G4
Barton-le-Street 176 C4
Barton-le-Willows 176 C3
Barton Mills 139 E1
Barton Moss 159 F4
Barton on Sea 76 A3
Barton-on-the-Heath 111 G5
Barton Seagrave 136 D1
Barton St David 84 A3
Barton Stacey 86 B4
Barton Turf 153 F1
Barton-under-Needwood 147 G1
Barton-upon-Humber 170 D3
Barway 138 C1
Barwell 135 G3
Barwick *Herts* 114 C3
Barwick *Som* 84 A1
Barwick in Elmet 169 E4
Baschurch 145 G1
Bascote 124 B4
Bascote Heath 124 B4
Basford Green 147 E4
Bashall Eaves 167 F5
Bashall Town 167 F5
Bashley 76 A4
Basildon 101 H4
Basingstoke 86 D5
Baslow 161 E2
Bason Bridge 83 F5
Bassaleg 94 D4
Bassenthwaite 178 D5
Bassett 86 B2
Bassingbourn 126 D2
Bassingfield 148 D3
Bassingham 149 G5
Bassingthorpe 149 G2
Basta 233 F4
Baston 137 F5
Bastwick 140 D5
Batchcott 121 H5
Batcombe *Dors* 74 B5
Batcombe *Som* 84 B4
Bate Heath 159 F2
Bath 96 B2
Bathampton 96 B2
Bathealton 82 D2
Batheaston 96 B2
Bathford 96 B2
Bathgate 207 E2
Bathley 149 E5
Bathpool *Corn* 70 D2
Bathpool *Som* 83 F3
Batley 168 D3
Batsford 111 F5
Battersby 182 C3
Battersea 100 C3
Batterstown 245 E1
Battisborough Cross 68 D2
Battisford 128 D3
Battisford Tye 128 C3
Battle *E Ssx* 89 H2
Battle *Pwys* 108 B4
Battlefield 133 E5
Battlesbridge 115 G1
Battlesden 113 F4
Battleton 82 B3
Battramsley 76 B4
Batt's Corner 87 F4
Bauds of Cullen 226 C5
Baugh 230 A4
Baughton 122 D2
Baughurst 98 C2
Baulking 97 H5
Baumber 163 G2
Baunton 110 D2
Baveney Wood 133 G1
Baverstock 85 F3
Bawburgh 140 B4
Bawdeswell 152 C1
Bawdrip 83 F4
Bawdsey 129 F2
Bawnboy 244 B4
Bawsey 151 G1
Bawtry 162 B4
Baxenden 167 G3
Baxterley 135 E3
Baybridge 189 G3
Baycliff 172 D4
Baydon 97 G3
Bayford *Herts* 114 B2
Bayford *Som* 84 C3
Bayles 189 E2
Baylham 128 D3
Baynard's Green 112 D4
Baysham 109 G4
Bayston Hill 133 F4
Baythorne End 127 H2
Bayton 122 B5
Bayworth 112 B1
Beachampton 112 D5
Beachamwell 139 E4
Beachans 225 G3
Beacharr 230 C2
Beachley 95 G5
Beacon 73 E5
Beacon End 116 A4
Beacon's Bottom 112 D1
Beaconsfield 99 G5
Beacrabhaic 231 F3
Beadlam 176 C5
Beadnell 203 G2
Beaford 81 F1
Beal *Northld* 203 E3
Beal *N Yorks* 169 G3
Béal an Mhuirthead 242 B4
Bealaclugga 239 E4
Bealaha 238 C2
Bealin 240 A5
Bealnablath 235 F2
Beamhurst 147 F3
Beaminster 74 A4
Beamish 190 B3
Beamsley 174 D2
Bean 101 F3
Beanacre 96 D2
Beanley 203 E1
Beare Green 88 B4
Bearley 123 G4
Bearna 239 E4
Bearpark 190 B2
Bearsbridge 189 E4
Bearsden 205 H2
Bearsted 102 A1
Bearwood *Herefs* 121 G3
Bearwood *Poole* 75 F4
Beattock 194 C4
Beauchamp Roding 115 E2
Beauchief 161 E3
Beaufort *BG* 108 C2
Beaufort *Kerry* 234 D4
Beaulieu 76 B4
Beauly 224 C3
Beaumaris 156 B2
Beaumont *Cumb* 188 A4
Beaumont *Esx* 116 C4
Beaumont Leys 135 H4
Beausale 123 H5
Beauworth 86 D3
Beaworthy 71 F4
Beazley End 115 F4
Bebington 158 B3
Bebside 197 H2
Beccles 140 D2
Becconsall 166 C3
Beckbury 133 H4
Beckenham 100 D2
Beckermet 178 B3
Beckermonds 174 B5
Beck Foot 179 H2
Beckfoot *Cumb* 178 D2
Beckfoot *Cumb* 187 F3
Beckford 110 D5
Beckhampton 97 E2
Beck Hole 183 E2
Beckingham *Lincs* 149 F4
Beckingham *Notts* 162 C3
Beckington 84 D5
Beckley *E Ssx* 90 B2
Beckley *Oxon* 112 B2
Beck Row 138 D1
Beck Side 172 C5
Beckton 101 E4
Beckwithshaw 175 F2
Becontree 101 F4
Bective 244 D1
Bedale 181 G1
Bedburn 181 F5
Bedchester 84 D2
Beddau 94 B4
Beddgelert 143 F4
Beddingham 89 E1
Beddington 100 D2
Bedfield 129 E4
Bedford 126 A2
Bedhampton 77 F5
Bedingfield 129 E4
Bedlar's Green 114 D3
Bedlington 197 H2
Bedlinog 108 B1
Bedmond 113 G2
Bednall 147 E1
Bedrule 201 H1
Bedstone 132 D1
Bedwas 94 C4
Bedworth 135 F2
Beeby 136 B4
Beech *Hants* 87 E4
Beech *Staffs* 146 D3
Beech Hill 98 D2
Beechingstoke 97 E1
Beedon 98 B3
Beeford 177 G2
Beeley 161 E1
Beelsby 163 G5
Beenacouma 234 B4
Beenham 98 C2
Beer 73 F3
Beer Crocombe 83 F2
Beer Hackett 74 B5
Beesands 69 F2
Beesby 164 C3
Beeson 69 F2
Beeston *Beds* 126 B2
Beeston *Ches* 145 H5
Beeston *Leeds* 168 D4
Beeston *Nflk* 139 G5
Beeston *Notts* 148 C3
Beeston Regis 152 D3
Beeswing 186 D5
Beetham 173 F4
Beetley 152 B1
Began 94 D4
Begbroke 112 A3
Begdale 138 B4
Begelly 105 H2
Beggar Hill 115 E1
Beguildy 132 B1
Behy Bridge 243 E4
Beighton *Nflk* 140 D4
Beighton *Sheff* 161 F3
Beinn Casgro 231 G4
Beith 198 C4
Bekan 243 E2
Bekesbourne 103 E1
Belaugh 153 E1
Belbins 86 B2
Belbroughton 123 E5
Belchamp Otten 128 A2
Belchamp St Paul 128 A2
Belchamp Walter 128 A2
Belchford 163 H2
Belcoo 244 A5
Belderg 242 D5
Belfast 248 B2
Belford 203 F2
Belgooly 235 G2
Belhelvie 227 F1
Belhinnie 226 B2
Bellabeg 226 B1
Bellacorick 242 D4
Bellaghy 247 H2
Bellahy 243 F3
Bellamore 192 B2
Bellanagare 243 G3
Bellanagh 244 B3
Bellanaleck 244 B5
Bellanamullia 239 H5
Bellanoch 204 A4
Bellanode 244 C5
Bellaty 220 B2
Bellavary 243 E3
Bell Bar 114 B2
Bell Busk 174 C2
Belleau 164 B2
Belleek *Arm* 245 E4
Belleek *Ferm* 246 C1
Belleheiglash 225 H3
Bell End 123 E5
Bellerby 181 F1
Bellever 69 E5
Bellewstown 245 E2
Bellfield 199 H2
Belliehill 220 D2
Bellingdon 113 F2
Bellingham 196 C2
Bellmount 240 A4
Belloch 230 B1
Bellsbank 193 E4
Bellshill *N Lan* 206 C1
Bellshill *Northld* 203 F2
Bellsmyre 205 G3
Bellspool 200 D3
Bellsquarry 207 F1
Bells Yew Green 89 G4
Belluton 95 H2
Belmaduthy 224 D4
Belmesthorpe 137 E5
Belmont *Bburn* 167 F2
Belmont *Shet* 233 G5
Belmullet 242 B4
Belnacraig 226 B1
Belowda 67 E4
Belper 148 A4
Belper Lane End 148 A4
Belsay 197 F1
Belsford 69 F3
Belsize 113 G1
Belstead 128 D2
Belston 198 C1
Belstone 71 G3
Belsyde 207 E3
Belthorn 167 F3
Beltinge 103 E2
Beltingham 189 E4
Beltoft 162 C5
Belton *Leics* 148 B1
Belton *Lincs* 149 G3
Belton *N Lincs* 162 C5
Belton *Nflk* 141 E4
Belton-in-Rutland 136 C4
Beltoy 248 B2
Beltra 242 D3
Beltring 89 G5
Belturbet 244 B4
Belvedere 101 E3
Belvoir 149 F2
Bembridge 77 E3
Bemersyde 201 H2
Bempton 177 H4
Benacre 141 E2
Benbuie 193 G3
Benburb 244 D5
Benderloch 210 C4
Bendish 113 H3
Bendooragh 247 H4
Benenden 90 A3
Benfield 185 F4
Benholm 221 F2
Beningbrough 176 A2
Benington *Herts* 114 B4
Benington *Lincs* 150 D4
Benllech 156 A3
Benmore *A & B* 204 D4
Benmore *Stir* 211 H3
Bennacott 70 D3
Bennan 230 C1
Bennecarrigan 230 C1
Bennettsbridge 240 C1
Benniworth 163 G3
Benover 89 H5
Benson 98 D5
Benstonhall 232 C4
Bent 221 E2
Benthall 133 G4
Bentham 110 C3
Benthoul 221 F5
Bentley *Donc* 169 G1
Bentley *E R of Yorks* 170 D4
Bentley *Hants* 87 F4
Bentley *Sflk* 128 D1
Bentley *Warks* 135 E3
Bentley Heath 134 D1
Benton 81 G4
Bentpath 195 F3
Bentworth 87 E4
Benvie 214 B4
Benville 74 A4
Benwick 138 A3
Beoley 123 F4
Beoraidbeg 217 F4
Bepton 87 G2
Beragh 247 F1
Berden 114 D4
Berea 104 D4
Bere Alston 71 E1
Bere Ferrers 68 C4
Berepper 64 D2
Bere Regis 74 D4
Bergh Apton 140 C4
Berinsfield 98 C5
Berkeley 110 A1
Berkhamsted 113 F2
Berkley 84 D5
Berkswell 135 E1
Bermondsey 100 D3
Bermuda 135 F2
Bernera 223 F2
Berners Roding 115 E2
Bernice 204 D4
Bernisdale 222 C4
Berrick Salome 98 D5
Berriedale 229 G3
Berrier 179 F5
Berriew 132 B4
Berrings 235 G3
Berrington *Northld* 203 E3
Berrington *Shrops* 133 E4
Berrow *Som* 95 E1
Berrow *Worcs* 122 C1
Berrow Green 122 C3
Berryfield 96 D2
Berry Hill 109 G2
Berryhillock 226 C5
Berrynarbor 81 F5
Berry Pomeroy 69 F4
Bersham 145 F4
Bersted 77 H4
Berwick 79 F5
Berwick Bassett 97 E3
Berwick Hill 197 G1
Berwick St James 85 F4
Berwick St John 85 E2
Berwick St Leonard 85 E3
Berwick-upon-Tweed 202 D4
Berwyn 144 D3
Besford *Shrops* 145 H1
Besford *Worcs* 123 E2
Besford Court 123 E2
Bessacarr 162 A5
Bessbrook 245 E4
Bessels Leigh *Oxon* 112 A1
Bessingham 152 D3
Best Beech Hill 89 G3
Besthorpe *Nflk* 139 H3
Besthorpe *Notts* 162 C1
Bestwood Village 148 C4
Beswick 170 D5
Betchworth 88 C5
Bethania *Cere* 119 F4
Bethania *Gwyn* 143 F4
Bethel *Anglsy* 155 G2
Bethel *Gwyn* 156 A1
Bethersden 90 B4
Bethesda *Gwyn* 156 B1
Bethesda *Pemb* 105 G3
Bethlehem 107 F4
Bethnal Green 100 D4
Betley 146 C4
Betsham 101 G3
Betteshanger 91 F5
Bettiscombe 73 G4
Bettisfield 145 G3
Betton *Shrops* 132 C4
Betton *Shrops* 146 B3
Bettws *Brid* 93 H4
Bettws *Mon* 108 D3
Bettws *Nwprt* 94 D5
Bettws Cedewain 132 A3
Bettws Gwerfil Goch 144 C4
Bettws Newydd 109 E2
Bettyhill 229 E5
Bettystown 245 F2
Betws 107 E2
Betws Bledrws 119 F3
Betws Garmon 143 E5
Betws Ifan 118 D2
Betws-y-Coed 143 H5
Betws-yn-Rhos 157 E2
Beulah *Cere* 118 C2
Beulah *Pwys* 120 B3
Bevendean 78 D5
Bevercotes 162 B2
Beverley 170 D4
Beverston 96 C5
Bevington 96 A5
Bewaldeth 187 G1
Bewcastle 195 H1
Bewdley 122 C5
Bewerley 175 E3
Bewholme 177 H1
Bexhill 89 H1
Bexley 101 E3
Bexleyheath 101 E3
Bexwell 138 D4
Beyton 128 B4
Bhatarsaigh 231 F1
Bibury 111 E2
Bicester 112 B4
Bickenhall 83 F2
Bickenhill 134 D2
Bicker 150 B3
Bickershaw 159 E5
Bickerstaffe 166 C1
Bickerton *Ches* 145 H4
Bickerton *N Yorks* 175 H2
Bickham Bridge 69 E3
Bickington *Devon* 69 F5
Bickington *Devon* 81 F3
Bickleigh *Devon* 68 C4
Bickleigh *Devon* 72 C5
Bickleton 81 F3
Bickley 101 E2
Bickley Moss 145 H4
Bickley Town 145 H4
Bicknacre 115 G2
Bicknoller 82 D4
Bicknor 102 B1
Bickton 85 G1
Bicton *Shrops* 132 C2
Bicton *Shrops* 132 D5
Bidborough 89 F4
Biddenden 90 B4
Biddenham 126 A3
Biddestone 96 C3
Biddisham 95 E1
Biddlesden 124 D2
Biddlestone 197 E4
Biddulph 146 D5
Biddulph Moor 146 D5
Bideford 81 E3
Bidford-on-Avon 123 G3
Bielby 176 D1
Bieldside 221 G5
Bierley 76 D2
Bierton 113 E3
Big Balcraig 185 F2
Big Sand 228 A1
Bigbury 69 E2
Bigbury-on-Sea 69 E2
Bigby 171 E1
Biggar *Cumb* 172 C3
Biggar *S Lan* 200 B3
Biggin *Derbs* 147 G5
Biggin *Derbs* 147 H4
Biggin *N Yorks* 169 G4
Biggin Hill 101 E1
Biggings 233 E3
Biggins 173 G4
Biggleswade 126 B2
Bighouse 229 F5
Bighton 86 D3
Bignor 87 H1
Bigods 115 E4
Bigrigg 178 B3
Bigton 233 F1

GAZETTEER

523
BOOLA–BRIDGE OF OICH

Boola 236 C3
Boolakennedy 236 B5
Booley 146 A2
Boor 228 A1
Boosbeck 182 D4
Boot 178 D2
Boothby Graffoe 149 G5
Boothby Pagnell 149 G2
Booth of Toft 233 F4
Boothstown 159 F5
Booth Wood 168 B2
Bootle *Cumb* 178 C1
Bootle *Seft* 158 B4
Booton 152 D1
Boquhan 205 H4
Boraston 122 B4
Borden 102 B2
Bordley 174 C3
Bordon 87 F3
Bordon Camp 87 F4
Boreham *Esx* 115 G2
Boreham *Wilts* 84 D4
Boreham Street 89 G1
Borehamwood 100 B5
Boreland *D & G* 185 F5
Boreland *D & G* 194 D3
Boreland *Stir* 212 B4
Borgh 231 E1
Borghastan 231 F5
Borgie 229 E5
Borgue *D & G* 186 A3
Borgue *Hghld* 229 G3
Borley 128 A2
Borley Green 128 C4
Bornais 231 E2
Borneskeitaig 222 C5
Borness 186 A3
Boroughbridge 175 G3
Borough Green 101 G1
Borras Head 145 F4
Borreraig 222 A4
Borris 240 D1
Borris in Ossory 240 B3
Borrisokane 239 H3
Borrisoleigh 239 H2
Borrowash 148 B2
Borrowby *N Yorks* 182 A1
Borrowby *N Yorks* 183 E4
Borrowfield 221 F4
Borstal 102 A2
Borth 130 D2
Borthwick 201 F5
Borthwickbrae 195 G5
Borthwickshiels 195 G5
Borth-y-Gest 143 F3
Borve 222 C4
Borwick 173 F4
Bosavern 64 A3
Bosbury 122 B2
Boscastle 70 B3
Boscombe *Bmth* 75 G3
Boscombe *Wilts* 85 G4
Bosham 77 G5
Bosham Hoe 77 G4
Bosherston 105 F1
Boskednan 64 B3
Bosley 160 A1
Bossall 176 C3
Bossiney 70 B3
Bossingham 91 E5
Bossington 82 B5
Bostadh 231 F5
Bostock Green 159 F1
Boston *Clare* 239 E3
Boston *Lincs* 150 C3
Boston Spa 169 F5
Boswednack 64 B3
Boswinger 67 E2
Botallack 64 A3
Botany Bay 114 B1
Botcheston 135 G4
Botesdale 128 C5
Bothal 197 G2
Bothamsall 162 B2
Bothel 187 G2
Bothenhampton 73 H3
Bothwell 206 C1
Botley *Bucks* 113 F2
Botley *Hants* 86 C1
Botley *Oxon* 112 A2
Botloes Green 110 A4
Botolph Claydon 112 D4
Botolphs 78 C5
Bottacks 224 C4
Bottesford *Leics* 149 F3
Bottesford *N Lincs* 162 D5
Bottisham 127 F4
Bottomcraig 214 B3
Botton 182 D2
Botton Head 173 H3
Botusfleming 68 B4
Botwnnog 142 C2
Bough Beech 89 E5
Boughrood 120 D1
Boughspring 109 G1
Boughton *Nflk* 138 D4
Boughton *Northants* 125 F4
Boughton *Notts* 162 B1
Boughton Aluph 90 C5
Boughton Lees 90 C5
Boughton Malherbe 90 B5
Boughton Monchelsea 89 H5
Boughton Street 102 D1
Bouladuff 240 A2
Boulby 183 E4
Bouldnor 76 B3
Bouldon 133 E2
Boulmer 197 H5
Boulston 105 F3
Boultenstone 220 C5
Boultham 163 E1
Bourn 126 D3
Bourne 150 A1
Bourne End *Beds* 125 H2
Bourne End *Bucks* 99 F4
Bourne End *Herts* 113 G2
Bournemouth 75 G3
Bournes Green 110 C2
Bournheath 123 E5
Bournmoor 190 C3
Bournville 134 C2
Bourton *Dors* 84 C3
Bourton *N Som* 95 E2
Bourton *Oxon* 97 G4
Bourton *Shrops* 133 F3
Bourton on Dunsmore 124 B5
Bourton-on-the-Hill 111 F5
Bourton-on-the-Water 111 F3
Bousd 216 C2
Bouth 172 D5
Bovedy 247 G3
Boveney 99 G3
Boveridge 85 F1
Boverton 94 A2
Bovey Tracey 72 B2
Bovingdon 113 G2
Bovington Camp 74 D3
Bow *Devon* 71 H4
Bow *T Ham* 100 D4
Bowbank 180 D4
Bow Brickhill 113 F5
Bowburn 190 C2
Bowcombe 76 C3
Bowd 73 E3
Bowden *Bdrs* 201 H2
Bowden *Devon* 69 F2
Bowden Hill 96 D2
Bowderdale 180 A2
Bowdon 159 G3
Bower 196 C2
Bowerchalke 85 F2
Bowerhill 96 D2
Bower House Tye 128 C2
Bowermadden 229 H5
Bowers Gifford 102 A4
Bowershall 207 F4
Bowertower 229 H5
Bowes 180 D3
Bowgreave 166 D5
Bowland 201 G3
Bowland Bridge 179 F1
Bowley 122 A3
Bowlhead Green 87 G4
Bowling 205 G2
Bowling Bank 145 F4
Bowling Green 122 D3
Bowmanstead 179 E2
Bowmore 230 B2
Bowness-on-Solway 187 G4
Bowness-on-Windermere 179 F2
Bow of Fife 214 B2
Bowsden 202 D3
Bow Street 130 D2
Bowthorpe 140 B4
Box *Glos* 110 C1
Box *Wilts* 96 C2
Boxbush 110 A3
Box End 125 H2
Boxford *Sflk* 128 C2
Boxford *W Berks* 98 B3
Boxgrove 87 G1
Box Hill 96 C2
Boxley 102 A1
Boxted *Esx* 128 C1
Boxted *Sflk* 128 A3
Boxted Cross 128 C1
Boxworth 126 D4
Boyle 243 G3
Boylestone 147 G3
Boyndie 226 D5
Boyndlie 227 F5
Boynton 177 G3
Boysack 221 E1
Boyton *Corn* 70 D3
Boyton *Sflk* 129 G2
Boyton *Wilts* 85 E4
Boyton Cross 115 E2
Bozeat 125 G3
Braaid 154 B2
Brabling Green 129 F4
Brabourne 90 D4
Brabourne Lees 90 D4
Brabster 229 H5
Bracadale 222 B3
Bracara 217 F4
Braceborough 137 F5
Bracebridge Heath 163 E1
Braceby 149 H3
Bracewell 174 B1
Brackenfield 148 A5
Bracklamore 227 E4
Brackletter 218 B3
Brackley *A & B* 230 C2
Brackley *Hghld* 225 E4
Brackley *Northants* 124 D1
Bracklin 244 C1
Brackloch 220 D3
Brackloon 243 G2
Bracknagh *Ofly* 240 C4
Bracknagh *Rosc* 243 H1
Bracknell 99 F2
Braco 212 D1
Bracobrae 226 C4
Bracon Ash 140 B3
Bracorina 217 F4
Bradbourne 147 G4
Bradbury 190 C1
Bradda 154 A1
Bradden 124 D2
Braddock 67 G4
Bradenham *Bucks* 113 E1
Bradenham *Nflk* 139 G4
Bradfield *Devon* 72 D5
Bradfield *Esx* 116 C4
Bradfield *Nflk* 153 E2
Bradfield *W Berks* 98 D3
Bradfield Combust 128 B3
Bradfield Green 146 B5
Bradfield Heath 116 C4
Bradfield St Clare 128 B3
Bradfield St George 128 B3
Bradford *Brad* 168 C4
Bradford *Devon* 81 E1
Bradford *Northld* 203 F2
Bradford Abbas 84 A1
Bradford Leigh 96 C2
Bradford-on-Avon 96 C2
Bradford-on-Tone 83 E2
Bradford Peverell 74 C3
Brading 77 E3
Bradley *Derbs* 147 G4
Bradley *Hants* 86 D4
Bradley *NE Lincs* 171 F1
Bradley *Staffs* 146 D1
Bradley *Wrex* 145 F4
Bradley Green 123 E4
Bradley in the Moors 147 F3
Bradley Stoke 95 H4
Bradmore 148 C2
Bradninch 72 D5
Bradnop 147 E5
Bradpole 74 A4
Bradshaw 167 F2
Bradstone 71 E2
Bradwall Green 159 G1
Bradwell *Derbs* 160 D3
Bradwell *Esx* 115 G4
Bradwell *MK* 113 E5
Bradwell *Nflk* 141 E4
Bradwell Grove 111 F2
Bradwell on Sea 116 B2
Bradwell Waterside 116 A2
Bradworthy 80 D1
Brae *Hghld* 224 D5
Brae *Hghld* 228 A1
Brae *Hghld* 228 D2
Brae *Shet* 233 F3
Braeantra 228 D1
Braedownie 220 B3
Braefield 224 B2
Braegrum 213 F3
Braehead *Angus* 221 E1
Braehead *D & G* 185 G3
Braehead *Ork* 232 B3
Braehead *Ork* 232 B5
Braehead *S Lan* 199 H2
Braehead *S Lan* 200 B4
Braehoulland 233 E4
Braemar 220 A4
Braemore *Hghld* 228 C1
Braemore *Hghld* 229 G3
Brae of Achnahaird 228 B3
Braes of Enzie 226 B4
Braes of Ullapool 228 C2
Braeside 205 E3
Braeswick 232 C5
Braeval 205 H5
Braewick 233 F3
Brafferton *Darl* 181 G4
Brafferton *N Yorks* 175 H4
Brafield-on-the-Green 125 F3
Bragar 231 F5
Bragbury End 114 B3
Bragenham 113 F4
Bragleenmore 210 C3
Braides 173 F2
Braidley 174 D5
Braidwood 199 H4
Braigo 230 A2
Brailsford 147 H3
Braintree 115 G4
Braiseworth 128 D5
Braishfield 86 B3
Braithwaite *Cumb* 178 D4
Braithwaite *Donc* 169 H2
Braithwell 161 G4
Bramber 78 C5
Brambridge 86 C2
Bramcote *Notts* 148 C3
Bramcote *Warks* 135 G2
Bramdean 86 D3
Bramerton 140 C4
Bramfield *Herts* 114 B3
Bramfield *Sflk* 140 D1
Bramford 128 D2
Bramhall 159 H3
Bramham 169 F5
Bramhope 168 D5
Bramley *Hants* 98 D1
Bramley *Roth* 161 G4
Bramley *Sry* 87 H5
Bramley Green 98 D1
Bramling 103 F1
Brampford Speke 72 C4
Brampton *Cambs* 126 C5
Brampton *Cumb* 180 A4
Brampton *Cumb* 188 C4
Brampton *Lincs* 162 C2
Brampton *Nflk* 153 E1
Brampton *Roth* 161 F5
Brampton *Sflk* 140 D2
Brampton Abbotts 109 H4
Brampton Ash 136 C2
Brampton Bryan 132 D1
Brampton en le Morthen 161 G3
Brampton Street 140 D2
Bramshall 147 F2
Bramshaw 85 H2
Bramshill 99 E2
Bramshott 87 F3
Branault 217 E2
Brancaster 151 H3
Brancaster Staithe 151 H3
Brancepeth 190 B2
Branchill 225 G4
Brandesburton 171 E5
Brandeston 129 F4
Brand Green 110 A4
Brandis Corner 71 E4
Brandiston 152 D1
Brandon *Dur* 190 B2
Brandon *Kerry* 234 B5
Brandon *Lincs* 149 G4
Brandon *Northld* 203 E1
Brandon *Sflk* 139 E2
Brandon *Warks* 135 G1
Brandon Bank 138 D2
Brandon Creek 138 D3
Brandon Parva 139 H4
Brandsby 176 B4
Brandy Wharf 163 E4
Brane 64 B2
Bran End 115 F4
Branksome 75 G3
Branksome Park 75 G3
Brannockstown 240 D4
Bransby 162 D2
Branscombe 73 E3
Bransford 122 C3
Bransgore 75 H4
Bransholme 171 E4
Branson's Cross 123 F5
Branston *Leics* 149 F2
Branston *Lincs* 163 E1
Branston *Staffs* 147 G1
Branston Booths 163 F1
Branstone 76 D2
Brant Broughton 149 G4
Brantham 128 D1
Branthwaite *Cumb* 178 C4
Branthwaite *Cumb* 187 H2
Brantingham 170 C3
Branton *Donc* 162 A5
Branton *Northld* 197 E5
Branxholme 195 G5
Branxton 202 C3
Brassington 147 G4
Brasted 101 E1
Brasted Chart 101 E1
Brathens 221 E4
Bratoft 164 C1
Brattleby 162 D3
Bratton 85 E5
Bratton Clovelly 71 F3
Bratton Fleming 81 G4
Bratton Seymour 84 B3
Braughing 114 C4
Braughing Friars 114 C4
Braunston 124 C4
Braunstone Town 135 H4
Braunston-in-Rutland 136 C4
Braunton 81 E4
Brawby 176 C4
Brawl 229 F5
Brawlbin 229 G5
Bray *Wklw* 241 F4
Bray *W & M* 99 G3
Braybrooke 136 C2
Braye 75 E1
Brayford 81 G3
Bray Shop 70 D2
Braystones 178 B3
Brayton 169 H4
Brazacott 70 D3
Brea 194 A1
Breach 91 F5
Breachwood Green 113 H4
Breacleit 231 F5
Breadsall 148 A3
Breadstone 110 A1
Bready 247 E3
Breage 64 D2
Breakachy 224 C3
Bream 109 H2
Breamore 85 G2
Brean 94 D1
Breanais 231 F4
Brearton 175 G3
Breascleit 231 F4
Breaston 148 B2
Brechfa 106 D4
Brechin 220 D2
Breckan 232 A3
Breckles 139 G3
Breckrey 222 C5
Brecon 108 B4
Bredbury 160 A4
Brede 90 A2
Bredenbury 122 B3
Bredfield 129 F3
Bredgar 102 B2
Bredhurst 102 A2
Bredicot 123 E3
Bredon 123 E1
Bredons Hardwick 123 E1
Bredon's Norton 123 E1
Bredwardine 121 F2
Breedon on the Hill 148 B1
Breich 207 E1
Breighton 170 A4
Breiwick 233 F2
Bremhill 96 D3
Brenchley 89 G4
Brenchoillie 210 D1
Brendon 81 H5
Brent Eleigh 128 B2
Brentford 100 B3
Brentingby 149 E1
Brent Knoll 83 F5
Brent Pelham 114 C4
Brentwood 101 F5
Brenzett 90 C3
Brereton 134 C5
Brereton Green 159 G1
Brereton Heath 159 G1
Bressingham 140 A2
Bressingham Common 140 A2
Bretby 147 H1
Bretford 124 B5
Bretforton 123 F2
Bretherdale Head 179 H2
Bretherton 166 D3
Brettabister 233 F3
Brettenham *Nflk* 139 G2
Brettenham *Sflk* 128 C3
Bretton 158 C1
Brewlands Bridge 220 B2
Brewood 134 A4
Briantspuddle 74 D3
Brickendon 114 B2
Bricket Wood 113 H2
Bricklehampton 123 E2
Bride 154 D5
Bridekirk 187 F1
Bridell 118 B2
Bridestowe 71 F3
Brideswell *Aber* 226 C3
Brideswell *Rosc* 243 H1
Bridford 72 B3
Bridge 103 E1
Bridge End *Lincs* 150 A3
Bridge End *Londy* 247 E4
Bridge End *Northld* 189 G4
Bridgefoot *Angus* 214 B4
Bridgefoot *Cumb* 187 F1
Bridge Green 127 E1
Bridgehampton 84 A2
Bridgehaugh 226 B3
Bridge Hewick 175 G4
Bridgeland 241 F2
Bridgemary 76 D4
Bridgend *A & B* 204 A4
Bridgend *A & B* 230 B2
Bridgend *A & B* 230 C1
Bridgend *Aber* 220 D5
Bridgend *Aber* 226 C3
Bridgend *Angus* 220 D2
Bridgend *Brid* 93 H4
Bridgend *Cere* 118 B2
Bridgend *Cumb* 179 F3
Bridgend *Fife* 214 B2
Bridgend *Glos* 110 B2
Bridgend *Moray* 226 B2
Bridgend *N Lan* 206 B2
Bridgend *W Loth* 207 F3
Bridgend of Lintrathen 220 B1
Bridge of Alford 226 C1
Bridge of Allan 206 D5
Bridge of Avon 225 H3
Bridge of Balgie 212 B5
Bridge of Brown 225 H2
Bridge of Cally 220 A1
Bridge of Canny 221 E4
Bridge of Craigisla 220 B1
Bridge of Dee 186 B4
Bridge of Don 227 F1
Bridge of Dun 221 E1
Bridge of Dye 221 E3
Bridge of Earn 213 G2
Bridge of Ericht 218 D1
Bridge of Feugh 221 E4
Bridge of Forss 229 G5
Bridge of Gairn 220 C4
Bridge of Gaur 218 D1
Bridge of Muchalls 221 G4
Bridge of Muick 220 C4
Bridge of Oich 218 C5

GAZETTEER

524
BRIDGE OF ORCHY–BURGHFIELD HILL

Bridge of Orchy 211 F4
Bridge of Tilt 219 G2
Bridge of Walls 233 E2
Bridge of Weir 205 F2
Bridge Reeve 81 G1
Bridgerule 70 D4
Bridges *Corn* 67 F3
Bridges *Shrops* 132 D3
Bridge Sollers 121 G2
Bridge Street 128 B2
Bridgetown *Corn* 70 D3
Bridgetown *Som* 82 B3
Bridgetown *Wex* 237 G4
Bridge Trafford 158 D2
Bridge Yate 96 A3
Bridgham 139 G2
Bridgnorth 133 G3
Bridgtown 134 B4
Bridgwater 83 F4
Bridlington 177 H3
Bridport 73 H3
Bridstow 109 G4
Brierfield 167 G4
Brierley *Barns* 169 F2
Brierley *Glos* 109 H3
Brierley *Herefs* 121 H3
Brierley Hill 134 B2
Brierton 191 E1
Brigdefoot 220 C5
Brigg 163 E5
Brigh 247 G1
Brigham *Cumb* 187 F1
Brigham *E R of Yorks* 177 G2
Brighouse *Cald* 168 C3
Brighouse *D & G* 186 A3
Brighstone 76 C2
Brightgate 147 H5
Brighthampton 111 H2
Brightling 89 G2
Brightlingsea 116 B3
Brighton 67 E3
Brighton and Hove 78 D5
Brightons 207 E3
Brightwalton 98 B3
Brightwell 129 E2
Brightwell Baldwin 98 D5
Brightwell-cum-Sotwell 98 C5
Brignall 181 E3
Brig o' Turk 212 A1
Brigsley 163 H5
Brigsteer 179 G1
Brigstock 136 D2
Brill 112 C3
Brilley 121 F2
Brimfield 122 A4
Brimington 161 F2
Brimley 69 F5
Brimpsfield 110 C3
Brimpton 98 C2
Brimpton Common 98 C2
Brims 232 A2
Brimscombe 110 C2
Brimstage 158 B3
Brind 170 A4
Brindister *Shet* 233 E3
Brindister *Shet* 233 F2
Brindle 167 E3
Brindley 146 A4
Brindley Ford 146 D4
Brineton 133 H5
Bringhurst 136 C3
Brington 137 F1
Brinian 232 B4
Briningham 152 C2
Brinkhill 164 B2
Brinkley 127 G3
Brinklow 135 G1
Brinkworth 97 E4
Brinmore 224 D2
Brinscall 167 E3
Brinsley 148 B4
Brinsop 121 G2
Brinsworth 161 F3
Brinton 152 C3
Brisco 188 B3
Briska 236 D4
Brisley 152 B1
Brislington 95 H3
Bristol 95 G3
Briston 152 C2
Britannia 167 H3
Britford 85 G3
Brithdir 143 H1
Briton Ferry 93 F5
Brittas 241 E4
Britway 236 B3
Britwell Salome 98 D5
Brixham 69 G3
Brixton *Devon* 68 D3
Brixton *Lamb* 100 D3
Brixton Deverill 84 D4
Brixworth 125 E5
Brize Norton 111 G2
Broad Blunsdon 97 F5
Broadbottom 160 B4
Broadbridge 77 G5
Broadbridge Heath 88 B3
Broad Campden 111 F5
Broad Chalke 85 F3
Broadclyst 72 C4
Broadfield 88 C3
Broadford *Clare* 239 F2
Broadford *Hghld* 222 D2
Broadford *Lim* 235 F5
Broadford Bridge 88 A2
Broad Green *Esx* 115 H4
Broad Green *Cambs* 127 G3
Broad Green *Worcs* 122 C3
Broadhaugh 195 G4
Broad Haven 105 E3
Broadheath 159 G3
Broad Heath 122 B4
Broadhembury 73 E5
Broadhempston 69 F4
Broad Hill 138 C1
Broad Hinton 97 F3
Broadholme 162 D2
Broadland Row 90 A2
Broadlay 106 C2
Broad Layings 98 B2
Broadley *Lancs* 167 H2
Broadley *Moray* 226 B5
Broadley Common 114 C2
Broad Marston 123 G2
Broadmayne 74 C3
Broadmeadows 201 F2
Broadmere 86 D5
Broadmoor 105 G2
Broadnymett 71 H4
Broadoak 73 H4
Broad Oak *Carm* 107 E4
Broad Oak *Cumb* 178 C1
Broad Oak *Dors* 84 C1
Broad Oak *E Ssx* 89 G2
Broad Oak *E Ssx* 90 A2
Broad Oak *Herefs* 109 F3
Broad Oak *Kent* 103 E2
Broad's Green 115 F3
Broadstairs 103 G2
Broadstone *Poole* 75 F4
Broadstone *Shrops* 133 E2
Broad Street 102 B1
Broadstreet Common 95 E4
Broad Street Green 115 H2
Broad Town 97 E3
Broadwas 122 C3
Broadwater 78 C5
Broadway *Carm* 106 B2
Broadway *Carm* 106 C2
Broadway *Sflk* 140 D1
Broadway *Som* 83 F2
Broadway *Wex* 237 G4
Broadway *Worcs* 111 E5
Broadwell *Glos* 109 G2
Broadwell *Glos* 111 F4
Broadwell *Oxon* 111 G2
Broadwell *Warks* 124 C4
Broadwey 74 C2
Broadwindsor 73 H4
Broadwoodkelly 71 G5
Broadwoodwidger 71 E3
Brobury 121 F2
Brochel 222 D3
Brochloch 193 E3
Brochroy 210 D4
Brockbridge 86 D2
Brockdish 140 B1
Brockenhurst 76 A4
Brocketsbrae 199 H3
Brockford Street 128 D4
Brockhall 124 D4
Brockham 88 B5
Brockhampton *Glos* 110 D4
Brockhampton *Herefs* 109 G5
Brock Hill 101 H5
Brockholes 168 C2
Brocklesby 171 E2
Brockley 95 F2
Brockley Corner 128 A5
Brockley Green 128 A3
Brockton *Shrops* 132 C2
Brockton *Shrops* 132 C4
Brockton *Shrops* 133 F3
Brockton *Shrops* 133 G4
Brockweir 109 G1
Brockworth 110 C3
Brocton 147 E1
Brodick 230 C1
Brodsworth 169 G1
Brogaig 222 C5
Brogborough 113 F5
Broken Cross *Ches* 159 F2
Broken Cross *Ches* 159 H2
Brokenborough 96 D4
Bromborough 158 C3
Brome 128 D5
Brome Street 129 E5
Bromeswell 129 F3
Bromfield *Cumb* 187 G3
Bromfield *Shrops* 133 E1
Bromham *Beds* 125 H3
Bromham *Wilts* 96 D2
Bromley 101 E2
Bromley Green 90 C4
Brompton *MT* 102 A2
Brompton *N Yorks* 177 E5
Brompton *N Yorks* 182 A2
Brompton Ralph 82 D3
Brompton Regis 82 C3
Brompton-on-Swale 181 G2
Bromsash 109 H4
Bromsberrow Heath 122 C1
Bromsgrove 123 E5
Bromyard 122 B3
Bromyard Downs 122 B3
Bronaber 143 G2
Brongest 118 D2
Bronington 145 G3
Bronllys 120 D1
Bronnant 119 G4
Bronwydd Arms 106 C4
Bronydd 121 E2
Bronygarth 145 E3
Brook *Carm* 106 B2
Brook *Hants* 85 H1
Brook *Hants* 86 A3
Brook *IOW* 76 B3
Brook *Kent* 90 D4
Brook *Sry* 87 G4
Brook Street *Esx* 101 F5
Brook Street *W Ssx* 88 D3
Brooke *Nflk* 140 C3
Brooke *Rut* 136 C4
Brookeborough 244 B5
Brookenby 163 G4
Brookfield 205 G1
Brookhouse *Ches* 160 A2
Brookhouse *Lancs* 173 F3
Brookhouse Green 146 C5
Brookland 90 C3
Brooklands 193 H1
Brookmans Park 114 B2
Brooks 132 A3
Brooks Green 88 B3
Brookthorpe 110 B3
Brookville 139 E3
Brookwood 99 G1
Broom *Beds* 126 B2
Broom *Warks* 123 F3
Broom Hill 75 F4
Broom of Dalreoch 213 F2
Broombrae 226 C1
Broome *Nflk* 140 D3
Broome *Shrops* 132 D2
Broome *Worcs* 134 B1
Broome Park 197 F5
Broomedge 159 F3
Broomer's Corner 88 B2
Broomfield *Aber* 227 F2
Broomfield *Esx* 115 F2
Broomfield *Kent* 102 B1
Broomfield *Kent* 103 E2
Broomfield *Som* 83 E3
Broomfleet 170 C3
Broomhill 197 H4
Brooms Green 122 C1
Brora 229 F2
Broseley 133 G4
Brosna *Kerry* 235 E5
Brosna *Ofly* 240 A3
Brotherhill 105 G2
Brothertoft 150 C4
Brotherton 169 F3
Brotton 182 D4
Broubster 229 G5
Brough *Cumb* 180 B3
Brough *Derbs* 160 D3
Brough *E R of Yorks* 170 C3
Brough *Hghld* 229 G5
Brough *Notts* 149 F5
Brough *Shet* 233 F2
Brough *Shet* 233 G3
Brough Sowerby 180 B3
Broughal 240 A4
Broughall 145 H3
Broughshane 248 A3
Broughton *Bdrs* 200 C3
Broughton *Cambs* 126 C5
Broughton *Flint* 158 B1
Broughton *Hants* 86 A3
Broughton *Lancs* 166 D4
Broughton *MK* 113 E5
Broughton *N Lincs* 170 D1
Broughton *Northants* 136 C1
Broughton *N Yorks* 174 C2
Broughton *N Yorks* 176 D4
Broughton *Ork* 232 B5
Broughton *Oxon* 124 B1
Broughton *Salf* 159 G5
Broughton *V of G* 93 H3
Broughton Astley 135 H3
Broughton Beck 172 D5
Broughton Gifford 96 C2
Broughton Hackett 123 E3
Broughton in Furness 178 D1
Broughton Mills 178 D1
Broughton Moor 187 F1
Broughton Poggs 111 F2
Broughtown 232 C5
Broughty Ferry 214 C4
Browland 233 E2
Brown Candover 86 D4
Brown Edge *Lancs* 166 C2
Brown Edge *Staffs* 146 D4
Brownhill *Aber* 226 D3
Brownhill *Aber* 227 E3
Brownhill *Bburn* 167 F4
Brownhills *Fife* 214 D2
Brownhills *Wals* 134 C4
Brownieside 203 F1
Browninghill Green 98 C1
Brownlow Heath 146 C5
Brownmuir 221 F3
Brownston 69 E3
Brownstown *Kild* 240 D4
Brownstown *Wat* 237 E4
Browsburn 206 C1
Brow Top 173 F2
Broxa 183 F1
Broxbourne 114 C2
Broxburn *E Loth* 209 E3
Broxburn *W Loth* 207 F2
Broxholme 162 D2
Broxted 115 E4
Broxton 145 G4
Broxwood 121 G3
Broyle Side 89 E1
Brù 231 G5
Bruachmary 225 F3
Bruairnis 231 E1
Bruan 229 H4
Bruera 145 G5
Bruern Abbey 111 G3
Bruff 239 F1
Bruichladdich 230 A2
Bruisyard 129 F4
Brumby 170 C1
Brund 147 F5
Brundall 140 C4
Brundish 129 F4
Brundish Street 129 F5
Bruntingthorpe 136 A3
Brunton *Fife* 214 B3
Brunton *Northld* 203 G1
Brunton *Wilts* 97 G1
Bruray 233 G3
Bruree 235 G5
Brushford *Devon* 81 G1
Brushford *Som* 82 B3
Bruton 84 B3
Bryansford 245 F4
Bryanston 75 E5
Brydekirk 187 G5
Brymbo 145 E4
Bryn *Carm* 107 E1
Bryn *Ches* 159 E2
Bryn *N & PT* 93 G5
Bryn *Shrops* 132 C2
Bryn *Wig* 159 E5
Brynamman 107 F3
Brynberian 118 B1
Bryncae 94 A4
Bryncethin 93 H4
Bryncir 143 E3
Bryn-coch 107 F1
Bryncroes 142 B2
Bryncrug 130 D4
Bryn Du 155 G2
Bryneglwys 144 D4
Brynford 157 H2
Bryn Gates 159 E5
Bryn Glas 143 F3
Bryn Golau 94 B4
Bryngwran 155 G2
Bryngwyn *Cere* 118 C2
Bryngwyn *Mon* 109 E2
Bryngwyn *Pemb* 105 E4
Bryngwyn *Pwys* 121 E2
Bryn-henllan 105 G5
Brynhoffnant 118 D3
Brynithel 108 D1
Bryn Iwan 106 B4
Brynmawr 108 C3
Brynmenyn 93 H4
Brynna 94 A4
Brynnay Gwynion 94 A4
Brynrefail 156 A3
Bryn Rhyd-yr-Arian 157 F1
Brynsadler 94 B4
Bryn Saith Marchog 144 C4
Brynsiencyn 156 A1
Brynteg *Anglsy* 156 A3
Brynteg *Wrex* 145 F4
Bryn-y-maen 156 D2
Buaile na h-Ochd 231 G5
Buaile nam Bodach 231 E1
Bualintur 222 C2
Bualnaluib 228 A1
Bubbenhall 135 F1
Bubwith 170 A4
Buccleuch 195 F5
Buchanan Smithy 205 G4
Buchanty 213 E3
Buchlyvie 206 A4
Buckabank 188 A3
Buckden *Cambs* 126 B4
Buckden *N Yorks* 174 C4
Buckenham 140 D4
Buckerell 73 E4
Buckfast 69 E4
Buckfastleigh 69 E4
Buckhaven 208 B5
Buckholm 201 G3
Buckhorn Weston 84 C2
Buckhurst Hill 101 E5
Buckie 226 B5
Buckies 229 G5
Buckingham 125 E1
Buckland *Bucks* 113 E3
Buckland *Devon* 69 E2
Buckland *Glos* 111 E5
Buckland *Herts* 126 D1
Buckland *Kent* 91 F4
Buckland *Oxon* 97 H5
Buckland *Sry* 88 C5
Buckland Brewer 81 E2
Buckland Common 113 F2
Buckland Dinham 84 C5
Buckland Filleigh 81 E1
Buckland in the Moor 69 E5
Buckland Monachorum 71 F1
Buckland Newton 74 C5
Buckland St Mary 83 F1
Bucklebury 98 C3
Bucklerheads 214 C4
Bucklers Hard 76 C4
Bucklesham 129 E2
Buckley 158 B1
Bucklow Hill 159 F3
Buckminster 149 F1
Buckna 248 B3
Bucknall *C of Stoke* 146 D4
Bucknall *Lincs* 163 G1
Bucknell *Oxon* 112 B4
Bucknell *Shrops* 132 D1
Bucksburn 227 F1
Buck's Cross 80 D2
Bucks Green 88 A3
Bucks Hill 113 G1
Bucks Horn Oak 87 F4
Buck's Mills 80 D2
Buckspool 105 F1
Buckton *E R of Yorks* 177 H4
Buckton *Herefs* 132 D1
Buckton *Northld* 203 E3
Buckton Vale 160 B5
Buckworth 137 F1
Budbrooke 123 H4
Budby 162 A2
Bude 70 C5
Budlake 72 C4
Budle 203 F3
Budleigh Salterton 72 D2
Budock Water 65 E3
Buerton 146 B3
Bugbrooke 125 E3
Bugle 67 F3
Bugthorpe 176 D2
Buildwas 133 F4
Builth Road 120 C3
Builth Wells 120 C3
Bulby 149 H2
Buldoo 229 F5
Bulford 85 G4
Bulford Camp 85 G4
Bulgaden 235 G5
Bulkeley 145 H4
Bulkington *Warks* 135 F2
Bulkington *Wilts* 96 D1
Bulkworthy 80 D1
Bullaun 239 F4
Bullbridge 148 A4
Bulley 110 B3
Bullpot Farm 173 H5
Bull's Green 114 B3
Bullwood 204 D2
Bulmer *Esx* 128 A2
Bulmer *N Yorks* 176 C3
Bulmer *Tye* 115 G5
Bulphan 101 G4
Bulverhythe 90 A1
Bulwell 148 C3
Bulwick 137 E3
Bumble's Green 114 C2
Bun a Mhuillinn 231 E1
Bunacaimb 217 F4
Bunacurry 242 B3
Bunarkaig 218 B4
Bunbeg 246 C4
Bunbrosna 244 B1
Bunbury 145 H5
Bunclody 241 E2
Buncrana 247 E4
Bundalloch 223 F2
Bundoran 246 C1
Bunessan 230 B4
Bungay 140 C2
Bunker's Hill 150 C4
Bunlahy 244 B2
Bunlarie 230 C1
Bunloit 224 C2
Bun Loyne 218 B5
Bunmahon 236 D4
Bunnahabhain 230 B2
Bunnanaddan 243 F4
Bunny 148 C2
Bunnyconnellan 243 E4
Bunratty 239 F2
Buntait 224 B2
Buntingford 114 C4
Bunwell 140 A3
Bunwell Hill 140 A3
Burbage *Derbs* 160 B2
Burbage *Leics* 135 G3
Burbage *Wilts* 97 G2
Burchett's Green 99 F4
Burcombe 85 F3
Burcot 98 C5
Burcott 113 E4
Burdale 177 E3
Burdrop 124 B1
Bures 128 B1
Bures Green 128 B1
Burford *Oxon* 111 G2
Burford *Shrops* 122 A4
Burg 216 D1
Burgate 128 D5
Burgess Hill 88 D2
Burgh *A & B* 230 B4
Burgh *Sflk* 129 E3
Burgh by Sands 188 A4
Burgh Castle 141 E4
Burghclere 98 B2
Burghead 225 G5
Burghfield 98 D2
Burghfield Common 98 D2
Burghfield Hill 98 D2

525

BURGH HEATH–CAREBY

Burgh Heath 100 C1
Burghill 121 H2
Burgh le Marsh 164 C1
Burgh next Aylsham 153 E2
Burgh on Bain 163 G3
Burgh St Peter 141 E3
Burghwallis 169 G2
Burham 101 H2
Buriton 87 E2
Burland 146 A4
Burlawn 67 E5
Burlescombe 82 D2
Burleston 74 D4
Burley *Hants* 75 H4
Burley *Rut* 136 D5
Burleydam 146 A3
Burley Gate 122 A2
Burley in Wharfedale 175 E1
Burley Street 75 H5
Burlingjobb 121 F3
Burlow 89 F2
Burlton 145 G2
Burmarsh 90 D3
Burmington 111 G5
Burn 169 G3
Burnage 159 H4
Burnaston 147 H2
Burnby 176 D1
Burnchurch 240 C1
Burncourt 236 B5
Burnend 227 E3
Burneside 179 G2
Burness 232 C5
Burneston 175 G5
Burnett 96 A2
Burnfoot *Bdrs* 195 G5
Burnfoot *Bdrs* 195 H5
Burnfoot *Dngl* 247 E4
Burnfoot *P & K* 213 F1
Burnfort 235 G4
Burnham *Bucks* 99 G4
Burnham *N Lincs* 171 E2
Burnham Deepdale 151 H3
Burnham Green 114 B3
Burnham Market 152 A3
Burnham Norton 152 A3
Burnham-on-Crouch 102 C5
Burnham-on-Sea 83 F5
Burnham Overy Staithe 152 A3
Burnham Overy Town 152 A3
Burnham Thorpe 152 A3
Burnhead *D & G* 194 A3
Burnhead *D & G* 194 B2
Burnhervie 226 D2
Burnhill Green 133 H4
Burnhope 190 B3
Burnhouse 198 C4
Burniston 183 G1
Burnley 167 H4
Burnmouth 202 D5
Burn of Aultmore 226 B4
Burn of Cambus 212 C1
Burnopfield 190 B4
Burnsall 174 D3
Burn's Green 114 B4
Burnside *Aber* 227 E3
Burnside *Angus* 220 C2
Burnside *Angus* 220 D1
Burnside *E Ayr* 193 F5
Burnside *P & K* 213 H1
Burnside *Shet* 233 E4
Burnside *W Loth* 207 F2
Burnside of Duntrune 214 C4
Burnswark 194 D1
Burntcliff Top 160 B1
Burntcommon 99 H1
Burnt Houses 181 F4
Burntisland 207 H4
Burnton 198 D1
Burntwood 134 C4
Burnt Yates 175 F3
Burpham *Sry* 99 H1
Burpham *W Ssx* 78 A5
Burradon *Nthld* 197 E4
Burradon *N Tyne* 190 C5
Burrafirth 233 G5
Burraland *Shet* 233 E2
Burraland *Shet* 233 F4
Burras 64 D3
Burraton 71 E1
Burravoe *Shet* 233 F3
Burravoe *Shet* 233 F4
Burray Village 232 B3
Burrells 180 A4
Burrelton 213 H4
Burren *Clare* 239 E4
Burren *Down* 245 F4
Burridge 76 D5
Burrill 175 F5
Burringham 170 B1
Burrington *Devon* 81 G2
Burrington *Herefs* 132 D1
Burrington *N Som* 95 F1
Burrough Green 127 G3
Burrough on the Hill 136 C5
Burrowbridge 83 G3
Burrowhill 99 G2
Burry Green 92 C5
Burry Port 106 C1
Burscough 166 C2
Burscough Bridge 166 C2
Bursea 170 B4
Burshill 177 G1
Bursledon 76 C5
Burslem 146 D4
Burstall 128 D2
Burstallhill 128 D2
Burstock 73 H4
Burston *Nflk* 140 A2
Burston *Staffs* 146 D2
Burstow 88 D4
Burstwick 171 F3
Burtersett 180 C1
Burthorpe 127 H4
Burtle 83 G4
Burton *Ches* 158 B2
Burton *Ches* 158 D1
Burton *Dors* 74 C3
Burton *Dors* 75 H4
Burton *Lincs* 163 E2
Burton *Nthld* 203 F2
Burton *Pemb* 105 F2
Burton *Som* 83 E4
Burton *Wilts* 96 C3
Burton *Wrex* 145 F5
Burton Agnes 177 G3
Burton Bradstock 74 A3
Burton Fleming 177 G4
Burton Green Warks 135 E1
Burton Green *Wrex* 145 F5
Burton Hastings 135 G3
Burton-in-Kendal 173 F4
Burton in Lonsdale 173 H4
Burton Joyce 148 D3
Burton Latimer 136 D1
Burton Lazars 136 C5
Burton-le-Coggles 149 G2
Burton Leonard 175 G3
Burton on the Wolds 148 C1
Burton Overy 136 B3
Burton Pedwardine 150 A3
Burton Pidsea 171 F4
Burtonport 246 B3
Burton Salmon 169 F3
Burton upon Stather 170 C2
Burton upon Trent 147 G1
Burtonwood 159 E4
Burwardsley 145 H5
Burwarton 133 F2
Burwash 89 G2
Burwash Common 89 G2
Burwash Weald 89 G2
Burwell *Cambs* 127 F4
Burwell *Lincs* 164 B2
Burwen 155 H4
Burwick 232 B2
Bury *Bury* 167 G2
Bury *Cambs* 137 H2
Bury *Som* 82 B3
Bury *W Ssx* 87 H1
Bury Green 114 D3
Bury St Edmunds 128 B4
Burythorpe 176 D3
Busbridge 87 H4
Busby *E Ren* 199 E5
Busby *P & K* 213 F3
Buscot 111 F1
Bush Bank 121 H3
Bushbury 134 B4
Bush Crathie 220 B4
Bushey 100 B5
Bush Green 140 B2
Bushey Heath 100 B5
Bushley 122 D1
Bushmills 247 H4
Bushton 97 E3
Busta 233 F3
Butchers Cross 89 F3
Butcombe 95 G2
Butleigh 83 H3
Butleigh Wootton 83 H4
Butlers Bridge 244 B4
Butlers Cross 113 E2
Butlers Marston 124 A2
Butlerstown 235 G1
Butley 129 G3
Butsfield 190 A3
Butt Green 146 B4
Butterburn 196 B1
Buttercrambe 176 C2
Butterknowle 181 F5
Butterleigh 72 C5
Butterley 148 B4
Buttermere *Cumb* 178 D4
Buttermere *Wilts* 98 A2
Buttershaw 168 C3
Butterstone 213 G5
Butterton 147 F5
Butterwick *Lincs* 150 D4
Butterwick *N Yorks* 176 C4
Butterwick *N Yorks* 177 F4
Buttevant 235 G4
Buttington 132 C4
Buttonoak 122 C5
Butt's Green 86 A3
Buxhall 128 C3
Buxted 89 E2
Buxton *Derbs* 160 C2
Buxton *Nflk* 153 E1
Bwlch 108 C4
Bwlch-derwin 143 E4
Bwlchgwyn 145 E4
Bwlch-Llan 119 F3
Bwlchnewydd 106 C4
Bwlchtocyn 142 C2
Bwlch-y-cibau 144 D1
Bwlchyddar 144 D1
Bwlch-y-fadfa 119 E2
Bwlch-y-ffridd 131 H3
Bwlchygroes 118 C1
Bwlch-y-sarnau 120 C5
Byers Green 190 B1
Byfield 124 C3
Byfleet 100 A2
Byford 121 G2
Bygrave 126 C1
Byker 190 C4
Bylane End 68 A3
Bylchau 157 F1
Byley 159 F1
Byrness 196 C4
Bythorn 137 F1
Byton 121 G4
Byworth 87 H2

C

Cabharstadh 231 G4
Cabourne 163 F5
Cabrach *A & B* 230 B2
Cabrach *Moray* 226 B2
Cacrabank 201 E1
Cadamstown *Kild* 240 D5
Cadamstown *Offy* 240 B4
Cadbury 72 C5
Cadbury Barton 81 G2
Cadder 206 B2
Caddington 113 G3
Caddonfoot 201 G2
Caddy 248 A2
Cadeby *Donc* 161 G5
Cadeby *Leics* 135 G4
Cadeleigh 72 C5
Cade Street 89 G2
Cadgwith 65 E1
Cadham 214 A1
Cadishead 159 F4
Cadle 93 E5
Cadley 97 G2
Cadmore End 99 E5
Cadnam 86 A1
Cadney 170 D1
Cadole 145 E5
Caeathro 143 E5
Caehopkin 107 G3
Caenby Corner 163 E3
Caerau *Brid* 93 G5
Caerau *Crdff* 94 C3
Caerdeon 143 F1
Caerfarchell 104 D4
Caergeiliog 155 G2
Caergwrle 145 F5
Caerhun 156 D2
Caer-Lan 107 G3
Caerleon 95 E5
Caer Llan 109 F2
Caernarfon 156 A1
Caerphilly 94 C4
Caersws 131 H3
Caerwent 95 F5
Caerwys 157 G2
Caethle 130 D3
Caheny 247 G3
Caher *Clare* 239 F3
Caher *Tipp* 236 C5
Caherconlish 239 G1
Caherdaniel 234 C2
Cahersiveen 234 B3
Caim 217 E2
Caio 107 F5
Cairinis 231 E3
Cairminis 231 F3
Cairnargat 226 B3
Cairnbaan 204 A4
Cairnborrow 226 B3
Cairnbrogie 227 E2
Cairncross *Angus* 220 D3
Cairncross *Bdrs* 209 G1
Cairndow 211 F2
Cairness 227 G5
Cairneyhill 207 F4
Cairngaan 184 D1
Cairngarroch 184 C3
Cairnhill *Aber* 226 D2
Cairnhill *Aber* 227 F2
Cairnie 226 C3
Cairnorrie 227 E3
Cairnpark 227 F1
Cairnryan 184 C5
Caisteal Ormacleit 231 E2
Caister-on-Sea 141 E5
Caistor 163 F5
Caistor St Edmund 140 B4
Caistron 197 E4
Calanais 231 F4
Calbourne 76 C3
Calceby 164 B2
Calcot *Glos* 111 E2
Calcot *W Berks* 98 D3
Caldarvan 205 G4
Caldback 233 G5
Caldbeck 187 H2
Caldbergh 174 D5
Caldecote *Cambs* 126 D3
Caldecote *Cambs* 137 F2
Caldecote *Herts* 126 C1
Caldecote *Warks* 135 F3
Caldecott *Northants* 125 H4
Caldecott *Rut* 136 D3
Calderbank 206 C1
Calder Bridge 178 B3
Calderbrook 168 A2
Caldercruix 206 D2
Calder Mains 229 G5
Caldermill 199 F3
Calder Vale 166 D5
Caldhame 220 D1
Caldicot 95 F4
Caldwell *Derbs* 135 E5
Caldwell *N Yorks* 181 F3
Caldy 158 A3
Caledon 244 D5
Caledrhydiau 119 E3
Calfsound 232 C5
Calgary 216 D1
Calgow 185 G5
Califer 225 G4
California *Falk* 207 E3
California *Nflk* 141 E5
Calke 148 A1
Callaghansmills 239 F3
Callakille 223 E4
Callaly 197 F4
Callan 240 B1
Callander 212 B1
Callestick 65 E5
Calligarry 217 E5
Callington 71 E1
Callow *Herefs* 109 F5
Callow *Mayo* 243 E3
Callow *Rosc* 243 G3
Callow End 122 D2
Callow Hill *Wilts* 97 E4
Callow Hill *Worcs* 122 C5
Callow Marsh 122 B2
Calmore 86 A1
Calmsden 110 D2
Calne 96 D3
Calow 161 F2
Calshot 76 C4
Calstock 71 E1
Calstone Wellington 97 E2
Calthorpe 152 D2
Calthwaite 188 B2
Calton *N Yorks* 174 C2
Calton *Staffs* 147 F4
Caltra 239 G5
Calveley 146 A5
Calver 160 D2
Calverhall 146 A3
Calver Hill 121 G2
Calverleigh 82 B1
Calverley 168 D4
Calverstown 240 D4
Calvert 112 C4
Calverton *MK* 112 D5
Calverton *Notts* 148 D4
Calvine 219 F2
Calvo 187 F3
Cam 110 B1
Camas-luinie 223 G2
Camasnacroise 217 G1
Camastianavaig 222 C3
Camault Muir 224 C3
Camb 233 F4
Camber 90 C2
Camberley 99 F2
Camberwell 100 D3
Camblesforth 169 H3
Cambo 197 E2
Cambois 197 H2
Camborne 64 D4
Cambourne 126 D4
Cambridge *Cambs* 127 E3
Cambridge *Glos* 110 B2
Cambus 206 D4
Cambusbarron 206 C4
Cambuskenneth 206 D4
Cambuslang 199 F5
Camden Town 100 C4
Camelford 70 B2
Camelon 206 D3
Camelsdale 87 G3
Camer 101 G2
Camerory 225 G2
Camers Green 122 C1
Camerton *B & NE Som* 96 A1
Camerton *Cumb* 187 E1
Camghouran 218 D1
Camlough 245 F4
Cammachmore 221 G4
Cammeringham 162 D3
Camolin 241 E1
Campbelton 198 A4
Campbeltown 230 C1
Campile 237 E5
Cample 194 A3
Campmuir 213 H4
Campsall 169 G2
Campsea Ashe 129 F3
Camps End 127 G2
Camps Heath 141 E3
Campton 126 B1
Camptown 196 B5
Camrose 105 F3
Camross 240 B3
Camserney 219 F1
Camus Croise 223 E1
Camusnagaul *Hghld* 218 A3
Camusnagaul *Hghld* 228 B1
Camusteel 223 E3
Camusterrach 223 E3
Camusvrachan 219 E1
Canada 86 A2
Canal Foot 172 D4
Candacraig 220 C4
Candlesby 164 C1
Candle Street 128 C5
Candy Mill 200 C3
Cane End 98 D3
Canewdon 102 C5
Canford Magna 75 F4
Canisbay 229 H5
Cann 84 D2
Cannards Grave 84 B4
Cann Common 84 D2
Cannich 224 B2
Canningstown 244 C3
Cannington 83 F4
Cannock 134 B5
Cannock Wood 134 C5
Canonbie 195 F1
Canon Bridge 121 G2
Canon Frome 122 B2
Canon Pyon 121 H2
Canons Ashby 124 D3
Canon's Town 64 C3
Canterbury 103 E1
Cantley *Donc* 162 A5
Cantley *Nflk* 140 D4
Cantlop 133 E4
Canton 94 C3
Cantraybruich 225 E3
Cantraydoune 225 E3
Cantraywood 225 E4
Cantsfield 173 G4
Canvey Island 102 A4
Canwick 163 E1
Canworthy Water 70 C3
Caol 218 A3
Caolas *A & B* 216 A1
Caolas *W Is* 231 E1
Caolas Scalpaigh 231 F4
Caolas Stocinis 231 F3
Caolasnacon 218 B2
Caol Ila 230 B2
Cape Castle 248 A4
Capel *Bangor* 130 D2
Capel *Kent* 89 G4
Capel *Sry* 88 B4
Capel Betws Lleucu 119 G3
Capel Carmel 142 B2
Capel Coch 155 H3
Capel Curig 143 G5
Capel Cynon 118 D2
Capel Dewi Cere 119 E2
Capel Dewi Cere 130 D2
Capel Dewi 106 D3
Capel Garmon 143 H5
Capel Gwyn *Anglsy* 155 G2
Capel Gwyn 106 D4
Capel Gwynfe 107 F3
Capel Hendre 107 E2
Capel Isaac 107 E4
Capel Iwan 118 C1
Capel Llanilltern 94 B4
Capel Parc 155 H3
Capel Seion 130 D1
Capel St Andrew 129 G2
Capel St Mary 128 D1
Capel Tygwydd 118 C2
Capel Uchaf 142 D4
Capelulo 156 C2
Capel-y-ffin 108 D4
Capenhurst 158 C2
Capernwray 173 F4
Capheaton 197 E2
Cappagh *Lim* 239 E1
Cappagh *Tyr* 247 G1
Cappagh White 239 G1
Cappalinnan 240 B2
Cappamore 239 G1
Cappataggle 239 G5
Cappeen 235 F2
Cappercleuch 200 D1
Cappoquin 236 C4
Capstone 102 A2
Capton 69 F3
Caputh 213 G4
Carbellow 199 F1
Carbis Bay 64 C3
Carbost *Hghld* 222 B2
Carbost *Hghld* 222 C4
Carbrooke 139 G4
Carburton 162 A2
Carbury 240 D5
Carcary 221 E1
Carclew 65 E3
Carco 193 H5
Car Colston 149 E3
Carcroft 169 G1
Cardenden 207 H5
Cardeston 132 D5
Cardiff 94 C3
Cardigan 118 B2
Cardington *Beds* 126 A2
Cardington *Shrops* 133 E3
Cardinham 70 B1
Cardow 225 H3
Cardrona 201 E3
Cardross 205 F3
Cardurnock 187 G4
Careby 137 E5

GAZETTEER

Coppenhall 146 D1
Copperhouse 64 C3
Coppingford 137 G2
Copplestone 72 A4
Coppull 167 E2
Copsale 88 B2
Copster Green 167 F4
Copston Magna 135 G2
Copt Heath 134 D1
Copt Hewick 175 G4
Copthorne 88 D4
Copt Oak 135 G5
Copy Lake 81 G1
Copythorne 86 A1
Coralstown 244 C1
Corbally *Clare* 238 C2
Corbally *Sligo* 243 E4
Corbay Upper 244 B2
Corbet Milltown 245 F5
Corbridge 189 G4
Corby 136 D2
Corby Glen 149 H1
Corclogh 242 B5
Cordal 235 E4
Coreley 133 F1
Corfe 83 E2
Corfe Castle 75 F2
Corfe Mullen 75 F4
Corfton 133 E2
Corgarff 220 B5
Corhampton 86 D2
Cork 235 G3
Corkey 248 A4
Corlae 193 G3
Corlea 244 A1
Corlee 243 E3
Corley 135 F2
Corley Ash 135 G2
Corley Moor 135 E2
Cornaa 154 D3
Cornabus 230 B2
Cornafulla 239 H5
Cornaigbeg 216 A1
Corney 178 C1
Cornforth 190 C1
Cornhill 226 C4
Cornhill on Tweed 202 C3
Cornholme 167 H3
Cornish Hall End 115 F5
Cornriggs 189 F2
Cornsay 190 A2
Corntown 224 C4
Cornwell 111 G4
Cornwood 68 D3
Cornworthy 69 F3
Corpach 218 A3
Corpusty 152 D2
Corran *Hghld* 217 H2
Corran *Hghld* 223 F1
Corranbuie 204 A2
Corrany 154 D3
Corravachie 228 D1
Corrie 230 C2
Corrie Common 195 E2
Corriedoo 193 G2
Corriemoillie 224 B3
Corrievorrie 225 E2
Corrimony 224 C4
Corringham *Lincs* 162 D4
Corringham *Thurr* 101 H4
Corris 131 E4
Corris Uchaf 131 E4
Corrofin *Clare* 239 E3
Corrofin *Gal* 239 F5
Corrour Station 218 C2
Corrow 204 D5
Corry 222 D2
Corrykinloch 228 D3
Corrymuckloch 213 E4
Corrynachenchy 230 B4
Corry of Ardnagrask 224 C4
Corscombe 74 A5
Corse *Aber* 226 C3
Corse *Glos* 110 B4
Corsebank 193 H5
Corse Lawn 110 B4
Corsewall 184 C5
Corsham 96 C3
Corsindae 221 E5
Corsley 84 D5
Corsley Heath 84 D5
Corsock 193 H1
Corston *B & NF Som* 96 A2
Corston *Wilts* 96 D4

Corstorphine 207 H2
Cortachy 220 C2
Corton *Sfk* 141 E3
Corton *Wilts* 85 E4
Corton Denham 84 B2
Corunna 231 E3
Corwen 144 C3
Cosby 135 H3
Cosford 135 G1
Cosgrove 125 F2
Cosham 77 E5
Cosheston 105 G2
Cossall 148 B3
Cosses 192 A2
Cossington *Leics* 136 A5
Cossington *Som* 83 G4
Costa 232 B4
Costessey 140 B5
Costock 148 C2
Coston *Leics* 149 F1
Coston *Nflk* 139 H4
Cote 111 H2
Cotebrook 159 E1
Cotegill 180 A2
Cotehill 188 B3
Cotes *Leics* 148 C1
Cotes *Staffs* 146 C2
Cotesbach 135 H2
Cotgrave 148 D3
Cothall *Aber* 227 E1
Cothall *Moray* 225 H5
Cotham 149 E4
Cothelstone 83 E3
Cothercott 132 D4
Cotherstone 181 E4
Cothill 112 A1
Cotleigh 73 F4
Coton *Cambs* 127 F3
Coton *Northants* 125 E5
Coton *Staffs* 147 E2
Coton Clanford 146 D1
Coton in the Elms 135 E5
Cott 69 F4
Cottam *Lancs* 166 D4
Cottam *Notts* 162 C2
Cottartown 225 G2
Cottenham 127 F4
Cotterdale 180 C1
Cottered 114 B4
Cotterstock 137 E3
Cottesbrooke 125 E5
Cottesmore 136 D5
Cottingham *E R of Yorks* 171 E4
Cottingham *Northants* 136 C3
Cottingley 168 C4
Cottisford 112 B4
Cotton *Sfk* 128 D4
Cotton *Staffs* 147 F4
Cotton End 126 A2
Cotton Stones 168 B3
Cottown *Aber* 226 C2
Cottown *Aber* 227 E1
Cottown *Aber* 227 B2
Cottown *P & K* 213 H3
Cotwalton 146 D2
Couchs Mill 67 G3
Coughton *Herefs* 109 G3
Coughton *Warks* 123 F4
Coulaghailtro 230 C2
Coulags 223 G3
Coulby Newham 182 B3
Coulderton 178 B3
Coull 220 D5
Coulport 205 E4
Coulsdon 100 C1
Coulston 96 D1
Coulter 200 B2
Coultershaw Bridge 87 H2
Coultings 83 E4
Coulton 176 B4
Coultra 214 B3
Cound 133 F4
Coundon 190 B1
Coundon Grange 181 G5
Countersett 180 D1
Countess Cross 115 H4
Countess Wear 72 C3
Countesthorpe 136 A3
Countisbury 81 H5
Coupar Angus 213 H5

Coupland 202 D2
Cour 230 C2
Court *Herefs* 121 G2
Court *Pwys* 120 D1
Court-at-Street 90 D4
Courteenhall 125 F3
Court Henry 107 E4
Courtmacsherry 235 G1
Courtown 241 F2
Courtsend 102 D5
Courtway 83 E3
Cousland 208 B2
Cousley Wood 89 G3
Coustonn 204 C2
Cove *A & B* 205 E3
Cove *Devon* 82 C2
Cove *Hants* 99 F1
Cove *Hghld* 228 A1
Cove Bay 221 G5
Covehithe 141 E2
Coven 134 B4
Coveney 138 B2
Covenham St Bartholomew 164 A4
Covenham St Mary 164 A4
Coventry 135 F1
Coverack 65 E1
Coverham 175 E5
Covesea 225 H5
Covington *Cambs* 126 A5
Covington *S Lan* 200 B3
Cowan Bridge 173 G4
Cowbeech 89 G1
Cowbit 150 C1
Cowbridge 94 A3
Cowden 89 E4
Cowdenbeath 207 G4
Cowers Lane 147 H4
Cowes 76 C4
Cowesby 182 B1
Cowfold 88 C2
Cowgill 180 B1
Cowie *Aber* 221 F4
Cowie *Stir* 206 D4
Cowley *Devon* 72 C4
Cowley *Glos* 110 D3
Cowley *Hilln* 100 A4
Cowley *Oxon* 112 B2
Cowling *N Yorks* 174 C1
Cowling *N Yorks* 175 F5
Cowlinge 127 H3
Cowpen 197 H1
Cowpen Bewley 182 B4
Cowplain 87 E1
Cowshill 189 F2
Cowstrandburn 207 F4
Cowthorpe 175 H2
Coxbank 146 B3
Coxbench 148 A3
Cox Common 140 D2
Coxford 152 A2
Coxheath 89 H5
Coxhoe 190 C2
Coxley 84 A4
Coxtie Green 115 E1
Coxwold 176 A4
Coychurch 94 A3
Coylton 198 D1
Coylumbridge 225 F1
Coynach 220 C5
Coynachie 226 C3
Coytrahen 93 G4
Craanford 241 E2
Crabbet Park 88 D4
Crabbs Cross 123 F4
Crabtree 88 C3
Crabtree Green 145 F3
Crackenthorpe 180 A4
Crackington Haven 70 A4
Cracklebank 133 H5
Crackpot 180 D2
Cracoe 174 C3
Craddock 82 D1
Cradhlastadh 231 F4
Cradley 122 C2
Crafthole 68 B3
Cragabus 230 B2
Craggan *Hghld* 225 G2
Craggan *Moray* 225 H2
Craggie *Hghld* 225 E2
Craggie *Hghld* 229 F3
Cragg Vale 168 B3
Craghead 190 B3
Crai 107 H4
Craibstone 226 C4
Craichie 214 D5

Craichie Mill 214 D5
Craig *Aber* 227 F2
Craig *D & G* 186 B5
Craig *D & G* 193 G1
Craig *Hghld* 223 G4
Craig *S Ayr* 192 D4
Craig *Tyr* 247 F3
Craigavon 247 H1
Craig-cefn-parc 107 F2
Craigdallie 214 A3
Craigdam 227 E2
Craigdarroch *D & G* 193 G3
Craigdarroch *E Ayr* 193 F4
Craigearn 226 D1
Craigellachie 226 A3
Craigend 213 G3
Craigendive 204 C3
Craigendoran 205 F3
Craigends 205 G2
Craigenputtock 193 H2
Craigens *A & B* 230 B2
Craigens *E Ayr* 199 E1
Craigfad 192 D4
Craighall 220 A1
Craighat 205 G3
Craighead *Fife* 215 E1
Craighead *Hghld* 225 E5
Craighlaw Mains 185 F4
Craighouse 230 B2
Craighu 224 C3
Craigie *Aber* 227 F2
Craigie *P & K* 213 G5
Craigie *S Ayr* 198 D2
Craiglockhart 207 H2
Craiglug 221 F4
Craigmalloch 193 E3
Craigmaud 227 E4
Craigmillar 208 A2
Craignant 145 E2
Craigneuk *N Lan* 199 G5
Craigneuk *N Lan* 206 C2
Craignure 210 A4
Craigo 221 E2
Craigow 213 G1
Craigrothie 214 B2
Craigroy 225 H4
Craigruie 212 A2
Craigs 248 A3
Craigsimmie 214 B3
Craigton *Angus* 214 D4
Craigton *Angus* 220 C1
Craigton *C of Aber* 221 F5
Craigton *Hghld* 229 E2
Craigton *Stir* 206 B4
Craigtown 229 F4
Craig-y-nos 107 G3
Craik *Aber* 226 B2
Craik *Bdrs* 195 F4
Crail 215 E1
Crailing 202 A1
Crailinghall 202 A1
Crakehall 181 G1
Crakehill 175 H4
Crambe 176 C3
Cramlington 197 H1
Cramond 207 G3
Cramond Bridge 207 G3
Cranage 159 G1
Cranberry 146 C3
Cranborne 85 F1
Cranbourne 99 G3
Cranbrook 90 A4
Cranbrook Common 90 A4
Crane 241 E1
Cranfield 125 H2
Cranford *Devon* 80 D2
Cranford *Dngl* 246 D4
Cranford *Hours* 100 B3
Cranford St Andrew 136 D1
Cranford St John 136 D1
Cranham *Glos* 110 C3
Cranham *Haver* 101 F4
Crank 158 D4
Cranleigh 88 A4
Cranmore *IOW* 76 B3
Cranmore *Som* 84 B4
Cranna 226 D4
Crannoch 226 C4
Cranoe 136 C3
Cransford 129 F4
Cranshaws 209 E1
Cranstal 154 D5
Cranstoun Riddel 208 B2
Crantock 66 C4

Cranwell 149 H4
Cranwich 139 E3
Cranworth 139 G4
Craobh Haven 210 A1
Crapstone 68 C4
Crarae 204 B5
Craskins 220 D5
Crask of Aigas 224 C3
Craster 203 G1
Craswall 108 D5
Cratfield 129 F5
Crathes 221 F4
Crathie *Aber* 220 B4
Crathie *Hghld* 219 E4
Crathorne 182 A3
Craughwell 239 F4
Craven Arms 132 D2
Crawcrook 190 A4
Crawford *Lancs* 166 D1
Crawford *S Lan* 200 B1
Crawfordjohn 200 A1
Crawfordsburn 248 C2
Crawick 193 H5
Crawley *Hants* 86 B3
Crawley *Oxon* 111 G3
Crawley *W Ssx* 88 C4
Crawley Down 88 D4
Crawleyside 189 G2
Crawshawbooth 167 G3
Crawton 221 F3
Cray *N Yorks* 174 C4
Cray *P & K* 220 A2
Crayford 101 F3
Crayke 176 B4
Crays Hill 101 H5
Cray's Pond 98 D4
Crazy Corner 244 C1
Creacombe 82 A2
Creagan 210 C5
Creaganterve Mhòr 204 A5
Creagh 244 B5
Creag Ghoraidh 231 E2
Creaguaineach 210 A4
Creaton 125 E5
Creca 187 G5
Crecora 239 F1
Credenhill 121 H2
Crediton 72 B4
Creebank 192 D1
Creech Heathfield 83 F3
Creech St Michael 83 F3
Creed 67 E2
Creedy Park 72 B4
Creegh 238 D2
Creekmoor 75 F3
Creekmouth 101 E4
Creeslough 246 D4
Creeting St Mary 128 D3
Creeton 149 H1
Creetown 185 G4
Creeves 239 F1
Creggan *Arm* 245 E4
Creggan *Tyr* 247 F2
Cregganbaun 242 C2
Creggans 210 D1
Creggs 243 G1
Cregneash 154 A1
Cregrina 120 D3
Creich 214 B3
Creigiau 94 B4
Cremyll 68 C3
Creslow 113 E4
Cressage 133 F4
Cressbrook 160 D2
Cresselly 105 G2
Cressing 115 G5
Cresswell *Northld* 197 H3
Cresswell *Staffs* 147 E3
Cresswell Quay 105 G2
Creswell 161 G2
Cretingham 129 E4
Cretshengan 230 C2
Crewe 146 B5
Crewe-by-Farndon 145 G4
Crewgreen 132 C5
Crewe Hall 146 B4
Crewkerne 83 G1
Crianlarich 211 G3
Cribyn 119 F3
Criccieth 143 E3
Crich 148 A4
Crichie 227 F3
Crichton 207 F5
Crick *Mon* 95 F5
Crick *Northants* 124 D5
Crickadarn 120 D2

Cricket Malherbie 83 G1
Cricket St Thomas 83 G1
Crickheath 145 E1
Crickhowell 108 D3
Cricklade 97 F5
Cridling Stubbs 169 G3
Crieff 213 E3
Criggion 132 C5
Crigglestone 169 E2
Crilly 244 D5
Crimond 227 G4
Crimonmogate 227 G4
Crimplesham 138 D4
Crimscote 123 H2
Crinan *A & B* 230 C3
Crindle 247 F4
Cringleford 140 B4
Crinow 105 H3
Cripplesease 64 C3
Cripp's Corner 90 A2
Crix 115 G2
Croasdale 178 C4
Crock Street 83 F1
Crockenhill 101 F2
Crockernwell 72 A3
Crockerton 84 D4
Crocketford 186 C5
Crockets Town 243 E4
Crockey Hill 176 B3
Crockham Hill 89 E5
Crockhurst Street 89 G4
Crockleford Heath 116 B4
Croesau Bach 145 E2
Croeserw 93 G5
Croes-goch 105 E4
Croes-lan 118 D2
Croesor 143 F3
Croesyceiliog *Trfn* 109 E1
Croesyceiliog *Carm* 106 C3
Croes-y-mwyalch 95 E5

Croes y pant 109 E2
Croft *Herefs* 121 H4
Croft *Leics* 135 H3
Croft *Lincs* 151 E5
Croftamie 205 G4
Croftgarrow 212 C5
Croftinloan 219 G1
Crofton *Wfield* 169 E2
Crofton *Wilts* 97 G2
Croft-on-Tees 181 G3
Croft *Warr* 159 E4
Crofts of Benachielt 229 G4
Crofts of Haddo 227 E3
Crofty 106 D1
Croggan 210 A3
Croghan *Offly* 240 C5
Croghan *Rosc* 243 G3
Croglin 100 C3
Crogo Mains 193 H1
Croick 228 D1
Cromarty 225 E5
Crombie *Angus* 214 D4
Crombie *Fife* 207 F4
Cromblet 227 E3
Cromdale 225 G2
Cromer Hyde 114 A3
Cromer *Herts* 114 B4
Cromer *Nflk* 153 E3
Cromford 147 H5
Cromhall 96 A5
Cromhall Common 96 A4
Cromlin 244 A4
Cromor 231 G5
Cromwell 149 E5
Cronberry 199 F1
Crondall 87 F5
Cronkedonney 154 A2
Cronk-y-Voddy 154 B3
Cronton 158 D3
Crook *Cumb* 179 G1
Crook *Dur* 190 B2
Crook of Devon 207 F5
Crookedholm 198 D3
Crookedwood 244 C1
Crookgate Bank 190 B4
Crookham *Northld* 202 D3
Crookham *W Berks* 98 C2
Crookham Village 99 E1
Crookhaven 234 D1
Crookhouse 202 B2
Crooklands 173 F3

D

533

EAST ORO–EYTON UPON THE WEALD MOORS

East Oro 202 D4
East Panson 71 E3
East Peckham 89 G5
East Pennard 84 A4
East Perry 126 B4
East Portlemouth 69 E1
East Prawle 69 F1
East Preston 78 B4
East Putford 80 D2
East Quantoxhead 82 D4
East Rainton 190 C3
East Ravendale 163 G4
East Raynham 152 A2
Eastrea 137 H3
Eastriggs 187 G5
Eastrington 170 B3
East Rudham 152 A2
East Runton 153 E3
East Ruston 153 F2
Eastry 103 G1
East Saltoun 208 C2
East Shefford 98 A3
East Sleekburn 197 H2
East Somerton 153 G1
East Stockwith 162 C4
East Stoke *Dors* 75 E3
East Stoke *Notts* 149 E4
East Stour 84 D2
East Stourmouth 103 F2
East Stratton 86 C4
East Studdal 91 F5
East Taphouse 67 G4
East-the-Water 81 E3
East Thirston 197 G3
East Tilbury 101 G3
East Tisted 87 E3
East Torrington 163 F3
East Tuddenham 140 A5
East Tullyfergus 220 B1
East Tytherley 86 A3
East Tytherton 96 D3
East Village 72 B5
Eastville 150 D5
East Wall 133 E3
East Walton 139 E5
Eastwell 149 E2
East Wellow 86 A2
East Wemyss 208 B5
East Whitburn 207 E2
East Whitefield 213 H4
Eastwick 114 C2
East Williamston 105 G2
East Winch 138 D5
East Winterslow 85 H3
East Wittering 77 F4
East Witton 175 E5
Eastwood *Cald* 168 A3
Eastwood *Notts* 148 B4
Eastwood *S on Sea* 102 B4
East Woodburn 196 D2
East Woodhay 98 B2
East Worldham 87 E4
East Worlington 82 A1
Eathorpe 124 B4
Eaton *Ches* 159 E1
Eaton *Ches* 159 H1
Eaton *Leics* 149 E2
Eaton *Nflk* 140 B4
Eaton *Notts* 162 B2
Eaton *Oxon* 112 A2
Eaton *Shrops* 132 D2
Eaton *Shrops* 133 E2
Eaton Bishop 109 F5
Eaton Bray 113 F3
Eaton Constantine 133 F4
Eaton Hall 145 G5
Eaton Hastings *Oxon* 111 G1
Eaton Hastings 111 G1
Eaton Socon 126 B3
Eaton upon Tern 146 B1
Eavestone 175 F3
Ebberston 177 E5
Ebbesbourne Wake 85 E2
Ebbw Vale 108 C2
Ebchester 190 A4
Ebford 72 C3
Ebrington 111 F5
Ecchinswell 98 B1
Ecclaw 209 F2
Ecclefechan 194 D1
Eccles *Bdrs* 202 B3
Eccles *Kent* 101 H2
Eccles *Salf* 159 G4
Ecclesfield 161 F4
Ecclesgreig 221 F2
Eccleshall 146 C2
Ecclesmachan 207 F2
Eccles on Sea 153 G2
Eccles Road 139 H3
Eccleston *Ches* 158 C1
Eccleston *Lancs* 166 D2
Eccleston *St Hel* 158 D4
Eccup 168 D5
Echt 221 E5
Eckford 202 B2
Eckington *Derbs* 161 F2
Eckington *Worcs* 123 E2
Ecton 125 F4
Edale *Derbs* 160 C3
Edale 160 C3
Edburton 78 C5
Edderside 187 F3
Edderton 229 E1
Eddington 103 E2
Eddleston 200 D4
Eden 248 B2
Edenbridge 89 E5
Edenderry 240 C5
Edenfield 167 G2
Edenhall 188 C1
Edenham 149 H1
Eden Park 100 D2
Edensor 161 E2
Edentaggart 205 F4
Edenthorpe 169 H1
Ederline 210 B1
Edern 142 C3
Ederny 247 E1
Edgarley 83 H4
Edgbaston 134 C2
Edgcote 124 C2
Edgcott 112 C4
Edgcumbe 65 E3
Edge *Glos* 110 B2
Edge *Shrops* 132 D4
Edgebolton 146 A1
Edge End 109 G3
Edgefield 152 D2
Edgefield Street 152 C2
Edgehill 124 B2
Edgerley 145 F1
Edgeworth 110 C2
Edgeworthstown 244 B2
Edgmond 146 B1
Edgmond Marsh 146 B1
Edgton 132 D2
Edgware 100 C5
Edgworth 167 F2
Edinample 212 B3
Edinbane 222 B4
Edinbarnet 205 H2
Edinburgh 208 A2
Edingale 135 F5
Edingley 148 D5
Edingthorpe 153 F2
Edington *Som* 83 G4
Edington *Wilts* 96 D1
Edistone 80 C2
Edithmead 83 F5
Edith Weston 136 D4
Edlesborough 113 F3
Edlingham 197 F4
Edlington 163 G2
Edmondsham 85 F1
Edmondsley 190 B3
Edmondthorpe 136 D5
Edmonstone 232 B4
Edmonton *Corn* 67 E5
Edmonton *Enf* 100 D5
Edmundbyers 189 H3
Ednam 202 B3
Ednaston 147 G3
Edney Common 115 F2
Edradynate 219 G1
Edrom 202 C5
Edstaston 145 H2
Edstone 123 G4
Edvin Loach 122 B3
Edwalton 148 C3
Edwardstone 128 B2
Edwinsford 107 E5
Edwinstowe 162 A1
Edworth 126 C2
Edwyn Ralph 122 B3
Edzell 221 E2
Efail Isaf 94 B4
Efailnewydd 142 D3
Efail-rhyd 144 D2
Efailwen 105 H4
Efenechtyd 144 D5
Effingham 100 B1
Effirth 233 E2
Efford 72 B4
Egbury 86 B5
Egerton *Bolt* 167 F2
Egerton *Kent* 90 B5
Egerton Forstal 90 B5
Egerton Green 145 H4
Eggborough 169 G3
Eggington 113 F4
Egginton 147 H2
Egglescliffe 182 A3
Eggleston 181 E4
Egham 99 H3
Egleton 136 D4
Eglingham 203 F1
Eglinton 247 F4
Eglish 247 G1
Egloshayle 67 F5
Egloskerry 70 D3
Eglwysbach 156 D2
Eglwys-Brewis 94 B2
Eglwys Cross 145 G3
Eglwys Fach 130 D3
Eglwyswen 118 B1
Eglwyswrw 118 B1
Egmanton 162 B1
Egremont 178 B3
Egton 183 E3
Egton Bridge 183 E3
Egypt 99 G4
Eight Ash Green 116 A4
Eilanreach 223 F1
Eilean Darach 228 B1
Einacleit 231 F4
Eisingrug 143 F2
Elan Village 120 B4
Elberton 95 H4
Elburton 68 C3
Elcho 213 H3
Elcombe 97 F4
Eldernell 137 H3
Eldersfield 110 B4
Elderslie 198 D5
Eldroth 174 A3
Eldwick 168 C5
Elford *Northld* 203 F2
Elford *Staffs* 134 D5
Elgin 225 H5
Elgol 222 D1
Elham 91 E4
Elie 208 C5
Elim 155 G3
Eling 76 B5
Eliock 193 H4
Elishaw 196 D3
Elkesley 162 B2
Elkstone 110 D3
Ellan 225 F2
Elland 168 C3
Ellary 230 C2
Ellastone 147 F3
Ellemford 209 F1
Ellenabeich 210 A2
Ellenhall 146 C2
Ellen's Green 88 A4
Ellerbeck 182 A2
Ellerby 183 E3
Ellerdine Heath 146 A1
Elleric 218 A1
Ellerker 170 C3
Ellerton *E R of Yorks* 170 A4
Ellerton *Shrops* 146 B2
Ellesborough 113 E2
Ellesmere 145 G2
Ellesmere Port 158 C2
Ellingham *Hants* 85 G1
Ellingham *Nflk* 140 D3
Ellingham *Northld* 203 F2
Ellingstring 175 E5
Ellington *Cambs* 126 B5
Ellington *Northld* 197 H3
Ellisfield 86 D5
Ellishadder 222 C5
Ellister 230 A2
Ellistown 135 G5
Ellistrin 246 D3
Ellon 227 F2
Ellonby 188 B2
Ellough 140 D2
Elloughton 170 C3
Ellwood 109 G2
Elm 138 B4
Elmbridge 123 E4
Elmdon *Esx* 127 E1
Elmdon *Soli* 134 D2
Elmdon Heath 134 D2
Elmesthorpe 135 G3
Elmhurst 134 D5
Elmley Castle 123 E2
Elmley Lovett 122 D4
Elmore 110 B3
Elmore Back 110 B3
Elm Park 101 F4
Elmscott 80 C2
Elmsett 128 D2
Elmstead Market 116 B4
Elmsted 90 D4
Elmstone 103 F2
Elmstone Hardwicke 110 C4
Elmswell *E R of Yorks* 177 F2
Elmswell *Sflk* 128 C4
Elmton 161 G2
Elphhillock 226 C1
Elphin *Hghld* 228 C2
Elphin *Rosc* 243 G3
Elphinstone 208 B2
Elrick *Aber* 221 F5
Elrick *Moray* 226 B2
Elrig 185 F3
Elsdon 196 D3
Elsecar 161 F5
Elsenham 114 D4
Elsfield 112 B2
Elsham 170 D2
Elsing 139 H5
Elslack 174 C1
Elsrickle 200 C3
Elstead 87 G4
Elsted 87 F2
Elsthorpe 149 H1
Elstob 181 H4
Elston *Lancs* 167 F4
Elston *Notts* 149 E4
Elstone 81 G2
Elstow 126 A2
Elstree 100 B5
Elstronwick 171 F4
Elswick 166 C4
Elsworth 126 D4
Elterwater 179 E2
Eltham 101 E3
Eltisley 126 C3
Elton *Cambs* 137 F3
Elton *Ches* 158 D2
Elton *Derbs* 147 G5
Elton *Glos* 110 A3
Elton *Herefs* 121 H5
Elton *Lim* 235 G5
Elton *Notts* 149 E3
Elton *S on Tees* 182 A4
Elvanfoot 194 B5
Elvaston 148 B2
Elveden 139 F1
Elvingston 208 C2
Elvington *Kent* 91 F5
Elvington *York* 176 C1
Elwick *Hpool* 191 E1
Elwick *Northld* 203 F3
Elworth 146 B5
Elworthy 82 D3
Ely *Cambs* 138 C1
Ely *Crdff* 94 C3
Emberton 125 G2
Embleton *Cumb* 178 D5
Embleton *Northld* 203 G1
Embo 229 F2
Emborough 84 B5
Embsay 174 D2
Emeraconart 230 B2
Emery Down 76 A5
Emley 168 D2
Emley Moor 168 D2
Emly 239 G1
Emmer Green 99 E3
Emmington 112 D2
Emneth 138 B4
Emneth Hungate 138 C4
Emo 240 C4
Empingham 136 D4
Empshott 87 F3
Emsworth 77 F5
Emyvale 244 D5
Enborne 98 B2
Enchmarsh 133 E3
Enderby 135 H3
Endmoor 173 F5
Endon 146 D4
Enfield 100 D5
Enford 85 G5
Engine Common 96 A4
Englefield 98 D3
Englefield Green 99 G3
English Bicknor 109 G3
Englishcombe 96 B2
English Frankton 145 G2
Engollan 66 D4
Enham-Alamein 86 B5
Enmore 83 E3
Ennerdale Bridge 178 C4
Ennis 239 E3
Enniscorthy 241 E1
Enniskean 235 F2
Enniskerry 241 F4
Enniskillen 244 B5
Ennistimon 238 D3
Enochdhu 219 H2
Ensay 216 C1
Ensbury 75 G4
Ensdon 132 D5
Ensis 81 F3
Enstone 111 H4
Enterkinfoot 194 A4
Enville 134 A2
Eòlaigearraidh 231 E1
Eorabus 230 B4
Eoropaidh 231 G5
Epperstone 148 D4
Epping 114 D2
Epping Green *Esx* 114 C2
Epping Green *Herts* 114 B2
Epping Upland 114 C2
Eppleby 181 F3
Epsom 100 C2
Epwell 124 B2
Epworth 162 C5
Erbistock 145 F3
Erbusaig 223 E2
Erchless Castle 224 B3
Erdington 134 D3
Eredine 210 C1
Eriboll 228 D4
Ericstane 194 C5
Eridge Green 89 F4
Erines 204 A3
Eriswell 139 E1
Erith 101 F3
Erlestoke 96 D1
Ermington 68 D3
Erpingham 152 D2
Errill 240 B3
Errogie 224 C2
Errol 214 A3
Erskine 205 G2
Ervie 184 B5
Erwarton 129 E1
Erwood 120 D2
Eryholme 181 H3
Eryrys 145 E5
Escomb 181 F5
Escrick 176 B1
Esgair 106 C4
Esgairgeiliog 131 E4
Esh 190 B2
Esher 100 B2
Esholt 168 C5
Eshott 197 G3
Eshton 174 C2
Esh Winning 190 B2
Eskadale 224 C3
Eskbank 208 B2
Eskdale Green 178 C2
Eskdalemuir 195 E3
Esker 239 F5
Esker South 244 A2
Eskham 164 B4
Esknish 230 B2
Esprick 166 C4
Essendine 137 E5
Essendon 114 B2
Essich 224 D3
Essington 134 B4
Esslemont 227 F2
Eston 182 C4
Etal 202 D3
Etchilhampton 97 E2
Etchingham 89 H3
Etchinghill *Kent* 91 E4
Etchinghill *Staffs* 147 E1
Etherley 181 F5
Ethie Mains 221 E1
Eton 99 G3
Etteridge 219 E4
Ettersgill 180 C5
Ettington 123 H2
Etton *E R of Yorks* 170 D5
Etton *Pbro* 137 F4
Ettrick 195 E5
Ettrickbridge 201 F1
Ettrickdale 204 C2
Ettrickhill 195 E5
Etwall 147 H2
Euston 139 F1
Euxton 167 E2
Evanton 224 D5
Evedon 150 A4
Evelix 229 E1
Evenjobb 121 F4
Evenley 124 D1
Evenlode 111 F4
Evenwood 181 F5
Everbay 232 C4
Evercreech 84 B4
Everdon 124 D3
Everingham 176 D1
Everleigh 97 G1
Everley 183 G1
Eversholt 113 F5
Evershot 74 B5
Eversley 99 E2
Eversley Centre 99 E2
Eversley Cross 99 E2
Everthorpe 170 C4
Everton *Beds* 126 C3
Everton *Hants* 76 A3
Everton *Notts* 162 B4
Evertown 195 F1
Evesbatch 122 B2
Evesham 123 F2
Evington 136 A4
Ewart Newtown 202 D2
Ewden Village 161 E4
Ewell 100 C2
Ewell Minnis 91 F4
Ewelme 98 D5
Ewen 97 E5
Ewenny 93 H3
Ewerby 150 A4
Ewerby Thorpe 150 A4
Ewes 195 F3
Ewhurst 88 A4
Ewhurst Green *E Ssx* 90 A2
Ewhurst Green *Sry* 88 A4
Ewloe 158 B1
Eworthy 71 F4
Ewshot 87 F5
Ewyas Harold 109 E4
Exbourne 71 G4
Exbury 76 C4
Exebridge 82 B2
Exelby 175 F5
Exeter 72 C3
Exeter Cross 69 F5
Exford 82 B4
Exhall *Warks* 123 G3
Exhall *Warks* 135 F2
Exlade Street 98 D4
Exminster 72 C3
Exmouth 72 D2
Exnaboe 233 F1
Exning 127 G4
Exton *Devon* 72 C3
Exton *Hants* 86 D2
Exton *Rut* 136 D5
Exton *Som* 82 B3
Eyam 160 D2
Eydon 124 C3
Eye *Herefs* 121 H4
Eye *Pbro* 137 G4
Eye *Sflk* 128 D5
Eye Green 137 G4
Eyemouth 209 H1
Eyeries 234 C2
Eyeworth 126 C2
Eyhorne Street 102 B1
Eyke 129 F3
Eynesbury 126 B3
Eynort 222 C2
Eynsford 101 F2
Eynsham 112 A2
Eype 73 H3
Eyre 222 C4
Eyrecourt 239 H4
Eythorne 91 F5
Eyton *Herefs* 121 H4
Eyton *Shrops* 132 D2
Eyton *Wrex* 145 F3
Eyton upon the Weald Moors 133 G5

GAZETTEER

534

FACCOMBE–FORMAL

F

Faccombe 98 A1
Faceby 182 B2
Faddiley 146 A4
Fadmoor 182 D1
Faebait 224 C4
Faerdre 107 F1
Faha Glen 236 D4
Fahamore 234 C5
Fahan *Dngl* 247 E4
Fahan *Kerry* 234 B4
Faifley 205 H2
Failand 95 G3
Failford 198 D2
Failsworth 160 A5
Fain 228 C1
Fairbourne 130 D5
Fairburn 169 F3
Fairfield *Worcs* 123 E5
Fairfield *Worcs* 134 A1
Fairford 111 E1
Fair Green 138 D5
Fairlands 99 G1
Fairlie 198 B5
Fairlight 90 B1
Fairlight Cove 90 B1
Fairmile 72 D4
Fairmilehead 207 H2
Fairnington 202 A2
Fair Oak 86 C2
Fairoak 146 C2
Fair Oak Green 98 D2
Fairseat 101 G2
Fairstead 115 G3
Fairwarp 89 E3
Fairy Cross 81 E2
Fakenham 152 B2
Fakenham Magna 139 G1
Fala 208 C1
Fala Dam 201 F5
Falahill 201 F5
Falcarragh 246 C4
Faldingworth 163 F3
Falfield *Fife* 214 C1
Falfield *S Glos* 96 A5
Falkenham 116 D5
Falkirk 206 D3
Falkland 214 A1
Falla 196 B5
Fallgate 161 F1
Fallin 206 D4
Falmer 79 E5
Falmouth 66 D1
Falstone 196 B2
Fanagmore 228 C4
Fancott 113 G4
Fangdale Beck 182 C1
Fangfoss 176 D2
Fans 201 H3
Farcet 137 G3
Far Cotton 125 E3
Farden 133 F1
Fardrum 240 A5
Fareham 76 D5
Farewell 134 C5
Far Forest 122 C5
Farforth 164 A2
Far Gearstones 174 A5
Faringdon 111 G1
Farington 166 D3
Farlam 188 C4
Farlary 229 E2
Farleigh *N Som* 95 F2
Farleigh *Sry* 100 D2
Farleigh Hungerford 96 C1
Farleigh Wallop 86 D5
Farlesthorpe 164 C2
Farleton *Cumb* 173 F5
Farleton *Lancs* 173 G3
Farley *Shrops* 132 D4
Farley *Staffs* 147 F3
Farley *Wilts* 85 H3
Farley Green 88 A5
Farley Hill 99 E2
Farleys End 110 B3
Farlington 176 B3
Farlow 133 F2
Farmborough 96 A2
Farmcote 111 E4
Farmington 111 E3
Farmoor 112 A2
Farmtown 226 C4
Farnagh 240 A5
Farnaght 244 A3
Farnborough *Brom* 101 E2
Farnborough *Hants* 99 F1
Farnborough *W Berks* 98 B4
Farnborough *Warks* 124 B2
Farncombe 87 H5
Farndish 125 G4
Farndon *Ches* 145 G4
Farndon *Notts* 149 E4
Farnell 221 E1
Farnham *Dors* 85 E2
Farnham *Esx* 114 D4
Farnham *N Yorks* 175 G3
Farnham *Sflk* 129 G4
Farnham *Sry* 87 F5
Farnham Common 99 G4
Farnham Green 114 D4
Farnham Royal 99 G4
Farningham 101 F2
Farnley 168 D5
Farnley Tyas 168 C2
Farnsfield 148 D5
Farnworth *Bolt* 159 F5
Farnworth *Halton* 158 D3
Farr *Hghld* 219 F5
Farr *Hghld* 224 D3
Farr *Hghld* 229 E5
Farran 235 G3
Farranfore 234 D4
Farringdon 72 D3
Farrington Gurney 96 A1
Farsley 168 D4
Farthinghoe 124 C1
Farthingloe 91 F4
Farthingstone 124 D3
Farway 73 E4
Fasach 222 A4
Fascadale 217 E2
Fasnacloich 210 D5
Fasque 221 E3
Fassfern 217 H3
Fatfield 190 C3
Fattahead 226 D4
Faugh 188 C3
Fauldhouse 207 E1
Faulkbourne 115 G3
Faulkland 96 B1
Fauls 146 A2
Faversham 102 D2
Favillar 226 A3
Fawdington 175 H4
Fawfieldhead 160 C1
Fawkham Green 101 F2
Fawler 111 H3
Fawley *Bucks* 99 E4
Fawley *Hants* 76 C4
Fawley *W Berks* 98 A4
Fawley Chapel 109 G4
Fawsyde 221 F3
Faxfleet 170 C3
Faygate 88 C3
Fazeley 135 E4
Feakle 239 F3
Fearby 175 E5
Fearn 229 F1
Fearnan 212 C5
Fearnbeg 223 E4
Fearnhead 159 E4
Fearnmore 223 E4
Featherstone *Staffs* 134 B4
Featherstone *Wfield* 169 F3
Feaval 232 A4
Feckenham 123 F4
Fedamore 239 F1
Fedderate 227 F4
Feeard 238 C1
Feenagh 235 F5
Feeny 247 F3
Feering 115 H3
Feetham 180 D2
Feizor 174 A3
Felbridge 88 D4
Felbrigg 153 E3
Felcourt 88 D4
Felden 113 G2
Felindre *Carm* 107 E3
Felindre *Carm* 107 F4
Felindre *Carm* 118 D1
Felindre *Pwys* 121 E1
Felindre *Pwys* 132 B2
Felindre *Swan* 107 E2
Felindre Farchog 118 B1
Felinfach *Cere* 119 F3
Felinfach *Pwys* 120 D1
Felinfoel 106 D2
Felingwmuchaf 106 D4
Felixkirk 175 H5
Felixstowe 117 E5
Felkington 202 D3
Felldownhead 71 E2
Fell End 180 B2
Fellgate 190 C4
Felling 190 C4
Fell Side 187 H2
Felmersham 125 H3
Felmingham 153 E2
Felpham 77 H4
Felsham 128 B3
Felsted 115 F3
Feltham 100 B3
Felthorpe 152 D1
Felton *Herefs* 122 A2
Felton *Northld* 197 G4
Felton *N Som* 95 G2
Felton Butler 132 D5
Feltwell 139 E3
Fenagh 244 A3
Fenay Bridge 168 C2
Fence 167 G4
Fence Houses 190 C3
Fencott 112 B3
Fen Ditton 127 E4
Fen Drayton 126 D4
Fen End 135 E1
Fenhouses 150 C3
Feniscowles 167 E3
Fenit 234 C5
Feniton 72 D4
Feniton Court 73 E4
Fennagh 240 D2
Fennor *Wat* 237 E4
Fennor *Wmth* 244 C1
Fenny Bentley 147 G4
Fenny Bridges 73 E4
Fenny Compton 124 B3
Fenny Drayton 135 F3
Fenny Stratford 113 E5
Fenrother 197 G3
Fenstanton 126 D4
Fenstead End 128 A3
Fenton *Barns* 208 D3
Fenton *Cambs* 137 H1
Fenton *C of Stoke* 146 D3
Fenton *Lincs* 149 F4
Fenton *Lincs* 162 C2
Fenton *Northld* 202 D2
Fenwick *Donc* 169 G2
Fenwick *E Ayr* 198 D3
Fenwick *Northld* 197 F1
Fenwick *Northld* 203 E3
Feochaig 230 C1
Feock 66 D1
Feohanagh *Kerry* 234 B4
Feohanagh *Lim* 235 F5
Feolin Ferry 230 B2
Ferbane 240 A5
Ferindonald 217 F5
Feriniquarrie 222 A4
Fermoy 236 B4
Fern 220 D2
Ferndale 94 A5
Ferndown 75 G4
Ferness 225 F3
Fernham 97 G5
Fernhill Heath 122 D3
Fernhurst 87 G3
Fernie 214 B2
Ferniegair 199 G4
Fernilea 222 B3
Fernilee 160 B2
Ferns 241 E1
Ferrensby 175 G3
Ferriby Sluice 170 D3
Ferring 78 B4
Ferrybridge 169 F3
Ferryden 221 E1
Ferryhill 190 C1
Ferryside 106 C2
Fersfield 139 H2
Fersit 218 C3
Feshiebridge 219 G5
Fetcham 100 B1
Fethard *Tipp* 240 B1
Fethard *Wex* 237 F4
Fetterangus 227 F4
Fettercairn 221 E3
Fews 236 D4
Fewston 175 E2
Ffairfach 107 E3
Ffair-Rhos 119 H4
Ffaldybrenin 119 G2
Ffarmers 119 G2
Ffawyddog 108 D3
Ffordd-las 157 G1
Fforest 107 E2
Fforest-fach 93 E5
Ffoshelyg 119 G4
Ffostrasol 118 D2
Ffridd Uchaf 143 F4
Ffrith 145 E5
Ffynnon-ddrain 106 C3
Ffynnongroyw 157 G3
Fidden 230 B4
Fiddes 221 F3
Fiddington *Glos* 110 C4
Fiddington *Som* 83 E4
Fiddleford 84 D1
Fiddlers Green 227 G4
Fiddlers Hamlet 114 D1
Fiddown 236 D5
Field 147 E2
Field Broughton 173 E5
Field Dalling 152 C3
Field Head 135 G4
Fieries 234 D4
Fifehead Magdalen 84 C2
Fifehead Neville 74 D5
Fifield *Oxon* 111 F3
Fifield *W & M* 99 G3
Fifield Bavant 85 F3
Figheldean 85 G5
Filby 141 E5
Filching 79 G4
Filey 177 G5
Filgrave 125 G2
Filkins 111 F2
Filleigh *Devon* 72 A5
Filleigh *Devon* 81 G3
Fillingham 162 D3
Fillongley 135 E2
Filmore Hill 87 E3
Filton 95 H3
Fimber 177 E3
Finavon 220 D1
Finchairn 210 C1
Fincham 138 D4
Finchampstead 99 E2
Finchdean 87 E1
Finchingfield 115 F5
Finchley 100 C5
Findern 147 H2
Findhorn 225 G5
Findhorn Bridge 225 E2
Findo Gask 213 F3
Findochty 226 B5
Findon *Aber* 221 G4
Findon *W Ssx* 78 B5
Findon Mains 224 D4
Findrassie 225 H5
Finedon 136 D1
Fingal Street 129 E5
Fingask 227 E2
Fingest 99 E5
Finghall 181 F1
Fingland *Cumb* 187 H4
Fingland *D & G* 199 G1
Finglesham 103 G1
Fingringhoe 116 B3
Finlarig 212 B4
Finlaystone 205 F2
Finmere 124 D1
Finnart 218 D1
Finnea 244 B2
Finningham 128 D4
Finningley 162 B4
Finnis 245 F5
Finnygaud 226 C4
Finsbury 100 D4
Finsthwaite 179 F1
Finstock 111 H3
Finstown 232 B3
Fintona 247 F1
Fintry *Aber* 226 D4
Fintry *Stir* 206 B4
Finuge 234 D5
Finvoy 247 H3
Finzean 221 E4
Fionnphort 230 B4
Fionnsabhagh 231 F3
Firbank 179 H1
Firbeck 161 H3
Firgrove 167 H2
Firle 89 E1
Firsby 151 E5
Firs Road 85 H3
Firth 233 F3
Fir Tree 190 A1
Fishbourne *IOW* 76 D3
Fishbourne *W Ssx* 77 G5
Fishburn 190 D1
Fishcross 206 D5
Fisherford 226 D3
Fisher's Pond 86 C2
Fisherstreet 87 H3
Fisherton *Hghld* 225 E4
Fisherton *S Ayr* 192 C5
Fisherton de la Mere 85 F4
Fishguard 105 F5
Fishlake 169 H2
Fishleigh Barton 81 F3
Fishpond Bottom 73 G4
Fishpool 167 G1
Fishtoft 150 D3
Fishtoft Drove 150 C4
Fishwick 202 D4
Fiskavaig 222 B3
Fiskerton *Lincs* 163 F2
Fiskerton *Notts* 149 E4
Fitling 171 G4
Fittleton 85 G5
Fittleworth 87 H2
Fitton End 138 B5
Fitz 145 G1
Fitzhead 82 D3
Fitzwilliam 169 F2
Fiunary 217 E1
Fivealley 240 A4
Five Ashes 89 F2
Fivehead 83 G2
Fivelanes 70 C2
Fivemilebourne 243 G5
Fivemiletown 244 C5
Five Oak Green 89 G5
Five Oaks 88 A3
Five Roads 106 D2
Flackwell Heath 99 F5
Fladbury 123 E2
Fladda 233 F4
Fladdabister 233 F2
Flagg 160 C1
Flamborough 177 H4
Flamstead 113 G3
Flansham 77 H4
Flasby 174 C2
Flash 160 B1
Flashader 222 B4
Flaunden 113 G1
Flawborough 149 E3
Flawith 176 A3
Flax Bourton 95 G2
Flaxby 175 G2
Flaxley 110 A3
Flaxpool 82 D4
Flaxton 176 C3
Fleckney 136 A3
Flecknoe 124 C4
Fleet *Dors* 74 B2
Fleet *Hants* 99 F1
Fleet *Lincs* 150 D1
Fleet Hargate 150 D2
Fleetwood 172 D1
Fleggburgh (Burgh St Margaret) 140 D5
Flemingston 94 B3
Flemington 199 F5
Flempton 128 A4
Fleoideabhagh 231 F3
Fletchertown 187 G2
Fletching 89 E2
Flexbury 70 C5
Flexford 87 G5
Flimby 187 F1
Flimwell 89 H3
Flint 158 A2
Flint Cross 127 F1
Flintham 149 E4
Flint Mountain 158 A2
Flinton 171 F4
Flitcham 151 G2
Flitton 113 G5
Flitwick 113 G5
Flixborough 170 C2
Flixborough Stather 170 C2
Flixton *N Yorks* 177 F4
Flixton *Sflk* 140 C2
Flixton *Traff* 159 F4
Flockton 168 D2
Flodden 202 D3
Flodigarry 222 C3
Flookburgh 173 E4
Flordon 140 B3
Flore 124 D4
Flotterton 197 E4
Flowton 128 D2
Flurrybridge 245 E4
Flush House 160 C5
Flushing *Aber* 227 G4
Flushing *Corn* 65 E2
Flushing *Corn* 66 D1
Flyford Flavell 123 E3
Fobbing 101 H4
Fochabers 226 B4
Fochriw 108 C2
Fockerby 170 B2
Fodderty 224 C4
Foel 131 G5
Foffarty 214 C5
Foggathorpe 170 B4
Fogo 202 B4
Fogorig 202 B4
Fogwatt 226 A4
Foindle 228 C4
Folda 220 B2
Fold Hill 151 E4
Fole 147 E3
Foleshill 135 F2
Folke 84 B1
Folkestone 91 E4
Folkingham 149 H2
Folkington 79 G4
Folksworth 137 F3
Folkton 177 G4
Folla Rule 226 D3
Follifoot 175 G2
Folly Gate 71 G4
Fonthill Bishop 85 E3
Fonthill Gifford 85 E3
Fontmell Magna 84 D2
Fontstown 240 D4
Fontwell 87 G1
Foodieash 214 B2
Foolow 160 D2
Foots Cray 101 E3
Forbestown 226 B1
Force Forge 179 E1
Forcett 181 F3
Ford *A & B* 210 B1
Ford *Bucks* 112 D2
Ford *Devon* 69 F2
Ford *Devon* 81 E2
Ford *Glos* 111 E4
Ford *Northld* 202 D3
Ford *Seft* 158 B4
Ford *Shrops* 132 D5
Ford *Staffs* 147 F4
Ford *Wilts* 85 G3
Ford *Wilts* 96 C3
Ford *W Ssx* 78 A4
Ford 82 D3
Fordcombe 89 F4
Fordell 207 G4
Forden 132 B4
Ford End *Esx* 115 F3
Ford End *Esx* 127 E1
Forder Green 69 F4
Fordham *Cambs* 127 G5
Fordham *Esx* 116 A4
Fordham *Herts* 114 A3
Fordham *Nflk* 138 D3
Fordingbridge 85 G1
Fordington 164 B2
Fordon 177 G4
Fordoun 221 F3
Fordstown 244 D2
Ford Street 83 E2
Fordstreet 115 H4
Fordton Mill 72 B4
Fordwells 111 G3
Fordwich 103 E1
Fordyce 226 C5
Fore 244 C2
Foremark 148 A2
Forestburn Gate 197 F3
Forest Coal Pit 108 D3
Forest Gate 101 E4
Forest Green 88 B4
Forest Head 188 C4
Forest Hill 112 B2
Forest-in-Teesdale 180 C5
Forest Mill 207 E4
Forest Row 89 E4
Forestside 87 F1
Forest Town 148 C5
Forfar 220 C1
Forgandenny 213 G2
Forge 131 E4
Forge Side 108 D2
Forgie 226 B4
Forgue 226 C3
Forkill 245 E4
Formal 220 B1

535

FORMBY–GILSTON PARK

Formby 166 B1
Forncett End 140 A3
Forncett St Mary 140 B3
Forncett St Peter 140 B3
Forneth 213 G5
Fornham All Saints 128 A4
Fornham St Genevieve 128 A4
Fornham St Martin 128 B4
Fornighty 225 F4
Forres 225 G4
Forrestfield 206 D2
Forry's Green 115 G5
Forsbrook 147 E3
Forse 229 H3
Forsinard 229 F4
Forston 74 C4
Fort Augustus 218 C5
Forter 220 A2
Forteviot 213 G2
Fort George 225 E4
Forth 200 A4
Forthampton 122 D1
Forthill 244 A1
Forth Road Bridge 207 G3
Fortingall 212 C5
Forton *Hants* 86 B4
Forton *Lancs* 173 F2
Forton *Shrops* 132 D5
Forton *Som* 83 F1
Forton *Staffs* 146 C1
Fortrie *Aber* 226 D3
Fortrie *Aber* 227 F3
Fortrose 225 E4
Fortuneswell 74 C1
Fort William 218 A3
Forty Green 112 D2
Forty Hill 100 D5
Forward Green 128 D3
Fosbury 97 H1
Foscot 111 F3
Fosdyke 150 C2
Fosdyke Bridge 150 C2
Foss 219 F1
Fossebridge 111 E2
Foss-y-ffin 119 E4
Foster Street 114 D2
Foston *Derbs* 147 G2
Foston *Lincs* 149 F3
Foston *N Yorks* 176 C3
Foston on the Wolds 177 G2
Fotherby 164 A4
Fotheringhay 137 F3
Foubister 232 B3
Foulden *Bdrs* 202 D5
Foulden *Nflk* 139 E3
Foulkesmill 237 F5
Foul Mile 89 G2
Foulridge 174 B1
Foulsham 152 C1
Fountainhall 201 F4
Four Ashes *Sflk* 128 C5
Four Ashes *Staffs* 134 B4
Four Crosses *Denb* 145 E4
Four Crosses *Pwys* 131 H4
Four Crosses *Pwys* 145 E1
Four Crosses *Staffs* 134 B4
Four Elms 89 E5
Four Forks 83 E4
Four Gotes 138 B5
Four Lanes 64 D3
Fourlanes End 146 C5
Four Marks 87 E4
Four Mile Bridge 155 F2
Four Mile House 243 G2
Four Oaks *Bham* 134 D3
Four Oaks *E Ssx* 90 B2
Four Oaks *Soli* 135 E2
Fourpenny 229 F2
Four Roads 243 G1
Fourstones 189 F5
Four Throws 90 A3
Fovant 85 F3
Foveran 227 F2
Fowey 67 G3
Fowlis 214 B4
Fowlis Wester 213 E3
Fowlmere 127 E2
Fownhope 109 G5
Foxash Estate 116 B4
Foxcombe Hill 112 A2
Fox Corner 99 G1
Foxcote 110 D3
Foxdale 154 B2
Foxearth 128 A2
Foxfield *Cumb* 172 C5
Foxfield *Leit* 244 A3
Foxford 243 E3
Foxham 96 D3
Foxhole 67 E3
Foxholes 177 F4
Foxhunt Green 89 F2
Fox Lane 99 F1
Foxley *Nflk* 152 C1
Foxley *Northants* 124 D3
Foxley *Wilts* 96 C4
Fox Street 116 B4
Foxt 147 E4
Foxton *Cambs* 127 E2
Foxton *Dur* 181 H4
Foxton *Leics* 136 B3
Foxup 174 B4
Foxwist Green 159 E1
Foy 109 H4
Foyers 224 C2
Foynes 239 E1
Fraddon 67 E3
Fradley 134 D5
Fradley South 134 D5
Fradswell 147 E2
Fraisthorpe 177 H3
Framfield 89 E2
Framingham Earl 140 C4
Framingham Pigot 140 C4
Framlingham 129 F4
Frampton *Dors* 74 B4
Frampton *Lincs* 150 C3
Frampton Cotterell 96 A4
Frampton Mansell 110 C2
Frampton on Severn 110 B2
Frampton West End 150 C3
Framsden 129 E3
Framwellgate Moor 190 C2
Franche 133 H1
Frankby 158 A3
Frankford 240 A4
Frankley 134 B2
Frankton 124 B5
Frant 89 F4
Fraserburgh 227 F5
Frating Green 116 B4
Fratton 77 E4
Freathy 68 B3
Freckenham 138 D1
Freckleton 166 C3
Freeby 149 F1
Freeland 111 H3
Freemount 235 F5
Freethorpe 140 D4
Freiston 150 D3
Freiston Shore 150 D3
Fremington *Devon* 81 F3
Fremington *N Yorks* 181 E2
Frenchbeer 71 H3
Frenchpark 243 G3
Frenich 211 H1
Frensham 87 F4
Fresgoe 229 F5
Freshfield 166 B1
Freshford *B & NE Som* 96 B2
Freshford *Kilk* 240 B2
Freshwater 76 B3
Freshwater East 105 G1
Fressingfield 129 F5
Freston 129 E1
Freswick 229 H5
Fretherne 110 A2
Frettenham 153 E1
Freuchie 214 A1
Freystrop 105 F2
Friar's Gate 89 E3
Friday Bridge 138 B4
Friday Street *E Ssx* 79 G4
Friday Street 88 B5
Fridaythorpe 177 E2
Friern Barnet 100 C5
Friesland 216 B1
Friesthorpe 163 F3
Frieth 99 E5
Frilford 98 B5
Frilsham 98 C3
Frimley 99 F1
Frindsbury 101 H2
Fring 151 G2
Fringford 112 C4
Frinsted 102 B1
Frinton-on-Sea 116 D3
Friockheim 220 D1
Frisby on the Wreake 148 D1
Friskney 151 E5
Friskney Eaudyke 151 E5
Friskney Tofts 151 E4
Friston *E Ssx* 79 F4
Friston *Sflk* 129 G4
Fritchley 148 A4
Fritham 85 H1
Frith Bank 150 C4
Frith Common 122 B4
Frithelstock 81 E2
Frithelstock Stone 81 E2
Frithville 150 C4
Frittenden 90 A4
Fritton 140 B3
Fritwell 112 B4
Frizinghall 168 C4
Frizington 178 B4
Frocester 110 B2
Frodesley 133 E4
Frodsham 158 D2
Froggatt 160 D2
Froghall 147 E4
Frogham 85 G1
Frogmore *Devon* 69 F2
Frogmore *Hants* 99 F2
Frogmore *Herts* 113 H2
Frog Pool 122 D4
Frogpool 65 E3
Frolesworth 135 H3
Frome 84 C5
Fromebridge 110 B2
Frome St Quintin 74 B4
Fromes Hill 122 B2
Fron *Gwyn* 142 C3
Fron *Pwys* 120 D4
Fron *Pwys* 132 B3
Fron *Pwys* 132 B4
Froncysyllte 145 E3
Frongoch 144 B3
Frosses 246 C2
Frostenden 141 E2
Frosterley 189 H2
Frotoft 232 B4
Froxfield 97 G2
Froxfield Green 87 E3
Fryerning 115 F1
Fryton 176 C4
Fuerty 243 G1
Fulbeck 149 G4
Fulbourn 127 F3
Fulbrook 111 G3
Fulford *Som* 83 E3
Fulford *Staffs* 147 E3
Fulford *York* 176 B1
Fulham 100 C3
Fulking 78 C5
Full Sutton 176 C2
Fuller's Moor 145 H4
Fuller Street 115 F3
Fullerton 86 B4
Fulletby 163 H2
Fullwood 198 D4
Fulmodeston 152 B2
Fulnetby 163 F2
Fulready 124 A2
Fulstow 164 A4
Fulwell *Oxon* 111 H4
Fulwell *Sund* 190 D4
Fulwood *Lancs* 166 D4
Fulwood *Sheff* 161 E3
Fundenhall 140 B3
Funtington 87 F1
Funtley 76 D5
Funzie 233 G4
Furley 73 F5
Furnace *A & B* 204 C5
Furnace *Cere* 130 D3
Furness Vale 160 B3
Furneux Pelham 114 C4
Furraleigh 236 D4
Furzebrook 75 E2
Furzehill 81 H5
Furzey Lodge 76 B4
Fyfett 83 E1
Fyfield *Esx* 115 E2
Fyfield *Glos* 111 F2
Fyfield *Hants* 86 A5
Fyfield *Oxon* 111 H1
Fyfield *Wilts* 97 F2
Fylingthorpe 183 F3
Fyvie 227 E3

G

Gablon 229 E1
Gabroc Hill 198 D4
Gaddesby 136 B5
Gadfa 155 H3
Gaer 108 C3
Gaer-fawr 109 F1
Gaerllwyd 109 F1
Gaerwen 156 A2
Gagingwell 111 H4
Gailey 134 B5
Gainestown 244 C1
Gainford 181 F4
Gainsborough 162 C4
Gainsford End 115 F5
Gair 195 E4
Gairloch 228 A1
Gairlochy 218 B3
Gairney Bank 207 G5
Gaisgill 180 A3
Gaitsgill 188 A3
Galashiels 201 G3
Galbally *Lim* 236 B5
Galbally *Wex* 237 F5
Galgate 173 F2
Galhampton 84 B3
Gallachoille 230 C3
Gallanach *A & B* 210 B3
Gallanach *A & B* 216 B2
Gallatown 208 A4
Galley Common 135 F3
Galleywood 115 F2
Gallowfauld 214 C5
Gallowstree Common 90 D4
Galltair 223 F2
Galmisdale 216 D3
Galmoy 240 B2
Galmpton *Devon* 69 E2
Galmpton *Tby* 69 G3
Galphay 175 F4
Galston 199 E3
Galtrigill 222 A4
Galway 239 E5
Gamblesby 188 D2
Gamble's Green 115 G3
Gamesley 160 B4
Gamlingay 126 C3
Gammaton 81 E3
Gammersgill 174 D5
Gamston *Notts* 148 D3
Gamston *Notts* 162 B2
Ganarew 109 G3
Ganavan 210 B4
Ganllwyd 143 G1
Gannochy 220 D2
Ganstead 171 E4
Ganthorpe 176 C4
Ganton 177 F4
Gaodhail 230 B4
Gaoth Sáile 242 C4
Garadice 244 D1
Garbally 239 G5
Garbat 224 B5
Garbhallt 204 C5
Garboldisham 139 H2
Gardenstown 227 E5
Gare Hill 84 C4
Garelochhead 205 E4
Garford 98 B5
Garforth 169 F4
Gargrave 174 C2
Gargunnock 206 C4
Garlieston 185 G3
Garlogie 221 F5
Garmond 227 E4
Garmony 230 B4
Garmouth 226 A5
Garn 142 C2
Garnant 107 F3
Garnavilla 236 C5
Garndolbenmaen 143 E3
Garnett Bridge 179 G2
Garnkirk 206 B2
Garn-yr-erw 108 D2
Garpel 199 F2
Garrabost 231 G4
Garraburn 226 B4
Garrachra 204 C4
Garra Eallabus 230 A2
Garrane 235 F3
Garranlahan 243 F2
Garraron 210 B1
Garras 65 E2
Garraun 239 G4
Garreg 143 F3
Garreg Bank 132 C5
Garrick 212 D2
Garrigill 189 E2
Garrison 243 H5
Garristown 245 E1
Garroch 193 F2
Garros 222 C5
Garrow 212 D5
Garrycloonagh 242 D4
Garryfine 235 G5
Garrygualach 218 B5
Garryhorn 193 E3
Garryvoe 236 B3
Garsdale 180 B1
Garsdale Head 180 B1
Garsdon 96 D4
Garshall Green 147 E2
Garsington 112 B2
Garstang 166 D5
Garston 158 C3
Gartachoil 205 H4
Gartbreck 230 A2
Gartcosh 206 B2
Garth *Brid* 93 G5
Garth *IOM* 154 B2
Garth *Pwys* 120 C2
Garth *Shet* 233 E3
Garth *Wrex* 145 E3
Garthatra 230 B2
Garthbrengy 120 C1
Gartheli 119 F3
Garthmyl 132 B3
Garthorpe *Leics* 149 F1
Garthorpe *N Lincs* 170 B2
Gartly 226 C2
Gartmore 205 H5
Gartnagrenach 204 A1
Gartness *N Lan* 206 C1
Gartness *Stir* 205 H4
Gartocharn 205 G4
Garton 171 G4
Garton-on-the-Wolds 177 F2
Gartymore 229 G3
Garvagh *Leit* 244 A3
Garvagh *Londy* 247 G3
Garvaghy 247 F1
Garvald 208 D2
Garvard 230 B3
Garve 224 B5
Garvestone 139 H4
Garvock *Aber* 221 F2
Garvock *Invclyd* 205 E2
Garwaldwaterfoot 195 E4
Garway 109 F4
Garway Hill 109 F4
Gask 227 G3
Gass 192 D4
Gastard 96 C2
Gasthorpe 139 G2
Gatcombe 76 C3
Gatebeck 173 F5
Gate Burton 162 C3
Gateford 161 H3
Gateforth 169 G3
Gatehead 198 C3
Gate Helmsley 176 C2
Gatehouse 196 C2
Gatehouse of Fleet 186 A4
Gatelawbridge 194 B3
Gateley 152 B1
Gatenby 175 G5
Gateshead 190 C4
Gatesheath 145 G5
Gateside *Aber* 226 D1
Gateside *Angus* 214 C5
Gateside *E Ren* 198 D5
Gateside *Fife* 213 H1
Gateside *N Ayr* 198 C4
Gathurst 166 D1
Gatley 159 G3
Gattabaun 240 B2
Gattonside 201 G3
Gaufron 120 C4
Gaulby 136 B4
Gauldry 214 B3
Gauls 213 G4
Gauntons Bank 145 H4
Gaunt's Common 75 F5
Gautby 163 G2
Gavinton 202 B4
Gawber 169 E1
Gawcott 112 C4
Gawsworth 159 H1
Gawthrop 180 A1
Gawthwaite 172 D5
Gaybrook 244 C1
Gaydon 124 B3
Gayhurst 125 G2
Gayle 180 C1
Gayles 181 F3
Gay Street 88 A2
Gayton *Nflk* 151 G1
Gayton *Northants* 125 E3
Gayton *Staffs* 147 E2
Gayton *Wir* 158 B3
Gayton le Marsh 164 B3
Gayton Thorpe 151 G1
Gaywood 151 F1
Gazeley 127 H4
Gearraidh Bhaird 231 G4
Gearraidh na h-Aibhne 231 F4
Geary 222 B5
Geashill 240 C4
Gedding 128 C3
Geddington 136 D2
Gedintailor 222 D3
Gedney 150 D1
Gedney Broadgate 150 D1
Gedney Drove End 151 E2
Gedney Dyke 150 D2
Gedney Hill 138 A5
Gee Cross 160 B4
Geevagh 243 G4
Geilston 205 F3
Geirinis 231 E2
Geise 229 G5
Geisiader 231 F4
Geldeston 140 D3
Gell *Cnwy* 157 E1
Gell *Gwyn* 143 E3
Gelli 105 G3
Gellifor 144 D5
Gelligaer 94 C5
Gellilydan 143 G3
Gellioedd 144 B3
Gellyburn 213 G4
Gellywen 106 B4
Gelston 186 C4
Gembling 177 G2
Genesis Green 127 H3
Genoch Mains 184 D4
Gentleshaw 134 C5
Georgeham 81 E4
George Nympton 81 H2
Georgia 64 B3
Germansweek 71 E4
Germoe 64 C2
Gerrans 66 D1
Gerrards Cross 99 G4
Gestingthorpe 115 G5
Geuffordd 132 B5
Geufron 131 F2
Gibbieston 213 F4
Gibraltar *Bucks* 112 D2
Gibraltar *Lincs* 151 F5
Gibraltar *Sflk* 129 E3
Gidea Park 101 F4
Gidleigh 71 H3
Gifford 208 D2
Giffordland 198 B4
Giffordtown 214 A2
Giggleswick 174 B3
Gilberdyke 170 B3
Gilchriston 208 C2
Gilcrux 187 F2
Gildersome 168 D3
Gildingwells 161 H3
Gileston 94 B2
Gilfach Goch 94 A4
Gilfachreda 119 E3
Gilford 245 E5
Gilgarran 178 B4
Gill 198 B4
Gillamoor 182 D1
Gillan 65 E2
Gillen 222 B4
Gilling East 176 B4
Gilling West 181 F2
Gillingham *Dors* 84 D3
Gillingham *MT* 102 A2
Gillingham *Nflk* 140 D3
Gill of Garth 232 B3
Gillow Heath 146 D5
Gills 229 H5
Gill's Green *Kent* 89 H3
Gill's Green *Kent* 90 A4
Gilmanscleuch 201 E1
Gilmerton *C of Edin* 208 A2
Gilmerton *P & K* 213 E3
Gilmilnscroft 199 F2
Gilmonby 180 D3
Gilmorton 135 H2
Gilsland 188 D5
Gilston *Bdrs* 201 F5
Gilston *Herts* 114 C3
Gilston Park 114 C3

GAZETTEER

537

GREAT HAUTBOIS–HAMPSTEAD

Great Hautbois	153	E1
Great Haywood	147	E1
Great Heck	169	G3
Great Henny	128	B1
Great Hinton	96	D1
Great Hockham	139	G3
Great Holland	116	D3
Great Horkesley	116	A4
Great Hormead	114	C4
Great Horwood	112	D4
Great Houghton *Barns*	169	F1
Great Houghton *Northants*	125	F3
Great Hucklow	160	D2
Great Kelk	177	G2
Great Kimble	113	E2
Great Kingshill	113	E1
Great Langton	181	G2
Great Leighs	115	F3
Great Limber	171	E1
Great Linford	125	G2
Great Livermere	128	B5
Great Longstone	160	D2
Great Lumley	190	C3
Great Lyth	133	E4
Great Malvern	122	C2
Great Maplestead	115	G5
Great Marton	166	B4
Great Massingham	151	H1
Great Milton	112	C2
Great Missenden	113	E1
Great Mitton	167	F4
Great Mongeham	91	F5
Great Moulton	140	B2
Great Munden	114	C4
Great Musgrave	180	B3
Great Ness	145	F1
Great Notley	115	F3
Great Oakley *Esx*	116	C4
Great Oakley *Northants*	136	D2
Great Offley	113	H4
Great Ormside	180	B4
Great Orton	188	A3
Great Ouseburn	175	H3
Great Oxendon	136	B2
Great Palgrave	139	F5
Great Parndon	114	C2
Great Paxton	126	C4
Great Plumstead	140	C5
Great Ponton	149	G2
Great Preston	169	F3
Great Raveley	137	H2
Great Rissington	111	F3
Great Rollright	111	G4
Great Ryburgh	152	B2
Great Ryle	197	E5
Great Ryton	133	E4
Great Saling	115	F4
Great Salkeld	188	C2
Great Sampford	115	E5
Great Sankey	159	E3
Great Saxham	128	A4
Great Shefford	98	A3
Great Shelford	127	E3
Great Smeaton	181	H2
Great Snoring	152	B2
Great Somerford	96	D4
Great Stainton	181	H4
Great Stambridge	102	B5
Great Staughton	126	B4
Great Steeping	164	B1
Great Stonar	103	G1
Greatstone-on-Sea	90	D2
Great Strickland	179	H4
Great Stukeley	126	C5
Great Sturton	163	G2
Great Sutton	133	E2
Great Swinburne	196	D1
Great Tew	111	H4
Great Tey	115	H4
Great Thirkleby	175	H4
Great Thurlow	127	G3
Great Torrington	81	E2
Great Tosson	197	E4
Great Totham *Esx*	115	H2
Great Totham *Esx*	115	H3
Great Urswick	172	D4
Great Wakering	102	C4
Great Waldingfield	128	B2
Great Walsingham	152	B3
Great Waltham	115	F3
Great Warley	101	F5
Great Washbourne	110	D5
Great Welnetham	128	B3
Great Wenham	128	D1
Great Whittington	189	H5
Great Wigborough	116	A3
Great Wilbraham	127	F3
Great Wishford	85	F3
Great Witchingham	152	D1
Great Witcombe	110	C3
Great Witley	122	C4
Great Wolford	111	F5
Greatworth	124	D2
Great Wratting	127	G2
Great Wymondley	114	A4
Great Wyrley	134	B4
Great Wytheford	145	H1
Great Yarmouth	141	E4
Great Yeldham	115	G5
Greeba	154	B3
Green	226	D4
Greenacres	200	D4
Greenan *S Ayr*	198	C1
Greenan *Wklw*	241	F3
Greenanstown	245	E2
Greenburn	207	E1
Greencastle *Dngl*	247	F4
Greencastle *Tyr*	247	F2
Greendykes	203	E2
Green End	114	B4
Greenfield *Beds*	113	G5
Greenfield *Flint*	157	H2
Greenfield *Hghld*	218	B4
Greenfield *Oldm*	160	B5
Greenfield *Oxon*	99	E5
Greenford	100	B4
Greengairs	206	C2
Greenham *Som*	82	D2
Greenham *W Berks*	98	B2
Green Hammerton	175	H2
Greenhaugh	196	C2
Greenhead	188	D5
Green Hill	97	E4
Greenhill *Brent*	100	B4
Greenhill *E Ssx*	89	F3
Greenhill *Falk*	206	D3
Greenhill *Kent*	103	E2
Greenhill *Sheff*	161	E3
Greenhithe	101	F3
Greenholm	199	E3
Greenholme	179	H3
Greenhouse	201	H1
Greenhow	175	E3
Greenisland	248	B2
Greenland	229	H5
Greenlands	99	E4
Green Lane *Herefs*	122	B2
Green Lane *Pwys*	132	B3
Greenlaw	202	B4
Greenloaning	212	D1
Greenmeadow	109	E1
Greenmount	167	G2
Greenmow	233	F1
Greenock	205	E3
Greenodd	172	D5
Green Ore	84	A5
Greenside	190	A4
Greensidehill	197	E5
Greenskares	227	E5
Greens Norton	125	E2
Greens of Bogside	225	H4
Greenspot	227	E2
Greenstead Green	115	G4
Greensted	114	D2
Green Street *Glos*	110	C3
Green Street *Herts*	114	A1
Green Street Green	101	E2
Green Tye	114	C3
Greenway	83	E3
Greenwich	100	D3
Greet	110	D4
Greete	122	A5
Greetham *Lincs*	164	A2
Greetham *Rut*	136	D5
Greetland	168	B3
Gregson Lane	167	E3
Greinetobht	231	E3
Greinton	83	G4
Gremista	233	F2
Grenaby	154	B2
Grenagh	235	G3
Grendon *Northants*	125	G4
Grendon *Warks*	135	E3
Grendon Common	135	E3
Grendon Green	122	A3
Grendon Underwood	112	C3
Grenofen	71	F1
Grenoside	161	E4
Greosabhagh	231	F3
Gresford	145	F4
Gresham	152	D3
Greshornish	222	B4
Gressenhall	139	G5
Gressingham	173	G3
Greta Bridge	181	E3
Gretna	187	H5
Gretna Green	187	H5
Gretton *Glos*	110	D4
Gretton *Northants*	136	D3
Gretton *Shrops*	133	E3
Grewelthorpe	175	F4
Greyabbey	248	C1
Greyfriars	88	A5
Greygarth	175	E4
Greylake	83	G3
Greynor	107	E2
Greys Green	99	F4
Greysouthen	187	F1
Greystoke	179	F5
Greystone *Aber*	220	C4
Greystone *Angus*	214	D5
Greystone *Lancs*	174	B1
Greystone *Tyr*	247	G1
Greystones	241	F4
Greywell	87	E5
Grianan	231	G5
Gribthorpe	170	B4
Griff	135	F2
Griffithstown	108	D1
Grimeford Village	167	E2
Grimethorpe	169	F1
Griminis	231	E2
Grimister	233	F4
Grimley	122	D4
Grimmet	192	C5
Grimness	232	B3
Grimoldby	164	B3
Grimpo	145	F2
Grimsargh	167	E4
Grimsby	171	G2
Grimscote	125	E3
Grimscott	70	D5
Grimsthorpe	149	H1
Grimston *E R of Yorks*	171	G4
Grimston *Leics*	148	D1
Grimston *Nflk*	151	G1
Grimstone	74	B4
Grindale	177	G4
Grindiscol	233	F2
Grindle	133	H4
Grindleford	160	D2
Grindleton	167	G5
Grindley	147	E2
Grindley Brook	145	H3
Grindlow	160	D2
Grindon *Northld*	202	D3
Grindon *Staffs*	147	F4
Gringley on the Hill	162	B4
Grinsdale	188	A4
Grinshill	145	H1
Grinton	181	E2
Griomsidar	231	G4
Grisedale	180	B1
Grishipoll	216	B2
Gristhorpe	177	G5
Griston	139	G3
Gritley	232	C3
Grittenham	97	E4
Grittleton	96	C4
Grizebeck	172	C5
Grizedale	179	E1
Grobister	232	C4
Groby	135	H4
Groes *Cnwy*	157	F1
Groes *N & PT*	93	F4
Groes-faen	94	B4
Groesffordd	142	C3
Groeslon	143	E5
Grogan	240	B5
Grogport	230	C2
Gromford	129	G3
Gronant	157	G3
Groombridge	89	F4
Groomsport	248	C2
Grosmont *Mon*	109	F4
Grosmont *N Yorks*	183	E3
Groton	128	C2
Grouville	75	H1
Grove *Dors*	74	C1
Grove *Kent*	103	F2
Grove *Notts*	162	B2
Grove *Oxon*	98	B5
Grove End	134	D3
Grove Park	101	E3
Grovesend	107	E1
Grudie	224	B5
Gruids	228	D2
Gruinart Flats	230	A2
Grula	222	C2
Gruline	230	B4
Grumbla	64	B2
Grunasound	233	F2
Grundisburgh	129	E3
Gruting	233	E2
Gualachulain	211	E5
Guardbridge	214	C2
Guarlford	122	D2
Guay	219	H1
Gubbergill	178	C2
Guestling Green	90	B1
Guestwick	152	C2
Guestwick Green	152	C2
Guide Post	197	H2
Guilden Morden	126	C2
Guilden Sutton	158	C1
Guildford	87	H5
Guildtown	213	G4
Guilsborough	125	E5
Guilsfield	132	B5
Guineaford	81	F4
Guisborough	182	C4
Guiseley	175	E1
Guist	152	B2
Guiting Power	111	E4
Gulladuff	247	G3
Gullane	208	C3
Gulval	64	B3
Gumfreston	105	H1
Gumley	136	B3
Gunby *E R of Yorks*	170	A4
Gunby *Lincs*	149	G1
Gundleton	86	D3
Gunn	81	G3
Gunnerside	180	D2
Gunnerton	196	D1
Gunness	170	B2
Gunnislake	71	E1
Gunnista	233	F2
Gunthorpe *Nflk*	152	C2
Gunthorpe *Notts*	148	D3
Gunwalloe	64	D2
Gunwalloe Fishing Cove	64	D2
Gurnard	76	C4
Gurney Slade	84	B5
Gurnos	107	G2
Gurteen	243	G5
Gussage All Saints	85	F1
Gussage St Michael	85	E1
Gusserane	237	F5
Guston	91	F4
Gutcher	233	G5
Guthram Gowt	150	B1
Guthrie	220	D1
Guyhirn	138	A4
Guyhirn Gull	138	A4
Guy's Head	151	E2
Guy's Marsh	84	D2
Guyzance	197	G4
Gwaelod-y-Garth	94	C4
Gwaenysgor	157	G3
Gwalchmai	155	G2
Gwarallt	106	D5
Gwardafolog	119	E2
Gwaun-Cae-Gurwen	107	F2
Gwbert	118	B2
Gweek	65	E2
Gweesalia	242	B4
Gwehelog	109	F2
Gwenddwr	120	D2
Gwennap	65	E3
Gwenter	65	E1
Gwernaffield	158	A1
Gwernafon	131	G3
Gwernesney	109	F1
Gwernogle	106	D5
Gwernymynydd	145	E5
Gwersyllt	145	F4
Gwespyr	157	G3
Gwinear	64	C3
Gwithian	64	C4
Gwndwn	106	D5
Gwyddelwern	144	C4
Gwyddgrug	119	F1
Gwystre	120	D4
Gwytherin	144	A5
Gyfelia	145	F4
Gyffin	156	D2
Gyleen	236	B2
H		
Habberley *Shrops*	132	D4
Habberley *Worcs*	122	D5
Habrough	171	E2
Haccombe	72	B1
Haceby	149	H3
Hacheston	129	F3
Hacketstown	241	E3
Hackford	139	H4
Hackforth	181	G1
Hackland	232	B4
Hackleton	125	F3
Hackness *N Yorks*	183	G1
Hackness *Ork*	232	B2
Hackney	100	D4
Hackthorn	163	E3
Hackthorpe	179	G4
Haconby	150	A2
Hade Edge	160	C5
Hadden	202	B3
Haddenham *Bucks*	112	D2
Haddenham *Cambs*	127	F5
Haddington *E Loth*	208	D2
Haddington *Lincs*	162	D1
Haddiscoe	140	D3
Haddon	137	F3
Hademore	134	D4
Hadfield	160	B4
Hadham Cross	114	C3
Hadham Ford	114	C3
Hadleigh *Esx*	102	B4
Hadleigh *Sflk*	128	C2
Hadleigh Heath	128	C2
Hadley	133	G5
Hadley End	147	F1
Hadlow	89	G5
Hadlow Down	89	F2
Hadnall	145	H1
Hadstock	127	F2
Hadzor	123	E4
Haffenden Quarter	90	B4
Hafod-Dinbych	144	A4
Hafod-y-Green	157	F2
Haggbeck	195	G1
Haggerston	203	E3
Haggrister	233	F3
Hagley *Herefs*	122	A2
Hagley *Worcs*	134	B2
Hagworthingham	164	A1
Haigh	167	E1
Haighton Green	167	E4
Haile	178	B3
Hailes	110	D4
Hailey	111	H3
Hailsham	89	F1
Hail Weston	126	B4
Hainault	101	E5
Hainford	153	E1
Hainton	163	G3
Haisthorpe	177	G3
Halam	148	D4
Halberton	82	C1
Halcro	229	H5
Hale *Halton*	158	D3
Hale *Hants*	85	G2
Hale *Sry*	87	F5
Hale *Traff*	159	G3
Hale Bank	158	D3
Halebarns	159	G3
Hales *Nflk*	140	D3
Hales *Staffs*	146	B2
Hales Place	103	E1
Halesowen	134	B2
Hale Street	89	G5
Halesworth	140	D1
Halewood	158	C3
Halford *Shrops*	132	D2
Halford *Warks*	123	H2
Halfpenny Green	133	H3
Halfway *Carm*	107	E4
Halfway *Carm*	107	G5
Halfway *W Berks*	98	B2
Halfway House *Shrops*	132	C5
Halfway House *Wat*	237	E4
Halfway Houses	102	C3
Halifax	168	B3
Halistra	222	B4
Halket	198	D4
Halkirk	229	G5
Halkyn	158	A2
Hall	198	D5
Halland	89	F2
Hallaton	136	C3
Hallatrow	96	A1
Hallbankgate	188	C4
Hall Cross	166	C4
Hall Dunnerdale	178	D2
Hallen	95	G4
Hall Green	134	D2
Halliburton	202	A4
Hallin	222	B4
Halling	101	H2
Hallington *Lincs*	164	A3
Hallington *Northld*	197	E1
Hall of the Forest	132	B2
Halloughton	148	D4
Hallow	122	D3
Hallrule	196	A5
Halls	209	E2
Hallsands	69	F1
Hall's Green	114	B4
Hallthwaites	172	C5
Hallworthy	70	C3
Hallyne	200	D3
Halmer End	146	C4
Halmore	110	A2
Halmyre Mains	200	D4
Halnaker	87	G1
Halsall	166	C2
Halse *Northants*	124	D2
Halse *Som*	82	D3
Halsetown	64	C3
Halsham	171	G3
Halsinger	81	F4
Halstead *Esx*	115	G4
Halstead *Kent*	101	E2
Halstead *Leics*	136	C4
Halstock	74	A5
Haltham	163	G1
Haltoft End	150	D4
Halton *Bucks*	113	E2
Halton *Halton*	158	D3
Halton *Lancs*	173	F3
Halton *Northld*	189	G5
Halton *Wrex*	145	F3
Halton Camp	113	E2
Halton East	174	D2
Halton Gill	174	B4
Halton Holegate	164	B1
Halton Lea Gate	188	D4
Halton West	174	B2
Haltwhistle	189	E4
Halvergate	140	D4
Halvosso	65	E3
Halwell	69	F3
Halwill	71	E4
Halwill Junction	71	E4
Ham *Glos*	110	A1
Ham *Hghld*	229	H5
Ham *Kent*	103	G1
Ham *Rich*	100	B3
Ham *Som*	83	F3
Ham *Wilts*	98	A2
Hambleden	99	E4
Hambledon *Hants*	86	D1
Hambledon *Sry*	87	H4
Hamble-le-Rice	76	C5
Hambleton *Lancs*	173	E1
Hambleton *N Yorks*	169	G4
Hambridge	83	G2
Hambrook *S Glos*	96	A3
Hambrook *W Ssx*	77	F5
Hameringham	164	A1
Hamerton	137	F1
Ham Green *N Som*	95	G3
Ham Green *Worcs*	123	F4
Hamilton	199	G5
Hamiltonsbawn	245	E5
Hammersmith	100	C3
Hammerwich	134	C4
Hammond Street	114	B2
Hammoon	84	D1
Hamnavoe *Shet*	233	E4
Hamnavoe *Shet*	233	F2
Hamnavoe *Shet*	233	F3
Hamnavoe *Shet*	233	F4
Hampden Park	79	G4
Hampen	111	E3
Hamperden End	115	E4
Hampnett	111	E3
Hampole	169	G2
Hampreston	75	G4
Hampstead	100	C4

GAZETTEER

539

HEMSBY–HOLT HEATH

Hemsby	141	E5
Hemswell	162	D4
Hemswell Cliff	162	D3
Hemsworth	169	F2
Hemyock	82	D1
Henbury *Ches*	159	H2
Henbury *C of Bris*	95	G3
Henderland	194	A1
Hendersyde Park	202	B3
Hendon *Barn*	100	C4
Hendon *Sund*	190	D4
Hendra	65	E3
Hendre	157	H1
Hendreforgan	94	A4
Hendy	107	F2
Heneglwys	155	H2
Henfield	88	C2
Henford	71	E4
Henghurst	90	C4
Hengoed *Caer*	94	C5
Hengoed *Pwys*	121	E3
Hengoed *Shrops*	145	E2
Hengrave	128	A4
Henham	114	D4
Henlade	83	F2
Henley *Sflk*	129	E3
Henley *Shrops*	133	E1
Henley *Som*	83	G3
Henley *W Ssx*	87	G3
Henley-in-Arden	123	G4
Henley-on-Thames	99	E4
Henley Park	99	G1
Henley's Down	89	H1
Henllan *Cere*	118	D2
Henllan *Denb*	157	F1
Henllan Amgoed	106	A3
Henllys	94	D5
Henlow	126	B1
Hennock	72	B2
Henny Street	128	B1
Henryd	156	D2
Henry's Moat	105	G4
Hensall	169	G3
Henshaw	189	E4
Henstead	141	E2
Henstridge	84	C2
Henstridge Marsh	84	C2
Henton *Oxon*	112	D2
Henton *Som*	83	H5
Henwood *Corn*	70	D1
Henwood *Oxon*	112	A2
Heogan	233	F2
Heol Senni	108	A4
Heol-y-Cyw	94	A4
Hepburn	203	E1
Hepple	197	E4
Hepscott	197	G2
Heptonstall	168	A3
Hepworth *Kirk*	160	D5
Hepworth *Sflk*	128	C5
Herbertstown	239	G1
Herbrandston	105	E2
Herdicott	70	D4
Hereford	121	H2
Heriot	201	F4
Hermiston	207	G2
Hermitage *Bdrs*	195	H3
Hermitage *Dors*	74	B5
Hermitage *W Berks*	98	C3
Hermitage *W Ssx*	77	F5
Hermon *Anglsy*	155	G1
Hermon *Carm*	106	C4
Hermon *Pemb*	106	A4
Herne	103	E2
Herne Bay	103	E2
Herne Common	103	E2
Herner	81	F3
Hernhill	102	D2
Herodsfoot	67	H4
Herongate	101	G5
Heronsford	192	A2
Heronsgate	100	A5
Herriard	87	E5
Herringfleet	141	E3
Herrings Green	126	A2
Herringswell	127	H5
Hersden	103	F2
Hersham	100	B2
Herstmonceux	89	G1
Herston	232	B2
Hertford	114	B3
Hertford Heath	114	B2
Hertingfordbury	114	B2
Hesketh Bank	166	C3
Hesketh Lane	167	E5
Hesket Newmarket	188	A2
Heskin Green	166	D2
Hesleden	190	D2
Hesleyside	196	C2
Heslington	176	B2
Hessay	176	A2
Hessenford	68	A3
Hessett	128	B4
Hessle	170	D3
Hest Bank	173	F3
Heston	100	B3
Heswall	158	B3
Hethe	112	B4
Hethersett	140	B4
Hethersgill	188	B5
Hethpool	202	C2
Hett	190	C2
Hetton	174	C2
Hetton-le-Hole	190	D3
Heugh	197	F1
Heugh-head *Aber*	220	C5
Heugh-head *Aber*	220	D4
Heveningham	140	C1
Hever	89	E4
Heversham	173	F5
Hevingham	152	D1
Hewas Water	67	E2
Hewelsfield	109	G2
Hewelsfield Common	109	G2
Hewish *N Som*	95	F2
Hewish *Som*	83	G1
Hexham	189	G4
Hextable	101	F3
Hexton	113	H4
Hexworthy	69	E5
Heybridge *Esx*	115	E1
Heybridge *Esx*	115	H2
Heybridge Basin	115	H2
Heybrook Bay	68	C2
Heydon *Cambs*	127	E2
Heydon *Nflk*	152	D2
Heydour	149	H3
Heylipol	230	A4
Heylor	233	E4
Heysham	173	E3
Heyshott	87	G2
Heytesbury	85	E4
Heythrop	111	H4
Heywood *Roch*	167	G2
Heywood *Wilts*	96	C1
Hibaldstow	163	E5
Hickleton	169	F1
Hickling *Nflk*	153	G1
Hickling *Notts*	148	D2
Hickling Green	153	G1
Hickling Heath	153	G1
Hickling Pastures	148	D2
Hickstead	88	C2
Hidcote Boyce	123	G2
High Ackworth	169	F2
Higham *Derbs*	148	A5
Higham *Kent*	101	H3
Higham *Lancs*	167	G4
Higham *Sflk*	127	H4
Higham *Sflk*	128	C1
Higham Dykes	197	F1
Higham Ferrers	125	H4
Higham Gobion	126	B1
Higham on the Hill	135	F3
Higham Wood	89	G5
Highampton	71	F5
High Bankhill	188	C2
High Banton	206	C3
High Beach	101	E5
High Beaumont Hill	181	G4
High Bentham	173	H3
High Bickington	81	G2
High Birkwith	174	A4
High Blantyre	199	F5
High Bonnybridge	206	D3
High Bradfield	161	E4
High Bray	81	G3
Highbridge *Hghld*	218	B3
Highbridge *Som*	83	F5
Highbrook	88	D3
High Bullen	81	F2
Highburton	168	C2
High Buston	197	G4
High Callerton	190	B5
High Catton	176	C2
Highclere	98	B2
Highcliffe	75	H3
High Cogges	111	H2
High Coniscliffe	181	G4
High Cross *Hants*	87	E3
High Cross *Herts*	114	C3
High Dougarie	230	C1
High Easter	115	E3
High Ellington	175	E5
High Enoch	194	A4
Higher Ansty	74	D4
Higher Ashton	72	B3
Higher Ballam	166	C4
Higher Bockhampton	74	C3
High Ercall	133	F5
Higher Cheriton	73	E4
Higher Clovelly	80	D2
Higher Crackington	70	C4
Higher Downs	64	C3
Higher End	166	D1
Higher Folds	159	F5
Higher Kingcombe	74	A4
Higher Kinnerton	145	F5
Higher Penwortham	166	D3
Higher Poynton	160	A3
Higher Prestacott	71	E4
Higher Tale	72	D4
Higher Tideford	69	F3
Higher Town	64	A5
Higher Walreddon	71	F1
Higher Walton *Lancs*	167	E3
Higher Walton *Warr*	159	E3
Higher Whitley	159	E3
Higher Wincham	159	F2
Higher Wych	145	H3
High Ferry	150	D4
Highfield *E R of Yorks*	170	A4
Highfield Gate	190	A4
Highfield *N Ayr*	198	C4
Highfields *Cambs*	126	D3
Highfields *Donc*	169	G1
High Garrett	115	G4
Highgate	100	C4
High Grange	181	F5
High Grantley	175	F3
High Green *Nflk*	140	A4
High Green *Sheff*	161	E4
High Green *Worcs*	122	D2
High Halden	90	B4
High Halstow	102	A3
High Ham	83	G3
High Harrington	178	B5
High Hatton	146	A1
High Hauxley	197	H4
High Hawsker	183	F3
High Heath	146	B2
High Hesket	188	B2
High Houses	180	C1
High Hoyland	168	D1
High Hunsley	170	D4
High Hurstwood	89	F3
High Hutton	176	D3
High Keil	230	B1
High Kelling	152	D3
High Lane *Herefs*	122	B4
High Lane *Stock*	160	B3
Highlane *Ches*	159	H1
Highlane *Derbs*	161	F3
High Laver	114	D2
Highlaws	187	F3
Highleadon	110	B4
High Legh	159	F3
Highleigh	77	G4
Highley	133	G2
High Littleton	96	A1
High Melton	169	G1
Highmoor Cross	99	E4
Highmoor Hill	95	F4
Highnam	110	B3
High Newton	173	E5
High Newton-by-the-Sea	203	G2
High Offley	146	C2
High Ongar	115	E2
High Onn	134	A5
High Risby	170	C2
High Roding	115	E3
High Salvington	78	B5
High Shaw	180	C1
High Shincliffe	190	C2
High Spen	190	A4
Highsted	102	C2
High Street *Corn*	67	E3
High Street *Kent*	89	H3
High Street *Sflk*	129	G3
High Street *Sflk*	140	D2
High Street Green	128	C3
Highstreet	240	A4
Hightae	194	C1
Hightown *Ches*	146	D5
Hightown *Seft*	166	B1
Hightown Green	128	C3
High Toynton	163	H1
High Trewhitt	197	E4
High Wardses	180	A2
Highway *Corn*	67	G3
Highway *Wilts*	97	E3
Highwood	82	D1
Highworth	97	G5
High Wray	179	F2
High Wych	114	D3
High Wycombe	99	F5
Hilborough	139	F4
Hilcote	148	B5
Hilcott	97	F1
Hildenborough	89	F5
Hildersham	127	F2
Hilderstone	146	D2
Hilderthorpe	177	H3
Hilfield	74	B5
Hilgay	138	D3
Hill *S Glos*	96	A5
Hill *Warks*	124	C4
Hillam	169	G3
Hillberry	154	C2
Hillborough	103	F2
Hillbrae *Aber*	226	C4
Hillbrae *Aber*	227	E2
Hillbrae *Aber*	227	E3
Hill Brow	87	F3
Hilldyke	150	C4
Hill End *Dur*	189	H2
Hill End *Fife*	207	F5
Hillend *Fife*	207	G3
Hillend *Midln*	208	A2
Hillerton	72	A4
Hillesden	112	C4
Hillesden Hamlet	112	C4
Hillesley	96	B4
Hillfarrance	83	E2
Hill Head	76	D4
Hillhead *Aber*	226	C3
Hillhead *Devon*	69	G3
Hillhead *S Ayr*	198	D1
Hillhead of Auchentumb	227	F4
Hillhead of Cocklaw	227	G3
Hilliard's Cross	134	D5
Hillingdon	100	A4
Hillington	151	G2
Hillmorton	124	C5
Hill Mountain	105	F2
Hillockhead	220	C5
Hill of Beath	207	G4
Hill of Fearn	229	F1
Hill Ridware	134	C5
Hillsborough	248	B1
Hillside *Aber*	221	G4
Hillside *Angus*	221	E2
Hillside *Ork*	232	B3
Hillside *Shet*	233	F3
Hill Street	243	H3
Hillswick	233	E4
Hill Top	76	C4
Hilltown *Down*	245	F4
Hilltown *Wex*	237	F5
Hillway	77	E3
Hillwell	233	F1
Hill Wootton	124	A4
Hilmarton	97	E3
Hilperton	96	C1
Hilsea	77	E4
Hilston	171	G4
Hiltingbury	86	B2
Hilton *Cambs*	126	C4
Hilton *Cumb*	180	B4
Hilton *Derbs*	147	G2
Hilton *Dors*	74	D4
Hilton *Dur*	181	F4
Hilton *Shrops*	133	H3
Hilton *S on Tees*	182	B3
Hilton of Cadboll	229	F1
Himbleton	123	E3
Himley	134	A3
Hincaster	173	F5
Hinckley	135	G3
Hinderclay	128	C5
Hinderwell	183	E4
Hindford	145	F2
Hindhead	87	G4
Hindley	159	E5
Hindley Green	159	E5
Hindlip	122	D3
Hindolveston	152	C2
Hindon	85	E3
Hindringham	152	B3
Hingham	139	H4
Hinstock	146	B2
Hintlesham	128	D2
Hinton *Hants*	75	H4
Hinton *Herefs*	109	E5
Hinton *Northants*	124	C3
Hinton *S Glos*	96	B3
Hinton *Shrops*	132	D4
Hinton Ampner	86	D3
Hinton Blewett	95	G1
Hinton Charterhouse	96	B1
Hinton-in-the-Hedges	124	D1
Hinton Martell	75	F5
Hinton on the Green	123	F2
Hinton Parva	97	G4
Hinton St George	83	G1
Hinton St Mary	84	C2
Hinton Waldrist	111	H1
Hints *Shrops*	133	F1
Hints *Staffs*	134	D4
Hinwick	125	G4
Hinxhill	90	D4
Hinxton	127	E2
Hinxworth	126	C2
Hipperholme	168	C3
Hipswell	181	F2
Hiraeth	105	H3
Hirn	221	E4
Hirnant	144	C1
Hirst	197	H2
Hirst Courtney	169	H3
Hirwaen	144	D5
Hirwaun	108	A2
Hiscott	81	F3
Histon	127	E4
Hitcham	128	C3
Hitchin	114	A4
Hither Green	101	E3
Hittisleigh	72	A4
Hixon	147	E2
Hoaden	103	F1
Hoaldalbert	109	F4
Hoar Cross	147	F1
Hoarwithy	109	G4
Hoath	103	F2
Hobarris	132	C1
Hobbister	232	B3
Hobkirk	196	A5
Hobson	190	B4
Hoby	148	D1
Hockering	140	A5
Hockerton	149	E5
Hockley	102	B5
Hockley Heath	134	D1
Hockliffe	113	F4
Hockwold cum Wilton	139	E2
Hockworthy	82	C2
Hoddesdon	114	C2
Hoddlesden	167	F3
Hodgeston	105	G1
Hodnet	146	A2
Hodsock	162	A3
Hodthorpe	161	G2
Hoe	139	G5
Hoe Gate	86	D1
Hoff	180	A4
Hoffleet Stow	150	B3
Hoggeston	113	E4
Hoggrills End	135	E3
Hogha Gearraidh	231	E3
Hoghton	167	E3
Hognaston	147	G4
Hogsthorpe	164	C2
Holbeach	150	D1
Holbeach Bank	150	D2
Holbeach Clough	150	C2
Holbeach Drove	138	A5
Holbeach Hurn	150	D2
Holbeach St Johns	150	C1
Holbeach St Marks	150	D2
Holbeach St Matthew	150	D2
Holbeck	161	G2
Holberrow Green	123	F3
Holbeton	68	D3
Holborn	100	D4
Holborough	101	H2
Holbrook *Derbs*	148	A4
Holbrook *Sflk*	129	E1
Holburn	203	E3
Holbury	76	C4
Holcombe *Devon*	72	C2
Holcombe *Som*	84	B5
Holcombe Rogus	82	D2
Holcot	125	F4
Holden	174	A1
Holdenby	125	E4
Holder's Green	115	E4
Holdgate	133	F2
Holdingham	149	H4
Holditch	73	G4
Hole in the Wall	109	H4
Holemoor	71	E5
Hole Park	90	A3
Holestane	194	A3
Hole Street	88	B1
Holford	83	E4
Holker	173	E4
Holkham	152	A3
Hollacombe	71	E4
Holland *Ork*	232	B5
Holland *Ork*	232	C4
Holland-on-Sea	116	D3
Hollandstoun	232	D5
Hollee	187	H5
Hollesley	129	G2
Hollinfare	159	F4
Hollingbourne	102	B1
Hollington *Derbs*	147	G3
Hollington *E Ssx*	90	A1
Hollington *Staffs*	147	F3
Hollingworth	160	B4
Hollins	159	G5
Hollinsclough	160	C1
Hollinwood	145	H3
Hollocombe	81	G1
Holloway	148	A5
Hollowell	125	E5
Hollybush *Caer*	108	C2
Hollybush *E Ayr*	192	D5
Hollybush *Worcs*	122	C1
Holly End	138	B4
Hollyfort	241	E2
Hollym	171	G3
Hollymount	243	E2
Hollywood *Wklw*	241	E4
Hollywood *Worcs*	134	C1
Holmbury St Mary	88	B4
Holme *Cambs*	137	G2
Holme *Cumb*	173	F4
Holme *Kirk*	160	C5
Holme *Notts*	149	F5
Holme Chapel	167	H3
Holme Green	169	G5
Holme Hale	139	F4
Holmehead	193	G2
Holme Lacy	109	G5
Holme Marsh	121	F3
Holme next the Sea	151	G3
Holme on the Wolds	170	D5
Holme Pierrepoint	148	D3
Holme-on-Spalding Moor	170	B4
Holmer	121	H2
Holmer Green	113	F1
Holmes Chapel	159	G1
Holmesfield	161	E2
Holmeswood	166	C2
Holmewood	161	F1
Holmfirth	168	C1
Holmhead	199	E1
Holmpton	171	H3
Holmrook	178	C2
Holmsgarth	233	F2
Holmside	190	B3
Holne	69	E4
Holnest	74	C5
Holsworthy	70	D5
Holsworthy Beacon	71	E5
Holt *Dors*	75	F5
Holt *Nflk*	152	C3
Holt *Wilts*	96	C2
Holt *Worcs*	122	D4
Holt *Wrex*	145	G4
Holthy	176	C2
Holt End *Worcs*	123	F4
Holt End	87	E4
Holt Fleet	122	D4
Holt Head	168	B2
Holt Heath *Dors*	75	G5
Holt Heath *Worcs*	122	D4

GAZETTEER

Innellan 204 D2
Innerhadden 219 E1
Inner Hope 69 E1
Innerleithen 201 E3
Innerleven 208 B5
Innermessan 184 C4
Innerwick *E Loth* 209 F2
Innerwick *P & K* 212 B5
Innfield 240 D5
Innsworth 110 C3
Insch 226 D2
Insh 219 F5
Inshegra 228 C4
Inshore 228 C5
Inskip 166 D4
Instow 81 E3
Inver *Aber* 220 B4
Inver *Hghld* 229 F1
Inver *Hghld* 229 G3
Inver *P & K* 213 F5
Inverailort 217 F3
Inveralligin 223 F4
Inverallochy 227 G5
Inveramsay 226 D2
Inveran *Gal* 238 D4
Inveran *Hghld* 229 E2
Inveraldie 214 C4
Inveraray 210 D1
Inverardran 211 G3
Inverarish 222 D3
Inverarity 214 C5
Inverarnan 211 G2
Inverasdale 228 A1
Inverbervie 221 F2
Inverbrough 225 E2
Invercassley 228 D2
Invercharnan 218 B1
Inverchoran 224 A4
Invercreran 210 D5
Inverdruie 225 F1
Inverebrie 227 F3
Inveresk 208 B2
Inverey 220 A4
Inverfarigaig 224 C2
Invergarry 218 C5
Invergelder 220 B4
Invergeldie 212 C3
Invergordon 225 E5
Invergowrie 214 B4
Inverguseran 217 F5
Inverharroch 226 B2
Inverherive 211 G3
Inverie 217 F4
Inverinan 210 C2
Inverinate 223 F2
Inverkeilor 221 E1
Inverkeithing 207 G3
Inverkeithny 226 D4
Inverkip 205 E2
Inverkirkaig 228 B3
Inverlael 228 C1
Inverlaidnan 225 F2
Inverlauren 205 F4
Inverlochlarig 211 H2
Inverlochy 211 E3
Invermoidart 217 F3
Invermoriston 224 B1
Invernaver 229 E5
Inverneill 204 A3
Inverness 224 D3
Invernoaden 204 D5
Inverquharity 220 C1
Inverquhomery 227 F3
Inverroy 218 B3
Invershiel 223 G2
Invershin 229 E2
Inversnaid 211 G1
Inverugie 227 G4
Inveruglas 211 G1
Inverurie 227 E2
Invervar 219 E1
Inverythan 226 D3
Inwardleigh 71 G4
Inworth 115 H3
Iochdar 231 E2
Iping 87 G2
Ipplepen 69 F4
Ipsden 98 D4
Ipstones 147 E4
Ipswich 129 E2
Irby 158 B3
Irby in the Marsh 164 C1
Irby Upon Humber 171 F1
Irchester 125 G4
Ireby *Cumb* 187 G2
Ireby *Lancs* 173 H4

Ireland 233 F1
Ireleth 172 C4
Ireshopeburn 189 F2
Irishtown 243 E2
Irlam 159 F4
Irnham 149 H2
Iron Acton 96 A4
Ironbridge 133 G2
Iron Cross 123 F3
Ironmacannie 193 G1
Ironside 227 E4
Ironville 148 B4
Irstead 153 F1
Irthington 188 C4
Irthlingborough 125 G5
Irton 177 F5
Irvine 198 C3
Irvinestown 247 E1
Isauld 229 F5
Isbister *Ork* 232 A4
Isbister *Ork* 232 B4
Isbister *Shet* 233 F4
Isbister *Shet* 233 G3
Isfield 89 E2
Isham 136 D1
Isle Abbotts 83 G2
Isle Brewers 83 G2
Isleham 138 D1
Isleham Marina 138 D1
Isle of Dogs 100 D3
Isle of Whithorn 185 G2
Isleornsay or Eilean
  Iarmain 223 E1
Islesburgh 233 F3
Islesteps 187 E5
Isleworth 100 B3
Isley Walton 148 B2
Islibhig 231 F4
Islington 100 D4
Islip *Northants* 137 E1
Islip *Oxon* 112 B3
Istead Rise 101 G2
Isycoed 145 G4
Itchen Abbas 86 C3
Itchen Stoke 86 C3
Itchingfield 88 B3
Itchington 96 A4
Itteringham 152 D2
Itton 71 H4
Itton Common 109 F1
Ivegill 188 B2
Ivelet 180 D2
Iver 100 A4
Iver Heath 99 H4
Iveston 190 A3
Ivinghoe 113 F3
Ivinghoe Aston 113 F3
Ivington 121 H3
Ivington Green 121 H3
Ivybridge 60 D3
Ivychurch 90 C3
Ivy Hatch 101 F1
Ivy Todd 139 F4
Iwade 102 C2
Iwerne Courtney
  or Shroton 84 D1
Iwerne Minster 84 D1
Ixworth 128 B5
Ixworth Thorpe 139 G1

J

Jack Hill 175 F2
Jackstown 226 D2
Jackton 199 E4
Jacobstow 70 C4
Jacobstowe 71 G4
Jacobs Well 99 G1
Jameston 105 G1
Jamestown *D & G* 195 F3
Jamestown *Hghld* 224 G4
Jamestown *Laois* 240 C4
Jamestown *Leit* 243 H3
Jamestown *W Dun* 205 F3
Janefield 225 E4
Jarrow 190 C5
Jarvis Brook 89 F3
Jawcraig 206 D3
Jayes Park 88 B4
Jaywick 116 C3
Jedburgh 202 A1
Jeffreyston 105 G2
Jemimaville 225 E5
Jerrettspass 245 E4

Jersay 206 D1
Jesmond 190 C5
Jevington 79 G4
Jewells Cross 70 D4
Jockey End 113 G3
Jocks Lodge 170 D4
Jodrell Bank 159 G2
Johnby 188 B1
John o' Groats 229 H5
John O'Gaunt 136 B4
John's Cross 89 H2
Johnshaven 221 F2
Johnston 105 F2
Johnstone 205 G1
Johnstonebridge 194 C3
Johnstown *Kild* 241 E4
Johnstown *Kilk* 240 B2
Johnstown *Meath* 244 D2
Johnstown *Wklw* 241 F2
Johnstown Bridge 240 D5
Johnstownbridge 244 A2
Johnswell 240 C2
Jonesborough 245 E4
Jordans 99 G5
Jordanston 105 F5
Julianstown 245 F2
Jump 161 F5
Juniper 189 G4
Juniper Green 207 H2
Juniper Hill 124 D1
Jurby East 154 C4
Jurby West 154 C4

K

Kaber 180 B3
Kaimes 208 A2
Kames *A & B* 204 B2
Kames *E Ayr* 199 F2
Kanturk 235 F4
Kate Kearney's
  Cottage 234 D3
Katesbridge 245 F5
Kea 66 D2
Keadby 170 B2
Keadew 243 H4
Keady 244 D5
Keal Cotes 150 D5
Kealkill 235 E2
Kearsley 159 F5
Kearstwick 173 G5
Kearton 180 D2
Kearvaig 228 C5
Keasden 174 A3
Kebholes 226 D4
Keddington 164 A3
Kedington 127 H2
Kedleston 147 H3
Keelby 171 F2
Keele 146 C4
Keeley Green 125 H2
Keenagh 244 A2
Keeres Green 115 E3
Keeston 105 F3
Keevil 96 D1
Kegworth 148 B2
Kehelland 64 D4
Keig 226 C2
Keighley 168 B5
Keilarsbrae 206 D4
Keilhill 226 D4
Keillmore 230 C3
Keillor 214 A5
Keillour 213 F3
Keills 230 B2
Keils 230 B2
Keinton
  Mandeville 84 A3
Keir Mill 194 A3
Keisby 149 H2
Keiss 229 H5
Keith 226 B4
Keithock 221 E2
Kelbrook 174 C1
Kelby 149 H3
Keld *Cumb* 179 H3
Keld *N Yorks* 180 C2
Keldholme 176 C5
Kelfield 169 G4
Kelham 149 E5
Kellan 230 B4
Kellas *Angus* 214 C4
Kellas *Moray* 225 H4
Kellaton 69 F1

Kelleth 180 A3
Kelleythorpe 177 F2
Kelling 152 C3
Kellingley 169 G3
Kellington 169 G3
Kelloe 190 C2
Kells *Ant* 248 A3
Kells *Kilk* 240 C1
Kells *Meath* 244 D2
Kelly 71 E2
Kelly Bray 71 E1
Kelmarsh 136 B1
Kelmscott 111 F1
Kelsale 129 G4
Kelsall 158 D1
Kelshall 126 D1
Kelsick 187 G3
Kelso 202 B2
Kelstedge 161 E1
Kelstern 163 H4
Kelston 96 B2
Keltneyburn 219 F1
Kelton *D & G* 187 E5
Kelton *Dur* 180 D4
Kelty 207 G4
Kelvedon 115 H3
Kelvedon Hatch 115 E1
Kelynack 64 A2
Kemacott 81 G5
Kemback 214 C2
Kemberton 133 G4
Kemble 96 D5
Kemerton 123 E1
Kemeys
  Commander 109 E2
Kemnay 226 D1
Kempley 109 H4
Kempley Green 109 H4
Kempsey 122 D2
Kempsford 111 F1
Kempston 126 A2
Kempston
  Hardwick 126 A2
Kempton 132 D2
Kemp Town 78 D5
Kemsing 101 F1
Kemsley 102 C2
Kenardington 90 C3
Kenchester 121 G2
Kencot 111 G2
Kendal 179 G1
Kendram 222 C5
Kenfig 93 G4
Kenfig Hill 93 G4
Kenilworth 135 F1
Kenknock 211 H4
Kenley *Shrops* 133 F4
Kenley *Sry* 100 D1
Kenmare 234 D3
Kenmore *Hghld* 223 E4
Kenmore *P & K* 212 D5
Kenn *Devon* 72 C3
Kenn *N Som* 95 F2
Kennacraig 204 A1
Kennerleigh 72 B5
Kennet 207 E4
Kennethmont 226 C2
Kennett 127 G4
Kennford 72 C3
Kenninghall 139 H2
Kennington *Kent* 90 C5
Kennington *Oxon* 112 B2
Kennoway 214 B1
Kenny Hill 138 D1
Kennythorpe 176 D3
Kenovay 216 A1
Kensaleyre 222 C4
Kensington 100 C3
Kensworth 113 G3
Kentallen 217 H1
Kentchurch 109 F4
Kentford 127 H4
Kentisbeare 72 D5
Kentisbury 81 G4
Kentisbury Ford 81 G4
Kentmere 179 G2
Kenton *Brent* 100 B4
Kenton *Devon* 72 C3
Kenton *Sflk* 129 E4
Kentra 217 F2
Kents Bank 173 E4
Kentsboro 86 A4
Kent's Green 110 A4
Kent's Oak 86 A2
Kentstown 245 E2
Kenwick 145 G2

Kenwyn 66 D2
Kenyon 159 E4
Keoldale 228 D5
Keppanach 217 H2
Keppoch 223 F2
Keprigan 230 C1
Kepwick 182 B3
Keresley 135 F2
Kerne Bridge 109 G3
Kerridge 160 A2
Kerris 64 B2
Kerry 132 A2
Kerrycroy 204 D1
Kerrymenoch 204 C1
Kerrysdale 228 A1
Kerry's Gate 109 E5
Kersall 149 E5
Kersey 128 C2
Kershopefoot 195 G2
Kersoe 123 E2
Kerswell 72 C5
Kerswell Green 122 D2
Kesgrave 129 E2
Kesh *Ferm* 246 D1
Kesh *Sligo* 243 G4
Keshcarrigan 243 H3
Kessingland 141 E2
Kestle Mill 66 D3
Keston 101 E2
Keswick *Cumb* 179 E4
Keswick *Nflk* 140 B4
Keswick *Nflk* 153 E2
Kettering 136 D1
Ketteringham 140 B4
Kettins 214 A4
Kettlebaston 128 C3
Kettlebridge 214 B1
Kettlebrook 135 E4
Kettleburgh 129 F4
Kettlehill 214 B1
Kettleholm 194 D1
Kettleness 183 E4
Kettleshulme 160 B2
Kettlesing Bottom 175 F2
Kettlestone 152 B2
Kettlethorpe 162 C2
Kettlewell 174 C4
Ketton 137 E4
Kew 100 B3
Kew Bridge 100 B3
Kewstoke 95 E2
Kexbrough 169 E1
Kexby *Lincs* 162 D3
Kexby *York* 176 C2
Keybridge 67 F5
Keycol 102 B2
Key Green 159 H1
Keyham 136 B4
Keyhaven 76 B3
Keyingham 171 F3
Keymer 88 D2
Keynsham 96 A2
Keysoe 126 A4
Keysoe Row 126 A4
Keyston 137 E1
Keyworth 148 D2
Kibblesworth 190 B4
Kibworth Beauchamp 136 B3
Kibworth Harcourt 136 B3
Kidbrooke 101 E3
Kiddal Lane End 169 F4
Kiddemore Green 134 A4
Kidderminster 122 D5
Kiddington 111 H4
Kidlington 112 A3
Kidmore End 98 D3
Kidsgrove 146 C4
Kidstones 174 C5
Kidwelly 106 C2
Kielder 196 A3
Kilbaha 238 C1
Kilbane 239 F2
Kilbarchan 205 G1
Kilbeg 217 F5
Kilbeggan 240 B5
Kilbeheny 236 B5
Kilberry *A & B* 230 C2
Kilberry *Kild* 240 C3
Kilberry *Meath* 244 D2
Kilbirnie 198 C4
Kilbricken 240 B3
Kilbride *A & B* 204 C2
Kilbride *A & B* 210 B3
Kilbride *Hghld* 222 D2
Kilbride *Meath* 244 D1
Kilbride *Wklw* 241 E4

Kilbride *Wklw* 241 F3
Kilbrien 236 C4
Kilbrin 235 F4
Kilbrittain 235 G2
Kilburn *Derbs* 148 A4
Kilburn *N Yorks* 176 A4
Kilby 136 A3
Kilcaimin 239 E4
Kilcar 246 B2
Kilcash 236 D5
Kilcavan 240 B4
Kilchamaig 204 A1
Kilchattan 230 B3
Kilchattan Bay 204 C1
Kilchenzie 230 B1
Kilcheran 210 B4
Kilchiaran 230 A2
Kilchoan 216 D2
Kilchoman 230 A2
Kilchreest 239 F4
Kilchrenan 210 D3
Kilclief 245 G5
Kilclonfert 240 C5
Kilcock 240 D5
Kilcogy 244 B2
Kilcolgan 239 E4
Kilcolman 239 E1
Kilcomin 239 H3
Kilcommon *Tipp* 236 C5
Kilcommon *Tipp* 239 H2
Kilcon 242 D4
Kilconly 243 E1
Kilconnell 239 G5
Kilconquhar 214 C1
Kilcoo 245 F4
Kilcoole 241 F4
Kilcormac 240 A4
Kilcornan 239 E1
Kilcorney 235 F4
Kilcot 110 A4
Kilcotty 241 E1
Kilcoy 224 D4
Kilcreggan 205 E3
Kilcrohane 234 D1
Kilcullen 240 D4
Kilcummin *Kerry* 234 C4
Kilcummin *Kerry* 235 E4
Kilcurly 245 E3
Kildale 182 C3
Kildalkey 244 D1
Kildalloig 230 C1
Kildangan 240 D4
Kildare 240 D4
Kildary 229 E1
Kildavanan 204 C2
Kildavin 240 D2
Kildonan 230 C1
Kildonnan 216 D3
Kildoney 235 H4
Kildrummy 226 B1
Kildwick 174 D1
Kilfeakle 239 H1
Kilfearagh 238 C2
Kilfenora 238 D3
Kilfinan 204 B3
Kilfinnan 218 B4
Kilfinnane 235 G5
Kilfinny 239 F1
Kilflyn 234 D5
Kilgarvan 235 E3
Kilgetty 105 H2
Kilglass 243 E4
Kilgobnet *Kerry* 234 D4
Kilgobnet *Wat* 236 C4
Kilgowan 240 D4
Kilgwrrwg
  Common 109 F1
Kilham
  E R of Yorks 177 G3
Kilham *Northld* 202 C2
Kilkea 240 D3
Kilkeasy 237 E5
Kilkee 238 C2
Kilkeel 245 F5
Kilkelly 243 F3
Kilkenneth 230 A4
Kilkenny *Glos* 110 D3
Kilkenny *Kilk* 240 C2
Kilkenny West 244 A1
Kilkerran 192 C4
Kilkerrin 243 F1
Kilkhampton 70 D5
Kilkieran 238 C5
Kilkishen 239 F2
Kill *Cav* 244 C3
Kill *Kild* 241 E4

547

MAERDY–MERRIFIELD

Maerdy *RCT* 108 A1
Maesbrook 145 F1
Maesbury Marsh 145 F1
Maes-glas 95 E4
Maeshafn 145 E5
Maesllyn 118 D2
Maesmynis 120 C2
Maes Pennant 157 H2
Maesteg 93 G5
Maesybont 107 E3
Maesycrugiau 119 E2
Maesycwmmer 94 C5
Maganey 240 D3
Magdalen Laver 114 D2
Maggieknockater 226 A3
Maghaberry 248 A1
Magham Down 89 G1
Maghera *Down* 245 G5
Maghera *Londy* 247 G3
Magherafelt 247 G2
Magheralin 248 A1
Magheraveely 244 B4
Maghery 246 B3
Maghull 166 C1
Magor 95 F4
Maguiresbridge 244 B5
Maiden Bradley 84 D4
Maidencombe 72 C1
Maidenhead 99 F4
Maiden Law 190 B3
Maiden Newton 74 B4
Maidens 192 B4
Maiden's Green 99 F3
Maidensgrove 99 E4
Maidenwell 70 B1
Maiden Wells 105 F1
Maidford 124 D3
Maids Moreton 125 E1
Maidstone 102 A1
Maidwell 125 E5
Maigh Cuilinn 239 E5
Mail 233 F1
Main 224 C3
Mainham 240 D5
Mains of Abergeldie 220 B4
Mains of Ardestie 214 D4
Mains of Balhall 220 D2
Mains of Ballindarg 220 C1
Mains of Balnakettle 221 E3
Mains of Balthayock 213 H3
Mains of Burgie 225 G4
Mains of Clunas 225 F3
Mains of Craigmill 225 G4
Mains of Crichie 227 F3
Mains of Dalvey 225 G2
Mains of Dellavaird 221 F3
Mains of Drum 221 F4
Mains of Kildrummy 226 B1
Mains of Kirktonhill 221 E2
Mains of Laithers 226 D4
Mains of Mayen 226 C4
Mains of Melgund 220 D1
Mains of Thornton 221 E2
Mainsriddle 186 D4
Mainstone 132 C2
Maisemore 110 B3
Majors Green 134 C1
Makerstoun 202 A2
Malacleit 231 E3
Malahide 245 F1
Malborough 69 E1
Maldon 115 G2
Malham 174 C3
Maligar 222 C5
Malin 247 F5
Malin Beg 246 A2
Mallaig 217 F4
Mallaig Bheag 217 F4
Mallaranny 242 C3
Malling 206 A5
Mallow 235 G4
Malltraeth 155 H1
Mallusk 248 B2
Mallwyd 131 F5
Malmesbury 96 D4
Malmsmead 82 A5
Malpas *Ches* 145 G4
Malpas *Corn* 66 D2
Malpas *Nwprt* 95 E5
Maltby *Lincs* 164 A3
Maltby *Roth* 161 G4
Maltby *S on Tees* 182 B3
Maltby le Marsh 164 C3
Maltman's Hill 90 B4
Malton 176 D4
Malvern Link 122 C2
Malvern Wells 122 C2
Mamble 122 B5
Manaccan 65 E2
Manafon 132 A4
Manais 231 F3
Manaton 72 A2
Manby 164 B3
Mancetter 135 F3
Manchester 159 G4
Mancot 158 B1
Mandally 218 C4
Manea 138 B2
Maneight 193 E4
Manfield 181 G3
Mangaster 233 F3
Mangotsfield 96 A3
Mangurstadh 231 F4
Mankinholes 168 A3
Manley 158 D2
Manmoel 108 C2
Mannal 230 A4
Manningford Bohune 97 F1
Manningford Bruce 97 F1
Mannings Heath 88 C3
Mannington 75 G5
Manningtree 116 C4
Mannofield 221 G5
Manorbier 105 G1
Manorbier Newton 105 G1
Manorcunningham 247 E3
Manordeilo 107 F4
Manorhamilton 243 G5
Manorowen 105 F5
Manquhill 193 G3
Mansell Gamage 121 G2
Mansell Lacy 121 G2
Manselstown 240 A2
Mansergh 173 G5
Mansfield *E Ayr* 193 F5
Mansfield *Notts* 148 C5
Mansfieldstown 245 E3
Mansfield Woodhouse 161 G1
Mansriggs 172 D5
Manston *Dors* 84 D2
Manston *Kent* 103 G2
Manswood 85 E1
Manthorpe 137 F5
Manton *N Lincs* 162 D5
Manton *Rut* 136 D4
Manton *Wilts* 97 F2
Mantua 243 G3
Manuden 114 D4
Maplebeck 149 E5
Maple Cross 100 A5
Mapledurham 98 D3
Mapledurwell 87 E5
Maplehurst 88 B2
Mapleton 147 G4
Mapperley 148 B3
Mapperton 74 A4
Mappleborough Green 123 F4
Mappleton 171 F5
Mappowder 74 C5
Màraig 231 F4
Marazion 64 C3
Marbury 145 H4
March 138 B3
Marcham 98 B5
Marchamley 146 A2
Marchington 147 F2
Marchington Woodlands 147 F2
Marchlands 200 B2
Marchwiel 145 F4
Marchwood 76 B5
Marcross 94 A2
Marden *Herefs* 122 A2
Marden *Kent* 89 H4
Marden *Wilts* 97 E1
Marden Thorn 89 H4
Mardu 132 C2
Mardy 109 E3
Marefield 136 B4
Mareham le Fen 150 C5
Mareham on the Hill 163 H1
Marehill 88 A2
Maresfield 89 E2
Marfleet 171 E3
Marford 145 F5
Margam 93 F4
Margaret Marsh 84 D2
Margaret Roding 115 E3
Margaretting 115 F1
Margate 103 G3
Margnaheglish 230 C1
Margreig 194 A1
Marham 139 E4
Marhamchurch 70 C4
Marholm 137 F4
Marian Cwm 157 G2
Marian-glas 156 A3
Mariansleigh 81 H2
Marishader 222 C5
Mark 83 G5
Markbeech 89 E4
Markby 164 C2
Mark Causeway 83 G5
Mark Cross 89 F3
Market Bosworth 135 G4
Market Deeping 137 F5
Market Drayton 146 B2
Market Harborough 136 B2
Market Lavington 97 E1
Market Overton 136 D5
Market Rasen 163 F3
Market Stainton 163 G2
Market Warsop 161 H1
Market Weighton 170 C5
Market Weston 128 C5
Markethill *Arm* 245 E5
Markethill *P & K* 214 A4
Markfield 135 G5
Markham 108 C1
Markham Moor 162 B2
Markinch 208 A5
Markington 175 F3
Marksbury 96 A2
Marks Tey 115 H4
Markwell 68 B3
Markyate 113 G3
Marlborough 97 F2
Marlbrook 123 E5
Marlcliff 123 F3
Marldon 69 G4
Marlesford 129 F3
Marley Green 146 A4
Marley Hill 190 B4
Marlfield 236 C5
Marlingford 140 A4
Marloes 104 D2
Marlow 99 F4
Marlow Bottom 99 F4
Marlpit Hill 89 E5
Marnhull 84 C2
Marnoch 226 C4
Marnock 206 C2
Marple 160 B3
Marr 169 G1
Marrick 181 E2
Marrister 233 G3
Marros 106 A2
Marsden 168 B2
Marsett 174 C5
Marsh 83 F1
Marshalsea 73 G4
Marsham 152 D1
Marshaw 173 G2
Marsh Baldon 112 B1
Marshborough 103 G1
Marshbrook 132 D2
Marshchapel 164 B4
Marshfield *Nwprt* 94 D4
Marshfield *S Glos* 96 B3
Marshgate 70 C3
Marsh Gibbon 112 C4
Marsh Green *Devon* 72 D3
Marsh Green *Kent* 89 E4
Marsh Green *T & W* 133 F5
Marsh Green 133 F5
Marshland St James 138 C4
Marsh Lane *Derbs* 161 F2
Marsh Lane *Glos* 109 G2
Marshside *Kent* 103 F2
Marshside *Seft* 166 B2
Marshwood 73 G4
Marske 181 F2
Marske-by-the-Sea 182 C4
Marston *Ches* 159 F2
Marston *Herefs* 121 G3
Marston *Lincs* 149 F3
Marston *Oxon* 112 B2
Marston *Staffs* 134 A5
Marston *Staffs* 146 D2
Marston *Warks* 135 E3
Marston *Wilts* 96 D1
Marston Doles 124 C3
Marston Green 134 D2
Marston Magna 84 A2
Marston Meysey 111 E1
Marston Montgomery 147 F3
Marston Moretaine 125 H2
Marston on Dove 147 G2
Marston St Lawrence 124 C2
Marston Stannett 122 A3
Marston Trussell 136 B2
Marstow 109 G3
Marsworth 113 F3
Marten 97 G1
Marthall 159 G2
Martham 141 E5
Martin *Hants* 85 F2
Martin *Kent* 91 F5
Martin *Lincs* 150 A5
Martindale 179 F4
Martin Dales 163 G1
Martin Drove End 85 F2
Martinhoe 81 G5
Martin Hussingtree 122 D4
Martin Mill 91 F5
Martinscroft 159 E3
Martinstown *Ant* 248 A3
Martinstown *Dors* 74 C3
Martlesham 129 F2
Martlesham Heath 129 E2
Martletwy 105 G2
Martley 122 C4
Martock 83 H2
Marton *Ches* 159 H1
Marton *Cumb* 172 C4
Marton *Lincs* 162 C3
Marton *Midbro* 182 B4
Marton *N Yorks* 175 H3
Marton *N Yorks* 176 C5
Marton *Shrops* 132 C4
Marton *Warks* 124 B4
Marton Abbey 176 B3
Marton-le-Moor 175 G4
Martyr Worthy 86 C3
Marwood 81 F4
Marybank 224 C4
Maryburgh 224 C4
Marygold 209 G1
Marykirk 221 E2
Marylebone *C of W* 100 C4
Marylebone *Wig* 159 F5
Marypark 225 H3
Maryport *Cumb* 187 E2
Maryport *D & G* 184 D1
Marystow 71 E2
Mary Tavy 71 F2
Maryton *Angus* 220 C1
Maryton *Angus* 221 E1
Marywell *Aber* 220 D4
Marywell *Aber* 221 G4
Marywell *Angus* 215 E5
Masham 175 F5
Mashbury 115 F2
Masongill 173 H4
Mastrick 221 G5
Matching 114 D2
Matching Green 114 D2
Matching Tye 114 D2
Matehy 235 G3
Matfen 189 H5
Matfield 89 G4
Mathern 95 G5
Mathon 122 C2
Mathry 105 E4
Matlaske 152 D2
Matlock 147 H5
Matlock Bath 147 H5
Matson 110 C3
Matterdale End 179 F4
Mattersey 162 B3
Mattingley 99 E1
Mattishall 139 H5
Mattishall Burgh 139 H5
Mauchline 198 D2
Maud 227 F4
Maugersbury 111 F4
Maughold 154 D4
Mauld 224 B3
Maulden 113 G5
Maulds Meaburn 179 H4
Maunby 175 G5
Maund Bryan 122 A3
Maundown 82 D3
Mauricesmills 239 E3
Mautby 141 E5
Mavesyn Ridware 134 C5
Mavis Enderby 164 B1
Mawbray 187 F3
Mawdesley 166 D2
Mawdlam 93 G4
Mawgan 65 E2
Mawgan Porth 66 D4
Mawla 65 E4
Mawnan 65 E2
Mawnan Smith 65 E2
Mawsley Village 125 F5
Mawthorpe 164 C2
Maxey 137 F4
Maxstoke 135 E2
Maxton 201 H2
Maxwellheugh 202 B2
Maxworthy 70 D3
Maybole 192 C4
Mayfield *E Ssx* 89 F3
Mayfield *Midln* 208 B1
Mayfield *Sry* 99 H1
Mayfield *Staffs* 147 G4
Mayford 99 G1
Mayglass 237 G4
Mayland 115 H1
Maylandsea 115 H1
Maynard's Green 89 F2
Maynooth 241 E5
Mayo 243 E2
Mayobridge 245 F4
Maypole *Is OS* 64 A4
Maypole *Kent* 103 E2
Maypole *Mon* 109 F3
Maypole Green 140 D3
Maywick 233 F1
Mazetown 248 B1
McGaffins Corner 245 E5
McGregor's Corner 248 A3
McLaughlins Corner 247 H3
Mead End 85 F2
Meadle 113 E2
Meadowtown 132 C4
Mealabost 231 G4
Mealabost Bhuirgh 231 G5
Mealasta 231 F4
Meal Bank 179 G2
Mealsgate 187 G2
Meanus 239 F1
Mearbeck 174 B3
Meare 83 H4
Meare Green 83 F3
Mears Ashby 125 F4
Measham 135 F5
Meathop 173 F5
Meaux 171 E4
Meavy 68 C4
Medbourne 136 C3
Medburn 190 A5
Meddon 80 C2
Meden Vale 161 H1
Medlam 150 C5
Medmenham 99 F4
Medomsley 190 A3
Medstead 87 E4
Meelick 239 H4
Meelin 235 F4
Meenaclady 246 C4
Meenglass 246 D2
Meerbrook 147 E5
Meer End 135 E1
Meesden 127 E1
Meeth 81 F1
Meggethead 200 D1
Meidrim 106 B3
Meifod 132 B5
Meigle 214 A5
Meikle Earnock 199 G4
Meikle Grenach 204 C1
Meikle Obney 213 F4
Meikleour 213 H4
Meikle Rahane 205 E4
Meikle Strath 221 E2
Meikle Tarty 227 F2
Meikle Wartle 226 D2
Meikle Whitefield 213 H4
Meinciau 106 D2
Meir 146 D3
Meir Heath 146 D3
Melbourn 126 D2
Melbourne *Derbs* 148 A2
Melbourne *E R of Yorks* 176 C1
Melbury Abbas 84 D2
Melbury Bubb 74 B5
Melbury Osmond 74 B5
Melbury Sampford 74 B5
Melby 233 E3
Melchbourne 126 A4
Melcombe Bingham 74 D4
Meldon *Devon* 71 G3
Meldon *Northld* 197 F2
Meldreth 126 D2
Melfort 210 B2
Melgarve 218 D4
Meliden 157 G3
Melinbrynrhedyn 131 F3
Melincourt 107 G1
Melin-y-coed 143 H5
Melin-y-ddol 132 A4
Melin-y-Wig 144 C4
Melkinthorpe 179 H5
Melkridge 189 E4
Melksham 96 D2
Melldalloch 204 B2
Melling *Lancs* 173 G4
Melling *Seft* 158 C5
Mellis 120 D5
Mellon Charles 228 A1
Mellon Udrigle 228 A2
Mellor *Lancs* 167 F4
Mellor *Stock* 160 B3
Mellor Brook 167 E4
Mells *Sflk* 140 D1
Mells *Som* 84 C5
Melmerby *Cumb* 188 D2
Melmerby *N Yorks* 174 D5
Melmerby *N Yorks* 175 G4
Melplash 74 A4
Melrose 201 G2
Melsetter 232 A2
Melsonby 181 F3
Meltham 168 B2
Melton 129 F3
Meltonby 176 D2
Melton Constable 152 C2
Melton Mowbray 149 E1
Melton Ross 171 E2
Melvaig 228 A1
Melverley 132 C5
Melverley Green 145 F1
Melvich 229 F5
Membury 73 F4
Memsie 227 F5
Memus 220 C2
Menabilly 67 F3
Menai Bridge 156 B2
Mendham 140 C2
Mendlesham 128 D4
Mendlesham Green 128 D4
Menheniot 68 A4
Menithwood 122 C4
Menlough *Gal* 239 E5
Menlough *Gal* 239 F5
Menna 67 E3
Mennock 193 H4
Menston 175 E1
Menstrie 206 D5
Mentmore 113 F3
Meoble 217 G4
Meole Brace 133 E4
Meonstoke 86 D2
Meopham 101 G2
Meopham Station 101 G2
Mepal 138 B2
Meppershall 126 B1
Merbach 121 F2
Mercaston 147 H3
Mere *Ches* 159 F3
Mere *Wilts* 84 D3
Mere Brow 166 C2
Mereclough 167 H4
Mere Green 134 D3
Mereworth 101 G1
Mergie 221 F4
Meriden 135 E2
Merkadale 222 C2
Merkland *D & G* 193 G1
Merkland *S Ayr* 192 B3
Merley 75 F4
Merlin's Bridge 105 F3
Merridge 83 E3
Merrifield 69 F2

GAZETTEER

550

NEWBIGGIN–NORTHEND

Newbiggin *Dur* 180 D5
Newbiggin *Northld* 173 G4
Newbiggin *N Yorks* 174 D5
Newbiggin *N Yorks* 180 D1
Newbiggin-by-the-Sea 197 H2
Newbigging *Angus* 214 A5
Newbigging *Angus* 214 C4
Newbigging *Angus* 214 C4
Newbigging *S Lan* 200 B4
Newbiggin-on-Lune 180 B3
New Birmingham 240 B1
Newbliss 244 C4
Newbold *Derbs* 161 F2
Newbold *Leics* 148 B1
Newbold on Avon 124 C5
Newbold-on-Stour 123 H2
Newbold Pacey 124 A3
Newbold Verdon 135 G4
New Bolingbroke 150 C5
Newborough *Pbro* 137 G4
Newborough *Staffs* 147 F2
Newbottle 124 C1
Newbourne 129 F2
New Brancepeth 190 B2
Newbridge *Caer* 94 D5
Newbridge *C of Edin* 207 G2
Newbridge *Corn* 64 B3
Newbridge *Corn* 70 D1
Newbridge *D & G* 194 B1
Newbridge *Hants* 86 A2
Newbridge *IOW* 76 C3
Newbridge *Kild* 240 D4
Newbridge *Lim* 239 E1
Newbridge *Oxon* 111 H1
Newbridge *Wrex* 145 E3
Newbridge-on-Usk 109 E1
Newbridge-on-Wye 120 C3
New Brighton Flint 158 B1
New Brighton Wir 158 B4
New Brinsley 148 B4
Newbrough 189 F5
New Broughton 145 F4
New Buckenham 140 A3
New Buildings 247 E3
Newbuildings 72 A4
Newburgh *Aber* 227 F2
Newburgh *Aber* 227 F4
Newburgh *Bdrs* 201 E1
Newburgh *Fife* 214 A2
Newburgh *Lancs* 166 D2
Newburn 190 B5
Newbury 98 B2
Newby *Cumb* 179 H4
Newby *Lancs* 167 G5
Newby *N Yorks* 173 H3
Newby *N Yorks* 182 B3
Newby Bridge 173 E5
Newby East 188 B4
New Byth 227 E4
Newby West 188 A3
Newby Wiske 175 G5
Newcastle *Down* 245 G4
Newcastle *Dub* 241 E5
Newcastle *Gal* 239 F5
Newcastle *Mon* 109 F3
Newcastle *Shrops* 132 B2
Newcastle *Tipp* 236 C5
Newcastle *Wklw* 241 F4
Newcastle Emlyn 118 D2
Newcastleton or Copshaw Holm 195 G2
Newcastle-under-Lyme 146 D4
Newcastle upon Tyne 190 B5
Newcastle West 239 E1
Newcestown 235 F2
Newchapel *Pemb* 118 C1
Newchapel *Sry* 88 D4
Newchapel *Staffs* 146 D4
Newchapel *Tipp* 236 C5
New Cheriton 86 D3
Newchurch *Carm* 106 C4
Newchurch *IOW* 76 D3
Newchurch *Kent* 90 D3
Newchurch *Mon* 109 F1
Newchurch *Pwys* 121 E3
Newchurch in Pendle 167 G4
New Clipstone 148 C5
New Costessey 140 B5
Newcott 83 E1
Newcraighall 208 B2
New Cross 130 D1
New Cumnock 193 F5
New Deer 227 E4
Newdigate 88 B4
New Duston 125 E4
New Earswick 176 B2
New Edlington 161 G4
New Ellerby 171 F4
Newell Green 99 F3
New Eltham 101 E3
New End 123 F3
Newenden 90 A3
Newent 110 A4
New Farnley 168 D4
New Ferry 158 B3
Newferry 247 H3
Newfield *Dur* 190 B1
Newfield *Hghld* 229 E1
New Fryston 169 F3
Newgale 105 E4
New Galloway 193 F1
Newgate 152 C3
Newgate Street 114 B2
New Gilston 214 C1
New Grimsby 64 A5
Newhall *Ches* 146 A4
Newhall *Derbs* 147 H1
Newham 203 F2
New Hartley 197 H1
Newhaven *Derbs* 147 G5
Newhaven *E Ssx* 79 E4
New Hedges 105 H2
New Herrington 190 C3
Newhey 168 A2
New Holland 171 E3
Newholm 183 F3
New Horndean 202 C4
New Houghton *Derbs* 161 G1
New Houghton *Nflk* 151 H2
Newhouse 206 C1
New Houses 174 B4
New Hutton 179 H1
New Hythe 101 H1
Newick 89 E2
Newington *Kent* 102 B2
Newington *Oxon* 98 D5
Newington Bagpath 96 C5
New Inn *Carm* 106 D5
New Inn *Cav* 244 C3
New Inn *Gal* 239 G5
New Inn *Laois* 240 C4
New Inn *Mon* 109 E1
New Inn *Mon* 109 F1
Newinn 236 C5
New Invention 121 F5
New Kelso 223 G3
New Kildimo 239 F1
New Lanark 200 A3
Newland *Glos* 109 G2
Newland *N Yorks* 170 A3
Newland *Worcs* 122 C2
Newlandrig 201 F5
Newlands *Bdrs* 195 H3
Newlands *Hghld* 225 E3
Newlands *Moray* 226 A4
Newlands *Northld* 190 A4
Newlands of Geise 229 G5
Newlands Park 155 F3
New Lane 166 C2
New Leake 150 D5
New Leeds 227 F4
New Longton 166 D3
Newlot 232 B4
New Luce 184 D4
Newlyn 64 B2
Newmachar 227 E2
Newmains 199 H5
New Malden 100 C2
Newmans Place 121 F2
Newmarket *Cork* 235 F4
Newmarket *Kilk* 240 C1
Newmarket *Sflk* 127 G4
Newmarket *W Is* 231 G5
Newmarket-on-Fergus 239 E2
New Marske 182 C4
New Marton 145 F2
New Micklefield 169 F4
New Mill *Corn* 64 B3
New Mill *Herts* 113 F3
New Mill *Kirk* 168 C1
Newmill *Aber* 221 F3
Newmill *Aber* 227 E2
Newmill *Bdrs* 195 G5
Newmill *Moray* 226 B4
New Mill End 113 H3
Newmill of Inshewan 220 C2
New Mills *Ches* 159 G3
New Mills *Corn* 66 D3
New Mills *Derbs* 160 B3
New Mills *Mon* 109 G2
New Mills *Pwys* 132 A4
Newmills 247 G1
Newmiln 213 G4
Newmilns 199 E3
New Milton 76 A4
New Moat 105 G4
Newnham *Glos* 110 A2
Newnham *Hants* 99 E1
Newnham *Herts* 126 C1
Newnham *Kent* 102 C1
Newnham *Northants* 124 D3
Newnham *Warks* 123 G4
Newnham *Worcs* 122 B4
Newnoth 226 C2
New Ollerton 162 B1
New Park 105 G2
New Pitsligo 227 E4
New Polzeath 67 E5
Newport *Devon* 81 F3
Newport *E R of Yorks* 170 C4
Newport *Esx* 114 D5
Newport *Glos* 110 A1
Newport *Hghld* 229 G3
Newport *IOW* 76 D3
Newport *Mayo* 242 D3
Newport *Nflk* 141 E5
Newport *Nwprt* 95 E4
Newport *Pemb* 105 G5
Newport *T & W* 146 B1
Newport *Tipp* 239 G2
Newport-on-Tay 214 C3
Newport Pagnell 125 G2
Newpound Common 88 A3
New Quay 118 D3
Newquay 66 D4
New Rackheath 140 C5
New Radnor 121 E4
New Ridley 189 H4
New Romney 90 D2
New Ross 237 E5
New Rossington 162 A4
New Row 167 F4
Newry 245 E4
Newseat *Aber* 226 D2
Newseat *Aber* 227 G4
Newsells 126 D1
Newsham *N Yorks* 181 F3
Newsham *Northld* 197 H1
Newsholme *E R of Yorks* 170 A3
Newsholme *Lancs* 174 B2
New Silksworth 190 D3
New Skelton 182 D4
New Stanton 148 B3
Newstead *Bdrs* 201 H2
Newstead *Northld* 203 F2
Newstead *Notts* 148 C4
New Stevenston 206 C1
Newthorpe 169 F4
Newtimber Place 88 C1
Newtoft 163 E3
Newton *A & B* 204 C5
Newton *Aber* 226 C3
Newton *Bdrs* 201 H1
Newton *Brid* 93 G3
Newton *Cambs* 127 E2
Newton *Cambs* 138 B5
Newton *Ches* 145 H5
Newton *Ches* 158 D2
Newton *Crdff* 94 D3
Newton *Cumb* 172 C4
Newton *D & G* 194 D3
Newton *Dors* 84 C1
Newton *Herefs* 109 E5
Newton *Herefs* 121 H3
Newton *Hghld* 224 D4
Newton *Hghld* 225 E4
Newton *Hghld* 225 E5
Newton *Hghld* 228 C3
Newton *Hghld* 229 H4
Newton *Lancs* 173 G4
Newton *Lancs* 173 H2
Newton *Lincs* 149 H3
Newton *N Ayr* 230 C2
Newton *Nflk* 139 F5
Newton *Northants* 136 D2
Newton *Northld* 189 H4
Newton *Notts* 148 D3
Newton *P & K* 213 E4
Newton *Sflk* 128 B2
Newton *S Lan* 199 F5
Newton *S Lan* 200 A2
Newton *Staffs* 147 E2
Newton *Swan* 93 E4
Newton *Warks* 124 C5
Newton *Wilts* 85 H2
Newton *W Loth* 207 F3
Newton Abbot 69 G5
Newtonairds 194 A2
Newton Arlosh 187 G4
Newton Aycliffe 181 G4
Newton Bewley 182 B5
Newton Blossomville 125 G3
Newton Bromswold 125 H4
Newton Burgoland 135 F4
Newton by Toft 163 F3
Newton Ferrers 68 D2
Newton Flotman 140 B3
Newtongrange 208 B1
Newton Harcourt 136 A3
Newtonhill 221 G4
Newton Kyme 169 F5
Newton-le-Willows *N Yorks* 181 G1
Newton-le-Willows *St Hel* 159 E4
Newton Linford 135 H4
Newton Longville 113 E4
Newton Mearns 199 E5
Newtonmill 221 E2
Newtonmore 219 F4
Newton Morrell 181 G3
Newton of Ardtoe 217 F2
Newton of Balcanquhal 213 H2
Newton of Falkland 214 A1
Newton-on-Ouse 176 A3
Newton-on-Rawcliffe 183 E1
Newton on the Moor 197 G4
Newton on Trent 162 C2
Newton Poppleford 72 D3
Newton Purcell 112 C4
Newton Regis 135 E4
Newton Reigny 188 B1
Newton Solney 147 H2
Newton St Cyres 72 B4
Newton St Faith 153 E1
Newton St Loe 96 B2
Newton St Petrock 81 E1
Newton Stacey 86 B4
Newton Stewart 185 G5
Newton Tony 85 H4
Newton Tracey 81 F3
Newton under Roseberry 182 C3
Newton upon Derwent 176 C1
Newton Valence 87 E3
Newton-with-Scales 166 C4
New Town *E Loth* 208 C2
New Town *E Ssx* 89 E2
New Town *Glos* 110 D5
Newtown *A & B* 210 D1
Newtown *Cumb* 188 C4
Newtown *Derbs* 160 B3
Newtown *Glos* 110 A2
Newtown *Hants* 76 A5
Newtown *Hants* 86 A2
Newtown *Hants* 86 D1
Newtown *Hants* 98 B2
Newtown *Herefs* 122 B2
Newtown *Hghld* 218 C5
Newtown *IOM* 154 B2
Newtown *IOW* 76 C3
Newtown *Kild* 240 D5
Newtown *Laois* 240 C3
Newtown *Meath* 245 E2
Newtown *Northld* 197 E4
Newtown *Northld* 203 E2
Newtown *Ofly* 239 H4
Newtown *Poole* 75 F3
Newtown *Pwys* 132 A3
Newtown *Rosc* 243 G2
Newtown *Shrops* 145 G2
Newtown *Staffs* 146 D5
Newtown *Staffs* 160 C1
Newtown *Tipp* 236 B5
Newtown *Tipp* 240 A3
Newtown *Wat* 236 D4
Newtown *Wilts* 85 E3
Newtownabbey 248 B2
Newtownards 248 C2
Newtown Bellew 243 F1
Newtownbutler 244 B4
Newtown Cashel 243 H1
Newtown Cloghans 243 E4
Newtown-Crommelin 248 A3
Newtown Cunningham 247 E3
Newtown Forbes 244 A2
Newtown Gore 244 B4
Newtownhamilton 245 E4
Newtown-in-St Martin 65 E2
Newtownlow 240 B5
Newtownlynch 239 E4
Newtownmount-kennedy 241 F4
Newtown St Boswells 201 H2
Newtown-Sandes 238 D1
Newtownshandrum 235 G5
Newtownstewart 247 E2
Newtown Unthank 135 G4
New Tredegar 108 C2
New Trows 199 H3
New Twopothouse Village 235 G4
Newtyle 214 A5
New Ulva 230 C3
New Waltham 171 G1
New Whittington 161 F2
New Winton 208 C2
New Yatt 111 H3
New York *Lincs* 150 B5
New York *N Tyne* 190 C5
Neyland 105 F2
Nibley 96 A4
Nicholashayne 82 D2
Nicholaston 92 D4
Nidd 175 G3
Nigg *C of Aber* 221 G5
Nigg *Hghld* 225 E5
Nigg Ferry 225 E5
Nightcott 82 B3
Nilig 144 C4
Nine Ashes 115 E2
Ninebanks 189 E3
Nine Mile Burn 200 D5
Ninemilehouse 240 B1
Ninfield 89 H1
Ningwood 76 B3
Nisbet 202 A2
Niton 76 D2
Nitshill 199 E5
Niwbwrch 155 H1
Noak Bridge 101 G5
Noak Hill 101 F5
Nobber 244 D2
Nobold 133 E5
Nobottle 125 E4
Nocton 163 F1
Nohaval 235 H2
Noke 112 B3
Nolton 105 E3
Nolton Haven 105 E3
No Man's Heath *Ches* 145 H4
No Man's Heath *Warks* 135 E4
Nomansland *Devon* 82 A1
Nomansland *Hants* 85 H2
Noneley 145 G2
Nonington 91 F5
Nook *Cumb* 173 F5
Nook *Cumb* 195 G1
Noranside 220 D2
Norbury *Derbs* 147 F3
Norbury *Shrops* 132 D3
Norbury *Staffs* 146 C1
Norbury Common 145 H4
Norby 233 E3
Norchard 122 D4
Nordelph 138 C4
Norden *Dors* 75 E2
Norden *Roch* 167 H2
Nordley 133 G3
Norham 202 D4
Norley 159 E2
Norleywood 76 B4
Normanby *N Lincs* 170 C2
Normanby *N Yorks* 176 C5
Normanby-by-Spital 163 E3
Normanby le Wold 163 F4
Norman Cross 137 G3
Normandy 87 G5
Norman's Green 72 D4
Normanton *C of Derby* 148 A2
Normanton *Leics* 149 F3
Normanton *Lincs* 149 G4
Normanton *Notts* 149 E5
Normanton *Rut* 136 D4
Normanton *Wfield* 169 E3
Normanton le Heath 135 F5
Normanton on Soar 148 C1
Normanton on Trent 162 C1
Normanton-on-the-Wolds 148 D2
Normoss 166 B4
Norrington Common 96 C2
Norris Hill 135 F5
Northacre 139 G3
Northallerton 181 H1
Northam *Devon* 81 E3
Northam *Sotton* 86 B1
Northampton 125 F4
North Ascot 99 G3
North Aston 112 A4
Northaw 114 B2
North Baddesley 86 B2
North Ballachulish 218 A2
North Balloch 192 C3
North Barrow 84 B3
North Barsham 152 B2
North Benfleet 102 A4
North Berwick 208 D4
North Blyth 197 H2
North Boarhunt 77 E5
Northborough 137 F4
Northbourne 91 F5
North Bovey 72 A2
North Bradley 96 C1
North Brentor 71 F2
North Brewham 84 C4
Northbridge Street 89 H2
Northbrook 112 A3
North Buckland 81 E4
North Burlingham 140 D5
North Cadbury 84 B3
North Cairn 184 B5
North Carlton 162 D2
North Cave 170 C4
North Cerney 110 D2
North Chailey 88 D2
Northchapel 87 H3
North Charford 85 G2
North Charlton 203 F1
North Cheriton 84 B3
North Chideock 73 H3
Northchurch 113 F2
North Cliffe 170 C4
North Clifton 162 C2
North Cockerington 164 B4
North Coker 84 A1
North Connel 210 C4
North Cornelly 93 G4
Northcote Manor 81 G2
North Cotes 164 B5
Northcott 70 D3
North Cove 141 E2
North Cowton 181 G2
North Cranna 226 D4
North Crawley 125 G2
North Cray 101 E3
North Creake 152 A3
North Curry 83 F3
North Dalton 177 E2
North Deighton 175 G2
North Duffield 170 A4
North Dykes 188 C2
North Elkington 163 H4
North Elmham 152 B1
North Elmsall 169 F2
North End *Esx* 114 D5
North End *Esx* 115 F3
North End *Hants* 98 B2
North End *N Som* 95 F2
North End *Ptsmth* 77 E4
North End *W Ssx* 78 B5
Northend *Bucks* 99 E5

551
NORTHEND–OTTERBURN CAMP

Northend
B & NE Som 96 B2
Northend *Warks* 124 B3
North Erradale 228 A1
North Fambridge 102 B5
North Fearns 222 D3
North Ferriby 170 D3
Northfield *Bdrs* 209 H2
Northfield *Bham* 134 C1
Northfield
C of Aber 227 F1
Northfleet 101 G3
North Flobbets 227 E3
North Frodingham 177 G2
Northgate 150 B2
North Gluss 233 F4
North Gorley 85 G1
North Green 140 B2
North Greetwell 163 E2
North Grimston 176 D3
North Halley 232 C3
North Hayling 77 F4
North Hazelrigg 203 E2
North Heasley 81 H3
North Heath 88 A2
North Hill *Cambs* 127 E5
North Hill *Corn* 70 D2
North Hinksey
Village 112 A2
North Holmwood 88 B5
North Huish 69 E3
North Hykeham 162 D1
Northiam 90 A3
Northill 126 B2
Northington 86 D4
North Kelsey 163 E5
North Kessock 224 D4
North Killingholme 171 E2
North Kilvington 175 H5
North Kilworth 136 A2
North Kyme 150 B4
North Lancing 78 C5
Northlands *Cav* 244 D3
Northlands *Lincs* 150 C4
Northleach 111 E3
North Lee 113 E2
North Leigh 111 H3
Northleigh 73 E4
North Leverton with
Habblesthorpe 162 C3
Northlew 71 F4
North Littleton 123 F2
North Lopham 139 H2
North Luffenham 136 D4
North Marden 87 F2
North Marston 112 D4
North Middleton 201 F5
North Molton 81 H3
Northmoor 111 H2
Northmoor Green
or Moorland 83 F3
North Moreton 98 C4
Northmuir 220 C1
North Mundham 77 G4
North Muskham 149 E5
North Newbald 170 C4
North Newington 124 B1
North Newnton 97 F1
North Newton 83 F3
North Nibley 96 B5
North Oakley 98 C1
North Ockendon 101 F4
Northolt 100 B4
Northop 158 A1
Northop Hall 158 B1
North Ormsby 163 H4
Northorpe *Lincs* 137 F5
Northorpe *Lincs* 150 B3
Northorpe *Lincs* 162 D4
North Otterington 181 H1
North Owersby 163 F4
Northowram 168 C3
North Perrott 83 H1
North Petherton 83 F3
North Petherwin 70 D3
North Pickenham 139 F4
North Piddle 123 E3
Northpunds 233 F1
North Queensferry 207 G3
North Radworthy 81 H3
North Rauceby 149 H4
Northrepps 153 E3
North Reston 164 B3
North Rigton 175 F1
North Ring 235 F1
North Rode 159 H1
North Roe 233 F4
North Runcton 138 D5
North Sandwick 233 G5
North Scale 172 C3
North Scarle 162 D1
North Seaton 197 H2
North Shian 210 C5
North Shields 190 D5
North Shoebury 102 C4
North Shore 166 B4
North Side 137 H3
North Skelton 182 D4
North Somercotes 164 B4
North Stainley 175 F4
North Stainmore 180 C4
North Stifford 101 F4
North Stoke
B & NE Som 96 B2
North Stoke
Oxon 98 D4
North Stoke
W Ssx 78 A5
North Street
Hants 86 D3
North Street *Berks* 98 D3
North Street *Kent* 102 D1
North Sunderland 203 G2
North Tamerton 70 D4
North Tawton 71 H4
North Thoresby 163 H4
North Tidworth 85 H5
North Tuddenham 139 H5
Northwall 232 C5
North Walsham 153 E2
North Waltham 86 D5
North Warnborough 87 E5
North Water
Bridge 221 E2
North Watten 229 H5
Northway *Devon* 80 D2
Northway *Glos* 123 F1
North Weald Bassett 114 D2
North Wheatley 162 C3
North Whilborough 69 G4
Northwich 159 F2
North Wick 95 G2
Northwick 95 G4
North Widcombe 95 G1
North Willingham 163 G3
North Wingfield 161 F1
North Witham 149 G1
Northwold 139 E3
Northwood *Derbs* 161 E1
Northwood *Hilln* 100 A5
Northwood *IOW* 76 C3
Northwood *Wrex* 145 G2
Northwood Green 110 A3
North Wootton
Dors 84 B1
North Wootton
Nflk 151 F1
North Wootton
Som 84 A4
North Wraxall 96 C3
Norton *Derbs* 161 F3
Norton *Donc* 169 G2
Norton *Glos* 110 C4
Norton *Halton* 159 E3
Norton *Herts* 126 C1
Norton *IOW* 76 B3
Norton *Northants* 124 D4
Norton *Notts* 161 H2
Norton *Pwys* 121 F4
Norton *Sflk* 128 C4
Norton *Shrops* 133 E2
Norton *Shrops* 133 F4
Norton *Shrops* 133 G4
Norton *S on Tees* 182 A4
Norton *Wilts* 96 C4
Norton *Worcs* 122 D3
Norton *Worcs* 123 F2
Norton *W Ssx* 77 H5
Norton Bavant 85 E4
Norton Bridge 146 D2
Norton Canes 134 C4
Norton Canon 121 G2
Norton Disney 149 F5
Norton East 134 C4
Norton Ferris 84 C4
Norton Fitzwarren 83 E3
Norton Green 76 B3
Norton Hawkfield 95 G2
Norton Heath 115 E2
Norton in Hales 146 B3
Norton-in-the-
Moors 146 D4
Norton-Juxta-
Twycross 135 F4
Norton-le-Clay 175 H4
Norton Lindsey 123 H4
Norton Malreward 95 H2
Norton Mandeville 115 E2
Norton-on-Derwent 176 D4
Norton St Philip 96 B1
Norton sub
Hamdon 83 H2
Norton Subcourse 140 D3
Norwell 149 E5
Norwell
Woodhouse 149 E5
Norwich 140 B4
Norwick 233 G5
Norwood 161 G3
Norwood Green 100 B3
Norwood Hill 88 C4
Noseley 136 B3
Noss 233 F1
Noss Mayo 68 C2
Nosterfield 175 F5
Nostie 223 F2
Notgrove 111 E3
Nottage 93 G3
Nottingham 148 C3
Nottington 74 C2
Notton *Wfield* 169 E2
Notton *Wilts* 96 D2
Nounsley 115 G2
Noutard's Green 122 C4
Nowton 128 B4
Nox 132 D5
Nuffield 98 D4
Nunburnholme 176 D1
Nuneaton 135 F3
Nuneham Courtenay 112 B1
Nun Monkton 176 A2
Nunney 84 C5
Nunnington 176 C4
Nunnykirk 197 F3
Nunthorpe 182 B3
Nunton 85 G3
Nunwick 196 D1
Nurney *Carl* 240 D2
Nurney *Kild* 240 D4
Nursling 86 B2
Nursted 87 F2
Nutbourne *W Ssx* 77 F5
Nutbourne *W Ssx* 88 A2
Nutfield 88 D5
Nuthall 148 C4
Nuthampstead 127 E1
Nuthurst *W Ssx* 88 B3
Nuthurst *Warks* 123 G5
Nutley *E Ssx* 89 E3
Nutley *Hants* 86 D4
Nutwell 162 A5
Nyadd 206 C5
Nybster 229 H5
Nyetimber 77 G4
Nyewood 87 F2
Nymet Rowland 81 H1
Nymet Tracey 72 A4
Nympsfield 110 B1
Nynehead 82 D2
Nyton 77 H5

O

Oadby 136 A4
Oad Street 102 B2
Oakamoor 147 F3
Oakbank 207 F2
Oak Cross 71 F4
Oakdale 108 C1
Oake 83 E3
Oaken 134 A4
Oakenclough 166 D5
Oakengates 133 G5
Oakenshaw *Dur* 190 B2
Oakenshaw *Kirk* 168 C3
Oakerthorpe 148 A4
Oakford *Cere* 119 E3
Oakford *Devon* 82 B2
Oakfordbridge 82 B2
Oakgrove 160 A1
Oakham 136 D4
Oakhanger 87 F4
Oakhill 84 B5
Oakington 127 E4
Oaklands *Cnwy* 143 H5
Oaklands *Herts* 114 A3
Oakle Street 110 B3
Oakley *Beds* 125 H3
Oakley *Bucks* 112 C3
Oakley *Fife* 207 F4
Oakley *Hants* 86 D5
Oakley *Poole* 75 F4
Oakley *Sflk* 129 E5
Oakley Green 99 G3
Oakridge Lynch 110 C2
Oaks 132 D4
Oaksey 96 D5
Oakthorpe 135 F5
Oakwood 189 G5
Oakworth 168 B4
Oare *Kent* 102 D2
Oare *Som* 82 A5
Oare *Wilts* 97 F2
Oasby 149 H3
Oatfield 230 B1
Oath 83 G3
Oathlaw 220 D1
Oban 210 B3
Oborne 84 B2
Occlestone
Green 159 F1
Occold 129 E5
Ochiltree 199 F1
Ochtermuthill 212 D2
Ochtertyre 212 D3
Ockbrook 148 B3
Ockham 100 A1
Ockle 217 E2
Ockley 88 B4
Ocle Pychard 122 A2
Ocraquoy 233 F2
Odcombe 83 H2
Odd Down 96 B2
Oddendale 179 H3
Oddingley 123 E3
Oddington 112 B3
Odell 125 H3
Odie 232 C4
Odiham 87 E5
Odstock 85 G3
Odstone 135 F4
Offchurch 124 B4
Offenham 123 F2
Offerton Green 160 A3
Offham *E Ssx* 88 D1
Offham *Kent* 101 G1
Offord Cluny 126 C4
Offord D'Arcy 126 C4
Offton 128 D2
Offwell 73 E4
Ogbourne Maizey 97 F3
Ogbourne
St Andrew 97 F3
Ogbourne
St George 97 F3
Ogden 168 B4
Ogil 220 C2
Ogle 197 F1
Ogmore 93 G3
Ogmore-by-Sea 93 G3
Ogmore Vale 94 A5
Oilgate 237 G5
Okeford Fitzpaine 74 D5
Okehampton 71 G4
Okehampton
Camp 71 G3
Okewood Hill 88 B4
Olantigh 90 D5
Old 125 F5
Old Aberdeen 227 F1
Old Alresford 86 D3
Old Arley 135 E3
Old Basing 98 D1
Old Beetley 152 B1
Old Belses 201 H2
Oldberrow 123 G4
Old Bewick 203 E1
Old Bolingbroke 164 B1
Oldborough 72 A5
Old Brampton 161 E2
Old Bridge of Urr 186 C5
Old Buckenham 139 H3
Old Burghclere 98 B1
Oldbury *Shrops* 133 G3
Oldbury *Swell* 134 B2
Oldbury *Warks* 135 F3
Oldbury-on-Severn 95 H5
Oldbury on
the Hill 96 C4
Old Byland 176 B5
Oldcastle *Meath* 244 C2
Oldcastle *Mon* 109 E4
Oldcastle Heath 145 G4
Old Castleton 195 H3
Old Cleeve 82 C4
Old Colwyn 157 E2
Oldcotes 161 H3
Old Court 121 F2
Old Craighall 208 B2
Oldcroft 109 H2
Old Crombie 226 C4
Old Dailly 192 B3
Old Dalby 148 D1
Old Deer 227 F4
Old Denaby 161 G4
Old Down 95 H4
Old Duffus 225 H5
Old Ellerby 171 F4
Old Felixstowe 117 E5
Oldfield *Brad* 168 B4
Oldfield *Worcs* 122 D4
Oldford 84 C5
Old Gore 109 H4
Oldham 160 A5
Oldhamstocks 209 F2
Old Head 235 G2
Old Heath 116 B4
Old Hunstanton 151 G3
Oldhurst 126 C5
Old Hutton 179 H1
Old Kea 66 D2
Old Kilcullen 240 D4
Old Kildimo 239 F1
Old Kilpatrick 205 G2
Old Kinnernie 226 D1
Old Knebworth 114 A3
Oldland 96 A3
Old Leake 150 D4
Oldleighlin 240 C2
Old Malton 176 D4
Oldmeldrum 227 E2
Old Micklefield 169 F4
Old Milverton 124 A4
Old Monkland 206 C1
Old Newton 128 C4
Old Park 133 G4
Old Philpstoun 207 F3
Old Radnor 121 F3
Old Rattray 227 G4
Old Rayne 226 D2
Old Romney 90 C3
Old Ross 237 F5
Old Scone 213 G3
Old Shields 206 D3
Oldshore Beg 228 C5
Oldshoremore 228 C5
Old Sodbury 96 B4
Old Somerby 149 G2
Oldstead 176 A4
Old Stratford 125 F2
Old Swarland 197 G4
Old Town *Cumb* 173 G5
Old Town *Is OS* 64 A4
Old Town *Laois* 240 B3
Old Town *Rosc* 239 H5
Oldtown *Aber* 226 C2
Oldtown *Dub* 245 F1
Oldtown of Ord 226 D4
Oldwalls 92 C5
Old Warden 126 B2
Oldways End 82 B3
Old Weston 137 F1
Oldwhat 227 E4
Old Whittington 161 F2
Old Windsor 99 G3
Old Wives Lees 102 D1
Oldwood 122 A4
Olgrinmore 229 G4
Oliver 200 C3
Oliver's Battery 86 C3
Ollaberry 233 F4
Ollerton *Ches* 159 G2
Ollerton *Notts* 162 B1
Ollerton *Shrops* 146 B2
Olney 125 G3
Olton 134 D2
Olveston 95 H4
Omagh 247 F1
Ombersley 122 D4
Omeath 245 F4
Ompton 162 B1
Onaght 238 C4
Onchan 154 C2
Onecote 147 F5
Onehouse 128 C3
Ongar Hill 151 F1
Ongar Street 121 G4
Onibury 133 E1
Onich 217 H2
Onllwyn 107 G2
Onneley 146 C3
Onslow Village 87 H5
Oola 239 G1
Opinan *Hghld* 223 E5
Opinan *Hghld* 228 A2
Orange Lane 202 B3
Oranmore 239 E5
Orbliston 226 A4
Orbost 222 B3
Orby 164 C1
Orchard Leigh 113 F2
Orchard Portman 83 E2
Orcheston 85 F4
Orcop 109 F4
Orcop Hill 109 F4
Ord 222 D1
Ordhead 221 E5
Ordie 220 C5
Ordiquish 226 A4
Ordley 226 D3
Ord Muir 224 C4
Ore 90 A1
Oreham Common 88 C1
Oreton 133 G2
Orford *Sflk* 129 G2
Orford *Warr* 159 E4
Organford 75 E3
Orgreave 134 D5
Oristown 244 D2
Orlestone 90 C3
Orleton *Herefs* 121 H4
Orleton *Worcs* 122 B4
Orlingbury 136 D1
Ormesby 182 B4
Ormesby
St Margaret 141 E5
Ormesby
St Michael 141 E5
Ormidale 204 C3
Ormiscaig 228 A1
Ormiston 208 C2
Ormsaigmore 216 D2
Ormsary 230 C2
Ormskirk 166 C1
Orphir 232 B3
Orpington 101 E2
Orrell 166 D1
Orritor 247 G2
Orrock 227 F2
Orroland 186 C3
Orsett 101 G4
Orslow 133 H5
Orston 149 E3
Orton *Cumb* 179 H3
Orton *Moray* 226 A4
Orton *Northants* 136 C1
Orton Longueville 137 G3
Orton-on-the-Hill 135 F4
Orwell 126 D3
Osbaldeston 167 E4
Osbaston 135 G4
Osbournby 149 H3
Oscroft 158 D1
Ose 222 B3
Osgathorpe 148 B1
Osgodby *Lincs* 163 F4
Osgodby *N Yorks* 169 H4
Osgodby *N Yorks* 177 G5
Oskaig 222 D3
Oskamull 230 B4
Osmaston 147 G3
Osmington 74 C2
Osmington Mills 74 C2
Osmotherley 182 B2
Ospisdale 229 E1
Ospringe 102 D2
Ossett 168 D2
Ossington 162 C1
Ostend *Essx* 102 C5
Ostend *Nflk* 153 F2
Oswaldkirk 176 B4
Oswaldtwistle 167 F3
Oswestry 145 E2
Otford 101 F1
Otham 102 A1
Othery 83 G3
Otley *Leeds* 168 D5
Otley *Sflk* 129 E3
Otterbourne 86 C2
Otterburn
N Yorks 174 B2
Otterburn
Northld 196 D3
Otterburn Camp 196 D3

GAZETTEER

552

OTTER FERRY–PERRY BAR

Otter Ferry 204 B3
Otterham 70 C3
Otterhampton 83 E4
Ottershaw 99 H2
Otterswick 233 F4
Otterton 72 D3
Ottery St Mary 73 E4
Ottringham 171 G3
Oughterard 238 D5
Oughterby 187 H4
Oughtershaw 174 B5
Oughtibridge 161 E4
Oulart 241 E1
Oulston 176 A4
Oulton *Cumb* 187 G3
Oulton *Leeds* 169 E3
Oulton *Nflk* 152 D2
Oulton *Sflk* 141 E3
Oulton *Staffs* 146 D3
Oulton Broad 141 E3
Oulton Street 152 D2
Oundle 137 E2
Ousby 188 D1
Ousdale 229 G3
Ousden 127 H3
Ousefleet 170 B3
Ouston 190 C3
Outeragh 236 C5
Outer Hope 69 E2
Outertown 232 A3
Outgate 179 F2
Outhgill 180 B2
Outlands 146 C2
Outlane 168 B2
Out Newton 171 H3
Out Rawcliffe 166 C5
Outwell 138 C4
Outwood *Sry* 88 D5
Outwood *Wfield* 169 E3
Outwoods 146 C1
Ovenden 168 B3
Ovens 235 G3
Over *Cambs* 126 D5
Over *S Glos* 95 G4
Overbister 232 C5
Overbury 123 E1
Overcombe 74 C2
Over Compton 84 A2
Over Green 134 D3
Over Haddon 160 D1
Over Kellet 173 F4
Over Kiddington 111 H4
Over Norton 111 G4
Over Peover 159 G2
Overseal 135 E5
Over Silton 182 B1
Oversland 102 D1
Oversley Green 123 F3
Overstone 125 F4
Overstrand 153 E3
Over Stratton 83 G2
Overthorpe 124 C2
Overton *Aber* 226 D1
Overton *C of Aber* 227 E1
Overton *D & G* 187 E4
Overton *Hants* 86 C5
Overton *Lancs* 173 E2
Overton *Shrops* 121 H5
Overton *Swan* 92 C4
Overton *Wrex* 145 F3
Overtown *N Lan* 199 H4
Overtown *Swin* 97 F3
Over Wallop 86 A4
Over Whitacre 135 E3
Over Worton 112 A4
Oving *Bucks* 112 D3
Oving *W Ssx* 77 H5
Ovingdean 79 E4
Ovingham 190 A4
Ovington *Dur* 181 F3
Ovington *Esx* 127 H2
Ovington *Hants* 86 D3
Ovington *Nflk* 139 G4
Ovington *Northld* 189 H4
Owenbeg 243 E4
Ower 86 A2
Owermoigne 74 D3
Owler Bar 161 E2
Owlswick 112 D2
Owmby-by-Spital 163 E3
Owning 236 D5
Owslebury 86 C2
Owston 136 C4
Owston Ferry 162 C5
Owstwick 171 G4
Owthorpe 148 D2
Owton Manor 191 E1
Oxborough 139 E4
Oxcombe 164 A2
Oxen End 115 F4
Oxenholme 179 G1
Oxenhope 168 B4
Oxen Park 172 D5
Oxenton 110 D4
Oxenwood 97 H1
Oxford 112 B2
Oxhill 124 A2
Oxley 134 B4
Oxley's Green 89 G2
Oxnam 202 B1
Oxshott 100 B2
Oxspring 161 E5
Oxted 88 D5
Oxton *Bdrs* 201 G4
Oxton *Notts* 148 D4
Oxwich 92 C4
Oxwich Green 92 C4
Oxwick 152 B2
Oykel Bridge 228 D2
Oyne 226 D2
Oystermouth 93 E4
Ozleworth 96 B5

P

Pabail Iarach 231 G4
Packington 135 F5
Padbury 112 D4
Paddington 100 C4
Paddlesworth 91 E4
Paddockhaugh 225 H4
Paddock Wood 89 G5
Paddolgreen 145 H2
Padeswood 145 E5
Padiham 167 G4
Padside 175 E2
Padstow 67 E5
Padworth 98 D2
Pagham 77 G4
Paglesham Churchend 102 C5
Paglesham Eastend 102 C5
Paignton 69 G4
Pailton 135 G2
Painscastle 121 E2
Painshawfield 189 H4
Painswick 110 C2
Painter's Forstal 102 C1
Paisley 205 G1
Pakefield 141 E3
Pakenham 128 B4
Palatine 240 D3
Pale 144 B3
Palestine 85 H4
Paley Street 99 F3
Palgrave 140 A1
Pallas Grean (New) 239 G1
Pallas Green 239 G1
Pallaskenry 239 E2
Palmerstown 94 C2
Palnackie 186 C4
Palnure 185 G4
Palterton 161 G1
Pamber End 98 D1
Pamber Green 98 D1
Pamber Heath 98 D2
Pamington 123 E1
Pamphill 75 F4
Pampisford 127 E2
Panborough 83 H5
Panbride 214 D4
Pancrasweek 70 D5
Pandy Mon 109 E3
Pandy Pwys 131 G4
Pandy Wrex 144 D3
Pandy Tudur 157 E1
Panfield 115 F4
Pangbourne 98 D3
Pannal 175 G2
Pant 145 E1
Pantasaph 157 H2
Panteg 105 F5
Pant-glas 131 E3
Pant Glâs 143 E4
Pantgwyn 118 C2
Pant-lasau 107 F1
Pant Mawr 131 F2
Pant-Meredith 107 F4
Panton 163 G2
Pantperthog 131 E4
Pant-y-dwr 120 C5
Pant-y-ffridd 132 B4
Pantyffynnon 107 E2
Panxworth 140 D5
Papcastle 178 C5
Papple 208 D2
Papplewick 148 C4
Papworth Everard 126 C4
Papworth St Agnes 126 C4
Par 67 F3
Parbold 166 D2
Parbrook 84 A4
Parc 144 A2
Parc-Henri 107 E4
Parcllyn 118 C3
Parc Seymour 95 F5
Pardshaw 178 C4
Parham 129 F4
Parish Holm 199 G2
Park 194 B3
Park Bernisdale 222 C4
Park Corner 98 D4
Park End 196 D1
Parkend 109 H2
Parkeston 116 D4
Park Farm 90 C4
Park Gate 76 D5
Parkgate *Ant* 248 B2
Parkgate *Ches* 158 B2
Parkgate *D & G* 194 C2
Parkgate *Sry* 88 C4
Parkham 80 D2
Parkham Ash 80 D2
Parkhill 213 H5
Parkhouse 109 G2
Parkhurst 76 C3
Park Lane 145 G3
Parkmill 92 D4
Parkside 226 B2
Parkstone 75 F3
Parley Cross 75 G4
Parracombe 81 G5
Parrog 105 G5
Parsley Hay 160 C1
Parsonby 187 F2
Parson Cross 161 E4
Parson Drove 138 A4
Partick 206 A2
Partington 159 F4
Partney 164 B1
Parton *Cumb* 178 B4
Parton *D & G* 186 B5
Partridge Green 88 B2
Partrishow 108 D4
Partry 242 D2
Parwich 147 G4
Passage East 237 E4
Passage West 236 A3
Passenham 112 D5
Passfield 87 F3
Passingford Bridge 114 D1
Paston 153 F2
Patcham 78 D5
Patching 78 B5
Patchole 81 G4
Patchway 95 H4
Pateley Bridge 175 E3
Pathe 83 G3
Pathfinder Village 72 B3
Pathhead *E Ayr* 193 F5
Pathhead *Fife* 208 A4
Pathhead *Midln* 208 B1
Pathlow 123 G3
Patmore Heath 114 C4
Patna 192 D5
Patney 97 E1
Path of Condie 213 G2
Patrick 154 B3
Patrick Brompton 181 G1
Patrickswell 239 F1
Patrington 171 G3
Patrixbourne 103 E1
Patterdale 179 F4
Pattingham 133 H3
Pattishall 125 E3
Pattiswick 115 G4
Patton Bridge 179 H2
Paul 64 B2
Paulerspury 125 E2
Paull 171 F3
Paulstown or Whitehall 240 D2
Paulton 96 A1
Pauperhaugh 197 F3
Pavenham 125 H3
Pawlett 83 F4
Pawston 202 C2
Paxford 111 F5
Paxton 202 D4
Payhembury 72 D4
Paythorne 174 B2
Peacehaven 79 E4
Peak Dale 160 C2
Peak Forest 160 C2
Peakirk 137 G4
Pean Hill 103 E2
Pearsie 220 C2
Peasedown St John 96 B1
Peasemore 98 B3
Peasenhall 129 G4
Pease Pottage 88 C3
Peaslake 88 A5
Peasmarsh 90 B2
Peaston 208 C2
Peastonbank 208 C2
Peathill 227 F5
Peat Inn 214 C1
Peatling Magna 136 A3
Peatling Parva 136 A2
Peaton 133 E2
Peats Corner 129 E4
Pebmarsh 115 H5
Pebworth 123 G2
Pecket Well 168 A3
Peckforton 145 H5
Peckleton 135 G4
Pedmore 134 B2
Pedwell 83 G4
Peebles 201 E3
Peel 154 B3
Peggs Green 135 G5
Pegsdon 113 H4
Pegswood 197 G2
Peinchorran 222 D3
Peinlich 222 C4
Pelaw 190 C4
Pelcomb Cross 105 F3
Peldon 116 A3
Pelsall 134 C4
Pelton 190 B3
Pelutho 187 F2
Pelynt 67 H3
Pembrey 106 C1
Pembridge 121 G3
Pembroke 105 F1
Pembroke Dock 105 F2
Pembury 89 G4
Penallt 109 G2
Pen-allt 109 G4
Penally 105 H1
Penare 67 F2
Penarth 94 C3
Pen-bont Rhydybeddau 130 D2
Penbryn 118 C3
Pencader 119 E1
Pencaitland 208 C2
Pencarreg 119 F2
Pencelli 108 B4
Pen-clawdd 106 D1
Pencoed 94 A4
Pencombe 122 A3
Pencoyd 109 G4
Pencraig *Herefs* 109 G3
Pencraig *Pwys* 144 C2
Pencroesoped 109 E2
Pendas Fields 169 E4
Pendeen 64 A3
Penderyn 108 A2
Pendine 106 A2
Pendlebury 159 G5
Pendleton 167 G4
Pendock 122 C1
Pendoggett 70 A2
Pendomer 74 A5
Pendoylan 94 B3
Penegoes 131 E4
Penelewey 66 D2
Penffordd 105 G4
Penffridd 143 E5
Penge 100 D3
Pengenffordd 108 C4
Pengorffwysfa 155 H4
Pengover Green 68 A4
Pengwern 157 F2
Penhale 67 E3
Penhallick 65 E1
Penhallow 65 E5
Penhalurick 65 E3
Penhow 95 F5
Penhurst 89 G2
Penicuik 200 D5
Peniel 157 F1
Penifiler 222 C3
Peninver 230 C1
Penisa'r Waun 156 B1
Penistone 160 D5
Penjerrick 65 E3
Penketh 159 E3
Penkill 192 B3
Penkridge 134 B5
Penley 145 G3
Penllech 142 B2
Penllergaer 107 E1
Penllyn 94 A3
Pen-llyn 155 G3
Penmachno 143 H4
Penmaen Caer 94 C5
Penmaenmawr 156 C2
Penmaenpool 143 G1
Penmaen Swan 92 D4
Penmark 94 B2
Penmon 156 B3
Penmorfa 143 E3
Penmynydd 156 A2
Penn 99 G5
Pennal 131 E4
Pennan 227 E5
Pennant *Cere* 119 F4
Pennant *Cnwy* 144 A5
Pennant *Pwys* 131 F3
Pennant Melangell 144 C2
Pennard 92 D4
Pennerley 132 D3
Pennington 172 D4
Pennorth 108 C4
Penn Street 113 F1
Penny Bridge 172 D5
Pennycross 230 B4
Pennygate 153 F1
Pennygown 230 B4
Pennymoor 72 B5
Pennyvenie 193 E4
Penparc 118 C2
Penparcau 130 C2
Penperlleni 109 E2
Penpillick 67 F3
Penpol 66 D1
Penpoll 67 G3
Penponds 64 D3
Penpont 194 A3
Penre-bach 119 F2
Penrherber 118 C1
Penrhiwceiber 94 B5
Penrhiw-llan 118 D2
Penrhiwpal 118 D2
Penrhos *Anglsy* 155 F3
Penrhos *Gwyn* 142 C2
Penrhos *Mon* 109 F2
Penrhos *Pwys* 107 G2
Penrhyn Bay 156 D3
Penrhyn-coch 130 D2
Penrhyndeudraeth 143 F3
Penrhyn-side 156 D3
Penrhys 94 B5
Penrice 92 C4
Penrith 188 C1
Penrose 66 D5
Penruddock 179 F5
Penryn 65 E3
Pensarn 157 E2
Pen-sarn *Gwyn* 142 D3
Pen-sarn *Gwyn* 143 F2
Pensax 122 C4
Pensby 158 B3
Penselwood 84 C3
Pensford 95 H2
Pensham 123 E2
Penshaw 190 C3
Penshurst 89 F4
Pensilva 70 D1
Penston 208 C2
Pentewan 67 F2
Pentir 156 B1
Pentire 66 C4
Pentlow 128 A2
Pentney 139 E5
Penton Mewsey 86 A5
Pentraeth 156 A2
Pentre *Pwys* 131 H2
Pentre *Shrops* 132 D5
Pentre *Wrex* 144 D2
Pentre *Wrex* 145 E3
Pentrebach *MT* 108 B2
Pentrebach *Swan* 107 E2
Pentre-bach 120 B1
Pentre Berw 155 H2
Pentre-bont 143 G4
Pentrecagal 118 D2
Pentre-celyn *Denb* 144 D4
Pentre-celyn *Pwys* 131 F4
Pentreclwydau 107 G2
Pentre-cwrt 118 D1
Pentre Dolau Honddu 120 C2
Pentredwr 145 E4
Pentre-dwr 93 E5
Pentrefelin *Cnwy* 156 D2
Pentrefelin *Gwyn* 143 E3
Pentrefelin *Pwys* 144 D1
Pentrefelin 107 E4
Pentrefelin 145 E3
Pentrefoelas 144 A4
Pentre Galar 106 A4
Pentregat 118 D3
Pentre-Gwenlais 107 E3
Pentre Gwynfryn 143 F2
Pentre Halkyn 158 A2
Pentreheyling 132 B3
Pentre Isaf 157 E1
Pentre-Llanrhaeadr 144 C5
Pentre Llifior 132 B3
Pentre-llwyn-llwyd 120 C3
Pentre-llyn 130 D1
Pentre-llyn-cymmer 144 B4
Pentre-mawr 157 F2
Pentre-Morgan 106 C4
Pentre'r beirdd 132 B5
Pentre'r-felin 107 H4
Pentre-tafarn-y-fedw 156 D1
Pentre-ty-gwyn 107 G5
Pentrich 148 A4
Pentridge 85 F2
Pentwyn 94 D4
Pentyrch 94 C4
Penuwch 119 F4
Penwithick 67 F3
Penwyllt 107 H3
Pen-y-banc 107 E4
Penybont 120 D4
Pen-y-bont *Carm* 106 B4
Pen-y-bont *Pwys* 145 E1
Pen-y-Bont 145 E1
Penybontfawr 144 C1
Penybryn 94 C5
Pen-y-bryn *Gwyn* 143 G1
Pen-y-bryn *Pemb* 118 B2
Penycae 145 E4
Pen-y-cae 107 G3
Pen-y-cae-mawr 109 F1
Pen-y-cefn 157 G2
Pen-y-clawdd 109 F2
Pen-y-coedcae 94 B4
Penycwm 105 E4
Pen-y-fai 93 G4
Penyffordd 145 F5
Pen-y-ffordd 157 G3
Pen-y-garn 107 E4
Penygarnedd 144 D1
Pen-y-garnedd 156 A2
Penygraig 94 A5
Pen-y-graig 142 B2
Penygroes 143 E4
Pen-y-groes 107 E3
Pen-y-lan 94 A3
Pen-y-Mynydd 106 D2
Pen-y-Park 121 F2
Pen-yr-heol 109 F2
Penysarn 155 H4
Pen-y-stryt 144 D4
Penywaun 108 A2
Penzance 64 B2
Peopleton 123 E3
Peover Heath 159 G2
Peper Harow 87 G4
Peplow 146 A1
Perceton 198 C3
Percie 220 D4
Percyhorner 227 F5
Perham Down 85 H5
Perivale 100 B4
Perkhill 220 D5
Perlethorpe 162 B2
Perranarworthal 65 E3
Perran Downs 64 C3
Perranporth 65 E5
Perranuthnoe 64 C2
Perranwell 65 E3
Perranzabuloe 65 E5
Perry Barr 134 C3

553

PERRY GREEN–PRESTON

Perry Green	114	C3
Perrystone Hill	109	H4
Pershall	146	C2
Pershore	123	E2
Pert	221	E2
Pertenhall	126	A4
Perth	213	G3
Perthy	145	F2
Perton	134	A3
Pertwood	84	D4
Peterborough	137	G4
Peterburn	228	A1
Peterchurch	109	E5
Peterculter	221	F5
Peterhead	227	G3
Peterlee	190	D2
Petersfield	87	E2
Peter's Green	113	H3
Peters Marland	81	E1
Peterstone Wentlooge	94	D4
Peterston-super-Ely	94	B3
Peterstow	109	G4
Peter Tavy	68	C5
Petertown	232	A3
Petham	90	D5
Petrockstowe	81	F1
Pett	90	B1
Pettaugh	129	E3
Pettigoe	246	D1
Pettinain	200	B3
Pettistree	129	F3
Petton *Devon*	82	C2
Petton *Shrops*	145	G2
Petts Wood	101	E2
Petty	227	E3
Pettycur	208	A4
Pettymuick	227	F2
Petworth	87	H2
Pevensey Bay	79	H5
Pewsey	97	F1
Philham	80	C2
Philiphaugh	201	F2
Phillack	64	C3
Philleigh	66	D1
Philpstoun	207	F3
Phocle Green	109	H4
Phoenix Green	99	E1
Phorp	225	G4
Pica	178	B4
Piccadilly Corner	140	C2
Piccotts End	113	G2
Pickerells	115	E2
Pickering	176	D5
Picket Piece	86	B3
Picket Post	75	H5
Pickford Green	135	E2
Pickhill	175	G5
Picklescott	132	D3
Pickletillem	214	C3
Pickmere	159	F2
Pickney	83	E3
Pickstock	146	B1
Pickwell *Devon*	81	E4
Pickwell *Leics*	136	C5
Pickworth *Lincs*	149	H2
Pickworth *Rut*	137	E5
Picton *Ches*	158	C2
Picton *N Yorks*	182	A3
Piddinghoe	79	E4
Piddington *Bucks*	113	E1
Piddington *Northants*	125	F3
Piddington *Oxon*	112	C3
Piddlehinton	74	C4
Piddletrenthide	74	C4
Pidley	126	D5
Piercebridge	181	G4
Piercetown	237	G5
Pierowall	232	B5
Pigdon	197	G2
Pike	239	H4
Pikehall	147	G5
Pilgrims Hatch	115	E1
Pilham	162	D4
Pill	95	G3
Pillaton	68	B4
Pillerton Hersey	124	A2
Pillerton Priors	124	A2
Pilleth	121	F4
Pilley *Barns*	161	E5
Pilley *Hants*	76	B4
Pilling	173	E1
Pilling Lane	173	E1
Pilning	95	G4
Pilsbury	160	C1
Pilsdon	73	H4
Pilsgate	137	F4
Pilsley *Derbs*	160	D2
Pilsley *Derbs*	161	F1
Pilton *Northants*	137	E2
Pilton *Rut*	136	D4
Pilton *Som*	84	A4
Pilton Green	92	C4
Piltown	236	D5
Pimperne	85	E1
Pinchbeck	150	B2
Pinchbeck West	150	B1
Pinfold	166	C2
Pinhay	73	G3
Pinhoe	72	C4
Pinley Green	123	H4
Pin Mill	129	E1
Pinminnoch	192	B3
Pinmore	192	B3
Pinn	73	E3
Pinner	100	B4
Pinvin	123	E2
Pinwherry	192	B2
Pinxton	148	B5
Pipe and Lyde	121	H2
Pipe Gate	146	B3
Piperhall	204	D1
Piperhill	225	F4
Pipe Ridware	134	C5
Pipers Pool	70	D3
Pipewell	136	C2
Pippacott	81	F4
Pipton	121	E1
Pirbright	99	G1
Pirnmill	230	C2
Pirton *Herts*	113	H4
Pirton *Worcs*	122	D2
Pisgah	130	D1
Pishill	99	E4
Pistyll	142	C3
Pitagowan	219	F2
Pitblae	227	F5
Pitcairngreen	213	G3
Pitcalnie	225	E5
Pitcaple	226	D2
Pitchaish	225	H3
Pitchcombe	110	C2
Pitchcott	112	D3
Pitchford	133	E4
Pitch Green	112	D2
Pitch Place	99	G1
Pitcombe	84	B3
Pitcox	209	E3
Pitcur	214	A4
Pitfichie	226	D1
Pitforthie	221	F3
Pitgrudy	229	F1
Pitkennedy	220	D1
Pitkevy	214	A1
Pitlessie	214	B1
Pitlochry	219	G1
Pitmachie	226	D2
Pitmedden	227	E2
Pitminster	83	E2
Pitmunie	226	D1
Pitney	83	H3
Pitscottie	214	C2
Pitsea	101	H4
Pitsford	125	F4
Pitsford Hill	82	D3
Pitstone	113	F3
Pitstone Green	113	F3
Pittendreich	225	H5
Pittentrail	229	E2
Pittenweem	214	D1
Pittington	190	C2
Pitton *Swan*	92	C4
Pitton *Wilts*	85	H3
Pittulie	227	F5
Pityme	67	E5
Pixey Green	129	E5
Place Newton	177	E4
Plaidy	226	D4
Plains	206	C2
Plaish	133	E3
Plaistow	87	H3
Plaitford	85	H2
Plas	106	D4
Plas Brondanw	143	F3
Plas Esgair	131	F4
Plas Gogerddan	130	D2
Plas Gwynant	143	F4
Plas Llysyn	131	G3
Plas Nantyr	144	D3
Plas-rhiw-Saeson	131	G4
Plastow Green	98	C2
Platt	101	G1
Plawsworth	190	C3
Plaxtol	101	G1
Playden	90	B2
Playford	129	E2
Play Hatch	99	E3
Playing Place	66	D2
Plealey	132	D4
Plean	206	D4
Pleasington	167	E3
Pleasley	161	G1
Pleinmont	75	F1
Plenderleith	196	B5
Plenmeller	189	E4
Pleshey	115	F3
Plâs Llwyngwern	131	E4
Plockton	223	F3
Plowden	132	D2
Ploxgreen	132	D4
Pluck	247	E3
Pluckley	90	B5
Pluckley Thorne	90	B4
Plumbland	187	G2
Plumbridge	247	F2
Plumley	159	F2
Plumpton *Cumb*	188	B2
Plumpton *E Ssx*	88	D1
Plumpton *Lancs*	166	C4
Plumpton Green	88	D2
Plumpton Head	188	C2
Plumpton Rocks	175	G2
Plumstead *Green*	101	E3
Plumstead *Nflk*	152	D2
Plumtree	148	D2
Plungar	149	E2
Plush	74	C4
Plwmp	118	D3
Plymouth	68	C3
Plympton	68	C3
Plymstock	68	C3
Plymtree	72	D4
Pockley	176	B5
Pocklington	176	D1
Pockthorpe	151	H2
Pode Hole	150	B1
Podimore	84	A3
Podington	125	G4
Podmore *Nflk*	139	G5
Podmore *Staffs*	146	C3
Point Clear	116	B3
Pointon	150	A2
Pokesdown	75	G3
Pol a' Charra	231	E1
Polapit Tamar	70	D3
Polbae	192	C1
Polbain	228	B2
Polbathic	68	B3
Polbeth	207	F1
Poldean	194	D4
Polebrook	137	F2
Polegate	79	G5
Poles	229	E2
Polesworth	135	E4
Polglass	228	B2
Polgooth	67	E3
Poling	78	A5
Polkerris	67	F3
Polla	228	D4
Pollagh	240	A5
Pollington	169	H2
Pollo	225	E5
Polloch	217	G2
Pollokshaws	199	E5
Pollokshields	206	A1
Polmassick	67	E2
Polmont	207	E3
Polnessan	192	D5
Polperro	67	H3
Polruan	67	G3
Polsham	83	H4
Polskeoch	193	G4
Polstead	128	C1
Polstead Heath	128	C2
Poltalloch	204	A5
Poltimore	72	C4
Polton	208	B2
Polwarth	202	B4
Polyphant	70	D2
Polzeath	67	E5
Pomeroy	247	G1
Ponde	120	D1
Pondersbridge	137	H3
Ponders End	100	D5
Pond Street	127	E1
Ponsanooth	65	E3
Ponsongath	65	E1
Ponsworthy	69	E5
Pont Aberglaslyn	143	F4
Pontamman	107	E3
Pontantwn	106	C3
Pontardawe	107	F2
Pontarddulais	107	E2
Pontarsais	106	C4
Pontblyddyn	145	E5
Pont Creuddyn	119	F3
Pont Crugnant	131	F3
Pont Cyfyng	143	G5
Pontdolgoch	131	H3
Pontefract	169	F3
Ponteland	197	G1
Ponterwyd	131	E2
Pontesbury	132	D4
Pontesford	132	D4
Pontfadog	145	E3
Pontfaen	105	G5
Pont-faen	120	C1
Pontgarreg	118	D3
Pont Henri	106	D2
Ponthir	95	E5
Ponthirwaun	118	C2
Pontllanfraith	94	C5
Pont Llanio	119	G3
Pontlliw	107	E1
Pont Llogel	131	H5
Pontllyfni	142	D4
Pontlottyn	108	C2
Pontneddfechan	107	H2
Pontoon	243	E3
Pont Pen-y-benglog	143	G5
Pontrhydfendigaid	119	H4
Pont Rhyd-y-cyff	93	G4
Pontrhydyfen	93	F5
Pont-rhyd-y-groes	131	E1
Pontrilas	109	E4
Pontrobert	132	A5
Pont-rug	156	A1
Ponts Green	89	G2
Pontshill	109	H4
Pont-Sian	119	E2
Pontsticill	108	B2
Pontyates	106	D2
Pontyberem	106	D2
Pontybodkin	145	E5
Pontyclun	94	B4
Pontycymer	93	H5
Pontymister	94	D4
Pont-y-pant	143	H4
Pontypool	108	D1
Pontypridd	94	B5
Pont-yr-hafod	105	F4
Pontywaun	94	D5
Pooksgreen	76	B5
Pool *Corn*	64	D4
Pool *Leeds*	168	D5
Poole	75	F3
Poole Keynes	97	E5
Poolewe	228	A1
Pooley Bridge	179	G4
Poolhill	110	A4
Pool of Muckhart	207	E5
Pool Quay	132	C5
Poorton	74	A4
Pootings	89	E5
Pope Hill	105	F3
Popeswood	99	F2
Popham	86	D4
Poplar	100	D4
Porchfield	76	C3
Poringland	140	C4
Porkellis	64	D3
Porlock	82	B5
Porlock Weir	82	B5
Port	245	F3
Portachoillan	230	C2
Portacloy	242	C5
Portadown	245	E5
Portaferry	245	G5
Portaleen	247	F5
Port-an-eorna	223	E2
Port Ann	204	B4
Port Appin	210	C5
Portarlington	240	C4
Port Askaig	230	B2
Portavadie	204	B2
Portavogie	240	C1
Portballintrae	247	H5
Port Bannatyne	204	C2
Portbury	95	G3
Port Carlisle	187	G4
Port Charlotte	230	A2
Portchester	77	E5
Portclair	224	B1
Port Driseach	204	B2
Port Durlainne	242	C5
Portelet	75	G1
Port Ellen	230	B2
Port Elphinstone	227	E2
Portencalzie	184	C5
Portencross	198	A4
Port Erin	154	A1
Portesham	74	B3
Port e Vullen	154	D4
Port-Eynon	92	C4
Portfield Gate	105	F3
Portgate	71	E3
Port Gaverne	70	A2
Port Glasgow	205	F2
Portglenone	247	H3
Portgordon	226	B5
Portgower	229	F2
Porth	94	B5
Porthallow	65	E2
Porthcawl	93	G3
Porthcothan	66	D5
Porthcurno	64	A2
Port Henderson	228	A1
Porthgain	105	E5
Porthkerry	94	B2
Porthleven	64	D2
Porthllechog	155	H4
Porthmadog	143	F3
Porthmeor	64	B3
Porth Navas	65	E2
Portholland	67	E2
Porthoustock	65	F2
Porthpean	67	F3
Porthtowan	64	D4
Porthyrhyd *Carm*	106	D3
Porthyrhyd *Carm*	107	F5
Porth-y-waen	145	E1
Portincaple	205	E4
Portington	170	B4
Portinnisherrich	210	C2
Portinscale	178	D4
Port Isaac	70	A2
Portishead	95	F3
Portknockie	226	C5
Portland	239	G4
Portlaoise	240	C3
Portlaw	236	D5
Portlethen	221	G4
Portlethen Village	221	G4
Portloe	67	E1
Port Logan	184	C2
Portmagee	234	B3
Portmahomack	229	F1
Portmarnock	241	F5
Portmeirion	143	F3
Portmellon	67	F2
Port Mholair	231	G5
Port Mõr	216	D3
Portmore	76	B4
Port Mulgrave	183	E4
Portnablagh	246	D4
Portnacroish	210	C5
Portnahaven	230	A2
Portnalong	222	B3
Portnaluchaig	217	F4
Portnancon	228	D5
Port nan Giuran	231	G5
Port nan Long	231	F3
Portnashangan	244	B1
Port Nis	231	G5
Portnoo	246	B3
Portobello	208	B2
Port of Menteith	206	A5
Porton	85	G4
Portpatrick	184	C3
Port Quin	70	A2
Portraine	245	F1
Port Ramsay	210	B5
Portreath	64	D4
Portree	222	C3
Portroe	239	G3
Portrush	247	G4
Portrye	204	D1
Port St Mary	154	A1
Portsalon	247	E4
Portscatho	66	D1
Portsea	77	E4
Port Sgiogarstaigh	231	G5
Portskerra	229	F5
Portskewett	95	F4
Portslade	78	D5
Portslade-by-Sea	78	D5
Portslogan	184	B4
Portsmouth	77	E4
Portsoy	226	C5
Portstewart	247	G4
Port Sunlight	158	B3
Portswood	86	B1
Port Talbot	93	F5
Portuairk	216	D2
Portumna	239	G4
Portway	123	F5
Port Wemyss	230	A2
Port William	185	F2
Portwrinkle	68	B3
Poslingford	127	H2
Postbridge	71	H2
Postcombe	112	D1
Postling	90	D4
Postwick	140	C4
Potarch	221	E4
Potsgrove	113	F4
Potten End	113	G2
Potterhanworth	163	F1
Potterhanworth Booths	163	F1
Potter Heigham	153	G1
Potterne	96	D1
Potterne Wick	96	D1
Potters Bar	114	B1
Potters Corner	90	C4
Potters Crouch	113	H2
Potters Forstal	90	B5
Potterspury	125	F2
Potter Street	114	D2
Potterton	227	F1
Potto	182	B2
Potton	126	C2
Pottore	244	A4
Pott Row	151	G1
Pott Shrigley	160	A2
Poughill *Corn*	70	C5
Poughill *Devon*	72	B5
Poulnamucky	236	C5
Poulshot	96	D1
Poulton	111	E1
Poulton-le-Fylde	166	B4
Pound Bank	122	C5
Poundgate	89	E3
Pound Hill	88	C4
Poundland	192	B2
Poundon	112	C4
Poundsgate	69	E5
Poundstock	70	C4
Powburn	197	F5
Powderham	72	C3
Power's Cross	239	G4
Powerstock	74	A4
Powfoot	187	G5
Powick	122	D3
Powmill	207	F5
Poxwell	74	C3
Poyle	100	A3
Poynings	88	C1
Poyntington	84	B2
Poynton	160	A3
Poynton Green *T & W*	133	F5
Poynton Green *T & W*	145	H1
Poyntzfield	225	E5
Poyntz Pass	245	E5
Poystreet Green	128	C3
Praa Sands	64	C2
Pratt's Bottom	101	E2
Praze-an-Beeble	64	D3
Predannack Wollas	64	D1
Prees	145	H2
Preesall	173	E1
Prees Green	145	H2
Preesgweene	145	E3
Prees Heath	145	H3
Prees Higher Heath	145	H3
Prendwick	197	E5
Pren-gwyn	119	E2
Prenteg	143	F3
Prenton	158	B3
Prescot	158	D4
Prescott	145	G1
Pressen	202	C3
Prestatyn	157	G3
Prestbury *Ches*	160	A2
Prestbury *Glos*	110	D4
Presteigne	121	F4
Presthope	133	F3
Prestleigh	84	B4
Preston *B & H*	78	D5
Preston *Bdrs*	209	F1
Preston *Devon*	69	G5
Preston *Dors*	74	C2

GAZETTEER

555

RHOSLEFAIN–RUTHVENFIELD

Rhoslefain 130 C4
Rhosllanerchrugog 145 F4
Rhosmaen 107 E4
Rhosmeirch 155 H2
Rhosneigr 155 G2
Rhosnesni 145 F4
Rhôs-on-Sea 156 D3
Rhossili 92 C4
Rhosson 104 D4
Rhostryfan 143 E5
Rhostyllen 145 F4
Rhosybol 155 H3
Rhos-y-brithdir 144 D1
Rhos-y-gwaliau 144 B2
Rhos-y-llan 142 B3
Rhos-y-mawn 157 E1
Rhos-y-meirch 121 F4
Rhu *A & B* 204 A1
Rhu *A & B* 205 E3
Rhuallt 157 G2
Rhuddlan 157 F2
Rhue 228 B2
Rhugarbh 210 C5
Rhulen 120 D2
Rhunahaorine 230 C2
Rhuvoult 228 C4
Rhyd *Gwyn* 143 F3
Rhyd *Pwys* 131 G4
Rhydargaeau 106 C4
Rhydcymerau 107 E5
Rhydd 122 D2
Rhyd-Ddu 143 F4
Rhydding 107 F1
Rhydlewis 118 D2
Rhydlios 142 B2
Rhydlydan 144 A4
Rhydowen 119 E2
Rhyd-Rosser 119 F4
Rhydspence 121 E2
Rhydtalog 145 E5
Rhyd-uchaf 144 B3
Rhydwyn 155 G3
Rhyd-y-clafdy 142 C2
Rhydycroesau 145 E2
Rhydyfelin *Cere* 130 C1
Rhydyfelin *RCT* 94 B4
Rhyd-y-foel 157 E2
Rhyd-y-fro 107 F2
Rhydymain 143 H1
Rhyd-y-meudwy 144 D4
Rhydymwyn 158 A1
Rhyd-yr-onen 130 D4
Rhydywrach 105 H3
Rhyl 157 F3
Rhymney 108 C2
Rhynd 213 H3
Rhynie *Aber* 226 C2
Rhynie *Hghld* 229 F1
Ribbesford 122 C5
Ribblehead 174 A4
Ribbleton 167 F4
Ribchester 167 F4
Riber 147 H5
Ribigill 229 E4
Riby 171 F1
Riccall 169 H4
Riccarton 198 D3
Richards Castle 121 H4
Richborough Port 103 G2
Richill 245 E5
Richings Park 100 A3
Richmond *N Yorks* 181 F2
Richmond *Rich* 100 B3
Rickarton 221 F4
Rickinghall 128 C5
Rickling 114 D4
Rickmansworth 113 G1
Riddell 201 G1
Riddlecombe 81 G1
Riddlesden 174 D1
Ridge *Dors* 75 E3
Ridge *Herts* 114 A1
Ridge *Wilts* 85 E3
Ridge Lane 135 E3
Ridgemarsh 102 D5
Ridgeway 161 F3
Ridgeway Cross 122 C2
Ridgewell 127 H2
Ridgewood 89 E2
Ridgmont 113 F5
Ridgway 132 D2
Riding Mill 189 H4
Ridley 101 G2
Ridleywood 145 F4
Ridlington *Nflk* 153 F2
Ridlington *Rut* 136 C4
Ridsdale 196 D2
Riechip 213 G5
Rienachait 228 B3
Rievaulx 176 B5
Rigg 187 H5
Riggend 206 C2
Rigside 200 A3
Rileyhill 134 D5
Rilla Mill 70 D1
Rillington 177 E4
Rimington 167 G5
Rimpton 84 B2
Rimswell 171 G3
Rinaston 105 F4
Ringaskiddy 236 A2
Ringford 186 B4
Ringland 140 A5
Ringles Cross 89 E2
Ringmer 89 F1
Ringmore 69 E2
Ring's End 138 A4
Ringsend 247 G4
Ringsfield 140 D2
Ringsfield Corner 140 D2
Ringshall *Bucks* 113 F3
Ringshall *Sflk* 128 C3
Ringshall Stocks 128 C3
Ringstead *Nflk* 151 G3
Ringstead *Northants* 137 E1
Ringville 236 D3
Ringwood 75 H5
Ringwould 91 G5
Rinmore 226 B1
Rinnigill 232 B3
Rinsey 64 C2
Riof 231 F4
Ripe 89 F1
Ripley *Derbs* 148 A4
Ripley *Hants* 75 H4
Ripley *N Yorks* 175 F3
Ripley *Sry* 100 A1
Riplingham 170 D4
Ripon 175 G4
Rippingale 150 A2
Ripple *Kent* 91 F5
Ripple *Worcs* 122 D1
Ripponden 168 B2
Rireavach 228 B2
Risabus 230 B2
Risbury 122 A3
Risby 128 A4
Risca 94 D5
Rise 171 F5
Risegate 150 B2
Riseley *Beds* 126 A4
Riseley *Hants* 99 E2
Rishangles 129 E4
Rishton 167 F4
Rishworth 168 B2
Rising Bridge 167 G3
Risley *Derbs* 148 B3
Risley *Warr* 159 F4
Risplith 175 F3
Rispond 228 D5
Rivar 97 H2
Rivenhall *Cambs* 127 F2
Rivenhall *Esx* 115 G3
Rivenhall End 115 G3
River *Hants* 87 G2
River *Kent* 91 F4
River Bank 127 F4
Riverchapel 241 F2
Riverhead 101 F1
Riverstick 235 G2
Riverstown *Cork* 235 H3
Riverstown *Sligo* 243 G4
Riverstown *Tipp* 239 H4
Rivington 167 E2
Roachill 82 B2
Roade 125 F3
Roadhead 195 H1
Roadmeetings 199 H4
Roadside of Catterline 221 F3
Roadside of Kinneff 221 F3
Roadwater 82 C4
Roag 222 B3
Roa Island 172 C3
Roath 94 D3
Roberton *Bdrs* 195 G5
Roberton *S Lan* 200 A2
Robertsbridge 89 H2
Robertstown 226 A3
Roberttown 168 C3
Robeston Cross 105 E2
Robeston Wathen 105 G3
Robeston West 105 E2
Robin Hood *Derbs* 161 E2
Robin Hood *Leeds* 169 E3
Robinhood End 115 F5
Robin Hood's Bay 183 G3
Robins 87 F2
Robinstown 244 D1
Roborough *C of Plym* 68 C4
Roborough *Devon* 81 F2
Robroyston 206 B2
Roby Mill 166 D1
Rocester 147 F3
Roch 105 E3
Rochallie 220 A1
Rochdale 167 H2
Roche 67 E4
Rochester *MT* 102 A2
Rochester *Northld* 196 C3
Rochford *Esx* 102 B5
Rochford *Worcs* 122 B4
Rochfortbridge 240 C5
Rock *Caer* 108 C1
Rock *Corn* 67 E5
Rock *Northld* 203 G1
Rock *Worcs* 122 C5
Rockbeare 72 D4
Rockbourne 85 G2
Rockchapel 235 E5
Rockcliffe *Cumb* 188 A4
Rockcliffe *D & G* 186 C3
Rockcorry 244 C4
Rock Ferry 158 B3
Rockfield *Hghld* 229 F1
Rockfield *Mon* 109 F3
Rockhampton 96 A5
Rockhill *Shrops* 132 C1
Rockhill *Tipp* 235 G5
Rockingham 136 D3
Rockland All Saints 139 G3
Rockland St Mary 140 C4
Rockland St Peter 139 G3
Rockley 97 F3
Rockmills 235 H4
Rockwell End 99 E4
Rockwell Green 82 D2
Rodbourne 96 D4
Rodd 121 F4
Roddam 203 E1
Rodden 74 B3
Roddymoor 190 B2
Rode 96 C1
Rode Heath 146 C5
Rodeheath 159 H1
Roden 133 F5
Rodhuish 82 C4
Rodington 133 F5
Rodley 110 A2
Rodmarton 110 C1
Rodmell 79 E5
Rodmersham 102 C2
Rodney Stoke 83 H5
Rodsley 147 G3
Roecliffe 175 G3
Roehampton 100 C3
Roesound 233 F3
Roffey 88 B3
Rogart 229 E2
Rogate 87 F2
Rogerstone 94 D4
Rogerton 199 F5
Roghadal 231 F3
Rogiet 95 F4
Roke 98 D5
Roker 190 D4
Rollesby 140 D5
Rolleston *Leics* 136 B4
Rolleston *Notts* 149 E4
Rolleston on Dove 147 G2
Rolston 171 F5
Rolstone 95 E2
Rolvenden 90 A3
Rolvenden Layne 90 B3
Romaldkirk 180 D4
Romanby 181 H1
Romannobridge 200 D4
Romansleigh 81 H2
Romford *Dors* 85 F1
Romford *Haver* 101 F4
Romiley 160 A4
Romsey 86 B2
Romsley *Shrops* 133 H2
Romsley *Worcs* 134 B1
Ronague 154 B2
Rookby 180 C3
Rookery Hill 79 F4
Rookhope 189 G2
Rookley 76 D3
Rooks Bridge 95 E1
Roonah Quay 242 C2
Roos 171 G4
Roosebeck 172 C3
Roosecote 172 C3
Roosky *Mayo* 243 F3
Roosky *Rosc* 244 A3
Rootpark 200 B4
Ropley 86 D3
Ropley Dean 86 D3
Ropsley 149 G2
Rora 227 G4
Rorandle 226 D1
Rorrington 132 C4
Rosarie 226 B4
Roscommon 243 G2
Roscrea 240 A3
Rose 65 E5
Roseacre 166 C4
Rose Ash 82 A2
Rosebank 199 H4
Rosebrough 203 F2
Rosebush 105 G4
Rosedale Abbey 182 D2
Roseden 203 E1
Rosefield 225 F4
Rosegreen 240 A1
Rosehall 228 D2
Rosehearty 227 F5
Rosehill *Aber* 220 D4
Rosehill *Shrops* 146 B2
Roseisle 225 H5
Rosemarket 105 F2
Rosemarkie 225 E4
Rosemary Lane 83 F1
Rosemount *P & K* 213 H5
Rosemount *S Ayr* 198 C2
Rosenallis 240 B4
Rosenannon 67 E4
Rosepool 105 E2
Rosewell 201 F5
Roseworthy 64 D3
Rosgill 179 G4
Roshven 217 F3
Roskhill 222 B3
Rosley 187 H3
Roslin 208 A1
Rosliston 135 E5
Rosmult 239 H2
Rosnakill 247 E4
Rosneath 205 E3
Ross *D & G* 186 A2
Ross *Meath* 244 C2
Ross *Northld* 203 F3
Ross *P & K* 212 D3
Rossbrin 234 D1
Ross Carbery 235 F1
Rossett 145 F5
Rossie Ochill 213 G2
Rossington 162 A4
Rossinver 243 H5
Rosskeen 224 D5
Rossland 205 G2
Rosslare 237 G5
Rosslare Harbour 237 G4
Rosslea 244 C4
Rossmore 235 F2
Ross-on-Wye 109 H4
Ross Port 242 C5
Rostellan 236 B2
Roster 229 H4
Rostherne 159 F3
Rosthwaite 179 E3
Roston 147 F3
Rostrevor 245 F4
Rosudgeon 64 C2
Rosyth 207 G3
Rothbury 197 F4
Rotherby 136 B5
Rotherfield 89 F3
Rotherfield Greys 99 E4
Rotherfield Peppard 99 E4
Rotherham 161 F4
Rothersthorpe 125 E3
Rotherwas 109 G5
Rotherwick 99 E1
Rothes 226 A4
Rothesay 204 C1
Rothiebrisbane 226 D3
Rothienorman 226 D3
Rothiesholm 232 C4
Rothley *Leics* 136 A5
Rothley *Northld* 197 E2
Rothmaise 226 D3
Rothwell *Leeds* 169 E3
Rothwell *Lincs* 163 G4
Rothwell *Northants* 136 C2
Rotsea 177 G2
Rottal 220 C2
Rottingdean 79 E4
Rottington 178 B3
Roud 76 D2
Rougham *Nflk* 152 A1
Rougham *Sflk* 128 B4
Rougham Green 128 B4
Roughburn 218 C3
Rough Close 146 D3
Rough Common 103 E1
Rough Haugh 229 E4
Roughlee 167 G5
Roughley 134 D3
Roughsike 195 H1
Roughton *Lincs* 163 G1
Roughton *Nflk* 153 E3
Roughton *Shrops* 133 H3
Roundbush Green 115 E3
Roundhay 169 E4
Roundstone 238 B5
Roundstreet Common 88 A3
Roundway 97 E2
Roundwood 241 F4
Rounton 182 A2
Rousdon 73 F3
Rousham 112 A4
Rousky 247 F2
Rous Lench 123 F3
Routdaneburn 198 B5
Routenburn 204 D1
Routh 171 E5
Row *Corn* 67 F5
Row *Cumb* 179 G1
Rowanburn 195 G1
Rowde 96 D2
Rowen 156 D2
Rowfoot 188 D4
Rowhedge 116 B3
Rowhook 88 B3
Rowington 123 H4
Rowington Green 123 H4
Rowland 160 D2
Rowlands Castle 87 E1
Rowlands Gill 190 B4
Rowledge 87 F4
Rowlestone 109 F4
Rowley *Devon* 81 H2
Rowley *Dur* 190 A3
Rowley *Shrops* 132 C4
Rowley Regis 134 B2
Rowly 88 A4
Rowney Green 123 F5
Rownhams 86 B2
Rowrah 178 C4
Rowsham 113 E3
Rowsley 161 E1
Rowston 150 A5
Rowton *Ches* 158 C1
Rowton *Shrops* 132 D5
Rowton *T & W* 146 A1
Roxburgh 202 B2
Roxby *N Lincs* 170 C2
Roxby *N Yorks* 183 E4
Roxton 126 B3
Roxwell 115 E2
Royal British Legion Village 101 H1
Royal Leamington Spa 124 A4
Royal Tunbridge Wells 89 F4
Royals Green 146 A3
Roybridge 218 B3
Roydon *Esx* 114 C2
Roydon *Nflk* 140 A2
Roydon *Nflk* 151 G1
Royston *Barns* 169 E2
Royston *Herts* 126 D2
Royton 167 H1
Rozel 75 H1
Ruabon 145 F3
Ruaig 216 A1
Ruan Lanihorne 66 D2
Ruan Major 65 E1
Ruan Minor 65 E1
Ruardean 109 H3
Ruardean Woodside 109 H3
Rubane 248 C1
Rubery 123 E5
Rubha Ghaisinis 231 E2
Ruckcroft 188 C2
Ruckhall 109 F5
Ruckinge 90 C3
Ruckland 164 A2
Rucklers Lane 113 G2
Ruckley 133 E4
Ruddington 148 C2
Rudford 110 B3
Rudge 84 D5
Rudgeway 96 A4
Rudgwick 88 A3
Rudhall 109 H4
Rudheath 159 F2
Rudheath Woods 159 F2
Rudley Green 115 G2
Rudloe 96 C2
Rudry 94 C4
Rudston 177 G3
Rudyard 147 E5
Rufford 166 D2
Rufforth 176 A2
Rugby 124 C5
Rugeley 147 E1
Ruilick 224 C4
Ruishton 83 F2
Ruisigearraidh 231 F3
Ruislip 100 A4
Ruislip Common 100 A4
Rumbling Bridge 207 F5
Rumburgh 140 C2
Rumford 66 D5
Rumney 94 D3
Rumwell 83 E2
Runcorn 158 D3
Runcton 77 G4
Runcton Holme 138 D4
Runfold 87 G5
Runhall 139 H4
Runham 141 E5
Runnington 82 D2
Runswick Bay 183 E4
Runtaleave 220 B2
Runwell 115 G1
Ruscombe 99 E3
Rushall *Herefs* 122 B1
Rushall *Nflk* 140 B2
Rushall *Wals* 134 C4
Rushall *Wilts* 97 F1
Rushbrooke 128 B4
Rushbury 133 E3
Rushden *Herts* 114 B4
Rushden *Northants* 125 H4
Rushford 139 G2
Rush Green 101 F4
Rushlake Green 89 G2
Rushmere 141 E2
Rushmere St Andrew 129 E2
Rushmoor 87 G4
Rushock 122 D5
Rusholme 159 G4
Rushton *Ches* 159 E1
Rushton *Northants* 136 C2
Rushton *Shrops* 133 F4
Rushton Spencer 146 D5
Rushwick 122 D3
Rushyford 190 C1
Ruskie 206 B5
Ruskington 150 A4
Rusland 179 E1
Rusper 88 C4
Ruspidge 109 H3
Russell's Water 99 E4
Rustington 78 A4
Ruston Parva 177 G3
Ruswarp 183 F3
Rutherend 199 F4
Rutherford 202 A2
Rutherglen 199 E5
Ruthernbridge 67 F4
Ruthin 144 D5
Ruthrieston 221 G5
Ruthven *Aber* 226 C4
Ruthven *Angus* 220 B1
Ruthven *Hghld* 219 F4
Ruthven *Hghld* 225 E3
Ruthvenfield 213 G3

GAZETTEER

Stainby 149 G1
Staincross 169 E1
Staindrop 181 F4
Staines 100 A3
Stainfield *Lincs* 150 A2
Stainfield *Lincs* 163 F2
Stainforth *Donc* 169 H2
Stainforth *N Yorks* 174 B3
Staining 166 B4
Stainland 168 B2
Stainsacre 183 F3
Stainton *Cumb* 173 F5
Stainton *Cumb* 188 B1
Stainton *Donc* 161 H4
Stainton *Dur* 181 E4
Stainton *Midbro* 182 B3
Stainton *N Yorks* 181 F2
Stainton by Langworth 163 F2
Stainton Grove 181 E4
Stainton le Vale 163 G4
Stainton with Adgarley 172 D4
Staintondale 183 G2
Stair *Cumb* 178 D4
Stair *S Ayr* 198 D1
Stairhaven 185 E3
Staithes 183 E4
Stake Pool 173 E1
Stakeford 197 H2
Stalbridge 84 C2
Stalbridge Weston 84 C2
Stalham 153 F2
Stalham Green 153 F1
Stalisfield Green 102 C1
Stalland Common 139 H3
Stalling Busk 174 C5
Stallingborough 171 F2
Stalmine 173 E1
Stalybridge 160 B4
Stambourne 115 F5
Stambourne Green 115 F5
Stamford *Lincs* 137 E4
Stamford *Northld* 203 G1
Stamford Bridge 176 C2
Stamfordham 190 A5
Stamullin 245 F2
Stanborough 114 A2
Stanbridge *Beds* 113 F4
Stanbridge *Dors* 75 F5
Stanbury 168 B4
Stand 206 C2
Standburn 207 E2
Standeford 134 B4
Standen 90 B4
Standford 87 F3
Standish 167 E2
Standlake 111 H2
Standon *Hants* 86 B3
Standon *Herts* 114 C4
Standon *Staffs* 146 C3
Stane 206 D1
Stanfield 152 B1
Stanford *Beds* 126 B2
Stanford *Kent* 90 D4
Stanford Bishop 122 B3
Stanford Bridge 122 C4
Stanford Dingley 98 C3
Stanford in the Vale 98 A5
Stanford-le-Hope 101 G4
Stanford on Avon 136 A1
Stanford on Soar 148 C1
Stanford on Teme 122 C4
Stanford Rivers 114 D1
Stanghow 182 D4
Stanhoe 151 H3
Stanhope *Bdrs* 200 C2
Stanhope *Dur* 189 H2
Stanion 136 D2
Stanley *Derbs* 148 B3
Stanley *Dur* 190 B3
Stanley *P & K* 213 G4
Stanley *Staffs* 146 D4
Stanley *Wfield* 169 E3
Stanley Common 148 B3
Stanley Crook 190 B2
Stanmer 78 D5
Stanmore *Harw* 100 B5
Stanmore *W Berks* 98 B3
Stannersburn 196 B2
Stanningfield 128 B3
Stannington *Northld* 197 G1
Stannington *Sheff* 161 E3
Stannington Station 197 G2
Stansbatch 121 G4

Stansfield 128 A3
Stanstead 128 A2
Stanstead Abbots 114 C2
Stansted 101 G2
Stansted Mountfitchet 114 D4
Stanton *Derbs* 147 H1
Stanton *Glos* 111 E5
Stanton *Mon* 109 E3
Stanton *Northld* 197 F2
Stanton *Sflk* 128 C5
Stanton *Staffs* 147 F4
Stanton by Bridge 148 A2
Stanton-by-Dale 148 B3
Stanton Drew 95 G2
Stanton Fitzwarren 97 F5
Stanton Harcourt 111 H2
Stanton Hill 148 B5
Stanton in Peak 160 D1
Stanton Lacy 133 E1
Stanton Long 133 F3
Stanton-on-the-Wolds 148 D2
Stanton Prior 96 A2
Stanton St Bernard 97 E2
Stanton St John 112 B2
Stanton St Quintin 96 D3
Stanton Street 128 C4
Stanton under Bardon 135 G5
Stanton upon Hine Heath 145 H1
Stanton Wick 95 H2
Stanwardine in the Fields 145 G1
Stanway *Esx* 116 A4
Stanway *Glos* 111 E5
Stanwell 100 A3
Stanwick 125 H5
Stanwick-St-John 181 F3
Stanydale 233 F2
Staoinebrig 231 E2
Stape 183 E1
Stapehill 75 G4
Stapeley 146 B4
Stapenhill 147 H1
Staple 103 F1
Staplecross 90 A2
Staplefield 88 C3
Staple Fitzpaine 83 F2
Stapleford *Cambs* 127 E3
Stapleford *Herts* 114 B3
Stapleford *Leics* 149 F1
Stapleford *Lincs* 149 F5
Stapleford *Notts* 148 B3
Stapleford *Wilts* 85 F4
Stapleford Abbotts 114 D1
Stapleford Tawney 114 D1
Staplegrove 83 E3
Staplehay 83 F2
Staplehurst 90 A4
Staplers 76 D3
Staplestown 240 D5
Stapleton *C of Bris* 95 H3
Stapleton *Cumb* 188 C5
Stapleton *Herefs* 121 F4
Stapleton *Leics* 135 G4
Stapleton *N Yorks* 181 G3
Stapleton *Shrops* 133 E4
Stapleton *Som* 83 H2
Stapley 83 E1
Staploe 126 B4
Staplow 122 B2
Star *Fife* 214 B1
Star *Pemb* 118 C1
Star *Som* 95 F1
Starbotton 174 C4
Starcross 72 C2
Stareton 124 A5
Starlings Green 114 D4
Starston 140 B2
Startforth 181 E4
Startley 96 D4
Stathe 83 G3
Stathern 149 E2
Station Town 190 D2
Staughton Highway 126 B4
Staunton *Glos* 109 G3
Staunton *Glos* 110 B4
Staunton Harold Hall 148 A1
Staunton in the Vale 149 F3
Staunton on Arrow 121 G4
Staunton on Wye 121 G2
Staupes 175 F2

Staveley *Cumb* 179 G2
Staveley *Derbs* 161 F2
Staveley *N Yorks* 175 G3
Staveley-in-Cartmel 173 E5
Staverton *Devon* 69 F4
Staverton *Glos* 110 C4
Staverton *Northants* 124 C4
Staverton *Wilts* 96 C2
Stawell 83 G4
Stawley 82 D2
Staxigoe 229 H4
Staxton 177 F4
Staylittle 131 F3
Staynall 173 E1
Staythorpe 149 E4
Stean 174 D4
Steane 124 D1
Stearsby 176 B4
Steart 83 F5
Stebbing 115 F4
Stebbing Green 115 F4
Stedham 87 G2
Steel Cross 89 F3
Steele Road 195 H3
Steen's Bridge 122 A3
Steep 87 E3
Steeple *Dors* 75 E2
Steeple *Esx* 116 A2
Steeple Ashton 96 D1
Steeple Aston 112 A4
Steeple Barton 112 A4
Steeple Bumpstead 127 G2
Steeple Claydon 112 C4
Steeple Gidding 137 F2
Steeple Langford 85 F4
Steeple Morden 126 C2
Steeton 174 D1
Stein 222 B4
Steinis 231 G4
Steinmanhill 227 E3
Stelling Minnis 90 D5
Stembridge 83 G2
Stemster 229 G5
Stenalees 67 F3
Stenhousemuir 206 D3
Stenigot 163 H3
Stenness 233 E4
Stenscholl 222 C5
Stenso 232 B4
Stenson 148 A2
Stenson Fields 148 A2
Stenton 209 E2
Stepaside *Corn* 67 E3
Stepaside *Dub* 241 H5
Stepaside *Pemb* 105 H2
Stepney 100 D4
Steppingley 113 G5
Stepps 206 B2
Sterndale Moor 160 C1
Sternfield 129 G4
Stert 97 E1
Stetchworth 127 G3
Stevenage 114 A4
Stevenston 198 B3
Steventon *Hants* 86 C5
Steventon *Oxon* 98 B5
Stevington 125 H3
Stewartby 125 H2
Stewarton *A & B* 230 C1
Stewarton *E Ayr* 198 D4
Stewartstown 247 G1
Stewkley 113 E4
Stewton 164 B3
Steyning 78 C5
Steynton 105 F2
Stibb 70 C5
Stibb Cross 81 E1
Stibb Green 97 G2
Stibbard 152 B2
Stibbington 137 F3
Stichill 202 B3
Stickford 150 D5
Sticklepath *Devon* 71 G4
Sticklepath *Devon* 81 F3
Stickney 150 C5
Stiffkey 152 B3
Stifford's Bridge 122 C2
Stillingfleet 169 G5
Stillington *N Yorks* 176 B3
Stillington *S on Tees* 181 H4
Stillorgan 241 F5
Stilton 137 G2

Stinchcombe 110 A1
Stinsford 74 C3
Stirchley 133 G4
Stirling *Aber* 227 G3
Stirling *Stir* 206 D4
Stisted 115 G4
Stithians 65 E3
Stivichall 135 F1
Stixwould 163 G1
Stoak 158 C2
Stobieside 199 F3
Stobo 200 D3
Stoborough 75 E3
Stoborough Green 75 E3
Stobshiel 208 C1
Stobswood 197 G3
Stobwood 200 B4
Stock 115 F1
Stock Green 123 E3
Stock Wood 123 F3
Stockbridge *Brad* 174 D1
Stockbridge *Hants* 86 B4
Stockbriggs 199 G3
Stockbury 102 B2
Stockcross 98 B2
Stockdalewath 188 A3
Stockerston 136 C3
Stocking Pelham 114 D4
Stockingford 135 F3
Stockland 73 F5
Stockland Bristol 83 E4
Stockleigh English 72 B5
Stockleigh Pomeroy 72 B4
Stockley 97 E2
Stocklinch 83 G2
Stockport 159 H3
Stocksbridge 161 E4
Stocksfield 189 H4
Stockton *Herefs* 121 H4
Stockton *Nflk* 140 D3
Stockton *Shrops* 133 G3
Stockton *Warks* 124 B4
Stockton *Wilts* 85 E4
Stockton Heath 159 E3
Stockton on Teme 122 C4
Stockton on the Forest 176 C2
Stockton-on-Tees 182 A4
Stodday 173 F2
Stodmarsh 103 F2
Stody 152 C2
Stoer 228 B3
Stoford *Dors* 84 A1
Stoford *Wilts* 85 F4
Stogumber 82 D4
Stogursey 83 E4
Stoke *Devon* 80 C2
Stoke *Hants* 77 F4
Stoke *Hants* 86 B5
Stoke *MT* 102 B3
Stoke Abbott 73 H4
Stoke Albany 136 C2
Stoke Ash 128 D5
Stoke Bardolph 148 D3
Stoke Bliss 122 B4
Stoke Bruerne 125 E2
Stoke by Clare 127 H2
Stoke-by-Nayland 128 C1
Stoke Canon 72 C4
Stoke Charity 86 C4
Stoke Climsland 71 E2
Stoke D'Abernon 100 B1
Stoke Doyle 137 E2
Stoke Dry 136 D3
Stoke Ferry 139 E4
Stoke Fleming 69 G2
Stokeford 75 E3
Stoke Gabriel 69 G3
Stoke Gifford 95 H3
Stoke Golding 135 F3
Stoke Goldington 125 F2
Stokeham 162 C2
Stoke Hammond 113 E4
Stoke Heath *Shrops* 146 B2
Stoke Heath *Worcs* 123 E4
Stoke Holy Cross 140 B4
Stokeinteignhead 72 C1
Stoke Lacy 122 B2
Stoke Lyne 112 B4
Stoke Mandeville 113 E2
Stokenchurch 112 D1
Stoke Newington 100 D4
Stokenham 69 F2
Stoke on Tern 146 A2

Stoke-on-Trent 146 D4
Stoke Orchard 110 C4
Stoke Poges 99 G4
Stoke Prior *Herefs* 121 H3
Stoke Prior *Worcs* 123 E4
Stoke Rivers 81 G4
Stoke Rochford 149 G2
Stoke Row 98 D4
Stoke St Gregory 83 G3
Stoke St Mary 83 F2
Stoke St Michael 84 B5
Stoke St Milborough 133 F2
Stokesay 132 D2
Stokesby 140 D5
Stokesley 182 B3
Stoke sub Hamdon 83 H2
Stoke Talmage 112 C1
Stoke Trister 84 C3
Stolford 83 E5
Stondon Massey 115 E1
Ston Easton 95 H1
Stone *Bucks* 112 D3
Stone *Glos* 96 A5
Stone *Kent* 101 F3
Stone *Staffs* 146 D2
Stone *Worcs* 122 D5
Stone Allerton 83 G5
Stone Bridge 244 C4
Stonebroom 148 B5
Stone Cross 79 G5
Stone-edge Batch 95 F3
Stonegate 89 G3
Stonegrave 176 C4
Stonehaugh 196 C1
Stonehaven 221 F3
Stone House 174 A5
Stonehouse *Glos* 110 B2
Stonehouse *Northld* 188 D4
Stonehouse *S Lan* 199 G4
Stone in Oxney 90 B3
Stoneleigh 135 F1
Stonely 126 B4
Stoner Hill 87 E3
Stonesby 149 F1
Stones Green 116 C4
Stonesfield 111 H3
Stone Street *Kent* 101 F1
Stone Street *Sflk* 140 D2
Stonethwaite 179 E3
Stoney Cross 76 A5
Stoneygate *Aber* 227 F3
Stoneygate *C of Leics* 136 A4
Stoneyhills 102 C5
Stoneykirk 184 C3
Stoney Middleton 160 D2
Stoney Stanton 135 G3
Stoney Stoke 84 C3
Stoney Stratton 84 B4
Stoney Stretton 132 D4
Stoneywood *C of Aber* 227 E1
Stoneywood *Falk* 206 C3
Stonganess 233 G5
Stonham Aspal 128 D3
Stonnall 134 C4
Stonor 99 E4
Stonton Wyville 136 B3
Stonyfield 229 E1
Stonyford *Ant* 248 B1
Stonyford *Kilk* 240 C1
Stony Houghton 161 G1
Stonyhurst College 167 F4
Stony Stratford 125 F2
Stoodleigh 82 B2
Stopham 88 A2
Stopsley 113 H4
Storeton 158 B3
Stormont 248 B2
Stormontfield 213 G3
Stornoway 231 G4
Storridge 122 C2
Storrington 88 A1
Storrs 179 F1
Storth 173 F4
Stotfield 126 C1
Stotfold 126 C1
Stottesdon 133 G2
Stoughton *Leics* 136 A4
Stoughton *Sry* 87 H5
Stoughton *W Ssx* 87 F4
Stoulton 123 E2
Stour Provost 84 C2

Stour Row 84 D2
Stourbridge 134 B2
Stourpaine 75 E5
Stourport-on-Severn 122 D5
Stourton *Staffs* 134 A2
Stourton *Warks* 111 G5
Stourton *Wilts* 84 C3
Stourton 134 A2
Stourton Caundle 84 C2
Stove 232 C4
Stoven 140 D2
Stow *Bdrs* 201 G3
Stow *Lincs* 162 D3
Stow Bardolph 138 D4
Stow Bedon 139 G3
Stow cum Quy 127 F4
Stow Longa 126 B5
Stow Maries 115 G1
Stowbridge 138 D4
Stowe *Glos* 109 G2
Stowe *Shrops* 132 C1
Stowe-by-Chartley 147 E2
Stowell *Som* 84 B2
Stowell 111 E3
Stowey 95 G1
Stowford 71 E3
Stowlangtoft 128 C4
Stowmarket 128 C3
Stow-on-the-Wold 111 F4
Stowting 90 D4
Stowupland 128 D3
Straad 204 C1
Strabane 247 E3
Strachan 221 F3
Strachur 204 C5
Stradbally *Kerry* 234 C4
Stradbally *Wat* 236 D4
Stradbroke 129 E5
Stradishall 127 H3
Stradone 244 C3
Stradsett 138 D4
Straffan 241 E5
Stragglethorpe 149 G4
Strahart 241 E1
Straid 248 B2
Straide 243 E3
Straith 194 A2
Straith Salach 242 C1
Straiton *Midln* 208 A2
Straiton *S Ayr* 192 D4
Straloch *Aber* 227 F2
Straloch *P & K* 219 H2
Stramshall 147 F3
Strand 235 F5
Strandhill 243 F5
Strang 154 C2
Strangford 245 G5
Strangways 85 G4
Stranocum 247 H4
Stranorlar 246 D2
Stranraer 184 C4
Stratfield Mortimer 98 D2
Stratfield Saye 98 D2
Stratfield Turgis 98 D1
Stratford *Newm* 100 D4
Stratford *Worcs* 122 D1
Stratford 240 D3
Stratford St Andrew 129 G4
Stratford St Mary 128 C1
Stratford Tony 85 F3
Stratford-upon-Avon 123 G3
Strath 228 A1
Strathan *Hghld* 217 H4
Strathan *Hghld* 228 B3
Strathaven 199 G3
Strathblane 206 A3
Strathcanaird 228 C2
Strathcarron 223 G3
Strathcoil 230 B4
Strathdon 226 B1
Strathkinness 214 C2
Strathmiglo 213 H2
Strathpeffer 224 C4
Strathrannoch 228 D1
Strathtay 219 G3
Strathy 229 F5
Strathyre 212 B2
Stratton *Corn* 70 C5
Stratton *Dors* 74 C3
Stratton *Glos* 110 D2
Stratton Audley 112 C4
Stratton St Margaret 97 F4
Stratton St Michael 140 B3
Stratton Strawless 153 E1

561
TELLISFORD–TITTENSOR

Tellisford 96 C1
Telscombe 79 E4
Templand 194 C2
Temple *C of Glas* 205 H2
Temple *Corn* 70 B1
Temple *Midln* 201 E5
Temple Bar 119 F3
Templebar 105 H2
Templeboy 243 F4
Temple Cloud 95 H1
Templecombe 84 C2
Templederry 239 H2
Temple End 128 A2
Templeetney 236 C5
Temple Ewell 91 F4
Temple Grafton 123 G3
Temple Guiting 111 E4
Temple Herdewyke 124 B3
Temple Hirst 169 H3
Templemartin 235 G2
Templemore 240 A2
Templenoe 234 D3
Temple Normanton 161 F1
Templeshanbo 240 D1
Temple Sowerby 188 D1
Templeton *Devon* 82 B1
Templeton *Pemb* 105 H2
Templeton Bridge 82 B1
Templetouhy 240 A2
Templetown 237 F4
Tempo 244 B5
Tempsford 126 B3
Ten Mile Bank 138 C3
Tenbury Wells 122 A4
Tenby 105 H1
Tendring 116 C4
Tenterden 90 B3
Terling 115 G3
Termon Rock 247 F1
Termonbarry 244 A2
Termonfeckin 245 F2
Ternhill 146 A2
Terregles 194 B1
Terrington 176 C4
Terrington St Clement 151 F1
Terrington St John 138 C5
Terryglass 239 G4
Terwick Common 87 F2
Teston 101 H1
Testwood 86 A1
Tetbury 96 C5
Tetbury Upton 96 C5
Tetchill 145 F2
Tetcott 70 D4
Tetford 164 A2
Tetney 164 A5
Tetney Lock 171 G1
Tetsworth 112 C1
Tettenhall 134 A4
Teversal 148 B5
Teversham 127 E3
Teviothead 195 G4
Tewel 221 F3
Tewin 114 B3
Tewin Wood 114 B3
Tewkesbury 122 D1
Teynham 102 C2
Thakeham 88 B2
Thame 112 D2
Thames Ditton 100 B2
Thames Haven 102 A4
Thamesmead 101 E3
Thanington 103 E1
Thankerton 200 B3
Tharston 140 B3
Thatcham 98 C2
Thatto Heath 158 D4
Thaxted 115 E4
The Aird 222 C4
Theakston 175 G5
Thealby 170 C2
Theale *Som* 83 H5
Theale *W Berks* 98 D3
Thearne 171 E4
The Bage 121 F2
The Balloch 212 D2
The Barony 232 A4
Theberton 129 G4
The Birks 221 F5
The Blythe 147 E2
The Bog 132 D3
The Braes 222 D3
The Bratch 134 A3
The Bryn 109 E2
The Burf 122 D4
The Burn 220 D2
The Bush 245 F3
The Butts 240 C2
The Camp 110 C2
The Chequer 145 G3
The City 112 D1
The Cock 245 G5
The Common *Bucks* 112 D4
The Common *Wilts* 85 H3
The Craigs 228 D1
The Cronk 154 C4
The Cross 247 F3
Thedden Grange 87 E4
Theddingworth 136 B2
Theddlethorpe All Saints 164 C3
Theddlethorpe St Helen 164 C3
The Den 198 C4
The Diamond *Ant* 248 A2
The Diamond *Tyr* 247 H2
The Down *Kent* 89 G4
The Down 89 G4
The Downs 244 C1
The Drums 220 C2
The Fence 109 G2
The Flatt 195 H1
The Grange 182 C2
The Green *Cumb* 172 C5
The Green *Wilts* 84 D3
The Grove 152 D1
The Harrow 241 E1
The Haughs 226 C4
The Haven 88 A3
The Headland 191 E1
The Heath 152 D1
The Herberts 94 A3
The Hermitage 100 C1
The Hill 172 C5
The Howe *Cumb* 179 G1
The Howe *IOM* 154 A1
The Hundred 122 A4
The Isle 133 E5
Thelbridge Barton 82 A1
The Lee 113 F2
The Leigh 110 C4
The Lhen 154 C5
Thelnetham 139 H1
The Loup 247 H2
Thelveton 140 B2
Thelwall 159 F3
The Marsh 132 C3
Themelthorpe 152 C1
The Middles 190 B3
The Moor 89 H3
The Mumbles 93 E4
The Mythe 122 D1
The Narth 109 G2
The Neuk 221 E4
Thenford 124 C2
The Old Byre 216 D1
The Pigeons 244 A1
The Pike *Tipp* 239 H3
The Pike *Wat* 236 B3
The Pike *Wat* 236 D4
The Polchar 225 F1
The Pole of Itlaw 226 D4
The Quarry 96 B5
Therfield 126 D1
The Rhos 105 G3
The Rock 247 G1
The Sheddings 248 B3
The Spa 245 G5
The Stocks 90 B3
The Sweep 236 D5
The Temple 248 B1
Thetford 139 F2
The Towans 64 C3
The Town 64 A5
The Vauld 122 A2
The Village 134 A3
The Wyke 133 G4
Theydon Bois 114 D1
Thick Hollins 168 C2
Thickwood 96 C3
Thimbleby *Lincs* 163 G1
Thimbleby *N Yorks* 182 B2
Thirlby 176 A5
Thirlestane 201 H4
Thirn 175 F5
Thirsk 175 H5
Thistleton 149 G1
Thistley Green 138 D1
Thixendale 176 D3
Thockrington 197 E1
Tholmair 231 E2
Tholomas Drove 138 B4
Tholthorpe 176 A3
Thomas Chapel 105 H2
Thomas Street 243 G1
Thomastown *Aber* 226 C3
Thomastown *Kilk* 240 C1
Thomastown *Meath* 244 D2
Thomastown *Tipp* 239 H1
Thompson 139 G3
Thomshill 225 H4
Thong 101 G3
Thoralby 174 D5
Thoresby 162 A2
Thoresthorpe 164 C2
Thoresway 163 G4
Thorganby *Lincs* 163 G4
Thorganby *N Yorks* 176 C1
Thorgill 182 D2
Thorington 140 D1
Thorington Street 128 C1
Thorlby 174 C2
Thorley Street 76 B3
Thormanby 176 A4
Thornaby-on-Tees 182 B4
Thornage 152 C3
Thornborough *Bucks* 112 D5
Thornborough *N Yorks* 175 F4
Thornbury *Devon* 81 E1
Thornbury *Herefs* 122 B3
Thornbury *S Glos* 96 A5
Thornby 125 E5
Thorncliffe 147 E5
Thorncombe 73 G4
Thorncombe Street 87 H4
Thorncote Green 126 B2
Thorndon 128 D4
Thorndon Cross 71 F3
Thorne 170 A2
Thorne St Margaret 82 D2
Thorner 169 E5
Thorney *Notts* 162 D2
Thorney *Pbro* 137 H4
Thorney 83 G2
Thorney Hill 75 H4
Thorney Toll 138 A4
Thornfalcon 83 F2
Thornford 84 B1
Thorngumbald 171 F3
Thornham 151 G3
Thornham Magna 128 D5
Thornham Parva 128 D5
Thornhaugh 137 F4
Thornhill *Caer* 94 C4
Thornhill *Cumb* 178 B3
Thornhill *D & G* 194 A3
Thornhill *Derbs* 160 D3
Thornhill *Sotton* 86 C1
Thornhill *Stir* 206 B5
Thornhill Edge 168 D2
Thornholme 177 G3
Thornicombe 75 E4
Thornley *Dur* 190 A2
Thornley *Dur* 190 D2
Thornliebank 199 E5
Thorns 127 H3
Thornthwaite *Cumb* 178 D5
Thornthwaite *N Yorks* 175 E2
Thornton *Angus* 214 B5
Thornton *Brad* 168 B4
Thornton *Bucks* 112 D5
Thornton *E R of Yorks* 176 D1
Thornton *Fife* 208 A5
Thornton *Lancs* 172 D1
Thornton *Leics* 135 G4
Thornton *Lincs* 163 G1
Thornton *Midbro* 182 B3
Thornton *Northld* 202 D4
Thornton *Seft* 158 B5
Thornton Curtis 171 E2
Thornton Hough 158 B3
Thornton le Moor 163 F4
Thornton Park 202 D4
Thornton Rust 180 D1
Thornton Steward 175 E5
Thornton Watlass 175 F5
Thorntonhall 199 E5
Thornton-in-Craven 174 C1
Thornton-le-Beans 182 A1
Thornton-le-Clay 176 C3
Thornton-le-Dale 176 D5
Thornton-le-Moor 182 A1
Thornton-le-Moors 158 C2
Thornton-le-Street 175 H5
Thorntonloch 209 F2
Thornwood Common 114 D2
Thoroton 149 E3
Thorp Arch 169 F5
Thorp St Peter 151 E5
Thorpe *Derbs* 147 G4
Thorpe *Dur* 181 F3
Thorpe *Lincs* 164 C3
Thorpe *N Yorks* 174 D3
Thorpe *Nflk* 140 D3
Thorpe *Notts* 149 E4
Thorpe *Sry* 99 H2
Thorpe Abbotts 140 B1
Thorpe Acre 148 C1
Thorpe Arnold 149 E1
Thorpe Audlin 169 F2
Thorpe Bassett 177 E4
Thorpe Bay 102 C4
Thorpe by Water 136 D3
Thorpe Constantine 135 E4
Thorpe Culvert 151 E5
Thorpe End 140 C5
Thorpe Fendykes 151 E5
Thorpe Green 128 B3
Thorpe Hesley 161 F4
Thorpe in Balne 169 G2
Thorpe Langton 136 B3
Thorpe Larches 182 A5
Thorpe le Fallows 162 D3
Thorpe-le-Soken 116 C4
Thorpe le Street 176 D1
Thorpe Malsor 136 C1
Thorpe Mandeville 124 C2
Thorpe Market 153 E3
Thorpe Marriot 140 B5
Thorpe Morieux 128 B3
Thorpeness 129 H3
Thorpe on the Hill 162 D1
Thorpe St Andrew 140 C4
Thorpe Salvin 161 G3
Thorpe Satchville 136 B5
Thorpe Thewles 182 A4
Thorpe Underwood 175 H2
Thorpe Waterville 137 E2
Thorpe Willoughby 169 G4
Thorrington 116 B3
Thorverton 72 C4
Thrandeston 128 D5
Thrapston 137 E1
Threapland *Cumb* 187 G2
Threapland *N Yorks* 174 C3
Threapwood 145 G4
Three Bridges *Lincs* 164 B3
Three Bridges *W Ssx* 88 C4
Three Chimneys 90 A4
Three Cocked Hat 140 D3
Three Cocks 121 E1
Three Crosses 92 D5
Three Cups Corner 89 G2
Three Holes 138 C4
Three Leg Cross 89 G3
Three Legged Cross 75 G5
Three Mile Cross 99 E2
Threekingham 150 A3
Threemilestone 65 E4
Threlkeld 179 F5
Threshers Bush 114 D2
Threshfield 174 C3
Threxton Hill 139 F3
Thrigby 141 E5
Thringarth 180 D4
Thringstone 135 G5
Thrintoft 181 H1
Thriplow 127 E2
Throckenholt 138 A4
Throcking 114 B4
Throckley 190 B5
Throckmorton 123 E2
Throop 75 G4
Throphill 197 F2
Thropton 197 E4
Throsk 206 D4
Througham 110 C2
Throwleigh 71 H3
Throwley 102 C1
Thrumpton 148 C2
Thrumster 229 H4
Thrunton 197 F5
Thrupp *Glos* 110 C2
Thrupp *Oxon* 112 A3
Thrushelton 71 F3
Thrushgill 173 H3
Thrussington 136 A5
Thruxton *Hants* 86 A5
Thruxton *Herefs* 109 F5
Thrybergh 161 G4
Thulston 148 B2
Thundergay 230 C2
Thundersley 102 A4
Thundridge 114 C3
Thurcaston 135 H5
Thurcroft 161 G3
Thurdon 70 D5
Thurgarton *Nflk* 152 D2
Thurgarton *Notts* 148 D4
Thurgoland 161 E5
Thurlaston *Leics* 135 H3
Thurlaston *Warks* 124 C5
Thurlbear 83 F2
Thurlby *Lincs* 137 F5
Thurlby *Lincs* 149 G5
Thurlby *Lincs* 164 C2
Thurleigh 126 A3
Thurles 240 A2
Thurlestone 69 E2
Thurloxton 83 F3
Thurlstone 160 D5
Thurlton 140 D3
Thurmaston 136 A4
Thurnby 136 A4
Thurne 140 D5
Thurnham *Kent* 102 B1
Thurnham *Lancs* 173 F2
Thurning *Nflk* 152 C2
Thurning *Northants* 137 F2
Thurnscoe 169 F1
Thurnscoe East 169 F1
Thursby 188 A3
Thursford 152 B2
Thursford Green 152 B2
Thursley 87 G4
Thurso 229 G5
Thurstaston 158 A3
Thurston 128 B4
Thurston End 128 A3
Thurstonfield 187 H4
Thurstonland 168 C2
Thurton 140 C4
Thurvaston 147 G3
Thuxton 139 H4
Thwaite *N Yorks* 180 C2
Thwaite *Sflk* 128 D4
Thwaite Head 179 F1
Thwaite St Mary 140 C3
Thwing 177 F4
Tibbermore 213 G3
Tibberton *Glos* 110 B4
Tibberton *T & W* 146 B1
Tibberton *Worcs* 123 E3
Tibbie Shiels Inn 200 D1
Tibenham 140 A2
Tibohine 243 G3
Tibshelf 148 B5
Tibthorpe 177 F2
Ticehurst 89 G3
Tichborne 86 D3
Tickencote 137 E4
Tickenham 95 F3
Tickhill 161 H4
Ticklerton 133 E3
Ticknall 148 A1
Tickton 171 E5
Tidcombe 97 G1
Tiddington *Oxon* 112 C2
Tiddington *Warks* 123 H3
Tidebrook 89 G3
Tideford 68 A3
Tidenham 109 G1
Tideswell 160 D2
Tidmarsh 98 D3
Tidmington 111 G5
Tidpit 85 F2
Tidworth 85 H5
Tidworth Camp 85 H5
Tiers Cross 105 F2
Tiffield 125 E3
Tifty 227 E3
Tigerton 220 D2
Tigh-na-Blair 212 D2
Tighnabruaich 204 B2
Tighnafiline 228 A1
Tigley 69 F4
Tikincor 236 C5
Tilbrook 126 A4
Tilbury 101 G3
Tilbury Juxta Clare 127 H2
Tile Cross 134 D2
Tile Hill 135 F1
Tilehurst 98 D3
Tilford 87 G4
Tillathrowie 226 B3
Tillers Green 122 B1
Tillicoultry 207 E5
Tillingham 116 A2
Tillington *Herefs* 121 H2
Tillington *W Ssx* 87 H2
Tillington Common 121 H2
Tillyarblet 220 D2
Tillybirloch 221 E5
Tillydrine 221 E4
Tillyfour 220 D5
Tillyfourie 226 D1
Tillygarmond 221 E4
Tillygreig 227 E2
Tillykerrie 227 E2
Tillylodge 220 D5
Tilmanstone 91 F5
Tilney All Saints 151 F1
Tilney cum Islington 138 C5
Tilney Fen End 138 C5
Tilney High End 138 C5
Tilney St Lawrence 138 C5
Tilshead 85 F5
Tilstock 145 H3
Tilston 145 G4
Tilstone Fearnall 145 H5
Tilsworth 113 F4
Tilton on the Hill 136 B4
Tiltups End 96 C5
Timahoe *Kild* 240 D5
Timahoe *Laois* 240 C3
Timberland 150 A5
Timbersbrook 146 D5
Timberscombe 82 C4
Timble 175 E2
Timoleague 235 G1
Timolin 240 D3
Timperley 159 G3
Timsbury *B & NE Som* 96 A1
Timsbury *Hants* 86 A2
Timsgearraidh 231 F4
Timworth Green 128 B4
Tinahely 241 E2
Tincleton 74 D3
Tindale 188 D4
Tingewick 125 E1
Tingley 168 D3
Tingrith 113 G5
Tingwall 232 B4
Tinhay 71 E3
Tinshill 168 D4
Tinsley 161 F4
Tintagel 70 B3
Tintern Parva 109 G1
Tintinhull 83 H2
Tintwistle 160 B4
Tinwald 194 C2
Tinwell 137 E4
Tipperary 239 G1
Tipperty 227 F2
Tipps End 138 C3
Tiptoe 76 A4
Tipton 134 B3
Tipton St John 72 D3
Tiptree 115 H3
Tiptree Heath 115 H3
Tirabad 120 B2
Tirkane 247 G3
Tirley 110 B4
Tirphil 108 C2
Tirril 179 G5
Tisbury 85 E3
Tisley Green 88 C4
Tisman's Common 88 A3
Tissington 147 G4
Titchberry 80 C3
Titchfield 76 D5
Titchmarsh 137 F1
Titchwell 151 H3
Tithby 148 D3
Titley 121 F4
Titlington 197 F5
Titson 70 C4
Tittensor 146 D3

GAZETTEER

Twyford *Nflk* 152 C1
Twyford *Wokm* 99 E3
Twyford Common 109 G5
Twynholm 186 B3
Twyning 122 D1
Twyning Green 123 E1
Twynllanan 107 G4
Twyn-yr-odyn 94 C3
Twyn-y-Sheriff 109 F2
Twywell 137 E1
Ty Mawr Cwm 144 B4
Ty Rhiw 94 C4
Tyberton 109 E5
Tyburn 134 D3
Tycroes 107 E2
Tycrwyn 144 D1
Tydd Gote 151 E1
Tydd St Giles 138 B5
Tydd St Mary 150 D1
Tye Green 115 G3
Ty-hen 142 B2
Tylas 245 E1
Tyldesley 159 F5
Tyler Hill 103 E2
Tylers Green 113 F1
Tyler's Green 114 D2
Tylorstown 94 B5
Tylwch 131 G2
Tynagh 239 G4
Tynan 244 D5
Ty-nant *Cere* 119 F3
Ty-nant *Cnwy* 144 B3
Ty-nant *Gwyn* 144 B2
Tyndrum 211 G4
Tyne Tunnel 190 C5
Tyneham 75 E2
Tynehead 201 F5
Tynemouth 190 D5
Tynewydd 93 H5
Tyninghame 209 E3
Tynron 193 H3
Tyn-y-ffridd 144 D2
Tynygongl 156 A3
Tynygraig 119 G2
Tyn-y-graig 120 C3
Ty'n-y-groes 156 D2
Tyrie 227 F5
Tyringham 125 G2
Tyrrellspass 240 B5
Tythegston 93 G3
Tytherington *Ches* 160 A2
Tytherington *S Glos* 96 A4
Tytherington *Som* 84 C5
Tytherington *Wilts* 85 E4
Tytherleigh 73 G4
Tytherton Lucas 96 D3
Tywardreath 67 F3
Tywardreath Highway 67 F3
Tywyn *Cnwy* 156 D2
Tywyn *Gwyn* 130 C4

U

Uachdar 231 E2
Ubbeston 140 C1
Ubbeston Green 129 F5
Ubley 95 G1
Uckerby 181 G2
Uckfield 89 E2
Uckington 110 C4
Uddingston 206 B1
Uddington 199 H2
Udimore 90 B2
Udny Green 227 G2
Udny Station 227 F2
Udstonhead 199 G4
Uffcott 97 F3
Uffculme 82 D1
Uffington *Lincs* 137 F4
Uffington *Oxon* 97 H4
Uffington *Shrops* 133 G5
Ufford *Pboro* 137 F4
Ufford *Sflk* 129 F3
Ufton 124 B4
Ufton Nervet 98 D2
Ugadale 230 C1
Ugborough 69 E3
Uggeshall 140 D1
Ugglebarnby 183 F3
Ugley 114 D4
Ugley Green 114 D4

Ugthorpe 183 E3
Uig *A & B* 204 D3
Uig *A & B* 216 B2
Uig *Hghld* 222 A4
Uig *Hghld* 222 C5
Uiginish 222 B4
Uigshader 222 C3
Uisken 230 B4
Ulbster 229 H4
Ulceby *Lincs* 164 B2
Ulceby *N Lincs* 171 E2
Ulceby Cross 164 B2
Ulcombe 90 A5
Uldale 187 H2
Uley 110 B1
Ulgham 197 G3
Ullapool 228 B2
Ullenhall 123 G4
Ullenwood 110 C3
Ulleskelf 169 G4
Ullesthorpe 135 H2
Ulley 161 G3
Ullingswick 122 A2
Ullinish 222 B3
Ullock 178 C4
Ulpha 178 D1
Ulrome 177 H2
Ulsta 233 F4
Ulting 113 G2
Ulverston 172 D4
Ulwell 75 F2
Ulzieside 193 H4
Umberleigh 81 G2
Unapool 228 C3
Underbarrow 179 G1
Underhoull 233 G5
Underriver 89 F5
Underwood *Notts* 148 B4
Underwood *Nwprt* 95 E4
Undy 95 F4
Unifirth 233 E3
Union Hall 235 C1
Union Mills 154 C2
Unstone 161 F2
Unstone Green 161 F2
Unthank 188 B2
Unthank End 188 B2
Upavon 97 F1
Up Cerne 74 C4
Upchurch 102 B2
Upcott 121 F3
Upend 127 G3
Up Exe 72 C4
Uphall 207 F2
Upham *Devon* 72 B5
Upham *Hants* 86 C2
Uphampton 122 D4
Up Hatherley 110 C3
Uphill 95 E1
Up Holland 166 D1
Uplawmoor 198 D5
Upleadon 110 B4
Upleatham 182 C4
Uplees 102 C2
Uploders 74 A3
Uplowman 82 C2
Uplyme 73 G3
Up Marden 87 F1
Upminster 101 F4
Up Nately 87 E5
Upottery 83 E1
Upper Affcot 132 D2
Upper Ardchronie 229 E1
Upper Ardoscadale 204 C1
Upper Arley 133 H2
Upper Arncott 112 C3
Upper Aston 133 H3
Upper Astrop 124 C1
Upper Badcall 228 C4
Upper Basildon 98 C3
Upper Beeding 78 C5
Upper Benefield 137 E2
Upper Bentley 123 E4
Upper Boddington 124 C3
Upper Borth 130 D2
Upper Brailes 111 G5
Upper Breinton 121 H2
Upper Broadheath 122 D3
Upper Broughton 148 D2
Upper Bucklebury 98 C2
Upper Bullington 86 C4
Upper Burgate 85 G2
Upper Burnhaugh 221 F4
Upper Caldecote 126 B2
Upper Camster 229 H4
Upper Castle Combe 96 C3

Upper Catesby 124 C3
Upper Catshill 123 E5
Upper Chapel 120 C2
Upperchurch 239 H2
Upper Chute 97 G1
Upper Clatford 86 B4
Upper Coberley 110 D3
Upper Cokeham 78 C5
Upper Colwall 122 C2
Upper Dallachy 226 B5
Upper Dean 126 A4
Upper Denby 160 D5
Upper Derraid 225 G3
Upper Dicker 89 F1
Upper Dowdeswell 110 D3
Upper Dunsforth 175 H3
Upper Eathie 225 E5
Upper Elkstone 147 F5
Upper End 160 C2
Upper Farringdon 87 E4
Upper Framilode 110 B2
Upper Froyle 87 F4
Upper Glenfintaig 218 B4
Upper Godney 83 H4
Upper Gravenhurst 126 B1
Upper Green 98 A2
Upper Hackney 147 H5
Upper Hale 87 F5
Upper Halling 101 G2
Upper Hambleton 136 D4
Upper Hardres Court 91 E5
Upper Hartfield 89 E3
Upper Haugh 161 F4
Upper Heath 133 F2
Upper Helmsley 176 C2
Upper Hergest 121 F3
Upper Heyford *Northants* 125 E4
Upper Heyford *Oxon* 125 E3
Upper Heyford *Oxon* 112 A4
Upper Hill 121 H3
Upper Hindhope 196 C4
Upper Hopton 168 C2
Upper Hulme 147 E5
Upper Inglesham 111 F1
Upper Killay 92 D5
Upper Knockando 225 H3
Upper Lambourn 97 H4
Upperlands 247 G3
Upper Layham 120 C2
Upper Lochton 221 E4
Upper Longdon 134 C5
Upper Longwood 133 F4
Upper Ludstone 133 H3
Upper Lydbrook 109 H3
Upper Maes-coed 109 E5
Upper Midhope 160 D4
Uppermill 160 B5
Upper Milovaig 222 A4
Upper Minety 97 E5
Upper North Dean 113 E1
Upper Obney 213 F4
Upper Oddington 111 F4
Upper Olach 222 C3
Upper Poppleton 176 B2
Upper Quinton 123 G2
Upper Rissington 111 F3
Upper Rochford 122 B4
Upper Sanday 232 C3
Upper Sapey 122 B4
Upper Seagry 96 D4
Upper Shelton 125 H2
Upper Sheringham 152 D3
Upper Skelmorlie 204 D2
Upper Slaughter 111 F4
Upper Soudley 109 H2
Upper Stoke 140 C4
Upper Stondon 126 B1
Upper Stowe 124 D3
Upper Street *Hants* 85 G2
Upper Street *Nflk* 140 B2
Upper Street *Nflk* 140 D5
Upper Street *Nflk* 153 E3
Upper Sundon 113 G4
Upper Swainswick 96 B2
Upper Swell 111 F4
Upper Tean 147 E3
Upperthong 168 C1
Upper Tillyrie 213 G1
Upperton 87 H2
Upper Tooting 100 C3
Upper Tote 222 D4
Uppertown 229 H5
Upper Tysoe 124 A2
Upper Upham 97 G3

Upper Upnor 102 A3
Upper Wardington 124 C2
Upper Weald 112 D5
Upper Weedon 124 D3
Upper Wield 86 D4
Upper Winchendon 112 D3
Upper Woodford 85 G4
Upper Woolhampton 98 C2
Upper Wootton 98 C1
Upper Wyche 122 C2
Uppingham 136 D3
Uppington *Dors* 75 F5
Uppington *Shrops* 133 F4
Upsall 182 B1
Upsettlington 202 C4
Upshire 114 C1
Up Somborne 86 B3
Upstreet 103 F2
Up Sydling 74 B4
Upthorpe 128 C5
Upton *Bucks* 112 D2
Upton *Cambs* 137 G1
Upton *Ches* 158 C1
Upton *Cork* 235 G2
Upton *Corn* 70 D1
Upton *Dors* 73 E4
Upton *Dors* 75 F3
Upton *Hants* 86 B2
Upton *Hants* 98 A1
Upton *Leics* 135 F3
Upton *Lincs* 162 D3
Upton *Nflk* 140 D5
Upton *Northants* 125 E4
Upton *Notts* 149 E4
Upton *Notts* 162 B2
Upton *Oxon* 98 C4
Upton *Pbro* 137 F4
Upton *Slough* 99 G3
Upton *Som* 82 C3
Upton *Wfield* 169 F2
Upton *Wir* 158 B3
Upton Bishop 109 H4
Upton Cheyney 96 A2
Upton Cressett 133 G3
Upton Cross 70 D1
Upton Grey 87 E5
Upton Hellions 72 B4
Upton Lovell 85 E4
Upton Magna 133 F5
Upton Noble 84 C4
Upton Pyne 72 C4
Upton Scudamore 84 D5
Upton Snodsbury 123 E3
Upton St Leonards 110 C3
Upton upon Severn 122 D2
Upton Warren 123 E4
Upwaltham 87 G1
Upware 127 F4
Upwell 138 C4
Upwey 74 C3
Upwood 137 H2
Urafirth 233 E4
Uragaig 230 B3
Urchfont 97 E1
Urdimarsh 122 A2
Ure 233 E4
Urgha 231 F4
Urlay Nook 182 A3
Urlingford 240 B2
Urmston 159 G4
Urquhart *Hghld* 224 D4
Urquhart *Moray* 226 A5
Urra 182 C2
Urray 224 C4
Usan 221 E1
Ushaw Moor 190 B2
Usk 109 E1
Usselby 163 F4
Utkinton 158 D1
Utley 174 D1
Uton 72 B4
Utterby 164 A4
Uttoxeter 147 F2
Uwchmynydd 142 B2
Uxbridge 100 A4
Uyeasound 233 G5
Uzmaston 105 F3

V

Vaila Hall 233 E2
Valley 155 F2
Valley Truckle 70 B2
Valleyfield 207 F4
Valleymount 241 E4
Valley Park 86 B2
Valsgarth 233 G5
Valtos 222 C5
Vange 101 H4
Varteg 108 D2
Vatten 222 B3
Vaul 216 A1
Vaynol Hall 156 A1
Vaynor 108 B2
Vellow 82 D4
Veness 232 C4
Venn 69 E2
Venn Ottery 72 D3
Vennington 132 C4
Venny Tedburn 72 B4
Ventnor 76 D2
Ventry 234 B4
Vernham Dean 98 A1
Vernham Street 98 A1
Vernolds Common 133 E2
Verwood 85 F1
Veryan 67 E1
Veryan Green 67 E2
Vicarage 73 F3
Vicarscross 158 C1
Vickerstown 172 C3
Victoria 67 E4
Vidlin 233 F3
Viewfield 202 B3
Viewpark 206 C1
Vigo Village 101 G2
Villavin 81 F2
Villierstown 236 C4
Vinehall Street 89 H2
Vines Cross 89 F2
Virginia 244 C3
Virginstow 71 E3
Vobster 84 C5
Voe *Shet* 233 F3
Voe *Shet* 233 F4
Vowchurch 109 E5
Voxter 233 F3

W

Waberthwaite 178 C1
Wackerfield 101 F4
Wacton 140 B3
Wadborough 123 E2
Wadcrag 178 D5
Waddesdon 112 D3
Waddingham 163 E4
Waddington *Lancs* 167 F5
Waddington *Lincs* 163 E1
Wadebridge 67 E5
Wadeford 83 F1
Wadenhoe 137 E2
Wadesmill 114 C3
Wadhurst 89 G3
Wadshelf 161 F2
Wadworth 161 H4
Waen 157 G1
Waen-fûch 145 E1
Wag 229 G3
Wagbeach 132 D4
Wainfleet All Saints 151 E5
Wainfleet Bank 151 E5
Wainfleet St Mary 151 E5
Wainfleet Tofts 151 E5
Wainhouse Corner 70 C4
Wainscott 102 A3
Wainstalls 168 B3
Waitby 180 B3
Wakefield 169 E3
Wakerley 137 E3
Wakes Colne 115 H4
Walberswick 141 E1
Walberton 78 A5
Walcot *Lincs* 149 H3
Walcot *Shrops* 132 C2
Walcot *T & W* 133 F5
Walcot *Warks* 123 G3
Walcote 135 H2
Walcott *Lincs* 150 A5
Walcott *Nflk* 153 F2
Walden 174 D5

Walden Head 174 C5
Walden Stubbs 169 G2
Walderslade 102 A2
Walderton 87 F1
Walditch 74 A3
Waldley 147 F3
Waldridge 190 C3
Waldringfield 129 F2
Waldron 89 F2
Wales 161 G3
Walesby *Lincs* 163 F4
Walesby *Notts* 162 B2
Walford *Herefs* 109 G3
Walford *Herefs* 132 D1
Walford *Shrops* 145 G1
Walgherton 146 B4
Walgrave 136 C1
Walkden 159 F5
Walker 190 C4
Walkerburn 201 F3
Walker Fold 167 F5
Walkeringham 162 C4
Walkerith 162 C4
Walkern 114 B4
Walker's Green 121 H2
Walkerville 181 G2
Walkhampton 68 C4
Walkington 170 D4
Walk Mill 167 H4
Wall *Northld* 189 G5
Wall *Staffs* 134 D4
Wall Bank 133 E3
Wall under Heywood 133 E3
Wallaceton 194 A2
Wallacetown *S Ayr* 192 C4
Wallacetown *S Ayr* 198 C1
Wallasey 158 B4
Wallingford 98 D4
Wallington *Hants* 76 D5
Wallington *Herts* 126 C1
Wallington *Sutt* 100 C2
Wallis 105 G4
Walliswood 88 B4
Wallridge 197 F1
Walls 233 E2
Wallsend 190 C5
Wallyford 208 B2
Walmer 91 G5
Walmer Bridge 166 D3
Walmersley 167 G2
Walmley 134 D3
Walpole 140 D1
Walpole Cross Keys 151 E1
Walpole Highway 138 C5
Walpole Marsh 151 E1
Walpole St Andrew 151 E1
Walpole St Peter 138 B5
Walsall 134 C3
Walsall Wood 134 C3
Walsden 168 A3
Walsgrave on Sowe 135 F2
Walsham
Walshford 175 H2
Walshtown 236 B3
Walsoken 138 B4
Walston 200 C4
Walter's Ash 113 E1
Walterstone 109 E4
Walterstown 245 E1
Waltham *Kent* 90 D5
Waltham *NE Lincs* 171 G1
Waltham Abbey 114 C1
Waltham Chase 86 D2
Waltham Cross 114 C1
Waltham on the Wolds 149 F2
Waltham St Lawrence 99 F3
Walthamstow 100 D4
Walton *Cumb* 188 C4
Walton *Derbs* 161 F1
Walton *Leeds* 169 F5
Walton *Leics* 136 A2
Walton *MK* 113 E5
Walton *Pwys* 121 F3
Walton *Sflk* 117 E5
Walton *Som* 83 H4
Walton *T & W* 146 A1
Walton *Warks* 124 A3
Walton *Wfield* 169 F2
Walton Cardiff 123 E1

WALTON EAST–WEST KNAPTON

WILDWOOD–WORTLEY

Acknowledgments

The following abbreviations are used throughout the photography credits: t top; c centre; b bottom; l left; r right. © RD indicates images that are copyright of The Reader's Digest Association Limited.

60 Collections/Barry Hitchcox 61 Collections/Gena Davies 249 The Skyscan Photolibrary 350-351 The Jason Hawkes Aerial Collection 354-355 Construction Photography.com 358-359 Construction Photography.com 408 Scotland in Focus/M Miller 409 Collections/Jonathan Hodson 410 www.eden-project.co.uk 411 Collections/Philip Craven 412 Collections/Gordon Hill 413 Collections/Paul Watts 414 Collections/Peter Thomas 415 Collections/George Wright 416 Tom Mackie 417 Collections/Oliver Benn 418 Tom Mackie 419 t Collections/George Wright b Tom Mackie 420 t Tom Mackie b Tom Mackie 421 Collections/Iain McGowan 422 Tom Mackie 423 Collections/Ray Farrar 424 Colin Molyneux 425 Colin Molyneux 426 Collections/Fay Godwin 427 Collections/Robert Pilgrim 428 t Collections/Philip Craven b Collections/Oliver Benn 429 Collections/Michael St Maur Sheil 430 Collections/Oliver Benn 431 t Collections/Brian Shuel b Colin Molyneux 432 Collections/Archie Miles 433 t Mick Sharp and Jean Williamson b Collections/Oliver Benn 434 Collections/Ray Farrar 435 Tom Mackie b Tom Mackie 436 Collections/Alain le Garsmeur 437 t Colin Molyneux b Mick Sharp and Jean Williamson 438 Tom Mackie 439 t Neil Holmes b Neil Holmes 440 Neil Holmes 441 Neil Holmes 442 Colin Molyneux 443 Colin Molyneux 444 Collections/Robin Weaver 445 Neil Holmes 446 t Tom Mackie b Neil Holmes 447 Collections/John Beldom 448 Colin Molyneux 449 Colin Molyneux 450 t Collections/Robin Weaver b Mick Sharp and Jean Williamson/Jean Williamson 451 Collections/Mike Weston 452 Neil Holmes 453 t Collections/Robert Hallmann b Neil Holmes 454 Collections/Roger Scruton b Collections/Lawrence Englesberg 455 Colin Molyneux 456 tl Collections/Lawrence Englesberg br Collections/John D Beldom 457 Tom Mackie 458 Collections/Gary Smith 459 cl Collections/Mike St Maur Sheil b Collections/Sam Walsh 460

Collections/Roger Scruton 461 The Skyscan Photolibrary 462 cl Collections/Ashley Cooper b Collections/Sam Walsh 463 Collections/Robin Weaver 464 Collections/Liz Stares 465 Tom Mackie 466 l Tom Mackie r Collections/Philip Nixon 467 Scotland in Focus/R Weir 468 Scotland in Focus/S J Whitehome 469 Collections/Graeme Peacock 470 Collections/Gaeme Peacock 471 Collections/Jarrold The Still Moving Picture Company/Andy Shennan 472 Collections/Graeme Peacock 473 tl Scotland in Focus/A Firth br The Still Moving Picture Company/Harvey Wood 474 l The Still Moving Picture Company/Doug Corrance r Collections/Nigel Burgess 475 Collections/Graeme Peacock 476 t The Still Moving Picture Company/Doug Corrance b The Still Moving Picture Company/Doug Corrance 477 The Still Moving Picture Company/David Robertson 478 Tom Mackie 479 The Still Moving Picture Company/David Robertson 480 The Still Moving Picture Company/Doug Corrance 481 The Still Moving Picture Company/David Robertson 482 tc Collections/Fay Godwin br The Still Moving Picture Company/David Robertson 483 Tom Mackie 484 The Still Moving Picture Company/Doug Corrance 485 Tom Mackie 486 The Still Moving Picture Company/G Satterly 487 tr Scotland in Focus/R Schofield bl Scotland in Focus/R Elliott 488 Charles Tait 489 Collections/Alain Le Garsmeur 490 Collections/Michael Diggin 491 Christopher Hill Photographic 492 Collections/Gerry Gavigan 493 Collections/John Lennon 494 © RD/Neil Holmes 495 Christopher Hill Photographic 496-497 Alvey & Towers Picture Library 497 tl © RD/John Freemen tr Alvey & Towers Picture Library cl (upper) © RD/Planet 3 cl (lower) © RD/John Freemen bl Bubbles Photo Library br © RD 498-499 © RD/(all) John Freemen 500 © RD/John Freeman 501 l © RD/John Freeman c © RD/Howard Jones cr © RD/John Freeman bc © RD/Howard Jones br © RD/John Freeman 502 tc © RD/Howard Jones cl © RD/Howard Jones c © RD/John Freeman r © RD/John Freeman bl © RD/Howard Jones bc © RD/Howard Jones 503 l © RD/John Freemen r © RD 506 © RD/Planet 3 508 Bubbles Photo Library 510 Alvey & Towers Picture Library 514-515 © RD 516 Collections/Bob Estall

Contributors

Cartographic editor Alison Ewington

Road mapping PSmapping: Philip Storey

All other mapping Mapping Ideas Limited:
Dave Brooker, Rob Clynes and James Macdonald

Cartographic assistance Mike Adams, Ben
Bowles, Paul Hopgood, Christine Johnston,
Belinda Kane, James Sherwood, Andrew
Thompson

Photography John Freeman

Illustration Planet Three Publishing Network
Limited

Ordnance Survey® This product includes mapping
data licensed from Ordnance
Survey® with the permission of the Controller
of Her Majesty's Stationery Office.
© Crown copyright 2004.
All rights reserved. Licence number 100018100.

The maps of Northern Ireland are reproduced
by permission of the Ordnance Survey of
Northern Ireland, on behalf of the Controller of
Her Majesty's Stationery Office © Crown
copyright 2004 (Permit No 40367)

The maps of the Republic of Ireland are based
on Ordnance Survey, Ireland by permission of
The Government (Permit No 7591)

The Reader's Digest Association Limited would
like to thank the following for their contribution to
this book:

Automobile Association
John Callanan for the town plan of Sligo
Estate Publications for town plans of Boulogne
  and Calais
Global Mapping Ltd for help with ferry ports maps
Good Pub Guide (20th edition) edited by Alistair
  Aird, published by Ebury
  © Random House Group Ltd
  for recommended pubs in Britain and
  Northern Ireland
Highways Agency, Peter Morgan for information
  about traffic congestion
Instant Library, Susan Field for research
Institute of Advanced Motorists,
  Ted Clements
Sheena Meredith for advice on first aid
Mountain High Maps copyright © Digital Wisdom
  Publishing for topographic relief maps
Royal Automobile Club
Royal Society for the Prevention of Accidents
Thales Avionics Aerad for help with
  airports maps
Tourist information centres and **local authorities**
  from all over Great Britain and Ireland
Trafficmaster, Michele Murphy and Graham
  Smith   for information on congestion blackspots

**The Complete Driver's Atlas of Britain and
Ireland** was edited and designed by
The Reader's Digest Association Limited, London.

First edition Copyright © 2003
The Reader's Digest Association Limited
11 Westferry Circus, Canary Wharf,
London E14 4HE
www.readersdigest.co.uk

Reprinted with amendments 2005

The contents of this book are believed to be
accurate at the time of printing. However Reader's
Digest accepts no responsibility or liability for any
errors or omissions.

We are committed to both the quality of our
products and the service we provide
to our customers. We value your comments,
so please feel free to contact us on
08705 113366 or via our web site at:
www.readersdigest.co.uk
If you have any comments about the content
of our books you can contact us at
gbeditorial@readersdigest.co.uk

Origination
Colour Systems Limited, London

Printing and Binding
MOHN Media, Germany

Visit our web site at
www.readersdigest.co.uk

Concept code UK1341/L
Book code 400-063-07
ISBN 0 276 42723 8

READER'S DIGEST

Editor
Lisa Thomas

Art Editor
Julie Bennett

Assistant Editors
Caroline Boucher
Liz Edwards

Designer
Kate Harris

Production Editor
Rachel Weaver

Picture Researcher
Rosie Taylor

Proofreaders
Ken Vickery
Rosemary Wighton

Editorial Director
Cortina Butler

Art Director
Nick Clark

Executive Editor
Julian Browne

Managing Editor
Alastair Holmes

Picture Resource Manager
Martin Smith

Style Editor
Ron Pankhurst

Book Production Manager
Fiona McIntosh

Pre-press Accounts Manager
Penny Grose

Road distances in Ireland (miles)

Triangular distance chart. Each row gives the distance from the named place to the places listed above it (ARMAGH, ATHLONE, BALLYMENA, BANGOR, BELFAST, COLERAINE, CORK, DONEGAL, DUBLIN, ENNIS, ENNISKILLEN, GALWAY, KILKENNY, KILLARNEY, LARNE, LIMERICK, LONDONDERRY …).

From ↓ / To →	ARMAGH	ATHLONE	BALLYMENA	BANGOR	BELFAST	COLERAINE	CORK	DONEGAL	DUBLIN	ENNIS	ENNISKILLEN	GALWAY	KILKENNY	KILLARNEY	LARNE
ATHLONE	98														
BALLYMENA	55	152													
BANGOR	55	153	41												
BELFAST	41	139	28	14											
COLERAINE	62	154	27	68	57										
CORK	242	135	293	279	265	304									
DONEGAL	78	112	90	125	111	78	249								
DUBLIN	81	78	132	118	105	143	163	138							
ENNIS	167	68	221	221	208	223	85	164	146						
ENNISKILLEN	50	84	82	98	84	92	218	37	100	153					
GALWAY	149	58	203	203	190	207	128	129	137	43	116				
KILKENNY	159	75	210	196	182	220	93	187	80	98	152	106			
KILLARNEY	239	142	298	284	270	295	56	255	192	91	225	134	122		
LARNE	62	160	21	34	22	49	287	113	126	230	105	212	203	292	
LIMERICK	…	…	…	…	…	…	…	…	…	…	…	…	…	…	…

Road distances in Great Britain (miles)

Triangular distance chart. Each row gives the distance from the named place to the places listed across the top (LONDON, ABERDEEN, ABERYSTWYTH, AYR, BARNSTAPLE, BERWICK, BIRMINGHAM, BLACKPOOL, BOURNEMOUTH, BRIGHTON, BRISTOL, CAMBRIDGE, CARDIFF, CARLISLE, DOVER, EDINBURGH, EXETER, FISHGUARD, FORT WILLIAM, GLASGOW, GLOUCESTER, HARWICH, HOLYHEAD, INVERNESS, KENDAL, KINGSTON UPON HULL, LEEDS, LINCOLN, LIVERPOOL, MANCHESTER, MIDDLESBROUGH, NEWCASTLE, NORWICH …).

ABERDEEN: 547
ABERYSTWYTH: 239, 466
AYR: 418, 183, 338
BARNSTAPLE: 216, 603, 211, 474
BERWICK: 349, 187, 321, 139, 453
BIRMINGHAM: 121, 431, 124, 302, 178, 267
BLACKPOOL: 246, 335, 166, 206, 304, 191, 131
BOURNEMOUTH: 108, 573, 210, 444, 121, 416, 162, 271
BRIGHTON: 59, 606, 285, 477, 208, 414, 171, 304, 99
BRISTOL: 120, 514, 128, 385, 100, 363, 88, 212, 81, 169
CAMBRIDGE: 60, 463, 216, 360, 267, 294, 98, 221, 159, 120, 171
CARDIFF: 152, 532, 110, 403, 127, 381, 106, 230, 125, 201, 44, 203
CARLISLE: 314, 232, 234, 103, 372, 87, 199, 102, 341, 375, 283, 257, 300
DOVER: 78, 587, 326, 504, 272, 418, 208, 331, 179, 82, 206, 124, 238, 401
EDINBURGH: 413, 125, 333, 83, 471, 57, 298, 201, 440, 474, 381, 334, 399, 98, 458
EXETER: 200, 587, 195, 458, 55, 437, 162, 286, 85, 175, 84, 251, 111, 355, 244, 454
FISHGUARD: 259, 522, 56, 393, 234, 377, 213, 220, 232, 308, 151, 310, 112, 290, 344, 388, 218
FORT WILLIAM: 524, 156, 444, 139, 582, 192, 409, 312, 551, 585, 492, 467, 510, 209, 591, 133, 566, 500
GLASGOW: 411, 147, 331, 36, 469, 105, 296, 199, 438, 472, 380, 354, 397, 97, 479, 48, 453, 387, 102
GLOUCESTER: 102, 479, 112, 350, 126, 328, 54, 178, 100, 155, 36, 150, 61, 247, 192, 346, 110, 169, 457, 344
HARWICH: 82, 547, 300, 445, 312, 378, 182, 306, 206, 132, 216, 69, 248, 342, 136, 419, 296, 355, 551, 438, 191
HOLYHEAD: 283, 460, 105, 331, 341, 315, 168, 158, 310, 344, 251, 260, 207, 228, 370, 327, 325, 161, 438, 325, 216, 344
INVERNESS: 572, 106, 492, 209, 630, 219, 458, 360, 600, 633, 541, 515, 558, 258, 640, 157, 614, 548, 65, 173, 506, 600, 486
KENDAL: 268, 279, 188, 150, 326, 134, 153, 56, 295, 329, 237, 251, 254, 47, 356, 146, 310, 244, 257, 144, 202, 335, 181, 305
KINGSTON UPON HULL: 187, 375, 225, 273, 321, 186, 134, 141, 283, 260, 231, 139, 249, 170, 264, 247, 305, 281, 380, 267, 196, 224, 219, 428, 164
LEEDS: 198, 331, 171, 228, 302, 162, 116, 87, 264, 263, 213, 147, 230, 126, 271, 202, 286, 335, 222, 178, 231, 165, 384, 71, 60
LINCOLN: 143, 387, 217, 285, 276, 218, 99, 153, 224, 216, 187, 95, 204, 182, 220, 259, 260, 311, 392, 279, 152, 180, 204, 440, 176, 47, 72
LIVERPOOL: 216, 358, 108, 228, 274, 213, 102, 56, 244, 277, 185, 193, 202, 126, 304, 224, 258, 164, 335, 222, 150, 276, 101, 384, 79, 128, 74, 140
MANCHESTER: 204, 353, 129, 224, 262, 209, 89, 51, 231, 265, 172, 160, 190, 121, 291, 219, 246, 185, 330, 217, 137, 244, 122, 379, 74, 97, 43, 85, 35
MIDDLESBROUGH: 254, 276, 242, 198, 358, 102, 172, 134, 320, 319, 269, 199, 286, 95, 323, 148, 342, 298, 281, 191, 234, 283, 235, 308, 84, 89, 63, 123, 144, 114
NEWCASTLE: 285, 234, 272, 160, 389, 65, 203, 152, 351, 350, 299, 229, 317, 60, 353, 106, 373, 328, 239, 154, 264, 313, 266, 266, 102, 142, 94, 154, 175, 144, 38
NORWICH: 115, 488, 278, 385, 329, 319, 159, 253, 220, 169, 233, 63, 264, 282, 173, 359, 313, 372, 492, 379, 212, 84, 321, 540, 276, 150, 172, 103, 240, 185, 223, 254

(Further rows, labels cut off at right edge of page:)
131, 394, 161, 291, 235, 225, 53, 125, 197, 195, 145, 86, 163, 188, 218, 265, 219, 216, 398, 285, 110, 170, 175, 446, 148, 92, 74, 38, 109, 71, 129, 160, 119
514, 182, 433, 128, 572, 182, 399, 301, 541, 574, 482, 457, 499, 199, 581, 123, 556, 489, 49, 92, 447, 541, 427, 115, 246, 369, 321, 381, 325, 320, 270, 229, 482
56, 503, 160, 374, 170, 322, 68, 202, 93, 109, 74, 81, 105, 271, 146, 370, 154, 213, 481, 368, 48, 145, 239, 529, 225, 189, 171, 130, 173, 161, 226, 257, 144
310, 697, 305, 568, 110, 547, 272, 396, 197, 287, 194, 361, 221, 465, 356, 564, 110, 328, 675, 562, 219, 406, 433, 723, 419, 414, 396, 369, 367, 355, 451, 482, 423
460, 87, 380, 97, 518, 104, 346, 248, 488, 521, 429, 380, 446, 146, 504, 42, 503, 436, 102, 62, 394, 464, 374, 114, 194, 277, 245, 305, 272, 267, 193, 151, 405
86, 433, 205, 331, 263, 264, 86, 198, 184, 158, 174, 38, 191, 228, 162, 305, 248, 299, 437, 324, 139, 122, 248, 486, 222, 110, 118, 51, 186, 130, 169, 200, 77
241, 628, 236, 499, 63, 478, 203, 327, 128, 218, 125, 292, 152, 396, 287, 495, 45, 259, 606, 493, 150, 337, 364, 654, 350, 345, 327, 300, 298, 286, 382, 413, 353
74, 588, 240, 459, 162, 406, 153, 286, 52, 53, 97, 131, 155, 356, 140, 454, 129, 263, 565, 453, 117, 168, 324, 614, 310, 274, 256, 214, 258, 245, 311, 342, 204
169, 364, 164, 274, 273, 195, 76, 102, 235, 233, 183, 122, 201, 171, 247, 235, 257, 220, 381, 268, 148, 207, 158, 429, 125, 66, 36, 47, 79, 38, 99, 130, 147
163, 415, 75, 287, 221, 272, 48, 115, 190, 224, 132, 140, 109, 185, 251, 283, 205, 129, 394, 281, 97, 224, 104, 443, 138, 162, 122, 141, 65, 74, 192, 223, 202
80, 569, 221, 440, 142, 388, 134, 268, 32, 66, 77, 131, 137, 337, 152, 436, 109, 244, 547, 434, 99, 729, 305, 595, 291, 255, 237, 196, 239, 227, 293, 324, 193
44, 534, 273, 451, 256, 365, 155, 278, 164, 90, 179, 71, 211, 348, 94, 406, 229, 318, 558, 445, 154, 63, 316, 606, 302, 211, 219, 167, 250, 238, 270, 301, 99
161, 387, 113, 258, 219, 243, 46, 86, 188, 222, 130, 138, 147, 156, 249, 254, 219, 169, 365, 252, 95, 222, 124, 414, 109, 128, 93, 91, 58, 45, 163, 194, 200
420, 232, 340, 51, 478, 169, 306, 208, 448, 481, 389, 363, 406, 106, 488, 133, 463, 396, 188, 86, 354, 448, 334, 258, 153, 276, 228, 288, 232, 227, 201, 163, 389
189, 569, 70, 440, 164, 418, 143, 267, 162, 238, 81, 240, 41, 337, 275, 435, 148, 72, 546, 433, 98, 285, 174, 595, 291, 285, 267, 241, 175, 226, 322, 353, 302
627, 160, 547, 263, 685, 274, 512, 415, 654, 688, 595, 570, 613, 312, 694, 212, 669, 603, 112, 228, 560, 654, 540, 57, 359, 483, 435, 495, 438, 433, 362, 321, 595
675, 208, 595, 311, 733, 322, 560, 463, 702, 736, 643, 618, 661, 360, 742, 260, 717, 651, 168, 276, 608, 702, 588, 105, 407, 531, 483, 543, 486, 481, 410, 369, 643
212, 322, 199, 220, 316, 147, 129, 114, 278, 276, 226, 156, 243, 117, 280, 193, 300, 255, 326, 191, 240, 192, 375, 91, 38, 24, 80, 102, 71, 50, 88, 181